W9-BZQ-455

Contemporary

Contemporary

Courtland L. Bovée / William F. Arens

1982

RICHARD D. IRWIN, INC. Homewood, Illinois 60430

ISBN 0-256-02736-6

Library of Congress Catalog Card No. 81–84890

Printed in the United States of America

1 2 3 4 5 6 7 8 9 0 D 9 8 7 6 5 4 3 2

Text and cover design by
Stuart D. Paterson

Cover lettering by
Tim Girvin / Seattle

Part calligraphy by
Tim Botts

Cover photo by
Jim L. Ballard

To my parents;
Gary and Marilyn;
Kevin and Lynelle;
and John

—C.L.B.

To William
and Christian

—W.F.A.

Foreword

The marketing concept holds that the central focus of the firm should be the maximization of customer satisfaction. The marketing manager has control of a number of factors, called the marketing mix, in attempting to satisfy customer desires. One of these factors is the firm's promotion activities, and one of the most important elements of the overall promotion effort is *advertising.*

Advertising has traditionally been taught from at least two perspectives. The one perspective emphasizes the advertising management function. It addresses such issues as the objectives for advertising, the amount of money that should be spent on it, how that money should be allocated among alternative media and geographical areas, how the advertising should be timed to best stimulate demand, and so on.

The other perspective emphasizes the practice of advertising. The thrust here is on the planning and creation of advertising that accomplishes the goals set for it. The topics typically addressed include the creation of advertising copy, the use of various media, the planning and evaluation of the effectiveness of specific advertising campaigns, and so on.

Contemporary Advertising is a blend of these perspectives. The objective of the text is to teach advertising, and this book offers a complete and thorough survey of the field of advertising as it is practiced today. The text is loaded with the information needed to understand advertising. It covers the procedures for creating and using advertising. Yet the book also treats advertising in the broader marketing context that suggests its use. Throughout, there are strong connections between the purposes specified for the advertising function, and the creation and execution of advertising that address these purposes.

This union of perspectives makes the book particularly exciting, an excitement which is enhanced by a crisp, direct writing style, and the practitioner/teacher orientations of the authors. Bovée is a college professor with extensive experience in communications and advertising; Arens is the creative director of his own advertising agency and has supervised a wide variety of award-winning local, national, and international campaigns. The book is apt testimony to their teaching, advertising, and communication skills.

Gilbert A. Churchill, Jr.
Advisory Editor
Donald C. Slichter Professor
in Business Research
University of Wisconsin/Madison

Preface

Everyone living and working in the world today is under the influence of advertising. In fact, according to some, America is an "overcommunicated society." Thus, the study of advertising has taken on new importance, not only for the student of business or journalism—who may one day be a practitioner—but also for the student of liberal arts or science—who will continue to be a consumer of advertising.

There are six reasons why students profit from studying advertising. It can help them to:

Understand the impact of advertising on our economy.

Comprehend its role in fashioning our society.

See how it fits into the broader discipline of business and marketing.

Learn how it relates to journalism and the field of communication.

Discover what advertising people do and the career opportunities the field offers.

Appreciate the creativity and technical expertise required in advertising.

We set out to present advertising as it is actually practiced. This text combines a strong managerial approach with a hands-on production orientation and includes the application of consumer behavior theory to marketing strategy and to effective copywriting and graphic techniques. In short, we believe advertising should be taught as it really is—as a business, as a marketing tool, as a creative process, and as a hybrid discipline that employs elements of the various arts and sciences—in a manner and a style relevant to the student of the 80s.

We wanted to develop a realistic work which would personally involve students with practical experiences while simultaneously giving them a solid understanding of advertising's role in marketing management.

Contemporary Advertising follows the traditional organization of topical material:

The historical, economic, and social aspects of advertising (two chapters).

The three major business segments of advertising—the advertisers, the agency, and the media and suppliers (three chapters).

The marketing plans and strategies of advertising (four chapters).

The creative processes involved in copywriting, art direction, print and broadcast production, and packaging (five chapters).

The media alternatives available to advertisers (five chapters).

The special types of advertising (four chapters).

The all-important evaluation of advertising.

We wanted this text to put flesh on the bones of academic theory. To capture and hold student interest, the opening story of each chapter, written in narrative style, describes an actual situation which illustrates a basic concept in the study of advertising. Numerous real-life, behind-the-scenes vignettes tell what really happens in the advertising business. Each of the 24 chapters is heavily illustrated with award-winning advertisements and campaigns. All media are represented—print, broadcast, and outdoor. Original artwork from the advertising agencies, much of it in full color, is used for most of the print ad illustrations. Actual frames from television commercials, along with the dialogue, are shown. A soundsheet of award-winning radio commercials is included. Several complete case histories—from concept through final production—are developed. And in-depth captions give the illustrations a real-life tie-in to the basic concepts presented in each chapter. All these features are aimed at giving the student a familiar handle for understanding the application and integration of advertising theory.

Active participation enhances learning, so we have introduced several "Advertising Laboratories" into every chapter. These highlighted sections of supplemental information serve as unique sidebars to the world of advertising. They include discussion questions which stimulate critical thinking and develop understanding of the concepts studied.

We believe that a text for a survey course must be both thorough and substantive, and that it must be built upon a sound academic foundation. *Contemporary Advertising* has been thoroughly reviewed by both the educational and professional communities. It has been classroom tested in several regions of the country. Students have cited several things they like about this text: the interest and enjoyment they experience from the material; the ease of reading and learning; and the career orientation of the book which even discusses job opportunities and prerequisites, as well as descriptions of specific positions in advertising or affiliated fields. Instructors and students alike have found that the many checklists are a valuable teaching and learning aid in organizing thinking and facilitating decision making.

Contemporary Advertising is intended for the undergraduate student in business or journalism schools. Because of its approach, depth of coverage, and marketing management emphasis we believe it will also be appropriate in courses on advertising management. The wealth of award-winning advertisements makes it a resource guide for students in art and graphic design courses as well as for professionals in the field. While the text is itself a complete introduction to the field of advertising, we have developed supplemental materials to assist the instructor and benefit the student.

Student supplement This *illustrated* companion to the text contains learning objectives for each chapter, subject outlines, exercises, do-it-yourself glossary builders, supplemental readings, debatable issues, and advertising workshops—all designed to complement the text and reinforce the concepts.

Teacher's manual This complete manual for the instructor offers a wealth of opportunities for classroom lectures and discussions. Included are text-keyed references and answers to all discussion questions, course and subject outlines, and a complete testing program to facilitate the administration of examinations.

Many of the materials and techniques included in this text come from our own personal experiences as a college classroom teacher and a current full-time advertising executive. Others come from the experiences of professional friends. We hope that this book will be a valuable resource guide, not only in the study of advertising, but later on in the practice of it as well. In all cases, we hope that students feel like they are there—that they experience the feel of the advertising world—whether they intend to become professionals in the business, to work with those who are practitioners, or simply to become more sophisticated consumers.

Acknowledgments

Naturally, the writing of a comprehensive textbook is a mammoth undertaking. And frankly, this project might never have been completed without the personal and professional assistance of many, many people. While we cannot begin to list them all here, there are some whose contributions to our efforts must be acknowledged.

In the early formative stages of this book, we were assisted and encouraged unselfishly by Sandy Brown, David Mellinger, Steve Bottfeld, Harriet Bredal Young, Paul Aass, Ginette Gentier, Connie Robinson, Lou Magnani, and Jim Stevenson.

During the writing and rewriting, when authors' conversation became dreadfully dreary and friendships were put to the test, there were those who helped by reviewing, typing, editing, researching, criticizing, discussing, and just being there. Thank you all: Gary Burke, David Kreitzer, Cyndee Sabetti, Karen Bierstedt, Wallace Capel, Meryam Pickard, Jim Hughes, Lucy Huddell, Stan Urlaub, David Schwartz, Marian Kohlepp, and Terry Sherf.

The several hundred illustrations for this book could not have been gathered without the interest and response from the many people in the advertising business we talked to in assembling the materials—people like Klaus Schmidt of Young & Rubicam; Susan A. Irwin and Evelyn Sassoon of Dancer Fitzgerald Sample; Judy Williams Krut of Needham, Harper & Steers; Jacqueline Kilgour of Ogilvy & Mather; Harold Gully of Leo Burnett; Larry Spagnola and Chip White of Doyle Dane Bernbach; Steve Eaker of D'Arcy-MacManus & Masius; Richard Evans of Eva-Tone Soundsheets, Inc.; and Rob Kennedy of the Coca-Cola Company. They, and all of the people we contacted, gave us their best—the mark of true professionals in any industry.

Finally, when the project had taken form and the manuscript was nearing completion, the need for assistance became monumental. A very special thank you goes to the academic reviewers who kept us on track: Richard Joel, University of Tennessee; Charles Patti, Arizona State University; David Furse, Vanderbilt University; Edward Riordan, Wayne State University; John Sutherland, University of Florida; Cecil V. Hynes, University of Maryland; Robert Settle, San Diego State University; Kenneth Shanley, Sinclair Community College, Dayton, Ohio; and Gustav V. Primosigh, Prairie State College and Communication Workshop, Inc.

We are grateful for the contributions from all of these people. Whatever shortcomings remain in this book are ours alone.

Finally, we received much time-consuming assistance and invaluable professional advice from Tom Michael, Dennis Gillaspy, and Ken Longman. Martha Vasquez and Ellen Flentye kept the typewriters humming, and the personal guidance and encouragement of Ann and Don Ritchy, Olivia Reyes Verdugo, and John V. Thill cannot be overstated.

To all of you and, of course, to our immediate families, thank you.

Courtland L. Bovée
William F. Arens

Contents

Part I

Advertising Perspectives

Part II

The Advertising Business

3

The advertisers 90

4

Advertising agencies 114

5

The media and suppliers 142

Part III

Marketing and Advertising Plans and Strategies

11

Creative art direction

12

Creative production: Print media

13

Creative production: Broadcast media 396

14

Creative packaging, labeling, and trademarks 428

Part V

Advertising Media

15

Media planning and selection 460

Part VII

Advertising Testing

Contemporary

Part I

Advertising

Perspectives

1

The evolution of advertising

A hundred years ago in Atlanta, Georgia, there was a pharmacist named John S. Pemberton. He was not particularly successful financially, but in those days pharmacists usually did not make much money. As a rule they found pleasure tinkering in their laboratories to develop new patent medicines or other products that could be sold in their drugstores. However, Dr. Pemberton was destined to develop something that would later become the most popular consumer packaged product in the world. In fact, it would revolutionize the beverage industry and create a new chapter in the history of marketing and advertising.

As legend goes, Dr. Pemberton was working over a three-legged pot in his backyard in 1886 when he produced a sweet-tasting brown syrup from the juices of certain plants and nuts. Mixed with soda fountain water, the syrup produced a remarkable sparkling taste. Pemberton's new elixir was placed on sale as a soda fountain drink for five cents a glass at Jacobs Pharmacy in downtown Atlanta. It was immediately popular. The date was May 8, 1886. On May 29 a newspaper ad in the *Atlanta Journal* invited Atlantans to try "the new and popular soda fountain drink." The ad also proclaimed that Coca-Cola, as Pemberton called it, was "Delicious and Refreshing," a theme that continues today (Figure 1–1).

You are probably familiar with many advertising themes and slogans—perhaps even more than you think—for soft drinks, automobiles, fast-food chains, clothing stores, movies, radio stations, banks, insurance companies, and cosmetic lines, just to name a few.

Following is a list of possible advertising slogans and headlines for Coca-Cola. Test your knowledge of advertising by trying to determine which ones were actually used by the Coca-Cola Company at one time.

The drink of quality.

The great national temperance beverage.

Whenever you see an arrow, think of Coca-Cola.

Thirst knows no season.

Around the corner from anywhere.

The pause that refreshes.

Universal symbol of the American way of life.

Midsummer magic.

Enjoy Coca-Cola.

In fact all nine slogans have been used by Coca-Cola. For the whole 94-year list of slogans, campaigns, and themes, see the Ad Lab. The list chronicles not only the history of the world's most successful product but also the history of modern advertising and the American free enterprise system itself (Figure 1–2).

As an introduction to the study of advertising, this history is very appropriate. Therefore, our first chapter will examine the evolution of advertising and the economic impact it has had on the products it serves and on the society in which it exists. But first it is important to understand what advertising is. That definition should explain what advertising does and what it tries to do. And it should introduce some of the terminology used to describe various types and classifications of advertising.

Advertising defined

What is advertising? According to McCann Erickson Inc., the advertising agency that develops Coca-Cola's national campaigns, advertising is "truth well told." This philosophy is echoed by Coke's vice president of advertising, William Sharp, who says that a commercial for Coca-Cola should have the properties of the product itself.

> (Coke's advertising) should be a pleasurable experience, refreshing to watch and pleasant to listen to. It should reflect quality by being quality. And it should make you say, I wish I'd been there. I wish I had been drinking Coke with these people.[1]

That's what advertising is to Coca-Cola. But can the same be said for other products and services in the marketplace today? How do we define the advertising we see for those commodities?

COCA-COLA.

DELICIOUS!
REFRESHING!
EXHILARATING!
INVIGORATING!

The New and Popular Soda Fountain Drink, containing the properties of the wonderful Coca plant and the famous Cola nuts. For sale by Willis Venable and Nunnally & Rawson.

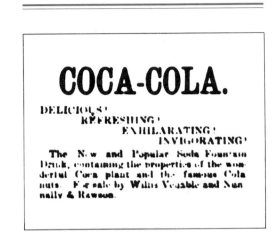

Figure 1—1 The first ad for Coca-Cola, in the *Atlanta Journal,* May 29, 1886, promised virtually the same attributes as ads today . . . Delicious! Refreshing!

Figure 1—2 The 1920s ushered in the "flapper" era. Sales of Coke spread and the slogan, "Thirst knows no season," became a reality.

Albert Lasker, who has been called the father of modern advertising, said that advertising is "salesmanship in print." That may well be. But he gave us that definition long before the advent of radio and television and at a time when the nature and scope of advertising were considerably different from what they are today.

From today's mass communications we all have a strong concept of what advertising is, and we also tend to have very strong opinions and prejudices about it (Figure 1–3). Thus the definitions of advertising are many and varied. It may be defined as a communication process, a marketing process, an economic and social process, a public relations process, or an information and persuasion process, depending on the point of view.

In this text we shall use the following working definition of advertising:

> Advertising is the nonpersonal communication of information usually paid for and usually persuasive in nature about products,

It had to be good to get where it is!

1886	Drink Coca-Cola.
1904	Delicious and refreshing.
1904	Coca-Cola . . . satisfies.
1905	Coca-Cola revives and sustains.
1905	Wherever you go . . . you'll find Coca-Cola.
1906	The drink of quality.
1906	The great national temperance beverage.
1907	Coca-Cola is full of vim, vigor and go—is a snappy drink.
1908	Get the genuine.
1909	Whenever you see an arrow, think of Coca-Cola.
1911	Enjoy a glass of liquid laughter.
1917	Three million a day.
1920	Coca-Cola . . . good things from 9 climes poured into a single glass.
1922	Thirst knows no season.
1923	Enjoy thirst.
1925	It has the charm of purity.
1925	With a drink so good . . . 'tis folly to be thirsty.
1925	Six million a day.
1926	Coca-Cola is the shortest distance between thirst and refreshment.
1927	It had to be good to get where it is.
1927	Around the corner from anywhere.
1927	At the little red sign.
1928	Coca-Cola . . . a pure drink of natural flavors.
1929	The best served drink in the world.
1929	The pause that refreshes.
1932	Ice-cold sunshine.
1932	Thirst come, thirst served.
1933	Bounce back to normal.
1933	Don't wear a tired, thirsty face.
1935	Coca-Cola . . . the pause that brings friends together.
1937	America's favorite moment.
1938	The best friend thirst ever had.
1938	Thirst asks nothing more.
1939	Coca-Cola goes along.
1939	Coca-Cola has the taste thirst goes for.
1939	Whoever you are, whatever you do, wherever you may be, when you think of refreshment, think of ice-cold Coca-Cola.
1940	Within easy reach of your thirst.
1940	America's year-round answer to thirst.
1941	Work refreshed.
1941	Coca-Cola belongs . . .
1942	The only thing like Coca-Cola is Coca-Cola itself.
1942	Coca-Cola has that extra something.
1942	The best is always the better buy.
1942	It's the real thing.
1943	Universal symbol of the American way of life . . . Coca-Cola.
1943	With a taste all its own.
1945	The happy symbol of a friendly way of life.
1945	Why grow thirsty?
1946	The world's friendliest club . . . admission 5¢.

services, or ideas by identified sponsors through the various media.

Let's take this definition apart and analyze its components.

Nonpersonal communication of information . . .

Advertising is not personal or face-to-face communication. Rather it is directed to groups of people and is therefore nonpersonal in nature. The group might be teenagers who enjoy rock music or men and women who watch soap operas or sporting events.

In direct-mail advertising an attempt is often made to personalize the message by inserting the receiver's name one or more times in the letter. But direct mail is still nonpersonal; the computer inserted the name. And the signature on the direct-mail advertisement is written electronically.

1946 Yes.
1947 Coca-Cola . . . continuous quality.
1947 Continous quality is quality you trust.
1947 The quality of Coca-Cola is a friendly quality you can always trust.
1948 Where there's Coke there's hospitality.
1949 Coca-Cola . . . along the highway to anywhere.
1950 Thirst, too, seeks quality.
1951 For home and hospitality.
1951 You taste its quality.
1952 What you want is a Coke.
1952 Coke follows thirst everywhere.
1953 Drive safely . . . Drive refreshed.
1953 Midsummer magic.
1955 Bright and bracing as sunshine.
1956 Coca-Cola . . . makes good things taste better.
1956 The friendliest drink on earth.
1956 Gives a bright little lift.
1956 Coca-Cola puts you at your sparkling best.
1957 Sign of good taste.
1958 The cold, crisp taste of Coke.
1959 Cheerful life of Coke.
1959 Relax refreshed with ice-cold Coca-Cola.
1959 Be really refreshed.
1959 The cold, crisp taste that so deeply satisfies.
1961 Coca-Cola refreshes you best.
1963 The big bold taste that's always just right.
1963 Things go better with Coke.
1963 Go better refreshed.
1964 Coca-Cola gives that special zing . . . refreshes best.
1965 Enjoy Coca Cola.
1965 For extra fun—take more than one! Take an extra carton of Coke!
1966 Coca-Cola has the taste you never get tired of.
1968 Tells your thirst to go fly a kite.
1968 Wave after wave—drink after drink.
1968 For twice the convenience, bring home two cartons of Coke.
1968 It's twice time.
1970 It's the real thing.
1971 I'd like to buy the world a Coke.
1972 Coke . . . goes with the good times.
1975 Look up America, see what we've got.
1976 Coke adds life . . .
1980 Have a Coke and a smile.

Laboratory applications

1. Which slogans would no longer be appropriate?
2. What slogan might Coca-Cola use to reflect the 1980s?

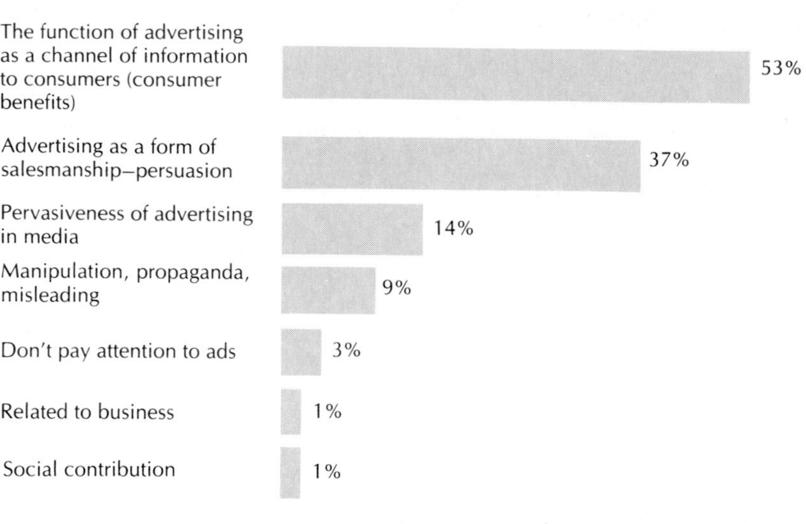

Figure 1–3 How consumers define advertising.

Usually paid for . . .

Most advertising is paid for by sponsors. General Motors, K mart, Schlitz, and the local record shop pay for the advertisements we read, hear, and see. But some advertisements are not paid for by their sponsors. The American Red Cross, United Way, and American Cancer Society are only three of hundreds of organizations that sponsor advertisements but do not pay for the time or space used to present them. Customarily their messages are presented at no charge by the print and broadcast media as a public service.

Usually persuasive in nature . . .

Persuasive means urging people to do something. It involves convincing people that the product advertised will benefit them. Most advertising tries to be persuasive—to win converts to a product, service, or idea. Some advertising, though, such as legal announcements, is intended merely to inform, not to persuade.

About products, services, or ideas . . .

Advertising is not restricted to the promotion of tangible products such as soap and cereal, however. Advertising is also used extensively to help sell services such as hair styling and motorcycle repairs. And increasingly advertising is used to sell economic, political, religious, and social ideas.

By identified sponsors . . .

For a message to be an advertisement the sponsor must be identified. For obvious reasons, the sponsor usually wants to be identified—or else why advertise? Most advertising is sponsored by commercial or profit-seeking enterprises. However, noncommercial organizations—churches, schools, political parties, charitable groups—may also sponsor advertising.

Through various media

Most advertising reaches us through what is called the "mass media"—that is, billboards, newspapers, magazines, radio, and television. But much advertising also reaches us through direct mail. Some advertising even reaches us through flyers placed under our windshield wipers at the shopping center or hung on our doors.

Functions of advertising

As soon as Dr. Pemberton had developed his new drink, he and his partner, Frank M. Robinson, came up with a name for it. They also decided to write the name in a unique way, using the flowing Spencerian script of the day. Later the name and script were trademarked with the U.S. Patent Office to ensure their sole usage by the Coca-Cola Company in its advertising and packaging. This demonstrates perhaps the most basic function of advertising—*to identify products and differentiate them from others.*

No sooner had they named the product than they ran an ad to tell people about it and where they could get it. Within a year, as more soda fountains began to sell the product, handpainted oilcloth signs with "Coca-Cola" began to appear, attached to store awnings (Figure 1–4). Then the word "Drink" was added to inform passersby that the product was a soda fountain beverage. Thus we see another basic

Figure 1–4 Oilcloth signs were often used in advertising Coca-Cola. In the 1890s they hung over the front doors of drugstores that dispensed the product.

function of advertising—*to communicate information about the product, its features, and its location of sale.*

In 1889 the rights to Coca-Cola were bought for $2,300 by Asa G. Candler. Unfortunately, Pemberton was in ill health and desperately needed the money. He was destined not to see the success his product would achieve.

Candler was a firm believer in advertising. He printed and distributed thousands of coupons offering a complimentary glass of Coca-Cola (Figure 1–5). As more and more people saw the advertisements and received free coupons, they tried the product and then tried it again. Another function of advertising is *to induce consumers to try new products and to suggest reuse.*

Figure 1–5 Coupons encouraged people to try the new soft drink in its early years. These are examples of some used in the 1890s.

After more people tried the soft drink, liked it, and requested it, more pharmacies bought the product to sell to their customers. *Stimulating the distribution of a product* is yet another basic function of advertising.

To this time Coca-Cola had been sold only at soda fountains. One of the many functions of advertising, though, is *to increase product usage.* In 1899 the first bottling plant opened in Chattanooga, Tennessee. The second opened the following year in Atlanta. In 30 years these first 2 bottling plants increased to 1,000, with 95 percent of them locally owned and operated.

As with anything popular, however, there were many imitators, and the battle against these competitors has been continuous. Another major function of advertising is *to build brand preference and loyalty,* and Candler's use of a constant and consistent promotional campaign helped to do this.

In 1916 the famous Coca-Cola bottle with its distinctive contour design was introduced. This helped identify Coke and differentiate it from competitors to such an extent that the company was granted registration of the bottle as a trademark by the U.S. Patent Office. In the meantime the bottle helped merchandise the company's other promotional efforts and also assure the public of the standardized quality of Coke with every purchase (Figure 1–6).

We see from this brief history of the beginnings of the Coca-Cola Company that advertising has many and varied functions. Generally these functions could be grouped and categorized as follows: marketing functions, communication and education functions, economic functions, and social functions. We shall discuss each of these briefly.

Marketing function

To make money, companies manufacture and sell products that compete in the marketplace. To increase their sales or profits, companies develop marketing strategies. The marketing strategy is determined by how companies want to combine and use various marketing elements, which are generally referred to as product, price, place, and promotion. Each of these will be discussed in Chapter 6.

Advertising falls in the promotion category and is part of the promotional mix along with personal selling, sales promotion, and public relations—all of which are used to sell or win acceptance for the company's products, services, or ideas.

1894 1899–1902 1900–1916 1915 1923 1937 1957 1961 1975

Figure 1–6

Putting Coca-Cola in a bottle greatly widened its distribution. Bottles have evolved over the years from the straight Hutchinson style used in 1899, and they have enjoyed decades of public acceptance. Management had great fear when it was suggested to add sizes larger than the traditional 6½-ounce container. Today, however, Coke is available in a wide variety of sizes.

Advertising involves presenting the message to a mass audience (large groups of people) using mass media. The cost of reaching a thousand prospects through advertising is usually far less than the cost of reaching one prospect through personal selling. For example, if you wanted to make a personal sales call on every football fan who watched the Super Bowl game in an effort to sell each a bottle of Coke, it would be unbelievably expensive. The McGraw-Hill Laboratory reports that the average personal sales call now costs well over $90. If we multiply that times the 40+ million people who watched the Super Bowl, the cost is mind-boggling. However, you could buy a 30-second television commercial on the Super Bowl and tell those same 33 million people about Coca-Cola for only $300,000. That's a lot less. In fact, you would be talking to prospects through advertising for only $7.50 per thousand, less than 10 percent of what it costs to talk to one prospect through personal selling.

Figure 1–7 From a wall in Pompeii, this inscription was promoting a contest of gladiators.

Communication function

All forms of advertising communicate some message to a group of people. As a communication function, advertising had its beginnings in ancient civilizations. Most historians believe the outdoor signs carved in clay, wood, or stone and used by ancient Greek and Roman merchants were the first form of advertising. Since the population was unable to read, the signs were symbols of the goods for sale, such as a boot for a shoemaker's shop (Figure 1–7).

Because early artisans took pride in their work, they placed their own marks on goods such as the cutlery, cloth, and pottery they produced. These trademarks enabled buyers to identify the work of a particular artisan, just as trademarks do today, thus assuring consumers that they were getting the goods they wanted.

Today the communication of information is still one of the basic functions and objectives of advertising. Examples of advertising used primarily for communication are ads in telephone directories, newspaper classified ads, and legal ntoices published by various organizations and government bodies.

Functions of advertising

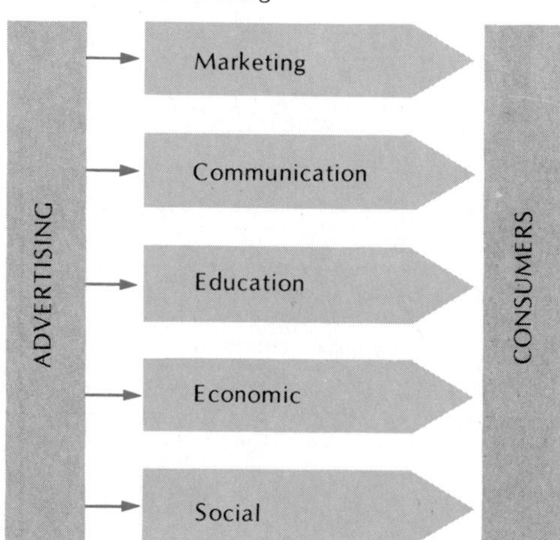

Education function

People learn from advertising. They learn about the products that are available to them, and they learn how they can better their lives. Ulanoff speaks of advertising as an instrument of education:

> Advertising, as an educator, speeds the adoption of the new and untried and, in so doing, accelerates technological advances in industry and hastens the realization of a fuller life for all. It helps reduce accidents and waste of natural resources and contributes to building a better understanding and appreciation of American ideologies.[2]

He goes on to say, though, that advertising must be more than educational to be successful. It must also be persuasive to move people to action, whether that action is the purchase of a different brand of breakfast cereal or regular attendance at church. This persuasiveness, he points out, usually has little in common with the impartiality of education.

What educational function do you think Coca-Cola advertising performs or has performed?

Economic function

By making people aware of products, services, and ideas, advertising promotes sales and thereby commerce as well. As a buyer's guide, it provides consumers with news of new products or prices, and it gives industrial buyers important information about new equipment and technology.

By informing many people at once about available products and services, advertising greatly reduces the cost of distribution and eases the task of personal selling. This leads to lower costs and higher profits, which can be invested in more capital equipment and jobs.

The freedom to advertise enables competitors to enter the marketplace. This encourages the improvement of existing products and the development of new, improved models. These actions translate into increased productivity, higher quality, and the disappearance of products that don't measure up. Thus as advertising invites people to try new products, it accelerates the success of good products and the failure of unacceptable products.

We shall discuss some of these far-reaching economic aspects of advertising later in this chapter.

Social function

Advertising is one of the major forces that has helped improve the standard of living in this country and around the world. By publicizing the material, social, and cultural opportunities of a free enterprise, consumer society, advertising has encouraged increased productivity by both management and labor.

If you earn even a small amount of money, you can buy an automobile. It may be secondhand, but from advertising you know that it is available. If you earn more money, you can buy a new car or one with more luxury features. You also have the opportunity to make a statement about yourself as an individual by the automobile you purchase. Advertising has created a personality for each automobile make and model on the market. You, as a free individual, have the opportunity to select the product that best matches your functional or social needs.

Advertising serves other social needs besides simply stimulating sales. Newspapers, magazines, radio, and television all receive their primary income from advertising. This facilitates freedom of the press.

Public services by advertising organizations also foster growth and understanding of important social causes. The Red Cross, Community Chest, United Way, and other noncommercial organizations receive continuous financial support and volunteer assistance because of the power of advertising.

Finally, advertising's effect on society has led to important social and legal changes. But, as we shall see in Chapter 2, advertising itself has been greatly affected by the very laws it has brought about.

Classifications of advertising

The word *advertising* is often preceded by an adjective that indicates the kind of advertising being discussed. To understand what advertising is, it is helpful to classify it—and thereby learn some basic terminology.

Classification by target audience

Advertising is always aimed at a particular segment of the population. When you see ads that don't appeal to you, sometimes it is because the ad is aimed at a group of people to which you do not belong. For example, an advertisement in *Aviation Week* magazine for technical military products might have no meaning to you. On the other hand, the reader of *Aviation Week* may have very little interest in an advertisement for a new clothing store in town. The target audience is generally defined as that group of individuals to whom the advertising message is directed.

There are many classifications of target audiences. The two major ones, though, are consumers and businesses.

Consumer advertising

This is advertising aimed at individuals or ultimate consumers who buy products for personal or nonbusiness reasons. Most television, radio, newspaper, and magazine ads are consumer advertisements. They are sponsored by the manufacturer of the product or the dealer who sells the product. They are usually directed at the ultimate consumer of the product or at the person who will buy the product for someone else's use. For example, a magazine advertisement for Coca-Cola may be aimed at both the purchaser and the consumer. A commercial for dog food on Johnny Carson's "Tonight Show," however, is aimed at the purchaser, not the consumer, of the product.

Business advertising

This is advertising aimed at people in business who buy products for business use. There are four distinct types of business advertising; industrial, trade, professional, and agricultural.

Industrial advertising This type of advertising is directed toward industrial companies that buy products to use in operating manufacturing plants, transportation companies, utilities, and a host of other industrial businesses. Most advertising in such magazines as *Iron Age* and *Electronics* is industrial advertising, although radio and television are used as well. This advertising is designed to stimulate the purchase of products like computers, electronic machinery, bottling machines, and construction equipment (Figure 1–8).

Figure 1–8

FLYING LETTER
30-second

(MUSIC UNDER AND THROUGHOUT.)
VO: How fast can you send a letter coast to coast?
VO: Watch. New York . . .
VO: Chicago . . .
VO: The Mississippi River.
VO: This is how fast—with the new IBM 6670 Information distributor.
VO: Los Angeles
VO: Delivered in 15 seconds. Printed by a laser . . . typewriter quality.
Cost: about eight cents.
VO: The IBM 6670.

People in advertising

John O'Toole

President and Chief Creative Officer
Foote, Cone & Belding Communications, Inc.

John O'Toole, born in Chicago in 1929, began his writing career at 15 when his first poem was published. He went on to obtain his B.S. degree in journalism at Northwestern University and then served a tour of active duty in the Marines. After his discharge he interviewed with Foote, Cone & Belding (FCB) first and he has been there ever since. He started as a copywriter under the guidance of the legendary Fairfax Cone, one of the agency's partners. He was promoted to creative director and then rose through the ranks to become president and chief creative officer of Foote, Cone & Belding Communications, Inc.

Today, headquartered at FCB's executive offices in New York City, he directs the company's four major subsidiaries: (1) Foote, Cone & Belding Advertising, which includes all U.S. advertising agency activities east of the Rockies; (2) Foote, Cone & Belding/Honig, representing all FCB advertising agency activities in the western United States; (3) FCB International, comprising all advertising agency operations outside the United States; and (4) Carl Byoir & Associates, which encompasses all FCB public relations operations.

The four FCB subsidiaries that O'Toole oversees consist of 33 full-service advertising agencies and 18 public relations offices in 19 countries. More than 3,300 employees, who speak a total of 14 languages, serve over 1,000 clients.

In a recent interview, portions of which were quoted in advertisements for *The Wall Street Journal,* O'Toole shared the following insights on advertising:

On today's consumers:

If I want to write to individual consumers, then I must know how they think, and live, and buy. So I believe it's essential to go beyond the statistics of public opinion, to look at what's happening in the real world. For example, you might see today as a time of reassuring quiet after the turbulence of the sixties. But that's only the surface. There's a new spirit of individualism, people seeking to satisfy their own goals, serve their ambitions, feed their individual appetities, find lifestyles to suit their needs. Small wonder there's such distrust of advertising that treats people as a homogeneous mass. Today's great advertising speaks to individual needs—to the strong drive to be yourself.

On visibility:

There's an enormous amount of advertising and communication fighting for attention. So visibility is difficult to achieve. Yet, you must gain the eyes of the people you want to reach, or you haven't a chance of winning their minds. But making an ad visible means running risks. If an ad is provocative, interesting, intriguing, it's apt to create some adverse comments. Consider the alternative: advertising so bland there's no bite.

On information:

Information sells. Perhaps some products can't be sold with information, but they're few in number—you have to work and dig and think to find out why they're different. Today's consumers are hungry for information. They want to know as much as possible about your product, your service, your company. Advertising writers are blessed with thousands of gifted products about which to write. Our problem, very simply, is to make sure we're as gifted as the products we're assigned.

(continued)

FCB is the third oldest, and fourth largest, advertising agency in the United States, and the ninth largest agency in the world. It has helped to turn Sunkist organges, Hallmark cards ("When you care enough to send the very best"), Clairol hair coloring ("Does she or doesn't she?"), Dial soap ("Aren't you glad you use dial?"), Zenith TV ("The quality goes in before the name goes on"), S. C. Johnson ("Raid kills bugs dead"), and hundreds of other products into universal habits.

In 1963 Foote, Cone & Belding made advertising industry history by offering its stock for public sale. Today FCB shares are held by some 4,000 stockholders throughout the world.

A quiet, reflective man, O'Toole is deeply dedicated to his trade. He is a member of the boards of directors of the American Association of Advertising Agencies and the Advertising Council. He is also a trustee of the American Ballet Theater. His poems have appeared in a number of magazines.

Trade advertising Manufacturers use trade advertising to stimulate wholesalers and retailers to buy goods for resale to their customers. An example of trade advertising is an ad promoting Coca-Cola to food store managers in a trade publication like *Progressive Grocer*.

Professional advertising This advertising is aimed at individuals who are normally licensed and operate under a code of ethics or a set of professional standards. Teachers, accountants, doctors, dentists, architects, and lawyers are examples.

Farm or agricultural advertising The nation's farmers are the audience for agricultural advertising. It is also directed at the growers, producers, and dealers of agricultural products. Publications such as *California Farmer* and *American Vegetable Grower* serve these markets.

Classification by geographic area covered

Advertising for a dress shop is run in the local area near the store. On the other hand, advertising for many American consumer products is seen in foreign countries from Africa to Asia. There are four classifications of advertising based on geography.

International advertising

Travel to Europe and you'll see advertisements for Crest in Norwegian. Go to Russia and you'll find the virtues of Pepsi-Cola extolled. Visit Brazil and watch an ad for Levi's on television (in Portuguese). International advertising is advertising directed at foreign markets (Figure 1–9).

National advertising

Advertising aimed at customers throughout the country is called national advertising, and its sponsors are called national advertisers.

Regional advertising

Many products are sold in only one area or region of the country, which might cover several states but not the entire nation. Publications such as *The Wall Street Journal* and *Time* sell space on either a national or a regional basis. Thus an airline that operates in only one part of the nation can purchase space in a regional edition of certain publications.

Local advertising

Many advertisers such as department stores, automobile dealers, and restaurants have customers in only one city or local trading area. Local advertising is often called retail advertising simply because most of it is paid for by retailers. It must be remembered, however, that not all retail advertising is local. Increasingly, retailers such as Sears, Roebuck and K mart are advertising beyond the local areas where their stores are located.

Although national and regional advertisements usually explain the merits and special features of a product, most local advertising tells consumers where to buy it. National and regional automobile commercials explain the durability, gas mileage, design, and other product qualities. Local advertising by automobile dealers emphasizes price, friendly salespeople, and other reasons to visit their dealership.

Figure 1–9 Mohammed Ali is not only a celebrity in the United States but in the Arab world as well. For that reason Toyota retained his services to help sell the Japanese car in Saudi Arabia. Ali's well-publicized, professional personality comes out in the headline: "The 1981 Corolla, like me, an international star."

Classification by medium

An advertising *medium* is any paid means used to present an advertisement to its target audience. It does not include "word-of-mouth" advertising. The principal media used in advertising are newspapers, magazines, radio, television, direct mail, and out-of-home, such as outdoor (signs, billboards) and transit (ads on buses, trucks). So advertising can be classified on the basis of the medium used to transit the message. Thus there is newspaper advertising, magazine advertising, and so on.

Classification by function or purpose

Another way to classify advertising is on the basis of the sponsor's general objectives. Some advertising, for example, is designed to sell a product; some is not.

Product versus nonproduct advertising

Product advertising is intended to sell products and services. Nonproduct advertising is designed to sell ideas. When Exxon places an advertisement for the petroleum products it sells, it is a product ad. Advertising by companies that offer insurance services are also product advertisements. It should be pointed out here, by the way, that in this text the term *product* will refer to both products and services.

Now if Phillips Petroleum tells about its ability to drill for oil without disturbing or polluting the environment, the advertisement is selling the company rather than a particular product. This form of advertising is called *corporate, nonproduct,* or *institutional* advertising. Corporate advertising can have various objectives. Sometimes referred to as "image" advertising, it can be used in an effort to counter public criticism (Figure 1–10). In other instances it is designed to promote noncontroversial causes, such as support for the arts or charities.

Too pretty to get its feet wet.
Shaving by shaving, feather by feather, a wood block takes on life. The shaping of decoys has been a skill in Louisiana for as long as Cajun has been spoken. But this beauty will never flirt with a duck. Her charms are saved for the artistic, the art collector, for all the admirers of things carved by hand. We at Phillips Petroleum are captivated, too. We try to take as much care when the work we do touches the habitats of wildfowl, as these artists take with their birds. To every last feather.

Figure 1–10 In this corporate advertisement for Phillips Petroleum the company promises to be a good environmentalist while drilling for oil. The company no doubt hopes such advertising will blunt the criticisms of environmental groups, which frequently fight their exploration efforts.

Commercial versus noncommercial advertising

A *commercial* advertisement sells goods, services, or ideas for a business with the expectation of making a profit. A *noncommercial* advertisement is sponsored by or for a charitable institution, civic group, or religious or political organization. Many noncommercial advertisements seek money and are run to raise funds. Others hope to change consumer behavior ("Buckle up for safety"). In Chapter 23 we will discuss noncommercial advertising.

Direct action versus indirect action advertising

Some advertisements are intended to bring about immediate action on the part of the reader. Mail-order advertisements, for example, fall into this category of direct action advertising. Likewise, some advertisements include a coupon for the reader to send in for catalogs or additional information. Again they are seeking an immediate, direct action from the reader (Figure 1–11).

Advertisements that attempt to build the image of a product or familiarity with the name and package are seeking an indirect action. Their objective is to influence the reader to purchase a specific brand the next time he or she is in the market for that product.

Most advertisements on television and radio are indirect action. Some, however, are a mixture of the two. It is not uncommon to see 60-second television commercials that devote 50 seconds to image building and the last 10 seconds to a local phone number for a free demonstration.

Evolution of modern advertising

As the world's industrial output has grown, so has the use of advertising. In the United States it is now a significant industry in relation to the total U.S. economy. In 1980 it made up 1.98 percent of the gross national product and represented a total expenditure of $54.6 billion (Figures 1–12 and 1–13). The media that had the most advertising expenditures (from high to low) were: newspapers, television, direct mail, radio, magazines, and outdoor. How did this industry grow to be so large?

Throughout history the purpose of advertising—to inform and persuade—has not changed. Although many people think of advertising as a modern process, it actually dates back many centuries. We have already seen how advertising as a communication function was born thousands of years ago. However, ancient civilizations had to depend on hand tools to produce goods. Because goods weren't produced in great quantity, the use of advertising to stimulate mass purchases of merchandise was not really necessary. At the same time, there were no mass media for possible advertisers to use.

Impact of printing and photography

The Chinese invented paper and Europe had its first paper mill by 1275.

Perhaps the most important event that ushered in the era of modern advertising was the invention of movable type by Johannes Gutenberg in 1440. His invention made possible new advertising media and the first forms of mass advertising, including printed posters,

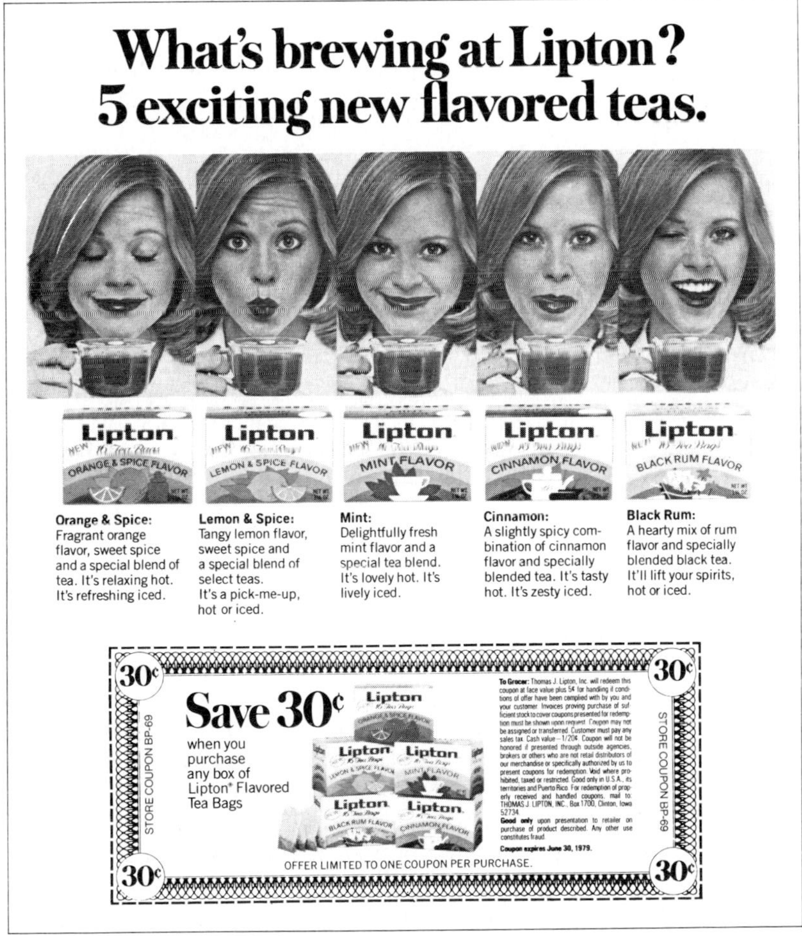

Figure 1–11 An offer to try Lipton's new flavored teas is contained in this direct action advertisement. Other companies may offer free catalogs or premiums at a discount for the return of their coupon.

Figure 1–12 Leaders in national advertising in the 1890s

Adams Tutti Frutti Gum	Gramophone
American Express Traveler's Cheques	Great Northern Railroad
Armour Beef Extract	Hamburg American Line
Baker's Cocoa	Hartford Bicycle
Battle Ax Plug Tobacco	Heinz's Baked Beans
Beardsley's Shredded Codfish	Hires' Root Beer
Beeman's Pepsin Gum	Hoffman House Cigars
Burlington Railroad	Ives & Pond Piano
California Fig Syrup	Ivory Soap
Caligraph Typewriter	Kirk's American Family Soap
Castoria	Kodak
Chicago Great Western	Lipton's Teas
Chicago, Milwaukee & St. Paul Railroad	Lundborg's Perfumes
Chicago Great Western Railway	Dr. Lyon's Toothpowder
Chickering Piano	Mason & Hamlin Piano
Columbia Bicycles	Mennen's Talcum Powder
Cleveland Baking Powder	Michigan Central Railroad
Cook's Tours	J. L. Mott Indoor Plumbing
Cuticura Soap	Munsing Underwear
Derby Desks	New York Central Railroad
Dixon's Graphite Paint	Oneita Knitted Goods
Dixon's Pencils	Pearline Soap Powder
Edison Mimeograph	Pearltop Lamp Chimneys
Earl & Wilson Collars	Pears' Soap
Elgin Watches	Pittsburgh Stogies
Edison Phonograph	Pond's Extract
Felt & Tarrant Comptometer	Postum Cereal
Ferry's Seeds	Prudential Insurance Co.
Franco American Soup	Quaker Oats

handbills, and newspaper advertisements. In London in about 1472 the first printed advertisement in English, tacked on church doors, announced a prayerbook for sale. The first newspaper advertisement appeared on the back of a London newspaper in 1650 offering a reward for the return of 12 stolen horses. Later, ads appeared for coffee, chocolate, tea, real estate, and medicines as well as "personal ads." The advertising was directed to a limited number of people who were customers of coffee houses where the newspapers were read. Periodical advertising was dealt a blow in England in 1712 when the government imposed a tax on newspapers in order to silence their criticisms. Eventually, the tax was abolished and newspapers flourished.

Another major technological breakthrough was the invention of photography in the late 1880s. Before this time products in printed advertisements could be illustrated only by drawings. As photography improved, newspapers and magazines used it more and more. Photography added credibility to advertising because it showed products as they are, rather than as visualized by an artist.

Figure 1–13 The 100 leading national advertisers in the United States
(total ad dollars in millions, 1980)

1	Procter & Gamble Co.	$649.6	51	Kellogg Co.	$95.7
2	Sears, Roebuck & Co.	599.6	52	Sterling Drug Co.	89.6
3	General Foods Corp.	410.0	53	Trans World Corp.	89.0
4	Philip Morris Inc.	364.6	54	Toyota Motor Sales U.S.A.	87.6
5	K mart Corp.	319.3	55	Mattel Inc.	87.1
6	General Motors Corp.	316.0	56	American Brands	85.6
7	R. J. Reynolds Industries	298.5	57	Eastman Kodak Co.	83.9
8	Ford Motor Co.	280.0	58	Mars Inc.	83.7
9	American Telephone & Telegraph	259.2	59	Warner Communications	82.3
10	Warner-Lambert Co.	235.2	60	Nestle Enterprises	82.0
11	Gulf & Western Industries	233.8	61	H. J. Heinz Co.	81.9
12	PepsiCo Inc.	233.4	62	SmithKline Corp.	81.4
13	Colgate-Palmolive Co.	225.0	63	CPC International	77.9
14	McDonald's Corp.	207.0	64	Clorox Co.	74.6
15	Ralston Purina Co.	206.8	65	Union Carbide Corp.	74.3
16	American Home Products	197.0	66	MCA Inc.	74.0
17	Bristol-Myers Co.	196.3	67	Miles Laboratories	73.0
18	Mobil Corp.	194.8	68	Volkswagen of America	70.0
19	Esmark Inc.	189.9	69	Nissan Motor Corp.	69.9
20	Coca-Cola Co.	184.2	70	Squibb Corp.	69.0
21	Anheuser-Busch	181.3	71	Jos. Schlitz Brewing Co.	66.4
22	Johnson & Johnson	177.0	72	Brown-Forman Distillers Co.	65.0
23	Beatrice Foods Co.	175.0	73	Greyhound Corp.	63.6
24	U.S. Government	173.0	74	American Express Co.	63.0
25	General Mills	171.1	75	UAL Inc.	60.2
26	Heublein Inc.	170.0	76	Campbell Soup Co.	58.0
27	RCA Corp.	164.3	77	Beecham Group Ltd.	56.6
28	Unilever U.S. Inc.	158.3	78	Kimberly-Clark	54.5
29	General Electric Co.	156.2	79	American Honda Motor Co.	54.3
30	Seagram Co. Ltd.	152.0	80	Eastern Air Lines	54.1
31	Gillette Co.	151.0	81	Wm. Wrigley Jr. Co.	51.8
32	Chrysler Corp.	150.3	82	Borden Co.	51.7
33	Nabisco Inc.	150.0	83	S. C. Johnson & Son	51.4
34	Consolidated Foods Corp.	149.2	84	MortonNorwich	50.2
35	Norton Simon Inc.	149.0	85	Pfizer Inc.	49.7
36	International Telephone & Telegraph Corp.	143.0	86	Polaroid Corp.	49.3
37	Time Inc.	141.9	87	Levi Strauss & Co.	48.7
38	Richardson-Vicks	134.0	88	ABC Inc.	46.8
39	Loews Corp.	132.8	89	American Airlines	46.3
40	CBS Inc.	132.4	90	American Motors Corp.	45.9
41	Chesebrough-Pond's	128.3	91	Columbia Pictures	43.0
42	Dart & Kraft	128.3	92	Standard Brands	42.1
43	American Cyanamid Co.	125.0	93	Noxell Corp.	41.3
44	Pillsbury Co.	124.0	93	Hershey Foods	41.3
45	J. C. Penney Co.	108.0	95	A. H. Robins Co.	41.1
46	Revlon Inc.	105.4	96	Delta Air Lines	38.7
47	Schering-Plough Corp.	100.0	97	Carnation	37.2
48	Quaker Oats Co.	99.7	98	Liggett Group	36.0
49	DuPont	98.3	99	Jeffrey Martin Inc.	35.7
50	B.A.T. Industries Ltd.	95.8	100	Mazda Motors of America	31.1

Note: The 100 largest national advertisers spent $13 billion in 1980. That amounts to over 23.8 percent of the total measured U.S. advertising expenditures that year.

Early U.S. advertising

The first newspaper advertisements in the American colonies appeared in the *Boston Newsletter* in 1704. Later Benjamin Franklin made advertisements more readable by using large headlines and by surrounding the advertisements with considerable white space. He is credited with being the first American to use illustrations in advertisements.

The first advertising agency

Historians consider Volney B. Palmer, who started business in Philadelphia in 1841, to be the earliest advertising agent in the United States. He contracted for large volumes of advertising space at discount rates from newspapers and then resold this space to advertisers at a higher rate. The advertisers usually prepared the advertisements themselves. In 1890 N. W. Ayer & Son, another Philadelphia advertising organization, offered its services to advertisers. This company was the first advertising agency to operate as agencies do today—planning, creating, and executing complete advertising campaigns for clients in return for a commission paid by the media or for fees received from advertisers. Thus advertising in newspapers led to the emergence of space sellers, whose services were ultimately expanded and refined into the modern advertising agency of today.

Influence of the Industrial Revolution

The Industrial Revolution in the United States started in the early 1800s. This gave manufacturers the ability to mass produce goods with uniform quality for the first time. In order to mass produce, however, they needed mass consumption, which required vast numbers of people to purchase their products. They could no longer be content to sell only in their local area. Manufacturers soon realized the tremendous value of advertising as an aid in selling to the exciting frontier markets in the West as well as the growing industrial markets in the East.

First national advertising medium

The Civil War and the victory of the industrial North over the agricultural South spurred on the Industrial Revolution. In July 1844, the first magazine advertising had appeared in the *Southern Messenger,* edited for a short while by Edgar Allen Poe. Magazines were the first medium used by manufacturers to reach the mass market and to stimulate mass consumption. Magazines made possible national advertising and thus the sale of products nationwide.

Other important developments

Other developments during the 19th century directly affected the growth of advertising. The population was growing rapidly, which provided an increasingly large market for manufacturers. At the same time there was a substantial increase in the number of people who could read. The literacy rate was up to 90 percent by the late 1800s. This large reading public provided an audience that could understand advertising messages.

A nationwide railroad transportation system was developing, which quickly moved the United States into a period of spectacular growth. In 1896 the federal government inaugurated rural free delivery (RFD). Direct-mail advertising and mail-order selling flourished with mass production. Manufacturers had an ever-increasing variety of products for their catalogs. There was now a means of delivering to the public their advertising (via newspaper and magazines) as well as their goods.

The invention of important communications devices, including the telegraph, telephone, and typewriter as well as the phonograph and motion pictures, enabled people to communicate as never before. In short, advertising was growing with the country and helping establish its marketing system.

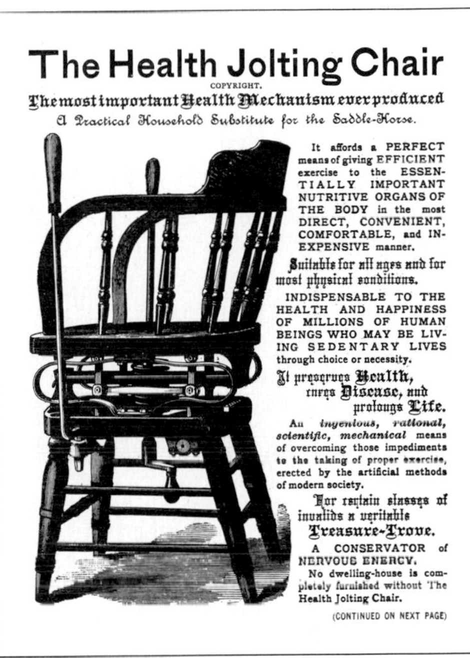

Figure 1–14 Advertisements for health gimmicks and patent medicines in weekly newspapers in the 1880s were typical of the era. They exemplified the attitude of manufacturers at that time known by the Latin expression *Caveat emptor* ("Let the buyer beware"). The result was the first consumer movement in this country leading to regulatory legislation. (See Chapter 2.)

Advertising enters the 20th century

In 1800 the United States was agricultural, but it ended the century as a great industrial nation. During the first two decades of the 1900s, advertising underwent an era of reexamination. Unsubstantiated advertising claims, which caused widespread resentment, resulted in a consumer revolt. The focal point of the attack was patent medicine advertising. Regulation began from within the advertising industry and from the government (Figure 1–14).

In the 1920s, after World War 1, the "era of salesmanship" had arrived and advertising became "salesmanship in print" (Figures 1–15 and 1–16). Full-color printing was used lavishly by magazine advertisers. Testimonial advertising by movie stars became popular.

On October 29, 1929, the stock market crashed, and advertising expenditures dropped dramatically. Because of an increasing amount of false and misleading advertising, several best-selling books exposed advertising as an unscrupulous exploiter of consumers. Thus the consumer movement took root and resulted in further government regulation.

Because of the sales resistance of consumers during the depression, advertising turned to research to regain effectiveness. A. C. Nielsen and George Gallup founded research organizations to delve into the minds of consumers.

Rise of broadcast advertising

A major, powerful new advertising medium, radio, started on November 2, 1920, in Pittsburgh, Pennsylvania. National advertisers used radio extensively because they could reach large, captive audiences that tuned into popular programs. At first advertising agencies produced radio shows. Radio became the primary means of mass communication. News direct from the scene and a whole new world of family entertainment became possible.

The most unusual expansion of any medium occurred after television was broadcast publicly in 1941. When World War II ended the use of television grew rapidly. Color TV was born in 1955. Today television is the second largest advertising medium in terms of total dollars spent by advertisers.

Postwar advertising

Since World War II the growth of both advertising and the money spent on it has been phenomenal. Postwar prosperity brought a boom of war babies eager to consume the products of the nation's manufacturers. As the war economy changed to a peacetime economy, the

Figure 1–15 If you ever wondered where the name "Palmolive" (of Colgate-Palmolive) came from, here's the answer. A 1922 Palmolive shampoo ad says results come from "palm and olive oils, the softening, soothing cleansers discovered 3,000 years ago in ancient Egypt." The company had not yet merged into Colgate-Palmolive.

manufacturers of war equipment reverted back to producing consumer products, offering greater luxury, greater style, and greater convenience through greater advertising.

The late 40s and early 50s were marked by a consumptionist society vigorously chasing up the social ladder in an effort to keep up with the Joneses. Ads of this era stressed social acceptance, style, luxury, and success until there were so many imitations that consumers couldn't take any more (Figure 1–17).

"Look... they gave me a map!"
GULF REFINING COMPANY

Figure 1–16 In 1934, Gulf was stressing its service of pioneering free road maps. Today many oil companies spend more on corporate advertising, telling people how they protect the environment or develop new energy resources, than on product advertising.

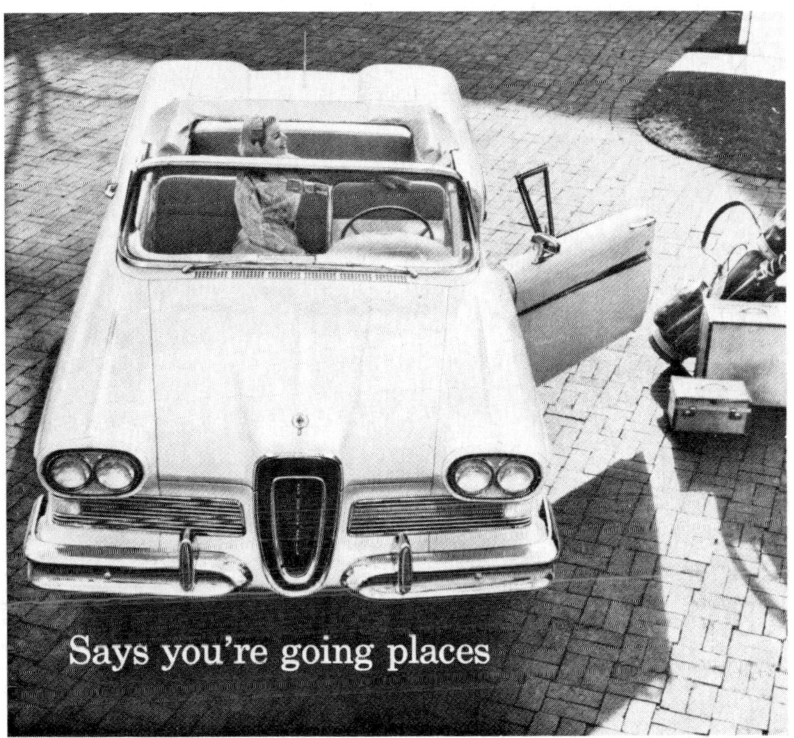

Slide onto the special seat reserved for the Edsel driver and glance out over that long, powerful hood. You get the feeling: *this is the way to look at the world.*

Just touch a Teletouch Drive button on the steering-wheel hub. The Edsel glides forward, gaining momentum instantly from America's most advanced engine. And you get the feeling: *this is the way to travel.*

You're right. Only Edsel offers the originality, power and handling ease that clearly says you're going places.

Yet there's less than fifty dollars difference between Edsel and V-8's in the Low-Priced Three.*

So put away all your old ideas about cars and see your Edsel Dealer for a demonstration drive.

Above: Edsel Citation Convertible. Engine: the E-475, with 10.5 to one compression ratio, 345 horsepower, 475 ft.-lb. torque. Transmission: Automatic with Teletouch Drive. Brakes: Self-adjusting.

**Based on comparisons of manufacturers' suggested retail delivered prices.*

EDSEL DIVISION · FORD MOTOR COMPANY

The EDSEL LOOK is here to stay—and 1959 cars will prove it!

1958 **EDSEL**

Figure 1–17 Ford Motor Company told us hopefully that the Edsel look was here to stay. They were wrong. To the tune of $350 million, it was perhaps the largest single product marketing disaster in U.S. history.

The transition to the image era of the 60s, therefore, was only natural. The Marlboro man created a macho image for male smokers, and Marlboro soared to the top of the sales charts, where it has stayed for over 20 years (Figure 1–18). Cadillac became the *Cadillac* of luxury and the bourgeois symbol of success surpassed only by the aristocratic snootiness of Rolls Royce.

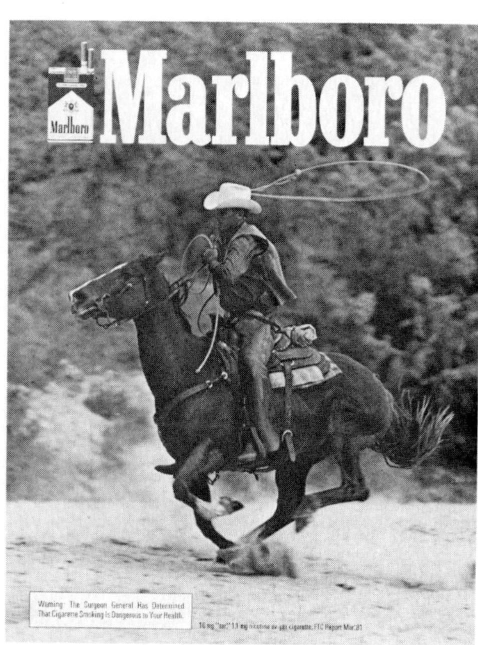

Figure 1–18 Until 1954 Marlboro had been a pink-tipped "women's" cigarette with sales to a restricted market. The ad claim had been "Mild as May," and the name Marlboro was written in delicate script. The restaged product included a flip-top box and a series of ads featuring rugged men, each with a tattoo on the back of his hand. Eventually the campaign settled on the now-famous cowboy theme.

The positioning era

As Jack Trout and Al Ries pointed out in their famous treatise on this subject, just as the me-too (imitative) products of the 50s killed the product era, the me-too images of the 60s killed the image era.

The 70s saw a new kind of advertising strategy, where the competitor's strengths became as important as the advertiser's. This was called the *positioning era,* and Trout and Ries were its greatest advocates. Acknowledging the importance of product features and image, they insisted that what was really important was how the product was ranked in the consumer's mind against the competition.

The most famous ads of the positioning era were Volkswagen ("Think small"), Avis ("We're only no. 2"), and 7-Up ("The un-cola"). But many other manufacturers tried it with great success, including Lincoln Continental ("Beats the other make of luxury car again"), Honeywell ("The other computer company"), and Vaseline (Intensive Care Skin Lotion) (Figure 1–19). Trout and Ries also pointed to product disappointments of the period and suggested that poor positioning was the reason; these included NCR ("The computer company"), Life Savers (Life Saver Gum), and Miles Laboratories (Alka Seltzer Plus).

The me decade

Trout and Ries did not address the consumer movement, which had received its greatest impetus from the disillusioning setbacks of the Vietnam War, the Watergate scandals, and the sudden shortage of vital natural resources. These fostered cynicism and distrust of the establishment and everything traditional, and they gave rise to a paradoxical quasi-morality that defended individual irresponsibility in the name of self-fulfillment and attacked corporate self-fullfillment in the name of social accountability.

By the beginning of the 80s Americans had already witnessed an avalanche of ads, especially in the toiletry and cosmetics industries, stressing the correctness of self-fulfillment to the me generation ("Kinda young. Kinda now. Charlie. Kinda free. Kinda wow. Charlie"). At the same time the nation's largest industrial concerns were spending millions on corporate advertising to extol their own virtuosity at cleaning up after themselves and otherwise protecting the world we live in (Figure 1–20). Likewise a new phenomenon called *demarketing* had appeared, as producers of energy and energy-consuming goods used marketing and advertising techniques to slow the demand for their products (Figure 1–21). Their strategy was to maintain the goodwill of their customers even though the demands of their customers could not be met.

Advertising today

This brief history shows that advertising reflects the world we live in. The last 20 years have seen an explosion in technology, which will probably more than double again in the next 20 years. As technology changes our lives, so will the actions and attitudes of special-interest groups from big business to big labor, from pro-growth advocates to

© VOLKSWAGEN OF AMERICA, INC.
Think small.
Our little car isn't so much of a novelty any more.
A couple of dozen college kids don't try to squeeze inside it.
The guy at the gas station doesn't ask where the gas goes.
Nobody even stares at our shape.
In fact, some people who drive our little flivver don't even think that about 27 miles to the gallon is going any great guns.
Or using five pints of oil instead of five quarts.
Or never needing anti-freeze.
Or racking up about 40,000 miles on a set of tires.
That's because once you get used to some of our economies, you don't even think about them any more.
Except when you squeeze into a small parking spot.
Or renew your small insurance. Or pay a small repair bill. Or trade in your old VW for a new one.
Think it over.

Figure 1–19 Jack Trout and Al Ries called this "probably the most famous ad of the 60s." In their view it helped usher in the positioning era of the 70s. By opting for the "small" position, Volkswagen assumed a leadership rank that took many years and millions of competitors' dollars to overcome.

environmentalists, from big religion to big cults. And fighting progress all the way, as some of them will, they will all use the tools of progress to effect their aims. One of these will be advertising and the most modern advertising media yet to be conceived.

Growth and status of international advertising

As U.S. companies entered world markets after World War II, consumption of American products grew tremendously. Today U.S. advertising expenditures account for over 50 percent of the world total. However, in the last 15 years expenditures by other countries have increased even more rapidly than American expenditures due to their own improved economic conditions and their desire to grow outward.

As national economies have expanded and personal incomes have increased, so has the use of advertising. In Korea, for example, exports have increased from $500,000 in 1955 to over $12 billion in 1980. The average annual wage is now $958 per year. The result is that

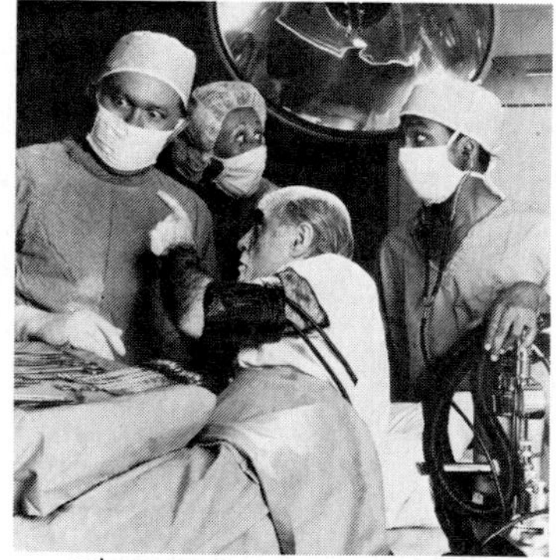

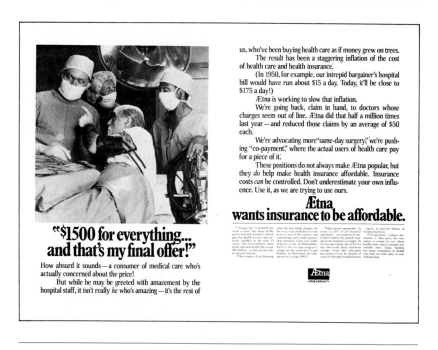

Figure 1–20 *Outrageous* was the term first used to describe Aetna's accountability campaign against soaring medical costs and insurance premiums. As the nation's leader in multiple-line insurance (life, group, and casualty), Aetna believed it was in its own interest to speak up on behalf of the consumer. Aetna was the first to make a large commitment to advertising its social responsibility, but other insurance companies rapidly followed suit. Aetna was also one of the first to use facts and figures in citation style to back up all claims made in their copy.

over 70 percent of households in Seoul now have television sets that carry commercial advertising.

For many years J. Walter Thompson was unchallenged as the largest agency in the world. But as the economies of previously underdeveloped countries have boomed, so has competition. By 1980 Dentsu Advertising, based in Tokyo, was the largest advertising agency in the world, with billings of over $2.5 billion.

Status of international advertising

Advertising in one form or another is practiced in every country of the world. Actual figures are not available, but recent estimates of worldwide advertising expenditures outside the United States exceed $40 billion per year. The emphasis placed on advertising in individual countries, though, depends on their level of development and the national attitude toward promotion. Figure 1–22 shows the per capita advertising expenditures in various countries. From this chart we can see that, generally, in those countries where personal income is higher, so are the levels of advertising expenditures. Moreover, advertising expenditures rise faster than do income levels. However, a saturation point seems to be reached when advertising expenditures approach 3 percent of average national income; at that point they tend to plateau.

It is interesting to note the major deviations from this pattern—namely, in France and Germany. This is probably caused by the aversion to promotion in some countries. In many societies "selling" has a very low status and is associated with hawkers in the streets. Also, in countries where there is no economic development, there is little purpose for advertising. Normally, though, as product lines and markets expand, distribution techniques become more complex and personal selling costs increase. Thus, the need for advertising grows, and that explains the general trend shown in Figure 1–22.

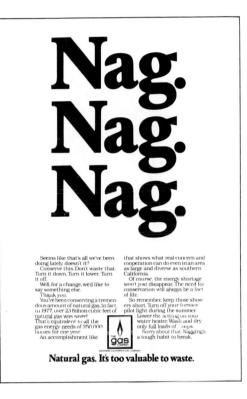

Figure 1–21 *Demarketing* was a new term in the 70s used to describe the efforts by utility companies and other energy providers to slow the demand for their limited products. The Southern California Gas Company won numerous advertising awards for its creativity in encouraging conservation.

Changing attitudes toward advertising

Today advertising is used worldwide to sell ideas, policies, and attitudes as well as products. Even the socialist countries, which once condemned advertising as an evil of capitalism and still frequently adhere to their theories of advertising as economic waste, are beginning to admit the benefits of advertising in developing their planned economies. Most are even encouraging advertising in their trade and technical journals.

Certainly one effect of international advertising has been the shrinking of the world. And one benefit has been increased understanding among people as foreign products, values, and ideas have been introduced to new markets around the world. The worldwide energy shortages of 1974 and 1979 caused a flurry of advertising campaigns by governments and private enterprises in every country, all working together to try to solve a single international problem.

Figure 1–22 Global ad expenditures

Country	Total (in millions)	Per capita*
Western Europe		
Switzerland	702	109.59
Denmark	507	99.41
Sweden	753	91.81
Finland	386	82.19
Netherlands	1,122	81.28
Norway	291	72.73
Austria	421	56.13
West Germany	2,986	48.56
France	2,502	47.31
United Kingdom	2,250	40.25
Spain	1,322	36.73
Iceland	—	35.50
Belgium	294	29.73
Luxembourg	11	28.25
Ireland	60	18.69
Italy	601	10.69
Malta	3	8.00
Portugal	69	7.24
Greece	62	6.70
Turkey	254	6.32
Africa		
South Africa	342	13.11
Libya	—	4.36
Rhodesia	—	2.79
Zambia	11	2.24
Mauritius	2	1.89
Egypt	58	1.52
Sudan	—	0.95
Kenya	13	0.93
Nigeria	53	0.82
Morocco	—	0.71
Liberia	1	0.39
Ghana	3	0.25
Ethiopia	1	0.03
Middle East		
Bahrain	12	41.00
Kuwait	18	17.70
Israel	58	16.74
Lebanon	35	11.63
Saudi Arabia	89	9.63
Syria	21	2.72
Jordan	—	2.46
Iraq	—	1.70
UAE	—	—
North America		
United States	54,600	156.69
Canada	2,378	103.40

Country	Total (in millions)	Per capita*
South Asia		
Iran	54	1.58
Sri Lanka	5	0.33
India	138	0.23
Pakistan	15	0.20
Bangladesh	—	0.13
Nepal	1	0.05
Afghanistan	—	—
Bhutan	—	—
Southeast Asia		
Singapore	51	22.04
Hong Kong	88	20.00
Taiwan	169	10.36
Malaysia	42	3.42
Thailand	131	3.04
Philippines	59	1.35
Indonesia	64	0.45
Australasia		
Australia	1,116	82.06
New Zealand	122	39.52
South America		
Venezuela	240	19.36
Argentina	432	16.80
Brazil	1,260	11.54
Peru	95	5.89
Chile	57	5.44
Uruguay	—	5.07
Ecuador	35	4.78
Colombia	93	3.79
Surinam	2	3.75
Bolivia	—	1.79
Paraguay	—	1.30
Central America		
Bermuda	7	110.00
Puerto Rico	96	30.09
Jamaica	36	17.24
Costa Rica	20	9.95
Trinidad & Tobago	11	9.91
Mexico	480	7.71
Panama	13	7.47
Dominican Republic	31	6.38
Nicaragua	—	2.50
Guatemala	—	1.95
El Salvador	—	1.20
Honduras	—	1.03
Northeast Asia		
Japan	4,856	43.05
Korea	187	5.21

A.

Figure 1–23 A. Coca-Cola was already in wide distribution "at all (soda) fountains," before the Ford name became a household word. In those days only the wealthy could afford an automobile, and it was still considered quite avant-garde. Thus, it was an attractive and interesting association for Coke illustrated in this 1905 advertisement.

B.

Figure 1–23 B. With the "charm of purity," a single Coke, one of 6,000,000 per day, was served by a white uniformed bellhop in this classic 1925 advertisement.

C.

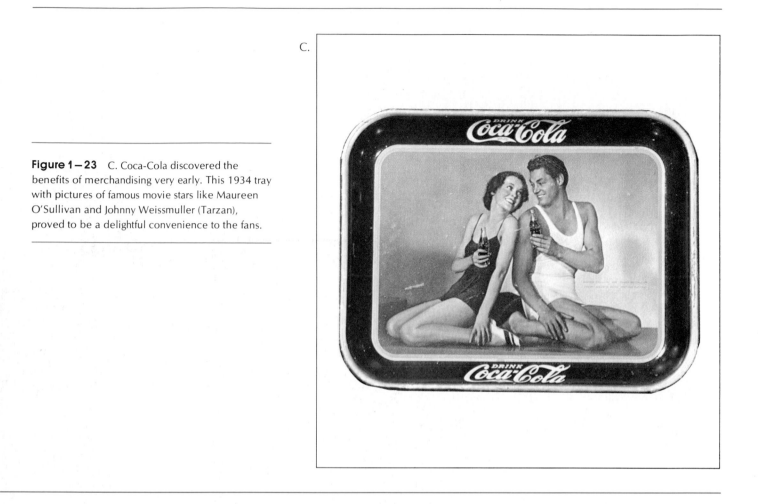

Figure 1—23 C. Coca-Cola discovered the benefits of merchandising very early. This 1934 tray with pictures of famous movie stars like Maureen O'Sullivan and Johnny Weissmuller (Tarzan), proved to be a delightful convenience to the fans.

D.

Figure 1—23 D. While many ads of the 30s showcased movie stars, later advertising such as this 1943 ad reflected World War II. At the same time Coke followed the troops with a total of 64 bottling plants shipped abroad during the war and set up as close as possible to combat areas in North Africa, Europe, and the Pacific. An order from Coca-Cola's president gave the assurance that "every man in uniform gets a bottle of Coke for 5¢ wherever he is and whatever it costs the company."

E.

Figure 1–23 E. As Coca-Cola spread around the world, ads and news coverage in major American magazines continued to echo the themes of refreshment and availability. This *Time* magazine cover which appeared in the 1950s describes Coke as the world's "friend."

Figure 1–23 F. A product such as Coca-Cola doesn't change; society, though, is constantly changing. Consequently, the advertising must change to reflect current lifestyles. An indication of Coke's success as the world's number one consumer product was the flashing sign at Times Square that greeted the Apollo astronauts returning from their moonflight: "Welcome Back to Earth, Home of Coca-Cola."

I'd like to teach the world to sing in perfect harmony. I'd like to buy the world a Coke and keep it company.

F.

G.

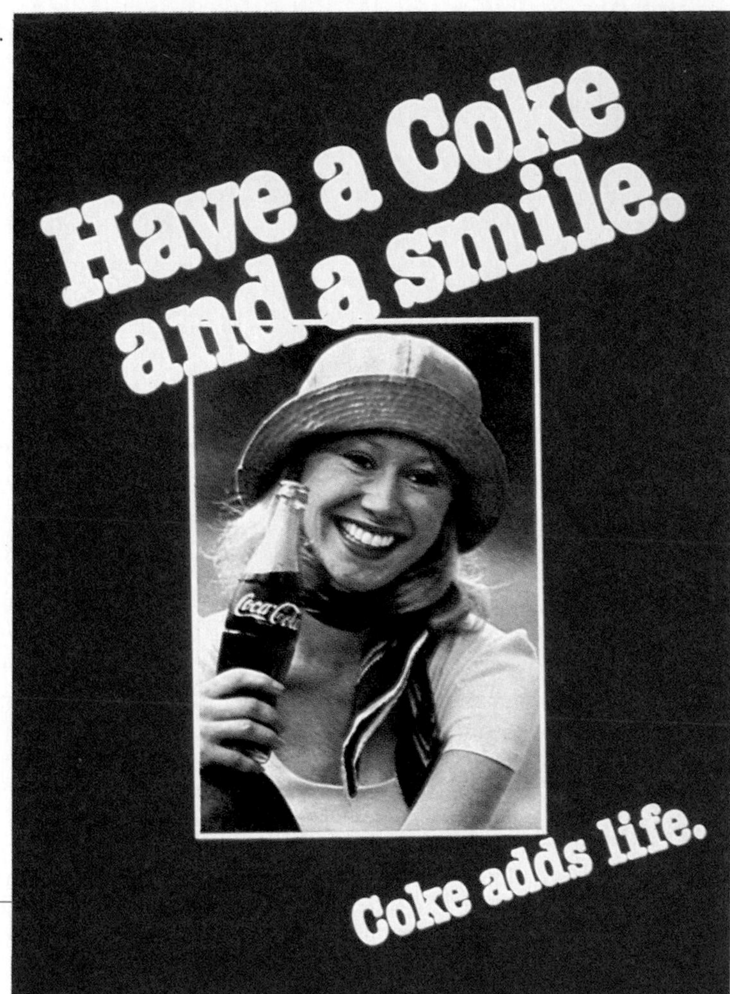

Figure 1–23 G. The campaign of the 1980s captures the warm moments of everyday life with the "Have a Coke and a Smile" series.

H.

Figure 1–23 H. Trademarks for Coca-Cola used around the world. Notice the similarities of letterforms, color, and style even when different alphabets are used. The Coca-Cola Company has subscribed to a unified worldwide advertising philosophy referred to as: "one sight, one sound, one sell."

As technology progresses, thereby improving communications in the less developed areas of the world, we anticipate that international advertising will continue to flourish. As a creative director for Ogilvy & Mather, Paris, has said, "Nous n'avons pas mal de budgets." Loosely translated, "We're not hurting for business."

The economic impact of advertising

Earlier in this chapter we mentioned that one function of advertising is an economic one. By making people aware of new products and services, or by reminding people to repurchase existing products, advertising promotes sales and thus commerce.

The billiard ball principle

The moment a company begins to advertise, like the opening shot in pool or billiards, a chain reaction of economic events takes place. Usually the extent of this chain reaction is impossible to measure. And, because it inevitably occurs at the same time as a host of other economic events, even the direction of the chain reaction is often in dispute.

For example, does advertising promote competition or discourage it? Does advertising raise or lower prices? What is the effect of advertising on the total demand for a product category? Does advertising affect consumer choice by widening it or narrowing it? How does advertising influence the business cycle? These are just some of the many questions frequently asked (and seldom resolved) that relate to the chain of economic events caused by advertising. The discussion of these questions in this section should give deeper insight into the overall economic impact of advertising.

Microeconomic impact of advertising

What happened when Dr. Pemberton ran that first advertisement for his new soft drink back in 1886? Perhaps by focusing on this tiny microscopic event we can understand some broader concepts about the economic impact of advertising.

Impact on the product and medium

First, there was an impact on the product itself. Some people were made aware of something new at Jacob's Pharmacy, and they decided to try the new drink the next time they were there. Others might have forgotten about the ad but, when told at the pharmacy about the new drink, may have thought, "Oh, yes, I've heard about that." Others may have been interested only in selling the new drink:

"What does Jacob's have that we don't have?" In all cases the initial impact on the product is sales, or at least a new market attitude that did not exist prior to the advertisement, with the accompanying additional sales.

There is also an economic impact on the medium that carries the advertisement for the product—in this case the newspaper. Pemberton may have spent only $10 on his advertisement, but that was $10 the *Atlanta Journal* did not have before. That $10, mixed with the thousands of dollars from other advertisers, paid for the salaries, paper, and ink used by the newspaper that month. In short, the advertisers' dollars enable the free press to continue operating.

Impact on the company

The second step in the chain reaction might be the impact on the company that advertises the product. Pemberton was able to sell the stock in his company because investors were able to see sales occurring. As he advertised more and sold more, the company's stock became more valuable. At the same time, by advertising the availability of this new product, Jacob's Pharmacy was able to attract new customers. This might have translated into increased sales of other products in the store, increased salaries for employees, and increased profits for the company.

Impact on competitors

Next is the impact on competitors. Other soft drink companies, seeing the advertisement for Coca-Cola, might have felt threatened by this newcomer. Their reaction might have been to lower their prices, to change their product, to advertise more, or to do nothing and just watch. In reality, as Coca-Cola achieved more and more success, imitators appeared on the scene. This spurred Coca-Cola to concentrate on standardizing the quality of its prooduct and to use more advertising designed to create brand loyalty.

Impact on customers

As competitors are influenced, so is the community of consumers in which the advertising takes place. Before Coca-Cola was advertised, consumers were limited in their choice to whatever soft drinks were currently available. By advertising Coke, Pemberton created wider consumer choice. And, as imitators arrived, there was even greater consumer choice.

Impact on the business community

Finally, advertising has an impact on the general business environment and on the business cycle. In a recent annual report, the Coca-Cola Company pointed out the effect on the local business environment of building a new bottling plant in some less developed countries:

> . . . setting up a bottling plant means virtually creating a system of local suppliers—putting into business everything from con-

> struction firms to build the plant to truck service garages to glass manufacturing plants. Mechanics and salesmen must be trained, and in many cases local craftsmen must be recruited to set up plants to make cases for bottles.
>
> A glass plant set in motion to produce bottles for Coca-Cola may also eventually produce bottles for milk, medicine and many other products that make contributions to the local economy.

On this microeconomic level, we can readily see the results of advertising and the freedom to advertise. For Coca-Cola to make such a capital investment in a new area, there must be a promise of potential profits. This is possible, of course, only if the company has the freedom to advertise its product after the new bottling plant is built and operating.

How would you apply the principles discussed above to the situation of a new shopping center opening and beginning to advertise in your area?

Macroeconomic view of advertising

Looking at the economic impact of advertising by one firm as we have just done gives us some simple answers to the complex questions raised earlier. But let's see if these answers are realistic in the larger world of national and international economics.

Importance of mass distribution

Most economists agree that mass production has been a great stimulus to the success of our free enterprise system. Mass production has been credited with making tremendous selection alternatives available to American consumers, with maintaining low prices for most consumer goods, and with making possible the highest standard of living in the world.

However, the success of mass production is dependent on a system of mass distribution. It requires a huge network of warehouses, transportation facilities, wholesalers, distributors, dealers, packaging plants, advertising media, salespersons, clerks, and stores to deliver the low-priced, mass-produced goods from the manufacturer to the consumer. It is this mass distribution system, which includes promotional activities like advertising, that has drawn the most fire from critical groups of consumers, legislators, and economists. The dirty words so often spoken are "middlemen's profits" which convey the implication of overpriced goods. Of course, the most conspicuous activity in the mass distribution system is advertising, and that visibility alone makes advertising a likely target for criticism.

Thus, while most people concede that advertising helps the individual firm, there is great disagreement about the benefits of advertising to the economy as a whole. The questions raised earlier, therefore, should be discussed from a macroeconomic point of view.

Effect of advertising on competition

The criticism is often heard that small businesses can't possibly compete with the huge advertising budgets of big businesses. A new automobile manufacturer could never compete, for instance, because the big-four American auto companies with their massive network of advertising have a monopolistic stranglehold on the consumer. Or the small beer companies have been driven out of business by the big breweries with their huge advertising expenditures.

The tune is familiar. Small is good; big is bad. And the consumer suffers at the hands of big business because the big companies' advertising kills the small companies. There is no doubt some truth to these criticisms.

For example, one of the most highly advertised products is beer. And the number of breweries has indeed been declining for more than a generation. It may be that intense competition tends to reduce the number of businesses in an industry, but those that remain compete vigorously for consumer patronage. One must also wonder whether firms that were eliminated through competition were those that served the consumers least effectively.

It is true, in industries characterized by heavy advertising, that advertising may act as a barrier to market entry by new competitors. However, the necessity for heavy spending on plants and machinery is also a barrier to entry and usually a far more significant one than marketing costs. This is certainly borne out by the automobile industry. There are only four auto manufacturers in the United States, but the number of automobiles successfully marketed here by foreign manufacturers has steadily increased since 1950. The barrier to entry, therefore, has *not* been marketing costs but rather manufacturing costs.

Economists such as Galbraith and Samuelson have held that advertising creates industrial concentration. They point to the fact that those companies that dominate particular industries invariably have the largest advertising budgets. We are faced, though, with the question of which came first, the chicken or the egg? Studies by Aaker and Myers to discover the relationship of advertising expenditures and industrial concentration concluded that "there is a positive relationship, but it is weaker than might be expected."[3]

Statements that attribute such great power to advertising have to be considered overly simplistic since they fail to admit the importance of other significant influences such as product quality, price, convenience, and customer satisfaction. Hershey chocolate candy bars, for instance, achieved and maintained market dominance for many years before spending any money on advertising.

Competition is highly valued in our economic system. As we shall discuss in Chapter 2, we have many laws and regulations designed to preserve it when it best serves the public interest. When competition would obviously be wasteful—two electric, gas, telephone, or water utilities serving the same people—regulated monopolies are permitted.

Businesses compete in many ways—for example, for personnel, plant and distribution locations, materials, and customers. The most obvious and most public form of competition is advertising. But does intensely competitive advertising actually result in increased or decreased competition? As we have seen, this is a tangled question with no simple answer.

Competition occurs not only among companies in the same industry but also among companies in all industries. An auto manufacturer is obviously competing with other auto makers for consumer patronage. But the firm is also competing for the consumer dollar with companies that market boats, air travel, new homes, and other products. As the number and variety of products increase, interindustry competition also increases.

Moreover, no advertiser is large enough to dominate the whole country geographically. Regional brands of beer outsell national brands in many areas. Local oil companies compete very successfully with national oil companies on the local level. And nonadvertised store brands of food compete with nationally advertised brands on the very same shelves (Figure 1–24).

Therefore, in some cases, heavy advertising actually encourages competition. In others, it discourages it.

"Our industrial concentration strategy seems to be working, Mr. Ford. I recommend we increase the Edsel advertising budget."

Effect of advertising on the value of products

Why do most people prefer Coca-Cola to some other cola? Nationally, many more Cokes are sold, for instance, than Pepsis. Similarly, why do more women prefer Chanel No. 5 to some other unadvertised, inexpensive perfume? Is it because the advertised products are better products? Probably not.

Dr. Ernest Dichter, a psychologist known as the father of motivational research, has supported the view that the image of a product, which is produced partially by advertising and promotion, is an inherent feature of the product itself. This image can add value to a product, making it more desirable to the consumer.

This fact was borne out in a famous court case between the Federal Trade Commission (FTC) and the Borden Company in the 1960s. The FTC accused Borden of selling milk of "physically identical and equal quality" at different prices. The Borden Company justified the price differences by pointing out that the higher priced milk was sold under a nationally branded label and the rest was sold under private labels. In 1967 the U.S. Circuit Court of Appeals issued a decision saying, in effect, that the price differential represented the added value that had been given to the branded product through extensive advertising and promotion.[4]

Advertising can show consumers new uses for products. Arm & Hammer Baking Soda has done this effectively. Television commercials demonstrating its air-purifying qualities in refrigerators and its water-purifying qualities in swimming pools have added a new dimension to an old product.

Advertising can add value to a product in the consumer's mind. For example, what do you think most people would prefer: to buy an unadvertised brand of denim pants or Levi's?

Advertising can also add an economic value to goods and services. Brand quality can produce higher price levels for manufacturers. If all aspirin is the same, why do people pay more for Bayer than for an unadvertised house brand (Figure 1–25)?

One advantage of our free market system is that consumers can choose the values they want in the products they buy. If price is important, for example, they can buy an inexpensive economy car. If image and luxury are more important, they can buy a fancy sedan or a racy sports car. Many of our wants are emotional, social, or psychological rather than functional. Advertising allows us, as free people, the opportunity to satisfy those wants.

Effect of advertising on prices

If advertising adds value to products, then it follows that advertising also adds costs. Right? And if companies would stop all that expensive advertising, then products would cost less. Right? Wrong.

What a way to run a "monopoly!"

COLONIAL MINUTEMAN

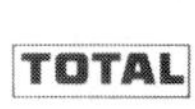

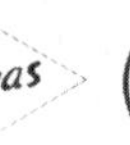

You're looking at some of the brands and names of companies that sell gasoline. Some people say oil companies are a monopoly. If so, it's the world's most inept "monopoly."

This "monopoly" is so inept that it offers the world's richest country some of the world's most inexpensive gasoline.

This "monopoly" is so inept that it lets everybody and his brother horn in on the action. Did you know that of the thousands of American oil companies, none has larger than an 8.5% share of the national gasoline market?

In fact, this "monopoly" is so inept that you probably wouldn't recognize that it is a monopoly because it looks so much like a competitive marketing system.

People who call us a monopoly obviously don't know what they're talking about.

union 76
Union Oil Company of California

Figure 1–24 During the two major energy crises of the 70s, the oil companies were frequently accused of "rigging" the crisis for monopolistic purposes. In one of the most effective issue-ads of the time, Union Oil pointed out the ineptitude of this "monopoly," which has given "the world's richest country some of the world's most inexpensive gasoline" and has let thousands of companies "horn in on the action" so that none has larger than an 8.5 percent share of the national gasoline market.

As we have just shown, there is no question that in some cases advertised products cost more than unadvertised products. However, there are probably just as many cases where the opposite is true. Timex watches, which are heavily advertised, cost less than most less advertised brands.

For years Tylenol was not advertised. As an over-the-counter pain reliever, it was sold as a substitute for people who could not tolerate the side effects of aspirin. It sold for $2.85 per 100 tablets. Datril was then introduced and advertised as having an identical formula with identical results. It was offered at $1.85 for 100 tablets. Tylenol immediately dropped its price and began to advertise. For some time thereafter the two engaged in heavy, competitive promotion, and prices continued to fall (Figure 1–26).

In recent years the Federal Trade Commission and the Supreme

Figure 1–25 As prices have climbed steadily upward, many consumers have switched to unadvertised house brands to save money. Many others, though, prefer the convenience and confidence of buying nationally advertised brands. One of the benefits of our system is this freedom of choice.

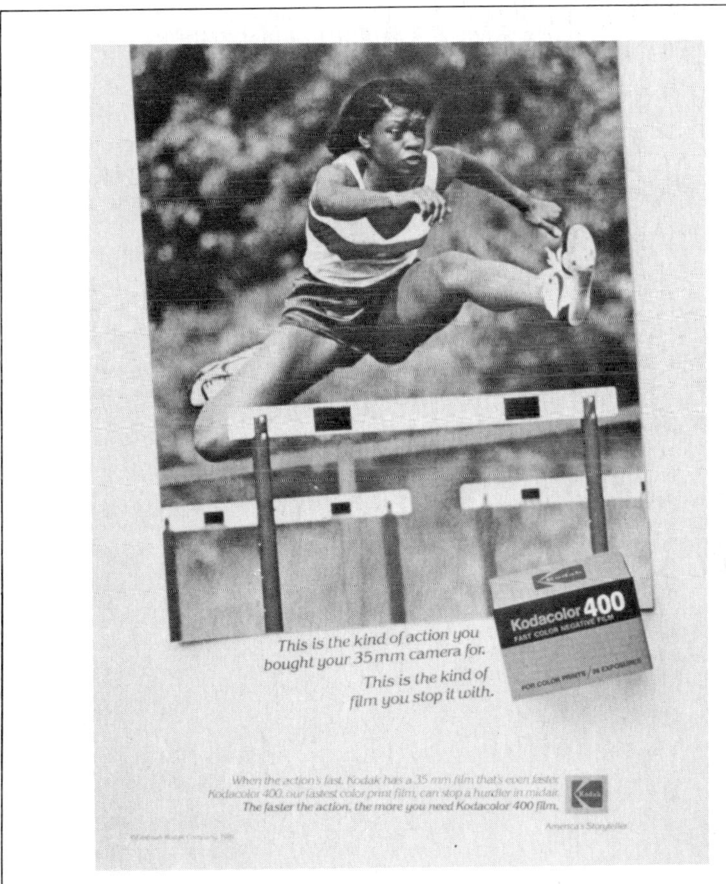

Figure 1–26 Eastman Kodak spent a phenomenal $84 million in 1980 advertising its photographic equipment and supplies. This accounts for only .9 percent of Kodak's $10 billion of sales. For every dollar spent on Kodak products, less than 1¢ pays for advertising costs. In this case, advertising probably plays a very constructive role in keeping prices down.

Court have ruled that professional people such as attorneys must be allowed to advertise because advertising has the competitive effect of keeping prices down. Thus any broad, sweeping statements about the positive or negative effects of advertising on prices is likely to be too simplistic. There are several important points to understand, though, about the relationship of advertising and prices:

1. As one of the many costs of doing business, advertising is indeed paid for by the consumer who buys the product. The amount spent on advertising, though, is usually very small compared with total sales. Nevertheless, it may increase the cost of some products.

2. As pointed out earlier, advertising is just one element of the mass distribution system. This system enables many manufacturers to engage in mass production. The long, uninterrupted runs used in mass production lower the unit cost of products. These economies of scale can be passed on to consumers in the form of lower prices. Thus overall prices may be made lower through the use of advertising.

3. Many industries, like agriculture, utilities, and oil, have had their prices so heavily regulated by the government that advertising has had no effect on them whatsoever.

4. Our economic system is complex and dynamic. We have a whole dictionary full of different market structures, including pure competition, pure monopoly, monopolistic competition, monopsony, discriminating monopoly, bilateral monopoly, and oligopoly. Marketing and advertising practices differ widely from one market structure to another. Thus the impact of advertising on prices also varies.

5. Price competition is perhaps most evident in retailing. However, even though prices are featured in many advertisements, there is less price competition than most laypeople realize. Price is only one basis for competition. In retailing, store location, service, size of selection, reputation, clientele, and image are also very important. In manufacturing, the attempt is to market products that are different from those of competing firms. As a result, the main subject of competition and advertising is *product differentiation*—"Why our product is superior"—not price. In price competition advertising forces prices down; in nonprice competition advertising tends to hold prices up.

Effect of advertising on consumer demand

Critics of advertising sometimes accuse marketers of foisting unwanted products on the public—of creating consumer demand where none existed before—through massive advertising expenditures. The question of what effect advertising has on total consumer demand is extremely complex. Economists and advertising professionals both have puzzled over this relationship. Numerous studies have produced general agreement that promotional activity has some effect on aggregate consumption but no agreement as to the extent. More significant, though, has been the effect of numerous other social and economic forces. These include great improvements in technology, education of the masses, increases in population and per capita income, and revolutionary changes in lifestyle. These have had a dynamic impact on the demand for different products.

For example, the demand for automobiles, mopeds, televisions, instant foods, and pocket calculators has expanded at a tremendous rate thanks in part to advertising but especially to favorable market conditions. At the same time, advertising has been able to do little to slow the decline in popularity of such things as men's and women's hats, train travel, fur coats, and home permanents.

We might conclude, therefore, that advertising can help to get new products off the ground by stimulating total consumer demand for the product class. But in declining markets, the most advertising can hope to do is slow the rate of decline. Thus we can also conclude that in growing markets advertisers generally compete for shares of that growth. In declining markets they compete for one another's shares.

Effect of advertising on consumer choice

As we pointed out earlier, the greatest area of competition is product differentiation. Manufacturers are always looking for ways to make their products different, or at least seem different, to appeal to a greater number of consumers. As a result, we see an endless list of automobile models, sizes, colors, and features to attract the most discriminating buyers. Grocery shelves may carry 15 to 20 different brands of breakfast cereals—something for everybody.

The freedom to advertise has given manufacturers an incentive to create new brands and improve old ones. When one brand has reached a point of market dominance, smaller brands may disappear for a short time. But inevitably the moment a better product comes along and is advertised skillfully, the tables are suddenly turned and the dominant brand rapidly loses to the new, better product. Invariably, as Walter Taplin points out, the consumer is the master and "the producer and advertiser is the slave."[5]

Effect of advertising on the business cycle

The relationship between advertising and the gross national product (GNP) has been debated for years. Friends of advertising point with pride to the growth this century in GNP, disposable income (DI), and personal consumption expenditures (PCE). They boast that advertising has been the primary cause of all these blessings. Critical economists tend to see advertising as wasteful expenditures with little relationship to the overall business cycle.

Both sides make very strong points and back up their claims with numerous studies. The problem with most of these studies, however, is that there are so many uncontrollable social and economic factors that constantly push and pull on the economic system that studying the effects of one small element like advertising is nearly impossible. The results are always questionable.

The most positive study to date was conducted by Charles Y. Yang and published in 1964. He concluded that an increase of 1 percent in advertising expenditures over the rate of increase in the gross national product can produce an increase in consumption of 0.1 percent. Subsequent increases in investment and income are then generated, which finally result in $16 of increased income generated by each $1 of increased advertising expenditure.[6]

This, of course, assumes increases in GNP. What about when GNP decreases? And, if what he says is true, why would GNP ever decrease if all we have to do is spend more advertising dollars? Again, we're left with the chicken and egg syndrome.

Historically, when business cycles dip, advertising expenditures are the first items cut by worried executives. Numerous studies have proven that those businesses that cut their advertising expenses least during a recession inevitably fare better after the recession. But no study has ever shown that if everybody just kept advertising, the recessionary cycle would be turned around.

We must conclude, therefore, that when business cycles are up, advertising contributes to the increase. When business cycles are down, advertising may act as a stabilizing force but the extent is currently impossible to measure.

Economic impact of advertising in perspective

To individual businesses like Coca-Cola, Procter & Gamble, Sears, Roebuck, and the little appliance store on the corner, advertising pays more in results than it costs. If advertising did not pay, businesses and other institutions would not use it.

For the consumer, advertising costs less than most people believe. The various media that carry the advertisements we see are amazingly efficient. A bottle of Coke contains about a penny's worth of advertising. An automobile that costs $7,000 includes an advertising cost of less than $100.

To the economy as a whole the importance of advertising may best be demonstrated by the *abundance principle*. This states that in an economy that produces more goods and services than can be consumed, advertising serves two important purposes: (1) to keep consumers informed of their selection alternatives, and (2) to allow companies to compete more effectively for consumer dollars.

The American economy produces an enormous selection for consumers. There are more than 10,000 different items on the average supermarket shelf. Each of the four American automobile manufacturers markets dozens of models. Clothing and shelter alternatives are seemingly endless. In short, the American economy is characterized by many suppliers competing for the consumer dollar. This competition generally tends to produce more and better products at similar or lower prices.

As a competitive tool, advertising has stimulated this phenomenon. Moreover, because American consumers have more income to spend after their physical needs have been satisfied, advertising has also stimulated the innovation and sale of new products to satisfy the consumer's social and psychological needs.

However, no amount of advertising can achieve long-term acceptance for products that do not meet consumer approval. Less than a dozen of the 50 best-known automobile brands developed in this century are still with us despite major advertising expenditures. Only 2 of the nation's 10 largest industrial firms in 1900 remain in the top 10 today despite massive advertising.

As advertising has stimulated a healthy economy, it has also stimulated a financially healthy consumer who is more informed, better educated, and more demanding. One of these demands has been accountability by manufacturers and advertising. That has led to an unprecedented level of social and legal regulation (see Chapter 2).

Summary

Advertising is defined as nonpersonal communication of information, usually paid for and usually persuasive in nature, about products, services, or ideas by identified sponsors through various media.

As a marketing tool, advertising serves several functions:

1. To identify products and differentiate them.
2. To communicate information about the product.
3. To induce the trial of new products by new users and to suggest repurchasing by existing users.
4. To stimulate a product's distribution.
5. To increase product use.
6. To build brand preference and loyalty.

Aside from marketing, advertising may also serve a communication function, an education function, an economic function, and a social function.

There are many different types of advertising. It may be classified by target audience (e.g., consumer, industrial), by geography (local, international), by the medium (radio, television) used, and by its function or purpose (e.g., product advertising, noncommercial advertising, direct action advertising).

The history of advertising began in very early times when most people could not read or write. The post–World War II era has been marked by the growth of television advertising, intense marketing competition, and increased attempts to differentiate products through positioning strategies or other techniques.

Around the world, as national economies have expanded and personal incomes have increased, so has the use of advertising. Recent estimates of worldwide advertising expenditures outside the United States exceed $40 billion a year. International attitudes toward advertising have also changed. Today even socialist countries use advertising techniques in the development of their planned economies.

The economic impact of advertising can be likened to the opening shot in billiards—a chain reaction that affects the company that advertises as well as its competitors, customers, and the business community.

On a broader scale advertising is often considered the trigger on America's mass distribution system that enables manufacturers to produce the products Americans want in high volume, at low prices, with standardized quality. There is disagreement, however, about whether advertising encourages or discourages competition, adds value to products, makes products more or less expensive, affects total consumer demand, narrows or widens consumer choice, and whether it has any real effect on national business cycles.

While controversy surrounds most of these economic issues, the importance of advertising can best be understood by accepting the abundance principle. This states that, in an economy that produces more goods and services than can be consumed, advertising keeps consumers informed of their selection alternatives and assists companies to compete more effectively.

As a result of advertising, today's consumer is more informed, better educated, and more demanding. These demands have led to an almost overwhelming amount of social and legal restraints on advertising.

Questions for review

1. How does advertising for the Red Cross compare with the standard definition of advertising?
2. What are the primary functions of advertising today? Give examples that serve these basic functions.
3. What is the difference between industrial advertising and professional advertising?
4. What is the difference between local and regional advertising? How do the media differ for each?
5. What was the earliest form of advertising, and what function did it serve?
6. What is demarketing? What examples can you cite of companies employing this concept?
7. As a consumer are you more likely to save money by buying at a store that doesn't spend a lot of money on advertising? Explain.
8. How does advertising increase a product's value?
9. What is the overall effect of advertising on consumer choice?
10. How does retail advertising affect the local economy? Are retailers in your area advertising more or less because of present economic conditions?

2

The social and legal impact of advertising

On a recent flight from New York to Chicago, John O'Toole (profiled in Chapter 1), the president of Foote, Cone & Belding advertising agency, sat next to a woman who inquired what he did for a living. When he responded that he was in advertising, she stated somewhat disdainfully, "I think advertising is destroying our language."

Because this is a common attack on the social impact of advertising, O'Toole debated whether to launch into his "case for national advertising as a preserver of clear, concise, colorful, and correct (to say nothing of alliterative) English." He refrained from that. Nor did this well-known poet tell her that advertising is "a portal for introducing new constructions and expressions into a constantly evolving language to enrich and renew it." He felt the flight would be far too short for such a long dissertation.

As he reported in one of his semiregular Memos to the Organization, he decided simply to cite an institution that, in his thinking, has done a far more thorough job of debasing language than advertising.

> Regular readers of these memos will assume that I took out after the federal government, or Harvard Business School, or that perennial favorite, the legal profession. Not so.
>
> I didn't have to look beyond the vehicle we were in to find a first-class miscreant: the airline industry.
>
> I showed her this paragraph I had just read in the in-flight magazine.
>
> "TWA is required by the federal government to ensure compliance with the regulations concerning smoking on board its flights. For the comfort and safety of all, we earnestly solicit each passenger's cooperation in strictly observing these rules. Persistent disregard could result in the offending passenger's disembarkation."
>
> What I think they're saying, amidst all the passive and conditional gobbledygook (I like that one, too), is this:
>
> "The government makes us enforce the no-smoking rules. Please obey them or we'll have to throw you off the plane."
>
> Now being thrown off a plane, presumably in flight, is a disquieting prospect. So perhaps they deliberately obscured the thought with gratuitous verbiage to soften its impact. Whatever the motive, comprehension is the victim.
>
> Pompous as it sounds, "disembarkation" is a more accurate word to describe getting off an airplane than the one they normally use: "de-planing." "We will be de-planing tonight," says the stewardess, "through the forward exit." I have an image of passengers standing at the forward exit picking tiny planes off their persons and dropping them out into the darkness. We are not de-planing. Actually the plane is de-peopling. But what's wrong with just "getting off"? Then there's the matter of redundancy in airline talk. "For your own personal safety and convenience," for example. Or, "Be sure your seat backs and tray tables are returned to their original upright positions."
>
> Compare that kind of language, which is the airline itself speaking, to the precision of advertising speaking for the airline: "Fly the friendly skies." "You're going to like us." "Doing what we do best."

Anyone who concludes advertising is the offender deserves to be disembarked.[1]

John O'Toole happens to be one of the most articulate "defenders of the faith" in advertising. However, the advertising industry has had to deal with a growing number of equally articulate critics who condemn it for a wide variety of cardinal sins far worse than the simple misuse of the English language (Figure 2–1). These attacks have led to a stream of actions on the part of consumer groups, business, and governmental bodies to regulate what advertisers say and do (Figure 2–2).

Social criticism of advertising

Advertising is the most visible activity of business. What a company may have been doing privately for many years suddenly becomes public the moment it starts to advertise. By publicly inviting people to try their products, companies invite public criticism and attack if their products do not live up to the promised benefits. Defenders of advertising say it is therefore safer to buy advertised articles than unadvertised products. By putting their names behind the goods, the makers of advertised articles have stuck their necks out and will try harder to fulfill their promises.

Because advertising is so public it is subjected to wide criticism, not only for the role it plays in selling products but also for the way it influences our society. As a selling tool, advertising is attacked for its excesses. Some critics charge that, at its worst, advertising is downright untruthful and, at best, it presents only positive information about products. Others charge that advertising manipulates people psychologically to buy things they can't afford by promising greater sex appeal, improved social status, or other unrealistic expectations. Still others attack advertising for being offensive or in bad taste. Many argue that there is just too much advertising and that this overwhelming quantity is one reason it has such an impact on our society.

As a social influence, advertising is often charged, on the one hand, with contributing to crime and violence and, on the other hand, with making people conform. Critics attack advertising for perpetuating stereotypes of people, for making people want things they don't need and can't afford, and for creating insecurity in order to sell goods. Advertising, they say, debases our language, takes unfair advantage of our children, makes us too materialistic, and encourages wastefulness (Figure 2–3). Finally, by influencing the media, critics charge, advertising interferes with freedom of the press.

To adequately detail all the pros and cons of the charges against advertising would require volumes. However, it is important for the beginning advertising student to understand the essence of these attacks and the impact they have on advertising as it is performed today and tomorrow. Let us therefore examine some of the more common criticisms as they are usually expressed.

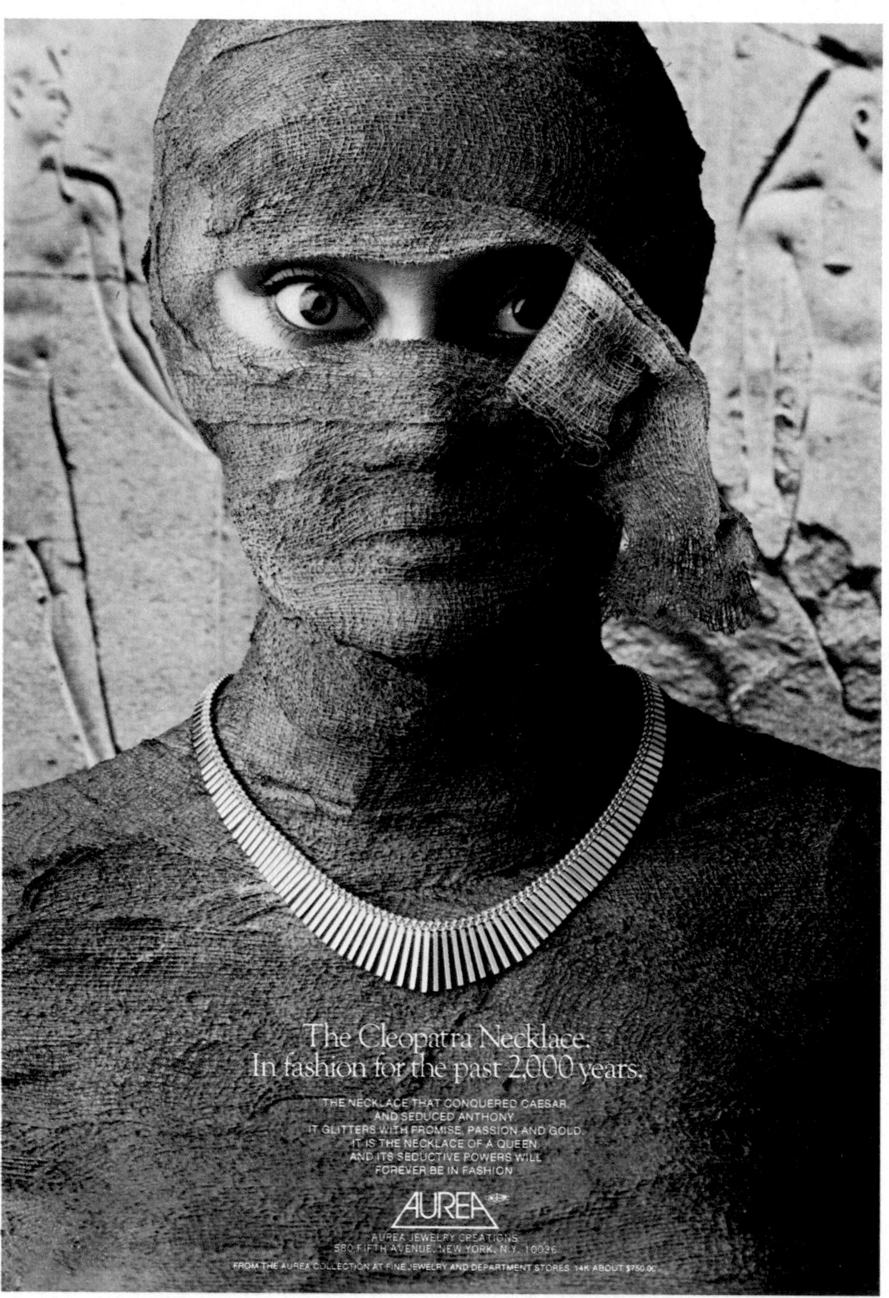

Figure 2–1

"The Cleopatra Necklace" contains seven lines of copy, six periods, five sentence fragments, and only two grammatically correct sentences. Critics of advertising might be appalled at this "debasement" of correct English usage. But study the effect. What does the ad really convey in meaning and feeling? Are you surprised to learn that the Cleopatra necklace costs $650? Would you have expected it to cost more? This is an excellent example of how effective copywriting can build value for a product. Of course, that too is a subject of criticism.

Figure 2–2

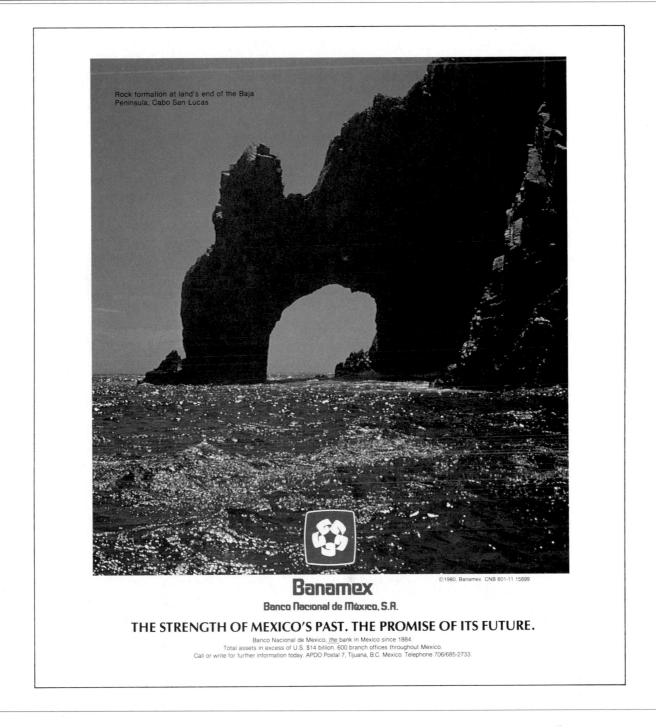

Advertising restrictions are sometimes intended to protect American business as well as to regulate it. Banco Nacional de México, that country's oldest and most prestigious bank, was prohibited from advertising the high interest they pay on savings. In fact, they are not allowed to even solicit accounts in the United States. The most they can do is institutional advertising to create awareness of their name. To open an account, you would have to go to Mexico. (See the discussion on the legal aspects of international advertising at the end of this chapter.)

Advertising debases our language

The very reasons John O'Toole likes advertising are the reasons defenders of traditional English usage don't like it. They feel advertising copy is too breezy, too informal, too casual, and therefore improper. Advertising, they believe, has destroyed the dignity of the language.

Grammar rules and especially punctuation rules are commonly broken by advertising copywriters, and this truly infuriates the critics. R. J. Reynolds Tobacco Co. introduced the line: "Winston tastes good like a cigarette should." The academic community created such a

Figure 2–3

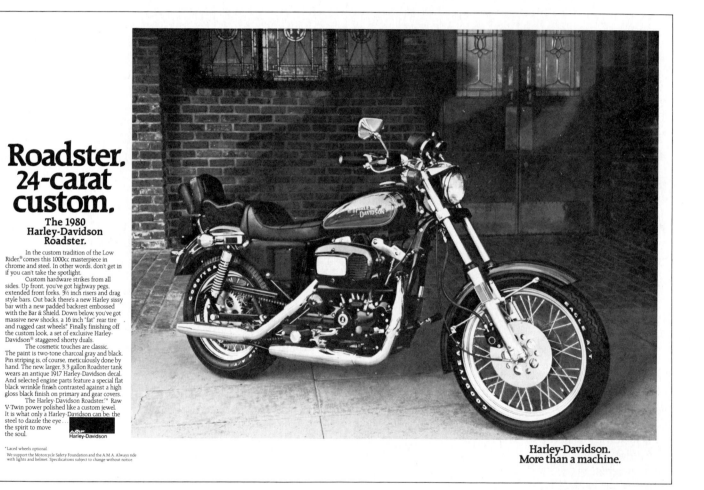

Indicative of American materialism, say the critics, is the amount of money spent on recreation and other unnecessary "things." The growth of the motorcycle market might reflect this. Note the appeals in the copy to status, macho exhibitionism, and material exclusivity: ". . . don't get in if you can't take the spotlight"; "Raw V-Twin power polished like a custom jewel"; ". . . the steel to dazzle the eye . . . the spirit to move the soul."

flap that the advertiser followed up with another commercial filmed on the steps of a university. When the student in the commercial voiced the famous slogan, another student in cap and gown quickly corrected her, saying: "Winston tastes good *as* a cigarette should." This temporarily quieted the critics, but the company continued to use the "like a cigarette should" slogan for many years.

English critics attack the heavy use of punctuation (hyphens, dashes, periods, exclamation points, dots, and quotation marks) used by copywriters and are further offended by the use of multiple adjectives ("rich, full-bodied, heavy texture," etc.). What the critics perhaps fail to realize is that today's advertising copywriters use the same license that has been allowed in poetry for centuries. Examine any of Shakespeare's plays and note the use of alliteration, double adjectives and adverbs, broken sentences, and unusual punctuation:

> O! That this too too solid flesh would melt,
> Thaw and resolve itself into a dew;
> Or that the Everlasting had not fix'd
> His canon 'gainst self-slaughter! O God! O God!
> How weary, stale, flat, and unprofitable
> Seem to me all the uses of this world.*

To do its job, advertising must speak to people. Therefore it must be understandable and readable. Advertisers have found that people respond better to a down-to-earth, conversational tone than to a more dignified, correct tone. Thus the best copywriters have developed a style that is descriptive, colorful, and even picturesque, as well as warm, human, and personal. Because of the need for brevity, the words are simple, lively, and full of personality, and punctuation is used to build a conversational tone rather than to construct grammatical sentences.

Advertising makes us too materialistic

Critics claim that advertising adversely affects our value system because it portrays the acquisition of more things as the means to a happier life instead of the acquisition of more spiritual or intellectual enlightenment. Advertising, they say, encourages people to buy more automobiles, more clothing, and more appliances than they need, all with the promise of greater status, greater social acceptance, and greater sex appeal. For example, they point to the fact that millions of Americans own 20 or more pairs of shoes, several TV sets, and several vehicles.

There is no doubt that we are the most materialistic society in the world. So the basic question concerning materialism is this: Is there a relationship between happiness and materalism? Does the acquisition of more goods and services contribute to contentment and the joy of living?

*W. Shakespeare, *Hamlet,* Act I, Scene II.

Philosophers and social scientists have debated the relationship between happiness and affluence for centuries but have reached no conclusions. Many people think that material comfort is necessary before a person can devote time to higher cultural and spiritual values. Therefore the stress on material things doesn't rule out spiritual and cultural values. In fact it may create a greater opportunity for it since the satisfaction of a person's higher desires is possible only after that person's lower, more basic desires have been met. Moreover, through its support of the media, advertising has brought literature, opera, drama, and symphonies to millions who would never had seen them otherwise.

The first responsibility of advertising is to aid its sponsor by informing, persuading, and reminding the sponsor's customers and prospects. Most sponsors are interested in selling goods and making profits, not in bringing about cultural changes or improvements. However, to achieve their objectives, sponsors have found that advertising is most effective when it reflects the society in which it exists. Thus, if culturally uplifting advertising copy would sell goods, advertisers would use it. Likewise, if people wanted a more cultural approach to advertisements and would respond to them, advertisers would be delighted to comply because it would be in their self-interest. Ultimately, the bottom line must prevail. The profit and loss in dollars and cents determine the advertising approach (Figure 2–4).

Advertising manipulates people psychologically to buy things they don't need

Advertising is often criticized for its power to make people do irrational things. The following are some suggestions based on variations of this criticism:

1. Advertising should be informative but not persuasive.
2. Advertising should report only factual, functional information.
3. Advertising shouldn't play to people's desires, emotions, fears, or anxieties.
4. Advertising should deal only with people's functional needs for products not their psychological needs for status, appeal, security, sexual attractiveness, or health.
5. Advertising makes us too materialistic.

Underlying all these criticisms is evidently either (1) a belief in some mystical, black magic power of advertising to hypnotically control customers, or (2) an equally strange attitude that consumers are poor, helpless, ignorant lambs who have no power of rational thinking or choice in the face of advertising's persuasive wolves.

Persuasion is a fact of life, and so is our need to confront persuasion on a daily basis. We see it in every avenue of our existence, not just in advertising. Teachers try to persuade students to study. Students try to persuade teachers to give them better grades. Girlfriends persuade boyfriends; preachers persuade congregations; charities persuade donors; borrowers persuade lenders; stockbrokers persuade investors; kids persuade parents; and advertising persuades people. In short, we are all busy persuading or being persuaded in one way or another. We need to recognize that advertising is persuasive by definition. Then we can become better consumers and critics of advertising.

A second reality is that when we persuade, we usually use a variety of tactics depending on the subject matter and the response of the

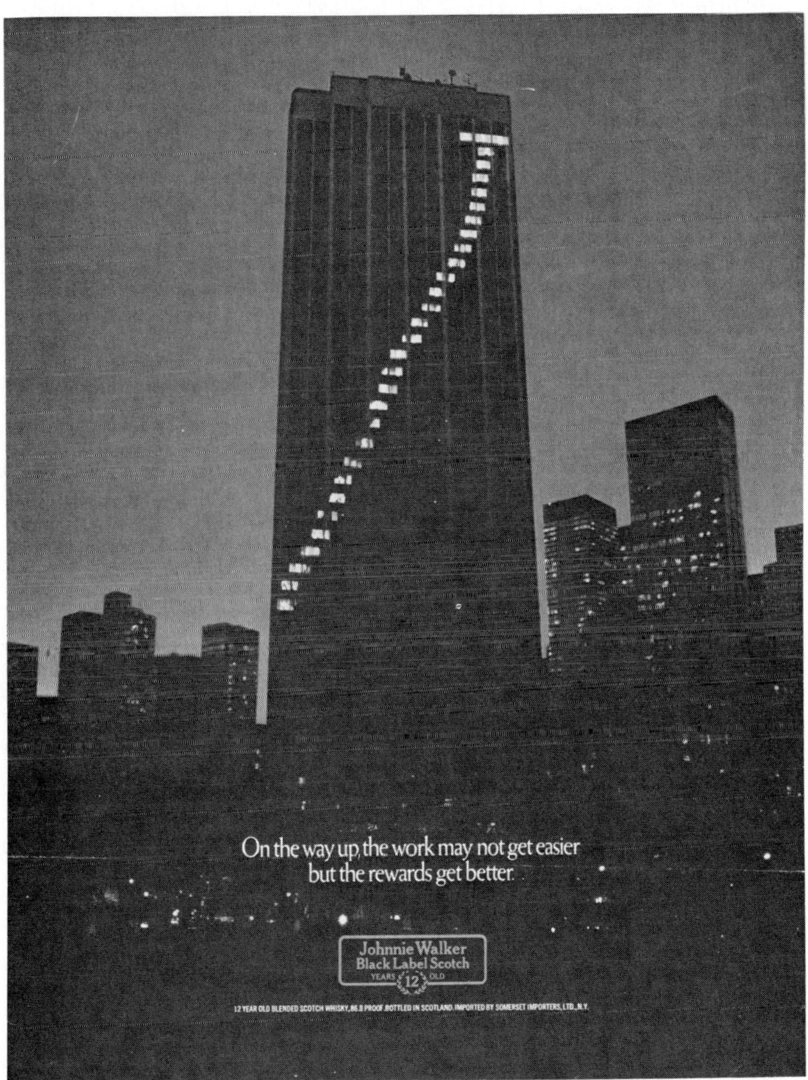

Figure 2–4 Johnnie Walker Black Label Scotch successfully appealed to status-seeking, upwardly mobile scotch drinkers in this award-winning magazine ad. "On the way up the work may not be easier, but the rewards get better." This brief headline encourages ambition and rewards status while it builds an image for Johnnie Walker. Critics condemn this subtle form of persuasion as being psychologically manipulative.

listener. Sometimes the simple facts of our case are overwhelmingly persuasive. Other times we appeal to some other need or motive of our listener because the facts alone aren't persuasive enough. Is it wrong or bad to use emotional appeals in persuasion? If so, then we are all wrong and bad because we all do it.

All of us have needs and desires beyond the basics of food, clothing, and shelter. Otherwise we would still live in caves, wear bearskins, and eat berries. One benefit of a free society is that we can choose to what degree we wish to indulge our desires, needs, and fantasies. Some people prefer a simple life without mortgage payments, fancy cars, and trips abroad. Others enjoy the material pleasures of a modern, technological society. There are advertising sponsors at both ends of that spectrum. Food companies offer natural products as well as convenience packaged goods. Shoe companies offer simple sandals as well as formal footwear.

All companies attempt to persuade consumers to try their products. Not all are successful, though. In spite of the fact that advertising techniques have become far more effective and efficient in recent years, there is still no black magic. The final reality is that far more products fail than succeed in the marketplace.

Advertising is excessive

One of the most common complaints about advertising is simply that there is too much of it. Consumer organizations protest "billboard blight" on the nation's highways. Local politicians criticize sign pollution in their communities. Advertisements reach us in cars, elevators, parking lots, hotel lobbies, subways, and our homes on radio and television, in newspapers, and through the mail. According to most experts, the average American is exposed to over 500 commercial messages a day. Some give even higher figures. According to the advertising critics, we are awash in a sea of commercials that make life less pleasant than it might otherwise be.

There is no doubt that we live in an overcommunicated society. There are so many products from which to choose (over 10,000 in the average supermarket); and in a highly competitive society, goods must move in order to survive. Therefore companies must shout to be heard, and advertising is their megaphone.

Advertising professionals themselves are concerned about this. In an effort to control the noise level and make their advertisements more effective, voluntary restrictions on advertising volume have been imposed by most media. This, of course, limits the supply of space and time and contributes to the rising cost of media.

Consumers' tolerance of advertising in the print media seems to be greater than in the broadcast media. Readers can simply turn the pages and ignore the advertising if they so desire. Broadcast media tend to be more intrusive and therefore receive greater criticism.

The fact is, though, that because mass distribution supports our free enterprise system, advertising volume is here to stay and is the price we must pay for free television, freedom of the press, and our high standard of living.

Advertising is offensive or in bad taste

Many people find advertising offensive to their religious convictions, morality, or political perspective. Others find the use of advertising techniques that emphasize sex, violence, or body functions to be in bad taste. Certainly this is one of the most controversial issues. (See the Ad Lab.)

Taste is highly subjective. What is good taste to some is bad taste to others. And tastes change. What is considered offensive today may not be offensive in the future. There was outrage when the first advertisement for underarm deodorant was published in the *Ladies Home Journal,* but today no one would question such an advertisement. Some people find liquor ads offensive, while others find them simply informative. There has been some experimentation with advertising birth control products on television. Some feel this is an important advancement and badly needed consumer information. Others feel it is not a proper subject for a mass medium.

In the not-so-distant past, nudity was rarely seen in print advertisements. Today it is often featured in ads for grooming and personal hygiene products. Where nudity is relevant to the product being advertised, such as a therapeutic tub, it is less likely to be regarded as obscene or offensive. However, the National Association of Broadcasters requires its member stations to ban ads for intimate products if sexual themes or connotations are used.

Often the products themselves are not offensive; only the way in which they are advertised may be open to criticism. The sensational aspects of a product, particularly a book or motion picture, are frequently emphasized in advertising. Shock value is used to gain attention, particularly by inexperienced copywriters. This is often a reflection of the tastes and interests of the American people, however. If the advertisements don't attract the readers and viewers they seek, the advertising campaign will falter and die. The reader, listener, or viewer has the ultimate veto authority by ignoring offensive material.

It is unrealistic to assume that advertising, particularly mass advertising, will ever be free of this criticism. But reputable advertisers are acutely aware of what the public considers to be tasteful advertising.

Advertising perpetuates stereotypes of people

Groups such as the National Organization for Women (NOW) protest that many of today's advertisements do not acknowledge the changing role of women in our society (Figure 2–5). One feminist says:

> Advertising is an insidious propaganda machine for a male supremacist society. It spews out images of women as sex mates, housekeepers, mothers, and menial workers—images that perhaps reflect the true status of women in society, but which also make it increasingly difficult for women to break out of the sexist stereotypes that imprison them.[2]

Consumer charges of ethnic and racial bias and of animal abuse in advertising have also been made in increasing numbers to federal and business regulatory agencies. The targets of these complaints have included ads that show a Japanese gardener at work and floor wax commercials that feature a black scrubwoman. Charges of animal abuse have been made against beer commercials in which a dray horse is seen hauling a huge, old-fashioned brewery wagon. While none of these advertisements were illegal, all were objects of consumer efforts to halt their use, even to penalizing the advertisers.

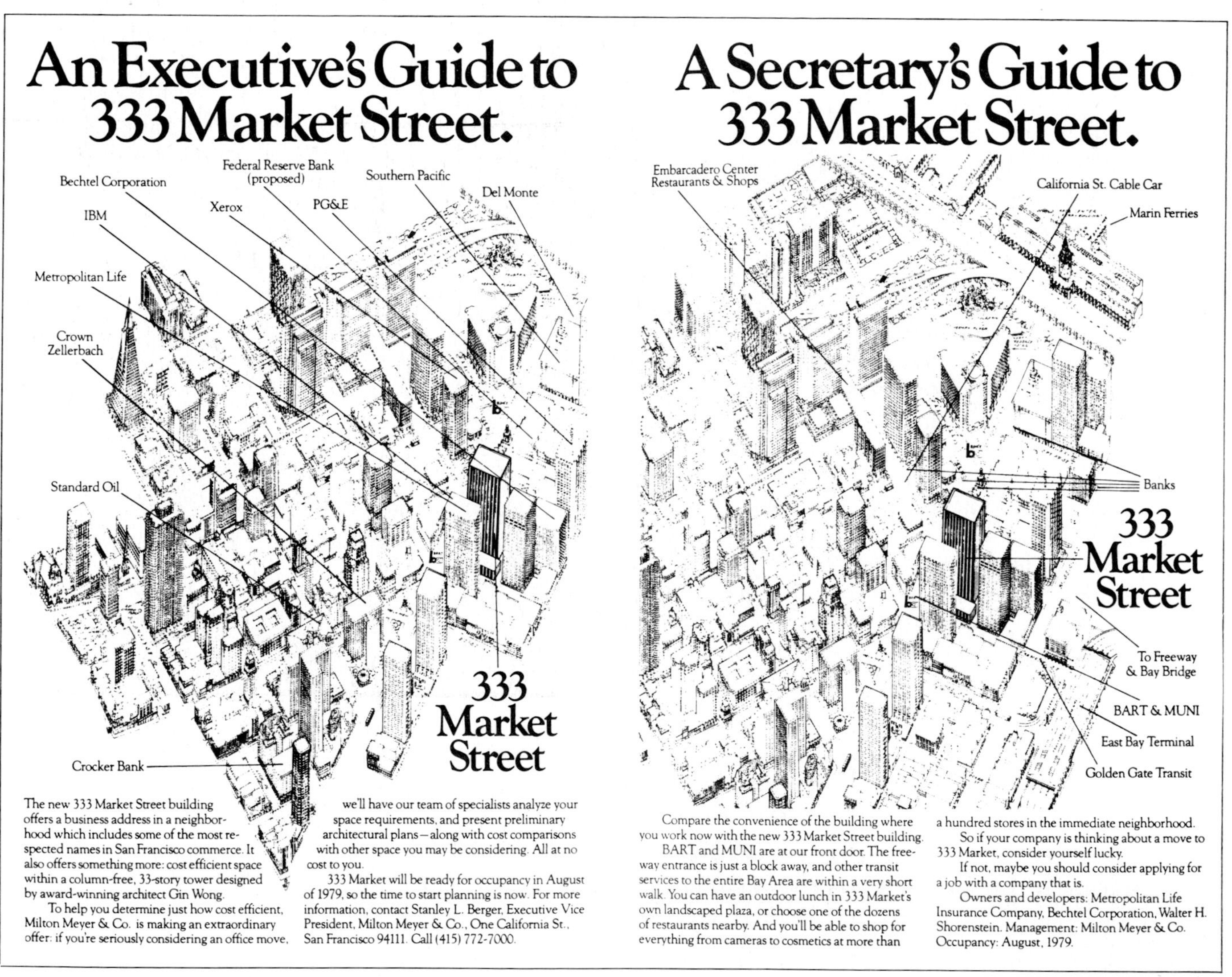

Figure 2–5 Some women might take offense at the suggestion that their interest is in street car terminals while men's interests are in corporate and financial centers. One writer to *Advertising Age* did and sent these two ads in as examples of ads we can do without. She wondered how many employers would want to hire the "simple-minded secretaries" that the ad on the right might appeal to.

Jury duty: Judge the guilt or innocence of these ads

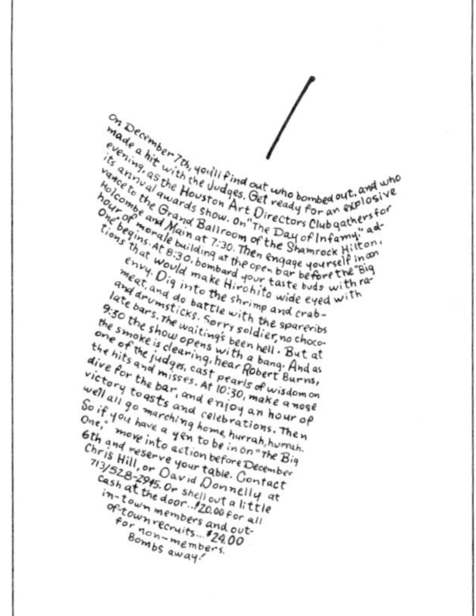

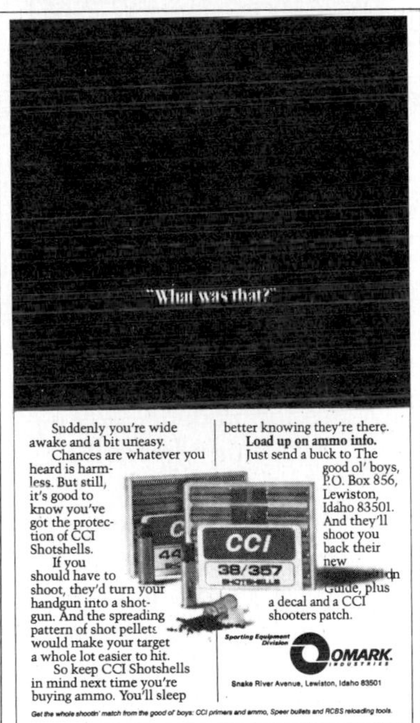

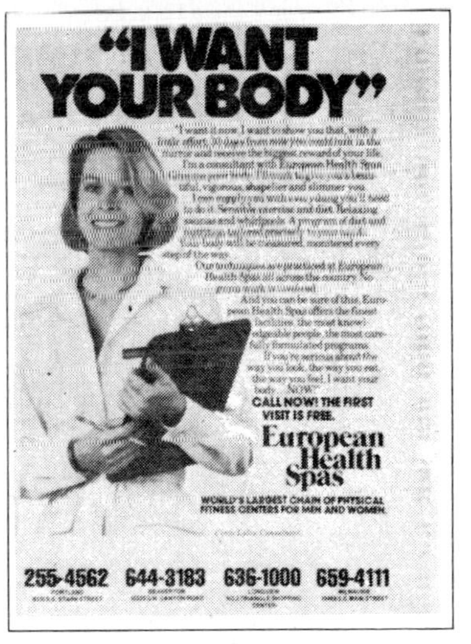

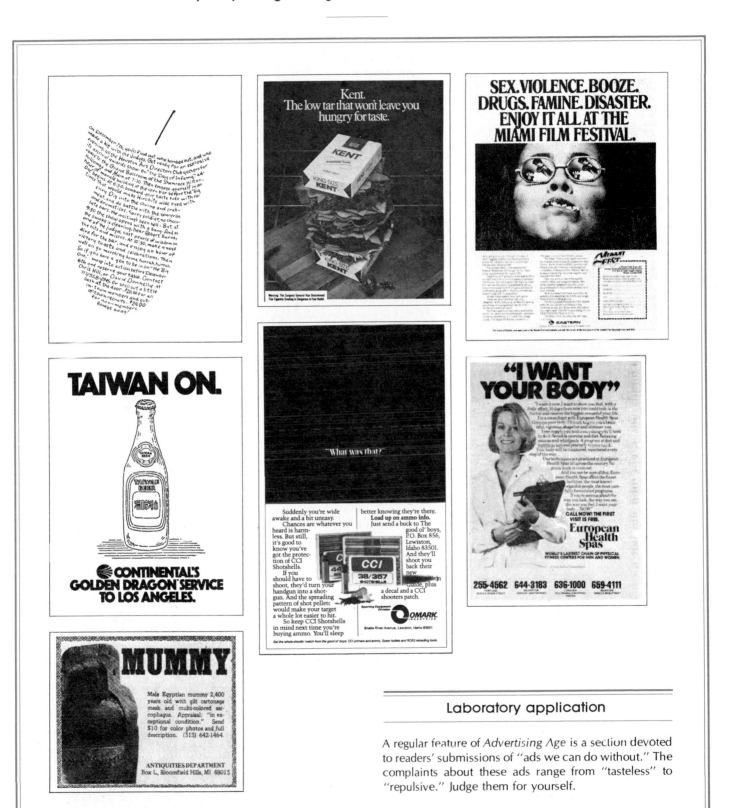

Laboratory application

A regular feature of *Advertising Age* is a section devoted to readers' submissions of "ads we can do without." The complaints about these ads range from "tasteless" to "repulsive." Judge them for yourself.

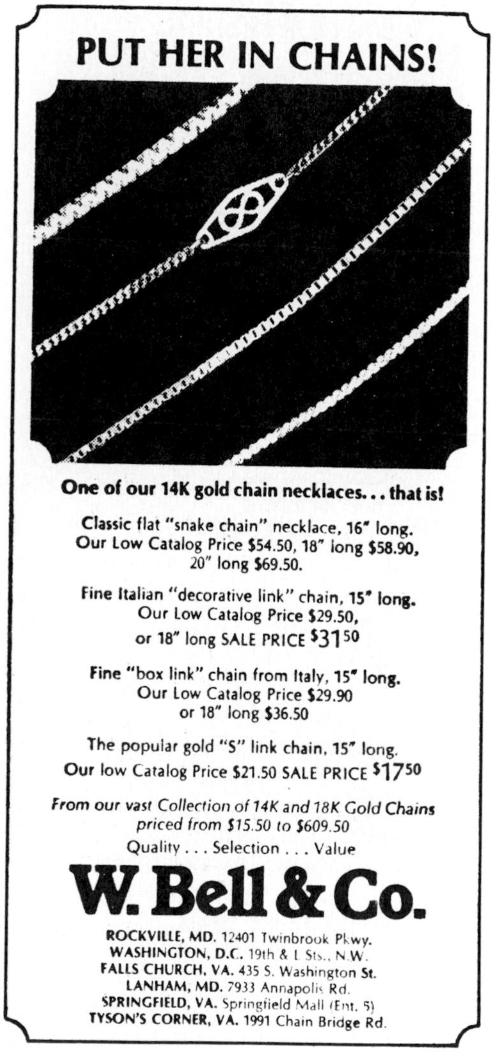

Unfortunately, despite the efforts of many, there is still too much bias and sexism in advertising (Figure 2–6). The proper portrayal of women and minorities is still open to debate, however, and changes with the times.

Today it has become especially important to portray women realistically, since they make so many important purchasing decisions. An area of vast change is the representation of minorities. Blacks, Hispanics, Italians, Chinese, American Indians, and others are now shown in favorable environments as a result of their upward mobility as well as organized pressure and threats of boycotts. New advertising agencies staffed with essentially minority personnel have been successful in reaching minority markets. Likewise, advertisers are taking special care to create advertisements that will neither offend nor alienate minority groups.

PUT HER IN CHAINS!

One of our 14K gold chain necklaces. . . that is!

Classic flat "snake chain" necklace, 16" long.
Our Low Catalog Price $54.50, 18" long $58.90,
20" long $69.50.

Fine Italian "decorative link" chain, 15" long.
Our Low Catalog Price $29.50,
or 18" long SALE PRICE $31.50

Fine "box link" chain from Italy, 15" long.
Our Low Catalog Price $29.90
or 18" long $36.50

The popular gold "S" link chain, 15" long.
Our low Catalog Price $21.50 SALE PRICE $17.50

From our vast Collection of 14K and 18K Gold Chains
priced from $15.50 to $609.50
Quality . . . Selection . . . Value

W. Bell & Co.

ROCKVILLE, MD. 12401 Twinbrook Pkwy.
WASHINGTON, D.C. 19th & L Sts., N.W.
FALLS CHURCH, VA. 435 S. Washington St.
LANHAM, MD. 7933 Annapolis Rd.
SPRINGFIELD, VA. Springfield Mall (Ent. 5)
TYSON'S CORNER, VA. 1991 Chain Bridge Rd.

Figure 2–6 Feminists railed at the sight of this advertisement for chain necklaces, which appeared in the *Washington Post.* Ads that suggest subservient roles for women have been their primary target since the beginning of the women's movement.

Advertising is deceptive

Perhaps the greatest attack on advertising has been and continues to be against the deceptive practices of some advertisers. This is the area that has also received the greatest regulatory scrutiny, as we shall see in the next section.

Critics define deceptiveness not only as false and misleading statements but also as any false impression conveyed, whether intentional or unintentional. Advertising deception can take a number of forms, and many of these are highly controversial with no hard and fast rules. The common practices that are considered deceptive include those listed in the Ad Lab.

Advertising must have the confidence of consumers if it is going to be effective. What is "truth"? What is "deception"? Sometimes the terms are hard to define. Deception will cause consumers to turn against a product and is therefore self-defeating. This is especially true for products for which the ad claims are easily verifiable.

Advertising puts the advertiser on record for all who care to look. Because of greater scrutiny by the government and by consumers, it is in the self-interest of advertisers to be honest and to avoid trouble. The company that wants to stay in business knows it can do so only with a reputation for honest dealing.

Defense of advertising

Advertising professionals admit that advertising has indeed been used irresponsibly many times over the years. They point out that, like a high-powered automobile, if you put a drunk at the wheel, you're going to get a lot of damage. The problem, though, is the drunk at the wheel, not the car.

In other words, they admit that advertising has been and still can be misused. But the abuse that has been heaped on advertising as a marketing tool and as a social influencer is no longer justified and is so excessive that it makes all advertising appear evil. To support this, they point out that of all the advertising reviewed by the Federal Trade Commission in a typical year, 97 percent is found to be satisfactory. Moreover, the critics who attack advertising's excesses use advertising techniques themselves to sell their books and further their points of view.

The sins of the past still come back to haunt advertising today. What was once an unchecked, free-swinging business activity is now such a closely scrutinized and heavily regulated profession that it

Deception or permissible lies?

Advertising critics have broadened the definition of deception to include many practices that were previously considered obvious and permissible exaggerations. Some of these practices are listed here:

False promises. Making an advertising promise that cannot be kept, such as "restores youth" or "prevents cancer."

Claims of uniqueness. Asserting that a product is "unique," "unparalleled," or "the first of its kind," among other things.

Incomplete description. Stating some, but not all, of the contents of a product, such as advertising a "solid oak" desk without mentioning that only the top is solid oak and that the rest is made of hardwoods with an oak veneer.

Misleading comparisons. Making meaningless comparisons, such as "a genuine antique reproduction" or "as good as a diamond," if the claim cannot be verified.

Bait-and-switch offers. Advertising an item at an unusually low price to bring people into the store, and then "switching" them to a higher priced model than the one advertised by stating that the advertised product is "out of stock" or "poorly made."

Visual distortions. Making a product look larger than it really is—for example, a TV commercial for a "giant steak" dinner special showing the steak on a miniature plate that makes it appear extra large. Or, showing a "deluxe" model that is not the same as the one offered at a "sale" price.

Testimonials. Implying that a product has the endorsement of a celebrity or an authority who is not a bona fide user of the product.

False comparisons. Demonstrating one product as superior to another without giving the "inferior" item a chance or by comparing it with the least competitive product available. For example, comparing the road performance of a steel-belted radial tire with an average "economy" tire.

Superlative words. Using absolute words such as "the finest" or "the greatest value," or verbal claims such as "cures," "halts," "defeats," or "eliminates forever."

Partial disclosures. Stating what a product can do but not what it cannot do. For example, claiming that an electrically powered automobile will go "60 miles per hour without gasoline" and not mentioning that it needs an eight-hour battery recharge every 100 miles. Or showing an angler with a lightweight plastic fishing rod beside a huge fish he could not possibly have landed with it.

Small-print qualifications. Making a statement in large print (Any new suit in stock—$50 off!) only to qualify or retract it in smaller type elsewhere in the ad ("With the purchase of a suit at the regular price").

Underselling claims. Making claims like "lowest prices in town," "highest trade-in allowances," or "never undersold."

Laboratory applications

1. Would you consider the practices described above deception or permissible "white lies"?
2. What examples have you seen of deception?

appears frightening to the novice entering the field. The excesses with which advertising has been rightfully or wrongfully charged have created layer upon layer of laws, regulations, and regulatory bodies. These are used by consumer groups, government, special-interest groups, and even other advertisers to review, check, control, and change advertising.

Regulators of advertising

A substantial amount of voluntary self-regulation has been achieved by the nation's advertisers in recent years. This reflects their desire for acceptance and growth in a competitive marketplace where consumer confidence is essential. Most large advertisers maintain careful systems of advertising review and gather strong data to substantiate their claims. Of all the regulators of advertising practices today, the greatest is, has been, and always will be voluntary self-regulation by the advertisers themselves.

There are several major types of advertising regulators that we will discuss here. These include: regulation by government on the federal, state, and local levels; self-regulation by advertisers; regulation by the advertising profession and the media; self-regulation by industrial organizations; regulation by the business community; and regulation by consumers and consumer protection organizations.

Mom's Bread

"Hello, Mom's? We think the FTC might let us run this one. We've cut the copy claims substantially."

Regulation by the federal government

The strictest advertising controls are imposed by federal and state laws and by judicial interpretations of these laws. Enforcement is the task of various government agencies. They must determine the scope and application of these laws and then act accordingly.

Federal Trade Commission

The FTC controls all national advertising used to promote products sold in interstate commerce. Its efforts are largely directed toward consumer protection by policing the marketing done through the media. This includes monitoring false and misleading product advertising, which is defined as advertising that misleads through untrue statements or implications or by the omission of material facts. The FTC is concerned not only with truth in advertising but also with how consumers interpret such truth—and the effect particular advertising statements have on consumers. Because these efforts call for highly subjective judgments, FTC attempts to regulate the advertising industry are often controversial.

Federal regulations of advertising largely grew out of efforts to control unfair business practices through enactment of the Sherman Antitrust Act of 1890 and amended by the Clayton Act of 1914. (See Figure 2–7.) The Federal Trade Commission Act was also passed in

1914. It provided for the establishment of a five-member Federal Trade Commission which has the power to enforce the act. Today the commission is the leading federal regulatory agency for advertising.

The Sherman Antitrust Act of 1890. Prohibited monopolies or attempts to monopolize and any "contract, combination, or conspiracy" in restraint of trade.

The Pure Food and Drug Act of 1906. Outlawed shipment of misbranded or adulterated food and drugs in interstate commerce. Amended later by *The Pure Food, Drug, and Cosmetics Act of 1938,* which required disclosure of material facts on labels and in literature accompanying products.

The Federal Trade Commission Act of 1914. Made unfair methods of competition illegal. Established the Federal Trade Commission to enforce the law by identifying "unfair business practices."

The Communications Act of 1934. Established the Federal Communications Commission (FCC) and empowered it to monitor, regulate, and control the nation's growing interstate communications system in the "public interest, convenience and necessity." Gave the FCC power to award and withdraw licenses for radio and television stations, which indirectly gives it power over advertising and program content.

The Robinson-Patman Act of 1936. Prohibited price discrimination that lessens competition or tends to create a monopoly. For example, anyone in interstate commerce cannot charge different customers different prices for products of like grade or quality unless such discounts are intended to meet competition or are based on the actual costs of servicing the customer.

The Wheeler-Lea Act of 1938. Expanded FTC jurisdiction over practices that injure the public even though they do not necessarily injure a competitor. Prior to this act, only action that harmed competitors was considered unlawful. The commission's authority was strengthened so that cease and desist orders become final 60 days after being served, with a fine to increase daily for failure to obey. The act also declared false advertising of food, drugs, cosmetics, and therapeutic devices illegal.

The Wool Products Labeling Act of 1939. Required that each product be labeled to show the total fiber weight of the wool; whether it is new, processed, or reused; the percentage of nonwool filling; and the name of the manufacturer.

The Lanham Trade-Mark Act of 1947. Passed to protect slogans and brand names from infringement by competitors. Appointed the U.S. Patent Office to register slogans, brand names, corporate or store names, and identifying symbols for brands or companies.

The Fur Products Labeling Act of 1952. Required that the correct

Figure 2–7 Major legislation affecting advertising.

name of the animal, as well as manufacturing details, appear on the label of each item offered for sale.

The Automobile Information Disclosure Act of 1958. Required the manufacturer to show the suggested retail price of each new car itemized for base cost, extras, and freight.

The Textile Fiber Products Identification Act of 1960. Required that labels on fiber items show the percentage of natural and synthetic fibers used in the manufacture of cloth and other materials.

The Fair Packaging and Labeling Act of 1966. Established a "truth-in-labeling" law, requiring manufacturers to state the contents of the package, who made it, and how much it contains. Appointed the FTC and the FDA to enforce its provisions.

The Truth-in-Lending Act of 1968. Required creditors to make full disclosure of the cost of consumer credit.

The Magnuson-Moss Warranty—Federal Trade Commission Improvement Act of 1975. Was adopted because of consumer pressure for clearer warranties. It gives the FTC power to protect consumers from deceptive warranties given by a manufacturer, wholesaler, or dealer relating to the material or workmanship in any product. The act specifies conditions for the refund, repair, and replacement of merchandise.

The Copyright Act of 1978. Provided for the protection of copyrights during the lifetime of the author plus 50 years after his or her death. Also extended existing copyrights to a maximum of 75 years from the previous 56 years.

Figure 2–7 *(concluded)*

The procedure of the FTC in monitoring claims is to compare the advertised product with what the advertising represents it to be. The FTC frequently asks advertisers to submit documentation and other proof of performance to substantiate their advertising claims. These include not only claims of product quality or performance, but also claims about product safety, value, and uniqueness, as well as claimed contributions to the user's health or well-being. An FTC request for documentation prohibits further use of unverified claims by the advertiser. The FTC requires that advertising claims be adequately substantiated and that the advertiser possess such proof before these claims are made in advertising (Figure 2–8).

Consider the case of Acne-Statin (Figure 2–9). This product was endorsed by singer Pat Boone. He said: "With four daughters, we've tried the leading acne medication at our house, and nothing ever seemed to work until our girls met a Beverly Hills doctor and got some real help through a product called 'Acne-Statin.' " The FTC said the advertising claims could not be substantiated and held that celebrities, like companies that place the ads, must verify the advertising claims before they go on the air or into print. In settlement of the case, an agreement was made with the FTC for Boone, Boone's production company, the doctor, and the advertising agency to make a partial restitution ($275,000 versus $8 million in sales) to consumers who requested a refund.

In another case, Campbell's Soup had a television commercial in which marbles were placed at the bottom of a bowl of soup. The marbles held the solid ingredients at the top so they would be more

Figure 2–8 **Decision points in FTC deceptive advertising matters**

	Issue	Possible actions	What should be done	Action
Step 1	Did the ad create erroneous beliefs?			
Step 2	Is the ad running now?		Should an injunction be obtained?	Obtain injunction
Step 3	Do the erroneous beliefs still exist?	How can the erroneous beliefs be corrected?	Should the erroneous beliefs be corrected?	Design the corrective action
Step 4	Might this company use this deceptive practice again?			Obtain cease and desist order
Step 5	Is the problem common to the industry?	What industry wide action can be taken? 1. Advertising substantiation 2. Trade regulation rule 3. Generalized cease and desist	Should industrywide actions be taken?	Initiate appropriate industrywide actions

visible, giving the impression that the soup contained more ingredients than it actually did. Campbell's defense was that if they didn't use the marbles the ingredients would sink to the bottom; this would lead someone watching the commercial to believe that there were fewer ingredients than was actually the case. Campbell's agreed to stop the practice.

In recent years the FTC has given increasing attention to bait-and-switch advertising. For example, the FTC filed a complaint stating that Sears, Roebuck & Company was using bait-and-switch tactics to sell its sewing machines. Sales people made disparaging remarks about an advertised model of sewing machine. They said there would be long delays in delivery, the sewing machines were noisy and had shorter guarantees than more expensive models, and they could not do certain types of stitching. The company agreed to halt the practice.

The FTC has also expanded its emphasis on affirmative disclosure, whereby advertisers must disclose not only the positive qualities of their products but also the negative aspects, such as limitations or deficiencies. Examples of this are EPA estimates of gas mileage for automobiles, pesticide warnings, and statements that soft drinks made with saccharin may be hazardous to the consumer's health.

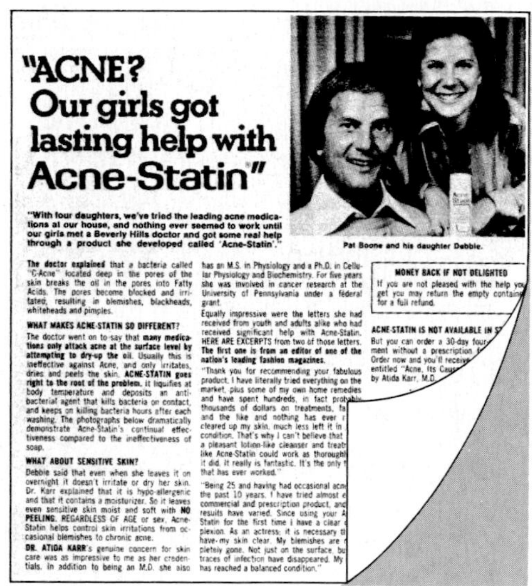

Figure 2–9 Actors and celebrities who endorse products became liable for their advertising claims after the Pat Boone–Acne-Statin case was settled with the FTC. This caused a great deal of consternation within the advertising industry as talent began to seek clauses in their contracts that would hold them harmless from suits by disgruntled consumers.

Also, endorsement of a product by an "expert" must be based on actual use by that expert. The endorser must be a bona fide user of the product. If an ad implies that the endorser has superior qualifications for making the judgment stated, the endorser's qualifications must bear this out.

Complaints against advertisements usually come from consumers, brand competitors, and the FTC's monitors. After an investigation, the FTC may decide to issue a complaint against the advertiser. This may take any of several forms. For example, a cease and desist order may be issued, prohibiting further use of the objectionable advertising. The advertiser may then sign an agreement to comply voluntarily. In other cases a consent decree may be issued. The advertiser may then agree to halt the advertising and not to indulge in such practices again without admitting guilt. The FTC may also require corrective advertising, whereby a portion of the company's advertising for a period of time must be devoted to explaining that the previous advertising was inaccurate or misleading (Figure 2–10).

This occurred in the case of Profile bread advertising, which claimed that each slice contained fewer calories than slices of other brands. However, it did not mention that slices of Profile were thinner than those of other brands. The company was ordered to devote 25 percent of its advertising for one year to correct this misleading statement. Ocean Spray Cranberry Juice used the words "high-energy food" to describe its product. The FTC charged that the words were misleading because, technically, high-energy food means calories, which is not recognized by many consumers. The company was required to spend 25 percent of its advertising for one year to explain the meaning of "high-energy food" and to confess that it means calories. In another case, Warner-Lambert had advertised Listerine for many years as a cold and sore-throat remedy based on tests they had conducted (Figure 2–11). The FTC proved the tests were invalid. Not only was Listerine required to stop making such claims, but it was called on by the court to run $10.2 million of advertising stating that

"Listerine will not help prevent colds or sore throats or lessen their severity."

Finally, in rare instances, the FTC may ask the Attorney General to try the advertiser on a misdemeanor charge. Conviction carries a fine of not more than $5,000 or not more than six months in jail.

The advertiser has 30 days to respond to any of these actions. The company can agree to the action or contest it by requesting a hearing

ADVERTISEMENT

FTC NOTICE

As a result of an investigation by the Federal Trade Commission into certain allegedly inaccurate past advertisements for STP's oil additive, STP Corporation has agreed to a $700,000 settlement. With regard to that settlement, STP is making the following statement:

It is the policy of STP to support its advertising with objective information and test data. In 1974 and 1975 an independent laboratory ran tests of the company's oil additive which led to claims of reduced oil consumption. However, these tests cannot be relied on to support the oil consumption reduction claim made by STP.

The FTC has taken the position that, in making that claim, the company violated the terms of a consent order. When STP learned that the test data did not support the claim, it stopped advertising containing that claim. New tests have been undertaken to determine the extent to which the oil additive affects oil consumption. Agreement to this settlement does not constitute an admission by STP that the law has been violated. Rather, STP has agreed to resolve the dispute with the FTC to avoid protracted and prohibitively expensive litigation.

February 13, 1978

Figure 2–10 Admitting that lab tests did not support its claims of oil consumption reduction, STP agreed to run this ad to appease the FTC. Part of the agreement with the FTC included a $700,000 settlement.

Figure 2–11 Listerine advertised for 50 years as a germ killer. In this 1941 scare approach, readers were admonished to gargle Listerine quick! The FTC held in the 1970s that the product did not relieve colds or sore throats and forced the company to include a corrective statement which said that the product was of no value in preventing colds and sore throats.

before a trial examiner retained by the FTC. The findings of the examiner are considered by the full five-member commission, which rules on them by affirming or modifying the order or by dismissing the case. If the decision is adverse, the advertiser may appeal it again through the federal court system (see Figures 2–12 and 2–13).

To prevent problems, the FTC is readily available to review advertising before it runs and to render "advance clearance" to the advertiser in an advisory opinion. The FTC also establishes advertising standards for the protection of consumers. To promote compliance with these standards, the FTC supplies advertisers, agencies, and the media with ongoing information about the regulations governing advertising in its *Industry Guides* and *Trade Regulation Rules*.

Federal Communications Commission

The seven-member Federal Communications Commission (FCC) was established as a result of the Communications Act of 1934. It has jurisdiction over the radio, television, telephone, and telegraph industries. Through its authority to license broadcasting stations and to remove a license or deny license renewal, the FCC has indirect control over broadcast advertising. This authority derives from the right of public domain over the airwaves and the mandate of broadcasting stations to operate in the public interest. The FCC stringently controls the airing of obscenity and profanity. It has imposed restrictions on both advertising content and what products may be advertised on radio and television. Even before the passage of the Public Health Cigarette Smoking Act by Congress in 1970, which banned cigarette advertising on television and radio, the FCC required stations to run antismoking commercials. The FCC disapproves of the broadcast advertising of liquor, contraceptives, and lotteries. It has openly opposed commercials by medical doctors, clerics, and marriage and family counselors. Although this disapproval does not prevent stations from running such commercials, it exerts major influence. Stations that do not comply with FCC policies may risk losing their licenses.

The FCC monitors only commercials that have been the subjects of complaints. However, individual stations are required to maintain daily logs of their commercials, and these may be examined by the commission at the time of license renewal. The FCC also exchanges confidential information with the FTC, particularly with regard to commercials that may involve false or deceptive advertising. When the FTC determines that a given commercial is deceptive or otherwise objectionable, it advises the FCC, which then informs the station of this cause for federal action.

Food and Drug Administration

A unit of the Department of Health and Human Services, the Food and Drug Administration (FDA) has authority over the advertising, labeling, packaging, and branding of packaged foods and therapeutic devices. It requires manufacturers to disclose all the ingredients on product labels, in all product advertising featured in stores, and in all accompanying or separately distributed product literature. The label must accurately state the weight or volume of the contents. Labels on

FIRST OF A SERIES

FTC Revolt

You've heard of the tax revolt. It's about time for an FTC revolt. Here's my story and why we've got to stop federal bureaucratic regulation.

My story is only one example of how the FTC is harassing small businesses but I'm not going to sit back and take it.

By Joseph Sugarman, President, JS&A Group, Inc.

I'm pretty lucky. When I started my business in my basement eight years ago, I had little more than an idea and a product.

The product was the pocket calculator. The idea was to sell it through advertisements in national magazines and newspapers.

Those first years in the basement weren't easy. But, we worked hard and through imaginative advertising and a dedicated staff, JS&A grew rapidly to become well recognized as an innovator in electronics and marketing.

THREE BLIZZARDS

In January of 1979, three major blizzards struck the Chicago area. The heaviest snowfall hit Northbrook, our village—just 20 miles north of Chicago.

Many of our employees were stranded—unable to get to our office where huge drifts made travel impossible. Not only were we unable to reach our office, but our computer totally broke down leaving us in even deeper trouble.

But we fought back. Our staff worked around the clock and on weekends. First, we processed orders manually. We also hired a group of computer specialists, rented outside computer time, employed a computer service bureau, and hired temporary help to feed this new computer network. We never gave up. Our totally dedicated staff and the patience of many of our customers helped us through the worst few months in our history. Although there were many customers who had to wait over 30 days for their parcels, every package was eventually shipped.

WE OPENED OUR DOORS

During this period, some of our customers called the FTC (Federal Trade Commission) to complain. We couldn't blame them. Despite our efforts to manually notify our customers of our delays, our computer was not functioning making the task extremely difficult.

The FTC advised JS&A of these complaints. To assure the FTC that we were a responsible company, we invited them to visit us. During their visit we showed them our computerized microfilm system which we use to back up every transaction. We showed them our new dual computer system (our main system and a backup system in case our main system ever failed again). And, we demonstrated how we were able to locate and trace every order. We were very cooperative, allowing them to look at every document they requested.

The FTC left. About one week later, they called and told us that they wanted us to pay a $100,000 penalty for not shipping our products within their 30-day rule. (The FTC rule states that anyone paying by check is entitled to have their purchase shipped within 30 days or they must be notified and given the option to cancel.)

NOT BY CONGRESS

The FTC rule is not a law nor a statute passed by Congress, but rather a rule created by the FTC to strengthen their enforcement powers. I always felt that the rule was intended to be used against companies that purposely took advantage of the consumer. Instead, it appears that the real violators, who often are too difficult to prosecute, get away while JS&A, a visible and highly respected company that pays taxes and has contributed to our free enterprise system, is singled out. I don't think that was the intent of the rule.

And when the FTC goes to court, they have the full resources of the US Government. Small, legitimate businesses haven't got a chance.

We're not perfect. We do make mistakes. But if we do make a mistake, we admit it, accept the responsibility, and then take whatever measures necessary to correct it. That's how we've built our reputation.

BLOW YOUR KNEE CAPS OFF

Our attorneys advised us to settle. As one attorney said, "It's like a bully pulling out a gun and saying, 'If you don't give me a nickel, I'll blow your knee caps off.'" They advised us that the government will subpoena thousands of documents to harass us and cause us great inconvenience. They warned us that even if we went to court and won, we would end up spending more in legal fees than if we settled.

To settle would mean to negotiate a fine and sign a consent decree. The FTC would then issue a press release publicizing their victory.

At first we tried to settle. We met with two young FTC attorneys and agreed in principle to pay consumers for any damages caused them. But there were practically no damages, just a temporary computer problem, some late shipments, and some bad weather. The FTC then issued a massive subpoena requesting documents that will take us months to gather and which we feel was designed to harass or force us to accept their original $100,000 settlement request.

Remember, the FTC publicizes their actions. And the higher the fine, the more the publicity and the more stature these two attorneys will have at the FTC.

If this all sounds like blackmail—that's just what it appeared to be to us.

We did ship our products late—something we've admitted to them and which we publicly admit here, but we refuse to be blackmailed into paying a huge fine at the expense of our company's reputation—something we've worked hard eight years to build.

We're not a big company and we realize it would be easier to settle now at any cost. But we're not. If this advertisement can attract the attention of Congressmen and Senators who have the power to stop the harassment of Americans by the FTC, then our efforts will be well spent.

ALL AMERICANS AFFECTED

Federal regulation and the whims of a few career-building bureaucrats is costing taxpayers millions, destroying our free enterprise system, affecting our productivity as a nation and as a result is lowering everybody's standard of living.

I urge Congressmen, Senators, businessmen and above all, the consumer to support legislation to take the powers of the FTC from the hands of a few unelected officials and bring them back to Congress and the people.

I will be running this advertisement in hundreds of magazines and newspapers during the coming months. I'm not asking for contributions to support my effort as this is my battle, but I do urge you to send this advertisement to your Congressmen and Senators. That's how you can help.

America was built on the free enterprise system. Today, the FTC is undermining this system. Freedom is not something that can be taken for granted and you often must fight for what you believe. I'm prepared to lead that fight. Please help me.

Note: To find out the complete story and for a guide on what action you can take, write me personally for my free booklet, "Blow your knee caps off."

One JS&A Plaza, Northbrook, Ill. 60062

©JS&A Group, Inc., 1979

Figure 2–12 Many companies have been stung by the actions of the FTC. One direct-mail house decided to fight back. Joseph Sugarman became a hero of the small and big businessperson alike who felt the federal bureaucracy had overstepped its bounds in too many instances. In time the President and Congress agreed and severely limited the jurisdiction of the FTC in 1980.

Should the government re-write this copy to protect itself from the FTC?

Jefferson, Hancock & Wythe, Inc.

INDEPENDENCE HALL, PHILA., PENNSYLVANIA

Client	House	*Date*	7/4/76
Job No.	1	*Space*	--
Medium	Parchment	*Publ. Date*	ASAP

Copy

A DECLARATION
By the Representatives of the United States of America
In General Congress Assembled.

When in the Course of human of Events, it becomes necessary for one People to dissolve the Political Bands which have connected them with another, and to assume among the Powers of the Earth, the separate and equal Station to which the Laws of Nature and of Nature's God entitle them, a decent Respect to the Opinions of Mankind requires that they should declare the causes which impel them to the Separation.

We hold these Truths to be self-evident, that all Men are created equal, that they are endowed by their Creator with certain unalienable Rights, that among these are Life, Liberty and the Pursuit of Happiness--That to secure these Rights, Governments are instituted among Men, deriving their just Powers from the Consent of the Governed, that whenever any Form of Government becomes destructive of these Ends, it is the Right of the People to alter or to abolish it, and to institute new Government, laying its Foundation on such Principles, and organizing its Powers in such Form, as to them shall seem most likely to effect their Safety and Happiness. Prudence, indeed, will dictate that Governments long established should not be changed for light and transient Causes; and accordingly all Experience hath shewn, that Mankind are more disposed to suffer, while Evils are sufferable, than to right themselves by abolishing the Forms to which they are accustomed. But when a long Train of Abuses and Usurpations, pursuing invariably the same Object, evinces a Design to reduce them under absolute Despotism, it is their Right, it is their Duty, to throw off such Government, and to provide new Guards for their future Security. Such has been the patient Sufferance of these Colonies; and such is now the Necessity which constrains them to alter their former Systems of Government. The History of the present King of Great Britain is a History of repeated Injuries and Usurpations, all having in direct Object the Establishment of an absolute Tyranny over these States. To prove this, let Facts be submitted to a candid World.

He has refused his Assent to Laws, the most wholesome and necessary for the public Good.

Continued. . . .

OK only if everybody showed up
Must prove existence of such laws No copies on file!
No! Must be substantiated
This is an implied guarantee. Copy must state that we don't guarantee it.
Are we prepared to disclose others?
Can't say 'all'. Qualify.
Someone may challenge this!!
Can't substantiate
Need a signed release
Since when are your opinions facts?
Disparaging! Do we have adequate research to back up?

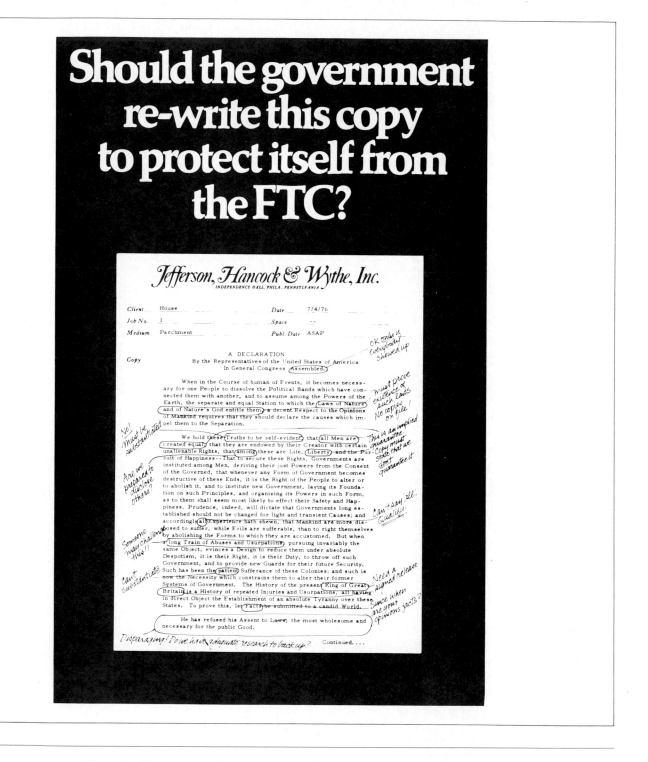

Figure 2–13 The actions of the FTC caused many in the advertising industry to react with alarm to the restrictions on their creativity. In this famous ad, Scali, McCabe, Sloves, suggests that the Declaration of Independence would probably be considered misleading and deceptive by the FTC's standards.

therapeutic devices must give clear instructions for use. The FDA is authorized to require warning and caution statements on packages of poisonous or otherwise hazardous products. It regulates "cents off" and other promotional statements on package labels. The FDA also has jurisdiction over the use of accurate words (such as "giant" or "family") to describe package sizes. It regulates the size and placement of type to indicate the weight or volume of a package.

Patent and Trademark Office

A *trademark,* according to the Lanham Trade-Mark Act (1947), is "any word, name, symbol, or device or any combination thereof adopted and used by a manufacturer or merchant to identify his goods and distinguish them from those manufactured or sold by others." Present trademark laws expand this to include titles, designations, slogans, character names, and distinctive sounds, features, and personalities used in advertising. Ownership may be designated in advertising or on a label, package, or letterhead by the word "Registered," the symbol R, or the symbol TM. None of these marks must be shown on a product, however. If a trademark is used illegally by another, the trademark owner can complain by notifying the violator in writing. If the illegal use continues, the trademark owner can ask the courts to order the violator to refrain from further infringement.

Library of Congress

All copyrighted material, including advertising, is registered and protected by the Library of Congress. A copyright issued to an advertiser grants the exclusive right to print, publish, or reproduce the protected ad for a period of time equal to the life span of the copyright owner plus 50 additional years. An advertisement can be copyrighted only if it contains original copy or illustration. Slogans, short phrases, and familiar symbols and designs cannot be copyrighted. Although a copyright prevents a whole advertisement from being legally used by another, it does not prevent others from using the general concept or idea of the ad or from paraphrasing the copy and expressing it in another way.

The use of any original creative written, musical, illustrative, or other material by an outside source in an advertisement without the express written consent of its creator is an infringement of copyright that may constitute grounds for legal action. For this reason, advertisers and agencies obtain permission before they use creative material from any outside source.

Copyright is indicated in an advertisement by the word "Copyright," the abbreviation "Copr.," or the copyright symbol © near the name of the advertiser. An advertisement that has foreign or international copyright protection usually contains the year of copyright as well. These copyright marks are also used to denote protection in other forms of print advertising, including booklets, sales brochures, and catalogs.

See Figure 2–14 for a summary of federal regulators of advertising. The jurisdiction of these agencies is often overlapping which makes the advertiser's task even more difficult.

Figure 2–14 Federal regulators of advertising

Agency	Function
Federal Trade Commission	Regulates all commerce between the states. Formed in 1914, the FTC is the leading federal regulatory agency for advertising practices and is the subject of the greatest criticism by the advertising profession.
Federal Communications Commission	Formed by the Communications Act of 1934, has jurisdiction over the radio, television, telephone, and telegraph industries. It maintains indirect control over advertising through its authority to license or revoke the license of all broadcast stations.
Food and Drug Administration	Has authority over the advertising, labeling, packaging, and branding of all packaged goods and therapeutic devices. It requires full disclosure labels, regulates the use of descriptive words on packages, and has jurisdiction over the packaging of poisonous or otherwise hazardous products.
Patent and Trademark Office	Regulates registration of patents and trademarks. It enforces the Trade-Mark Act of 1947.
Library of Congress	Registers and protects all copyrighted material including advertisements, music, books, booklets, and other creative material.
Alcohol and Tobacco Tax Division.	Has almost absolute authority over liquor advertising through its powers to suspend, revoke, or deny renewal of manufacturing and sales permits for distillers, vintners, and brewers found to be in violation of regulations.
Office of Consumer Affairs	Is the chief consumer protection department in the federal government. Established in 1971, the OCA coordinates, maintains, and publicizes information on all federal activities in the field of consumer protection. Publications produced and circulated by the OCA include consumer education guidelines, monthly newsletters, and a consumer services column that is released to some 4,500 weekly newspapers.
U.S. Postal Service	Has authority to halt mail delivery to any firm or person guilty of misusing the mails. The U.S. Postal Service maintains control over false and deceptive advertising, pornography, lottery offers, and guarantees which deceive or defraud.

Department of Agriculture	Closely monitors the distribution of misbranded or unregistered commercial poisons. The Department of Agriculture (USDA) works with the FTC to enforce regulations governing certain products.
USDA Grain Division	Has regulatory authority over false and deceptive advertising for seeds and grain products. The Grain Division of the U.S. Department of Agriculture is also empowered to initiate action against violators.
Civil Aeronautics Board	Regulates air traffic and advertising of all air carriers engaged in interstate commerce.
Securities and Exchange Commission	Was established in 1934 and has jurisdiction over all advertising of stocks, bonds, and other securities sold via interstate commerce. The SEC requires that public offerings of such issues contain full disclosure of all pertinent information on the company and the securities offered so that the prospective investor can make an informed buying decision. This disclosure must mention any negative elements that may affect the investment.
Department of Justice	Normally does not initiate legal action against persons or firms charged with violating the federal laws governing advertising. Instead, the Department of Justice enforces these laws and represents the federal government in the prosecution of cases referred to it by other federal agencies.
Consumer Product Safety Commission	Was established in 1972 to develop and enforce standards for potentially hazardous consumer products. It derives its power from four acts: the Flammable Fabrics Act of 1954, the Federal Hazardous Substances Act of 1960, the Children Protection Act of 1966, and the Standard for the Flammability of Children's Sleepwear of 1972. It has jurisdiction over the placement of warning statements in advertisements and other promotional materials for products covered under these acts. Its authority extends to household products, toys, and hazardous substances that cause accidental poisoning. The Consumer Product Safety Commission actively investigates product advertising and labeling violations brought to its attention by consumers and consumer protection groups. Continued violations by product makers are grounds for prosecution and punitive action by the Attorney General.

Regulation by state government

Most media advertising falls into the category of interstate commerce and is therefore regulated by federal agencies. Intrastate advertising, however, including local newspaper, radio, and television advertising, is under the jurisdiction of state laws and enforcement agencies. Most state legislation governing advertising is based on the "truth-in-advertising" model statute developed by *Printer's Ink,* the pioneer trade paper of the industry, which is no longer published. The statute holds that any maker of an advertisement that is found to contain "untrue, deceptive, or misleading" material shall be guilty of a misdemeanor. Today 46 states—with the exception of Arkansas, Delaware, Mississippi, and New Mexico—enforce laws patterned after this statute to control fraudulent and deceptive advertising.

Regulation by local government

Many counties and cities, notably large population centers like New York and Chicago, enforce laws regulating local advertising practices. At least 50 cities, including Los Angeles, Dallas, and Cleveland, also maintain consumer protection agencies to enforce these laws. Similarly, certain counties, like Westchester County (New York) and Harris County (Texas), have consumer protection agencies. These agencies function chiefly to protect local consumers against unfair and misleading practices by area merchants.

Self-regulation by advertisers

Most large advertisers reflect a sense of social responsibility in their advertising. Falstaff Brewing Company, for example, specifically avoids implying that beer will give people "a lift." It also rejects any appeals to adolescents and children as well as any references to sex. While efforts like these have improved the levels of advertising taste and integrity, they have not accomplished enough to satisfy the critics of advertising—notably some consumers and consumer advocate groups. They also have raised the following questions about consumer demands for self-regulation by advertisers:

1. Does self-regulation conflict with the free enterprise right of advertisers to conduct business as they see fit?
2. Does self-regulation impair free, open business competition?
3. Does the creation of consumer complaint departments encourage valid complaints or merely invite frivolous ones?
4. Does compliance with consumer demands result in excessive costs to advertisers that ultimately require higher product costs?

Despite these considerations, self-regulation has increased in recent years. Today it is widely conducted by industry trade associations, professional organizations, advertising agencies, advertising associations and publications, media trade organizations and publications, business organizations, and the National Advertising Review Board (NARB), which together include every segment of the industry.

Self-regulation by industries and professions

Many industries maintain their own advertising codes. These reflect an agreement by companies in the same industry to abide by certain advertising standards and practices. The codes establish a basis for complaint, whereby a member may ask the executive board of the association to review existing competitive conditions in terms of the advertising code to which all members have subscribed.

Some industry codes reflect a high degree of social conscience. The code of the national distilling industry prohibits liquor advertising on television and radio, outdoor advertising near a military or naval base, and advertising in any publication that bears a Sunday dateline. The Wine Institute code bars references to athletes, appeals to children, and inferences that wine is associated with religion.

Certain professions, such as legal, medical, and dental, also maintain advertising codes through their national, state, or local organizations. Until recently, most such groups strictly prohibited advertising by their members except for announcements that a new practice had been established, a new partner added, or an office location changed. After the 1977 U.S. Supreme Court decision declaring state bar association bans on member advertising to be in violation of the First Amendment right of free speech, attorneys are permitted to advertise their legal services, specialties, education and professional honors, office hours, fees, and credit arrangements (Figure 2–15). In some states dentists are also permitted to advertise. Recent actions by the Justice Department and the FTC may remove the bans on advertising by physicians, opticians, architects, and engineers. There has already been a relaxing of state laws that prohibit the advertising of eyeglasses and prescription drugs.

Codes like these are only as effective as the powers of enforcement vested in individual trade associations. Since enforcement may conflict with antitrust laws that prohibit interference with open competion, trade associations usually exert peer pressure on member companies that violate their codes rather than resorting to hearings or penalties.

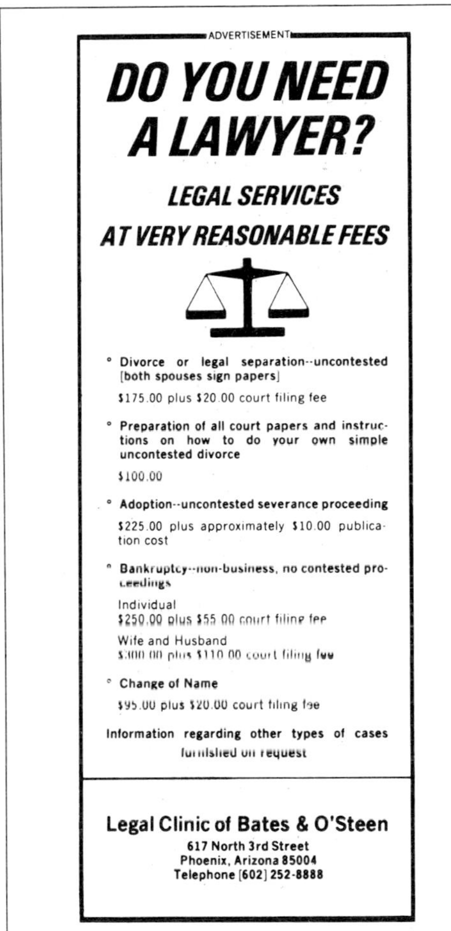

Figure 2–15 The ad that changed history. Prior to the Bates ad, attorneys were not allowed to advertise. The case went all the way to the U.S. Supreme Court, which determined that state bar associations could not prohibit their members from advertising their services. Unfortunately, the moment the ban was lifted, we were treated to a plethora of attorney ads using some of the most deceptive advertising techniques known, including bait and switch. This caused great alarm among various professional advertising groups and prompted some to take action.

Self-regulation by business

Several business-monitoring organizations provide effective controls over advertising practices, particularly at the local level. The largest of these organizations is the Better Business Bureau. Established in 1916, the Better Business Bureau (BBB) evolved from an earlier truth-in-advertising campaign conducted by the American Advertising Federation. Today national and local BBB offices funded by dues from over 100,000 member companies operate to protect consumers against fradulent and deceptive advertising and sales practices. These bureaus, composed of advertisers, agency and media representatives, and laypeople, monitor advertising in their communities. They receive and investigate complaints from consumers and other advertisers. Violators are contacted and asked to revise their advertising. In many cases this is sufficient. The BBB also maintains files on violators, which are open to the public. Records of violators who do not comply are sent to appropriate government agencies for further action. The BBB often works with local law enforcement agencies to prosecute advertisers guilty of fraud and misrepresentation. Each year the BBB investigates more than 40,000 advertisements for possible violations of truth and accuracy. All members of the BBB are pledged to uphold its stringent advertising standards.

The Council of Better Business Bureaus, Inc., is the parent organization of the Better Business Bureau and part of the National Advertising Review Council. One of its functions is helping new industries to develop standards for ethical and responsible advertising. It also provides ongoing information about advertising regulations and recent court and administrative rulings that affect advertising in "Do's and Don'ts in Advertising Copy," a looseleaf advisory bulletin mailed each month to advertisers, agencies, and the media.

Self-regulation by the advertising profession

Most advertising agencies monitor their own practices. In addition, professional advertising associations oversee the activities of their agency members to prevent any problems that may trigger government intervention. Advertising publications actively report issues and actions before the courts in an effort to educate agencies and advertisers about possible legal infractions. Many media require data and test results confirming product claims before they accept advertising. Efforts like these are designed to prevent infractions.

Advertising agencies

Although information about a product or service is supplied to the agency by the advertiser, it is the responsibility of the agency to research and verify all product claims and comparative product data before using them in advertising. The media may require such documentation before accepting the advertising. Substantiation also may be needed if government or consumer agencies challenge the caims. Agencies can be held legally liable for fraudulent or misleading advertising claims. For these reasons, most advertising agencies have legal counsel and regularly submit their advertisements for review. If any aspects of the advertising are challenged, the advertiser's attorneys are asked to again review the advertising and to either confirm it is true or advise that unverified material be replaced.

Advertising associations

The American Association of Advertising Agencies (AAAA) and two other national organizations—the Association of National Advertisers

People in advertising

Morton J. Simon

Attorney-at-Law

Morton J. Simon is one of the nation's foremost authorities on advertising and public relations law. A member of the Philadelphia Bar Association, he has served as counsel to the American Marketing Association, the Advertising Federation of America, the League of Advertising Agencies, and Eastern Industrial Advertisers.

In his private law practice, Simon almost exclusively represents advertising, public relations, marketing agencies and their clients, the communications media, and advertisers. He is a specialist in "copy screening" for advertisers to help prevent legal improprieties.

Simon is the author of *Public Relations Law*, *The Advertising Truth Book*, and other reference texts as well as of hundreds of published articles. In his book, *The Law for Advertising and Marketing*, Simon makes the important point that "the law of advertising and marketing is a vast and deceptive morass, holding many pitfalls for the unwary who may be more concerned with creative problems than with the strictures of the law."

Simon first became interested in advertising law shortly after his graduation from Harvard Law School. As he represented his first advertising clients, he discovered that little research had been done on the legal aspects of advertising, public relations, and corporate communications. Simon devoted himself to this pursuit, and now 95 percent of his clients are advertising agencies, public relations firms, and publishers.

In an interview, Simon said that he is "continually impressed" by the efforts at self-regulation among advertisers. Citing the manuals, rule books, and guidelines that companies produce for their advertising departments or agencies, Simon observed, "These internal restrictions, arising from the social responsibility of the company, are frequently much tougher than the rules of the FTC or any other government regulation."

On the massive proliferation of government controls in recent years, Simon reflected, "It's as though the government has come to believe that the great majority of the American people are completely incompetent to run their own lives."

Despite these regulatory increases, said Simon, the feedback he has received from many in the advertising industry indicates there is "an honest desire to improve, change, and eliminate inequities." From the questions addressed to him by professional audiences, he concludes, "The majority are doing their best to improve all the time."

Still, Simon emphasizes, "Advertising students should be aware that virtually every one of their daily activities, while working in the advertising field, may well involve some legal ramification under both federal and state laws." Nevertheless, he cautions, "advertising people should not attempt to be lawyers. The important thing is that they *recognize* the legal potentials of a particular ad, program, promotion, or campaign. Having recognized this, they should seek competent legal advice and follow it. After all, they are advertising people—not lawyers. *Alertment*, not solution, should be their personal target." In advertising, Simon concludes, "I have found one premise to be basic: 'If in doubt, *don't*.' " In keeping with this attitude, Simon also recommends that advertising agencies not accept legal liability for their clients' media bills.

Simon is a frequent speaker on communication law at association conferences and advertising industry conventions, and he has also been a lecturer at Temple University and the University of Pennsylvania. He teaches a course on the legal aspects of advertising, public relations, and communication at the Charles Morris Price School.

and the American Advertising Federation—are actively engaged in monitoring industrywide advertising practices.

The AAAA, an association of advertising agencies throughout the United States, controls agency practices by denying membership to any agency judged unethical. The AAAA *Standards of Practice* and *Creative Code* set forth advertising principles for member agencies (Figure 2–16).

The American Advertising Federation (AAF) is also a nationwide association of advertising people. The AAF helped to establish the Federal Trade Commission, and its early "vigilance" committees were the forerunners of the Better Business Bureaus. The AAF "Advertising Code of American Business" establishes standards for truthful and responsible advertising. Since most local advertising clubs belong to the AAF, it has been instrumental in influencing agencies and advertisers to abide by these principles.

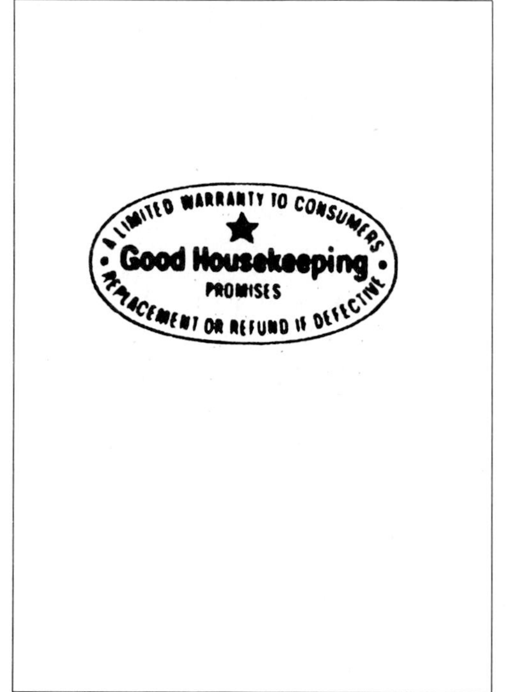

The Association of National Advertisers (ANA) is composed of 400 major manufacturing and service companies which are clients of member agencies of the AAAA. These companies, which are pledged to uphold the ANA code of advertising ethics, work with the ANA through a joint Committee for Improvement of Advertising Content.

Advertising publications

Magazines and newspapers that serve the advertising industry maintain close watch over advertising practices. *Advertising Age,* the industry's leading trade publication, continually champions the cause of more ethical and responsible advertising. Ads deemed objectionable by readers are regularly featured as "advertising we can do without" in the letters to the editor, "Voice of the Advertiser," section.

The media

After an advertisement is approved by agency and advertiser, it is submitted to the media. Almost all media maintain some form of advertising review. They reserve the right to reject any material they regard as objectionable, even if it is not deceptive.

The strictest review is by the television networks. Advertisers are required to submit all commercials intended for a network or affiliated station to the broadcast standards department of that network. Commercial copy then goes simultaneously to each of the three networks for independent review.

The networks are guided by the Broadcast Code, which is published, administered, and continually updated by the Code Authority of the National Association of Broadcasters (NAB). Designed to provide self-regulation to prevent any government regulation of broadcast advertising, the Code Authority is particularly stringent in such areas as its "Children's Television Advertising Guidelines," which govern practices like host selling, toy advertising, and premium offers.

Individual TV and radio stations also screen commercials, but local standards vary widely. One reason is that only about 76 percent of all U.S. television stations and an even smaller proportion of radio stations are members of the National Association of Broadcasters.

CREATIVE CODE

American Association of Advertising Agencies

The members of the American Association of Advertising Agencies recognize:

1. That advertising bears a dual responsibility in the American economic system and way of life.

To the public it is a primary way of knowing about the goods and services which are the products of American free enterprise, goods and services which can be freely chosen to suit the desires and needs of the individual. The public is entitled to expect that advertising will be reliable in content and honest in presentation.

To the advertiser it is a primary way of persuading people to buy his goods or services, within the framework of a highly competitive economic system. He is entitled to regard advertising as a dynamic means of building his business and his profits.

2. That advertising enjoys a particularly intimate relationship to the American family. It enters the home as an integral part of television and radio programs, to speak to the individual and often to the entire family. It shares the pages of favorite newspapers and magazines. It presents itself to travelers and to readers of the daily mails. In all these forms, it bears a special responsibility to respect the tastes and self-interest of the public.

3. That advertising is directed to sizable groups or to the public at large, which is made up of many interests and many tastes. As is the case with all public enterprises, ranging from sports to education and even to religion, it is almost impossible to speak without finding someone in disagreement. Nonetheless, advertising people recognize their obligation to operate within the traditional American limitations: to serve the interests of the majority and to respect the rights of the minority.

Therefore we, the members of the American Association of Advertising Agencies, in addition to supporting and obeying the laws and legal regulations pertaining to advertising, undertake to extend and broaden the application of high ethical standards. Specifically, we will not knowingly produce advertising which contains:

a. False or misleading statements or exaggerations, visual or verbal.

b. Testimonials which do not reflect the real choice of a competent witness.

c. Price claims which are misleading.

d. Comparisons which unfairly disparage a competitive product or service.

e. Claims insufficiently supported, or which distort the true meaning or practicable application of statements made by professional or scientific authority.

f. Statements, suggestions or pictures offensive to public decency.

We recognize that there are areas which are subject to honestly different interpretations and judgment. Taste is subjective and may even vary from time to time as well as from individual to individual. Frequency of seeing or hearing advertising messages will necessarily vary greatly from person to person.

However, we agree not to recommend to an advertiser and to discourage the use of advertising which is in poor or questionable taste or which is deliberately irritating through content, presentation or excessive repetition.

Clear and willful violations of this Code shall be referred to the Board of Directors of the American Association of Advertising Agencies for appropriate action, including possible annulment of membership as provided in Article IV, Section 5, of the Constitution and By-Laws.

Conscientious adherence to the letter and the spirit of this Code will strengthen advertising and the free enterprise system of which it is part. *Adopted April 26, 1962*

Endorsed by

Advertising Association of the West, Advertising Federation of America, Agricultural Publishers Association, Associated Business Publications, Association of Industrial Advertisers, Association of National Advertisers, Magazine Publishers Association, National Business Publications, Newspaper Advertising Executives Association, Radio Code Review Board (National Association of Broadcasters), Station Representatives Association, TV Code Review Board (NAB)

Figure 2–16 The American Association of Advertising Agencies *Creative Code.*

National magazines monitor all advertising, particularly those by new advertisers and for new products. While newer publications that are eager to sell space may not be so vigilant, some established magazines, including *Time* and *Newsweek*, are highly scrupulous. *Good Housekeeping* tests every product before accepting advertising. If the tests do not substantiate the claims made, the ad is rejected. Products that are accepted, however, may feature the *Good Housekeeping* "Seal of Approval" on their labels and in advertising. If any such product is later found to be defective, *Good Housekeeping* promises to refund the money paid for it. A similar product seal and warranty are offered by *Parents Magazine*. *The New Yorker* will not accept discount retail store advertising or advertisements for feminine hygiene products or self-medication products. *Reader's Digest* will not accept tobacco advertising.

Newspapers also monitor and review advertising. Larger newspapers have clearance staffs that read every ad submitted. Most smaller newspapers rely on the advertising manager, sales personnel, or proofreaders to check ad copy. The advertising policies followed by most newspapers, set forth in *Newspaper Rates and Data* (Standard Rate and Data Service, Inc.), include such restrictions as "No objectionable medical, personal, matrimonial, clairvoyant, or palmistry advertising accepted; no stock promotion or financial advertising, other than those securities of known value, will be accepted." Another rule prohibits the publication of any advertisement that simulates reading matter that cannot be readily recognized as advertising unless such an ad features the word "advertisement" or "advt."

Although some small newspapers have less stringent policies, large dailies like the *New York Times* and the *Chicago Tribune* are known for their strictness. Most newspapers closely monitor the comparative price claims made by their retail advertisers. A new-car dealer who advertises "greatest values anywhere" may be asked to change it to "compare our values."

Media trade organizations

The most stringent media regulations govern network affiliate broadcast advertising. These regulations are based on the Code of the National Association of Broadcasters (NAB). Special code provisions apply to advertising in such areas as commercial messages to children, toys, nonprescription drugs, and personal hygiene products.

Advertising on sensitive subjects is reviewed by the NAB Code Board in accordance with the following procedures: (1) the agency submits the script or storyboard to the Code Board: (2) the material is reviewed and the agency is notified of any contents that violate the code; (3) the agency and advertiser are invited to meet with NAB representatives to discuss the violation; (4) the material may be revised and resubmitted until approved; and (5) if approval is not forthcoming, the agency can request a hearing before the board of the NAB to appeal the ruling. Even material that is approved by the Code Board may not necessarily be accepted for broadcast by the network. If a commercial is not approved by the board, however, and is thereafter accepted and aired by a television or radio station, that station may be denied future membership in the NAB.

National Advertising Review Council

In 1971 the National Advertising Review Council (NARC) was established by the Council of Better Business Bureaus, Inc., in conjunction with the American Association of Advertising Agencies, the American Advertising Federation, and the Association of National Advertisers. Its primary purpose is to promote and enforce standards of truth, accuracy, taste, morality, and social responsibility in advertising. Composed of eight members drawn from the leadership of these four organizations, NARC is regarded as the most comprehensive and effective regulatory mechanism in the advertising industry.

Under its direction, two regulatory divisions were established: the National Advertising Division (NAD), an investigative body, and the National Advertising Review Board (NARB), an appeals board for NAD decisions (Figure 2–17). The NAD monitors advertising industry prac-

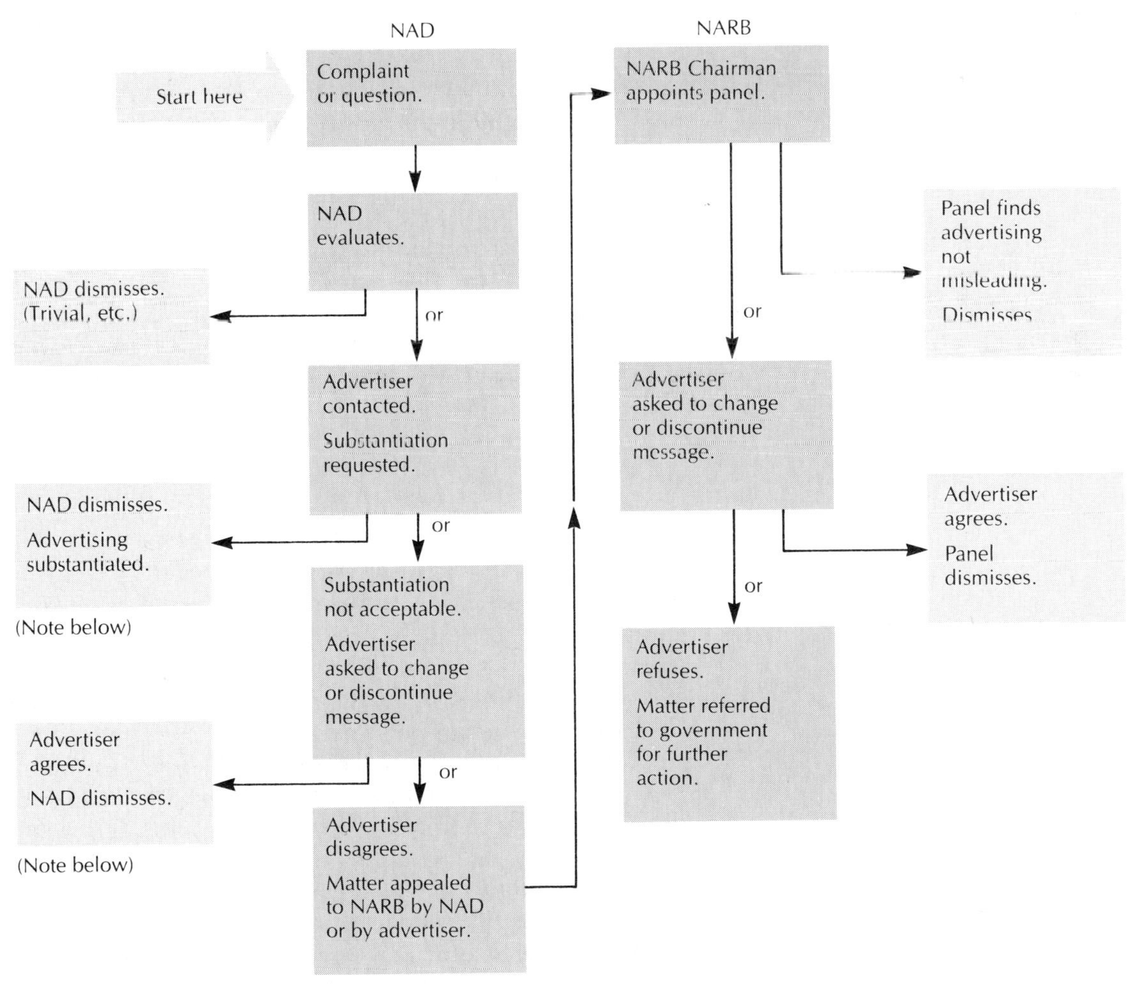

Figure 2–17 Advertising self-regulation procedure.

tices. It reviews complaints received from consumers and consumer groups, brand competitors, Better Business Bureaus, NAD monitors, and others about objectionable advertisements. These complaints are chiefly about false or misleading advertising claims and about ads that depart from taste, morality, or social responsibility. When a complaint is found to be valid, the NAD contacts the advertiser. If false or misleading claims are charged, the NAD requests substantiation or other justification. Advertisers who cannot provide this are asked to modify their advertisements or to withdraw them from the media. Nearly half the national advertising cases reviewed by the NAD to date have resulted either in substantially revised advertising or in withdrawal of advertising by the advertiser.

If an advertiser refuses to modify or withdraw the advertising, the case is referred to the National Advertising Review Board (NARB) for adjudication (Figure 2–18). The NARB consists of a chairperson and 50 volunteer members: 30 national advertisers, 10 agency representatives, and 10 laypeople from the public sector. A five-member panel, composed of three advertisers, one agency representative, and one layperson, is then selected from this board to review the complaint. Panel members may elect to uphold, modify, or reverse the earlier decision of the NAD. If the panel decides to uphold the decision, the advertiser is again asked to revise or withdraw the advertising. Failure to do so will result in the NARB releasing the facts of the case to the media. The NARB will then forward the case to the Federal Trade Commission or other appropriate government agency for further action (Figure 2–19).

Both the NARB and the NAD issue monthly reports to help establish practicable standards for the advertising industry. The NARB also sponsors advisory panels to study such specialized topics as comparative advertising and women in advertising. The NAD is available to evaluate and render decisions about proposed advertising campaigns prior to their completion and placement in the media.

Regulation by consumer control

The greatest recent growth among the regulatory forces governing advertising has been that of consumer protection organizations. Starting in the 1960s, the consumer movement began to play an increasingly active role in fighting fraudulent and deceptive advertising. Consumers demanded not only that products perform as advertised but also that more product information be provided so that people can compare and make better buying decisions. The impact of the consumer movement and its growing pressure for more stringent advertising regulation soon gave rise to a new word: *consumerism,* or social action designed to dramatize the rights of the buying public. Since then, one fact has become clear to both advertisers and agencies: The American consumer has power.

Consumerism: Impact on advertising.

The growing consumer movement has caused advertisers and agencies to pay more attention to product claims, especially those related to energy use (such as the estimated miles per gallon of a new auto) and the nutritional value of processed foods (such as sugar-coated breakfast cereals). Consumerism has fostered the growth of consumer advocate groups and regulatory agencies. It has also promoted more consumer research by advertisers, agencies, and the media in an effort to learn what consumers want—and how to provide it. Many advertisers agree that the creation of customer relations departments

"I think that ad is lying."
If you think that an advertisement is misleading or untruthful, here's what you can do about it.
Most advertisers work very hard to make sure their advertising is completely honest and truthful. But if you ever see an advertisement or a commercial that you think takes liberties with the truth or makes questionable claims, there's something you can do about it.
Write to the National Advertising Review Board.
If truth or accuracy in a national ad or commercial is your concern (not matters of taste or matters of editorial or program content), the advertiser will be asked for substantiation of the claims made.
Where justified, advertisers will be requested to modify or discontinue any claim for which there is not adequate support.
You will be notified of the results of the investigation and they will be reported in a monthly press release.
NARB IS SELF-REGULATION
The NARB was formed in 1971 out of the conviction that self-regulation of advertising is preferable to government regulation. It is faster. No tax dollars are required to support it.
The NARB is sponsored by four leading advertising and business organizations: The American Association of Advertising Agencies, the American Advertising Federation, the Association of National Advertisers, and the Council of Better Business Bureaus. Its board of directors consists of representatives of advertiser companies, advertising agencies, and members representing the public sector.
Since its inception, more than 1,300 inquiries regarding national advertising have been reviewed.
Advertisers have cooperated in providing substantiation of the advertising in question.
More important, not one advertiser has refused to modify or discontinue advertising found to be misleading.
NARB is self-regulation that works.
If you would like further information or if you see advertising that you feel is untruthful...
write to:
National Advertising Review Board, 845 Third Avenue, New York, New York 10022.

Figure 2–18 The NARB urges consumers to report advertisements they think are misleading, untruthful, or deceptive. They point out that the "NARB is self-regulation that works" since "not one advertiser has refused to modify or discontinue advertising found to be misleading."

and investment in public goodwill ultimately will pay off in improved consumer relations and sales. This trend is particularly evident among financial institutions, such as banks and savings-and-loans, and the public utilities.

Consumer information networks

Several large organizations serve as mass communication networks for the exchange of consumer information. They enable consumers to express their views on advertising and marketing infractions. These organizations include the Consumer Federation of America (CFA), the National Council of Senior Citizens, and the National Board of the Young Women's Christian Association (YWCA). They have the following functions: (1) serves as a central clearinghouse for the exchange and dissemination of information among its members; (2) aids the development of state, regional, and local consumer organizations; (3) works with and provides services to national, regional, county, and municipal consumer groups. The National Consumer League, though originally conceived to improve working conditions for labor, now concentrates increasingly on issues that affect consumers.

Figure 2–19 NARB panels: Complaints and decisions

Complaint	That Carte Blanche Corporation used potentially misleading advertising in claiming that, "A lot of restaurants and hotels don't take American Express. But do take Carte Blanche. Because as good as American Express is, it isn't enough." NAD reviewed substantiation submitted by the advertiser and found it inadequate. With no promise of revision of the claim, the matter was appealed to NARB.
Decision	The panel found the substantiation submitted by the advertiser to be geographically limited and therefore inadequate. It also ruled that the consumer would interpret the phrase "a lot" as used in the advertising to mean "a substantial number," and the facts submitted did not support this conclusion. The panel, therefore, found the advertising claim to be misleading and recommended that it be changed or discontinued.
Advertiser Response	Carte Blanche Corporation accepted the decision of the panel, but termed the action "moot" since the advertising had been discontinued.
Complaint	That Zenith Radio Corporation used misleading advertising in claiming in a television commercial that: "Every color TV Zenith makes is built right here in the United States by Americans like these." (The video showed Zenith employees at work.) At issue was the use of foreign-made components which investigation by NAD placed at as much as 14.5 percent of total components/parts, and approximately 9.5 percent of the value of a representative Zenith set. NAD, therefore, found the advertising

misleading. Though the company cooperated fully throughout the investigation, it declined to change the advertising. NAD appealed to NARB. In the interim, Zenith reversed its earlier decision, and notified NAD that the commercial in question was being withdrawn from further use.

Decision In light of the above cooperative action by the advertiser, NAD asked the NARB panel to dismiss. The panel concurred and dismissed the matter.

Complaint That Volkswagen of America, Inc., used false and misleading advertising in selecting a single point from its warranty (i.e., a term of 24 months or 24,000 miles) and in comparing it with 12-month/12,000-mile terms in a selected list of 94 other cars. Complainant argued that the omission of other points in the warranties implied to the consumer that all were the same except for the terms compared. NAD had dismissed the complaint.

Decision The panel's unanimous decision stated that while an advertiser has the privilege of selecting one or more points in his warranty to feature in advertising, if he does so he has the responsibility to point out that warranties differ in many respects, and that other features not cited may be of importance to the purchaser. Since this was not done in the subject advertising, the panel found it to be misleading and recommended that it be either modified or discontinued.

Advertiser Statement The advertiser did not agree with the findings of the panel, but stated that the advertising had run its planned media course prior to the initial complaint, and the panel proceedings were felt to be "moot."

Complaint This action, initiated by NAD, deemed advertising by Ralston-Purina Company for "Chuck Wagon Dinner for Dogs" to be misleading in that it photographically depicted "tender juicy chunks" which appeared to be meat, but in actuality were made from soybeans. NAD referred the matter to NARB after a period of time in which it felt the advertiser had been given ample time to respond but had not. Subsequent to the referral, however, the advertiser did respond to NAD, stating that the advertising in question had been replaced with new copy removing the elements judged to be deceptive.

Decision With assurances from the advertiser that the old advertising would no longer be used, and in the belief that the new advertising eliminated elements of possible misrepresentation, NAD requested that the matter be dismissed by the NARB. After a thorough review of the matter, the panel accepted the NAD recommendation and dismissed the complaint.

Consumer interests also are served by several private, nonprofit testing organizations like Consumers Union, Consumers' Research, and Underwriters Laboratories.

Consumer advocates.

Consumer advocate groups focus on issues that involve advertising and advertisers. These groups act on complaints received from consumers as well as on those that grow out of their own research. Their normal procedures are to: (1) investigate the complaint; (2) if warranted, contact the advertiser and ask that the objectionable advertisement or practice be halted; (3) if the advertiser does not comply, release publicity or criticism about the offense to the media; (4) submit complaints with substantiating evidence to appropriate government agencies for further action; and (5) in some instances, file a lawsuit and seek to obtain from the courts a cease and desist order, or a fine or other penalty, against the violator.

Legal restraints on international advertisers

No discussion of the social and legal aspects of advertising is complete without some consideration of the restrictions imposed by foreign cultures and governments on what may or may not be said, shown, or done in an ad. Some restrictions are legal ones; others are moral and ethical ones which determine the boundaries of good taste (Figure 2–20).

Advertising claims are strongly regulated in many countries. Superlatives of any kind are frequently outlawed. In Germany, for example, superlatives may be used only if they are scientifically provable, and no reference may be made to a competitive product. In the U.S. the seller is often in a more favorable position than the buyer. In many European countries just the reverse is true. Many countries bar practices such as two-for-the-price-of-one offers, one-cent sales, box-top gimmicks, and free tie-in offers.

Some countries have taxes on advertising, and they are not always standardized even within a single country. Austria charges a 10-percent tax on newspaper and magazine advertising in all states except two. The 10-percent tax is also charged on radio and television ads in all but one state where the radio tax is 20 percent.

These restrictions can cause problems in international advertising. McCann-Erickson tried to translate the old Coca-Cola slogan, "Refreshes you best," into foreign languages. This slogan in the United States would merely be considered harmless exaggeration. In Germany, however, it was outside the boundaries of the law. The agency, therefore, substituted "Das erfrischt richtig," or "Refreshes you right."

In Europe there are "Official Sales Periods," which are the only times price cuts may be advertised. These periods vary from country to country, but control is very strict and fines are extremely high. And before a sale ad may be published, it frequently must be approved by a government-controlled agency.

The only solution to these and the myriads of other legal problems encountered by international advertisers is to have a lawyer on retainer.

Figure 2–20 Advertising regulations in selected countries of Western Europe

Country	General regulations		Limitations on specific products			Media regulations	
	Comparative Advertising	Advertising to children	Alcoholic beverages	Tobacco	Drugs and medicine	Restricted or banned media	Limitations on commercials
Austria	Banned if denigrating	Direct appeal forbidden	None	Voluntary ban on television ads	Ads need approval of government	None	Maximum length of 30 seconds
Belgium	Banned if denigrating	See drugs	Ads for absinthe drinks banned	Cigarette ads banned in cinema, television, and radio	Banned by law in all general media	No commercial television or radio	Not applicable
Denmark	Minor restrictions	None	None	Voluntary control over cigarette ads	Banned in all general media	No commercial television or radio	Not applicable
Finland	None	None	Banned on TV	Banned on TV and media directed at youth	Voluntary control over copy	No domestic radio	No television commercials on certain days
France	Banned	Prebroadcast screening of commercials	Hard liquor banned on all media, others on radio and TV	Cigarettes banned on TV and radio	Copy clearance needed	Total receipts from one advertiser limited to 8% of total TV	Blocks, or groups, of commercials only (no spots)
Germany	Banned	Voluntary for TV and radio	Voluntary limits by industry	Banned on TV and radio	Banned in all media	None	TV commercials between 6 and 8 P.M.; none on Sunday
Italy	Direct comparisons banned; indirect OK if substantiated	Cannot show children eating	Some restrictions on TV ads	All tobacco banned in all media	Copy clearance needed	None	Sold in broadcast packages
Netherlands	OK if comparison is fair, detailed	Voluntary restraints	Voluntary restraints on TV and radio	Voluntary restraints on TV and radio	None	None	No more than two TV commercials per week per product
Sweden	Banned if denigrating	Ban on showing children in danger	Voluntary control on ads for wine and hard liquor	Banned in all media	Prescription drug ads banned	No commercial TV or radio	Not applicable
Switzerland	None	None	Banned in all media	Banned in all media	Banned in all media	No commercial radio	No more than two TV commercials per week per product
United Kingdom	Banned if denigrating	Voluntary rules designed to protect children	No commercials before 9 P.M.	Cigarette ads banned on TV and radio	Voluntary control	None on major media	None

Summary

As advertising has proliferated in the media, the criticism of advertising has also intensified. Detractors say that advertising debases our language, makes us too materialistic, and manipulates people unethically. Furthermore, they say, advertising is not only excessive but also offensive or in bad taste, it is frequently deceptive, and it perpetuates unrealistic stereotypes of people.

Defenders of advertising admit that advertising has been and sometimes still is misused. However, they point out that the abuse heaped on advertising is no longer justified and is itself excessive. Moreover, the very critics who attack advertising, they say, use basic advertising techniques to sell their books and further their points of view.

One result of this criticism is the large body of laws and regulations that has swelled in recent decades to restrict the use of advertising. Regulation comes in several forms: self-regulation by advertisers; regulation by the advertising profession and the media; regulation by local, state, and federal government agencies; self-regulation by industrial associations and the business community; and regulation by the consumer protection organizations.

The strictest advertising controls are those imposed by laws. Enforcement of these laws may come from the Federal Trade Commission (FTC), the Federal Communications Commission (FCC), the Food and Drug Administration (FDA), the Securities and Exchange Commission (SEC), and a host of other bureaucracies. The actions of the FTC have been criticized so much that Congress limited its jurisdiction in 1980. However, the growth of consumer advocacy groups in the last decade almost ensures continued pressure to further restrict what advertisers can say, show, and do.

The most effective body for self-regulation has been the National Advertising Review Council, which was formed by the Council of Better Business Bureaus, Inc., in conjunction with the American Association of Advertising Agencies, the American Advertising Federation, and the Association of National Advertisers. Through its investigative body, the National Advertising Division (NAD), complaints received from consumers, brand competitors, or local Better Business Bureaus can be reviewed and corrective measures suggested. Advertisers that refuse to comply are referred to the council's appeals body, the National Advertising Review Board (NARB), which may uphold, modify, or reverse the NAD's findings. It may also direct the advertiser to modify or withdraw the advertisement in question.

Because of restrictions imposed by foreign cultures and governments, international advertisers must deal with an entirely different set of laws from those of domestic advertisers. The only solution to this extremely complex legal environment is to consult with knowledgeable local attorneys in each country where advertising is to be placed.

Questions for review

1. Is it the responsibility of advertising to lead or to reflect society?
2. How is the NARB structured? What is its importance to consumers and advertisers?
3. What is the relationship between the FTC and the advertising industry? Do you feel the FTC has overstepped its authority? Explain. Can you cite recent examples of FTC action against advertisers?
4. What are the provisions of the Wheeler-Lea Act? Why is it important for advertisers to be aware of the provisions of this act?
5. Does advertising tend to create monopolies? Justify your answer with examples.
6. What are the major organizations involved in the self-regulation of advertising?
7. How does the FCC exert control over advertising?
8. Why do most large agencies employ lawyers to "clear" advertising?
9. Why is the trademark law important?
10. Why are feminists so upset about advertising today? Is their displeasure reasonable?

Part II

The Advertising Business

The fruit of labor is GENIUS

3

The advertisers

Frank Perdue was being interviewed for an article in *Esquire* magazine. "I could say I planned all this," he says, "but I was just back there with my father and a couple of other guys working my ass off every day. I wasn't even sure for a long time that I even liked the chicken business. But my advantage is that I grew up having to know my business in every detail. I dug cesspools, made coops and cleaned them out. I know I'm not very smart, at least from the point of view of pure IQ, and that gave me one prime ingredient of success—fear. I mean a man should have enough fear so that he's always second-guessing himself."

He pulls out a wrinkled clipping from his wallet. The words are Alexander Hamilton's: "Men give me credit for some genius. All the genius I have lies in this. When I have a subject in hand, I study it profoundly. Day and night it is before me. I explore it in all its bearings. My mind becomes pervaded with it. Then the effort I have made is what people are pleased to call the fruit of genius. It is the fruit of labor and thought."

Chickens are not a very glamorous business. And Frank Perdue didn't know anything about advertising. But when Madison Avenue learned that this chicken farmer from the Delmarva Peninsula (located between the Chesapeake Bay on the west and the Atlantic Ocean on the east) was ready to take a big plunge into advertising, everybody scrambled for the account. So many people were fawning all over Perdue that it made him uncomfortable. He pulled back for awhile.

To make sure that nobody put him at that disadvantage again, Perdue pervaded himself with advertising day and night. He devoured great volumes on the subject, and he can still drop quotes by people like David Ogilvy and Rosser Reeves the way other people cite the Bible or Shakespeare. He haunted an advertising institute, studying all the pamphlets and textbooks. He called up advertising journalists and radio and TV station managers in New York, systematically trying to pick brains. Almost nobody knew him, but many helped simply because they were impressed by his inventive industry.

By the time he set himself up to be courted again by Madison Avenue, Perdue was an expert. Altogether, he interviewed almost 50 agencies. Eventually, he narrowed his list down to a championship flight of nine. Then he really went on the offensive, grilling, double-checking, interviewing. He called one very prominent agency and asked them to have lunch with him in the Oak Room of the Plaza Hotel. The whole top executive force trooped over to the Plaza, licking their chops, convinced Perdue was going to tell them that he had selected their agency for his chickens. Instead, as soon as they settled at the table, Perdue informed them that they hadn't even made his final list, but he would appreciate it if they would rank the nine agencies that were still left in the running. Stunned and flabbergasted, the agency boys dived into another round of martinis and patiently did as he requested.

The losers were really the lucky ones. When Perdue called up Ed McCabe, the copy chief at Scali, McCabe, Sloves, for about the 800th time in a week, McCabe finally blew his cork. "You know, Frank," he said, "I'm not even sure that we want your account anymore because you're such a pain in the ass." McCabe recalls, "You know all he said to that? He just said, 'yeah, I know I'm a pain in the ass, and now that we've got that settled, here's what I want to ask you this time.' "

Sometime later Perdue picked McCabe's agency. One of the first commercials they shot, in a campaign built around Perdue himself (another idea he never cottoned to), won an award (Figure 3–1). Ed McCabe won more honors for his work on the Perdue campaign than any other copywriter in the nation that year. Frank Perdue became the biggest chicken man in the nation's biggest city, and a celebrity to boot. "I could write a book about advertising," he says matter of factly.[1]

Companies that advertise

Virtually every successful business uses advertising, and the majority of people who work in advertising are in the companies that use advertising. These range in size from small retail shops to huge, multinational manufacturing firms, from small industrial concerns to large service organizations. All these companies have an advertising department of some sort, even if it is just one person like Frank Perdue who shares his company's advertising responsibility with many other job functions.

Naturally the importance of the advertising person in the company depends on several factors: who the person is, the size of the company, the type of business in which the company operates, the size of the advertising program, the role of advertising in the company's other marketing activities, and the degree of involvement of top management in the advertising function.

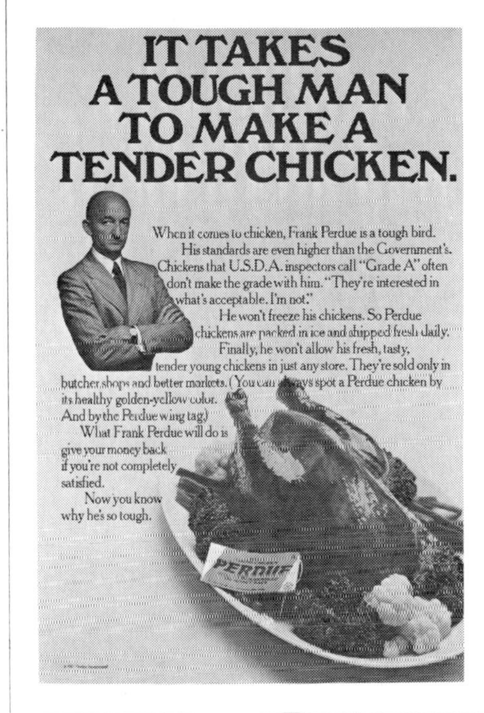

Figure 3–1 The Perdue campaign has been revolutionary in the business since it demonstrated that fresh meat could be branded and sold like packaged products. A large supermarket chain put Perdue side by side against a house brand selling for six cents a pound less. Incredibly, 40 percent of the customers chose Perdue at the premium price.

Company people involved in advertising

Most of us think of advertising people as copywriters, art directors, or account executives—the people who work for advertising agencies. In fact, the people who work for the companies that advertise are also very much a part of the advertising business.

Company presidents and other top executives are usually very interested in how their advertising represents the company. Many are directly involved in the advertising decisions that have to be made, especially those in smaller companies.

Sales and marketing personnel have a direct relationship to advertising. They frequently provide input to the creative process and make decisions regarding which advertising agency to use and their proposed advertising programs.

In large companies, there may be a separate advertising department headed by an advertising manager or marketing director. This department may include one person or several hundred.

Product people, engineers, designers, and production personnel often are asked to make recommendations about product features or provide information about competitive products that can help advertising.

Administrative people in finance, purchasing, or accounting are asked to consider the impact of advertising programs on the company's financial status. Often they are involved in evaluating a campaign in progress or in determining appropriate budgets for the next campaign.

Even clerical people get involved. Many receptionists, secretaries, typists, and file clerks take part in the advertising process by virtue of their position within the company. It is not unusual to see a secretary in a small firm move up to an administrative assistant position and eventually become a manager of the company's advertising activities.

Just about everybody who works for a firm that advertises feels that the company's advertising represents him or her in some way and therefore has some feeling about it. As a result, the more we can learn about advertising, how it works, and why it is prepared the way it is, the better help we can be to the companies that employ us.

What company advertising departments do

The ways advertising departments function are as varied as the companies that operate them. Many companies perform all their advertising activities themselves, whereas others hire outside advertising agencies or specialists to help them. Regardless of the way responsibilities are divided, there are certain things all advertisers must do.

Functions common to all advertisers

Every successful advertiser, large or small, must have understanding and expertise in communications to perform the basic functions necessary to have a successful advertising program. These functions are administration, planning, budgeting, and coordination with other company departments and with outside advertising services. We shall discuss each function briefly.

Administration

The advertiser's administrative functions include organizing and staffing the advertising department, supervising and controlling the department's activities, and selecting the advertising agencies to be used. An advertising manager is normally responsible for recommending specific advertising programs based on the company's marketing plans and budgets. It is imperative, therefore, that the advertising manager have a thorough understanding of all the major factors influencing the company's marketing activities. The advertising manager should also establish an efficient procedure for handling inquiries, analyzing competitive advertising, and evaluating his or her own ads. It is usually the advertising manager's responsibility to sell the campaign to top management. Some companies have a committee system to oversee the work of the advertising department. In this way the expertise of the entire firm can be applied to the formation and execution of advertising policy.

People in advertising

William Sharp

Vice President/Advertising Manager
Coca-Cola USA

William Sharp is vice president and advertising manager for Coca-Cola USA, the domestic soft drink division of the Coca-Cola Company. He directs and coordinates the development and implementation of advertising materials for all the company's soft drink products.

A native Chicagoan, Sharp began his career as the owner of a Chicago-based advertising agency. He went on to become a copywriter for Tatham-Laird and Kudner, then copy supervisor of Leo Burnett Advertising Agency/Chicago, and finally group creative supervisor of J. Walter Thompson/Chicago.

During this time Sharp developed and directed the Basic Advertising Course, an educational program sponsored by the American Association of Advertising Agencies to train young, disadvantaged persons for entry-level professional positions in advertising. Sharp recruited faculty and students and served as instructor and administrator of the program for two years at Northwestern University. The course, the first of its kind, is still used today.

Sharp then was appointed director of communications for the Office of Economic Opportunity in Washington, D.C. He was directly involved in developing policies, strategies, and experimental programs to improve national communications resources as a means to better the quality of life for all Americans, and particularly the disadvantaged. He was also instrumental in influencing regulations and legislation toward achieving this objective.

Sharp joined Coca-Cola USA as Allied Brands advertising manager in 1972. Only two years later, he was named advertising manager of Coca-Cola. He was elected to the position he presently occupies in 1976.

As advertising manager for Coca-Cola USA, Sharp works with brand managers to provide the company's various advertising agencies with sufficient insights into its marketing plans to enable them to create effective advertising. "My job," said Sharp, "is to help develop and have a clear understanding of what our advertising goals and objectives are, and to work with all our resources to help in the development of advertising that meets these goals and objectives." Toward this end he confers with the company's market research people daily, with its legal officers several times a week, and with the brand managers and advertising agency representatives "every day, all day."

In his handsome executive office surrounded by tapes, storyboards (a series of drawings used in a proposed television commercial), a television, and other symbols befitting the professional home of an advertising manager, Sharp reflects the success of his distinguished career. He has served as chairman of the American Advertising Federation and as a member of the board of directors of the Association of National Advertisers. He has also been chairman of the National Academy of Engineering's Telecommunication Subcommittee on Education and of the Urban System Subcommittee of the Federal Interagency Media Committee.

A lecturer of note, Sharp is also the author of *How to Be Black and Get a Job in the Advertising Agency Business Anyway.* He has received numerous awards both in the advertising industry and in recognition of his outstanding achievements in motivating minority youth. Sharp is listed in *Who's Who in America.*

Planning

Although it is only periodically necessary to draw up formal advertising plans for the approval of management, the planning process is ongong. Planning is actually a process of defining and redefining goals and objectives, outlining and reoutlining advertising strategies and campaigns, scheduling and rescheduling specific advertisements, and evaluating and reevaluating advertising results. The way advertising plans are developed will be discussed in Chapter 9.

Budgeting

The advertising budget is usually determined annually or semiannually. The advertising manager has the task of formulating the budget and selling it to top management, but top management usually has the last word on how much will actually be allocated to advertising functions. The budget includes the cost of advertising and the operating expenses of the advertising department (Figure 3–2). It is also the advertising department's responsibility to see that the budget is followed and not squandered away before all the advertising tasks are performed.

Coordination with other departments

The fact that advertising may be set up as a separate department does not mean it operates independently of the firm's other functions. The activities of business are usually divided into three categories: production, finance, and marketing. Advertising, like sales, is a marketing activity. Thus, the advertising manager must coordinate the department's activities with other marketing functions. The advertising department must also coordinate its work with the various departments involved in production and finance.

For example, the advertising department may give the company input on the size, style, color, and operation of products that might increase customer satisfaction. Both the sales and advertising departments should find out and communicate to the production departments what consumers want in products and packaging.

The accounting department should be consulted for detailed cost figures. Records are kept on expenditures for research, overhead, ad production, and media. Controlling costs is a joint responsibility of both these departments.

The legal department works with the advertising department to protect the company from trademark and copyright infringement and to keep it from inadvertently violating truth-in-advertising laws.

In short, a close relationship between advertising personnel and other company departments is vital.

Coordination with outside advertising services

Finally, it is necessary for every advertising department to coordinate and supervise the work of any outside advertising services it employs. These may be companies or individuals that assist in the production of advertisements, such as advertising agencies or art studios. Or they may be companies that publish or broadcast the company's advertisements, such as newspapers, magazines, and television stations.

The advertising department is the liaison between the firm and the outside service. It has the responsibility of screening and analyzing the various services available, making recommendations to management, and frequently deciding which outside services to use. (See the Agency Review Checklist.) The advertising manager is then responsible for supervising and evaluating the work performed.

Space and time costs in regular media
Advertising consultants
Ad-pretesting services
Institutional advertising
Industry directory listings
Readership or audience research
Media costs for consumer contests, premium and sampling promotions
Ad department travel and entertainment expenses
Ad department salaries
Advertising association dues
Local cooperative advertising
Direct mail to consumers
Subscriptions to periodicals and services for ad department
Storage of advertising materials

Catalogs for consumers
Classified telephone directories
Space in irregular publications
Advertising aids for salesmen
Financial advertising
Dealer help literature
Contributions to industry ad funds
Direct mail to dealers and jobbers
Office supplies
Point-of-sale materials
Window display installation costs
Charges for services performed by other departments
Catalogs for dealers
Test-marketing programs
Sample requests generated by advertising
Costs of exhibits except personnel
Ad department share of overhead
House organs for customers and dealers
Cost of cash value or sampling coupons
Cost of contest entry blanks
Cross-advertising enclosures
Contest judging and handling fees
Depreciation of ad department equipment
Mobile exhibits
Employee fringe benefits
Catalogs for salesmen
Packaging consultants
Consumer contest awards

Premium handling charges
House-to-house sample distribution
Packaging charges for premium promotions
Cost of merchandise for tie-in promotions
Product tags
Showrooms
Testing new labels and packages
Package design and artwork
Cost of non-self-liquidating premiums
Consumer education programs
Product publicity
Factory signs
House organs for salesmen
Signs on company-owned vehicles
Instruction enclosures
Press clipping services
Market research (outside produced)
Samples of middlemen
Recruitment advertising
Price sheets
Public relations consultants
Coupon redemption costs
Corporate publicity
Market research (company produced)
Exhibit personnel
Gifts of company products
Cost of deal merchandise
Share of corporate salaries
Cost of guarantee refunds
Share of legal expenses
Cost of detail or missionary men
Sponsoring recreational activities
Product research
House organs for employees
Entertaining customers and prospects
Scholarships
Plant tours
Annual reports
Outright charity donations

This chart is designed to simplify the assignment of expenses to the advertising budget by identifying items that should be charged (white list), items that are debatable (gray list), and items that should not be charged (black list).

Figure 3–2

Agency Review Checklist

The following agency review form is only a sample. It will need to be expanded, reduced or revised to suit your individual needs. You may wish, for example, to use a weighting or you may prefer to make comments on every point rather than use a grading system.

Nevertheless, this sample will give you some idea of the areas to cover. Use it as a checklist when you develop the review format that is right for you.

Company reviewer ______________________

Title ______________________

Agency representative ______________________

Title ______________________

Period under review from __________ to __________

Division, department or product, if applicable ______________________

	UNACCEPTABLE 1	MARGINAL 2	3	SATISFACTORY 4	5	EXCELLENT 6
Art						
1. Overall quality of work						
2. Well thought out to meet the creative strategy						
3. More effective than competitive work						
Production						
1. Faithful to creative concept and creative execution						
2. Prepared on time, within budget.						
3. Control of outside services.						
Media						
1. Soundness of media research.						
2. Effective and efficient media strategy and alternatives.						
3. Achieve objectives within budget.						
4. Negotiates and executes program smoothly.						
5. Periodic review of plan and budget.						
Account management						
1. Motivates and involves all agency resources.						
2. Continuity and professionalism.						
3. Adequate meaningful contact.						
4. Knowledge of account/product-market.						
5. Working relationships.						
Financial/Administrative						
1. Competitive bids obtained and submitted.						
2. Maintains adequate files/submits detailed invoices.						
3. Billing is timely/reflects smooth accounting.						
4. Administratively and financially stable.						
Research						
1. Internal capabilities meet needs.						
2. Control of outside services.						
3. Utilizes existing research.						
4. Adequate testing of creative product.						
Performance						
1. Continues to grow with company.						
2. Keeps schedules.						

	UNACCEPTABLE 1	MARGINAL 2	3	SATISFACTORY 4	5	EXCELLENT 6
3. Reacts well to criticism.						
4. Takes initiative and speaks out.						
5. Performs efficiently and effectively.						
Staffing						
1. Depth and professionalism throughout agency.						
2. Depth and professionalism on the account.						
3. Management spends time and effort on account.						
General						
1. Background knowledge of markets and products.						
2. Understanding of advertising fundamentals						
3. Adherance to company policy.						
4. Responsive to requests.						
Strategy						
1. Knowledge of company business.						
2. Knowledge of competition.						
3. Ability to define problems.						
Planning						
1. Assistance in establishing objectives.						
2. Contribution to marketing plans.						
3. Presentation of plans and programs.						
Creative						
1. Innovative and successful creative concepts.						
2. Accurate interpretation of problems/solutions in creative product.						
3. Ability to stay within established criteria.						
4. Cost consciousness.						
Copy						
1. Overall quality of work.						
2. Well thought out to meet the creative strategy.						
3. More effective than competitive work.						

Functions performed by some advertisers

If you owned a small retail television and appliance store you might have one person as your advertising department. That person would be responsible for performing the various administrative, planning, budgeting, and coordinating functions. But what else might be done? In most cases the person would also lay out the ads to be run in the newspaper, write much of the advertising copy, and handle all the media placement, too. However, it is unlikely that that person would actually create the physical advertisements unless he or she was also a commercial artist or graphic designer. For that reason many manufacturers of consumer goods prepare advertisements in advance and supply them to the retailers who sell their products. The retail advertising department inserts the store name, address, and telephone number at the bottom of the advertisement and gives it to the newspaper.

On the other hand, if you owned a large retail chain you might have a complete advertising department staffed and equipped to provide a wide range of advertising services in-house. These activities generally fall into the categories of advertising production, media placement, and marketing support services.

Figure 3–3 Revlon's in-house agency is called the 50th Floor Workshop. Several Revlon products, including Ciara, Charlie perfumes, and Revlon lipsticks and nail enamels, are served by this department, which is responsible for creating and producing all advertising materials.

Advertising production

When a firm does not use an advertising agency, the advertising department may be responsible for creating and preparing all advertising materials. The department would then have its own staff of artists, copywriters, and production specialists to produce the work (Figure 3–3).

Media placement

Some advertising departments are responsible for the media function. They have to analyze all potential media and rate them according to space cost, services to advertisers, market potential, advertiser acceptance, publication or broadcast image, circulation or reach, editorial policy, editorial format, and editorial content. The department is also responsible for developing media schedules, purchasing space and airtime, and verifying affidavits of performance.

Other marketing support services

Frequently a company's advertising agency is responsible for the preparation of product and corporate advertisements, while the company's own advertising department is responsible for other marketing support services such as the collateral printed materials that are distributed to management, salespeople, dealers, and distributors.

Some advertisers purchase their own product photography, develop sales contests, and produce trade show exhibits, technical films, or direct-mail campaigns.

There are many other functions performed by advertising departments and advertising agencies. The degree of responsibility of each varies from company to company.

How large advertisers work

Just as the size and the function of the advertising department depend on a variety of factors, so does the way in which the department is organized. No two firms, product lines, or markets are exactly alike. Therefore the method or organization depends on the unique circumstances of each company.

In this section we will discuss how most large advertisers operate in centralized and decentralized departments. Then we will briefly discuss the in-house advertising agency, its advantages, and its disadvantages.

Centralized organization

What do Wheaties, Cheerios, Betty Crocker, Parker Games, and Foot-Joy golf shoes have in common? For one thing, they are just a few of the many products marketed by General Mills, Inc., in Minneapolis, Minnesota. One of the 20 largest national advertisers, General Mills reportedly increased its advertising budget 10 percent in 1979 in response to an improved marketing environment. This strategy had been paying off for several years, and it paid off again in 1979 in increased sales and a 14 percent boost in profit.

It also paid off for some in personal promotions. The largest dollar contribution to company profits in 1976 had come from General Mills's Craft, Game and Toy Group headed by F. C. Waller, that division's director of business development and marketing planning. Waller was then promoted to General Mills's vice-president–director of marketing services. Since then he has supervised the company's vast advertising and marketing services department, 330 employees, and a $189 million media advertising budget (up from $111 million in 1976).

Located at corporate headquarters in Minneapolis, Marketing Services (as the department is called) is much more than just an advertising department. It is really many departments within a department. As a centralized advertising department, it has the basic responsibilities of administration, planning, budgeting, and coordination for the promotion of more than 50 different brands. In the process it supervises 26 outside advertising agencies and operates its own in-house agency for new or smaller brands.

Organized around functional specialties (e.g., market research, media, graphics, copy advisory), Marketing Services consults with General Mills brand managers and consolidates many of their expenditures for maximum efficiency. The Media Department, for example, is involved daily in all media plans and dollar allocations with the various marketing divisions. The Production and Art Services Department handles the graphic requirements of the in-house agency as well as package design for all brands. And Betty Crocker Kitchens provides promotional services for the various Betty Crocker marketing programs (see Figure 3–4).

However, Marketing Services is more than just a staff service department. It is also a profit center. Its Consumer Promotions Department handles money-making coupon programs for flatware, crystal, and other products. And Betty Crocker Enterprises develops, produces, and sells recipe books and cookbooks, another money-making venture.

The result is a highly effective series of mostly unrelated advertising programs for a wide variety of products and brands, all directed from one central spot. According to Waller, this organization has the disadvantage of making it more difficult to provide a general overview of marketing strategies and execution. At the same time, however, it gives General Mills great efficiency in its advertising programs and facilitates the process of delivering savings.

Now suppose you have a chain of stores that requires a large amount of advertising support. You consider hiring additional advertising personnel. But how do you organize them? Do you assign an advertising manager to each store and allow each to handle its own promotion? Or do you assign your new personnel to work under your existing advertising manager at the main store?

The oldest and still most common advertising department is the centralized organization like the one at General Mills. In smaller companies the advertising manager may report directly to the president. In larger firms the advertising manager usually reports to a marketing vice president. (See the Ad Lab.)

There are several advantages to a centralized advertising depart-

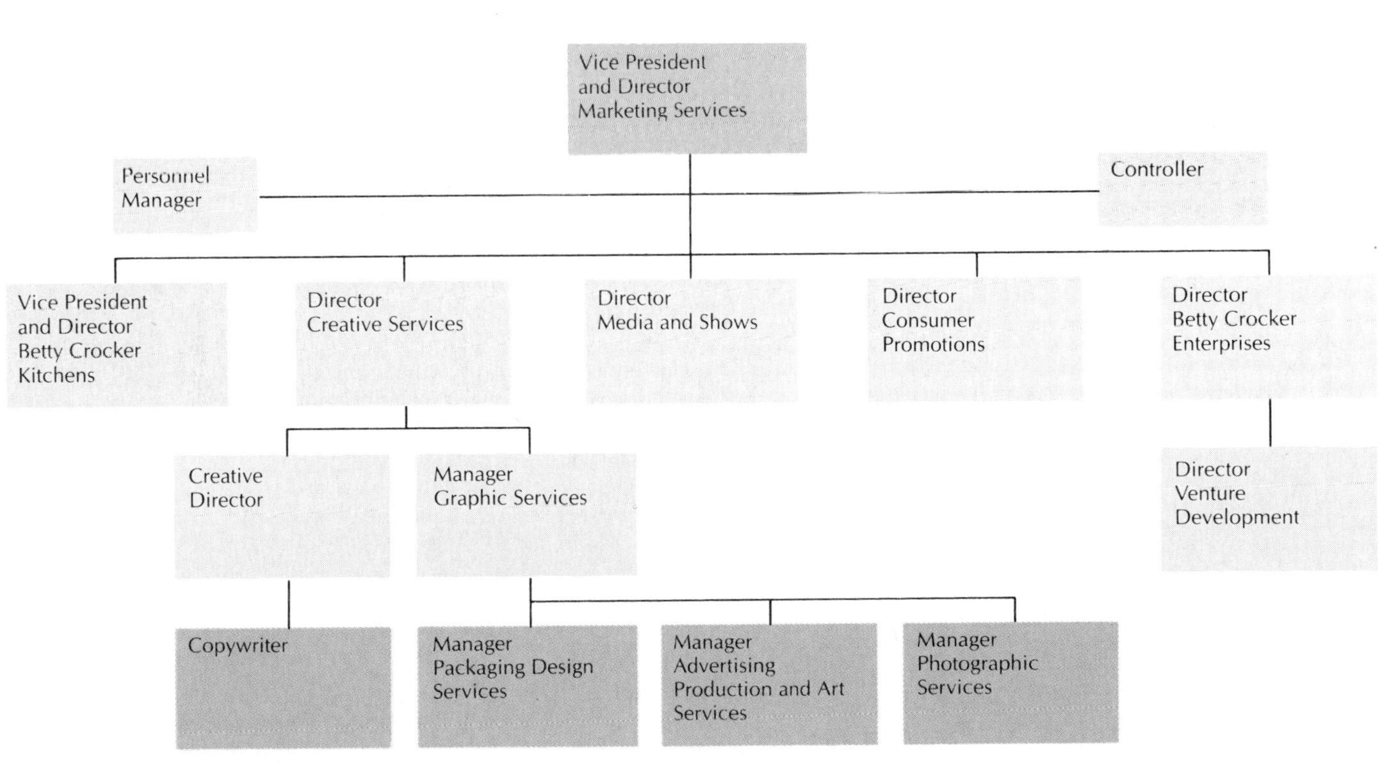

Figure 3–4 General Mills's organization chart.

ment. Communications flow more easily within the organization. The need for a large staff of advertising specialists is reduced. Lower level personnel do not need to be exceptional because the firm's top management can take part in advertising decision making. And, unlike decentralized organizations, complete continuity can be built into

Career opportunities in company advertising departments

Employment of advertising personnel is expected to increase faster than the average for all occupations through the 1980s. The growing number of consumer and industrial goods and increasing competition in many product and service markets will cause advertising expenditures to rise, thereby creating a need for more advertising employees. Because of the sheer number of advertising departments, the opportunities here are greater than with advertising agencies.

Company advertising departments need managerial personnel, but some need creative, media, and research people, too. Listed on the chart below are the titles of jobs commonly found in companies, the educational preparation required, the occupational experience helpful for gaining entry into the position, and salary information. The salaries vary considerably depending on the applicant's educational background and experience, the size of the company, and its geographic location.

Job title	Educational preparation	Occupational or related experience	Extracurricular activities	Salary
Advertising manager	College degree required with emphasis in marketing; some positions require M.B.A.	Advertising and/or marketing department of a manufacturer or large retailer	Participation in advertising and marketing clubs; membership in off-campus organizations in contact with business community helpful	$17,000+
Public relations specialist	College degree required with emphasis on liberal arts courses; English, journalism, and marketing courses helpful	Journalism jobs even with small newspapers or specialized magazines can be useful; selling, marketing, and advertising experience helpful; military experience as a public information officer or writing experience with military publication or broadcasting	Free-lance writing, community organization work, election and fund campaigning, and public speaking are good supporting experience	$17,000+

the communications programs—and at a substantial cost savings.

Every centralized advertising department is unique in its internal structure. For example, if your TV store chain merges with another appliance chain, you might decide to have one advertising manager supervise all the advertising for radios and television sets. Then you

Job title	Educational preparation	Occupational or related experience	Extracurricular activities	Salary
Copywriter for retail advertising department	B.A. preferred with courses in advertising, English, sociology, psychology, and languages	Retail store sales or advertising; newspaper, magazine, or broadcast writing	Advertising or marketing clubs; writing for school and community publications	$12,000 (entry level)
Artist for retail advertising department	Commercial art courses; B.A. desirable	School newspaper or magazine experience doing layout illustration, or printing production	Participation in community projects doing posters, brochures, direct mail, and advertising	$12,000 (entry level)

Other opportunities: Product managers, market researchers, production specialists, house organ editors/writers, audiovisual managers, marketing assistants, marketing directors, technical writers, technical illustrators, and sales promotion managers.

Laboratory application

Select one of the "other opportunities" listed or choose an occupation not included in this box. Discuss what educational preparation, occupational or related experience, and extracurricular activities might assist you in obtaining such a job.

might have another manager supervise the advertising for washers, dryers, and refrigerators. Each manager might have a staff of employees including artists, copywriters, and people to plan media expenditures. Most centralized organizations are structured in one of five ways:

1. By product.
2. By subfunction of advertising (sales promotion, print production, TV/radio buying, outdoor advertising, etc.).
3. By end user (i.e., consumer products, industrial products).
4. By media.
5. By geography (i.e., western advertising, eastern advertising).

There are also numerous other ways that large advertisers with centralized departments can work, depending on the character of the management, the firm's marketing needs, and the nature of the company's customers and products.

Decentralized organization

As companies become larger and larger, take on new brands or products, acquire subsidiaries, and establish divisions in several parts of the country, a centralized advertising department becomes highly impractical. A company then begins to decentralize its advertising and establish new departments assigned to the various divisions, subsidiaries, products, countries, regions, brands, or whatever other categories most suit the firm's needs. The final authority and responsibility for each divisions' advertising rest with the product manager or the general manager of the particular division.

Imagine that you are one of the over 50 college graduates to be hired this year for the advertising department of the king of American advertisers, Procter & Gamble Co. in Cincinnati. Fresh out of college, with your degree under your belt, you are entering the legendary Marine Corps of marketing, P&G's brand manager development program.

Commonly referred to as the nation's number one marketing practitioner, this $6-billion company manufactures and sells over 70 different consumer products. These include many brands that are the leaders in their fields: Tide, Ivory soap, Crest toothpaste (Figure 3–5), Pampers diapers, Duncan Hines cake mixes, Crisco shortening, and Charmin paper products, just to mention a few. As a new recruit, you are on your way (you hope) to becoming the brand manager for one of these perennial favorites of American families.

But at first you're not sure where you are headed. Procter & Gamble has 15 separate operating divisions. Only six of these are consumer product divisions: packaged soaps and detergents, bar soaps and household cleaning products, food products, coffee, toilet goods, and paper products. In addition, there are five industrial product divisions and four international divisions. Each division is set up almost like a separate company with five functional areas of operation. Each has its own research and development department, manufacturing plant, advertising department, sales force, and finance and accounting staff. Likewise, every brand within each division has a brand manager, two assistant brand managers, and one or two staff assistants. The brand managers report to brand-group supervisors, who report to the division managers, who report to P&G's corporate management.

So let's pretend you arrive in Cincinnati and you find that you have been assigned to the advertising department of the paper products division as a staff assistant for one of the division's brand managers. You also learn what to expect in your effort to become a P&G brand manager. Your job for the next couple of years will be to learn everything you possibly can about your brand and about this giant company that spends over $649 million per year advertising its products. That's more than any other company in the world spends. As P&G's chair-

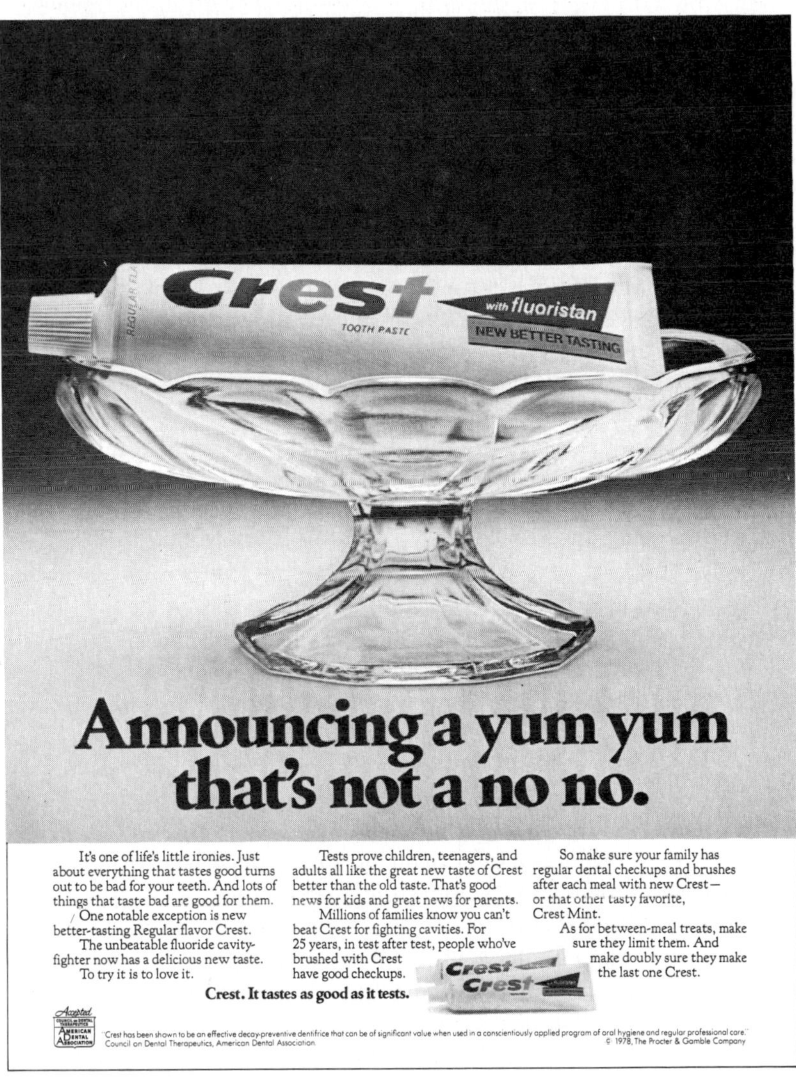

Figure 3–5 Procter & Gamble is not known for winning many advertising awards. This example, though, is a classic that has won the approval of the professional advertising community.

Figure 3–6 Procter & Gamble brand managers are responsible for the advertising of their brands as well as their overall marketing success. Some critics, though, say they have more responsibility than authority.

man once said, "We're as much in the advertising business as we are in the manufacturing business."

As an apprentice brand manager, you will live with and learn the statistics of your brand's performance against competitors. You will be assigned to work on store displays. You will develop sales projections for your brand, help plan advertising budgets, and coordinate with other sections of the division's advertising department: media, copy, art and packaging, sampling and couponing, and legal. You will learn how market research helps determine the packages, scents, sizes, and colors people want; how product research improves the brand in response to competition; and how the division's sales force tries to muscle more shelf space for the brand in the supermarket.

After a year of this you will be sent out into the field to sell for six months. At that time you will be promoted to assistant brand manager. You will meet with wholesalers, rack jobbers, and grocers. You will check shelf facings, store displays, and couponing volume to make sure your division's brands are getting the retail attention they deserve.

When you return to Cincinnati, you will be assigned to another brand within your division. Here you will follow through on the detail work required by your brand manager, administer market research field studies, keep close to advertising activities for your new brand, work with your brand's advertising agency, and coordinate special brand promotions. Your most important assignment at this point is to get ready to take over your boss's job. Eventually, as your boss is moved up or out, you will become a P&G brand manager.

This brand manager system has kept P&G ahead as the nation's leading consumer products marketer. The brand manager is, in effect, the general, and behind the general is an army of personnel, talent, brains, and money to make the brand go. Each manager has his or her own advertising agency, which creates and places the brand's media advertising. The manager has the help of the division's advertising department for coordinating sales promotion and merchandising programs, and the support of the corporate advertising department's media and research supervisors who give statistical information and guidance.

Some say brand managers are frustrated by having more responsibility than authority since they need divisional approval for most of their decisions (Figure 3–6). Nevertheless, brand managers are in the unique position of being close to their market, close to their product, and close to their management, all at the same time. This gives Procter & Gamble both the up-to-date, detailed information it needs to make tough marketing decisions and the follow-through it requires to execute those decisions.

When advertising is decentralized in large multidivision companies, it more easily conforms to the specific problems and needs of the division. Flexibility is increased, allowing quicker and easier adjustments in campaigns and media schedules. New approaches and creative ideas are introduced more easily. And the results of each division's advertising may be measured independently of the others.

Ford Motor Company, for example, is organized on a highly decentralized basis, and consequently the advertising is also decentralized. Each of its principal product divisions has its own advertising activity. These include the Ford, Lincoln-Mercury, Ford Tractor, and

Checklist for ways to be a better client

The more effective you are as a client, the better the work you will get from your agency.

☐ Look for the big idea. Concentrate first on positioning and brand personality. Too few products have either. Do not allow a *single* advertisement—no matter how brilliant—to change your positioning or your brand personality.

☐ Learn the fine art of conducting a creative meeting. Deal with the important issues first. Strategy. Consumer benefit. Reason why. State clearly whether you think the advertisement succeeds in these areas. And if not, why not.

☐ Cultivate honesty. Tell your agency the truth. Make sure your advertising tells the truth, and *implies* the truth as well. And never let creative people get away with excuses that honesty is "dull."

☐ Be enthusiastic. When you like the advertising, let the creative people know you like it. Applause is their staff of life. After a really good presentation, send the copywriter a note. You may be amazed at the results.

Be frank when you *don't like the advertising*. Copy writers won't hate you for turning down an idea if you give them a *reason*. They may even agree with you.

☐ Be human. Try to react like a person, not a corporation. Be human enough to laugh at a funny advertisement, even if it is off-strategy.

☐ Be willing to admit you aren't sure. Don't let your agency press you by asking for the order *immediately* after a new copy presentation. You may need time to absorb what they've been thinking about for a long while.

☐ Insist on creative discipline. Professionals don't bridle at discipline. A strategy helps creative people zero in on a target. But remember that rules are only a *starting* point.

☐ Keep the creative people involved in your business. Successful copywriters want to know the latest market shares just as much as you do. Tell them what's happening, good *and* bad. Sales figures, consumer letters, a crazy idea from your research chemist—all can help.

☐ Don't insulate your top people from the creative people. Agency creative people want to receive objectives *directly*—not filtered through layers. While most projects need not involve your top management, a valuable perspective can be provided by those not tied up in the day-to-day work. Good work is done in an atmosphere of involvement, not insulation.

☐ Make the agency feel responsible. Be a leader, not a nitpicker. *Tell them what you think is wrong, not how to fix it.*

☐ Don't be afraid to ask for great advertising. Let your agency know you have confidence in them to deliver more than just "good solid advertising." Aiming for greatness involves trying new directions—and some risks. It is *safer* to go for singles than home runs. Sometimes the situation calls for more.

☐ Set objectives. If you expect action and results, you must know where you want to go. Set objectives—for your advertising and your business.

☐ Switch people, not agencies. Candor prevents minor disagreements from becoming major rifts. If there are problems, ask for new people to work on your account. A different copywriter or account executive on your business may provide a fresh approach, without depriving the business of necessary continuity.

☐ Be sure the agency makes a profit on your account. Clients who demand more service than the income can cover are shortsighted. The agency can't afford to put its best people to work on that account and may end up looking for a profitable new account to replace it. In a good relationship, the agency grows as the client grows.

☐ Avoid insularity. Don't isolate yourself with the same people—at work, on the tennis court, at cocktail parties. Force yourself to go beyond the comfortable world of your own lifestyle.

☐ Care about being a client. Creative people do their best work on accounts they like, for clients they like to work with. *Good clients*. That doesn't mean *easy* clients. There is even competition within an advertising agency to work for certain clients. That's why good clients wind up with the best writers and the best account executives.

☐ Suggest work sessions. Set up informal give and take discussions, where copywriters can air rough ideas, and you can talk about your objectives. These sessions are especially helpful just before the agency starts a complex assignment.

Ford Parts and Service divisions as well as the Ford Motor Credit Company subsidiary. The divisional advertising managers report to divisional marketing managers who report to the divisional general manager.

Some companies that work in a decentralized manner like Ford also have an advertising department at the corporate level. It might assist the divisional advertising managers in any of a variety of different ways such as technical advice, media buying, research, or TV production.

The advertising department at Ford's headquarters is responsible for only corporate advertising that is designed to support the product advertising of its various divisions.

There are certain drawbacks to decentralized advertising departments. Individual department heads sometimes tend to be more concerned with their budgets, problems, and promotions than with determining what will benefit the firm as a whole. The potential power of repetitive advertising is often diminished because there is no uniformity in the advertising among divisions. Rivalry between brand managers may become fierce and may further deteriorate into secrecy and jealousy. It is virtually impossible to standardize styles, themes, or approaches. After one multidivision company decentralized, it had difficulty just getting the product brand managers to use the same logo in their ads.

Of course there are advantages to both centralized and decentralized advertising departments. What works successfully in one market, though, may not work in the next. There are no constants in determining which form or organization is best. And no organization is pure. They are all different and individually designed to fit the needs of the particular company.

Most large companies end up with a combination of both centralized and decentralized control. Eastman-Kodak, for example, is organized by end-user markets and has individualized advertising operations for each. All these departments are located in Rochester, New York, however. Each advertising and promotion manager reports to his or her particular division's general manager. Kodak's director of advertising and promotion acts as an across-the-board coordinator and supervisor for all advertising activities of the various markets divisions and provides for centralized needs such as media, printing production, and advertising research. (See the Ad Lab.)

In-house agencies

Some companies, in an effort to save money and centralize all their advertising activities, have fired their advertising agencies and set up their own in-house advertising agencies, wholly owned by the company. The "full-service house agency" is set up and staffed to do all the work of an independent full service agency. Being fully self-contained, it is capable of developing and accomplishing every type of publicity, sales promotion, and advertising required by the typical manufacturing company.

The in-house advertising agency is basically a total-capability advertising department. All aspects of advertising creativity and production are performed in-house, and the ads are placed by the same in-house department. Operating as an advertising agency for the company, this department also retains any media commissions that are allowed it.

One of the most successful in-house agencies is in Phoenix, Arizona, and is registered under the name of COMM Advertising. COMM AD is the Marketing Communications Department of Motorola, a subsidiary of Motorola, Inc. (Figure 3–7). Within this department are eight groups, which provide the whole range of promotional services necessary to the company. The Technical Communications Department-

Which ad would you select?

1.

2.

3.

4.

Laboratory application

Assume you are the advertising manager for Hathaway shirts and your advertising agency brought you the pictured ad layouts for a new campaign. Which ad would you select? Why?

It takes courage to be a good advertising person. Mike Turner, the senior vice president of Ogilvy & Mather and managing director of OM's Houston office, offered this fictitious example of how a fearful agency account team systematically botched up a marvelous advertisement. Creating great advertising requires trust between the advertising manager and the creative team. Both must possess the courage to give the advertiser what is needed, rather than what he or she wants. The agency needs the courage to present it. The advertiser needs the vision to recognize its greatness and the courage to buy it.

In this example, ad 1 is the famous Hathaway shirt ad as it originally was conceived in the mid-1950s. The ad created an outstanding image for Hathaway and made the agency, Ogilvy & Mather, famous. However, an account team terrified of taking risks nearly destroyed it at its birth.

When the ad was presented to an account executive at the agency, he added the ugly panel at the left (ad 2) and changed the strong, simple statement to a lackluster headline. Next in came a woman (ad 3) to add sex appeal. Then (ad 4) off went the "risky" eyepatch. Why? Because people might associate it with unpleasant eye diseases.

As Turner says, "this account team was so busy trying to outguess what the client wanted that they never gave one moment's thought to what was needed, and in the process a great advertisement was destroyed."

But what would you have done if the agency had presented these four layouts? Would you have had the courage to buy the "risky" ad? Or would you have taken the "safe" route?

Turner suggests that if an account person wants safety, he should go quickly and sign up as a tour guide on a cruise ship since he's great at the "at your pleasure" bit.

ment prepares all data sheets, handbooks, technical brochures, application notes, technical public relations, and product news releases. The Advertising and Sales Promotion Department prepares media ads and sales support material and performs the media buying function. The Graphic Arts and Technical Arts Departments produce all art materials needed by the other groups. In addition, Motorola has a manager of Advertising and Sales Promotion responsible for all trade show activity, sales of technical information to the public, meeting site planning, open houses, promotional literature, and audio visual productions. The manager of the Marketing Communications Department reports to the Director of Marketing Programs, who is one of six divisional marketing managers reporting to Motorola's director of worldwide marketing.

COMM AD has a long record of successes. Originally formed in 1976 to give the company greater control and economy, the department grew to its present size of 63 people in 1981.

The possible loss of objectivity or creativity that might be offered by an outside agency is admitted by the company. Another possible disadvantage is the required fixed level of staffing, which is not easily variable during business fluctuations, unlike outside agencies.

Nevertheless, COMM AD is respected in industrial advertising circles as being one of the most capable, creative, and successful in-house advertising agencies, and Motorola indicates every intention of maintaining it (Figure 3–8).

There are several reasons advertisers set up their own agencies. Usually the most important is the hope of realizing savings by cutting overhead expenses and saving the 15 percent commission on space advertising that would normally be given to an advertising agency. With a house agency the company is not charged the standard print

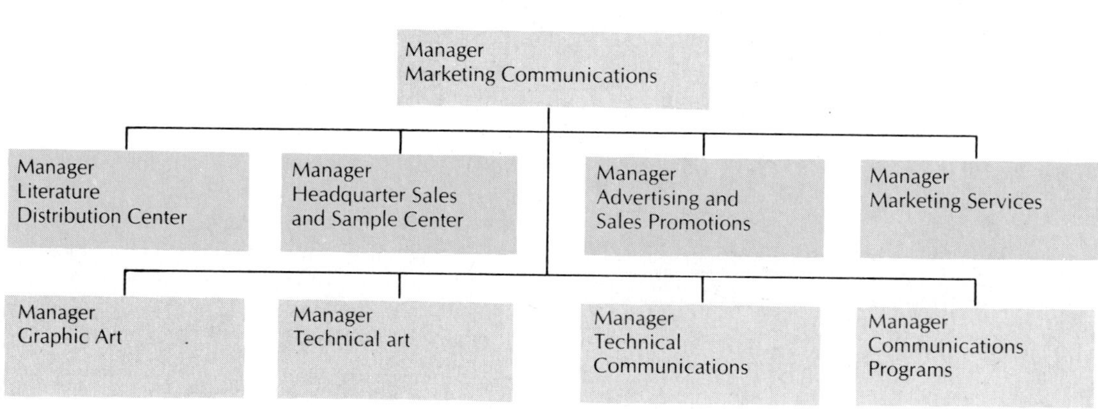

Figure 3–7 This is an organization chart for COMM AD, Motorola's in-house advertising agency. It is able to provide the whole gamut of advertising activities from producing its own technical artwork to developing ads and placing them in the various trade media used to promote the company's vast line of products.

or art production markup, which ranges from 17.65 to 25 percent when such items are purchased through an outside agency. Advertisers likewise feel they can receive more attention from their agency if the company is its only client.

The fact is that in-house agencies usually can respond better to pressure deadlines because they can focus their full resources on the project. Although outside agencies may be able to produce just as quickly, they often have to hire free-lance help, thereby potentially incurring enormous overtime charges. Likewise, house agencies tend to have a greater depth of understanding of the company's products

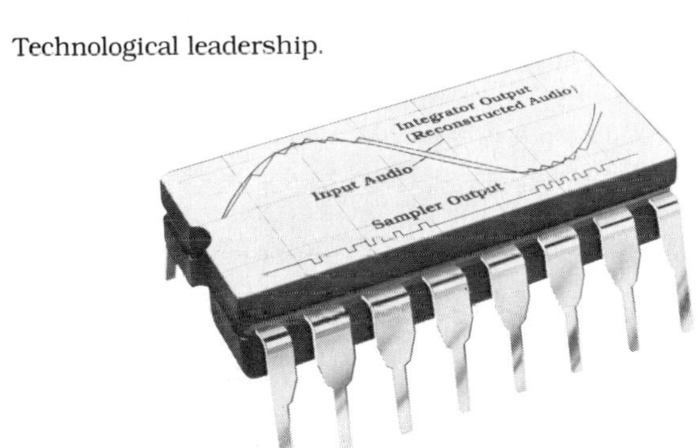

Figure 3–8 Through its in-house agency, COMM AD Advertising, Motorola is able to produce highly technical advertisements for its semiconductor products. A few outside agencies have the technical expertise to create such ads, but most have difficulty even understanding them, much less writing them.

and markets. Also, services rendered to departments outside the normal advertising functions may be easily charged to those departments. This is particularly important for retailers. It enables the other departments to benefit from the talents of the in-house agency, and yet the true cost of the agency can be established. Finally, many companies feel they have better management control of and involvement in the advertising when it is done in-house. (See Figure 3–9.)

Despite these advantages, many full-service house agencies have not succeeded. In attempting to save as much of the independent agency's commission as possible, some companies have sacrificed more than they anticipated. The benefit of the independent agency's objectivity is often lost along with much of its talent. Large, independent agencies provide experience, versatility, and a diversity of talent usually not available in in-house agencies. In-house agencies usually find it extremely difficult to attract the best creative talent. Part of this might be because of the slower wage-raise policy of some corporations. But also some creative people fear getting trapped in what they think might be a stagnant environment without the incentive and vitality that result from the stiff competition in the agency world. In addition, advertising production may suffer by becoming excessively company-oriented rather than consumer-oriented. By overly reflecting company policies and views, it can become too self-serving.

Some media, such as consumer magazines, do not give the 15 percent commission to in-house agencies because they do not consider them true advertising agencies. If that occurs too often, the in-house agency will not save the company money at all.

One other drawback is that management may feel stuck with the in-house agency when things do not go well. Companies that have independent agencies can easily replace them if the work is not satisfactory.

For years advertisers and agencies have squabbled over the pros and cons of in-house advertising agencies. The independent agencies consider in-house agencies as interlopers and harbor a degree of bitterness toward the media that allow them the commission. It's not likely that the argument will be settled in the near future.

There's no question that some in-house agencies have been highly successful. Many retailers have used house agencies successfully for years, especially for their broadcast advertising (Figure 3–10). (See Chapter 20 for an in-depth look at retail advertisers.) Some companies, though, have had good advertising agencies, fired them, set up their own in-house agencies, and eventually reverted back to the independent agency saying they had not saved a penny and had lost creativity. In short, it depends on the needs and circumstances of the particular company.

Managing international advertising

Put yourself in the position of the advertising manager of an American company that is beginning to market its products abroad. You are aware of the obvious problem—in foreign markets you have to use a different creative strategy. You will be speaking to a different market with a different system of values, a different environment, and probably a different language. The media you generally use may not be available or as effective. As a result of these and other factors, your advertising message must be different, too. Foreign customers more than likely have different purchasing abilities, different purchasing habits, and different motivations.

You are also faced with another problem. How will the advertising be managed and physically produced? Will your in-house advertising department do it? Will your domestic advertising agency do it? Or will you have to go into the foreign market, set up a foreign advertising department, or hire a foreign advertising agency?

The subject of foreign agencies will be addressed in the next chapter. However, the answer to all these questions depends basically on two factors: (1) how the company tends to structure its foreign marketing operations, and (2) within that structure, what are the most effective and economical means to conduct advertising activities.

Just as in the domestic situation, how to manage the advertising in foreign markets depends to a great extent on the foreign marketing structure of the company. Does the company intend to market its

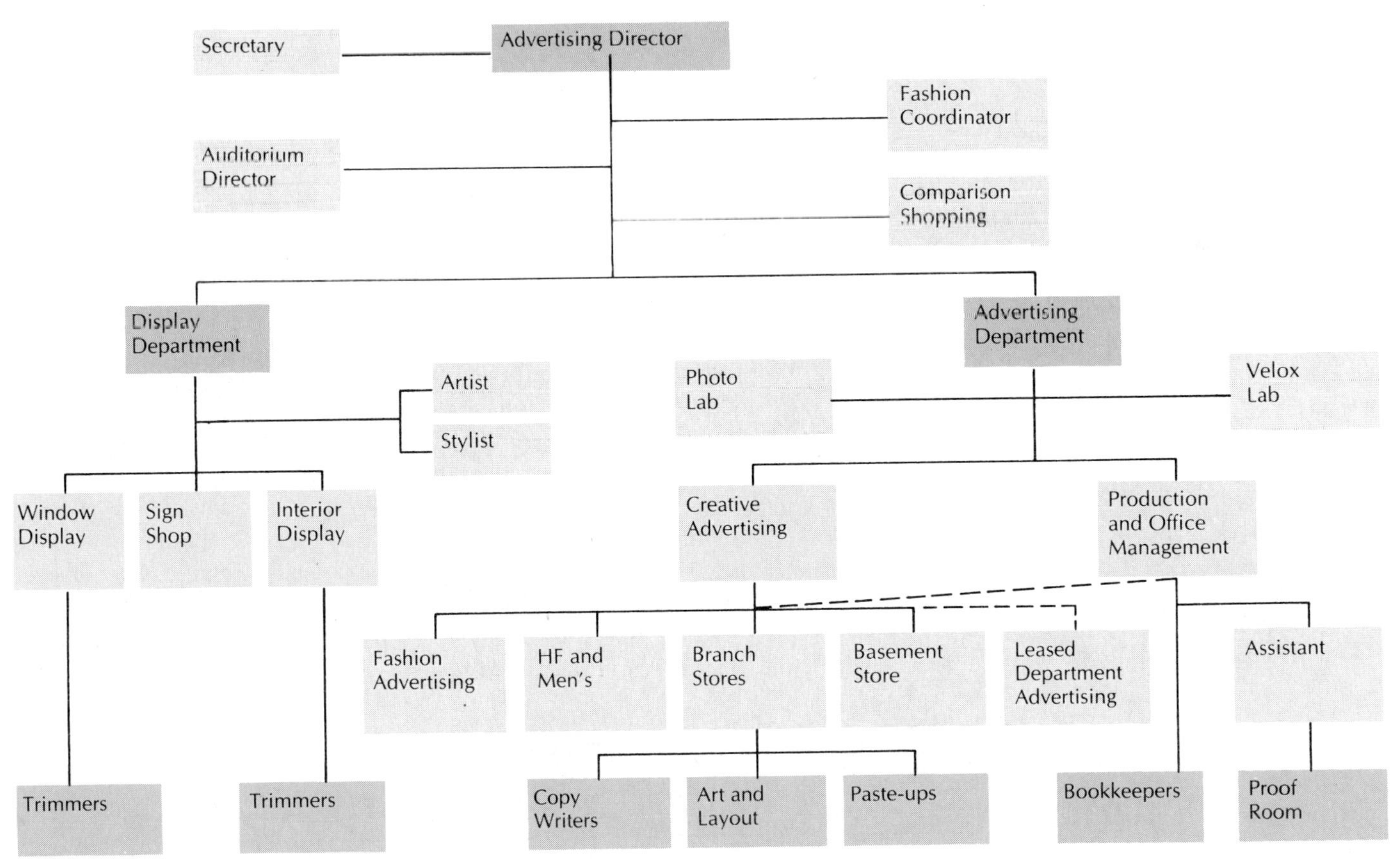

Figure 3–9 Organization chart for a typical in-house retail advertising department.

products *internationally* or *multinationally?* What is the difference? These words are frequently used interchangeably. However, the difference relates to the degree of centralized coordination. Multinational firms like Coca-Cola have strong direction and coordination from one central headquarters. The chairman of Coca-Cola has called this strategy, "One sight, one sound, one sell." On the other hand, 3M Company operates internationally with virtually autonomous units in various countries around the world. Similarly, many large retailers have foreign operations responsible for their own product lines, their own marketing organizations, and their own profits and losses.

The direction a company takes depends on many variables, among them the breadth of its product line, the availability of qualified management, the similarity of usable marketing techniques, and the economic impact of particular marketing strategies. It goes without saying, though, that the decision to operate internationally or multinationally has a strong influence on the advertising decisions that follow.

Figure 3–10 Retail print ad created by Bloomingdale's in-house agency. Performing the work in-house gives some advertisers greater control as well as cost effectiveness.

Summary

The advertising a company uses affects virtually every person in the company. And many more people have an impact on the company's advertising program than just the artists or copywriters who produce it. For that reason, some understanding of how advertising works can be beneficial to every employee irrespective of his or her position in the firm.

All advertising departments are responsible for planning, administration, budgeting, and coordination with other departments or outside advertising services. In addition, some advertising departments take responsibility for ad production, media placement, and other marketing support services. The degree of responsibility depends on the size and needs of the firm, the nature of its business, and the characteristics of the markets it serves.

Large advertisers may organize their departments on a centralized or a decentralized basis. Centralized organizations boast efficiency, economy, advertising continuity, and a high degree of corporate control. Decentralized organizations, on the other hand, tend to be more flexible and more responsive to changing market conditions. New approaches are introduced more easily, and advertising effectiveness can be more readily measured.

Drawbacks to the decentralized organization include lack of corporate control, potential loss of advertising continuity, and increased cost.

Some firms have developed in-house advertising agencies to offer the firm total capabilities and attention. Companies with in-house shops often hope to save money by keeping the normal agency commissions for themselves. However, some firms have found they have saved money but lost creativity. The advantage or disadvantage of an in-house agency really depends on the needs and circumstances of the particular company.

Managing international advertising campaigns presents new and complex problems. Markets, media, and languages differ. Multinational companies tend to centralize their advertising management, while companies organized internationally tend to decentralize it. The direction a particular company takes depends on many variables including the product mix, management availability, marketing strategy, and economics.

Questions for review

1. What are the responsibilities of the advertising manager? Why does a company that has an advertising agency need an advertising manager?
2. In what ways are advertising departments organized? What are their different organizational structures?
3. What are five primary functions common to all advertising departments? Describe them.
4. Specifically, what tasks are involved in advertising production, media placement, and marketing support services?
5. Enumerate some career opportunities which would be available in company advertising departments.
6. How can you obtain information about a company for which you might like to work?
7. What are some important questions to ask in selecting or working with an advertising agency?
8. How does the P&G brand manager system operate? Why has this system been so successful?
9. What is an in-house agency? What are its advantages and disadvantages?
10. What should be the advertising manager's role in working with the advertising agency?

4

Advertising agencies

Coors, the magic name in beer; Coors, the account every U.S. advertising agency was smacking its corporate lips over. Coors was looking for a new agency, and Ted Bates & Co. was invited to pitch the business. It would be their first beer account in years, but somehow they knew they were going to get it. They knew it because "that's the only attitude to have when you're pitching new business."

From the very first briefing sessions, the rapport was good. The prospective client knew what they wanted: a national advertising program that would help Coors expand throughout the country and offset the market domination of the three or four nationally distributed beers. Coors management also knew what they didn't want—a speculative, or free, creative presentation.

Apparently Coors was going to base the choice more on the agency's track record and approach than on a subjective creative evaluation. This made the Bates people think the Coors folks were going to be a special kind of client—if they could land them. They knew, however, that even though they couldn't rely on a creative pitch, they would have to be more creative than ever. So the creative department was pulled in on the project from the beginning. John Moss, the agency's vice president and account supervisor, assembled his team and worked until the wee hours of many mornings, rehearsing the presentation of Bates successes for its clients.

As the nation's sixth largest agency, billing over $1 billion per year, Bates had many client successes to choose from. With clients like Kava coffee, Wyler's iced tea, Breck shampoo, Kool cigarettes, Schweppes tonic water, Arrid deodorant, Colgate toothpaste, and Panasonic, the problem was as much what not to tell as what to tell.

Coors didn't want a speculative media presentation, either; that is, they weren't looking for a rationale for what media they should use. That meant the media department had to work for two solid weeks pulling together case histories.

Finally, they were ready. Bates winged its Coors task force out to Golden, Colorado.

The client was sharp, on the ball. John Moss and his team had six solid hours of presenting to get through. It all went without a hitch. The Coors reaction seemed good. They all spoke the same language. But in the "new account" game, you never know. The next agency might talk their language even better, and they were talking to several other top agencies, including Ogilvy & Mather and Foote, Cone & Belding. Exhausted, the Bates team flew back to New York. They were ready to hear from Coors; ready to get to work.

Suspense was high around the agency. They waited. The suspense ended on April 22. The call came in, and the message was:

> We are pleased to announce that the Adolph Coors Company has appointed Ted Bates as our agency.

Party. Party. Big Coors party—the call echoed through the halls—and Coors beer flowed like golden spring water.

But, servicing a $20-million-plus account doesn't leave a lot of time for partying. The next day 22 members of the new Coors team left for a three-day orientation in Colorado. The new client wanted a campaign on the air by June 1, one that would help them achieve their rightful share of the market. And that's just what Bates wanted to give them with their new campaign theme, "Taste the high country"[1] (Figure 4–1).

The role of the advertising agency

Why would a large company like Adolph Coors, which spends over $20 million a year advertising its beer, want to hire an advertising agency? Couldn't they afford to hire their own advertising people and save money by doing their own advertising in-house? And why would they go all the way to New York to find an agency? Couldn't they work a lot more efficiently and inexpensively with a company in Denver? What does the New York advertising agency do that's so special anyway? How did Ted Bates & Co. get in on the act? How do they get to work on a $20-million advertising account? Do all the agency's accounts have to be that big for an agency to make money? How do smaller agencies make money?

These and many other questions are logical ones for the beginning advertising student. We hope a discussion of the agency side of the advertising business will shed some light on these issues and give a clearer understanding of the important role agencies play. We shall first discuss what an advertising agency is and why so many advertisers use one.

An *advertising agency* is an independent organization of creative and business people who specialize in the development and preparation of advertising plans, advertisements, and other promotional tools. The agency also arranges or contracts for the purchase of advertising space and time in communications media. It does all this on behalf of different sellers, who are referred to as its *clients,* in an effort to find customers for their goods and services.[2]

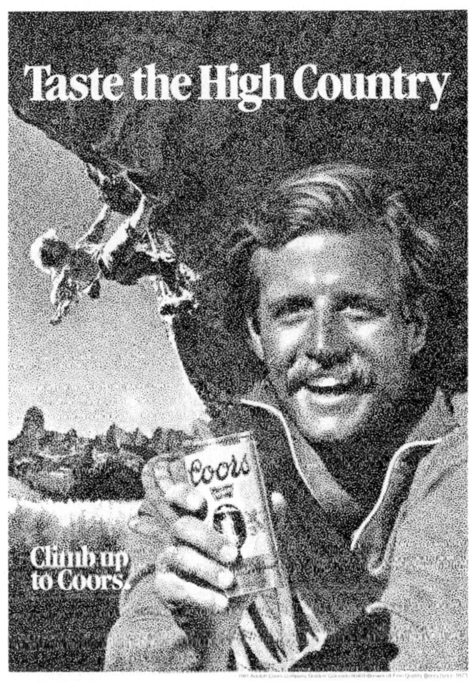

Figure 4–1 A. Coors's new campaign inviting beer drinkers to "Taste the high country" uses a series of male-macho themes from cowboys to mountain climbers to skiers to communicate the brand's masculine, active image.

This definition gives us some good clues as to why so many advertisers hire advertising agencies. For one thing, they are *independent,* not owned by the advertiser, the media, or the suppliers. This independence allows them to bring an outside, objective viewpoint to the advertiser's business. That viewpoint is valuable because of the agency's depth of experience in working with a variety of marketing problems for their clients. This independence also enables them to serve their clients' needs better when dealing with the media because their allegiance is to the client rather than to any particular medium. (See the Ad Lab.)

The agency employs a combination of *creative people* and *business people* who are specialists in applying the complex art and science of advertising to business problems. They include writers, artists, market analysts, media analysts, research people, salespeople, and advertising specialists of all sorts who apply their skills and talents to help make their clients successful. For much the same reason that a well-run business seeks professional help from an attorney, accountant, banker, or management specialist, advertisers use agencies because they are equipped to create more effective advertising—and select more effective media—than the advertisers themselves can do.

Advertising agencies develop and prepare advertising plans, ad-

How big is the agency business?

Although New York, Los Angeles, and Chicago are the three leading advertising centers in the United States, few cities with at least 100,000 people are without an advertising agency. Indeed, many small cities and towns support one or more agencies. Of 8,000 agencies, however, only 80 or 1 percent, have gross incomes of $5 million or more. These agencies represent approximately $20 billion in domestic billing—that is, the amount of client money the agency spends on media and equivalent activities. Interestingly, the top 10 agencies (which account for approximately one tenth of 1 percent of all agencies) handle 28 percent of the total volume of business.

An estimated 82,000 people are employed by United States–based advertising agencies today. Most agencies, however, have a low "body count" compared with that of other professions. When an agency staff is well balanced in skills and versatility, only five or six people can easily handle $1 million in annual billing. In agencies that bill $20 million or more per year, this ratio is usually even lower.

Top ten agencies in U.S. income

(U.S. Agencies: Gross income in $ millions)

Rank	Agency	1980
1	Young & Rubicam	$200.0
2	J. Walker Thompson Co.	137.8
3	Ogilvy & Mather	125.5
4	Foote; Cone & Belding	109.1
5	Leo Burnett Co.	108.2
6	Ted Bates & Co.	108.0
7	BBDO Int'l.	105.8
8	Doyle Dane Bernbach	98.1
9	Grey Advertising	78.7
10	Benton & Bowles	73.8

Top ten agencies in world income

(U.S. Agencies: Gross income in $ millions)

Rank	Agency	1980
1	Young & Rubicam	$340.8
2	J. Walter Thompson Co.	322.5
3	McCann Erickson	268.7
4	Ogilvy & Mather	245.9
5	Ted Bates & Co.	210.6
6	BBDO Int'l.	175.6
7	Leo Burnett Co.	169.7
8	SSC&B	166.7
9	Foote, Cone & Belding	164.3
10	D'Arcy-MacManus & Masius	156.0

Laboratory applications

1. How many agencies are listed on both tables? How many are on only one table? Can you explain why this is so?
2. How many agencies are there in the town where you live? Which is the largest? What accounts (with which you are familiar) do they handle? What is your opinion of their work?

vertisements, and other promotional tools for a wide variety of clients. They have day-to-day contact with outside specialists and suppliers who illustrate advertisements, take photographs, set type, retouch art, make plates, film commercials, and record sound, which are required for producing quality work. They are therefore able to stay abreast of the latest advances in technology, the most recent changes in prices, and the most current problems in production quality. This all benefits their clients (Figure 4–2).

By arranging and contracting for the purchase of broadcast time and magazine or newspaper space, the agency provides yet another service to the client. For one thing it saves the client money. Most media allow the agency to keep 15 percent of the gross amount of money placed in their medium. This agency commission reduces the amount of money the advertiser would otherwise have to pay the agency for its services. For this commission, the agency is expected to maintain an expertise in the various media available to the advertiser. This is a large task. There are thousands of magazines, business publications, newspapers, national TV and radio networks with hundreds of different programs, local TV and radio stations, not to mention all the outdoor advertising companies, transit and car card advertising companies, and direct-mail lists available to carry their clients' messages. Media are constantly changing, and they require continuing study by agency media specialists and researchers who do nothing else. For this reason, agencies are considered media specialists, and even the largest advertisers turn to them for advice.

Finally, agencies work for a variety of different sellers to find customers for their goods and services. Agencies work for their clients, not for the media and or the suppliers. Their moral, ethical, financial, and sometimes even legal obligation is to their clients to find them the best prices, give them the best quality work, and help them grow and prosper. Today almost all sizeable advertisers rely on an advertising agency for expert, objective counsel and unique creative skills.[3]

There are still many agency switches made every year. Likewise, many advertisers determine that it is in their best interest to work without an agency. Why is this so, if the agencies have all that independence, skill, expertise, and talent we just discussed?

Besides the obvious problems of personality conflicts and lack of communication that sometimes enter every human relationship, not every agency has all that much independence, skill, expertise, or talent. Likewise, an agency may produce outstanding results for one type of client and then be totally incapable of grasping the problem or devising an appropriate solution for a different type. Some agencies lack the strength to remain truly independent and end up only trying to please the client rather than give what is needed. Others are so arrogant in their approach that they forget to listen to the client. Some clients outgrow their agencies and need additional services offered only by larger firms. Some clients fail to see the expertise that is being offered to them and try to force their agencies to give them safe, but unexciting, advertising. Others might make the honest mistake of giving their agencies incorrect information about their products, their markets, or their competitive strengths and weaknesses. In any of these cases the agency's work will invariably suffer, the results

Figure 4–1 B.

HIGH COUNTRY 60-second

(MUSIC THROUGHOUT)

CHORUS: Taste the high country. Taste the high country.

(SFX: BEER BEING POURED)

MAN SINGS (VO): There's a place where the hawk soars free, where a man can be what he wants to be. Where the air is crisp and the water's clear and there's just one beer that's brewed up here.

CHORUS: Taste the high country. Taste the high country. Taste the high country. Taste Coors.

ANNCR (VO): Coors is born high in the Rockies and the quality never comes down. It's brewed with pure Rocky Mountain Spring Water and its own special high country barley.

MAN (OC): That's no flatland beer.

WOMAN (OC): It's not city beer.

MAN 2 (OC): It's Coors.

CHORUS: Taste the high country.

(MUSIC OUT) Climb up to Coors.

received by the advertiser will be less than desired, and either the agency or the client may become restless and desire a change.

Types of agencies

Advertising agencies are normally classified by one of two criteria: (1) the type of business they handle, such as consumer goods, industrial products, financial services, retail, and real estate, and (2) the range of services they offer, such as full-service, media buying services, or creative services. We shall discuss the major categories briefly.

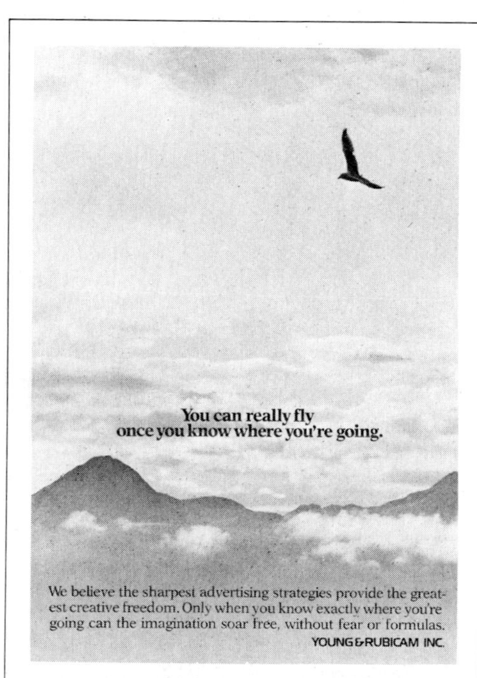

You can really fly
once you know where you're going.
We believe the sharpest advertising strategies provide the greatest creative freedom. Only when you know exactly where you're going can the imagination soar free, without fear or formulas.
YOUNG&RUBICAM INC.

Figure 4–2 Young & Rubicam Inc., the largest American advertising agency, uses beautiful imagery to illustrate a basic truth about advertising . . . and life.

General consumer agencies

A *general agency* is one that is willing to represent the widest variety of accounts. In practice, however, it concentrates on *consumer* accounts—that is, companies that make goods purchased chiefly by consumers. Soaps, cereals, automobiles, pet foods, and toiletries are examples. Most of the advertising produced by a general agency is placed in consumer media—television, radio, billboards, newspapers, and magazines—which are commissionable to the agency. As a result, the general agency obtains most of its income from media commissions.

A general agency may be either domestic (based in the United States) or international (based in the United States with branches abroad). Many of the nation's larger general agencies have shifted their focus from domestic advertising to the world market. Each country in which they operate is, in effect, a distinct market. People in other lands have their own attitudes, buying habits, business systems, and laws. (See the Ad Lab.) Thus it is seldom practical simply to translate American advertising into the languages of other countries. It is often more effective to have a foreign-based staff of advertising specialists transform and adapt basic concepts to the needs of people in their countries, adding the verbal and visual appeals to which they most readily respond.

To conduct international activities, there are several types of agencies available to advertisers beside the regular domestic or U.S. international agency.

Export agencies

Some agencies specialize in creating ads for American companies that are engaged in international advertising. These *export agencies* may work in association with domestic agencies on particular accounts in addition to having clients of their own for whom they perform this same speciality.

Export agencies will usually specialize in preparing ads for particular language groups or geographic areas and will employ native-born writers in those languages and specialists familiar with the foreign media opportunities.

Foreign agencies

Companies may also select local *foreign agencies* to coordinate their activities in particular markets. The foreign agencies, of course, boast local talent who understand local attitudes and customers as well as local media. When Banamex (Banco Nacional de México, mentioned in Chapter 2) wanted to promote an awareness of its bank to Americans, it selected a local California agency to handle its advertising in the border areas from California to Texas. Banamex already had an agency in Mexico City and another for its worldwide banking services in New York. But they knew that most American customers lived within a couple hundred miles of the border.

Advertising in the Soviet Union

Who ever would have thought that more than 100 advertising agencies would be plying their trade today in the Soviet Union? Certainly not Marx! According to traditional Marxist-Leninist doctrine, advertising is a tool of capitalistic exploitation. It siphons off the surplus value belonging to underpaid workers and puts it in the hands of overpaid white-collar workers who are nonproductively employed writing jingles.

Yet there has been an impressive growth of advertising agencies in the Soviet Union. The initial argument was that these agencies exist to develop advertising to support Soviet goods in export markets where it is necessary to compete against Western and other nations. But many advertisements also appear in print and broadcast media reaching Russian consumers. Another rationale was established at the 1957 Prague Conference of Advertising Workers of Socialist Countries, which made three points as to how advertising was to be used: (1) to educate people's tastes, develop their requirements, and thus actively form demand; (2) to help the consumer by providing information about the most rational means of consumption; and (3) to help to raise the culture of trade. Furthermore, Soviet advertising is to be ideological, truthful, concrete, and functional. The Soviets claim that their advertising does not indulge in devices used in the West. Their ads will not use celebrities—only experts will be used to promote a product. They will not use mood advertising. They will not create brand differentiation when none exists.

Experts think that the main use of Soviet advertising is to help industry move products that come into excess supply where the Soviets do not want to do the logical thing, cut prices.

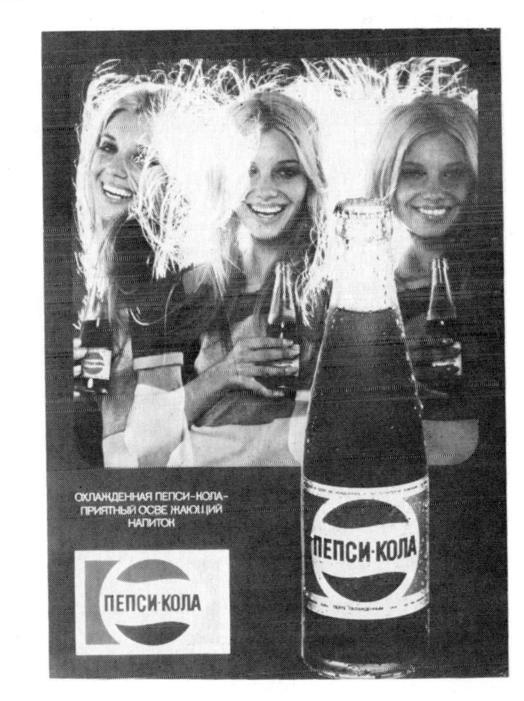

Laboratory application

How does the Pepsi-Cola advertisement illustrated succeed in satisfying Soviet policies on the use of advertising?

For many consumer accounts it might be beneficial to seek a local agency in key markets. However, using a variety of local agencies in different markets can make it hard to coordinate a multinational advertising program.

If a company is planning a multinational campaign with all activities centralized and coordinated from one location, it is usually advantageous to use one international advertising agency. On the other hand, if a company is planning an international program promoting differently to the various markets it serves, it is better to appoint local agencies who understand the needs of those particular markets. In selecting agencies, companies normally choose those that correspond in size to their service needs. In this way, a client will not pay for services that are not required.

Foreign international agencies

Even though Banco Nacional de México selected a local foreign agency (from their perspective), many international advertisers find that only a large *foreign agency* with offices or affiliates in many markets can do the job adequately. For American companies, many of these are based in Brussels, which has been called the capital of Europe. The agencies are staffed with multilingual, multinational personnel in both creative and administrative positions. Others are in Tokyo, Hong Kong, and Mexico City. Through such agencies, campaigns can be coordinated and controlled under one roof for a series of countries or markets. These agencies usually have branch offices or affiliates in countries throughout a given area upon whom they can call for specialized services such as arranging local press conferences or trade fairs. Many of these foreign international agencies are similar in size to the largest American international agencies. In fact, Dentsu Advertising in Tokyo, a foreign international agency, is now the largest advertising agency in the world (Figure 4–3).

Figure 4–3 **Top ten agencies outside the United States**

(billings in $ millions)

Agency	Billings
Dentsu	$2,437.0
Hakuhodo	896.3
Eurocom (France)	519.7
Naito Issue Sha	370.3
Daiko Advertising	491.8
Dai-Ichi Kikaku	272.6
Tokyu	239.9
Publicis-Conseil (France)	201.2
Yomiko	172.9
Asahi Kokoku Sha	165.4

All agencies are Japanese unless otherwise indicated. 1979 data.

Industrial agencies

An *industrial agency* represents client companies that make goods to be sold to other companies. Computer hardware, smelting furnaces, locomotives, and radium counters are examples of such goods.

Although business and industrial advertising may not seem as glamorous as consumer advertising, it is extremely important and requires highly developed technical knowledge as well as the ability to translate this knowledge into precise and persuasive advertising. (See Chapter 21 on business advertising.)

Most industrial advertising is placed in trade magazines and other business publications. These are generally commissionable, but their rates are far lower than those of consumer media. The result is that commissions are not large enough to cover the costs of the agency's services, so industrial agencies normally charge the client an additional service fee.

Full-service agencies

The modern *full-service advertising agency* is equipped to serve its clients in all areas of communication and promotion. Its services are essentially grouped in two categories—advertising and nonadvertising.

Advertising services include planning, creating, and producing advertisements, as well as performing research and media selection services. Nonadvertising functions include producing sales promotion materials, publicity articles, annual reports, trade show exhibits, and sales training materials.

The range of agency services will be discussed more fully in the section on what agency people do, later in this chapter.

Media buying services

In recent years, as the tendency toward specialization has increased, the number of offshoots from the agency business has also increased. Among these are *media buying services,* which are organizations of media specialists experienced in purchasing and packaging radio and television time. Such companies owe their success, in part, to the fact that radio and TV time is "perishable"; that is, a 60-second radio spot at 8 P.M. cannot be sold after that hour has arrived. For that reason, radio and television stations try to presell as much advertising time as possible and discount their rates to anyone who buys a large amount of time. Thus, the media buying service can negotiate a special discount rate with radio and TV stations. It then sells this time to advertising agencies or advertisers.

As part of their service, media buying firms provide the prospective customer with a detailed analysis of the media buy. Once the media package is sold, the buying service orders the spots on each of the stations involved, verifies performance, sees to it that stations "make good" for any spots missed, and even pays the media bills.

The method of compensation used by media buying services varies. Some receive a set fee. Others operate on an incentive basis, receiving a prescribed percentage of the money they save the client.

Creative boutiques

Just as some media specialists have set up media buying services, some creative specialists have set up creative services with directors, artists, and writers, called *creative boutiques*. Working in teams, they work for advertisers and occasionally advertising agencies. Their mission is normally to develop central advertising themes and produce fresh, distinctive advertising messages.

Because advertising effectiveness largely depends on originality in conception, design, and writing, advertisers tend to value this quality highly. However, the creative services of the boutique are provided without the marketing and sales direction that full-service agencies offer. This therefore actually limits the boutique to the role of a creative supplier. (See the Ad Lab.)

What do agency people do?

The American Association of Advertising Agencies (AAAA) is the national organization of the advertising agency business. Its standards for membership are very high, and it has endeavored to be the most

How to find out about agencies and their clients

Basic information about advertising agencies in the United States can be obtained from the *Standard Directory of Advertising Agencies*. Known as the "Red Book" because of its cover color, this guide to the industry lists the names and addresses of most of the nation's agencies by state. It names the associations to which they belong, if any, and the media associations that recognize them for credit purposes. It also lists each agency's annual billings by media classification, the names and titles of its executives, and the names of its current accounts.

A related volume, *The Standard Directory of Advertisers,* lists the names of thousands of U.S. companies that advertise and the names and titles of their executives. Also cited are the names of their advertising agencies, their total annual advertising budget, and the principal media they use.

Laboratory applications

1. From your library, obtain a copy of the agency Red Book. Compare your local Yellow Pages listing of advertising agencies to the Red Book listing. Are most of the agencies in your town listed in the Red Book? Which ones are not? Why do you suppose those are not listed?
2. Of the local agencies, call one of the clients they have listed in the Red Book. Ask to speak to the advertising manager. From him or her, see what information you can obtain about the agency—its size, number of employees, type of work, quality, price, and other factors.

responsible speaker for the advertising industry. With almost 400 members, it is composed of the largest and oldest agencies in the business, which place almost 80 percent of all advertising handled by all agencies in the United States.

In its Agency Service Standards, the AAAA explains that the purpose of an agency is to interpret to an advertiser's audience, or to that part of it which it is desired to reach, the advantages of a product or service. To accomplish this, the agency provides the following services:

1. A study of the client's product or service in order to determine the advantages and disadvantages inherent in the product itself, and in its relation to competition.
2. An analysis of the present and potential market for which the product or service is adapted, as to: location, extent of possible sales, season, trade and economic conditions, and the nature and amount of competition.
3. A knowledge of the factors of distribution and sales and their methods of operation.
4. A knowledge of all the available media and means which can profitably be used to carry the interpretation of the product or service to the consumer, wholesaler, dealer or contractor.

This knowledge covers: the character, the influence, the audience, the physical requirements, and the costs of the various media.

Acting on the study, analysis, and knowledge as explained in the preceding paragraphs, recommendations are made and the following procedure ensues:

5. Formulation of a definite plan and presentation of this plan to the client.
6. Execution of this plan:
   a. Writing, designing, illustrating of advertisements, or other appropriate forms of the message.
   b. Contracting for the space, time, or other means of advertising.
   c. The proper incorporation of the message in mechanical form and forwarding it with proper instructions for the fulfillment of the contract.
   d. Checking and verifying of insertions, display, or other means used.
   e. Auditing and billing for the service, space, and preparation.
7. Cooperation with the client's sales force, to insure the greatest effect from advertising.[4]

The AAAA goes on to explain that these basic elements of agency service have remained virtually unchanged since the Agency Service Standards were written and adopted in 1918. All the agency people fit into this pattern: account executives who maintain contact with the clients; art directors; copywriters; media planners; space and time buyers; print, radio, and TV production people; market analysts; advertising researchers; and all the others.

In addition to the services outlined above, many agencies perform a variety of other nonadvertising tasks for their clients. These might include package design, sales research and training, sales literature, displays, and public relations activities (Figure 4–4).

To understand more fully the various functions outlined above, look at the agency people involved in the Perdue Chicken story presented in Chapter 3. Scali, McCabe, Sloves is the agency Frank Perdue selected to handle his account. It was not one of New York's largest agencies. In fact, at the time it was one of the smaller shops, but it had piled up an impressive record with several other accounts such as Volvo and Dictaphone. As a full-service agency, Scali, McCabe, Sloves provides all the services outlined by the AAAA Service Standards (Figure 4–5).

Research

Before any advertising is created, research must be undertaken to study the uses and advantages of the product or service, to analyze the present and potential customers, and to determine what will influence them to buy. At Scali, McCabe, Sloves, the research department is headed by a senior vice president who is bent on getting information. Is price important? How do people perceive the product? What kind of person would be attracted to buy it? How familiar is the brand name to consumers? Sam Scali, the agency's creative director, has said, "We can't create on intuition. Give artists all the information they need to do a job—because advertising is based on information."[5]

Planning

The planning process actually begins before research and continues afterward. In the case of Perdue, Sam Scali, Ed McCabe, and Alan Pesky, the director of account services, were responsible for initiating this process with the client to determine his marketing and advertising objectives. They then met with the agency's market analysts, media

Public relations	Sales promotion and collateral material	Marketing & research	Media advertising
Annual reports	Booklets	Ad effectiveness	Business publications
Editorial sevices	Catalogs	Attitude studies	Consumer magazines
Feature articles	Dealer sales aids	Market development	Farm papers
House organ	Direct mail	Market planning	Newspapers
Newsletters	Displays	Market research	Outdoor and transit
News releases	Fact sheets	Media research	Radio
Open house events	Films & slides	Product evaluation	Television
Press conferences	Meetings, speeches		Trade magazines
Special events	Point-of-purchase		
Planning & policy dev.	Posters		
	Sales meetings		
	Sales presentations		
	Sales training		
	Technical literature		
	Identity programs		
	Graphic styling		
	Interior design		
	Signage		
	Design evaluation		
	Packaging & labels		

Figure 4–4 The range of services typically offered by a full-service advertising agency. Many agencies offer a shorter menu, and some have established subsidiaries for specialty areas.

Award-winning advertising doesn't sell?

Advertising prepared by Scali, McCabe, Sloves won four first-place awards at the Copy Club of New York's recent Gold Key Awards presentation. More than any other agency.

In the Advertising Club's upcoming Andy Awards, Scali, McCabe, Sloves has more finalists than agencies billing ten, twenty, thirty times more than we do. In fact, we have more finalists than anybody. 23 in all.

During the five years we've been in business we've won *hundreds* of awards for our work.

So if you're an advertiser in the market for an agency, you now have all the evidence you need to justify steering clear of us. After all, everybody knows award-winning advertising doesn't sell anything, right?

One of the most successful campaigns in the history of automobile advertising.

We're happy that the Volvo magazine campaign has won first place in the Copy Club Awards, two years in a row.

And we're grateful that William Tyler of Advertising Age picked it as one of the "Ten Best" again this year.

But we're proud of the fact that our advertising has helped Volvo realize more than a 100% growth in sales in the five years we've been together.

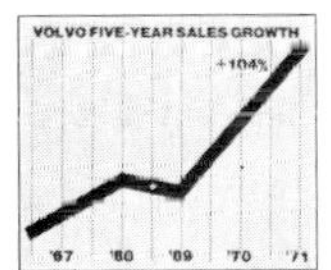

During the same period, incidentally, domestic cars in Volvo's price category experienced virtually no increase.

Lately, Volvo has had a string of sixteen months in which they broke their own previous sales records.

Mr. James C. LaMarre, Vice President of Marketing at Volvo says: *"Next to the excellence of our product, the effectiveness of our advertising is the most important factor in Volvo's success in the United States."*

Quite a tribute.

But the client and the agency aren't the only ones who like Volvo advertising.

One of the "big three" Detroit automobile companies has run some new ads that read like last year's Volvo ads.

We're only a little flattered. It's the smallest of the big three.

When is a chicken not a chicken?

When Perdue Incorporated was looking for an advertising agency to help sell their chickens, they interviewed 48 of them (agencies, not chickens) before deciding upon Scali, McCabe, Sloves.

The advertising we created for them won three first place awards the other night. In the television, radio and trade advertising categories.

Better yet, research shows that in just nine months Perdue has won a higher brand awareness than all other brands of chicken sold in New York *combined*.

Perdue is happy. Their product, long considered an un-brandable commodity, now commands a premium price. And they've had to increase production by more than 30% to meet the increased demand.

Consumers are also happy. The fan mail for the product, and of all things, the advertising, is overwhelming.

A Pennsylvania woman went the farthest in her praise. She wrote to say she'd been driving 100 miles to buy a Perdue chicken.

Once upon a time, it was asking a lot to get someone to walk a mile for a camel.

An as yet unheralded success.

Our first ad for the Dictaphone Corporation appeared too late to qualify for this year's awards competitions.

And because it's so recent, we'd be the first to admit that our efforts on their behalf are still only a qualified success.

But so far our work has confirmed a lot of people's faith in the power of advertising, including our own. And including the President of Dictaphone, Mr. E. Lawrence Tabat, who recently said: *"In the history of the Corporation, we have never had such spectacular results from advertising."*

Bad News For IBM.

We're far from sanguine. In this case, our own first act could prove difficult to follow.

The business of advertising. An overview.

Scali, McCabe, Sloves is not naive enough to ask you to believe that winning awards is necessarily an indication of effective selling.

Nor would we ever claim that not winning them is proof of our efficacy.

As we've seen, it's possible to do both.

The fact that our advertising works is what makes our business grow.

The fact that it wins awards makes it a little more fun.

And if you don't have fun at what you do, how can you be good at it?

We work for these companies

American Can Company
Columbia Broadcasting System
Dictaphone Corporation
Funk & Wagnalls, Inc.
[illegible]
Hornblower & Weeks-Hemphill, Noyes
Perdue, Incorporated
Swift & Co.
Time, Inc.
The Village Voice
Volvo, Inc.
Volvo (Canada) Ltd.
Whitehall Tobacco Products, Inc.
Xerox Corporation

Public Service
Citizens for a Quieter City
Department of Health, Education & Welfare
Lincoln Center for the Performing Arts
National Audubon Society

SCALI, McCABE, SLOVES, INC.
345 Park Avenue, New York, N.Y. 10022 *212-421-2050*

If your company would like to see a reel of our television commercials or a portfolio of our print advertising, just write or call Marvin Sloves, President

Figure 4–5 Many advertisers and agencies claim that award-winning advertising doesn't sell. Scali, McCabe, Sloves, Inc., answers with the facts of Volvo's growth, Perdue's sales success, and testimonials from Dictaphone, all of whom had many award-winning ads. As they say, it's possible to do both. (Photo left to right: Sam Scali, Edward McCabe, Marvin Sloves, J. Leonard Hultgren, Alan Pesky.)

planners, and other creative people to determine the appropriate advertising strategy. The results of research were considered, and the evaluation of the agency's planning team was then distilled into a detailed marketing and advertising plan. After the client approves this plan, it becomes the blueprint for the agency's creative and media program.

WE'RE LOOKING FOR AN ART DIRECTOR BETTER THAN ANYBODY AT CHIAT/DAY.

Which is perfectly alright for us to say, since we're Chiat/Day.

We're saying it because we just got past $75 million with no politics, no bad clients, and no excuses for ordinary work. And this would be a helluva time to start making compromises.

So if you don't have a lot of experience, impeccable standards, and blazing speed, you're in the wrong ad. Goodbye.

But if you're qualified—really, really qualified—there are two things you could do.

The first thing is, don't call.

The second thing is, send no more than six non-returnable examples of your best work, along with a resume, to Mark Doyle at the address below.

And don't think six ads aren't enough.

Around here, that's a whole morning's work.

CHIAT/DAY

517 South Olive Street, Los Angeles, California 90013

Figure 4–6 This recruitment advertisement for Chiat/Day, the winner of *Advertising Age's* 1980 Agency of the Year award, suggests why they were the first West Coast agency to win the honor.

Creative services

Most advertising relies heavily on *copy*—those words that make up the headline and message of the ad. People like Ed McCabe who create these words are called *copywriters.* Their work requires skill, since they must be able to condense all that can be said about a product or service into just those points that are salient and pertinent to a given advertisement. Thus, what a copywriter doesn't say is just as important as what he or she says. Copywriters usually work closely with the agency artists and production staff.

The agency art department is composed of art directors, like Sam Scali (see Figure 4–6), and graphic designers whose primary job is to *lay out* advertising—that is, to illustrate in sketches how the various components of an ad will fit together. When their assignment is to conceive a television commercial, the artists lay it out in a comic-strip series of sequential frames called a *storyboard.*

Most large agencies have their own art departments. Others prefer to purchase art services from independent studios or outside freelance designers.

Print and broadcast production

After Sam Scali and Ed McCabe designed and wrote the advertisement and Frank Perdue approved it, it went into production. This is the responsibility of the agency's print production manager or broadcast producers and directors.

For print advertising, the production department buys type, photographs, illustrations, and other components needed for the finished art. Production personnel then work with photoengravers, color separators, and other graphic arts suppliers to obtain the plates or prints needed for the media scheduled. When printing is required for brochures or other literature, the production staff assigns and supervises the work and then arranges to have it shipped to the client.

If the ad is a broadcast commercial, the broadcast production personnel take the approved script or the storyboard and set about producing the finished product. They work with actors, camera people, and production specialists to convert the commercial into a tape or record (for radio) or a film or videotape (for television). Often requiring many hours of rehearsal and labor, broadcast production is an exacting job that demands great patience and the ability to work well with others.

Traffic

One of the greatest sins in the advertising agency business is to miss a deadline; and the whole business revolves around deadlines. If Scali, McCabe, Sloves, intends to run an ad in a monthly trade magazine read by Perdue's grocers and they miss the deadline, they will have to wait another whole month to show that ad. That does not please clients.

The job of the agency traffic department therefore is to make sure that the work flow is smooth and efficient. It coordinates all phases of production and checks to see that everything is completed on time and that all ads and commercials are received by the media before the deadline.

Media

When Frank Perdue started advertising, the agency recommended subway posters as an initial medium for three reasons: it requires a small budget, the art could be used again in butcher shop windows, and the message is read by working mothers and lower to middle income groups. Later, as the campaign developed and more money became available, other more expensive media were considered and used.

The job of the media director is to match the profile of the desired target market with the profiles of the audiences of a wide range of media. The media are then evaluated according to efficiency and cost, and the media director recommends the best medium or media combination to use.

The agency media department maintains up-to-date files of reference data that detail the special characteristics of each medium, its circulation or reach, its costs, advertiser services, and so forth. Sources of information such as the *Standard Rate & Data* directories and A. C. Nielsen reports offer the media specialist detailed statistics on the thousands of radio, TV, magazine, newspaper, and outdoor media available. Additional information is offered by media sales representatives. For the client, unbiased and authenticated media information is one of the most valuable services an agency can offer.

Account management

Scali, McCabe, Sloves's account management team is an essential part of the agency's organization. The account executive is the liaison between the agency and the client. Responsible on the one hand for mustering all the agency's services for the benefit of the client and on the other hand for representing the agency's point of view to the client, the account executive is often caught in the middle. The AE, therefore, must be tough, tactful, diplomatic, creative, persuasive, knowledgeable, sensitive, honest, and courageous all at once (Figure 4–7). (See the Ad Lab., pages 130–131.)

Scali, McCabe, Sloves, and other large agencies have many account executives who report to management (or account) supervisors. The management supervisors report to the agency's directors of account services.

New business

To survive, agencies must grow. The best creative people always want to work for the "hot shops," the ones that are growing. Growth requires a steady flow of new business. Often this comes from new products developed by existing clients. In other cases agencies are sought by new clients who know their work. Scali, McCabe, Sloves receives 15 to 20 calls per week, for example, because they are well known for the work they have done on Perdue, Volvo, and Maxell recording tape, to mention just a few.

Most agencies keep a constant eye open for new business and have either "new business representatives" or agency principals assigned to target prospective clients and sell the agency's services.

Causes of friction

Client respondents: What do you feel are some of the more common "bad habits" of agencies and clients which can cause trouble in the relationship?

Agency	
Personnel turnover, understanding	13%
Lack of interest in client business	8
Tend toward blind defensiveness	8
Inexperienced account people	8
Unresponsive to client problems (late delivery, etc.)	8
Too loose, unstructured	6
Too much politics	6
Poor communication	6
Tendency not to listen, inflexibility	6
Client	
Not giving enough information	19
Expecting too much	15
Multiple approval levels	13
Lack of client direction, objectives, strategy, etc.	13
Not sharing total marketing approach	10
Arbitrary changes in direction, indecisiveness, lack of direction	8
Not being candid—Flo: problems	6

Agency respondents: What do you feel are some of the more common "bad habits" of agencies and clients which can cause trouble in the relationship?

Agency	
Poor follow-through, speed/flexibility, failure to meet deadlines	23%
Not cost conscious, wasteful of time, production money	
Personnel turnover	14
Poor communication	14
Don't share all the facts	11
Take client for granted	11
Consistent diversion of staff to new business pros.	11
Politics	9
Lack of written reports, estimates, etc.	9
Client	
Lack of client corp. strategy	17
Lack of top management involvement	14
Failure to level with agency	14
Indecisiveness	11
Lack of concern/understanding of agency finances	9
Expect magic answers	9
Fingering agency for product failure	9
Inconsistency of advertising funds	6

Figure 4–7 Clients change agencies for a variety of reasons. Likewise agencies may feel uncomfortable with a client and resign the account. Some reasons for agency-client strains are outlined in this survey.

Accounting

Scali, McCabe, Sloves receives invoices every day from radio and TV stations, magazines, newspapers, billboard companies, transit companies, type houses, photoengravers, free-lance artists and illustrators, talent agencies, photographers, television production companies, sound studios, music producers, and printers, just to mention a few. These bills are totaled by the accounting department on periodic statements to the clients. Client payments are received and recorded, and the accounting department pays all these outside suppliers.

Dealing with variations in media commissions, agency markups, errors in invoices, cash discounts, and the complex flow of large amounts of cash for dozens of clients requires a highly competent accounting staff. At the same time, they must monitor the agency's income and expenses and keep management informed of the company's financial status.

Additional services

What has just been described might be considered basic to the advertising agency business. Many agencies, however, provide a variety of other services and employ specialists to perform these tasks. Scali, McCabe, Sloves, for instance, has a highly regarded sales promotion department which is used by most of the firm's clients to produce dealer ads, window posters, point-of-purchase displays, dealer contest materials, and sales material.

Other agencies maintain public relations specialists, direct marketing specialists, home economics experts, package designers, or economists depending on the nature and needs of their clients.

How do agencies work?

How an advertising agency organizes its functions, operations, and personnel may vary greatly according to its size (gross billings or number of large accounts), the types of accounts it serves, and whether it is local, regional, national, or international.

Small agency structure

In small agencies, daily business operations are usually supervised by the owner or president, who may be in charge of new business development as well (Figure 4–8). Client contact is generally handled by account executives. The account executive may also produce creative concepts for the clients and even write their copy. Artwork is done by an inside art director or purchased from an independent studio or free-lance designer. Most small agencies have a production and traffic department or an employee who fulfills these functions. They also may have a media buyer, but in very small agencies the

Career opportunities in advertising agencies

Why work for an advertising agency? In an agency you can specialize or work on a variety of accounts, plan a client's entire marketing program, or create the advertising itself. And because each project meets a challenge—to make your client's investment profitable, usually in the form of increased sales—you'll be competing with other bright people and cooperating with highly talented, experienced staff members.

Furthermore, unlike most other businesses, your work in an agency need not be limited to the affairs of one company or one industry. You could get involved in (and learn about) fields as diverse as food manufacturing and financial institutions, the auto industry and air travel, retailing and restaurants. Thus, you can quickly gain a breadth of knowledge and experience about a variety of businesses.

Your own functions at an agency are determined partly by its size. In a small one with few accounts, you might handle several types of assignments. In a large international agency with hundreds of accounts, thousands of employees, and millions of dollars in business every year, you are likely to be assigned to one role at a time.

No matter what size agency you work for, you can be sure of one thing. If you are imaginative and quick-thinking, can work under pressure, and have a bent for solving problems, you'll find endless stimulation and satisfaction in agency work.

There aren't many businesses a person can hope to run while still young. Advertising agencies are different. In fact, more than one fifth of the agencies that belong to the American Association of Advertising Agencies are run by executives who were under 40 when they stepped up to the chief executive's chair. If you want responsibility and are willing to work, you'll find faster advancement in an advertising agency than in many other businesses.

Major positions of responsibility in an advertising agency

Job title	Educational preparation	Occupational experience	Extracurricular activities	Average salary
Account executive	B.A. in business; M.B.A. desirable	Advertising and/or marketing department of a manufacturer or large retailer; intern in an agency	Participation in campus and community business organizations, advertising club	$25,500
Copywriter	B.A. with courses in advertising and marketing, English literature, sociology, psychology, philosophy, languages	Retail store sales or writing advertisements for newspapers, magazines, or broadcasters (portfolio required*)	Literary groups, press club, public relations club, journalism society, and communication arts group	$16,000 (junior) $26,000 (senior)
Art director	B.A. desirable but not required; degree from professional art school preferred; community college courses; visual arts courses	Retail store advertising; visual arts studio (portfolio required*)	Art director club; communication arts group; graphic arts group	$27,000

Job title	Educational preparation	Occupational experience	Extracurricular activities	Average salary
Media buyer	B.A. with emphasis on marketing, economics, English, mathematics and statistics; M.B.A. desirable	Retail store sales, media sales, media research, assistant media buyer, media trainee	Ad club and media organizations	$34,500 (media director) $22,000 (media supervisor) $16,000 (buyer of time and space)
Traffic manager	B.A. helpful but not required (This is commonly an entry-level position in an agency because it provides an acquaintance with the agency's functions and personnel. A degree would normally be highly desirable for promotional purposes.)	Work experience in company advertising department, media advertising departments	Ad club, marketing organization	$16,000
Production manager	B.A. helpful but not essential; emphasis on graphic arts courses, visual arts courses, typography, design and layout	Work experience with printers, photoengravers, paper merchants, typesetters, photostat houses, and art studios	Printing club, graphic arts group, art directors club	$24,000 (production manager) $18,000 (production assistant)
Other agency positions:	Market researcher, office manager, treasurer, secretary, billing clerk, bookkeeper, sales promotion specialist, film and television commercial producer, personnel manager, art buyer, casting specialist, television business affairs manager, talent reuse specialist.			

*A portfolio is a collection of your best work which you show during the job interview.

Note: For further information about advertising programs in four-year colleges and universities, write to Advertising Education Publications, 3429 Fifty-Fifth Street, Lubbock, TX 79413, enclose $1, and ask for a copy of *Where Shall I Go to Study Advertising.* Also available, free of charge, is *Advertising: A Guide to Careers in Advertising* from the American Association of Advertising Agencies, 200 Park Avenue, New York, NY 10017.

Laboratory applications

1. From the list of positions, select one you might like to fill. Call a local advertising agency and see what you can find out about their requirements for that position, including salary paid, expected responsibilities, and other factors of importance.
2. Which of the positions offer, in your view, the greatest opportunity for growth and success? Why?

account executives also purchase media time and space for their accounts.

In medium and large agencies, organization is generally more formal. Larger agencies are structured according to one of two systems: the departmental system or the group system.

Departmental system

In this system each of the agency's varied functions—account management, creative services, media, traffic, and production—is set up as a separate department. Each department is called on as needed to perform its specialty. The account executive handles the client contact, the creative department writes the ad and lays it out, and so forth (Figure 4–9).

The group system

As agencies get larger they tend to use the group system, in which the agency is divided into a number of "little" agencies or groups. A group is composed of an account executive, a copywriter, an artist, a media buyer, and any other specialists that are needed. The group may be assigned to serve only one account—if the account is very large—or, as in most cases, three or four accounts. A very large agency may have up to a dozen or more groups. It may even have separate production and traffic units to serve each one (Figure 4–10).

Each of these systems has its advantages. The system used in small and medium-size agencies requires personnel to wear more than one hat since the volume of billings is not large enough to support a team of specialists in each department. On the other hand, this system tends to promote operating economy and efficiency as well as more personal—and effective—client relations.

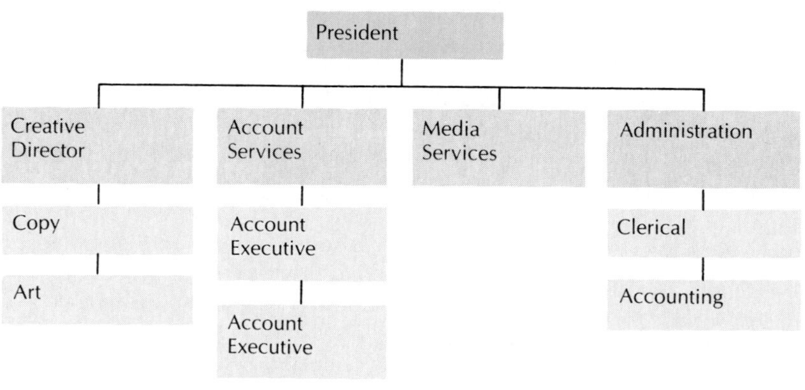

Figure 4–8 Typical organization of a small advertising agency.

The departmental system is good because it offers agency personnel new, challenging opportunities. Through this variety of experiences, they can expand their knowledge and skills. Thus they are able to bring both depth and breadth of experience to each new client account.

The group system enables the agency employees in each group to become thoroughly familiar with the accounts they are serving. This continuing exposure equips them to apply knowledge and experience to account problems. Continuity also allows them to monitor advertising campaigns and to make adjustments as needed for increased effectiveness. This system encourages harmonious interaction among group members and between the group and the client organization through frequent exchanges of ideas as they work together to achieve a common goal. The group is a collection of experts joined together by a sense of responsibility and governed by accountability.

The form of agency organization that best enables the agency to provide its services effectively, efficiently, and profitably is the one that should be implemented.

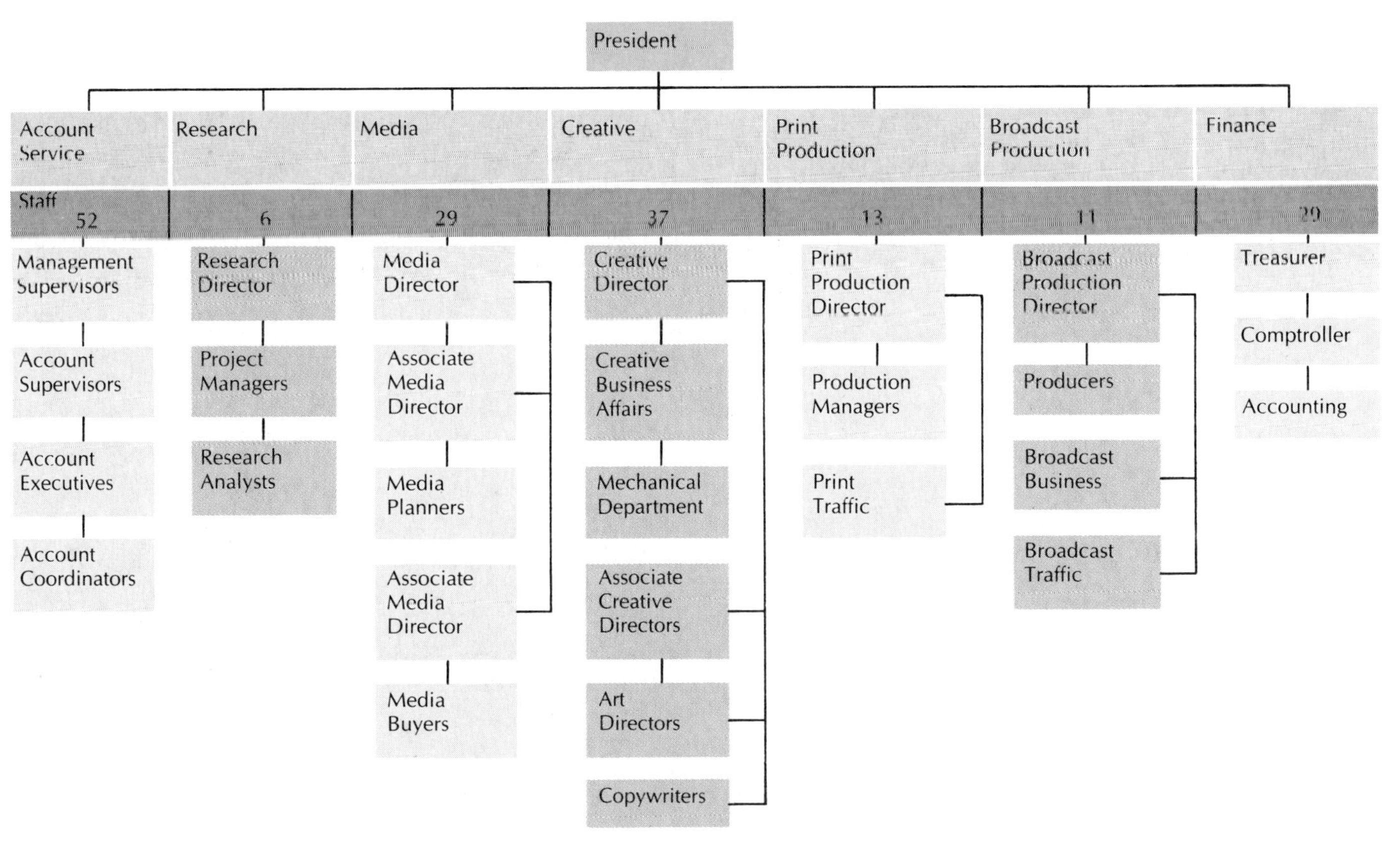

Figure 4–9 Advertising agency organization chart (departmental structure).

How do agencies make money?

Like any other business, an advertising agency must make a fair profit on the services it renders. Inasmuch as the amount of service typically varies from client to client, agencies use a variety of compensation methods to arrive at an equitable financial arrangement. Basically, agencies make money from three sources: (1) media commissions, (2) markups on outside purchases, and (3) fees or retainers. We shall discuss each of these briefly.

Media commissions

Historically, the major media have allowed recognized agencies to retain a commission on any space or time they purchase. This is because the agencies save the media a lot of expense in sales and collections. For most major media, the commission allowed is 15 percent. With outdoor advertising, it is usually 16⅔ percent. The way this system works is simple. Assume you wish to spend $1,000 for a magazine ad for your company. Your agency works with you, arranges

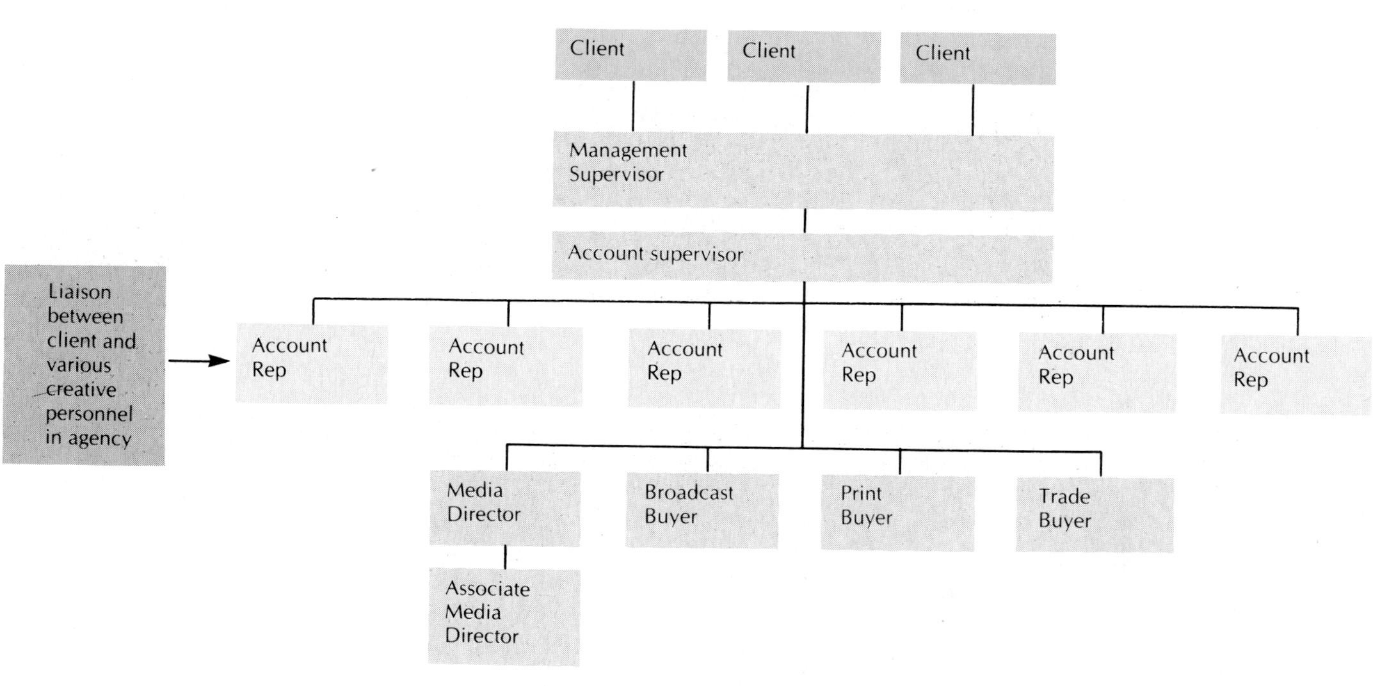

Figure 4–10 Advertising agency organization chart (group structure).

with the magazine to buy the space, places the order for you, and delivers the ad to the magazine. When the ad appears, the magazine bills the agency $1,000. The agency then bills you $1,000. You pay the agency this gross amount, and the agency remits the money to the magazine *less* its 15 percent commission, as follows:

$$\$1,000 - (1,000 \times 0.15) = \$850$$

If you spent $1 million, the agency's commission would be $150,000, and it would remit $850,000 to the media. For large accounts, the agency normally provides its creative services, media services, and accounting and account management services for this fee. For smaller accounts, though, the commission is usually not enough to cover the cost of all these services, so additional compensation is required. (See the Ad Lab.)

Pay the bill and get your two cents worth

Many media allow a 2 percent discount for prompt payment of their invoices (normally within 10 days). Most agencies pass this savings on to their client in the form of a bill reduction. Here's how it works.

Assume a $10,000 ad is placed by the agency in a national magazine.

1. The magazine bills the agency $10,000, less 15 percent commission, less two percent for prompt payment.
2. The agency computes the amount due the medium as follows:

$10,000	
x0.85	(15 percent agency commission)
$ 8,500	
x0.98	(2 percent prompt payment discount)
$ 8,330	Amount due the medium

3. The agency then bills the client as follows:

$10,000	Media cost
−170	2 percent prompt payment discount
$ 9,830	Billed to client

4. The client pays the agency promptly and the agency remits the amount due to the medium.

$9,830	Paid by client
1,500	15% retained by the agency
$8,330	Cash to the medium

In the advertising business, when the medium quotes rates to the agency, it describes this policy simply by saying: "The ad cost is $10,000, less 15 and 2."

Laboratory applications

1. Procter & Gamble spent over $649 million in advertising in 1980. If they were able to save 2 percent on all their advertising expenses by paying their bills on time, what would that have amounted to in 1980? How important do you believe the 2 percent is to P&G? Discuss.
2. Assume an ad for $47,500 is placed by an agency in a national magazine, and the client is invoiced by the 31st. What will the client pay if payment is sent by the 5th of the following month? What will the client pay if payment is sent by the 15th? What will be the agency commission?

Markups

To create your ad for the magazine, the agency normally has to buy type, photography, illustrations, photoengravings, or a variety of other services from outside suppliers. These suppliers do not normally give the agency a commission, so the agency buys these services and adds a markup to the client.

Traditionally agencies have added a 17.65 percent markup to outside purchases. The reason for this figure goes back to the 15 percent commission practice. When 17.65 percent is added to a net invoice, that amount becomes 15 percent of the new total gross, as follows:

$$\$8.50 \times 17.65\% = \$1.50$$
$$\$8.50 + \$1.50 = \$10.00$$
$$\$1.50 = 15\% \times \$10.00$$

Thus, the agency ends up with 15 percent of the total bill, which is the traditional agency commission. Some media, especially local newspapers, do not allow for an agency commission in their local rates. Therefore, agencies that use these media frequently use the markup formula to receive their commission. In this case, when you run an ad for $1,000, the agency will bill you $1,176.50, keep the $176.50, and remit the $1,000 to the medium.

In recent years many agencies have found that the 17.65 percent markup is not sufficient to cover the cost of services performed in buying from outside suppliers. This is especially true on smaller accounts where the sums spent are minor. As a result, some agencies now charge as much as 20–25 percent markup. (See Figure 4–11.)

Fees

Assume you are a small advertising agency with several local advertising clients. Perhaps your largest advertiser spends only $10,000 per month in commissionable media, yet it requires a lot of your time to service the account, provide in-depth media plans, stage in-store promotions, supervise press interviews, and develop posters and displays for windows and counters. Obviously the $1,500 per month you receive from the media commissions does not cover the amount of work you, your secretary, your artist, and your media person have to devote to this client. Nor does the $100–$200 extra you might pick up in markups offset the tremendous amount of time required plus the cost of your office overhead. You are going to have to charge your client an additional fee for your work. How do you determine a reasonable amount?

Agencies that serve their clients on a fee basis frequently use one of two pricing methods. The first is a fee-commission combination. With this method, the agency establishes a fixed monthly fee for all its services to the client. If, during a given month, the agency earns any media commissions for time or space purchased for the client, it may retain the total of these commissions in addition to the fee.

The second method is a straight fee arrangement. This is frequently used for accounts in which the services needed—research or public relations, for example—produce no commission income, or in which any media commissions received are credited to the client against the fee. The straight fee is frequently called a *retainer* and is similar to the retainers paid to attorneys or accountants.

The retainer system is based on a cost plus fixed fees arrangement. It assures the agency that it will receive a fair profit. Under this system the agency estimates the amount of personnel time required by the client, determines the cost of that personnel, adds a factor of 2.5–3 for overhead and another factor (e.g., 0.5) for profit, and that total becomes the fee charged. (Figure 4–12).

Number of agencies represented	242
Rent, light and depreciation	7.22%
Taxes (other than U.S. income)	4.11
Other operating expenses	16.89
Total payroll	61.02
Payments into retirement plans	2.32
Insurance for employee benefit	1.71
Total expenses	93.27
Profit before U.S. income tax for all agencies	6.73
U.S. income taxes	1.64
Net profit	5.09
Profit before U.S. income tax for incorporated agencies	6.58
U.S. income tax for incorporated agencies	1.84
Net profit for incorporated agencies	4.74
Net profit for incorporated agencies (as percentage of sales—i.e., billing)	0.99

Figure 4–11 Survey of costs and profits for 242 agencies.

Figure 4–12 How to compute a monthly retainer

Employee	Annual salary	Hourly rate*	Billable rate†		Est. hours/ month	Total
1	$12,000	$ 7.50	$22.50	×	10	$ 225
2	$25,000	$15.00	$45.00	×	20	$ 900
3	$30,000	$20.00	$60.00	×	15	$ 900
4	$20,000	$17.00	$42.00	×	20	$ 840
						$2,865

*Assuming approximately 130 hours a month.
†Using 3 as total factors.

Using the data in Figure 4–12, you might determine to handle your client's work for a total monthly retainer of $3,000 and credit commissions against that fee. Or you might determine that the retainer will have to be over and above commissions since most of the time estimated above will be for noncommissionable work in public relations and sales promotion. In either case, it will be up to you to sell your client on the value of your services and to negotiate a compensation arrangement that will be fair for both.

How do agencies get clients?

To succeed, advertising agencies must have clients. But where do those clients come from? What can a small agency do when it has a staff of artists, copywriters, account executives, media people, secretaries, and bookkeepers, but not enough billing to pay the salaries?

Della Femina Travisano and Partners is one of the largest and most successful advertising agencies in the business. But it wasn't always that way. Jerry Della Femina started with four people. They all had excellent backgrounds working for other agencies in New York, but they wanted to have their own business. So they set up shop, but they didn't have any clients. They called on prospective advertisers. They did some odd jobs and projects for friends, but the money was going quickly. Finally they decided to give one last try before closing the doors. They took all the money they had left and blew it on a big bash cocktail party, inviting everybody they could think of to their offices. The town was so impressed with this bright, aggressive, new "hot shop" that Jerry ended up landing three new clients from the party; they were on their way.

An advertising agency, like any other business, has a product or a service to sell. Clients come to an advertising agency, therefore, in much the same way as they come to an attorney, a doctor, a hairdresser, or a clothier: by referral, through advertising, because they were solicited, or because of reputation (Figure 4–13).

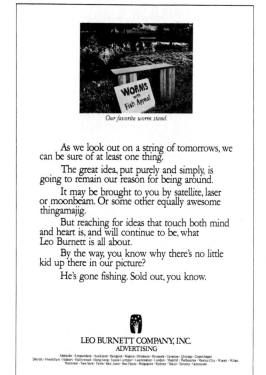

Our favorite worm stand.

As we look out on a string of tomorrows, we can be sure of at least one thing.

The great idea, put purely and simply, is going to remain our reason for being around.

It may be brought to you by satellite, laser or moonbeam. Or some other equally awesome thingamajig.

But reaching for ideas that touch both mind and heart is, and will continue to be, what Leo Burnett is all about.

By the way, you know why there's no little kid up there in our picture?

He's gone fishing. Sold out, you know.

LEO BURNETT COMPANY, INC.
ADVERTISING

Adelaide · Amsterdam · Auckland · Bangkok · Bogota · Brisbane · Brussels · Caracas · Chicago · Copenhagen
Detroit · Frankfurt · Hobart · Hollywood · Hong Kong · Kuala Lumpur · Launceston · London · Madrid · Melbourne · Mexico City · Miami · Milan
Montreal · New York · Paris · San Juan · Sao Paulo · Singapore · Sydney · Tokyo · Toronto · Vancouver

Figure 4–13 The simplest ideas are often the biggest ideas. That message from Leo Burnett, offered with the sublime humor of understatement, makes an effective statement of this agency's philosophy of advertising.

Referrals

Most good advertising agencies get their clients by referral. The president of one company asks the president of another company who does those great ads, and the next week the agency gets a call. Sometimes the agency getting the call feels the prospective client might pose a conflict of interest with an existing client. In this case the business might be referred by one agency to another.

In the case of local advertisers, representatives of the media frequently refer clients to an agency with whom they have a working relationship. It helps, therefore, for agencies to maintain good relationships with their existing clients, with the media, and with other agencies, and it is common practice for them to "put the word out" when they are looking for new business (Figure 4–14).

Solicitations for new business

An agency may decide to openly solicit new business by (1) advertising, (2) writing solicitation letters, (3) making "cold" calls on clients of other agencies, or (4) following up leads from sources within the business. Few agencies advertise their services. Considering the business they are in, one survey turned up some amusing answers as to why they don't advertise. Among the most common responses were:

"Advertising is not very effective."
"We have never been able to agree on an advertising theme."
"We have never budgeted for advertising."[6]

Most agencies prefer to have clients referred to them. Others take a more aggressive approach, seeking new business through direct solicitation or any other means available.

The task of soliciting new business usually falls to one of the agency's principals, since the rest of the staff is normally assigned to the work of existing clients. Once a new business prospect has been found, however, staffers may be called in to assist on the presentation.

People in advertising

Mary Wells Lawrence

Chairman of the Board, President, and Chief Executive Officer
Wells, Rich, Greene, Inc.

Mary Wells Lawrence, one of the highest paid executives in advertising today, is founder, president, and chief executive officer of Wells, Rich, Greene, Inc. WRG is the fastest growing agency in industry history and commands annual billings of $400 million.

Lawrence was born in Youngstown, Ohio, where she began her career as a department store copywriter. She attended New York's Neighborhood Playhouse School Theatre and then studied at Carnegie Tech. At 23 she became fashion advertising manager for Macy's. A year later Lawrence joined McCann Erickson as copy group head. In 1957 she was named a vice president of Doyle Dane Bernbach. She later became a senior partner at Jack Tinker & Partners, where she created advertising for Alka-Seltzer and Braniff.

In 1966, with associates Dick Rich and Stewart Greene, Lawrence left Tinker to launch her own advertising agency. The firm soon signed such accounts as Braniff, Benson & Hedges 100s, and Alka-Seltzer. Within a year, Wells, Rich, Greene became one of the nation's 50 largest agencies, with billings of $30 million. By 1973 it had acquired the Gardner Agency of St. Louis and created a subsidiary, WRG-Dragoti. Today Wells, Rich, Greene has offices in nearly a dozen cities, including New York, London, Dallas, Atlanta, Chicago, and Los Angeles. Among its clients have been Procter & Gamble, Ralston, and Standard Brands.

As chief administrator, Mary Wells Lawrence still often handles the presentation of the firm's advertising campaigns to its clients. She regards this as critical for an effective agency-client relationship. And she is one of the best presenters in the business. "I'm not brilliant at anything except selling," she admits, "and at being incredibly organized."

Explaining WRG's success, Lawrence says, "We innovated the concept of fewer people for every dollar of billing. Our senior art directors and writers are *working* talents who come up with campaigns themselves, instead of coaxing them out of less experienced people. Our top management works on client problems. Our vice chairman writes copy. Our president personally directs the Account Services Department." And everyone still calls Mary by her first name.

Her management philosophy centers on hiring exceptionally talented people, then providing them with an environment and strong motivations that stimulate their best creative ideas. She emphasizes that such ideas must adapt and change in today's economic environment. "The answer today, no matter how clever," says Lawrence, "probably will not work tomorrow."

Named to the Copywriters' Hall of Fame in 1969, Lawrence is the recipient of the Colgate Award of the National Business Leaders Hall of Fame. She received an honorary doctor of laws degree from Babson College in 1970 and from Carnegie Mellon University in 1974. That same year she was named by Governor Nelson Rockefeller to the Commission on Critical Choices for America. She was later appointed by President Gerald R. Ford to the President's Council on Inflation and was chosen to represent American business at the economic summit in Washington, D.C.

Mary Wells Lawrence is a member of the boards of directors of the Ralston Purina Company and of Junior Achievement, Inc. She also serves on the Services Policy Advisory Committee, which operates to remove barriers in international trade.

Lawrence has been called "today's woman, completely tuned to today and doing all the just-right things." She is a hard-driving professional ("The prime force in my life is work") who has become a symbol of success in the industry. Lawrence is aware of her influence. "Ten years ago," she notes, "men would have been scared of me—but not today. Nowadays, it doesn't make any difference if you're a man or a woman. I've got a successful track record so far, and that's all that interests people."

Public relations

Agencies frequently find that their best source of business is simply their good reputation. This normally comes after a long time in the business, but most agencies participate in activities that will help raise their profile in the business community. Some work on charitable committees; others assist local politicians; and some are active in the arts, education, religion, or social circles. Some give seminars; others write articles in magazines; and many others become active in advertising clubs or other professional organizations. All these activities contribute to getting the agency known and respected in the community. From this respect come business opportunities.

XEROX
THIS COMMERCIAL RAN JUST 17 TIMES. AND THAT'S GOSPEL.
Some people believe that in order for a commercial to be really effective, it has to run hundreds of times.
That's true. For most commercials.
The original 60-second Xerox "Monk" commercial ran a mere 17 times the first year.
After the very first airing the response began to be felt. We call that High Profile Advertising.
The kind of advertising we do for such clients as McDonald's, Honda, Parkay margarine and many, many more.
Call Joel Baumwoll in New York, Keith Reinhard in Chicago, or Brad Roberts in Los Angeles to find out how we do it.
NEEDHAM, HARPER & STEERS
High Profile Advertising

Figure 4–14 In Latin countries, there is an amusing expression about people who greet their friends by "tipping their neighbor's hat." This practice is quite common for American advertising agencies who find it most effective to explain who they are by telling you who their clients are.

Presentations

Once an advertiser becomes interested in an agency, the agency may be asked to make a presentation. This may mean anything from a simple discussion of the agency's philosophy, experience, personnel, and track record to a full-blown audiovisual show, complete with slides, films, sample commercials, or even proposed campaigns. In the vernacular of the trade, this latter is commonly, and somewhat disdainfully, referred to as a "dog and pony show."

Some advertisers ask or imply that they want the agency to make a *speculative presentation*. This means they want to see what the agency would do for them before they hire them. Most reputable agencies refuse to do "spec" presentations, because it is generally considered unethical and unprofessional. Smaller agencies think it gives larger, wealthier agencies an unfair advantage. Large agencies, however, do not want to invest their money in presentations that allow clients to pick their brains for free. And larger advertisers do not like agencies to use the money they are paying, and the talent they are paying for, to be wasted on presentations to other clients. Thus, the practice is generally frowned on. However, when business gets tough and clients are scarce, spec presentations invariably start appearing.

Most agencies try to build their nonspeculative presentations around the work they have performed for other advertisers. In this way, they can demonstrate their versatility, philosophy, expertise, and depth of understanding of the marketplace and the client's business. At the beginning of this chapter, we saw how Ted Bates & Company got the Coors beer account. They were not asked to give a speculative presentation. Rather, the client was interested in the agency's philosophical approach to marketing problems and their track record with other clients.

A simple fact, often overlooked, is that in the process of this type of presentation, both the agency and the advertiser can get to know one another and find out if they like each other. Advertising is a people-oriented business, and the advertiser-agency relationship is a peculiar kind of marriage. As in any marriage, though, there must be mutual liking, trust, and communication.

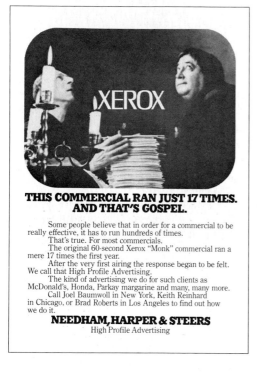

Summary

Advertising agencies are independent organizations of creative and business people who specialize in the development and preparation of advertising plans, advertisements, and other promotional tools. The agency also arranges for the purchase of advertising space and time in the media. It does all this on behalf of its clients in an effort to find customers for their goods and services.

Agencies may be classified by the types of clients they handle (e.g., financial, retail, industrial) or by the range of services they offer (e.g., full-service, media buying services, domestic or foreign advertising).

To accomplish their task, agencies provide a wide range of services to their clients. These include research, planning, creative services, print and broadcast production, coordination of media and suppliers, account management, and accounting services, to name a few. In addition, the agency may provide public relations assistance, sales promotion counseling, direct marketing assistance, package design, and even economic research.

Agencies, like their clients, may be organized in several ways. Some use the departmental system in which each agency function (media, creative, production, etc.) operates as a separate department. Others use the group system in which the agency is divided into a number of little "agencies" or groups composed of the particular specialists needed for each account.

To make money, agencies may charge fees or retainers, receive commissions from the media, or markup outside purchases of type, photography, or printing that they buy for their clients. Usually some combination of these systems is negotiated with the client. There are advantages and disadvantages to each method.

Most agencies get their clients through referral or personal solicitation. Considering the business they are in, it is surprising that most advertising agencies do very little advertising of their own services.

Questions for review

1. What are the functions of a full-service advertising agency? Describe.
2. What are some of the most important points for an advertiser to consider in selecting an agency?
3. What are the advantages and disadvantages to an advertiser in changing agencies on a regular basis?
4. What is the relationship between the agency's creative department and its research department?
5. The following is a list of tasks an advertiser might request an agency to perform. Which person in the agency would do the work? Are there any tasks an agency might not be able to perform?
   a. Develop a company slogan.
   b. Design a study for test-marketing a new product.
   c. Take a photograph for an advertisement.
   d. Choose an actress for a television commercial.
   e. Provide advice on pricing a new product.
   f. Come up with an idea for a contest.
6. How is new business generated for an advertising agency? Who is responsible for this task?
7. Why do even good agencies lose accounts to other agencies?
8. How are agencies compensated? Why are there a variety of methods?
9. How are agencies organized? What are the advantages and disadvantages of each plan?
10. What is the usual policy regarding an agency handling competing accounts?

5

The media and suppliers

As a rambunctious sophomore at Brown University, Robert Edward Turner III was suspended for getting caught in a women's dormitory room at nearby Wheaton College. After spending six months of active duty in the Coast Guard, he returned to Brown, where he majored in the classics and excelled at sailing as well as debating. In his senior year he was suspended again for entertaining a Wheaton girl in *his* room. He was also barred from his fraternity for burning down its homecoming float.[1]

When Turner was 24, his father suffered a nervous breakdown and committed suicide. The tragedy made a man out of a playboy. Obsessed by a fervor to conquer and enraptured by the grand ideas of building the Parthenon or the pyramids, Ted Turner took his father's failing billboard business and multiplied it into one of the largest private empires in advertising in less than 20 years.

When Ted was nine years old, the family moved from Cincinnati to Savannah, Georgia, where his father, Ed Turner, bought the outdoor advertising company that became the Turner Advertising Company. During summers, Ted worked a 40-hour week cutting grass and painting poles.[2] During college he was offered the chance to work and sail for the Noroton (Connecticut) Yacht Club, but his father, a strict disciplinarian who had often beaten Ted as a child, insisted he continue to work for the family business. By this time it had expanded to several cities in the South. Turner complied and worked as an account executive for the flagship company in Savannah, selling billboard space to local advertisers and advertising agencies. By the time he was 22, he was general manager of the Turner Advertising Company's branch in Macon.

Two years later his father overextended himself buying the General Outdoor Advertising Company in Atlanta, the biggest in the country. In the ensuing financial struggle to stay afloat, Ed Turner initiated plans to sell out, which greatly agitated Ted who had already developed a zealot's taste for the business.

When his father shot himself, Ted immediately halted the sell-out transactions and, against the advice of his financial consultants, set about to bring the debt-ridden business back to health. Through a series of complex financial dealings he rescued the company and regained the parts of the family business that had already been sold.

A few years later he again rejected his consultants' warnings and branched out into television, buying an independent UHF-TV station that was losing more than $500,000 a year. He immediately grabbed up five network shows that were not being shown on the local network affiliate station, sold sponsorships to local advertisers, and within three years turned Channel 17 into one of the first profitable independent stations in the nation.

Turner wanted to televise major league sports, but he didn't want to pay broadcast rights. So he bought the Atlanta Braves baseball team and the Atlanta Hawks basketball team, both of which were in the cellar in their respective leagues and suffering from dismal attendance. As the teams' number one fan, Turner used his flair for promotion and bombast to boost attendance, sell advertising sponsorships, and catapult himself to national prominence as the "Mouth of the South" (Figure 5–1).

Turner's boldest stroke came in 1975 when RCA launched the Satcom satellite. He quickly built a $750,000 transmission antenna, formed a company to operate it, and in December 1976 began to distribute his local station's signal to cable TV systems in other states. With his "superstation that serves the nation," Turner immediately quadrupled his audience, picked up revenue from subscribing cable systems, and attracted the first of WTBS's 150 national advertisers. Moreover, he was paying only local station rates for the programs he was buying from Hollywood's program suppliers. By 1980 Turner's WTBS superstation was reaching nearly 9 million cable homes in 48 states and, combined with Turner's other ventures, creating annual revenues of $38 million.

To market his station's cable audience, Turner opened offices in Chicago and New York, where national advertisers vied for the opportunity to sponsor the televised games of the Braves and the Hawks. He also bought the rights to many reruns of network shows, built a library of 3,000 motion pictures, and expanded the programming to include news, special events, prime-time adult programs, and children's shows.

In June 1980 Turner struck again. *Newsweek* magazine reported the occasion:

> As usual, Ted Turner couldn't wait to start talking. Minutes before the camera's ruby light flashed on, cable TV's garrulous impresario was already well into his inaugural address before a gathering of Atlanta VIP's. By the time he actually went on the air, Turner was proudly reciting from an ode to himself composed by his public-relations man ("To act upon one's convictions while others wait/To create a positive force in a world where cynics abound . . ."). At last, he proclaimed: "I dedicate this news channel for America." Drums rolled, flags ascended and three military bands blared the national anthem. As the last notes faded, Turner whooped out a lusty "Awwriiight!" With that, he thrust into motion an historic television breakthrough—the world's first 24-hour-a-day network devoted entirely to news.[3]

Figure 5–1 The "Mouth of the South," Ted Turner has entrepreneurial spirit and flair for bombast, braggadocio, and promotion, which have catapulted him to riches and national prominence. As *Newsweek* says, his style may be the antithesis of boardroom decorum, but his formidable business acumen and knack for bringing off the near-miraculous have brought him wide professional respect. In 1977 he even found the time to win yacht racing's most prestigious America's Cup. But his antics earned him the title "Captain Outrageous."

Turner's Cable News Network (CNN) was launched, and 2.2 million homes were suddenly able to plug into the state of the world at their convenience through television's first news-on-demand station. With seven domestic and three foreign news bureaus, a corps of network TV news veterans like Daniel Schorr and Reese Shonfield, and a wide variety of provocative commentators from Barry Goldwater to Ralph Nader, CNN was taking on the networks. Even more significantly, Turner was providing an early demonstration of what is still to come in the 1980s and 1990s (Figure 5–2).

Within the next decade, it is predicted that the number of U.S. homes wired to receive cable systems will surge from one in five to more than half. As the dial becomes clogged with as many as 50 channels, broadcasters may survive only by emulating Turner and offering highly specialized fare—becoming, in effect, "narrowcasters" instead of broadcasters. Even the three major networks may be forced into cable casting as advertisers seek specialized markets for their products.

Turner is showing the way. He receives a monthly fee from the cable-system operators who carry his service (about 20 cents per subscriber), and he reserves 12 minutes of time for advertisers (10 for CNN and 2 for the local cablecaster). With heavyweight sponsors such as General Mills, Sears, Time, Inc., and Bristol-Myers helping Turner launch the system, it's no wonder that this flamboyant southern folk hero boasts, "This will be the most significant achievement in the annals of journalism."

A sign on Turner's desk epitomizes his competitive drive: "Either Lead, Follow, or Get Out of the Way."

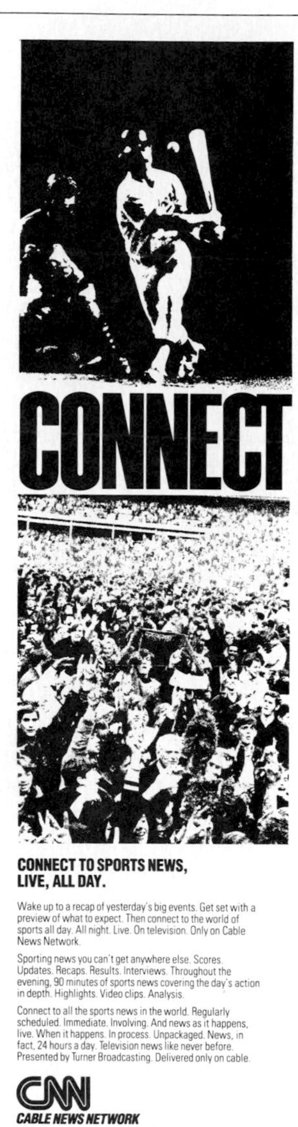

Figure 5–2 Ads in newspapers and magazines were used to launch the historic CNN news network. Within two weeks of beginning, Turner landed the nation's biggest advertiser, Procter & Gamble, for sponsorship of the cable newscasts.

Media

The medium that carries the advertiser's message is the vital connection between the company that manufactures a product and the customer who might wish to buy it. It is the third link in the communication chain.

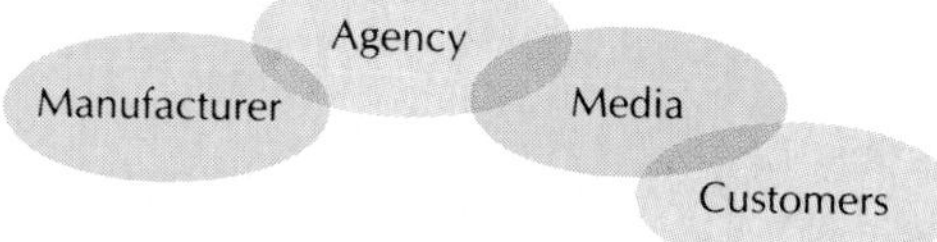

Cable television, like Ted Turner's, is one of the newest media to be used by advertisers and their agencies in this constant struggle to reach customers with product news.

The media that are available today include the traditional broadcast, print, direct mail, and out-of-home media and an increasing variety of new, often untried, sometimes esoteric media that have been born in the recent years of exploding technology.

For the student of advertising, it is important to understand the various traditional media, their relationship to the advertising business, and the significance of current trends in the media world. For the person seeking a career in advertising, the media have often offered the first door to employment, and, for some like Ted Turner who started by cutting grass, they have offered the greatest opportunity for financial reward.

What are the media?

The media may be divided into several major categories: print, broadcast, out-of-home, direct mail, and other media. Due to recent media trends, there are beginning to be some overlaps. We shall mention these in passing along with a brief description of each major category.

Print media

Traditionally *print media* refers to newspapers and magazines. In the United States today there are 1,745 daily and 7,602 weekly newspapers. Most of these are local. Some national newspapers such as *The Wall Street Journal, Barron's,* and trade publications like *Electronic*

News and *Supermarket News* have become quite successful. We are seeing the emergence of certain regional consumer newspapers like the *Los Angeles Times,* which has branched throughout southern California, and the *New York Times,* which covers several eastern states.

Magazines, on the other hand, have long been national, and the trend is toward localization and specialization. According to the *Standard Directory of Periodicals,* there are 64,000 different magazines published in the United States alone. These include national consumer publications like *Time, Newsweek, Sports Illustrated, Cosmopolitan,* and *TV Guide;* national trade publications like *Electronic Design, Broadcasting,* and *Advertising Age;* local city magazines like *Palm Springs Life, New York* magazine, *Chicago* magazine, and *Arkansas Times;* regional consumer magazines like *Sunset;* and local or regional trade and farm publications such as *California Farmer, Prairie Farmer, New England Grocer,* and *Grit* (Figure 5–3). Also included are a variety

Figure 5–3 This ad, "Big Frog in Small Towns," is one of dozens in a series that run in the advertising trade press. The ads are designed to increase awareness among advertisers and agencies of this 99-year-old national publication.

of special-interest newsletters such as the *Kiplinger Washington Letter* and the *Januz Direct Marketing Letter.*

Aside from the newsletters, which normally do not carry advertising, this vast array of periodicals and publications make it possible for advertisers to pinpoint their messages to highly select markets in any of a variety of fields or geographic locations.

The term *print media* also includes directories such as the Yellow Pages, *Hotel Travel Index,* and the *Thomas Register;* school or church newspapers and yearbooks; and programs used at sporting events and theatrical performances. The term is used generally to describe any commercially published medium that sells advertising space to a variety of advertisers.

Broadcast media

The broadcast media of radio and television are frequently referred to as *electronic media.* They include 726 local television stations; 7,000 local radio stations; several radio and TV networks including ABC, CBS, NBC, Mutual, Westinghouse, and others; and the 4,000 local cable systems now blanketing the country and still growing.

As *Marketing Communications* reports, "There is a revolution in the air—and it comes from outer space."[4] What was just a lightweight medium yesterday is rapidly becoming a heavyweight contender; cable TV offers the potential for big problems as well as opportunities for the nation's advertisers. Today, due to satellites, cable has become the main tool of programmers who want to start new TV networks (Figure 5–4). Home Box Office shows movies and sports for a fee with no commercials. Ted Turner shows news, movies, and sports for free with commercials. Calliope shows children's programs without commercials. UPI and Reuters both broadcast news, one via still photos and the other via alphanumeric readouts. There are also religious networks, sponsored film networks, and even a network with live coverage of Congress.

The eventual impact of this proliferation is nearly impossible to assess. One thing seems certain, though. The competition for viewers is increasing at an alarming pace for the major networks. The number of viewers determines the rates than can be charged for advertising time, and that determines the revenues the networks receive. As audiences become more fragmented and turn to noncommercial stations, the major networks will face new challenges to create revenue.

Out-of-home media

The major categories of out-of-home media are outdoor advertising (billboards), point-of-purchase displays (counter cards), and transit advertising (bus and car cards). Most U.S. outdoor advertising plants like the Turner Advertising Company are local firms, but much of their revenue comes from national advertisers such as tobacco companies and liquor distillers. Transit advertising has been an effective, inexpensive medium to reach people out of their homes and in the buying community. Convenient "take-one" pads inside buses have facilitated the direct action possibilities of this medium. Likewise, point-of-purchase displays in stores and supermarkets have proved beneficial to manufacturers of items bought on impulse.

Recent innovations in out-of-home media include colorful Beetle-board advertising and Ad-Vans, posters in bus shelters and train stations, and creative billboards in airport lounges from directional clocks to courtesy phone centers. Also included as out-of-home media are stadium scoreboard ads, flashing signs such as in Times Square, flying banners and lights, and skywriting.

Direct mail

When companies mail their advertisements directly to prospective customers without using one of the commercially published media, this is called *direct-mail advertising*. Often prepared by agencies that specialize in direct mail, advertisements may be a simple letter with an offer or solicitation, or a complex package with coupons, brochures, samples, or other devices designed to stimulate response. Direct mail is the most expensive medium on a cost-per-exposure basis. But it is also usually the most effective because the advertiser can target the customer directly and doesn't have to compete with other advertisers for attention like in a magazine or newspaper.

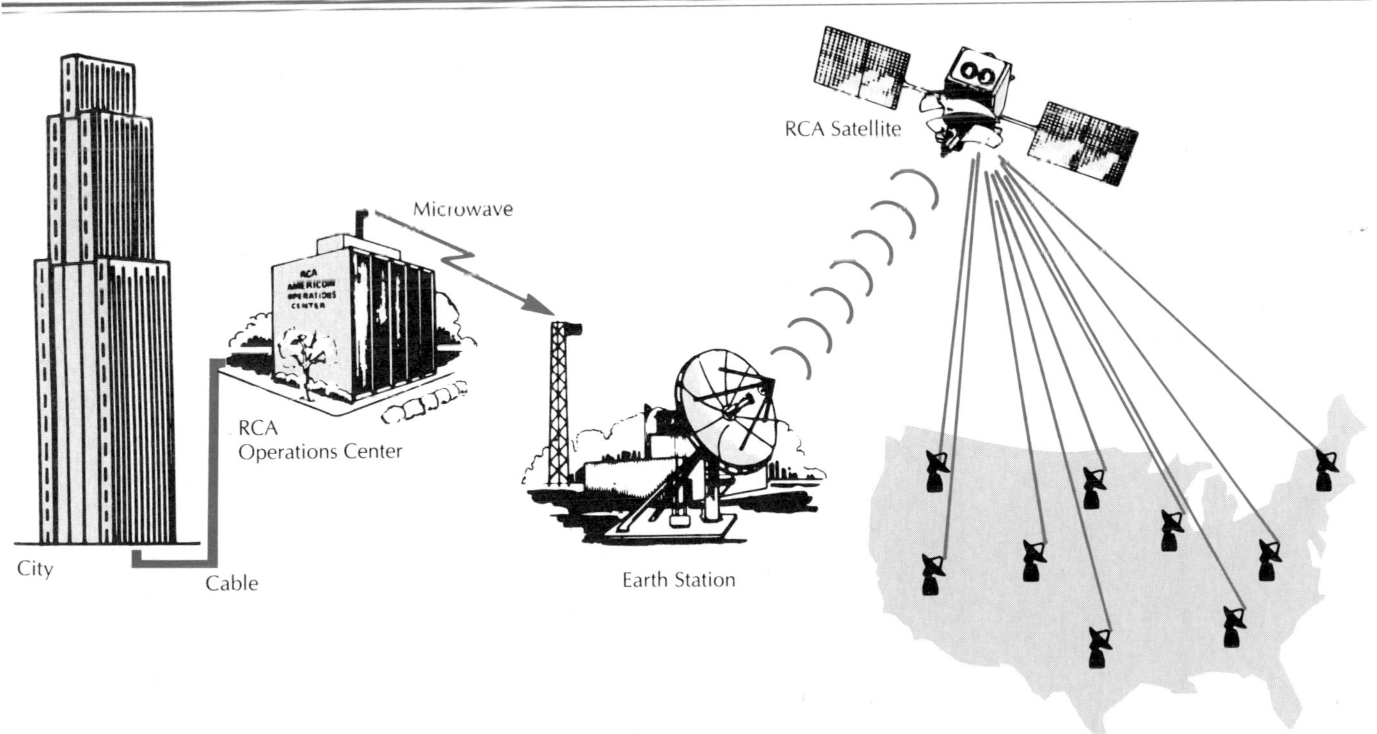

Figure 5–4 How a TV satellite works.

Other media

With recent technological progress has come a host of new advertising media to confound even the most knowledgeable media planners and buyers. (See the Ad Lab.) Cinema advertising, long a favorite in European countries, has recently begun to appear between movies in theaters around the country. Automatic telephone-dialing devices with recorded messages are another new direct advertising medium. Coptermedia offers new opportunities for nighttime out-of-home advertisers. By suspending a 40-by-8-foot billboard with thousands of light bulbs on it, the helicopter flies the message overhead to the surprise of those on the ground. Even records can now be pressed into plastic sheets and inserted in magazines or mailed via direct mail to prospective customers to give sound and music to the message (see Chapter 13).

As progress continues, so will the proliferation of new media that are not even thought of today, and so will the opportunities for those seeking their fortunes in the media.

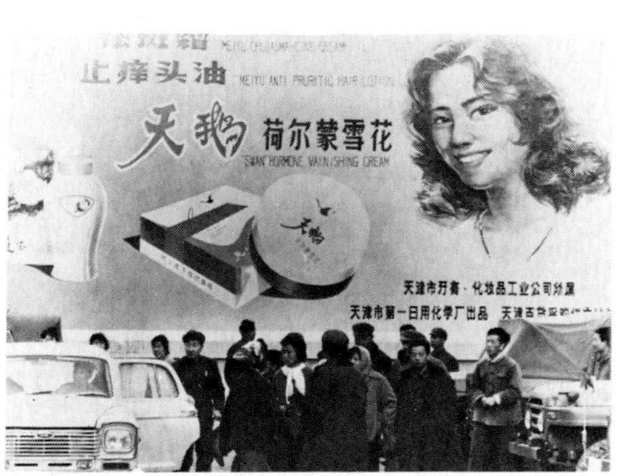

Figure 5–5 A new billboard at the Peking No. 1 Department Store shows a Chinese girl with Western-style hair and lipstick touting the virtues of "Swan" hormone vanishing cream. New billboards are cropping up around Peking and are directed at Western and Chinese buyers.

Media in foreign markets

It has been said that American advertising people can get used to the foreign styles of advertising faster than they can get used to foreign media. In the United States, if you want to promote a popular soft drink as a youthful, fun refresher, you use television. In several European countries, you are not able to. The same is true in Asia, South America, and Africa. Around the world, most broadcast media are owned and controlled by the government, and many governments do not allow commercials on radio or television.

In countries that do allow television advertising, you have another problem. How many people own television sets, and who are they? In Europe the majority of the population now owns TVs. But in less developed nations TVs are found only among the upper income groups. The result is a different media mix in foreign markets than in the United States.

Types of media available

The same media we find here exist around the world. Virtually every country has radio, television, newspapers, magazines, outdoor, and direct mail (Figure 5–5). However, as we have pointed out, it may not always be legal to use all these media for advertising. In addition, cinema advertising is a very popular medium in many countries, as are some other selective specialty media that either do not exist or are not widely used here.

Generally the media available to the international advertiser can be categorized as either international media or foreign media, depending on the audience the particular medium serves.

International media Several large American publishers like Time, Inc., McGraw-Hill, and Scientific American circulate international editions of their magazines abroad. Often written in English, they tend to be read by well-educated, upper income consumers and are therefore good vehicles for reaching this audience. The *Reader's Digest* is distributed to 170 foreign countries. However, it is printed in the local language of each country.

Recently there has been an increase in the number of international trade or specialty publications. *European Business* is published in

Off-the-wall media that pull customers off the fence

Advertising via telephone

You can purchase 30-second messages in which the advertiser supplies the company with relevant sales points. They can be taped, introduced by a live-pitch person, or both. "Where to Buy" telephone services identify retailers of specific products from consumers' inquiries.

Aerial banners and lights

Banners, usually more than 30 feet long, are pulled by low-flying planes. After dark, traveling aerial lights can display messages of up to 90 characters.

Balloons

The advertiser's message is imprinted on the balloons. Airborne heights vary from 200 to 800 feet.

Coptermedia

This method uses thousands of light bulbs mounted on a 40-by-8-foot billboard frame on a slow-flying helicopter. The effect is that of a brilliant flying electric sign floating about 500 feet above the ground.

Handbills

Handbills are simple sheets of paper with brief advertising messages which may be slipped under windshield wipers or hung on door knobs. Distributed by agents, they are one of the least expensive methods of advertising a local service or retail business.

Litter receptacles

Some major cities offer space on concrete litter receptacles at major commercial intersections.

Paper-book advertising

Bound-in inserts are available. Approximately 350 million pocket books are sold annually. The audience can be pinpointed by book title.

Shopping bags

Bags are offered to grocery chains on a regionally exclusive basis. A shopper's checklist is printed on both sides, and advertisers can have their names printed on the list next to or in place of the category designation.

Taxicab advertising

The back panel of front seats, the outside rear, and displays built on the roof provide day and night exposure. Rear-screen slide projectors facing riders are also available in some major markets.

Theater-screen advertising

Commercials ranging from 30 seconds to 2½ minutes are screened at performances in most indoor and drive-in theaters. The average national movie audience consists of approximately 500 million people per week, with women and younger people dominant.

Laboratory applications

1. What other off-the-wall media can you think of that might help pull customers off the fence?
2. How effective do you think the off-the-wall media described here are for advertisers?

Switzerland in English but is distributed throughout Europe. *Electronic Product News* is printed in English, published in Belgium, and distributed throughout Europe.

International media have for the most part been limited to newspapers and magazines. However, the Voice of America (VOA) and Radio Luxemburg are examples of international broadcast media. In recent years, in an effort to correct our trade deficit, the VOA has carried spots for American products on its broadcasts.

Figure 5–6 English and Chinese are the two official languages in Hong Kong. McDonald's advertises its golden arches in both. Note the similarity in layout.

Foreign media Due to the scarcity of effective international media, international advertisers are usually obliged to use the local media of the countries in which they are marketing. Foreign media cater to their own local national audience. This, of course, requires advertisers to produce advertisements in the language or languages of each country. In some countries there is more than one official language. In Belgium, ads are prepared in both Dutch and French, and some magazines produce two separate versions (Figure 5–6).

Overspill media In addition to international and foreign media, a recent phenomenon is overspill media. This is actually foreign media aimed at a local national population that is inadvertently received by a substantial portion of the population of a neighboring country. In Europe, for example, where the major languages are French, German, and English, the keys areas of overspill are Belgium, Switzerland, and Austria. There is also overspill into countries that are short on publications, particularly specialized ones, in their own native languages. English and German media have a large circulation in Scandinavian countries. French and English media are popular in Spain, Italy, North Africa, and the Middle East. And a wide variety of foreign language media are spilling into the Eastern Bloc countries.

According to a study by the Foote, Cone & Belding advertising agency on overspill media in Europe, multinational advertisers are now faced with the danger that these media may carry both international and local campaigns for the same product or service. This may confuse potential buyers. As this media area develops, local subsidiaries or distributors must coordinate their programs to avoid confusion. However, overspill media offer the potential to save money by regionalizing campaigns.

Within the broad categories of international, foreign, and overspill media are the various types of media with which we are familiar in the United States—namely, radio, magazines, television, newspapers, and so on. The difference lies not so much in the availability of the media as in the coverage offered and the economics of using one medium over another.

Media coverage

Whereas in the United States the broad middle class may be reached by any of innumerable media, this is not necessarily true in many foreign markets. For one thing, lower literacy rates and general education levels may restrict the coverage of mass press media. Furthermore, where income levels are low, ownership of televisions is similarly low. What occurs, therefore, is a natural segmentation of the market by the selective coverage of the various media.

In countries dominated by national newspapers, circulation may be primarily to upper class, well-educated people. On the other hand, both Pepsi and Coca-Cola have reached the lower income markets successfully through the use of radio, which enjoys almost universal ownership. Moreover, in some countries many stores and bars allow their radios to blare onto the street, making the sound available to any passersby. Auto manufacturers use television and magazines successfully to reach the upper class. And cinema advertising is used to reach whole urban populations where television ownership is low, since motion picture attendance there is still very high. However, there may be some selectivity by simply restricting the showing of commercials to upper income areas or to slum theaters, depending on a particular product's market.

Economics of foreign media

As pointed out in Chapter 1, a major purpose of advertising is to communicate with customers less expensively than through the use of personal selling. In many underdeveloped countries, however, this is not necessarily true. Colgate-Palmolive has found that in some countries where labor is extremely cheap, they can send people around with baskets of samples twice a year. This kind of personal contact would be impossible in the United States where Colgate has had to use advertising to do the entire consumer selling job.

In the United States the cost of labor has also inhibited the growth of outdoor advertising. In most foreign markets, though, outdoor enjoys far greater coverage, since it costs less to have people paint the signs. In Mexico, for example, almost every street seems to have a "Disfrute Coca-Cola" sign. In Nigeria billboards with the slogan "Guiness gives you power" next to the bulging biceps of an African arm have kept Guiness stout ale the best seller for many years. This despite an 80 percent illiteracy rate.

Of course, just as economics determine which medium is used, economics also determine the availability of media. We have just seen this in the case of outdoor advertising. Likewise, one factor that inhibits the growth of TV is its cost. This same factor, however, causes some countries to consider opening TV to commercial use to help pay for it. We may expect, therefore, that as more countries allow commercial broadcasts, the proliferation of television will increase. On the other hand, as labor rates increase, we may expect to see reductions in the number of press and outdoor media available in foreign markets. Likewise, the use of personal selling and sales promotion may similarly become more restricted due to the costs involved.

Figure 5–6 *(concluded)*

Functions of the media

Ted Turner's billboard company had one purpose—to carry advertising for its customers. Other media may provide a variety of functions. These would include the communication of news or interesting information, the offering of mass or specialized entertainment, and the dissemination of advertising messages.

News and information

When we speak of the news media, we think of newspapers, newsmagazines, and radio or television reporters. Some of these have a stronger news orientation than others. The primary purpose of newspapers is to carry news. Most radio and tevision stations, however, devote only a small portion of their programming to news. The three major networks have historically presented only 22 minutes of news in prime evening time. Thus, some people like Ted Turner feel there is a potential for all-news broadcast stations like CNN.

Some media may be referred to as news media, but the news they carry is very specialized. Weekly newspapers specialize in local community news events, social notes, and high school sports. Fashion magazines specialize in fashion news. Trade publications specialize in news that is pertinent to that trade.

In most cases the news we receive is gathered and reported to us in a very economical form. For only $5 we might receive hundreds of pages of daily newspaper news every month. Many weekly papers, in fact, are distributed at no charge at all, as are many colorful trade publications. The reason for this is advertising. The rates paid by advertisers enable the free press to operate without government interference. This more than anything else characterizes the news media in the United States.

Entertainment

Television and radio, motion pictures, many magazines, and even some newspapers might be classified as primarily entertainment media. Prime-time network movies, country western radio stations, and detective story magazines are all designed to entertain us; that is their primary function. In the attempt to entertain, they hope to attract a large audience to help them substantiate the rates they charge advertisers. If the rate is reasonable, advertisers are eager to pay for the opportunity to deliver their message to that audience. In most cases, again, the entertainment comes to us at a very low price.

Some entertainment media charge for the entertainment and carry little or no advertising. Home Box Office, for example, charges subscribers for movies and entertainment and carries no advertising. This allows the consumer to choose between free TV and fee TV.

Advertising

The out-of-home media (billboards, transit, point-of-purchase) tend to be strictly advertising media. Companies erect billboards and sell the space, or they contract for buses and sell that space. There is no entertainment or news value associated with these media, as their audiences are intrinsically captive.

Some print media are strictly advertising also. Weekly shoppers carry no editorials or entertainment, only advertising. Customers hoping to find bargains browse through the pages and advertisers gain exposure.

Recently some effort has been made to begin all-advertising cable stations similar to CNN, and we expect these attempts to multiply in the future with the increased availability of cable.

Media people in advertising

Inasmuch as advertising is one of the major functions of most media, most media people are involved to some extent in advertising. Television stations, for example, have camera people, directors, engineers, and audio technicians who spend as much or more time producing television commercials for local advertisers as they do preparing the nightly local newscast.

Radio stations similarly employ disc jockeys and production managers who often spend their off-air time producing local radio commercials. It is common to see successful D.J.'s quitting their station jobs to free-lance as commercial voices.

Broadcast media also employ copywriters, continuity writers, promotion directors, and traffic managers who write commercials, promote station activities, and schedule commercials within the daily programming. In addition, they all have sales staffs who regularly call on advertisers and agencies, sell airtime, and frequently write and produce commercial announcements.

Newspapers and magazines employ writers, graphic designers, production artists, sales promotion specialists, merchandising personnel, researchers, and printers. All these people are involved with the medium's sales staff in writing, designing, or producing advertisements and promotions for the publication and its advertisers.

There are vast opportunities for people interested in advertising on the media side. Many of today's top advertising executives began by working in the traffic department of a local radio station or by cutting grass around the billboards of a local outdoor advertising company. (See the Ad Lab.)

Networks

The salespeople (account executives) who work for the networks concentrate on the national advertisers and their agencies who regularly purchase network radio or television time. In addition to selling network time, they frequently sell spot radio and TV time in individual markets or regions. That way, a company that doesn't have its product distributed nationwide can still buy television or radio time from the network on a per market basis.

To facilitate the sales effort, the network rep normally has a host of tools available. These include research data on the programs being offered, packaged programs for advertisers who are seeking sponsorships, time clearances (agreements from local stations to use the programs being sold), and merchandising services.

Magazines

Most national magazines are headquartered in New York or Chicago and have extensive advertising departments to assist advertisers with personal calls, research information, and occasionally merchandising assistance. In addition, the magazines usually have additional sales offices in major U.S. cities or else a rep firm with nationwide offices to call on agencies and advertisers wherever they are located.

The magazine's sales force is frequently assisted by an in-house staff of writers, art directors, and sales promotion specialists who are constantly preparing direct-mail pieces, research reports, and other promotional tools for media buyers and advertising managers (Figure 5–7).

Most major publications spend a substantial sum for the services of outside research firms like W. R. Simmons and Mediamark Research Inc., which conduct extensive media audience studies. These studies are used by the sales staff to prove the worth of their publication to the agency's media buyers who also depend on these studies to justify their media recommendations.

Career opportunities with the media and suppliers

A tremendous number of employment opportunities are available with the media and suppliers. The advertising departments of the media are strongly sales-oriented. The suppliers need personnel who generally have technical backgrounds and specialized skills.

The lists below give some idea of the types and variety of positions for which employees are need.

Media	Suppliers	
Sales representatives	Free-lance artists	Retouchers
Sales managers	Free-lance copywriters	Paper merchants
Copywriters	Jingle creators	Film processing specialists
Artists	Mailing list brokers	Convention display artists and designers
Production specialists	Typesetters	Printers
Market researchers	Photographers	Market researchers
Sales promotion specialists	Premium promoters	Film and videotape producers and directors
	Photoengravers	Free-lance public relations writers
	Casting specialists	
	Packaging designers	
	Illustrators	

Job title	Educational preparation	Occupational experience	Extracurricular activities	Average salary
Sales representative	B.A. preferred but not required; emphasis on business courses	Retail sales, direct sales	Sales and marketing clubs, ad club, print and broadcast organizations	Variable; commission against draw or guarantee; often highest paid position in the company
Jingle creator	B.A. preferred but not required; emphasis on music and business	Recording studio, jingle production house	Ad club, band, rock group, glee club or church choir	$25,000

Selling media advertising

Every advertising medium has an advertising sales department, which is responsible for selling the medium's space or time. The way these departments are structured and the manner in which they function depend on the type of medium. Needless to say, these departments are very important since they are normally the primary source of income to the medium.

Job title	Educational preparation	Occupational experience	Extracurricular activities	Average salary
Market researcher	B.A., M.B.A., Ph.D. desirable, emphasis on writing, mathematics, statistics, sociology, and psychology	Interviewer for research organization, research trainee, research assistant; experience in company research department or	Research organizations	\$15,000 (research analyst) \$29,300 (research director)
Photographer	B.A. from a professional art school preferred	Photography studio, school newspaper, magazine, yearbook	Photography club, photo exhibit shows, and graphic arts club	\$20,000
Film and video tape producer or director	B.A. preferred but not required	Film studio, tape studio, television station, photography studio	National Academy of Television Arts and Sciences, telecommunications and film organizations	\$15,300 (associate producer) \$22,600 (broadcast producer or director)

Laboratory applications

1. Do any of these jobs look interesting to you as a career opportunity? Which ones? Why?
2. Choose one of the positions. What could you do to learn more about that job? Outline a plan to research the opportunities for obtaining such a job.

"I don't know who you are.
I don't know your company.
I don't know your company's product.
I don't know what your company stands for.
I don't know your company's customers.
I don't know your company's record.
I don't know your company's reputation.
Now—what was it you wanted to sell me?"
MORAL: Sales start before your salesman calls—with business publication advertising.
McGRAW-HILL MAGAZINES
BUSINESS • PROFESSIONAL • TECHNICAL

Figure 5–7 This classic advertisement by McGraw-Hill Magazines tells of the benefit of magazine advertising with a series of negative headlines familiar to every industrial salesperson.

Newspapers

Newspaper advertising departments vary in size from one person for a small weekly to several hundred people for a large metropolitan daily (Figure 5–8). Normally the advertising department is divided into retail advertising, general (or national) advertising, and classified, with a manager heading each group.

A newspaper offers a wide variety of services to entice advertisers. These include art and copy and also special promotions, publicity, market research, and planning assistance. To promote itself to advertisers, a newspaper frequently has a sales promotion department, an outside advertising agency, and a corps of salespeople to visit and assist advertisers and agencies. A merchandising department may even be staffed to assist national advertisers with local store promotions.

However, virtually no newspaper can maintain enough salespeople to call on national advertisers and agencies outside the medium's immediate geographic area. It would be too costly. So newspapers normally contract with independent media representative firms to sell for them on the national level.

Rep firms provide three basic functions: (1) to promote the medium itself, in this case newspapers; (2) to promote the market in which the particular newspaper publishes; and (3) to sell the particular newspaper over competitive publications. Rep firms handle only one newspaper per market and receive the exclusive right to represent that paper nationally.

To sell their newspapers' space, reps have to demonstrate to national advertisers that (1) the newspaper's audience has the right demographic profile for the advertiser's product, (2) the newspaper offers an economical alternative to competitive media, (3) the newspaper has excellent coverage of the market, and (4) fringe benefits, such as merchandising assistance, are available from the newspaper. For this service, newspapers normally pay 10–15 percent commission or an agreed-upon fee for large publications.

Broadcast stations

Local radio and television advertising departments are structured much like newspapers, with a local sales manager and a national sales manager. However, these sales departments are normally much smaller than those of daily newspapers.

Broadcast rep firms are also used, and they earn 5–15 percent of the sales they make to national advertisers (Figure 5–9, page 158).

To assist their advertisers, all broadcast stations offer copy, art, and production services; many also offer merchandising and research.

Out-of-home

Local billboard company owners (called plant operators) lease promising sites from property owners, construct billboards on these sites, and then sell the space to local advertisers such as banks and shopping centers.

Similarly, transit operators have a sales staff or contract with an independent sales organization to sell the space available on the sides and interiors of buses, taxicabs, and stations.

Local plant operators will assist their customers with copy and art if needed as well as research data showing the most visible sites.

National advertising is normally sold to agencies and advertisers through an industrywide organization.

Suppliers

To round out our discussion of the organizations involved in the advertising business, it is important to consider the group commonly referred to as *suppliers*. These are people or organizations that specialize in one aspect of the business. Without their services it might be impossible to produce the $54.6 billion worth of advertising placed every year.

Although it is impossible to mention them all, we shall briefly discuss at least some of the important ones here. These are art studios, typesetters, printers, film and video production houses, and research companies.

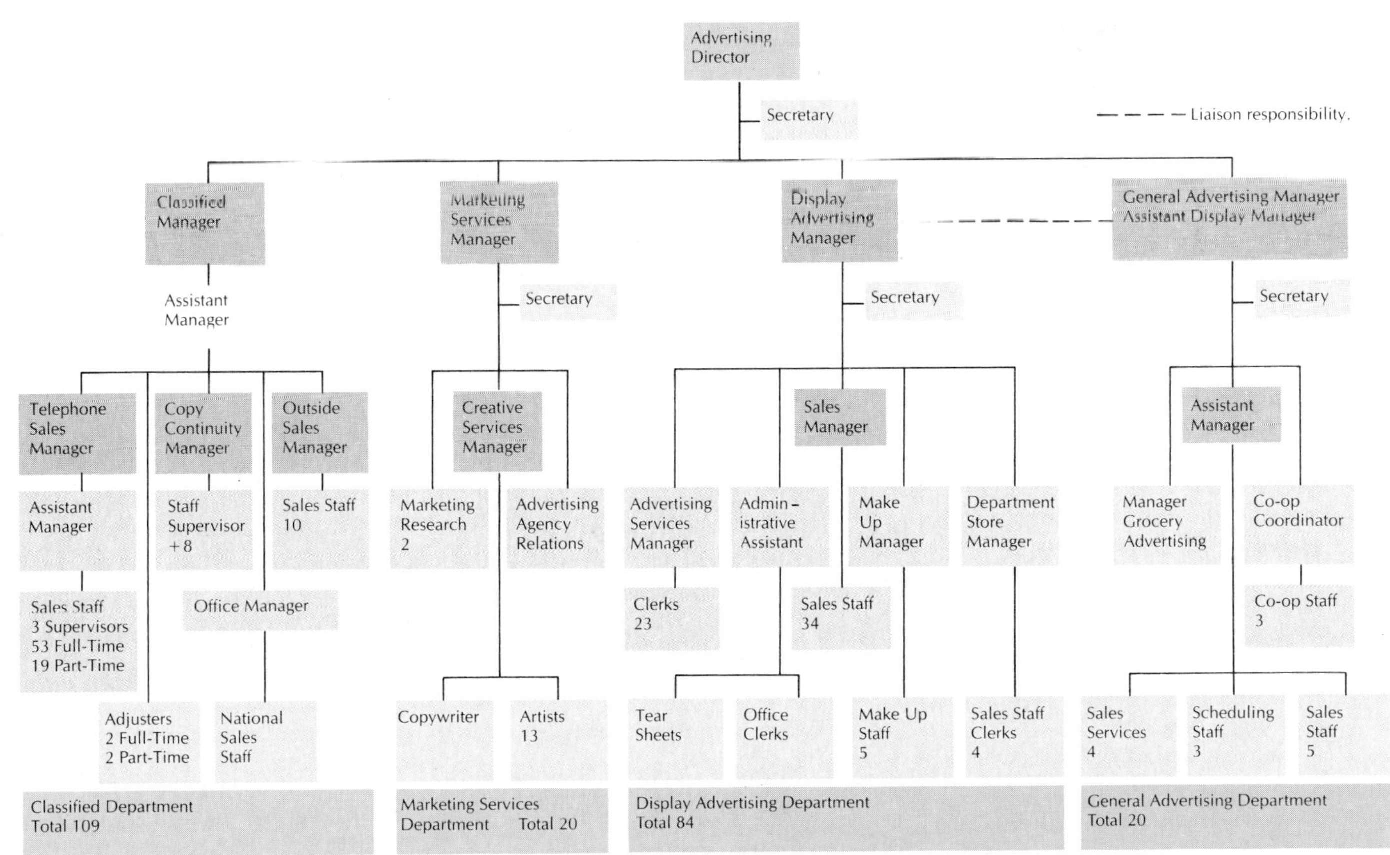

Figure 5–8 Advertising Department of Union-Tribune Publishing Co., San Diego.

Art studios

Art studios produce finished artwork and illustrations for advertisements. They may take the place of an art department for small agencies or supplement the work of a large agency's art department. Normally art studios are very small organizations with as few as three or four employees. Some large studios, though, employ several art directors, graphic designers, layout artists, production artists, sales reps, illustrators, and even photographers and photo retouchers. These last three, however, usually prefer to work independently in their own specialized organizations.

Inasmuch as most studios are started, owned, and managed by an artist or art director, that person frequently is also the organization's only salesperson. By calling on agencies and advertising managers, the artist attempts to sell the studio's services, take projects back to the office to be produced, and then deliver them for the client's approval. Thus it requires a great deal of time-consuming work, a large amount of responsibility, and a talent for organization and management to be successful in the studio business (Figure 5–10).

Figure 5–9 Blair Radio, a major national rep firm for radio stations, promises to "beat the competition to the punch." As one of the largest rep firms, Blair is able to provide its station clients with programming consulting services and computerized media planning services.

Typesetters

Virtually every printed advertisement we see has been to a type house. The typesetter is responsible for taking the copywriter's words and the art director's layout and translating them into what appears in the ad. This requires a high degree of technical knowledge and skill and some artistic talent, too. (See Chapter 12, "Creative Production: Print Media.")

Type houses are probably required to have the greatest speed of any business involved in advertising. It is common for art directors to call in orders for type in the morning and to request delivery by noon. The large typesetters are therefore highly computerized and systematized to function efficiently and economically (Figure 5–11). This, of course, requires large capital investments and has resulted in increased labor and material costs as well as soaring prices for type.

As an exercise, make a photocopy of this page, find the typesetter closest to you, and take the page there for a price estimate. Be sure to say you want it set exactly as it is here. Then ask the typesetter how much it would cost to have just one of the sentences set and delivered to your residence. You might be surprised at what you discover. Many unsophisticated advertisers are surprised the first time they encounter advertising production charges.

Printers

Vital to the advertising business are the printers who produce brochures, stationery, business cards, direct-mail pieces, handbills, sales promotion materials, point-of-purchase displays, and the various print media in which advertisements are placed. Printers employ highly trained specialists who prepare artwork for reproduction, make plates,

People in advertising

Richard Avedon

Photographer

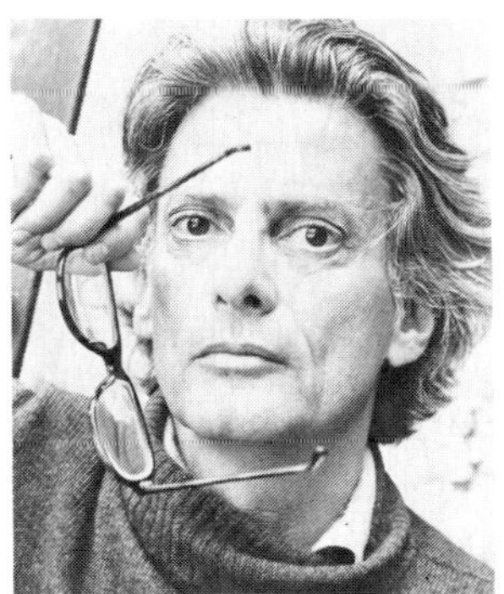

Possibly the world's highest paid photographer, commanding up to $5,000 a sitting to produce ads for companies like Polaroid and Revlon, the famed Richard Avedon has revolutionized advertising and fashion photography. He has also turned these photographs into art forms.

Even as a boy, Avedon was intrigued by photography. The son of an immigrant dress store owner, he collected photos from the fashion magazines his father read. One of the first photographs he took, using a box camera, was of composer Sergei Rachmaninoff.

Avedon's first job was as an errand boy for a photography firm. After World War II began, he entered the Merchant Marines. His father's going-away gift was a Rolleiflex camera—it was to change the course of Avedon's life. He applied to the Merchant Marines' photography branch and was assigned to Sheepshead Bay in Brooklyn. While there, he took an unusual photo portrait of two brothers. One was captured in sharp detail in the foreground and the other was out of focus in the background—the first of the "blurred image" photos that were to become an Avedon trademark.

After resuming civilian life, Avedon persuaded New York's elite Bonwit Teller department store to let him borrow some clothes in exchange for a series of free fashion shots. Then he hired the most expensive model in town. Bonwit Teller liked the photos so much that they were displayed in the store, and Avedon landed his first paying assignments.

Avedon submitted these works, along with the portrait of the two brothers, to Alexey Brodovitch, art director of *Harper's Bazaar*. Brodovitch was instantly impressed by the out-of-focus portrait and hired Avedon. The young photographer's works, he said later, "reflected freshness—and individuality."

This was apparent when Avedon drove some models to a beach and photographed them running barefoot, romping, playing leapfrog, and scampering over the sand on stilts. Although *Harper's* had never featured barefoot models before, Brodovitch was delighted and ran the shots. Soon Avedon shattered another long-time convention by photographing models in bizarre settings, including junkyards, the zoo, the circus, the pyramids of Egypt, and even NASA's Cape Kennedy launch pads. He also did away with models' frozen, mannequin-like expressions. Instead, his models laughed, danced, and flirted, combining glamour and theatrics. Many of them, like Twiggy and Suzy Parker, soared to fame as top-name models.

At 33 Avedon inspired the Paramount hit musical *Funny Face* (1957), in which Fred Astaire, as a leading fashion photographer, used many of Avedon's novel camera techniques.

Avedon left *Harper's Bazaar* in 1965. A year later he became a staff photographer for *Vogue Magazine*. Meanwhile, major advertising agencies began flocking to Avedon. He applied the same unique ideas he had used in fashion photography and began creating revolutionary advertising art. He was soon producing photographs for top-name agencies and clients like Revlon, Du Pont, Cartier, and Douglas Aircraft. By the mid-1960s, Avedon's studio was reportedly billing over $250,000 a year. Today his clients include DeBeers, Lebanthal & Co., First Boston Bank, Calvin Klein, Gianni Versace, and Procter & Gamble. Avedon does many television commercials as well as still photography.

One Avedon ad series, hailed as "the most famous testimonial campaign of the 70s—perhaps of all time," was for Blackglama. Avedon photographed celebrities so famous that their names are not even mentioned in the ads. Instead the Jane Trahey (see Chapter 20 on local advertising) copyline ("What becomes a legend most?")

(continued)

is all that is needed to convey that superstars choose Blackglama minks.

Avedon's photo portraits have been shown at New York's Museum of Modern Art and the Smithsonian Institution in Washington, D.C. They are also featured in *Observations* (New York: Simon & Schuster, 1959) and in *Nothing Personal* (New York: Atheneum Publishers, 1964.) Other Avedon works are in *Avedon: Photographs 1947–1977* (New York: Farrar, Straus & Giroux, 1978.) Photographs and articles by Richard Avedon have appeared in *Life, Look, This Week, Graphis,* and *U.S. Camera Annual.*

Called "one of the world's 10 greatest photographers" by *Popular Photography* (1958) and "the most influential man in his field" by *Newsweek* (1978), small, intense, urbanely handsome Avedon continues to work actively at his art. He was the first photographer ever to be featured on the cover of *Newsweek* magazine.

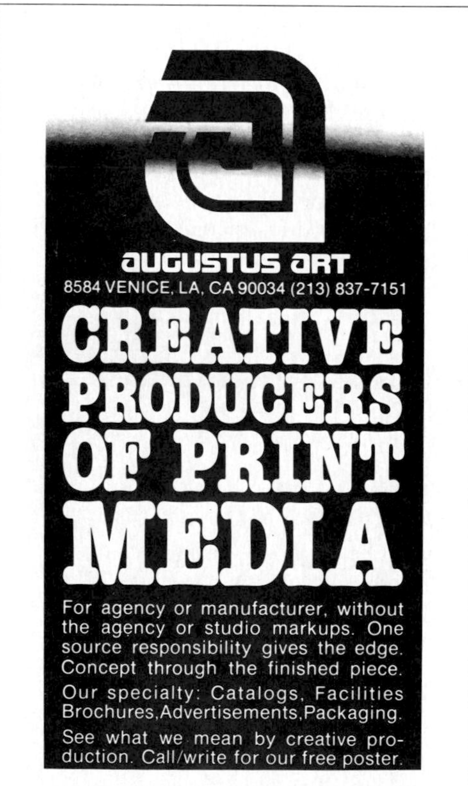

Figure 5–10 Augustus Art is one of the thousands of art studios that work for advertisers and agencies by producing graphic displays, ads, brochures, package designs, and catalogs. These studios range in size from little one-person shops to huge organizations with as many as 100 employees. They are therefore great training grounds for young artists out of school.

operate presses and collating machines, and run binderies. In addition, large printers employ salespeople who work with advertisers and agencies to sell their service. They sometimes earn very large commissions.

Types of printers range from small insta-printers to large web offset printers. Some specialize in offset lithography, rotogravure, letterpress, engraving, or other techniques. (See Chapter 12, "Creative Production: Print Media.")

Film and video production houses

Very few agencies have in-house television production capabilities. Small agencies often work with a local TV station to produce commercials, but all the large agencies work with independent production houses (Figure 5–12). Some of these may specialize in film making, others in videotape production, and some in both. Their services are usually contracted for on a bid basis, but some are specially sought out for their unique talent or capabilities (Figure 5–13). As we shall discuss in Chapter 13, Levi's went to a special production house in Hollywood to produce its innovative, award-winning animated commercials.

Research companies

Most major advertisers, agencies, and media include a research function as part of their marketing efforts. Advertisers are concerned about the attitudes of their customers, the size of potential markets, and the acceptability of their products.

Agencies, on the other hand, are anxious to know what advertising approaches to use, which concepts communicate most efficiently, and how effective past campaigns have been.

The media are concerned with the reading and viewing habits of their audiences, the desired markets of their advertiser-customers, and the perceptions of the public toward their own particular medium.

Research, therefore, is a closely allied field to advertising and an important tool of the marketing professional.

However, inasmuch as most firms do not maintain a fully staffed research department, there are thousands of independent research companies and consultants that can be employed to help (Figure 5–14). The range of services available from these suppliers is extensive as shown below.

1. Advertising research, including:
   Motivation research.
   Copy research.
   Media research.
   Studies of ad effectiveness.
2. Business economics and corporate research, including:
   Forecasting business trends.
   Pricing studies.
   Product mix studies.
3. Corporate responsibility research, including:
   Studies of legal constraints on advertising.
   Social values and policies studies.
4. Product research, including:
   New product acceptance.
   Competitive product studies.
   Packaging research.
5. Sales and market research, including:

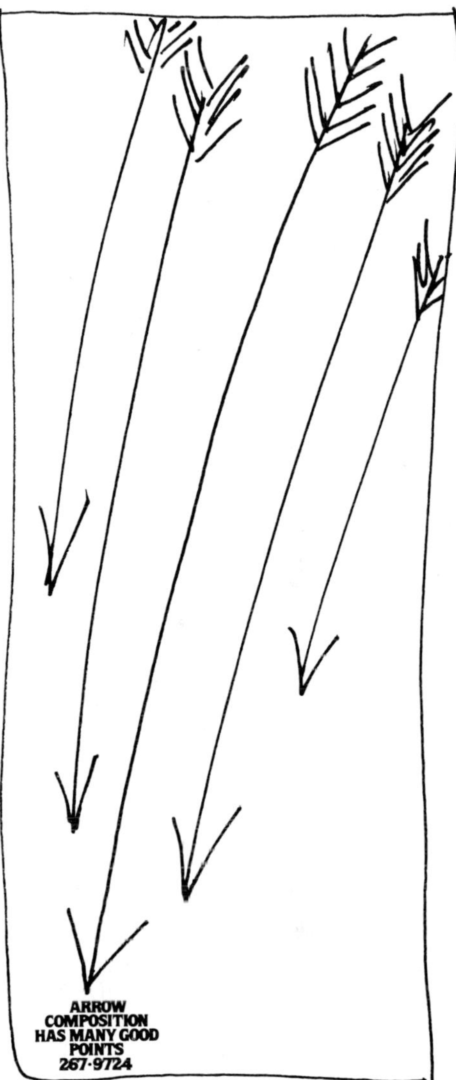

Figure 5–11 Arrow Composition reminds readers of its services in this simple but eye-catching advertisement. Typesetters are selected because of the availability of various styles of type as well as the quality of their work, speed of delivery, and price.

Figure 5–12 Quality advertisements require a great deal of behind-the-scenes work, which is usually done by production houses and free-lance photographers.

Market share analysis.
Determination of market characteristics.
Test markets and store audits.
Promotional studies of premiums, coupons, and sampling.
Measurement of market potentials.[5]

Research firms come in all sizes, shapes, and specialties. They employ analysts with advanced degrees in psychology, sociology, anthropology, economics, and marketing as well as staff statisticians, field interviewers, and computer programmers.

★
CONCEPT
WRITING
STORYBOARDS
DESIGN
PRODUCTION
RECORDING
★
VIDEOTAPE
FILM

SUPERCOLOSSAL

SUPERCOLOSSAL PICTURES
3413 CAHUENGA BLVD. WEST
HOLLYWOOD·CA. 90068
(213) 876-6770.

Figure 5–13 Supercolossal Pictures is one of the many film production houses used by agencies to produce commercials. This ad soliciting business appeared in *Commercials Monthly*.

Figure 5–14 A clever ad for a market research company suggests that it is smarter to discover the facts of a situation before committing large amounts to a project rather than afterward.

Summary

The medium that carries the advertising message from the advertiser to the customers is the third and vital link in the communication chain. The major mass media available today are broadcast, print, out-of-home, and direct mail.

Print media are normally newspapers and magazines. However, there are also directories, school or church newsletters, and programs at sporting events. Broadcast media are radio, television, and other electronic message carriers like cable TV. Out-of-home is a broad term used to describe outdoor advertising (billboards), point-of-purchase displays (counter cards), and transit advertising (bus and car cards). Direct mail refers to the mailing of advertisements by companies directly to their customers without the use of the commercially published media. Other media include cinema advertising, beetleboards, copter media, and scoreboard advertising.

In foreign markets some media that we use in the United States are not available. On the other hand, other selective specialty media are more available and more economical. Advertisers may use international media, local foreign media, or overspill media in foreign markets. However, they must study those markets carefully to determine how to get the best coverage. The media strategy is almost certain to be different from that in the United States.

Other functions, like news, entertainment, and information, assist the media in performing their advertising function. As a result, there are many career opportunities on the media side, and many of today's most successful advertising people started by working for the media.

Every medium has a sales department, which calls on local advertisers and agencies to sell them space or time. In addition, most media can help the advertiser with production assistance, market research, sales promotion, or merchandising services. Most major media contract with a rep firm to sell their space or time to national advertisers.

In addition to the media, advertising suppliers are crucial to the growth of the industry. These suppliers include, but are not limited to, art studios, typographers, printers, photographers, film and video production companies, and market research firms. These companies, too, offer opportunities for specialized advertising careers.

Questions for review

1. What are the media of advertising? What is meant by media proliferation, and how does that affect the future of advertising?
2. What are some unusual advertising media? Which do you believe are likely to gain in popularity in the future?
3. What is a rep firm? Describe its functions.
4. Who are the media people in advertising? Briefly describe their jobs.
5. What are the functions of the media? How do these functions interrelate with advertising?
6. What are some types of organizations that are suppliers to advertisers and advertising agencies? Why don't more advertisers and advertising agencies develop the capability of performing the functions of suppliers?
7. What are the primary sales tools used by a person representing an advertising medium?
8. What do advertisers and agencies learn when they meet with media representatives?
9. What does a medium really sell to an advertiser or to an advertising agency?
10. How should an advertiser or advertising agency go about locating suppliers and evaluating their services?

Part III

Marketing and Advertising: Plans and Strategies

Advertising and the marketing mix

A quarter of a century ago, after nine years of work, the Ford Motor Company introduced what was not destined to be one of its better ideas—the Edsel. Named after one of Mr. Ford's sons, the car was touted by Mercury Division general manager F. C. Reith as the latest in engineering design, complete with safety rim wheels, self-adjusting brakes, and even an automatic transmission with push-button controls in the middle of the steering wheel. The Ford Motor Company had spent over $250 million designing, engineering, and producing the Edsel. Eventually 110,000 cars were produced and shipped to dealers across the country. The company then spent over $30 million advertising the Edsel in magazines, newspapers, and national radio and TV. No effort and certainly no dollars were spared. After all, as Reith had predicted, the Edsel was destined to be a success.

Within two years the Ford Motor Company had discontinued production and lost $350 million on the Edsel model. What went wrong? Why did Edsel fail? After so many years of experience and success, how could Ford have flopped so miserably?

Ford's market research department had asked some basic questions prior to the development decision and again prior to the production decision: (1) Does the car-buying public want this car? Does it appeal to them? (2) Do they need this car? Or are there already other cars that fill the same need? (3) At the price customers will be able or willing to pay for this car, can we sell enough to cover all the costs of manufacturing, distribution, advertising, and sales? (4) After covering all those costs, can we still make a worthwhile profit on this car?

These questions embrace the most basic issues in marketing. When Ford asked them, they were answered with weak affirmatives in 1954 and negatively in 1956. Unfortunately, top management ignored the answers, no doubt assured of their product's superiority and their company's ability to push the product through its nationwide network of dealers with its $30 million advertising budget.

In April 1980 *Advertising Age* reported that in a survey of advertising professionals across the country, Edsel had been voted the biggest product failure in history. They reported the comment of one advertising person who said, "I happen to think that was a pretty good ad campaign. Mismarketing, to be sure. But okay advertising."[1]

What is marketing?

Management usually divides the functions of business into three areas: production, finance, and marketing. Students who major in business administration study many subjects that relate to one or all of these areas. For instance, courses in accounting relate to the finance area. Purchasing or manufacturing courses relate to the production area. And advertising is a specialty area of marketing.

To be a good specialist in advertising, a person must also have a good general understanding of the marketing framework within which advertising operates. Marketing also includes such activities as market research, product distribution, pricing, and sales, all of which also relate to advertising. The purposes of this chapter are to outline the subject of marketing and to discuss advertising's role in the marketing function.

Growth of the marketing concept

Unfortunately *marketing* may be one of the most misunderstood terms in business. In the past it was defined as "those various business activities which are used to direct the flow of products from the company that makes them to the people who use them." However, this definition tends to emphasize the activities of distribution and transportation, and today the field of marketing includes many other equally important activities.

A hundred years ago, when there were few products and many consumers, companies had to worry only about creating and producing more products to satisfy the huge demand. This was called the *production-oriented period,* and the emphasis in marketing was indeed on distribution and transportation.

After the introduction of mass production techniques, the marketplace was glutted with products. So business began to emphasize the selling function. The *sales-oriented period* was marked by extravagant advertising claims and an attitude of *caveat emptor* ("let the buyer beware") as companies tried to unload their products on the public.

The saturation point was eventually reached, and many companies found that no amount of high-pressure selling or slick advertising could move any more products. In the end, many companies lost substantial sums because of unsold inventories or falling sales.

In recent years companies have found it more profitable to determine in advance what customers want and then make products that will satisfy those desires. This is called the *marketing-oriented period.* Of course, many companies still operate under the sales-oriented concept or even the production-oriented concept. But they are constantly courting failure, and they risk experiencing their own Edsels.

Edsel failed because the company did not adequately determine the wants and the desires of the public when the new car was introduced. At a Ford executive committee meeting in 1954, Robert S. McNamara asked, "What is this new car intended to offer the car-buying public?" Unfortunately, his question was not fully answered. Many marketing experts feel that at the time the Edsel was introduced, the American public already had a variety of chrome-filled, medium-priced cars from which to choose. They didn't want or need another one, and no amount of advertising could convince them differently.

In its broadest sense today, then, *marketing* refers to all business activities aimed at: (1) *finding out who customers are and what they want,* (2) *developing products to satisfy those customers' needs and desires,* and (3) *getting the products into the customers' hands.* The objective of marketing is to help the company make a profit by providing its customers with products or services that they want or need. Companies that operate under the marketing concept are concerned with shaping products to meet consumer needs rather than forcing consumers to buy what the manufacturer wants. As a result they are intensely interested in the consumer's point of view, and they allow that point of view to dictate many company activities.

The task of marketing and advertising

Under the marketing concept, the task of the marketing department is divided into three areas: (1) discover, locate, and measure the demand for products; (2) interpret this information for management so they can translate it into new services or products; and (3) develop and implement a plan that makes the product available and informs prospective customers about the product's need-satisfying capabilities (Figure 6–1). Advertising is primarily concerned with the informing function, as well as persuading and reminding customers about the product. But to be successful, advertising depends on the adequate performance of the other marketing activities as well.

As Edsel showed, a company can spend $30 million on advertising and still fail. The product must be what the consumer wants. The price must be acceptable. There must be a place where consumers

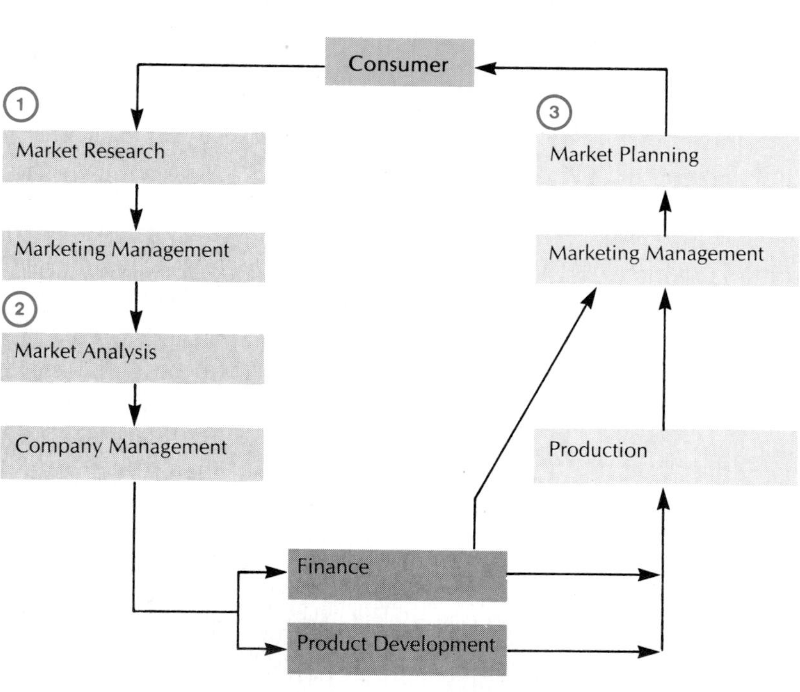

Figure 6–1 The consumer-marketing cycle. The tasks of marketing management under the marketing concept are: (1) locating and measuring the demand for products; (2) interpreting this demand for management, which then develops products to satisfy the need; and (3) developing and implementing a plan that makes the product available and informs consumers about the product's capabilities. Marketing therefore begins and ends with the consumer.

can buy the product conveniently. And there must be people ready and able to sell the product to the consumer and coordinate all these other activities adequately and successfully. (See the Ad Lab.)

To explain the importance of these activities, we shall briefly explore the ways in which markets are discovered, located, and measured. Then we shall discuss the *four Ps*—product, price, place, and promotion—which are referred to as the *elements of the marketing mix* and which are used to move the product from the company to the consumer. The way in which a company decides to coordinate these elements has a profound effect on the advertising it uses.

First let's be sure we understand what a market is and where it can be found.

What is a market?

At the annual convention of the Savings Institutions Marketing Society of America, delegates were shown a number of different advertisements that had been placed by savings institutions around the country. The savings bank officers in the audience were asked to grade each of the ads on a scale of 1 to 10. One ad presented was an outstanding example of tongue-in-cheek humor by Clearwater Federal Savings and Loan Association, a $450-million savings institution in Florida.

The ad pictured a millionaire standing in the hallway of his mansion before a large, ornately framed painting. The headline of the ad read: "I keep the family jewels in the safe behind the portrait of my first wife. I keep my money at Clearwater Federal." This was followed by a column of light, humorous copy, which told how rich the man was, how security-conscious, and how much he liked all the free services at Clearwater Federal that kept his money safe from his *second wife's* shopping sprees. The ad was signed: "Clearwater Federal. Where those who've made it keep it" (Figure 6–2).

Most savings and loan executives who viewed the ad gave it a very low rating, saying they felt it wouldn't appeal to everybody but only to the very rich.

The majority fallacy

Their reaction is an excellent illustration of the *majority fallacy*—a common misconception that in order to be successful, a product or service must appeal to the majority of people. Sophisticated marketing and advertising people know that this is just not true. Often several products or services compete for the same customers, and therefore each is able to attract only a fraction of all the business. A new competitive product might do better if it is specifically aimed at just one group of those customers (like wealthy people) rather than at the majority of customers.

Clearwater Federal did an admirable job of selecting a profitable minority market (wealthy people and those who would like to see themselves as wealthy) and catering to it. A market, therefore, does not have to include everybody. A market may include just one group of potential customers who share a common interest, need, or desire. This group of customers must be able to use the product or service which is offered to some advantage, and they must be able to afford

Marketing Charlie: A turning point in fragrance marketing

The strategies of many recent fragrance introductions are clearly designed to keep pace with, or even a half-step ahead of, women's evolving self-concept. Revlon's fragrance, "Charlie," broke with tradition in positioning and name when it was introduced in 1973. Within a year it was the largest selling fragrance nationally, and within three years it had become the largest selling in the world. When Charles Revson, company chief, suggested naming the new fragrance "Charlie," some staffers shook their heads skeptically, but research showed that women loved the name. The Charlie character was positioned as a career-oriented, athletic trendsetter—a socially active, independent, and adventurous woman. Ads by Revlon's 50th Floor Workshop show an "irreverent and unpretentious" young woman striding confidently through an urban setting. The marketing strategy has not undergone significant change since the introduction. Revlon added the tag "Now the world belongs to Charlie" in 1977, as they expanded distribution to international markets.

How did the marketing of women's fragrances change during the 1970s? "Fragrance was much more of a special occasion usage situation ten years ago," says Al Skolnik, Revlon fragrance vice president. "Therefore, it was much more directly related to romance and love than it is today. One of the successes of fragrance marketing in the last few years is that we've gotten women out of the idea that if they're staying around the house, or going to the office, they don't need fragrance. We've established the concept of a wardrobe of fragrances for different occasions or moods. The women's movement idea of doing things for your own satisfaction and gratification, rather than just to attract a man, contributed to the achievement of the marketing goal. It contributed in another way too: now 50 percent or more of women are working and earning an income. This is helpful when you're trying to get across the notion that fragrance is part of the basic ritual of grooming."

The Charlie line, introduced by Revlon in 1974, now includes about 50 items. The media mix remains predominantly TV, with large print support in magazines such as *Glamour, Self,* and *Cosmopolitan.* Charlie products are sold in department stores, drug units, and mass merchandisers. But there are variations: the "Charlie Limited Editions" collection, introduced in 1979, was sold in only "fine" department stores.

Fragrance sales gross over $50 million annually. Unlike Edsel, Revlon obviously discovered an area of demand the fragrance consumer wanted filled. Charlie filled it.

Charlie: A fragrance that's here to stay

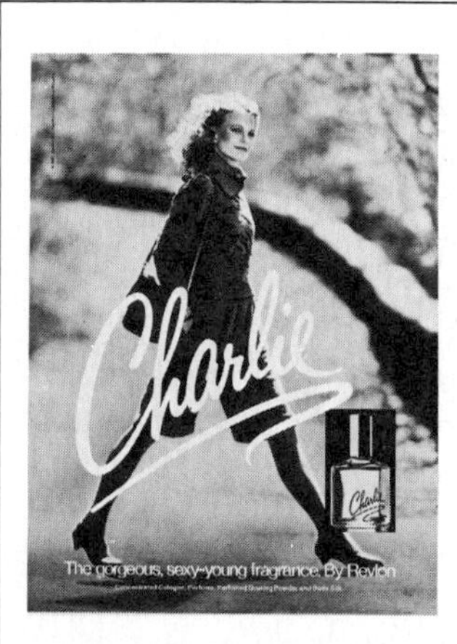
Charlie
The gorgeous, sexy-young fragrance. By Revlon

Laboratory application

From your reading of the text so far and your knowledge of the Charlie story, what need or needs do you think existed in the marketplace that Charlie is aimed at satisfying?

the purchase price. In its simplest terms, therefore, a market is people.

There are three broad classifications of markets to which companies advertise and sell:

1. *Consumer markets* are composed of people who buy products for their own personal use.
2. *Producer markets* are individuals or companies (like manufacturing companies) that buy products needed for the production of products or other services.

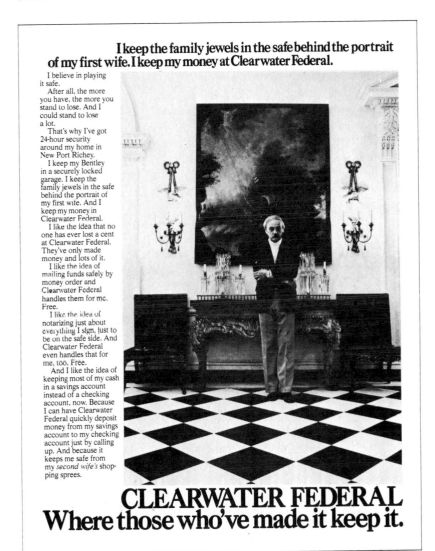

Figure 6–2 Clearwater Federal targeted a very profitable market segment in this tongue-in-cheek ad. Wealthy people can afford to laugh at themselves, and the not-so-wealthy can enjoy the joke, too. Unfortunately, most savings executives viewing this ad failed to understand the sophisticated humor and marketing strategy, fearing it would not appeal to everybody. That is called the *majority fallacy*.

3. *Reseller markets* are individuals or companies that buy products for the purpose of reselling them, like retail stores and car dealers.
4. *Government markets* are governmental bodies which buy products for the successful coordination of municipal, state, federal, or other governmental activities.
5. *International markets* are any of the previously mentioned markets which operate outside the boundaries of the United States.

Locating and measuring the market

The whole purpose of marketing and advertising is to find the right people and get them together with the right products. The advertisements we see every day are usually intended to appeal to a particular group of people called the company's target market. The better defined that market is, the better chance of success the company will have.

In the case of Clearwater Federal a target market was selected composed of that group of individuals who were wealthy or achieving wealth and, therefore, interested in security as well as high interest on their investments. A federally insured savings account, which pays high interest and comes complete with many free services, would probably be an attractive offer to this group.

Market segmentation

Markets for other products may be selected according to a variety of other classifications based on common characteristics of customers as Figure 6–3 shows. This process of dividing markets into meaningful groups is called market segmentation and will be fully discussed in Chapter 7, "Consumer Behavior and Market Segmentation."

By categorizing customers into meaningful segments, the company may determine which group would potentially be the most profitable market, design products for that segment, and then aim all of its marketing activities at that group.

Figure 6–3 Methods of segmenting markets

Variables	Typical breakdowns
Geographic	
Region	Pacific, Mountain, West North Central, West South Central, East North Central, East South Central, South Atlantic, Middle Atlantic, New England
County size	A, B, C, D
City or SMSA size	Under 5,000, 5,000–19,999, 20,000–49,999, 50,000–99,999, 100,000–249,999, 250,000–499,999, 500,000–999,999, 1,000,000–3,999,999, 4,000,000 or over

Variables	Typical breakdowns
Geographic	
Density	Urban, suburban, rural
Climate	Northern, southern
Demographic	
Age	Under 6, 6–11, 12–19, 20–34, 35–49, 50–64, 65+
Sex	Male, female
Family size	1–2, 3–4, 5+
Family life cycle	Young, single; young, married, no children; young, married, youngest child under six; young, married, youngest child six or over; older, married, with children; older, married, no children under 18; older, single; other
Income	Under $3,000, $3,000–$5,000, $5,000–$7,000, $7,000–$10,000, $10,000–$15,000, $15,000–$25 000, $25,000 and over
Occupation	Professional and technical; managers, officials, and proprietors; clerical, sales; craftsmen, foremen; operatives; farmers; retired; students; housewives; unemployed
Education	Grade school or less; some high school; graduated high school; some college; graduated college
Religion	Catholic, Protestant, Jewish, other
Race	White, black, oriental
Nationality	American, British, French, German, Scandinavian, Italian, Latin American, Middle Eastern, Japanese
Psychographic	
Social class	Lower lowers, upper lowers, lower middles, upper middles, lower uppers, upper uppers
Lifestyle	Straights, swingers, longhairs
Personality	Compulsive, gregarious, authoritarian, ambitious
Behavioristic	
Purchase occasion	Regular occasion, special occasion
Benefits sought	Economy, convenience, prestige
User status	Nonuser, exuser, potential user, first-time user, regular user
Usage rate	Light user, medium user, heavy user
Loyalty status	None, medium, strong, absolute
Readiness stage	Unaware, aware, informed, interested, desirous, intending to buy
Marketing-factor sensitivity	Quality, price, service, advertising, sales promotion

Market research

To select the most desirable segments, companies try to learn as much as they can about the various groups within the total market. Using market research techniques, companies first attempt to measure the size of the total market for the particular product. Then they try to estimate the size of the segments within the market. In the case of Clearwater Federal, they might have attempted to measure:

1. The total market for savings and loans and banks in the area.
2. The total size of the "wealthy people" segment.
3. The total size of the segment with "wealthy attitudes."

Next the company tries to measure the share of the market that it might attract. For example:

1. What is the potential share of the total market that Clearwater Federal might attract if it aimed at the majority market?
2. What is the potential share of the "wealthy people" segment that Clearwater Federal might attract if it aimed specifically at that market?

There are various methods used to measure the size of markets depending on the type of market being considered. For example, the methods used to measure consumer markets differ greatly from the methods used to measure producer markets. These methods will be more completely described in Chapter 8 on methods of research.

Target marketing

Once the size and potential of the wealthy people segment are determined and the company selects that group as its *target market,* the planning of other marketing activities is greatly facilitated. Special services catering to that segment may be designed, the price of services will be determined, the number and location of branches needed become apparent, and the most suitable type of advertising can be prepared. Everything can be aimed at appealing to that target market. (See Chapter 9, "Marketing and Advertising Planning.")

If the wealthy people segment of the total savings and loan market had not appeared sufficiently large to be profitable, Clearwater Federal would have had to select a different target market, and the other marketing activities would have been different, too. (See the Ad Lab.)

The marketing mix

Advertising, as the communications device in marketing, is just one of the many marketing tools which may be used to help move goods or services from the company to its target market. However, the importance of advertising varies from business to business, depending on the nature of the company and the other marketing activities it uses. Every company has the option of adding, subtracting, or changing four elements in its marketing program to achieve a desired marketing mix. These elements, which comprise the mix, are called the four Ps: product, price, place, and promotion.

Consider two vastly different examples. First, a medical doctor wishes to increase the size of his or her practice. Some marketing-related communications might be business cards, a sign on the door, formal announcements, and direct-mail reminders to patients to come in for a checkup. Overall, though, due to professional ethics which have traditionally barred the use of media promotion, advertising plays little or no part in the doctor's business. Of greater importance are the physician's medical skill, experience, the cost of service, the location of the office, the size of the staff, and the physician's bedside manner. On the other hand, how important is advertising in marketing a mail-order item? In this case, advertising may be the lifeblood of the business.

For 50 years Charles Atlas has marketed his body-building course and equipment through mail-order advertisements in magazines for boys and young men. In that time the company has made over $30 million in sales. Furthermore, the entire effort has been made through advertising, without the use of a single salesperson. In fact, Charles Roman, who created the series of ads first used in 1929, is still using basically the same ads today (Figure 6–4).

From these two examples, we can see that there are vast differences in the roles played by advertising in the marketing of various items. These differences are the result of company decisions about the appropriate mix of marketing activities that should be used to promote its products or services.

Marketing Charlie: Who is the target market?

Review the Charlie story cited earlier and relate that information to what you have read in the text about locating and measuring the market for products.

Charlie
The gorgeous, sexy-young fragrance. By Revlon

Laboratory applications

1. Is Charlie intended to appeal to all women or to just a particular group? What group?
2. Following the chart in Figure 6–3, what geographic, demographic, psychographic, and behavioristic segments do you think Revlon selected to be the target market for Charlie? Explain your reasoning.

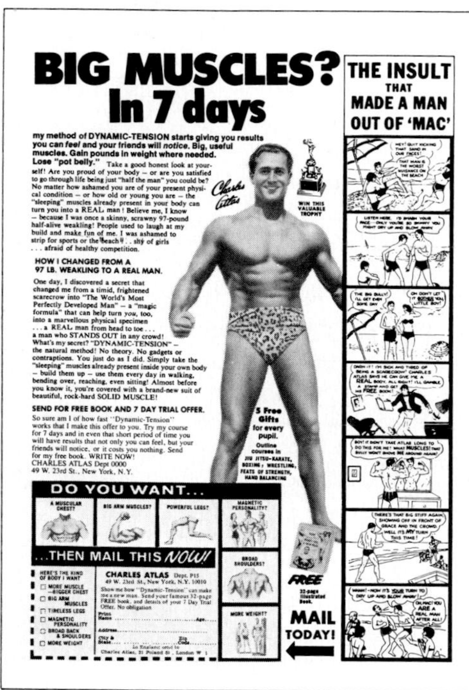

Figure 6–4 From this classic ad campaign came the famous question: "Do friends kick sand in your face?" Also came the classic concept of the "97-pound weakling." The basic ad remained virtually unchanged for 50 years, which reminds us of another famous line: "Stick with a winner."

In the case of the doctor, what would the marketing mix for the medical practice include? The doctor's product would be the healing service or particular specialty. The place element would be the location of the office and the decision on whether to make house calls. Price would also be a factor in marketing the services. Inasmuch as the doctor is not allowed by the profession to advertise, what permissible promotional activities would be most important to success? The sign on the door? Appointment cards? Or bedside manner? Now consider Charles Atlas. What do we already know about his marketing mix?

The remainder of this chapter will focus further on the relationship of each of these four Ps (product, price, place, and promotion) to the advertising a company may use.

Advertising and the product element

Companies use various means to distinguish their products from the products of their competitors. The way the product is advertised may be one of these.

Consider the ads for the Honda and the MGB in Figure 6–5. We see not only two very different styles of advertising but also two different ways of distinguishing products from one another. Look at the Honda ad first. What is the advertised uniqueness of the Honda? What features does the car have that make it stand out? How are those features important to the consumer? How would you answer the same questions for the MGB ad? Are they trying to sell something more than the functional superiority of the car? What?

What we learn from these two examples provides a clue to the answer to one of the most basic marketing questions: What is a product?

What is a product?

When you buy an automobile, what are you really buying? Is it the massive configuration of steel, plastic, rubber, and chrome you see? Is it the transportation it will deliver? Or is it the better gas mileage you will realize? On the other hand, is the product really the sleek, racy lines of the car, the sense of speed you experience, and the self-esteem and confidence you have as people look at you admiringly in your gleeming, sexy machine? What is this product you are buying?

Today's marketers know that a product may be any or all of these things. A product represents a bundle of values or satisfactions to the consumer, depending on the individual consumer's particular needs and desires. The satisfactions the consumer receives, known as the *benefits,* may be simply functional, such as transportation, better gas mileage, or larger size. Or the satisfactions may be social or psychological, such as beauty, self-esteem, pride, luxury, and sex appeal. By definition, therefore, *a product is a bundle of values encompassing functional, social, psychological, economic and other consumer needs.*

When companies develop new products for specific markets, they first try to determine the psychological and functional needs of that market. The new products are then developed as complete *product concepts* with corresponding bundles of functional and psychological satisfactions in mind. This product concept is carried over into the way the product is designed, named, packaged, labeled, displayed, classified, and advertised. (See the Checklist on page 179.)

Consider the names of various automobiles such as Volkswagen, Mazda, Mercedes Benz, and Ford. Do you consider these functional names, or do they have some psychological connotations? Now consider these names: Jaguar, Mustang, Barracuda, 280-ZX, Continental, El Dorado. Do these names imply functional benefits or psychological satisfactions?

The way a company classifies its product is important in defining

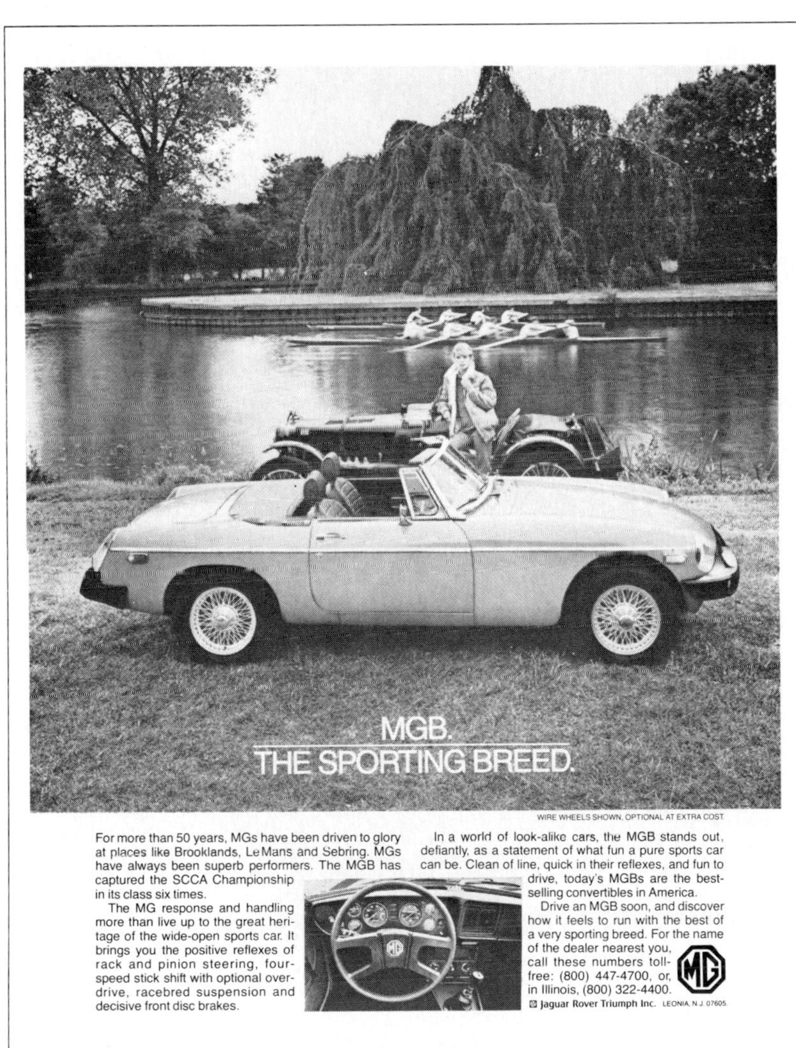

MGB.
THE SPORTING BREED.
WIRE WHEELS SHOWN, OPTIONAL AT EXTRA COST.
For more than 50 years, MGs have been driven to glory at places like Brooklands, LeMans and Sebring. MGs have always been superb performers. The MGB has captured the SCCA Championship in its class six times.
The MG response and handling more than live up to the great heritage of the wide-open sports car. It brings you the positive reflexes of rack and pinion steering, four-speed stick shift with optional overdrive, racebred suspension and decisive front disc brakes.
In a world of look-alike cars, the MGB stands out, defiantly, as a statement of what fun a pure sports car can be. Clean of line, quick in their reflexes, and fun to drive, today's MGBs are the best-selling convertibles in America.
Drive an MGB soon, and discover how it feels to run with the best of a very sporting breed. For the name of the dealer nearest you, call these numbers toll-free: (800) 447-4700, or, in Illinois, (800) 322-4400.
MG
Jaguar Rover Triumph Inc. LEONIA, N.J. 07605

Figure 6–5

the product concept and its marketing mix. There are many ways in which products may be classified. They may be grouped by markets—that is, by who buys them. They may be classified by how fast they are used up or by how tangible they are. They may be grouped according to the purchasing habits of the people who buy them. Or they may be classified according to some physical description.

Product differentiation

Henry Ford is reputed to have said, "They can have any color they want as long as it's black." Since that time marketers have come to realize that if they don't offer customers what they want, the competition will. Thus, the concept of product differentiation—building

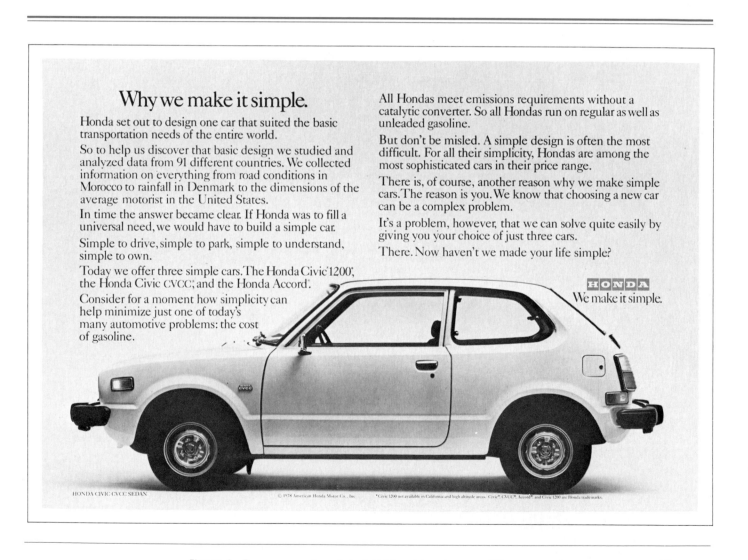

Why we make it simple.
Honda set out to design one car that suited the basic transportation needs of the entire world.
So to help us discover that basic design we studied and analyzed data from 91 different countries. We collected information on everything from road conditions in Morocco to rainfall in Denmark to the dimensions of the average motorist in the United States.
In time the answer became clear. If Honda was to fill a universal need, we would have to build a simple car.
Simple to drive, simple to park, simple to understand, simple to own.
Today we offer three simple cars. The Honda Civic 1200*, the Honda Civic CVCC*, and the Honda Accord*.
Consider for a moment how simplicity can help minimize just one of today's many automotive problems: the cost of gasoline.
All Hondas meet emissions requirements without a catalytic converter. So all Hondas run on regular as well as unleaded gasoline.
But don't be misled. A simple design is often the most difficult. For all their simplicity, Hondas are among the most sophisticated cars in their price range.
There is, of course, another reason why we make simple cars. The reason is you. We know that choosing a new car can be a complex problem.
It's a problem, however, that we can solve quite easily by giving you your choice of just three cars.
There. Now haven't we made your life simple?
HONDA
We make it simple.
HONDA CIVIC CVCC SEDAN
© 1978 American Honda Motor Co., Inc.
*Civic 1200 not available in California and high altitude areas. Civic®, CVCC®, Accord®, and Civic 1200 are Honda trademarks.

Figure 6–5 (*concluded*) MGB and Honda—Two different cars representing two very different product concepts. MGB, the traditional sports car, offers the primary benefit of fun along with good handling. Honda offers simplicity and practicality.

differences into products to satisfy consumer demand—has become a basic marketing strategy. The differences between products may be perceptible, imperceptible, or induced.

Perceptible differences Visibly apparent to the consumer are perceptible differences. Automobiles come in a variety of shapes, colors, and sizes. Refrigerators are designed with right- and left-hand doors, single doors, double doors, and varieties of colors and sizes.

Imperceptible differences Not readily apparent are imperceptible differences, even though they may certainly exist. For example, without getting underneath the Honda, the consumer cannot perceive that its engine has no catalytic converter. Nor can one tell without lifting up the hood that the engine sits sideways and the car has front-wheel drive. Likewise, cigarettes look pretty much alike from the outside, but once people buy a certain pack and open it up they may discover a different shaped filter or a different color of paper. Once they light up, they experience differences in taste. The same is true with chewing gum and many food products. The differences may be imperceptible, or hidden, at first, but they do exist, and they may greatly affect the desirability of the product.

Induced differences Between some products such as aspirin,

Checklist of product classifications

By market

☐ Consumer goods. Products and services we use in our daily lives (food, clothing, furniture, automobiles).

☐ Producer goods. Products used by companies for the purpose of producing other products (raw materials, agricultural commodities, machinery, tools, equipment).

By rate of consumption and tangibility

☐ Durable goods. Tangible products which are long-lasting and infrequently replaced (cars, trucks, refrigerators, furniture).

☐ Nondurable goods. Tangible products which may be consumed in one or a few uses and usually need to be replaced at regular intervals (food, soap, gasoline, oil).

☐ Services. Activities, benefits, or satisfactions offered for sale (travel, haircuts, legal and medical services, massages).

By purchasing habits

☐ Convenience goods. Purchases made frequently with a minimum of effort (cigarettes, food, newspapers).

☐ Shopping goods. Infrequently purchased items for which greater time is spent comparing price, quality, style, warranty (furniture, cars, clothing, tires).

☐ Specialty goods. Products with such unique characteristics that consumers will make special efforts to purchase them even if they're more expensive (fancy photographic equipment, special women's fashions, stereo components).

By product description

☐ Package goods. Cereals, hair tonics, etc.

☐ Hard goods. Furniture, appliances.

☐ Soft goods. Clothing, bedding.

☐ Services. Nontangible products.

gasoline, certain brands of cigarettes, and packaged foods induced differences are created by advertising. One of the most successful product introductions in recent years was L'eggs hosiery. The product itself was not differentiated other than through unique branding, packaging, distribution, merchandising, and advertising.

Product positioning

In 1959 the Avis Rent-a-Car Company stunned the advertising world and the general public by openly acknowledging that it was only number two. "Therefore," they said, "we try harder." The Avis campaign was immensely successful. Why? Was it because they tried harder? What was the real or perceived difference between Avis and the other car rental companies? The answer is one word: *positioning*.

Most products and services compete in a field of similar products and services. If the features or attributes of a particular product can be made distinct, it will tend to occupy a particular product space or *position* in the consumer's mind. Part of the marketing effort, therefore, must be to determine what positions are open in the consumer's mind and to develop products to fill them.

There are many different ways to position products. They may be ranked in the consumer's mind by the benefits they offer, by some perceptible difference, or by some imperceptible or even induced difference.

How was Avis positioned? Avis had no product features that were different from Hertz, National, or the other car rental companies. The product difference was, in effect, nonexistent. Hertz, on the other hand, was very distinct. Everyone knew it was the largest. Avis used this knowledge to position itself against Hertz as an alternative. By saying that it was number two, it made itself distinct and gained widespread recognition.

Product life cycle

Just as humans pass through stages in life from infancy to death, products go through a progression known as the *product life cycle.*[2] Marketing and advertising people have identified four major stages in this cycle: introduction, growth, maturity, and decline (Figure 6–6). The way in which a product is advertised depends to a great extent on where the product is in its life cycle.

When a company *introduces* a completely new product, the objective is to stimulate *primary demand*—that is, consumer demand for the whole product class. Advertising stresses information about the product's features—what it does and how it works—to educate the consuming public about the new product. Promotion to the trade is also used to encourage distributors and retailers to carry the new product. During the introductory phase, losses are common as companies spend an inordinate amount of money on research and development and on advertising and promotion to build demand for the growth stage.

As sales volume begins to rise rapidly, the product enters the *growth* stage. New customers are making their first purchases while earlier customers are already repurchasing. As the demand for the product

People in advertising

Al Ries and Jack Trout

Chairman of the Board and President
Trout & Ries Advertising

Al Ries and Jack Trout are widely known for developing the "positioning" approach to advertising. Ries is founder and chairman of the board of Trout & Ries Advertising, a $25-million New York agency whose clients include RCA, Western Union, and Monsanto. He was previously associated with Marstellar Advertising, Needham, Harper & Steers, and General Electric. Ries is a member of the boards of the Sales Executives Club and the Advertising Club of New York.

Jack Trout, president of Trout & Ries, joined the agency in 1968 after serving as divisional advertising manager for Uniroyal. He was formerly with General Electric. A recent *New York Times Magazine* article credited Trout with changing the entire direction of the advertising industry with his unique "positioning" concept.

Positioning has received widespread attention in business, consumer, and advertising publications. Articles have brought Trout and Ries more than 120,000 reprint requests and scores of speaking invitations. *Positioning* has become the buzzword of advertising and marketing people not only in this country but around the world.

What is positioning?

Positioning is a simple principle that can best be demonstrated by asking yourself some simple questions. Who was the first person to fly solo across the North Atlantic? Don't think it couldn't be Charles Lindbergh, because it was. Now who was the second person to fly solo across the North Atlantic? Not so easy to answer, is it? Who was the first person to walk on the moon? Neil Armstrong, right? Now who was the second? The first person, the first company to occupy the position in the prospect's mind is going to be awfully hard to dislodge: IBM in computers, Hertz in rent-a-cars, Coke in cola.

The mind: A memory bank

Like a memory bank, the mind has a slot or position for each bit of information it has chosen to retain. In its operation, the mind is a lot like a computer. But there is one important difference. A computer has to accept what is put into it, whereas the mind does not. In fact, it's quite the opposite. As a defense mechanism against the volume of today's communications, the mind screens and rejects much of the information offered it. In general, the mind accepts only new information that matches its prior knowledge or experience. It filters out everything else.

For example, when a viewer sees a television commercial that says, "NCR means computers," he doesn't accept it. IBM means computers; NCR means National Cash Register. The computer "position" in the minds of most people is filled by a company called IBM (International Business Machines Corp.). For a competitive computer manufacturer to obtain a favorable position in the prospect's mind, it must relate its company to IBM's position.

To cope with advertising's complexity, people have learned to rank products and brands in the mind. Perhaps this can best be visualized by imagining a series of ladders in the mind. On each step is a brand name, and each different ladder represents a different product category. For advertisers to increase their brand preference, they must move up the ladder.

This is difficult, especially if the new category is not positioned against an old one. The mind has no room for the new and different unless they are related to the

(*continued*)

old. Therefore, if you have a truly new product, it's often better to tell the prospect what the product is not rather than what it is.

The first automobile, for example, was called a "horseless" carriage, a name that positioned the concept against the existing mode of transportation. Words like "offtrack" betting, "lead-free" gasoline, and "tubeless" tires are examples of how new concepts can best be positioned against the old.

Number one strategy

Successful marketing strategy usually consists of keeping your eyes open to possibilities and then striking before the product ladder is firmly fixed. The marketing leader is usually the one who moves the ladder into the mind with his or her brand nailed to the one and only rung.

Once there, what can a company do to keep its top-dog position? As long as a company owns the position, there's no point in running ads that scream "We're No. 1." It is much better to enhance the product category in the prospects' minds. Notice the current IBM campaign that ignores competition and sells the value of computers—all computers, not just the company's types.

Number two strategy

Most companies are in the number two, three, four, or even worse category. What then? Hope springs eternal in the human breast. Nine times out of ten, the also-ran sets out to attack the leader. The result is disaster.

In the communication jungle, the only hope is to be selective, to concentrate on narrow targets, and to practice segmentation. For example, Anheuser-Busch found an opening for a high-priced beer and filled it with Michelob. Advertisers must assess the competitors. They must locate weak points in their positions and then launch marketing attacks against them. Savin developed small, inexpensive copiers and took advantage of a weakness in the Xerox product line.

Simply stated, the first rule of positioning is this: You can't compete head-on against a company that has a strong, established position. You can go around, under, or over, but never head to head. The leader owns the high ground, the top position in the prospect's mind, the top rung of the product ladder.

In positioning, the name of a company or product is important. Allegheny Airlines was regarded as "small" and "regional" in consumers' minds until it changed its name to USAir. Now, say Ries and Trout, "Watch them take off." Similarly, if your corporate name is inappropriate for a new product you plan to market, create a new corporate name—and a new position. Singer Company put its name on business machines and lost $371 million. They committed the ultimate positioning mistake by trying to transfer a brand name to a different product sold to a different market.

Importance of objectivity

To be successful in positioning, advertising and marketing people must be brutally frank. They must try to eliminate all ego from the decision-making process; it only clouds the issue. One critical aspect of positioning is objectively evaluating products and how they are viewed by customers and prospects. Successful companies get their information from the marketplace. That is where the program has to succeed, not in the product manager's office.

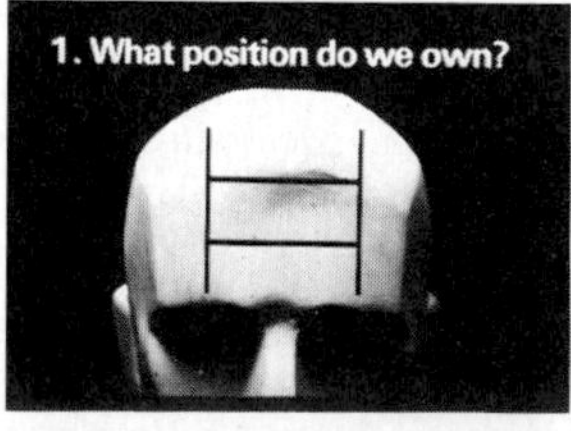

1. What position do we own?

The marketplace is where to find the answer

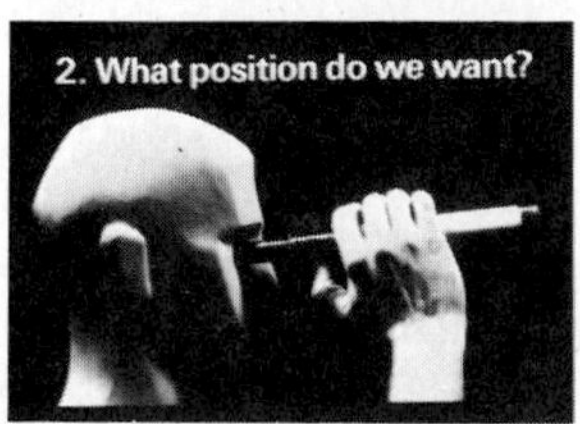

2. What position do we want?

Select a position that won't become obsolete

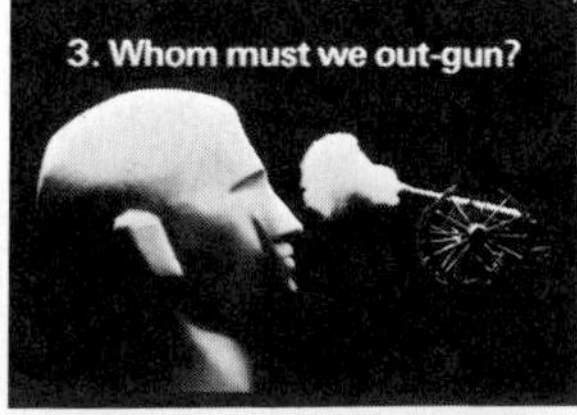

3. Whom must we out-gun?

Avoid a confrontation with marketing leaders

4. Do we have enough money?

Spend enough to accomplish the objective

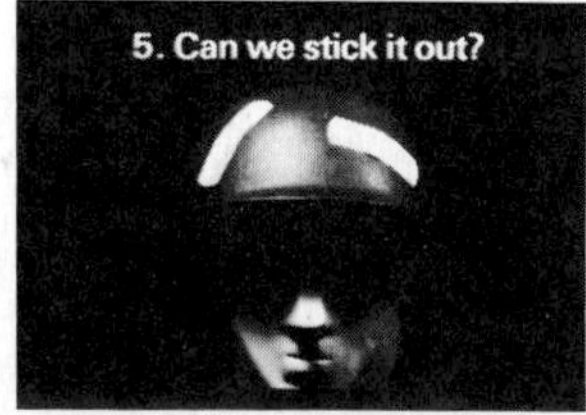

5. Can we stick it out?

Expect internal pressures for change

Creativity can often get in the way

class expands, stimulated by mass advertising and word of mouth, competitive products begin to emerge and create even more pressure on the marketplace.

At this point, as sheer momentum carries the product's sales upward, the ratio of advertising expenditures to total sales begins to decrease, and the firm begins to realize substantial profits. In 1978, for example, more than half a million videotape machines were sold. That was four times the number sold in the previous year. By 1980 as many as 10 percent of all U.S. homes had videotape machines, and more and more competitors were entering the scene.

In the *maturity* stage, industry sales reach a plateau as the marketplace becomes saturated and the number of new customers dwindles. As competition intensifies, profits also diminish. Promotional efforts are increased, but the emphasis is on *selective demand* to impress customers with the subtle advantages of one brand over another. Companies increase sales only at the expense of competitors. Therefore, product positioning becomes more important as companies fight for even the smallest increases in market share.

During the maturity stage, companies frequently take any of a variety of actions to try to extend the life cycle. These may be designed to (1) increase the frequency of use by existing customers, (2) add new users, (3) develop new uses for the product, or (4) change the size of packages, design new labels, or improve quality. Arm and Hammer baking soda, for example, has had its life cycle extended by promoting new uses for the product. It started as a cooking aid but then was promoted as a refrigerator deodorizer.

Finally, as products eventually enter the *decline* stage due to obsolescence or changing consumer tastes, companies may choose to

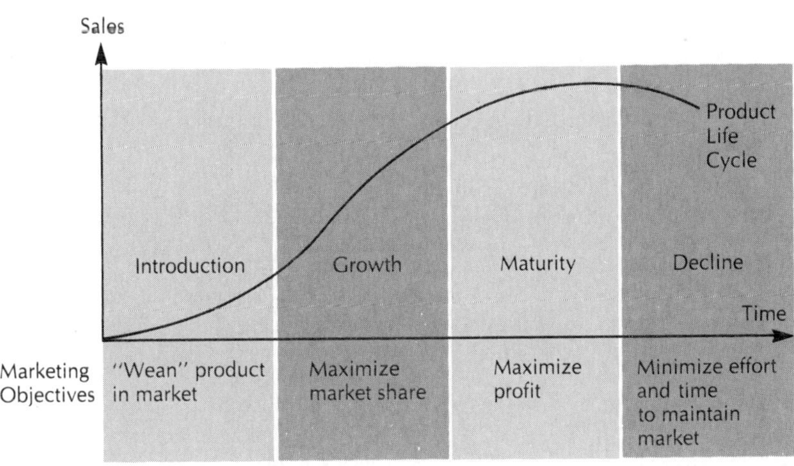

Figure 6–6 The product life cycle. Marketing objectives change as the product proceeds from one stage of the cycle to the next. So do marketing strategies. In the introductory and growth stages, promotional activities are aimed at creating product awareness and inducing trial. In later stages, efforts may be aimed at suggesting competitive comparison or maintaining brand loyalty.

cease all promotion and phase them out quickly as in the case of Edsel, or let them die slowly like old brands of cigarettes. They may attempt to revitalize the product, as in the case of Oxydol detergent, by designing into it some new perceptible or imperceptible product difference (See the Ad Lab.)

Advertising and the price element

The price of a product frequently has a tremendous bearing on the product's advertising. We see ads in newspapers regularly for retail goods that have been marked down for quick clearance. Advertising is used here to communicate the low price and motivate people to enter the store. On the other hand, many advertisements do not mention the price, but rather talk about other features of the product. And, finally, many premium-priced products are touted for the very fact that they do cost more. L'Oreal has excelled at promoting the expensive luxury of its hair products to the "me" generation.

Influential factors

Since price plays such an important role in product advertising, we must consider the factors that influence how a company determines

Marketing Charlie: Understanding the product

Charles Revson, the president of Revlon, has said, "In the factory we make cosmetics, and in the drugstore we sell hope." He was speaking of the product concepts of Revlon's vast line of beauty care products.

Laboratory applications

1. What besides hope do you think is the product concept of Charlie perfume?
2. How would this product be classified?
3. How is Charlie differentiated from other perfumes?
4. What competitive position does Charlie occupy?
5. What stage of the product life cycle is Charlie in? How can you tell?

Charlie
The gorgeous, sexy-young fragrance. By Revlon

the price for its products. Among the important considerations are market demand, production and distribution costs, competition, and corporate objectives. From these factors, companies may determine the appropriate pricing strategy. However, because of these factors, price is often the one element in the marketing mix over which the company has the least control.

Market demand Most people are familiar with the law of supply and demand. If the supply of a product stays the same and the desire (or demand) for it increases, the price will tend to rise. If the demand decreases below the available supply, then the price will tend to drop (Figure 6–7).

During the 1980 recession, automobile manufacturers were faced with a glut of unsold cars and low consumer demand. They offered factory rebates—in effect, a price cut. More cars were then bought because of the lower price. In this case no amount of advertising or promoting would have had the same effect as simply cutting the price.

Production and distribution costs As pointed out in Chapter 1, American mass production and mass distribution techniques have enabled more manufacturers to produce and deliver more products to more consumers more inexpensively than in any country. The price

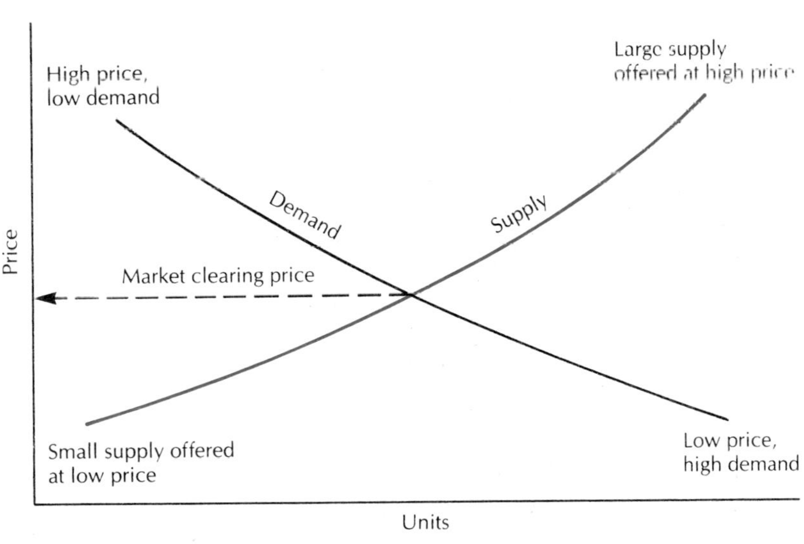

Figure 6–7 If you plot the demand versus price and the supply versus price together, you get this figure. The demand curve is a schedule of the amounts demanded at various prices. The supply curve is a schedule of the amounts offered for sale at various prices. The point where the two curves cross is called the *market clearing price,* where demand and supply are in balance. It is the price that clears the market of supply.

of goods depends largely on the cost of production and distribution. As these costs increase, they must be passed on to the consumer or the company will eventually be unable to meet its overhead and be forced to close its doors. If too many companies were forced to go out of business, products would become scarce and prices would soar even higher.

Competition Before the first energy shortage of 1974, price wars between gasoline service stations were common. As far as the consumer was concerned, gasoline was gasoline and the most important consideration was price. If one competing station lowered its prices, the consumer switched without hesitation. This all changed during the energy shortages. Suddenly competition was no longer over price but rather availability. With the short supply, long lines formed and prices skyrocketed. But the consumer didn't care as long as he or she could get a full tank of gas. Eventually, as prices doubled and tripled, demand dwindled, fuel consumption dropped, and price competition among service stations returned.

Corporate objectives Prices are also influenced by the objectives of the company. If a company is introducing a new product, it may set a high price to increase its short-term profits and thereby recover its start-up costs as quickly as possible. Or it may decide to enter the product as a premium or luxury-priced item aimed at a smaller target market.

As products enter the maturity stage of the life cycle, corporate objectives tend to be aimed at increasing the share of the market, which tends to lower the price charged.

Figure 6–8 shows two ads. What do you think the corporate objectives might be in each case?

Other factors Other factors that influence the price of products and thus the advertising for those products are: consumer income, consumer tastes, government controls and regulations, and the supply of raw materials. Only after taking all these into consideration can the marketing manager determine pricing strategy.

Pricing strategies

The options a company has for determining its pricing strategy are numerous. Assume you are opening a retail stereo shop. You plan to sell hi-fi equipment, tape decks, car stereos, and peripheral products. One of your first decisions has to be how to price your merchandise. Consider the following alternatives.

Competitive pricing strategy You could run ads declaring: "We won't be undersold!" Your ads could show or list a wide variety of products with a large, bold price next to each item. This would mean lower profit on each item and would require constant monitoring of competitive prices. It would also open you up to retaliatory actions by your competitors.

Comparative pricing You could run ads for a new stereo system showing the regular list price and your special low price. By always comparing your low price with "normal" list prices, you might give the impression that your store offers discount prices on everything.

Long before Tiffany, Cartier or Harry Winston...

1810, James Madison was President. The population of New York City was only 96,000. Still among those early Americans was a sprinkling of fashion conscious women, searching for jewelry to match their taste. They found it at a small shop on Middle Road, later to become 5th Avenue. The ancestor of today's Black, Starr & Frost.

Though we were the first, we never intended to become America's biggest jeweler. Nor even the flashiest or most expensive. Our name stands for quality, fashion and value.

Black, Starr & Frost has stores in Washington, D.C., Florida, California, Texas, Michigan, New Jersey and Nevada. Now we introduce our fine jewelry to Washington State with our newest store in Bellevue.

Our store is an ideal place to discover jewelry, diamonds, fine watches and one-of-a-kind heirloom pieces unavailable anywhere else. We also have a master jeweler on the premises who can custom make your own designs.

You'll find a wide range of merchandise, whether you want to spend one hundred dollars or one hundred thousand dollars. You'll find a refreshing attitude of genuine helpfulness. And you'll find what you've searched for—beautiful jewelry to match your taste.

Bellevue's Own

BLACK, STARR & FROST

FINE JEWELERS SINCE 1810

Now open at Bellevue Square.

AT 35,000 FEET, THOSE PURPLE MOUNTAINS LOSE A LOT OF THEIR MAJESTY.

That high up, you don't see America. You see the clouds that cover America. Travel Amtrak, though, and we'll give you down-to-earth travel at down-to-earth prices.

Just how low? Check the box below. And the truth is, if you haven't taken Amtrak lately, you're in for some very pleasant surprises.

Like plush, reclining seats. Why, even in coach they're first class, with lots of feet for your legs. We give you a first-class view, too, of where you're going, while you're getting there. Plus satisfying food for everyone's appetite. And everyone's budget.

Amtrak can take you to more than 500 cities, towns and out-of-the-way places, all across America. Including some you've always promised yourself you'd visit.

Do it—there's no better time.

A GREAT RIDE AND A GREAT DEAL

NEW YORK TO:	REGULAR ROUND TRIP	RIGHT NOW	YOU SAVE
Chicago	$116.00	$ 73.00	$ 43.00
St. Louis	136.00	83.00	53.00
Cleveland	85.00	52.50	32.50
Buffalo	66.00	43.00	23.00
Montreal	62.00	33.00	29.00
Orlando	152.00	96.00	56.00
Miami	172.00	106.00	66.00
Charleston, S.C.	116.00	73.00	43.00

NOTE: Fare not valid during peak hours at certain holiday periods, seats are limited; call for details, schedules and reservations.

And while seats are limited, call Amtrak or your travel agent. We can probably reserve the seats you need, the day you want to go.

Penn Station, 8th Ave., W. 31st-W. 33rd Sts., New York/Grand Central Terminal, E. 42nd St. & Park Ave., New York Amtrak City Ticket Office, 12 W. 51st St., New York/Call 736-4545 in New York City. In Nassau and Suffolk Counties, 981-9100. Elsewhere in New York State and New Jersey, call toll-free, 800-523-5700. In Connecticut, 800-523-5720.

Amtrak

WE'VE BEEN WORKING ON THE RAILROAD.

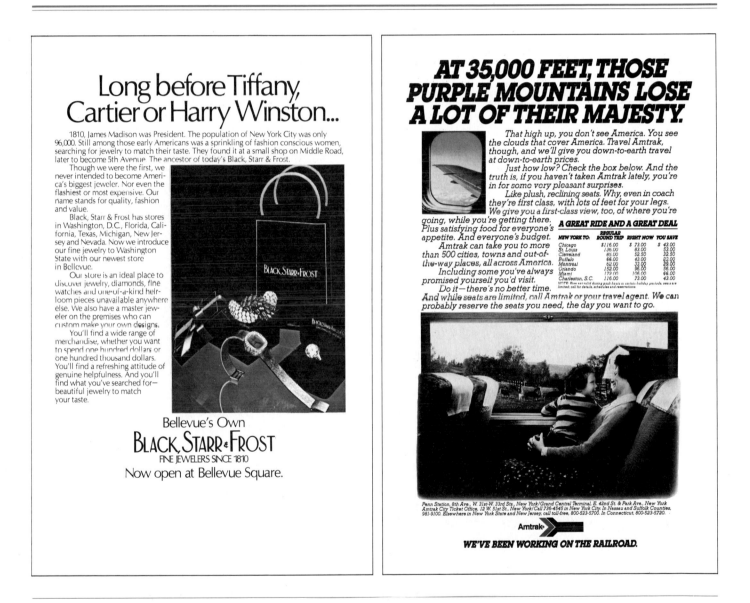

Black, Starr & Frost has been around since 1810. As this ad says, the name stands for quality, fashion, and value. What does that say about price? Amtrak, on the other hand, offers an on-the-ground view of America at ground-level prices. This is a head-on attack against soaring airline prices.

Figure 6–8

Skimming strategy If yours is the only stereo store in the area, you might decide to start with relatively high prices to quickly recover all the money you had to spend furnishing, decorating, stocking, and promoting the store. Your ads would probably feature convenience. Later you might decide to lower your prices if a competitive store opens up. What might be the problems or disadvantages with this policy?

Penetration pricing Some stores open and immediately offer prices lower than they intend to have later on. Their hope is to penetrate the market quickly by creating immediate traffic and sales. As they develop regular customers, they gradually raise their prices to a more profitable level. Initial advertising might feature low prices, whereas later ads would promote store services, quality products, wide selection, or convenience.

Promotional pricing To introduce a new line of equipment or to clear out old lines, you might use promotional pricing techniques. Two-for-one sales or end-of-month sales are typical of retail efforts to maintain traffic, stimulate demand, or make room for new merchandise.

Loss-leader pricing A special promotional strategy common to retail selling is the loss-leader strategy. You might select one stereo package and advertise it at $100 below your cost. The purpose is to create store traffic and sell other regularly priced merchandise. This presents the problem, though, of bait-and-switch advertising, which is illegal and unethical. If you offer loss leaders, you must have them in stock and be prepared to sell them without trying to talk customers out of them.

Prestige pricing Rather then competing on the basis of price, maybe you would rather offer the finest stereo equipment available, the best service, free delivery, and friendly clerks in plush surroundings. In this case your ads might not mention prices at all. They would be aimed at a select clientele who could afford to pay your higher prices in exchange for convenience, courtesy, and quality.

Which of these stragegies would you select for your stereo store? Why? What do you feel would be the advantages and disadvantages of each?

Advertising and the place element

If you manufacture a product, you must ask how and where the consumer or end user will buy it. At the factory? From a door-to-door salesperson? In a store? Before the first advertisement can be created, this question of place, or distribution, must be answered. There are two basic methods of distribution a company may use: direct or indirect.

Direct marketing

Avon cosmetics has used a direct marketing strategy successfully for many years. The company's large sales force of women call on neighbors and sell the firm's products directly without going through retail stores. Other direct marketers include local dairies that have residential milkmen, Tupperware, and mail-order houses that communicate directly with consumers through mail-order advertisements and catalogs.

Indirect marketing

Most cosmetic companies, unlike Avon, market their products through a distribution channel that includes a network of middlemen. A *middleman* is a business firm that operates between the producer and the consumer or industrial purchaser.[3] The term includes both wholesalers and retailers, as well as manufacturers' representatives, brokers, jobbers, and distributors. A *distribution channel* is composed of all the firms and individuals that take title, or assist in taking title, to the product as it moves from the producer to the consumer.[4]

To facilitate the massive flow of manufactured goods, various types of indirect distribution channels have developed to make products available to customers more economically than the manufacturers could accomplish through direct marketing. Appliance companies, for example, contract with exclusive distributors who buy the products from the factory and resell them to dealers, who in turn resell them to consumers. Many industrial companies market their products through reps or distributors to original equipment manufacturers (OEMs). The OEMs, in turn, may incorporate the product as a component in their own product, which is then sold to their customers.

Advertising and distribution strategy[5]

The advertising a company uses depends on its method of distribution. Much of the advertising we see is not prepared or paid for by the manufacturer but rather by the distributors or the retailer. Over the years the amount of promotional support given to manufacturers by members of the distribution channel cannot be overrated.

As part of their marketing strategy, manufacturers must determine what amount of market coverage is necessary for their products. Procter & Gamble, for example, defines adequate coverage for Crest toothpaste as almost every supermarket, discount store, drugstore, and variety store. Other products might need only one dealer for every 50,000 people. There are traditionally three types of distribution strategies used by consumer goods manufacturers: intensive, selective, and exclusive.

Intensive distribution Soft drinks, candy, Bic pens, Timex watches, and many other convenience goods are available to purchasers at every possible location. This enables the consumer to buy with a minimum of effort. The profit on each unit is usually very low, but the volume of sales is high. For this reason, the sales burden is usually carried by the manufacturer's national advertising program. Ads appear in trade magazines to *push* the product into the retail "pipeline" and in mass media to stimulate consumers to *pull* the products through the pipeline. As the manufacturer feels the need for either more push or more pull, special promotions may be used for the trade or for consumers.

Selective distribution By limiting the number of outlets, manufacturers can cut their costs of distribution and promotion. Many hardware tools, for example, are sold selectively through discount chains, home improvement centers, and hardware stores. Manufacturers may use some national advertising, but the sales burden is normally carried by the retailer. In this case the manufacturer may pay part of the retailer's advertising costs through a *cooperative advertising* program, and the retailer agrees to display the products prominently.

Exclusive distribution Some manufacturers grant exclusive rights to a wholesaler or retailer to sell in one geographic region. Automobile dealers are the best example of this. In a town of 50,000–100,000 population, there will be only one Datsun dealer or one Cadillac dealer. This is also common in the high-fashion business and in the marketing of some major appliance and furniture lines. What is lost in market coverage is often gained in the ability to maintain a prestige image and premium prices. Manufacturers and retailers also cooperate closely in advertising and promotion programs. (See the Ad Lab.)

Marketing Charlie: Price and distribution strategies

When Charlie perfume was introduced, the company had to determine the most appropriate price and distribution strategies. In setting the price, market demand had to be considered as well as the cost of producing and distributing the product. Competitive prices had to be analyzed, and, above all, Revlon's corporate objectives for this product had to be weighed. Only then could price and distribution strategy be designed.

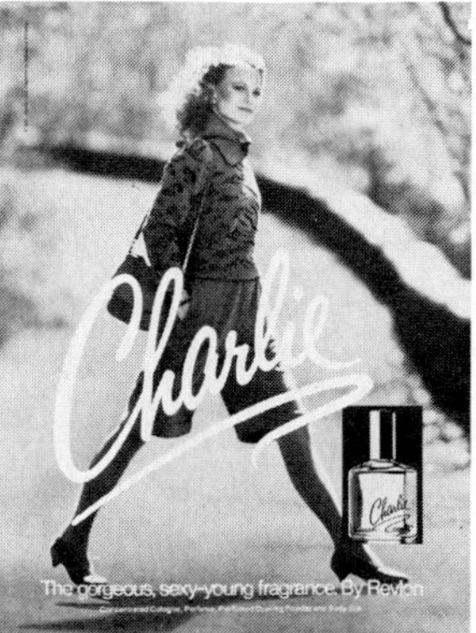
Charlie
The gorgeous, sexy-young fragrance. By Revlon

Laboratory applications

1. Visit two or three stores where Charlie is sold and see whether you can determine what strategies Revlon has used. Have they used a competitive pricing strategy? A skimming strategy? A prestige strategy? Or some other?
2. From a visit to a store, determine whether they chose to use intensive distribution, selective distribution, or exclusive distribution. Don't be afraid to ask the store manager for assistance. That could prove to be very informative.

Vertical marketing systems[6]

To be efficient, members of the distribution channel need to cooperate closely with one another. This need has given rise in recent years to the development of various types of vertical marketing systems. These include *corporate systems* like Sears, Roebuck, which owns the manufacturers of many products sold in their stores; *administered systems* like Magnavox, which gains strong retailer support because of the brand's reputation; and *contractual systems* like I.G.A. Food Stores, which is a voluntary chain of independent members sponsored by a single wholesaler. Other types of contractual systems include retail cooperatives, which set up their own wholesaling operations to better compete with chains, and franchises like McDonald's, in which dealers (franchisees) operate under the guidelines and direction of the manufacturer. (See Figures 6–9 and 6–10).

Figure 6–9 The five largest fast-food restaurants

Rank	Company	Sales ($ millions)	Number of units in chain	Chain's share of market*
1	McDonald's	$5,385	5,747	18.7%
2	Kentucky Fried Chicken	1,900	6,075	5.7
3	Burger King	1,680	2,584	5.3
4	Wendy's International	1,002	1,818	3.9
5	International Dairy Queen	926	4,860	3.7

*Based on Commerce Department figures for fast-food restaurants that franchise.

Figure 6–10 The Golden Skillet Companies have used this award winning ad in selected trade magazines to stimulate inquiries from businesspeople about purchasing a Golden Skillet franchise and thereby joining their vertical marketing system. By 1980 they had become the third largest fried-chicken chain.

Vertical marketing systems have enabled both manufacturers and retailers to achieve substantial savings as well as continuity in advertising. A common store name and similar inventories mean that a single newspaper ad can promote all of that chain's retailers in the particular trading area.

Advertising and the promotion element

After the other elements of the marketing mix have been determined, the company can add, subtract, or modify its promotional activities. *Promotion* has been defined as the marketing-related communication between the seller and the buyer. Those activities usually considered part of the *promotional mix* include personal selling, advertising, public relations, sales promotion, and collateral materials.

Personal selling

Selling is one of the oldest professions in the world; every product or service must be sold. However, the degree to which personal selling is used varies. Some products are sold by clerks in retail stores, others by direct salespeople, and others by no salespeople, as in the case of mail order, where advertising carries the entire sales burden.

Advertising

Advertising has been called mass or nonpersonal selling. As discussed earlier, advertising is used to inform, persuade, and remind customers about particular products and services. Some products, of course, lend themselves to advertising more than others. Some positive factors are:

1. High primary demand trend for the product.
2. Chance for significant product differentiation.
3. High relative importance to the consumer of hidden qualities as opposed to external qualities.
4. The opportunity to use strong emotional appeals.
5. Substantial sums to support advertising.

Where these conditions exist, as in the cosmetics industry, large advertising expenditures are favored, and the ratio of advertising to sales dollars is often quite high. For completely undifferentiated products, such as sugar, salt, and other raw materials or commodities, the importance of advertising is minimal. In this case price is usually the primary influence. This will be discussed further in Chapter 9, "Marketing and Advertising Planning." The role advertising should play depends on many factors and is a major decision in the marketing planning process.

Public relations

Whereas advertising is paid-for communication, public relations usually has no clear or overt sponsorship. Many firms use public relations and publicity as supplements to advertising to inform various audiences about the company and its products and to help build corporate credibility and image. Public relations, as we shall discuss in Chapter 22, is an extremely powerful tool that should always be considered in the design of a company's promotional mix.

Sales promotion

Sales promotion, the subject of Chapter 19, is a broad category that covers nonmedia advertising activities. Some items often included in sales promotion are free samples, displays, trading stamps, sweepstakes, cents-off coupons, and premiums. Grocery manufacturers print and distribute over 27 billion coupons per year. Of these, only 3 billion are ever redeemed. But this accounts for approximately $210 million annually that manufacturers give to their customers to try their products. Similarly, financial institutions spend millions on premiums to attract new accounts. *Reader's Digest,* for example, is famous for its annual sweepstakes designed to increase circulation.

Collateral materials

Collateral is a term used to refer to all the accessory advertising materials prepared by companies to help achieve sales or some other corporate objective. These may include sales literature, catalogs, brochures, annual reports, point-of-purchase displays, and booklets. (See the Ad Lab.)

Therefore, when we look at the promotional mix, we see that advertising is just one of the elements which companies have the option of using. The promotional mix itself is just one element of the whole marketing mix. These relationships are important to understand in order to keep the highly visible (and often controversial) subject of advertising in perspective.

Since most of the other promotional elements are so closely related to advertising, though, they are suitable topics for this text and will be treated as they concern our discussions of advertising principles and techniques. That includes all the promotional activities outlined above except personal selling.

In the process of marketing and advertising planning, the decision to use any or all of these promotional elements must be based on experience and judgment. Their degree of use is an appropriate subject of constant reevaluation in all companies.

As we shall discuss in Chapter 9, marketing and advertising planning should be a continuous process of analysis, planning, execution, review, and replanning.

Marketing Charlie: Promoting the sweet smell of success

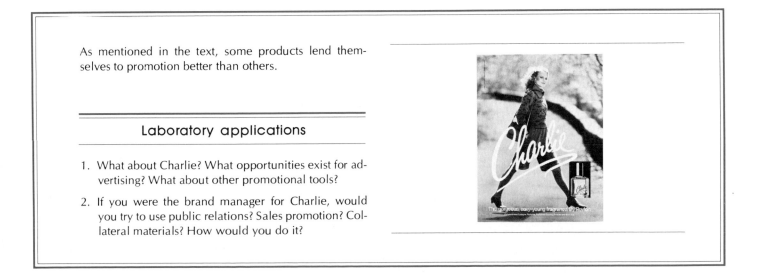

As mentioned in the text, some products lend themselves to promotion better than others.

Laboratory applications

1. What about Charlie? What opportunities exist for advertising? What about other promotional tools?
2. If you were the brand manager for Charlie, would you try to use public relations? Sales promotion? Collateral materials? How would you do it?

Summary

The term *marketing* refers to all business activities aimed at: (1) finding out who customers are and what they want, (2) developing products to satisfy those customers' needs and desires, and (3) getting those products into the customers' hands. In its simplest terms, marketing is the process companies use to satisfy their customer's needs and make a profit.

Advertising is concerned with the third step mentioned above. It is one tool marketers can use to inform, persuade, and remind customers about their products or services. To be successful, though, advertising depends on the adequate performance of the other marketing activities.

A *market* is a group of people who share a common need for a product or service and who can afford it. There are several classifications of markets: consumer, producer, reseller, government, and international.

To locate and measure potential markets, companies use market research and market segmentation. Based on common characteristics of customers, large markets are divided into smaller, more meaningful groups. Companies can then select from these groups a target market at which they will aim all their marketing activities.

Every company can add, subtract, or modify four elements in its marketing program to achieve a desired marketing mix. The elements of the marketing mix are referred to as the 4 Ps: product, price, place, and promotion.

Product, as a marketing term, refers to the bundle of values, encompassing functional, social, psychological, economic, or other consumer needs, that is offered to the customer. When offering new products to the market, companies first try to determine what needs will be satisfied by the product and then to carry that concept over into the design, packaging, displaying, and advertising. Thus, to satisfy their customers' needs and desires, marketers build perceptible, imperceptible, or induced differences into their products. They also try to build a position for their product against competitive products in the consumer's mind.

Just as humans go through a life cycle, so do products. The location of a product in its life cycle determines to a great extent how it is advertised.

Price refers to what a customer pays for a product and how that is paid. Some products compete on the basis of price, but many do not. The most common pricing strategies are competitive pricing, comparative pricing, skimming, penetration pricing, promotional pricing, loss-leader pricing, and prestige pricing.

The term *place* refers to how and where the product is distributed, bought, and sold. Companies may use either direct or indirect methods of distribution. Most products are distributed indirectly from the manufacturer to the ultimate customer by way of one or more middlemen. Consumer goods manufacturers use several types of distribution strategies. These include intensive, selective, and exclusive distribution as well as vertical marketing systems, retail cooperatives, and franchises.

Promotion refers to the marketing-related communication between the seller and the buyer. Elements of the promotional mix include personal selling, advertising, public relations, sales promotion, and collateral.

Advertising is considered nonpersonal selling and is most effective when there is a high demand for the product, a chance for significant product differentiation, an importance to the consumer of hidden product qualities, the opportunity to use strong emotional appeals, and substantial sums to support an advertising program.

Questions for review

1. How did the marketing concept evolve?
2. How does advertising relate to marketing?
3. What are the elements of the marketing mix?
4. What is a market? Gives examples of different kinds of markets.
5. What are examples of product positioning not discussed in this chapter?
6. What is the product life cycle?
7. What influences the price of a product?
8. How do corporate objectives relate to the product life cycle?
9. What are the basic methods of distribution?
10. What product characteristics encourage heavy advertising? Little advertising? Why?

7

Consumer behavior and market segmentation

Do you know Joe Shields? Chances are you do, although you may know him by another name. He's 21 years old, bigger than average, good looking, sports a well-trimmed moustache, and has medium-length sandy brown hair. Joe dresses casually but well, and he loves to have a good time. You have probably seen him at football games, on the beach playing volleyball, or at the local pub with a beer in one hand and a pretty woman on the other. Actually Joe likes women a lot, and they like him.

He's not only big physically but has a strong personality, too. He hopes to be a lawyer one day, and he is already opinionated and has a way with words. He's not afraid to say what he wants, and he usually gets it. His friends look for his approval and tend to follow his lead. Joe's parents are definitely upper middle class. His dad is a building contractor and knows everybody in town. And, of course, that helped the last time Joe was stopped for driving too fast.

With or without his parents, though, Joe does well. He's not at the top of his class, but his grades are well above average. He enjoys school and is conscientious about his work. But that doesn't stop him from having a good time.

He's not a loner or a homebody. He likes to go out with both men and women. And he always seems to have the time to do both. He likes parties where there are lots of music and talk, and he is generally regarded by women as a bit of a swinger. But he's not at all rowdy. Actually he can be very quiet at times.

Joe looks forward to going away to law school, although he hasn't decided where yet. And he doesn't seem too worried about it. Perhaps "casual" is the best way to describe Joe, because even his personal relationships seem to be light and easy rather than heavy and serious. Marriage and a family are a long way off, at least until after law school. And, besides, Joe is having too much fun to be thinking seriously about that.

Do you know Joe? Do you know him well enough to describe what kind of car he'd like to buy if money were no obstacle? Do you know him well enough to describe the kind of house he'd like? The kind of restaurant? The kind of food? Do you think he eats a lot of fast foods or do you think he prefers cooking for himself? What kind of beer does he drink? Or soft drink? Does he smoke? What brand of cigarettes? And what about clothes? What stores does he frequent? What brands does he buy? Does he own a stereo? What make?

In marketing and advertising, companies are constantly trying to match people with products. An understanding of what makes consumers like Joe Shields behave the way they do is important to the advertising professional.

Consumer behavior: Directional force in advertising

Some people regard advertising as an art. Others consider it a science. Actually it is a unique combination of the two. Advertising involves the effective blending of the behavioral *sciences* (anthropology, sociology, psychology) with the communicating *arts* (writing, drama, graphics, photography, etc.) to motivate, modify, or reinforce consumer perceptions, beliefs, attitudes, and behavior. To accomplish this, marketing and advertising people must constantly be aware of consumers' attitudes, beliefs, likes and dislikes, habits, fears, wants, and desires. And since these are always changing, steps must be taken to monitor them.

As societies change their attitudes toward dress, recreation, morals, religion, education, economics, or even other people, advertising techniques change, too. Why? Because the behavioral characteristics of large groups of people give the directional force to any advertising aimed at those groups. In short, advertising tries to use the trends in mass consumer behavior to effect changes in specific consumer behavior.

Look at the 1959 De Soto ad in Figure 7–1. What do you see? A young woman, white, affluent, dressed well and rather formally, concerned about stepping out of her new car "like a lady." Compare that with more recent automobile ads where we see young women, of various ethnic backgrounds, dressed according to modern trends, and enjoying the technical performance of their vehicles. Not only does the style of advertising reflect differences in accepted social behavior, but even the customer has changed considerably over the last 20 years. She thinks differently, acts differently, and seeks different product benefits than she used to.

There are two steps in understanding this relationship between consumer behavior and advertising. First, it is important to realize how complex human behavior is and how wide a variety of influences affect behavior. Second, we need to understand how these influences are used by marketers to categorize groups of consumers who tend to behave in the same way. At the same time, we shall see how the tendencies or characteristics of these behavioral groups become the basis for advertising campaigns.

The complexity of consumer buying decisions

When making even the simplest purchase, consumers go through a complicated mental process. The Ad Lab on page 199 illustrates the typical anatomy of a purchase.

For us to fully appreciate the complexity of the consumer's buying decisions, we need to understand the variety of individual influences on consumer behavior; the impact of environmental factors such as family, social, and cultural influences on the consumer; and how these components are integrated in the consumer's mind.

Individual influences on consumer behavior: The importance of your inner self

The effort of all advertising is to influence people's buying behavior, but it is difficult to foresee the success of planned advertising programs because human beings are all individuals. Each behaves differently, thereby making mass consumer behavior virtually unpredictable. Consider some of the contrasts in individual behavior patterns we see every day.

- People vary in their persuasibility. Some are easily persuaded to do something; others are skeptical and difficult to convince.
- Some people are "cool heads" and control their emotions. Others are "hot heads" and anger easily.
- Some people are loners, whereas others need the security of a crowd.
- Some people love their work and others hate it.
- Many people are oriented toward the acquisition of material things. Some people are motivated mainly by spiritual matters.
- Some people spend their money cautiously. Others spend their money recklessly.

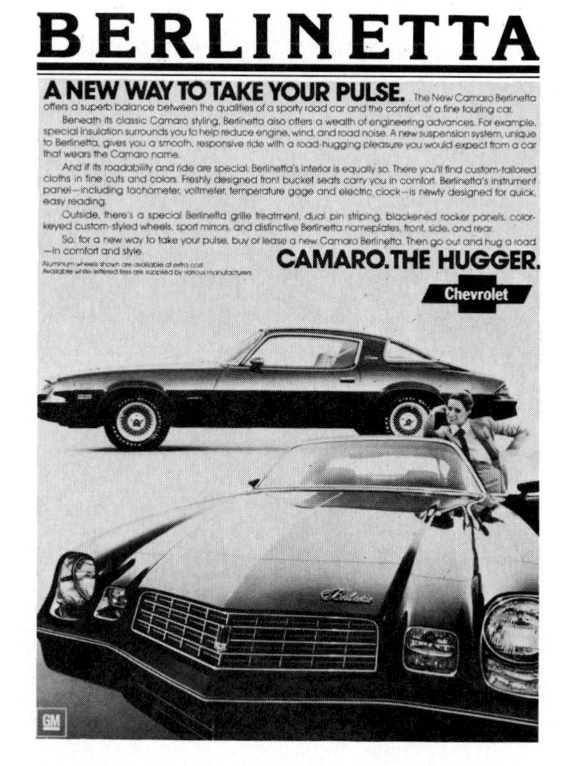

Figure 7–1 Automobile advertising then and now. Twenty years ago De Soto developed product attributes like swivel seats to suit feminine tastes of the day. Notice the way the model is dressed. Fashions have changed, with the pants-suited, necktied, sporty model advertising the Chevrolet Camaro.

Many other contrasts in the behavior of people could be noted such as sexual expression, interests in sports and hobbies, religious preferences, self-worth, goal orientation, color preferences, and musical expression. All affect consumers' buying decisions (Figure 7–2).

To further complicate the advertiser's goal of influencing consumer behavior, consider these observations. First, people's attitudes, beliefs, and preferences change. What we have liked for the last five years we may suddenly not like tomorrow or at some time in the future. That includes products, people, activities, and living conditions.

Second, individual behavior is inconsistent and difficult to predict from one day to the next. Joe Shields might react to an idea positively one day but negatively the next. He might enjoy going to a movie tonight, but he might prefer to stay home tomorrow.

Third, people are often unable to explain their behavior. A woman might say she bought a dress because she needed it and it was marked down 30 percent. The real reason might have been different.

To buy or not to buy: That is the question

A firm's marketing efforts act with noncommercial sources of information to stimulate the purchase decision process. This process is tempered by the individual influences of consumer behavior, including motivation, personality, learning, and perception. The process stops when the consumer loses interest or evaluates the product and decides not to make a purchase. If a purchase is made, the consumer has the opportunity to see whether the product satisfies his or her needs. If not, the consumer will discontinue the use of the product.

Laboratory applications

1. Using the chart and description above as a guide, explain in your own words how the purchase decision model works.
2. Consider a purchase you have recently made. Analyze the mental process you went through in making that purchase. Can you explain how the purchase decision model worked or didn't work in your case?

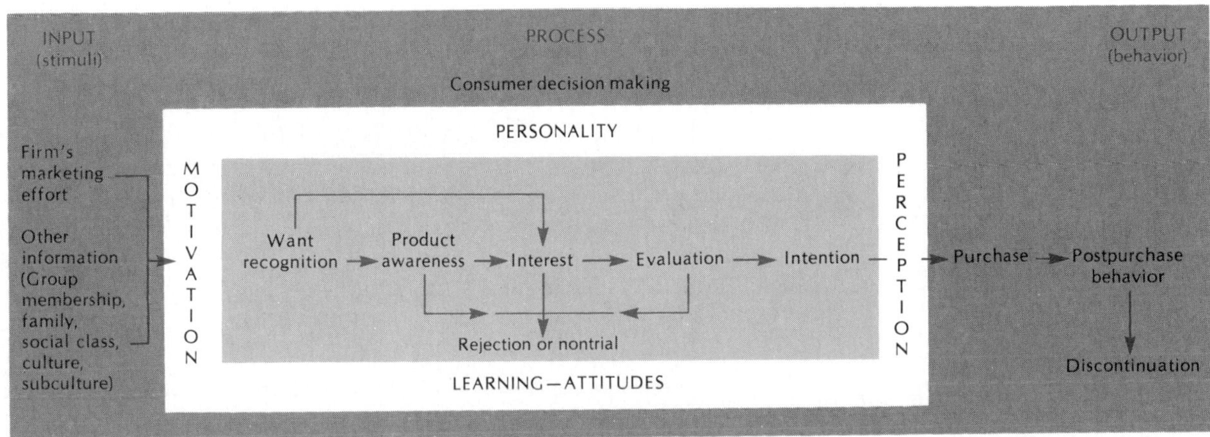

People often do not understand why they behave as they do. And if they do understand their true motivations, they may fear expressing them. For example, an executive who purchases a new Mercedes probably would be reluctant to admit that the real reason for the purchase was severe insecurity as a child.

Needs and motives

In the study of consumer behavior, *motivation* is understood to mean the underlying drives that contribute to the individual consumer's purchasing actions. These drives stem from some conscious or unconscious needs of the consumer. Unfortunately, though, motivations cannot be directly observed. When we see Joe Shields eat, we assume he is hungry, but that may not be correct. We eat for a variety of reasons besides hunger—to be sociable, because it is time to eat, because we are bored, or because we are nervous.

Often a combination of motives underlies our behavior in making a decision. The reasons (motives) a person switches an account from the City Bank to the Peoples Bank may be (1) the Peoples Bank is closer to work, (2) it does not charge for overdrafts, and/or (3) the personnel in the Peoples Bank are more friendly.

What becomes a Legend most?
Blackglama

Figure 7–2 Liv Ullman, the famous Norwegian actress, is one of a host of celebrities to pose for Blackglama fur ads. The campaign—simple and dogmatic—has itself become a legend. It has created an unequaled image of prestige and status not only for the company and its customers but also for its well-known models.

Thus, people have different needs and therefore different motivations. Understanding needs is very complex. One need might be satisfied in many ways. Likewise, the same product might satisfy different needs for different people, and it is not always clear which need or needs a product might be satisfying.

Psychologists have tried to categorize needs to understand them better. Abraham Maslow developed the following widely used *hierarchy of needs* on the theory that the lower biologic or survival needs are dominant in human behavior and must be satisfied before higher, socially acquired needs become meaningful (Figure 7–3).

1. Physiological needs—food, drink, oxygen, sex, and rest.
2. Safety needs—infantile dependency; avoidance of situations that are unfamiliar, threatening, or might lead to injury or illness; and economic security.
3. Social needs—friendship and affection, and a sense of belonging.
4. Esteem needs—self-respect, recognition, status, prestige, and success.
5. Self-actualization—living up to one's expectations (self-fulfillment).[1]

In affluent societies, such as the United States, Canada, Western Europe, and Japan, most individuals pay little attention to such physiological needs as the availability of food or the safety of drinking water and waste-treatment facilities. These needs are taken for granted. As a result, marketing and advertising campaigns for many premium products stress benefits related to self-esteem and self-fulfillment, and some even offer the rewards of better love relationships. (See the Ad Lab.)

Although Maslow's hierarchy is a convenient way to classify human needs, it would be a mistake to assume that needs occur one step at a time. Usually most people are motivated by a combination of needs.

The problem of analyzing motivations for marketing purposes is

Figure 7–3 Promotional appeals and hierarchy of needs

Need	Product	Promotional appeal
Physiological	Small home	Inexpensive housing for the family; small but well-built
Safety	Smoke alarm	Could save your family's lives; think of your children and your spouse
Social	Gold bracelet	Show your sweetheart you care on Valentine's Day
Esteem	Expensive luxury car	Picture car in front of "gracious" home or club
Self-actualization	Graphite golf clubs	For the three-day-a-week golfer; for the golfer who is looking for only two strokes

aggravated by the fact that people are admittedly moved by both conscious and unconscious needs. To explore the depths of the unconscious, psychologists like Ernest Dichter have developed a discipline called *motivation research,* which, although limited to very small samples of consumers and hampered by analytical subjectivity, has offered some insights into the underlying reasons for unexpected consumer behavior. We shall discuss this subject more thoroughly in Chapter 8 on marketing research.

Individual perception

While Joe Shields is motivated by his personal needs for self-esteem, love, or social recognition, his behavior is affected by his particular perception of himself and of the world around him.

Perception is the sensing of stimuli to which an individual is exposed—the act or process of comprehending the world in which the individual exists.[2] For example, when Joe looks at an automobile that he *needs* for transportation, he perceives more than a random collection of paint, tires, glass, and steel. He perceives an integrated entity designed to provide a variety of benefits—transportation, comfort, convenience, economy, and even status for the driver.

A person's perception of this integrated entity may be affected by the individual's self-concept, needs and motivations, knowledge, past experience, feelings, attitudes, and personality. As we suggested in Chapter 6 in the section on product concept, part of a person's past experience or attitude might be shaped by the advertising he or she has seen. Research has shown, for example, that the Grand Prix is generally perceived to be a highly masculine automobile and the Karman Ghia a feminine one.[3]

Self-concept and roles We all carry images in our minds of who we are and who we want to be. If Joe Shields wants to appear masculine and a bit racy, he may favor an automobile that supports that image. On the other hand, if he wants to be regarded as solid and respectable, he may choose a type of vehicle that represents good engineering, safety, and economy (Figure 7–4). From the preceding statements about the Karman Ghia and the Pontiac Grand Prix, we can understand why a woman who sees herself as young and attractive would be more inclined to favor the Karman Ghia over the more macho Pontiac Grand Prix.

Marketers are very concerned with the perceptions consumers have of their products, because, to the consumer, the perception *is* the reality. As marketing consultant and psychophysicist Howard Moskowitz says, if the consumer wants a "natural taste" and if the con-

Using needs to stimulate motivation

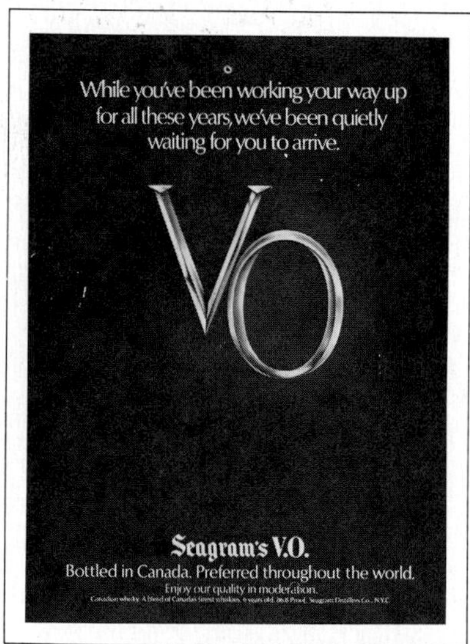

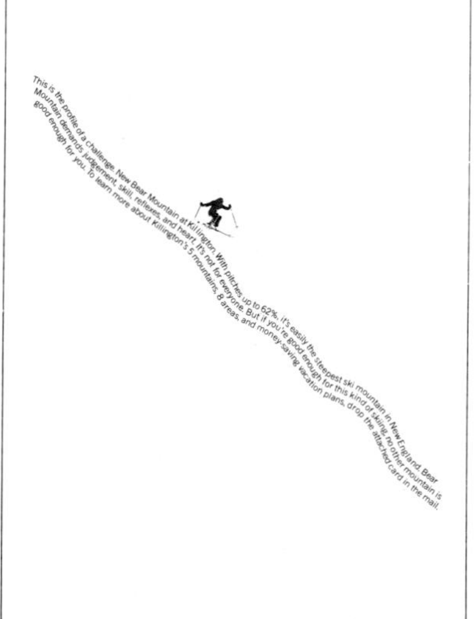

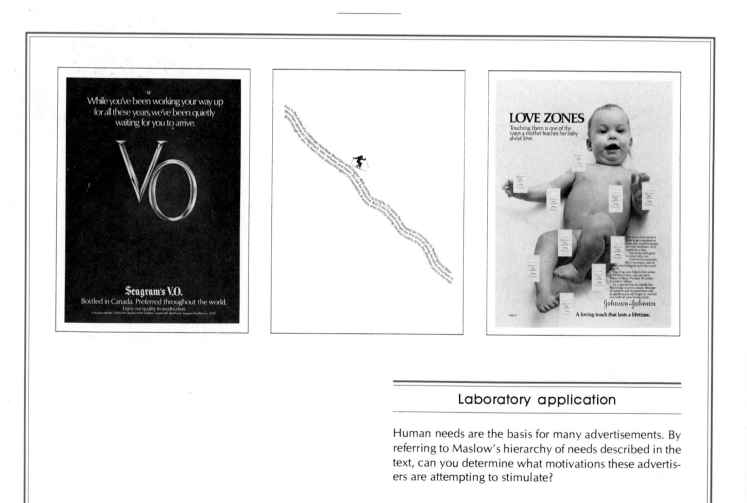

Laboratory application

Human needs are the basis for many advertisements. By referring to Maslow's hierarchy of needs described in the text, can you determine what motivations these advertisers are attempting to stimulate?

sumer thinks lemonade with additives tastes natural, that's what we'll give her.

> Lemon flavor is lemon flavor, whether you get it from a tree or from an artist flavorist. The constituents are different, but what is perceived as lemon flavor *is* lemon flavor. That's reality.[4]

Selective perception One of the major problems advertisers face is the fact that each of us exercises *selective perception.* As humans we have the ability to select from the many sensations bombarding our central processing unit those that relate to our previous experiences, needs, or desires. The average adult is exposed to nearly 20,000 messages a day—twice as many as we received 10 years ago. Yet most people are hardly aware of most of these. We are limited not only by the physical capacity of our senses but also by our interests. We focus attention on some things and avoid others. A single newspaper may contain hundreds of advertisements, but the average reader recalls only a small number of these and is influenced by even less. Thus, advertisers may spend millions of dollars on national media advertising, sales promotion, and point-of-purchase displays only to discover in later research that consumers have no knowledge of the product or promotion.

Moreover, research has shown that new automobile buyers are more likely to read advertisements about the brands of cars they have already purchased than about competitive makes.[5] This selectivity makes it important for marketers to obtain satisfied customers and build brand loyalty, and for the product to fit the image created by advertising. Satisfied customers will be less likely to seek new information about competing products and probably will not even notice it when it is forced on them.

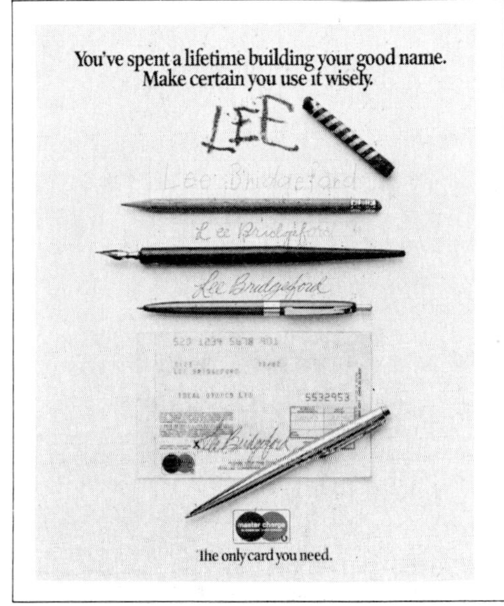

Figure 7–4 In an unusual and effective appeal to the credit customer's self-concept of being responsible, MasterCharge capitalizes on the idea of protecting your good name.

Theory of cognitive dissonance Selective perception serves us in a variety of ways. Besides saving us time by filtering out irrelevant or uninteresting data, it protects us from facing unpleasant realities. Leon Festinger developed a theory of *cognitive dissonance,* which states basically that people strive to justify their behavior by reducing the degree to which their impressions or beliefs are inconsistent with reality (dissonance).[6] For example, people who use Scope mouthwash because they believe that it's the most effective product on the market may see an ad that "proves" that Lavoris is even more effective. This exposure may create dissonance because of the gap between current thinking and the "new evidence." Advertisers such as Lavoris hope that consumers experience dissonance because the Scope buyer upon seeing the "proof" of greater effectiveness might then relieve the uncomfortable tension resulting from the dissonance by switching to Lavoris.

Consumer learning and habit development

Another individual influence on consumer behavior is the way in which consumers learn new information and develop purchasing habits. A major objective of advertising is to teach people about products and where to buy them. So advertisers are very interested in how people learn. Many psychologists consider learning to be the most fundamental process in human behavior. The advanced, "higher level" needs, for example, are learned. Learning produces our habits and skills. It also contributes to the development of attitudes, beliefs, preferences, prejudices, emotions, and standards of conduct.

Learning is a relatively permanent change in behavior that occurs as a result of reinforced practices. Theories of learning are numerous, but most can be classified into two broad categories: cognitive theory and stimulus-response theory. *Cognitive theory* views learning as a mental process of memory, thinking, and the rational application of knowledge to practical problem solving.[7] This theory may be an accurate description of the way we learn in school. *Stimulus-response theory,* on the other hand, treats learning as a trial-and-error process whereby needs, motives, or drives are triggered by some cue or *stimulus* to cause the individual to *respond* in an effort to satisfy the need. Satisfaction, then, rewards or reinforces the response by reducing the drive and producing repeat behavior the next time the drive is aroused.[8] A simple schematic of these two theories is presented in Figure 7–5.

Let us examine how the stimulus-response theory works in marketing. An advertisement is a stimulus, or *cue,* while a purchase is a response. The motivation is to satisfy various needs. If the product

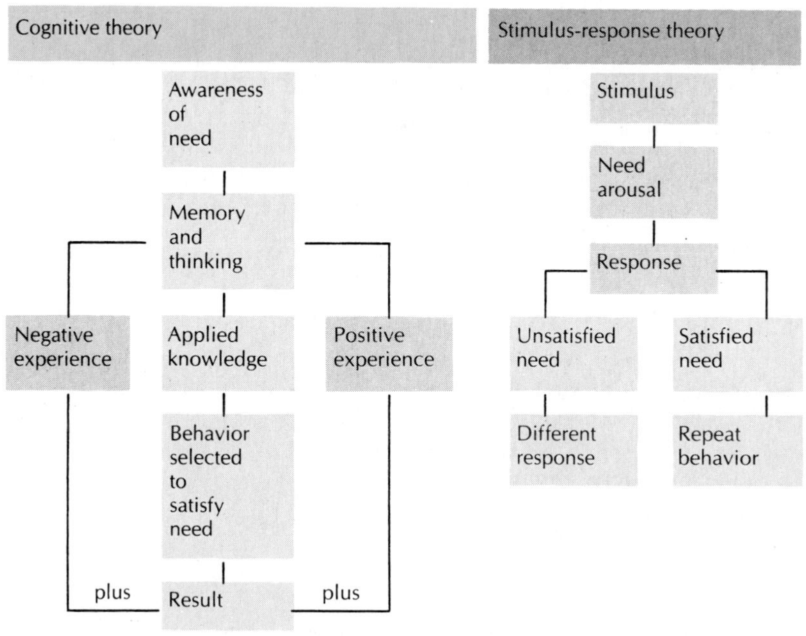

Figure 7–5 Two theories of learning.

that the consumer purchases gives satisfaction, then there is some reinforcement. Additional reinforcement may be given through superior product performance, good service, and reminder advertising.

Through *repetition* of the cues (advertisements), the learning process, including memory, may be reinforced and repeat behavior encouraged. Learning may be further enhanced by engaging the consumer's *participation* in the process through the use of free samples or free in-home trials of the product. Finally, if learning is reinforced enough and repeat behavior is produced, a purchasing *habit* may result.

Habit is the natural extension of learning. It is the acquired or developed behavior pattern that has become nearly or completely involuntary. The old cliché "People are the creatures of habit" is true.

Why most consumer behavior is habitual There are three reasons why most consumer behavior is habitual. First, we resort to habit when we select products because it is *easy*. When we consider an alternative to an existing brand choice, we are forced to think, evaluate, compare, and then decide—and this is difficult for most of us, not to mention risky. We may be dissatisfied with a new choice.

Second, we rely on habit because of *necessity*. Consider the person who purchases 50 items in a supermarket. To read all the labels of competitive brands would require hours of concentration, which almost no one has the time—or inclination—to do.

Third, we resort to habit because it is usually the *rational* thing to do. As we learn through trial and error which brands serve us well and which do not, we also learn which stores and service outlets satisfy us and which do not. When we find a product or a store to our liking, we continue to buy the product, or patronize the store, because it is the intelligent thing to do.

Interest of advertisers in habit Advertisers have three habit-related goals.

1. *Habit breaking.*—To get consumers to *break* an existing purchase habit—that is, to stop buying their habitual brand and try a new brand. Many devices are used to get consumers to try a different product or visit a store at least once (Figure 7–6). These include giving away free samples of the product, announcing something new about the product, giving limited-time price reductions, and holding grand openings.

2. *Habit acquisition.*—To get consumers to *acquire* the habit of buying their brand or patronizing their establishment. To build a product preference habit, advertisers may use "reassurance" advertising to remind customers of an earlier purchase response. Examples of advertising themes designed to build purchasing habits are: "Have it your way—at Burger King," "Try it, you'll like it" (Alka Seltzer), and "Once in the morning does it" (Scope).

3. *Habit reinforcement.*—Once consumers are won over, to get them to *remain* habitual users or patrons. Each time a consumer uses the product and is satisfied, the habit of buying the product is reinforced. Continued satisfaction may reinforce the purchase habit to such a degree that the purchase decision is virtually automatic.

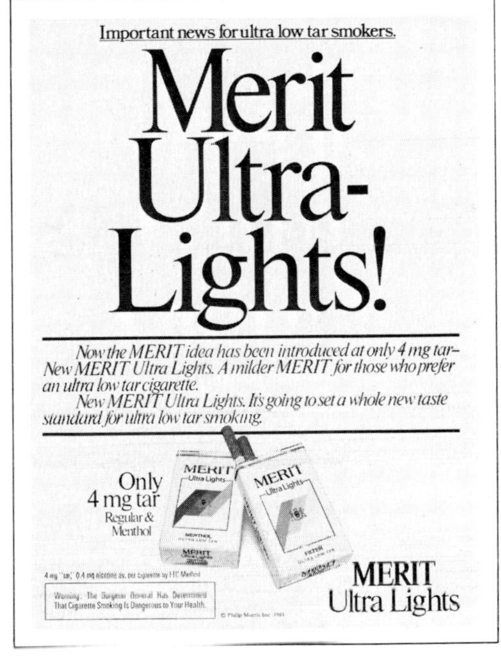

Figure 7–6 Cigarette smoking is a habit, and so is the brand smoked. Philip Morris uses the statistical approach to try to help consumers break their current brand habit and acquire the Merit habit.

Much advertising is aimed at reminding consumers that a product they use is good for them. Examples of slogans used to help reinforce a positive image in the minds of consumers are: "Coke. It's the real thing," "The king of beers for one hundred years. Budweiser," and "I'd rather fight than switch" (Tareyton).

Of course, the overall objective is to produce the consumer behavior phenomenon known as *brand loyalty.* Brand loyalty is the consumer's decision to repurchase a brand continually because the consumer perceives that the brand has the right product features or quality at the right price.[9] Measuring brand loyalty, or even defining its characteristics, is very difficult since so many aspects may be involved: consumer attitudes, perceptions, family pressure, friendship with the salesperson, and other factors. However, this is the usual long-term objective of marketers and one goal in studying consumer behavior.

Environmental influences on consumer behavior: The importance of what's around you

In addition to the numerous internal, individual influences we have just discussed, there are many external, environmental factors that influence consumer behavior. The most important are the consumer's family, social, and cultural environments.

Family

Our attitudes toward right and wrong, religion, work, male and female roles, political philosophy, sexual behavior, other races, ethical values, and economics are given their initial direction in the family setting. This influence is usually strong and long-lasting. Few people, for example, who were brought up in one religion switch to another when they mature. Nor are people easily persuaded to accept a radically different political outlook or social philosophy. If one is reared in a capitalist or socialist environment, one will likely die a capitalist or a socialist.

The family setting also affects our attitudes toward many products and our purchasing habits. Food preferences in particular are shaped to a considerable extent by what people eat when growing up. If Joe Shields grows up eating turnip greens and corn bread, he will probably continue to enjoy them as an adult. Many other product preferences are formed in the family environment. Being programmed at an early age to know that the "right" headache relief is St. Joseph and the "right" name for appliances is General Electric goes a long way toward shaping the purchasing behavior of adults.

Society

The social community in which we live also influences the way we live. The social class we belong to, the leaders whose opinions we value, and the groups with which we identify all affect our views on life and the products we buy.

People in advertising

Rena Bartos

Senior Vice President and Director of Communications Development
J. Walter Thompson Company

Rena Bartos is perhaps advertising's best-known authority on the changing role of women and the effects these changes have on product marketing. Her major responsibility as a senior vice president and director of communications development for J. Walter Thompson Company, America's second largest advertising agency, is to track these social changes and identify their impact on marketing strategies. Bartos works with all JWT offices in implementing her findings, and she consults with company clients worldwide. JWT clients include Eastman Kodak, Quaker Oats, Ford Motor Company, and Chevron.

This unique function grew out of a research program initiated by Bartos in 1972 to measure the changing roles of women. Her goal since then has been to forge a research link between female consumers and the advertising they see. Identifying women as "the moving target," Bartos declares that advertisers would be "better off aiming at where she's going than where she's been." Though many TV commercials portray women as idyllic housewives bent on achieving "the whitest, brightest wash in town" and dishes "you can see your face in," Bartos points out that 50 percent of the nation's women are employed and many others are in school or retired. Only 36 percent of American women are full-time homemakers. This makes traditional housewives a "minority group."

Bartos, a trained sociologist and professional researcher, also found that the women's market contains four distinct segments: career women, "just-a-job" working women, homemakers who plan to remain at home, and homemakers who plan to seek employment later. Women in each of these groups, she found, favor different products, shop differently, and use the media differently. They also have far more say about how family funds are spent than women did two decades ago. In fact, the major changes in women's lives over the past 20 years may have caused marketing programs to miss their mark, says Bartos, for these changes are not reflected in most of the ads we see today. They continue to portray women as full-time housewives, mothers, shoppers, cleaners, and cooks, and they minimize their roles in the working world and in community affairs.

In a recent article, Bartos said, "Marketing procedures and tools have never been more sophisticated and complex than they are today. Yet there is a curious gap between the realities of social change and the picture of society reflected in most marketing plans and advertising campaigns. Many marketing specialists who pride themselves on their pragmatism and realism have not related their day-to-day marketing activities to the facts of social change. The potential contribution of these sophisticated marketing tools," she said, "may be limited by the social perspective of the marketing specialists who use them."

It is this "social perspective" that Bartos is seeking to sharpen. "The first marketers who meet the challenge and close the gap between the realities of social change and their procedures," she declares, "will reap the benefits of discovering new marketing opportunities. The tools are available to all."

Bartos obtained her bachelor's degree from Rutgers University and did graduate work in sociology at Columbia University. She then joined McCann-Erickson as a research representative, became director of research for Fletcher-Richards Agency, and was named associate research director at Marplan. After serving two tours of duty with Interpublic, Bartos joined J. Walter Thompson Co. in 1966. She was named vice president in 1969 and became director of communications research the following year. In 1975 she was elected senior vice president.

(continued)

A recipient of the Matrix Award for outstanding achievement in advertising, Bartos has also been presented the WEAL Achievement Award in advertising and many other industry tributes. She serves on the boards of directors of the Advertising Research Foundation, the American Marketing Association, the Educational Foundation of the American Association of Advertising Agencies, and the Travel Research Association. She is a member of the board of advisors of the American Woman's Economic Development Corporation.

Bartos is the author of *Advertising and Consumers—New Perspectives,* published by the American Association of Advertising Agencies. Her articles have appeared in *Harvard Business Review, Madison Avenue, Marketing Times,* and *The Journal of Marketing.*

Social class Our society can be divided into social classes. People in the same social class tend to have similar attitudes, status symbols, and spending patterns. Which of the social classes outlined in Figure 7–7 do you believe Joe Shields falls into?

We are a socially mobile society; that is, it is possible for members of our society to move upward or downward. Many middle-aged Americans have moved up one or two classes. Few, however, have moved up three or more. Some people fall back a class or two but not many. It is significant that, with the exception of the upper-upper class and the lower-lower class, people in the other four classes are motivated to move up (Figure 7–8). The "get ahead," "better than your peers," "move up," and "win greater admiration" philosophy is a strong part of the American culture. Advertising people capitalize on the broad-based desire to "be the best you can."

Reference groups Whenever we are concerned with how we will appear in the eyes of another group, or whenever we attempt to emulate members of another group, we are demonstrating the significance of reference groups. Reference groups can be personal (family, fellow workers, neighbors) or impersonal (movie stars, professional athletes, business executives). A special form of reference group—our peers—exerts a great influence on what we believe or at least on the way we behave. To win acceptance by our peers (fellow students, fellow workers, colleagues, etc.) we purchase the right style of clothing, choose the appropriate place to live, and acquire habits that will earn us their approval.

Often an individual is influenced by two reference groups in opposite directions and has to choose between them. For example, to win peer approval, some young people may engage in behavior they believe (because of family influence) is wrong, such as taking drugs, smoking, or drinking.

Opinion leaders An *opinion leader* is someone whose beliefs or attitudes are considered right by people who share an interest in a specific activity. All fields (sports, religion, economics, fashion, finance, etc.) have opinion leaders. Our minds reason that "if so-and-so believes Spalding is the right tennis racket, then it must be. She knows more about the game than I do." Or if Mr. Smith says natural fur is in again, then the consumer may reason, "I'm going to buy a coat made of real fur. After all Mr. Smith is the expert on fashion."

Culture

The influence of culture on the consumer is immeasurable. Americans eat hot dogs, peanut butter, and apple pie. In Europe you may

The widely studied social classification system was developed by W. Lloyd Warner. According to Warner, six social classes can be identified.

Upper-upper class. The upper-upper class is the social elite. It consists of prominent people whose families have been wealthy for generations. Less than 1 percent of the population belongs to this privileged class. People in this class live graciously and quietly. They have great power but tend to use it inconspicuously.

Lower-upper class. This class is also small, consisting of less than 2 percent of the population. Sometimes referred to as the "Nouveau riche," members of this class include well-to-do industrialists, business, and professional people. People in the lower-upper class are not yet fully accepted as the social peers of the people in the upper-upper class.

Upper-middle class. The upper-middle class consists of about 10 percent of the population. Its members are successful small business people, middle and upper level managers in business and government, and professional people who are moderately successful. Many people who make up suburbia belong to this class. People in this class tend to be very success-oriented and want to improve their status in life.

Lower-middle class. This class consists of approximately 30 to 35 percent of the population. Members in it work in nonmanagerial jobs, own small business, and occupy low level positions in government. The lower-middle class is strongly motivated to win approval from their peers, has a strong family orientation, and tends to be very law-abiding.

Upper-lower class. This is the largest social class, consisting of an estimated 40 percent of the population. Its members are unskilled or semiskilled. Very few work in managerial positions or in the professions. When we think of the "working class," we think of people in this category. The upper-lower class strives less to "get ahead," "succeed," and "make more money" than the four classes above it.

Lower-lower class. This group consists of an estimated 15 percent of the population. It is characterized by low-level motivation, despair, living day to day, lack of concern for education and "getting ahead," and a whatever-will-be-will-be attitude.

Figure 7—7 American social classes.

find a few hamburger outlets, but hamburgers won't taste the same. And you probably won't get a chocolate milk shake either.

In the United States and Canada the populations are made up of many subcultures. Some subcultures are based on race, nationality, religion, or simply living in a particular geographic region. The advertiser must understand these subcultures because cultural differences affect responses to products as well as to advertising. From generation to generation, these subcultures transfer their beliefs and values. Racial, religious, and ethnic groups all have backgrounds that affect their preference for styles of dress, food, beverages, transportation, personal care products, and household furnishings, to name a few. These cultural customs, traditions, attitudes, and taboos cannot be ignored by advertisers. (See the Ad Lab on page 212.) Similarly, the social environment in a foreign country is based on language, culture, literacy rate, religion, and lifestyle.

Figure 7–8 Prestige of various occupations in the United States

Occupation	Rating*	Occupation	Rating*
U.S. Supreme Court Justice	94	Trained machinist	75
Physician	92	Police officer	72
Cabinet member	90	Carpenter	68
College professor	90	Traveling salesperson	66
Lawyer	89	Plumber	65
Banker	85	Truck driver	59
Instructor in public schools	82	Singer in nightclub	54
Accountant	81	Dock worker	50
Building contractor	80	Taxi driver	49
Electrician	76	Bartender	48
		Garbage collector	39
		Shoe shiner	34

*The effective scale ranges from 94 to 34.

In the United States we are coaxed (through advertising) to keep our mouths clean, our breath fresh, and our teeth healthy by brushing after every meal. In the Protestant culture, cleanliness is considered next to godliness. On the other hand, in France, only one person out of three brushes his teeth. In that culture, interfering too much with one's body by overindulging in toiletries or bathing has the opposite meaning. It is considered vain, immoral, and improper. To conform to their cultural concept of morality, it would be more appropriate to advertise toothpaste as something modern and chic rather than as a breath freshener or cavity preventer.

Integrating the components of consumer behavior

We have seen in this chapter the wide array of influences on every consumer's purchasing decision. If Joe Shields needs a new shirt, his decision will be affected by both internal and external factors. Look back now at the purchase decision model in the first Ad Lab in this chapter to see how Joe's purchase decision takes place.

The shirt manufacturer may advertise or a local retail store may announce a sale on shirts. A friend of Joe's may have just bought a new shirt, or Joe's mother may have said she didn't like the shirt he was wearing. Any of these external influences might trigger the recognition by Joe that he needs or wants a new shirt. These external influences also influence the type or brand of shirt that Joe selects.

At this point, however, Joe's decision on whether to purchase a shirt and, if so, which shirt is further influenced by internal forces. These include his needs (which may be physiologic, psychological, or, most likely, a combination), his personality, his self-concept, his perception of the features or benefits of particular types of shirts, and his own education or experience, which have contributed to his normal purchasing habits.

As all these forces converge within Joe's mental computer, he progresses through realizing a need, becoming aware of shirts and ads for shirts, developing an interest, evaluating what he believes he should do, forming an intention to buy, and eventually selecting a shirt. This process may take several days or it may occur in a few seconds if Joe happens to be in a store or passing a store window. It stands to reason that if we knew all the forces influencing an individual and could weigh the effect of each force, we would be able to predict the individual's probable purchase behavior.

A simplified decision matrix whereby we can look at all the factors influencing Joe Shield's decision to buy a new car and determine his probable course of action is shown in the Ad Lab on page 214. Before testing your understanding of Joe's purchase behavior, though, reread the introduction to this chapter about Joe's personality and environment. Then see if you can figure out what car Joe would buy.

From the marketer's point of view, the more that is known about both the internal and external forces that influence Joe, the easier it is to create advertisements that will communicate with him (Figure 7–9).

Market segmentation

As we defined it in Chapter 6, *market segmentation* is the process of dividing a company's total market into smaller groups or segments to (1) locate target markets, (2) identify the needs of those target markets, (3) design products to fill those needs, and (4) promote the products specifically to those target markets. Major tasks of the marketing manager, therefore, are to (1) determine what segments within the total market offer the greatest potential for profit after considering the

How understanding consumer behavior helps create effective advertising

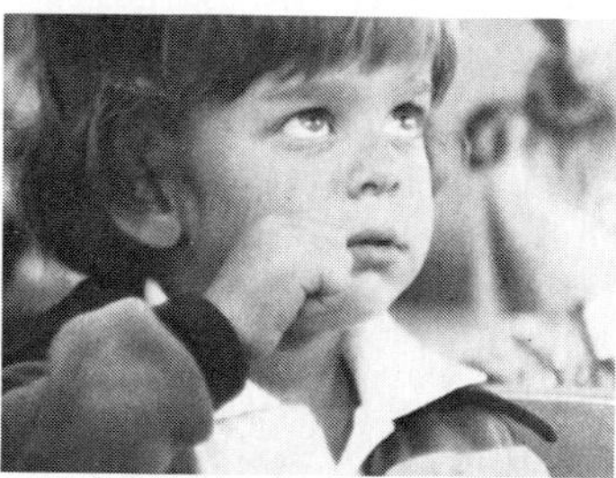

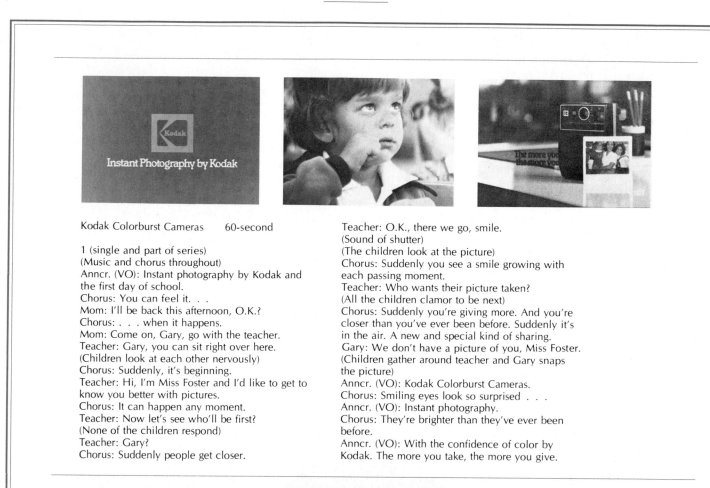

Kodak Colorburst Cameras 60-second

1 (single and part of series)
(Music and chorus throughout)
Anncr. (VO): Instant photography by Kodak and the first day of school.
Chorus: You can feel it. . .
Mom: I'll be back this afternoon, O.K.?
Chorus: . . . when it happens.
Mom: Come on, Gary, go with the teacher.
Teacher: Gary, you can sit right over here.
(Children look at each other nervously)
Chorus: Suddenly, it's beginning.
Teacher: Hi, I'm Miss Foster and I'd like to get to know you better with pictures.
Chorus: It can happen any moment.
Teacher: Now let's see who'll be first?
(None of the children respond)
Teacher: Gary?
Chorus: Suddenly people get closer.
Teacher: O.K., there we go, smile.
(Sound of shutter)
(The children look at the picture)
Chorus: Suddenly you see a smile growing with each passing moment.
Teacher: Who wants their picture taken?
(All the children clamor to be next)
Chorus: Suddenly you're giving more. And you're closer than you've ever been before. Suddenly it's in the air. A new and special kind of sharing.
Gary: We don't have a picture of you, Miss Foster.
(Children gather around teacher and Gary snaps the picture)
Anncr. (VO): Kodak Colorburst Cameras.
Chorus: Smiling eyes look so surprised . . .
Anncr. (VO): Instant photography.
Chorus: They're brighter than they've ever been before.
Anncr. (VO): With the confidence of color by Kodak. The more you take, the more you give.

Yamahopper 30-second

MUSIC UNDER THROUGHOUT.
SFX: CHICKEN CLUCKING.
FARMER: All week long I watch my crop.
But Saturday night I Yamahop.
SON: If I can ever stop my pop.
(FATHER LAUGHING LOUDLY IN B.G.)
I'll get a chance to Yamahop.
SHOPPER: It's more fun shoppin'
when you're Yamahoppin'.
COP: When I'm not a cop, I Yamahop.
(LAUGHS)
ANNCR (VO): Yamaha's versatile new Yamahopper gets over
100 miles per gallon. And you can Yamahop for $429 a pop.
HOPPY: They call me Yamahoppy.

The Echo
of an interesting
woman.
Echo Scarfs. Always smart, Always special. At fine stores always

Laboratory application

Study the advertisements pictured here. What principles of consumer behavior does each exemplify? Discuss each ad from the viewpoint of individual influences on consumer behavior—namely, needs and motives, individual perception, or learning and habit development. Then discuss them from the viewpoint of environmental influences—namely, family, society, and culture.

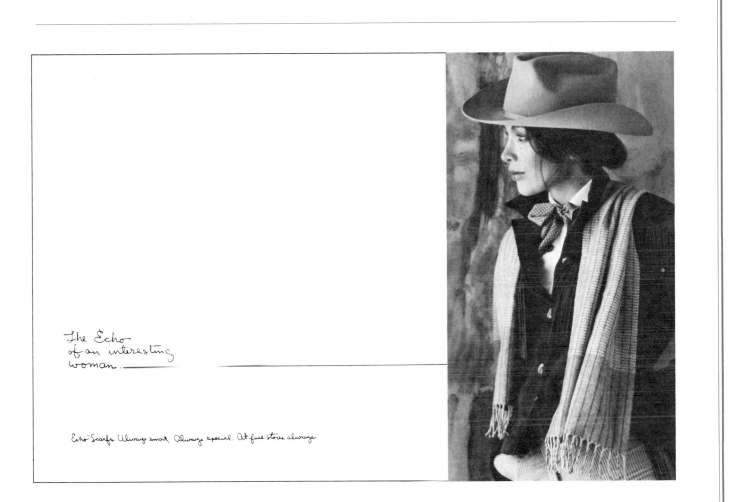

company's capabilities and objectives, and (2) find more effective means of communicating with each segment. An understanding of consumer behavior will assist in both tasks.

General Foods conducted a study to determine which types of

The decision matrix: Can you predict consumer behavior?

Do you know Joe Shields well enough to predict what car he would be inclined to buy?

If we knew consumers well enough, we could theoretically construct a decision matrix to see what products they would be likely to purchase based on their personality and the forces that influence them. In the case of Joe Shields, we probably have some idea of the amount of influence each of the six decision forces would have on him. If we score those influences on a scale of 1 to 3 against different types of automobiles, we get a picture of how Joe might behave (1 = weak; 2 = moderate; 3 = strong).

Decision Forces		Considerations	Family Sedan	Economy Car	Sports Car	Van or Pick-up
Internal	Needs or Motives	Maslow's hierarchy: physiological, safety, security; belongingness, love, self-esteem, status; self-fulfillment				
	Perceptions	The way external stimuli are sensed when modified by needs, personality, experience, attitude and feelings. Selective perception.				
	Learning & Habits	How we learn in school and in life, what we learn; what we have experienced; the importance of habit in our lives				
External	Family	Attitudes toward right and wrong, morality, ethics, religion. Male and female roles, safety; politics; sexual behavior; food, work; economy				
	Social	Social class and class mobility; importance of reference groups: family, neighbors, peers; influence of opinion leaders				
	Cultural	American customs, traditions, attitudes, subcultural influences based on race, religion, ethnicity, or geography, influences on taste and style				
		Totals				

Laboratory application

What needs do you suppose Joe has for transportation, economy, safety, sex appeal, self-esteem, status, or self-fulfillment? Which of these needs would be greatest? How strong would these needs be as motives in selecting the family sedan? An economy car? A personal sports car? A pickup or a van?

In the spaces provided on the chart, score each car on a scale from 1 to 3. Then total each column. Which car has the highest total? Is this result consistent with the Joe Shields you know? Why?

consumers were likely to buy dog food and what kind of product would be most appealing to them. General Foods already manufactured Gaines and Gainesburger products, but it had no canned dog food in that $2-billion market.

Of the six basic types of dog owners classified by the study, two were found most likely to buy the most expensive kind of dog food. One of these groups tended to regard dogs as baby substitutes, were generally women, and tended to live in small apartments in the city. The other group included well-educated, high-income people concerned about nutrition who were willing to spend a lot of money to keep their dogs healthy.

General Foods targeted these two groups and introduced Cycle dog food in four different nutritional formulations. Cycle 1 is for puppies up to 18 months, Cycle 2 for young adult dogs, Cycle 3 for overweight dogs, and Cycle 4 for dogs over seven years old. Ads featured the differing nutritional needs of dogs as they grew older. Indications are that General Foods has successfully reached the market segments it targeted.[10]

Segmenting consumer markets

The Cycle dog food case is an interesting example of psychographic segmentation. The dog owners targeted by General Foods all held a similar loving *attitude* toward their pets that implied that nothing was too good for them and that nutrition was a very important consideration. Marketers use a variety of methods to segment markets and identify behavioral groups. (See Figure 6–3 in Chapter 6.) These methods generally fall into four categories:

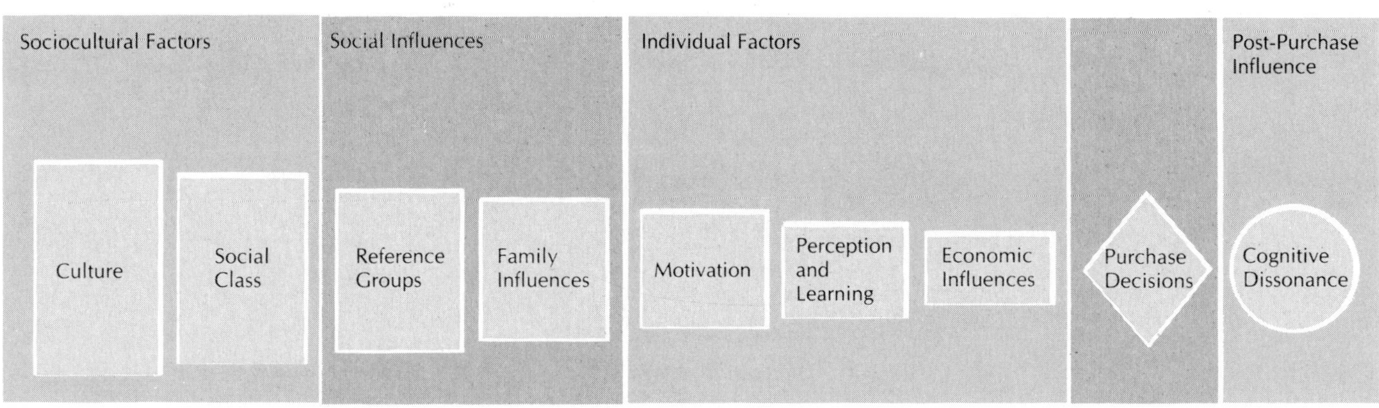

Figure 7–9 Model of consumer behavior.

1. Geographic.
2. Demographic.
3. Psychographic.
4. Behavioristic.

Geographic

One of the simplest methods of segmenting markets is by their geographic location. People who live in one region of the country frequently have purchasing habits that differ from those in other regions (Figure 7–10). People in the Sunbelt states, for example, purchase

Figure 7–10 Did you ever wonder? The best markets . . . and the worst

It's no secret that air conditioners and snow shovels sell better in some cities than others. The same is also true of just about every kind of product, from popcorn to deodorants. Below are the most and least promising markets for a number of consumer products, based on a survey of 20 key cities.

	The best	The worst
Beer and ale (percent of drinkers who consume)	Milwaukee (67.9)	Dallas/Fort Worth (44.2)
Canned chili (percent of homemakers who use)	Dallas/Fort Worth (72.7)	Boston (6)
Insecticides (percent of homemakers who use at least once a month)	Houston (61.9)	New York (26.4)
Life insurance (percent of adults who currently have)	Pittsburgh (80.3)	Miami (53.4)
Lipstick (percent of women using at least twice a day)	Seattle/Tacoma (58.2)	Cincinnati (35.6)
Panty hose (percent of women who bought in past month)	Houston (61.1)	Miami (39.7)
Popcorn (percent of adults who buy for home use)	Minneapolis/ St. Paul (54.3)	Miami (26.5)
Scotch whisky (percent of drinkers who consume)	New York (35.9)	Cincinnati (9.6)

more suntan lotions than people in the North or Midwest. Those in the North, though, purchase heavy winter clothing as well as special equipment for dealing with rain, snow, ice, sleet, and sub-zero temperatures. Even in local markets, geographic segmentation is important. A local retailer may attract people from one part of town to his west-side store but have no store to serve people on the east side.

When marketers analyze geographic data, they study sales by region, county size, city size, specific locations, and the kind of stores where sales are made. Many products sell well in urban areas but poorly in suburban or rural areas, and vice versa. For instance, the market for a swimming pool contractor is very small in center-city areas, but it is considerably larger in suburban areas.

Demographic

Demographics is the study of the numerical characteristics of the population. It has long been used to divide or segment populations by sex, age, occupation, education, income, and other quantifiable factors. It is useful for a firm that sells products primarily to persons aged 65 and older to know how many people are in this market segment along with where they live and their incomes. How would you describe the demographic characteristics of the Cycle dog food market?

As consumers grow older, their behavior changes, as expressed by their demand for goods and services. The kind of products they buy therefore depends on what stage they are in in the human *life cycle.* Marketers have tried to chart this life cycle and draw some conclusions about product appeals for each stage (Figure 7–11). However, these charts usually make assumptions that do not necessarily reflect the real world. For example, the widely used Wells-Gubar chart assumes all people marry and have children. This is not true, especially today. Nevertheless, we can assume that as people grow older their responsibilities do change, and so do their interests in various products (Figure 7–12).

Demographics give us useful statistical information about markets, but they fail to provide us with much information about the psychological makeup of people who constitute markets. Not all people in one sex, one age group, or one income group have the same wants, attitudes, or beliefs. In fact, people in the same demographic segment may have widely differing product preferences.

Psychographic

Psychographics is a relatively new term which means the classification of consumers into market segments on the basis of psychological makeup—namely, personality, attitude, and lifestyle. Psychographics seeks to determine why they maintain their present attitudes. It classifies people according to their attitude toward life (workers, achievers, traditionalists) and their purchasing patterns (What newspapers do they read? Which magazines? Which brand of cigarettes do they buy? Which TV programs do they watch? What records do they buy?)

Marketers have attempted to categorize consumers by personality types in the hope of finding a common basis for making product

Figure 7–11 Swinging singles to solitary survivors: An overview of the life cycle

Bachelor stage: young, single, not living at home	Newly married couples: young, no children	Full nest I: youngest child under 6	Full nest II: youngest child 6 or over	Full nest III: older married couples with dependent children	Empty nest I: older married couples, no children living with them, head in labor force	Empty nest II: older married couples, no children living at home, head retired	Solitary survivor, in labor force	Retired survivor, retired
Few financial burdens Fashion opinion leaders Recreation-oriented Buy: Basic kitchen equipment, basic furniture, cars, vacations	Better off financially than they will be in near future Highest purchase rate and highest average purchase of durables Buy: Cars, refrigerators, stoves, convertible and durable furniture, vacations	Home purchasing at peak Liquid assets low Dissatisfied with financial position and amount of money saved Interested in new products like advertised products Buy: Washers, dryers, TV, baby food, chest rubs and cough medicine, vitamins, dolls, wagons, sleds, skates	Financial position better Some wives work Less influenced by advertising Buy larger-sized packages, multiple-unit desks Buy: Many foods, cleaning materials, bicycles, music lessons, pianos	Financial position still better More wives work Some children get jobs Hard to influence with advertising High average purchase of durables Buy: New, more tasteful furniture, auto travel, nonnecessary appliances, boats, dental services, magazines	Home ownership at peak Most satisfied with financial position and money saved Interested in travel, recreation, self-education Make gifts and contributions Not interested in new products Buy: Vacations, luxuries, home improvements	Drastic cut in income Keep home Buy: Medical appliances, medical care, products that aid health, sleep, and digestion	Income still good but likely to sell home	Same medical and product needs as other retired group: drastic cut in income Special need for attention, affection, and security

appeals. Rogers studied consumer personalities by the way they adopt new products. He came up with five groups:

1. Innovators—Highly venturesome, cosmopolitan people who are eager to try new ideas and willing to accept the risk of an occasional bad experience with a new product.
2. Early adopters—People in the community with whom the average man or woman checks out an innovation; a successful and careful innovator, the early adopter is influential with those who follow.
3. Early majority—A group that tends to deliberate before adopting a product; its members are seldom leaders, but they are important in legitimizing and innovating.
4. Late majority—A cautious group that adopts ideas after the bulk of public confidence is already in favor of an innovation.
5. Laggards—Past-oriented people who are suspicious of change and of those who bring it; by the time they adopt a product, it may already have been replaced by yet another.[11]

This method of classification might be criticized as an oversimplification of consumer personalities and purchase behavior. There are so many influencing factors on the consumer's adoption process that an early adopter for one product might well be a laggard for some other, and vice versa.

Figure 7–12 Heavy usage patterns of various age groups

Age	Name of age group	Merchandise purchased
0–5	Young children	Baby food, toys, nursery furniture, children's wear
6–19	School children (including teenagers)	Clothing, sports equipment, phonograph records, school supplies, food, cosmetics, used cars
20–34	Young adult	Cars, furniture, houses, clothing, recreational equipment, purchases for younger age segments
35–49	Younger middle-aged	Larger homes, better cars, second cars, new furniture, recreational equipment
50–64	Older middle-aged	Recreational items, purchases for young marrieds and infants
65 and over	Senior adult	Medical services, travel, drugs, purchases for younger age groups

Marketers have been able to create psychological profiles of the heavy users of various types of products, ranging from beer to air travel. For example, women who are heavy users of bank credit cards have been described as leading an active lifestyle, belonging to various social organizations, and being concerned with their appearance. They view the homemaking role more as managing and purchasing than the traditional concept of cleaning, cooking, and caring for children. They tend to be liberal and liberated, and they could be categorized as innovators, willing to take some risks and try new things.[12]

When marketers understand the attitudes, lifestyle, and personalities of people who tend to buy their products or services, the implications are considerable. It should enable companies to better select potential target markets and match the image of their products with the type of consumer using the product.

Behavioristic

Many marketers believe that the best starting point for determining market segments is by dividing consumers into product-related groups based on their knowledge, attitude, use, or response to actual products or product attributes.[13] This is generally called *behavioristic* (or product-related) *segmentation.* Behavioristic segments might be defined by any of a large number of variables.

Purchase occasion Buyers might be distinguished by *when* they use a product or service. Air travelers, for example, might fly for business or for vacation. Thus, one airline might promote itself as a business flyer while another targets the tourist market.

Benefits sought By determining the major benefits consumers seek in a product (high quality, low price, status, speed, sex appeal, good taste, etc.), marketers may design products and advertising especially around those particular benefits (Figure 7–13). (See the Ad Lab.)

User status There are many types of product users into which markets can be segmented, including nonusers, exusers, potential users, new users, and regular users. By targeting one or another of these groups, marketers might develop new products or new users for old products.

Usage rate Also called *volume segmentation,* usage rates are used to define consumers as light, medium, or heavy users of products. In many product categories, 80 percent of the product may be sold to only 20 percent of the people (Figure 7–14). Marketers are usually interested in defining that 20 percent as closely as possible. For example, 67 percent of the population don't even drink beer. On the other hand, 17 percent drink 88 percent of all the beer sold. Logially, a beer company would rather attract one heavy user to its brand than one light user.

Marketers try to find common characteristics among heavy users of their products. In this way product differences may be more easily defined and advertising strategies more simply drawn. For example, heavy beer drinkers have been found to be primarily working-class men between the ages of 25 and 50, who watch more than three and one-half hours of television per day and prefer to watch sports programs.[14] What implications can a beer advertiser draw from that in determining an advertising plan?

Marketers of one product sometimes find that their customers are heavy users of other products, too. Therefore they can define their target markets in terms of the usage rates of those other products. Bowling alleys, for example, can target their markets to heavy beer drinkers and their families. Women who are heavy users of eye makeup have also been found to be heavy users of face makeup, lipstick, hair spray, perfume, cigarettes, and gasoline.[15]

By determining as many descriptive qualities of their markets as possible, marketers hope to end up with rich profiles that enable them to target all their marketing activities efficiently. In Figure 7–15 we

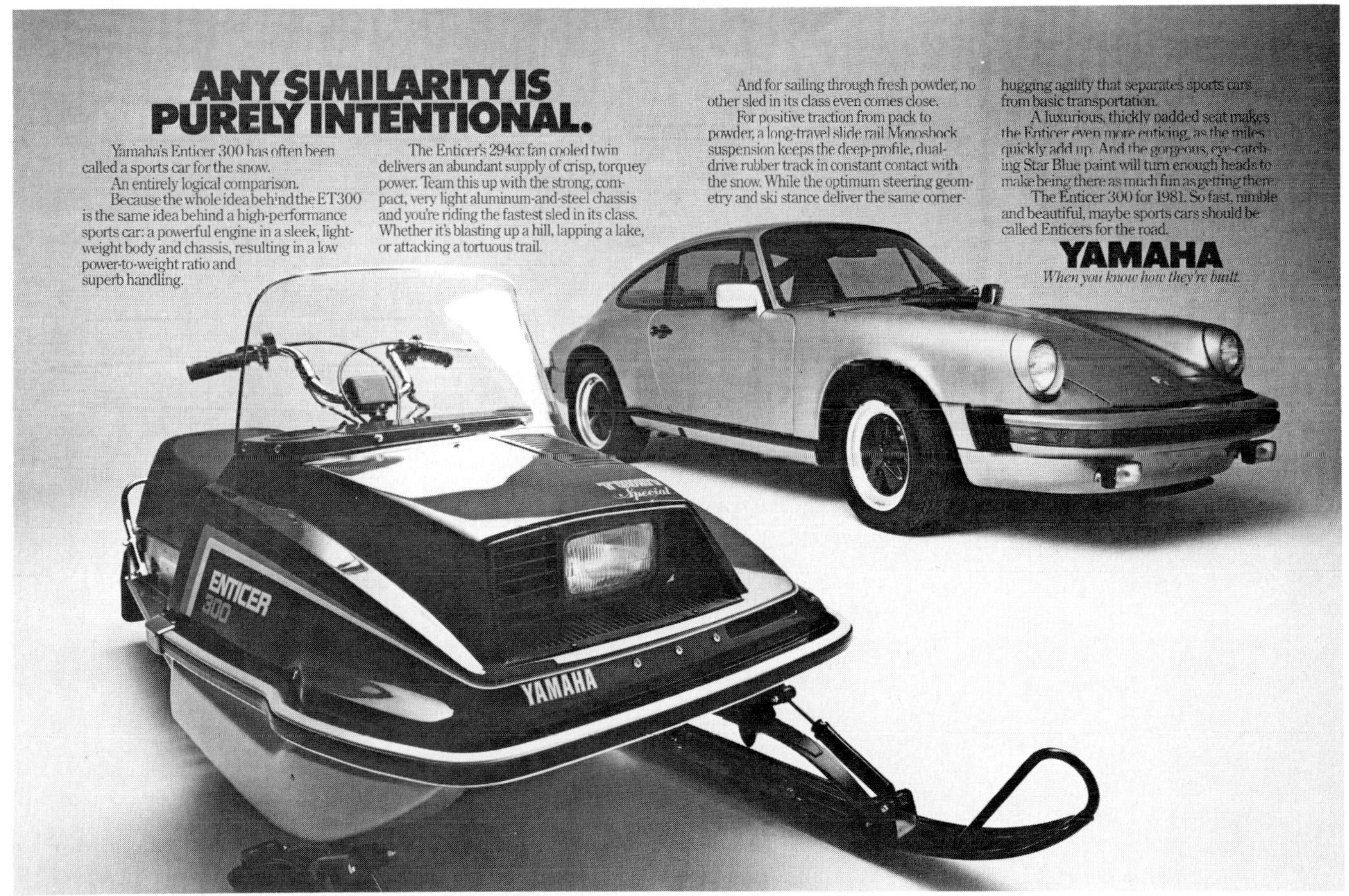

Figure 7–13 For the snowmobiler seeking the benefits of power, speed, and handling, Yamaha offers its Enticer 3000 model and, through not-so-subtle advertising, suggests the additional benefit of Porsche prestige.

can see how users of different toothpaste brands are segmented by benefits sought, demographics, behavioristics, and psychographics. Try making a similar chart for the four vehicles Joe Shields was considering.

Sports car benefits: Choosing the right appeal

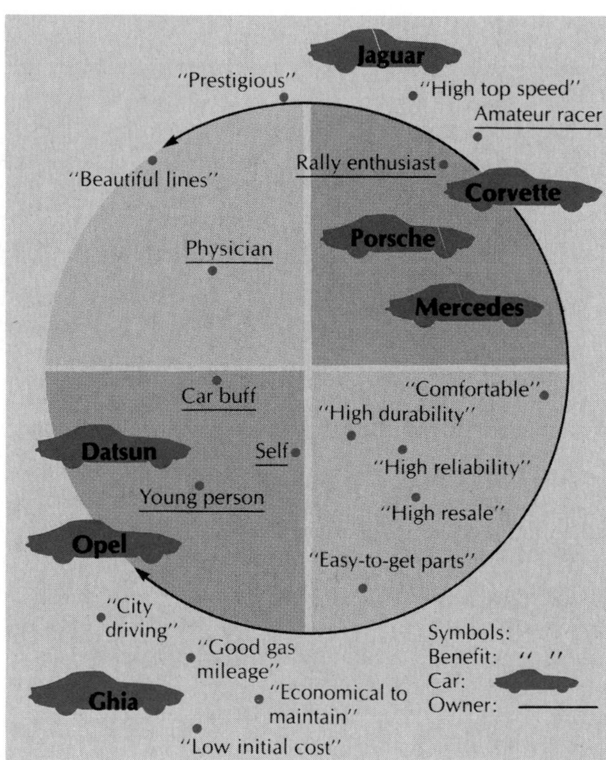

In using benefit segmentation, the task is to determine the major benefits that people might be looking for in the product class, the kinds of people who might be looking for each benefit, and the existing brands that come close to delivering each benefit. Researchers are increasingly using "perceptual mapping" to accomplish this. Perceptual mapping involves interviewing consumers with special questions and applying advanced statistical techniques to the data. A perceptual mapping of the sports car market is illustrated below. Various benefits sought by sports car buyers are shown in quotation marks; various sports cars are shown in small polygons; and various stereotyped owners are shown underlined. Note the Corvette and Jaguar sports cars in the upper right of the figure. They are close to the benefit "high top speed" and to the stereotyped car owners "amateur racer" and "rally enthusiast." Also note the benefits "prestigious" and "beautiful lines" in the upper left. None of the studied sports cars quite fits these descriptions, which means that there is an opportunity to design an even more "prestigious" and "beautiful lines" car than those studied. Also look at the Opel and the Ghia in the lower left. Their benefits are "city driving," "good gas mileage," "economical to maintain," and "low initial cost." No particular stereotyped owner is shown. Note also the cluster of benefits at the lower right called "high durability," "high reliability," and "high resale," and the surprising absence of an existing sports car matching those benefits. This might be another opportunity for a sports car manufacturer.

Laboratory applications

1. What benefits does Joe Shields seek in a car?
2. Would any of the cars on the perceptual map fit the benefits he seeks? Which ones?

Segmenting business markets

Business, or industrial, markets are composed of manufacturers, utilities, government agencies, contractors, wholesalers, retailers, banks, insurance companies, and institutions that buy goods and services to help them in their own business. These may be raw materials or parts that go into the product they manufacture, or they might be desks, office equipment, vehicles, or a variety of business services that are used in conducting their business. The products sold to business markets are often intended for resale to the public, as in the case of retail goods.

In all these situations, identifying prospective business market segments is just as important as identifying consumer market segments. In most cases we can use many of the same variables we discussed for consumer markets. Most organizations may be segmented by geographic location and by several behavioristic variables, such as benefits sought, user status, usage rate, and purchase occasion. Business markets have several distinctive characteristics, however—geographic concentration, a relatively small number of buyers, and a systematic procedure for making purchases.[16] These offer considerable implications for the companies seeking ways to segment their markets.

		NON-USERS	USERS	
			"Light half"	"Heavy half"
Lemon-lime	Households	42%	29%	29%
	Volume	0	9%	91%
Colas	Households	22	39	39
	Volume	0	10	90
Dog food	Households	67	16	17
	Volume	0	13	87
Hair tonic	Households	52	24	24
	Volume	0	13	87
Ready-to-eat cereals	Households	4	48	48
	Volume	0	13	87
Beer	Households	67	16	17
	Volume	0	12	88

Figure 7–14 Annual purchase concentration in several product categories.

Market concentration

The market for industrial goods is heavily concentrated in the east north central and the mid-Atlantic states. The stylized map in Figure 7–16 shows that for manufactured goods, more than 50 percent of U.S. industry is located east of the Mississippi and north of the Mason-Dixon line. This reduces greatly the geographic target of most industrial marketing efforts made by companies.

Moreover, industrial marketers deal with a very limited number of buyers. Less than 2 percent of all the companies in the United States account for over 50 percent of all the manufacturing dollars. Thus, customer size is a critical basis for market segmentation. Companies may decide to concentrate all their marketing efforts on a few large customers or to target their products to the more numerous smaller customers. Steelcase, for example, manufactures office furniture and divides its marketing efforts between major accounts, on which its sales force calls directly, and dealer accounts, which resell their products to many small purchasers.

Business marketers can further break their markets down into who the end users are. Computers are now used in virtually every kind of business. If a firm develops a new computer-related product, it may decide to design it for use in one particular industry or field—banking, for instance.

Business purchasing procedures

The process businesses use to evaluate new products and make purchases is frequently far more complex and rigid than the consumer purchase process described at the beginning of this chapter. Marketers must design their communications programs with this in mind.

Large firms invariably have a purchasing department, which acts as a professional consumer, evaluating the need for products, analyzing proposed purchases, seeking approvals and authorizations, making requisitions, placing purchase orders, and generally supervising all the product purchasing in the firm. The purchase decision, there-

Figure 7–15 Segmenting the U.S. toothpaste market

Benefit segments	Demographics	Behavioristics	Psychographics	Favored brands
Economy (low price)	Men	Heavy users	High autonomy, value-oriented	Brands on sale
Medicinal (decay prevention	Large families	Heavy users	Hypochondriac, conservative	Crest
Cosmetic (bright teeth)	Teens, young adults	Smokers	High sociability, active	Macleans, Ultra Brite
Taste (good tasting)	Children	Spearmint lovers	High self-involvement, hedonistic	Colgate, Aim

fore, may take weeks, months, or even years before a sale is finally consummated. This is especially true in government agencies. Frequently, the purchase decisions also depend on factors besides product quality—delivery time, terms of sale, service requirements, certainty of continuing supply, and others.

When analyzing market segments, many marketers consider the purchase decision process of various segments before determining the appropriate target market. Many new companies, for instance, target other small companies where the purchase decision can be made quickly, and contract with commission-only representatives to call on larger firms that require more time to consummate the sale.

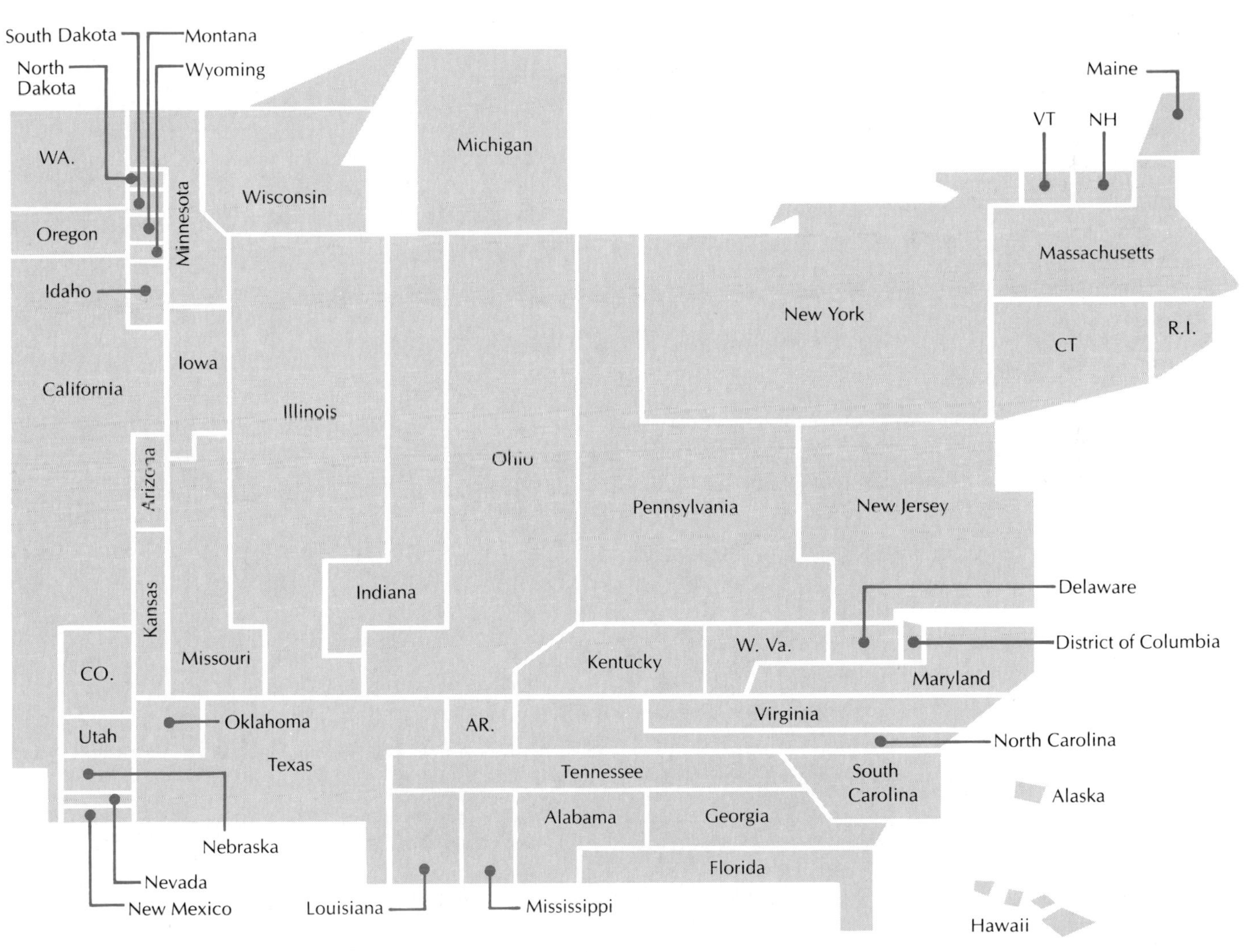

Figure 7–16 The United States in proportion to the value of manufactured products.

Summary

The objectives of advertising are to motivate, modify, or reinforce consumer attitudes, perceptions, beliefs, and behavior. This requires the effective blending of the behavioral sciences (anthropology, sociology, psychology) with the communicating arts (writing, drama, graphics, photography, etc). Marketing and advertising people constantly monitor consumer attitudes, beliefs, likes and dislikes, habits, wants, and desires. The behavioral characteristics of large groups of people give the directional force to any advertising aimed at those groups. Thus, advertising uses changes in mass consumer behavior to affect changes in specific consumer behavior.

To be successful, advertising people must understand the complexity of human behavior and the variety of influences on behavior. As marketers become aware of group behavioral characteristics, they can use those characteristics to define new markets and develop advertising campaigns for those markets. Consumer behavior is affected by both internal, individual influences and external, environmental influences. Individual influences include the consumer's personal needs and motives, the consumer's perception of the world, the way the consumer learns, and the habits that consumer has developed. External environmental influences include the consumer's family, social structure, and culture. The way these influencing factors are integrated within the consumer determine how that consumer behaves.

The keen interest in consumer behavior today stems from the desire of marketers to find more effective means of communicating with their customers and to use common purchase behavior patterns as the basis for market segmentation. Market segmentation is the process of dividing a company's total market into smaller groups or segments for the purpose of (1) locating target markets, (2) identifying the needs of those target markets, (3) designing products to fill those needs, and (4) promoting products specifically to those target markets. Marketers use a variety of methods to segment markets and identify behavioral groups. The most common bases for segmenting markets are (1) geographic, (2) demographic, (3) psychographic, and (4) behavioristic.

Business markets are often segmented in the same way as consumer markets: by geographic location and by several behavioristic variables. In addition, they may be grouped by market concentration or by business purchasing procedures.

Questions for review

1. Why is consumer behavior called the directional force in advertising?
2. What are the individual influences on consumer behavior?
3. What is the significance of Maslow's theory of human behavior?
4. What is meant by the phrase, "the perception is the reality"?
5. What is the theory of cognitive dissonance? What is its importance to advertising?
6. What is the significance of habit to advertisers?
7. What are five environmental influences on consumer behavior?
8. What is market segmentation? Why is it important to advertisers?
9. What is the difference between geographic, demographic, psychographic, and behavioristic segmentation?
10. How is the segmentation of business markets different from that of consumer markets?

8

Marketing research: Inputs to the planning process

Pat Cunningham had a serious problem. The senior vice president of N. W. Ayer advertising agency in New York was supposed to produce a phrase that would revolutionize an $11-billion-a-year industry. Cunningham slipped a yellow piece of paper into his typewriter, adjusted the margin and tab, and waited for a brainstorm. His assignment was to come up with a new image for 7up, one good enough to propel the clear, lemon-lime liquid into a battle with Coke and Pepsi for soft-drink supremacy in the United States. After suffering from a series of identity problems for five decades—including the dubious reputation of being the soft drink that relieves hangovers—Seven-Up wanted a simple, compelling advertising slogan that would make their product irresistible to consumers. The ad agency that came up with the best candidate would win the 7up account and the lucrative commissions that go with placing millions of dollars of advertising—maybe $40 million in this case.

Cunningham's colleagues at Ayer had provided him with reams of market research about the soft-drink industry and 7up. They had analyzed sales data, tested consumer attitudes, and studied product attributes and liabilities, trying to find the best way to change 7up's image and boost its sales. They had agreed that 7up should somehow be tied to the active, outdoor lifestyle of Americans. Make 7up the drink of active Americans. Hitch it to hiking, jogging, biking, tennis, swimming. Even though Coke and Pepsi seemed to have monopolized that appeal, imitation is a grand tradition on Madison Avenue. Anyway, the brains at Ayer were convinced that 7up, with its clear, zesty appearance, fits the outdoor scene better than the colas. Even the name 7up lends itself to a bouncy, active theme.

It wasn't the first time Cunningham had worked on a high-stakes bid. At age 35, despite his thinning, prematurely gray hair, Cunningham was an advertising whiz kid. He was good at creating slogans—the poetry of promotion. "Teflon, for people who have to eat and run" was a Cunningham product. So was "Avon, you make me smile." But what can you say about carbonated water, sugar, citric acid, sodium citrate, and natural lemon and lime flavors? How do you make that stuff sing? If he could hit just the right note for 7up, who knows how far he could go. A kingdom for a great slogan!

From his 41st-floor office on the north side of the Burlington building on the Avenue of the Americas, Cunningham stared out at a majestic, unobstructed view of upper Manhattan, New Jersey, and the Bronx. Central Park was spread out below like a green carpet. Suddenly he had an idea. He tapped it out: "America's turning 7up." That's it, thought Cunningham. By God, that's it! AMERICA'S TURNING 7UP[1] (Figure 8–1).

The need for marketing research

As we discussed in Chapter 7, advertising people want to know what makes you tick. When a company like Seven-Up plans to spend $20 million or $40 million on advertising, it doesn't want to risk losing it on ads or commercials that you won't look at or respond to. They don't want to waste time and money putting their messages on TV shows you don't watch, or in magazines you don't read, or on billboards if you don't drive a car. Advertising is expensive. A TV commerical might cost $100,000 a minute. A national magazine color page might cost over $75,000. This is too much money to risk if you're not going to be there to see it, or don't pay attention to it, or don't like it, or don't believe it, or forget it two minutes after it's gone. That's why advertising people need research—to cut the risks.[2]

Armed with Pat Cunningham's slogan and the marketing know-how of its new owner, Philip Morris, Inc., Seven-Up launched an audacious assault on the dominance of Coke and Pepsi in the soft-drink business. The goal was to change the drinking habits of America.

Big bucks were at stake. Americans like soft drinks. In fact, we spend more on soft drinks than many countries spend on food or national defense. We consume an average of 359 cans or bottles a year for every man, woman, and child. Cola sales account for 62 percent of that market; lemon-lime flavors, only 12 percent. An increase of just 1 percent in market share means an added $110 million in sales.[3] A decrease of just 1 percent means a similar loss. There are high stakes; and the higher the stakes, the greater is the marketer's need to know.

Figure 8–1 Tying the product to the active American lifestyle was the task of Seven-Up's agency and the rationale behind its new slogan, "America's turning 7up."

The scope of marketing research

The American Marketing Association defines *research* as "the systematic gathering, recording, and analyzing of data about problems relating to the marketing of goods and services."[4] (See the Ad Lab.)

Many decisions advertising people are forced to make cannot be made merely from intuition or knowledge of the product. Pat Cunningham, for example, would have had no knowledge of what attitudes consumers had toward 7up or any of the colas without research data. Before he sat down to develop his now-famous slogan, Cunningham needed to know how consumers perceive 7up, what they think are the product's strong points or liabilities, how that compares with competitive brands, and what image would be most credible for the product.

As Longman says, "To be of benefit to us, research must be designed to maximize the probability of uncovering the facts about the marketplace that will affect our judgment about what to do."

> We will want to know whether people are aware of the existence of our brand or, in some cases, aware of the product class in which we compete. We would like to know whether those who are aware of our brand have a favorable opinion of it, and whether they think as favorably of our competitors. We will want to know how often our brand and competing brands are used, and whether they are used regularly or erratically. We will want to know what kinds of people use our brand and what kinds of people use competing brands. We will want to know

how different kinds of people characterize our brand and competing brands. And we will want to know which consumers buy the product in which channels of distribution, what different uses are made of the product and on what different occasions the product is used.[5]

The importance of this information depends on the amount of risk involved in the decisions that are made. In Chapter 6 we discussed the colossal failure of the Edsel. The mistake of ignoring research findings cost Ford Motor Company $350 million and earned for them the dubious award of the greatest marketing failure in history.

Marketing research is useful in all stages of the management process. For firms that operate under the marketing concept (discussed

Market research versus marketing research: Xerox knew the difference

The difference between market research and marketing research is more than a semantic one. They can be distinguished on at least two substantive grounds. In the first place, they differ in scope. Market research is research about the market: its size, composition, structure, and so on. In contrast, marketing research is research about any problem in marketing, not just the market—for example, for sales personnel, compensation or channels of distribution. Thus, the term "marketing research" is much broader in scope, and is therefore preferable.

Another basis for distinction is that market research emphasizes measurement; it concentrates on quantitative dimensions. In contrast, marketing research emphasizes creativity; it concentrates on qualitative aspects. It seeks to discover unsatisfied consumer needs and wants; it tries to ferret out unsolved problems in the marketplace, the so-called holes in the market that offer significant opportunities for bringing innovation and change to it. The objective is to disturb the equilibrium in the market in the company's favor. The resulting increase in market share rebounds to the innovator as a reward for detecting problems, frustrations, difficulties or dissatisfactions, and then providing solutions which are perceived by the market as true solutions. This is the heart of the developmental type of research referred to previously. It focuses on what could be, rather than on what is.

The dramatic and successful entry of Xerox into the copying market of the late 50s is a classic example of the use of creative marketing research to discover and develop a huge, unexploited market opportunity. The two principal companies then in the market, Kodak (Verifax) and 3M (Thermofax), not only had inferior technology but required users to purchase their machines outright and to use only paper made exclusively by them. Defined this way, the market for copying machines (and copying) remained relatively small. If Xerox had used mere market research, it might have concluded, "The market is too small; why bother?"

However, its marketing research revealed the true potential for a company which could bring real innovation to the market, not only in technology (xerography), but in marketing strategy as well. It said, "We'll lend you our machine, and you can use any paper you wish!" The wedding of superior technology and superior marketing produced a striking synergistic effect; when copying was made easy, the market exploded! Xerox was not interested in what the market was but what it could be as a result of the constructive contribution Xerox could bring to it.

Laboratory application

Explain how you could do market research for a fast-food chain in your area. Then explain how you could do marketing research.

in Chapter 6), marketing research plays a key role in identifying consumer needs, developing new products and communication strategies, and assessing the effectiveness of marketing programs and promotional activities. Figure 8–2 shows the wide range of applications for which marketing research is used in a cross section of U.S. companies.

Figure 8–2 Marketing research activities of 1,322 companies

Research activity	Percent doing
Advertising research	
Studies of ad effectiveness	49%
Media research	44
Copy research	37
Motivation research	33
Business economics and corporate research	
Short-range forecasting (up to one year)	63
Long-range forecasting (over one year)	61
Studies of business trends	61
Pricing studies	56
Acquisition studies	53
Product-mix studies	51
Plant- and warehouse-location studies	47
Company-employee studies	45
Export and international studies	41
Corporate-responsibility research	
Studies on legal constraints on advertising and promotion	38
Ecological impact studies	27
Social values and policies studies	25
Consumers' "right to know" studies	18
Product research	
Competitive product studies	64
New product acceptance and potential	63
Testing of existing products	57
Packaging research: design or physical characteristics	44
Sales and market research	
Measurement of market potentials	68
Determination of market characteristics	68
Market share analysis	67
Sales analysis	65
Establishment of sales quotas, territories	57
Distribution channels studies	48
Sales compensation studies	45
Test markets, store audits	38
Consumer panel operations	33

Our objective in this chapter is to outline the basic research procedures used today and to look specifically at the way these procedures affect marketing and advertising plans and strategies.

Basic steps in the research procedure

The president of Seven-Up was John Kidwell. He came to Seven-Up in 1965 as a brand manager for one of the company's other products. Later he was sent to Canada to become president of Seven-Up's Canadian subsidiary. In a short time 7up sales in Canada took off under Kidwell. The drink even outsold Coke and Pepsi in some places.

> Kidwell was a natural at marketing. Though he had never taken a business course in his life—he was a philosophy and English major as an undergraduate at St. John's University in Minnesota and completed his course work for an M.A. in English literature at Catholic University, in Washington, D.C.—Kidwell instinctively knew how to sell a product. He also understood the value of market research and planning, something the top brass at Seven-Up at that time did not. Kidwell took a career risk when he accepted the appointment as senior vice president for marketing at Seven-Up headquarters in St. Louis.[6]

In 1976 Kidwell was summoned back to St. Louis to analyze and halt a sagging brand share condition. The number three soft drink had lost its sales momentum, was feeling pressure from fourth place Dr. Pepper, and had already slipped eight tenths of a share point—a substantial piece of business.

Research objectives and problem definition

Kidwell knew that the first step in the marketing research process is to define the problem and set research objectives (Figure 8–3). He discovered on his return to St. Louis that there was no ongoing market

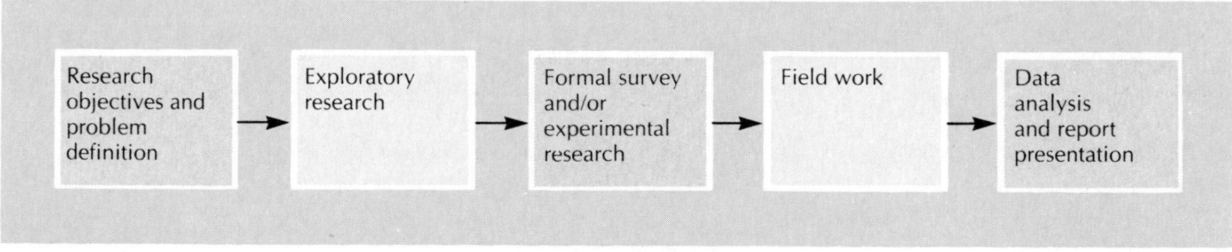

Figure 8–3 Marketing research process.

research or marketing information system at Seven-Up and that the company's survival was threatened by this. The company was running blind. It had no idea why 7up's position in the market was deteriorating.

Moreover, Kidwell discovered the company was in trouble with its bottlers. In the soft drink business, the local bottlers have the franchise to produce and sell the product in their area, and they have a lot of clout. In the United States there are more than 470 bottlers that produce 7up. They were upset over the brand's eroding market share and impatient with the company's hesitancy in mounting an aggressive marketing effort.[7]

Thus, Kidwell was confronted with several problem *symptoms*. His first objective was to discover the *causes*, so the problem could be accurately defined and understood.

Schultz and Martin recommend that at the beginning of any research project, a concise statement of the research problem and objectives should be written. The statement should contain three basic elements:

1. The information to be gathered must be measurable.
2. It must be relevant to the problem.
3. The various pieces of information or knowledge to be gained must be related.[8]

For example, the statement of Seven-Up's problem and research objectives might have been written as follows:

> Sales of 7up, while still increasing, seem to have lost their momentum. Our share of the market has slipped 8/10 of 1 percent in the last year. Is this slippage due to a decline in the total lemon-lime category, is it due to increased competition from the colas, or are sales lost to another brand? If sales are lost to another brand, which is it and why?

This problem is specific and measurable, the questions asked are relevant to the problem, and the information requested is directly related.

Exploratory research

The second step in the research process is to assess current knowledge through a number of information procedures. The objective of exploratory research is simply to learn more about the market, the competition, the business environment, and the problem before any formal research is undertaken. This may consist of discussing the problem with informed sources inside the firm; with wholesalers, distributors, or retailers outside the firm; with customers; or even with competitors. The two main tasks of the exploratory research stage are to analyze internal data and to collect outside secondary data.

Utilizing internal data

Many valuable sources of information usually exist within the company's records. Some types of internal data that might prove useful to the marketing manager are product shipment figures, billings to customers, warranty card records, advertising expenditures, sales expenses, correspondence from customers, and records of meetings with sales staffs. (See Figure 8–4.)

Certainly in the case of Seven-Up, an analysis of sales data, Nielsen retail audits, and records of correspondence from bottlers might have signaled the problem faced by the company. In another situation the marketing manager might discover from marketing expense data that certain customers or territories offer an unprofitable relationship of sales produced to the cost incurred to produce them.

Collecting secondary data

Secondary data are data that already exist somewhere, having been collected for another purpose.[9] Much information is available—usually free—if the researcher just knows where to look for it. It might be government-issued materials, such as census data or publications from the Department of Commerce, or published information from market research companies, trade associations, or various trade publications.

Generally, collecting secondary data is less costly than collecting primary data, and it requires less time. Problems with secondary data are: (1) they may be obsolete; (2) they may not be relevant to the problem at hand; (3) they may not be valid or reliable information, depending on the way they were collected; or (4) the very wealth of information available to be reviewed may be overpowering relative to the size of the problem being studied. (See the Ad Lab.)

Some of the most frequently used sources of secondary data are the following.

Library reference materials The logical place to begin secondary research is in a library. The card catalog of books will lead researchers to endless avenues of information. Some helpful library reference aids are the *Business Periodicals Index* (for business magazines), *Reader's Guide to Periodical Literature* (for consumer magazines), *Public Information Service Bulletin,* and the *New York Times Index* (Figure 8–5). Libraries also have many other sources of factual and statistical information such as the *World Almanac and Book of Facts.*

Government publications The federal government is one of the most profuse sources of secondary data, including specialized information for marketing personnel such as the *Statistical Abstract of the United States.*

Trade association publications More than 2,000 trade associations are listed in the *Directory of National Trade Associations,* which is published by the Department of Commerce. There is at least one trade association for virtually every industry, and most of them issue a wealth of printed literature. Many publish annual fact books containing both government data of interest to their industries and information gathered by the associations themselves.

Research organizations publications Numerous research organizations make it their business to sell data of interest to advertisers and agencies on a subscription basis. Also, many universities operate bureaus of business research that issue helpful information.

People in advertising

Joseph G. Smith

President
Oxtoby-Smith, Inc.

Joseph G. Smith is founder and president of Oxtoby-Smith, Inc., one of the nation's foremost consumer research organizations. The firm provides advertisers and agencies with information and skillful guidance regarding consumer behavior to help them optimize marketing decisions. Among its clients are American Motors, Continental Baking Company, Coca-Cola Foods, General Electric, and Xerox. It has served as a spawning ground and a model for an extraordinary number of gifted people in the consumer research business.

Before founding Oxtoby-Smith in 1956, Smith served on the staffs of the Rand Corporation and the National Research Council in Washington, D.C. A certified psychologist, he obtained B.S., M.A., and Ph.D. degrees in psychology from the University of Iowa, where he was elected to Phi Beta Kappa.

Discussing the work of his organization, Smith cites its use of incisive research tools together with imaginative and flexible interpretation. "They are essentially the tools of a social scientist," he explains. The research process starts with "a good, relevant sampling." Next, he reports, "is adequate statistical analysis with emphasis on reliable coding." Since turning an interview into a bunch of holes punched in cards can facilitate error, says Dr. Smith, "we are obsessive about reliability—the need for quality control in every one of these initial functions." "Of particular pride," says Smith, "is that our company has been successful in applying the disciplines and skills of social science in the marketing community without in any way demeaning its commitment to the highest standards of professional skill and integrity."

Despite the care taken in conducting research, he adds, there are several major problems to overcome. One is to assure that the personality of the interviewer or the methods in which information is collected do not influence the results of the survey. A way to prevent this, says Smith, is to design questionnaires that aren't vulnerable to the interviewer's lack of skill or personal prejudice.

Another potential problem, notes Smith, "is in what information we get." He explains that it is easy to develop "precise but sterile arrays of data" that offer little real or meaningful guidance to the client. "Here is where wit and flexibility are critically needed," he reports. "We've got to stay loose—and be willing to explore new approaches to get the kind of information resource which will really help a client to accurately solve a problem."

It is this innovative approach that has enabled Oxtoby-Smith to develop continuing, long-term relationships with clients like TWA and American Motors. Rather than simply working on a job-shop basis, the company is involved in all aspects of the research and in its applications. Smith tries to make market research a contributing resource for management decision making. He contributes at various times of the year, he designs the studies, he thinks through the problems, he executes, and he interprets the results.

As examples, Smith cites "demand scheduling" at TWA—the first systematic and responsive discount fare program—and the American Motors "Buyer Protection Plan." Through research, Oxtoby-Smith determined the desire of consumers for lower air fares and better protection when purchasing an automobile. "I think," says Smith, "these programs offer reasonably good evidence that consumer responsiveness is really enlightened self-interest."

Summing up the value of consumer research to successful marketing, Smith observes, "If you take the proper thermometers, use them in the proper places, and read them with concern, sensitivity, and empathy for the businessperson, consumer research can be an immensely powerful weapon. Surprisingly, in many corporate cor-

(continued)

ridors, it's still a secret weapon. Maybe it takes as much wit, courage, and passion to use it well as it takes to do it well."

Joseph Smith has published and speaks extensively on subjects related to consumer research. He has served as an expert witness in proceedings of the Federal Trade Commission and other regulatory agencies as well as in trademark litigation. A Fellow of the American Psychological Association, Smith is listed in *American Men of Science*. He is a member of the American Marketing Association, the American Association for Public Opinion Research, the Market Research Council, and the Copy Research Council.

When John Kidwell finished reviewing all his internal data and the outside secondary research on 7up's problems, he found that 7up was *not* losing sales to Coke and Pepsi, but rather to diet drinks and to Sprite and Mountain Dew. In the wake of its successful 10-year-old Uncola campaign, it was no longer a specialty drink or a mixer as it had once been regarded (Figure 8–6). But it was still not a first-choice soft drink. 7up's popularity was mostly with older people and with women. This all meant one thing to Kidwell. The brand's image needed a facelift. It needed a more "macho" feeling to appeal to the youth market, since young people are the major source of soft drink sales.

Collecting primary data

By this time the N. W. Ayer advertising agency was in the picture. It too had analyzed all of Seven-Up's secondary data. Of particular interest were the company's records of competitive taste tests for various soft drink brands. When consumers drank identified brands, they said they preferred 7up to all the others. When the bottles were unmarked, 7up still won. This caused Ayer to wonder why, if the 7up taste was indeed preferable, consumers didn't buy it in greater quantities than the colas. Perhaps the product had some problems or liabilities in the consumers' perception that didn't relate to taste but rather to the product's image or personality. The agency decided to do some primary research to get the answer.

Basic methodology

Once the researcher has concluded the exploratory research phase, it may be discovered that there is still a need to gain additional information directly from the marketplace. There are basically three alternatives in collecting this primary data: observation, experiment, and survey.

Observational method This is used when researchers actually monitor the overt actions of the person being studied. This may take the form of a traffic count by outdoor billboard companies, a television

1. *A. C. Nielsen Company.* Audits 1,600 supermarkets, 750 drugstores, and 150 mass merchandisers every two weeks to determine share of market, prices, displays, inventory, and promotional efforts of selected product categories. Also audits warehouse movement of new products through 150 food chains and independent warehouses. Estimates audience size, characteristics, viewing habits, and switching for individual television programs.
2. *IMS International.* Research services include (*a*) retail outlet measures of ethical pharmaceutical sales; (*b*) panels of doctors reporting on diagnosis and treatment of patients; (*c*) customized audits of purchases by hospitals and laboratories; and (*d*) custom studies, including surveys.
3. *SAMI.* Collects warehouse withdrawal data to produce continuous movement information for thousands of individual brand items in each of the U.S. market areas. Captures continuous store movement data from UPC scanner-equipped stores with their Scanner Store Data Service. Electronic Consumer Panels link specific store purchases to individual households.
4. *The Arbitron Company.* Measures television viewing and radio listening audiences at the local market level with diaries placed in homes (supplemented by telephone interviewing). About 2 million households are contacted each year.
5. *Burke International Research.* Custom research in marketing and advertising, especially day-after recall of TV commercials on-air, all of which is done by telephone surveys.
6. *Market Facts.* Activities include (*a*) field surveys, (*b*) Marketest store audit system, (*c*) national telephone center (CRT interviewing via WATS), (*d*) consumer mail panels, and (*e*) Consumer Opinion Forum.
7. *Westat Inc.* Market research studies conducted via personal interview, telephone, or mail for civilian agencies of the U.S. government.
8. *Audits & Surveys.* Services include Retail Census of Product Distribution (a study of products and brands in some 40,000 retail outlets); National Total-Market Audit (provides data on market size/market shares); sales by outlet type, region, and size of city; inventory levels and percentage of distribution and out-of-stock situations; National Restaurant Market Index (samples 6,000 restaurants to determine purchasing habits); Selling-Areas Distribution Index (reports on package facings, shelf price, and promotional activity using 2,375 supermarkets as its sample).
9. *Marketing and Research Counselors.* A full-service, custom research house, using telephone survey WATS facility.
10. *ASI Market Research.* Specializes in controlled audience pretesting of TV commercials, print advertising pretesting, surveys, and focus group interviews.

Figure 8–4 Leading research companies and what they do. Listed in order of rank according to revenue received for research services.

Using marketing research for new-product development

You are a marketing manager for a major manufacturer of ethical drug products, and management has indicated an interest in marketing a line of products to the proprietary market. After considerable brainstorming, you determine that your company has the research and development capability to produce a superior line of proprietary vitamin products which could be sold through your normal distribution channels.

The problem is to assess the opportunities to get into the over-the-counter vitamin business and to obtain volume share and profit levels consistent with corporate criteria.

The first step in obtaining the required information on the vitamin market is to consult available reference guides (see the chart). These will lead you to most of the important sources specific to the normal market. Additional information can be obtained through direct contact with qualified persons at the sources. In most cases they will lead you to less obvious data sources, which may turn up information of key significance to your overall findings. At this stage you will also reach the "industry experts" who may confirm (or deny) your assessment of the opportunities to participate in the vitamin market. Having systematically gone through all these steps, your search is completed. With 50 pounds of data, however, your real job has just begun.

A guide to obtaining information on the vitamin market

	U.S. government	Trade and other organizations	Consumer/ business press	Business and medical indexes and services and directories
Reference guides	U.S. Government Organizational Manual Federal Statistical Directory Government reports and announcements	Encyclopedia of Associations	Business Standard Rate & Data Service Consumer Standard Rate & Data Service	Business Periodicals Index Funk & Scott Index of Corporations & Industries Index Medicus Thomas Register of American Corporations Pharmaceutical News Index
Sources specific to the vitamin market				
Issues				
Nature of the product Vitamins and how they are used New products and/or external issues influencing the market	National Technical Information Service (Department of Commerce) National Center for Health Statistics (HEW)	Vitamin Information Bureau American Dietetic Association National Science Foundation	Consumer Reports Today's Health Drug Topics Prevention Magazine American Druggist Product Marketing	Specific articles appearing in: Consumer Reports Today's Health Drug Topics Prevention Magazine American Druggist Product Marketing Journal of the AMA New England Journal of Medicine FDA Reports (newsletter)

	U.S. Government	Trade and other organizations	Consumer/business press	Business and medical indexes and services and directories
Sources specific to the vitamin market				
Role of government				
Impact of existing and potential government rules and regulations	Food & Drug Administration (HEW) Reports of congressional committees	The Proprietary Association Pharmaceutical Manufacturing Association Consumer groups	Articles appearing in business magazines, drug trade books, and medical journals	Pharmaceutical News Index FDA Reports
Competition				
Nature of the competition and extent of leverage in the market	Form 10-k's (SEC)		Articles appearing in business magazines and drug trade books	Moody's Industrial Manual Standard & Poor's corporation records Value Line Investment Survey Dun & Bradstreet Reports National Investment Library annual report Disclosure, Inc. annual report Thomas Register of American Corporations
Advertising				
Kinds and levels of advertising support Creative strategies employed by advertisers			Advertising Age Marketing Communications	Leading National Advertisers Publishers Information Bureau
Consumer behavior				
Level of vitamin usage by consumers Consumers' perceptions and attitudes concerning vitamins	National Technical Information Service (Department of Commerce) National Center for Health Statistics (HEW)	Consumer groups	Prevention Magazine Readership studies of general consumer and trade magazines	Findex-Directory of Market Research Reports, Studies & Surveys

Using marketing research *(continued)*

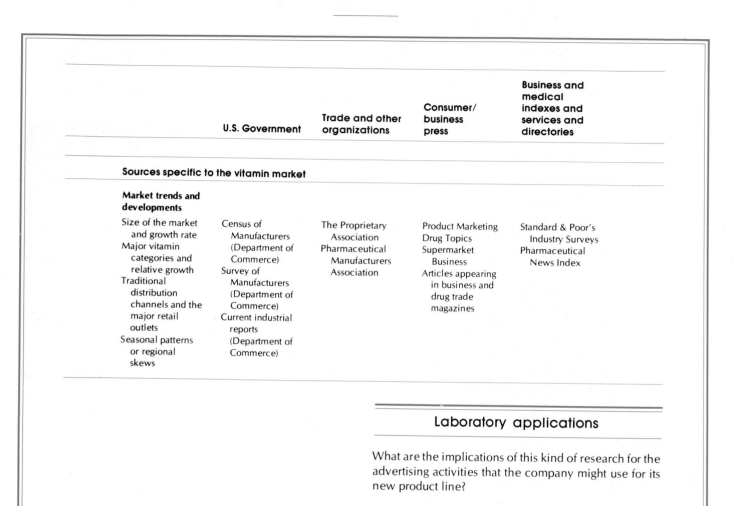

	U.S. Government	Trade and other organizations	Consumer/ business press	Business and medical indexes and services and directories
Sources specific to the vitamin market				
Market trends and developments				
Size of the market and growth rate Major vitamin categories and relative growth Traditional distribution channels and the major retail outlets Seasonal patterns or regional skews	Census of Manufacturers (Department of Commerce) Survey of Manufacturers (Department of Commerce) Current industrial reports (Department of Commerce)	The Proprietary Association Pharmaceutical Manufacturers Association	Product Marketing Drug Topics Supermarket Business Articles appearing in business and drug trade magazines	Standard & Poor's Industry Surveys Pharmaceutical News Index

Laboratory applications

What are the implications of this kind of research for the advertising activities that the company might use for its new product line?

audience count by means of an instrument hooked to TV sets, or a study of the way consumers react to products displayed in the supermarket.

The Pet Milk Company at one point radically changed its evaporated milk label and introduced the new label in the Detroit market. Researchers posted themselves near the evaporated milk section of supermarkets and observed how customers responded to the new label. Since it was apparent from observation that the label was causing a great deal of consumer confusion, and since retail orders were severely depressed, the label was withdrawn from distribution.[10]

Experimental method This is a type of research designed to measure actual cause-and-effect relationships. Strict controls are used so that the variable that causes the effect can be determined. This method is used primarily in test marketing new products in isolated markets and in testing new advertising campaigns prior to national introduction. However, the method is expensive and not easy to use, since it is very difficult to control all the marketing variables. (See the Ad Lab.)

Survey method This is the most common way to gather primary research data. By asking questions of current or prospective customers,

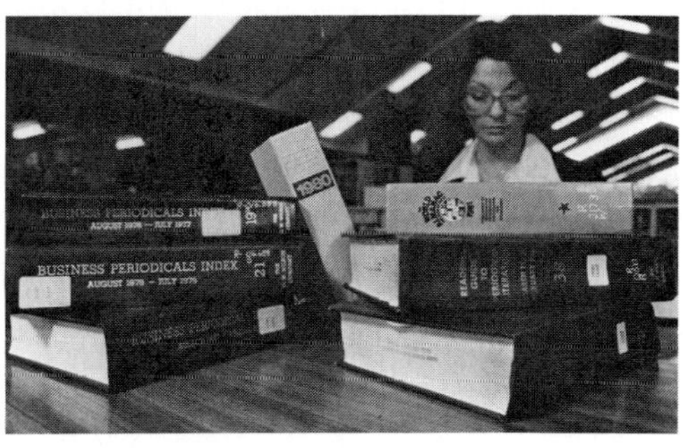

Figure 8–5 The *Business Periodicals Index* is among the most useful reference guides for advertisers who wish to conduct secondary research. It is available at most libraries.

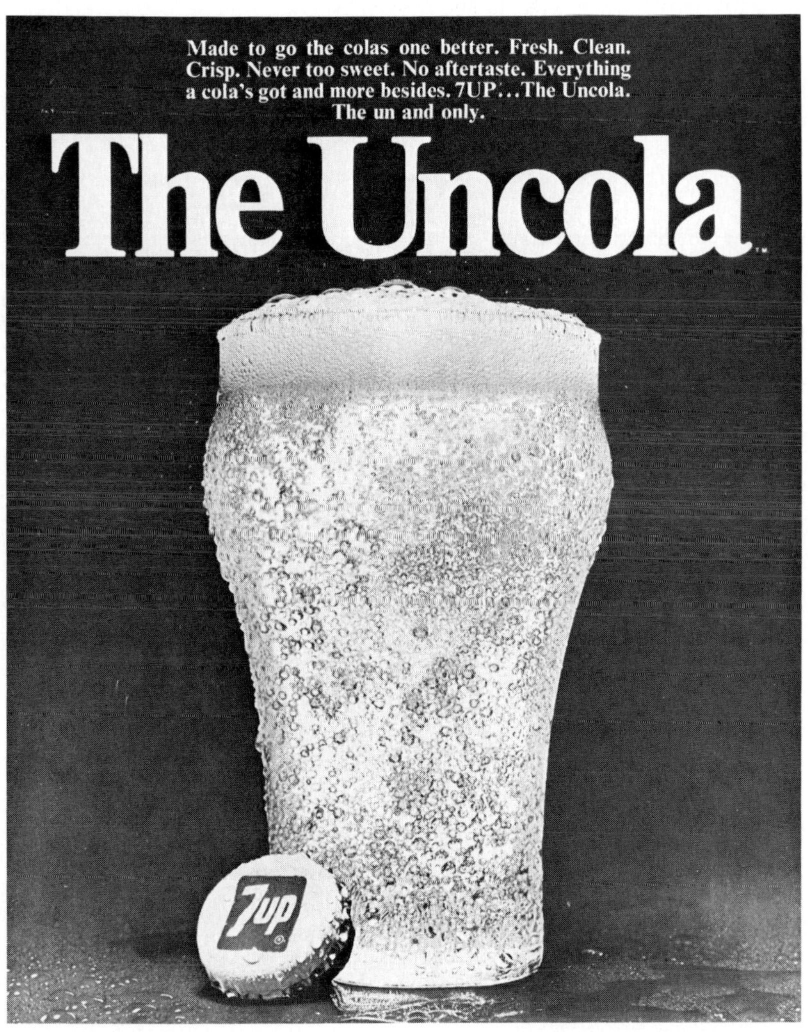

Figure 8–6 Seven-Up's famous Uncola campaign successfully positioned the product as an alternative to the cola drinks. The company, though, wanted more than just a Number 3 position, so it mounted its aggressive, new "lifestyle" campaign to take on the leaders. Only time will tell the merits of that idea.

the researcher hopes to obtain information on attitudes, opinions, or motivations. The political poll is one of the most common surveys with which consumers are familiar. The three common ways of conducting surveys are by telephone, by mail, and by personal interview. Each of these has distinct advantages and disadvantages (Figure 8–7).

N. W. Ayer decided to run what is known as a problem-analysis survey to determine the relative liabilities of 7up versus the cola drinks. Ayer asked consumers to rate the soft drinks according to several issues:

1. Contains ingredients that are not good for you.
2. Tastes too syrupy.
3. Tastes too sweet.
4. Leaves an aftertaste.
5. Is too heavy or filling after exercise.
6. Is not in tune with the lighter way people eat and drink today.

In every case the colas were rated worse than 7up, especially in the category of unhealthy ingredients.[11]

A simple experimental design using control and experimental stores

A simple example of a marketing experiment would be an in-store test to determine the effectiveness of a product display in generating additional sales. One approach to such an experiment would be to use two groups of stores, a group of *control* stores and a group of *experimental* stores. The control and experimental stores might be given the treatment shown. Unit sales of the product would be measured during the pretest, the test, and the posttest periods in both control and experimental stores. In the control stores, the conditions would be the same in all three periods. By contrast, in the experimental stores, the display would be erected during the test period. The effectiveness of the display in generating additional sales would be determined by comparing the sales patterns in the control versus the experimental stores and testing the significance of the statistical differences found.

Laboratory applications

1. What is the purpose of the control store?
2. Do you think a similar method could be used to test advertisements or media?

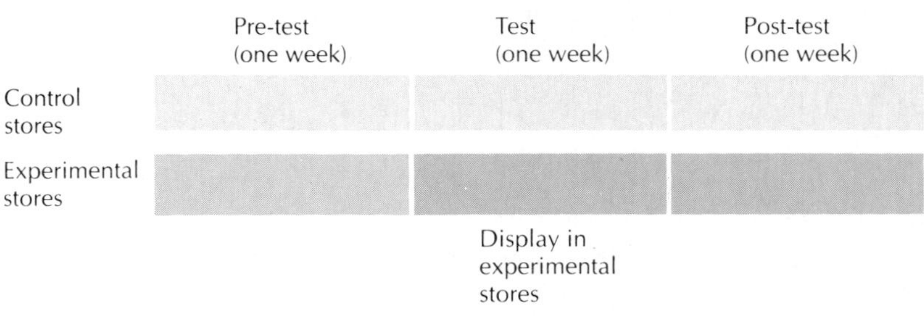

Elements of quantitative research

The three methods of data collection just described are used by market researchers primarily to develop hard numbers so they can completely and accurately measure a particular market situation. These *quantitative,* or descriptive, methods require formal design and rigorous standards for collecting and tabulating information. Only in this way can inaccuracies be minimized and the data be reliable for future decision making.

The success of these research projects, therefore, depends on several key elements. The most important are the sampling method used

Figure 8–7 Advantages and disadvantages of telephone, mail, and personal surveys

Survey method	Advantages	Disadvantages
Telephone	Fast, convenient method of obtaining even large numbers of responses in a short time	Poor for obtaining large amount of information or for asking difficult questions
	Relatively low cost per interview	Securing cooperation not always possible
	Sometimes good for reaching important people who are inaccessible	Obtaining a random sample may be difficult
	Respondents can be contacted at specific times of the day	Respondents cannot be observed while giving answers
Mail	Interviewer bias is eliminated since no interviewer is present	Extensive or complex questionnaires usually yield poor results
	Questionnaire may be answered more accurately since respondents can fill out the forms at their leisure	Respondent's interest in the subject under investigation has a direct effect on returns
	Good for reaching people who are sometimes otherwise inaccessible	Good possibility of biased or nonrepresentative returns
	Comparatively low cost for reaching small and widely scattered groups	Respondents may be unable or unwilling to give answers without probing or stimulation from the interviewer
Personal interview	Most reliable of the survey methods because of face-to-face contact	Most costly method
	Questions can be longer and more complex than with other methods	Some respondents such as high-level business executives may be difficult to contact
	With skilled observation and probing, respondent can be encouraged to answer questions fully	Personal bias of individual interviewers can affect results
	Representativeness of sample can be well controlled	Reliability of face-to-face interviewing depends on integrity and skill of interviewers, which in some cases may be lacking

and the way the survey questionnaire is designed. We shall discuss these briefly.

Sampling theories When 7up wants to know what consumers think about its taste or its image, it cannot possibly ask everybody in the country. That would be too expensive and time-consuming. However, it is important that the results of the research accurately reflect the *universe,* or the entire target population, of soft drink consumers. Market researchers therefore select a *sample* of the population that they hope will represent the whole population. To accomplish this, they must make several basic decisions. Who is to be surveyed? How many people should be surveyed? How should the respondents be chosen?

A sample can be representative only if it reflects the pertinent characteristics of the universe the researcher wants to measure. Naturally, if we survey people who normally do not vote in an election, we are not going to get a result representative of the voters. The *sample unit,* or whom we survey, therefore, is very important.

Theories of sampling are drawn from the mathematical theories of probability. If nine voters in the same town say they favor Reagan and five say they favor Carter, what do you think the next voter you ask will probably say? If 99 voters say Reagan and 5 say Carter, the question might be easier to answer. Thus, if a sample is to be considered adequate, it must be large enough to achieve satisfactory precision or stability. Naturally, the larger the *sample size,* the more reliable are the results. However, adequate sample size has nothing to do with the size of the population. Good reliability can often be obtained with samples representing only a fraction of 1 percent of the population if the proper procedure is used. (See the Ad Lab.)

The two most commonly used *sampling procedures* are random probability samples and nonprobability samples.

Probability samples This procedure gives every unit in the universe an equal and known probability of being selected for the research. If a researcher wishes to know the opinions of a community regarding a particular issue, all members of the community would constitute the universe. Selecting various members of the community at random produces an unbiased sample and the most accurate results, but it also presents certain difficulties. It requires that every unit be known, listed, and numbered so that each has an equal chance of being selected. This is often prohibitively expensive, and sometimes impossible, especially in the case of customers for nationally distributed products.

Nonprobability samples This procedure does not provide every unit in the universe with an equal chance of being included. As a result, there is no guarantee that the sample will be representative. Moreover, the probable magnitude of the sampling error cannot be measured as it can with random sampling. Nonetheless, nonprobability samples are used extensively because they are less expensive, and less time-consuming and because random sampling is often not feasible. When only a general measure of the data is needed, nonprobability sampling can be very useful. Most advertising and marketing research studies use the nonprobability method.

How does sampling work?

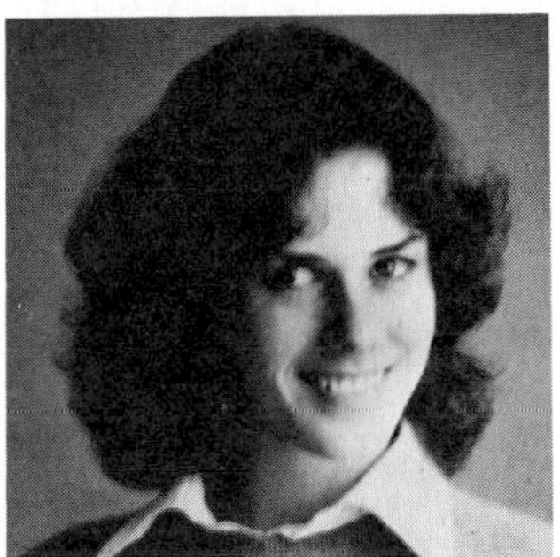

Most expert statisticians could give you some very comprehensive answers to that question. Probably too comprehensive, in fact, for anyone but another expert statistician. So let's explain sampling by using a photograph of a woman.

Picture No. 1 is composed of several hundred thousand dots. Let's consider these dots as our total population and draw several samples.

The three smaller pictures represent samples of 250, 1,000, and 2,000 dots. These samples represent a specific kind of sample design called "area probability sampling" because the black and white dots in the samples are distributed in proportion to their distribution in the original picture (more black dots in the hair, more white dots in the face, etc.). Think of homes (which add up to our population) instead of dots (which add up the pictures), and you have the sampling method used by Nielsen for arriving at national TV ratings.

Now . . . if you put the book down and step back a few feet, you'll notice a very interesting thing as you look at these small pictures. Your eye will adjust to the overall image and stop trying to "read" the dots. See how the 250-dot sample provides a recognizable picture? Recognizable, yes, but obviously not much detail. So, let's take a look at the 1,000 dot sample . . . again from a few feet away.

Now we find that the woman is *very* recognizable; in fact, if all we wanted was a reliable idea of what she looked like, this sample would be quite adequate.

Another interesting thing about sampling. The 1,000-dot photograph is about twice as sharp as the 250-dot photograph because it has *four times* as many dots. And so it is with sampling: to double the accuracy, one must *quadruple* sample size.

These are some of the basic sampling laws followed in constructing Nielsen's 1,200-home television sample. Just as the 1,000-dot photograph provides a reliable idea of what the woman looks like, the television industry regards the Nielsen sample as adequate in size to provide a reliable estimate of national TV viewing habits and trends.

250

1,000

2,000

Laboratory application

Under what circumstances could area probability sampling be used other than in determining TV ratings?

In the case of 7up, the nonprobability method was sufficient to determine taste preferences and product liability features.

Questionnaire design The construction of a good questionnaire requires considerable expertise (Figure 8–8). Much research bias is blamed on poorly designed questionnaires. Typical problems include asking the wrong types of questions, asking too many questions, using the wrong form for a question which makes it either too difficult to answer or too difficult to tabulate, and using the wrong choice of words.

Consider the simple question: "What kind of soap do you use?" The respondent doesn't know what the word "soap" means. Is it hand soap, shampoo, laundry detergent, dishwashing soap, cleansing cream, or dishwaster detergent? And take the word "kind." Does that mean what brand, what size, or what use? Finally, what constitutes "use"? Does that mean what do I buy? I might buy one "kind" for me and another "kind" for my husband. I certainly "use" several different "kinds." Answering the question accurately is impossible. Worse, if the question is answered, the researcher doesn't know what the answer signifies and will likely draw an incorrect conclusion. (See the Checklist.)

There are many ways to ask essentially the same question. Figure 8–9 shows four commonly used methods that might elicit responses about the taste of cola drinks. There are many variations even within these four methods. For example, additional choices might be added to the multiple-choice format. Neutral responses might be added to the scale format. And there is obvious bias in the dichotomous question.

What is important is that the questions elicit a response that will be both accurate and useful to the researcher's needs. For this reason, it is advisable that all questionnaires be tested on a small subsample to detect any confusion, bias, or ambiguities.

Elements of qualitative research

At this point in the research, Ayer wanted to know why 7up had such a sales problem when it was rated better in quality and taste than colas. They devised a questionnaire to determine whether the brand's appeal was hurt by the consumers' perception of who drinks it. They developed a list of celebrities. Then in a series of shopping center intercepts, they asked people to tell what soft drink they thought each of these celebrities drank—7up or Coke. Do Telly Savalas, Baretta, and the Fonz drink 7up? Not on your life. They drink Coke. That's what people thought. 7up was perceived as a drink for women and white-collar workers.

Now Ayer knew. They had to give 7up a more macho image, or at least get rid of the effeminate perception. It was time to start creating and turn to other *qualitative* research techniques.

A variety of indirect research methods are used by marketers to understand the "why" of consumer behavior. Some questions, no matter how skillfully posed, create a problem for the consumer to answer. As we discussed in Chapter 7, it is especially difficult for consumers to give the real reasons for their product choices. Thus qualitative research is used more and more to enable marketers to

Hello! I'm from National Research, Inc. We're conducting a survey on soft drinks, and I'd like to speak to the member of your household who normally purchases soft drinks for this household.

1a. Do you or does any member of your household work for a soft drink company or bottling company?

Yes 1 (*terminate interview*) No 2

1b. Do you or does any member of your household work for an advertising agency or marketing research company?

Yes 3 (*terminate interview*) No 4

1c. Do you or does any member of your household work for a radio or television station, newspaper, or magazine?

Yes 5 (*terminate interview*) No 6

2a. Have you purchased any soft drinks for this household to drink at home in the past week or two?

Yes 7 No 8

2b. How many purchases of soft drinks have you made in the past week?

None 1 2 3 4 5 6 7 (or more)

2c. What soft drink brand do you usually purchase?

2d. *For each listed brand not mentioned in question 2c ask:* Do you purchase ______ for household consumption frequently, occasionally, or hardly ever?

	Frequently	Occasionally	Hardly ever
Canada Dry	1	2	3
Coca-Cola	4	5	6
Diet Pepsi	7	8	9
Diet-Rite	10	11	12
Pepsi-Cola	13	14	15
Royal Crown Cola	16	17	18
7up	19	20	21
Tab	22	23	24

Figure 8–8 Personal interview questionnaire. A questionnaire designed to collect information about consumer purchasing habits and attitudes toward soft drinks. Seven-Up may have used a similar survey to discover its competitive position in the minds of consumers. Note the variety of questions asked and the simple layout to facilitate use.

get a general impression of the market, the consumer, or the product. Some marketers refer to it as *motivation* research.

Qualitative research, according to Sampson, is usually exploratory or diagnostic in nature, involving small numbers of people surveyed on a nonprobability basis to gain impressions rather than defintions.[12]

Checklist for developing an effective questionnaire

One of the major frustrations of inexperienced market researchers is the development of a sound questionnaire. Too often the questionnaire is prepared, the survey is started, and about halfway through the third or fourth interview, it becomes apparent that respondents don't understand what information is being sought. Even worse is the case where the survey is completed and it is then learned that an important piece of information was inadvertently left out. In either case, the problem usually lies with the questionnaire.

Entire books have been written about how to develop questionnaires. The following is simply a checklist of those things which are often overlooked or neglected by beginning researchers.

☐ Explain the research objectives. Be sure the reason for the study is clear. Listing the objectives helps to prevent the inclusion of extraneous material or questions that "would be interesting to know the answers to" but are not germane to the actual study.

☐ Write the actual points to be determined by the questionnaire. Again, be sure the description of the desired information is clear and concise. Avoid long questionnaires that tax the patience of the respondent. When this happens, careless or flip answers often result, or the respondent finds reasons not to answer the questions fully.

☐ Break the items to be determined down into specific questions. Questions must be stated so that they are clear to respondents and there is no chance for misunderstanding. Avoid generalities and ambiguous terms.

☐ Write a rough draft first. Polish it after you've made all your points.

☐ Use a short opening statement. Include your name, the name of your organization, and the broad purpose of the questionnaire.

☐ Open with one or two easily answered, interesting, and inoffensive questions. This tends to put the respondent at ease.

☐ Structure the questions so they flow logically and easily from one to another. Ask general questions before the more detailed ones.

☐ Have as few "closed" questions as possible. Use open-ended questions where possible, although there are some problems with them:

- Open-ended questions let the respondent answer whatever comes to mind, but answers are difficult to tabulate.
- Most open-ended questions can be closed by providing a list of anticipated answers for the interviewer to check off. This simplifies tabulation.

☐ Avoid questions that suggest an answer or that could be considered "leading" questions. Let the respondent answer fully and honestly. Don't use words with strong favorable or unfavorable connotations. They tend to bias results.

☐ Make the questions easy to answer. Don't use long, detailed questionnaires which may confuse the respondent.

☐ When possible, include a few questions which will serve as a cross-check on earlier answers. This aids in ensuring validity.

☐ Put the demographic questions (e.g., age, income, education) and other personal questions at the end of the questionnaire.

☐ Pretest the questionnaire to get out the bugs. Your primary concern is to make sure the questions are being interpreted as intended and that all information being sought is included. Twenty to 30 persons in the proposed respondent group are usually a sufficient sample for a pretest.

The methods used in qualitative research usually may be described as intensive or projective in nature.

Projective techniques The idea behind this approach is to get an understanding of people's underlying or subconscious feelings, attitudes, opinions, needs, and motives by asking indirect questions or otherwise involving the consumer in a situation in which he or she can "project" feelings about the problem or product.

The survey Ayer conducted in shopping center interviews was one type of projective technique. These techniques have long been used by psychologists for clinical diagnosis, and they have now been adapted to marketing use. There are also many other types of projective techniques. All require highly experienced researchers to be used correctly.

Intensive techniques Using this approach requires great care in administering the questions as it is an extension of the interview method of research. One type, called the *depth interview,* uses carefully planned, but loosely structured questions to enable the interviewer to probe the deeper feelings of the respondents. The interviewer may talk to the subject for an hour or more in an informal setting to give the impression of an unstructured conversation and to set the subject at ease. Although these interviews are very helpful at discov-

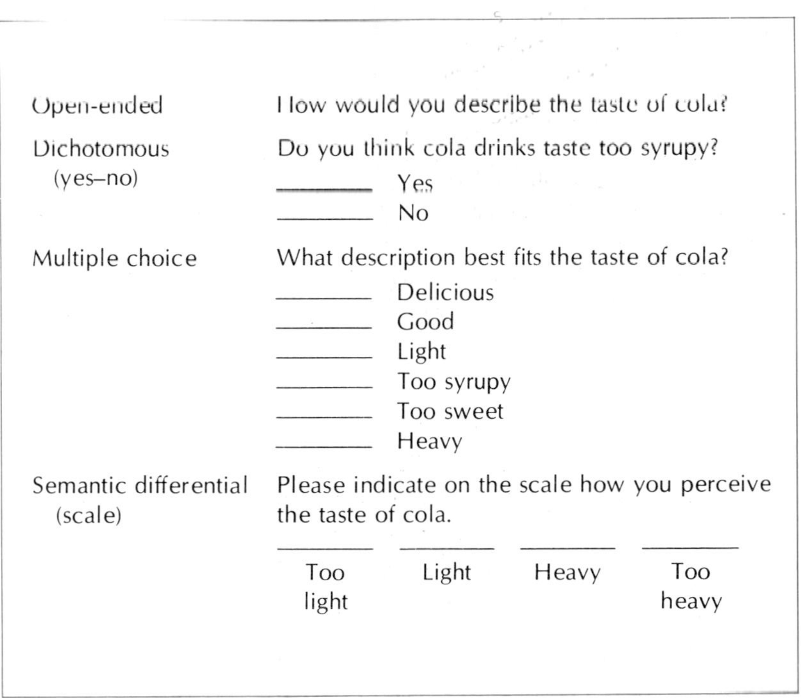

Open-ended	How would you describe the taste of cola?
Dichotomous (yes–no)	Do you think cola drinks taste too syrupy? ________ Yes ________ No
Multiple choice	What description best fits the taste of cola? ________ Delicious ________ Good ________ Light ________ Too syrupy ________ Too sweet ________ Heavy
Semantic differential (scale)	Please indicate on the scale how you perceive the taste of cola. ________ ________ ________ ________ Too light / Light / Heavy / Too heavy

Figure 8–9 Different ways to phrase research questions.

ering individual motivations, they are also very expensive, extremely time-consuming, and limited by the lack of skilled interviewers. For this reason, many organizations use group techniques.

The *focus group* method is one of the most useful. Six to twelve people, "typical" of the target market, are invited in to discuss the product, the service, or the marketing situation (Figure 8–10). A trained leader guides the often free-wheeling discussion for an hour or more, and the group interaction reveals the group's true feelings or behavior toward the product. These meetings are usually recorded and may even be viewed or videotaped from behind a one-way mirror. These groups do not offer sampling validity, but their thinking can often be used prior to a subsequent formal survey to assist in questionnaire construction.[13]

Figure 8–10 Focus group sessions are usually held in comfortable settings where participants can feel relaxed about discussing their attitudes and beliefs. The one-way mirror conceals recording or videotaping equipment and often agency or advertiser personnel viewing the proceedings.

Compiling and tabulating data

After all the research data have been collected, they must be organized, verified, edited, and tabulated. Answers must be checked to eliminate errors or inconsistencies. For instance, one person might answer a question "two years" while another says "24 months." These must be changed to the same units for correct tabulation. Some questionnaires may be rejected because the answers are obviously the result of misunderstanding. Finally, the data must be counted and summarized. For small studies, tabulation may be manual. But most research projects today require the use of sophisticated data processing equipment to count the answers and produce cross tabulations of the data.

For example, many researchers want a cross tabulation of product use by age group or other important demographic information. The researcher may take the raw data, apply advanced statistical techniques to them, and pass them through the computer again to seek additional findings. At this point, the cost of the research study can go through the ceiling if an unskilled marketer becomes enamored with the idea of seeing all the cross tabulations possible (Figure 8–11). The researcher must use skill and imagination to select only those crosstabulations that will show significant relationships.

Interpreting the findings

Marketing research is used to help solve management problems. The researcher, therefore, must prepare a complete report on the information that has been discovered and what it means. Tables and graphs may be used, but it is important that these be explained in words management can understand. The use of technical jargon (such as "multivariate analysis of variance model") should be avoided or at least confined to the appendix. The report should state the problem and research objective, a summary of the findings, and the researcher's conclusions drawn from an unbiased analysis of the data. The researcher's recommendations for management action should also be described, and the whole report should be offered with an oral presentation to allow management feedback and to highlight important points. A description of the methodology, statistical analysis, and the raw data on which the report is based constitute the report's appendix. (See the Checklist.)

Figure 8–11 How much does research cost?

(outside firm versus do-it-yourself)

Telephone:	
500 20-minute interviews, with report	
Outside firm	$4,500–$6,000
Do-it-yourself	$2,000–$2,500
Mail:	
500 returns, with report—33 percent response rate	
Outside firm	$5,000–$6,000
Do-it-yourself	$1,000–$1,500
Intercept:	
500 interviews, four or five questions, with report	
Outside firm	$5,000
Do-it-yourself	$350–$500
Executive interviews (talking to business administrators):	
20 Interviews, with report	
Outside firm	$2,500–$7,500
Do-it-yourself	Your time
Focus group:	
One group, 8 to 10 people, with report	
Outside firm	$1,500–$2,500
Do-it-yourself	$650–$800

Applying research to the advertising strategy

Thus far, we have seen how Seven-Up and N. W. Ayer, in a step-by-step process, discovered the product's problem of sagging sales, evaluated the competitive strengths and weaknesses of the brand, and measured consumer attitudes toward it. All this information was important for the development of the company's advertising strategy.

Overholser separates the objectives of advertising strategy research into three categories.[14] We shall call these:

1. Product concept definition.
2. Target market selection.
3. Message-element selection.

Faison refers to these three categories as Stage 1 of advertising research. Stage 2, he suggests, is research designed for concept development; and Stage 3 includes the pretesting of ads and commercials.[15] We add a fourth stage—campaign evaluation—which is research designed to measure the effectiveness of a campaign after it has run (Figure 8–12).

We shall discuss stages 3 and 4 in Chapter 24, "Evaluation of Advertising." At this point it is important to understand how advertisers apply the marketing research procedures we have discussed to basic advertising strategy and concept development.

Developing advertising strategy

We have already seen how Seven-Up used its initial marketing research results to discover which consumers were currently buying

Checklist for conducting a consumer survey

☐ Develop a list of specific survey objectives. Exactly what do you want to learn?

☐ Project a research timetable. How long will it take to get the information? Is the time span practical for your needs?

☐ Determine the method of sampling. Should you use a probability or nonprobability sample? How precise should the results be? What level of error can you accept in a trade-off with costs?

☐ Develop the questionnaire.

☐ Determine the sampling frame. In other words, on what basis will the sample be selected? Telephone directory? Subscriber list? Service station owners? Another basis?

☐ Develop the sample. Be sure that, if a probability sample is chosen, you encompass the entire universe. If nonprobability, what is the basis on which you select the respondents?

☐ Do the field work. In some instances, if you are directing the study, your job may include hiring, training, and supervising the field force or the group that will gather the data.

☐ Verify the field work. Be sure arrangements are made for verification of a certain amount of the data gathered from the sample. This step is crucial if the results are to be used for decision making.

☐ Tabulate the data.

☐ Analyze the results. What are the major findings? Any important new information, or further confirmation of what was suspected?

☐ Prepare the report. What form should it take? What charts and graphs should be included?

☐ Present the survey results. To whom will the material be presented? How formal will the presentation be?

7up and how the general soft-drink-consuming market perceived 7up as a product concept. Let's review for a moment the results of the Stage 1 research.

Product concept definition

Following its successful Un-cola campaign, 7up was positioned in the consumer's mind as an alternative to the colas. It was seen as more of a specialty drink, slightly effeminate, something for the white-collar class. As Faison points out, it is usually easier to position a product in a manner consistent with consumer attitudes and perceptions than to reposition it by emphasizing other uses or attributes.[16] Trout and Ries, the positioning gurus, would agree. In fact, they had complimented Seven-Up for years for their effective campaign positioning the drink as the Un-Cola. And it is likely that Trout and Ries would disagree with Seven-Up's decision to change strategy. They believe it is virtually fruitless to try to dislodge a market leader unless the leader is making serious positioning mistakes.

Seven-Up, though, wanted to reposition the product to compete

Figure 8–12 Advertising research at stages of advertising development

	Stage 1 Research: Strategy determination	**Stage 2 Research: Concept development**	**Stage 3 Research: Rough production**	**Stage 4 Research: Post-testing**
Timing	Before creative work begins	Before agency production begins	Before finished artwork and photography	After the campaign has run
Research problem	Product-class definition Prospect-group selection Message-element selection	Concept testing Name testing Slogan testing	Print pretesting Television storyboard pretesting Radio commercial pretesting	Advertising effectiveness Consumer attitude change Sales increases
Techniques	Consumer-attitude and usage studies	Free-association tests Qualitative interviews Statement-comparison tests	Consumer jury Matched samples Portfolio tests Storyboard test Mechanical devices Psychological rating scales	Aided recall Unaided recall Sales tests Inquiry tests Attitude tests

head-to-head with the colas. For this reason, they were willing (and knew they had) to commit many more dollars to their new campaign. Through the expensive and time-consuming process of repositioning the brand, Seven-Up hoped they could change the consumer perception of the product concept. Of course, only time will tell the correctness of their decision.

Target market selection

Seven-Up's studies showed that the product's heavy users were mostly women and older people. Similarly, the user profile studies we mentioned showed that people didn't perceive 7up as a drink for the active, outdoor, rugged, two-fisted set. Yet taste and quality tests showed 7up to be appropriate for that more active lifestyle, and the company knew that was where the big market was. Again, the product needed to be repositioned if it was going to be attractive to the 15–34 age group, which the company wanted to target.

Message-element selection

According to Faison, studies on message-element selection are "concerned with the likes and dislikes of the consumers in relation to the brands and products being considered, focusing on the particular themes and claims that may be promising."[17] The attitude studies Ayer had conducted pointed up numerous possible message-elements that might be used: colas were too sweet and syrupy, 7up left no after-taste, etc. The agency decided to begin concept testing in order to discover which of the message-element options might prove most successful in the repositioning effort. This would be the company's Stage 2 research aimed at advertising concept development.

Concept testing

Ayer prepared five tentative advertising layouts, each with an illustration and a headline stressing a different 7up appeal, as listed in Figure 8–13.[18] The agency then gathered numerous focus groups of volunteer consumers into their unique "developmental lab," which combines intensive qualitative interviews with certain quantitative techniques. While a discussion leader moderated the conversation, each group was shown the series of ads and their reactions were measured as well as taped and observed by Ayer staff behind a one-way mirror.

The focus groups were nearly unanimous in their choice: active lifestyle. Two thirds of the participants liked that theme compared with an approval rating of only 35 percent for the runner-up—carbonation. The reason for their choice was clear. They spoke about their desire to enjoy a more active life, one that was more in tune with nature. 7up fit that desire, they said, using words like "clear," "crisp," "clean," "sparkling," and "light" to describe the product. They also liked the illustration that Ayer used with the theme. It

Carbonation: Studies had shown that consumers thought there was more carbonation in 7up than in colas. To blunt that criticism, Ayer tried to transform carbonation into an attribute. Copy: "The bubbling soft drink that bursts into taste."

Not syrupy: This would take advantage of 7up's less syrupy taste compared to the colas. Copy: "I was raised on syrupy soft drinks, but now I feel like a 7up."

Active lifestyle: The goal here was to couple 7up with words like healthy, energetic, informal, casual, and natural. Copy: "7up fits the way Americans are today."

Thirst: Research had shown that soft-drink users prefer 7up over the colas as a thirst quencher. This would work off that appeal. Copy: "For the big thirst, America puts the grip on 7up."

Taste: This pitch cut back to the marked and unmarked bottle tests, which revealed drinker preference for the taste of 7up. Copy: "In taste tests, six out of ten people had a 'clear' favorite."

Figure 8–13 Five models for 7up.

showed people of various ages and races enjoying themselves together, outdoors, with a refreshing 7up.

To confirm their findings, Ayer used another technique. Taking the same illustration, they removed the name 7up from the cans and changed the headline to read "____ fits the way Americans are today." They then asked consumers to fill in the blank with either 7up or one of the colas. Three quarters named 7up.

That was it. That was the day Pat Cunningham retired to his office and came up with the hit slogan that John Kidwell would later approve and on which the company would stake its future: "America's Turning 7up."

Summary

Marketing research is defined as the systematic gathering, recording, and analyzing of data about problems relating to the marketing of goods and services. Marketing research is useful in identifying consumer needs, developing new products and communication strategies, and assessing the effectiveness of marketing programs and promotional activities.

In conducting research, the first step is to define the problem and set research objectives. The problem should be specific and measurable. The questions should be relevant to the problem. The information requested should be directly related.

The second step is to conduct exploratory research by analyzing internal data and collecting secondary data.

The third step in the research process is to collect primary data. This may be done by observation, experiment, or survey. Primary research projects may be either quantitative or qualitiative in nature.

Quantitative research is used to accurately measure a particular market situation. The success of these projects depends on the sampling methods used and the way the survey questionnaire is designed. The two most commonly used sampling procedures are random probability sample and nonprobability sample. Questionnaires must be designed to be both accurate and useful to the researcher's needs. It is advisable, therefore, that all questionnaires be tested on a subsample to detect any confusion, bias, or ambiguity.

Qualitative research is used to enable marketers to get a general impression of the market. It normally involves small numbers of people sampled on a nonprobability basis to gain impressions rather than definitions. The methods used in qualitiative research may be projective techniques or intensive techniques.

The final steps in the research process are compiling and tabulating the data and interpreting the findings in a way they can be understood.

The results of marketing research are used to develop advertising strategy and to test advertising concepts. Research results help the marketer define the product concept, select the target market, and develop the primary advertising message elements.

Questions for review

1. If marketing research is so important to advertisers, why are so many able to succeed without using it?
2. What is the difference between marketing research and market research?
3. What are the advantages and disadvantages of using secondary data rather than primary data?
4. When have you used observational research personally? Describe the situation.
5. What is the difference between quantitative and qualitative research?
6. When have you used experimental research personally? Describe the situation.
7. What are the major methods of surveying? Which is the most costly?
8. What are the advantages and disadvantages of the two most common sampling procedures?
9. What are the five major pitfalls in designing a questionnaire?
10. How does research help in the development of advertising strategy?

9

Marketing and advertising planning

It was 1971 and the war was getting tougher—not the war in Vietnam, or in the Mideast, or in Africa, but the war in New York. The giant axis forces of P&G and C/P together had annihilated most of the insurgent guerrillas. Every year they captured more hostages. By 1971 they controlled 73 percent of the territory and bodies were strewn everywhere. The little army of L.B. held only 17 percent of the land and they were being squeezed on all sides. They had to fight or run.

With their backs to the wall down on Park Avenue, they decided to attack with new forces, reinforcements, and millions of dollars worth of armaments. C/P's generals were only a few blocks down the street, and they watched with dismay as the new L.B. recruits started marching . . . and marching. Suddenly the generals lost their foothold on some prime territory. P&G's generals meanwhile were a thousand miles away in Cincinnati, and before they knew it their forces too lost some important real estate.

The battle waged on year after year. And year after year the little army from L.B. kept pouring in more reinforcements, more money, more armaments. By 1980 it had captured enough of P&G's and C/P's territory to be battling with C/P for the number two spot. The stakes were high and the competition fierce. Even today the battle goes on. After all, the toothpaste market is worth close to $400 million in sales every year, and every share point is tantalizing territory.

Marketing is war and the marketplace is the battlefield. (See the Ad Lab.) The consumer toothpaste market is no exception. Indeed, the 70s saw a very significant battle between the rival forces of Procter & Gamble, Colgate-Palmolive, and Lever Bros. for the dentrifice market.

Let's look at the condition of the battlefield in 1971 to see what really took place. The market was dominated by Procter & Gamble with its Crest and Gleem brands and by the Colgate-Palmolive Company with Ultra-Brite and Colgate. Together these giants controlled 73 percent of the total toothpaste market. Lever Bros., with its Close-up and Pepsodent brands, had only 17 percent (Figure 9–1, page 263). Their problem was how to tackle the leaders.

In the toothpaste field two benefit segments historically divided the market: the dental health segment and the cosmetic segment. The dental health segment is characterized by cavity prevention claims. The cosmetic segment includes fresh breath and whitening claims. P&G's Gleem and Crest were both in the dental health group. Lever's brands were both in the cosmetic segment.

The opportunity was in the growing dental health segment. In 1971 that represented 65 percent of the total toothpaste market. That's where all the P&G brands were, Colgate had one, and Lever had no entry at all. To make matters worse, Crest had made the first therapeutic claim in 1956 and had continued with consistent and effective advertising programs. In addition, the seal of approval of the American Dental Association in 1960, substantial consumer loyalty, and the largest advertising budget in the field (over $12 million a year at that time) made it a well-entrenched market leader. Colgate was dominant also, spending only slightly less than Crest. Lever wanted to join in this huge "profit party" but noted the number of recent product failures strewn about the battlefield: Cue, Fact, Ipana-Plus, and Stripe, to mention just a few.[1]

To tackle the leaders, therefore, would require a new product, very careful planning, an excellent advertising campaign, enough money to accomplish the objectives, and time.

The next year, Lever's new entry, AIM with Stannous Fluoride Anti-Cavity Ingredient, went into test areas and immediately achieved its objective of a 10 percent share of market. By 1974 the company reached its objective of national distribution and immediately took a significant share of the *national* market. By 1980, thanks to AIM, Lever was beginning to rival Colgate-Palmolive, which held the number two spot with 27 percent of the market. AIM had been a marketing and advertising success.

For our purposes, the AIM story demonstrates that advertising success usually depends less on creativity and more on strategy. Good advertising strategy depends on careful marketing planning. The process of marketing and advertising planning is the subject of this chapter and the means whereby we can bring together the topics of the last three chapters: marketing research, consumer behavior, market segmentation, advertising, and the marketing mix.

The marketing plan

What did Lever Bros. do to successfully enter the dental health care segment of the toothpaste market and carve out such a large share in so short a time? They didn't have nearly so much money to spend as either Procter & Gamble or Colgate-Palmolive; how did they do it?

Was it because of great advertising? Partly. But where did the ideas for the advertising come from? How did they decide what to write the ads about, where to run them, and what to say?

The answer lies in one word: *planning*. Successful advertising campaigns come from good promotional plans. Good promotional plans are based on solid marketing plans.

Yet, according to Richard Stansfield, author of *The Advertising Manager's Handbook*, "more money is poured down the drain—absolutely wasted—on advertising that doesn't have a ghost of a chance of doing its assigned job because of a dismal lack of adequate planning than for any other reason."[2]

Stansfield believes that an incredible number of companies are "afflicted with the debilitating Orville and Wilbur Wright syndrome—flying by the seat of the pants when it comes to marketing in general and advertising in particular."[3]

What is a marketing plan? And what is an advertising plan? What is the difference, and what is their relationship? Let's deal with the first question first so we can better understand the overall success of the Lever Bros. campaign.

What is a marketing plan?

Stansfield believes the written marketing plan is like a road map to the tourist. "It helps him find the right route, and once found, helps him stay on it." Inasmuch as marketing is the *only* source of income

The 80s: An era of marketing warfare*

The language of marketing has been borrowed from the military.

We launch a marketing campaign. Hopefully, a breakthrough campaign.

We promote people to higher positions. In divisions, companies, units. We report gains and losses. Sometimes we issue uniforms.

From time to time we go into the field to inspect those uniforms and review the progress of the troops. We have been known to pull rank.

In short, we have borrowed so many things from the military that we might as well go all the way.

We might as well adopt the strategic principles of warfare which have guided military thinking for centuries.

Military science is thousands of years old. Before the birth of Christ, professional armies led by professional soldiers met on the battlefields around the world.

Marketing, as a scientific discipline, is less than 50 years old. Marketing is long on "seat of the pants" thinking and short on theory.

Military principles can help bridge the gap.

"On War"

Our theoretical cornerstone and "textbook" for marketing warfare is the classic book on military strategy, "On War."

Written in 1831 by a Prussian general, Carl von Clausewitz, the book outlines the strategic principles behind all successful wars.

Two simple ideas dominate Clausewitz' thinking.

First is the principle of force. Says Clausewitz, "The greatest possible number of troops should be brought into action at the decisive point."

Clausewitz studied all of the military battles of recorded history and found only two where the victory went to the side inferior in manpower by a factor of more than two to one.

The vast majority of the time, the larger force prevailed. "God," said Napoleon, "is on the side of the big battalions."

The second principle is related to the first. It's superiority of the defense.

Take Napoleon at Waterloo. Napoleon actually had a slight superiority in numbers. 74,000 men versus Wellington's 67,000.

But Wellington had the advantage of being on the defense. Napoleon knew he had to attack before Blulcher's Prussians arrived. And, of course, the defense prevailed.

So this year we predict that Chevrolet will be the largest selling car, Crest will be the largest selling toothpaste, and McDonald's the largest fast-food company. Regardless of what the competition does and how much money it spends.

A well-established defensive position is extremely strong and very difficult to overcome.

The strategic square

So how do the principles of warfare apply to the marketing arena? It all comes down to what we call a "strategic square."

Look at this strategic square from the point of view of an entire industry: the U.S. automotive industry.

General Motors	Ford
Chrysler	American Motors

There are four major companies in the field. In broad general terms, what type of warfare should General Motors, Ford, Chrysler, and American Motors wage?

General Motors is the leader, gets more than half the business. Their primary concern ought to be defense.

Ford, on the other hand, is a strong number two. They are the only automobile company in a position to mount offensive attacks against GM.

Out of every 100 companies	
One should play defense	Two should play offense
Three should flank	And 94 should be guerrillas

Chrysler is a distant third and should avoid direct attacks, rather they should try flanking moves. Smaller, bigger, cheaper, more expensive, etc.

What can you say about poor American Motors? Head for the hills and become a guerrilla. The company should find a market segment small enough to defend. For AMC, the broad area of, say, "small cars" would be too overwhelming. American Motors simply doesn't have the force to defend such a large market segment. But Trout believes that the Jeep business is distinctive and important enough to protect and make the most of. AMC's claim to that portion of the market should be further extended to include other four-wheel-drive vehicles.

Offensive warfare

Let's look more closely at each of the four types of marketing warfare starting with offensive warfare.

Of course, the big question you're probably asking yourself is can you successfully attack a leader?

Colgate had a strong number one position in toothpaste. But Procter & Gamble knew a thing or two about Carl von Clausewitz.

"Many assume that half efforts can be effective," said Clausewitz "A small jump is easier than a large one, but no one wishing to cross a wide ditch would cross half of it first."

Translation: The ditches are filled with companies saving money for a rainy fiscal year.

P&G launched Crest toothpaste not only with a massive $20-million advertising budget, but also with a Cincinnati version of the English longbow.

The American Dental Association "seal of approval."

Crest went over the top and is now the number one selling toothpaste in the country.

Overtaking the leader is not that common. Most companies are happy if they can establish a profitable number two position.

How can anybody topple Listerine, the king of halitosis hill?

Let's see if Clausewitz has anything to suggest.

"The battle is more a killing of the enemy's courage than his soldiers. Blood is always its price and slaughter its character as well as name."

Which is what Scope is doing with its "medicine breath" attacks on Listerine.

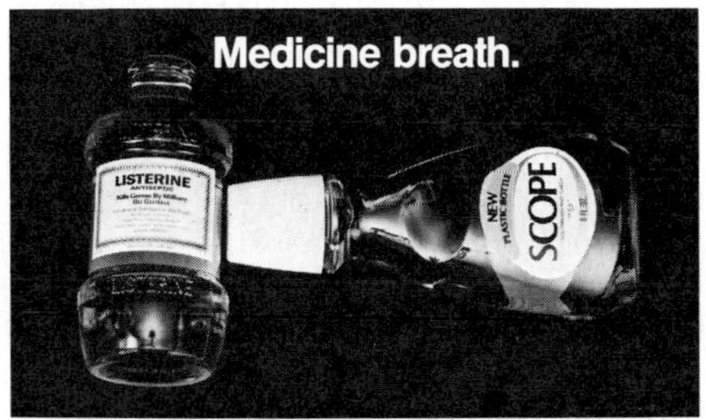

This attack was successful because they launched it at Listerine's weakest position. It improved Scope's position and secured its long-term position.

But, we should point out, Listerine is still the leader, by a long margin. A well-established defensive position is extremely strong and very difficult to overcome.

To sum up, here are the rules of the road in waging offensive marketing warfare.

1. The main consideration is the strength of the leader's position. Too many companies consider only their own strengths and weaknesses. No matter how strong a number two or three company is in a certain category or attribute, it cannot win if this also is where the leader is strong.

2. The attack should be launched on as narrow a front as possible. The "full line" is a luxury only for leaders. Offensive war should be waged with narrow lines, preferably single products.

3. The attack should be launched at the leader's weakest position. The only success that American Motors has enjoyed in recent years was with the "Buyer's Protection Plan" which was an attack against the poor serservice reputation of most General Motors dealers.

Defensive warfare

The battle of migraine mountain is an example of the advantages of quick response on the part of the leader.

Datril, as you might remember, opened up a war on Tylenol with a price attack.

But the Johnson & Johnson people obviously had read Clausewitz.

The 80's: An era of marketing warfare* *(continued)*

"Power used at the right moment against the right adversary brings more power."

Johnson & Johnson immediately cut Tylenol's price. Even before Datril started its price advertising.

Result: They repelled the Datril attacks and inflicted heavy losses on the Bristol-Myers entry which ended up with nothing to show for their efforts except a terrific headache.

Here are the principles of defensive marketing warfare.

1. Defensive marketing warfare is a game only market leaders should play.

2. The best defense is a good offense. A leader should introduce new products and services before the competition does. It's better to take business away from yourself than have someone else do it for you.

Says Clausewitz: "The statesman who, seeing war inevitable, hesitates to strike first is guilty of a crime against his country."

3. Strong competitive moves should always be "blocked." In a word, move rapidly and copy the competitive move. Too many companies let their egos get in the way. They "pooh-pooh" the competitor until it's too late to save the situation.

Flanking warfare

The third type of marketing warfare is flanking warfare. This is where the action is for most companies. Let's see why flanking moves are usually much more successful than head-on attacks.

Let's see if Clausewitz has any suggestions.

"Where absolute superiority is not attainable, you must produce a relative one at the decisive point by making skillful use of what you have."

In practice, this means attacking IBM where IBM is weak, not where they are strong.

As Amadahl is doing successfully on the high end and Digital Equipment Corporation is doing successfully on the low end.

Orville Redenbacher is successfully flanking the popcorn market leader with a high-priced brand.

Other examples of high-price flanking moves include Michelob and Mercedes.

Or as one wag put it: Who won the marketing battle between Cadillac and Lincoln Continental?

Answer: Mercedes.

Here are the principles of flanking marketing warfare:

1. Good flanking moves must be made into uncontested areas. DEC introduced a small computer before IBM did. Michelob was the first domestic premium-priced beer.

2. Tractical surprise ought to be an important element. Those Harvard Business School types with their phalanx of research experts often will snatch defeat from the jaws of victory by wasting time, the critical element in any successful flanking attack.

3. The pursuit is as critical as the attack itself. (Too many companies quit after they're ahead.)

Guerrilla warfare

The fourth type of marketing warfare is guerrilla warfare. Most of America's four million corporations should be waging guerrilla warfare.

As a glittering generality, out of every 100 companies, one should play defense, two should play offense, three should flank, and 94 should be guerrillas.

The key attribute of successful guerrilla wars is flexibility. A guerrilla should not hestiate to abandon a given product or market if the tide of battle changes.

"Capitulation is not a disgrace," says Clausewitz. "A general can no more entertain the idea of fighting to the last man than a good chess player would play an obviously lost game."

Here are the principles of guerrilla marketing warfare.

1. Find a market segment small enough to defend. It could be small geographically. Or in volume.

2. No matter how successful you become, never act like the leader. (No Cadillac limousine for the head honcho.)

3. Be prepared to "bug-out" at a moment's notice. A company that runs away, lives again to fight another day.

*In Chapter 6, Jack Trout and Al Ries presented the concept of positioning. In this chapter, they share their latest advice—approach the marketplace as though it were a battlefield!

Laboratory applications

1. Think of a successful product and explain its success in terms of marketing warfare.
2. Select a product and explain how marketing warfare strategy might be used to gain greater success.

for a company (except possibly for investments), the marketing plan may be the most important document a company can possess. The marketing plan triggers everything—production, selling, advertising, and research and development. It is the "how to," the key to the future of the company.

The marketing plan serves a number of very important company functions. First, it assembles all the pertinent facts about a company, the markets it serves, its products, services, customers, competition, and so on, in one spot. It also brings all these facts up to date. Second, it forces all the functions within the company to work together: product development, selling, credit, transportation, and so on. Third, it sets goals and objectives to be attained within specified periods of time and lays out the precise strategies that will be used to achieve them. Thus, it musters the company's forces for the marketing battlefield (Figure 9–2).

Effect of the marketing plan on advertising

If it truly does all these things, the marketing plan should have a profound effect on the company's advertising programs. For one thing, the marketing plan enables analysis, criticism, and improvement of all company operations including past marketing and advertising programs.

Second, it dictates the future role of advertising in the marketing

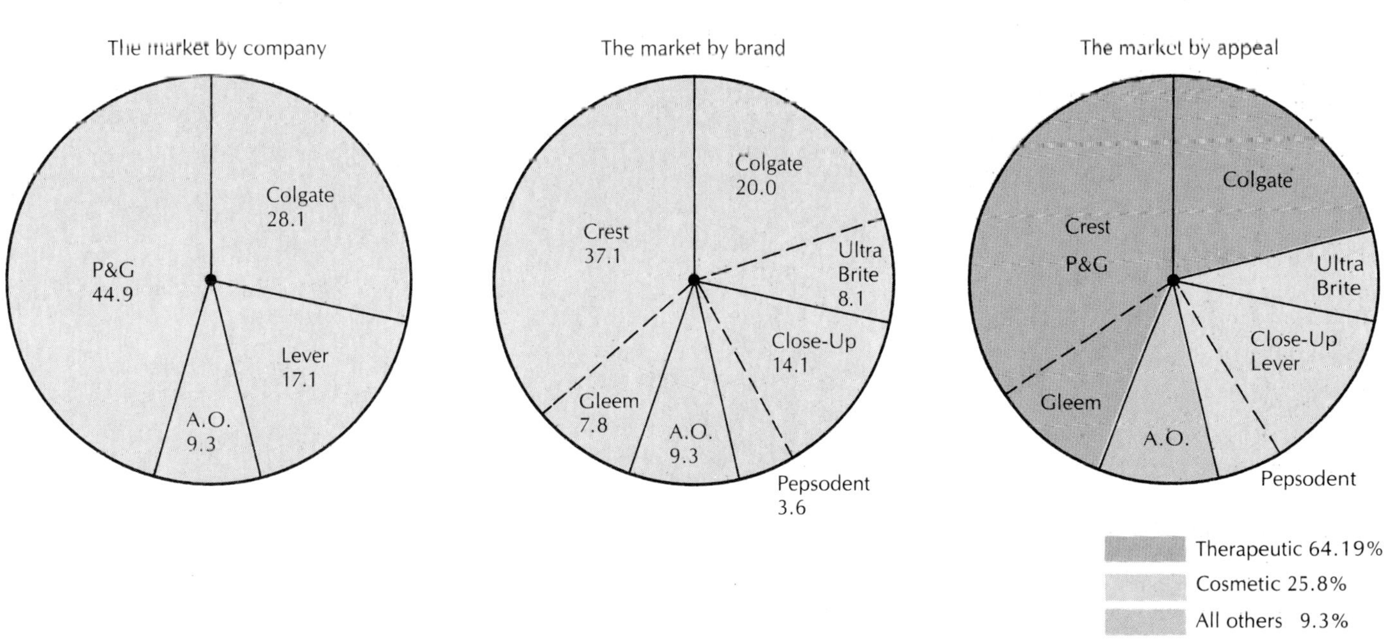

The toothpaste market in 1971 by company, by brand, and by appeal (in percentages).

Figure 9–1

mix. It determines those marketing activities that will require advertising support as well as those advertising programs that will need marketing support.

Finally, it gives direction to advertising creativity, enables better implementation of advertising programs, and ensures continuity of all advertising activities.

Elements of the marketing plan

The written marketing plan must reflect the goals of the company's top management and still be consistent with the capabilities of the company's various departments. The plan should be prepared with four principal sections: situation analysis, marketing objectives, marketing strategy, and action programs.

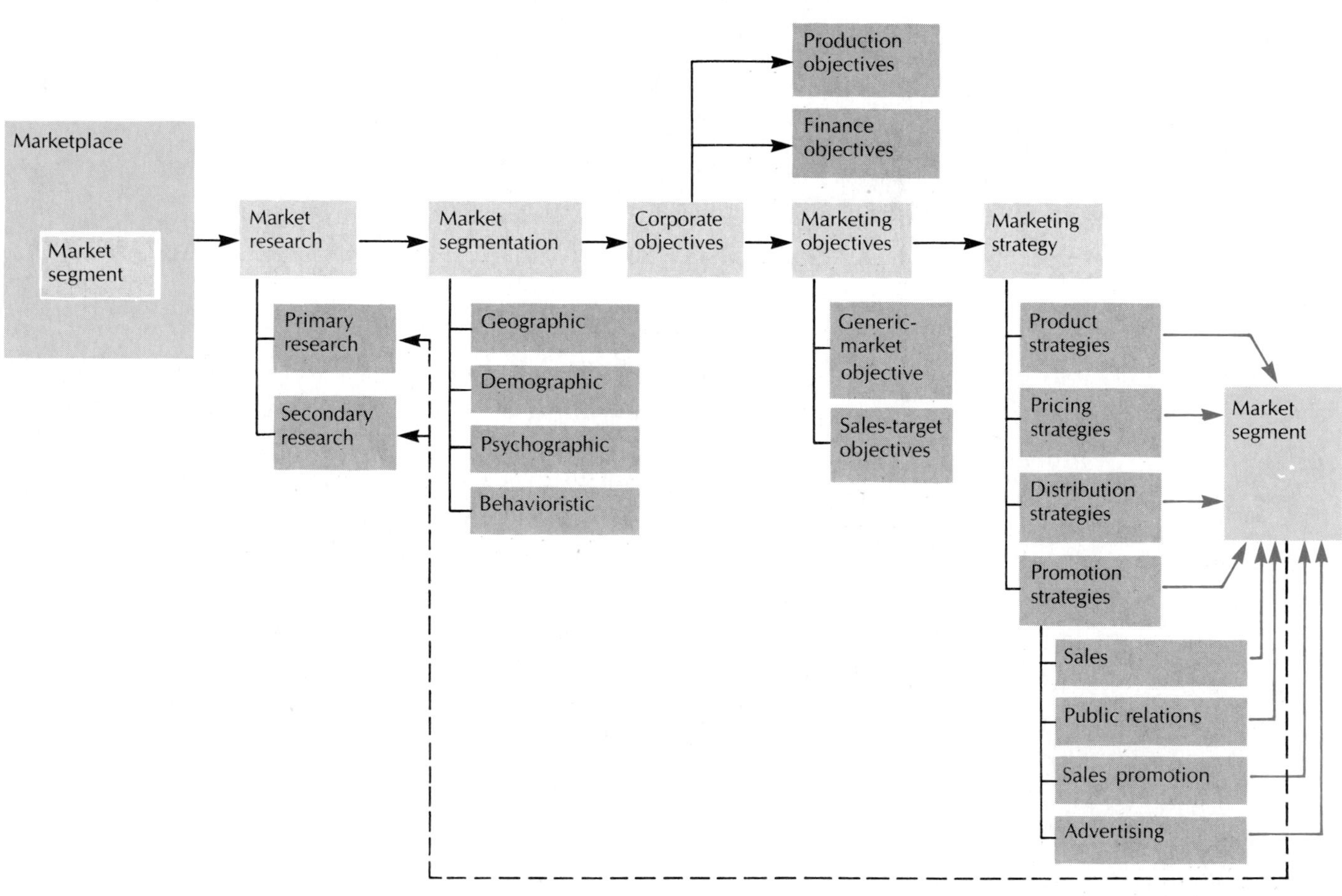

Figure 9–2 This "mustering your forces for the battlefield" model illustrates the marketing planning process. The process is a continuous cycle that begins and ends with the consumer.

Situation analysis

The situation analysis section is usually the longest portion of the marketing plan. It is a statement of where the company is today and how it got there. It should include all relevant facts about the company's history, growth, products or services, sales volume, share of market, competitive status, markets served, distribution system, past advertising programs, results of market research programs, company capabilities, and strengths and weaknesses.

The Checklist for Situation Analysis suggests some of the most important elements to be included. In addition, information should be gathered on key factors outside the company's immediate control. These might include facts on the economic, political, social, technological, or commercial environment in which the company operates. Only when these facts are completely gathered and agreed upon can management hope to plan for the future successfully.

The introduction to this chapter presented many of the facts included in Lever Bros.' analysis of their situation in 1971. In addition, Lever knew it had won consumer approval of the patented clear-gel toothpaste process used in its Close-Up brand in the cosmetic segment of the market. The question remained how to use what they had learned in the cosmetic segment to gain success in the dental health care segment.

Marketing objectives

Once the situation analysis is completed, the company can lay down specific marketing objectives to be attained within the time covered by the marketing plan.

Lever Bros., for example, determined specific marketing objectives for AIM for the first several years after its introduction. These might have been expressed as follows:

1. Introduce the product to test markets and achieve a 10 percent share of market by the end of the first year.
2. Achieve total national distribution by the end of the second year.
3. Achieve a 10 percent share of market nationally by the end of the third year.

These objectives must be based on the amount of money the company has to spend, its knowledge of the marketplace, and its analysis of the competitive environment.

The marketing objectives a company sets should be logical deductions from the review of its current situation, its prediction of future trends, and its understanding of corporate objectives. *Corporate objectives* are usually stated in terms of profit or return on investment. Or they may be stated in terms of net worth, earnings ratios, growth, or corporate reputation. *Marketing objectives,* on the other hand, should relate to (1) the needs of specific target markets and (2) specific sales objectives. Kotler refers to the first as *generic-market objectives* and the second as *sales target objectives.*[4]

The concept of a generic market is an attempt to shift management's view of the company from a producer of products to a satisfier of market needs. For example, many people feel that one reason the

Penn Central Railroad went bankrupt was because it viewed itself as a railroad company rather than a provider of transportation. If it had adopted the latter view, it might have been able to diversify into other more profitable techniques for providing transportation for people or

Checklist for situation analysis

1. **The industry**
   ☐ Companies in industry: dollar sales, strengths, etc.
   ☐ Growth patterns within industry: primary demand curve, per capita consumption, growth potential.
   ☐ History of industry: technological advances, trends, etc.
   ☐ Characteristics of industry: distribution patterns, industry control, promotional activity, geographic characteristics, profit patterns, etc.
2. **The company**
   ☐ The company story: history, size, growth, profitability, scope of business, competence in various areas, reputation, strengths, weaknesses, etc.
3. **The product or service**
   ☐ The product story: development, quality, design, description, packaging, price structure, uses (primary, secondary, potential), reputation, strengths, weaknesses, etc.
   ☐ Product sales features: exclusive, nonexclusive differentiating qualities, product's competitive position in mind of consumer, etc.
   ☐ Product research: improvements planned.
4. **Sales history**
   ☐ Sales and sales costs by product, model, sales districts, etc.
   ☐ Profit history.
5. **Share of market**
   ☐ Sales history industrywide: share of market in dollars and units.
   ☐ Market potential: industry trends, company trend, demand trends.
6. **The market**
   ☐ Who and where is market, how has market been segmented in the past, how can it be segmented in future, what are consumer needs, attitudes, and characteristics? How, why, when, and where do consumers buy?
   ☐ Past advertising appeals which have proved successful or unsuccessful in speaking to consumer needs.
   ☐ Who are our customers, past customers, future customers? What characteristics do they have in common? What do they like about our product? What don't they like?
7. **Distribution**
   ☐ History and evaluation of how and where product is distributed, current trend.
   ☐ Company's relationship with and attitudes of members of the distribution channel toward product/company.
   ☐ Past policies regarding trade advertising, deals, co-op advertising programs, etc.
   ☐ Status of trade literature, dealer promotions, point-of-purchase, displays, etc.
8. **Pricing policies**
   ☐ Price history: trends, relationship to needs of buyers, competitive price situation.
   ☐ Past price objectives: management attitudes, buyer attitudes, channel attitudes, etc.
9. **Competition**
   ☐ Who is the competition? Primary, secondary, share of market, products, services, goals, attitudes. What is competition's growth history and size?
   ☐ Strengths of competition: sales features, product quality, size, etc. Weaknesses of competition.
   ☐ Marketing activities of competition: advertising, promotions, distribution, sales force, etc. Estimated budget.
10. **Promotion**
    ☐ Successes and failures of past promotion policy, sales force, advertising, publicity.
    ☐ Promotion expenditures: history, budget emphasis, relation to competition, trend.
    ☐ Advertising programs: strategies, themes, campaigns.
    ☐ Sales force: size, scope, ability, cost/sale.

freight. The broader view allows management to consider additional options for the company besides what it has done in the past. Good examples of this are the oil companies, which now see themselves as producers of energy, not just gasoline.

As for sales-target objectives, they should be specific, quantitative, and realistic. If Lever Bros. had made the statement that their marketing objective was to sell more toothpaste than anybody, it would have been considered nonspecific, unquantified, and downright foolhardy. Rather their objective should be stated in precise terms such as "attaining a 10 percent share of the $256-million dental health segment of the national toothpaste market within three years." This objective is specific as to product and market, quantified as to time and amount, and, judging by the results, realistic.

Objectives may be expressed in a number of ways. For instance, many marketing organizations set objectives by the following criteria:

1. Total sales volume.
2. Sales volume by product, market segment, customer type.
3. Market share in total or by product line.
4. Growth rate of sales volume in total or by product line.
5. Gross profit in total or by product line.

Many other objectives are used as well, including: addition of new products; deletion of old products; development of new distribution channels or new policies regarding inventory control, pricing, and research; addition of marketing personnel; and retraining of field sales staff. Some firms today include objectives relating to social responsibility: statements concerning the preservation of natural resources, participation in community projects, and support of educational programs or institutions.[5] Regardless of what types of objectives are set, specificity is the key to their attainment and to the subsequent development of appropriate marketing activities.

As we shall see in the section of this chapter on the advertising plan, specific marketing objectives also have an important impact on the way advertising objectives are set. Only by setting specific objectives can management measure the degree of marketing and advertising success it is achieving.

Marketing strategy

The next section of the marketing plan is the statement of how the company is going to accomplish its marketing objectives. The strategy is the total directional thrust of the company, the "how to" of the marketing plan. For example, if you decide you must travel from New York to Los Angeles, your objective is to get to Los Angeles. Your strategy might be to take the train, to take the plane, or to go around the Horn on a square-rigged schooner. The last choice might be the most fun, but it would hardly be considered the most profitable or efficient strategy.

The strategy a company develops depends on the company's marketing objectives and the particular market being approached. The first step therefore is the selection of the *target market*. This will have already been accomplished to some extent through the market segmentation process before even setting corporate objectives. But the marketing director may pick more tightly defined target markets within the broader scope of the market segment.

For instance, Lever Bros. determined that it wanted to serve the health care segment of the dentrifice market with a new product. The marketing manager for AIM then had to select the appropriate target market within that segment. It might have been appropriate to select urban people concerned about the high cost of dental care. Or older people concerned about losing their teeth. Instead, AIM chose to target children "in the cavity-prone years." In a typical market segmentation strategy, AIM was designed specifically for the health care segment (because it contained stannous fluoride) *and* for the target market within the segment (because it was made to taste better to children).

The second step in the development of the marketing strategy is to determine a cost-effective marketing mix for each target market the company pursues. The mix will consist of particular levels of the four Ps (see Chapter 6): product, price, place, and promotion.[6]

What was Lever Bros.' marketing mix for AIM? First, a superior product, a clear gel with stannous fluoride, a well-designed package, and a memorable name AIM (Figure 9–3). Second, a competitive price and distribution system. Next, a promotional program that involved distribution of free samples to consumers, distribution of samples and explanatory materials to dentists, and a heavy advertising program consistent with share and volume targets.

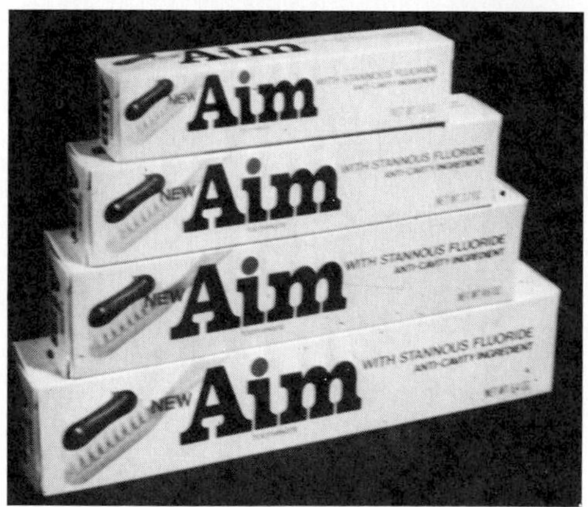

Figure 9–3 The clear gel toothpaste had won consumer approval with the earlier success of Close-Up. With a highly communicative package and a memorable name—AIM, with Stannous Fluoride Anti-Cavity Ingredient—Lever was ready to tackle the leaders.

There are many common types of marketing strategies. For example, a company might decide to increase distribution, initiate new uses for a product, increase or change the product line, develop entirely new markets, or go into discount pricing. Each of these tends to emphasize one or more particular elements of the marketing mix.

To determine the appropriate marketing mix, Kotler suggests that the company must first examine the wants of the market, and the position of competitors, and then decide on the competitive position it wants to occupy in the target market.[7]

David Ogilvy has said the first decision in marketing and advertising is also the most important: *how to position your product.* Ogilvy's agency developed the advertising for AIM and another Lever product, Dove. When Lever introduced Dove in 1957, the company decided to position the new product as a complexion bar for dry skin, not as a soap to get you clean.

> Dove's print and television advertising contrasted the effects of Dove and soap by showing pretty women taking the "Dove Face Test." Advertising promised that Dove "creams your skin while you wash," and supported that promise with a demonstration of the cleansing cream pouring into the bar.[8]

Dove had maintained its position for a quarter of a century, and the strategy had never changed. Every commercial still uses the same cleansing cream demonstration.

Companies usually have two choices in selecting a position. One is to pick a similar position next to a competitor and battle it out for the same customers. Another is to find a position that is not currently held by a competitor, a hole in the market, and quickly move to fill it.

Lever Bros. decided to position AIM against Crest and Colgate in the health care market segment and to use a *product differentiation* strategy to distinguish itself in the eyes of potential customers. Product differentiation, as we discussed in Chapter 6, is the efforts companies make to build unique differences or improvements into their products. AIM is an excellent example of product differentiation because it was the first really different fluoride toothpaste to take on Crest and Colgate. In the gel formulation, fluoride ion activity is significantly higher than in Crest. AIM disperses faster in the mouth than Crest. It is less abrasive than Crest, and taste tests show a preference of two to one over both Crest and Colgate.[9] In short, Lever Bros. had come up with a significantly different product, so their primary task was to tell people about it and get them to try it.

Instead of positioning itself against the competition through product differentiation, a company might elect to position itself through *price/quality differentiation.* It could offer a better quality product at a higher price, like L'Oreal, and use the theme: "You deserve the best." Or it could advertise the same quality at a lower price, like Suave, saying: "Why pay more for the same?"

There are many variations of product differentiation strategies, price/quality strategies, positioning strategies, and segmentation strategies. Finding the best strategy calls for generating creative alternatives. These must then be evaluated in terms of satisfying the needs of the marketplace, securing advantages over the competition, and creating company profits.

The particular marketing strategy a company selects will dramatically affect the advertising it uses. It will determine (1) the amount of advertising to be used (2) the creative thrust of advertisements, and (3) which advertising media to use. In short, the marketing strategy will determine the advertising strategy. To be effective, a marketing strategy must stand the test of time. It must be an ingenious design for achieving a desired goal, and it must be result-oriented.

Action programs

Once the overall marketing objectives and marketing strategy have been set, the company may determine what specific actions should be undertaken, by whom, and when, regarding each element within the marketing mix.

The *objectives* of a company indicate where it wants to go; the *strategy* indicates the general method and the intended route; and the *tactics* (or action programs) determine the precise details of the particular methods and routes it will use to get there.

In the case of a shoe company, a strategy may be to elect to produce a high-quality product, charge a premium price, sell only through better department stores, and rely heavily on advertising to promote the products. The action programs might then be to develop a shoe that will give two years of normal wear, be available at Bullocks and Macy's, sell for $55.95, and be supported by a $1.5-million advertising budget divided equally between television and magazines. On the other hand, the firm might determine that it would be more profitable to use a different set of action programs that would still be in keeping with the overall objectives and strategy.[10]

It is in this world of action programs that advertising campaigns live. In the next section, therefore, we shall discuss the process used for planning advertising.

In addition to the four sections of the marketing plan already discussed, most marketing plans include a section on measurement, control, and review, a section on resource allocation, and an executive summary at the beginning to briefly state the contents of the whole plan. Where these subjects relate purely to marketing, they are beyond the scope of this text. As they relate to advertising, they will be discussed later in this chapter and in Chapter 24, "Evaluation of Advertising."

The advertising plan

Richard Stansfield has decried the pervasive mediocrity of advertising. The fault, he feels, lies with inadequate planning, first on the marketing level and second on the advertising level. Advertising, he points out, is a natural outgrowth of the marketing plan. Once the marketing objectives and strategy have been determined, the advertising manager can begin to plan.

In fact, a company's communications or advertising plan is prepared in much the same way as the marketing plan. The same process of performing analysis, setting objectives, and determining strategy is followed. From that strategy, specific tactics or advertising programs are conceived and created.

Review of the marketing plan

The advertising manager's first task is to review the marketing plan. It is important to understand where the company is going, how it intends to get there, and the intended role of advertising in the marketing mix. The first section, therefore, of the advertising plan is a premises or situation analysis section. This briefly restates the company's current situation, target markets, long- and short-term marketing objectives, and decisions regarding market positioning and the marketing mix. From this information the corresponding advertising objectives and strategy may be determined.

Setting advertising objectives

Understanding the sales and profit objectives for particular products sold to particular market segments is essential to advertising planning. These are designated as marketing objectives, not advertising or communications objectives. These marketing objectives must be set before the advertising manager can determine the specific tasks assigned to advertising.

Due to poor planning policies, some executives of large corporations that annually spend substantial advertising dollars have little

People in advertising

Barbara Gardner Proctor

President/Creative Director
Proctor & Gardner Advertising, Inc.

The impressive career of Barbara Gardner Proctor, founder and president of Chicago's Proctor & Gardner Advertising, Inc., has been shaped by a series of "firsts." In 1963 she was the first black person in agency advertising in Chicago. Seven years later she was granted the first service loan ever issued by the Small Business Administration. She transformed it into the nation's first full-service advertising agency specializing in marketing to black communities, with a black woman as president. She built that agency into a $12.2-million business. Her client roster includes Kraft Foods and Sears, Roebuck and Co.

Before making her mark in advertising, Proctor gained acclaim as the person who brought the Beatles to the United States while employed by VeeJay Records. She had joined the firm as a public relations writer and then became an international director. She developed as an international jazz critic, feature writer, and record reviewer for *Downbeat* magazine.

Proctor started in advertising in the early 1960s as a copywriter for Post-Keyes-Gardner/Chicago. Five years later she joined North Advertising Agency as a copy supervisor. During this period she realized advertising was not only challenging and rewarding but also a way to create positive changes in the lives of black people. In 1970 she decided to form her own agency.

Proctor has directed the advertising for dozens of accounts, including Gillette, Paper Mate, FTD Florists, Maybelline, and Jewel Food Stores. Everything that goes out the door of her chic, ultramodern silver and white office, high above the Chicago River, is written by her. Before launching her agency, Proctor had never worked on promotion specifically for the black consumer market. Now most of her agency's output is directed to specialized black markets. But Proctor does not agree with the idea of a homogeneous black market. "There is no such thing as *the* black market," she says. "The black community is not one lump market, and that is the thing my agency deals with—segmenting the black community."

As to the advertising directed at blacks today, Proctor adds, "You would think that all we do is drink and smoke, that we eat only fast foods, and don't have much of a family life." Although these things are true of many Americans, she says, "It's all we get. You would not think from the ads, for instance, that a lot of blacks fly, despite the fact that we spend over $30 million a year going to conventions and meetings."

Likening her agency to an achievement in which all blacks can take pride, Proctor states, "I'm building a solid symbol, and black people are welcome to use it. I will be the best advertising agency in the business and I will be black. I will have one of the best offices in the country—and I will be black."

When asked what advice she would give to students on how to succeed in business, Proctor said, "Concentrate your energies on developing curiosity, self-discipline, and flexibility. The ability to succeed in the future will require these characteristics as our world continues to demand incisive analysis, concentrated expertise, and rapid adaptation."

The recipient of nearly 40 awards, including the American TV Commercial Award and the International Film Festival Award, Proctor was named by *Business Week* as one of the "100 Top Corporate Women in America." In 1976 she was presented an Honorary Doctorate of Humane Letters by Southern Methodist University. She is a member of the boards of directors of nearly a dozen national and regional organizations.

In a recently published anthology of elite black Americans, Proctor was the only self-made millionairess included. All the other women had either inherited or married money, but Barbara Gardner Proctor has worked for her success.

idea of the specific tasks or objectives of their advertising programs. Often heard are vague expressions such as "keeping our name out in front" and "giving ammunition to the sales force." Part of the fault for this lies with advertising managers, who have been historically fearful of defining specific, measurable objectives for advertising to accomplish. By stating misty, generalized objectives, like "creating a favorable impression of the product in the marketplace in order to increase sales and maximize profits," the manager protects the program from ever being measured for effectiveness. Such vague gobbledygook serves only to reinforce the negative attitude shared by many executives about the large amount of money "wasted" in advertising. The statement commonly attributed to John Wanamaker is typical of this misunderstanding of advertising objectives: "I know half of my advertising dollars are being wasted. I just don't know which half."

Understanding what advertising can do

To define advertising objectives, we must have a clear understanding of what advertising can do. Albert Lasker, who has been called the father of modern advertising, referred to advertising as "salesmanship in print" (see Chapter 1). He was a master of direct-action, mail-order advertising, where advertising actually closed the sale. *Direct-action advertising* attempts to induce the prospective customer to act immediately. This usually means clipping a coupon and mailing it in to order the product from the manufacturer.

On the other hand, *delayed-action advertising* seeks to inform, persuade, or remind its intended audience over an extended time about the company, product, service, or issue being advertised. This is the type of advertising generally used by retailers, manufacturers, banks, insurance companies, services, and associations.

The Waterford ad in Figure 9–4 is an interesting combination of a delayed-action/direct-action advertisement. The delayed-action objective of the ad is to inform and persuade the reader that a Waterford water goblet is actually a luxurious, decorative objet d'art, not just a water glass, and that it can be put to a wide variety of uses. To drive this point home, the ad solicits a direct-action response for imaginative ideas on how to use a pet Waterford goblet and offers a reward to the 100 best entries.

Advertising pyramid

Most advertising programs hope to eventually cause some action on the part of prospective customers. However, only a very small percentage of those exposed to particular advertisements are ever expected to act right away. A number of very important steps must be accomplished before customers can be expected to act. Numerous models of how the advertising process works have been created by advertising researchers. The Dagmar, Lavidge-Steiner, and AIDA models all begin and end essentially the same way, differing only in the intermediate steps (Figure 9–5).

A simple method of understanding the tasks advertising performs in preparing customers to act might be to think of advertising as building a pyramid (Figure 9–6). Before a new product is introduced, the universe of prospective customers is in the desert of unawareness, totally oblivious to the product's existence. Thus, the first step for the pharoah of advertising is to lay the foundation of the pyramid by making people aware of the product or service.

The next step is to give a portion of that foundation group enough information in order that they are not only aware of the product but that they also understand what it does and perhaps some of its features. The general objective of the second step is to increase comprehension.

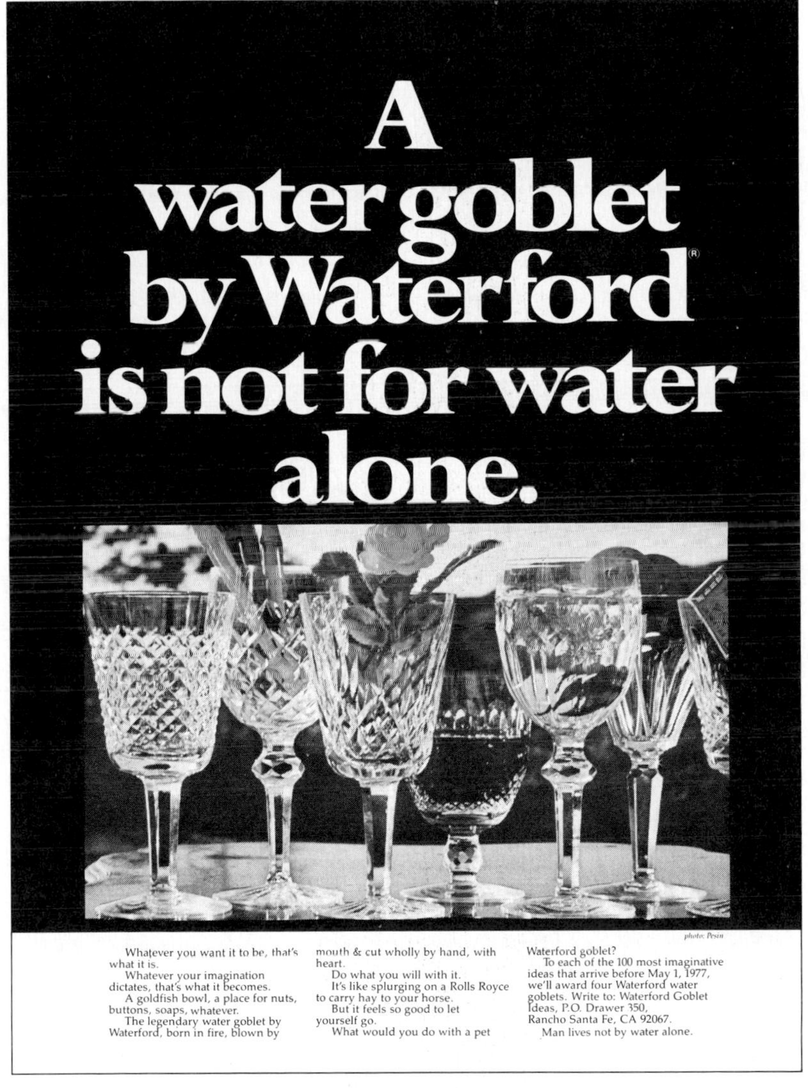

Figure 9–4 This beautiful ad for Waterford crystal includes a direct-action device to solicit responses. However, the primary objective of the ad is obviously not direct action. Had it been, the company would have included a coupon, bold-face type, or a similar device, in the headline.

Next it is necessary to communicate enough about the product and its features so that a certain number of people will actually believe in its value. This is called the conviction block. Of those who become convinced, some can be moved to the block of people who actually desire the product.

Finally, and only after all the preceding steps have been accomplished, the advertiser might expect a certain percentage of those who desire the product to actually go out and purchase it.

It's important to realize that this pyramid is not static. The advertiser is actually working in three dimensions: numbers, dollars, and time. Over an extended time, as more and more dollars are spent in advertising, the number of people who become aware of the product increases. Likewise, more and more comprehend the product, believe in it, desire it, and make the final action of purchasing it.

The objectives of delayed-action advertising, therefore, will change. At first the greatest effort might be spent to simply create awareness of the product. Later it might be centered more on creating desire or stimulating action.

In his book, *Defining Advertising Goals for Measured Advertising Results,* Russell H. Colley suggests that advertisers set "goals" that are specific as to time and degree and that could be based on research studies and tests.[11] For example: "to increase among 30 million housewives who own automatic washers the number who identify brand X as a low-sudsing detergent and who are persuaded that it gets clothes cleaner—from 10 percent to 40 percent in one year."

The problem with this is that it requires benchmark studies prior to the campaign and testing after the campaign, and it assumes that before and after results are simple and clear. This is rarely the case in the real world. Furthermore, major changes in attitude and awareness can be created by many events besides advertising, and sometimes, *cannot* be affected by advertising at all. For our purposes here in understanding the nature of advertising communication and the importance of trying to make advertising accountable, however, we will apply Colley's principles to Acme footwear.

Specific advertising objectives for the first-year introduction of the

Figure 9–5 Traditional models used to describe the advertising process

Dagmar	Lavidge-Steiner	AIDA	Adoption process
Awareness	Awareness	Attention	Awareness
Comprehension	Knowledge	Interest	Interest
Conviction	Liking	Desire	Evaluation
Action	Preference	Action	Trial
	Conviction		Adoption
	Purchase		

hypothetical Acme Company's new casual footwear line might read as follows:

1. Communicate the existence and availability of the Acme Casual Footwear line to 25 percent of the 10 million annual consumers of women's casual footwear between the ages of 15 and 49 years old who spend an average of $25 on each pair of shoes.
2. Inform 50 percent of the Aware group that Acme footwear is positioned as a high-quality, premium-priced line available from select local retailers.
3. Convince 50 percent of the Informed group that the Acme line is very high quality, comfortable, stylish, and worth the price.
4. Stimulate the desire within 50 percent of the Convinced group to try on a pair of Acme casual shoes.
5. Motivate 50 percent of the Desire group to actually go to their local Acme dealer and test a pair of Acme shoes.

It's important to note here that these advertising objectives are both specific as to time and degree and quantified like marketing objectives. That means that at the end of the first year, a consumer attitude study could be performed to determine *how many* people are *aware* of the Acme Company; *how many* people *know* what Acme makes; *how many* people *understand* the primary features of Acme casual footwear; and so on. If these results can be measured statistically, so can the effectiveness of the advertising program.

If Acme's advertising objectives are all achieved, and if we assume that all those who try them buy them, Acme would gain approximately a 1.5 percent share of the targeted women's casual footwear market (or $3.75 million in sales) by the end of year one.

The second-year objectives might be to increase the percentage of women who are aware of the product, perhaps to 35 percent. Then

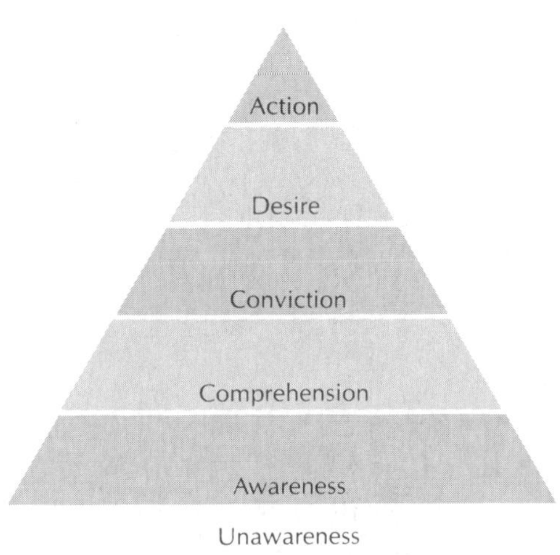

Figure 9–6 The advertising pyramid.

greater emphasis could be placed on persuading more of them to believe in the product and eventually to try it.

Lever Bros. speeded up this process in the introduction of AIM. By using heavy sampling of the product, they were able to convert many people from being totally unaware one day to being users of the product the next. This is extremely expensive. However, many manufacturers use couponing and other sales promotion devices to accelerate the long-term effects of advertising (see Chapter 19).

The marketing objectives Lever Bros. set were very aggressive. They had a new, unknown product. They were attacking a very loyal Crest market. Advertising objectives therefore had to be equally aggressive, including moving a lot of people into the action block right away.

When a certain percentage of people have actually made the purchase decision once, a new advertising objective may be introduced: to stimulate some percentage of past purchasers to repurchase the product. As more and more people make the purchase and repurchase decision, our pyramid diagram can be changed (Figure 9–7). A new inverted pyramid can be drawn on top of the old pyramid to represent the growing number of people who join the action block and develop the habit of purchasing and repurchasing the product.

The problem with this type of a model in real life is that it tends to oversimplify several complex phenomena of human behavior: how communication takes place, how learning is achieved, how needs and desires are stimulated, and how consumer purchasing actually happens. It also pays no attention to the dynamics of changing consumer tastes and preferences, to the activities of competitors, or to the fact that people can come into and leave the market continuously

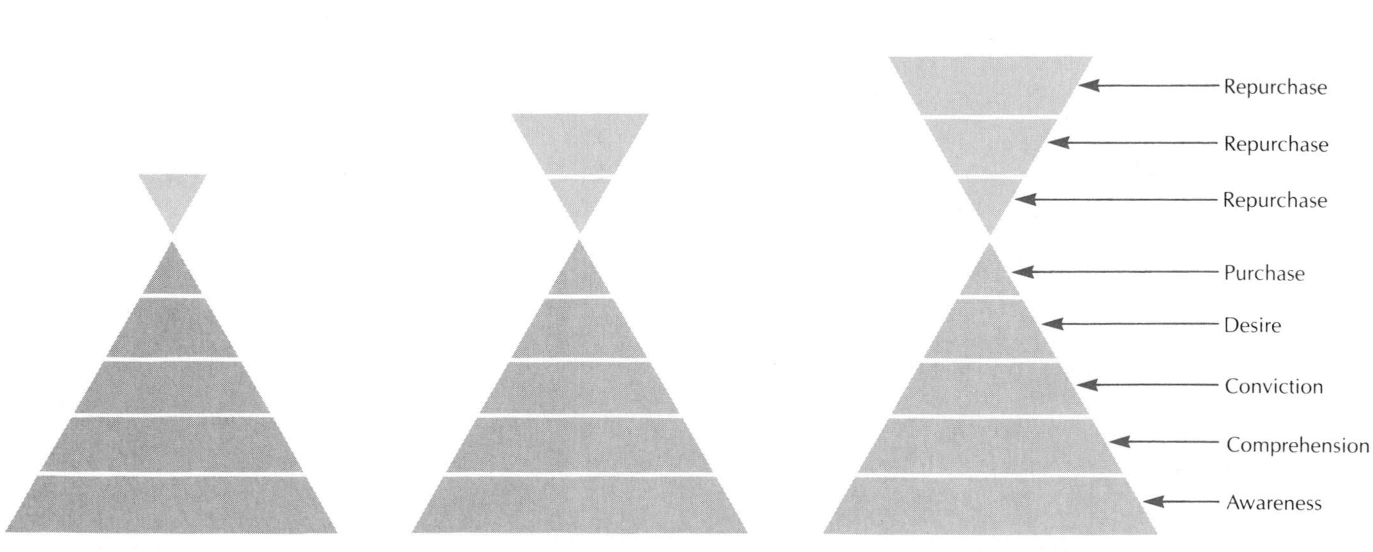

Figure 9–7 The advertising pyramids. As more and more advertising impressions are made, and as more and more people purchase and repurchase the product, new blocks of ever-expanding numbers of customers may be built on top of the original pyramid.

Checklist of advertising tasks

This checklist is a "thought starter" in developing specific advertising objectives. It can be applied to a single ad, a year's campaign for each product, or it can aid in developing a company's entire advertising philosophy among all those who create and approve advertising.

1. **To what extent does the advertising aim at closing an *immediate sale?***
   ☐ Perform the complete selling function (take the product through all the necessary steps toward a sale).
   ☐ Close sales to prospects already partly sold through past advertising efforts ("Ask for the order" or "clincher" advertising).
   ☐ Announce a special reason for "buying now" (price, premium, etc.)
   ☐ Remind people to buy.
   ☐ Tie in with some special buying event.
   ☐ Stimulate impulse sales.

2. **Does the advertising aim at *near-term* sales by moving the prospect, step by step, closer to a sale (so that when confronted with a buying situation the customer will ask for, reach for, or accept the advertised brand)?**
   ☐ Create awareness of existence of product or brand.
   ☐ Create "brand image" or favorable emotional disposition toward the brand.
   ☐ Implant information or attitude regarding benefits and superior features of brand.
   ☐ Combat or offset competitive claims.
   ☐ Correct false impressions, misinformation, and other obstacles to sales.
   ☐ Build familiarity and easy recognition of package or trademark.

3. **Does the advertising aim at building a "long-range consumer franchise"?**
   ☐ Build confidence in company and brand which is expected to pay off in years to come.
   ☐ Build customer demand which places company in stronger position in relation to its distribution (not at the "mercy of the marketplace").
   ☐ Place advertiser in position to select preferred distributors and dealers.
   ☐ Secure universal distribution.
   ☐ Establish a "reputation platform" for launching new brands or product lines.
   ☐ Establish brand recognition and acceptance which will enable the company to open up new markets (geographic, price, age, sex).

4. **Specifically, how can advertising contribute toward increased sales?**
   ☐ Hold present customers against the inroads of competition?
   ☐ Convert competitive users to advertiser's brand?
   ☐ Cause people to specify advertiser's brand instead of asking for product by generic name?
   ☐ Convert nonusers of the product type to users of product and brand?
   ☐ Make steady customers out of occasional or sporadic customers?
   ☐ Advertising new uses of the product?
   ☐ Persuading customers to buy larger sizes or multiple units?
   ☐ Reminding users to buy?
   ☐ Encouraging greater frequency or quantity of use?

5. **Does the advertising aim at some specific step which leads to a sale?**
   ☐ Persuade prospect to write for descriptive literature, return a coupon, enter a contest.
   ☐ Persuade prospect to visit a showroom, ask for a demonstration.
   ☐ Induce prospect to sample the product (trial offer).

6. **How important are "supplementary benefits" of end-use advertising?**
   ☐ Aid salespeople in opening new accounts.
   ☐ Aid salespeople in getting larger orders from wholesalers and retailers.
   ☐ Aid salespeople in getting preferred display space.
   ☐ Give salespeople an entree.
   ☐ Build morale of company sales force.
   ☐ Impress the trade (causing recommendation to their customers and favorable treatment to salespeople).

7. **Is it a task of advertising to impart information needed to consummate sales and build customer satisfaction?**
   ☐ "Where to buy it" advertising.

Checklist for advertising tasks *(continued)*

- ☐ "How to use it" advertising.
- ☐ New models, features, package.
- ☐ New prices.
- ☐ Special terms, trade-in offers, etc.
- ☐ New policies (guarantees, etc.).

8. To what extent does the advertising aim at building confidence and good will for the corporation among:

- ☐ Customers and potential customers?
- ☐ The trade (distributors, dealers, retail people)?
- ☐ Employees and potential employees?
- ☐ The financial community?
- ☐ The public at large?

9. Specifically what kind of images does the company wish to build?

- ☐ Product quality, dependability.
- ☐ Service.
- ☐ Family resemblance of diversified products.
- ☐ Corporate citizenship.
- ☐ Growth, progressiveness, technical leadership.

at various levels of the pyramid due to any of a million internal or external stimuli.

The hypothetical pyramid model does give a simple way of looking at the long-term building effects of media advertising. It also gives us the realization that as we find consumers at various levels of the pyramid, our communication needs, the objectives we can expect, and our strategies for achieving them all change. For new products building awareness will probably be our primary objective. For well-known, established products we will want to focus on building appeal. For well-known and well-liked products facing stiff competitive activity we will want to promote additional use with ads that stress action. (See the Checklist of Advertising Tasks.)

Advertising strategy

In the section on marketing planning, we learned that the marketing objective is where the company wants to be, whereas the marketing strategy indicates how it is going to get there. Similarly, the advertising or communications objective tells us where we want to be with respect to consumer awareness, attitude, and preference, whereas the advertising or creative strategy tells us how we are going to get there. Creative strategy is determined by the advertiser's use of the creative mix.

Creative mix

Marketing strategy refers to the way in which the marketing mix (product, price, place, promotion) is used. Promotional strategy (see Chapter 6) refers to the way the promotional mix (personal selling, advertising, public relations, sales promotion, and collateral) is used.

Similarly, the *creative mix* is composed of those advertising elements that the company controls to achieve its advertising objectives. These elements include:

1. The product concept.
2. The target audience.
3. The communications media.
4. The advertising message.

The *product concept* refers to the "bundle of values" the product might represent to the consumer. As discussed in Chapter 6, both the MGB and the Honda are medium-priced automobiles aimed at the American small-car market. However, the product concepts differ. One is conceived as a wide-open, fun, traditional sports car, whereas the other is conceived as sophisticated simplicity, practical, and easy to own.

When writing the advertising plan, the advertising manager should develop a simple statement to describe the product concept. To create this statement, the advertiser must consider the company's marketing strategy as it relates to the product. What is the product's intended position in the market? What is the company's intention relative to using a product differentiation or price/quality differentiation strategy? What stage of the product life cycle is the product in? How is the product classified, packaged, branded? All these influence the product concept.

What was the product concept for AIM? Functionally, it was a clear gel toothpaste containing stannous fluoride. Conceptually, it was a "modern, therapeutic toothpaste containing the world-famous cavity fighting ingredient stannous fluoride and offering more brushing incentives, color, texture, taste, and appearance, than any competing brand."[12]

The *target audience* refers to the specific people the advertising will approach. In the marketing plan for AIM, the target market was described as children in the dental health segment of the toothpaste market. In the advertising plan, however, the target audience is different from the target market. The intended audience for AIM was *mothers* who had children at home, as well as every dentist in the United States (Figure 9–8).

Figure 9–8 Lever broke its campaign with a call to mothers who had "cavity-prone children." Not long after, Colgate followed with its claims about "the cavity-prone years." What a coincidence!

In determining the target audience, it is important to consider not only who the end user is but also who makes the purchasing decision and who influences the purchasing decision. Children, for example, exert a strong influence on where the family decides to eat. So McDonald's concentrates much of its spending on children as a target audience.

The *communications media* refer to the method or vehicles used to transmit the advertiser's message. These may include radio, television, newspapers, magazines, or billboards. They may include direct mail, publicity, and certain sales promotion techniques such as sample packs or coupons. Media considerations will be discussed more fully in Chapter 15. It's important to understand here, though, that the media to be used are determined by considering audience or readership statistics, potential communications effectiveness, relevance to the rest of the creative mix, and cost at the time the advertising plan is developed. (See the Ad Lab.)

The *advertising message* is what the company plans to say in its advertisements and how it plans to say it. Lever Bros. developed what they called an "omnibus" message strategy to answer all the questions that might arise in the mind of a Crest user. They also decided to use

Creative use of the creative mix

Some advertisements emphasize one element of the creative mix more than any other to achieve a creative blockbuster. Pictured here are several award-winning advertisements that illustrate this point.

A. Market segmentation for Jewish dogs seems to be the strategy for Mother Klein's Kosher Style Dog Food. This is a classic example of a target audience creative strategy complete with inside ethnic humor.

B. Metzdorf Advertising also needed a sharp new employee. This out-of-focus message strategy drives the point home and earned the agency many kudos for its creative idea.

C. The Westbury Hotel used inexpensive, small-space newspaper advertisements with modern-day hieroglyphic graphics to pique the reader's curiosity in their effort to entice visitors to New York to see the King Tut exhibit.

D. Art directors love the elegant simplicity of the Eaton Stores ad from Montreal. The message strategy here is based not on *what* is said (which is very little) but on *how* it is said (which is a lot). Imagine the dynamics of this ad in its original full-page newspaper format.

E. Classified advertising is used commonly for personnel hiring, but rarely is a classified ad written as humorously and as bluntly. Response to this advertisement was overwhelming.

A.

Mother knows best.

Of course the mother we refer to is none other than the very same lady whose picture adorns our can.

And if you think a Jewish mother can be difficult to live with, you should only live long enough to work for one some time.

It isn't easy.

She worries about our liver. She babies our beef. And watches over our chicken like a mother hen.

And keeps our kosher style kitchen so spotless and clean, your dog could eat off the floor. (We keep one set of books and two sets of dishes.)

Why you ask? Why should someone be so concerned about running a dog food concern? It would take over 5700 years to answer.

But when you buy a can of Mother Klein's Kosher Style Dog Food, you can rest assured she cares enough to send her very best.

Not because her picture's on the label in front. But because she stands behind every can.

You don't have to be Jewish to love Mother Klein's Kosher Style Dog Food.

B.

We're looking for a sharp operator who can get our photo lab back in focus. Must have 2-4 years' experience and not be afraid of the dark. For a clearer picture call Randy Ivey at Metzdorf Advertising. 526-5361. (We're an equal oppurtunity employer)

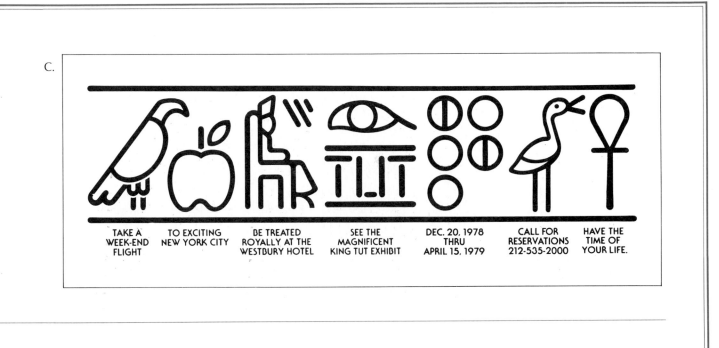

C.

TAKE A WEEK-END FLIGHT
TO EXCITING NEW YORK CITY
BE TREATED ROYALLY AT THE WESTBURY HOTEL
SEE THE MAGNIFICENT KING TUT EXHIBIT
DEC. 20, 1978 THRU APRIL 15, 1979
CALL FOR RESERVATIONS 212-535-2000
HAVE THE TIME OF YOUR LIFE.

D.

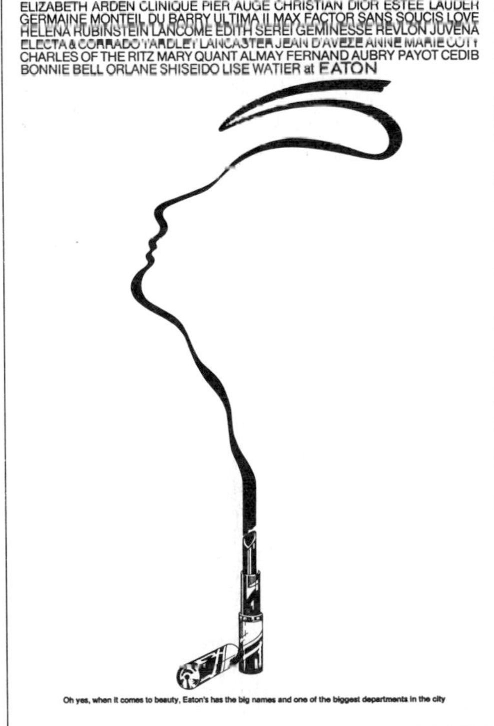

ELIZABETH ARDEN CLINIQUE PIER AUGE CHRISTIAN DIOR ESTEE LAUDER
GERMAINE MONTEIL DU BARRY ULTIMA II MAX FACTOR SANS SOUCIS LOVE
HELENA RUBINSTEIN LANCOME EDITH SEREI GEMINESSE REVLON JUVENA
CHARLES OF THE RITZ MARY QUANT ALMAY FERNAND AUBRY PAYOT CEDIB
BONNIE BELL ORLANE SHISEIDO LISE WATIER at EATON
Oh yes, when it comes to beauty, Eaton's has the big names and one of the biggest departments in the city

E.

WAREHOUSE PERSON

Unambitious individual for work in warehouse moving furniture & other heavy objects. Absolutely no chance for advancement. No vac. or any other fringe benefits. 48 hr. work week. May be adjusted from time to time to interfere with your personal plans. Pay $3.00 per hr. Persons interested in doing a good job need not apply. Call Mr. Ruddy. 213/373-6744

Laboratory application

Select other advertisements used to illustrate this text. Describe which elements of the creative mix are being emphasized.

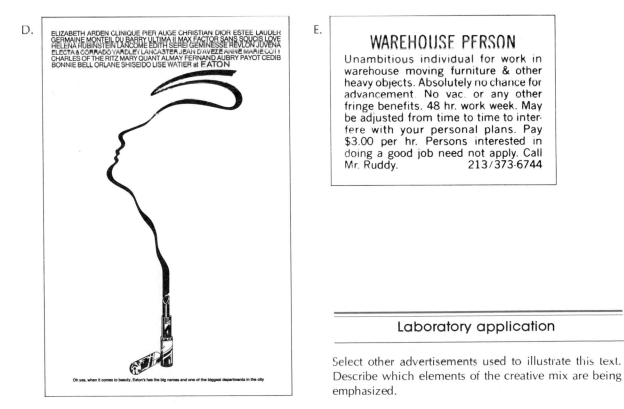

a slice-of-life technique to create as nearly as possible the situation that was likely to occur in many Crest homes. They developed a great theme line, "Take Aim against cavities." That was the message strategy.

The advertising plan lays out the general direction of the campaign for the allotted time period. Then when it comes to creating the individual advertisements or commercials, the same process is repeated. The same questions are asked: What is the overall objective of the campaign? What is the overall strategy? What is the specific objective of this ad? What is the best way to do it? Whom are we talking to? What media are we going to use? What do we want to say? How do we want to say it?

Look at the ads in Figure 9–9 and see how Lever Bros. decided to say it. Can you see how the advertisement is a rational outgrowth of the marketing and advertising plan?

Advertising investment

In the winter of 1973–74, and five years later in 1979, the country experienced the first throes of the energy shortage. Cars lined up for blocks, sometimes miles, to buy gasoline at the one station in town that was open. Lights on Christmas trees were turned off. City halls and utility company buildings were dark at night. Plastics were in short supply. In fact, virtually everything made from petroleum or petrochemicals was back-ordered, and prices for energy-related items skyrocketed. Companies called their suppliers, begging for products. Suddenly everybody started taking his or her favorite salesperson to lunch—anything to get the necessary materials and supplies so business could continue.

Many executives marched into their company advertising departments and ordered the immediate cancellation of all ads. The cry was the same everywhere: "Stop advertising! For God's sake, we don't need any more orders. Our customers hate us enough as it is! Besides, at this point it's just a waste of money!" Many advertising budgets were cut to zero.

As little as 12 months later, the salespeople for many of these same companies were back buying lunch again. The executives were behind their desks worrying over their financial statements. And the stockholders were wondering how their companies had just lost several percentage points in their share of the market.

Advertising as an investment

Accountants and Internal Revenue Service agents consider advertising a current business expense. Consequently many executives treat advertising as an item on the budget that can be trimmed or eliminated like other expense items when sales are either at an extremely high or extremely low level. Although this is certainly understandable, it is also regrettable.

FATHER: Hi, Son.
Hey! What's that?
Helen! . . Helen! What's with this blue stuff.

MOTHER: Oh, it's a new toothpaste — — AIM. I just got it.

FATHER: Have you flipped? What about fluoride? And you know what the dentist said. The kid's cavity-prone.

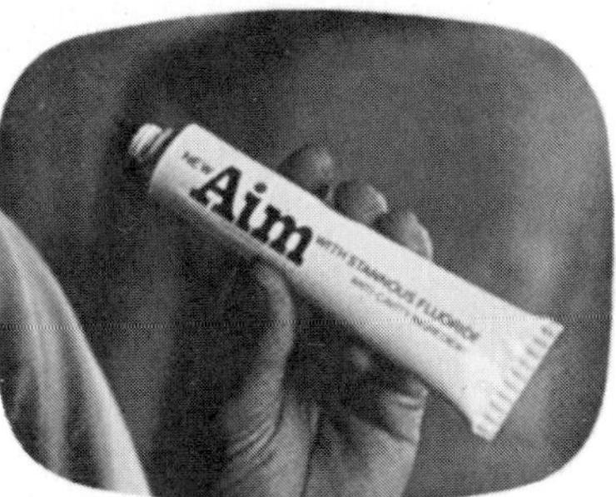

MOTHER: Henry, AIM has stannous fluoride just like our old toothpaste.

FATHER: O.K., so it has fluoride. So, what's wrong with the fluoride we've been using?

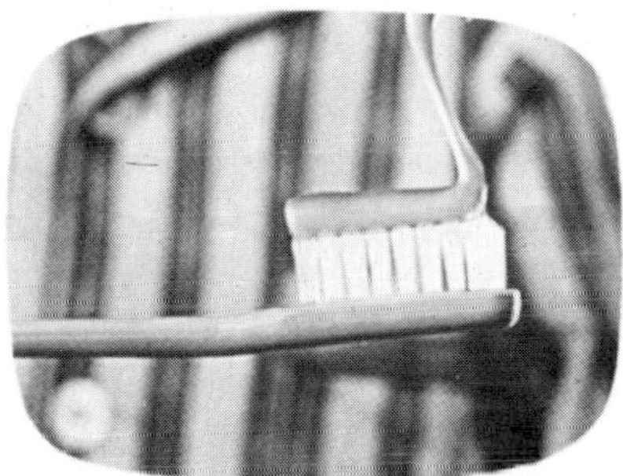

MOTHER: Look, Henry. AIM is a gel And they say this gel formula spreads faster than paste in normal brushing time. . .

and AIM is also less abrasive than the leading fluoride paste.

SON: I like It! It tastes good!

MOTHER: He likes it, Henry.

FATHER: Well, I don't know . . . our old toothpaste . . .

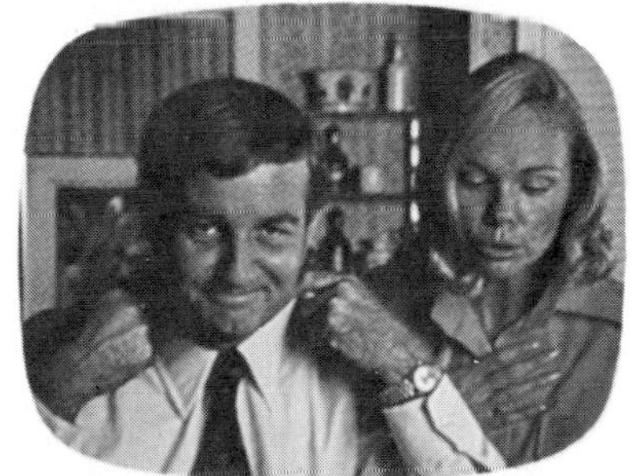

MOTHER: Oh, Henry. Our old toothpaste has been around since I was a girl. Look AIM is new. It's got stannous fluoride, it's less abrasive and he likes it.

FATHER: You know, maybe he'll brush longer.

ANNCR(VR): If your children are in the cavity prone years, have them brush often, see the dentist regularly and take AIM against cavities.

Figure 9—9

An investment in future sales

The cost of a new plant or of a distribution warehouse is considered an investment in the future ability of the company to produce and distribute products. Similarly, advertising, as one element of the promotion mix, should be considered an investment in future sales. Of course, advertising is used on a short-term basis to stimulate immediate sales, but it also has a cumulative long-range effect.

Advertising builds a consumer franchise and prompts goodwill. This in turn enhances the reputation and value of the company name. At first advertising may move a person to buy a new kind of potato chip, but it also affects his next purchase of potato chips, and the one after that, and the one after that. This same advertising may also influence the consumer to try other of the firm's snacks.

Thus, while advertising may be treated as a current expense for accounting purposes, it could also be considered a long-term capital investment. For management to consider advertising as an investment, however, it must understand the relationship between advertising and sales and profits.

Relationship of advertising to sales and profits

Unfortunately, no one has come up with a reliable, exact method of precisely determining the effect of advertising on sales. As we have shown in the last four chapters, there are many internal and external variables that influence a company's marketing and advertising efforts. Therefore, the research methodology that has been developed to measure the relationships between advertising and sales and sales and profit are far from perfect and can give only rough estimates. However, enough data are available to verify certain facts:

1. Sales will increase if there is additional advertising. At some point, however, the rate of return will decline. (See the Ad Lab.)
2. Sales response to advertising is spread out over a long period of time.
3. There are minimum levels below which advertising expenditures will have no effect on sales.
4. There will be some sales even if there is no advertising.
5. There are saturation limits imposed by culture and competition above which no amount of advertising could push sales.

To management, these facts, verified by numerous studies, might be interpreted into the following advice on how to allocate funds for advertising: Don't advertise at all unless you are willing to spend enough to have some effect on sales. If you do decide to advertise, be willing to continue spending for an extended time. Do not expect immediate results, but keep your eye on the sales curve. Increase the advertising budget in stages until the effect on sales is noticed. At the point at which this effect is noticed, determine the effect on profits of the additional sales realized at this level of advertising expenditure. Next, continue increasing the level of advertising in gradual stages. At each stage, notice the volume of sales and determine the profitability. Continue increasing the advertising expenditure until (1) sales cease to be affected by additional advertising, or (2) the additional sales realized cease to be profitable. This is the upper limit and the

How economists view the effect of advertising on sales

Normally, the quantity sold will depend on the number of dollars the company spends advertising the product. And within reasonable limits (if its advertising program is not too repugnant), the more dollars spent on advertising, the more a company will sell—up to a point. Yet, even the most enthusiastic advertising agency will admit, reluctantly, that it is possible to spend too much on advertising.

To decide rationally how much to spend on this part of its marketing effort, management obviously should know just how quantity demanded is affected by advertising expenditure—how much more it will be able to sell per additional dollar of advertising, and when additional advertising dollars cease being effective. It needs to have, not a fixed number representing potential demand, but a graph or a statistical equation describing the relationship between sales and advertising.

Notice that in our illustration most of the curve goes uphill as we move to the right (it has a positive slope). This means that additional advertising will continue to bring in business until (at a budget of x million dollars) people become so saturated by the message that it begins to repel them and turn them away from the product.

Even in cases in which the saturation level cannot be reached within the range of outlays the firm can afford, the curve is likely to level off, becoming flatter and flatter as the amount spent on advertising gets larger and larger, and saturation is approached. The point at which the curve begins to flatten is the point at which returns from advertising begin to diminish. When the total advertising budget is small, even a $1 addition to the campaign may bring in as much as $10 in new sales and so be very much worthwhile to the firm. But when the market approaches saturation, each additional dollar may contribute only 30 cents in new sales, and that is not sound business.

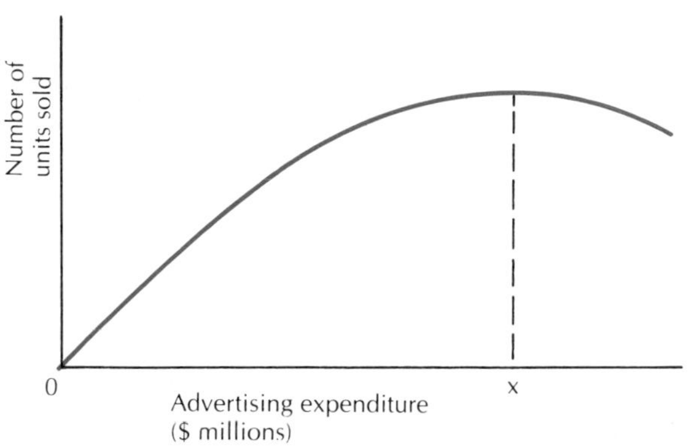

Laboratory application

1. Can you give an example of when the advertising expenditure curve would have a negative slope?

2. Economists suggest that the quantity sold depends on the number of dollars the company spends on advertising. Is that a safe assumption? Discuss.

point at which the advertising expenditures should then be maintained.

This seemingly simple advice on how to set the appropriate level of advertising is actually full of complexities. It assumes, for instance, that advertising is the only marketing activity that affects sales. In reality, we know that the increased advertising expenditure may not be the cause of the increased sales at all. Rather the increased sales may be due to a better job of personal selling or to seasonal changes in the general business cycle. Furthermore, it assumes the company has a clear-cut way of determining the relationship of sales to profit. This is rarely true.

Moreover, what if the company is selling a multiplicity of products? Then we have the problem of determining which advertising is contributing to which product, since all the company's advertising may help all the products.

One thing remains clear. Since the response to advertising is spread out over such an extended time, advertising should be viewed as a long-term investment in the future profits of the company. Unfortunately, as long as management views advertising as a current expense, it attempts to keep those funds to a minimum. Naturally, like all expenditures, advertising should be evaluated for wastefulness. But, historically, those companies that make advertising the scapegoat during periods of economic fluctuation invariably end up losing some share of market when the economy returns to stable growth.

Allocating funds for advertising

No advertising or marketing plan is complete without a discussion of what the program is going to cost and how the money is to be spent. Management must be convinced by the advertising department that the method used to arrive at the suggested level of expenditure makes good business sense. Our purpose here is to discuss some of the influences on the advertising appropriation and to present some common methods companies use to arrive at an advertising budget.

Inexact science

Allocating funds to advertising is a very difficult task. It's risky to predict the advertising expenditure that will be necessary to create a certain volume of sales. The effects of advertising are spread out over a long time. A person who buys a car in the spring may have been prompted by last fall's advertising. So how do you accurately measure the effect of past advertising? A person who buys a competitive food product and likes it may continue to purchase it over several years. How do you know, therefore, that the money you continue to spend advertising to this person is profitable?

Small-appliance purchases are often affected by the familiarity of the brand name. That makes it very difficult to gauge the amount of the firm's sales that are a direct result of present advertising expenditures and of future advertising. So, how do you know when you hit that point of diminishing returns?

These are just some of the problems facing advertising managers as they sit down to figure out their annual advertising budget.

The variable environments of business

Every business operates in several environments simultaneously. The way the company relates to these environments may determine its success or failure. Before attempting to determine the advertising allocation, therefore, the advertising manager must consider the status of the following:

1. Economic, political, social, and legal environment. The level of general economic activity, social customs and attitudes, as well as the structure of tax rates affect both total industry sales and corporate profits on sales.
2. Institutional environment. What is the level of sales within the

industry? The company can expect only a share of the total market demand.
3. Competitive environment. The various activities of competitors may either help or hinder the company from making sales and achieving profits.
4. Internal environment. The activities of the company itself in relation to its competitors and its markets will have a bearing on the effectiveness of advertising expenditures.[13]

A thorough reappraisal of these factors at the time the advertising allocation is determined may have a profound effect on how much the company feels it can or should spend.

Methods of allocating funds

Business executives' attitudes toward the advertising budget are relatively simple to understand. They will spend more money as long as they can be assured it will bring in a profit. If it takes a dollar in advertising to produce one more penny of profit, it is worth the expense. The trick, however, is to determine when the dollar spent in advertising is not going to bring in a profit but rather will result in a loss. That is hard to predict in advance, and advertising budgets must always be developed in advance.

In an effort to reduce the risk of overspending or underspending, a number of methods have been developed over the years that companies use in determining how much to spend on advertising. Some businesspeople rely solely on one technique, while others use several in combination. Recently there has been a tendency to shy away from the simpler methods of the past, such as percentage of sales, and to use more sophisticated methods. However, no technique for allocating advertising funds is adequate for all situations. The methods discussed in this section are those used primarily to arrive at national advertising budgets. Additional techniques used by retailers who operate under a different set of variables are discussed in Chapter 20, "Local Advertising."

Percentage of sales

The percentage of sales method is one of the most popular techniques used to set the advertising appropriation. It may be based on a percentage of last year's sales, anticipated sales for next year, or a combination of the two. Businesspeople like this method because it is the most simple, it doesn't cost them anything, it is related to revenue, and it is considered safe (Figure 9–10).

Usually the percentage is based on an industry average or on company experience (Figure 9–11). Unfortunately, though, it is too often determined arbitrarily. The problem of basing the percentage on an industry average is that it assumes that the whole industry has similar objectives and faces the same marketing variables. When the percentage is based on company history, it assumes that the market is highly static, which is rarely the case.

There are some advantages to this method. When applied against

Figure 9–10

50 leaders' advertising as percent of sales

(covering total 1980 ad expenditures, including measured and unmeasured media)

	Ad rank	Company	Advertising	Sales	Advertising percentage of sales
Appliances, Tv, Radio	27	RCA Corp.	164,328,300	8,011,300,000	2.1
	29	General Electric Co.	156,196,300	24,959,000,000	0.6
Automobiles	6	General Motors Corp.	316,000,000	57,728,500,000	0.5
	8	Ford Motor Co.	280,000,000	37,085,500,000	0.8
	32	Chrysler Corp.	150,300,000	9,225,300,000	1.6
Chemicals	43	American Cyanamid Co.	125,000,000	3,453,934,000	3.6
	49	DuPont	98,300,000	13,652,000,000	0.7
Communications, Entertainment	37	Time Inc.	141,851,000	2,881,783,000	4.9
	40	CBS Inc.	132,372,000	4,062,052,000	3.3
Drugs	38	Richardson-Vicks	134,000,000	1,211,151,000	11.1
	47	Schering-Plough Corp.	100,000,000	1,740,000,000	5.7
Food	3	General Foods	410,000,000	6,601,300,000	6.2
	14	McDonald's Corp.	206,962,100	6,266,000,000	3.3
	15	Ralston Purina Co.	206,794,860	4,886,000,000	4.2
	19	Esmark Inc.	189,907,000	2,956,422,000	6.4
	23	Beatrice Foods	175,000,000	8,772,804,000	2.0
	25	General Mills	171,114,790	4,852,400,000	3.5
	33	Nabisco Inc.	150,000,000	2,568,700,000	5.8
	34	Consolidated Foods Corp.	149,221,000	5,600,000,000	2.7
	35	Norton Simon Inc.	149,000,000	3,012,772,000	4.9
	41	Dart & Kraft	128,283,000	9,411,000,000	1.4
	44	Pillsbury Co.	124,025,700	3,301,700,000	3.8
	48	Quaker Oats Co.	99,666,700	2,405,200,000	4.1
Retail Chains	2	Sears, Roebuck & Co.	599,600,000	25,195,000,000	2.4
	5	K mart Corp.	319,311,000	14,200,000,000	2.2
	45	J. C. Penney Co.	108,000,000	11,353,000,000	0.9
Soaps, Cleansers (and Allied)	1	Procter & Gamble	649,624,200	11,416,000,000	5.7
	13	Colgate-Palmolive Co.	225,000,000	5,130,464,000	9.4
	28	Unilever U.S. Inc.	158,329,100	1,486,660,000	10.6

(continued)

	Ad rank	Company	Advertising	Sales	Advertising percentage of sales
Soft Drinks	12	PepsiCo Inc.	233,400,000	5,975,220,000	3.9
	20	Coca-Cola Inc.	184,185,000	5,912,600,000	3.1
Telephone Service, Equipment	9	American Telephone & Telegraph	259,170,000	50,791,200,000	0.5
	36	International Telephone & Telegraph	143,000,000	18,529,655,000	0.7
Tobacco	4	Philip Morris Inc.	364,594,700	9,822,300,000	3.7
	7	R. J. Reynolds Industries	298,524,100	10,354,100,000	2.9
	50	B.A.T. Industries	95,757,000	1,475,000,000	6.5
Toiletries, Cosmetics	10	Warner-Lambert Co.	235,202,000	3,479,207,000	6.8
	16	American Home Products Corp.	197,000,000	4,074,095,000	4.8
	17	Bristol-Myers Co.	196,286,400	3,158,300,000	6.2
	31	Gillette Co.	150,981,700	2,315,294,000	6.5
	41	Chesebrough-Pond's	128,316,000	1,377,484,000	9.3
	46	Revlon Inc.	105,430,400	2,203,324,000	4.8
Wine, Beer, and Liquor	21	Anheuser-Busch	181,278,500	3,822,400,000	4.7
	26	Heublein Inc.	170,000,000	1,921,879,000	8.8
	30	Seagram Co. Ltd.	152,000,000	2,534,952,000	6.0
Miscellaneous	11	Gulf & Western Industries	233,800,000	6,885,000,000	3.4
	18	Mobil Corp.	194,816,700	63,726,000,000	0.3
	22	Johnson & Johnson	177,000,000	2,633,600,000	6.7
	24	U.S. Government	172,964,514	—	—
	39	Loews Corp.	132,785,200	4,530,000,000	2.9

future sales, it often works well. It assumes that a certain number of dollars are needed to sell a certain number of units. If we know what that percentage is, the correlation between advertising and sales should remain constant if the market is stable and competitors' advertising remains relatively unchanged. Furthermore, management tends to think in terms of percentages whether it is income or outgo. They think of advertising in the same way, so this method is simple. Also, because this method is common throughout the industry, it diminishes the likelihood of competitive warfare.

The greatest shortcoming of the percentage of sales method is that it violates the basic marketing principle that marketing activities stimulate demand and thus sales; they do not occur as a result of them. This method tends to set advertising in a fixed mode and is unable to respond to changing conditions in the marketplace. If advertising automatically increases when sales increase and declines when sales decline, it automatically ignores all the other environments of business that might be suggesting a totally opposite move.

Percentage of profit

This method is similar to the percentage of sales method except that the percentage is applied to profit. It may be the past year's profits or profits expected in the coming year. Proponents of this method like it because they know they are dealing with profit dollars rather than with before-profit dollars. Furthermore, because they are working with only a percentage of the profit, they know there is an additional reservoir of profitable dollars to be used if necessary.

This method suffers the same deficiencies as the percentage of sales approach. Many forces other than current advertising affect profit, and it is even more difficult to evaluate profit effectiveness than sales effectiveness. A variation of this method was suggested at the beginning of this section where units of advertising funds were increased until the marginal return of the last unit did not equal the marginal cost. As we said then, it's a nice, simple theory, but current advertising effectiveness cannot be precisely measured in most cases.

Unit of sale

This method, also called the case-rate method, is another variation of the percentage of sales technique. It has many of the same deficien-

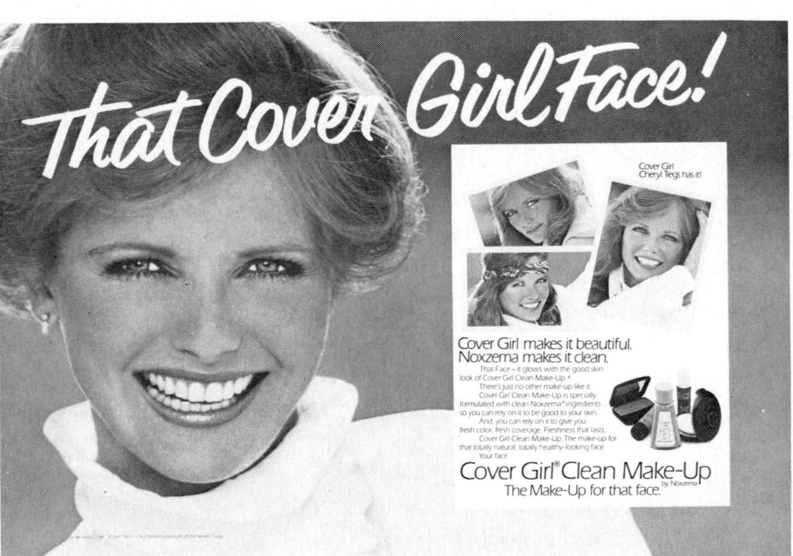

Figure 9–11 Noxell Corporation, which manufactures Cover Girl Make-Up and other products, had a budget of $41 million in 1980 and was the 93rd largest advertiser. But it was the number two spender of advertising as a percentage of sales—20.2 percent. Compare that to the major automobile manufacturers, which often spend less than 1 percent for advertising. That translates to as little as $50 a car.

cies. This method allocates a specific amount to each unit produced or to each unit anticipated to be produced. A specific dollar figure is set for each case, box, barrel, or carton. For example, some automobile manufacturers set a figure of $40–$45 per car to be spent on advertising.

The unit of sale method has its greatest advantage in assessing members of horizontal cooperative programs and trade associations. Each member contributes equitably according to production. For example, in an effort to stimulate demand for California beef, the Southern California Beef Association assessed cattle feeders and packers 25 cents to be used in advertising for each steer slaughtered.

Of course, this method cannot be used effectively for new product introductions. To overcome consumer inertia, spending must be much more than the usual unit of sale allocation. Another problem is that the amount assessed per unit often becomes set and the advertising program cannot respond to dynamic marketing problems.

Competitive parity

This method allocates advertising dollars according to the amounts spent by the firm's major competitors. We like to call it the self-defense method. It follows the line, "If they're spending that much, we'd better." Or conversely, "If that's all they're spending, there's no reason for us to spend any more."

Many businesspeople rationalize that if their leading competitors have been successful in capturing their share of the market, they will be successful by emulating them. Furthermore, many companies ascertain the relative efficiency of their operations by comparing their firm's statistics in production and finance with their competitors. It's only natural that this same technique should be applied to preparing advertising budgets.

The fallacies of this rationalization should be obvious. Your competitors' objectives are rarely the same as yours. When your competitors make a mistake, so do you. Finally, many industries maintain a relatively low "noise level" of advertising. Just a moderate increase in one firm's advertising expenses could enable that particular company to stand out above the rest. As long as it budgets defensively, however, it misses that opportunity.

Share of market

In industries where products are very similar, there is usually a high correlation between a company's share of the market and its share of industry advertising. Knowing this, some firms set a goal for a certain portion of the market and then apply the same percentage of industry advertising dollars to their budget.

This method has the advantage of aggressively attempting to achieve an objective. According to J. O. Peckham, the executive vice president of the A. C. Nielson Company, a company's best chance of maintaining its share of market is to maintain a share of advertising somewhat ahead of its share of market. For example, if you have a 50 percent share of the market, you should spend 55 percent of the industry's advertising dollars.

One shortcoming is that there is no guarantee that your competitors will not increase their advertising budgets.

For new products, share of market is a common method. According to Peckham's formula, when a new product brand is introduced, the advertising budget should be about one and a half times the brand's expected share of market in two years. This means that if the company's two-year sales goal is 10 percent of the market, it should spend about 15 percent of the industry's advertising during the first two years.[14]

The share of market method assumes that to gain share of market, you must first gain share of mind. This is a logical approach to budgeting strategy. However, one hazard of this method is the tendency to become complacent. Companies compete on more than one basis, and advertising is just one tool of the marketing mix. Therefore, simply maintaining a higher percentage of media exposure may not be enough to accomplish the desired results. Companies must maintain an awareness of all the marketing activities of their competitors besides advertising.

Task method

The task method is also known as the objective or budget buildup method. In recent years it has gained considerable popularity and is one of the few logical means of determining advertising allocations. It defines the objectives that are sought and how advertising is to be used to accomplish those objectives. It considers advertising one of the marketing tools used to generate sales rather than occurring as a result of sales.

The task method occurs in three steps: defining the objectives, determining strategy, and estimating the cost. After specific, quantitative marketing objectives have been set, the advertiser develops programs to be used in attaining them. If the objective is to increase the number of coffee cases sold by 10 percent, the advertiser will have to determine which advertising approach will work best, how often ads are to be run, and which media are to be used. The proposed cost of this program is determined, and this becomes the basis for the advertising budget. Naturally, it is necessary to consider this budget in light of the company's financial position. If the cost is too high, the objectives may have to be scaled down and the strategy adjusted accordingly. Likewise, after the campaign has run, if the results are better or worse than had been anticipated, the next budget may require appropriate revisions.

The task method forces companies to think in terms of goals and whether they are being accomplished. The effectiveness of this method is most apparent when the results of particular ads or campaigns can be readily measured. Due to its nature, this method is adaptable to changing conditions in the market and is easily revised as dictated by past results.

Of course, while it is much easier to look back and determine whether money has been spent wisely, it is often very difficult to determine in advance the amount of money that will be needed to reach a specific goal. This is the major drawback to the task method. Likewise, although techniques for measuring the effect of advertising are improving, they are still weak in many areas. As techniques become more exact, though, advertisers are using the task method more and more. Today it is probably the best basis for estimating the size of an advertising budget.

Additional methods

There are several other methods for allocating funds which advertisers use to varying degrees. The *empirical research method* uses experimentation to determine the best level of advertising expenditure. By running a series of tests in different markets with different budgets, companies determine which is the most efficient level of expenditure.

Since the introduction of computers, there has been a great deal of research interest in the use of *quantitative mathematical models* for budgeting. A number of sophisticated techniques have been developed (Figure 9–12). However, for the most part these equations are not easily understood by line executives, and each relies on assumptions of data that are frequently unavailable or very expensive for the average business.

Some companies determine their advertising budget in an arbitrary manner. The *arbitrary method* is used primarily by small, inexperienced advertisers who have not realized the advantages of planned advertising and marketing strategy.

Others use the *all available funds method.* This "go for broke" technique is generally used by advertisers with limited capital who are trying to introduce a new product. Fortunately, this method is not used often because the available funds eventually exceed what is needed for advertising. When this occurs, the advertiser seeks another method such as the task method.

The bottom line

All these methods potentially assume one of two fallacies. The first fallacy is more obvious—that advertising is a result of sales. We know that this is not true, and yet the widespread use of the percentage of sales method indicates that many businesspeople think that advertising should be a result of sales.

The second fallacy is that advertising creates sales. Only in rare circumstances (where direct-action advertising is used) can advertising be said to create sales. Advertising locates prospects and stimulates demand. It may even stimulate inquiries. Salespeople likewise may locate prospects and stimulate demand. They also close the sale. But in reality, only customers create sales. It is the customer's choice to buy or not to buy the product, not the company's choice.

The job of advertising is to inform, persuade, and remind. In that way, advertising affects sales. However, advertising is jut one part of the whole, and advertising managers must keep this in mind when preparing their plans and their budgets for management.

How much should you spend on advertising?

Ogilvy & Mather can often answer this question through the use of a new analytical tool.

For the last year, Ogilvy & Mather has been using a technique that reveals the relationship between advertising expenditure, market share and profit.

This technique makes use of a mathematical model developed by the Hendry Corporation, an independent group of marketing consultants.

Ogilvy & Mather is the only advertising agency with rights to use it.

Its validity has been demonstrated with many products in many categories of consumer goods.

The information needed for the model is available from the current files of most advertisers. No need for extensive market tests or elaborate market research.

Results can be obtained quickly, and inexpensively.

The technique is new. Some of our clients are using it in planning their advertising budgets. Others are testing it in the marketplace. Still others are considering how to apply it to their particular problems, or how best to translate what it tells them into marketing action.

We believe it is an important new tool for guiding strategic planning. It forces objective thinking.

The varying uses of the theory are reflected in the examples that follow. We put them forward to indicate how this new tool might help you clarify your own thinking about questions such as:

What is the optimum spending level for your product?

Analysis for one of our clients showed that he could cut advertising by $3,000,000 — with little decline in share of market but a *significant increase in profits.*

A similar analysis for another client showed that he should double his already large advertising budget if he wished to achieve optimum *profits.*

If you manufacture a product with a small share of market you may choose to advertise beyond the point of maximum profit — in order to maintain distribution. This analysis will indicate how much advertising should be used.

On the other hand, if your product enjoys a high share of market, you may wish to sacrifice some profit in order to sustain this high share — for competitive reasons. Again, our analysis will suggest the appropriate level of advertising to accomplish this.

Whatever your marketing objectives, we believe you can now determine the optimum level of advertising consistent with them.

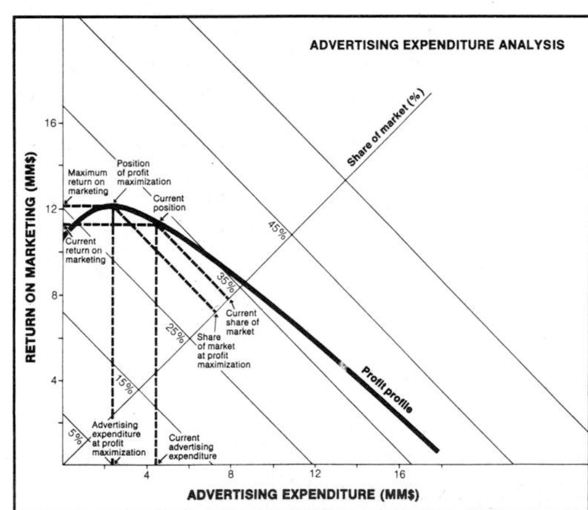

A schematic representation of the relationship between Advertising, Share of Market and Return on Marketing. (Return on Marketing = Profits + Allocated Costs; it excludes the cost of advertising.)

This analysis shows that a cut of $1,900,000 in Advertising (from $4.3 to $2.4 million) would result in maximization of return on marketing and an increase in returns (over and above the cut in advertising) of $900,000 (from $11,200,000 to $12,100,000). This, however, would result in a drop in share of market of 3.5 percentage points (from 33.5 to 30.0) which might be harmful to the momentum of the brand in a highly competitive market.

How much of your share of market is due to advertising?

For some products advertising accounts for a major part of their share of market; without any advertising their survival would be doubtful. For example, one brand studied had an 11 percent share of market. Analysis showed that its share would be only 6 percent in the absence of advertising.

For another brand, our analysis found that advertising contributed only one share point out of nine. However, unit margins were high enough to make this one share point very profitable.

We believe that for the first time it is possible to find out in dollars and cents what you are getting for your advertising dollars.

How can you best allocate your total advertising among different brands or among different forms of a single brand?

Most manufacturers who sell a number of products determine advertising budgets brand by brand. Total profits for the company can sometimes be increased by spending more on some brands and less on others than was determined on an individual basis; while the aggregate company advertising expenditure remains the same.

Ogilvy & Mather can now help you determine when this is the case — and how much to spend on each brand.

If your brand comes in more than one form you may be missing profit opportunities as a result of inefficient division of your advertising budget among the various forms.

One of our clients was marketing a product in four forms. All of the advertising was placed behind Form I. Our analysis showed that if he shifted a large part of his budget to Form III, he would increase his profit without affecting his total share of market.

How can you best allocate your advertising budget to different sales territories?

In the same way that brand shares can vary by sales territories, the productivity of advertising can also vary from territory to territory.

A regional analysis showed how one of our clients could realize $300,000 in additional profit if he would reallocate his $4,000,000 advertising budget.

The analysis showed him how to distribute the money so that, dollar for dollar, it was *equally productive in each of his marketing areas.*

How big an advertising budget to introduce new products?

For one of our clients we found that the marketing objectives for a new product could not be achieved at an affordable level of advertising. *So we advised them not to advertise at all.*

For another new product, a brief market test was used to obtain data for use in the mathematical model. We were then able to determine the optimum advertising budget. The analysis indicated that *less* advertising than was used in the test would yield the most profitable results.

N.B. This method of analysis reflects conditions in the market at the time it is made; it does not allow for subsequent major changes. If marketing conditions change substantially, the analysis must be repeated.

2 East 48th Street, New York, N.Y. 10017

Figure 9–12 Use of the Hendry model to relate advertising to sales and profits as used by Ogilvy & Mather.

Summary

The marketing plan may be the most important document a company has. It assembles all the pertinent facts about a company, the markets it serves, its products, and its competition in one place and brings all these facts up to date. It sets specific goals and objectives to be attained and describes the precise strategies that will be used to achieve them. Thus, it musters all the company's forces for the marketing battlefield, and in so doing dictates the role of advertising in the marketing mix.

The marketing plan should contain four principal sections: (1) situation analysis, (2) marketing objectives, (3) marketing strategy, and (4) action programs. A company's marketing objectives should be logical deductions from an analysis of its current situation, its prediction of future trends, and its understanding of corporate objectives. They should relate to the needs of specific target markets and sales objectives. The sales target objectives should be specific, quantitative, and realistic.

The first step in developing marketing strategy is to select the target market. The second step is to determine a cost-effective marketing mix for each target market the company pursues. The marketing mix is determined by how the company uses the four Ps: product, price, place, and promotion. Advertising is one of the promotional tools companies may use.

Advertising is a natural outgrowth of the marketing plan, and the advertising plan is prepared in much the same way as the marketing plan. It includes a section on analysis, advertising objectives, and strategy.

Advertising objectives may be expressed in terms of moving prospective customers up through the advertising pyramid (awareness, comprehension, conviction, desire, action). Or they may be expressed in terms of generating inquiries, coupon response, or attitude change.

The advertising (or creative) strategy is determined by the advertiser's use of the creative mix. The creative mix is composed of the (1) product concept, (2) target audience, (3) communications media, and (4) advertising message. The product concept refers to the bundle of values the product is intended to represent to the consumer. The target audience is the specific people the advertising will approach. It may or may not be the same as the target market. The communications media are the vehicles used to transmit the advertiser's message. The advertising message is what the company plans to say in its advertisements and how it plans to say it.

There are several methods commonly used for allocating funds to advertising. Historically, the most popular method has been the percentage of sales approach. A similar method is called the percentage of profit approach. The share of market method was developed because a high correlation has been found between a company's share of the market and its share of industry advertising. The task method has gained considerable popularity because it is considered a logical means of determining advertising allocation. It involves defining the advertising objective, determining the strategy, and estimating the cost to conduct that strategy. If the company cannot afford the cost, then it must scale down its objectives.

Questions for review

1. What is the importance of the marketing plan?
2. What is the difference between generic-marketing objectives and sales-target objectives? Give an example of each.
3. What are the steps in developing a marketing plan?
4. How is marketing strategy determined?
5. What are the steps in developing an advertising plan?
6. What is the difference between marketing objectives and advertising objectives?
7. What are the environmental factors that affect the company's expenditures for marketing and advertising?
8. What is the most common method of allocating funds for advertising? Why?
9. What does competitive parity mean? What is the fallacy behind this method?
10. How could a chain of retail shoe stores use the empirical research method for determining its advertising budget?

Part IV

Advertising Creativity: Communication Solutions to Marketing Problems

10

Creative copywriting

Suppose you are the advertising manager for one of the world's largest paper companies. Your boss, the marketing director, invites you in, asks you to sit down, and tosses a sheet of paper at you across the desk. You glance at it quickly. It's a summary of a recent consumer research study, and the bottom line is that people are reading less and less every year. Fewer books, fewer magazines, fewer newspapers. In fact, the study shows that literacy among America's youth is declining rapidly. Many who graduate from high school can barely read or write.

"Do you know what that means?" asks your boss.

You nod affirmatively. Your company is one of the leading suppliers of paper for books, magazines, newspapers, and commercial printing.

"I want you to give me a plan to attack this situation." And you are excused to start working on your problem. What would you do?

Unfortunately, this is not just a hypothetical situation. Literacy among youth has been declining for some years, and this problem has troubled parents, educators, and the International Paper Company. They decided to try to do something about it. Together with their agency, Ogilvy & Mather, they created an unusual advertising campaign called "The Power of the Printed Word." It was designed to help young people improve their verbal skills and thereby help IP's customers as well.

The campaign broke in the fall of 1979. At the time the agency's vice president/creative director said, "We did everything we could to make people want to read the ads." The language was simple and direct. Photos were used with captions to attract the reader's attention and add a bit of humor. And the ads were laid out in a very easy-to-follow style with editorial-type columns, several illustrations, boxes, bold type headings, and short paragraphs.

Consisting of seven "how-to" articles, each written by a well-known and respected wordsmith, the campaign ran in youth-oriented and general interest magazines, some large metropolitan newspapers, and many small community newspapers. During the first four months, the company received over 1,000 letters a day and requests for 1 million reprints. The campaign was a smashing success—not because it could eradicate America's verbal problems, but because it generated a lot of interest and some concern. In the long run this concern could lead to a drive to improve the reading and writing abilities of America's future generations[1] (Figure 10–1).

Copywriting and advertising strategy

International Paper's advertising objective was to create awareness of the problem of declining literacy and to stimulate interest on the part of teachers and young people to do something about it (at least for themselves). The success of their efforts was indicated by the number of inquiries they received for reprints of their ads. But what was the strategy that enabled them to achieve that success?

A review of Chapter 9 reminds us that advertising strategy involves four elements:

1. The product concept.
2. The target audience.
3. The communications media.
4. The advertising message.

The product concept, in this case, has seemingly little to do with International Paper's functional product. Instead of selling paper, they are selling an idea: the power of the printed word—the concept that reading and writing are important skills.

The target audience was young people—namely, high school students aged 15–18 and young adults aged 18–34. In the first year of the campaign, using print media like *Newsweek, Sports Illustrated, Rolling Stone, Ebony,* and *Seventeen,* International Paper reached 50 million young people with their message.

What was the message strategy? The message strategy is determined by what the company wants to say and how it wants to say it. International Paper wanted to say that reading and writing skills are important. They can help your career, provide new opportunities in life, give pleasure and enjoyment to yourself and others, and help those around you. How to say that involved developing a verbal and nonverbal presentation of the message that would be simple, interesting, informative, entertaining, enjoyable, and helpful. In Chapter 11, "Creative Art Direction," we will discuss the nonverbal, graphic side of message strategy. The subject of this chapter, copywriting, concerns the verbal element of message strategy. The combined product of the art director and the copywriter is the creative nucleus, which is then translated through the production process into the final advertisement or commercial.

Building the message strategy

Before the copywriter starts to think about writing an ad, he or she must understand the marketing and advertising strategies completely. This includes the message strategy. If the advertising plan has not spelled it out in detail (which is often the case), then the copywriter should immediately build a message strategy, with the art director if possible, and get it approved before going any further. The fastest way to have an advertisement rejected is to write a brilliant piece of work that is off-strategy.

Review the research; analyze the facts. Study the market, the product, the competition. (See the Checklist.) How is the market segmented? How is the product to be positioned? Who are the best prospects for the product? Is the target audience different from the target market? What is the key consumer benefit (Figure 10–2)? What support or reason does the consumer need to believe in that benefit? What support can you give? What is the product's image to be? The answers to these questions determine the message strategy.

At this point, research is important. As we saw in Chapter 8, N. W. Ayer tested all its ideas for 7up before writing the advertising.

Research identifies the best prospects; research identifies the best strategy; research can find the most important consumer appeals or product claims. *What* the advertising says is more important than *how* it is said. So test the strategy.

Copy platform

You are almost ready to start writing. Now review your strategy and write a brief general statement of what consumer needs we are ap-

How to write clearly

By Edward T. Thompson
Editor-in-Chief, Reader's Digest

International Paper asked Edward T. Thompson to share some of what he has learned in nineteen years with Reader's Digest, a magazine famous for making complicated subjects understandable to millions of readers.

If you are afraid to write, don't be.

If you think you've got to string together big fancy words and high-flying phrases, forget it.

To write well, unless you aspire to be a professional poet or novelist, you only need to get your ideas across simply and clearly.

It's not easy. But it *is* easier than you might imagine.

There are only three basic requirements:

First, you must *want* to write clearly. And I believe you really do, if you've stayed this far with me.

Second, you must be willing to *work hard*. Thinking means work–and that's what it takes to do anything well.

Third, you must know and follow some *basic guidelines*.

If, while you're writing for clarity, some lovely, dramatic or inspired phrases or sentences come to you, fine. Put them in.

But then with cold, objective eyes and mind ask yourself: "Do they detract from clarity?" If they do, grit your teeth and cut the frills.

Follow some basic guidelines

I can't give you a complete list of "dos and don'ts" for every writing problem you'll ever face.

But I can give you some fundamental guidelines that cover the most common problems.

1. Outline what you want to say.

I know that sounds grade-schoolish. But you can't write clearly until, *before you start*, you know where you will stop.

Ironically, that's even a problem in writing an outline (i.e., knowing the ending before you begin).

So try this method:

• On 3"x 5" cards, write–one point to a card–all the points you need to make.
• Divide the cards into piles–one pile for each group of points *closely related* to each other. (If you were describing an automobile, you'd put all the points about mileage in one pile, all the points about safety in another, and so on.)
• Arrange your piles of points in a sequence. Which are most important and should be given first or saved for last? Which must you present before others in order to make the others understandable?
• Now, *within* each pile, do the same thing–arrange the *points* in logical, understandable order.

There you have your outline, needing only an introduction and conclusion.

This is a practical way to outline. It's also flexible. You can add, delete or change the location of points easily.

2. Start where your readers are.

How much do they know about the subject? Don't write to a level higher than your readers' knowledge of it.

CAUTION: Forget that old–and wrong–advice about writing to a 12-year-old mentality. That's insulting. But do remember that your prime purpose is to *explain* something, not prove that you're smarter than your readers.

3. Avoid jargon.

Don't use words, expressions, phrases known only to people with specific knowledge or interests.

Example: A scientist, using scientific jargon, wrote, "The biota exhibited a one hundred percent mortality response." He could have written: "All the fish died."

4. Use familiar combinations of words.

A speech writer for President Franklin D. Roosevelt wrote, "We are endeavoring to construct a more inclusive society." F.D.R. changed it to, "We're going to make a country in which no one is left out."

CAUTION: By familiar combinations of words, I do *not* mean incorrect grammar. *That* can be *un*clear. Example: John's father says he can't go out Friday. (Who can't go out? John or his father?)

5. Use "first-degree" words.

These words immediately bring an image to your mind. Other words must be "translated" through the first-degree word before you see the image. Those are second/third-degree words.

"Outline for clarity. Write your points on 3"x 5" cards–one point to a card. Then you can easily add to, or change the order of points–even delete some."

First-degree words	Second/third-degree words
face	visage, countenance
stay	abide, remain, reside
book	volume, tome, publication

First-degree words are usually the most precise words, too.

"Grit your teeth and cut the frills. That's one of the suggestions I offer here to help you write clearly. They cover the most common problems. And they're all easy to follow."

6. Stick to the point.

Your outline– which was more work in the beginning–now saves you work. Because now you can ask about any sentence you write: "Does it relate to a point in the outline? If it doesn't, should I add it to the outline? If not, I'm getting off the track." Then, full steam ahead–on the main line.

7. Be as brief as possible.

Whatever you write, shortening–*condensing*–almost always makes it tighter, straighter, easier to read and understand.

Condensing, as *Reader's Digest* does it, is in large part artistry. But it involves techniques that anyone can learn and use.

• *Present your points in logical ABC order:* Here again, your outline should save you work because, if you did it right, your points already stand in logical ABC order–A makes B understandable, B makes C understandable and so on. To write in a straight line is to say something clearly in the fewest possible words.
• *Don't waste words telling people what they already know:* Notice how we edited this: "Have you ever wondered how banks rate you as a credit risk? ~~You know, of course, that it's some combination of facts about your income, your job, and so on. But actually,~~ Many banks have a scoring system...."
• *Cut out excess evidence and unnecessary anecdotes:* Usually, one fact or example (at most, two) will support a point. More just belabor it. And while writing about something may remind you of a good story, ask yourself: "Does it *really help* to tell the story, or does it slow me down?"

The biota exhibited a 100% mortality response

Writing clearly means avoiding jargon. Why didn't he just say: "All the fish died!"

(Many people think *Reader's Digest* articles are filled with anecdotes. Actually, we use them sparingly and usually for one of two reasons: either the subject is so dry it needs some "humanity" to give it life; or the subject is so hard to grasp, it needs anecdotes to help readers understand. If the subject is both lively and easy to grasp, we move right along.)

• *Look for the most common word wasters:* windy phrases.

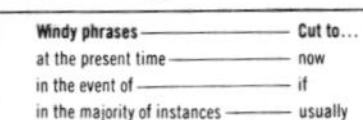

Windy phrases	Cut to...
at the present time	now
in the event of	if
in the majority of instances	usually

• *Look for passive verbs you can make active:* Invariably, this produces a shorter sentence. "The cherry tree *was* chopped down by George Washington." (Passive verb and nine words.) "George Washington *chopped* down the cherry tree." (Active verb and seven words.)
• *Look for positive/negative sections from which you can cut the negative:* See how we did it here: "The answer ~~does not rest with carelessness or incompetence. It lies largely in~~ is having enough people to do the job."
• Finally, to write more clearly by saying it in fewer words: when you've finished, stop.

Years ago, International Paper sponsored a series of advertisements, "Send me a man who reads," to help make Americans more aware of the value of reading.

Today, the printed word is more vital than ever. Now there is more need than ever before for all of us to *read* better, *write* better, and *communicate* better.

International Paper offers this *new* series in the hope that, even in a small way, we can help.

For reprints of this advertisement, write: "Power of the Printed Word," International Paper Co., Dept. , P.O. Box 900, Elmsford, New York 10523.

Figure 10–1 "How to write clearly," by Edward T. Thompson, Editor-in-Chief, *Reader's Digest,* was the subject of only one ad in International Paper's award-winning series directed to young people. Others included "How to write a business letter" by Malcolm Forbes; Tony Randall on "How to improve your vocabulary"; and Bill Cosby on "How to read faster." In all cases, the authors of the ads worked closely with the advertising agency's art director and copywriter to insure student readability and interest.

pealing to. What product features satisfy those needs? What support is there for the product claim? What is the product's position? What personality or image have you decided to create? What approach or tone will be used in the copy? And generally what will the copy say? This copy platform will be your guide for writing the ad.

When the first ad is written, review the strategy and copy platform again. See whether the ad measures up. If it doesn't, reject it, throw it away, and start again. As we said in Chapter 9, marketing is war. Wars are won and lost because of strategy.

Objectives of good copy

By 1910 Henry Ford had spent five years and thousands of dollars perfecting his new Model T. Now the first models were ready; it was time to advertise. But what sort of ad should he run? Ads at that time were mostly art or photos, with few, if any, words. But Ford believed art alone couldn't sell his Model T. It had to be described—in detail.

A few weeks later readers of the *Saturday Evening Post* were startled to see a black and white ad, two pages long, that contained no pictures. Instead, it was all words!

"When Ford speaks the world listens" (Figure 10–3).

"Buy a Ford car because it is better—not because it is cheaper."

"The reason why can be given in a very few words. . . ."

The "very few words" total about 1,200. They told how Henry Ford had invented the Model T. They detailed the financial condition of the Ford Company. And they listed its 28 factories, assembly plants, and branches.

The ad was a "first." It contained more words, or *copy,* than any ad of the day. It also caused some industry leaders to rebuke Ford. "Pictures sell cars," one said flatly, "not words." But Ford stood his ground and proved he was right. The ad soon produced more sales than any other auto ad in history. And it gave Henry Ford his first push toward what was to become 10 years later the largest and most profitable manufacturing company in the world.[2]

This example illustrates that few elements in advertising are subject to more misconceptions than the creative function and the objectives of good copy.

Advertising pyramid

We have discussed the general objectives of advertising: to inform, persuade, and remind. We have also discussed the specific tasks advertising tries to accomplish in pursuit of these general purposes. These specific tasks or objectives were explained in Chapter 9 by means of the advertising pyramid. Advertising attempts to make people aware first and then create understanding. Next it attempts to convince people, create desire, and finally motivate them to action. The objectives of good copywriting might be similarly explained by creating a copy pyramid.

Copywriter's checklist of product marketing facts

Identity
- ☐ Trade name
- ☐ Trademark
- ☐ Product symbol
- ☐ Other copyrighted or patented information

Performance
- ☐ What does it do?
- ☐ What might it be expected to do that it does *not?*
- ☐ How does it work?
- ☐ How is it made or produced?
- ☐ What is in it?
  - Raw materials
  - Preservatives
  - Chemicals
  - Special ingredients
  - Nutrients
- ☐ What are its physical characteristics?
  - Color
  - Appearance
  - Smell
  - Others
  - Taste
  - Texture

Life
- ☐ What is its life or use span?

Effectiveness
- ☐ Is there proof that it has been tested and works well?
- ☐ Are there any government or other regulations that need to be mentioned or observed?

Competitive information
- ☐ Who are the competitors?
- ☐ Does it have any advantages over them?
- ☐ Does it have any disadvantages?
- ☐ Are they all about the same?
- ☐ Do rival products present problems that this one solves?

Manufacturing
- ☐ How is it made?
- ☐ How long does it take?
- ☐ How many steps in the process?
- ☐ How about the people involved in making it?
- ☐ Are there any special machines used?
- ☐ Where is it made?

Packaging
- ☐ Unit size or sizes offered
- ☐ Package shape
- ☐ Package design
  - Styling
  - Color
  - Special protection for product
  - A carrier for product
- ☐ Package label

History
- ☐ When was it created or invented?
- ☐ Who introduced it?
- ☐ Has it had other names?
- ☐ Have there been product changes?
- ☐ Is there any "romance" to it?

Consumer use
- ☐ How is the product used?
- ☐ Are there other possible uses?
- ☐ How frequently is it bought?
- ☐ What type of person uses the product?
- ☐ Why is the product bought?
  - Personal use
  - Gift
  - Work
- ☐ What type of person uses the product most (heavy user)?
- ☐ What amount of the product is bought by the heavy user?
- ☐ Where does the best customer live?
- ☐ What kind of person is a heavy user or buyer?

Product image
- ☐ How do people view the product?
- ☐ What do they like about it?
- ☐ What do they dislike about it?
- ☐ Is it a luxury?
- ☐ Is it a necessity?
- ☐ Is it a habit?
- ☐ Is it self-indulgent?
- ☐ Do people have to have it but wish they didn't?

Distribution
- ☐ How widely is the product distributed?
- ☐ Are there exclusive sellers?
- ☐ Is there a ready supply or limited amount?
- ☐ Is it available for a short season?

Market position
- ☐ What is its share of the total market?

Research
- ☐ What research about the product does the supplier have?
- ☐ Is research available?

Copy pyramid

The purpose of copywriting is to persuade or remind a group or groups of individuals to take some action in order to satisfy some need or want of theirs. But first people need to be made aware—either of their problems or, if that's obvious, that a solution exists. To create awareness requires getting their attention.

Attention

Gaining attention is therefore the first objective of copywriting and is the foundation block of the copy pyramid (Figure 10–4). Copywriters have numerous devices at their disposal to gain attention.

The basic approach or consumer appeal of the advertisement normally determines how much attention the ad will receive. It also determines the success of the advertisement in moving its readers up through the other blocks in the pyramid.

There are innumerable type of appeals or approaches used by advertisers. The two broadest categories are rational appeals and emotional appeals. The former is an appeal to the consumer's practical, functional need for the product or service. The latter relates to the consumer's psychological, social, or emotional needs. Many other types of appeals used by advertisers may or may not fall into one of those two broad categories. (See Figure 10–5.) These include positive and negative appeals, fear and sex appeals, and humor appeals. Depending on the message strategy, any or all of these may be used to gain attention, create a personality for the product or service, and stimulate consumer interest, credibility, desire, and action.

Figure 10–2

EASY TO USE 30-second

ANNCR (VO): A lot of people think using Federal-Express is complicated but really, it's so simple, even a Vice-President can do it.

VP (OC): HELLOOOOOO FEDERAL

ANNCR (VO): All you do is pick up the phone and we come to your office and pick up the package.

Why, even a president can do that!

PRES (OC): HELLOOOOOO FEDERAL

ANNCR (VO): In fact, using Federal Express is so simple that even a Chairman of the Board can do it.

CHAIRMAN (OC): HELLOOOOOO . . .

(SFX: FINGERS SNAP, SNAP)

ANNCR (VO): Federal Express. When it absolutely, positively has to be there overnight.

There are some factors over which the copywriter has no control. Obviously, the size of the advertisement influences whether or not it will be noticed. The position in a publication determines who will see the advertisement. The copywriter must take all these factors into account before deciding on an attention-getting device. The attention-getting device must relate to the product, to the rest of the advertisement, and to the intended audience. Headlines that promise

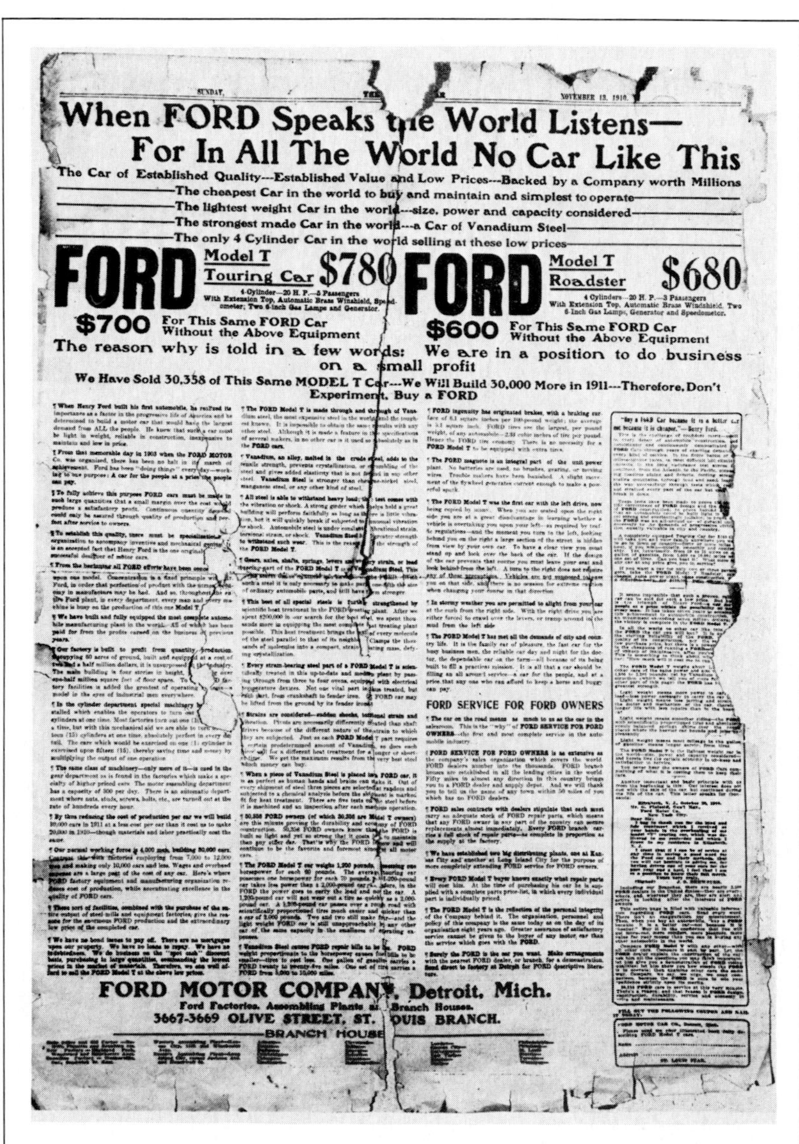

Figure 10–3 This 1910 advertisement written by Henry Ford might have been the inspiration for E. F. Hutton's famous campaign: "When E. F. Hutton Talks, People listen." Containing 1,200 words, the Ford ad contained the longest copy of any advertisement of its time. It also sold more autos than any previous ad in history.

something but fail to deliver it will not make a sale; in fact, the advertiser may alienate a potential customer. For example, ads that use nudes or salacious headlines that are unrelated to the product or sales ideas attract attention but often lose sales.

Figure 10–5 Selected advertising appeals

Appetite
Taste
Health
Fear
Humor
Security
Cleanliness
Sex attraction
Romance
Social approval/approval of others
Social achievement
Ambition
Personal comfort
Protection of others
Sympathy for others
Devotion to others
Guilt
Pride of personal appearance
Home comfort
Pride in appearance of property
Pleasure of recreation
Entertainment
Opportunity for more leisure time
Avoidance of a laborious task
Enhancement of earnings
Style (beauty)
Pride of possession
Curiosity
Novelty
Safety
Courtesy
Hedonism (pleasure for pleasure's sake)
Rest or sleep
Economy in use
Economy in purchase
Efficiency in operation or use
Dependability in use
Dependability in quality
Durability
Variety of selection
Simplicity
Sport/play/physical activity
Cooperation

Figure 10–4 The copy pyramid.

Interest

The second step in building the copy pyramid is to create interest. We have gotten our customer's attention. She's looking at our advertisement. But if we can't keep her interest, we're going to lose her. So we have to talk to her, about her, and about her problems and needs. We may use the word *you* frequently.

Interest is the bridge between attention and credibility. It is an important step. There are several effective ways to build and maintain interest. We might use cartoon characters, subheads, interior illustrations, storyline copy, or charts and tables. We shall discuss some of these later.

Credibility

As we work our way up the copy pyramid, the next block is very important because it is a stumbling block—credibility. Consumers today are more sophisticated than in years past. To them the proofs offered in some advertisments are not only unbelievable but also insulting. In such cases product sales frequently suffer. As a result, if the advertiser offers test data, they must give honest support to the product claim and not be statistical manipulation.

Credibility is sometimes added to advertisements through the use of presenters. As a spokesman, actor James Garner has lent great credibility to the ease of operating Polaroid's One-Step cameras. Juliet Prowse, the famous dancer, has the legs to demonstrate the staying power of L'eggs hosiery.

Suffice it to say that if the copy or the ad technique does not make the product's claim credible, then the next two blocks of the pyramid will surely crumble.

Desire

To heighten desire we need to inform the reader or the viewer of the benefits of our product or service. Each new benefit should heighten desire because it is matched with a real or perceived need of the customer. Even when only one benefit is presented, it must be done in such a way that the customer believes it and understands its application to his or her situation. This is why knowing the customer is so important.

Action

We now build the final block in the copy pyramid. It is the same as the final block in the advertising pyramid. We want to motivate the reader to take some action, to do something, or at least to agree with us. The action may be immediate or future. It may be a direct request: "Come to our sale May 15." It may be indirect or implied in the copy: "Make holiday cooking easier—start with PAM."

The request for action must be in the copy. You're asking for the order. You're asking that the reader agree with you. Too many advertisements have forgotten that readers are generally lazy or preoccupied; they need a course of action spelled out for them. That's the job of good copy.

Understanding copy terminology

All advertisements are made up of numerous elements or components. These elements may be moved, enlarged, reduced, reversed, changed, or eliminated until a new look or approach is achieved. To discuss copy we must understand what these elements are and what they do.

The key elements in print advertising are the headline, illustration, subhead, body copy, captions, boxes and panels, slogans, logotypes (logos), seals, and signatures.

In broadcast advertising, copy is normally spoken dialogue, so it is usually referred to as the "audio" portion of the commercial. The audio may be delivered as a *voice-over* by an announcer who is not seen but whose voice we hear. Or it may be *on-camera* dialogue by an announcer, a spokesperson, or actors playing out a scene. When words are shown on the screen, they are normally referred to by the same terms used in print advertising. Let us discuss each of those terms briefly.

Headlines

The headline is considered by many to be the most important element in a print advertisement. The term *headline* refers to the words in the leading position in the advertisement—that is, the words that will be read first or that are positioned to draw the most attention. As a result, headlines are usually set in larger type than other portions of the advertisement.

A headline has six important functions. First, the headline must attract attention to the advertisement. The entire message is usually lost if no one reads the headline. To promote the eternity ring, De-Beers uses a highly effective headline statement: "You once said 'I do.' Now you can say 'I'm glad I did.' " (Figure 10–6).

Second, the headline should select the reader; that is, it tells whether the subject matter of the ad interests the reader. "Should a gentleman offer a lady a Tiparillo?" excites interest and selects the audience. It is a headline for men that doesn't alienate women.

Audiences may be qualified by demographic (age, sex, income) or by psychographic criteria. A noted copywriter, Stan Freeburg, developed a headline for an airline advertisement that used psychographic qualification. The headline read: "Hey, you with the sweaty palms!" The campaign was short-lived. Research has since shown that airline passengers subconsciously are disturbed by airline advertisements which are concerned with safety. So advertising care is advisable;

psychographic qualification can backfire and the results can be devastating.

Third, the headline should lead the reader directly into the body copy. One good example is:

Headline: "What kind of man reads *Playboy?*"

Body copy: "He's a man who demands the best life has to offer. . . ."

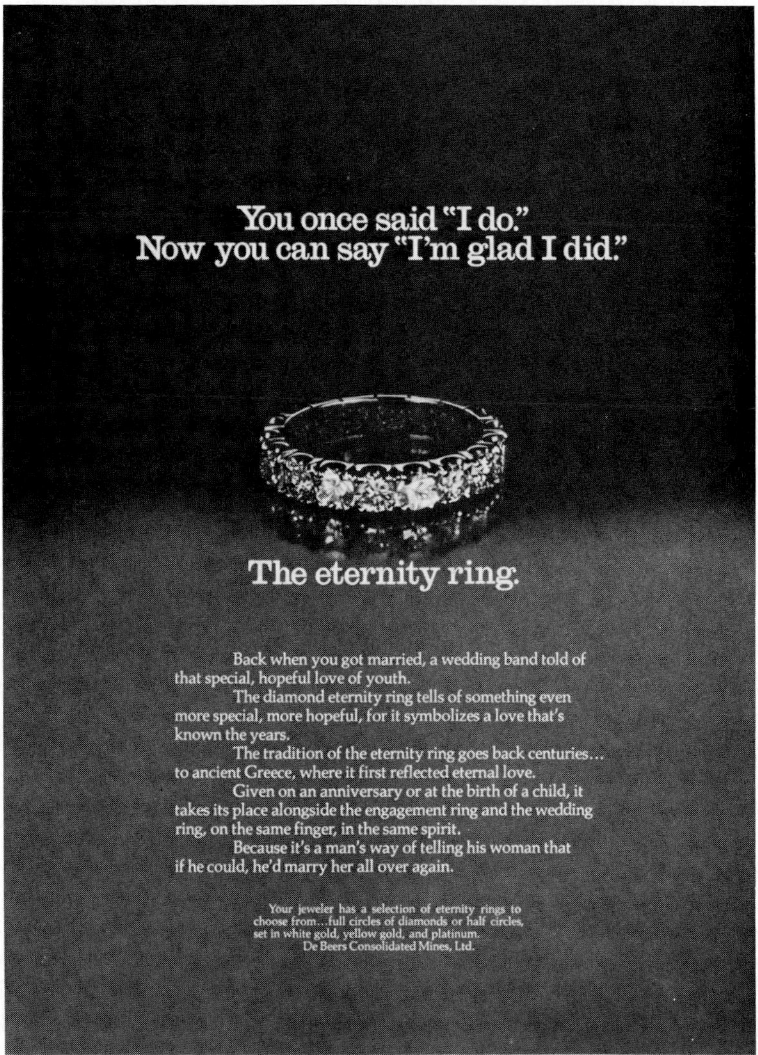

Figure 10–6 DeBeers Consolidated Mines controls the marketing of eighty percent of the world's diamond production through its Central Selling Organization in London. To support the retail jewelry trade to whom it sells, DeBeers conducts a massive international advertising campaign and has been responsible for such famous slogans as "A diamond is forever." Here, to promote its eternity ring, DeBeers speaks of the deep love that has "known the years." The headline not only attracts attention; it effectively tells the whole story.

People in advertising

John Caples

Vice President
Batton, Barton, Durstine & Osborn, Inc.

John Caples, famed master of advertising copy, is a vice president of Batten, Barton, Durstine & Osborn, America's seventh largest advertising agency. Creator of such classic ads as "They laughed when I sat down at the piano," Caples has written copy for scores of nationally advertised products in his more than 50 years of advertising. He has also taught advertising courses at Columbia University and at the Advertising Club of New York.

Noted for his research into scientific methods of testing advertising effectiveness, Caples has lectured extensively on these methods. He has also supervised advertising research for Du Pont, General Electric, U.S. Steel, Lever Bros., Goodrich Tire and Rubber, U.S. Navy, and other major organizations.

Born in New York City, Caples attended Columbia University. He was later nominated to the U.S. Naval Academy at Annapolis, where he earned a B.S. degree. While a student engineer with New York Telephone Company, Caples completed an advertising course at Columbia. He soon became a copywriter for Ruthrauff & Ryan. There he wrote the classic piano ad that was to launch an important new mail-order technique—and his advertising career.

In 1927 Caples joined Batten, Barton, Durstine & Osborn as a copywriter and account executive. He was named a vice president of BBDO in 1941, a position he still holds. In a recent interview, Caples made these observations about copywriting:

On word power: "Simple words are powerful words. Even the best educated people don't resent simple words. But they're the words many people understand. Write to your barber or mechanic or elevator operator. Remember, too, that every word is important. Sometimes you can change a word and increase the pulling power of the ad. Once I changed the word 'repair' to 'fix,' and the ad pulled 20 percent more!"

On humor: "Avoid it. What's funny to one person isn't to millions of others. Copy should sell, not just entertain. Remember there's not one funny line in the two most influential books ever written: the Bible and the Sears catalog."

On changing times: "Times change. People don't. Words like *free* and *new* are as potent as ever. Ads that appeal to a reader's self-interest still work. People may disagree about what self-improvement is important, but we all want to improve ourselves. Ads that offer news still work. The subjects that are news change, but the human curiosity to know what's new doesn't. These appeals worked 50 years ago. They work today. They'll work 50 years hence."

Praising these insights, David Ogilvy, chairman of the board of Ogilvy & Mather, International, said of John Caples, "He is not only an indomitable analyzer and teacher of advertising, he is also a first-rate copywriter—one of the most effective there has ever been."

Ogilvy hailed Caples' book, *Tested Advertising Methods,* as "the most useful book about advertising that I have ever read." Caples has authored three other books on advertising: *Making Ads Pay, Advertising Ideas,* and *Advertising for Immediate Sales.* Since 1972 he has been a featured monthly columnist in *Direct Marketing Magazine.*

Recipient of the annual award of the National Association of Direct Mail Writers and the Hundred Million Club Leadership Award, Caples was elected to the Copywriters Hall of Fame in 1973. Four years later he was named to the Advertising Hall of Fame. He is listed in *Who's Who in America.*

Slight and soft-spoken, Caples hardly fits the image of Madison Avenue's "man in the gray flannel suit." Yet, as his clients know, few surpass John Caples in the ability to induce people to buy products through skillful, persuasive advertising.

Fourth, the headline must present the complete selling idea. It may be intended merely to carry through a campaign theme, but it should tell the whole story (Figure 10–7). Marlboro accomplishes this in beautiful magazine and outdoor advertisements with nothing more than a western illustration, a cigarette pack, and the headline: "Come to where the flavor is. Marlboro Country." The headline creates the mood, suggests the image, asks for the sale, and states the brand name, all at once. Not only that, it is memorable and identifiable with the product. It therefore has the ability to trigger a recognition response in the consumer's mind. The DeBeers headline mentioned earlier accomplishes the same task.

David Ogilvy points out that on the average five times as many people read the headline as read the body copy. Therefore if you haven't done some selling in the headline, you've wasted 80 percent of your money. Ogilvy also suggests that advertisers should not be afraid of long headlines. Headlines that contain 6 to 12 words usually get the best results; and his best headline, he says, contained 18 words: "At sixty miles an hour the loudest noise in the new Rolls-Royce comes from the electric clock."[3]

Fifth, the headline should promise the customer a benefit. Ontario Pork tells consumers "How to save money by getting into hock" (Figure) 10–8). The benefit should be readily apparent to the reader and easy to get.

Sixth, the headline should present product *news* of interest to the reader. Consumers look for new products, new uses of old products, or improvements on old products. Therefore words that imply newness increase readership and should be used whenever applicable. Examples are *new, now, suddenly, announcing, introducing, it's here, improvement, revolutionary, just arrived, and important development.* (See the Checklist.)

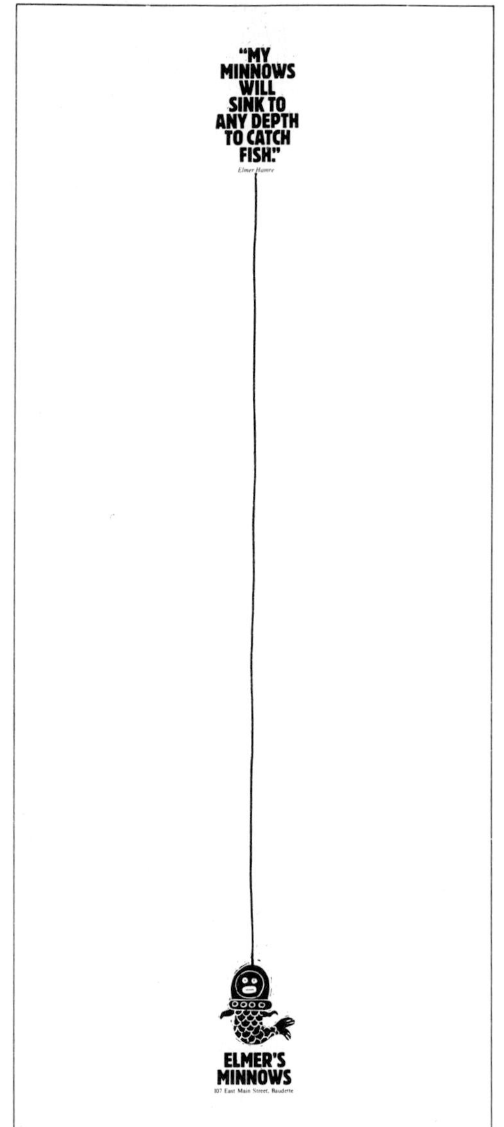

Figure 10–7 Small-space ads can be just as effective as full-color spreads. What is required is not big space but rather a big idea. Elmer's Minnows consistently hooks advertising awards with small-space newspaper ads in which the whole selling idea is wrapped up in the headline and the graphic.

Subheads

Subheads are misnamed because they can appear above or below the headline. They can also appear in the body copy or the text of the advertisement. A subhead that appears above the headline is called a "kicker."

Subheads usually appear in a smaller type size than the headline. They are almost invariably larger than the body copy or text type size. Subheads may appear in boldface (heavier) type or in lighter ink color.

The purpose of the subhead is to transmit key sales points—fast! Most individuals read only the headline and subheads. The subhead should be reserved for important facts that may not be as dramatic or memorable as the headline information. Some may require more space than a headline because they communicate more information in more words.

The subheads should reinforce the headline and advertisement theme. Mobil's "Save less time in the air" is a headline well reinforced by these subheads: "The oil that saves you gas," "The oil that saves you oil," "Better in hot and cold weather," and "Better engine protection" (Figure 10–9).

Body copy

Body copy, or *text,* as it is sometimes called, tells the complete sales story. It is a logical continuation of the headline and subheads. The body copy is set in a smaller typeface (size) than headlines or subheads. Body copy is also where the sale is closed.

The text should relate to the campaign appeal and to the reader's self-interest. It must explain how the product or service being advertised satisfies the customer's need. The text may concentrate on a single benefit or several benefits as they relate specifically to the target audience. Write it as if you were conversing with one person. Some pointers follow.

1. Don't beat around the bush. Get straight to the point.
2. Be specific, factual. Don't generalize.
3. Avoid superlatives (people usually don't believe them anyway).
4. Be truthful and make the truth fascinating. Don't be a bore.
5. Be enthusiastic, friendly, and memorable. Tell the whole story and no more. When finished, stop.[4]

There are four basic elements to body copy: the lead-in paragraph, interior, trial, and close.

Lead-in paragraph

The lead-in paragraph is a bridge between the headline, subheads, and the sales ideas presented in the text. It transfers reading interest to product interest.

Headline: "TV that puts itself to sleep."

Lead-in paragraph: "You don't have to get out of bed to turn off this Zenith portable TV. Just pre-set the time for up to 3 hours."

The lead-in paragraph may perform other functions as well. In short-copy advertisements (an increasing trend) the lead-in paragraph may also be the close. It may include both a promise and claim-support information.

Interior paragraphs

This is where we provide proof for claims and promises. Remember, a good advertisement must not only be truthful, it also has to be believable in order to be effective. With educational levels constantly rising and with increased consumer awareness, proofs must be offered carefully. The key to the interior paragraphs is credibility. The proof you offer may fall into the following categories:

1. Research: government or private studies.
2. Testing: by case history, testing firm, consumers, or the advertiser.
3. Usage: product market rank, case history, testimonial, endorsements.
4. Guarantee: trial offers, demonstration offers, free samples, warranty information.

Trial close

Interspersed in the interior paragraphs should be requests for the order. Good body copy asks for the order more than once in many cases. In mail-order advertisements particularly, it is necessary to ask for the order several times. Consumers may decide to buy without reading the entire body copy. The trial close gives them the option to make the buying decision before they get bored.

Close

An advertisement's close asks consumers to do something and tells them how to do it. This is the point in the advertisement when the sale is made. We use the word *sale* in its broadest sense. Not all

Figure 10–8 Clever copywriting and beautiful illustration characterize this ad tendered by the Ontario Pork Association. The copy is complete, informative, and helpful. The illustration is succulent. It's no wonder the ad won all the big awards and sold a lot of pork, too.

advertisements sell products or services. We may be looking for a change in attitude, an understanding of our point of view, or a new preference for our product or service.

The close can be direct or indirect, ranging from subtle suggestion to direct command. English Leather men's toiletries uses an indirect close in its headline: "My men wear English Leather or they wear nothing at all." The last sentence of the body repeats the same line, suggesting indirectly that if you want to please a woman you will wear English Leather or, conversely, if you want to please a man, you will buy him English Leather. A direct close seeks immediate consumer response. The response may be in the form of a purchase or a request for further details.

Checklist of what works best in print

Here is a checklist to help you create effective newspaper and magazine advertisements.

☐ Use simple layouts. One big picture works better than several small pictures. Avoid cluttered pages. (Layouts that resemble the magazine's editorial format are well read.)

☐ Always put a caption under a photograph. Readership of picture captions is generally twice as great as of body copy. The picture caption can be an advertisement by itself.

☐ Don't be afraid of long copy. The people who read beyond the headline are *prospects for your product or your service*. If your product is expensive—like a car, a vacation, or an industrial product—prospects are hungry for the information long copy gives them. Consider long copy if you have a complex story to tell, many different product points to make, or an expensive product or service to sell.

☐ Avoid negative headlines. People are literal-minded and may remember only the negatives. Sell the positive benefits in your product—not that it won't harm or that some defect has been solved. Look for emotional words that attract and motivate, like *free* and *new* and *love*.

☐ Don't be afraid of long headlines. Research shows that on the average long headlines sell more merchandise than short ones.

☐ Look for *story appeal*. Next to the headline, an illustration is the most effective way to get a reader's attention. Try for story appeal—the kind of illustration that makes the reader ask: "What's going on here?"

☐ Photographs are better than drawings. Research says that photography increases recall an average of 26 percent over artwork.

☐ Look at your advertisement in its editorial environment. Ask to see your advertisement pasted into the magazine in which it will appear. Or, for newspapers, photostated in the same tone as the newspaper page. Beautifully mounted layouts are deceptive. The reader will never see your advertisement printed on high-gloss paper, with a big white border, mounted on a board. It is *misleading* for you to look at it this way.

☐ Develop a single advertising format. An overall format for all print advertising can double recognition. This rule holds special meaning for industrial advertisers. One format will help readers see your advertisements as coming from one large corporation, rather than several small companies.

☐ Before-and-after photographs make a point better than words. If you can, show a visual contrast—a change in the consumer, or a demonstration of product superiority.

☐ Do not print copy in reverse type. It may look attractive, but it reduces readership. For the same reason, don't surprint copy on the illustration of your advertisement.

☐ Make each advertisement a complete sale. Your message must be contained in the headline. React to the overall impression, as the reader will. Only the advertiser reads all his advertisements. Any advertisement in a series must stand on its own. *Every one* must make a complete sale. Assume it will be the only advertisement for your product a reader will ever see.

The successful close simplifies the reader's response and makes it as easy as possible for the reader to order the merchandise, send for information, or visit a showroom. Make reader action easy! Provide a business reply card for mailing or include a toll-free telephone number. Make sure the close tells the consumer where to shop or what to send. In fact, everything the reader needs for action should be in the close or near it (Figure 10–10).

The final purpose of the close is to provide a memorable knife to cut through the last shreds of skepticism. The close should reinforce all the reader's positive thoughts and dispel any negative thoughts concerning the product or service.

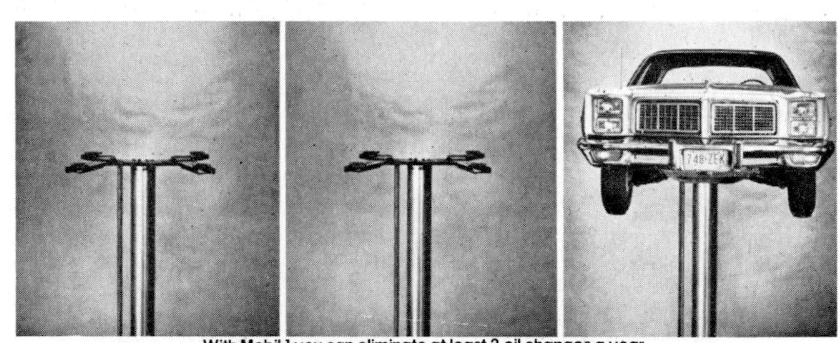

With Mobil 1 you can eliminate at least 2 oil changes a year.
Spend less time in the air.
Switching to Mobil 1 is a good way to keep your car where it belongs. On the ground.
If you've been changing your oil the way most people have (every 4 to 6,000 miles) Mobil 1 could take you much farther and eliminate at least 2 oil changes a year. You could rack up a total of 15,000 miles or go a full year, whatever comes first, before you have to put your car up on the rack for an oil change. (If your car is still under warranty, you should change your oil in accordance with warranty requirements.)
The oil that saves you gas.
Mobil 1 cuts friction so well it actually takes the average car up to 10 extra miles on a tankful of gas.
The oil that saves you oil.
Since Mobil 1 doesn't evaporate as rapidly as ordinary oil you should be using less oil. (Provided, of course, that your engine is in good mechanical condition.)
Better in hot and cold weather.
Mobil 1 is a synthesized engine lubricant that outperforms premium motor oil all seasons of the year. Since Mobil 1 doesn't thicken up as much as ordinary oil in cold weather, you'll be getting easier cold weather starts. Mobil 1 can actually help your car get started in temperatures as low as 35 degrees below zero.
Mobil 1 doesn't thin out the way ordinary oil does in hot weather, either. It continues to spread a better protective film over the moving parts of your engine, even in the hottest days of summer.
Better engine protection.
To prove how good our oil really is we ran Mobil 1 in a car for 15,000 miles, adding oil as needed. Incredible as it may seem, tests showed that after 15,000 miles of driving, used Mobil 1 still protected the engine as well as brand new premium motor oil!
So if you're up in the air about which oil to buy, come down to earth.
Buy Mobil 1.
Mobil 1
The oil that saves you gas ...saves you oil changes.

Figure 10–9 The subheads should reinforce the headline and advertisement theme. Mobil's headline is well reinforced by the subheads.

Boxes and panels

Boxes and panels are generally used in advertisements that contain coupons, special offers, contest rules, and order blanks. The boxes and panels are used to set these features apart from the rest of the advertisement.

Specifically, a *box* is copy around which a line has been drawn. A *panel* is an elongated box that usually runs the whole length or width of an ad. Sometimes it may be shaded or completely black with text or copy shown in reverse (white lettering).

Boxes and panels are used to draw greater attention to a specific element or message in your advertisement.

Figure 10–10 "Never go fishing without Mann-made worms" is the final close from Mann's Bait Company. Everything in this ad is designed to help the reader understand the product and buy it on the special limited offer.

Slogans

Slogans (or tag lines) are similar to headlines. In fact, many of them began as successful headlines. They become standard statements for salespeople and company employees. They become a battle cry for the company. In fact, the word *slogan* comes from the Gaelic term for "battle cry."

Slogans have two basic purposes. The first is to provide continuity for a campaign. The second is to reduce a key theme or idea the company wants associated with its product or itself to a brief, memorable statement. DeBeers ads still claim the famous promise in their tag line: "Diamonds are forever."

Slogans are like old friends who stay the same year after year. You recognize them instantly and you feel you understand them. Some slogans endure because they encapsulate a corporate philosophy: "Quality never goes out of style" (Levi's).

Effective slogans are short, easy to understand, memorable, and easy to repeat. Good slogans help set the product apart from its competitors ("When it rains, it pours"—Morton Salt). Rhyme, rhythm, and alliteration are valuable copy aids to use when writing slogans.

Seals, logotypes, and signatures

The term *seal* is the subject of much confusion among advertising students. For some, it indicates the seals offered by such organizations as the Good Housekeeping Institute, Underwriters' Laboratories, and Parents' Institute. These are given only when a product meets standards established by these institutions. Since they are all recognized authorities—and are trusted implicitly—it is beneficial to include them in an advertisement. These seals provide an independent, valued endorsement for the advertised product.

For others, the term *seal* refers to the company seal or trademark. These are actually called *logotypes.* Logotypes (logos) and signature cuts (sig cuts) are special designs of the advertiser's name or product name. They appear in all the advertisements and are like trademarks because they give the product individuality and provide quick recognition at the point of purchase.

Types of headlines and copy styles

Copywriters and advertising academicians have been trying to classify types of headlines and body copy for years. There are probably as many different classifications and types as there are authors on the subject. Richard Stansfield, for example, has come up with 23 "basic" types of headlines for which he has developed names that range from "Teaser" to "So what?"

The advertising practitioner would probably say "so what?" to the whole subject. However, for the student of advertising and the businessperson with limited experience in the field, it is helpful to briefly discuss certain common types of headlines and copy styles. This should facilitate understanding the role of copywriting and the skill required to write effective copy.

Headlines

Generally, we can classify good advertising headlines into five basic categories: benefit, provocative, news/information, question, and command.

Benefit headlines

Benefit headlines make a direct promise to the reader. Two good examples are "A Rabbit diesel could give you cheaper long-distance rates than your telephone" and "Everytime we race, you won" (Yamaha).

Provocative headlines

Some headlines are written to provoke the reader's curiosity. To learn more, the reader must read the body copy. Of course, the danger here is that the reader won't read on and the headline won't have sold anything. For that reason, provocative headlines are usually coupled with illustrations that offer clarification or some *story appeal.* Figure 10–11 is an example: "Dear American Tourister: I fell flat on my attache." The accompanying illustration shows the testimonial letter-writer tumbling down a flight of stairs and landing on his American Tourister briefcase. To know the rest of the story, the reader must read on.

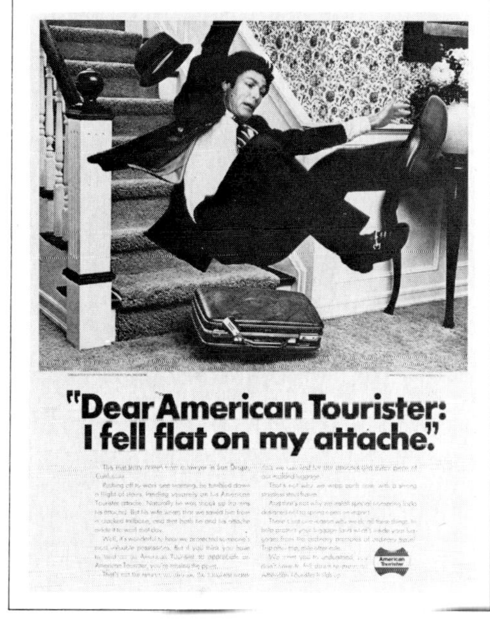

Figure 10–11 American Tourister has successfully used the testimonial approach with provocative headlines for years. Another well-known example is "You're great on unscheduled flights" with the ad showing a suitcase being thrown from the top of a car.

News/information headlines

This category includes many of the "how-to" headlines as well as headlines that seek to gain identification for their sponsors by announcing some news or providing some promise of information. Dunlop tennis rackets and balls, for example, are advertised in long-copy, instructive ads with the headline: "Improving your game is our game" (Figure 10–12). Another example is: "The Honda Civic. The car we designed around a shopping bag." Or Chivas Regal: "The most carefully poured Scotch in the world." This headline provides the reader with an enormous amount of information in a very short sentence. It tells the reader that Chivas Regal is precious and expensive. Neither of these facts is necessarily "hot news," but both provide information and are memorable.

Question headlines

Question headlines can be dangerous. If you ask a question that the reader can answer quickly, the rest of the advertisement may not get read. Imagine a headline that reads: "Do you like food?" The reader answers "of course" and turns the page.

An American Airlines' advertisement with the headline "If you don't show your kids where America began, who will?" did not fall into that trap. It was designed to motivate thoughtful parents about future travel plans. It accomplished that objective.

Command headlines

A headline that orders you to do something might seem negative, yet we pay attention to such headlines. They motivate us through fear or emotion, or because we understand the inherent correctness of the command. For example, "Drive safely. The life you save may be your own" is extremely well known and difficult to challenge as being a good idea. Similar appeals have extended to drunk driving: "Get the drunk driver off the road."

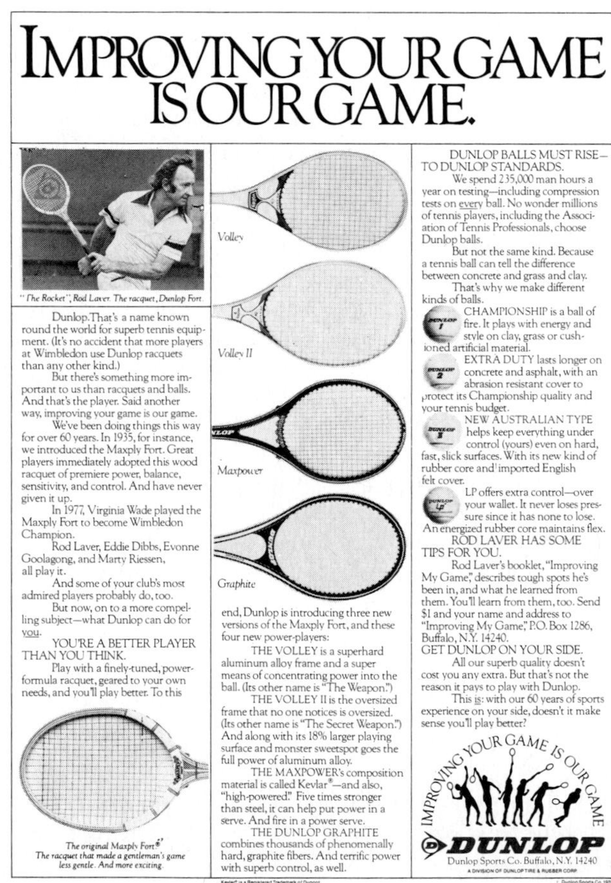

Figure 10–12 Long columns of informative copy in this Dunlop ad help the tennis enthusiast. Note the clean graphic design, the clear use of subheads to pull the reader through the copy, and the captioned illustrations. The whole ad comes off in a very credible, editorial fashion.

Other command headlines are more pleasant such as "Listen to what you've been missing in cassette sound" (3M Company).

Perhaps the best command headline ever written was: "Promise her anything but give her Arpege."

Classifying headlines into categories might take a lifetime and would serve little purpose. We have only touched on a few in this brief discussion. Many headline categories are easily combined. Some work better with illustrations than others. Provocative headlines and question headlines, for example, usually require more support from definitive illustrations. A good exercise for the beginning copywriter is to keep a checklist of headline types and try to write several different types for each new project. That is one way to find the best solution to the problem at hand.

Copy styles

In writing copy we look for the techniques that provide the greatest sales appeal for the idea we are presenting. The advertising plan gives the direction for *what* to say. Now we're concerned with *how* to say it.

Copy styles fall into several categories. These include straight-line, narrative, institutional, dialogue/monologue, picture-caption, and gimmick.[5]

Straight-line copy

The body copy begins immediately to explain or develop the headline and illustration in a clear attempt to sell the product. The product's sales points are ticked off in order of their importance.

Straight-line copy is advantageous in industrial situations and for consumer products that may be difficult to use. Many camera advertisements, for example, use this straight factual copy style to get the message across. The straight-line approach emphasizes the reason the consumer should buy something.

Narrative copy

Narrative copy tells a story. It sets up a problem and then creates a solution using the particular sales features of the product or service. It may then suggest that you use the same solution if you have that problem.

Institutional copy

Sometimes the advertiser tries to sell an idea or the merits of the organization or service rather than sales features of a particular product. Often institutional copy is also narrative in style because it lends warmth to the organization. Banks, insurance companies, public utilities and large manufacturing concerns are the most common users of institutional copy (Figure 10–13).

Dialogue/monologue copy

This technique can add the credibility that narrative copy sometimes lacks. The characters illustrated in the advertisement do the selling in their own words either through a testimonial or quasitestimonial technique or through a comic strip panel (Figure 10–14).

However, this style is not usually written well by the layperson. The copywriter who uses dialogue should have some playwriting experience. Unless it is done well, dialogue can be dull—not everything people say is interesting.

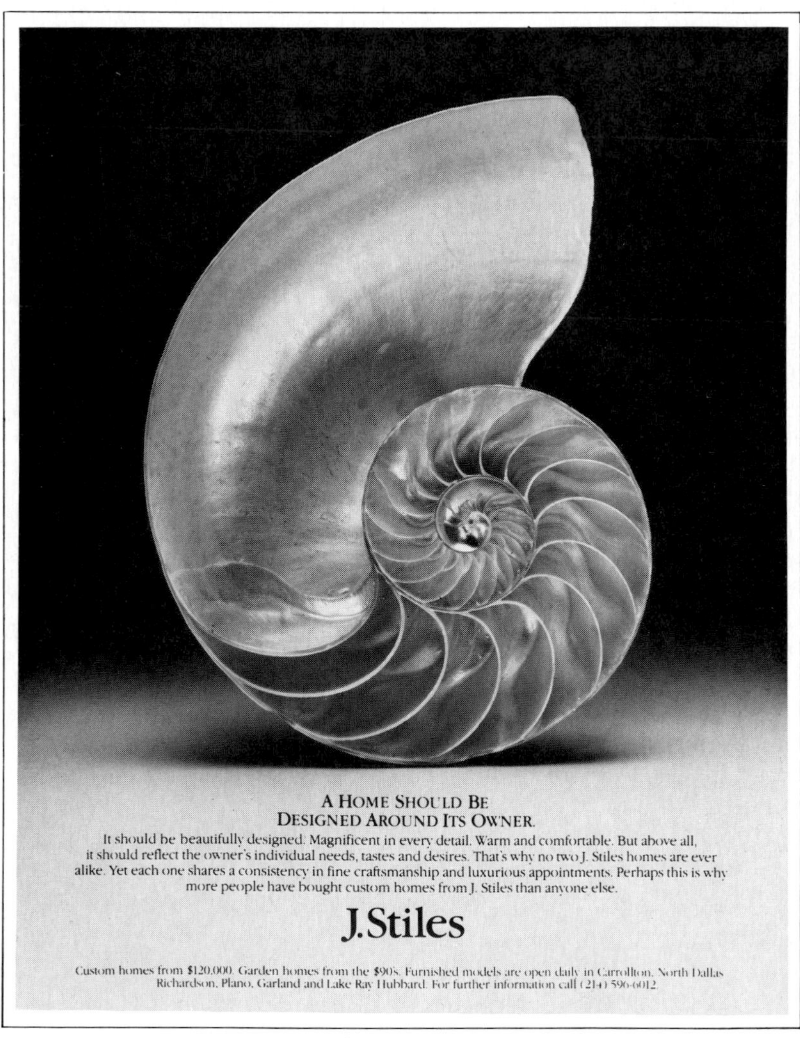

A HOME SHOULD BE
DESIGNED AROUND ITS OWNER.
It should be beautifully designed. Magnificent in every detail. Warm and comfortable. But above all, it should reflect the owner's individual needs, tastes and desires. That's why no two J. Stiles homes are ever alike. Yet each one shares a consistency in fine craftsmanship and luxurious appointments. Perhaps this is why more people have bought custom homes from J. Stiles than anyone else.
J.Stiles
Custom homes from $120,000. Garden homes from the $90's. Furnished models are open daily in Carrollton, North Dallas Richardson, Plano, Garland and Lake Ray Hubbard. For further information call (214) 596-6012.

Figure 10–13 J. Stiles runs an elegant campaign in various slick Texas magazines to enhance the company's image as a high-quality custom home builder. This institutional approach is probably far more effective as an image builder than a more promotional approach would be.

Picture-caption copy

Sometimes it is easier to tell the story through a series of illustrations and captions than through the use of a copy block alone. This is especially true when the product is shown in a number of different uses or when a variety of styles or designs of the product are available.

Gimmick copy

Gimmick copy depends on humor, poetry, rhyming, great exaggeration, gags, and other trick devices (Figure 10–15). Don't downgrade gimmick advertising. A gimmick carried out rationally is believable. One institutional campaign featured a pink elephant as a product's speaker. Once you accepted the pink elephant and laughed, you suddenly discovered you were thinking about the product and not the speaker.

Humor is a popular device, particularly in broadcast advertising. However, it is also very controversial.

As a general rule, observe the following principles with any kind of gimmick copy:

- Use it for low-priced products rather than for higher priced products.
- Humor may be used to destroy an outmoded attitude or use pattern that affects your product. The campaign "You've come a long way baby" used sophisticated humor to bring women back to smoking (more women have quit than men).
- Humor is effective when high memorability in a short time is needed.
- Don't use humor for serious subjects.
- Never use humor that is in questionable taste.

These rules have their exceptions, of course. The good copywriter learns the techniques and the principles so they can be used more effectively (and can be broken when necessary). (See the Ad Lab.)

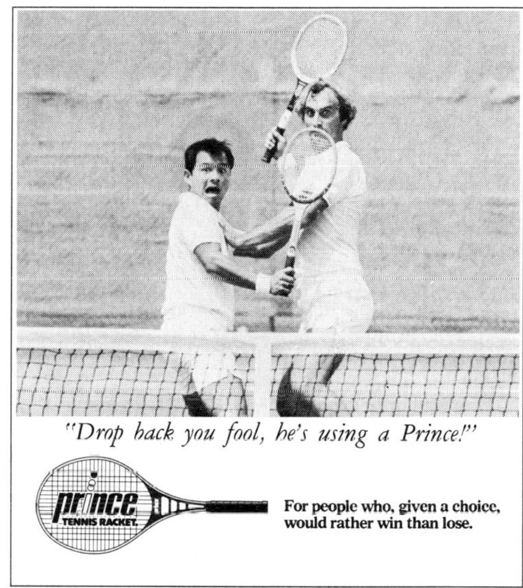

"Drop back you fool, he's using a Prince!"
prince TENNIS RACKET
For people who, given a choice, would rather win than lose.

Figure 10–14 The humor in this dialogue ad is instantaneous. The picture further emphasizes the message. Note, finally, the tongue-in-cheek tag line. It is a simple message, completely told, from beginning to end.

Common pitfalls in writing copy

The key point to remember about copy style is that it must reflect American tastes and values (assuming the advertisement is oriented to the American public). Today's consumer is intelligent, educated, and discriminating. Generalizations are not convincing. The consumer is looking for specific information to form judgments and make purchase decisions. Being specific means leaving out the fancy advertising buzz words. *Amazing, wonderful,* and *finest* all fall into that category.

Words cost money. A print advertisement may cost $50 a word or $5,000 a word, depending on the medium. Every word must count at those prices. Words that do not sell cost more money than words that do. So use the words that sell; and avoid the pitfalls that plague beginning copywriters and annoy customers.

Obfuscation

Readability is the fundamental requirement of any print advertisement. Avoid ten-dollar words (like *obfuscation*) that nobody understands. Write simply in the everyday, colloquial English that people use in conversation. (See the Ad Lab.) Use small words. You will get your point across better if you use words and phrases that are familiar to your reader. Use short sentences. The longer the sentence, the harder it is to understand. Compare these paragraphs:

The Armco vacuum cleaner not only cleans your rugs and

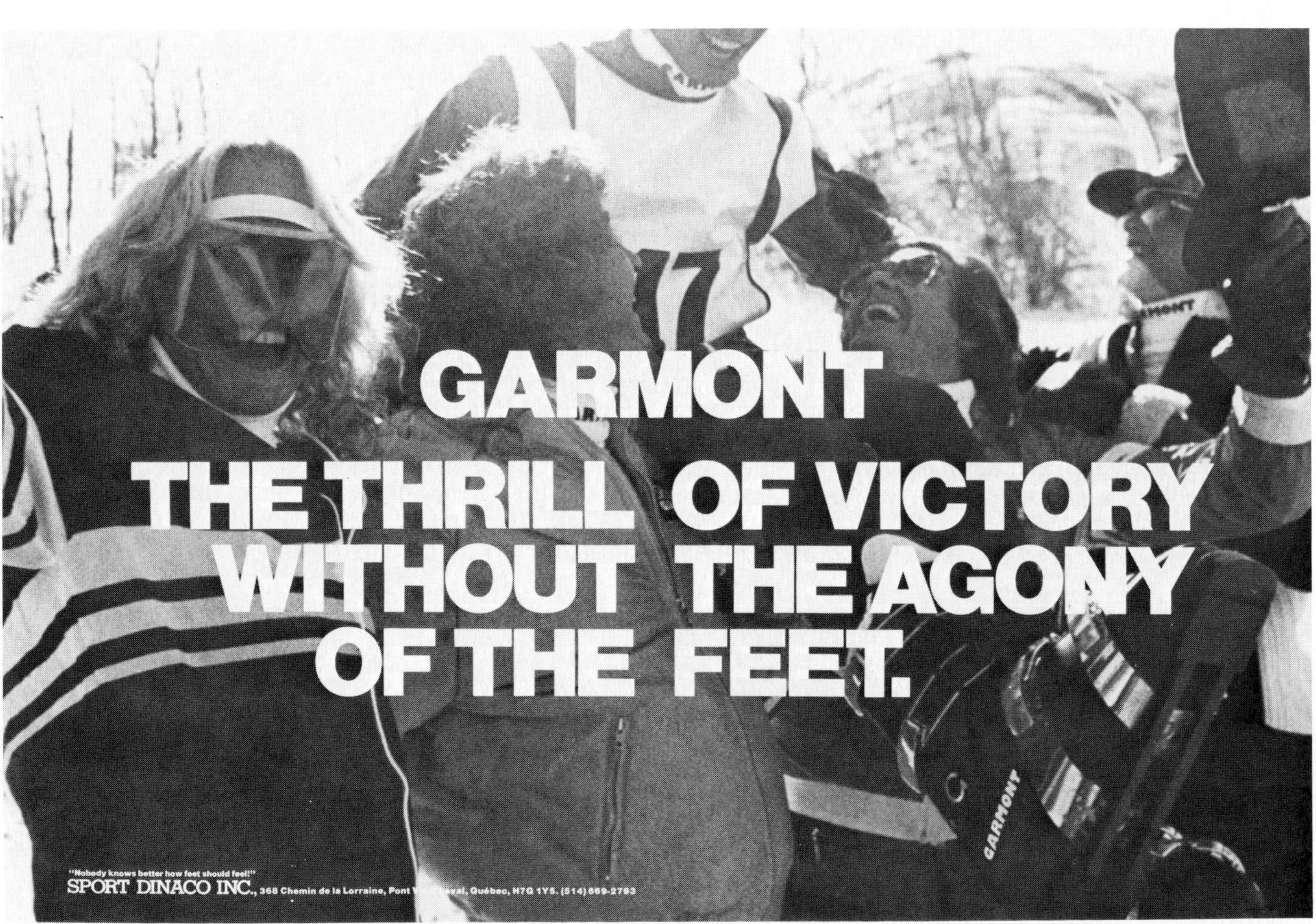

Figure 10–15 Garmont boots merchandises the famous ABC Wide World of Sports line in this gimmick headline designed to communicate the product's comfort.

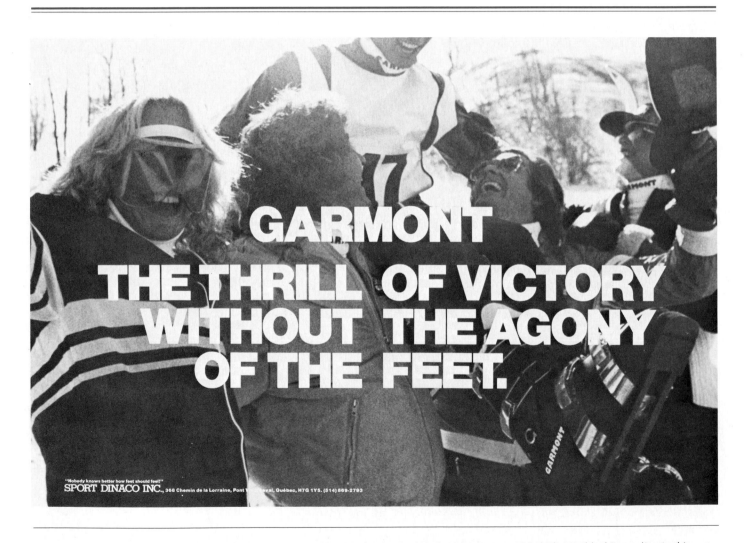

drapes, it's invaluable on hard surfaces such as vinyl floors, wood floors, even cement. You won't believe how incredibly smooth and quiet the machine is as it travels across your sparkling floors.

The Armco vacuum cleaner cleans rugs . . . drapes. It cleans hard surfaces like woods and vinyl floors. Even cement! The Armco vacuum cleaner is smooth . . . quiet. Try it! Make your floors sparkle with new cleanliness.

Thousands of advertisements compete for your reader. The more readable your advertisment, the more likely it will be read.

Filibustering

We have discussed the importance of brevity. Look at this headline: "Winston tastes good like a cigarette should." Now imagine if it weren't concise: "Winston cigarettes taste exceedingly fine, the way every cigarette manufacturer wishes his cigarettes would taste."

Long-winded filibusters should be confined to the Senate. They are not allowed in advertising. Be complete, but be concise.

Clichés/triteness/superlatives

Overused expressions do nothing for copy. In fact, at least one study suggests that they harm readability. Most superlatives and clichés were once exciting statements, but time has worn their value into rags.

Certainly clichés can communicate, and not all stock expressions are clichés. But clichés erode consumer confidence. They contribute to an out-of-date image.

Abstracts/vagueness

Abstract words are words that do not provide a specific measurement, such as *good, fine, OK*. They are not easily understood or evaluated. Concrete words are specific and understood.

Good copy is concrete and tied in with the experience of the audience to which it appeals. Words should have concrete dollars and cents value. For example, in an industrial ad for a new piece of equipment, it would be better to be specific and say the machine "performs the work of five people" rather than to simply mention that it's a "work-saving machine."

Me me me.

To be effective the advertisement must appeal to the reader's self-interest, not the advertiser's. If you want to get your message across and persuade the reader, use the "you" attitude. Talk in terms of his or her needs, hopes, wishes, and preferences. Talk about the reader

Test your understanding of headline types and copy styles

Laboratory application

Carefully read the advertisements in this section. Identify the headline type and copy style for each advertisement from the list below.

Headline types	Copy styles
Benefit	Straight-line
Provocative/curiosity	Narrative
News/information	Institutional
Question	Dialogue/monologue
Command/challenge	Picture-caption
	Gimmick

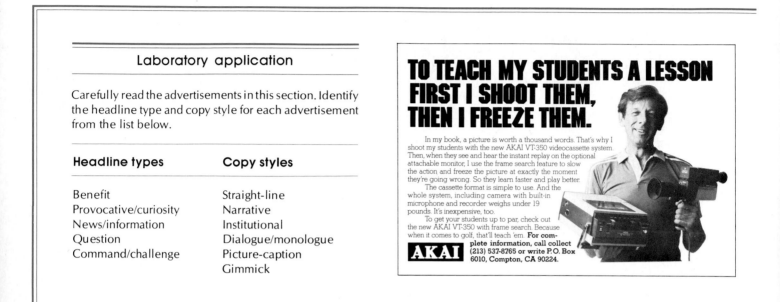

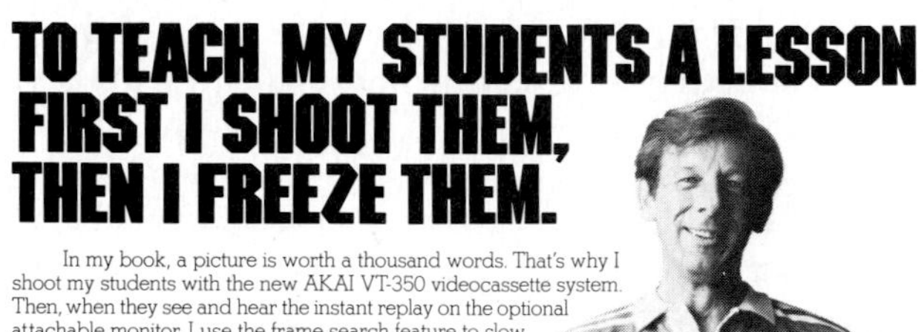

TO TEACH MY STUDENTS A LESSON
FIRST I SHOOT THEM,
THEN I FREEZE THEM.

In my book, a picture is worth a thousand words. That's why I shoot my students with the new AKAI VT-350 videocassette system. Then, when they see and hear the instant replay on the optional attachable monitor, I use the frame search feature to slow the action and freeze the picture at exactly the moment they're going wrong. So they learn faster and play better.

The cassette format is simple to use. And the whole system, including camera with built-in microphone and recorder weighs under 19 pounds. It's inexpensive, too.

To get your students up to par, check out the new AKAI VT-350 with frame search. Because when it comes to golf, that'll teach 'em. **For complete information, call collect (213) 537-8765 or write P.O. Box 6010, Compton, CA 90224.**

Are you paying filet prices but eating sole?

All steak today costs a small fortune.

But when was the last time you can remember eating a steak that was worth what you paid for it?

Our steaks cost a little more than you're paying now.

But you should know you cannot buy a more tender, better tasting steak than a Prime-Pak steak. At any price.

A fact we're willing to guarantee, unconditionally, in writing.

We can make this guarantee, fearlessly, because we buy only the best beef money can buy.

This means paying top-dollar for our steaks and charging top-dollar for them.

But in return, you get a steak that has been fed only expensive corn and grain.

A steak that is rich in crucial marbling.

A steak that has been through a costly aging process.

A steak that has been trimmed of all but a quarter-inch of fat, the proper amount for cooking.

A steak that is the best-eating piece of meat you've ever bought anywhere at any price.

In addition, each Prime-Pak steak we sell must not only meet USDA standards, it must meet our own. And our standards are a lot harder to meet than the government's.

We also *blast freeze* our steaks at 50° below zero to seal in all the tenderness, flavorfulness and juiciness we've paid so dearly for.

Then we ship them individually wrapped, vacuum sealed in heavy-gauge film and packed in a carton overstuffed with dry ice.

Naturally, all this adds up to a lot of money. But at least when you promise your friends the best steak they've ever tasted, you won't feel like you've put your foot in your mouth.

Prime-Pak

For a free copy of our catalog, call 800-645-9498 toll-free.

BEFORE

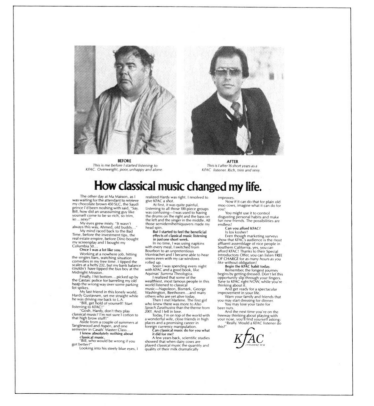

This is me before I started listening to KFAC. Overweight, poor, unhappy and alone.

AFTER

This is I after 16 short years as a KFAC listener. Rich, trim and sexy.

How classical music changed my life.

The other day at Ma Maison, as I was waiting for the attendant to retrieve my chocolate brown 450 SLC, the Saudi prince I'd been noshing with said, "Say, Bill, how did an unassuming guy like yourself come to be so rich, so trim, so…sexy?"

My eyes grew misty. "It wasn't always this way, Ahmed, old buddy…"

My mind raced back to the Bad Time, before the investment tips, the real estate empire, before Dino bought my screenplay and I bought my Columbia 50…

Once I was a lot like you.

Working at a nowhere job, hitting the singles bars, watching situation comedies in my free time. I tipped the scales at a hefty 232, but my bank balance couldn't have tipped the bus boy at the Midnight Mission.

Finally, I hit bottom…picked up by the Castaic police for barreling my old heap the wrong way over some parking lot spikes.

My last friend in this lonely world, Hardy Gustavsen, set me straight while he was driving me back to L.A.

"Bill, get hold of yourself! Start listening to KFAC!"

"Gosh, Hardy, don't they play classical music? I'm not sure I cotton to that high brow stuff!"

Aside from a couple of summers at Tanglewood and Aspen, and one semester in Casals' Master Class…

I knew absolutely nothing about classical music.

"Bill, who would be wrong if you got better?"

Looking into his steely blue eyes, I realized Hardy was right. I resolved to give KFAC a shot.

At first, it was quite painful. Listening to all those 100-piece groups was confusing—I was used to having the drums on the right and the bass on the left and the singer in the middle. All those semidemihemiquavers made my head spin.

But I started to feel the beneficial effects of classical music listening in just one short week.

In no time, I was using napkins with every meal, I switched from Bourbon to an unpretentious Montrachet and I became able to hear sirens even with my car windows rolled up.

Soon I was spending every night with KFAC and a good book, like Aquinas' *Summa Theologica.*

I realized that some of the wealthiest, most famous people in this world listened to classical music—Napoleon, Bismark, George Washington, Beethoven…and many others who are yet alive today.

Then I met Marlene. The first girl who knew there was more to *Also Sprach Zarathustra* than the theme from *2001.* And I fell in love.

Today, I'm on top of the world with a wonderful wife, close friends in high places and a promising career in foreign currency manipulation.

Can classical music do for you what it did for me?

A few years back, scientific studies showed that when dairy cows are played classical music the quantity and quality of their milk dramatically improves.

Now if it can do that for plain old moo cows, imagine what it can do for you!

You might use it to control disgusting personal habits and make fun new friends. The possibilities are endless!

Can you afford KFAC?

Is lox kosher?

Even though marketing surveys show that KFAC's audience is the most affluent assemblage of nice people in Southern California, yes, you *can* afford KFAC! Thanks to their Special Introductory Offer, you can listen FREE OF CHARGE for as *many hours as you like* without obligation!

Begin the KFAC habit today.

Remember, the longest journey begins by getting dressed. Don't let this opportunity slip through your fingers. Tune to KFAC right NOW, while you're thinking about it.

And get ready for a spectacular improvement in your life.

Warn your family and friends that you may start dressing for dinner.

You may lose your taste for beer nuts.

And the next time you're on the freeway thinking about playing with your nose, you'll find yourself asking:

"Really. Would a KFAC listener do this?"

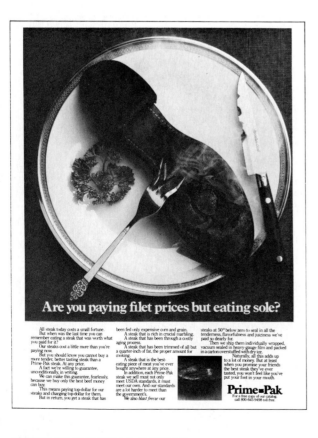

AZIZA DEMONSTRATES SHADOW WITH SEALER AND MASCARA WITH SEALER.
(THEY WON'T COME OFF TILL YOU TAKE THEM OFF.)
When you're busy all day long, the last thing you want to worry about is whether your eye shadow is creasing and fading or if your mascara is speckling and smudging.
That's why Aziza created Shadow with Sealer and Mascara with Sealer. Each contains a special blend of ingredients that gently seal themselves against moisture and skin oils once they're on your lid or lash. So the fresh, pretty look you put on in the morning still looks lovely at night.
This means that, at last, you won't have to check on your eye shadow every few hours. Because with crease-proof, fadeproof and waterproof Aziza Shadow with Sealer the color stays smooth and true all day. And you'll never have to wonder if your mascara is still on your lashes and not under your eyes because Aziza Mascara with Sealer is smudgeproof and smearproof, too.
We've also made Shadow with Sealer and Mascara with Sealer very easy to apply and full of lustrous color. There are 14 beautiful creme and frosted Shadow shades. And the Mascara comes in five rich colors as well as regular and extra-length formulas.
When you want to remove your makeup, both Sealer products will come off easily with Aziza Eye Makeup Remover Pads, Aziza Non-Oily Makeup Remover Lotion, or your favorite cold cream.
Do you have any questions about eye makeup? Write for our free book, "Aziza Demonstrates All About Eyes." Simply send 25¢ for postage and handling to Aziza, Dept. 844, 33 Benedict Place, Greenwich, Conn. 06830.
Because Aziza knows all about eyes.
Aziza by Prince Matchabelli

POLICE DEPT
08 15 78
B7864 1649
MEET THE EXPERT BEHIND OUR NEW COIN TELEPHONE
GTE AUTOMATIC ELECTRIC

Test your understanding of headline types and copy styles *(continued)*

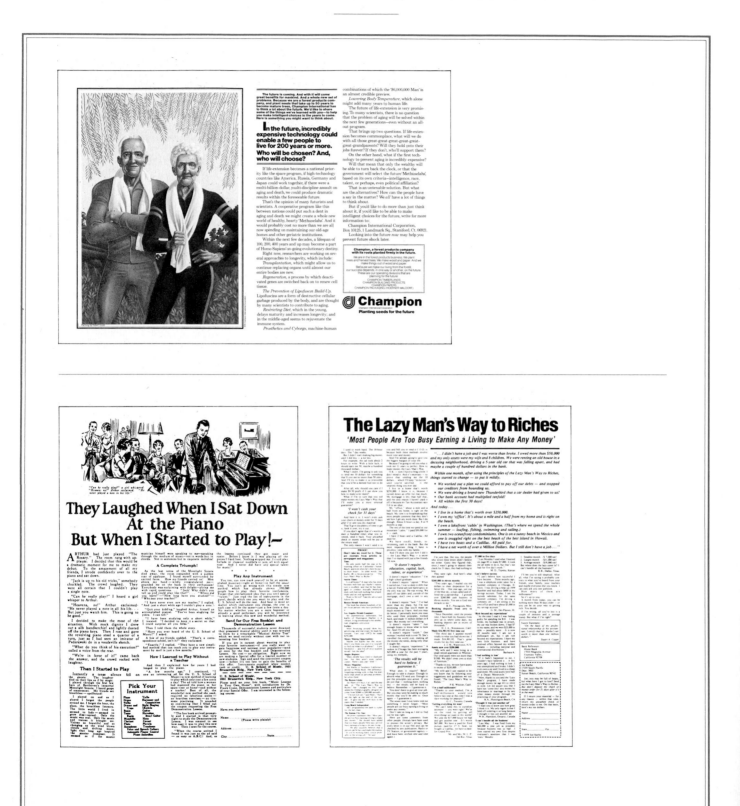

The future is coming. And with it will come great benefits for mankind. And a whole new set of problems. Because we are a forest products company, and plant seeds that take up to 50 years to become mature trees, Champion International has to think a lot about the future. We'd like to share some of the things we've learned with you—to help you make intelligent choices in the years to come. Here is something you might want to think about.

In the future, incredibly expensive technology could enable a few people to live for 200 years or more. Who will be chosen? And, who will choose?

If life-extension becomes a national priority like the space program, if high-technology countries like America, Russia, Germany and Japan could work together, if there were a multi-billion-dollar, multi-discipline assault on aging and death, we could produce dramatic results within the foreseeable future.

That's the opinion of many futurists and scientists. A cooperative program like this between nations could put such a dent in aging and death we might create a whole new world of healthy, hearty 'Methuselahs'. And it would probably cost no more than we are all now spending on maintaining our old-age homes and other geriatric institutions.

Within the next few decades, a lifespan of 100, 200, 400 years and up may become a part of Homo Sapiens' on-going evolutionary destiny.

Right now, researchers are working on several approaches to longevity, which include:

Transplantation, which might allow us to continue replacing organs until almost our entire bodies are new.

Regeneration, a process by which deactivated genes are switched back on to renew cell tissue.

The Prevention of Lipofuscin Build-Up. Lipofuscins are a form of destructive cellular garbage produced by the body, and are thought by many scientists to contribute to aging.

Restricting Diet, which in the young, delays maturity and increases longevity; and in the middle-aged seems to rejuvenate the immune system.

Prosthetics and Cyborgs, machine-human combinations of which the '$6,000,000 Man' is an almost credible preview.

Lowering Body Temperature, which alone might add many years to human life.

The future of life-extension is very promising. To many scientists, there is no question that the problem of aging will be solved within the next few generations—even without an all-out program.

That brings up two questions. If life-extension becomes commonplace, what will we do with all those great-great-great-great-great-great-grandparents? Will they hold onto their jobs forever? If they don't, who'll support them?

On the other hand, what if the first technology to prevent aging is incredibly expensive?

Will that mean that only the wealthy will be able to turn back the clock, or that the government will select the future 'Methuselahs', based on its own criteria—intelligence, race, talent, or perhaps, even political affiliation?

That is an untenable solution. But what are the alternatives? How can the people have a say in the matter? We *all* have a lot of things to think about.

But if you'd like to do more than just think about it, if you'd like to be able to make intelligent choices for the future, write for more information to:

Champion International Corporation, Box 10125, 1 Landmark Sq., Stamford, Ct. 06921.

Looking into the future *now* may help you prevent future shock later.

Champion, a forest products company with its roots planted firmly in the future.

We are in the forest products business. We plant trees and harvest trees. We make wood and paper. And we make things out of wood and paper.

Because we make our living from the forest, our success depends, in one way or another, on the future. These are our operating divisions that are planning for the future:

CHAMPION TIMBERLANDS
CHAMPION BUILDING PRODUCTS
CHAMPION PAPERS
CHAMPION PACKAGING (HOERNER WALDORF)

Champion
Champion International Corporation
Planting seeds for the future

They Laughed When I Sat Down At the Piano But When I Started to Play!—

A Complete Triumph!

Then I Started to Play

How I Learned to Play Without a Teacher

Play Any Instrument

Send for Our Free Booklet and Demonstration Lesson

Pick Your Instrument

Piano	'Cello
Organ	Harmony and Composition
Violin	Sight Singing
Drums and Traps	Ukulele
Banjo	Guitar
Tenor Banjo	Hawaiian Steel Guitar
Mandolin	Harp
Clarinet	Cornet
Flute	Piccolo
Saxophone	Trombone
Voice and Speech Culture	
Automatic Finger Control	
Piano Accordion	

U. S. School of Music, 1031 Brunswick Bldg., New York City.

Have you above instrument? ....

Name .... (Please write plainly)

Address ....

City .... State ....

The Lazy Man's Way to Riches

'Most People Are Too Busy Earning a Living to Make Any Money'

". . . I didn't have a job and I was worse than broke. I owed more than $50,000 and my only assets were my wife and 8 children. We were renting an old house in a decaying neighborhood, driving a 5-year old car that was falling apart, and had maybe a couple of hundred dollars in the bank.

Within one month, after using the principles of the Lazy Man's Way to Riches, things started to change — to put it mildly.

- *We worked out a plan we could afford to pay off our debts — and stopped our creditors from hounding us.*
- *We were driving a brand-new Thunderbird that a car dealer had given to us!*
- *Our bank account had multiplied tenfold!*
- *All within the first 30 days!*

And today . . .

- *I live in a home that's worth over $250,000.*
- *I own my 'office'. It's about a mile and a half from my home and is right on the beach.*
- *I own a lakefront 'cabin' in Washington. (That's where we spend the whole summer — loafing, fishing, swimming and sailing.)*
- *I own two oceanfront condominiums. One is on a sunny beach in Mexico and one is snuggled right on the best beach of the best island in Hawaii.*
- *I have two boats and a Cadillac. All paid for.*
- *I have a net worth of over a Million Dollars. But I still don't have a job . . ."*

and you are talking about the most interesting person in the world. For example:

Me	You
We are pleased to announce our new flight schedule from Cincinnati to Philadelphia which is any hour on the hour.	You can take a plane from Cincinnati to Philadelphia any hour on the hour.
We believe this vacuum cleaner to be technically superior to any other on the market.	Your house will be more beautiful because you'll be using the most powerful, easy-to-use vacuum we have ever offered.

The power of negative thinking

Think negatively, write negatively, and you may produce a negative response. Readers often respond more favorably to a positive viewpoint than to a negative one. Stress what things are or what they will be instead of what they are not or won't be. Remember that words have implications. They can provide a positive or negative response apart from literal meanings. Also, be aware that different people react

Cutting through the fog in copywriting

The Gunning Fox Index is a measure of your writing simplicity. Here's how it works:

Take 100-word samples from any given piece of writing—at least five or six samples if possible.

Count the number of words to the end of the sentence nearest the end of the 100-word sample (this could be more or less than 100) and enter in column 1.

Count the number of sentences in the sample and enter in column 2.

Count the number of sentences in that sample and enter in column 2.

Enter the total in column 3.

Do *not* count:

1. Proper nouns—Chicago, California, Throckmorton, Jonathan.
2. Compound words made of simple words—bookkeeper, furthermore, nevertheless.
3. Words that become three syllables because of an added *verb* ending such as -ing or -ed—bargaining, donating, recanted, accounted.

Total each column.

Find the average number of words per sentence; divide the total number of words (column 1) by the total number of sentences (column 2).

Find the average number of words with three syllables or more; divide the total of column 3 by the number of samples.

Add the two averages, then multiply by 0.4. The result is the reading grade level—the Fog Index—for that piece of writing.

Laboratory application

Select five or six pieces of your writing. Compute the Fox Index.

to the same word in different ways. *Love,* that most beautiful word, may have a positive note for a single person and a negative connotation for a divorced person.

Euphemisms

To *euphemize* is to substitute an inoffensive, mild word for a word that is offensive, harsh, or blunt. When a copywriter euphemizes, he or she puts a good face on something. Calling toilet paper "bathroom tissue" doesn't change its appearance or function, but it may soften the mental impression for people. Other euphemisms are "resale cars" (for used cars), "package store" (for liquor store), "underarm wetness" (for sweaty armpits), "irregularity" (for constipation), and "midriff bulge" (for fat gut). But be careful, euphemisms can be misleading and, if considered fraudulent, could invite FTC investigation.

Defamation

All advertising copy is governed by the laws of defamation. Making a false statement or allegation about a person or holding a person up to contempt is defamation. When this is done in print advertising it is called *libel.* In broadcast advertising or verbal statements it is called *slander.* Defamation occurs even when people's names are used or references are made to them in a libelous or slanderous manner. Size of audience is not a defense; a libelous statement, for example, need only be read by more than one person to be defamation.

Summary

Art is the visual presentation of the message strategy, and copy is the verbal presentation of the message. Before the copywriter begins to write, he or she must understand the intended marketing and advertising strategy. This usually requires a review of the marketing and advertising plan, an analysis of the facts, and an examination of the creative strategy. The copywriter should develop a brief, written copy platform that tells what the copy will say and how it will support the message strategy.

The objectives of advertising can be demonstrated through the use of the advertising pyramid. Similarly, the objectives of good copywriting can be explained by the use of a copy pyramid. To build the pyramid, the copywriter seeks to gain attention, create interest, achieve credibility, heighten desire, and stimulate action.

The key copy elements in print advertising are headlines, subheads, body copy, captions, boxes and panels, slogans, logotypes, seals, and signatures. In broadcasting advertising, copy is normally spoken dialogue and is referred to as the audio portion of the commercial. The copy may be delivered as a voice-over by an unseen announcer or on-camera by an announcer, spokesperson, or actor.

There are many types of headlines and copy styles. Good advertising headlines can generally be classified into five basic categories: (1) benefit, (2) provocative, (3) news/information, (4) question, and (5) command. Copy styles also fall into several categories. These are (1) straight line, (2) narrative, (3) institutional, (4) dialogue/monologue, (5) picture-caption, and (6) gimmick.

The pitfalls for unsuspecting copywriters are many and varied. The most common ones are obfuscation, filibustering, clichés/triteness/superlatives, abstract/vagueness, me me me, negative thinking, misleading euphemisms, and unintentional defamation.

Questions for review

1. Name five elements of message strategy.
2. What is the function of the copy pyramid? How is it built?
3. What are the elements of a print advertisement? Describe the function of each.
4. Choose an advertisement which you like and rewrite the headline using three different styles.
5. Find an advertisement with a tag line. What is its function, and what is your opinion of it?
6. What does *obfuscation* mean?
7. What are the six basic functions of a headline?
8. What are some of the most effective methods for making copy interesting?
9. Find an advertisement that you don't like. What is the message strategy? What type of headline is used? What is the copy style? Do you think the copy and headline reflect the strategy? What don't you like about the ad? Why?
10. What criteria should be applied in deciding which of the six types of copy should be used for a particular advertisement?

11

Creative art direction

From a small agricultural community in California's Imperial Valley, Earl Cavanah went to New York to become an art director. He was talented and before long found himself at Scali, McCabe, Sloves, the agency that does the ads for Volvo, Perdue Chickens, and Pioneer Electronics. Cavanah had worked on the Pioneer account for some time and had done a good job. When *Playboy* magazine retained the agency to help boost newsstand sales for some of its upcoming issues, the problem was given to Earl and Larry Cadman, a copywriter.

The agency's account team had already developed the basic advertising plan with the client. The intended audience would be 18–34-year-old men, middle to upper income, and upwardly mobile. This suggested a mixed media strategy using television as the primary vehicle supported by quarter-page newspaper ads in large-circulation newspapers and a short flight of supporting radio commercials. The product concept of *Playboy* magazine was well defined. It is *the* men's magazine, and everybody knows what's inside: beautiful girls. What typically differentiates one issue from another are the articles, feature stories, and interviews with famous people as well as the particular beautiful girl in that month's centerfold. That had to be the message.

One of their first projects was to work on the September 1979 issue, which was to feature pictures of women from the Ivy League colleges, the magazine's annual pigskin preview of professional football teams, and an interesting personal interview with baseball star Pete Rose. The question was how to tell this story in 30 seconds on television in an attention-getting, interesting, tasteful, memorable, and motivating way.

For Larry and Earl the first step in designing any advertisement or commercial is always the toughest. It's the long, tedious, difficult task of analyzing the problem, assembling any and all pertinent information, and developing some verbal or visual concept of how to communicate what needs to be said. This visualization process means establishing a mental idea or picture of the advertisement, commercial, or campaign before any copy is written or artwork begun.

The process may be called *visualization, conceptualization,* or *ideation.* It is the most important step in planning the advertisement. It is the creative point where the search for the "big idea" takes place. In this process, five, ten, twenty, a hundred, or more ideas may come up, be considered, and then rejected for any of a variety of reasons.

In searching for the big idea for the *Playboy* commercial, Earl Cavanah and Larry Cadman worked through a wide variety of concepts. At one point they thought of showing a scene with a father and son discussing what college the boy should attend. Then the *Playboy* pictures of the Ivy League coeds could be a humorous key to the boy's choice. They tried to work with that idea, but it was technically difficult. Finally, they rejected it. It was just too unwieldly, too complex. They liked the inherent humor, but it just took too long to get to the sales point of the message.

Back to the drawing board. Twenty more ideas. Some good, some not so good, some bad. No big ideas. Nothing clicked. They recalled the phrase: "Advertising is 10 percent inspiration, 90 percent perspiration." It was sure true this time. They went back over the plans. They restudied the information they had. They analyzed who would want to read this fall issue. What was the real differentiating feature?

What would have significance to those 18–34-year-old readers? And then how to present it? It was frustrating. "How about a fraternity house approach," said Larry.

"Animal House," said Earl. (The movie *Animal House,* about fraternity house high jinks, had come out the year before.)

"Yes," said Larry. "Maybe with two guys standing out in front looking at the September issue and discussing the articles while a party's going on in the background."

Earl jumped in, "No. We get a straight fraternity-president-type talking to a short, fat, animal-type who just ogles the magazine while the straight guy goes on and on talking about the interesting features and stories."

"Yeah, and they're both totally oblivious to what's going on in the background . . . like chairs flying through the windows, the roof caving in. . . ."

"I think we got it."

"We got it. Let's do it."

The big idea. That inspired creative nutshell, out of which grows all the visual and verbal details of every great advertisement (Figure 11–1).

In this chapter we will discuss those visual details, the art in advertising—what it is, where it comes from, how it's done.

What is art?

In advertising, *art* refers to more than what a cartoonist, a painter, or an illustrator does. The term refers to the whole visual presentation of the commercial or advertisement. That includes how the words in the ad are arranged, what size and style of type are used, whether photos or illustrations should be used, and, if so, how they should be organized. Art also refers to what style of photography or illustration is used, how color is used, and how these elements of an ad are arranged and relate to one another in size and proportion. This is true for both print ads and television commercials. Art directors are as involved in writing and producing the commercials we see on TV as copywriters are. In fact, many of the finest agencies have their art directors help write radio commercials. The feeling is that effective radio advertising combines sounds and words to create visual *word pictures* in the mind of the listener. To help orchestrate this visual side of the radio commercial, the art director can be very instrumental. Thus, every advertisement uses *art*—even if sometimes it is not good art.

Role of the advertising artist

There are several different types of people employed in advertising art. All of them may be called artists as a general description even though they may perform entirely different tasks. What is surprising to nonadvertising professionals is that so many of these "artists" cannot draw. They have been trained for other specialties.

Art directors

Art directors are responsible for the visual presentation of the ad. They are therefore normally involved in the initial concept of the ad, they work with a copywriter, and they may do the initial sketches, or layouts, of what the ad might look like. From that point on, they may

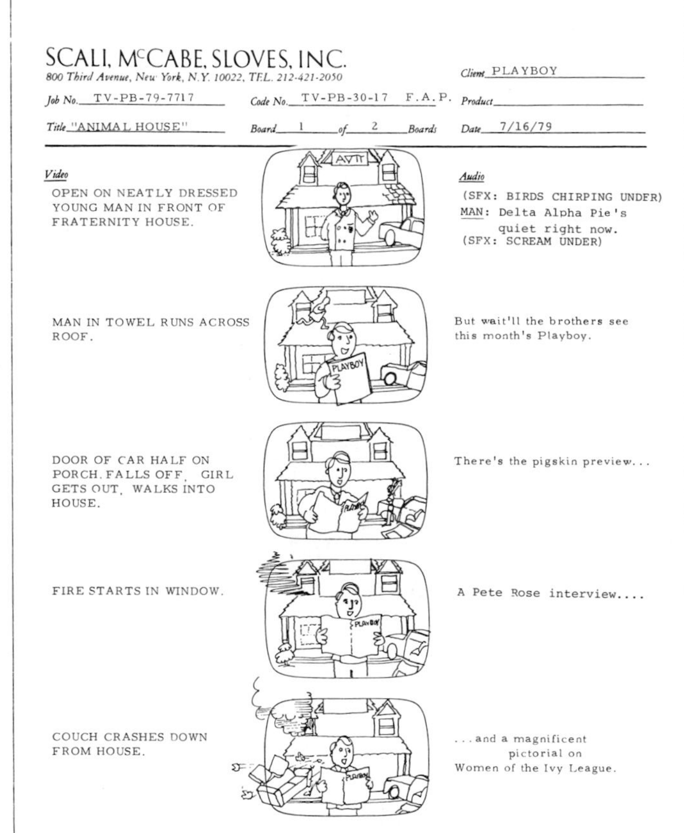

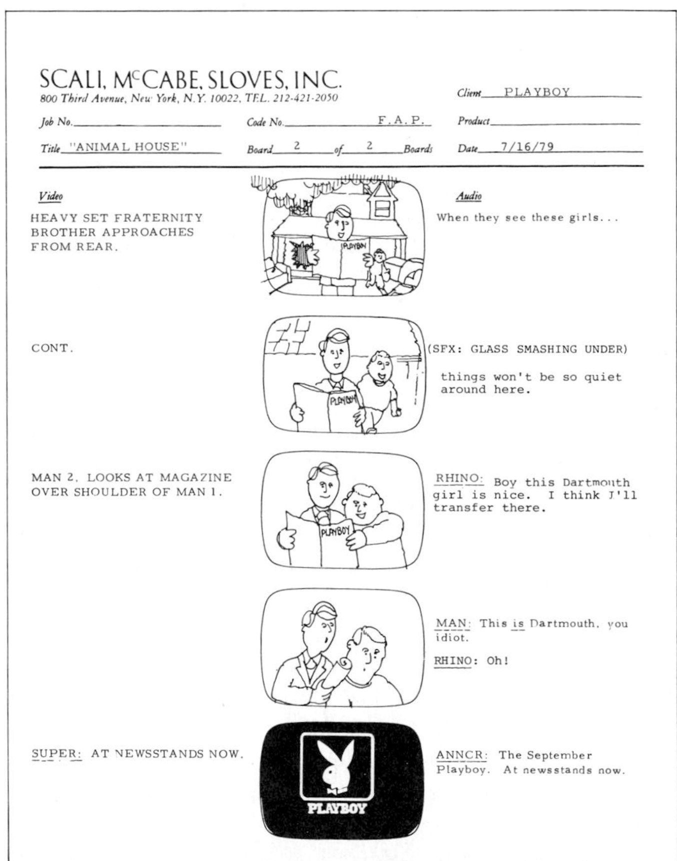

Figure 11–1 This storyboard serves as the layout for the television commercial. Creating storyboards requires the same skill and artistry as doing layouts. All the principles of design are considered for a national-quality television commercial. Of course, it is much more difficult to imagine what a finished commercial will look like by looking at a storyboard than to imagine a finished magazine ad by looking at a layout. But it allows the agency and the client an opportunity to appraise the commercial before proceeding with actual production.

not touch the ad again themselves, except to supervise its progress to completion.

The best art directors are strong conceptually in both words and pictures. They are also highly trained in pure graphic design and experienced in various aspects of advertising and art, and they are good managers of people. They may have a large or small staff under them, depending on the organization, or they may work free lance in which case they probably do more of the work normally handled by assistants on agency art department staffs.

Graphic designers

Graphic designers are responsible for the shape, dimension, and placement of the elements in an ad. The initial design of the ad dictates its artistic direction and eventually determines whether that ad is to be stunning, beautiful, a "work of art," or just another ad. To avoid the latter, graphic designers are employed.

Designers are precision specialists. They are preoccupied with the shape and form of things, and their effort in advertising is to arrange the form of the ad in the most attractive and effective way possible. Usually the art director acts as the designer, too. Sometimes, however, a separate designer is employed to offer a unique touch to a particular ad.

Illustrators

The artists who paint or draw the pictures we see in ads are called *illustrators*. One of the greatest illustrators in this century was Norman Rockwell, whose pictures brought to life the cover of the *Saturday Evening Post* every week.

Illustrators are specialists. They are so specialized, in fact, that many frequently concentrate on just one type of illustrating. Fashion illustrators, for example, specialize in drawing clothing. Their training enables them to catch a particular look and communicate the unique feel of a garment. Furniture illustrators do the same thing with home furnishings. They might draw a manufacturer's sofa, for example, in pencil or with watercolors, paying great attention to the fabric upholstery or wood veneer and showing it all off in a beautiful living room setting.

Illustration is such a specialty that most advertising illustrators work free lance. Very few agencies or advertisers retain full-time illustrators unless their work is also so specialized that they require the continuous efforts of one type of illustrator (Figure 11–2).

Production artists

Production or paste-up artists are responsible for assembling the various elements of an ad and mechanically putting them together the way the art director or designer indicated. Good production artists are fast, precise, and knowledgeable about the whole production process (see Chapter 12). In addition, they have the ability to stand the tedious task of bending over a drawing board all day assembling little pieces of type, drawing perfectly straight, clean lines with a pen, or cutting delicate photographs with a sharp knife.

Most art directors and designers start as production artists and work their way up. It's very difficult work, but it is also important, since this is where the ads actually come together in their finished form.

Figure 11–2 Nocona Boots uses a superb illustration in a photorealistic style to demonstrate the beauty of their product and create a super-macho image for the purchaser. Notice the detail of the snake's skin, the dry-cracked desert floor, the stitching on the boots, and even the subtle humor of the Let's Rodeo ring. Note also the graphic design, which leads the reader in a zigzag pattern down through the ad and ends right at the company logo. This is exceptional, award-winning advertising.

Designing the advertisement

The market for motorcycles in the United States and Canada is extremely large. It is also highly fragmented, with products from Germany, Italy, Sweden, England, and Japan successfully competing with American machines. To America's cyclists, many of these bikes might look alike. However, the manufacturers of Yamaha motorcycles felt that their Japanese bikes were superior to the rest in engineering, design, and performance. The question was how to communicate this.

Yamaha turned to its American agency, Botsford-Ketchum (San Francisco), for help. The agency responded with a campaign that not only won numerous awards for its excellent copy, art, and design, but also set a new international standard for motorcycle advertising.[1]

The campaign combined beautiful photography, sophisticated technical illustration, and straightforward, factual copy in a series of inviting, easy-to-read, full-color page ads and two-page spreads. Each ad supported the campaign theme: "When you know how they're built, you'll buy a Yamaha." The ads resembled the editorial format of slick specialty magazines. As such, the ads built great credibility with readers because of their familiarity with that editorial format in nonadvertising situations (Figure 11–3).

Over several years the ads grew in sophistication in both copy and illustration as readers became more familiar with the technical terminology associated with motorcycles. Unique features of Yamaha's superiority in engineering were shown with small *call-outs* or captions next to the photo illustrations. The illustrations became more intricate and diagrammatic as the agency introduced the design changes on new Yamaha models.

In test after test, the Yamaha ads consistently scored first or second in consumer memorability. Dealer feedback was excellent. And within two years Yamaha's share of market rose three points, placing them behind only Honda in the American market.

What set Yamaha's advertising apart was, again, the "big idea"— the same thing that sets all good advertising apart. In this case the big idea was the unique art direction, design, and execution in each ad in the campaign. Not only was the art concept unique and brilliantly executed, but, most important, it was also relevant to the subject matter, the audience, the objectives of the company, and the verbal presentation in the headline and the copy.

One of the most impressive features about the Yamaha ads is the

People in advertising

George H. Lois

President
Lois Pitts Gershon

George H. Lois, hailed by the *New York Times* as "perhaps the most outstanding art director in America," is president of Lois Pitts Gershon and has had an indelible influence on American advertising.

The son of Greek immigrant parents, born and raised in the upper Bronx, Lois attended P.S. 7, where his drawings were spotted by a teacher. She not only sent him to take the entrance exam for Manhattan's famed High School of Music and Art in 1945, but even gave him the dime for round-trip subway fare. Lois was accepted.

After high school Lois entered Pratt Institute to study art. A professor there decided Lois' talents were too advanced for what Pratt could offer and sent him to see design studio owner Reba Sochis. She examined Lois' portfolio and promptly hired him.

At 21 Lois became an art director at CBS. He then joined Lennen & Newell. That same year he created the first of the 92 brash, compelling covers he was to produce for *Esquire* magazine over the next 10 years. Lois was soon hired by Sudler & Hennessey. A year later he went on to Doyle Dane Bernbach. There his work captured three gold medals in the New York Art Directors Club annual competition.

Lois left DDB at age 28 to help found Papert, Koenig, Lois. When it grew into a $40 million agency—the first one ever to go public—George Lois became the first art director to launch a "big business." Four years later he left PKL with associates Ron Holland and Jim Callaway to form a new agency, Lois Holland Callaway. It repeated the rapid success of PKL. Then in 1977 Lois stunned Madison Avenue again. He left LHC to become president of the $55-million Creamer Lois agency network. Within a year he resigned to form Lois Pitts Gershon.

Heralded by *ANNY* as one of America's "most promising new agencies," Lois Pitts Gershon has already achieved $22 million in annual billing. Today it occupies an entire floor of New York's prestigious Piaget building. Agency clients include the Dreyfus Corporation, Qwip Systems, and Vitalis. According to the LPG philosophy, "Great advertising not only conveys what has to be said about a product, but does so with a sense of theater and style." These two qualities—theater and style—describe the maverick, often outrageous creative output of George H. Lois.

Explaining Lois' unorthodox style, Bill Pitts, executive vice president of Lois Pitts Gershon, wrote, "Headlines must sound like the words and cadences people use. Copy has to read like images, not abstractions. But above all else," Pitts emphasized, "coming up with the unexpected always matters most."

Lois confirmed this when he told an audience recently, "Advertising should aim to be seemingly outrageous." The reason? Advertising must be *visible* to be effective. It can be made visible, Lois said, by following these 10 rules:

1. Make advertising human.
2. Believe in advertising as though your life depended on it.
3. Talk in prose that everyone relates to.
4. Create concepts, not ads.
5. Never settle for *almost* perfect.
6. Never try to please the trade ahead of the consumer.
7. Never be defeated by government or industry regulations.
8. Relate to the *real* world.
9. Take risks.
10. Listen to your heart—and respect your instincts.

(*continued*)

"I aim for visibility," Lois declared, "through tenacious individuality—advertising with *chutzpah*—messages that grab a mass audience, that make brands household words, that enter the language, that enhance the very essence of the product."

Today Lois continues to create uncommon, often audacious campaigns. Arriving at his drawing table at 7:30 each morning, he works directly on every project, personally rendering each frame of his storyboards and tracing every word he sets in type.

Lois' 92 *Esquire* covers and numerous other triumphs of his prolific 30-year career are featured in his book, *The Art of Advertising: George Lois on Mass Communication.*

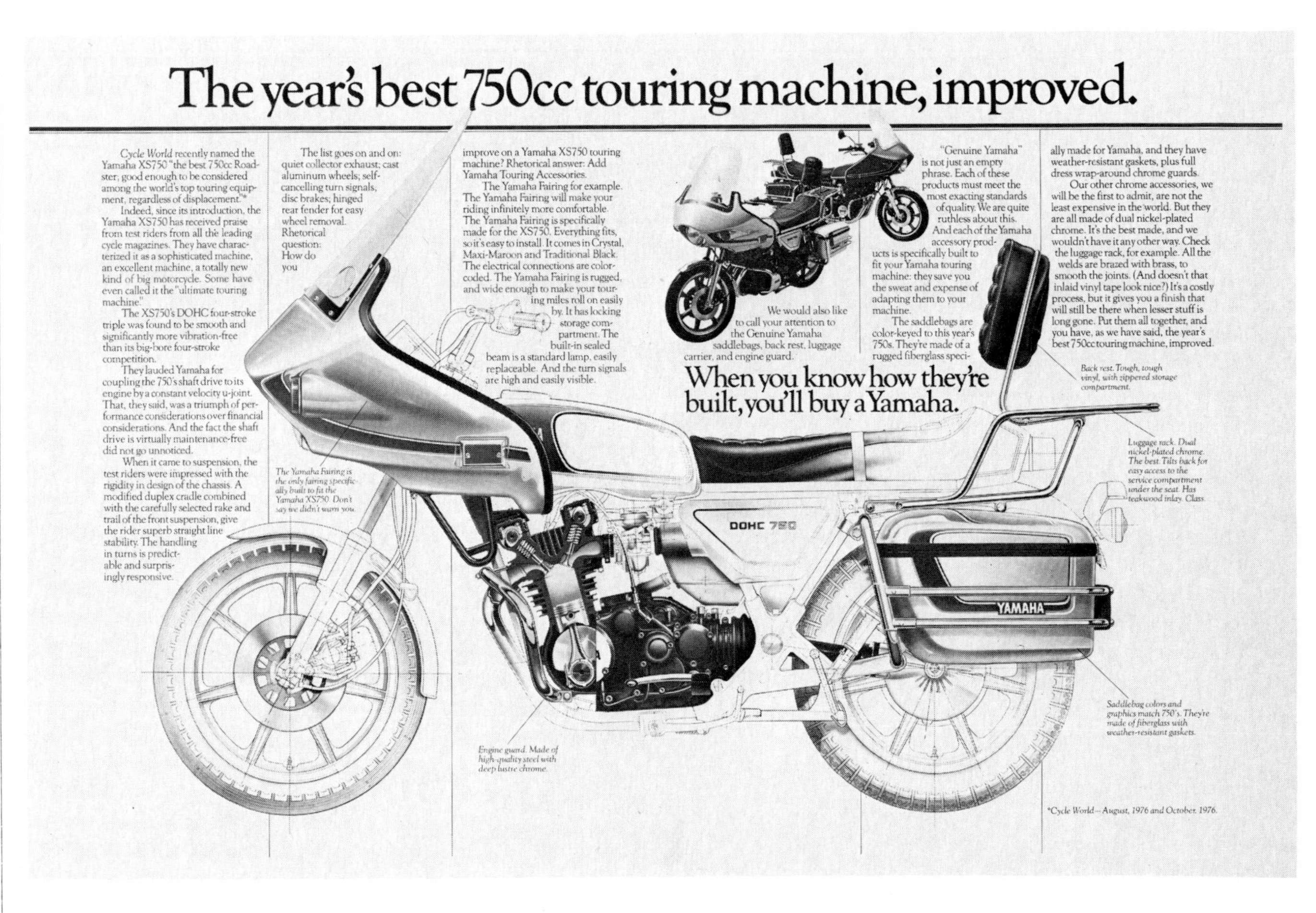

Figure 11–3 One of a series of award-winning ads for Yamaha motorcycles. Notice the lack of company signature at the bottom of the ad. This was intended to impart an editorial feeling in order to build credibility for the product's quality and the company's engineering skill. The volume and intricacy of work on the Yamaha campaign required the full-time efforts of three art directors, each of whom supervised a staff of other art specialists.

layout and design. Note how the copy is set in neat, easy-to-read columns and yet works in and around the central, dynamic illustration. Note the attractiveness of the style of type used in the headline and body copy and the effective use of rules and lines to structure the ad and organize the reading material. Finally, notice the total unity and balance in spite of the number of elements in the ad. The Yamaha campaign is an appropriate demonstration of the importance of layout and design to advertising.

Laying out the ad

For print media, the first work from the art department is seen in the form of a *layout,* which is a design of the advertisement within the specified dimensions. The term is used when referring to newspapers, magazines, and outdoor and transit advertisements. For direct-mail and point-of-purchase materials, which often require a three-dimensional presentation of the message, the layout is referred to as a *dummy.* For television, the script of a commercial is first seen as a layout in the form of a *storyboard,* which is a series of pictures or frames that correspond to the script.

The use of layouts

A layout is an orderly formation of the parts of the advertisement: headline, subheads, illustration, copy, picture captions, trademarks, slogans, and signature (or logotype).

The layout has two purposes. One is a mechanical function. It works as a blueprint, showing where the parts of the ad are to be placed. It guides the copywriter in determining the amount of copy to write. It helps the illustrator or photographer determine the size and style of pictures to be used. It helps the art director plan the size and style of type to be used. It is also helpful in determining costs.

The second purpose of the layout is a psychological or symbolic function. The ad's layout, as well as its execution, creates the feeling of the ad (Figure 11–4). Depending on the way the layout is designed, it can be crucial in determining the image a business or product will present. For example, many discount drugstores lay their ads out with a cluttered, busy look. This is typical of bargain-basement advertising and the purpose is to create the image of a store for bargain hunters. On the other hand, stores that offer high-quality merchandise, service, and status at high prices normally use large, beautiful illustrations, small blocks of copy, and ample white space.

Both these layouts communicate store image as well as provide blueprint directions for the production artist. The art director therefore must be very sensitive when designing the initial layout to use a format that is in keeping with the desired image of the product or business. (See the Ad Lab.) In the case of Yamaha, that was one of the primary reasons for the combination of editorial and picture-caption layout. It presented a highly credible image instantly.

Steps in advertising layout

Each step in the layout process serves a particular purpose. For a specific ad, all or some of the steps may be performed. Layouts are relied upon as guides in the development of the advertisement by those who are working on it and by those who must approve it.

Thumbnail sketches

These are miniature sketches approximately one-fourth to one-eighth the size of the finished ad. They are used for trying out ideas. The best sketch can be chosen for further development (Figure 11–5).

Rough layout

The next step is the rough layout, which is the size of the actual ad. The headlines and subheads are lettered onto the layout, the artwork and photographs are drawn, and the body copy is simulated with pencil lines.

If the advertisement is to be a television commercial, the proposed scenes in the commercial are drawn in a series of boxes shaped like TV screens. The copy corresponding to each scene is indicated underneath along with a description of sound effects and music.

Figure 11–1 shows the storyboard for the *Playboy* commercial as initially laid out by Earl Cavanah. This storyboard serves as the eventual layout or blueprint for producing the commercial.

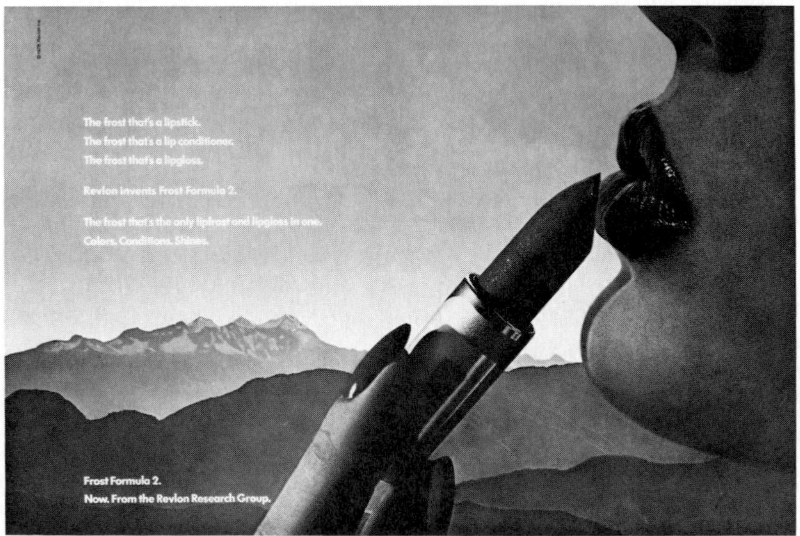

Figure 11–4 Stunning layout and graphic design from Revlon's in-house agency. Notice the center point of the fingers, luscious mouth, and glossy lipstick in extreme close-up against the frosty, snow-capped mountains in the distance.

Comprehensive layout

This is a facsimile of the finished advertisement and is prepared so a client can gauge the effect of the ad. Copy is set in type and pasted into position. The illustrations are very carefully drawn. If a photograph will be included, it is pasted into position as well. It's not uncommon for a client to be charged for the expense of a "comp" because it is for the client's benefit rather than for the agency's benefit. In national consumer advertising, the costs of other layouts are usually covered by the commission the agency receives from the media.

Mechanical

Once the type has been set and the illustrations created or photographs taken, these elements of the ad are pasted into the exact position in which they will appear in the final ad. This *mechanical* (or *paste-up*) is then used as a direct basis for the next step in the repro-

The psychological impact of color

Reaction to color, says Walter Margulies, is generally based on a person's national origin or race. For example, "warm" colors are red, yellow, and orange; "these tend to stimulate, excite, and create an active response." Those from a warmer climate, apparently, are most responsive to those colors.

Violet and "leaf green" fall right on the line between warm and cool. Each can be one or the other, depending on the shade used.

Here are some more Margulies observations:

Red Symbol of blood and fire. A runnerup to blue as man's "favorite color," but it is the most versatile; i.e., it's the hottest color with highest "action quotient." Appropriate for Campbell's Soups, Stouffer's frozen foods, and meats. Conveys strong masculine appeal—shaving cream, Lucky Strike, Marlboro.

Brown Another masculine color, associated with earth, woods, mellowness, age, warmth, comfort—i.e., the essential male; used to sell men anything (even cosmetics), for example, Revlon's Braggi.

Yellow High impact to catch "consumer's eye, particularly when used with black—psychologically right for corn, lemon, or sun tan products.

Green Symbol of health, freshness—popular for tobacco products, especially mentholated—i.e., Salem, Pall Mall menthol.

Blue Coldest color, with most appeal, effective for frozen foods (ice impression); if used with lighter tints becomes "sweet"—Montclair cigarettes, Lowenbrau beer, Wondra flour.

Black Conveys sophistication, high-end merchandise or used to simulate expensive products; good as background and foil for other colors.

Orange Most "edible" color, especially in browntinged shades, evokes autumn and good things to eat.

Laboratory applications

1. Based on Margulies' observations, explain the moods or feelings that are stimulated by specific color advertisements or packages illustrated in this text.
2. Name products for which a redesign using different color combinations might make the product or package more attractive.

A.

B.

C.

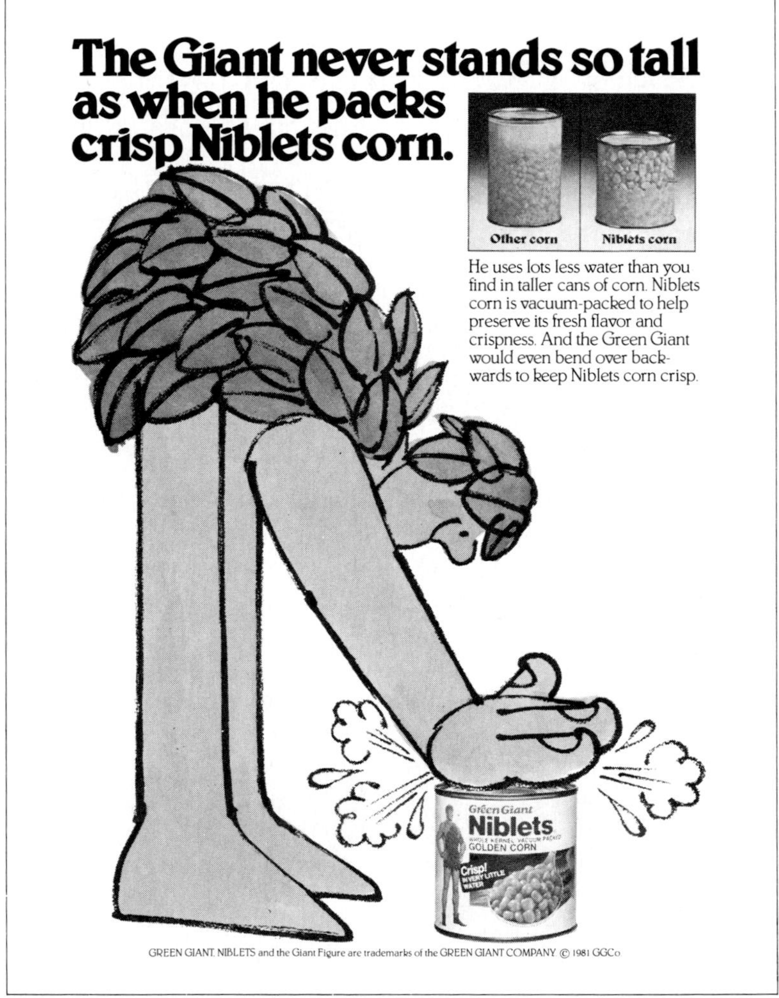

Figure 11–5 A. Thumbnail sketches. B. Rough layout. C. Finished advertisement.

duction process. (See Chapter 12, "Creative Production: Print Media.")

Dummy

For layouts of brochures and other multipage materials, a dummy is prepared. It is put together, page for page, just like the finished product will eventually appear. A dummy may go through the thumbnail, rough, comprehensive, and mechanical stages just as a regular layout. (See the Checklist.)

Checklist of design principles

There are no formulas that can assure effective layouts. However, there will be a great opportunity for successful layouts if the following factors are taken into consideration.

1. Balance

The reference point that determines the balance of a layout is the optical center. The optical center is about one eighth above the physical center, or five eighths from the bottom of the page. Balance is the arrangement of the elements as they are positioned on the page—the left side of the optical center versus the right, and above the optical center versus below. There are two kinds of balance, formal and informal.

☐ Formal balance. Perfect symmetry is the key to formal balance: *matched elements* on either side of line dissecting the ad have equal optical weight. This is used to strike a dignified, stable, conservative image.

☐ Informal balance. By placing elements of *different* size, shape, intensity of color, or darkness at different distances from the optical center, a visually balanced presentation can be achieved. Just like a teeter-totter, an object of greater optical weight near the center can be balanced by an object of less weight placed farther from the center. Most advertisements use informal balance because it makes the ad more interesting, imaginative, and exciting.

2. Movement

The principle of design that causes the reader of an advertisement to read the material in the sequence desired is called movement. This can be achieved through a variety of techniques.

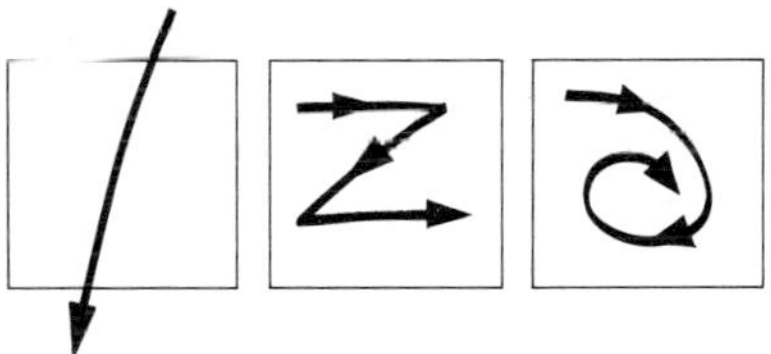

☐ Through the use of *gaze motion,* the placement of people or animals in the advertisement so that their eyes direct our eyes to the next important element to be read.

☐ By the use of mechanical devices such as pointing fingers, rectangles, lines, or arrows to direct attention from element to element or, in television, by moving the actors or the camera or by changing scenes.

☐ Through the use of comic-strip sequence and pictures with captions that force the reader to start at the beginning and follow the sequence in order to grasp the message.

☐ By using white space and color to emphasize a body of type or an illustration. Eyes will go from a dark element to a light, from color to noncolor.

☐ By taking advantage of the natural tendency of readers to start at the top left corner of the page and proceed on a diagonal Z motion to the lower right corner.

☐ By using size itself, which attracts attention because readers are drawn to the biggest and most dominant element on the page and then to the smaller elements.

Checklist of design principles *(continued)*

3. Proportion

Elements in an advertisement should be accorded space based on their importance to the complete advertisement. For best appearance, elements frequently use varying amounts of space in some proportion, such as three or two, to avoid the monotony of equal amounts of space for each element.

4. Contrast

An effective way of drawing attention to a particular element is with the use of contrast in color, size, or style. For example, reverse (white letters on a dark background), or a black and white ad with a red border, or an ad with an unusual type style creates contrast and draws attention.

5. Continuity

Continuity refers to the relationship of one ad to the rest of the campaign. This is achieved by using the same design format, style, and tone for all advertisements, by using the same spokesperson in commercials, by incorporating an unusual and unique graphic element in all ads, or by the consistent use of other techniques such as a logo, a cartoon character, or a catchy slogan.

6. Unity

Unity is the ad's bonding agent. It means that, although the ad is made up of many different parts, these elements relate to one another in such a way that the ad gives a harmonious impression. Balance, movement, proportion, contrast, and color may all contribute to unity of design. In addition, many other techniques can be used:

☐ Type styles from the same family.

☐ Borders around ads to hold elements together.

☐ Overlapping one picture or element over another.

☐ Judicious use of white space.

☐ Graphic tools such as boxes, arrows, or tints.

7. Clarity and simplicity

Any elements that can be eliminated without damaging the effect the advertiser is trying to achieve should be eliminated. Too many different type styles; type that is too small; too many reverses, illustrations, or boxed items; and unnecessary copy make layout complex and too busy. It makes the advertisement hard to read and hurts the overall effect desired.

8. White space (isolation)

Visit a local shopping center and notice the stores that stock lower-priced shoes. They normally display as many styles in the window as possible using virtually every foot of space available. Then go to a store carrying high-fashion, expensive shoes, and note how they selectively display a few shoes in their windows. Simply by looking at the window displays you get a certain image of the price of the merchandise carried by the store. The same image is conveyed by advertisements in their use of white space.

White space is the part of the advertisement that is not occupied by other elements (even though the color of the background may be black or some color other than white). White space can be used to focus attention to an isolated element. Put a vast amount of white space around a block of copy and it almost appears as if it's in a spotlight. White space has a great deal to do with the image the artist desires to create.

Which kind of layout works best?

Readership studies over the years indicate that the highest scoring advertisements usually use the standard layout with a single, dominant illustration that occupies between 60 and 70 percent of the ad's total area.[2] Next in ranking are ads that have one large picture and two more that are smaller. The illustration is there to stop the reader and arouse attention. Therefore, the content of the picture or pictures should also be interesting.

Headlines are also intended to stop the reader (Figure 11–6). Research shows that short statements in one line are best but that a second line is acceptable. The total headline area needs to fill only 10 to 15 percent of the ad, so the type does not have to be particularly huge. Headlines may appear above or below the photograph depending on the situation.

Copy blocks should not be too long. Although long-copy ads can certainly be effective, research shows that readership drops considerably if ads have more than 50 words. Therefore, if the motive is to attract a large number of readers, copy blocks should be kept to less then 20 percent of the ad.

Finally, company signatures do not have to be particularly large. Most people who read ads also read who placed the ad. So company signatures or logos do not need to occupy more than 5–10 percent of the area. For best results they should be placed in the lower-right-hand corner or across the bottom of the ad.

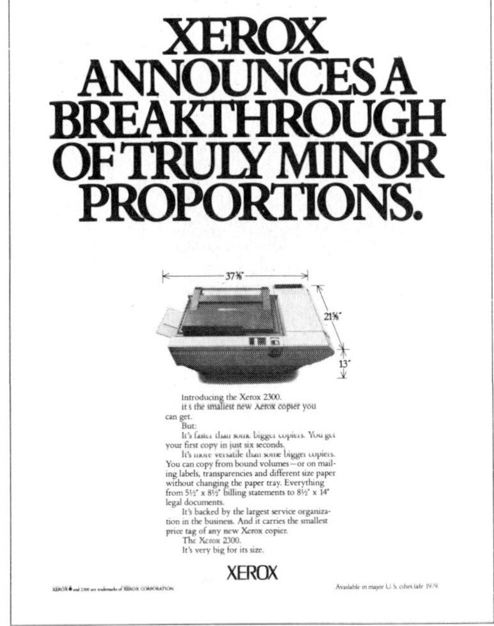

Figure 11–6 Xerox could have shown a big picture of its Model 2300 copier but chose instead to show a very small picture of it with a big headline. This counterpoint technique is so unexpected that it catches the reader's attention and arouses interest in reading the headline. By stating the physical dimensions of the product, credibility is enhanced and the smallness claim is further clarified. The graphic idea in this ad, as the last line in the copy states, is "very big for its size."

Advertising illustration

Most people who are unfamiliar with advertising think that an artist is someone who paints or draws. As we discussed at the beginning of this chapter, many advertising artists have no talent for drawing at all. Their talent lies in the area of design or art direction, or in the mechanical areas of paste-up and production.

The artists who paint, sketch, and draw in advertising are called *illustrators*. The artists who produce pictures with a camera are called *photographers*. Together they are responsible for all the illustrations or pictures we see in advertising.

Purpose of illustration

Most readers of advertisements (1) look at the illustration, (2) read the headline, and (3) read the body copy, in that order. If any one of these elements fails, the impact of the advertisement is decreased. A great deal of responsibility for the success of an advertisement, therefore, is placed on the illustration. Some advertisements have no illustrations because someone made a conscious decision that an illustration was not needed in order for effective communication to occur. However, if an illustration is used, it must do one or more of the following:

1. Capture the attention of the reader.
2. Identify the subject of the advertisement.
3. Qualify readers by stopping those who are legitimate prospects and letting others skip over your ad if they are so inclined.
4. Arouse interest in reading the headline.
5. Create a favorable impression of the product or the advertiser.
6. Clarify claims made by the copy.
7. Help convince the reader of the truth of claims made in the copy.

8. Emphasize unique features of the product.
9. Provide continuity for all advertisements in the campaign through the use of the same illustrative technique in each individual ad.[3]

Illustrative techniques

Illustrations are chosen on the basis of their need, cost, technical limitations of producing them, time required to obtain them, effect desired, printing process to be used, paper on which they are to be printed, and availability of the artist who can produce what is needed in the medium desired.

The two basic devices for illustrating an advertisement are photography and drawn or painted illustrations.

Don't I look super, man.
Diamonds. And suddenly you feel irresistible.

Figure 11–7 "Don't I look super, man?" Well, that may be debatable. But the Richard Avedon photograph of the jewel-laden model with the stringy hair gets the point across with a wallop: Diamonds make you *feel* irresistible.

Photography

There are several important contributions that a good photograph can make to an advertisement.

Realism People like to see the "real thing" in their ads. Good color photography does wonders for all kinds of products, from gleaming motor cars to steaming bowls of soup. Just look at the food photography in any homemaker's magazine.

The feeling of "it's happening now" Photographs—especially news-type photographs—put you right on the spot. You are standing on the goal line when the touchdown is scored. You get involved.

Making the "cartoon effect" come alive Photographers have done some wonderful things in taking cartoon situations and giving them the added dimension of realism. A drawing of the eye-patched Hathaway man, for instance, might be effective, but it would lack the dynamic realism of a photograph of the actual man.

Adding mood, beauty, and sensitivity Photographers are sometimes able to achieve a high artistic level with their pictures. A photograph can carry a tremendous emotional wallop (Figure 11–7).

Speed, flexibility, and economy A drawing or painting takes longer to complete than a photograph. In fact, several photographs can be taken at one session. And if the advertiser doesn't want to pay for custom photographs to be taken, *stock* photos of popular situations, people, and places can usually be purchased at reasonable cost.[4]

It is not unusual for a photographer to take hundreds of shots before being satisfied. The photographer may shoot a wide variety of poses at various angles and with various light settings. The negatives are then printed on a *contact sheet* in small size and in unretouched form. With the use of a magnifying glass, the art director finds the photo that is most suitable for use.

Photography offers flexibility, since photographs can be cropped to any size or shape and retouched with a paint brush or airbrush to improve the photograph.

When a photograph is sold, whether it is a stock photo or a photograph taken by a commissioned photographer, there must be a "legal release." In the case of stock photos, the stock photo house will have taken care of that. However, for photographs that are commissioned, any individuals who appear in the picture must sign a standard release available from most stationery stores, which grants permission to the advertiser for the photo's use. For children, the release must be obtained from the parent or guardian.

In addition, new copyright laws have restricted the rights of advertisers to use the work of photographers without compensating them equitably. The price a photographer charges, therefore, frequently depends on the intended use of the work. If the advertiser decides later to use the photograph in additional ways, the photographer usually has to be paid more money. These agreements are negotiable and should always be put in writing in advance.

Drawings

There are times when it is better to use drawn illustrations than photographs either because the advertiser wants to illustrate an event that has already taken place or one that will take place in the future, or because the drawing will produce greater impact.

An illustrator is limited only by his or her own skill. Unlike photographers, there is no need to find just the right setting or the right models. The artist has the freedom to create the impression or effect desired through his or her own personal style, such as exemplified by Norman Rockwell. In this way, drawings, like cartoons, can exaggerate in ways a photograph cannot.

The Yamaha campaign used technical illustrators, who have the ability to work from blueprints if necessary, to create a precise picture of a product and its intricate components.

There are a number of techniques (media) illustrators use to produce drawings. These include (1) line drawings, (2) wash drawings, (3) scratchboard, (4) pencil, crayon, and charcoal, and (5) oil, acrylic, tempera, and watercolor.

Line drawings These are excellent for providing clear detail and sharpness. There are no shades of gray; everything is either black or white. They are sometimes referred to as pen-and-ink drawings. Line drawings are less costly than drawings with tonal values. Cartoons are frequently done as line drawings. Line drawings are used quite often for small illustrations or in small ads.

Wash drawings Sometimes it is too expensive or too time-consuming to photograph a situation. A wash drawing might then be used. As a painting done in various shades of one color, it can be almost as realistic as a black and white photograph. Moreover, it can overcome the limitations of a camera. There are two types of wash drawings: tight and loose. A tight drawing is quite detailed and is much more realistic than a loose drawing. It comes closest to a photograph as an illustrative technique. A loose wash drawing is more impressionistic. This technique is used extensively by fashion illustrators.

Scratchboard On a special paper with a surface specifically made for this art form, black ink is applied to the area of the illustration. With the use of a scratching device (a stylus or other sharp instrument), the ink is removed and a white line remains. The artwork is distinctive and different, and gives the impression of fine workmanship. It is also quite expensive.

Other illustrative techniques There are numerous other media used to draw illustrations. These include pencil, crayon, and charcoal illustrations as well as oil, acrylic, tempera, and watercolor paintings (Figure 11–8). All these media are used for the individual effect each creates, but they are less common in advertising than either line or wash drawings. They are normally used when the artist wishes to convey an impressionistic feeling or create a solid, dignified image of quality.

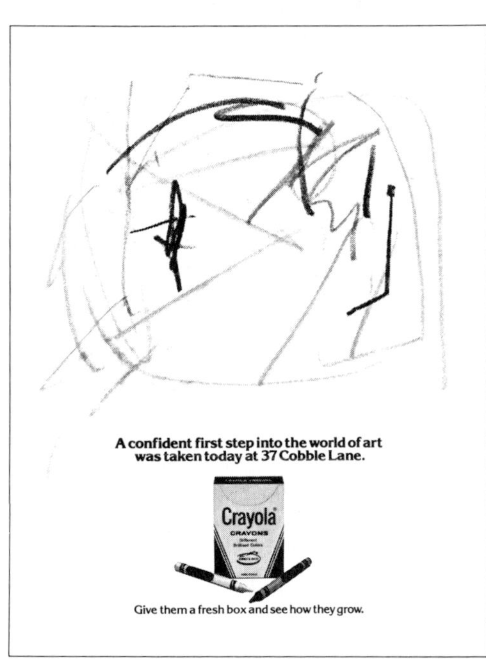

A confident first step into the world of art
was taken today at 37 Cobble Lane.
Crayola
Give them a fresh box and see how they grow.

Figure 11–8 A clever use of crayon illustration to help sell Crayola crayons. Also an equally clever and subtle tug at parents' heart strings.

Choosing the illustration

One dynamic aspect of advertising is the infinite number of illustrations that can be used to communicate the benefits of a product or service. The kind of illustration used is often determined during the visualization process. But frequently the kind of illustration is not determined until the art director or designer is laying out the ad. See the Checklist for the most common types of advertising illustrations used. Frequently advertising managers or art directors keep a similar checklist handy to help in the creative process of choosing the best type of illustration for their ad.

What if you're advertising a zipper? How exciting is a picture of a zipper? Do you show it on a man's pants or a lady's dress? Do you picture it opened or closed? Or do you picture something else, like the embarrassed face of a man whose zipper is broken? (See Figure 11–9.)

If you're doing an ad for Ferrari cars, what kind of illustration do you use? Do you show the car alone or with people around it? Do you use a picture of the car driving on the road or standing still? Do you show the interior or the exterior? Do you picture the car from the front, from the side, or from above? (See "Art Director's Portfolio.")

Selecting the appropriate photograph or illustration for an advertisement is a difficult creative task and is often what separates the great from the not-so-great.

Art directors have to deal with several basic issues in the selection of illustrations:

1. Is an illustration needed for effective communication to occur?
2. What should the subject of the illustration be and is that subject relevant to the advertiser's creative strategy?
3. Should an illustrator or a photographer be used?
4. What are the technical and budgetary requirements needed to accomplish the desired illustrative solution?

While these questions are very basic, they are also unfortunately the most overlooked. They should be asked and answered in the initial planning stages of the advertisement, and they should be asked again at the time the advertisement is being produced.

Just as an exercise, thumb through any chapter in this book and study any one of the advertisements shown. Ask yourself the questions listed above as they would apply to the ad which you have chosen. On any day, in any given agency, this exercise is performed routinely by top art directors.

Figure 11–9 Talon, Inc. has used a humorous approach for years to advertise its various zipper models to consumers and to the trade. Other ads include a photograph of a football with a zipper on it and one with a banana peel with a zipper on it, which uses an ingenious touch of humor to drive the product feature home: "A Talon zipper doesn't slip. Even on a banana peel."

Art director's portfolio

A.

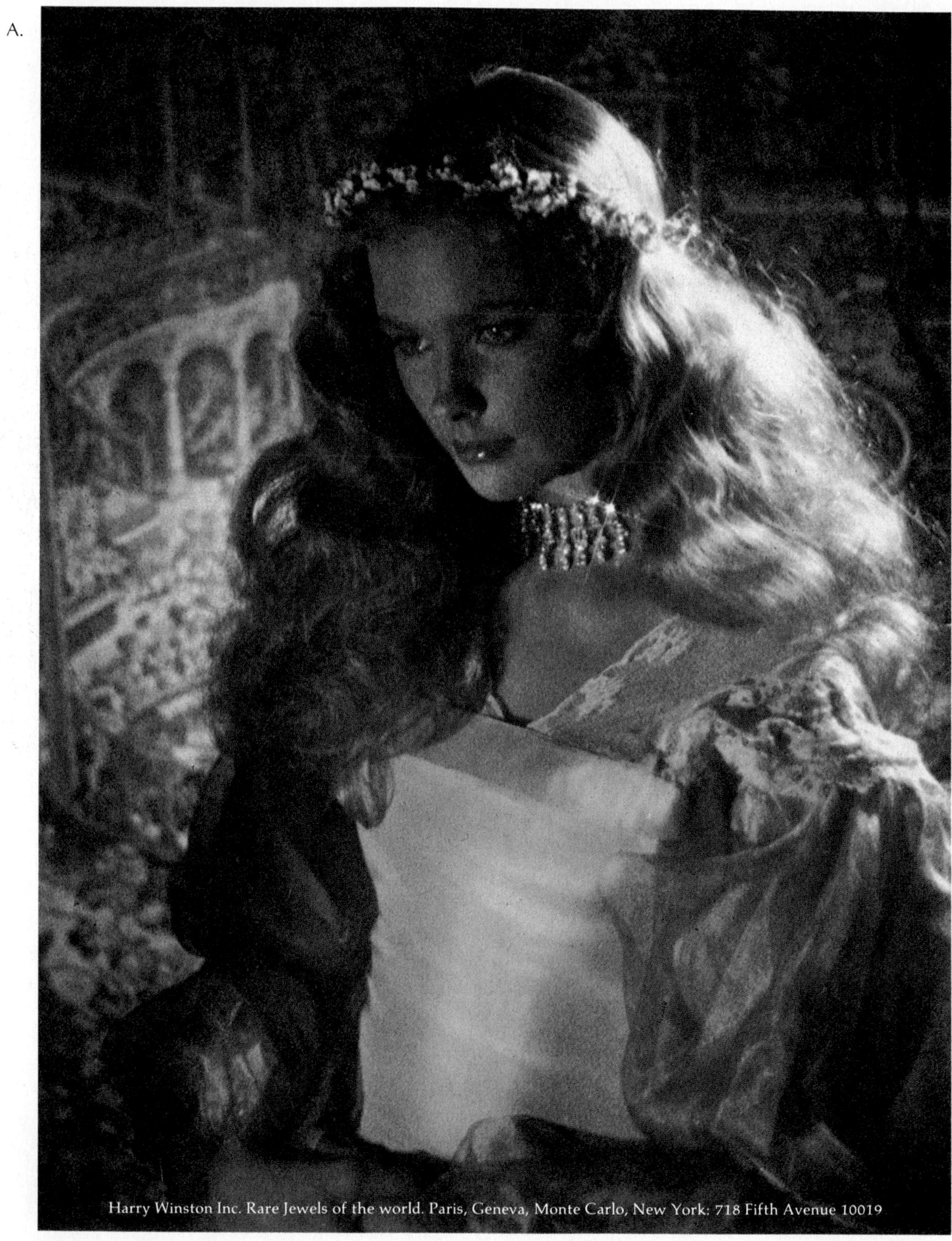

Harry Winston Inc. Rare Jewels of the world. Paris, Geneva, Monte Carlo, New York: 718 Fifth Avenue 10019

B.

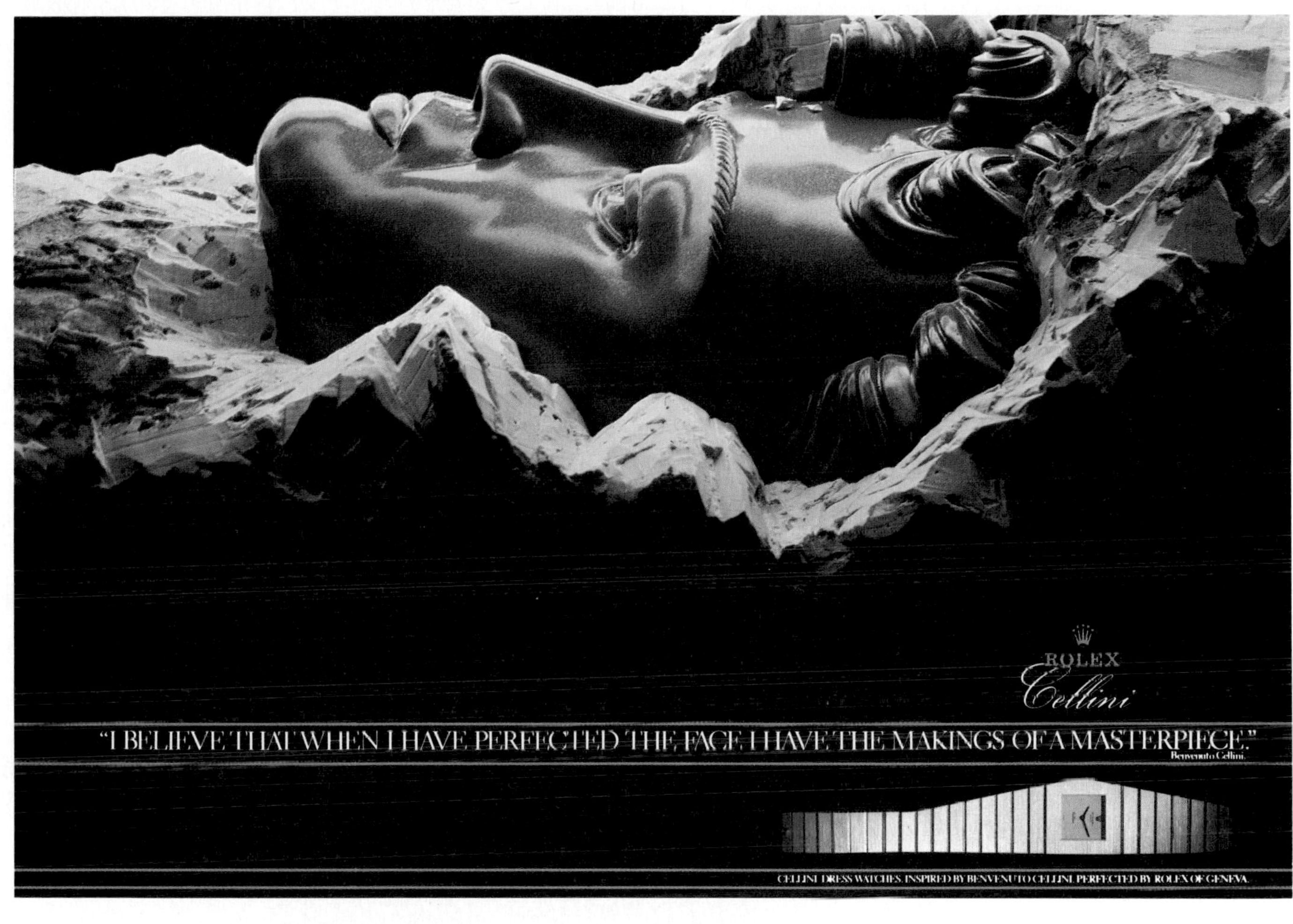

A. Poster-style layout with soft, sensitive photography. No real effort to show merchandise but rather to create a sensitive mood and a romantic feeling. Almost out of focus, the gentle beauty of the model allows readers to project into the advertisement what they want to see about the era of the ad, the story, and the message. This ad is a rare jewel from Harry Winston, Inc.

B. Sculpture in gold to symbolize the face of the Rolex watch is the big idea of this ad. Unusual poster-style layout quoting the words of sculptor Benvenuto Cellini achieves dynamic impact through the vast use of the gold face against a black background.

Art director's portfolio *(continued)*

C.

D.

E.

Why the beer from here is better than the beer from there.

If Oregon were like other places, you'd expect the beer here to be like other beers.

But in attitude as well as geography, our state is different from places like Wisconsin and Missouri. And that's why Portland-brewed Blitz-Weinhard is so different from the beers brewed in Milwaukee or St. Louis.

Natural beer, naturally brewed and naturally aged.

Over the last 30 years or so, science has revolutionized the art of brewing.

There are chemicals on the market which can shorten the time it takes to brew beer. And other chemicals which can preserve it once it's bottled. There are machines available to make beer ferment faster, and techniques to make it "age" quicker.

These are cost-saving innovations. But they're not a natural part of the brewing process, so they're not part of making Blitz-Weinhard beer.

At Blitz-Weinhard, we use no additives, no preservatives, no chemicals, and no shortcuts. Our product is naturally brewed, naturally fermented, and naturally aged.

This means it costs us more to make Blitz-Weinhard. But we believe natural country deserves nothing less than natural beer.

A small brewery

Once America's demand for beer was supplied by hundreds of small, local breweries. Today, brewing is heavily concentrated in the hands of a few large, national manufacturers with sizeable brewing plants located in different parts of the country.

But Blitz-Weinhard is made only at the original brewery in Portland. As a result, the total amount of beer we can produce is quite small by industry standards. This means we are able to brew with the extra time, care and attention required to produce the finest product possible.

The hops and barley are better here.

There's a type of barley which grows only in the Northwest, and it is held in high regard by brewers everywhere. It's safe to say that breweries in the East and Midwest would use more of this barley, but for the high cost of shipping it across the country.

Because we're close to the source, we are able to brew Blitz-Weinhard with more of this premium barley than any other beer we know of.

We also brew our beer with premium Cascade hops. This variety was developed by Oregon State University, and has been acclaimed throughout the industry as the equal of Bavaria's famed Hallertau hop. But the Willamette and Yakima valleys are the only areas suited to growing Cascade hops, and the relatively small crop assures a premium price—a price we are willing to pay in order to brew Blitz-Weinhard with the finest ingredients available.

Fresher beer is better beer.

Newly brewed beer must spend time in ageing vats to bring its flavor to maturity. Ageing is necessary to mellow the beer, and to bring out its sparkling clarity.

But once in the bottle, time is the enemy of good beer. In a matter of weeks, it can begin to lose its freshness. Eventually it will become stale and unappetizing.

Because our goal is to supply quality beer only to the people of Oregon, bottles of Blitz-Weinhard don't have to spend weeks or months being shipped long distances, or standing in warehouses. Brewery-fresh Blitz-Weinhard beer can reach the farthest point of our distribution within hours of leaving Portland.

Taste and tradition, guaranteed.

Blitz-Weinhard has been brewing premium beer for Oregonians since Territorial days. We are the oldest continuously operating brewery west of the Mississippi, and throughout our 122-year history, we have tried to follow the basic guiding principle laid down by our founder, pioneer brewer Henry Weinhard:

"Spare no time, effort, nor cost to give our customers a perfect glass of beer."

In the spirit of these words, every bottle and can of Blitz Weinhard beer carries a written guarantee of satisfaction. If you are ever displeased with our product, for any reason, your money will be refunded.

We're aware that other brewers don't offer a guarantee like ours. But when you think about it, there's no reason why they should.

After all, they're not the beer here.

The beer here.

Blitz-Weinhard Brewing Company, Portland, Oregon.

C. Picture-sequence layout shows the many sides of personality-model Cheryl Tiegs and demonstrates the versatility of the Clairesse product.

D. Surrealistic photo-illustration exemplifies the "bold look of Kohler." Notice how the ample use of white space around the headline again demonstrates boldness. Whole ad symbolizes Kohler's modern, state-of-the-art product line.

E. Two-page spread using color, whimsical illustration, and long, reason-why copy. Big illustration showing the beauty and freshness of Oregon nature attracts the reader's attention to the Blitz-Weinhard story.

Art director's portfolio *(continued)*

F.

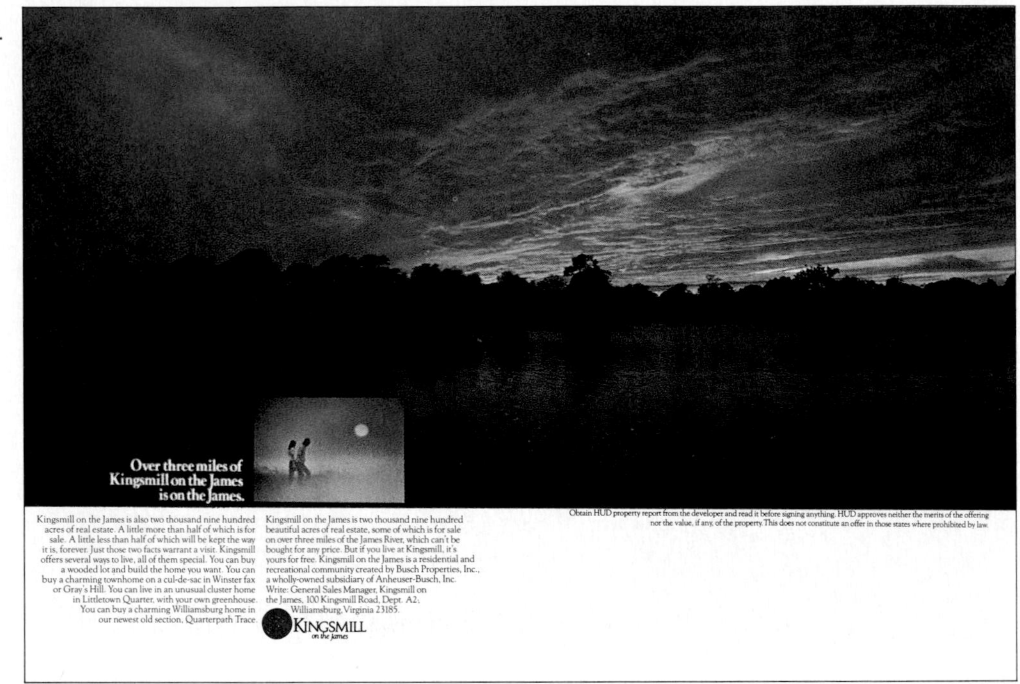

G.

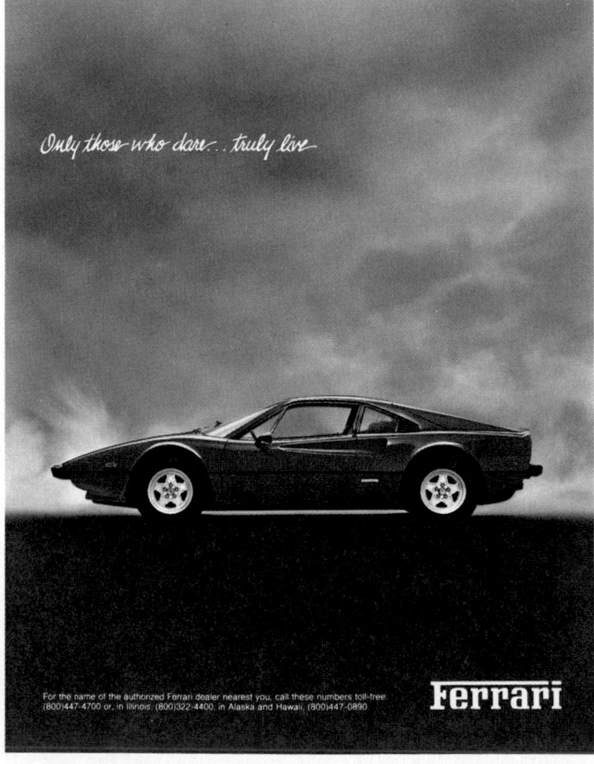

F. Kingsmill on the James is located on the James River. Could there be any doubt after seeing this ad? The picture tells the whole story.

G. The Ferrari mystique is accentuated by the poster layout with the stark photo of the car against an eerily colored sky. Striking contrast is punctuated by the simple headline: "Only those who dare . . . truly live."

H.

I.

H. Modified standard layout, neatly structured columns of copy, large central photographic illustration shot from interesting angle with mellow color to create the mood and feeling of a high-quality table wine. The copy gives all the details.

I. Fabulous photographic illustration of stunning jewels shot against the embossed Bulgari name. What more needs to be said to create the image of the best?

Art director's portfolio *(concluded)*

J.

K.

J. George Lois (profiled in this chapter) designed this striking multiple-illustration ad for Arm & Hammer. By cramming tons of information and visuals into one ad with skill and beauty, Lois achieved an extraordinary result ideal for the many uses of Arm & Hammer Baking Soda. Notice the eye-catching technique of relating visuals to each other (e.g., the teeth and the cake).

K. Elegant poster-style layout, stunning photographic treatment of sculpted candies. The ad tells the price without ever mentioning it and demonstrates a broad departure from typical candy advertising.

L. Technical treatment of a consumer product. Dynamic layout with a photo of a Porsche on a test track. Long explanatory copy, with bright technical illustration of turbine mechanism. Whole ad creates flash, flair, and credibility. One of a very successful series by Porsche.

L.

Consumer Orientation
No. 3 in a Series
Subject: Introduction of the Porsche 924 Turbo
3
Porsche 924 Turbo
Porsche+Audi
Nothing Even Comes Close
The Porsche 924 Turbo. On the track at Weissach, it covers the quarter mile from a standing start in 16.3 seconds. Its speed at the ¼-mile mark is 88 mph. Its maximum speed: 132 mph. The 924 Turbo is a direct descendant of the 917 Can-Am champion, the Porsche that made turbocharging practical for road racers. Prior to the 917, turbocharged automobiles suffered from poor throttle response and reliability. But the 917 Turbo solved these problems with its unique bypass valve and wastegate control system—standard equipment on the new 924 Turbo.
1. The KKK turbocharger draws in fresh air.
2. The compressor forces the air/fuel mixture into the engine cylinders under pressure. Because the turbocharged engine receives more air/fuel than a naturally-aspirated engine, its combustion is greater. And its horsepower is increased without increasing its engine displacement. Thus, while the 924 Turbo's engine displaces only 1984 cc, it develops 143 hp at 5500 rpm.
3. The 924 Turbo has almost instantaneous throttle response because of its bypass valve. When the throttle is closed, the valve opens and routes the pressurized air harmlessly back through the compressor in a closed loop. This maintains turbine speed. So when boost is demanded, the turbine does not have to be re-accelerated. Boost is available again in only 0.1 second.
4. Hot, normally-wasted, engine exhaust gases drive the turbine (6) which is connected by a common shaft to the compressor.
5. The gases vent by way of the exhaust line and muffler. A wastegate is located upstream of the turbine to control the excess gases not required to power the turbine.
At Porsche, we design a car as a total system. And so the 924 Turbo has a new cylinder head. A stronger driveshaft. New spoilers, front and rear. In fact, it has the lowest drag coefficient of any street Porsche: 0.35. And as a result of its total design efficiency, it requires only 16.5 horsepower to cruise at 55 mph.
For more information on the 924 Turbo, call toll free: (800) 447-4700. In Illinois, (800) 322-4400.
1 Fresh Air
2 Pressurized Air
3 Compressor
4 Exhaust Gases
5 Exhaust Outlet
6 Turbine

Checklist for choosing illustrations

Some common types of advertising illustrations are the following:

☐ The package containing the product. This is especially important for packaged goods because it helps the consumer identify the product on the grocery shelf.

☐ The product alone. Most advertising people point out the lower than average readership scores for ads that show the product alone. However, the Ferrari ad is an excellent example of how this technique can be used to advantage.

☐ The product in use. Automobile ads almost invariably show the car in use while talking about the ride, the luxury, the handling, or the economy. Cosmetic ads usually show the product in use with a close-up photograph of a beautiful woman wearing the mascara, the lipstick, or the eye shadow being advertised.

☐ How to use the product. For food products, recipe ads featuring a new way to use the product historically pull very high readership scores.

☐ Product features. The Yamaha campaign discussed at the beginning of this chapter is an excellent example of illustrating product features.

☐ Comparison of products. One mouthwash compares itself with another, or one electric razor claims a closer shave than competitors A, B, or C.

☐ User benefit. When Sylvania introduced its new 10-bulb flash cartridge, it illustrated user benefit through a series of 10 photographs of "Mona Lisa." The headline keyed the humor: "Now you have two more chances to get it right." It is often difficult to illustrate user benefits, especially intangible benefits. However, salespeople know that the best way to get a customer's attention is to show the customer a way to benefit from the product.

☐ Humor. There is no doubt that much advertising is entertainment. Humor in the right situations can make a positive, lasting impression. It can also destroy credibility if used incorrectly. Caution is always recommended when dealing with serious subjects. When appropriate, though, humor is like Pernod: "It grows on you."

☐ Testimonial. A most common type of illustration is the photo of a star or a real person such as a teenager touting the product.

☐ Before and after. This variation of the testimonial illustration has proved very effective for weight-loss products, skin care lotions, and body-building courses.

☐ Negative appeal. Sometimes it is stronger to point out what happens if you don't use the product than if you do use it. Electricity, for example, is something we all take for granted, and illustrating it in use might be very difficult. Illustrating it not in use, however, is very simple—and compelling.

Summary

Every advertisement uses art. In advertising *art* refers to the whole visual presentation of the commercial or advertisement. That includes how the words in the ad are arranged, what size and style of type are used, whether photographs or illustrations are used, and how actors are placed in a television commercial.

There are many types of artists involved in advertising. These include art directors, graphic designers, illustrators, and production artists, to name a few. Each has been trained to handle a particular specialty.

For print advertising, the first work from the art department is seen in the form of a layout, which is a design of the advertisement within specified dimensions. The layout has two purposes. One is a mechanical function to show where the parts of the ad are to be placed. The other is a psychological or symbolic function to demonstrate the visual image a business or product will present.

There are several steps used in laying out an ad. These include a thumbnail sketch, rough layout, comprehensive layout, and mechanical. For brochures and other multipage materials the layout is referred to as a dummy. For television the layout is referred to as a storyboard.

A great deal of responsibility for the success of an advertisement is placed on the illustration. The illustration may be used to capture the attention of the reader, to identify the subject of the advertisement, to create a favorable impression, or for a host of other reasons.

The two basic devices for illustrating an advertisement are photography and drawings. Photography can make several important contributions to an advertisement, including realism; a feeling of immediacy; a feeling of live action; the special enhancement of mood, beauty, and sensitivity; and speed, flexibility, and economy.

Drawings may be used if the art director feels they can achieve greater impact than photographs. There are a number of techniques used in producing drawings. These include (1) line drawings; (2) wash drawings; (3) scratchboard; (4) pencil, crayon, and charcoal; and (5) oil, acrylic, tempera, and watercolor.

Selecting the appropriate photograph or illustration for an advertisement is a difficult creative task. Some common types of advertising illustrations are the package containing the product, the product alone, the product in use, comparison of products, user benefit, before and after, and the negative appeal of showing what happens if you don't use the product.

Questions for review

1. What is art in advertising?
2. What is the contribution of the art director to an advertisement?
3. What is a layout? What is its purpose?
4. What is the best color to stimulate sales?
5. What is a mechanical?
6. What color is white space?
7. What is the purpose of an illustration in an advertisement? When would you not use an illustration?
8. What are the advantages and disadvantages of photography in advertising?
9. What are the advantages and disadvantages of drawn illustrations?
10. What are five criteria for selecting illustrations? Which do you think is the most important?

12

Creative production: Print media

Everyone is familiar with the efforts made by big cities to clean up their skid-row areas. If you gave a photograph of those slums to a retoucher like Louis Grubb, he could perform a miracle of urban renewal—transforming run-down shacks into freshly painted, beautifully renovated historic landmarks replete with green lawns, flowing gardens, and majestic trees.

The role of the retoucher, whose accomplishments, style, and sensitivity help make the art director look good, is surprising to many. Most people don't realize that, as Grubb reports it, "almost every photograph you see for a national advertiser these days has been worked on by a retoucher to some degree."

For example, after the original shot for the More ad (Figure 12–1) was inspected by the agency art directors at Leber Katz Partners and by the client, improvements to be made were noted on the print. The enlarged dye transfer was then delivered to Lou Grubb by the lab. The task in this case was relatively simple: make her a little slimmer and a little blonder, add a little color, smooth the wrinkles in her pants, lengthen one pant leg, and darken some shadows.

Other times the task is far more complex, requiring the skill of an experienced painter or illustrator. Warwick, Welsh & Miller, the agency for Air Canada, didn't think the river in Figure 12–2 was wide enough for an ad, so they asked Louis Grubb to add more river. A composite of four different negatives was "stripped" together as instructed by Louis Grubb and delivered as a single dye transfer. In that composite the river current was going in two or three different directions and reflected a wide variety of different colors and shades. It was a job for an illustrator. Grubb virtually repainted the river, turned the lights on all along the canal, and even changed the color of the sky to give an early evening nightfall effect.

Says Grubb, "Our job is to correct the basic deficiencies in the original photograph or, in effect, to improve upon the appearance of reality."[1]

The production process

The average person who reads advertisements has no concept of the intricate, detailed, technical stages those printed announcements go through from start to finish. Yet the entire advertising effort can be affected by the outcome of the production process. An otherwise beautiful ad can be destroyed by a poor selection of type, by a less-than-interesting photograph, by improper manufacture of printing plates, or simply by an incorrect procedure used to print photographs or artwork on a particular paper stock.

Any person who is connected with advertising, therefore, should have some basic knowledge and understanding of production procedures. A fundamental grasp of mechanical production will save a lot of money and disappointment in the long run.

In recent years it has become more difficult and complex to gain a thorough knowledge of these production procedures. Enormous technological progress has been made in the graphic arts. This is due in particular to the revolutionary application of electronics to the field. As a result, the knowledge of experienced print production professionals has become extremely important to today's major advertisers and advertising agencies.

In Chapter 11 we looked at the award-winning ads created for Yamaha motorcycles by Botsford-Ketchum. We discussed the editorial design of the ads, the interesting combination of illustration and photography, and the unity of the art concept with Yamaha's campaign theme: "When you know how they're built, you'll buy a Yamaha."

At the time Botsford-Ketchum handled the Yamaha motorcycle account, Joe Soca was the agency's production supervisor. He became intimately involved in the campaign after the concept was developed. His responsibility was to ensure that the final advertisement printed in the magazine reflected exactly what the art director had intended.

This was no small task inasmuch as each advertisement presented numerous production complexities. These included the reproduction of fine technical illustrations in full color, the precise specification and placement of type around the illustrations, and the need to have all printing materials checked, approved, duplicated, and shipped to the magazines in time for a specific deadline.

Planning print production

After an advertisement has been laid out and the artwork and copy approved, it is under the supervision of the print production manager and a staff of production artists and assistants. The print production department specifies type, creates camera-ready mechanicals and orders printing materials, and gives any necessary technical instructions to outside production specialists.

The manager must decide at the earliest possible time what is most important for a particular project: speed, quality, or economy. The answer may determine which production methods are used; one will surely be sacrificed at the expense of another. In the Yamaha ads, what do you think was considered most important?

Working backward from the closing dates (deadlines) of the publications, the production manager schedules when each step of the work must be completed in order to meet the deadline. These deadlines can vary from months to hours.

The production manager acquaints the art director and copywriter with the opportunities and limitations of various production techniques and keeps them abreast of the progress of each job. In the case of Yamaha, this meant coordinating with three teams of art directors and writers for just the one account.

Finally, the production manager must check all proofs for errors, obtain all necessary approvals from agency and client executives, and release the approved advertisements to the publications.

For the production process to run smoothly, it is important for all concerned to have a working knowledge and understanding of production procedures. Consider the problem of correcting errors. After the advertisement has been delivered to the typographer, photoplatemaker, printer, or publication, it costs substantially more to make any changes than before the actual production begins. For example, the cost of changing a single comma after the copy has been set in type is more than $10.

As a result, advertisers as well as the personnel in their agencies should develop a sensitivity to art, graphics, and type and learn all they can about typography, platemaking, printing, and color.

Typography

Turn back to Chapter 11 and look carefully at the Yamaha ad in Figure 11–4. Now look at the Yamaha ad in Figure 12–3. It was cre-

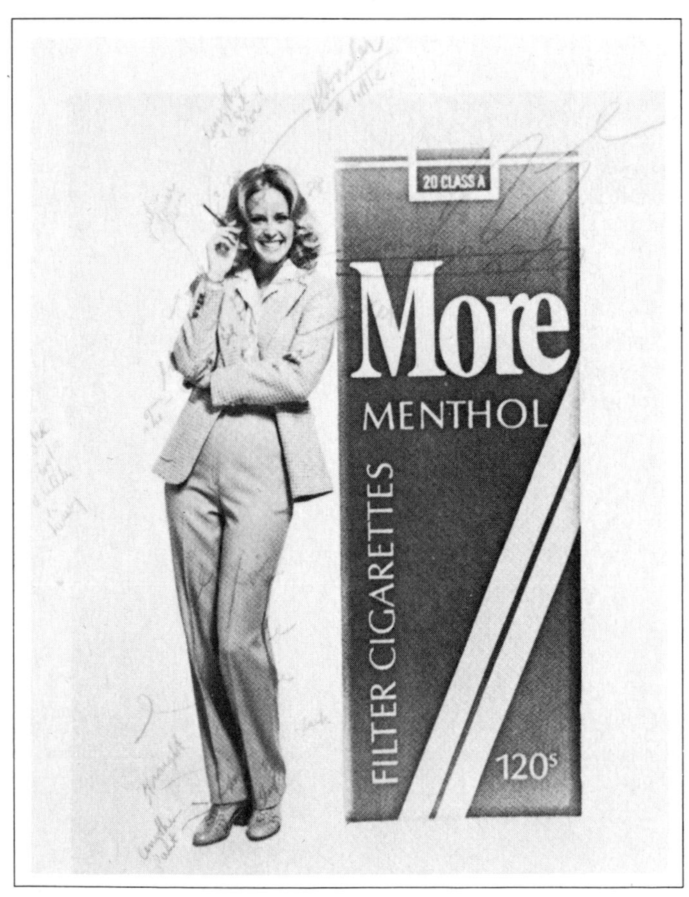

Figure 12–1 Print for a More ad has the art director's instructions. The model leans on a dummy pack created for the shoot. Final ad shows the cigarette package stripped in and the model "slimmed and smoothed." (Louis Grubb, retoucher.)

ated a year or two later by Chiat-Day Advertising in Los Angeles. What major differences do you notice between the two ads? Both use an illustrative technique to talk about the unique features of the bikes. Both use a somewhat similar design. Yet the ads look considerably different, and some people think they create a very different feeling.

The major difference, of course, is the use of typography. Figure 11–4 uses a headline set in a very pretty, traditional typeface called Goudy (pronounced "gow-dee") Old Style. Notice the characteristics of this typeface: delicate curved serifs (tails) on each letter; variation

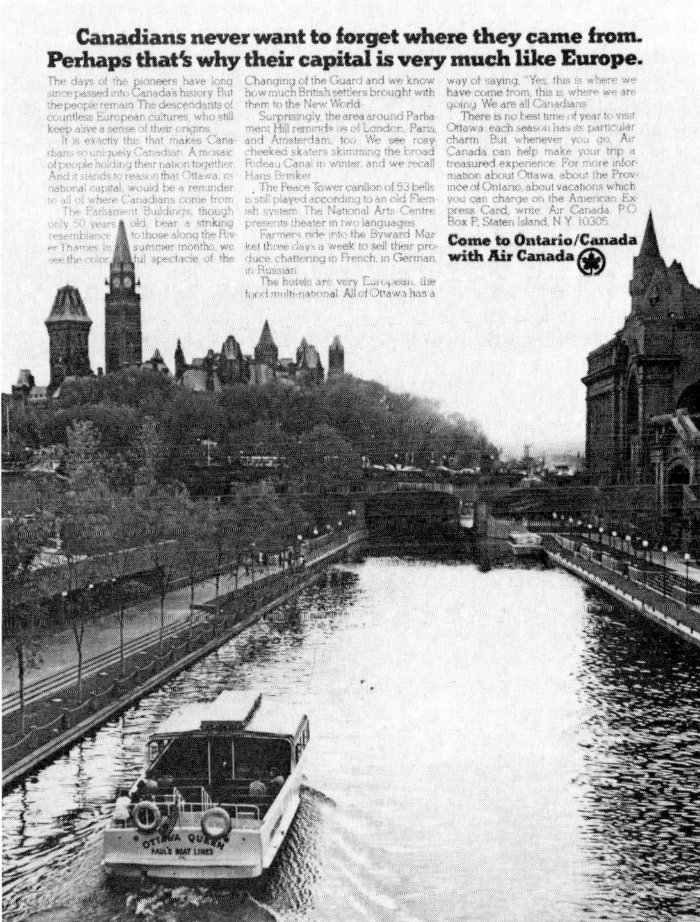

The river didn't seem wide enough in this photograph for an Air Canada ad so more river was added. This was done in the lab and called "stripping." A four-negative composite was delivered to Grubb. "In that composite, the river current was going in two or three different directions and reflecting an awful number of different colors and shades. It became a painting job, a work of illustration." Grubb also turned the lights on along the river and changed the color of the sky to give a nightfall effect. (Louis Grubb, retoucher.)

Figure 12–2

in the thickness of the letter strokes; and the clear, easy-to-read roundness of style.

Figure 12–3, on the other hand, uses a larger, sans serif (no tails) headline typeface called Futura Bold. This typeface is characterized by no serifs on the letters; uniform thickness of strokes; wide, thick letters; and a bold, round, "newsy," announcement-style presentation.

Consumers differ in the styles they prefer. Art directors therefore try to select type styles that suit the objectives and strategy of the campaign and communicate well with the target audience.

Which of these typestyles do you prefer? Do you find one easier to read? Is one more attractive than the other? Does one communicate news value better? Which attracts your attention more quickly?

Figure 12–3 The Yamaha campaign, as executed by Chiat-Day, features a continuation of the illustrative techniques already in use by Yamaha with the addition of bold, newsy, action-oriented headlines. Many art directors feel this is more in tune with the intended audience of the ads—motorcycle enthusiasts.

People in advertising

Klaus F. Schmidt

Vice President and
Director of Creative Support
Young & Rubicam Inc., New York

Klaus F. Schmidt is vice president and director of creative support at Young & Rubicam Inc., New York. In this capacity he is responsible for the company's print production, art buying, audiovisual facilities, and art studio. Prior to his appointment in 1968 Schmidt served as type director and then as director of print operations for Young & Rubicam.

Born in Germany, where he received his graphic arts training, Schmidt came to the United States in 1951 as a union compositor and printer. He obtained a B.A. in advertising and marketing at Wayne State University in Detroit. Schmidt went on to become type director of Mogul, Williams & Saylor, and then of Doyle Dane Bernbach Inc., both in New York, before joining Y&R in 1961.

Print production, says Schmidt, is the "vital step" that transforms an advertising concept into the final printed result. While account executives "need not become expert," he notes, in the technical complexities of typesetting, photoplatemaking, and printing, they "should understand at least the basics of graphic arts technology and print production procedures". Only with this working knowledge, Schmidt explains, can account executives expect to communicate successfully with their clients.

Emphasizing that print production people "are not merely technically knowledgeable purchasing agents assigned to buying typesetting, printing image carriers, paper, and other graphic arts services and commodities," Schmidt points out that "they are, beyond that basic purchasing function, you and your client's graphic arts consultants, production planners, and production liaison people—internally, with the creative, traffic, media, and account management areas, and externally with graphic arts vendors and with the print media."

Schmidt notes that, at Young & Rubicam, New York, the print production group includes the following:

1. *Art buyers,* who are versed in various forms of photographic/illustrative techniques. They know the available talent and make all business arrangements with photographers, illustrators, retouchers, photo labs, and others, in close cooperation with art directors.

2. *Type directors,* who are trained in the creative as well as the technical aspects of typography. They select, specify, mark up, and purchase all typesetting, working with the art directors.

3. *Print producers,* who coordinate all print production activities with the traffic, account management, and creative groups. They purchase image carriers for the various printed media from photoplatemaking and duplicating houses and provide the vital contact with publication production departments.

4. *Printing buyers,* who specialize in the production planning and buying of outdoor and transit advertising, newspaper and magazine inserts, as well as collateral printed material from brochures to elaborate die-cut direct-mail pieces. A printing buyer's knowledge reaches into properties of paper and ink and into the capabilities of printing, binding, and finishing equipment.

Schmidt, who has written numerous articles for American and European graphic arts magazines, has been the recipient of the Typomundus Award of the International Center for the Typographic Arts and the International Book Exhibition Award.

Cofounder and former board chairman of the International Center for the Typographic Arts, Schmidt has also served as chairman of the American Association of Advertising Agencies' Subcommittee on Phototypography and of the Customer Relations Committee of the Gravure Technical Association. He is a member of the AAAA Subcommittee on Newspaper Formats and the New York Advertising Production, Type Directors, and Art Directors Clubs.

How to use type as the major graphic design element

Type—and type directing—reaches its apex when the art director chooses it as the sole or major design element as illustrated in the following figures.

Type is used in many ways today, and nowhere is that more apparent than in headlines. Serifs, sans serifs, verticals, slants, condensed, expanded, across-the-gutter, loose, tight, all caps, upper and lowercase, small, huge, elegant, powerful, quiet, screaming, colored, dropped-out, plain, fancy—this is the type story today.

Art directors are not only using all possible headline styles, but they're also working *with* them—their directing reflects solid, effective judgment, with type matched to art to fulfill ad objectives.

Laboratory application

Discuss these ads with reference to the impact of type selection on the design concept and the execution.

A.

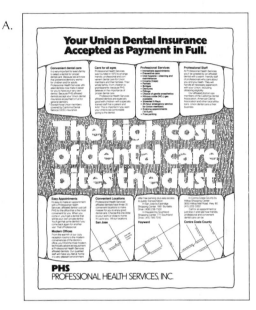

Your Union Dental Insurance Accepted as Payment in Full.

The high cost of dental care bites the dust.

PHS
PROFESSIONAL HEALTH SERVICES, INC.

B.

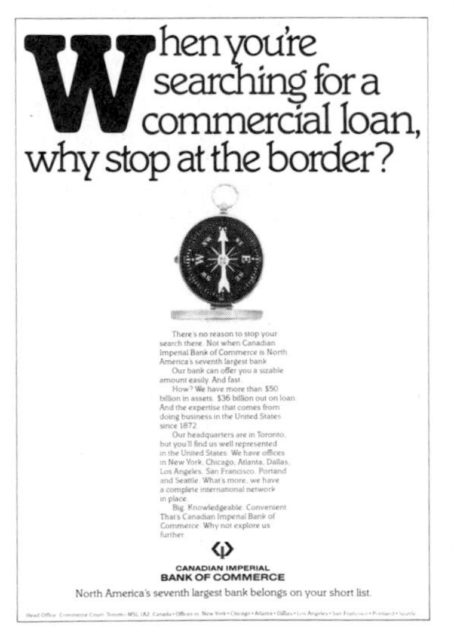

C.

WHY WE HAVE CHANGED OUR NAME

Peoples Gas Company's origins go back to 1850—to a small utility supplying manufactured gas in one neighborhood in the City of Chicago.

Over the years we've grown and branched out in many different energy directions. Our natural gas transmission and distribution operations, for instance, now constitute the fourth largest interstate system in the United States. We have potentially important programs moving ahead in liquefied natural gas and coal gasification.

We're in the business of exploring for oil and gas through our Texoma and Harper subsidiaries.

We're in the coal business through the acquisition of Industrial Fuels Corporation and additional mining properties which it has since acquired.

In recent weeks, we have signed a preliminary agreement to acquire Exeter Company, a leading onshore drilling contractor.

From a local utility in 1850, we are becoming a large and diversified energy company.

So, with some regrets, our stockholders have voted to change our name from Peoples Gas Company to *Peoples Energy Corporation*.

This new name more fully reflects the scope of our operations while retaining the widespread recognition and historic significance of the "Peoples" name, which has served us well.

Peoples Energy Corporation
Managing Energy is Our Business

Natural Gas Pipeline Company of America
Texoma Production Company • The Peoples Gas Light and Coke Company
Harper Oil Company • Industrial Fuels Corporation • North Shore Gas Company
For further information write: Peoples Energy Corporation, 122 South Michigan Ave., Chicago, IL 60603

D.

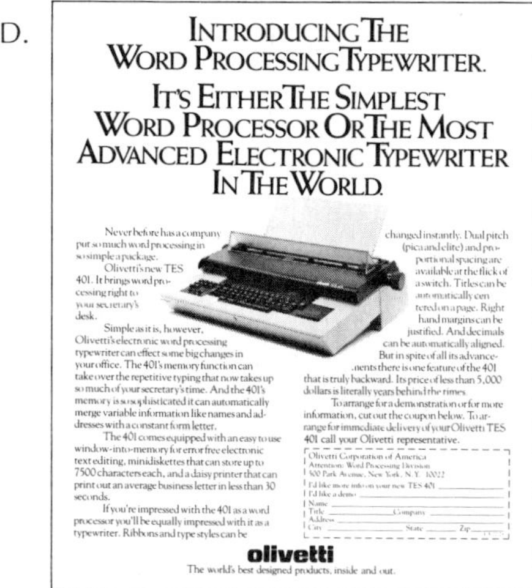

E.

Imagine a place where $1 billion in outside capital has been invested in the last six months.

Imagine a skyline of office buildings, hotels, shopping malls, convention facilities, and industrial parks that didn't exist the last time you looked.

Imagine a group of five vital counties and a vibrant city working hard, working together, to make your business a success.

Imagine 250 pages of answers to every question you have. Now, try to imagine not finding out more.

Write Donald D. Moyer, Director, Economic Development Council of Greater Baltimore, Suite 900, 2 Hopkins Plaza, Baltimore, Maryland 21201, or call (301) 727-0447.

BOOM

Baltimore City & Surrounding Counties

ANNE ARUNDEL
BALTIMORE
CARROLL
HARFORD
HOWARD

F.

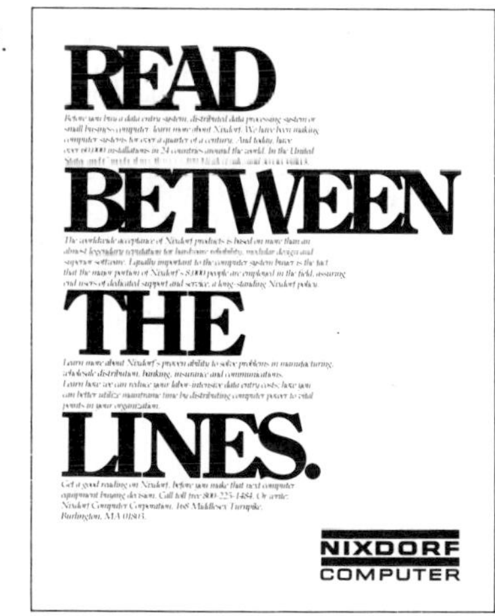

G.

H.

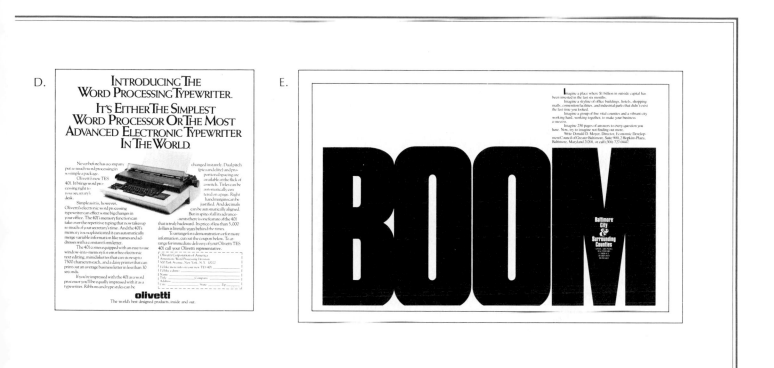

Do you get different feelings, or a different impression, from the two type styles? Does one offer a greater feeling of credibility than the other? Considering all these things, if you were the art director would you prefer one of these type styles over the other? (See the Ad Lab.)

Classes of type

Type can be divided into two broad classes: display type and text type. *Display type* is larger and usually heavier than text type. It is used in headlines, subheads, logos, addresses, and wherever there is a need for emphasis in an advertisement. For body copy in an advertisement, the smaller *text type* is used.

Type groups

There are thousands of typefaces available, and type designers are continually developing new ones. Typefaces are classified into various groups because of their similarity in design. There is no reason to learn the names of all the faces because each typesetting house or printer has only a limited number of typefaces, depending on requirements and the kind of equipment that has been purchased. Except for persons who wish to become specialists in the field, an understanding of the five major type groups is sufficient (Figure 12–4).

Roman

This is the most popular type group. It offers the greatest number of designs, which means that contrast can be achieved without a basic design change. It is also considered the most readable. The two most distinguishing characteristics of Roman type are (1) the small lines, tails, or serifs that cross the ends of the main strokes, and (2) variations in the thickness of the strokes. Roman type can be obtained in a variety of sizes and contains dozens of subclassifications that differ from one another on the basis of thickness of the strokes, the way the letters are designed (letterforms), and the size and regularity of the serifs.

Sans serif

This is the second most popular type group. It is also referred to as *block, contemporary,* or *gothic.* This large group of typefaces is characterized by (1) the lack of serifs (thus the name, sans serif) and (2) the uniform thickness of the strokes.

Sans serif typefaces are usually not so readable in text type as Roman faces. However, they are widely used because of the simple, clean lines, which give a modern appearance.

Square serif

A combination of sans serif and Roman, square serif faces have the same uniform thickness of strokes as sans serif faces. Square serif is similar to Roman in that it has serifs, but the serifs have the same weight and thickness as the main strokes of the letters.

Cursive or script

These typefaces resemble handwriting. They are rather difficult to read and are used primarily in headlines. The letters are often connected

ROMAN TYPE		Garamond (OLD STYLE)
		Plantin
		Caledonia (TRANSITIONAL)
		Baskerville
	ITC	Zapf Book (MODERN)
	ITC	Tiffany
SANS SERIF TYPE		Helvetica
		Spartan Book
		Eurostyle
		Franklin Gothic
SQUARE SERIF TYPE		Serifa 55
		Rockwell
	ITC	Lubalin Graph Medium
		Memphis Medium
SCRIPT TYPE		Snell Round Hand
		Bank Script
		Kaufman Bold
ORNAMENTAL TYPE		HELVIN
		Karnac
		NEON
		Orbit-B

Figure 12–4 The five major type groups.

Cheltenham
Cheltenham Italic
Cheltenham Bold
Cheltenham Bold Italic
Cheltenham Bold Condensed
Cheltenham Bold Condensed Italic
Cheltenham Bold Extra Condensed
Cheltenham Nova
Cheltenham Bold Nova
Cheltenham Light*
*Cheltenham Light Italic**
Cheltenham Book*
*Cheltenham Book Italic**
Cheltenham Bold*
Cheltenham Bold Italic*
Cheltenham Ultra*
Cheltenham Ultra Italic*
Cheltenham Light Condensed*
*Cheltenham Light Condensed Italic**
Cheltenham Book Condensed*
*Cheltenham Book Condensed Italic**
Cheltenham Bold Condensed*
Cheltenham Bold Condensed Italic*
Cheltenham Ultra Condensed*
Cheltenham Ultra Condensed Italic*

Figure 12–5 The Cheltenham family. Note the variety of looks available to be used without changing families. Art directors may use a boldface in the headline, lightface in the copy, as well as different sizes or even italics for emphasis. Most art directors try to avoid using more than one type family in a single ad.

and convey a feeling of femininity, formality, or beauty. They are commonly used in cosmetic and fashion advertising.

Ornamental

This group of typefaces includes designs that provide novelty and are ornamental or decorative. They are used for special effects but are also difficult to read.

Type families

Within each major type group, there are type families. A type family is made up of related faces identified by such names as Cheltenham, Futura, Goudy, Bodoni, and Caslon (Figure 12–5). The basic design remains the same within a family, but there are variations in the proportion, weight, and slant of the characters. These variations make up a family and commonly include light, medium, bold, extra bold, condensed, extended, and italic. All these variations may not be available in a particular type family. These differences, however, enable the typographer to provide contrast and emphasis in an advertisement without changing type styles. For any typeface and size of type, a font consists of a complete assortment of capitals, small capitals, lowercase letters, numerals, and punctuation marks.

In an effort to control the exclusivity of their advertising, some advertisers have a unique typestyle designed. The Volvo ad in Figure 12–6, for example, shows a bold, sans serif headline set in Volvo's own type style designed by John Danza, the creative director at Scali, McCabe, Sloves, Volvo's advertising agency.

Other advertisers might go in the opposite direction for uniformity. *Vogue, Glamour, McCalls,* and *Good Housekeeping* magazines all use different editorial typefaces. The Oil of Olay ads that appear in these publications are tailor-made to incorporate the same typography and design elements as in the magazines (Figure 12–7). In this way, a truly editorial look is given to these testimonial ads, and the company hopes credibility is thereby enhanced.

Type structure and measurement

Several terms must be explained in order to understand type structure and measurement.

Points

Points measure the depth (or height) of the type. There are 72 points to the inch, so one point equals $^1/_{72}$ of an inch. This term refers to the vertical measurement of a line of type measured from the bottom of the descenders, or extensions downward from the body of the type, to the top of the ascenders, or extensions upward from the body of the type.

The most common type sizes used in advertising are 6, 8, 10, 12, 14, 18, 24, 36, 42, 60, 72, 84, 96, and 120 points (Figure 12–8). The smaller sizes, 6 through 14 points, are used for text type. The larger sizes are used for display type.

Pica

The unit of measurement for the horizontal width of lines of type is the *pica*. There are six picas to the inch (Figure 12–9). The width of a single letter of type depends on the style of the typeface and whether it is regular or bold, extended or condensed. It also depends on the proportions of the letter. But averages for each type style and size have been established and are provided by the manufacturer of the type.

DO YOU HAVE THE FEELING YOUR CAR ISN'T WORTH WHAT YOU PAID FOR IT? YOU'RE NOT ALONE.

The average purchase price of a new car today is more than $6,000. And when people part with that kind of money they expect a lot in return.

But according to a national survey conducted by K. M. Warwick Marketing Research, apparently millions of car owners feel they don't get it.*

If you've been driven to this conclusion, give some thought to driving a new Volvo. Volvos start at $6,645.† And according to the same independent survey, more Volvo owners feel they get their money's worth than the owners of Sevilles, Cutlasses, Cordobas, Continentals and 53 other models from G.M., Ford, Chrysler and AMC.

Get behind the wheel of a Volvo and you'll immediately begin to understand what makes this car worth the money.

The feeling of solidity. The quality of workmanship. The sense that a Volvo wasn't designed to be here today and gone tomorrow. (Volvos are so well made that their average life expectancy in Sweden is now 16.7 years.)

In a Volvo, you'll also discover many standard features you have to pay extra for on other cars (if you can get them at all). Like paint that's four coats deep. Two separate undercoatings. Orthopedically designed front bucket seats that adjust to the contours of your back. Disc brakes on all four wheels. Fuel injection. Steel-belted radial tires. An electric rear window defroster. Tinted glass. And safety characteristics so advanced that more than 40 Volvos are being studied by the U.S. Government.

So if you're the kind of person who wants value for your money, remember one thing.

It's not how much money you pay for a car. It's how much car you get for your money.

VOLVO

VOLVO. A CAR YOU CAN BELIEVE IN.

Figure 12–6 The Volvo typeface. Designed by John Danza at Scali, McCabe, Sloves, Volvo has owned its own exclusive typeface for many years. Used in the headline and tag line of all ads, it guarantees an exclusive continuity to the company's advertising campaigns.

Upper and lowercase

Capital letters are called *uppercase* and small letters are called *lowercase.* The terms came about as a result of compositors in days past who set type by hand and stacked the two cases containing the capital and small letters one above the other.

Type can be set using all caps, caps and small caps, or caps and lowercase. Note from the material you are now reading how much easier it is to read a combination of upper and lowercase. Advertising copy set in lower case will invariably be more readable than copy set in all-capitals. That goes for headlines as well as body copy. Type set in solid capitals can be used for emphasis but this should be done so very sparingly.

A.

What Did Your Mirror Reveal This Morning?

This morning started out like any other. You put on the coffee and set out the juice glasses. Then, as always, you went to freshen up to greet the day and your family pleasantly. Looking in the mirror as you brushed

your hair, you suddenly realized that you looked older. Somehow you hadn't noticed before. But you couldn't help wondering if other people were aware of the change.

Now you and your mirror have come face-to-face with the truth, it's time you discovered a secret known to fortunate women from many parts of the world, the secret of a mysterious beauty fluid that can help you look younger by creating a moist climate for your skin. This skin-loving liquid is known in the United States as Oil of Olay beauty lotion.

Simply smooth Oil of Olay over your face and throat to let it begin to work so that it can help you look younger. Watch the precious fluid disappear into your skin. Oil of Olay penetrates remarkably quickly, bringing pure moisture, tropical oil and precious emollients to ease dryness. Dryness, of course, can so easily make you look older, as it makes little wrinkle lines more obvious. The very first day you use Oil of Olay, those lines can become less noticeable. Even though they may not comment, the change will be apparent to other people.

The skin-cherishing beauty fluid works mysteriously as a partner with nature to help maintain your skin's natural moisture balance and let your skin become softer, smoother, younger looking.

Within moments after applying the beauty fluid, your face takes on a renewed lustre and radiance, a kind of marvelously dewy glow. Remember that look? Isn't it a joy to see it again?

When will you choose to use the precious beauty fluid? Exposure to wind and sun, some cosmetics, even sudden temperature changes can cause your skin to feel dry and look older, just as certainly as the passing years do. So whenever your skin feels dry, it may be telling you that it would welcome Oil of Olay.

If you're like most dedicated users, you will want Oil of Olay to be part of your morning and evening beauty ritual. Oil of Olay faithfully every morning, either to let your skin live in its own moist climate or under your cosmetics. Because the beauty fluid penetrates so quickly and doesn't leave a greasy afterfeel, you'll find it marvelous under makeup. Again, faithfully every night, so that Oil of Olay can cherish and pamper your skin into quiet hours of night.

Remember what your mirror revealed this morning? How reassuring to know that with Oil of Olay your mirror can soon reflect a younger look. What a lovely way to face the day.

Beauty Secrets

Perhaps the sudden realization that you looked older than you realized has prompted you to plan an overall self-improvement program, complete with diet, exercise and time set aside for intensive grooming. When you're exercising, giving yourself a manicure or while you're figuring out your calorie count for the day, is a good time for an extra application of Oil of Olay.

* * *

When you've discovered Oil of Olay, you won't want a single drop to go to waste. After you've smoothed the beauty fluid on your face and throat, massage your elbows with Oil of Olay. You may not see that particular dry area, but others certainly do.

* * *

When you can take time for a leisurely bath, smooth Oil of Olay® on your face and throat while you're relaxing and unwinding in the tub. It feels marvelous, and the discreet fragrance that surrounds you is one more delicious addition to that peaceful time.

B.

What Have the Past Few Years Done to Your Looks?

Like so many women today you've changed over these past few years. With kudos from your husband and children you've gone back to school (you'd always wanted to). Or you've taken a job (you're terrific at it, too). Or you may have become involved in local politics (you can actually take the floor now without blushing).

Doing new things has given you a whole new perspective on yourself. In fact, you're simply not the same person that you were, and that's a very exciting feeling. But what about your looks? Perhaps you're having the first real conference with your mirror that you've had in years. Does it seem to be whispering, "Look at those little wrinkle lines... do you really think other people don't see them?" Or, "Tennis and golf are great for your figure but your skin is beginning to look dry and a little weatherbeaten. Don't you mind?" And guess what? You do mind...you mind quite a bit. Because once you became more aware of the world out there it made you feel younger. No wonder you say to yourself, "Why shouldn't I *look* younger, too?"

Bravo. Why shouldn't you indeed. So before another day goes by, discover for yourself the secret shared by fortunate women from Stockholm to Sydney to San Francisco and beyond...the secret of a mysterious beauty fluid that can help you look younger as it minimizes dryness.

Known in the United States as Oil of Olay beauty lotion, this incredibly light, silky and non-greasy fluid lets your skin live in its own moist climate.

Just smooth Oil of Olay on your face and throat. You'll be amazed at how quickly it penetrates, bringing a wealth of pure moisture, tropical oil and precious emollients to help your skin maintain its natural moisture balance.

Within moments your skin becomes softer and more supple. There's a luminous glow again. (Did you think it was lost forever?) Those little wrinkle lines can begin to show less...and yes, all that can help you look younger.

Think how you'll feel when others notice. Your husband, especially. He may tell you that you look marvelous, or you may read it in his eyes. Isn't that one of the small sweet moments in a marriage?

Like most Oil of Olay lovers you'll probably want to make a pleasurable little habit of the beauty fluid. At bedtime stroke it on to mist your skin into the night. Remember, it's so non-greasy, moments after it disappears into your skin all you feel is velvety softness, all you see is a dewy, radiant look.

In the morning gentle on Oil of Olay again. It's a fabulous first step before makeup (you barely have to wait to skim on your cosmetics). And on a day you'd like to take a makeup break, go ahead. With Oil of Olay you can still look fresh and glowy.

Any other time your skin seems thirsty, don't hestiate to treat it to extra helpings of Oil of Olay. Especially when the environment is punishing, let Oil of Olay create the moist climate your skin loves to live in.

Now that you know how Oil of Olay can care for your looks, shouldn't you welcome the beauty fluid into your life for the coming years.

Beauty Secrets

When your husband is stuck after hours at the office, plan a little late-night supper for two at the coffee table. Sleek on Oil of Olay, wear something long...and maybe light a fragrance candle. That's a home-coming to make him forget he's had a rough day.

* * *

For a brisk morning eye-opener, splash your face with cold water, towel not-quite-dry and smooth on Oil of Olay.® That's one of the nicer ways to start your day.

C.

WOULD YOU LOVE TO LOOK YOUNGER TO YOUR HUSBAND?

Ever since your husband started playing tennis again and his step became springier, was the secret wish there? When you found yourself suggesting little candlelit dinners and feeling almost absurdly romantic, you probably knew for sure that you'd love to look younger to

him, just as he's looking younger to you.

At a moment like this, how lucky to discover the secret of a mysterious beauty fluid that can help you look younger by creating a moist climate for your skin. The secret, shared by enlightened women around the world, is known in the United States as Oil of Olay beauty lotion.

Oil of Olay quickly penetrates your skin, without a greasy feeling, to help maintain its natural moisture balance and ease dryness. That's very important, of course, because dryness can make those age-telling little wrinkle lines more noticeable. (If you've glimpsed them in the mirror, you probably felt the pang every women feels at the thought of looking older than she likes.)

You gentle light and silky Oil of Olay on your face and throat. Almost at once, your skin drinks in the wealth of pure moisture, tropical oil and precious emollients. Your face becomes softer to the touch. The little lines show less. And, surprisingly, the luminous look you thought had vanished birthdays ago is back. Will others see the difference? Your husband may be the first to notice.

How will you look to him? How will he react? Those are pretty exciting things to find yourself wondering about.

If you're like most dedicated users, you'll want to make the mysterious beauty fluid a part of your beauty care twice a day. At night, smooth it on for a deliciously silky feeling as your skin benefits into the night. In the morning, apply Oil of Olay again for a fresh start under your cosmetics. (Because Oil of Olay is so fast-penetrating and non-greasy, you'll love it under makeup.) Use the beauty fluid at other times, too. Whenever your face feels as though it's having a dry spell, let Oil of Olay create a dewy climate for your skin and watch the bloom come back.

Would you love to look younger to your husband? It's easy to ask yourself that question when Oil of Olay is there to help.

BEAUTY SECRETS

If you're feeling and looking a little frazzled after a long day of shopping, take a break. Feet up, dampened pads on eyes, and a lovely sleeking of Oil of Olay on face and throat. Play a record, sip a cooling beverage and think romantic thoughts. What a pleasant prelude to his homecoming.

* * *

When you and your husband are on a weekend car jaunt exploring the countryside, your skin can begin to look dry. Why not pack a bottle of Oil of Olay in your tote bag. Smooth on the beauty fluid before you get to that charming inn for lunch. You'll arrive fresh-faced and radiant enough for lunching outdoors in the sunlight.

* * *

Being alone together, not even talking, can be the most intimate of times. The next evening he's listening to music and you're reading, pamper your face with an extra application of Oil of Olay. It's nice to know that because Oil of Olay® doesn't leave a greasy look, he'll see only a lovely, dewy glow.

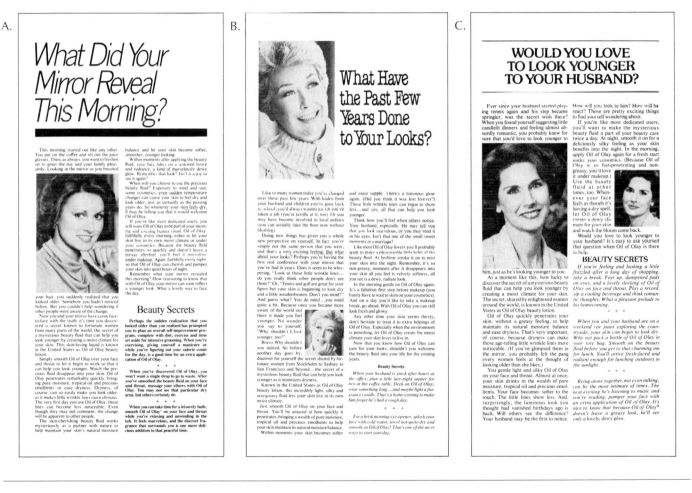

Figure 12–7 Ad A appeared in *Vogue*, ad B in *Good Housekeeping*, and ad C in *McCall's*. Because these advertisements so closely resemble the editorial matter of the publications in which they appear, the advertiser must allow the publisher to insert the word "Advertisement" at the top of each ad.

Type selection

The art of selecting and setting type is known as *typography*. Because almost every advertisement has some reading matter, type has tremendous importance in advertising. The typeface chosen affects the advertisement's general appearance, design, and legibility. Although type cannot compensate for a weak headline, poorly written body

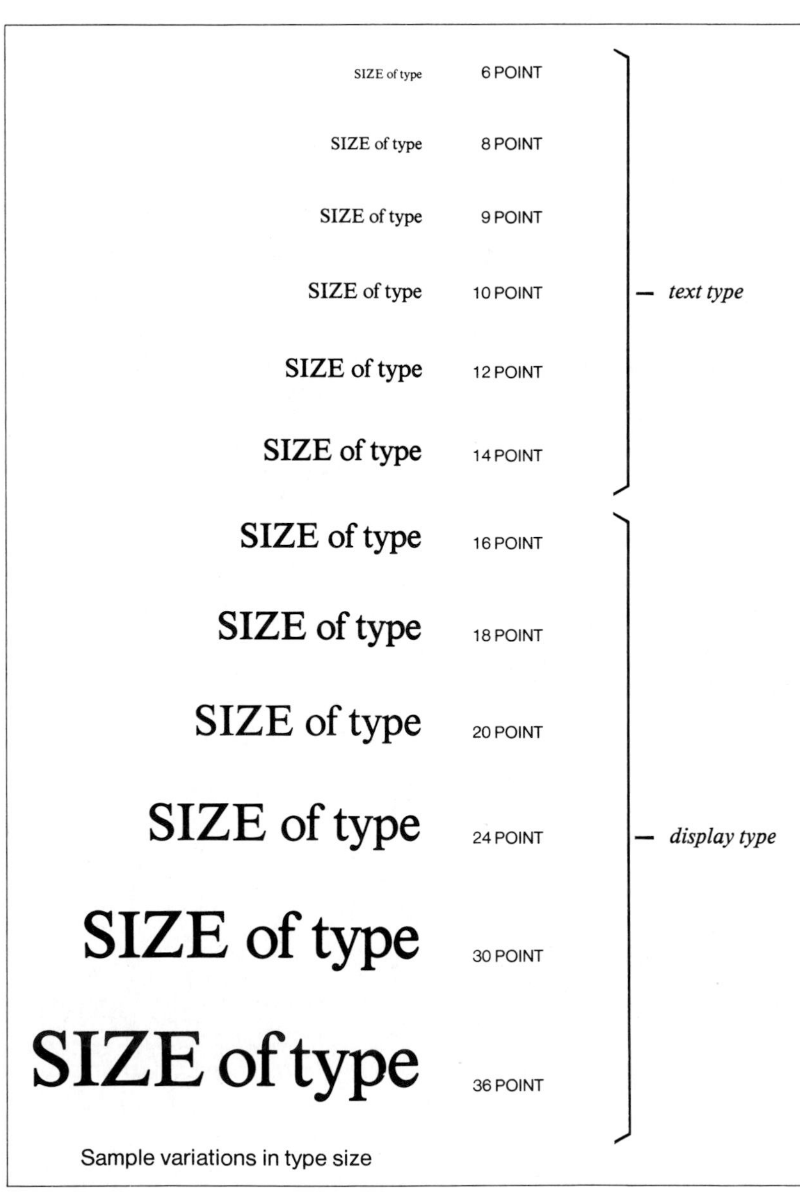

Figure 12–8 Sample variations in type size.

copy, or a lack of appropriate illustrations, it can create interest and attract readers to the advertisement.

Knowledge of the effects and symbolism of typefaces requires great expertise. There may be fewer experts who can accurately interpret how a typeface will influence an ad than any other kind of expert connected with the advertising business. This art requires experience and skill and should not be left to the layperson. Among local advertisers, however, it is often the most overlooked aspect of advertising creativity.

There are four important points to consider in type selection.

Legibility

Factors that contribute to legibility include type style, boldness, size, length of the line, and spacing between the words, lines, and paragraphs. An advertisement is printed to be read, and a reduction in legibility kills interest. Difficult-to-read typefaces should be used sparingly and only to create special effects.

Naturally, large, bold, legible typefaces are the easiest to read. However, we are limited by the amount of space in the advertisement and the amount of copy that must be written. Legibility is also affected by the length of the line in which the copy is set. Newspaper columns are usually less than 2 inches wide, magazine columns slightly wider. For advertisements, columns of copy less than 3 inches (18 picas) wide are usually recommended.

The way lines of type are spaced also influence legibility. Between lines of type there is always a small amount of space to allow for *descenders* (j's) and *ascenders* (d's). When this is the only space between lines, type is "set solid." Sometimes an art director decides to add extra space between the lines to give a slightly more "airy" feeling. In this case, *leading* (pronounced "ledding") between lines is called for. The term relates back to when thin metal strips were actually inserted between lines of metal type.

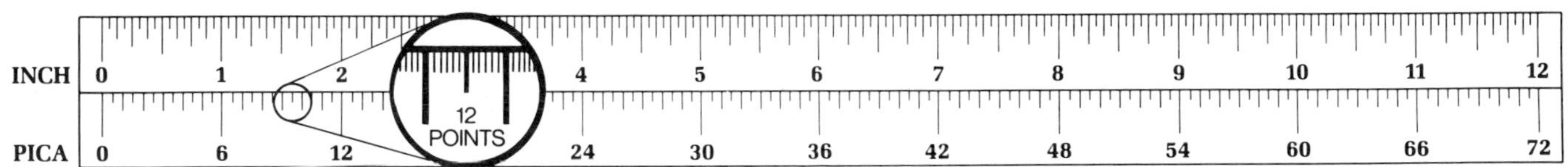

Figure 12–9

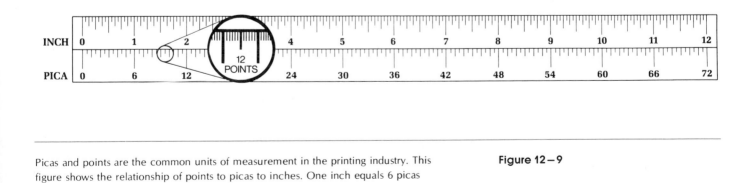

Picas and points are the common units of measurement in the printing industry. This figure shows the relationship of points to picas to inches. One inch equals 6 picas or 72 points. Thus, type set at 36 points would be 1/2 inch tall; and an 18 pica column of type would be 3 inches wide.

The most unforgettable characters you will ever meet

Laboratory application

Choose five of these type styles and discuss them from the standpoint of readability, appropriateness (give examples of products), harmony/appearance, and emphasis.

AIRKRAFT
Locomotive
STRIPES
FAT SHADOW
GALADRIEL
Magnificat
GOOD VIBRATIONS
Motter Ombra
Pluto Outline
ROCO
Shamrock
BUSTER

ELEFONT
MASQUERADE
BABY TEETH
GLASER STENCIL
oxford
SINALOA
PICCADILLY
YAGI LINK DOUBLE
Cathedral
Shatter
Neptun
L'Auriol

Knightsbridge
Harlow
CALYPSO
traffic
YANKEE
SUPERSTAR
Thalia
Octopuss
BLOCK UP
Fino
quartermaine
STOP

Type that is set in 10-point with 2 points of space (leading) between lines is specified as "10 on 12," or "10/12." This same terminology is used whether the type is set in metal or by photocomposition, to be discussed later.

Appropriateness

A typeface must be appropriate to the product being advertised. With many varieties of type available in terms of both style (typeface) and size, a host of moods and feelings can be conveyed quite apart from the meanings of the words themselves. Some typefaces suggest ruggedness and masculinity, while others give a feeling of delicateness and femininity. A typeface can whisper "luxury," while another can scream "bargain." A typeface that conveys the feeling of something old-fashioned obviously would be inappropriate in an advertisement for a space-age electronic watch. (See the Ad Lab.)

Harmony/appearance

The type should harmonize with other elements of the advertisement, including the illustration and the layout. This means choosing typefaces that are closely related or belong to the same family. Mixing too many typefaces results in disharmony and a feeling of clutter.

Emphasis

Emphasis with type selection can be achieved by using contrast. One method is to use more than a single type style, or to use italic versus roman or upright type, lowercase versus uppercase, or small-size versus large-size type. Care must be taken because an effort to emphasize *all* the elements in an advertisement will only result in emphasizing none of the elements.

Type specification and copy casting

Type must fit into the space designated for it in the layout. So before the type can be selected, the number of characters in the copy has to be determined, or "cast off."

There are two methods for fitting the copy to the space. With the word count method, the words in the copy are counted and divided by the number of words per square inch that can be set in a particular type style and size as given in a standard table.

With the character-count method, there is greater accuracy. An actual count is made of the number of characters (letters, word spaces, and punctuation marks) in the copy. In a type specimen book or chart provided by the typographer, the average number of characters per pica is given for each typeface and type point size. From this information it is relatively simple to determine how much space a given type will use.

Copy sent to a typographer or publication should be marked with the type specifications written beside the copy. Usually the copy is accompanied by a layout.

When specifying type, the typographer should be provided with at least the following information: (1) the typeface by name, (2) the type size and the leading, and (3) the type width in picas. The specification of type in advertising agencies is handled by art directors, type directors, or the print production staff. However, it is important for copywriters and account executives as well, to understand the basics of type specification and copycasting since copy must often be written to fit a particular space in an advertisement. Otherwise, the ad risks looking either overly crowded or too empty—thereby impairing its visual impact.

Typesetting methods

The last decade has seen a revolution in typesetting methods. The old methods of metal type composition (which caused letters to be formed by pouring molten lead into brass molds) is virtually obsolete. This "hot-type" era, which included composition processes with such names as hand-setting, Monotype, Linotype, and Ludlow, has yielded to a new era characterized by high-speed electronic photocomposition equipment and operators schooled in computer technology. The new "cold-type" era, which really began in the 1960s, has seen a technological explosion with tremendous changes in the tools available to art directors, designers, and writers and the effects they can achieve while at the same time saving time and money.

Today's typesetting methods generally fall into two broad classifications: strike-on composition and photocomposition.

Strike-on composition

Strike-on or *direct-impression composition* can be done on either a regular typewriter or the new breed of intelligent electronic typewriters, which have microprocessors, can perform basic text-editing functions automatically, and offer storage capabilities. Although there is only a limited range of typefaces available and these machines produce only text, not display type, this means of composition offers substantial savings and is primarily used when economy is the overriding consideration. Because the price of the equipment is relatively low, organizations can afford to have the equipment in-house, which offers the advantage of getting material set quickly when the need arises. This equipment is often used in typesetting direct-mail advertising, catalogs, and house organs.

Photocomposition

This is the most dominant method of producing advertising materials today. It is a combination of computer technology and electronics, which offers an almost unlimited number of typefaces and sizes, faster reproduction at lower cost, and improved clarity and sharpness of image.

The basic function of all phototypesetting machines is to expose photosensitive paper, or film, to a projected image of the character being set. This may be done photo-optically, by cathode-ray tube (CRT) technology, or by laser exposure (Figure 12–10).

Photo-optic typesetters

Most typesetters today fall into this category, which uses an electromechanical method of generating characters. Character fonts are stored on film grids, discs, drums, or film strip matrices. The matrix is usually rotated mechanically until the desired character is in the proper position. A xenon lamp is flashed and the light image of the character is projected through a lens, which magnifies it to the desired size. This image is then reflected off a mirror onto the photosensitive paper or film, and the character has been set.

CRT typesetters

In cathode-ray tube techniques, characters are stored digitally. When they are to be generated, they are retrieved from the computer's memory and passed to a print CRT (similar to a television receiver tube) where they are lined up and then exposed through a lens system onto the photosensitive paper or film. Since they are generated electronically, the characters can be modified (condensed, heavied, slanted, etc.) at the operator's command. These high-speed versatile machines are considerably more expensive than the photo-optic devices. However, they can store hundreds of fonts and have extremely high speed capabilities.

Laser typesetters

With new computer-laser technology, type fonts and software programs are stored digitally in a computer that also controls the on/off action of the laser beam as it "writes" onto (exposes) the output paper or film. No CRT is used. Extremely high speeds are possible as well as great reliability and versatility.

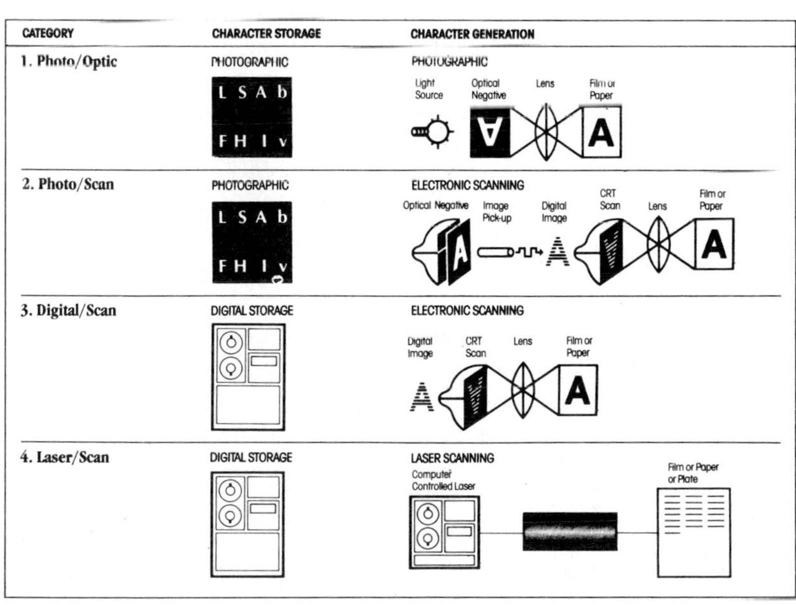

Figure 12–10

The typesetting process

Typesetting is a series of separate steps, including inputting (keyboarding), hyphenation and justification, typesetting by one of the processes explained above, developing the exposed photographic material, proofreading for errors and omissions, correcting and resetting, and makeup. Modern equipment available today ranges from equipment that performs only one step in the process to complete *direct-entry* systems, which have the input and output capabilities in one device (Figure 12–11).

These new direct-entry phototypesetters became affordable at the end of the 1970s. Now many advertising agencies, studios, and clients have them in-house, facilitating fast, cost-effective, do-it-yourself typesetting, which previously was provided by large, outside type houses.

Figure 12–11 The on-screen layout of the Comp/Edit from AM Varityper gives a visual presentation of the typeset layout before the type is set. The final typeset output has all elements in position so there is little or no need for paste-up in straight-copy advertisements.

The printing process

The transfer of an image from one surface to another is the objective of all printing methods. There are basically four major methods by which printed advertising materials are reproduced today: letterpress, rotogravure, offset lithography, and screen printing (Figure 12–12).

Letterpress

In letterpress printing the ink is applied to a raised (relief) surface and transferred to the paper. The process is similar to the way a rubber stamp works. Like a stamp, the image to be transferred is backward ("wrong reading"). The printing is done from a metal or plastic printing plate, usually on a rotary press.

The rotary press is designed for high-speed work and for economy in long press runs. Both the paper (in a continuous web) and the printing surface are on cylinders. The printing plate used is curved so that it will fit the cylinder. The printing takes place as the two cylinders strike against each other.

Letterpress is used in the reproduction of about 30 percent of this country's newspapers and a number of magazines that need good quality with sharp contrast. However, its use has been constantly shrinking with the advent of newer, higher quality methods.

Rotogravure

The process used in rotogravure is the reverse of letterpress. Instead of the printing design being raised above the printing plate, the rotogravure process prints from a depressed surface. The design is etched into a metal plate or cylinder, leaving depressions one or two thousandths of an inch deep. As the plate is inked and wiped clean with a metal blade, ink is left in tiny depressions. It is then transferred to the paper by pressure and suction.

Because preparing the printing plates or cylinders is time-consuming and costly, rotogravure is practical and economical only for long press runs. Sunday newspaper supplements, mail-order catalogs, many major magazines, packaging, and other material with a great number of photographs are well suited for this method. It is noted for its good reproduction of color on quality paper stocks as well as newsprint.

Offset lithography

In offset lithography the image on the printing plate appears to the

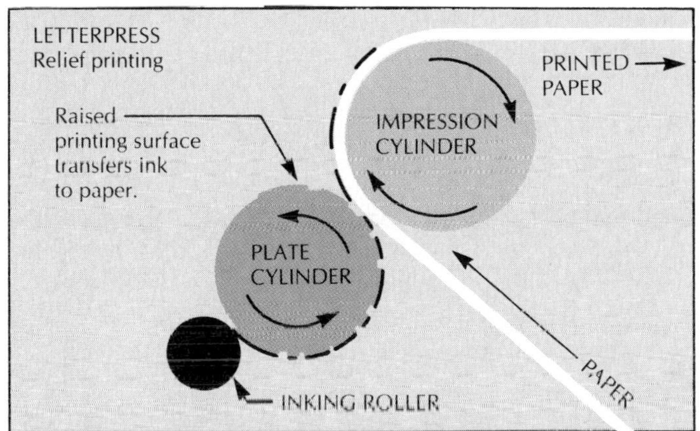

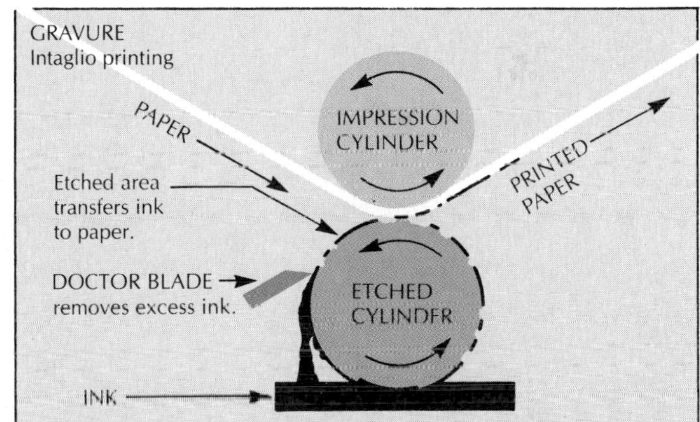

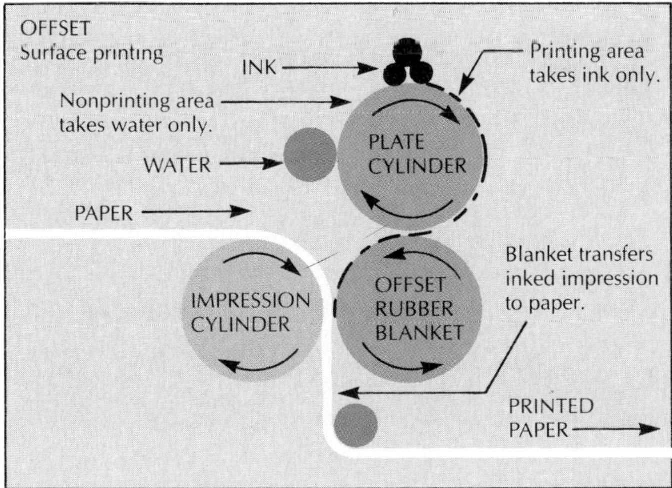

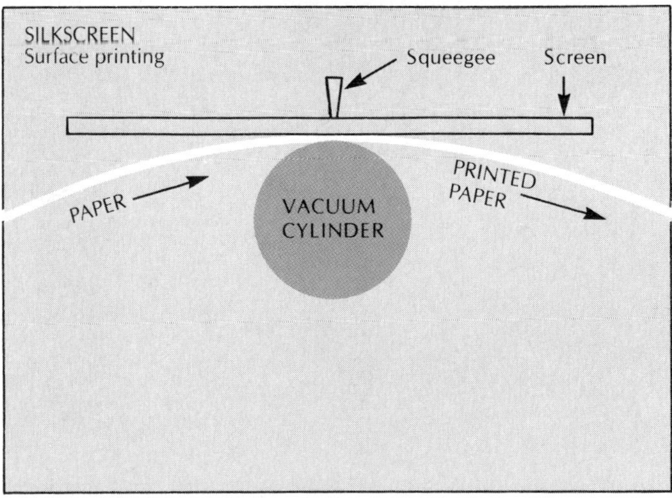

Figure 12–12 These are comparative illustrations of the major printing processes in use today. To complement your understanding of these processes, visit a local printer and ask to see the presses at work. It will be interesting and worthwhile.

naked eye to be on a flat surface instead of raised, as in letterpress, or depressed, as in rotogravure.

The principle underlying lithography is that oil and water do not mix. To start, a photograph is made of the material to be printed. The negative from the photograph is laid on top of a zinc or aluminum printing plate and exposed to light. Chemicals are applied to the plate after the exposure, and the image takes the form of a greasy coating. The plate is then attached to a cylinder on a rotary printing press and water is applied with a roller. The greasy coated image repels the water, but the blank portions of the plate retain it. As the plate is inked with an oily ink, the moist blank portions of the plate repel the ink. The greasy coated image retains the ink for transfer to an intermediate rubber surface called a blanket, which comes in contact with the paper and enables the image to be printed.

Today lithography is the most popular printing process in the United States. The printing plates cost less than for other printing methods, the printing can be done on rougher paper than can letterpress, and the preparation time is short. Because the process is photographic, it meshes well with the most popular form of typesetting, photocomposition. Advertisers simply have to provide camera-ready paste-ups or film.

Lithography is used extensively for inexpensive advertising materials prepared at "instant" printing shops. Most newspapers and magazines are printed by this process, as are most books (including this one), direct-mail materials, and catalogs (Figure 12–13). Because it is suitable for printing on metal, most packaging, including beer and soft drink cans, is also printed by lithography.

Figure 12–13 This high-speed Heidelberg five-color offset press is used for printing magazines. The first four units are used for four-color process printing, while the fifth may be used to varnish the printed page or to lay down a specific extra color. For example, some art directors may want a "company green" which is printed with a specific colored ink rather than through process colors.

Screen printing (serigraphy)

The billboards we see along the highway illustrate the use of screen printing. Billboards use sheets of paper that have historically been too large for many printing presses. Also the quantities required for many outdoor advertising campaigns, especially local ones, are so small that it is often uneconomical to use other printing processes, like offset, which might be used for national campaigns.

Screen printing is an old process based on the stencil principle and requires no plates. A special screen is stretched tightly on a frame. The frame is placed on the surface on which the message or image is to be printed. A stencil, either hand cut from film or photographically prepared, is used to block out areas that are not part of the image to be printed. Ink is squeezed through the screen by a squeegee (rubber rollers) sliding across the surface, which reproduces the desired image. For printing in color, a separate stencil is made for each color.

Printing stencils are made of nylon or stainless steel mesh. Originally, silk was used, hence the old term *silk screen.* Today automatic presses for screen printing are also available, which makes the process economical for even longer runs.

Preparing plates for the press

For all of today's modern, high-speed presses, whether the method is letterpress, rotogravure, or offset lithography, printing plates are required. A process called *photoplatemaking* is used to create the printing surface on the plates.

The photoplatemaking process can easily be compared to taking a picture with your own camera. When you take a picture, a negative is produced. The picture is then made by laying the negative on sensitized paper and exposing it to light. Photoplatemaking also begins with a picture. However the negative of the image photographed is printed in reverse on a sensitized metal plate rather than on paper.

Letterpress plates

The letterpress process requires a raised printing image on the surface of the printing plate. To produce this, the negative of the photographed image is laid on top of a sensitized plastic or copper plate and exposed to light. Since the light values of a negative are in reverse, the image areas in the negative are light and the light passes through to the plate. The plate has been treated with a light-sensitive emulsion. This emulsion hardens in the areas where the light passes through. The hardened emulsion forms an acid-resistant protective covering over the areas of the metal plate where there is an image. The plate is placed in an acid bath, which etches away the nondesign areas and leaves the desired raised printing image on the surface of the plate. The result is called a *line plate.* When a plastic plate is used, a photochemical process called *photopolymerization* followed by a simple washout is used to produce a relief plate.

Line plates Also known—in the letterpress printing process—as line cuts, line etchings, and line engravings, line plates reproduce only two tonal values, black and white. Thus, typeset copy, charcoal illustrations, and pen and ink drawings can be reproduced by a line cut. A photograph or other illustration requiring gradations in tone cannot be reproduced without using an additional engraving process—namely, a halftone screen.

65-line screen.

100-line screen.

150-line screen.

Figure 12–14 Halftone screens. Three examples of the same photograph show the effect of varying the screen fineness.

Halftones Whereas line plates print lines and solid areas, halftone plates print from dots. The key element in making such a plate is the halftone screen, which breaks up continuous-tone artwork into dots. The screen is glass or plastic, crisscrossed with fine black lines at right angles like a window screen. This screen is placed in the camera between the lens and the negative holder, which in effect converts the artwork into a series of black dots.

In the dark areas of the (halftone) photograph the dots are large; in the gray areas they are small; and in the white areas they almost disappear. The combination of big and little dots with a little or a lot of white space between them produces the shading in the photograph. The human eye, seeing minute dots of black and white, mixes them and perceives them as gradations of tone, but in fact this is an illusion. The screened illustration is made up of only two tones, black and white.

The fineness of the halftone screen determines the quality of the illusion. A fine screen has more lines and thus more dots per square inch. Screens generally range from 50 to 150 lines to the inch each way, and the printed halftone is described as a 65-line or a 110-line screen, for example. Variation in the fineness of the screen is necessary because the quality of the paper upon which the halftone is printed may be smooth and glossy or coarse and ink-absorbent. Halftones printed on newsprint must be screened coarsely, whereas fine-quality magazine paper can take fine-screen halftones (see Figure 12–14). Figure 12–15 demonstrates the effect different screens have on the reproduction of a photograph. Note that with a coarse screen the dots can be seen with the naked eye.

Stripping Before the plates are made, the type and line art illustrations are photographed separately from the halftone. The various negatives are then assembled through a process known as "stripping" into one single negative, which will be used to produce the combination plate.

Lithographic and gravure plates

The same line and halftone processes are used when making lithographic plates, except that the plates are not etched in relief as in letterpress.

For rotogravure, two separate films are similarly made—one for all type and line illustrations and the other for halftone illustrations. The negatives are combined into a single film "positive." The image is then transferred to a copper cylinder in a somewhat more complicated process than for letterpress plates. In the gravure process, even type and line art is screened.

Color-process plates

The method for printing full-color advertisements with tonal values such as photographs and paintings is the full-color process. This process is based on the principle that all colors can be printed by combining the three primary colors—yellow, red (magenta), and blue (cyan)—plus black (which provides greater detail and density as well as shades of gray).

All the printing processes we have discussed can print color. However, a press can print only one color at a time. Therefore, if a job is to be printed in full color, the printer must prepare four different printing plates, one for each color.

The artwork to be reproduced is photographed through color filters that eliminate all the colors except one. For example, one filter eliminates all colors except red and extracts every light ray of red to be blended into the final reproduced picture. An electronic scanning device may also be used to make these color separations.

Thus, four separate continuous-tone negatives are produced to make a set of four-color plates: one for yellow, one for red, one for blue, and one for black. The resulting negatives are in black and white and are called *color separation negatives.*

These color separations are photographed through a halftone screen to make a set of screened negatives from which the plates are made.

Straight-line.

Mezzo tint.

Etch tone.

Wavy line (dry brush).

Random line.

Two-color texture.

Figure 12–15

Special line screens. Many special effects are possible through the use of different screening processes. All these operate on the same principle as the dot screen. They use lines, scratches, or some other technique, and require much more careful photo work.

In photographing the color separations, the halftone screen is rotated to a different angle for each separation. As a result the dots do not completely overlap because the four plates superimpose the dots over one another during printing. Tiny clusters of halftone dots of the four colors in various sizes on the printed page give the eye the optical illusion of seeing different colors of the original photography or painting. In printing, transparent inks are used, which allow the person to see all colors through the four overlapping coatings of ink on the paper. For example, even though green ink is not used, green can be reproduced by a yellow and a blue dot, each overlapping their respective colors on paper in the form of halftone dots. Dark green would have larger blue halftone dots than yellow (see the Ad Lab.)

The recently developed laser scanners perform two- or four-color separations and screening in one process, along with enlargement or reduction. Highlight/shadow density changes, contrast modification, color change, or removal for an area or a whole piece are accomplished by the operator in a single operation. All this is done in several minutes instead of the hours or days spent on the camera work and hand-etching steps needed in the process camera operation described previously.

For letterpress printing, the four-color halftone plates are made the same as for black and white halftones, except four plates are sent to publication instead of one. For rotogravure and lithography, color-separated positive or negative film is furnished instead of plates. From this film, publications make their own printing plates or cylinders.

Preparing materials for publications

Most local media, newspapers, and magazines are very willing and able to work with their advertisers to help produce their advertisements. Frequently this service is free. The local dress shop or furniture store works with the newspaper's ad salesperson and provides the copy and illustrations, and the newspaper's production department will take care of the rest.

At some point in their growth, advertisers decide to exercise more control over the production process to assure consistency and quality. Major agencies always like to maintain complete control over the preparation of materials used for reproduction rather than giving the media that responsibility.

Production suppliers

Few agencies or advertisers maintain all the necessary capital equipment and personnel required for producing printed materials. As a result they hire outside print production companies who work at their direction. The suppliers may include a typesetting house, a photoplatemaker, a color separator, a gravure service, or a duplicating house for newspaper material. All these sources are particularly important when media schedules include publications that print by different processes or when it is desirable to convert material from one printing process to another to save time and money.

Making duplicate materials

Media schedules frequently contain numerous publications that will run the advertisement at about the same time. This requires the advertiser to provide materials to each publication.

Production specifications can be obtained directly from the publication. It is often more convenient, however, to use the Standard Rate and Data Service *Print Media Production Data* directory, which contains critical information on the printing material and mechanical measurements (dimensions of advertising space accepted) of every major publication.

For publications printed by letterpress, original or duplicate printing plates must be provided. There are two common kinds of duplicate plates: (1) *electrotypes* and (2) Cronapress duplicates (called *Cronars*) made by a special Du Pont process. Not long ago duplicate materials for letterpress newspapers consisted of *mats* (short for matrices), which were used to make *stereotypes* of the original plate. However, as the letterpress process has declined in use, so has the use of mats.

For publications printed by rotogravure or offset lithography, duplicate materials consist of duplicate sets of film positives (for gravure) or photographic copies of the mechanical and screened art (for offset lithography). These photographic copies may be in the form of *photoprints* (a screened print or a Velox) or contact *film negatives*, depending on the requirements of the particular publication. (See the Checklist.)

Selecting papers for printing

When preparing materials for printing, it is important to know the kind of paper on which the advertisement will be printed. Some advertisers are so concerned about the appearance of their advertisements that they will have them printed on a higher quality of paper stock than is used in the regular pages of a newspaper or magazine. They will then ship the printed material to the publication for insertion or binding.

Paper used in advertising can be broken down into three categories: writing, book, and cover stock.

Writing paper is commonly used in letters and other direct mail pieces. Bond writing paper is the most durable and also the most frequently used.

Book paper includes a large number of types. The major classifications are news stock, antique finish, machine finish, English finish, and coated. These range from the less expensive, very porous, course papers to the very smooth, expensive, heavier papers used for industrial brochures and fine quality annual reports.

Cover paper is used for softcover book covers and sometimes for direct mail pieces because of the tough, durable quality. Advertisers can choose from many finishes and textures.

From concept through production of a magazine advertisement

Marketing considerations

More than a decade ago, Eastern Airlines identified a trend among consumers toward several shorter vacations and a move away from traditional, longer holidays. A growing number of consumers can afford to live this way, and see the airplane as an ideal way to meet their travel needs.

These prospects who live in a northern region traditionally prefer winter vacations in sunny, warm places like Florida, Mexico, and the Caribbean. Since Eastern has a north-south route structure, they are positioned to maximize airfare revenue from this group of sun-seekers. But also because of this route structure, it is vital for Eastern's fiscal stability to keep planes full during this period.

Eastern identified two types of vacation prospects: the "planner," who is committed to the idea of a winter vacation and has merely to choose his airline, and the "impulse" prospects, who could be motivated to take a winter vacation but who is not currently planning one.

The challenge for Eastern and its advertising agency, Young & Rubicam Inc., was to identify an advertising strategy that would build demand for winter vacations by (1) maximizing Eastern's share of planners and (2) building demand among the impulse prospects.

Eastern's advertising approach has been to sell both the end benefit of a winter vacation (sun, relaxation, beach), which appeals to the impulse group, and Eastern's scope of destinations, which appeals to the planning segment.

One of the major message elements is the sun and its warm benefits during the cold winter months. The challenge of the winter campaign was to describe the scope of Eastern's sun destinations (in visual and copy treatment) in a manner that would motivate both the planning and impulse prospects.

Creative concept

In the past Eastern had appealed to winter vacationers with theme lines "We've got your sunshine" and "Eastern has a warm spot just for you."

Because of deregulation and increasing competition on these prime routes, Y&R felt a more competitive theme line was needed this year. The concept was developed "When you need the sun there's only one. Eastern."

The idea of incorporating Eastern's logo with the sun came from the same competitive environment. Now, with this visual device Eastern would really *own* the sun.

The art director decided to execute this logo-sized sun at sunset to try to add an element of drama, romance, and emotion. When the sun is low on the horizon, the light is magic and magnificent, and the earth, sky, and water become bathed in the warm golden colors. The sun itself goes from hot white to golden yellow and even looks oval—very much like the actual Eastern logo.

To enhance the emotional aspect even further, and to give the execution more personal focus, the close-up of the people was developed in layout form.

The ad (which became part of a magazine, newspaper, outdoor, and television campaign) had a concept of its own now. The top part was the close-up of the warm relationship of two people on vacation. The bottom was the long-shot panorama of that couple in the environment of the setting sun.

Shooting the ad

After the client approved layout, copy, and print cost estimates, the agency selected photographer Denny Tillman, to shoot the print campaign.

The photographer realized the most difficult part of this assignment would be that perfect, magnificent sunset. He could direct the models and choose the props, but the forces of nature were beyond his control.

After some quick research, it was decided that Miami would be the ideal place to shoot. Miami had model agencies to find the talent, palm trees, tropical water, and good weather reports (the shooting took place in August, and that's hurricane season), and unobstructed vistas for sunrises and sunsets.

The ad had to be shot in two parts (the top close-up and the bottom long shot). As it turned out, the ad was photographed in four parts (see A, four 35 mm slides).

While scouting locations, casting for models, and searching for sailboats and wardrobe during the day, the photographer was shooting sunrises and sunsets. (In print, you can't tell the difference between sunrise and sunset.)

The actual sunrise used in the ad was shot from a boat looking toward the lighthouse on Key Biscayne. The sunrise was golden and glorious. As specified by the client, the models were to be an attractive, wholesome young couple in their early 20s. After the sun rose high in the sky, the panorama long shot was completed.

Because the art director wanted to enhance the warm sunny feeling, she insisted that all props and wardrobe were to be in bright colors. Therefore the sail was in a rainbow of yellow, orange, and red, and the bathing suits were in red and magenta.

But the photographer was still only two-thirds finished. Now the close-up had to be photographed, and he even shot this two ways: first with the sun in front of the sail, then with the sun behind.

Preparation for production

After the photographer had submitted his 35-mm pictures, the art director and the art buyer selected those they wanted for reproduction and planned all preparatory steps.

The top illustration in the ad, showing the young couple on the catamaran, called for a dye transfer (see B, unretouched dye transfer). As much golden sun color as possible was forced into the illustration. This had the effect of taking all the blue out of the water and sky. When the retouching was done on the dye transfer print, the rich golden colors were left on the couple and the boat, but they were reduced in the sky and the water, which, in turn, had blue added (see C, retouched dye transfer). The cool blue had the effect of enhancing the golden color on the boat and the couple.

The bottom illustration in the ad presented other problems. Because of time and lighting limitations, the elements required for the illustration had been shot separately as 35-mm transparencies under as much control as possible. Variations of position and color had been exposed of the lighthouse and shore line, ocean and sun, and the sailboat.

The art director made black and white photostats of all elements and pasted them up in the desired sizes as a stripping guide. This guide and the three original 35-mm transparencies were given to a dye transfer laboratory. They produced four-color camera separations of each element. From these separations, four-color mats, combining all elements in scale and position, were prepared. They consisted of lighthouse and shore, sky with repositioned sun, and water with repositioned boat. A range of dye transfer prints from reddish gold to yellowish gold was pulled (see D, dye transfer).

The print selected by the art director was turned over to a retoucher who removed all strip lines, put detail into the lighthouse and water, and—last but not least—added the Eastern logo to the sun (see E, dye transfer).

Typesetting

Meanwhile the copy had been "marked up" by the agency type director. Together with a layout, the type specifications were turned over to a phototypesetting house. The headline was composed on photodisplay equipment, while the text was set on a computer-aided photounit. From the film output of the equipment, diazo photoproofs were prepared and delivered to Y&R (see F through H).

After some text alterations made by the client and the agency, the art director prepared a mechanical showing the exact position and sizing of artwork and typography (see I, mechanical). On the basis of that mechanical, the phototype shop stripped up all line film (headline, text, and logotype) in exact position. From this film mechanical, a negative line film was contacted, which was delivered to the photoplatemaker together with the mechanical.

Photoplatemaking

The photoplatemaker had to prepare both letterpress engravings and offset separation films in order to fill the needs of the magazines on the media list. He made continuous-tone and subsequently screened separations of the two illustrations delivered to him as retouched dye transfer prints.

Using the line negative sent by the type shop and his screened separations, the photoplatemaker produced sets of four-color letterpress and offset plates. Letterpress and offset proofs and progressives (a set of proofs showing each color single and in all combinations with others) were pulled and delivered to the agency print producer on the Eastern Airlines account (see J, progressive proofs).

Minor color corrections were accomplished by the photoplatemaker through dot etching of the offset film masters and re-etching of the letterpress plates.

After client and agency product group approval, the original letterpress plates and the necessary number of offset film sets contacted from the master films were released to several newsweeklies and travel magazines in which the advertisement had been scheduled to run. Together with the plates and films went photoplatemaker's proofs and progressives, which were to guide the publication press people in achieving a faithful color reproduction (see K, final photomaker's proof).

From concept through production of a magazine advertisement

A.

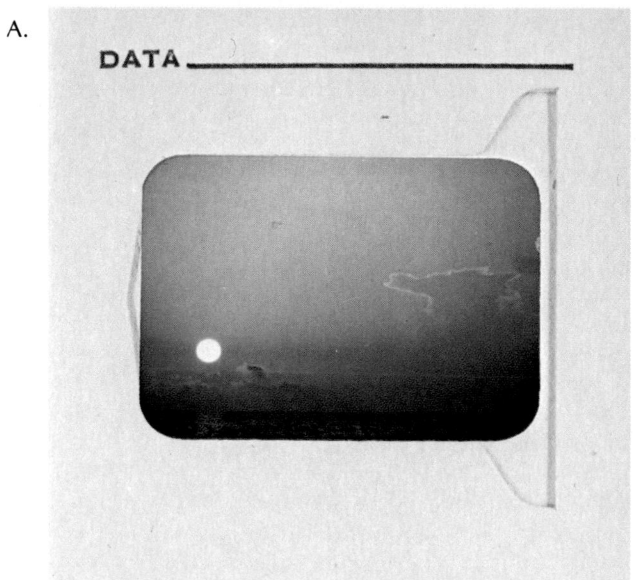

B.

C.

A. Four 35-mm slides developed from the shooting.

B. Unretouched dye transfer made from the fourth 35-mm transparency.

C. Retouched dye transfer.

From concept through production of a magazine advertisement *(continued)*

D.

E.

F.

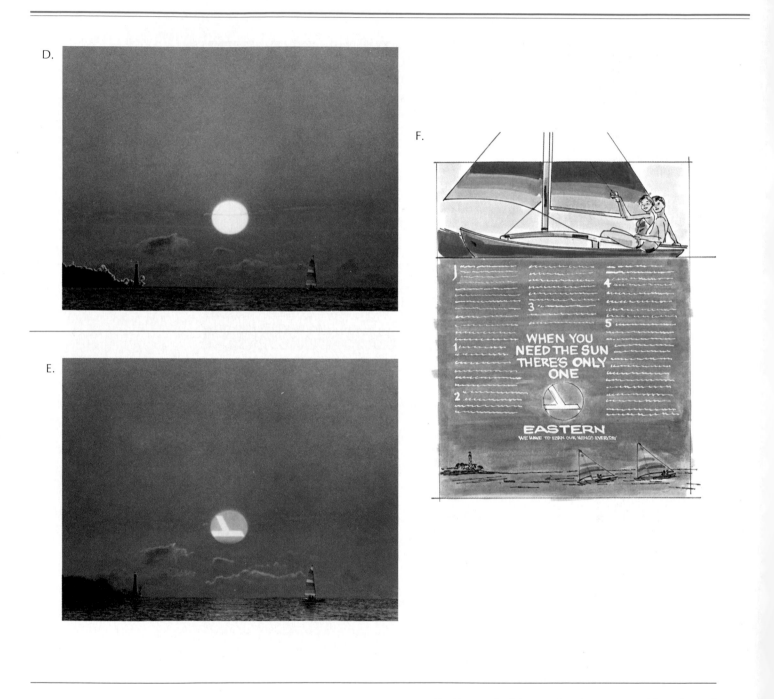

D. Unretouched dye transfer photocomposed from three of the four original 35-mm transparencies.

E. Retouched dye transfer.

F. Rough layout.

G.

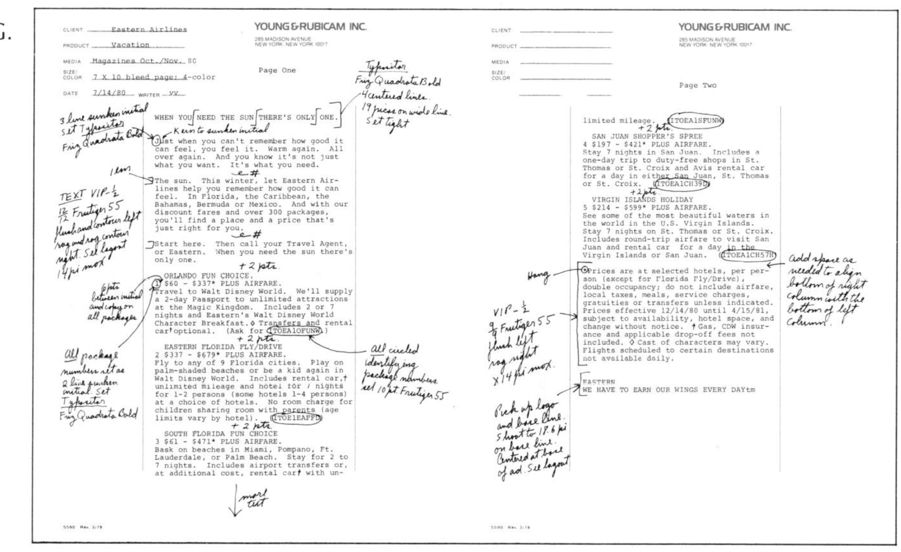

CLIENT Eastern Airlines
PRODUCT Vacation
MEDIA Magazines Oct./Nov. 80
SIZE/COLOR 7 X 10 bleed page: 4-color
DATE 7/14/80 WRITER VV

YOUNG & RUBICAM INC.
285 MADISON AVENUE
NEW YORK, NEW YORK 10017

Page One

WHEN YOU NEED THE SUN THERE'S ONLY ONE.

Just when you can't remember how good it can feel, you feel it. Warm again. All over again. And you know it's not just what you want. It's what you need.

The sun. This winter, let Eastern Airlines help you remember how good it can feel. In Florida, the Caribbean, the Bahamas, Bermuda or Mexico. And with our discount fares and over 300 packages, you'll find a place and a price that's just right for you.

Start here. Then call your Travel Agent, or Eastern. When you need the sun there's only one.

ORLANDO FUN CHOICE.
1 $60 - $337* PLUS AIRFARE.
Travel to Walt Disney World. We'll supply a 2-day Passport to unlimited attractions at the Magic Kingdom. Includes 2 or 7 nights and Eastern's Walt Disney World Character Breakfast.◊ Transfers and rental car† optional. (Ask for ITOEA1OFUNW.)

EASTERN FLORIDA FLY/DRIVE
2 $337 - $679* PLUS AIRFARE.
Fly to any of 9 Florida cities. Play on palm-shaded beaches or be a kid again in Walt Disney World. Includes rental car,† unlimited mileage and hotel for 7 nights for 1-2 persons (some hotels 1-4 persons) at a choice of hotels. No room charge for children sharing room with parents (age limits vary by hotel). (ITOE1EAFFD)

SOUTH FLORIDA FUN CHOICE
3 $61 - $471* PLUS AIRFARE.
Bask on beaches in Miami, Pompano, Ft. Lauderdale, or Palm Beach. Stay for 2 to 7 nights. Includes airport transfers or, at additional cost, rental car† with un-

Handwritten markup: 3 line sunken initial set Typositor Friz Quadrata Bold — Kern to sunken initial — Typositor Friz Quadrata Bold 4 centered lines. 19 picas on wide line. Set tight — 1 em — TEXT VIP-½ 12/12 Frutiger 55 flush and contour left rag and rag contour right. See layout 14 pi max — + 2 pts. — 6 pts between initial and copy on all packages — All package numbers set as 2 line sunken initial. Set Typositor Friz Quadrata Bold — All circled identifying package numbers set 10 pt. Frutiger 55 — more text

5590 Rev. 3/78

CLIENT
PRODUCT
MEDIA
SIZE/COLOR

YOUNG & RUBICAM INC.
285 MADISON AVENUE
NEW YORK, NEW YORK 10017

Page Two

limited mileage. (ITOEA1SFUNW)

SAN JUAN SHOPPER'S SPREE
4 $197 - $421* PLUS AIRFARE.
Stay 7 nights in San Juan. Includes a one-day trip to duty-free shops in St. Thomas or St. Croix and Avis rental car for a day in either San Juan, St. Thomas or St. Croix. (ITOEA1CH39D)

VIRGIN ISLANDS HOLIDAY
5 $214 - $599* PLUS AIRFARE.
See some of the most beautiful waters in the world in the U.S. Virgin Islands. Stay 7 nights on St. Thomas or St. Croix. Includes round-trip airfare to visit San Juan and rental car for a day in the Virgin Islands or San Juan. (ITOEA1CH57H)

*Prices are at selected hotels, per person (except for Florida Fly/Drive), double occupancy; do not include airfare, local taxes, meals, service charges, gratuities or transfers unless indicated. Prices effective 12/14/80 until 4/15/81, subject to availability, hotel space, and change without notice. †Gas, CDW insurance and applicable drop-off fees not included. ◊ Cast of characters may vary. Flights scheduled to certain destinations not available daily.

EASTERN
WE HAVE TO EARN OUR WINGS EVERY DAYtm

Handwritten markup: + 2 pts. — Hang — VIP-½ 9/9 Frutiger 55 flush left rag right x 14 pi max. — add space as needed to align bottom of right column with the bottom of left column. — Pick up logo and base line. Shoot to 17.6 pi on base line. Centered at base of ad. See layout

5590 Rev. 3/78

H.

WHEN YOU NEED THE SUN THERE'S ONLY ONE.

EASTERN
WE HAVE TO EARN OUR WINGS EVERY DAY.

I.

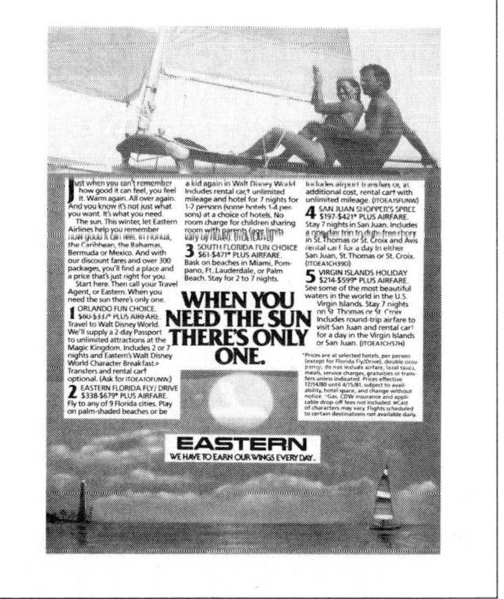

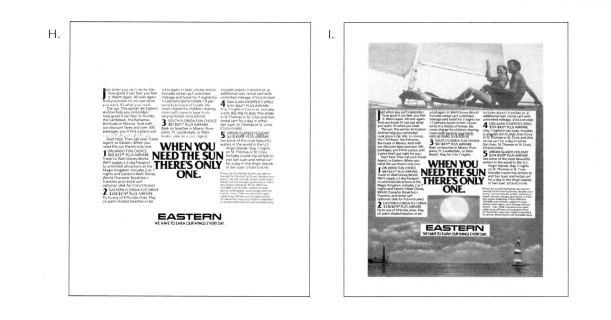

G. Copy with type director's markup for the phototypesetter.

H. Type proof with all copy in position.

I. Mechanical (keyline) consisting of repro type proof and photostats of unretouched artwork.

From concept through production of a magazine advertisement *(continued)*

J.

Yellow

Magenta

Yellow/magenta

Cyan

Yellow/magenta/cyan

Black

K.

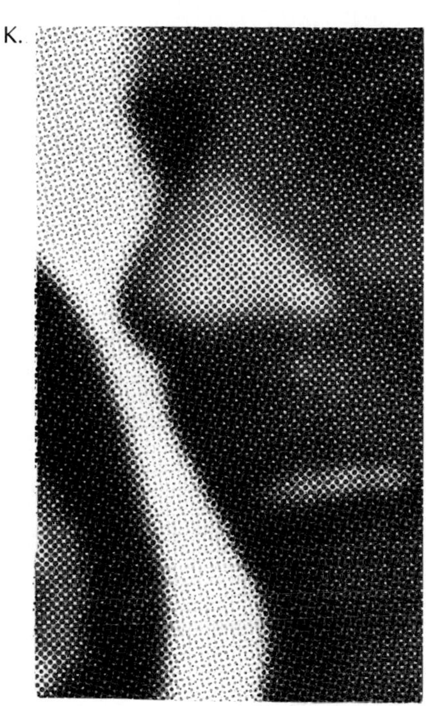

L.

J. Progressive proofs (color separations).

K. A greatly enlarged section of the final printed advertisement showing how the process colors are combined to produce continuous color tone.

L. Final photoplatemaker's proof.

Checklist of cost-cutting methods

The costs of print production have increased dramatically in the last 10 years. Some major advertising agencies have taken typesetting and other jobs in-house to save their clients the cost of outside suppliers. For novices in the advertising business, simple mistakes or oversights can be very costly to the agency or advertiser. For that reason beginners should thoroughly acquaint themselves with the production procedure required for each job and complete each step before proceeding to the next. Some of the ways costs can be cut include the following:

☐ Always make your instructions clear.

☐ Send your typographer, photoplatemaker, and duplicator clean copy.

☐ Avoid complicated telephone alterations.

☐ Get copy and layout approved before having the job set; get mechanicals approved before making separations or plates.

☐ Get a "style" approved before typesetting large jobs.

☐ Make your alterations on the manuscript before the job is set.

☐ Don't order more proofs than you need.

☐ Group large-quantity press proofs, if possible.

☐ Avoid super-rush jobs.

☐ For problem jobs, ask the advice of the color separator, platemaker, or duplicator and communicate what you are trying to accomplish.

Summary

The production process in print advertising is so critical that if it is not handled correctly, an otherwise beautiful ad can be destroyed. A fundamental understanding of production techniques therefore can save a lot of money and disappointment.

The print production manager's job is to ensure that the final advertisement reflects what the art director had in mind. That is often a difficult task as the print production manager must work within the limited, specified confines of time requirements, quality objectives, and acceptable budget.

The typeface chosen for an advertisement affects its appearance, design, and legibility. Type can generally be divided into two broad classes: display type and text type. In addition, typefaces can be classified by their similarity of design. The major type groups are Roman, sans serif, square serif, cursive or script, and ornamental. Within each group are many type families such as Bodoni, Futura, Goudy, and Caslon. In a type family the basic design remains the same, but variations of weight, slant, and size are available.

Type is measured in terms of points and picas. Points measure the vertical size of type (e.g., 6 pt., 8 pt., 10 pt.). There are 72 points to an inch. Picas measure the horizontal width of a line of type. There are 6 picas to an inch. So a column 18 picas wide is 3 inches wide. Type may further be referred to as uppercase (capital letters) and lowercase (small letters).

There are four important points to consider when selecting type: legibility, appropriateness, harmony or appearance, and emphasis. The process of determining how much type will fit a specified area in an advertisement is called copy casting. There are several methods used to cast copy today.

There are also several methods used to set type. The most important of these are the various photocomposition techniques. These include photo-optical methods, cathrode-ray tube (CRT) techniques, and laser scanning.

Printing processes have undergone great technological changes in recent decades. Today the most common printing methods are letterpress, rotogravure, offset lithography, and screen printing. Each method has its unique advantages and disadvantages.

Preparing plates for printing is much like taking a picture with a camera except that the image is exposed to a sensitized metal plate rather than photographic paper. Two types of plates are used for printing—line plates and halftone plates. Line plates print only two tonal values—black and white. When gradation of tone are required, as in an illustration or photograph, halftone plates are used. These print a series of black dots of various sizes, which produce an optical illusion of tonal grades.

When color is required, additional plates are needed for each color printed. For full-color photographs or illustrations, four halftone plates are used, one for each primary color plus black. These print the dots of various colors in tiny clusters, which create the illusion of full color.

Plates being sent to different publications need to be duplicated. The two kinds of duplicate plates commonly used are called electrotypes and cronapress duplicates. Rotogravure and offset publications simply require film positives and film negatives, respectively.

Questions for review

1. What are the characteristics of the five major type groups?
2. What is meant by type casting? Explain the ways in which it is done.
3. What is the importance of these terms: legibility, appropriateness, harmony/appearance, emphasis?
4. What do these terms mean: point, pica, uppercase, lowercase?
5. The two broad classifications of display type and text type have basic differences. Explain what they are. Give some examples in which display type may be used.
6. What are the types of photocomposition?
7. What are the major differences among these printing processes: letterpress, rotogravure, offset lithography, and screen printing?
8. What is a halftone? How is it produced?
9. How are color photographs printed?
10. What are some typical production suppliers and their role in the production of advertising?

13

Creative production: Broadcast media

Dick Wilson, at 63 years old, has been an actor for almost half a century. He has appeared in over 300 television roles and has played major parts in such well-known series as "Bewitched," "Hogan's Heroes," and "McHale's Navy." But it wasn't until he started playing the fussbudget store clerk telling customers not to "squeeze the Charmin" that people began asking for his autograph. By 1980, after 15 years as Mr. Whipple, Wilson was earning around $100,000 per year for 5 to 10 days of work and praying to live to 100. That's how long the advertiser had promised to keep using him (Figure 13–1).

When Virginia Kraft goes home to the little village in Iowa where she was born, she's the queen of the parade. The old water tower in the small Swedish community of 700 has been changed into a giant coffee pot with a spout, a handle, and painted flames at the bottom. They've painted it white with little flowers and a Swedish poem on it. All this to honor the lady who has the stage name of Virginia Christine but whom we all know and recognize as Mrs. Olsen of Folger's Coffee fame (Figure 13–2).

Dick Wilson and Virginia Christine are just two of the many continuing personalities seen on TV's commercial circuit. The list includes many others: Madge the manicurist for Palmolive Liquid, Old Lonely the Maytag repairman, Rosie the counter lady for Bounty paper towels, Maxwell House Coffee's Cora, and Pete the Butcher for Shake 'n' Bake, just to name a few.

These continuing commercial presenters, according to most advertisers, produce fantastic goodwill and product identification. They attract attention, identify the brand immediately by their familiarity, act as friendly authority figures for the consuming public, and guarantee advertising continuity over the years to the brands they support. As such, they are an important consideration in the development of product advertising campaigns and in the production of commercials for broadcast media.

Producing television commercials

Advertisers produce over 50,000 commercials every year in an effort to sell their products and services. No one knows exactly how much is spent in the production of these commercials, but most estimates are in the hundreds of millions of dollars.

Producing television commercials is expensive. A simple spot for a local advertiser might cost from $500 to $10,000. National-quality commercials cost considerably more. The lowest figure is probably around $10,000 with highs in the hundreds of thousands.

As the technology of broadcast commercial production has soared, so have the cost and complexity. This has necessitated the specialization of those involved in the production process. Whereas major agencies used to be able to maintain complete broadcast production facilities in-house, the trend in recent decades has been toward the increased use of outside producers, directors, production companies, and technical suppliers.

As a result, gaining expert knowledge of broadcast production has become more difficult. A broad understanding of basic production concepts, though, is a must for anyone involved in advertising today. This includes an understanding of the way commercials are written, which types of commercials are most effective and most commonly used, the basic techniques for producing a commercial, and the important steps in the production process.

For the advertising student, an understanding of these concepts will explain how commercials are made, why commercial production is so expensive, and what methods can be used to cut costs without sacrificing quality or effectiveness.

Writing the commercial

How did Dick Wilson, for instance, get to be Mr. Whipple and Virginia Christine become Mrs. Olsen? Where do those characters come from? To put it simply, they usually come right out of the heads of the art director and copywriter who conceptualized the commercial. The initial concept may call for an actor to play a part, or the creative team may decide they want to use a well-known celebrity to present the product. Casting the characters in a commercial is a major factor considered at the time the commercial is written, and the most important consideration in casting is relevance to the product. It might be unwise to use a comic to sell financial services, for example.

As the copy is written and the storyboard laid out, the creative team develops the personalities of their characters and usually writes a brief but detailed description of them. These descriptions are used in casting sessions as guides in the selection of prospective actors to be interviewed, auditioned, and considered for the roles. Sometimes a Dick Wilson or Virginia Christine will be discovered—solid, believable actors who go beyond a simple role and actually create a personality or image for the product.

Figure 13–1 Dick Wilson as Mr. Whipple.

Mechanics

A television script is divided into two portions. The right side is the *audio*—indicating sound effects, spoken copy, and music. The left side is the *video*—indicating camera action, scenes, and instructions. (See the script for Yoplait Yogurt later in this chapter.)

After the script has been approved by the person in charge of the account, the writer and art director prepare a storyboard. The typical storyboard is a sheet preprinted with a series of 8 to 20 blank television screens (frames). The frames are sketched in by the art director to represent the video. The audio, plus instructions for the video, are typed underneath. Due to space limitations, many abbreviations are used. See Figure 13–3 for some of the more common ones.

A storyboard helps in estimating the expense, visualizing the message, revealing any weakness in concept, presenting for client approval, and guiding the actual shooting. At best, the storyboard is an approximation of what the commercial will be. Actual production sometimes results in many changes in lighting, camera angle, focal point, and emphasis. The camera sees many things the artist didn't see, and vice versa.

Sometimes, to aid and supplement the storyboard, a commercial is roughly taped using the writers and artists as actors. Or the storyboard sketches may be photographed on a film strip and then accompanied by the audio portion synchronized on tape. This is called an *animatic.*

Figure 13–2 Virginia Christine as Mrs. Olsen.

CU:	Close-up. Very close shot of person or object.
ECU:	Extreme close-up. A more extreme version of the above. Sometimes designated as BCU (big close-up) or TCU (tight close-up).
MCU:	Medium close-up. Emphasizes the subject but includes other objects nearby.
MS:	Medium shot. Wide-angle shot of subject but not whole set.
FS:	Full shot. Entire set or object.
LS:	Long shot. Full view of scene to give effect of distance.
DOLLY:	Move camera toward or away from subject. Dolly in (DI), dolly out (DO), or dolly back (DB).
PAN:	Camera scans from one side to the other.
ZOOM:	Move rapidly in or out from the subject without blurring.
SUPER:	Superimpose one image on another—as showing lettering over a scene.
DISS:	Dissolve (also DSS). Fade out one scene while fading in another.
CUT:	Instant change of one picture to another.
WIPE:	Gradually erase picture from screen. (Many varied effects are possible.)

Frequently used audio instructions are: "voice-over" (VO)—an off-screen voice, usually the announcer's; "down and under"—sound effects fade as voice comes on; and its counterpart "up and over."

Figure 13–3 Cut, zoom, and wipe, please!

Writing effectively

In Chapter 10 the fundamentals of writing advertising copy were presented. The writing of television commercials demands that additional attention be given to credibility, believability, and relevance. That goes well beyond the use of words.

Millions of dollars spent on TV commercial research have resulted in the following principles:

The opening should be a short, compelling attention-getter—compelling in action, drama, humor, or human interest.

Situations should be believable—authentic and true to life. Demonstrations should never appear to be a camera trick.

The commercial should be in good taste—ethically and morally—and not offend or step on any toes.

The entertainment should be a means to an end and not interfere with the message.

The general structure of the commercial and the copy should be simple and easy to follow. The video should carry over half the weight, with the audio merely supporting.

Characters should be appealing and believable.

These are only some of the principles research has shown to be true. See the Checklist for more.

To illustrate these principles, look at the 30-second award-winning Jarman shoes commercial illustrated in Figure 13–4. Created by The Bloom Agency in Dallas, this is a classic example of a well-written, simple, interesting, credible, and entertaining commercial.

Checklist for writing effective TV commercials

☐ The opening should be pertinent, relevant, and not forced. It should permit a smooth transition to the balance of the commercial.

☐ The situation should lend itself naturally to the sales story—without the use of extraneous, distractive gimmicks.

☐ The situation should be high in human interest.

☐ The viewer should be able to identify with the situation.

☐ Generally hold the number of elements to a minimum.

☐ Present a simple sequence of ideas.

☐ The words should be short, realistic, and conversational, not "ad talk." Sentences should be short.

☐ Words should not be wasted describing what is being seen.

☐ The words should interpret the picture and prepare the viewer for the next scene.

☐ Don't jump too far ahead in the audio by describing one feature while showing another. Synchronize audio and video.

☐ Keep the audio copy concise—without wasted words. Fewer words are needed for TV than for radio. Less than two words per second is effective for demonstrations.

☐ Remember, 60-second commercials with 101 to 110 words are most effective. Those with more than 170 words are the least effective.

☐ Allow five or six seconds for the average scene, with none less than three seconds.

☐ Provide enough movement to avoid static scenes.

☐ Scenes should offer variety without "jumping."

☐ The commercial should look fresh and new.

☐ Any presenters should be properly handled—identified, compatible, authoritative, pleasing, and nondistracting.

☐ The general video treatment should be interesting.

JARMAN SHOES

"Manhole"

Comm'l. No.: XGEJ - 8033

SFX: CITY STREET SOUNDS.
ON CAMERA: At this level, it's easy to become an expert on shoe styles.

Know what I see a lot of? Jarman.

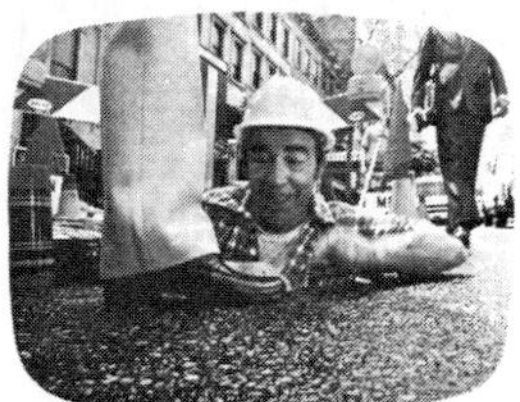

Take those.

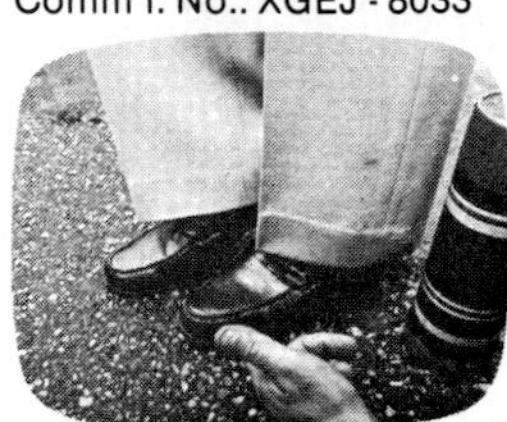

Look European?

They're Jarman.

Those boots and slip ons...

Both Jarman.

That one too. Looks comfortable doesn't it?

And they're not that expensive either.

Yes sir, when it comes to style,

I'd say Jarman's got a style to fit everybody.

Well, just about everybody.

Hello there, how are you?

You need a cab? (WHISTLES) Taxi!

Figure 13–4

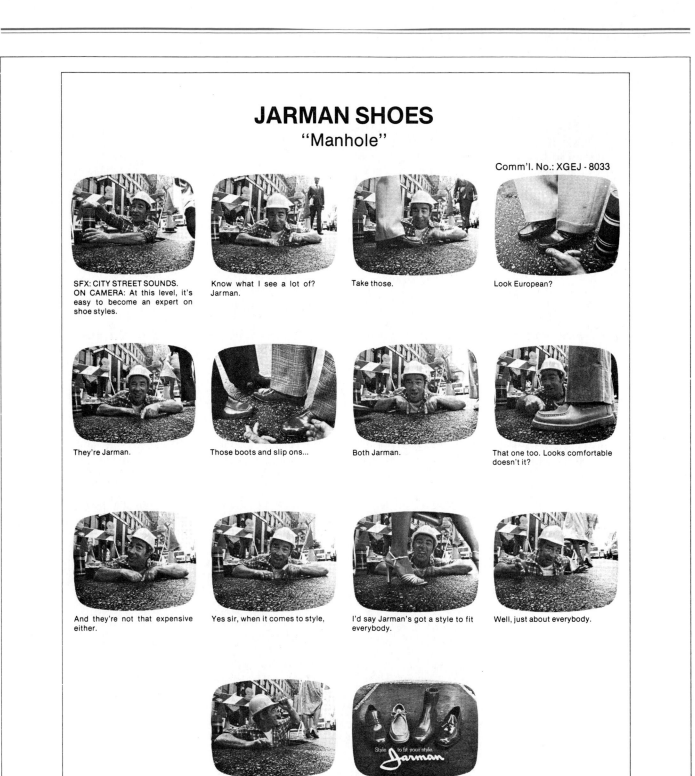

First, look at the commercial as a whole. There is one dominant mood throughout and a single, unified impression. The number of people is kept to a minimum. The whole commercial is shot in *close-up.* Everything not relevant to the commercial's objective has been deleted. The situation is high in human interest and believable. The structure is *simple* and easy to follow. The presenter is *appealing,* authoritative, and credible. The entertainment value is high, but perfectly *relevant.* The *sales points* are demonstrated smoothly, and the product *name* is given sufficient mention. Finally, there is a strong *closing identification* illustrating the name and the product.

Looking at some of the mechanics, note that there seems to be only one scene throughout. There are in fact four different camera setups. But the *unity* is so strong and the flow so smooth that the changes are hardly noticeable.

Examine the opening scene. Before one word is spoken, we know who the man is and what he's doing. He looks the part and acts the part. In 12 words he has established the whole context of the commercial and is into the sell. By the second frame of the storyboard he has already said the product name once and made a case for the popularity of the product. By the third frame he's proving his first sales point and is into the second—style. Then he hits the name again. Two frames later he hits it again and then there is a third sales point—comfort. One more frame and he hits the fourth sales point—price. Then he hits the name again and the fifth point—for men only. Finally, a touch of human interest humor is handled in exceptionally good taste, and the closing frame shows the shoes, the name, and the strong tag line: "Style to fit your style."

In all, the commercial contains only 76 words, yet it says so much. That's what makes a commercial memorable.

Types of television commercials

The advertisements we have discussed have all been "presenter" commercials, where one person or character presents the product and carries the whole sales message. Sometimes these presenters are celebrities, like Bill Cosby for Jell-O and Ford, James Garner for Polaroid, or O. J. Simpson for Hertz. Other times they are corporate officers of the sponsor, like Frank Perdue for Perdue Chicken or Lee Iacocca, the chairman of the board of Chrysler Corporation. In the case of Jarman, we see an actor playing a role and simultaneously acting as a spokesperson. Other commercials, like Bank of America, use an actor to play a straight, unidentified spokesperson. The variations are almost limitless.

There are many types of commercials in addition to the presenter format (Figure 13–5). Actually there may be as many ways of classifying television ads as there are television advertisers. The six basic categories, though, in addition to the presenter category, are: the straight announcement, demonstration, testimonial, slice of life, lifestyle, and animation. These groupings often overlap and should not be considered ironclad.

We will next discuss each of these types briefly before considering

Figure 13–5 Seven key factors in successful TV commercials

Product	Campaign results	Star	Continuing central character	"Look"	"Word"	Jingle	Story	Demo
Budweiser beer	No. 1 in United States; in world	Lou Rawls; Ed McMahon	"Clydes-dales"			"This Bud's for You"	Sport	
Contac	No. 1 in world			Tiny Time Pills				Pills in slow motion
Dr Pepper	Up 15 percent a year for last six years			Youthful	"Pepper"	"I'm a Pepper"		
Esso "Tiger"	Gained 12 percent; 28 percent in first year		"Tiger"			"Hold that Tiger"	"Lady & tiger"	
Kellogg's sugar flakes	Part of big no. 1; "Tony" 23 years old		"Tony" the Tiger		"Great"		Tony's stripe	
Kool-Aid powered drink	Passed 10 million packs a day		Face on pitcher			"Kool-Aid Kool-Aid"	Pitcher's arrival	
L'eggs hosiery	Won 30-percent share against 600 under 4-percent rivals	Juliet Prowse				"L'eggs! L'eggs!"		Gals show advantages
Levi's	Way out no. 1 again after 150 years		G	Sharp cartoon			Heritage/ youth	—as on label
Marlboro cigarets	Moved to no. 1 in United States		"Cowboy"	Western	Filter, Flavor, Flip Top	"Lot to like"	Lone hero	
Maxwell House coffee	No. 1 against rivals		"Cora"		"Good to last drop"		Cora convinces	
9 Lives cat food	Owns 25 percent of canned cat food market		Morris the Cat		Unique cat voice		"Finicky" fun	
Parkay Margarine	No. 1 in margarine				"Butter?" "Parkay!"			

Product	Campaign results	Star	Continuing central character	"Look"	"Word"	Jingle	Story	Demo
Pillsbury "Doughboy"	Valued at $20 million		"Doughboy"			"Nuthin' says lovin"		Baking time lapse
Pine-Sol cleanser	Has gone up to no. 1			Graffiti		Pine-Sol theme		Wipe-offs
Polaroid cameras	Sold 2 million "One Steps"	J. Garner and "Wife"					"Hubby-wife"	Camera at work
RCA TV	Has passed Zenith, no. 1	Leslie Caron + more						Color emphasis
Shake n'Bake	Quick national intro success		"Pete, the Butcher"				Pete's point	Moist results
Vaseline Intensive Care	Passed Jergens, 25-Year leader			Dry leaf			Leaf's dryness	Supple leaf
Visine Eye Wash	Passed Murine, 25-year leader			Frenetic edit	"Gets the red out"		Day's irritation	Red clears up
Winchester small cigars	Tripled market; then took 70 percent of it!		Winchester man			"Hero" wins gal	Farce situation	
Wisk detergent	Now no. 3 detergent; and no. 1 liquid!				"Ring around collar"		Problem/ solution	Results

the more practical subjects of production techniques and procedures.

Straight announcement

This is the oldest type of television commercial. An announcer delivers a sales message directly into the camera or off-screen while a slide or film is shown on screen. It is a safe method and can be effective if the script is well written and the announcer convincing. The appeal may be either "hard sell" or relaxed. It is a relatively simple approach, and the lack of elaborate facilities required saves money. It may be combined with a demonstration.

Few commercials are made this way today. The chief holdouts are late-night TV programs, local advertisers, and ads for nonprofit organizations.

Demonstration

Studies have shown that a demonstration convinces an audience better and faster than an oral message. Memorable demonstrations have been used to show the product advantages of car tires, ballpoint pens, and paper towels, to mention just a few. Such products may be demonstrated in three ways—in use, in competition, or before and after.

These techniques enable the viewer who sees the utility and quality of a product to project what its performance would be like if he or she owned it. Therefore, the theme of the demonstration should be as clear, simple, graphic, and *relevant* as possible. It doesn't make any sense to demonstrate a point that is not important to the customer.

Figure 13–6 James Garner and Mariette Hartley are frequent award-winners for their highly believable, often ad-libbed commercials for Polaroid. They have been so convincing, in fact, that many people assume they are husband and wife—which is not true.

Testimonial

People are most easily persuaded by the opinions of individuals they respect. This holds true whether the "product" is a political candidate or a bar of soap. It makes TV testimonials highly effective.

Figures from all walks of life endorse products—from big-name stars and personalities to unknowns and nonprofessionals. The person used usually depends on the product. One research firm found that a little girl's endorsement on a cake mix carried more weight than that of a chef. The viewer felt confident he or she could handle any cake mix a little girl could, but perhaps not one recommended by a chef.

Using celebrities to endorse a product gains attention. But they must be believable. The product and copy must fit their mannerisms and style (Figure 13–6).

Satisfied customers also provide excellent testimonials. They're often camera shy, but their natural sincerity is usually persuasive.

Slice of life (problem solution)

The slice-of-life commercial is a little play that portrays a real-life situation. It usually starts with just plain folks before they discover the solution to their problem. The situation is usually tense, often dealing with something of a personal nature—bad breath, dentures, dandruff, B.O., or yellow laundry. Usually a relative or a co-worker drops the hint, the product is tried, and the next scene shows the result—a happier, cleaner, more fragrant person off with a new date or finally able to bite into an apple. Such commercials are often irritating to viewers, but their messages still break through and sell, which is why you keep seeing them.

The key to effective slice-of-life commercials is simplicity. The ad should concentrate on one product benefit and make it memorable. Often a *mnemonic device* is used to dramatize the product benefit. Users of Imperial Margarine suddenly discover a crown on their head, or the doorbell rings for the Avon lady. Creative people as well as consumers find these corny, but they make a commercial memorable.

Believability is difficult to achieve in slice-of-life commercials.

People don't really talk about "ring around the collar," so the actors must be highly credible to put the fantasy across. For that reason, most local advertisers don't use the slice-of-life technique. Creating that believability takes very professional talent and money.

Lifestyle

When they want to present the user rather than the product, advertisers frequently use the lifestyle technique. Tijuana Smalls cigars targeted its message to young, contemporary men with the message: "You know who you are. Maybe you'll like Tijuana Smalls." Soft drink advertisers frequently target their messages to active, outdoorsy, young people, focusing on who drinks the brand rather than specific product advantages.

Animation

The use of cartoons, puppet characters, or animated demonstrations can be very effective in communicating especially difficult messages or with specialized markets like children.

Herbal Essence shampoo developed a unique art style for its packaging and print advertising, which it animated for its television commercials. This created a mood, personality, and unity, which were evident in every communication about the product.

Chevron USA used an animated dinosaur to creatively describe the source of fossil fuel and the energy problems we face today. The ads won the 1978 Clio for TV animation (Figure 13–7).

Figure 13–7 Chevron's famous animated dinosaur uses clever, whimsical humor to deliver the point that fossil fuels take a long time to develop and are rapidly disappearing.

The way in which aspirin or other medications affect the human system is difficult to explain. Animated pictures of headaches and stomachs, however, can simplify the subject and make a demonstration understandable.

Production techniques

Animation is more than just a category of commercial. It is also a major production technique that is experiencing startling technological progress today. When Levi's spent a quarter of a million dollars to produce a single animated TV commercial, it was called "a milestone in television advertising" by columnist Harry Wayne McMahan in *Advertising Age*.[1] The commercial did indeed make history—in more ways than one:

It set a new record for production cost of just one commercial.

It chalked up the highest test score in Burke's (a major advertising research company) experience, with a score of 59—two to four times as high as "normal" commercials.

It pioneered radically new and effective techniques in communication—especially with young people.

It continued to build the sales momentum of this 130-year-old firm, which in 1980 used more than 10 percent of all the cotton grown in this country.

The commercial—created by Levi's agency, Foote, Cone & Belding/Honig, San Francisco—was 60 seconds long and titled "Brand Name." When the Disney organization saw the storyboard, they turned down the production assignment at any price. Then the production house of Robert Abel & Associates, Hollywood, came into the picture. Their experience with new lighting and photography techniques convinced them they could produce the commercial for $250,000.

The resulting commercial must be seen to be appreciated because it is so visually outstanding. Part of its success is due to the use of technical and electronic effects described as "luminetics" or "drawing with light on film," an entirely new approach to film making. According to Robert Abel, the techniques are similar to some used in the feature film "Star Wars" that "stimulate the subconscious or dream levels of perception—the area of fantasy."[2]

One psychiatrist described the style and technique of the commercial as penetrating directly to the subconscious section of the brain, to become "reality" and to be retained in "permanent memory."

The commercial starred the red Levi's logo as the doggy blanket on a fantasized puppy on a leash, barking and leading its owner down a lengthy San Francisco street (Figure 13–8). Although the set was only 52 feet long, its unique design and perspective made it appear to stretch out to infinity.

The key to the effect was an intricate and specially built electronic crane and dolly. This made it possible for the camera to travel on a track. It could pan, tilt, stop, and go from scene to scene in what appeared to be one continuous take of the puppy "trademark" being walked down the street. The camera was automated electronically to totally repeat the same movements in identical continuous sequence time after time. As many as 42 separate exposures could be put on the same film negative. Thus one take could cover the puppy, another an old miner petting him, another a woman shopper, another a translucent "android," another a boy on a skateboard, and so on.

Animation was combined smoothly with live action in several scenes. In one, when the "puppy" jumped through a window, the strings holding the doggy blanket logo would of course not go through the window frame, and several frames of animation were added to bridge the gap.

In all, over 40 people took part in the production—in specialties ranging from choregraphy and costuming to optical design and puppeteering. It took six people for the ingenious system engineering and design.

Apparently the commercial was worth it, considering all the word-of-mouth publicity and image-building it brought to Levi's. After viewing the commercial during the Burke test, a number of people were heard to say, "Levi's must be better, the commercial is so well done."

While this Levi's masterpiece opened the door to untold innovations in commercials, there have historically been relatively few basic types of executions. Possibly this is because the selling idea is generally considered more important than the way it is presented.

FOOTE, CONE & BELDING/HONIG

Client: Levi Strauss & Co.
Product: Corporate
Title: "Brand Name"
Commercial No: LZMB 7621

MALE (VO): C'mon old Trademark, time for your walk. Where will you take me? Sure wish you could talk.

I know what you'd tell me. How your family began with

the same Levi's blue jeans worn by this man.

Hey, here come more Levi's; red, yellow and blue.

Free wheeling kiddos are wearing them, too!

And what a surprise! Look who's been window shopping for clothes.

Yeah, a gal in her Levi's instinctively knows of your special appeal. Enough of this kissing, little Register Mark.

Time that we meet some guys by the park. Dressed in your newest addition. Sums it up right there: Levi's Sportswear.

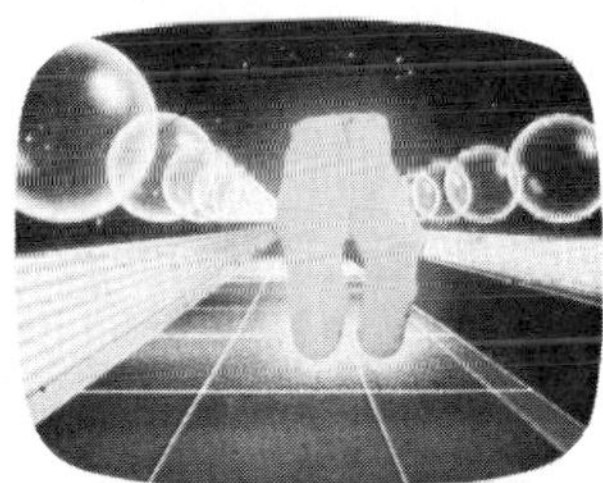

Hey, Trademark, this looks like the place where tomorrows begin.

Your family's future — sure looks like it should.

That's right, little Trademark —

Levi's don't have to be blue — just have to be good!

Figure 13–8

Animation techniques

The Levi's commercial is a modern example of computerized, laser light animation. However, the more standard animation techniques involve the use of cartoons, puppets, and photo animation.

Cartoons

This technique often has the highest viewer interest, the longest life, and the lowest cost per showing, but many viewers consider it childlike. There are several animation styles—Disney, contemporary, psychedelic, and others. Cartoons are sometimes supplemented by live action, especially when a serious purchase decision is to be made and the product benefits are described.

The cartoon technique is achieved by drawing individual illustrations of each step in the action and photographing them one frame at a time. There are 24 frames per second, so when they are projected there is the illusion of movement.

Puppets

Frequently puppets or dolls are used instead of illustrations. Special kinds of action, such as the journey of a drug through the body, can be portrayed.

Photo animation

This technique uses still photography instead of illustrations or puppets. By making slight movements of the photos from one frame to the next, the animated illusion is created. This is especially effective for making titles move. However, it is considered a very low-budget technique.

Stop-motion

This is another animation technique whereby objects and animals come to life—walk, run, dance, and do tricks—by means of stop-motion photography. One of the most famous special-effect creations is the charming, giggling Pillsbury Doughboy (Figure 13–9). The Doughboy is a flexible rubber figure with movable joints. The arms and legs can be bent to simulate walking or pointing. Each frame of film is shot individually. An arm may be moved only $^1/_{32}$ inch on each frame, but when the frames are assembled the effect is smooth and natural. Since film is projected at 24 frames per second, this means 1,440 frames must be shot for each minute of activity by the Doughboy.

Live action

The basic production technique that portrays people in everyday situations is called *live action*. It gives the greatest realism, but sometimes lacks the distinctiveness of animated commercials or commercials that use special effects.

Special effects

Memorability is often achieved by using dramatic sound, music, or photography. Pepsi-Cola, for example, used striking shots of the sun, unusual colors, slow motion, and new camera techniques to project the image of a youth-oriented drink. It was reinforced by young actors and a contemporary musical theme. Such special effects often attract viewers and win awards. But if the sales message is complex or based on logic, another technique would be more successful. The obvious precaution is not to let your technique so enthrall the audience that they don't remember your product.

Most special effects don't go this far. They are usually limited to one fantasy or mnemonic device: a jolly green giant, a white tornado, or the Imperial crown. In these cases the fantasy is directly related to the product's claims. Their heavy repetition makes strong impressions on the viewer.

Figure 13–9 Poppin' Fresh, the Pillsbury doughboy, has been the continuing central character of that company's commercials for many years. Made of rubber with flexible arms and legs, the doughboy can seemingly be made to walk, talk, laugh, and point, through the marvel of stop-motion photography.

The production process

The Tom Thumb-Page stores in Dallas planned a promotion to sell Thanksgiving turkeys and talk about the store's money-back guarantee. Its advertising agency, KCBN, had developed a very simple concept for a television commercial. A live turkey would be shown in an extreme tight close-up. As the announcer spoke off-screen, the camera would slowly zoom back, showing the turkey bobbing his head and occasionally gobbling at the announcer's words. Finally, as the announcer promised to give any unsatisfied customers their money back—or another turkey—the turkey was supposed to run offstage.

In concept it was a very simple spot, but in the production process it turned into a frustrating but hilarious farce reminiscent of the Keystone Cops. Many producers talk about the production problems of working with kids. They should try working with a turkey!

KCBN found a "trained" turkey in upstate New York. That was fine since they had already decided to go to New York to produce the commercial to assure top-quality production.

On the day of shooting everybody was at the studio. The agency account and creative people had flown in from Dallas, and the trained turkey had been trucked in from upstate. The agency had been assured that the turkey would gobble on command and, with a simple hand signal, would run off-stage.

The lighting was set up, tested, and checked. The announcer practiced his pitch in the sound booth. The audio and video levels were adjusted and checked. Everything was ready to go. The trainer picked up the turkey, carried him onto the set, and deposited him on the marked spot in front of the camera.

The lights blazed, the film rolled, the red camera lights went on, the director called for action, and the announcer read the script. At just the right instant, the trainer gave the turkey his cue to go. The turkey didn't move an inch.

"Cut!"

"OK. Let's try it again. Take two."

On the second try the turkey just sat there again.

"I don't understand it," said the trainer. "He's never done this before."

Five takes later, the turkey was still just sitting there. By this time the trainer had abandoned his hand signals and was starting to shout at the bird, clapping his hands, screaming, stamping his foot. The pitch of his hysteria was rising rapidly. But the turkey just sat there. And the lights were getting hotter and hotter.

Finally, the trainer came on the set with a long broom handle.

"This'll do it," he said. There seemed to be a slight tone of hostility in his voice.

"Action," shouted the director.

Just as the announcer got to the cue in the script, the trainer lunged with the broom handle, stabbing the unsuspecting fowl in the belly. With a horrendous squawk, the turkey bolted the set, crashed into one light stand and then another, toppling them over. He landed on top of one lamp, and as the searing heat scorched his wings, he squawked off in frenzied half-flight only to get tangled in more lights, cables, cameras, and props. All the while, the trainer and crew were chasing him around the set trying to capture him.

Finally they subdued the terrified bird and spent an hour calming him down while they relit the set. But, of course, when they were finally ready to start up again, the turkey now knew what was out there. And there was no way on earth he was going to move. He just sat absolutely still—terrified.

When all seemed lost, somebody got a bright idea. They decided to tie a line to his ankles and string the line off-camera. When the cue came, they gently jerked the line, pulling the bird's feet out from under him. Frightened by this sudden turn of events, the turkey flapped his wings, squawked, and struggled to regain his footing. In the process, he moved sideways just enough to go off-camera, and the effect was finally achieved. The director and crew, the agency, the trainer, and, most of all, the turkey all heaved a huge sigh of relief (Figure 13–10).

Figure 13–10 Profits jumped 27 percent for Cullum Companies thanks, in part, to Tom Thumb TV spots.

Costs

Roman and Maas list 14 factors that add to the cost of a commercial:[3]

1. Children and animals (including turkeys).
2. Location shooting.
3. Large cast.
4. Superstar talent.
5. Night or weekend filming.
6. Animation.
7. Involved opticals, special effects, stop-motion.
8. Both location and studio shooting for one commercial.
9. Expensive set decoration.
10. Special photographic equipment.
11. A second day of shooting.
12. Legal requirements.
13. A single word or sentence of dialogue.
14. An extremely simple, close-up commercial.

About the last factor, they point out that the extremely simple close-up is the kind of commercial that frequently requires a whole day just to get lighting right. We might add: "or to get the turkey to move."

There are three stages or steps in the process of producing a television commercial:

1. Preproduction—which includes all the work prior to the actual day of filming, including casting, arranging for locations, estimating costs, obtaining necessary permissions, selecting technical suppliers and production companies, and finding props and costumes.
2. Production—the actual day (or days) that the commercial is filmed or videotaped.
3. Postproduction—all the work done after the day of shooting to finish the commercial, including editing, processing film, recording sound effects, mixing audio and video, and duplicating final films or tapes.

Each step has a dramatic impact on the eventual quality of the commercial and its cost. We shall discuss each stage briefly (see Figure 13–11).

Preproduction

After the advertiser approves a storyboard and budget, the production begins. Few people have the background to handle the entire production from start to finish. For this reason the commercial is a group effort. The team includes a writer, art director, producer, director, and sometimes a musical composer and choreographer. The person responsible for completion on schedule and within the budget is the producer, either in-house or free lance.

The producer seeks competitive bids, usually sending copies of the storyboard to three studios. The bids include the services of a director, camera operators, electricians, and other technicians. The studio may edit the film or tape, or it may be sent elsewhere for editing.

After the studio has been chosen, the cast is selected by audition or through talent agencies, and an announcer, if needed, is chosen. Next the set is built, and the crew and cast rehearse under the director's supervision.

The greatest waste of money in commercial production inevitably occurs because of a lack of adequate preproduction planning. The converse is also true. The greatest savings can be effected by proper planning before the day of production.

Casting, for example, is a crucial decision and must be completely settled before the day of shooting. Children and animals are unpredictable and often cause production delays. Rehearsals before production, therefore, are a must.

Shooting days are expensive. The cost of studios, casts, crews, and equipment are normally figured on a full-day basis. Therefore, any unnecessary delays that could throw the production into an unexpected second shooting day must be avoided. This also suggests a problem for location shooting. Weather must be considered. Locations should be selected close to home whenever possible. Extra days on location are extremely expensive.

All these factors should be taken into consideration during the preproduction phase, and every aspect of the commercial production discussed, decided, and approved by the client, agency, and production company prior to the shooting day.

During these preparatory steps, a preproduction meeting should be held by the producer. It includes the agency account executive, the writer, art director, studio director, possibly the advertiser, and any-

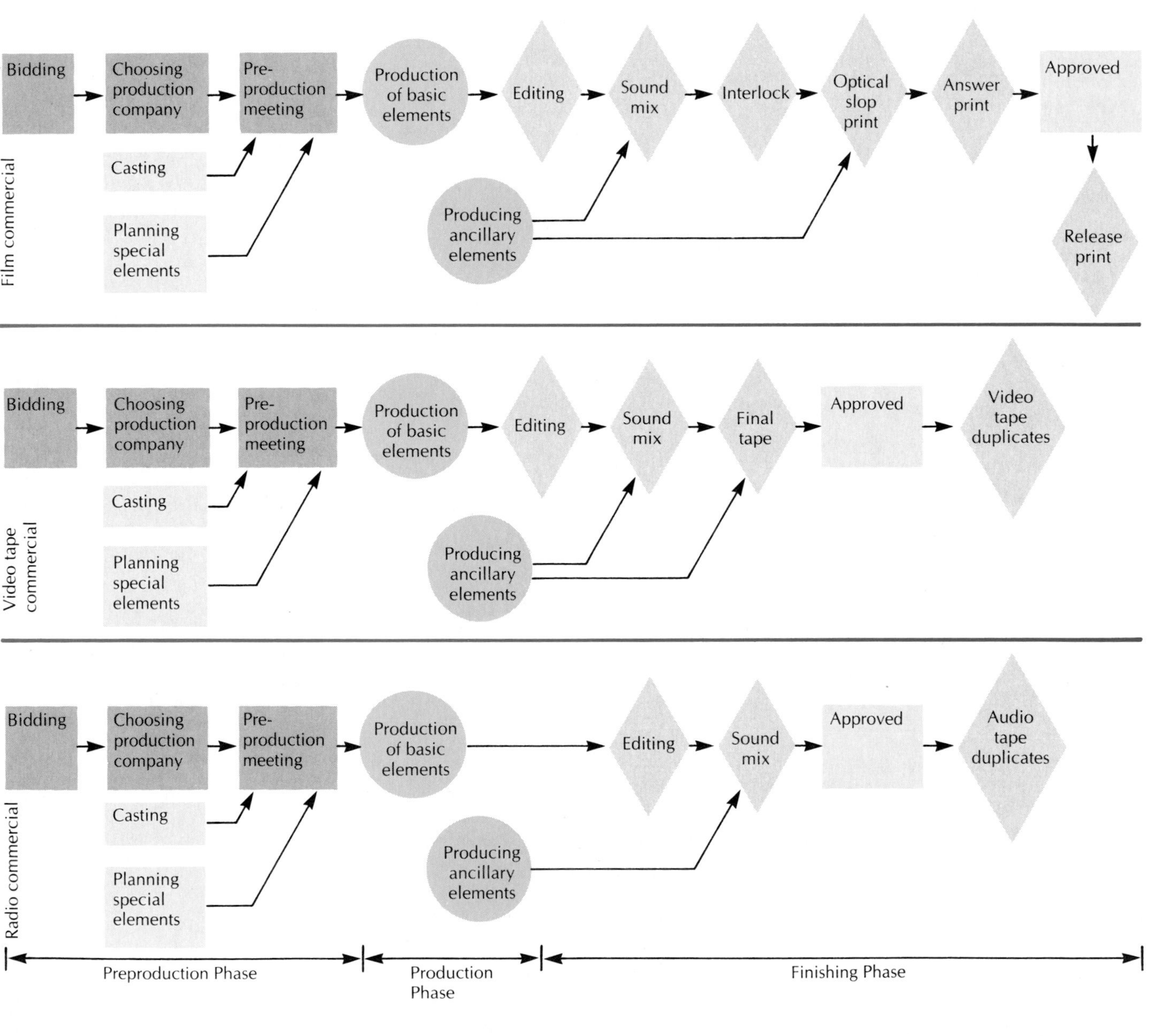

Figure 13–11 The process of broadcast production.

one else deemed important to the production. At this time they iron out any last-minute problems, review the storyboard, and make final decisions on the actors and announcer. The music, sets, action, lighting, and camera angles are all reviewed. The more details that are settled at this time, the better. A 60-second commercial takes only 90 feet of film, but the shooting often requires several days and from 3,000 to 5,000 feet of film.

The soundtrack may be recorded before, during, or after the actual production of the film or videotape. Recording the sound in advance assures that the commercial will be neither too long nor too short. This technique is used when the subject of the commercial has to move or dance to a specific rhythm. Sometimes, though, music or voice-over is recorded after the shooting.

Production

The actual shooting day (or days) of a commercial can be very long and tedious. Starting very early in the morning, the crew may take several hours just to light the set to the director's liking.

When the scenes are being shot, it may be necessary to try several "takes" to get them right. During this time the lighting may be readjusted several times as unexpected shadows pop up. The director usually requires two or three good takes of every scene. In addition each scene is probably shot from two or three different angles: one to establish the characters, one to show only the person speaking, and one to show the reaction of the person listening.

Scenes are not necessarily shot in order. For example, scenes with no synchronized sound are usually shot last since they don't require the full crew.

Between the shootings of each scene, a long interval may be required to move the camera, reset the lights, reposition the actors, and pick up the action, sound, and look to match the other scenes (Figure 13–12). This is extremely important since each piece of action must match what comes before and after. Otherwise the commercial will contain disconcerting jumps that can potentially destroy the credibility of the message.

Postproduction

The postproduction phase is where the commercial is actually put together. It is also the stage that usually determines how good a commercial is. The responsibility of the film editor, sound mixer, and director at this point is enormous.

The visual portion of the filmed commercial is first assembled on one piece of celluloid without the extra effects of dissolves, titles, or *supers* (words superimposed on the picture). The sound portion of the film is assembled on another piece of celluloid. This is called the *work print* stage (also called *rough cut* or *interlock*). At this time, scenes may be substituted, music and sound effects added, or other last-minute changes made.

Next the external sound is recorded. The announcer records the voice-over narrative. The music is recorded by the musicians and singers, or prerecorded stock music may be bought and integrated into the commercial. Sound effects such as doorbells ringing or doors slamming are mixed. This includes the actors' voices, the announcer, the music track, the singers, and the sound effects.

The finished sound is put on one piece of celluloid, which, combined with the almost-completed visual celluloid, is called the *mixed interlock*. When these two are joined, along with all the required optical effects and titles, a print is made called the *answer print*. This is the final commercial. If it receives all the necessary approvals, *dupes* (copies) are made and delivered to the networks or TV stations for airing.

Film versus tape

Today very few commercials are done live. Even those that look live are usually videotaped, and most commercials are made on color film. Film projects a soft texture that live broadcasts and videotape do not have. Because film is the oldest method of showing moving pictures, there is a large pool of skilled talent in this field. Also film is extremely flexible and versatile. It can be used for numerous optical effects, slow motion, distance shots, mood shots, fast action, and animation. The film size normally used for national commercials is

Figure 13–12 Preparing the set for a Whirlpool commercial may take hours to get the lights, products, and talent in the most attractive and effective positions. Each time the scene or camera angle changes, the lights may have to be reset to maintain continuity.

People in advertising

Rick Levine

President
Rick Levine Productions

Award-winning director Rick Levine is founder and president of Manhattan-based Rick Levine Productions, whose TV commercials have garnered an impressive array of industry honors. In 1979 these included seven Clios, an Andy, gold and silver NYAD medals, four Lions, and the coveted Gold Palm for sweeping the largest number of video commercial awards at the Cannes Film Festival. The Levine commercials that earned these impressive awards include TV campaigns for Pepsi, Xerox, Volkswagen, Lavoris, Pacific Telephone, BMW, Pan American World Airways, and Blitz Beer.

Rick Levine began his career at Parsons School of Design, where he graduated with honors. After two years in the U.S. Army, he joined NBC, then CBS. He went on to become an art director at Doyle Dane Bernbach, then Wells, Rich, Greene, and ultimately Carl Ally. His first directing assignment came while he was on the staff at Wylde Films.

"Fortunately," he recalls, "there were some people in ad agencies who realized that Rick Levine might do a good job because he had a good background as an art director. They came to me with some interesting concepts, and we won some awards in that first year." Rick Levine's commercials have been winning awards ever since.

While at Wylde Films, Levine met Chuck Pfeifer. In 1973 they formed Rick Levine Productions. Of their success, Levine says, "Chuck has the same attitude that I have. He insists on quality work. I will lose money on a job in order to make it come out right." Rick Levine Productions has profited from that premise and today has offices in New York and Los Angeles.

Also unique is Levine's approach to directing commercials. "I try to go for subtlety," he explains. "Some directors do commercials like cartoon comic books. I don't. I try not to be obvious." Does subtlety work? Levine believes it does. "Even if a spot doesn't give you a great big guffaw the first time you see it, the second or third time you'll see little touches of humor. I've been told that what people like about my work, is that I always capture the moment in a commercial."

Levine, whose commercials have a distinctive storytelling quality, notes that making such spots can be time-consuming. "Shooting Pepsi was almost like shooting a feature film," he says of his TV campaign for BBDO. "We were together for approximately eight weeks, during which we shot five commercials, each with a different look." The spots ultimately captured a Clio, a One Show gold award, and the Lion award at Cannes.

How does Levine feel about such awards? "It's really not the director who wins awards," he reflects. "It's the creative people who write the commercials and who then have to go out and sell their concepts to their clients in what is today a very rough market."

Levine shoots many of his commercials in Europe and has full production contacts in every major city. As to his favorite type of job, he says, "I like soft-sell commercials where the feelings get the message across. I did a spot for Welch's grape juice seven years ago that is still running. It shows an old man and a young boy walking through a vineyard. It is a great pastoral feeling with a reminiscing quality. The tag line, showing a can of Welch's grape juice, is: 'The closest you can get to Uncle Arthur's grapes without getting your feet wet.' "

Yet Levine adds, "Even though there is a note of humanity in all the commercials I do, I like to put on a different hat for each one. I do dialogue, humor, action—a variety of commercial types. I just try to avoid the repetitious, hard-sell spots that leave little room for creativity."

35 mm. If some rough-test commercials are to be run, 16 mm is sometimes used because it is much less expensive. Likewise, local commercials usually use 16 mm for lower cost. Duplicate film prints are also cheaper than videotape dupes.

On the other hand, recording a commercial on one- or two-inch magnetic videotape offers a more brilliant picture and better fidelity than film. It certainly looks more realistic and appears to have a "live" quality. Tape is also more consistent in quality than film stock. The chief advantage of tape, though, is that it can provide an immediate playback to the take. This permits the work to be checked and redone while the props and actors are still assembled. Computerization has cut editing time by up to 90 percent of that involved in film. Videotape can be replayed almost forever, but a film commercial can be run only about 25 times.

Some directors shoot their commercials on film to gain the advantages of texture and sensitive mood lighting. Then they dub their processed film onto videotape to do their editing. This is more costly, but it gives them the advantage of faster finishing and the opportunity to see the optical effects instantly as they are added. Most directors, however, still prefer to edit on film because of the wider range of effects possible, thereby achieving a higher level of "creative story telling." (See "From Concept Through Production of a Television Commercial.")

Producing radio commercials

Blue Nun was the best selling imported wine in the United States in 1980. But it wasn't always that way. In fact, until a few years ago, sales of Blue Nun were fairly static at about 70,000 cases per year. The wine was positioned as a gourmet selection and advertised only in sophisticated gourmet magazines via small-space ads.

Then Della Femina, Travisano & Partners got into the act. This agency was known for its highly creative and unusual approaches to marketing and advertising problems. In the case of Blue Nun, they lived up to their reputation.

The agency recommended repositioning the brand as an "all-purpose" wine that was perfectly suited to all meals and foods. They also suggested selling it as a packaged goods item rather than a specialty good. This strategy put them squarely against the leading all-purpose rosé wines such as Mateus and Lancers. The most interesting part of the strategy, though, was the suggestion to use radio exclusively to deliver Blue Nun's message. The agency felt that radio could be used best to target the intended market (men, high middle to upper class demographics) and simultaneously deliver the large audience numbers required for a packaged goods product.

Because of the uniqueness of the brand identification, it was decided to feature the Blue Nun name as the easiest way to order a premium wine for any meal.

The agency selected the husband/wife comedy team, Stiller and Meara, to deliver a series of humorous slice-of-life vignettes of the problems couples face while ordering and serving wine. The agency

From concept through production of a television commercial

Marketing background

General Mills acquired the rights to Yoplait Yogurt about three years ago. Yoplait is a superb French product that both looks and tastes different from American yogurts, and it is preferred by many who try it. In recent years yogurt has been a fast-growing business in the United States due to increasing health and fitness trends. However the category is cluttered with brands that offer essentially the same generic benefits: smooth, creamy taste, fruit, and natural ingredients. The challenge to Dancer Fitzgerald Sample, Yoplait's advertising agency, was to break through the clutter and separate Yoplait from its competition by making the idea of its great taste believable in a distinctive way.

Creative strategy

The first step was to pinpoint a target audience. Research showed that yogurt consumers are educated, upscale, urban adults on the leading edge of new trends. Second, all efforts had to be focused against that narrow target. Finally, the brand would be sold on image to distinguish it from other brands in an attribute-oriented category. Drawing on the brand's heritage, DFS chose the Yogurt of France image, and this became the key thought to be communicated in the advertising. In addition to the Yogurt of France image, the advertising had to convey Yoplait's unique taste experience in a way that would be appealing to the target audience and with a tone that positioned Yoplait as an important yogurt suited to the active, contemporary lifestyle of the target consumer.

The advertising would be exposed to the public via selectively targeted media vehicles, including superior prime-time television and upscale magazines.

Creative concept

Agency creative groups presented four different executions of the strategy developed by the account group. The one selected featured celebrities, instantly recognizable as "real Americans," who were unfamiliar with Yoplait at the opening of the commercial, but who, after tasting it, broke into French as a reaction to its great taste. The account group chose this campaign for its simplicity and sophistication, as well as its clear interpretation of the Yogurt of France strategy. In addition, the campaign was easily adaptable to print and radio.

Storyboard, script, and production estimate

DFS presented the four campaigns to the Yoplait brand group and recommended the celebrity execution, which the brand group approved. DFS then obtained estimates from several production companies based on the storyboard and made a recommendation that the brand group accepted. They chose the production house based on the high quality of its past work, the producer's previous experience with celebrities, and his ability to inject a sense of theater and comedy into his productions.

Preproduction

The next step was to select appropriate celebrities and negotiate the terms of their contracts. First, the account and creative groups chose several celebrities who would be instantly recognizable as "real Americans" and would appeal to Yoplait's upscale target. The DFS casting department contacted the agents of these celebrities, and after considering their cost, availability, and desirability, the agency and client agreed on three. Jack Klugman (of "The Odd Couple" and "Quincy") and Loretta Swit (of MASH) were selected on the basis of their overall appeal and recognizability, and Tommy LaSorda, manager of the Los Angeles Dodgers, was chosen specifically for the Los Angeles market, where Yoplait intended to introduce the campaign first.

DFS decided to shoot each of the three commercials on the West Coast, where all three celebrities lived, and to fly the director there. However, each commercial had different preproduction requirements. Each celebrity should appear in an environment natural to him or her. Jack Klugman and Loretta Swit would be shot wearing their own clothing. Jack would be in his kitchen, and Loretta would be on her patio. However, the stars' own homes could not be used, so the agency and production crews had to find houses near Los Angeles that met the shooting requirements, and whose owners were willing to allow the shoot to take place in their homes. In addition, a French coach was hired to tutor Klugman at his home two days before the shoot, and a wardrobe had to be purchased for Swit.

Unlike Klugman and Swit, LaSorda would appear in his Dodger uniform at his desk. A set designer known for his work in films was hired to design a set to represent LaSorda's office. The final set included a videotape machine, trophies, and other baseball memorabilia.

From concept through production of a television commercial *(continued)*

Shooting the commercial

The agency account and creative groups, the production team, and the brand group assembled for the shoots, each of which required only one day. In the case of Klugman and Swit, print shoots were scheduled as well as the television commercial productions. The creative group scheduled the print shoot early in the day, so that the performer would be fresh, and the shoot itself would serve as a warm-up for the television shoot.

For each commercial, the prerecorded announcer track introduced the product and described it. The track was played while the celebrity acted in the first part of the commercial. In the final section, the celebrity broke into French and was also recorded. Later the two tracks were spliced.

The director shot the commercial on 35-mm film, but also provided video playbacks. In so doing, these video playbacks allowed the creative group, the celebrity, and the client to see takes and evaluate or make corrections as necessary.

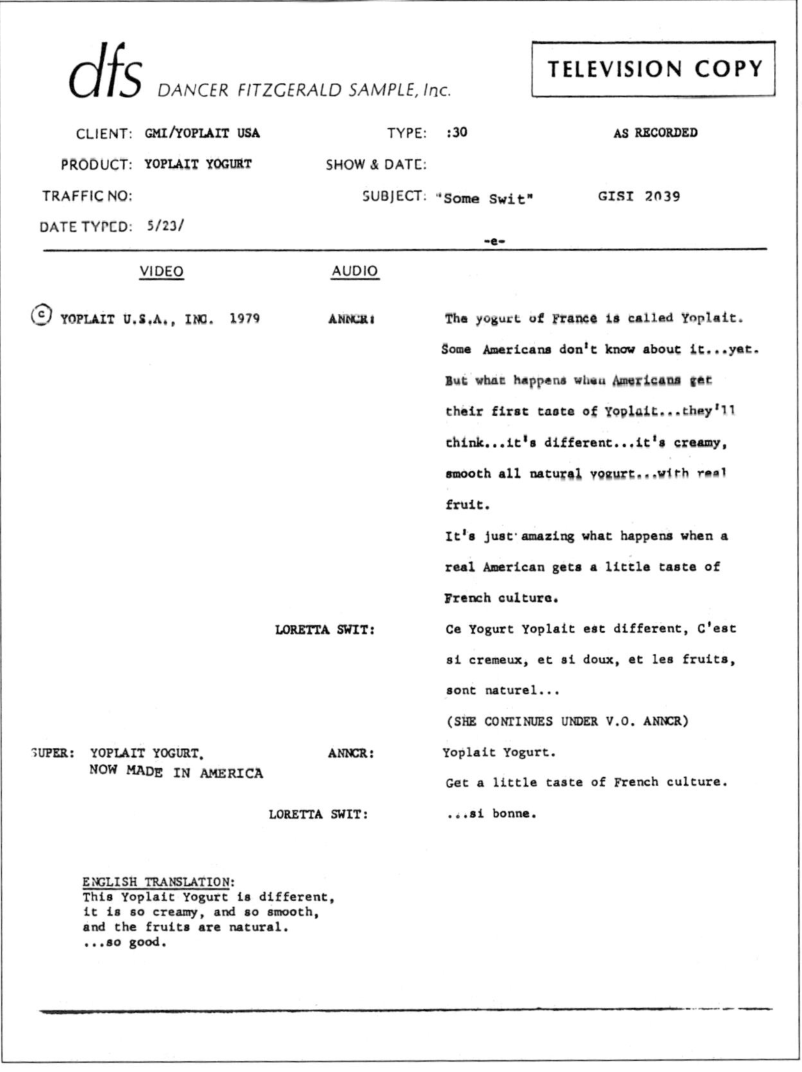

dfs DANCER FITZGERALD SAMPLE, Inc.

TELEVISION COPY

CLIENT: GMI/YOPLAIT USA TYPE: :30 AS RECORDED
PRODUCT: YOPLAIT YOGURT SHOW & DATE:
TRAFFIC NO: SUBJECT: "Some Swit" GISI 2039
DATE TYPED: 5/23/

-e-

VIDEO	AUDIO	
© YOPLAIT U.S.A., INC. 1979	ANNCR:	The yogurt of France is called Yoplait. Some Americans don't know about it...yet. But what happens when Americans get their first taste of Yoplait...they'll think...it's different...it's creamy, smooth all natural yogurt...with real fruit. It's just amazing what happens when a real American gets a little taste of French culture.
	LORETTA SWIT:	Ce Yogurt Yoplait est different, C'est si cremeux, et si doux, et les fruits, sont naturel... (SHE CONTINUES UNDER V.O. ANNCR)
SUPER: YOPLAIT YOGURT. NOW MADE IN AMERICA	ANNCR:	Yoplait Yogurt. Get a little taste of French culture.
	LORETTA SWIT:	...si bonne.

ENGLISH TRANSLATION:
This Yoplait Yogurt is different,
it is so creamy, and so smooth,
and the fruits are natural.
...so good.

From concept through production of a television commercial *(continued)*

Dailies to distribution prints

Following each shoot, the creative group and producer met to select the best *takes*. Since each commercial was shot many times, they selected the best versions for presentation to the account group and the brand group. They spliced the corresponding voice track onto the announcer track and combined the soundtrack with the film. The process included a *rough cut*, or a film that has action but no sound, a *soundtrack*, mentioned above, and an *interlock*, a preliminary version of the film with sound.

With account group and brand group approval of selected takes for each commercial, the agency made an *answer print*, or a 35-mm film of the final approved commercial, for each celebrity execution. They then made videotapes from the answer prints for distribution to television stations.

Campaign results

On the West Coast, where Yoplait was first introduced, the advertising exceeded every objective. After eight weeks Yoplait achieved 64 percent brand and 51 percent advertising awareness, and after six months Yoplait' share was estimated to be between 20 and 25 percent. It was the number one or two brand wherever sold. Shipments averaged 125,000 cases per week (or about +200 percent of objective). Yoplait's success helped to dramatically expand the entire category (by about +25 percent)—prompting a page one *Los Angeles Times* article on Yoplait's phenomenal appeal and success.

YOPLAIT YOGURT

"SOME SWIT"

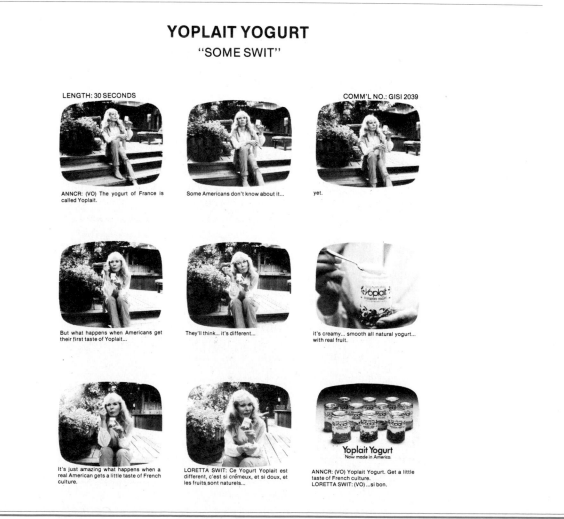

LENGTH: 30 SECONDS

COMM'L NO.: GISI 2039

ANNCR: (VO) The yogurt of France is called Yoplait.

Some Americans don't know about it...

yet.

But what happens when Americans get their first taste of Yoplait...

They'll think... it's different...

Yoplait

it's creamy... smooth all natural yogurt... with real fruit.

It's just amazing what happens when a real American gets a little taste of French culture.

LORETTA SWIT: Ce Yogurt Yoplait est different, c'est si crémeux, et si doux, et les fruits sont naturels...

Yoplait Yogurt
Now made in America.

ANNCR: (VO) Yoplait Yogurt. Get a little taste of French culture.
LORETTA SWIT: (VO) ...si bon.

assigned an art director and copywriter, Mark Yusting and Kay Kavanagh, to develop the scripts.

Locking themselves in an office for several days, Yusting and Kavanagh hammered out the first series of radio commercials, which would eventually catapult Blue Nun into market leadership. Simultaneously, these commercials repositioned radio as an action medium for advertisers in need of results.

The tone and manner of the commercials set a trend for the next decade of Blue Nun advertising by playing off the brand's name with sophisticated wit and humor (Figure 13–13).

Advertiser: Schieffelin & Co.
Product or service: Blue Nun Wine
Structure: Slice of life, with humor
Commercial length: 60 seconds

Stiller:	Excuse me, the cruise director assigned me this table for dinner.
Meara:	Say, weren't you the fella at the costume ball last night dressed as a giant tuna? With scales, the gills and the fins?
Stiller:	Yeah—that was me.
Meara:	I recognized you right away.
Stiller:	Were you there?
Meara:	I was dressed as a mermaid so I had to spend most of the night sitting down. Did you ever try dancing with both legs wrapped in aluminum foil?
Stiller:	No, I can't say I have. Did you order dinner yet?
Meara:	I'm having the filet of sole.
Stiller:	Hmmm. The filet mignon looks good. Would you like to share a bottle of wine?
Meara:	Terrific.
Stiller:	I noticed a little Blue Nun at the Captain's table.
Meara:	Poor thing. Maybe she's seasick.
Stiller:	No, Blue Nun is a wine. A delicious white wine.
Meara:	Oh, we can't have a white wine if you're having meat and I'm having fish.
Stiller:	Sure we can. Blue Nun is a white wine that's correct with any dish. Your filet of sole. My filet mignon.
Meara:	Oh, it's so nice to meet a man who knows the finer things. You must be a gourmet?
Stiller:	No, as a matter of fact, I'm an accountant. Small firm in the city. Do a lot of tax work. . . . [*fade out*]
Announcer:	Blue Nun. The delicious white wine that's correct with any dish. Another Sichel wine imported by Schieffelin & Company, New York.

Figure 13–13 Blue Nun radio commercial.

Blue Nun no longer sells 70,000 cases per year. By 1980 the figure exceeded 1.2 million cases per year and was still climbing. It had become this country's best selling imported wine, having beaten out Lancers and Mateus, and its brand image had become equal to or better than those two previous leaders in all its advertised markets.

Producing radio commercials is similar to producing television commercials in several aspects. It uses the same basic techniques as television—namely, testimonials, slice of life, straight announcements, or music, and generally follows the same developmental pattern as television. Only the details differ.

Writing radio copy

Radio listeners usually decide within the first five to eight seconds whether they want to pay attention to a commercial. Therefore radio copy must be intensive. It should get the listener's attention and hold it to the end. To accomplish this, many techniques and devices can be used. Creativity knows no limits. The wide range of possibilities was considered by Wallace Ross and Bob Landers who came up with 17 creative categories. (See the Ad Lab.)

The radio listener is often busy driving, washing dishes, or reading the paper. Therefore the message should be catchy, memorable, and never dull. In the effort to gain attention, though, care must be taken to avoid jarring the listener offensively. That can cause resentment. A friendly approach wins more friends than a bloodcurdling scream. The style should be kept personal, relaxed, and cheerful.

Humor can be one of the best attention-getting devices. It is being used increasingly with success. But beware! It is difficult to master. Poorly done humor is worse than none at all.

Some additional rules of thumb follow:

Mention the advertiser's name often—at least three times.

If the name is tricky, spell it—at least once.

Be conversational. Use easy-to-pronounce words and short sentences. Avoid tongue twisters.

Keep the message simple. Omit unneeded words.

Concentrate on one main selling point. Don't try to crowd in too many ideas. Make the *big* idea crystal clear!

Create a visual image. Paint pictures with the words. Use descriptive language. Familiar sounds such as a fire engine siren or a car engine can help paint the picture.

Stress action words rather than passive words.

Emphasize the product benefits repeatedly—with variations.

Make the script fit the available time. The average announcer normally reads about 125 words per minute, with the range running from 100 to 150 words.

A good rule of thumb for the number of words in a commercial is as follows:[4]

10 second	20–25 words	20 seconds	40–45 words

30 seconds 60–70 words 60 seconds 125–140 words

And be sure to *ask for the order.* Try to get the listener to *do* something. The story is told that Martin Block, an early announcer on radio station WNEW, once made a bet. Figuring that many women drove from New Jersey to New York to shop, he bet that he could persuade some of them by radio to turn around, go back through the tunnel, and buy their dresses from his New Jersey sponsor. He did, they did, and he won the bet. The women told his sponsor![5]

To hear some outstanding commercials, play the Eva-Tone Soundsheet included in this book.

Types of radio commercials

Although not all radio commercials can be rigidly cataloged, they fall into four basic types: musical, slice of life, straight, and personality.

Musical

A number of years ago Coca-Cola introduced a musical commercial to promote its campaign: "It's the Real Thing." The music from the commercial was so popular that it was later released as a single and became a hit song: "I'd Like to Teach the World to Sing." By that time the song was so well identified as the Coke song that every time the hit song was played people thought of Coca-Cola.

Today jingles, or musical commercials, are among the best and the worst advertising messages produced. If done well, they can bring enormous success—well beyond that of the average nonmusical commercial. Likewise, when done poorly, they can waste the advertising budget.

Musical commercials have several variations. The entire message may be sung, jingles may be interspersed throughout the copy, or orchestras may play symphonic arrangements. A growing number of producers use music that has no lyrics as a background theme. After hearing several such announcements, the listener gradually begins to associate the product with the music. This is called a *musical logotype.*

Advertisers have three principal sources of music. They can buy the use of a tune from the copyright owner, which is usually expensive. They can use a melody in the public domain, which is free. Or they can hire a composer to write an original tune. Several of these original tunes besides the Coke song have turned into hits.

Slice of life (problem solution)

Like in television, the slice of life is a situation commercial in which professional actors discuss a problem and propose the product as its solution. Played with the proper drama, it can get attention and create interest. "Slice" commercials can be produced straight or for humorous effect (Figure 13–14). In all cases the story should be relevant to the product and simply told.

Advertiser: Ohrbach's
Agency: In-House: Ohrbach's
Copy: Jerry Stiller & Ann Meara
Recording studio: The Audio Dept.
Agency producer: H. I. Leder
Studio producer: Gene Coleman
Director: H. I. Leder

Welcome to "last chance," the sensitivity group for people who are flunking life. Now who wants to share their problems? Speak up. Don't be afraid.

I'll share.

What's your name, dummy?

Sherman Doily . . . lately; my life is empty and drab. I'd be better off dead. My mother's a trumpet player. When she sees me; she plays taps.

Sherman, you're a victim. Look at you—you even dress like a loser. Nobody wears a noose for a necktie.

It's my hang-up. I'm hopeless. I've tried everything Yoga, Yogurt, Primal, Primal-Primal. . . .

Have you tried Ohrbach's?

Figure 13–14

Straight announcement

The straight commercial is probably the easiest to write. Delivered by one person, it can be designed as an *integrated commercial*—that is, woven into a show or tailored to a given program. There are no special sound effects as a rule. The only music, if any, is played in the background. It is adaptable to almost any product or situation and is therefore used frequently (Figure 13–15). Getting and holding the listener's attention is probably its greatest problem.

Personality

It is sometimes desirable to have a disc jockey or show host express the message in his or her own style. When such a commercial is done well, it is almost always better than anything the advertiser could supply.

Selling on radio: 17 creative ways

1. *Product demo*—telling how a product is used or the purposes it serves.
2. *Voice power*—where the power of the commercial is in the casting of a unique voice.
3. *Electronic sound*—synthetic sound-making machines create a memorable product-sound association.
4. *Customer interview*—a product spokesperson and customer discuss the product advantages—often spontaneously.
5. *Humorous fake interview*—variation of the customer interview in a lighter vein.
6. *Hyperbole or exaggerated statement*—overstatement arouses interest in legitimate product claims that might otherwise pass unnoticed; often a spoof.
7. *Sixth dimension*—compression of time and events into a brief spot involving the listener in future projections.
8. *Hot property*—commercial adapts a current sensation—a hit show, performer, or song.
9. *Comedian power*—established comedians do commercials in their own unique style, implying celebrity endorsement.
10. *Historical fantasy*—situation with historical characters revived to convey product message.
11. *Sound picture*—recognizable sounds used to involve listener by stimulating his or her imagination.
12. *Demographics*—music or references appeal to a particular segment of the population, as an age or interest group.
13. *Imagery transfer*—musical logo or other sound reinforces the effects of a television campaign.
14. *Celebrity interview*—famous person endorses product in an informal manner.
15. *Product song*—Music and words combine to create musical logo selling product in the style of popular music.
16. *Editing genius*—many different situations, voices, types of music, and sounds are combined in a series of quick cuts.
17. *Improvisation*—assigned a situation, performers work out the dialogue extemporaneously; may be post-edited.

Laboratory applications

1. Select three radio commercials with which you are familiar and discuss which creative techniques they use.
2. Select a radio commercial with which you are familiar and discuss how it could have been more effective by using a different creative technique.

The advertiser surrenders control of the commercial, however, and turns it over to the personality. The main risk, outside of occasional blunders, is that the personality may criticize the product. Even so, this sometimes lends a realism that is hard to achieve otherwise.

If the advertiser decides to go this route, the personality is supplied with a fact sheet. The fact sheet gives the main points to be stressed and the phrases to be repeated. However, most of the specific wording and its mode of delivery are left up to the personality.

The radio production process

A radio commercial is quicker, simpler, and less expensive to produce than a television commercial.

Live commercials are used when advertisers feel they can use local announcers or personalities or a local program format to their advantage. For example, some advertisers like to capitalize on the popularity and credibility of a local DJ in the community.

Live commercials require that the station be sent a script and a recording of music, or special effects, if any is to be used. Care must be taken to insure that the material has been accurately timed for length. A live commercial script should run about 100–120 words per minute. This will enable the announcer to deliver the message at a normal conversational pace. In some cases, only a fact sheet on the product, rather than a script, will be sent. The local announcer is then expected to ad-lib the actual selling message.

The disadvantage of live commercials is that announcers may not be consistent in their delivery. In addition, the use of sound effects is quite limited. Obviously, if uniformity of delivery of the commercial is crucial, a recorded commercial must be used.

An agency may assign a radio producer from its staff or, as is often the case, hire a free-lance producer to develop the commercial. The radio producer first estimates the costs and then presents a budget to the advertiser for approval. Next, for recorded commercials, the producer selects a studio and a casting director.

The casting director casts professional actors for roles if it is a slice-of-life commercial or finds the right "voice" if there is only an announcer. If the script calls for music, the producer decides whether to use music already recorded or to hire a composer. He or she may also hire a music director, musicians, and singers. This is often done after hearing auditon tapes of the recommended talent. Depending on the script, sound effects may be created or taken from prerecorded sources.

Next, a director supervises rehearsals until everything falls into place. Then the commercial is recorded several times and the best take is selected. Music, sound, and vocal are usually recorded separately and mixed. In any case, the final recording is referred to as the master tape.

From the master tape, duplicates of the commercials, called *dubs,* are recorded onto ¼-inch magnetic tape and sent to radio stations for broadcast.

Advertiser: Autotronics, Inc.
Dallas, Texas
Agency: Inglehart and Partners,
Inc. Chicago
Copywriter: Jerry Inglehart
Recording studio: Newjack, L.A. and Universal,
Chicago
Agency producer: Jerry Inglehart
Studio producer: Larry Huerta
Director: Jerry Inglehart

Anncr: If you listen carefully for the next 30 seconds, you may never have to pay another speeding ticket. This message is about a dependable little electronic device called "The Snooper XK." It sits on your dash like a watchdog. The moment it detects radar . . .

SFX: BEEP BEEP BEEP
(CONTINUES UNDER ANNCR) it flashes a warning and beeps, reminding you to check your speed. You get plenty of advance warning, whether the radar beaming device is on the roadside, in the sky, or hidden in a tree.

Figure 13–15

Summary

An understanding of broadcast production concepts includes knowing the way commercials are written, the types of commercials that are most effective and commonly used, the basic techniques for producing a commercial, and the important steps in the production process.

A television script is divided into two portions. The right side is the audio, indicating sound effects, spoken copy, and music, and the left side is the video, indicating camera action, scenes, and instructions. After the script is written, the writer and art director prepare a storyboard, which is a sheet preprinted with a series of blank television screens. These are sketched in by the art director to represent the video, and the audio, along with instructions for the video, is typed underneath.

Writing television commercials requires credibility, believability, and relevance, but that goes well beyond the use of words. It involves the way in which the commercial is produced.

The six basic types of television commercials are straight announcement, demonstration, testimonial, slice of life, lifestyle, and animation. Animation techniques can further be categorized by whether they use cartoons, puppets, photo animation, or the new computerized laser light methods.

Producing a television commercial involves three stages or steps: preproduction, production, and postproduction. The preproduction stage includes all the work prior to the actual day of filming—casting, arranging for locations, estimating costs, finding props and costumes, and other work. The production stage is the actual days that the commercial is filmed or videotaped. Postproduction refers to the work done after the day of shooting. This includes editing, processing film, recording sound effects, mixing, and duplicating final films or tapes.

Most commercials are shot on film. Film is extremely flexible and versatile, it can be used for numerous optical effects, and film prints are cheaper than videotape dubs. In recent years, though, many more commercials are shot on tape. Videotape offers a more brilliant picture and better fidelity than film, it looks more realistic, and tape quality is more consistent than film stock. The chief advantage of tape, though, is that it can provide an immediate playback of the scene that was shot.

Producing radio commercials is similar to producing television commercials in several aspects. It uses the same basic techniques and generally follows the same development pattern. Only the details and the cost differ.

Radio offers a wide range of creative possibilities. The radio listener is often busy doing something else while the radio is on, so the message should be catchy, memorable, and simple. Radio commercials should be written to create a visual image in the mind of the listener. Action words should be used rather than passive words. The copy should fit the available time. The four basic types of radio commercials are musical, slice of life, straight announcement, and personality.

The radio production process is similar to television production only simpler and less costly. The final commercial is dubbed onto ¼-inch tape for distribution.

Questions for review

1. What is the benefit to the advertiser of using a continuing commercial presenter?
2. Why is an understanding of broadcast production techniques important for people involved in advertising today?
3. What is an animatic and how it is used?
4. What is the importance of unity to a television commercial?
5. What are the seven key factors in successful television commercials?
6. What are the advantages and disadvantages of using animation in television advertising?
7. What leads to the greatest waste of money in broadcast commercial production? Explain.
8. Is it better to use film or tape in producing a television commercial?
9. Why is radio often described as theater of the mind? Explain.
10. What are the four basic types of radio commercials? Describe them. Which is most effective, and why?

14

Creative packaging, labeling, and trademarks

In the late 1960s more than 600 brands of ladies' hosiery were being sold in supermarkets and drugstores. Competition was based on price. Promotional displays were ordinary or nonexistent.

Hanes had historically sold its high-priced brand of hosiery exclusively through department stores and specialty shops. But with the passage of time and changes in merchandising techniques, Hanes was losing in the market-share battle. It decided to enter the mass retail market served by grocery and drug chains. When it did, it made packaging and promotional history.

The egg has been called the "perfect package." Taking a tip from this miracle of nature, the Hanes Corporation designed a distinctive package, a new brand name, and a merchandise display unit that boosted the sales of its women's pantyhose and made the company the dominant force in the $1.2-billion women's hosiery market.

The name adopted was L'eggs—a feminine, product-related term. The package was entirely new and attention-getting. It was created in the shape of a large plastic egg and came in a color-coded cylinder.

Next came a display of equally unusual design. It became a highly productive merchandising unit with outstanding sales results. It was a free-standing, boutique-type display. When originally introduced, it held 24 dozen egg-shaped container units. A later model held 35 dozen units (Figure 14–1).

Retailers liked the display. It proclaimed the product loudly but nicely. It was modern and could be placed anywhere in a store. Its popular design often won it a prized location near the checkout counter. Most important, it increased hosiery sales. At the end of the first 13 weeks in which L'eggs was in supermarkets and drugstores, market researchers determined that it had attained a brand awareness level of 85 percent. The company's hosiery lines contributed greatly to its total sales results and earnings. Sales increased 18 percent to $372 million by the mid-70s. Earnings rose 44 percent to over $18 million. It went on to win a 30-percent share against 600 under-four-percent rivals by 1980.

Hanes's experience with L'eggs dramatically demonstrates the importance of packaging. Packaging is often the most distinctive identification a product has. It can be the key reason for a product's success or failure. Competition in the marketplace is keen, and fickle shoppers develop favorites. In this chapter we will examine the role and function of packaging in the marketing process and the important elements of packaging design. We will then consider the closely related topics of labeling and trademarks as they affect the marketing of products.

Packaging: Its role and function in marketing

In the average supermarket more than 10,000 items compete for the customers' attention and dollars. Often the package is the major factor in this competition. Packaging is increasingly important because of the emphasis on self-service, not only in grocery stores but in drug, variety, and other retail establishments as well. The package helps sell the product because it quickly identifies the brand to current users and endeavors to convince nonusers to try its contents for the first time.

The five functions of packaging are (1) containment and protection, (2) identification, (3) convenience, (4) consumer appeal, and (5) economy.

Containment and protection

The successful package offers containment and protection. In fulfilling this function the container must be designed so that the product is protected from damage in shipping, prevented from becoming stale, and kept from deteriorating on dealers' shelves or while in the possession of the ultimate consumer. Packages must protect their contents from water vapor (frozen foods), grease, infestation, and odors. Consumers don't want contaminated food, leaky packages, or cut fingers. Protection requirements are established by both the government and trade associations.

Figure 14–1 This L'eggs merchandiser-display model boosted the Hanes Corporation hosiery line into the dominant position in the industry. Its huge success later led to the design of twin-tower models.

Identification

The package must quickly identify the product by using the trade name, trademark, or trade character, or a combination of these devices. Packaging has become so important as an identification device that companies such as Heinz have adhered to the same basic bottle and label designs for years.

Consumers require high visibility and clear legibility in packaging (Figure 14–2). Type should be easy to read. Color combinations should provide high contrast. (Shoppers seldom wear their reading glasses.)

The retailer also likes quick identification of a package. Distinctive packages are less likely to be mistaken on the shelves.

Convenience

On the retail level, packages must be able to survive storage and reshipment. They must be easy to stack and display. This is why you do not see very many pyramid-shaped bottles. Packages with odd sizes and shapes fall over and break easily. The retailer also looks for a full range of sizes to fit the customer's needs. Whether a store stocks an item is often influenced by these considerations.

Consumer requirements are similar. Consumers want packages that can be stored and opened easily. For this reason, when the package is designed it is important to know where the product will be stored. A package designed to fit on the shelf of a refrigerator will differ from those stored in the medicine cabinet or on a laundry room shelf. The Vaseline bottle, for example, was designed with a rectangular shape to fit on a medicine cabinet shelf. Products that will fit on a dresser table should have packages that do not permit them to spill or tip over easily. Shampoo bottles should be easy to grip (Figure 14–3).

Sometimes a customer's desire for convenience can interfere with protection. For example, cellophane wrappings permit easy inspection, but they may not always protect well. Spouts make pouring much easier, but they may limit the strength of the package.

Consumer appeal

How well the package appeals to consumers is the result of many factors, including size, color, material, and shape. Easy-to-read package instructions also appeal to consumers.

Sizes are important because consumers have differing use requirements and budgets. On the other hand, if a product is available in many sizes, the retailer may not be able to carry all of them.

Color, too, is an important consideration (Figure 14–4). Louis Cheskin, a well-known researcher, has completed several studies suggesting that certain colors have special meanings to consumers. General Foods changed the Sanka package when it learned its yellow label suggested weakness.

Package shape is also important (Figure 14–5). Containers of Janitor in a Drum and heart-shaped Valentine's Day candy packages tell what the product is and what it is supposed to do.

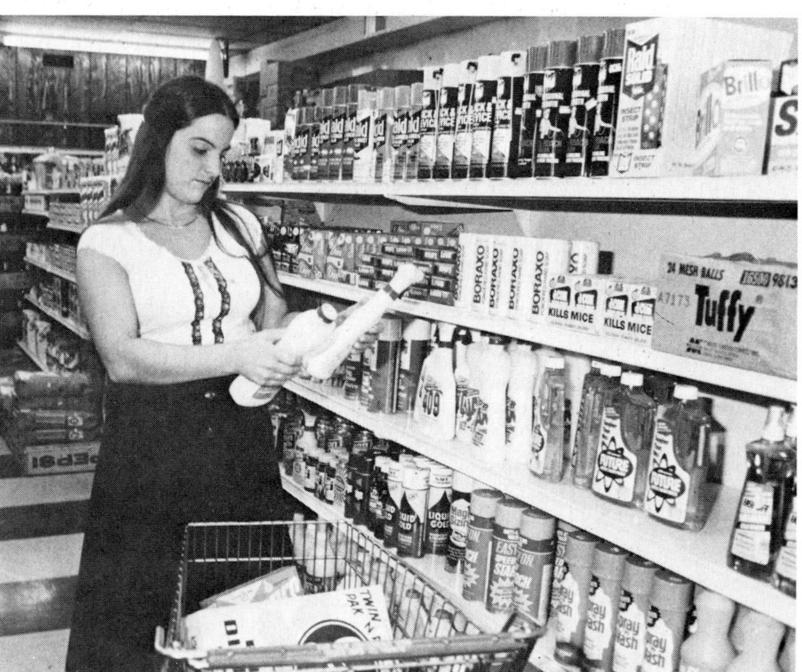

Figure 14–2 Product packages must be designed to be easily identifiable on grocery store shelves. Competing for space with perhaps 10,000 other products, they should be easy to display, offer eye appeal to the customer, and be available in sizes practical for consumer use.

Sometimes gift wrapping is used for special holidays. Although fairly successful, it increases the cost of packaging and poses problems if it doesn't sell out. Those remaining must be altered, offered at a discount, or displayed during the next holiday occasion.

The packaging of several items together offers convenience and usually a discount price. Combination packaging also limits the waste that occurs with unit packaging (Figure 14–6).

The convenience that comes from secondary use can also add to the appeal of a package. For example, Kraft manufactures a cheese glass that, once emptied, can be used for serving fruit juice. Or liquor bottles can sometimes serve as decanters or vases. These packages are really premiums that give the buyer of the product extra value for the dollars spent.

Figure 14–3 The trend is "back to nature" and convenience in shampoos. The bottle must be designed for gripping by wet, slippery hands.

Economy

Whether or not a package is used depends on its cost. Besides the obvious cost of materials and printing, the expense can vary according to the amount of protection, identification, convenience, and consumer appeal.

Sometimes a small increase in production costs may be more than offset by increased customer appeal. Aluminum foil and waxed paper boxes now come with cutting edges. Kleenex tissues become a hit with the introduction of a package that dispensed one tissue at a time. Now the law requires that many medicines be offered in "child-proof" plastic bottles. These benefits may make a considerable difference to the consumer.

Some of the factors that affect the cost of packaging are:

1. Cost of packaging materials.
2. Cost of manufacturing the package.
3. Cost of storage and shipping.
4. Cost of equipment used to manufacture and fill packages.
5. Cost of associated labor.

Packaging design

Perhaps the best way to emphasize the importance of the design of packaging is by pointing out the money spent on it. In 1980 it was over $50 billion. In fact, more money was spent on packaging than on advertising. A major reason for the heavy emphasis on packaging is the trend toward self-service. This requires the package to play a major role in both advertising and selling.

Packaging encompasses the physical appearance of the container and includes design, color, shape, labeling, and materials. In designing a package, consideration should be given to three factors: (1) how it communicates verbally and nonverbally, (2) the prestige desired, and (3) its stand-out appeal.

Packaging communicates both verbally and nonverbally. One bread manufacturer decided that a green wrapping would connote freshness. The only problem was that the customers associated it with fresh mold!

Even after consumers buy the product, they must continually be "sold" on it. A leading package designer, Walter P. Margulies, uses the cigarette package as a prime example. He stresses that it must be taken out 20 times and often placed in view of friends, intimates, co-workers, and strangers. Because of this, the design must "give consideration to what the user thinks others would regard as prestigious. Indeed cigarettes are a classic example of these so-called 'irrational products' in which fancy, whim, and mystique all operate in place of rational choice"[1] (Figures 14–7 and 14–8).

The package must be made to stand out from the others on the shelf. This can be done by using shape, color, or size to indicate in-use application or to just grab the attention of the shopper. The integrity of the manufacturer can be implied by the shape of the package. And regional preferences also play a role. For example, researchers determined in one study that people in the western part of the United States prefer margarine in an oblong package; the rest of the U.S. population prefers a square package.

Figure 14–4 This deodorant comes in a two-piece shadow box. Boxes and containers are color-keyed to the line's three scents.

Packages come in many forms

Packages come in many forms, including wrappers, cartons, boxes, crates, cans, bottles, jars, tubes, barrels, drums, and pallets. Packages are made of many substances, primarily paper, steel ("tin" cans), aluminum, plastic, wood, glass, burlap, and other fibers. Newer packaging materials include metal foils, which not only protect the contents but also add to the attractiveness of the package. Plastic provides a lightweight container as well as a safer one because it is unbreakable. Important improvements in packaging are occurring such as wax wraps that keep products like cereals fresh and amber-green glass wine bottles that protect the contents from damage by light. The relatively new, flexible plastic film pouch for food products has become a substitute for tin cans and makes packages even more flexible, light, and compact.

Packaging specialists

Management ultimately makes the final design decisions about packages and labels. However, because the right packages and labels have become increasingly important, numerous specialists have emerged to assist management in the decision-making process.

Because packaging is closely related to advertising, and because of the similar techniques used in advertising and packaging, the advertising department and the advertising agency usually play the most important role in package development. Advertising agencies design labels and packages and prepare the copy that goes on them. In many instances their help is vital because they coordinate their work with the overall theme of the advertising campaign that they have devised for the product. Most agencies consider packaging within the realm of their responsibilities. Packaging is now also considered part of the advertising and sales budgets of manufacturers, who previously viewed it as a facet of production.

However, packaging problems have become so complex in recent years that packaging specialists are being used increasingly by advertisers and their agencies.

1. Consulting firms are used to provide package designs. These companies are staffed by designers and artists who are acutely aware of the effect of colors and shapes on consumer buying practices.

2. Design departments of larger corporations have their own personnel to work on packaging. In this case the same people who design the package probably played a role in designing the product as well.

3. Container manufacturers often provide help with package design as a service to their present and potential customers. It is considered part of the service that goes along with the sale of the package manufacturer's products of metal, paper, plastic, or other packaging materials.

When should a package be changed?

There is an old saying: "If you build a better mousetrap, the world will beat a path to your door." Unfortunately, this is not always true.

Figure 14–6 This six-pack container can be used for storing and returning empty bottles for refund. A zipper-type opening is on both sides of the carton near the top. When both tabs are pulled, the top removes to reveal the carrying handles inside.

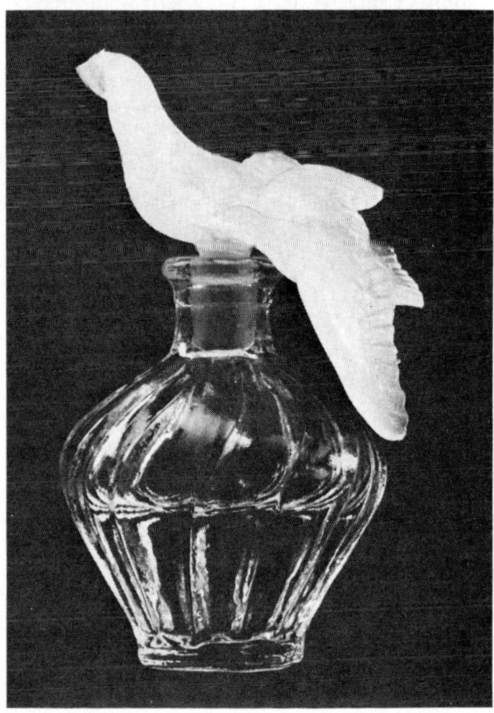

Figure 14–5 Distinctive packaging: Halston (*top*) and Nina Ricci's 43-ounce crystal bottle of L'Air du Temps Eau de Toilette that retails for $1,350.

A better Swedish mousetrap was introduced into the U.S. market in the late 1970s and immediately encountered problems. Called "The New Mousetrap," the product was packaged in a see-through polyurethane bag, but the graphics on the bag hid the product from view. In addition, the bag was difficult to handle and hard to open. The package was simply a poor marketing tool.

Selame Design Associates of Newton Lower Falls, Maine, was retained to develop new packaging for the product. First they wanted to create a catchy name (no pun intended). "Get 'm!" was approved by the client, Wicander Enterprises.

Then, since minimizing costs was an important consideration, they created a highly practical and visible package using as little material as possible and incorporating the bright orange product itself into the design (Figure 14–9).

The orange tent card matched the mousetrap color. A *die-cut* opening in the front panel served to show the product and also hold it in place with a single staple. The graphic design of the rear legs and tail of a mouse showed how the trap works. The card was made of coated material and printed in only two colors, orange and black (for economy). The name was reversed out in white.

Introduced in March 1979, the product immediately sold well. The self-selling, easily usable package apparently outweighed the mousetrap's higher price tag.

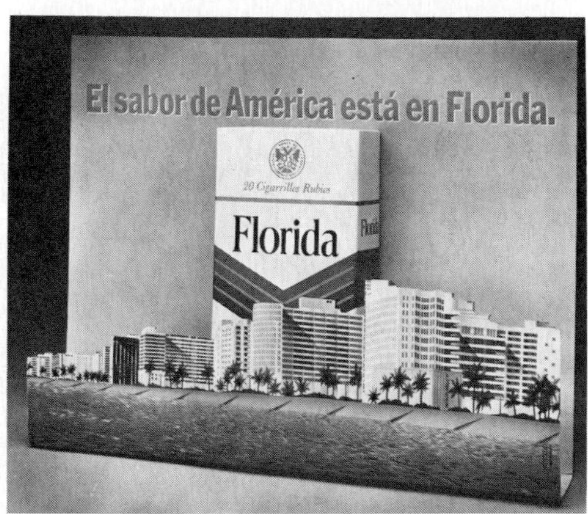

Figure 14–7 Translated, this point-of-purchase display proclaims: "America's taste is in Florida." Perhaps a strange-sounding line for Americans, but it seems to have been motivating for the Spanish public.

There are many reasons why even successful packaging gets changed (Figures 14–10 and 14–11). If a product is altered or improved, the packaging may change. New packaging may be necessitated by substitutions in materials, such as aluminum or plastic. Or competitors can influence alterations in the package.

A decision to stay with the present form can be as crucial as a decision to change it. Millions of dollars are spent in researching a new image and then promoting it. Margulies offers these caveats in determining whether packaging should be changed.[2]

1. Don't change because of a new brand manager's desire to innovate.
2. Don't change to imitate your competition.
3. Don't change for physical packaging innovation only.
4. Don't change for design values alone.
5. Don't change when product identification is strong.
6. Don change if it may hurt the branding.
7. Don't change if it will weaken the product's authenticity.
8. Don't change if it will critically raise the product's price.

When a decision to change has been made, designers often change the packaging very gradually so the consumer will feel comfortable and not suspect that something has happened to the product he or she has known and believed in for so many years.[3]

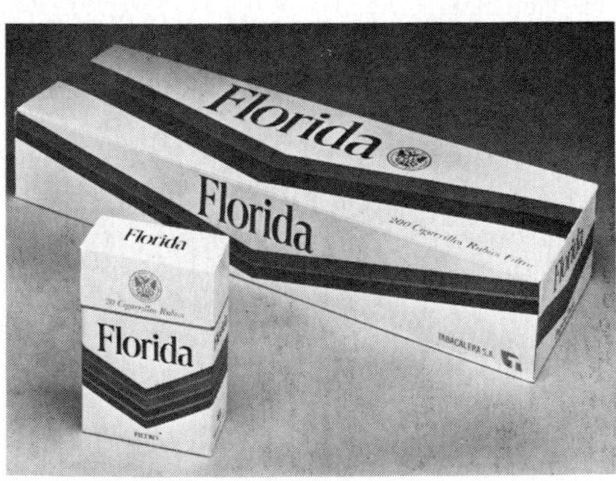

Figure 14–8 The Spanish tobacco industry, a government monopoly, decided to produce a new, high-quality cigarette with an American flavor that could compete with American cigarettes. Package colors are red, burgundy, and black—colors that suggest full-flavored American blends—on a white crush-proof box.

Innovations in package design

Package designs are constantly changing as new materials are developed or costs change. In recent years numerous innovations have been introduced with several purposes in mind: (1) aligning the package more closely with the product's marketing strategy; (2) emphasizing the product's benefits, (3) emphasizing the product's name; and (4) taking advantage of new materials. We will discuss each of these briefly.

Aligning packaging to marketing strategy

Packaging must fit in with the company's marketing strategy. This begins by identifying the segment of the market to which the product is directed. Then the challenge is to find the best packaging system to communicate with this market. That usually requires research. The basic package design might also be adaptable to the manufacturer's other products or to additional future products, so these considerations (and many others) must be weighed.

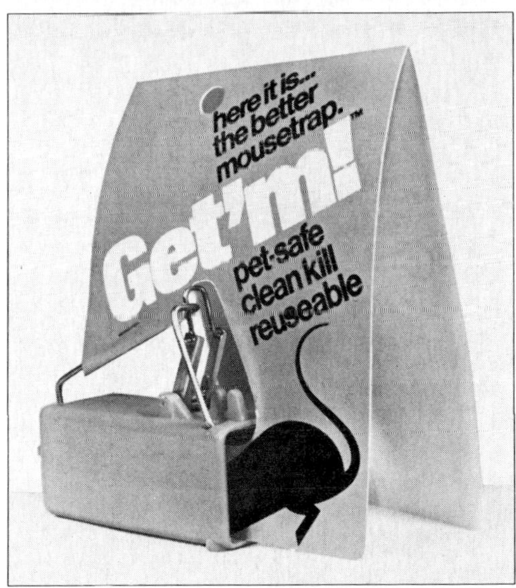

Figure 14–9 These two illustrations provide a comparison between the old and the new.

Emphasizing product benefits

Both copy and design should emphasize the product's benefits. Side panels should be used to sell because stacking procedures may differ from store to store. Perhaps a recipe may be included on the side or back panel (Figure 14–12). Recipes are strong selling tools. If they are used, decisions must be made about which one to use and whether the season will affect the choice of a recipe. If the product is to be sold in two packages, the inside package should convey the same impression and give the same benefit information as the outside package.

Emphasizing name identification

One problem with Wicander's better mousetrap was poor name identification on the package. The proper emphasis must be placed on the product's name. There are recent graphic innovations in how to depict names in words and type. "Get 'm" is an excellent example of the use of bold graphic words and type styles to convey immediate information to buyers and to identify the product briefly and accurately.

Using new materials

Plastic has created many new packaging ideas. It aids in controlling moisture for drinks, nuts, and candies. Odd-shaped products can be covered by stretchable "shrink" plastic. A small product mounted under a plastic dome on a card, called a *blister card,* is convenient and rackable and thwarts shoplifters.

The glass industry is working on an unbreakable bottle and on reducing costs by computerized glassmaking. Also, by electrostatic flocking, fabrics are being applied to glass. This not only is attractive but also offers protection.

In short, new materials are constantly being introduced. Costs of packaging are likewise continually rising. This forces professional package designers to stay current with the state of the art by studying the trends in material use and the new technological advancements in the field.

Testing package designs

About half of all major firms conduct some form of package research.[4] Packages are tested against competitors products and with alternative designs. Package testing is divided into two categories: visual and psychological.

Various instruments are used by researchers to obtain data for visual (or perceptual) research. One is a slide projector called a *tachistoscope* (T-scope), which shows the design for a fraction of a second. If the respondent can pick the package out at certain very short times, the package is a success. Other instruments are the *angle meter* and the *blur meter,* which measure how well a graphic element can be discerned at different angles, and the *polariscope,* which reveals how well a design can be read under poor lighting conditions. The *ocular camera* measures eye movements in response to specific design elements, and the *pupilometer* photographs pupil size. Research data have shown that pupil dilation reflects positive emotional response.

Psychological testing, on the other hand, generally uses projective techniques such as the Thematic Apperception Test or Semantic Differential Test. In the Semantic Differential Test, subjects are asked to pick from a list the various words and phrases they think best describe a package. The Thematic Apperception Test asks subjects to project their own interpretations of sketches and cartoons. Other testing techniques include interviews and in-store observations of consumer behavior.

Figure 14–10 Time passes, fashions change. The Morton Salt package with the umbrella girl has kept pace. With changing hair and wardrobe, the girl not only reflects current trends but also symbolizes Morton Salt's long history of advertising, which has helped capture and hold a larger share of the salt market than all other brands combined for about 60 years.

Other considerations in package design

In addition to the function, cost, and design of packaging, manufacturers must consider other factors. Two of the most important are the environment and the law.

Environment

The impact of various types of packages and containers on our environment has become a subject of heated debate in the hallways of American legislatures.

Plastic—particularly PVC (polyvinylchloride)—that is not biodegradable has been a subject of intense industry investigation.

Aerosol cans are being replaced because of the gaseous freon propellants in them. Freon is believed to reduce the earth's ozone layer, which allows the penetration of ultraviolet rays and causes skin cancer.

Packages are often blamed for much of the litter and waste on the nation's highways. Oregon and Michigan, in fact, have outlawed no-deposit, no-return cans and bottles. Yet industry spokespersons point out that the packaging industry is responsible for less than 15 percent of all solid wastes.[5] And many packagers support recycling programs and other waste disposal programs.

It's obvious, though, that the environment must be added to the list of considerations when any new packaging is developed.

People in advertising

Saul Bass

President
Saul Bass/Herb Yager & Associates

Saul Bass, creator of some of the world's best-known product and corporate symbols, is president of Saul Bass/Herb Yager & Associates, Los Angeles. Many of the logos and trademarks he has designed for Alcoa, United Airlines, the Bell System, Hunt-Wesson, and Quaker Oats are exhibited in the Library of Congress, the Museum of Modern Art, and the Smithsonian Institution.

Bass, whose trademarks include AT&T's bell within a circle and the big Celanese "C," was one of the first distinguished specialists in corporate identity. According to Bass, corporate identity consists of the challenge of determining what the best perception of a company should be, then developing design to reinforce the "good things" the public perceives and to eliminate any misperceptions. He found this same challenge in designing service symbols, like those he created for the Girl Scouts of America and United Way.

Yet Bass emphasizes that a company cannot project something that "isn't there." He explains, "There's nothing worse than to create an aura about a company that's not substantiated by fact. It's not only ineffective," he says, "but harmful to the company."

"Design must be responsive," says the New York–born designer, "to deeply felt but often unexpressed concerns." He cited his work for Continental Airlines as an example. "Air travelers," he says, "have a fear of flying, often unexpressed but real." The look of the plane affects people. Braniff, he reflects, "ignored this when they painted their planes one color. It made them look like balloons—not a good feeling. The basic concept of a plane is of a projectile. The idea of it continuing to move forward is rather important." For this reason, Bass painted the exteriors of Continental planes white, and added stripes to maintain an aerodynamic "high-tech" look.

From the beginning of his career, painting signs on Bronx store windows while in high school, Bass developed definite ideas about what design could and should do. In the late 1940s he moved to Los Angeles to create motion picture advertising logos for the Blaine-Thompson Agency. When the clients began coming to him instead of the agency, Bass requested a modest raise. The agency's answer was "be patient." So Bass went into business for himself. That was the beginning of Saul Bass & Associates.

Bass has been an art director, a package and poster designer, a photographer, an illustrator, and a film maker. Yet despite his broad and diverse talents, a sense of continuity pervades the celebrated achievements of his career. His association with producer-director Otto Preminger led him from designing film advertising logos to adapting these logos to film titles so the advertising campaigns and titles would have continuity. The most famous of his film titles, for *The Man with the Golden Arm,* launched a totally new look in title design.

Bass has also achieved distinction as a film maker. His film *Why Man Creates,* sponsored by Kaiser Aluminum, won him both an Academy Award and the Gold Medal at the Moscow Film Festival.

Bass is concerned about the "institutionalization of corporate identity" that he feels is occurring today. "There's a tendency toward sterility," he observes, "with symbols becoming cold, monolithic, and abstract. That is not sensing corporate requirements very well. I can't think of any corporation that can't use some expression of responsiveness to human needs."

Today nearly everyone encounters a Saul Bass design or logo. All who have seen a Warner Bros. movie, used a Dixie Cup, opened a box of Quaker Oats, visited a Security Pacific National Bank, or lit an Ohio Blue Tip match have seen his work. Says Bass, "The other day, a Bell System service van drove by, and my young son, Jeffrey, said, 'Look Daddy—there goes one of your trucks.' You know," Bass smiled, "I still enjoy hearing that."

Law

Legal restrictions on packaging are proposed in Congress in almost every session. The Fair Packaging and Label Act of 1966 enables consumers to obtain accurate information on the quality of a package's contents and to compare its values with those of other similar products. The Food and Drug Administration regulates the contents and labeling of packages of food, drugs, and cosmetics. The Federal Trade Commission also has jurisdiction over the packaging of consumer products. The FTC has promulgated rules to prevent misrepresentation in packaging. No package may say "economy" or "jumbo" unless the product is also available in a smaller size.

Many bills are proposed to increase product information and consumer safety. The proposed Federal Prevention Packaging Act would require mandatory safety closures on all household containers of toxic materials. Charges of "exploding pop bottles" and other dangers may

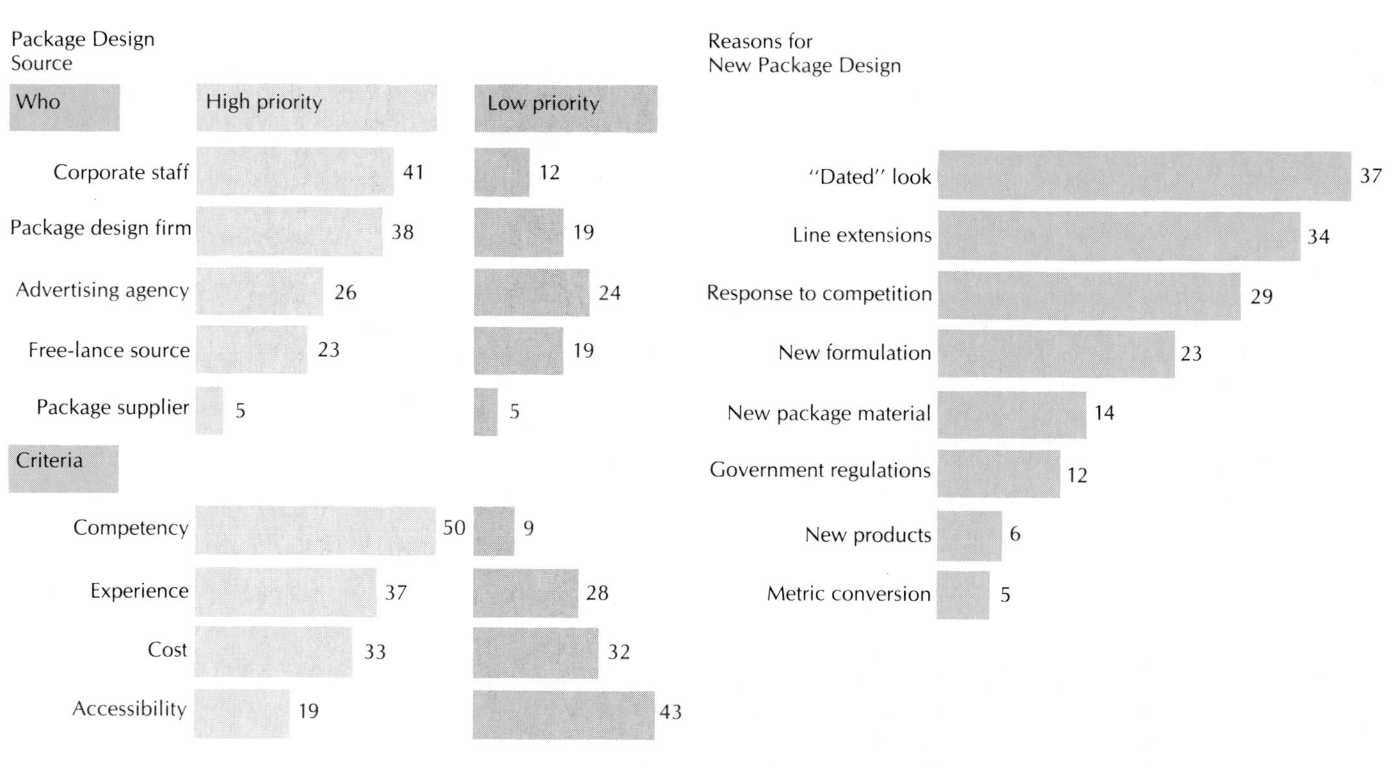

Figure 14–11

Advertising Techniques surveyed corporations to discover the reasons for adding or changing package designs, and the services most commonly used. For most companies the reason was either to give the product a newer, more current look, or because of a new product being added to the line. Almost half the companies responding use their own corporate staff for new package design. Most of the rest use a specialized package design firm.

lead to legislation requiring the product to ooze out slowly if the package is punctured.

Other bills propose that labels be positioned prominently and that all perishables carry an uncoded expiration date. One thing is for sure—labels and packages should always be reviewed by an attorney to verify that they conform to the law.

Labels in product marketing

As important as the product's package is the label that contains the brand name or symbol, the name and address of the manufacturer or distributor, the product composition and size, and recommended uses for the product. Labels serve a number of important functions: (1) identification and information, (2) disclosure of ingredients, (3) instructions on product use, and (4) persuasion and motivation. We will discuss each of these briefly in this section.

But first take a few moments to study the special color section, "Award-Winning Packaging, Labels, and Trademarks," which follows. It concludes some of the most outstanding examples to be seen in recent years. They demonstrate the numerous principles elaborated upon in this chapter.

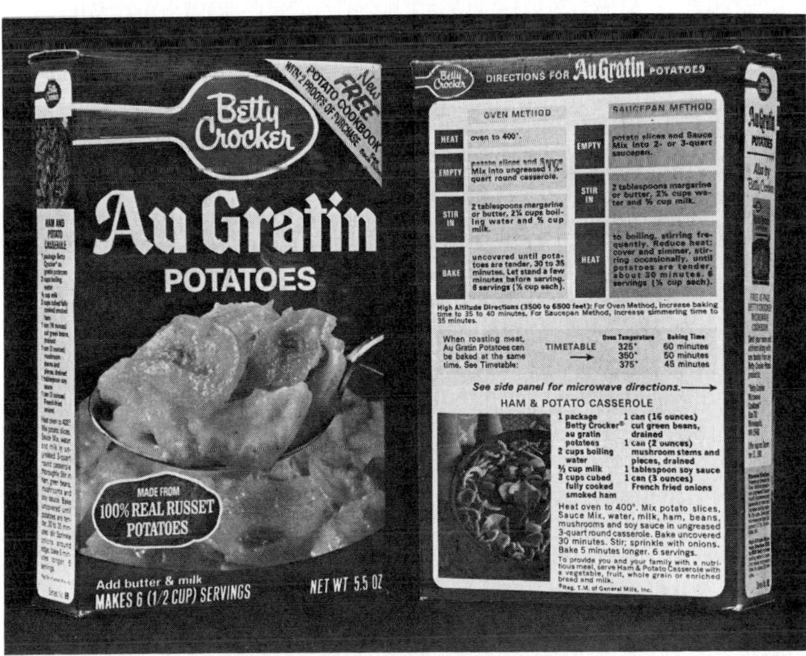

Figure 14–12 Package with recipe.

Award-winning packaging, labels, and trademarks

A.

B.

C.

D.

A. Shineido Co. Ltd. of Japan asked Sandgren and Murtha, Inc. to design these toiletry packages. The chunk-style bottles with an Oriental flair have rounded corners, which research has shown appeal to women (as opposed to square corners, which appeal to men).

B. Sunkist turned to the Schechter Group to design a bold, visually lively logotype to be adapted to a variety of bottles, cans, and cartons. The objective of the design was to communicate clearly the nature of the product while retaining the Sunkist heritage.

C. The Bruce Wolfe design for Sierra beer capitalizes on the romantic fantasy of the purity of the unspoiled mountains and wilderness by showing a painting (done by Joseph Bommerito) of an outdoor scene on its label. The gold color is stressed since it's perceived as masculine. The letter style reinforces a wholesome, old-fashioned appeal rather than the hard-sell look associated with some beers.

D. Spoken quickly enough, The Pushpinoff Ultimate pure milk chocolate and almond bar has the ring of a Russian import. The illustration, framed in gold foil to denote richness and quality, is reminiscent of the elegant lifestyles of the 20s. This package design by New York's Push Pin Studios (which became its own entrepreneur in the marketing of fine candies and nuts) combines offbeat nostalgia and art deco with the tongue-in-cheek humor typical of advertising creatives.

Award-winning packaging, labels, and trademarks *(continued)*

E.

F.

G.

H.

E. Bruce Wolfe used a single, dominant illustration to project freshness, quality, and home cooking. The label illustrations are each different, of course, but the shapes and lettering turn the shelf display into a dynamic billboard. Naming the product Home Brand was excellent trademark strategy because the line now has a generic rather than brand name sound. Note that the jars look like those used in home canning. The utter simplicity capitalizes on the trend toward "earth values" of doing it yourself.

F. For quick and easy identification, the graphic design department of Polaroid used the five-bar color-coding of their corporate symbol with the traditional News Gothic type style for the Polaroid name. The result is a family of packages that are at once simple, elegant, modern, and communicative.

G. Bloomingdale's pasta containers, designed by Steven Liska of Liska and Associates, Chicago, are decorative as well as functional. With their continental elegance and high-quality product imagery, they would display well in almost any kitchen. Note the use of type and color to show content. Consumers will enjoy the practicality of a canister that will keep the product fresh.

H. For these extremely perishable, high-quality roasted coffee beans, Chien/Hori Design created an attractive, highly visible package meant to portray a gourmet look. A color-code system is used behind the name of the variety of coffee bean, which helps in consumer identification, inventorying, and stocking. The cleverness of the product name, Coffee Bean, is unfortunately self-defeating, however. Since it is obviously a purely descriptive generic name, it most likely would not qualify to be trademarked and therefore cannot be protected.

Identification and information

Most products that go on the market have some form of identification. The label that informs the buyer of the product's brand name and its manufacturer is called a *brand label.* Even fresh fruits may carry a label, like Chiquita bananas.

Although some goods are adequately identified with only the name of the product and the seller, most products require a more extensive description of their nature and use. Cosmetics, processed foods, patent drugs, textiles, and a host of other goods are required by law to carry a fairly extensive list of their ingredients or components. Labels of some products, such as furs, may be required to provide information on their place of origin.

A new development in labeling is the Universal Product Code (UPC). It consists of a series of linear bars and a 10-digit number that identifies the product (Figure 14–13). With the use of optical scanning equipment, a computerized checkout system is possible. This speeds the checkout process and enables stores to have immediate inventory information. Important selling trends can be identified quickly in terms of which brands are selling, in what sizes, in what colors, and at what prices. This information can be particularly valuable because marketing research is greatly aided. Experiments about product modifications, labeling changes, and new-product introductions can be monitored daily. Also, the effects of special promotional efforts, point-of-purchase advertising, and displays can be accurately measured. Consumers are better served because it reduces the amount of human error in ringing up sales and in maintaining adequate inventories of the merchandise the consumer wants.

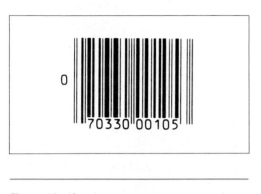

Figure 14–13 The Universal Product code for a ballpoint pen.

Disclosure of ingredients

Legislation has greatly affected the information on labels. For example, the Federal Food, Drug, and Cosmetic Act requires lables for certain products to include not only the product name and the manufacturer's name and address, but also the quantity and nature of the contents and whether any artificial flavoring or preservatives are included. The ingredients in food products must be listed by volume in descending order; that is, if sugar constitutes the largest share of the total volume of ingredients, then sugar has to be listed first.

The Food and Drug Administration has issued standards for nutritional lables for all food products. Labels for over-the-counter drugs must warn of any possible harmful effects that might result from using the product. Also, the percentage of alcohol content must be indicated on labels for beer, wines, and liquors.

Cigarette packages have to carry a health warning. Fabric content and washing instructions must be given on clothing labels as specified in the Wool Products Labeling Act and the Synthetic Fibers Act.

The disclosure of ingredients can increase favorable support through "word-of-mouth" advertising. Informational labeling can stimulate sales since product satisfaction can result from buyers having confidence in the wisdom of their purchase.

Instructions on product use

Instructions must be furnished on the use of many products. Commercial plant foods, for instance, must tell the buyer the amount to be used and the recommended frequency of feedings. Many manufacturers furnish instructions for additional uses of their products as a way of increasing sales. Manufacturers of food items, for example, often provide recipes and serving suggestions on the package.

Persuasion and motivation

Just as the function of advertising is to inform, persuade, and remind, the label is seen by most marketers as one more opportunity to talk to the consumer. The label can be very motivating in getting consumers to purchase a product. In addition to attractive artwork and interesting copy, instructions about the proper use and care of the product can be a persuasive selling tool. The label can reinforce the buyer's initial desire to purchase the product.

In view of the consumer movement, the wise manufacturer uses the label as an opportunity to provide vital information and to be as informative as possible. This is particularly important when the product is purchased in a self-service store.

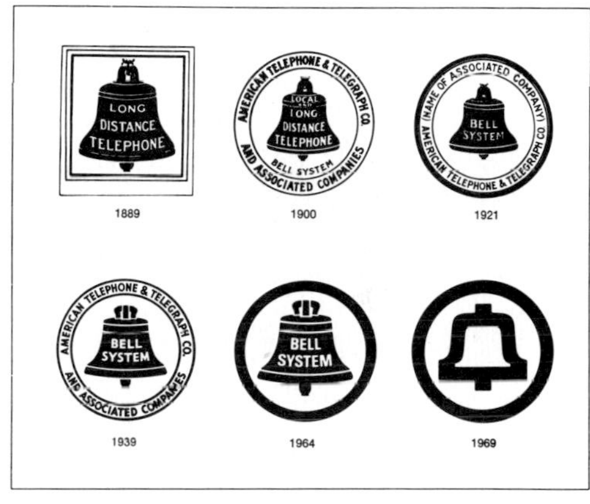

Figure 14–14 The long history of AT&T can be seen through its parade of logos during the last century. Note the utter simplicity of its current symbol. It is the most universally recognized American trademark.

Role and function of trademarks

It's hard to admit it if you look old fashioned, but sometimes the evidence is overwhelming. Such was the case in 1968 when American Telephone & Telegraph Company acknowledged the need for change as well as unification of the 23 regional companies that constitute its nationwide Bell System.[6]

At that time its 1964 trademark looked old-fashioned, and its fleet of 177,000 green vehicles looked like war surplus equipment. Telephone directories were confusing in their graphic design. Stationery and other business forms of the 23 companies had little or nothing in common. In fact, they looked like 23 different organizations.

AT&T hired Saul Bass & Associates, one of the country's foremost graphic design firms, to develop a new trademark and logotype (Figure 14–14).

A *trademark* is a word, term, name, number, symbol, letter, pictorial device, or any combination of these adopted and used by a manufacturer or merchant to identify the source of the goods and distinguish them from those manufactured or sold by others. Its purpose is to provide protection so the public will not be deceived by imitations. It also protects the owner of the trademark from unfair competition and the unlawful use of his or her property. There may be a number of pastry products, for example, but Pop Tart pastries come only from Kellogg.

When Saul Bass was given the AT&T project, the program was

structured into five phases of work, ranging from the initial situation analysis to the development of a new trademark system along with its various applications and the control documents that would help implement and maintain the program. The sheer physical size of the task was extraordinary. It was, in fact, one of the largest *corporate identification programs* ever undertaken, consuming many years and many millions of dollars of work. By 1976 the entire Bell System fleet displayed the new identification. By 1980 Bell System building identification and signage encompassed the exterior and interior designs of more than 30,000 buildings, and the implementation of the program was still going on.

Before the program was unveiled to the public, a research study determined that 70 percent of the American public knew that the old Bell symbol stood for AT&T. Three years later the recognition factor had grown to over 90 percent—making the new Bell symbol more universally recognized than any other American trademark.

Trademark terminology

In additional to trademarks, there are trade names, service marks, trade characters, certification marks, and collective marks. We shall discuss each of these briefly.

Trademarks and brands

A *trademark* or *brand* is a word or words such as Bell System or a symbol such as the bell for AT&T's products. It identifies one particular product or line of products from a single source. Products may also have more than one trademark, such as Coke and Coca-Cola.

Trade name

A *trade name* identifies the name under which a company does business. Two common examples are Maxim (brand name) for General Foods (trade name) and Cadillac (brand name) for General Motors (trade name).

In some instances, a company may use the same trade name and trademark, for example, Quaker Oats for the Quaker Oats Company. A *house mark* is a trademark used on all or most of the products emanating from a particular company, as, for example, Nabisco.

Service mark

When a service is being identified rather than a product, the name or symbol is known as a *service mark*. For example, the Greyhound dog identifies services rendered by the Greyhound Corporation.

Trade characters

Betty Crocker, the Green Giant, Tony the Tiger, Aunt Jemina, the Marlboro man, Chiquita, and the Pillsbury dough boy are all famous examples of *trade characters* (Figure 14–15). They can be people, birds, animals, or other objects that may or may not also be applied to the goods as a trademark. Trade characters are used because they identify sources of products or businesses more readily. They catch attention and sustain interest. (See the Ad Lab.)

Certification mark

Certificate marks guarantee origin, grade, or quality. Teflon II, for example, certifies that cookware treated with Teflon nonstick coating meets Du Pont manufacturing standards. Cookware manufacturers therefore may use the mark in advertising if their products are treated with Teflon nonstick coating.

Collective mark

Collective marks are used to indicate membership in an organization. Members of the National Association of Electrical Contractors, for instance, may use the NECA symbol in their advertising.

Figure 14–15 Trade characters such as the Green Giant and Chiquita are lifelike creatures and become known as symbols for the products they represent.

Importance of trademarks

Why is the trademark system so important? The United States Trademark Association (USTA) lists these seven reasons:[7]

1. *Encourages market competition.* Market and merchandise competition in America depends on the ability of competing producers to identify their goods and services. Without trademarks to differentiate the source of one product from another, an important incentive to offer superior quality is lost.
2. *Fixes responsibility.* Trademarks act as a major deterrent to care less manufacturing. Dissatisfied consumers can instantly identify products that fail to live up to claims or expected standards of quality.
3. *Stimulates innovation.* Continuous new-product development in a free society requires a trademark system to guarantee the innovator that his or her goods can be recognized and rewarded if they prove successful.
4. *Low costs.* The economics of mass production and mass distribution depend on trademarks to develop and hold large markets. Without trademarks, cost-saving distribution techniques such as self-service supermarket merchandising would be impaired. Nor would producers have the confidence of repeat sales to package products at the rate of millions of units per week.
5. *Saves consumer time.* Fast product identification saves valuable time for consumers. The average American food shopper spends only 30 minutes per week selecting 50 different products on a typical trip to the supermarket.
6. *Gives consumers a choice.* Trademarks make it possible for consumers to tell one product from another, choose their favorites, and reject the brands they don't like.
7. *Creates foreign markets.* American companies' foreign trade has a major role in building the U.S. economy. Trademarks make it pos-

Bringing up Betty

"She's an all-American girl with blue eyes. She's a good cook, a good administrator, a good mother, civic-minded, she's good at everything." So Jerome Ryan, the artist of a recent portrait of the world's most famous cake baker, describes Betty Crocker.

Over 70,000 visitors to the Betty Crocker Kitchens in Minneapolis learn every year that their favorite maker of frosting, super-moist cakes, muffins, and nearly 130 other products is fictional. "They react like children finding out about Santa Claus." says General Mills food publicist Claudia Regan.

Betty, as she is known to her artists and publicists, was born in 1921. Gold Medal Flour had run an ad that featured a jigsaw puzzle of a flour delivery at a corner store. Readers pasted down the completed picture to win a cookbook. The response was so large "they decided not to use the name of some researcher to answer the letters," Regan says.

Whence B.C.? William G. Crocker was a popular, recently retired director of the Washburn Crosby Company (later swallowed by General Mills). The first Minneapolis flour mill had been called Crocker. The name Betty was also popular and suggested warmth.

Home bakers heard Betty before they saw her. In 1924, the Betty Crocker "Cooking School of the Air" became the first daytime radio food service program. It continued for 24 years, with over 1 million registrations from listeners who received recipes.

Betty's grandmotherly features did not grace cake boxes, however, until her 25th birthday in 1936, when Washburn commissioned a portrait from artist Neysa McMein. The features of several Home Service Department members served for the composite likeness that remained in use for almost 20 years.

But as the market changed, so did Betty. General Mills began selling more and more convenience foods, which were aimed at the younger women who would use them. In 1955, the company invited six artists—among them Norman Rockwell—to paint a new portrait, and asked 1,600 women to pick their favorite. Illustrator Hilda Taylor's Betty was deemed the best.

In 1965 and 1968, artist Joe Bowler updated Betty, making her younger and more sophisticated. In 1972, Minneapolis illustrator Jerome Ryan, who had painted all the U.S. Presidents for the backs of General Mills cereal boxes, was asked to paint a new portrait. "I didn't think Betty should be too beautiful," Ryan says. "Bowler's was a slightly executive type, very polished. My Betty is more Midwestern and homespun. She's taller than his—about 5'8"—older and less slick. Bowler's eyes were exotic—curved upward on the outside. Mine fall downward a little on the outside corners, enough to keep her from looking like a real swisher."

Her hair, however, was a sticky problem. Mercedes Bates, head of the Kitchens, was given a hand in modeling the new Betty, since she had to live with large reproductions of the portrait all over her office. Betty's outfit had already been decided. She would wear a trademark red David Crystal suit and a Monet pin, both made by subsidiaries of General Mills.

"Mercedes took the model and had a wig made," Ryan says. "It was a matronly hairdo that didn't please me particularly. I would've softened the hair, shortened it, had a nice cap of curls, but I would not have swept it off the forehead. She looks 35 or 40, and I wanted her to look younger. The character was left completely up to me, but a part of my contract [which included a clause forbidding Ryan to reveal the identity of either of his models, one for the face and one for the eyes] was that it would be photographically painted, so those people who knew nothing about art would think it was a real person."

Publicist Regan disagrees. "We always make clear that she's not real. She doesn't sign letters. We don't personalize her or imply that she's responsible for the quality of the products."

Betty was changed again in 1980 so that her hairstyle and dress reflected the changing lifestyle of America's consumers. This version incorporates the features of the 1965 face with softened, more casual coiffure and clothing.

Laboratory applications

1. How would you compare the attributes of Betty Crocker with other trade characters currently used in the food field?
2. What do you feel are the benefits of using a trade character in food advertising?

A.

1936

B.

1955

C.

1965

D.

1968

E.

1972

F.

1980

sible for American producers to create worldwide markets for their products.

Source of trademarks and brand names

The company's marketing or research department is often called on to develop a name for a new product or a new name for an old product. Here are some ways in which names are invented.

Personal names

One of the most common ways of labeling your product is by naming it after yourself: Gerber baby foods, Hershey chocolate, Ford automobile. Problems occur, however, because people have similar names. They can be easily copied and it can be difficult to stop someone else from using his own name on his products (Figure 14–16).

Names can also be invented: Betty Crocker, Mr. Clean, Buster Brown. Often a mystique is built around a name. Betty Crocker has the reputation for getting things done right in the kitchen.

Mythical and historical figures have often had their names commercialized, as in the cases of Lincoln and Ajax.

Geographic names

If a geographic name is used in an arbitrary manner, it may function as a trademark. However, if it identifies a product's place of origin or suggests where the product may have come from, it may not function as a trademark.

Coined or invented names

Standard Oil of New Jersey spent more than $125 million in one year to change its name. The company replaced the three names it had used, Humble, Esso, and Enco (each in a different part of the country), and adopted a coined word, Exxon, as its new trademark and trade name.

The most distinctive names are often coined or invented. Kodak was coined by George Eastman because he wanted a name beginning and ending with an infrequently used letter. Kleenex and Xerox are two other examples. They have an advantage because they are short, pronounceable, and arbitrary. It's unlikely others will use anything similar.

When Exxon chose its name, the company decided they wanted something no longer than four or five letters. With the use of a computer, they developed a list of 10,000 coined words, which was finally narrowed to half a dozen. The remaining names were then tested in more than 100 languages to make sure that they didn't mean anything offensive or ridiculous. This search, which lasted more than three years and involved personal interviews of more than 7,000 persons throughout the world, ultimately led to the word Exxon as the best choice.

Initials and numbers

Some of the more common examples are IBM computers, RCA televisions, J&B scotch, 7-11 stores, and A-1 steak sauce.

Company name

The company name is sometimes used also as a brand name—for example, Texaco, Gulf, Shell.

The Curse of Benjamin Franklin Goodrich: His Name.

It's one of fate's cruel accidents that our biggest competitor's name turns out to be almost identical to our founder's.

Goodyear. Goodrich.

Awfully confusing. Especially since Goodyear has advertised more than we have.

The fact is, we even think a lot of people who've seen our ads have come away remembering their name. Just because they've seen it so often.

Sure, we could change our name. But we'd rather do ads like this to clear up the confusion.

Because we like our name.

We're proud of it.

After all, B. F. Goodrich introduced pneumatic passenger tires way back in 1896, not Goodyear. It was B. F. Goodrich who was first to introduce the tubeless tire for automobiles, too, back in 1947. And in 1965, B. F. Goodrich introduced the first American-made radial tire. For five years, nationally, our radial is the only tire we've advertised.

Why?

Because the radial is the biggest tire innovation in nearly a quarter century, that's why.

No conventional tire we've ever made, none, stops as fast, corners as well, and lasts as long as our Goodrich Lifesaver Steel Radial.

It's the result of our company's commitment, for ten years, to make the most advanced radial on the road.

Now, ever since the Goodrich company started, things we believed about tires have had a funny way of ending up being things everybody believed.

Even Goodyear.

You watch. We're almost certain that before too long, you'll see Goodyear advertising a steel radial, too. Along with all their other tires.

Old B. F. would be mighty proud.

Lifesaver® Steel Radials.

B.F.Goodrich
America's Premier Radial Tire Maker

If you want Goodrich, you'll just have to remember Goodrich.

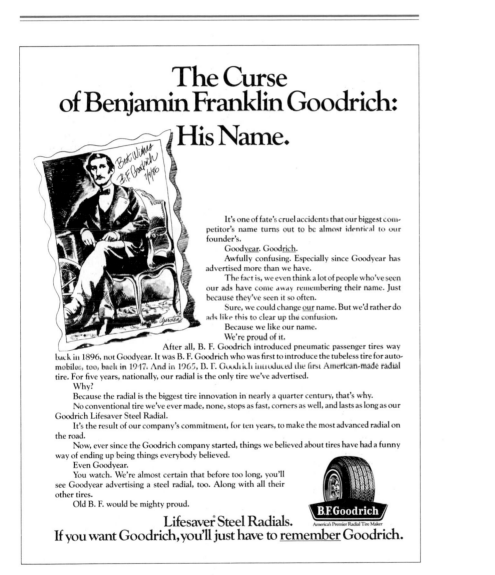

Figure 14–16 Goodrich has had an identity problem for years because of confusion with Goodyear. Recently, they have taken advantage of this confusion to position themselves against their big competitor. By poking fun at themselves, they've been able to gain attention, recognition, and memorability. But that has been a hard way to get it.

Foreign words

Perfume companies often use French words to project an image of romance (Vol De Nuit). Auto manufacturers use foreign words to add mystery and intrigue: Cordova, Biarritz.

Licensed names

Sometimes manufacturers license names for their marketability: Snoopy toothbrushes, Mickey Mouse watches. The prices are often steep, and the use of the name is subject to tight restrictions.

Dictionary words

Some of the most successful products have dictionary names: Tide detergent, Whirlpool appliances, Arrow shirts.

Arbitrary marks are dictionary words that have nothing to do with product identification and are more easily protected than words that have some relationship to the product. Examples of arbitrary marks are Cheer detergent and Camel cigarettes. Cars are often given names of animals: Mustang, Cougar.

Guidelines for creating trademarks

A trademark should be distinctive rather than commonplace. The purpose of the trademark is to distinguish and identify the source of the product. A distinctive trademark will accomplish that objective. Why adopt a mark like Gold, Royal, National, American, or Acme when others may be using the same name?

A trademark should be simple, crisp, short, and pleasant sounding. A trademark needs to be remembered to be effective. Think of Ritz crackers, Coors beer. To prevent confusion, the name should be spelled so that it can be pronounced only one way. Baume Bengue was changed to Ben Gay for just that reason.

A trademark should be appropriately designed. The mark should be adaptable for use in all media.

A trademark should have no unpleasant connotations. It should work in all countries and among all segments of society. If the trademark can be punned unpleasantly here or abroad it should be avoided.

A trademark may imply the satisfaction of a need. Pamper disposable diapers, Halo shampoo, Mum deodorant, and Eveready batteries are examples of such trademarks.

A trademark should be easy to spell, to learn, to read, to write, to recognize, to pronounce, and to remember. To associate the mark with the source of the goods, you must be able to remember it. Note how quickly Gleem toothpaste and Cheerios cereal come to mind.

A trademark should have attention value. Since there are approximately 10,000 products in a supermarket screaming for consumer action, your name has to be heard over 9,999 other loud voices.

A trademark should be international. Often companies expand rapidly. As they grow into the international market, they tend to be tied with the United States. Uniroyal had this problem as U.S. Rubber before the company changed its name. IBM, on the other hand, never had this problem.

A trademark should not describe the product or one of its characteristics. Suppose you were making a brand of coffee that was green because of its bean composition. To use the word *green* in your trademark would be a mistake, because anyone else making coffee with a similar appearance could then use the word *green* to describe its product.

A trademark should not be confusing or deceptive. The Patent and Trademark Office refuses to register trademarks that are confusingly similar to previously registered marks. Use of a trademark has also been enjoined by the courts because of deceptive similarity to a prior mark (Figure 14–17).

Red Cross Shoes was sued by the American Red Cross to enjoin its use of Red Cross as a trademark. The mark was temporarily changed to Gold Cross, but the company finally won the right to market its shoes under the name it had used for 50 years—as long as they included a suitable disclaimer in their ads.

The Holiday Inn motel chain failed in preventing another company from using Holiday Out as a trademark for a campground.

If you want to register a trademark, there are simple procedures to follow. Of course, just registering a trademark does not mean you own it. Trademark rights come from continuous proper use and protection.

A trademark registration can be obtained from the U.S. Patent and Trademark Office, which registers thousands of marks each year.

There are attorneys who specialize in trademark law. Such an attorney should be consulted to determine whether a newly created trademark infringes on anyone else's trademark.

Once the trademark is registered, registration should be indicated by printing under it (usually in smaller type), "Registered U.S. Patent and Trademark Office," or the abbreviation, "Reg. U.S. Pat. & T.M. Off." The symbol ® is also used to indicate registration. Registration may be sought in foreign countries as well as in the United States if the product is going to be exported or produced overseas.

A trademark name should always be set in capital letters or other distinguishing type. It should be affixed to the product or its container.

A trademark should be used in a consistent form. If the public develops an abbreviation such as Coke for Coca-Cola, it should be used and registered as a separate and additional brand name.

Importance of protecting trademarks

Ownership of a trademark can be lost for many reasons, or it can be abandoned voluntarily. International Harvester once owned some 250 trademarks, of which only 60 are kept current. Some are lost through neglect or improper assignment.

Probably the most bitter and spectacular method of losing a trademark comes in court decisions that declare the trademark "generic," which means the term has come into common use and is now the

Figure 14–17 **Trademarks in conflict**

Mark of successful party	Product	Name	Product
AWAKE	Frozen concentrate for imitation orange juice	ARISE	Liquid breakfast drink
BEER NUTS	Shelled and salted peanuts	BEER POTATO CHIPS	Potato chips
BIG BOY	Stick candy	BIG BOY!	Powder for soft drinks
BY GEORGE	Men's toiletries	GEORGE V	Toilet water
CONDITION	Beauty pack treatment for hair	CURL AND CON-DITION	Permanent waving lotion
CORVETTE	Automobile	VETTE	Fiberglass repair panels for automobiles
DUMPMASTER	Lifting mechanism for true dumping	TRASHMASTER	Heavy-duty vehicles
KENTUCKY FRIED CHICKEN COR-PORATION	Restaurants	OLD KENTUCKY HOME FRIED CHICKEN, INC.	Restaurants
MISTOMETER	Metered dose dispensers	METER MIST	Preparation for asthma
OCEAN FREEZE	Frozen seafood	SEA FREEZE	Frozen seafood
Q-TIPS	Swabs made of sanitary absorbent cotton	QUICK TIPS	Manicure finishing spray
VANISH	Toilet bowl cleaner	BANISH	Room deodorant
WHOPPER and HOME OF THE WHOPPER	Burger-type sandwiches and drive-in restaurant services	WHOPPABURGER	Sandwiches

dictionary name for the product. Advertising's very success may sometimes prove to be its failure. This is precisely what has happened to famous brand names like Thermos. They have become so thoroughly identified with a useful article or common function that the public uses them as the generic name. Whenever a trademark ceases to indicate that the product derives from one particular source, exclusive legal rights to it are in jeopardy. Among marks that have been lost are shredded wheat, yo yo, cube steak, and trampoline. The same fate may befall Scotch Tape and Formica, which are currently battling in the courts to keep their brand names exclusive.

Owners of most trademarks take particular care to prevent their marks from becoming generic (Figure 14–18). They always see that the trademark is distinguished from surrounding words and always followed by the generic name of the product (Glad disposable trash bags, Kleenex tissues, Jell-O brand gelatin). They never refer to the trademark in the plural. It is not three Kleenexes but three Kleenex tissues. They never use their trademark in the possessive form.

"But Mr. Carruthers, you said you needed forty Xeroxes."
Mr. Carruthers used our name incorrectly. That's why he got 40 Xerox copiers, when what he really wanted was 40 copies made on his Xerox copier.
He didn't know that Xerox, as a trademark of Xerox Corporation, should be followed by the descriptive word for the particular product, such as "Xerox duplicator" or "Xerox copier."
And should only be used as a noun when referring to the corporation itself.
If Mr. Carruthers had asked for 40 copies or 40 photocopies made on his Xerox copier, he would have gotten exactly what he wanted.
And if you use Xerox properly, you'll get exactly what you want, too.
P.S. You're welcome to make 40 copies or 40 photocopies of this ad. Preferably on your Xerox copier.
XEROX

Figure 14–18 Xerox advertises in order to protect its trade name and trademark.

Summary

Packaging can give a company the competitive edge in getting customers' attention and dollars. The package should help sell the product by identifying the brand to current users and attempt to convince nonusers to try it for the first time. The five key functions of packaging are (1) containment and protection, (2) identification, (3) convenience, (4) consumer appeal, and (5) economy.

More money is spent on packaging than on advertising primarily because of increasing emphasis on self-service. This requires the package to play an important role in both advertising and selling.

Packaging encompasses the physical appearance of the container and includes design, color, shape, labeling, and materials. Factors that should be considered in packaging design are (1) how the package communicates verbally and nonverbally, (2) the prestige desired, and (3) the stand-out appeal required.

Packaging specialists assist advertisers and their agencies. They may be found in consulting firms, company design departments, and container manufacturers.

Package design is often changed because of a desire to (1) align the package more closely with the product's marketing strategy, (2) emphasize the product's benefits, (3) emphasize the product's name, or (4) take advantage of new materials.

Visual and psychological tests are frequently used to test packages against competitors and with alternative designs. Devices used for visual testing include a tachistoscope, angle meter, blur meter, and polariscope. Psychological testing uses projective techniques.

Packagers must also be concerned about the environment. Although packaging accounts for less than 15 percent of all solid wastes, many packagers are involved in recycling and waste disposal programs. Restrictive legislation has made it necessary in some cases for packagers to use alternative materials.

The Fair Packaging and Label Act of 1966 makes it possible for consumers to get accurate information about the quality of a package's contents and to compare its values with those of other products. The Food and Drug Administration regulates the contents and labeling of packages of food, drugs, and cosmetics. The Federal Trade Commission also has jurisdiction over the packaging of consumer products and has instigated rules to prevent misrepresentation on packaging.

A vital part of a product's package is the label that gives the name of the product and the manufacturer. Labels serve several important functions: (1) identification and information, (2) dislosure of ingredients, (3) instructions on product use, and (4) persuasion and motivation.

Trademarks, trade names, service marks, trade characters, certification marks, and collective marks are devices available for advertisers to create an individual identity for themselves. Owners of trademarks are careful to prevent their marks from becoming generic. A trademark should be distinguished from surrounding words by capitalizing all its letters; it should be followed by the generic name of the product. It should never be referred to in the plural nor should it ever be used in the possessive form.

Questions for review

1. What are the five functions of packaging? Describe each.
2. Why is there an increasing emphasis on packaging today?
3. What are the most important factors to consider in designing a package?
4. What are packaging specialists? What role do they play in packaging? Where can such specialists be located?
5. What are the major reasons for a package to be redesigned?
6. What are some instruments used to test packages among consumers?
7. What are the most important provisions of the Fair Packaging and Label Act of 1966?
8. What functions do labels play in product marketing?
9. Define the following:
   a. Trademark.
   b. Trade name.
   c. Service mark.
   d. Trade characters.
   e. Certification mark.
   f. Collective mark.
10. Why is the trademark system so important?

Part V

Advertising

Media

Spreading the WORD

15

Media planning and selection

The market for cameras in the United States had historically been split between amateur and serious photographers. Until the mid-1970s the amateur market was the target for inexpensive snapshot cameras, among them the 110 "pocket" cameras and the Kodak and Polaroid "instant" cameras. These were advertised via mass media to the broad range of amateur snapshot consumers, while the more expensive 35-mm cameras were advertised predominantly in photo magazines to the small specialized market of serious and professional photographers.

In 1975 the tiny Japanese optics maker, Canon, had gone through hard times but was on its way to becoming a billion-dollar, diversified, precision instrument concern. However, it still lagged behind the other well-known 35-mm camera manufacturers in U.S. sales. These were Minolta, Olympus, and Pentax. In 1976 the Japanese camera maker introduced its new fully automatic AE-1 single-lens reflex (SLR) camera and made a historic shift in marketing strategy.

Less than 10 percent of U.S. consumers owned 35-mm cameras. Canon realized that the market was wide open for an aggressive marketing approach. Research showed that 80 percent of the people who buy SLR cameras are upscale, college-educated men between the ages of 18 and 45. Most are married and about half have children. Canon felt this group would make an ideal market for the new automatic camera if they could just see how easy it was to operate.

Canon decided to use network television to introduce its new product to the masses. Hiring Grey Advertising in New York to create the campaign, Canon spent a modest \$1.5 million in prime-time TV in the fourth quarter of 1976, just in time for Christmas. With tennis pro John Newcomb as the spokesman, Grey used the theme, "The Canon AE-1 is so advanced it's simple." Consumers could see the camera demonstrated, step by step, right on their TV screens in live action sequences that no form of print advertising had paralleled. The results were immediately successful.

In 1977 Canon increased its television spending to \$3 million, with heavy emphasis in the spring and fall months. Magazine spending likewise rose to \$1.7 million. In 1978 the total budget shot up to \$9.6 million with over \$6 million of that in network and spot TV. The magazine lineup, which was handled by Dentsu Advertising, but reflected the TV campaign, included regular insertions in leading consumer magazines with heavy male readership. These included *Time, Newsweek, Playboy, Sports Illustrated, Road and Track, Skiing, Golf, Tennis,* and *Esquire.*

The TV scheduling included heavy sports programming such as Monday Night Football and the World Series. Leading sports personalities such as Peggy Fleming, Jean-Claude Killy, Ben Crenshaw, and Tracy Austin (Figure 15–1) were hired to show how simple the AE-1 was to operate, even for a novice photographer.

To top it all off, Canon joined the host of other manufacturers sponsoring the Winter Olympics in 1980 by becoming the official camera of the games. The Lake Placid logo was used in all advertisements, and a special series of corporate Olympic ads featuring the whole Canon line was created.

The success of Canon's media plan was evidenced by the fact that within a year, Canon came from behind and took over the 35-mm sales lead. Immediately the other manufacturers jumped into the fray with new product introductions and hefty television buying. Network TV spending ballooned from $5 million in 1977 to $15.6 million in 1978. Spot TV rose from $5.6 million to $10.9 million in the same period. The next year total TV spending for 35-mm cameras exploded to $50 million.

By 1978 Minolta was the largest TV spender. But a year later they were still $50 million behind Canon in sales.[1] According to one of the biggest camera dealers in New York, Canon was still "outselling all other 35-mm cameras by far."[2] In three short years they had captured a 32 percent share of the market. And by 1979 their sales had swelled to 2.9 million units.

In short, Canon had scored a huge marketing success, not so much because of what people usually call advertising creativity, but because of extraordinary media planning and selection. The decisions made in media planning frequently involve as much creativity as the decisions made by senior art directors and copywriters. As we shall see in this chapter, media decisions, like good art and copy ideas, are based on sound marketing principles and research as well as experience and intuition.

Media planning

Each medium—newspapers, magazines, radio, television, direct mail, outdoor, transit advertising, and others—has unique capabilities (Figure 15–2). Each also has unique audience characteristics. The advertiser and agency must *plan* which media to use to convey their message to the consumers identified as the target audience. Then the task of the media planner is to *select* from those media the particular radio stations, TV programs, newspapers, etc., that will reach the target audience most effectively. The media function, therefore, involves two basic processes: media planning and media selection.

Media decisions are made in a larger marketing and advertising framework. Within this framework, we shall examine how a media plan is developed, what terms are used to express media objectives, and what alternative media strategies are available to the advertiser. Finally, we shall analyze the criteria used to select particular media vehicles, schedule the appearance of advertisements and commercials, and measure the relative effectiveness of one medium over another.

Role of media in the marketing framework

As we discussed in Chapters 6 and 9, advertising is a promotional activity, and promotion is just one of the four Ps that companies may use to achieve their marketing objectives. The others are product, price, and place.

Canon®

PRODUCT: CANON AE-1 "TRACY AUSTIN" :30 GREY ADVERTISING INC.

1. TRACY: I'm tennis pro Tracy Austin.

2. PHOTOGRAPHER: I'm pro photographer Arthur Grace.

3. TRACY: To some I'm still a school girl.

4. To others, I'm a tough competitor.

5. PHOTOGRAPHER: My Canon AE-1 captures the two Tracy Austins. (CLICK)

6. The telephoto lens

7. shows how hard she works. (CLICK)

8. The portrait lens shows how soft she is. (CLICK)

9. Here, your turn, Tracy.

10. ANNCR: The AE-1 makes it easy

11. to shoot like a pro. (CLICK)

12. The incomparable Canon AE-1. So advanced -- it's simple.

Figure 15–1

Figure 15–2 Advertising volume in the United States

($ millions, 1980)

Medium	Volume: Share	Volume: Total	Percent of share	Percent of total
Newspapers				
Local	13,188	15,541	85	28
National	2,353		15	
Television				
Network	5,130	11,366	45	21
Spot	3,269		29	
Local	2,967		26	
Direct mail		7,596		14
Magazines				
Business	1,674	4,953	34	9
Weeklies	1,418		29	
Monthlies	949		19	
Women's	782		16	
Farm	130		2	
Radio				
Local	2,823	3,777	75	7
Spot	774		20	
Network	180		5	
Outdoor				
National	390	600	65	1
Local	210		35	
Miscellaneous				
National	5,670	10,767	53	20
Local	5,097		47	
Total				
National	30,315	54,600	55	100
Local	24,285		45	

By the time Canon made the decision to try television advertising, it was already exercising a very new marketing plan with major changes in the product and price elements. The new, inexpensive Canon AE-1 automatic single-lens reflex camera was a great departure from the bigger, more complex, and more expensive 35-mm cameras of the past. In developing the marketing plan for this new product, Canon analyzed the marketing situation, determined realistic marketing objectives, and developed a unique marketing strategy.

Marketing objectives and strategy

Before media planning can begin, the marketing objectives for the product, brand, or service must be precisely determined by the advertiser and the agency. These may include a decision to expand the market for the product—by advertising 35-mm cameras not only to serious photographers but also to hobbyists. The marketer may seek to extend distribution into new geographic markets or income groups. Or the objectives may be to resell current users—by advertising a camera with "new, more advanced" capabilities to current camera owners.

Consider the risk that was involved for Canon. Less than 10 percent of the people in the United States owned a 35-mm camera. To most marketers that would indicate little interest in the product class and would discourage them from considering any mass marketing techniques. Obviously, at some point, some optimistic person at Canon looked at those figures in reverse and said, "If only 10 percent of the people have a 35-mm camera, then we still have 90 percent of the market that we can sell to. What a wonderful opportunity!" That was right. But in another situation it might have been wrong.

Consider the other related risks. How much would it cost to develop a new, untried camera for the small market that then existed? How would a lower priced camera fare in a market that was used to paying high prices for high quality? How much would it cost to manufacture enough of these untried cameras to make it profitable even if they did sell well? How would camera retailers accept these new 35-mm cameras that sold for less and gave them less profit? Would the beginning photographer pay even that much for his or her first camera?

All these questions had to be answered satisfactorily before marketing objectives or a marketing strategy could be developed. Once that was accomplished, advertising objectives could be determined and advertising strategies considered.

Advertising strategy

In Chapter 9, "Marketing and Advertising Planning," we described the advertising strategy as the manner in which the advertiser uses the elements of the creative mix. Those elements are: (1) the product concept, (2) the target audience, (3) the communications media, and (4) the advertising message. How did Canon combine these elements?

Canon's plan targeted a whole new market—upscale men between the ages of 18 and 45, amateur photographers buying their first or second cameras, upper income, active, educated, and family-oriented, for whom good photography would be a useful, enjoyable recreational activity. This was definitely a large, mass market and a new target audience for 35-mm camera advertising. This audience would be offered not just a new product but also a new product concept—a camera that offered ease and simplicity of operation, like the pocket cameras, along with the historic, professional quality of 35-mm cameras.

The price would be new, too—higher than the pocket cameras to be sure, but less than other 35-mm cameras and still affordable.

The message strategy was to be authoritative and positive, almost dogmatic, and as simple as the camera: "The Canon AE-1 is so advanced it's simple." And this would be demonstrated by well-known, believable personalitites who were not professional photographers.

By this time the media choice appeared obvious. A mass market, the ability to demonstrate in live action, the audience desired, and the opportunity to tie in to relevant sporting events all dictated using television as the mainstay of the media plan with the support of special-interest magazines. How this media plan was developed depended, like a marketing or advertising plan, on two things: objectives and strategy.

Defining media objectives

Development of the media plan begins with determining the primary target audiences and then setting goals for communicating with those audiences.

Target audience

In the initial stages of marketing planning the target market should be defined. Similarly defining the target audience is an essential step in determining media objectives and strategy, since the whole media effort is wasted if the right people are not exposed to the ads in the campaign.

As we shall see in the section on media selection and scheduling, media vehicles are selected based on how well they "deliver" an audience that closely parallels the described target audience. The advertiser is always concerned about wasting dollars by reaching consumers who are less likely to need or buy the product, or who are not important buying influences.

Research organizations that measure the size of various media audiences usually provide some breakdown of the demographic composition of a particular medium's audience. Audience data are usually segmented by area of residence as well as by sex and age. In addition, for most major media information is available on income, family size, and educational levels of the audience. This will be described more fully in the section on media selection and scheduling.

How media objectives are expressed

After the target market is defined, specific objectives may be set. These should be stated precisely so that, once the plan is under way, the results can be measured against the objectives. Sissors and Petray suggest that the purpose is to translate marketing objectives into goals that media can accomplish (Figure 15–3). Media objectives are often expressed in terms of reach, frequency, impressions, gross rating points, and continuity.

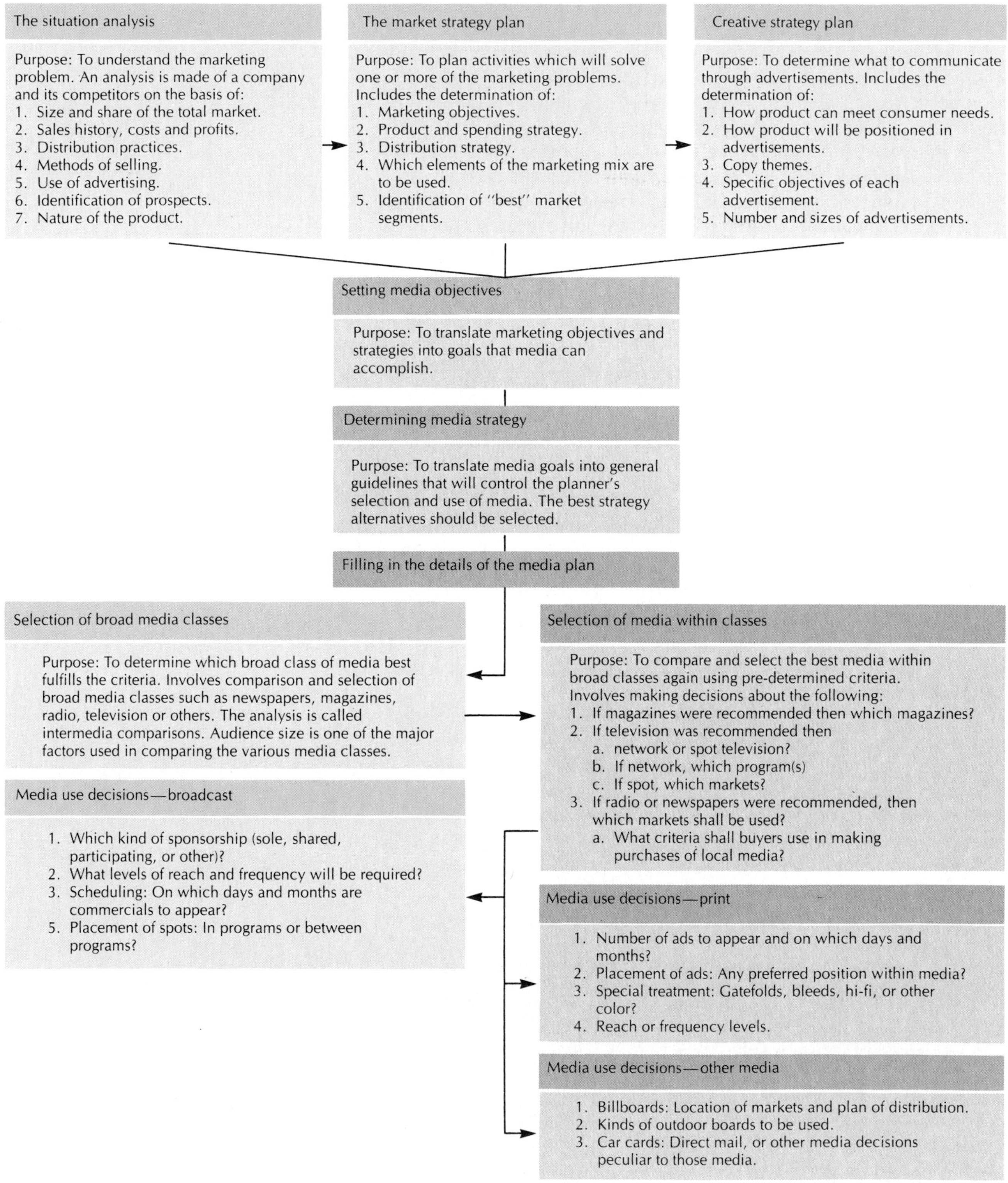

The situation analysis

Purpose: To understand the marketing problem. An analysis is made of a company and its competitors on the basis of:
1. Size and share of the total market.
2. Sales history, costs and profits.
3. Distribution practices.
4. Methods of selling.
5. Use of advertising.
6. Identification of prospects.
7. Nature of the product.

The market strategy plan

Purpose: To plan activities which will solve one or more of the marketing problems. Includes the determination of:
1. Marketing objectives.
2. Product and spending strategy.
3. Distribution strategy.
4. Which elements of the marketing mix are to be used.
5. Identification of "best" market segments.

Creative strategy plan

Purpose: To determine what to communicate through advertisements. Includes the determination of:
1. How product can meet consumer needs.
2. How product will be positioned in advertisements.
3. Copy themes.
4. Specific objectives of each advertisement.
5. Number and sizes of advertisements.

Setting media objectives

Purpose: To translate marketing objectives and strategies into goals that media can accomplish.

Determining media strategy

Purpose: To translate media goals into general guidelines that will control the planner's selection and use of media. The best strategy alternatives should be selected.

Filling in the details of the media plan

Selection of broad media classes

Purpose: To determine which broad class of media best fulfills the criteria. Involves comparison and selection of broad media classes such as newspapers, magazines, radio, television or others. The analysis is called intermedia comparisons. Audience size is one of the major factors used in comparing the various media classes.

Selection of media within classes

Purpose: To compare and select the best media within broad classes again using pre-determined criteria. Involves making decisions about the following:
1. If magazines were recommended then which magazines?
2. If television was recommended then
   a. network or spot television?
   b. If network, which program(s)
   c. If spot, which markets?
3. If radio or newspapers were recommended, then which markets shall be used?
   a. What criteria shall buyers use in making purchases of local media?

Media use decisions—broadcast

1. Which kind of sponsorship (sole, shared, participating, or other)?
2. What levels of reach and frequency will be required?
3. Scheduling: On which days and months are commercials to appear?
5. Placement of spots: In programs or between programs?

Media use decisions—print

1. Number of ads to appear and on which days and months?
2. Placement of ads: Any preferred position within media?
3. Special treatment: Gatefolds, bleeds, hi-fi, or other color?
4. Reach or frequency levels.

Media use decisions—other media

1. Billboards: Location of markets and plan of distribution.
2. Kinds of outdoor boards to be used.
3. Car cards: Direct mail, or other media decisions peculiar to those media.

Figure 15–3 The scope of media planning activities.

Reach *Reach* is the total number of different people or households exposed to an advertising schedule during a given time, usually four weeks. For example, if 8,000 out of 10,000 radio listeners heard the Super Soap commercials on radio stations CBA and XYZ at least once during a four-week period, then the reach was 8,000, or 80 percent of the 10,000 listeners. Reach, then, measures the *extent* of the audience exposure of a media vehicle.

Frequency *Frequency* is the total number of times an advertising message reaches the same person or household. Suppose 4,000 of the 10,000 radio listeners heard the Super Soap commercial *three* times during the four-week period, and 4,000 of the households heard it *five* times. The *average frequency* would be determined by using the following formula:

$$\begin{matrix}\text{Average}\\ \text{frequency}\end{matrix} = \frac{\text{Total exposures}}{\text{Audience reach}} = \frac{(4{,}000 \times 3) + (4{,}000 \times 5)}{8{,}000} = \frac{32{,}000}{8{,}000} = 4$$

Of the 8,000 listeners reached, the average number of exposures was four. Frequency, then, measures the *intensity* of a specific media schedule.

Impressions *Impressions* are the total number of messages delivered by a media plan. In the example above, it would be the same as *total exposures*. It is calculated by multiplying the number of people who receive a message by the number of times they receive it—in this case, 32,000. If the same schedule ran for another four weeks, what do you think would be the total number of impressions? What would be the average frequency?

Gross rating points The total weight of a specific media schedule might be expressed by counting the total number of impressions. However, today a more common method of expressing this is in *gross rating points*. They are equal to the reach, expressed as a percentage of the population, multiplied by the average frequency. In our example, 80 percent of the radio households heard the Super Soap commercial an average of four times during the four-week period. To determine the gross rating points of this radio schedule, we use the following formula:

$$\text{Reach} \times \text{Frequency} = \text{GRP} \qquad 80 \times 40 = 320 \text{ gross rating points}$$

Continuity *Continuity* is the length of time an advertising message runs over a given period. For example, the Super Soap commercial might be scheduled on radio stations CBA and XYZ for a four-week period and then sustained by occasional spot commercials on station XYZ for an additional nine weeks.

The reach, frequency, and continuity of a media plan depend on the advertiser's media budget. All budgets are limited and so are the media objectives that may be attained. It should also be understood that these objectives have an inverse relationship to one another within the limits of the budget (Figure 15–4). To achieve greater reach, some frequency must be sacrificed. Likewise, to gain greater continuity, some reach and/or frequency must be sacrificed. The goal of the media planner, therefore, is to optimize these objectives by getting enough reach, enough frequency, and the proper continuity to make the media plan work for the advertiser.

Determining the correct media objectives—that is, the best mix of reach, frequency, and continuity—is directly related to the media strategy discussed in the next section. (See the Checklist.)

Considerations in developing media strategy

The media strategy is determined by which classes of media the advertiser chooses to use and the manner in which those media are used. Should the advertiser, for example, run three commercials per week on network television for 52 weeks a year? Or should network radio be used for four weeks followed by four weeks of ads in local newspapers and national magazines? These decisions are based on a wide variety of factors, some of which we shall discuss here.

Market scope

A key strategic decision is the market scope of the media plan. Advertising should be limited to areas where the product is available.

When the product is available in only one city, a *local* plan is used. It may also be used to introduce or test-market a new product.

A *regional* plan is an extension of a local plan. It may cover several adjoining metropolitan areas, an entire state, or several neigh-

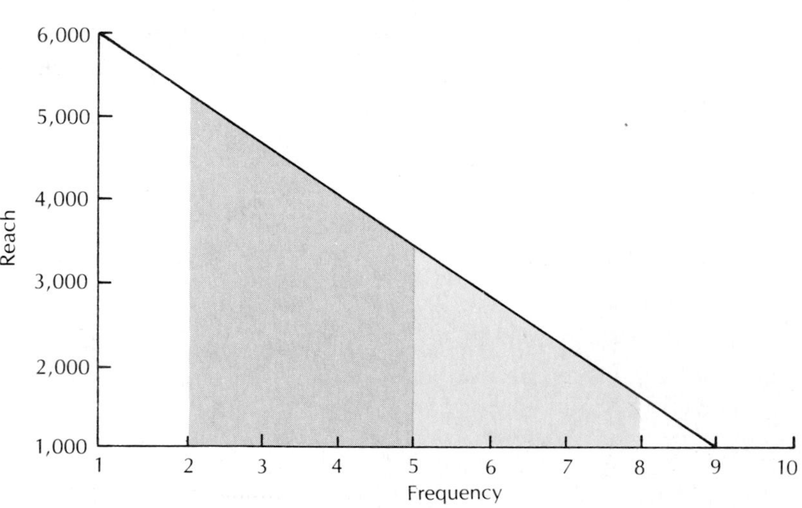

Figure 15–4 Reach and frequency have an inverse relationship to each other. For example, for the same budget, it might be possible to reach 6,000 people 2 times, 3,000 people 5.5 times, or 1,000 people 8 times.

Checklist for setting media objectives

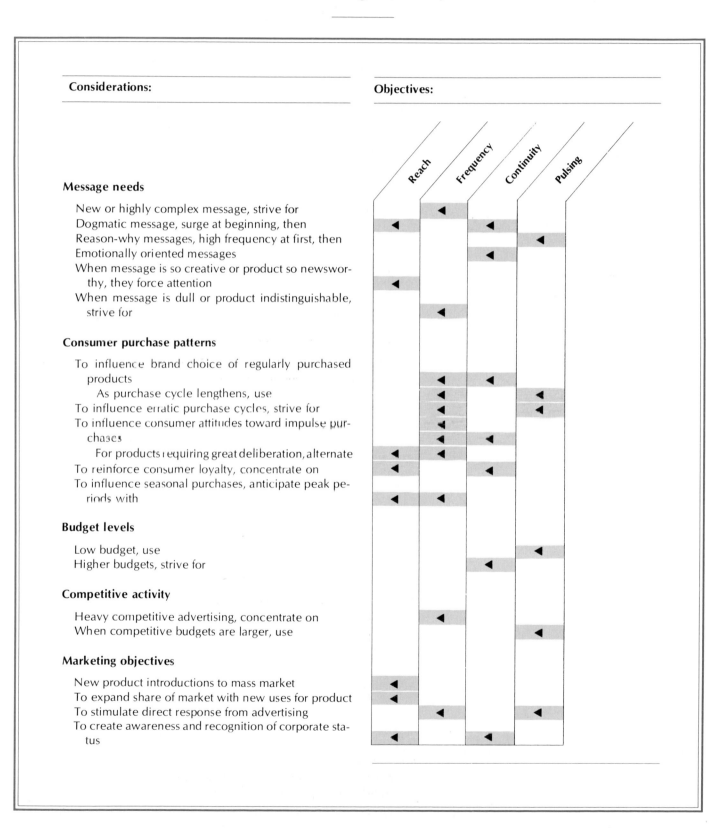

Considerations:

Objectives:

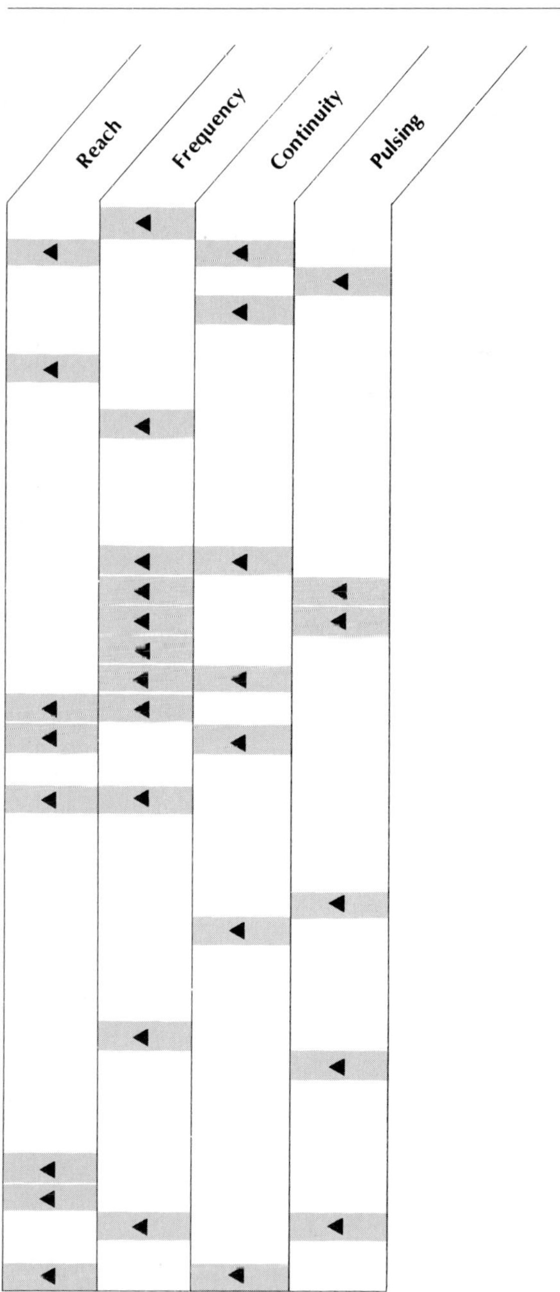

Message needs

- New or highly complex message, strive for
- Dogmatic message, surge at beginning, then
- Reason-why messages, high frequency at first, then
- Emotionally oriented messages
- When message is so creative or product so newsworthy, they force attention
- When message is dull or product indistinguishable, strive for

Consumer purchase patterns

- To influence brand choice of regularly purchased products
  - As purchase cycle lengthens, use
- To influence erratic purchase cycles, strive for
- To influence consumer attitudes toward impulse purchases
  - For products requiring great deliberation, alternate
- To reinforce consumer loyalty, concentrate on
- To influence seasonal purchases, anticipate peak periods with

Budget levels

- Low budget, use
- Higher budgets, strive for

Competitive activity

- Heavy competitive advertising, concentrate on
- When competitive budgets are larger, use

Marketing objectives

- New product introductions to mass market
- To expand share of market with new uses for product
- To stimulate direct response from advertising
- To create awareness and recognition of corporate status

boring states. Regional plans are often used to accommodate sectional differences in taste or preference that affect product sales. For example, more instant coffee is sold in the Midwest than in New England. Regional media objectives can be achieved by using local media, the regional editions of national magazines, and spot television and radio.

Advertisers who have nationwide product distribution and want to reach consumers throughout the country generally use a *national* plan. Their goal is usually to reach these prospects at the lowest cost per thousand (CPM). The media used in a national plan are usually network television, network radio, full-circulation national magazines, and nationally syndicated Sunday newspaper supplements. On the other hand, motion picture distributors may use local newspapers, tobacco companies use outdoor, and transit advertising may be used as well as direct mail. Figure 15–5 shows the media used by the 50 largest national advertisers.

The market scope might also be based on something other than geography. A selective plan might be designed to reach persons in specific income, educational, occupation, social, or ethnic groups or in certain special-interest groups, wherever they are located. The advertiser may want to reach electrical engineers or middle-income, black consumers. Or, as in the case of Canon cameras, the goal may be to reach sports enthusiasts. The media used in a selective plan may be magazines directed at specific markets, such as *Golf Digest, Popular Electronics,* or *Ebony*. Other possibilities include ethnic radio stations, direct mail, select TV programs, and special issues of Sunday newspapers devoted to specific topics.

Nature of message

Advertising messages differ in many ways. Some are very simple, dogmatic messages: "When E. F. Hutton talks, people listen." Others are based on an emotional attitude, appealing to people's need for safety, security, social approval, love, beauty, or fun: "Reach out and touch someone." Many advertisers use a reason-why approach to explain their product's advantages: "Lite. Everything you always wanted in a beer. And less." Some messages are complex, requiring considerable space or time for explanation. Others announce a new product or product concept and are therefore unfamiliar to the consuming public. In each of these circumstances, the media strategy will be considerably affected.

A message on radio or TV that is either new or highly complex, like the ad for Mobil oil, requires greater freqeuncy to be understood and remembered (Figure 15–6). A dogmatic message, like that for Bubblicious, may require a surge at the beginning to communicate the idea (Figure 15–7). Then it is usually advantageous to strive for greater reach and maintain low frequency.

Reason-why messages may be as complex to understand at first as IBM's Correcting Selectric typewriter. But once the explanation is understood, a pulsing of advertising exposures at irregular intervals is often sufficient to remind customers of the explanation (Figure 15–8).

On the other hand, emotionally oriented messages are usually more effective if spaced at regular intervals to create a continuing feeling about the product.[3]

Figure 15–5

The media expenditures of 50 leaders

(in measured media only, grouped by industries, ad dollars in thousands, 1980)

Rank		Company	Total	Percent of total dollars							
				News-papers	Genl. mags.	Farm pub.	Spot TV	Net TV	Spot radio	Net radio	Out-door
Appliances, TV, Radio	33	RCA Corp.	77,297.3	32.5	31.4	—	8.0	25.7	0.2	1.8	0.4
	35	General Electric Co.	74,296.3	16.3	22.1	—	11.3	44.4	1.9	3.7	0.3
Automobiles	4	General Motors Corp.	295,968.4	17.6	18.7	0.7	6.4	41.7	10.9	1.3	2.7
	6	Ford Motor Co.	247,310.5	9.9	14.5	1.0	12.8	50.8	7.9	2.3	0.8
	9	Chrysler Corp.	165,451.4	12.8	9.9	0.6	7.1	39.5	29.8	0.2	0.1
	34	Toyota Motor Co.	75,128.0	9.3	9.3	—	44.0	30.5	4.8	—	2.1
	49	Volkswagen of America	59,720.3	8.3	36.3	—	21.7	32.5	0.2	—	1.0
Communications, Entertainment	26	Time Inc.	79,042.6	7.9	34.5	—	48.4	6.6	0.8	1.7	0.1
	46	CBS Inc.	66,344.1	20.6	43.1	—	20.1	7.2	1.0	6.8	1.2
Drugs	28	Sterling Drug Co.	83,517.4	0.5	13.9	0.2	6.5	68.8	2.0	8.0	0.1
	38	Richardson-Vicks	59,108.4	0.4	19.0	0.5	9.4	59.6	2.1	6.7	2.3
	50	Schering-Plough Corp.	72,244.0	0.5	6.5	—	17.9	69.1	4.6	1.3	—
Food	2	General Foods Corp.	338,717.0	2.9	10.1	—	24.6	59.5	1.6	1.2	0.1
	10	General Mills	161,142.7	2.1	9.3	—	40.6	47.0	0.7	0.2	0.1
	14	McDonald's Corp.	130,862.1	—	1.8	—	54.0	41.0	0.7	0.1	2.4
	18	Dart & Kraft Inc.	122,841.5	5.4	22.4	0.6	27.1	39.2	4.5	0.9	0.5
	21	Ralston Purina Co.	114,887.7	1.9	11.8	—	17.5	63.8	4.3	—	0.1
	24	Pillsbury Co.	96,895.1	3.2	5.3	—	32.9	55.0	2.9	1.3	0.4
	25	Kellogg Co.	90,486.2	4.6	4.9	—	21.0	66.1	2.8	0.6	—
	30	Consolidated Foods	82,571.0	2.1	15.3	—	26.4	52.4	2.2	1.3	0.3
	36	Norton Simon Inc.	73,264.2	7.5	23.6	—	27.1	36.5	1.8	0.4	3.1
	37	Nestle Enterprises	72,949.6	5.5	7.1	—	35.1	49.4	1.2	1.4	0.3
	41	Quaker Oats Co.	68,575.1	1.4	13.8	—	16.4	68.0	0.4	—	—
	44	Esmark Inc.	64,819.1	3.2	13.9	—	14.2	64.6	1.9	2.1	0.1
	45	Nabisco Inc.	63,923.4	2.1	15.0	—	20.8	61.2	0.9	—	—
Gum, Candy	39	Mars Inc.	70,290.5	4.0	0.4	—	42.0	52.2	1.1	0.3	—
Retail chains	13	Sears, Roebuck & Co.	143,265.9	—	22.4	—	10.9	60.7	1.8	3.7	0.5
Soap, Cleansers (and allied)	1	Procter & Gamble Co.	545,723.2	1.4	6.8	—	24.8	66.1	0.8	—	0.1
	16	Unilever	129,329.1	1.3	11.2	—	29.8	57.3	0.2	—	0.2
	32	Colgate-Palmolive Co.	79,336.1	2.6	9.0	0.2	29.8	50.5	7.8	—	0.1
Soft drinks	11	PepsiCo Inc.	160,869.9	1.1	1.8	—	36.0	55.2	5.4	—	0.5
	15	Coca-Cola Co.	129,481.7	4.2	3.1	—	36.0	44.7	7.7	1.1	2.3

Figure 15–5 *(continued)*

Rank		Company	Total	Percent of total dollars: Newspapers	Genl. mags.	Farm pub.	Spot TV	Net TV	Spot radio	Net radio	Outdoor
Telephone service, Equipment	7	American Telephone & Telegraph Co.	180,665.6	10.6	19.1	—	28.1	31.8	6.7	3.3	0.4
	47	International Telephone & Telegraph Corp.	63,159.9	6.5	13.8	—	48.6	28.9	1.2	0.1	0.9
Tobacco	3	Philip Morris Inc.	319,594.7	24.2	24.8	—	7.1	30.5	3.5	—	9.9
	5	R. J. Reynolds Industries	294,124.1	38.5	40.3	—	2.8	3.7	0.2	—	14.5
	31	B.A.T. Industries	79,457.0	17.2	41.3	—	8.5	—	0.1	—	32.9
	40	American Brands	69,598.9	24.2	49.2	—	2.1	8.5	0.1	0.4	15.5
Toiletries, Cosmetics	8	American Home Products Corp.	180,288.2	0.8	5.2	0.3	20.2	68.7	2.9	1.9	—
	12	Bristol-Myers Co.	150,996.3	1.7	12.2	—	13.9	70.2	1.8	—	0.2
	19	Johnson & Johnson	120,409.1	4.2	15.3	0.2	4.1	75.1	0.5	0.6	—
	22	Loews Corp.	112,785.2	40.8	34.2	—	1.4	3.9	0.3	—	19.4
	23	Warner-Lambert Co.	98,202.0	2.9	5.8	—	21.7	64.3	0.1	5.0	0.2
	27	Gillette Co.	85,981.7	1.4	14.0	—	15.3	69.2	—	—	0.1
	42	Chesebrough-Pond's	68,428.7	2.8	16.6	—	8.8	71.7	0.1	—	—
	48	Revlon Inc.	61,897.9	1.1	17.7	—	36.1	40.9	1.7	2.5	—
Beer, Wine, Liquor	17	Anheuser-Busch	127,661.6	1.3	4.0	—	19.0	51.2	21.5	2.0	1.0
	20	Seagram Co.	117,339.9	15.4	60.2	—	4.6	9.6	0.3	—	9.9
	29	Heublein Inc.	82,959.3	6.1	19.8	—	21.6	36.5	7.7	—	8.3
Miscellaneous	43	U.S. Government	67,862.1	10.7	27.6	1.1	8.4	27.4	18.7	4.8	1.3

Consumer purchase patterns

As important as the nature of the message are the purchasing habits of customers for the product. Some products are purchased at very regular intervals, and the advertising function, illustrated by the brand-switching model, is to influence brand choice (Figure 15–9). If this is the case, we want to reach prospects quite regularly and especially just before they make their next purchasing decision. Situations of this type call for relatively high frequency and high continuity, depending on the length of time of the purchasing cycle. As the purchasing cycle gets longer, the pulsing of messages becomes more appropriate.

In some cases, the purchase cycle is erratic but susceptible to influence by advertising. In these situations we try to space advertising exposures, as in the purchase-cycle model, using periods of high frequency followed by periods of very low exposure (Figure 15–10). The purpose is to try to reduce the length of time between purchases.

Some products are bought on impulse and therefore require steady, high-frequency advertising. Others that are bought after great deliberation require pulsing with alternately high and low frequencies. This depends greatly on market conditions and on competitive activity.

Products with a high degree of brand loyalty can usually be served with lower levels of frequency, allowing the advertiser to achieve greater reach and continuity.

Seasonal products such as snow tires or suntan lotion require concentrated exposures just before peak buying periods.

Budget levels

As we mentioned earlier, the reach, frequency, and continuity of any media plan are greatly limited by the advertising budget. Of great importance to most small advertisers, therefore, is an understanding of how to use their budget most effectively. Generally the smaller the budget, the more pulsing is required. In this way, even with a low budget, the advertiser can sometimes attract as much attention as bigger competitors in the product class. As the budget grows larger, greater continuity can be sought by spreading advertising messages more evenly.

Mechanical considerations

Greater attention can usually be gained by running a full-color ad than by placing a black and white ad. Likewise a full-page ad attracts more attention than a quarter-page ad (Figures 15–11 and 15–12). Within the confines of limited advertising budgets, though, larger units of space or time cost dearly in terms of reach, frequency, and continuity.

Is it better for a small advertiser to run a full-page ad once a month or a quarter-page ad once a week? Should television advertisers use occasional 60-second announcements or a lot of 10-, 20-, and 30-second commercials? The answers to these questions are not simple. Some messages require more time and space to be explained. Competitive activity often dictates more message units. The nature of the product itself may demand the prestige of a full page or full color. On the other hand, the need for high frequency may demand smaller units. It is sometimes better to run several small ads consistently than to run one large ad occasionally.

Other mechanical considerations include using the preferred positions of magazine advertisements on front and back covers or sponsoring prime-time television shows. Special positions, sponsorships, and other mechanical opportunities are usually sold at a premium by the media. A full-color ad often costs twice the price of a black and white ad. Special "bleed" printing, where the advertisement extends to the edge of a page, often costs an additional 10 or 15 percent. Special inserts, gatefolds, unusual paper stocks, and consecutively numbered coupons all cost more. The media planner must therefore weigh the benefits of these extra costs in terms of the potential sales impact against the loss of reach and frequency.

Competitive strategy

Media strategy must also consider what competitive advertisers are doing, particularly if their advertising budgets are larger. The general

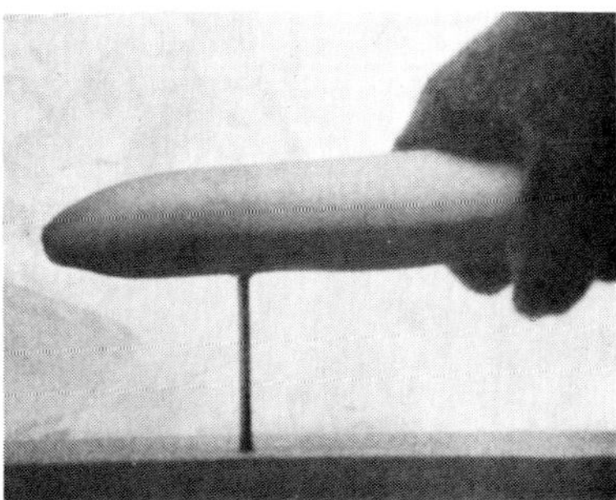

Figure 15–6

COLD WEATHER
30-second

ANNCR: (VO) at 35 degrees below zero,
this is what you can do with a banana.
This is what happens to a freshly cut rose.
And this is Premium Motor Oil.
At 35 degrees below zero,
this is what you can do with Mobil 1 Motor Oil.

MOBIL 1: The oil that saves you gas,
helps get you going,
even at 35 below.

rule is to bypass media that competitors dominate and to choose instead those that offer a strong or dominant position. An exception to this is when a campaign has such a unique creative approach that it will stand out, regardless of competitive advertising.

Merchandising factors

There must be special strategies for campaigns that feature merchandising incentives, such as cents-off coupons, introductory price reductions, premium offers, or prize contests. Such campaigns are usually designed to introduce new products, to increase sales among current users, to reinforce competitive standing, or to promote good dealer relations. An entire advertising program may be built around merchandising offers, so they require careful preparation by the media planner.

Nature of the medium

An important determinant in media strategy is the nature of the media themselves. Some media lend themselves better to certain messages than others. For an understanding of the advantages and disadvantages of each of the major media from the point of view of creative people, see the Ad Lab on page 478.

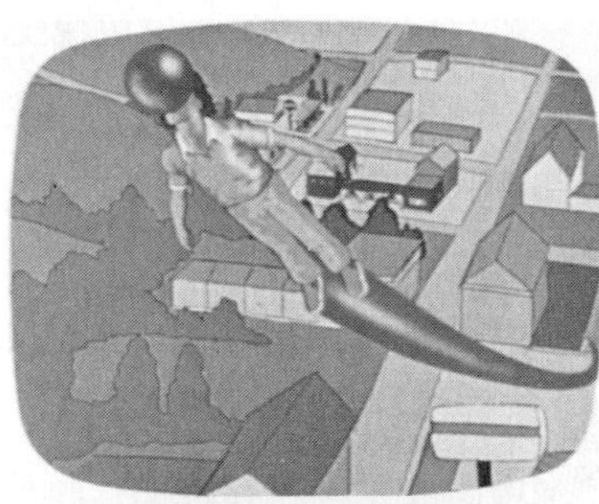

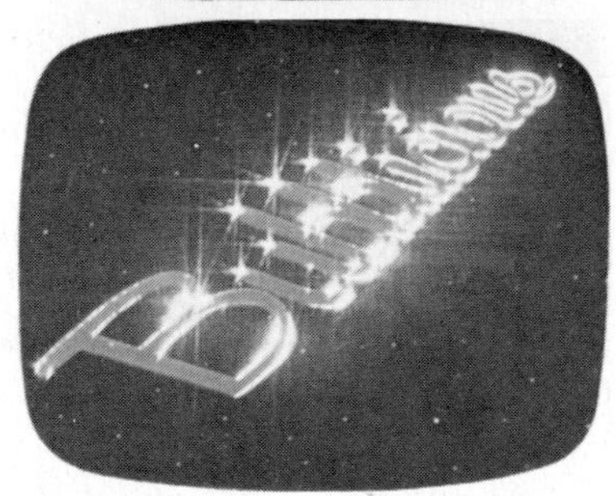

Figure 15–7

ULTIMATE BUBBLE
30-second

WHISPERED: Bubblicious.
It's the Ultimate Bubble,
Bubblicious.
(MUSIC)
SUNG: It's the Ultimate Bubble.
WHISPERED: Soft and Juicy.
SUNG: It's the Ultimate Bubble.
WHISPERED: So Delicious.
(MUSIC)
SUNG: It's the Ultimate Bubble.
(MUSIC)
SUNG: It's the Ultimate Bubble,
Bubblicious.
The Ultimate Bubble,
Bubblicious.
(MUSIC)

Stating the media strategy

A written statement of the media strategy is an integral part of any media plan. Without it, it is very difficult to analyze the logic and consistency of the overall media schedule that is recommended.

The strategy statement should not only tell what types of media will be used but also give the rationale for the choice. It should start with a brief definition of the target market, and it should outline specific reach, frequency, and continuity goals. The nature of the message should be explained as well as any related timing, merchandising, or mechanical considerations. The intended size of message units should be stated along with the effect of budget restrictions. Finally the strategy statement should provide a budget breakdown of the various types of media to be used over the period of the campaign as well as the cost of production and any collateral materials.

Media selection and scheduling

After the media strategy is developed, the task of selecting the specific media vehicles and scheduling their use falls to the media planner. In its media strategy statement, Canon decided to use sports programming to reach upscale, young men. But which sports programs should be used? Boxing? Bowling? Golf? Baseball? Football? Basketball? "Wide World of Sports"? The choices seem endless. Which golf tournaments? Which football games? Should ads also be run in horse show programs or baseball scorecards? How about an ad on the scoreboard at these events?

As always, budgets are limited. The media planner must take many factors into consideration to make the most efficient media selection and then weigh a variety of other criteria to schedule these media appropriately.

Considerations in media selection

The media planner's job is to match the right media vehicles with the right audience at the right time in the best environment and the most logical place so that the advertising message will not only achieve the desired exposure but also attract attention and motivate customers to some action. And the planner must do this with cost efficiency so that the reach, frequency, and continuity goals can be met. Therefore, in considering specific media vehicles for use, the planner studies several influencing factors: (1) campaign objectives and strategy; (2) audience size and characteristics; (3) geographic coverage; (4) attention, exposure, and motivation value of the media; (5) cost efficiency; and (6) various approaches available for media selection.

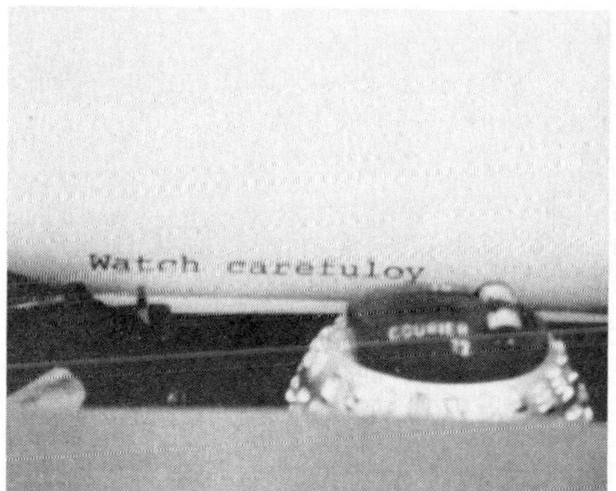

Figure 15–8

ERASING TYPEWRITER
30-second

In this IBM commercial the product speaks for itself. The only sound is that of the typewriter sending the message to the viewer and demonstrating its unique feature.

(TYPEWRITER SOUND THROUGHOUT)
Watch carefuloy.
Watch carefulo
Watch careful
Watch carefully.
See?

This typewriter
lifts off mistakes
with the touch
of a key.
The IBM Correcting
SELECTRIC Typewriter.
The typewriter
that also erases.

Campaign objectives and strategy

When the selection process begins, the media planner's first job is to review the nature of the product or service, the intended objectives and strategies that have been developed, and the primary and secondary target markets. These all influence what media he or she selects (Figure 15–13).

week	1	2	3	4	5	6	7	8	9	10	11	12	13	14	15	16	17	18	19	20	21	22
Advertising exposures			x	x x	x x x	x	x	x	x x x	x	x x	x x x	x	x x	x x x	x	x x	x x x	x	x x	x x x	
Brand X purchased	■																■					
Our brand purchased					■				■				■								■	

Figure 15–9 Brand-switching model for a four-week purchase cycle. In this cycle continuity is high and frequency is concentrated prior to normal purchase occasions. Note in week 17 that frequency was low and the brand was not purchased, perhaps due to high advertising exposure from the competition.

week	1	2	3	4	5	6	7	8	9	10	11	12	13	14	15	16	17	18	19	20	21	22	23	24	25
Advertising exposure				x x x	x x	x			x	x x	x x x	x x x	x x					x x	x x x	x x x	x x x	x x			
Normal purchase occasion	•				•	•	•						•	•								•	•		
Influenced purchase occasion				■	■	■					■	■	■						■	■	■	■			

Figure 15–10 Purchase-cycle model for erratic purchase cycle. In a 25-week period the customer might normally purchase the product eight times at irregular intervals. By increasing the frequency during media pulses, these purchase occasions might occur sooner and be extended. The intent here is to suggest reuse of the product to an already satisfied customer.

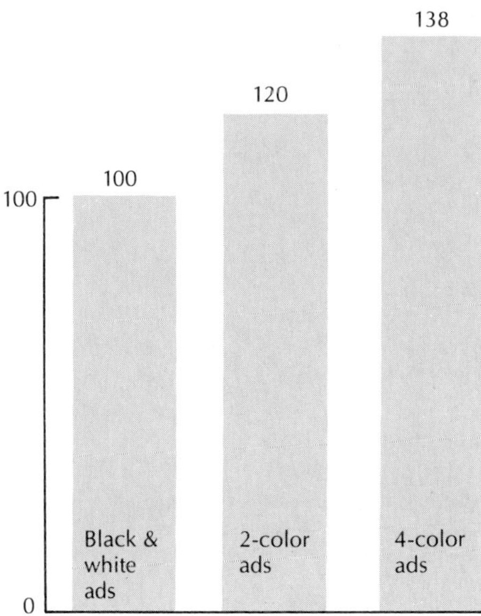

Figure 15–11 How advertising readership is influenced by the addition of four-color: The addition of four-color significantly increases the average advertising readership score beyond both two-color and black and white.

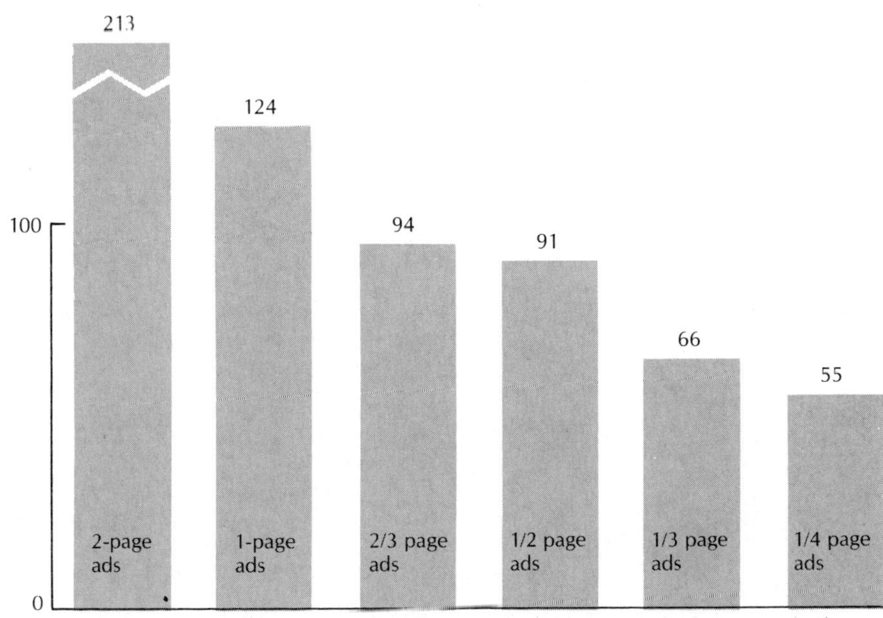

Figure 15–12 How advertising readership is influenced by ad size: As the size of an advertisement increases, the readership score increases.

Media selection: As the creative person sees it

	Creative disadvantages	Creative advantages
Newspapers	Loss of fidelity, especially in reproduction of halftone illustration. Too many ad-format variations among newspapers. Variance in column widths. Difficulty in controlling ad position on page.	Almost any ad size available. Impact of black against white (still one of the most powerful color combinations). Sense of immediacy. Quick response; easy accountability. Local emphasis. Changes possible at short notice.
Magazines	Size not as large as those of newspapers or posters. Long closing dates, limiting flexibility. Lack of immediacy. Tendency to cluster ads. Possible difficulties in securing favorable spot in an issue.	High-quality reproduction. Prestige factor. Accurate demographic information available. Graphic opportunities (use of white space, benday screen, reverse type). Color.
Television	No time to convey a lot of information. Air clutter (almost 25 percent of broadcasting is nonprogramming material). Intrusiveness (TV tops list of consumers' complaints in this respect). Capricious station censorship.	Combination of sight and sound. Movement. A single message at a time. Viewer's empathy. Opportunity to demonstrate the product. Believability: "What you see is what you get."
Radio	Lack of visual excitement. Wavering attention span (many listeners tune out commercials). Inadequate data on listening habits (when is the "listener" really listening?). Fleeting nature of message.	Opportunity to explore sound. Favorable to humor. Intimacy. Loyal following (the average person listens regularly to only about two stations). Ability to change message quickly.
Direct mail	Damper of state, federal, and postal regulations on creative experimentations. Censorship often unpredictable. Formula thinking encouraged by "proven" direct-mail track records.	Graphic and production flexibility, such as use of three-dimensional effect (folding, die-cuts, pop-ups). Measurable. As scientific as any other form of advertising. Highly personal.
Posters	Essentially a one-line medium with only a limited opportunity to expand on the advertising message. Inadequate audience research, especially in transit advertising.	Graphic opportunities. Color. Large size. High-fidelity reproduction. Simple, direct approach. Possibility of an entirely visual message.
Point of sale	Difficulty in pinpointing audience. Failure of retailers to make proper use of material submitted to them.	Opportunities for three-dimensional effects, movement, sound, and new production techniques.

Laboratory application

1. What creative disadvantages and advantages can you add to the list?
2. From the list of leading advertisers in Figure 15–5, select one, and explain why the primary medium they use is specifically advantageous for their product from a creative point of view.

Figure 15–13

Comparative evaluation of advertising media

	Spot television	Network television	Spot radio	Network radio	Consumer magazines	Business publications	Farm publications	Sunday supplements	Daily newspapers	Weekly newspapers	Direct mail	Outdoor	Transit	Point of purchase
Audience considerations														
Attentiveness of audience	++	++	++	++	++	++	++	++	++	++	++	+	+	+
Interest of audience	++	+++	++	++	+++	+++	+++	+++	+++	+++	+	+	+	+
Avoids excess selection by audience	++	++	++	++	+	+	+	+	+	+	+	+	+	+
Offers selectivity to advertiser	+	+	++	++	+++	+++	+++	+	+	+	+++	+	+	+
Avoids waste	+	+	+	+	+++	+++	+++	++	+	+	+++	+	+	+
Offers involvement	++	+++	++	++	++	+++	+++	++	++	++	+	+	+	+
Avoids distraction	++	+++	++	++	+++	+++	+++	++	++	++	+++	+	+	+
Avoids resistance	N	N	N	N	N	N	N	N	N	N	N	N	N	N
Provides impact	V	V	V	V	V	V	V	V	V	V	V	V	V	V
Offers prestige	++	+++	+	++	+++	+++	++	+++	++	+	+	+	+	+
Good quality of audience data	++	++	++	++	+++	+++	++	++	++	+	++	+	+	+
Timing factors														
Offers repetition	+++	+++	+++	+++	++	++	++	+	++	+	V	+++	+++	++
Avoids irritation	+	+	+	++	++	++	++	++	++	++	++	++	++	++
Offers frequency	+++	+++	+++	++	++	++	++	+	++	+	++	+++	+++	++
Offers frequency of issuance	+++	+++	+++	+++	V	V	+	+	++	+	V	N	N	N
Offers flexibility in scheduling	+++	+++	+++	+++	V	V	+	+	++	+	V	N	N	N
Long life	+	+	+	+	+++	+++	+++	++	+	++	+	+	+	+
Low mortality rate	+	+	+	+	+++	+++	+++	++	+	++	+	+	+	+
Avoids perishability	+	+	+	+	+++	+++	+++	++	+	++	+	+	+	+
Allows long message	++	++	++	++	+++	+++	+++	+++	+++	+++	+++	+	+	+
Provides product protection	V	++	V	++	++	++	++	++	V	V	+++	+	+	++
Geographic considerations														
Offers geographic selectivity	+++	+	+++	+	++	++	++	+++	+++	+++	+++	++	++	+++
Offers proximity to point of sale	+	+	+	+	+	+	+	+	+	+	++	++	++	+++
Provides for local dealer "tags"	++	+	++	+	++	++	++	++	+++	+++	+++	++	++	+++
Creative considerations														
Permits demonstration	+++	+++	+	+	++	++	++	++	++	++	+++	+	+	+++
Provides impact	+++	+++	++	++	++	++	++	++	++	++	+++	+	+	++
Permits relation to editorial matter	++	++	+	++	+++	+++	+++	++	++	++	+++	N	N	N
Competitive factors														
Light use of medium by competitors	+	+++	+	+++	+	+++	+++	++	++	+++	++	++	+++	+++
Low amount of total advertising	+	+	V	+++	++	V	+++	++	++	++	+++	++	+	+++
Control considerations														
Advertiser control of media content	+	++	+	++	+	+	+	+	+	+	+++	N	N	N
Favorable environment	+	++	+	++	+	+	+	+	+	+	+++	+	+	+++
Advertiser control of location	V	+++	V	+++	++	++	++	+	+	+	+++	+	+	++
Amount of government regulation	+	N	+	N	N	N	N	N	N	N	+	+	N	N
Number of other restrictions	+	+	+	+	V	V	V	V	V	V	+	+	+	+
Mechanical and production factors														
Ease of insertion	++	+++	++	+++	+++	+++	+++	++	++	+	+++	++	++	+
High reproduction quality	++	++	++	++	+++	+++	+++	+++	V	V	+++	V	V	+++
Flexibility of format	++	++	++	++	+++	+++	+++	+	+	+	+++	++	+	+
Avoids vandalism	N	N	N	N	N	N	N	N	N	N	N	+	+	+
Financial considerations														
Low total cost	++	+	++	+	+	+	+	++	+++	+++	+	++	++	++
High efficiency	++	+++	+++	++	++	++	++	++	++	+	+++	+++	+++	+

Note: N = not a factor for this medium, V = varies from one vehicle to another within the medium, + = weak, ++ = medium, +++ = strong.

Some media are better suited than others to express the unique attributes of certain products. Some products may be refused time or space by media because of their personal nature. Some magazines, for example, do not accept advertising for intimate-use products. Others reject advertising for cigarettes or liquor.

The nature of the product may also suggest the type of media to be used. For example, when a product—such as a fine perfume—has a distinct personality or image, it should be advertised in media that have personality traits that reinforce this image. Some magazines, for instance, are regarded as feminine or masculine, high-brow or low-brow, serious or frivolous.

If the objective of the advertising campaign is to gain product distribution in an area where it is weak or nonexistent, the media selected must be those that influence both consumers and potential dealers. If the goal is to stimulate sales of a nationally distributed product in certain isolated markets, the advertising must be concentrated in the local or regional media that penetrate these markets, rather than in national media. Where the objective is to elevate product image and reputation, the advertiser may elect to sponsor high-quality programs on network television rather than to use the popular consumer media known to generate product sales.

The price of the product and the pricing strategy may influence media choices, too. For example, pricing is often a key consideration in product positioning. Thus, a premium-priced product may require the use of prestigious or "class" media to support its market image. The media planner must then carefully assess the objectives of the campaign in order to fulfill them through the selection of the most suitable media.

Reviewing the target market for the product or service is a vital step in media selection. The more the media planner knows about this market, the better the media selections are likely to be. Data on the nature of the target market and the characteristics of potential product buyers should be obtained from the advertiser and the agency's account service staff. These data should include the size, location, and demographic profile of the intended market such as age, sex, education, occupation, income, and religion. They should also include their psychographic characteristics, such as lifestyle, personality, and attitudinal traits. Behavior characteristics should be studied, too, such as purchase cycles, benefits sought, and other product use habits. The task of the media planner is then (1) to select from these data the characteristics most relevant to the acceptance, purchase, and use of the product (e.g.; the most relevant characteristics for ladies dress shops are sex and age); and (2) to match these data to the characteristics of the audiences reached by the specific media vehicles under consideration.

Characteristics of media audiences

Audience denotes the total number of people who are reached by a given medium. In the case of print media, the term *circulation* is used to refer to the total number of copies of an average issue that are distributed through subscriptions and newsstand sales. *Readership* (circulation × the average number of readers per copy) denotes the total number of readers of an average issue of a publication. The total number of people reached is greater than the number of copies circulated due to pass-along readership. In addition, some publications are read more thoroughly than others, so the advertiser's message may be exposed to a larger *share* of readers in some publications than in others.

The media planner needs to know (1) how many people are reached by a station or a publication, (2) the degree of interest these people have in the publication or program, and (3) how closely the characteristics of the audience or circulation match the profile of the target market.

Data on the size of broadcast audiences are readily available. TV-Q and Simmons Market Research Bureau measure the degree of audience interest and attentiveness in programs. For print media, reader interest may be inferred from the trend of circulation. A consistently growing circulation may indicate greater reader interest, whereas a dwindling circulation may point to declining reader interest. Another way to assess this is to check the percentage of subscription renewals over the past several years.

Readership and audience studies conducted by various media have yielded information of special importance to media planners about the characteristics of their audience. These data enable the media planner to determine how closely the audience characteristics match the profile of the target market prospects.

For example, if the product is intended for tennis enthusiasts, it is essential that the medium selected is the one that reaches tennis players most efficiently. This information may be obtained from the media themselves or from media research organizations, media trade associations, media directories, and independent media buying services. Figure 15–14, for example, shows research data from the W. R. Simmons Company on a wide range of magazine readers, including their age, income, and occupational status and other factors (Figure 15–15). Simmons also publishes demographic and psychographic data on product usage among a varied group of consumers. Analyzing this data results in better media selections.

The *content* of a medium reflects the types of people in its audience. For instance, some radio stations emphasize in-depth news or sports, others jazz or rock, and still others symphonic music or operas. Each type of programming attracts a different audience, the character of which can be determined by analysis. Figure 15–15 gives Simmons data on the appeal of various radio formats to different age groups.

Geographic coverage

There is no point in advertising to people who don't live in an area where the product or service is sold. Therefore the geograhic coverage of a medium is often the determining factor in selection.

Many national brands face tougher competition in some regions than in others. Often extra advertising dollars are concentrated in those areas where competition is stiffer. Airlines select media that cover the cities they serve and omit media that are circulated in other areas.

CONSUMER MAGAZINES: READER CHARACTERISTICS

	READERS '000	READERS % Cov	READERS RPC	% M	% W	% Age 18-34	Age 18-34 Index	Median Age (Years)	$25,000 + HH Inc.	HH Inc. Index	College Grad.	College Grad. Index	Manger./Admin.	Manger./Admin. Index	In-Home Readers	In-Home Readers %	Cost Per M* Page B/W	Cost Per M* Page 4CLR
TOTAL ADULTS	(155,794)			(48.0)	(52.0)	(63,109)	(40.5)	(40.9)	(41,274)	(26.5)	(22,011)	(14.1)	(10,858)	(7.0)				
GENERAL EDITORIAL																		
Book Digest	2,678	.9	2.70E	36.9	63.1	1,278	82	43.0	1,309	128	1,262	231	567	209	1,984	74.1	$3.73	$5.28
National Geographic	28,290	18.2	2.76	53.9	46.1	10,988	96	42.1	10,138	135	7,875	198	3,589	181	21,480	75.9	1.92	2.63
New Yorker	3,044	2.0	6.10	51.6	48.4	1,487	121	35.5	1,276	158	1,326	309	423	199	1,600	52.6	2.50	3.94
People	19,057	12.2	8.24	42.0	58.0	12,346	160	29.6	4,994	99	3,443	128	1,316	99	10,419	54.7	1.00	1.28
Reader's Digest	39,807	25.6	2.20	42.7	57.3	13,154	82	45.6	9,230	88	5,993	107	3,293	119	33,847	85.0	1.62	1.95
Saturday Review	1,394	.9	2.65	45.7	54.3	73.4	130	33.7	432	117	642	328	102	104	847	60.8	3.52	4.84
Smithsonian	3,703	2.4	2.04	49.2	50.8	1,549	103	39.7	1,658	168	1,879	359	462	177	2,671	72.1	4.05	6.08
TV Guide	42,028	27.0	2.15	45.7	54.3	21,613	126	34.5	7,688	69	5,356	90	2,595	87	39,175	93.2	1.31	1.55
SELECTIVE EDITORIAL																		
New York/New West (Net)	2,266	1.5	3.21	51.5	48.5	1,137	120	35.9	837	135	852	259	317	194	1,384	61.1	$2.87	4.48
Psychology Today	4,254	2.7	3.62	43.3	56.7	2,914	169	29.2	1,327	117	1,594	265	257	84	2,587	60.8	3.42	4.93
Scientific American	2,487	1.6	3.63	70.4	29.6	1,504	149	31.6	1,148	174	1,576	448	335	191	1,378	55.4	3.54	5.31
NEWSWEEKLIES																		
Newsweek	18,015	11.6	6.14	58.4	41.6	9,053	124	34.9	6,128	129	5,335	211	2,330	186	10,230	56.8	$1.63	$2.53
Sports Illustrated	12,510	8.0	4.16	76.1	23.9	7,733	152	39.5	3,882	117	2,966	167	1,378	157	7,167	57.3	2.07	3.23
Time	20,664	13.3	4.79	56.7	43.3	10,051	120	35.8	7,149	131	6,003	206	2,449	169	13,397	64.8	1.98	3.09
U.S. News & World Report	9,239	5.9	4.47	67.1	32.9	3,274	87	43.3	3,451	141	3,367	259	1,624	257	5,333	57.7	2.14	3.38
SUPPLEMENTS																		
New York Times Magazine	4,319	2.8	3.01	53.8	46.2	2,115	121	35.7	1,688	147	1,795	294	592	196	3,479	80.6	$2.11	$3.25
NEWSPAPERS (Daily)																		
New York Times	2,428	1.6	2.81	56.1	43.9	1,124	114	38.2	1,020	158	1,186	345	383	224	1,833	75.5	$6.28	NA
The Star	11,250	7.2	3.56	38.3	61.7	5,746	126	34.4	1,580	70	615	39	375	54	8,523	75.8	.73	.86
TOTAL MEN	(74,722)					(31,256)	(41.8)	(39.6)	(22,470)	(30.1)	(12,880)	(17.2)	(8,348)	(11.2)				
BUSINESS																		
Barrons	650	.9	2.89	84.3	15.7	253	95	40.2	321	164	404	362	203	279	257	39.5	$9.17	NA
Business Week	3,151	4.2	3.91	74.0	26.0	1,313	100	38.6	1,597	168	1,634	301	995	282	1,378	43.7	4.94	7.41
Forbes	1,327	1.8	1.96	77.9	22.1	555	100	41.2	687	172	782	342	424	285	649	48.9	8.28	12.57
Fortune	1,386	1.9	2.45E	77.9	22.1	644	111	39.5	798	192	771	324	398	257	689	49.7	10.57	16.07
Money	2,442	3.3	2.89E	64.2	35.8	1,257	123	34.3	1,014	190	948	227	509	182	1,253	51.5	4.05	6.33
Wall Street Journal	3,133	4.2	1.92	72.3	27.7	999	76	43.7	1,909	202	1,804	334	1,168	332	949	30.2	11.58	NA
MEN'S																		
Esquire	1,519	2.0	2.33	65.5	34.5	796	126	34.0	425	93	332	127	237	139	827	54.4	$5.89	$8.82
Penthouse	8,604	11.5	1.85	83.1	16.9	6,384	178	27.9	1,897	73	1,349	91	883	92	4,475	52.0	2.62	3.96
Playboy	13,571	18.2	2.45	79.1	20.9	9,187	162	29.3	3,582	88	2,772	119	1,977	209	8,221	60.6	2.31	3.23
SPORTS																		
Golf Digest	1,940	2.6	2.00	83.6	16.4	798	98	40.1	800	136	653	195	482	221	1,122	57.8	$6.61	$9.91
Gold Magazine	1,028	1.4	1.45	78.1	21.9	463	108	37.9	463	150	325	184	179	155	530	51.6	9.02	13.54
Sport	2,551	3.4	2.01	78.6	21.4	1,933	181	26.5	711	93	360	82	317	111	1,293	50.7	4.30	6.28
World Tennis	570	.8	1.69	51.9	48.1	260	109	38.8	233	136	209	213	92	145	313	54.9	10.83	16.25
Zift Davis Net (Gross)	10,707	14.3	2.99	78.9	21.1	5,782	166	27.1	2,541	101	1,637	114	972	104	5,279	49.3	4.27	6.32
OUTDOOR																		
Field & Steam	6,505	8.7	3.15	76.9	23.1	3,520	118	35.3	1,500	70	1,046	85	800	101	4,382	67.4	$2.37	$3.53
Guns & Ammo	2,704	3.6	5.54	89.3	10.7	1,779	157	30.2	614	75	334	72	244	80	1,440	53.3	1.80	2.88
Outdoor Life	4,625	6.2	2.67	76.8	23.2	2,260	116	35.8	784	56	480	60	408	79	2,817	60.9	3.01	4.28
Sports Afield	2,301	3.1	4.35	86.3	13.7	980	101	39.5	609	88	325	82	295	114	1,260	54.8	2.39	3.41
MECHANICS AUTOMOTIVE																		
Car & Craft	1,933	2.6	5.14	95.2	4.8	1,641	202	26.0	330	57	108	33	112	52	945	48.9	2.32	3.72
Car & Driver	2,395	3.2	3.29	89.5	10.5	1,952	194	25.7	520	72	342	83	247	92	1,365	57.0	5.26	8.32
Hot Rod	4,214	5.6	4.81	86.5	13.5	3,469	197	25.0	714	56	256	35	281	60	2,140	50.8	3.65	5.45
Mechanix Illustrated	4,433	5.9	2.53	85.1	14.9	1,961	106	37.5	1,003	75	738	197	572	115	2,535	57.2	2.91	4.12
Motor Trend	2,517	3.4	3.32	94.5	5.5	1,683	159	29.2	772	102	300	69	230	81	1,364	54.2	4.47	7.15
Popular Mechanics	5,399	7.2	3.30	86.2	13.8	2,432	108	36.9	1,209	74	842	91	528	88	3,337	61.8	2.35	3.33
Popular Science	3,820	5.1	2.12	87.7	12.3	1,832	114	36.2	1,193	104	1,007	153	495	115	2,409	63.1	3.72	5.27
Road & Track	2,194	2.9	3.70	91.2	8.8	1,726	180	26.9	539	82	388	103	187	76	1,189	54.2	4.15	6.53
Peterson Action Group (Gross)	15,217	7.0	4.82	87.8	12.2	7,477	171	27.7	2,176	69	1,187	66	912	78	6,093	40.0	3.07	4.92
Motorcyclist	1,247	1.7	8.66	79.9	20.1	1,001	193	26.3	273	73	93	44	92	66	656	52.6	2.18	3.48
													WORKING WOMEN					
TOTAL WOMEN	(81,073)					(31,853)	(39.3)	(42.1)	(18,804)	(23.2)	(9,131)	(11.3)	(38,362)	(47.3)				
WOMEN'S																		
American Baby	1,841	2.3	1.85	13.5	86.5	1,578	216	26.6	217	50	311	148	789	90	1,200	65.2	$7.79	10.77
Ms.	1,295	1.6	2.58	19.5	80.5	1,041	198	27.8	321	104	396	263	1,010	160	777	60.0	4.56	5.81
Parents Magazine	3,257	4.0	2.26	20.5	79.5	2,245	175	29.9	515	68	383	104	1,646	107	2,123	65.2	4.54	5.81
WOMEN'S SERVICE																		
Better Homes & Garden	16,894	20.8	2.11	25.2	74.8	6,578	99	41.3	4,513	116	2,772	145	8,864	111	12,012	71.1	$2.84	3.43
Family Circle	17,051	21.0	2.24	13.7	86.3	7,321	110	38.5	3,719	94	2,313	120	8,721	108	13,522	79.3	2.63	3.15
Good Housekeeping	17,605	21.7	3.40	15.6	84.4	7,463	107	39.4	3,957	97	2,571	128	9,400	123	11,938	67.8	1.89	2.36
Ladies Home Journal	12,393	15.3	2.20	14.2	85.8	4,858	100	42.2	2,972	103	1,972	141	6,542	112	8,316	67.1	2.44	3.02
McCall's	16,648	20.5	2.56	15.8	84.2	7,156	109	39.3	3,813	98	2,179	116	3,915	113	11,469	68.9	2.32	2.85
Redbook	10,504	13.0	2.36	15.2	84.8	5,324	129	34.8	2,513	103	1,554	131	5,777	116	6,942	66.1	2.39	3.18
Woman's Day	17,257	21.3	2.29	9.8	90.2	7,164	105	39.3	3,762	94	2,195	112	8,817	108	13,884	80.5	2.61	3.12
Conde Nast Mag. (Gross)	25,732	31.7	4.88	14.8	85.2	9,721	140	31.4	4,584	112	3,144	157	102	123	10,011	38.9	2.27	3.23
FASHION BEAUTY																		
Cosmopolitan	8,937	11.0	3.23	18.2	81.8	6,089	173	28.5	2,014	97	1,447	143	5,841	138	5,708	63.9	$1.66	2.24
Glamour	7,485	9.2	4.02	6.9	93.1	5,026	170	27.5	1,956	112	1,296	153	4,623	130	3,874	51.8	1.56	2.19
Harper's Bazaar	2,923	3.6	4.70	14.7	85.3	1,553	136	33.4	881	130	564	171	1,655	120	1,133	38.8	2.50	3.60
Mademoiselle	3,469	4.3	3.73	8.2	91.8	2,525	186	27.4	996	124	635	163	2,346	143	1,751	50.5	2.13	3.11
Vogue	5,141	6.3	5.30	11.6	88.4	2,826	139	32.6	1,481	124	362	148	3,135	129	2,301	44.8	1.81	2.64
SHELTER																		
House Beautiful	4,260	5.3	4.93	18.5	81.5	1,868	102	39.7	1,355	125	877	166	2,686	121	2,446	57.4	$2.44	$3.57
House & Garden	7,142	8.8	6.90	25.1	74.9	3,121	111	38.4	1,780	107	1,345	165	3,984	117	3,979	55.7	1.78	2.62

E - Estimated.

* For page costs see Circulation and Rates table.

Figure 15–14 Consumer magazines: Reader characteristics.

Geographic considerations have given rise to the popularity of regional editions of magazines, the use of spot TV instead of network TV, and the use of local media instead of national media for national advertisers.

Exposure, attention, and motivational value

As we said at the beginning of this section, the job of the media planner is to match the right media with the target audience so that the advertisements not only achieve the desired *exposure* but also attract *attention* and *motivate* prospective customers to act. This is the art of media planning, and it is very difficult since little reliable data have ever been developed to measure the relative strength of one medium over another in terms of exposure, attention, or motivation. However, these are still important issues which experienced media planners are compelled to consider every day.

Exposure Think about exposure in terms of how many people your ad sees rather than the other way around. If you place an advertisement in a magazine with 3 million readers, how many of those 3 million will your ad actually see? If a given television program has an audience of 10 million viewers, how many people will your commercial actually see?

The figures are usually considerably less than the total audience or circulation. Some people read only one article in a magazine, set it aside, and never pick it up again. Others thumb through every page, pouring over the ads with as much or more interest than the articles. Many people watch television until the commercial, then jump up and change the channel, or go to another room to get a snack. Other programs keep people glued to their chairs but still have to contend with conversation about the show during the commercial break.

Assessing the exposure value of one publication, radio station, or TV program over another is a difficult task.

Attention The degree of attention paid to ads by those exposed to them is another consideration. If you are not interested in motorcycles or cosmetics, then you probably don't even notice ads for them when you see them. On the other hand, if you are in the market for a new automobile, you probably notice every new-car ad you see.

Thus, whereas exposure value relates only to the medium itself, attention value relates to the advertising message and copy just as much as to the medium. It is logical to assume that special-interest media, such as tennis magazines, offer good attention value to a tennis product. But what kind of attention value does the daily newspaper offer to a boating product? Will the boating enthusiast be thinking about a boat while reading the newspaper? There are no simple answers to these questions, and much research still needs to be done. But six factors have been found to positively affect the attention value of a medium:[4]

1. Audience involvement with editorial content or program material.
2. Specialization of audience interest or identification.
3. Number of competitive advertisers (the fewer, the better).

4. Audience familiarity with advertiser's campaign.
5. Quality of advertising reproduction.
6. Timeliness of advertising exposure.

Motivation These same factors affect a medium's motivation value. In some cases, though, they are a more important contributor to motivation than to attention, and vice versa. For instance, familiarity with the advertiser's campaign may affect attention significantly but motivation very little. On the other hand, good-quality reproduction and timeliness can be very motivating to someone interested in the product. Therefore, attention value and motivation value should be considered separately when assessing alternative media.

One simple method the media planner can use to assist in analyzing these values is the EAM model described in the Ad Lab. This is a weighting method, which forces the media planner to assign a specific number value to his or her judgment of a medium's potential strengths. This same weighting method can be used for evaluating other subjective considerations in media selection such as the relative importance of audience age demographics against income characteristics.

Cost efficiency

The final step in determining what media to select is to analyze the cost efficiency of each medium available.

A common term used in media buying is *CPM,* or *cost per thousand.* The media compare themselves with other media by the cost

Total adults in U.S. 6 A.M.–midnight, Monday–Friday	U.S. total	Total radio	Adult contemporary	All news	Beautiful music	Black	Classical/semiclassical	Country	Golden oldies	Middle of the road	Progressive	Soft contemporary	Standard	Talk	Top 40
18 to 24															
Percent of composite	18.3	21.7	38.8	6.6	5.7	37.0	9.1	11.8	49.8	14.9	39.0	41.1	9.3	5.0	39.1
Index	100	119	212	36	31	202	50	64	272	81	213	225	51	27	214
25 to 34															
Percent of composite	22.0	24.4	30.7	14.6	15.2	30.8	12.4	21.2	29.8	28.5	43.9	36.8	13.8	8.0	30.7
Index	100	111	140	66	69	140	56	96	135	130	200	167	63	36	140
35 to 44															
Percent of composite	15.6	17.4	10.5	13.3	23.1	18.6	28.6	27.8	11.9	18.3	8.1	6.5	21.3	14.1	14.9
Index	100	112	67	85	148	119	183	178	76	117	52	42	137	90	96
45 to 54															
Percent of composite	15.7	15.4	8.0	24.3	22.8	10.9	33.2	15.9	3.1	19.6	6.1	6.5	23.3	26.8	8.3
Index	100	98	51	155	145	69	211	101	20	125	45	41	148	171	53
55 to 64															
Percent of composite	13.6	12.0	6.9	19.0	20.3	1.6	11.2	15.2	2.8	10.6	2.3	6.9	16.6	21.1	3.9
Index	100	88	51	140	149	12	82	112	21	78	15	51	122	155	29
65 or over															
Percent of composite	14.8	9.1	5.1	22.2	12.8	1.2	5.4	8.2	2.3	8.2	0.7	2.6	15.7	25.3	3.2
Index	100	61	34	150	86	8	36	55	16	55	5	18	106	171	22
18 to 49															
Percent of composite	63.0	69.8	83.0	46.0	54.1	92.4	57.7	69.8	93.7	70.2	91.7	87.8	53.8	36.0	87.6
Index	100	111	132	73	86	147	92	111	149	111	146	139	85	57	139
35 to 49															
Percent of composite	22.7	23.7	13.6	24.8	33.2	24.7	36.1	36.8	14.1	26.8	8.8	9.8	30.7	22.9	17.9
Index	100	104	60	109	146	109	159	162	62	118	39	43	135	101	79

Figure 15–15 Average quarter-hour audiences by formats.

of reaching 1,000 people in their audience. The cost per thousand for a full-page ad in the daily newspaper that costs $5,000 and has 300 thousand subscribers would be calculated as:

$$\text{CPM} = \frac{\$5{,}000}{300} = \$16.67$$

Weekly newspapers that charge $3,000 for a full page would promote themselves as less expensive, because the cost per thousand for their combined circulation of 250 thousand would be considerably less on a full-page ad:

$$\frac{\$3{,}000}{250} = \$12.00/\text{M}$$

However, the media planner is more interested in *cost efficiency* in reaching the target audience, not the cost of reaching the medium's total circulation.

If we use the EAM model described in the Ad Lab on the next page, comparing the relative cost efficiency of each medium becomes a simple task. We divide the cost of the particular medium by the total index value we calculated for each medium.

In our example, the full-page ad in the financial section of the daily newspaper costs $5,000. Our cost efficiency based on our total index value for that medium would be calculated as follows:

$$\frac{\$5{,}000}{43{,}200} = 0.12$$

To run a full-page ad in the five weekly newspapers might cost only $3,000, but the cost would be higher to reach the target audience:

$$\frac{\$3{,}000}{21{,}000} = 0.14$$

Thus, the daily newspaper is definitely the better buy from a cost-efficiency standpoint, and the more attractive selection.

Selection approaches

In our analysis of media efficiency, we may discover that several media are attractive to use because each contains a segment of prospects for our product. The question may arise, therefore, as to how to reach the greatest number of prospects.

One consideration might be to use a *broadside approach,* sending an equal number of messages to each group and hoping for the best. Another approach, called *profile matching,* might be to split up the media schedule so that the messages are delivered to each segment in proportion to that segment's importance among all prospects. This would probably result in greater reach than the broadside approach. The third method would be to work the various market segments as a gold miner works several claims—start with the richest claim first. This method, called the *high-assay principle,* suggests starting with the medium that produces the best return and then moving to other media only when the first becomes unavailable or loses its effectiveness. According to Longman, unless prospects can be individually identified, this is the best method to maximize reach.[5]

When the rate of return (added new reach) of the daily newspapers falls below what the rate of return would be from the weekly newspapers, then it is time to switch or add other media.

These principles are very important for the media planner to understand. However, they are also highly theoretical and based on extremely simple hypothetical cases. In the real world many factors complicate the process. Cost factors must be considered. It is very difficult to weigh the actual sales potential of given market segments. And combination effects of media overlapping from the advertiser's media schedule produce distorted figures that make accurate measurement of results difficult. Other things being equal, though, if our objective is to reach the most prospects, we prefer the media with the largest audiences and the greatest number of prospects for concentrated scheduling.[6] If our objective is higher frequency, we prefer to select several media vehicles with smaller audiences.

The EAM model: How to evaluate exposure-attention-motivation values of media

Let us suppose you are selecting local media to advertise a bank's new interest rates. Your preliminary analysis indicates that the media available to you are: both the financial and sports sections of the daily metropolitan newspaper with 300,000 subscribers; five weekly community newspapers with a total of 250,000 readers; a slick, 66,000-circulation, monthly magazine concerned with local social events; and three local radio stations. One features all news; another offers pleasant, middle-of-the-road music; and the third is a hard-rock station. The rock station has 200,000 listeners, the news station, 100,000, and the MOR 80,000.

Your job is to select from this list the most effective media in terms of potential prospects by evaluating and ranking each medium's exposure, attention, and motivation value.

By constructing an EAM model, we can assign values to each factor we wish to consider. These values are very subjective, based on the media planner's best judgment from past experience with different media vehicles and product groups. This process of assigning a value to the planner's subjective judgment affords a clear basis for analysis and decision making. Here's how it works.

First, list the various media alternatives along with their stated circulation or audience figures. Assign a value from 0.1 to 0.9 to each factor being considered based on your judgment of that medium's value. Then, by multiplying the audience figures by each successive value listed, you arrive at a hypothetical index of total value.

For example, of all the readers of the daily newspaper, we might assume that only 2 out of 10 read the financial section. So we assign it 0.2 for exposure. Of those that read the financial section, though, 8 out of 10 might be very interested in banking news and notice the bank's advertisement. And for every 10 that notice it, we might assume that 9 might find this new interest rate very motivating because of its timeliness. So we assign 0.8 to attention and 0.9 to motivation. When we multiply 300,000 by 0.2, then by 0.8, and then by 0.9, we arrive at a total index value of 43,200.

Proceeding down the list we can perform the same task for each of the other media, considering the editorial content, the interests or predisposition of the particular audiences, potential for competitive advertising, capability for good reproduction quality, timeliness of exposure, familiarity with the advertiser, and so on.

When we are finished we have a group of numbers that we can then analyze against one another and against the cost of the various media involved. And we also possibly discover some startling results.

The EAM model in practice provides only relative estimates of effectiveness, and it is only as good as the media planner using it. One cannot predict the exact measure for the values, and therefore they should not be used to suggest the probable payoff of an advertisement in terms of new customers. It is, however, an effective method for making comparisons, and the actual effectiveness of the approach can sometimes be measured after a campaign from the return of coupons or other devices designed to *source* customers.

Scheduling criteria

After we have selected the media vehicles we wish to use, we must decide how many of each media vehicle's space or time units should be bought and over what period of time these units should be used.

As we mentioned earlier, reach and frequency objectives are normally considered for four-week periods. In other words, how many people do we want to reach and how many times do we want to reach them during a given four-week period? The next consideration, then, is how many four-week flights we want to use. Do we want to schedule a steady year-round campaign of 13 four-week flights achieving 120 gross rating points of reach and an average frequency of 3.5 during each month of the year? Or do we want to pulse our campaign, concentrating heavily at first for two months and then backing off and running only occasionally for the rest of the year?

EAM model

Medium	Audience/ circulation	Exposure value	Attention value	Motivation value	Total index value
Daily newspaper (financial)	300,000	0.2	0.8	0.9	43,200
Daily newspaper (sports)	300,000	0.3	0.5	0.5	22,500
Weekly newspapers	250,000	0.4	0.3	0.7	21,000
Monthly magazine (social)	66,000	0.5	0.3	0.7	7,000
Radio (all news)	100,000	0.5	0.7	0.8	28,000
Radio (middle of the road)	80,000	0.3	0.5	0.6	6,300
Radio (rock)	200,000	0.6	0.3	0.2	7,200

Laboratory applications

1. From the results of this laboratory experiment, would you suppose that a rock radio station would offer as interesting an alternative for bank advertising as a slick monthly magazine read by the social elite? Should these figures be reanalyzed?
2. Would you expect the financial section of the daily newspaper to be twice as effective as all the community newspapers combined? Discuss.

Types of schedules

There are many kinds of schedules in use today. The following are the six basic types most commonly used:[7]

1. *Steady.* These are the easiest types of schedules to prepare: one ad per week for 52 weeks, or one ad per month for 12 months.
2. *Seasonal pulse.* Suntan oil is rarely advertised in the winter; snow tires rarely in the summer. Seasonal buying patterns dictate heavy media use during peak selling periods.
3. *Periodic pulse.* When media pulses are scheduled at regular intervals but are not related to the seasons of the year, we have what is called a periodic pulse pattern.
4. *Erratic pulse.* When the advertising is spaced at irregular intervals, the company may be trying to cause changes in typical purchase cycles, as we discussed in the section on media strategy.
5. *Start-up pulse.* This is a common pattern designed to start off a campaign with a bang. It is very common to see this every year when the new atuomobile models are introduced. It is almost always used to introduce a new product.
6. *Promotional pulse.* Often the media schedule must be designed to support some special promotion of the manufacturer, so buying will be heavier during the time of the promotion than at other times.

As we can see, pulsing of some form characterizes all but the simplest media schedules, and the degree of continuity (or pulsing) is a function of the media strategy. Therefore, at the time the media planner is preparing the actual schedule, it is wise to review the strategy section of the media plan to be sure the final schedule actually reflects what was originally intended.

Analyzing reach, frequency, and continuity

It is up to the media planner to determine the right combination of reach, frequency, and continuity. It is not uncommon for media people to simply say, "match the competition . . . and then some." But, of course, if everybody did that a vicious circle would ensue. It is a little more scientific for the media planner to remember the basic findings of research:

1. Continuity is important because advertising is often quickly forgotten when consumers are not continually exposed to it. In most cases it is a waste of money for advertisers to spend money one week and then six weeks later run ads for another week. To develop continuity requires committing dollars to some continuous period of time.
2. Repeated exposures are needed to impress a message on the memories of a large proportion of consumers. The advertiser who runs only four or five radio spots per week gives up so much frequency (usually for the sake of continuity) as to make the schedule almost worthless.
3. As the number of exposures increases, both the number of persons who remember it and the length of time they remember it in-

People in advertising

Mark S. Oken

Senior Vice President
and Media Director
The Bloom Agency

Media specialist Mark S. Oken is senior vice president and media director of The Bloom Agency, Dallas, one of the 10 fastest growing full-service advertising agencies in the United States.

A graduate of Northwestern University, where he received a B.S. in business administration (accounting) in 1956, Oken went on to obtain an M.B.A. in marketing at the University of Michigan.

He launched his career in advertising as a media buyer for Kenyon & Eckhardt. Four years later Oken joined Needham, Louis & Brorby as a time buyer. He went on to Foote, Cone & Belding in 1963 as manager of network facilities. Within four years Oken became media supervisor at Needham, Harper & Steers. In 1971 he was named senior vice president and media director of The Bloom Agency, whose clients include Mitsubishi Aircraft International, Pet, Inc., Six Flags, and Southwest Airlines. The agency, which has more than doubled in size during the past five years, today has nearly 300 employees and annual billings of over $61 million.

The growing success of The Bloom Agency, according to Oken, is due in part to the fact that it performs media planning and selection for its clients not on the traditional 15 percent commission basis, as most agencies do, but on a fee basis. "This fee system," Oken reports, "has proven to make our media services for clients much more effective. It motivates better work," he explains, "and puts the emphasis in our work where the client wants it."

Oken also believes that the fee formula affords the agency greater flexibility in its approach to clients' media goals. For media people, he notes, the fee system "provides greater freedom to examine overall marketing objectives—and to offer useful suggestions for achieving them that might not otherwise be possible." These suggestions, says Oken, "might even recommend against media spending. We might urge heavier consumer or trade promotional activity instead." And where media use is indicated, Oken observes, "the fee system enables the agency to recommend certain unique types of media that might not be profitable for the agency were it compensated solely by media commissions."

Clients can help to make their agencies' media services even more effective, says Oken, by observing the following practices:

1. Formulate specific and realistic media objectives.
2. Share important data with your agency's media staff, including sales, budget, product development, and brand performance information.
3. Permit innovative media planning.
4. Be willing to look beyond "media numbers" to achieve more productive media plans.
5. Discuss and make media decisions with your agency rather than deviating from it or superseding it arbitrarily.
7. Avoid last-minute media buys or changes that can undermine the effectiveness of your media program.
8. Don't be drawn in by "bargain" buys that are not efficient.
9. Ask your agency to show you and your personnel how to understand and evaluate its media recommendations.

Oken is a frequent contributor to media trade publications and a member of the Newspaper Committee of the American Association of Advertising Agencies. He is active in numerous organizations and serves on the board of directors of the Advertisers Club, Chicago; the Association of Broadcast Executives of Texas; and the Dallas Advertising League.

crease. This is why so many media planners believe frequency is the most important media objective. It's the key to remembering.

4. An intensive "burst" of advertising is more likely to cause a large number of people to remember it, at least for a short time, than is spreading a schedule thinly over a 12-month period. This is the most common strategy for building frequency on a limited budget and the rationale behind pulsing advertising schedules.
5. Fewer exposures per prospect in a comparatively large group promote greater memory of the advertising than do more exposures per prospect in a smaller group. In other words, there's a point at which reach becomes more important than frequency to promoting memory.
6. As additional exposures per prospect are purchased, the dollar efficiency of advertising decreases. At some point, therefore, it is again more important to seek reach rather than additional frequency.

The media planner must decide how to weight reach, frequency, and continuity to maximize the impact and dollar efficiency of the advertising. Since no perfect scientific method has been devised to do that, this is the *art* of media planning.

Summary

The decisions made in media planning frequently involve as much creativity as the decisions made by art directors and copywriters. And like good art and copy ideas, media decisions should be based on sound marketing principles and research, not just experience and intuition.

The media function involves two basic processes: media planning and media selection. Media planning begins by determining primary target audiences and then setting goals or objectives for communicating with those audiences. Media objectives may be expressed in terms of reach, frequency, impressions, gross rating points, and continuity.

In developing the appropriate media strategy, the planner must consider many variables. These include the scope of the market, the nature of the message, consumer purchase patterns, budget levels, the mechanical limitations of the media, competitive strategy, the merchandising needs of the advertiser, and the basic nature of the medium itself.

After the media strategy is developed, the tasks of selecting specific media vehicles begins. Numerous factors influence the selection process: (1) campaign objectives and strategy; (2) the size and characteristics of each medium's audience; (3) geographic coverage; (4) the attention, exposure, and motivation value of each medium; (5) cost efficiency; and (6) the intended selection approach.

Once the particular media vehicles have been selected, the problem arises as to how to schedule their use; that is, how many of each medium's space or time units should be bought over what period of time? There are many ways to schedule a media campaign, from steady, continuous advertising to erratic pulses of commercials. This decision is usually a function of the media strategy.

The final result must be a logical weighting of reach, frequency, and continuity to maximize the effectiveness of the campaign and the efficiency of dollars spent. This is referred to as the *art* of media planning.

Questions for review

1. What must the media planner take into consideration before media planning can begin?
2. What are the first two steps in developing the media plan?
3. How are media objectives often expressed? Describe.
4. What is the primary factor that determines the level of reach, frequency, and continuity?
5. What are the six basic types of media schedules? Give details on how each is used.
6. Of what importance are the following considerations in developing media strategy?
   a. Market scope.
   b. Nature of message.
   c. Consumer purchase patterns.
   d. Budget levels.
   e. Mechanical considerations.
   f. Competitive strategy.
   g. Merchandising factors.
   h. Nature of the medium.
7. What are the major factors that influence the use of specific media vehicles? Justify the importance of each factor.
8. What method is used to determine media costs?
9. What is the difference among the following media selection approaches: (*a*) broadside approach, (*b*) profile matching, and (*c*) high-assay principle?
10. What have basic research findings revealed about the right combination of reach, frequency, and continuity?

16

Print media

It was the biggest advertising competition in history, with over 8,000 entries, sponsored jointly by the Newspaper Advertising Bureau and the International Newspaper Advertising Executives. There were six Creative Gold awards—each an ounce of pure gold—to recognize the best retail and general daily newspaper ads published in the past year—the state of the art. And there were money prizes! A total of $50,000, with a first prize of $25,000. These prizes were for either published ads or unpublished ideas or layouts that attempted to move ahead of current practice and explore innovative ways to use the versatile newspaper medium.

One of the major problems for advertising professionals is simply to be heard above the high noise level of competitive messages—to pierce the consumer's armor of apathy and skepticism. Two things seem to be called for. First, faster and more efficient communication, and second, truly relevant messages.

The $25,000 first-prize winner—the Volkswagen ad shown in Figure 16–1—broke new ground on both counts. Virtually instant communication is achieved by the novel device of a headline that is half words and half picture. The real headline is: "You can blow your brains out over the high price of gasoline, or buy a Volkswagen." That's 16 words. But by substituting a drawing for the first 12 words, communication becomes instant and total.

The ad is the creation of two luminaries of the advertising world: Bob Levenson, vice chairman of Doyle Dane Bernbach and a member of the Copywriter's Hall of Fame, and Charles Piccirillo, senior vice president and creative management supervisor of the same agency.

The ad also meets the criterion of relevance. When the fuel crisis was making headlines, Levenson and Piccirillo felt they could take advantage of it and maybe sell some cars for Volkswagen. "We have always put any ad we have done that way in newspapers," says Levenson. "Newspapers mean news, and when you have an event that affects the whole country, you expect to see that in newspapers. And we wanted to get the message out quickly, and where else can you get it in practically overnight?"[1]

Using newspapers in the creative mix

Advertising people are constantly looking for *creative* solutions to their clients' marketing problems. In fact, as we pointed out in Chapter 9, advertising strategy is alternately referred to as *creative strategy,* and it is determined by the advertiser's use of the *creative mix.*

The dictionary defines *creativity* as "artistic or intellectual inventiveness." That definition seems particularly applicable to advertising because advertising so often calls for a combination of artistic disciplines—illustration, photography, graphic design, creative writing—and the intellectual requirements of shrewd marketing and media planning, psychological empathy, and rational persuasion.

Some people maintain that advertising is "not creative unless it sells." While that is a useful buzz phrase for deflecting impractical suggestions from creative staff, most advertising professionals realize that it probably falls short of the truth. As we know, many factors besides advertising creativity are involved in sales: the product, value offered, price, availability, competitive pressures, timing, and even the weather, all have an impact on sales. Nevertheless, creative advertising can give the advertiser a chance to be heard, to present an offer. A fresh creative approach can do that superbly.

The printed page, in general, and the newspaper, in particular, provide a unique, flexible medium for the maker of advertising to express this creativity.

How newspapers assist creativity

The newspaper provides all the basics. It is read by almost everybody who can reasonably be thought of as a consumer, and it is read almost daily. According to research, most people read the newspaper in a reasonably ordered way. In the course of their reading they open and look at 84 percent of the pages—giving the advertiser a good opportunity to gain their attention if the method used is creative enough to merit it.

The newspaper offers great flexibility, which assists creativity. There is little limitation on ad size; there is black and white, spot color, full color; and through preprinted inserts, there is an endless variety of shapes, paper stocks, and printing methods. Finally, the advertiser's printed message lasts. It stands still for rereading and reconsideration, for clipping and for sharing. The newspaper can be shopped from because it is really news about the marketplace.[2]

What works best in newspapers?

Newspapers have inherent features that have traditionally set them apart from other media.[3] For example:

1. Newspapers are a *mass* medium, penetrating every segment of society.
2. Newspapers are a *local* medium, covering a specific geographic area, which is both a market and a community of people sharing common concerns and interests.
3. Newspapers are *comprehensive* in scope, covering an extraordinary variety of topics and interests.
4. Newspapers are read *selectively* as readers search for what is personally interesting and useful.
5. Newspapers are *timely* since they are primarily devoted to the news.
6. Newspaper readership is *concentrated* in time. Virtually all the reading of a particular day's paper is done that day.
7. Newspapers represent a *permanent* record that people use actively. Ads and articles are often saved for permanent reference.

These features give rise to a number of special attributes of newspapers that offer clues to the ad maker who is seeking what will work best creatively:

Figure 16–1 The $25,000 winner in the newspaper creativity competition. Says Bob Levenson, the writer: ". . . there was never any question that it should be a newspaper ad, and a full-page newspaper ad at that, because that's the kind of impact we wanted to have." Charles Piccirillo, the art director, was looking for an immediate way to express the frustration everyone felt with the fuel crisis. "This was my first sketch, with a big fat magic marker. It seemed the only way to do it was big and loud and get it in tomorrow's newspaper while the news was still in the newspaper. They ripped it off my pad and took it to the client, and it came back approved."

1. Newspapers provide the opportunity for massive same-day exposure of an advertising message to a large cross section of any market. That means very broad *reach*. For advertisers like Marlboro, newspapers are a valuable reminder medium for a campaign that has long been established in the consumer's mind (Figure 16–2).

2. Newspapers combine broad reach with highly *selective attention* from the very small number of active prospects who, on any given day, are interested in what the advertiser is trying to tell them or sell them. One Tuesday a full-page ad appeared in the general news section of the *New York Times*. The ad was completely blank except for a portion of a needle-like graphic element peeking up from the bottom of the page (Figure 16–3). The interest of all New Yorkers was aroused. From shipping clerks to housewives to company presidents, everybody talked about it.

The next day a second ad appeared, again in the general news section, which showed a little more of the graphic. Everybody instantly recognized it as the famous spire on top of the Chrysler Building. But curiosity towered. "Maybe it's a remake of King Kong?"

On the third day the ad appeared in the financial section to attract the target audience—businesspeople who were looking for prime commercial office space.

The ad worked beautifully, as planned. And it also won a Creative Gold award in the Ad Concepts '79 competition.

3. Newspapers provide great creative flexibility to the advertiser. The ad's physical size and shape can be chosen and varied to give the degree of dominance or repetition that suits the advertiser's purpose. The advertiser can use black and white, color, Sunday magazines, or custom inserts. The newspaper, therefore, is almost a media mix by itself.

The $10,000 second-prize winner in the newspaper competition was won by Ron Anderson and Tom McElligott of Bozell & Jacobs in Minneapolis. They created a two-color, speculative layout for their client United Way which played off the perception of the newspaper's physical nature and use apart from its primary "news" purpose: "If you still wonder why there's a United Way, try using this newspaper as a blanket some night on a park bench" (Figure 16–4).

4. With newspapers the advertiser can go where the customers are. That may mean concentrating the messages in one market or spreading them out over a national schedule. That may mean running the ad in one part of the paper or in several sections. The advertiser can place ads on short notice, localize copy, and work with retailers by using co-op programs.

5. The newspaper is an active medium rather than a passive one.[5] Readers turn the pages, clip and save, write in the margins, sort through the contents, screening out what they don't want from those things they want to concentrate on. This reader-involving quality of newspapers offers unlimited creative opportunities to advertisers. Coupon ads are an obvious example. Some Ad Concepts entries were built around the idea of pseudo-involvement, where the action requested was really an attention-getting device with no serious idea of the action being carried out.

The United Airlines layout of a kite serves its attention-getting purpose even if it's flown only in the friendly skies of the imagination (Figure 16–5).

Some drawbacks to newspapers

While newspapers offer the many advantages and opportunities mentioned above, like all media they also have their drawbacks.

Lack of audience selectivity

Newspapers enable advertisers to be geographically selective, but they do not isolate and cover specific socioeconomic groups. Instead, most newspapers reach broad, diverse groups of readers. The consumer desires and needs of these broad groups may not be compatible with the marketing segmentation objectives of the advertiser. For example, a newspaper sports section may be a good place to advertise general sports products or services, such as surfboards or football tickets, but it would be highly inefficient for advertising sports products to retail sporting goods dealers because of the tremendous waste of circulation.

Short life span

The life span of a daily newspaper is usually only a few hours. Unless a reader clips and saves a newspaper ad or coupon, it may be lost forever. Almost nobody reads yesterday's paper.

Poor production quality

Newspapers are produced quickly; there is no time to use quality reproduction techniques. And generally the coarse paper used for newspapers creates a finished product far less impressive than magazines with their slick, smooth paper stock.

Heavy advertising competition

So many advertisements appear in a single issue of a newspaper (63 percent of the average daily paper) that the potential of any one ad to capture major attention is minimized. Each ad competes for notice with every other ad on the same page or spread.

Potentially poor placement

The position in which an advertisement is placed on a newspaper page can determine how many readers will see it and how much attention they will give it. However, the advertiser has little or no control over this placement. Studies have found that ads placed above the horizontal fold of a newspaper are seen more frequently than those placed beneath the fold. Similarly, ads in the outside columns of a page are seen more frequently than those in the inside column.

Overlapping circulation

Many areas are served by newspapers that have overlapping circulation; that is, some residents read not one, but two or more different newspapers. Thus, an advertiser may be paying for circulation that his or her ad has already reached in a different newspaper.

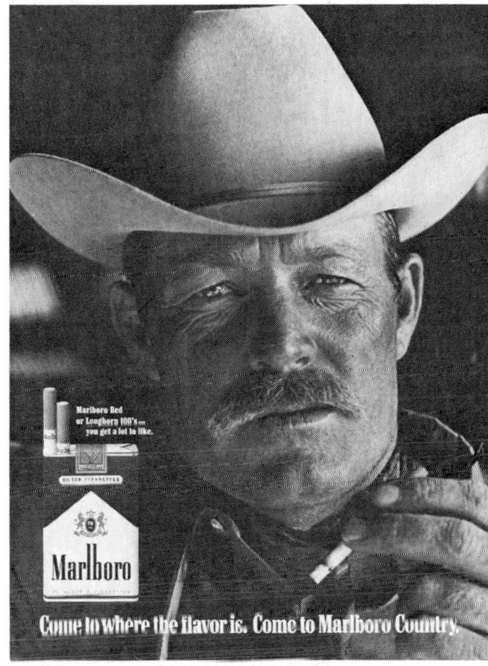

Figure 16–2 Marlboro illustrates the concept of creative continuity. Jim Morgan, executive vice president of Philip Morris, USA, comments on the creative content of the Marlboro newspaper ad. "The power lies in its utter simplicity—in the stark contrast a Marlboro ad in the newspaper has compared to other ads in that same issue." With no copy other than the name and the required "tar" information, the campaign is at a point, because of its consistency through the years, "where you can show a cowboy and not even say the name, and people will know it's a Marlboro ad."[4]

Who uses newspapers?

Early in our nation's history, three well-known Americans faced different, but similar, problems.

Governor William Penn, in 1681, wanted to attract hard-working European settlers to the new Pennsylvania colony. The Dutch and the Germans were likely prospects, he decided, but they needed to be informed.

A Boston silversmith named Paul Revere wanted to develop customers for his new engravings of the Boston Massacre. It was 1776 and his celebrated ride the year before had made his name known for miles around, but not his engravings.

In 1790 President George Washington decided the young American nation could reduce its dependency on England only by building up its infant textile industries. The people would have to be motivated to buy American-made clothes. Then he had an idea: he would wear them himself. As President and a man of fashion,

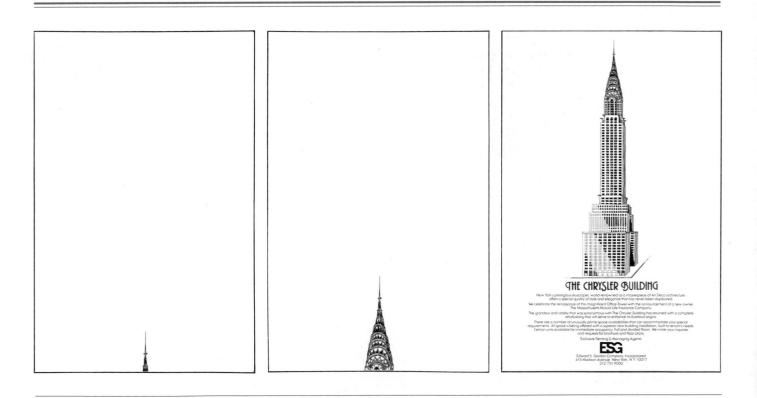

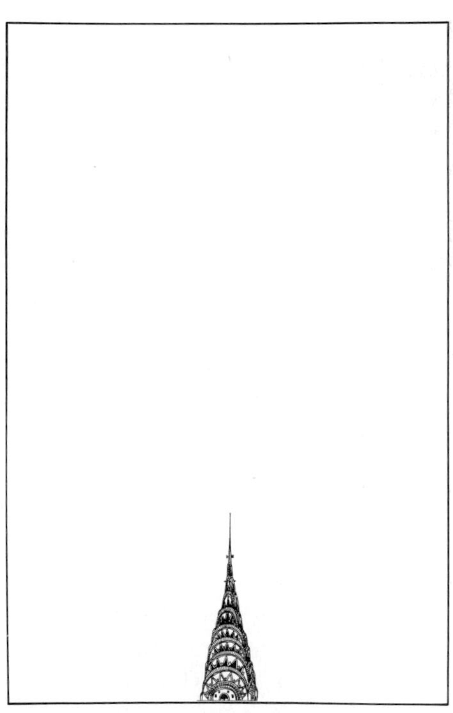

Figure 16–3

The Chrysler Building's success was easy. As a full-page ad, the first ad in this three-day series turned the town upside down when it appeared. Some of the newspaper's executives called down to find out if someone in the production department had forgotten to run an ad in the space. The campaign not only won tremendous attention, but it also created one of the most successful rental programs in real estate history. Occupancy of the Chrysler Building soared from 40 percent to 90 percent within three months.

he was sure to be imitated. But how could he assure that news of his new American-made garments would reach the people in areas outside Virginia?

All three of these notables achieved their objectives by using a common means: the newspaper. Governor Penn placed foreign-language advertisements in the newspapers of northern Europe and soon attracted hordes of new settlers. Paul Revere advertised his engravings in newspapers west of Boston and developed many new customers. And George Washington enlisted a leading newspaper of the day to publish what may have been one of the nation's first publicity stories.

The effectiveness of newspaper exposure has been similarly confirmed by thousands of other satisfied users. Today, as in 1776, newspapers are the nation's dominant medium in terms of advertising volume. They receive nearly 30 percent of the dollars spent by the nation's advertisers. In 1980 newspapers derived an estimated $15.6 billion from advertising revenues.[6]

Consider these important facts:

1. The average U.S. newspaper averages 72 pages for morning editions, 60 pages for evening editions, and 208 pages for Sunday editions.
2. The printed matter averages 64 percent for advertising and 36 percent for editorial matter.
3. The average U.S. metropolitan daily newspaper obtains about 75 percent of its income from sales of advertising space. The bulk of the remaining income comes from subscriptions and vendor sales. Estimates are that, without advertising income, the *New York Times* would have to sell its Sunday edition for $7 a copy to break even.

In 1980 there were 1,745 daily newspapers in the United States with a total circulation of 62 million. The nation's more than 7,602 semiweekly and weekly newspapers have a combined circulation of more than 40.9 million.

The newspaper is the major community-serving medium for both news and advertising. With the huge growth of radio and television over the past 20 years, more and more national advertising has shifted to these electronic media. The result is that radio and television today carry most of the national advertising, while 85 percent of newspaper advertising revenue comes from local advertising. The major national advertisers in newspapers are automobile manufacturers, tobacco companies, food processors, and airlines.

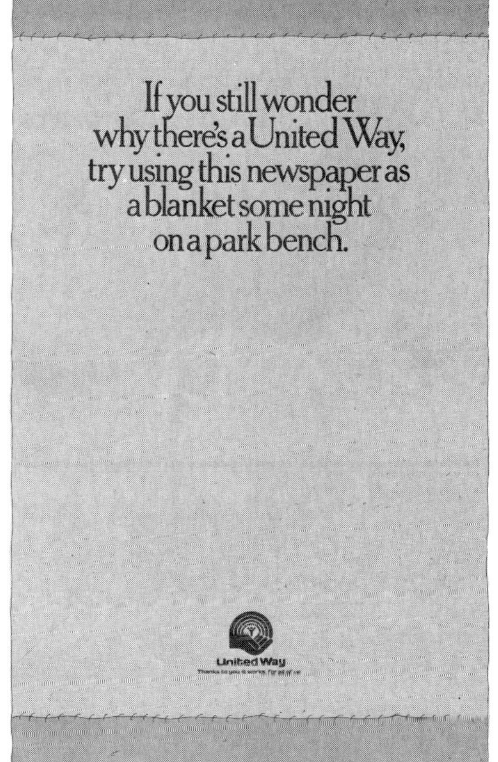

Figure 16–4 United Way works for all of us, especially the less fortunate. That's the message behind this simple, powerful layout of a blanket made from a newspaper page. The creators, Ron Anderson and Tom McElligott, also won a $1,000 award for a similar full-page layout for United Way that pictured a run-down shack in the ghetto. The headline, "If you want to know what living in a ghetto feels like, tape this to your window." The physical size of the newspaper page allows many such creative solutions.

How newspapers are classified

Newspapers may be classified by their frequency of delivery, by the type of audience they reach, or by their physical size.

Frequency of delivery

The two basic types of newspapers are *dailies* and *weeklies.* Dailies are published at least five times a week, Monday through Friday. Some are published on Saturday and Sunday as well. Dailies are produced as either morning or evening editions. Of the 1,805 dailies in the United States, 1,388 are evening papers, 387 are morning papers, and 30 are "all-day" newspapers. One recent study found that morning editions tend to have a broader geographic circulation and a larger male readership. Evening editions were found to be read more by women. Despite these broad characteristics, each daily newspaper has its own circulation traits, chiefly determined by the geographic region it serves and the demographic makeup of its readers.

The weekly newspaper characteristically serves readers in small urban or suburban areas or farm communities. One reason for the growth of readership among many weekly newspapers is their exclusive emphasis on local news and advertising. Weekly newspapers

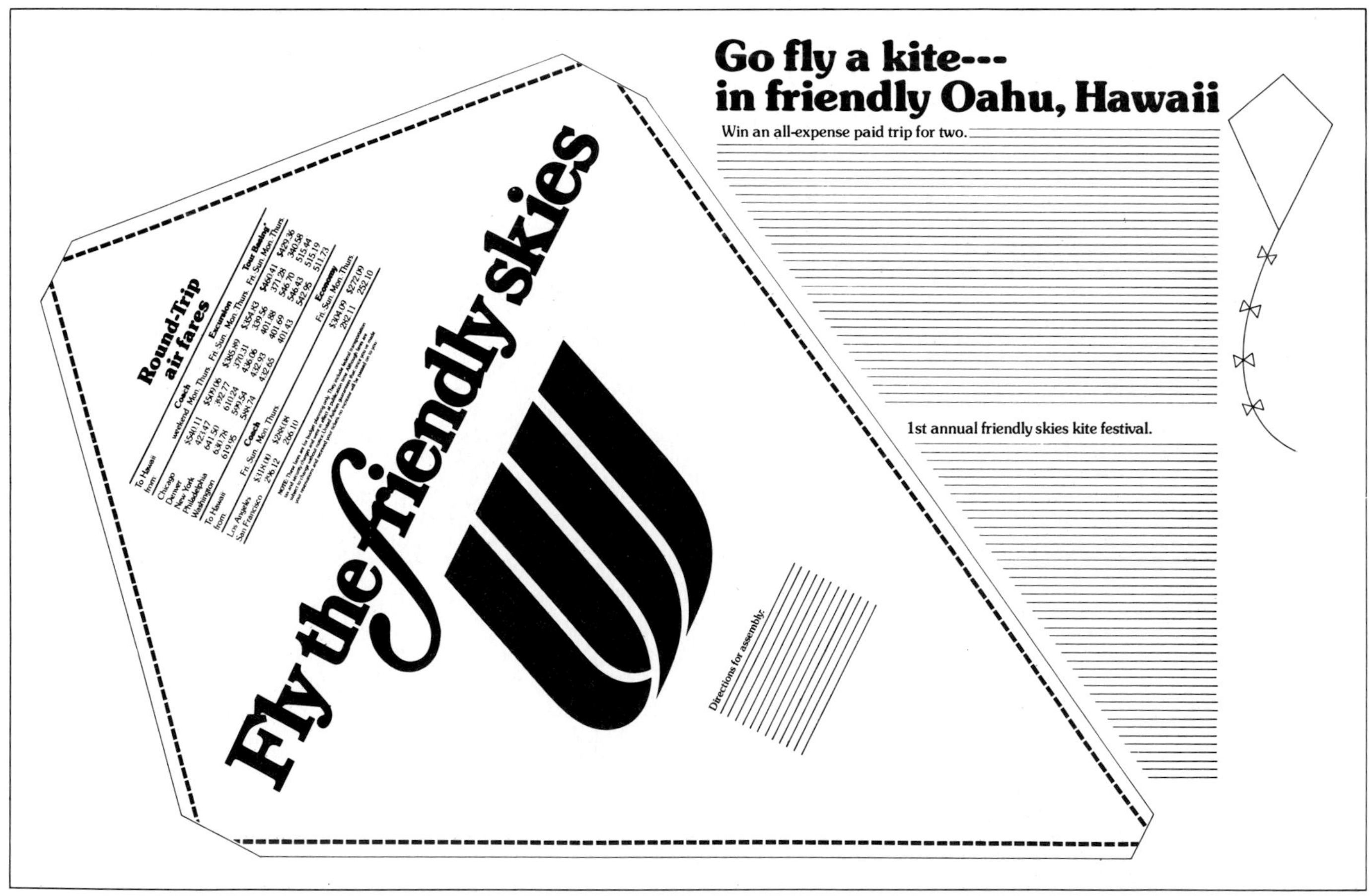

Figure 16–5 Fly the friendly skies in your imagination, as the text suggests. This layout for United Airlines won a $1,000 prize for its reader-involving concept. Newspapers offer advertisers the opportunity to actively involve their readers by clipping coupons, saving articles, working puzzles, or even constructing paper toys like this. Numerous Ad Concepts winners were selected for their attention-getting, reader-involving characteristics.

offer their readers relief from unsettling national and international crises in the form of familiar names, news of local personalities, and hometown sports, entertainment, and social coverage.

The weekly newspaper usually offers advertisers a high degree of readership but at a cost per thousand that is often higher than that of the daily paper. The rate may be justified since the weekly has a longer life than the daily and is often exposed to more readers per copy.

Specialized audience

Some dailies and weeklies are aimed at specific special-interest audiences such as military, ethnic, social, or religious groups. Some are published by fraternal, labor union, or professional organizations. Their specialized news and features enable them to achieve high readership. They generally contain advertising oriented to their special audiences, and they may have unique advertising regulations.

Among these newspapers, for example, are those that specifically serve black readers. Today 203 dailies and weeklies nationwide are oriented to blacks, such as the *Amsterdam News.* Still other specialized papers serve foreign-language ethnic groups, such as Spanish, German, Polish, Chinese, or Armenian readers. The U.S. has ethnic newspapers published in 43 languages other than English.

Specialized newspapers are also produced for business and financial audiences. *The Wall Street Journal* is the leading national business and financial daily, with a circulation of 1,838,891.

The leading U.S. military newspaper is *Stars and Stripes.* Its daily and Sunday European and Pacific editions are read by more than 1 million overseas armed services personnel.

Size

The two basic newspaper formats are standard and tabloid. The *standard-size* newspaper is generally 18–23 inches deep and 13 or more inches wide. This type of newspaper is usually eight columns wide, although a recent trend has been toward a six-column layout and a slightly reduced page size.

The *tabloid* newspaper is generally about half as deep as a standard-size newspaper and about 12–14 inches wide, though size varies from one tabloid to another. It is sold flat, without folding, and looks like an unbound magazine. Most tabloid pages have five columns, each about two inches wide. The *Christian Science Monitor* converted to a tabloid format and now has half the page size of its previous standard format with approximately twice the number of pages. This new format, four columns per page, was adopted to encourage advertisers who run full-page ads in national magazines to place these same ads in the *Monitor.*

Three national tabloid newspapers, all fighting with sensational news stories for single-copy sales through grocery supermarkets across the country, are the *National Enquirer, The Star,* and the *Midnight Globe.* Their combined circulation is 11 million a week.

In contrast, other tabloids emphasize "straight" news and features. The *New York Daily News,* for example, has the nation's largest daily and Sunday newspaper circulation—over 1.5 million readers daily and over 2.5 million on Sunday.

Other types of newspapers

Some 720 of the nation's daily newspapers publish Sunday editions. The combined circulation of these Sunday papers is more than 54 million. Sunday newspapers generally combine standard news coverage with their own special functions. These functions include:

1. Much greater classified advertising volume.
2. Much greater advertising and news volume.
3. In-depth coverage of developments in the arts, business, sports, housing, entertainment, and travel.
4. Review and analysis of the past week's events.

Most Sunday newspapers also feature a newspaper-distributed magazine, or *Sunday supplement.* Some publish their own supplement such as the *Los Angeles Times' "Home"* magazine. The remaining newspapers subscribe to a syndicated magazine supplement. These are compiled, edited, and printed by a central organization, then shipped to individual newspapers for insertion in their Sunday editions. Three examples of syndicated supplements are shown in Figure 16–6.

Sunday supplements are distinct from other sections of the newspaper, since they are printed on smoother paper stock. This heavier, higher quality paper is more conducive to color printing. Thus, it enables Sunday supplements to attract and feature higher quality national advertising.

Another type of newspaper is the independent shopping guide or free community newspaper. Sometimes called "pennysavers," newspapers (or shoppers) of this type carry little news and practically no features. Instead, they are distributed free of charge and are filled with advertising aimed at essentially the same audience as the weekly newspapers—urban and suburban community readers.

Shoppers may be published weekly, biweekly, or monthly. Readership is generally high, and the publisher strives to achieve maximum saturation of the circulation area.

Figure 16–6 Sunday supplements

			Black/white		Four-color	
Supplements	**Number of papers**	**Circulation**	**Page**	**Cost per thousand**	**Page**	**Cost per thousand**
Family Weekly	348	12,303,505	$ 82,030	$6.67	$ 93,420	$7.59
Parade	130	21,644,119	141,020	6.51	173,060	7.99
Sunday	51	21,488,586	164,522	7.66	200,372	9.32

Types of newspaper advertising

The major classifications of newspaper advertising are: display, classified, public notices, and preprinted inserts. The first classifications consist of a number of subclasses, as shown here:

- Display advertising.
  - General (national) advertising.
  - Retail (local) advertising.
    - Retail merchandise.
    - Local services.
    - Farm auction.
    - Political.
    - Miscellaneous.
  - Paid reading notices.
- Classified advertising.
  - Classified advertising.
  - Classified display advertising.
  - Business and professional cards.
  - Farm auction.
- Public notices.
  - Legal notices.
  - Public treasurers' reports and other public reports.
  - Public notices by private citizens and organizations.
  - Financial reports.
- Preprinted inserts.

Display advertising

The size of display advertising runs from small boxes to one- and two-page ads. Display ads are generally featured in all areas of the newspaper except on page one, the editorial page, the obituary page, the first page of major sections, and the classified section.

The two principal types of display advertising are *local* and *general* (national). Most newspapers charge the local advertiser and the national advertiser different rates. The national rate averages 51 percent higher than the local rate. Newspapers attribute these higher national rates to the added costs they incur in serving national advertisers. For instance, they point out that this advertising is usually placed by an advertising agency to which the newspaper gives a 15 percent commission. Some newspapers serve these agencies through media representatives, to whom they must also pay a commission. If the advertising comes from another city or state, still other costs are involved. Thus, newspaper publishers feel the higher national rates are justified.

This dual rate system, however, has been the topic of continuing controversy among advertisers. Many agencies and advertisers use every available means to qualify for the lower local rate. Some locally based agencies specialize in placing ads for national clients at the lower rate and then charge them a 3–4 percent commission for this money-saving service.

In 1980 about 85 percent of all newspaper display advertising was local. The largest source of newspaper display revenue is local retail merchants.

Newspaper display ads can be black and white, multicolored, or full-colored, with or without pictures. Most local display advertising is either black and white or some rudimentary colors, printed directly on the newspaper. In contrast, much national advertising is preprinted on magazine-supplement-type paper and fills an entire page. The opposite side of the page may then be left for the newspaper's own purposes.

One common variation of the display ad is the *reading notice*. This type of ad looks like editorial matter. It is sometimes charged at a higher space rate than normal display advertising. To prevent readers from mistaking it for editorial matter, the law requires that the word "advertisement" appear at the top of the reading notice. Many, but not all, newspapers accept reading notices.

Classified advertising

Classified advertisements are a unique and important feature of newspapers. They provide a community marketplace for goods, services, and opportunities of every type, from real estate and new-car sales to employment openings and business proposals of major magnitude. Such ads are usually arranged under subheads that describe the class of goods or the need that the ads seek to satisfy. For example, you would look for a job under the classification "Help Wanted" and for an employee in the listings headed "Situations Wanted." Classified rates are based on the amount of space purchased and how long the ad is to run. Most employment, housing, and automotive advertising run today is in the form of classified advertising.

Some newspapers also accept classified display advertising. Such ads are run in the classified section of the newspaper and are generally characterized by larger-size type, photos, art borders, abundant white space, and sometimes even color.

Preprinted inserts

Preprinted inserts are inserted into the fold of the newspaper and look like a separate, smaller section of the paper. The inserts are printed by the advertiser and then delivered to the newspaper plant to be inserted into a specific edition either by machine or by the newscarriers. Sizes range from a typical newspaper page to a piece no larger than a double postcard. Formats include catalogs, brochures, mail-back devices and perforated coupons.

A number of large metropolitan dailies allow advertisers to distribute their inserts to specific circulation zones only. Thus, a store that wants to reach shoppers in its immediate area only can place an insert in the local-zone editions. Retail stores, auto dealers, large national advertisers, and others have found it less costly to distribute their circulars in this manner than by mailing them or delivering them door to door. By 1979 advertising expenditures for printing and distributing these inserts reached $1.6 billion, 85 percent of it retail and 15 percent national.[8]

How to buy newspaper space

Newspapers serve different reader audiences in varying degrees. Thus, for effectiveness, it is important that the media buyer and advertiser know the characteristics of a newspaper's readership—the median age, sex, occupation, income, educational level, and buying habits of the typical reader.

In single-newspaper cities, the demographic characteristics of readers are likely to reflect some cross section of the population as a whole. In cities with two or more newspapers, however, these characteristics may vary widely. Los Angeles, for example, is served by the *Times,* noted for its moderate political outlook, and the *Herald-Examiner,* considered politically conservative. Each newspaper has a different readership.

Readership is also determined by the time of day a newspaper is published. An advertiser, for example, may have to decide between advertising a bedding sale in a morning newspaper that has a 70 percent male readership or an evening newspaper read by equal numbers of men and women. Each alternative has its advantage: The morning paper can advertise the sale that day and attract immediate shoppers, and the evening paper can be read by husband and wife together and motivate them to come to the sale the following day. The advertiser must decide about these and other factors to determine the optimum timing and placement for the ad.

Audience segmentation by section

In a sense, every reader of the newspaper reads a different newspaper. That's because every newspaper contains such a wide variety of material—international news, national and local politics, advice to the lovelorn, recipes for tomorrow's dinner, photos, crossword puzzles, and comics. From this wide assortment, readers can take only what they want and, in effect, can edit their own newspaper.

This offers opportunities to the advertiser who wants to target advertising to specific groups. The sports section offers heavy male readership; society sections offer heavy female readership. Business people, male and female, are normally interested in the business or finance section. And children love to read the comics. Figure 16–7 shows traditional male-female readership figures by editorial content.

Reading rate cards

Newspapers provide potential advertisers with a printed information form called a *rate card.* This card lists the newspaper's advertising rates, mechanical and copy requirements, advertising deadlines, and other information the advertiser needs to know before placing an order. Some of the common terms used on rate cards are described here.

Agate lines versus column inches

Newspaper space is sold by *agate lines* (a unit of measurement for depth) or by *column inches*. The agate line measures 1/14-inch deep by one standard column wide. A standard column is usually two inches wide, but many editors use different column widths to enhance their paper's layout. Buyers and sellers of newspaper space refer to agate lines as "linage."

The increasing trend among smaller newspapers is to sell advertising space by the column inch. A column inch is one inch deep by one column wide. It is equivalent to 14 agate lines. Can you compute how many agate lines an ad would be that is eight inches tall and four columns wide?* (See the Ad Lab.)

Retail versus general rates

National advertisers, as noted earlier, are usually charged a higher rate than local advertisers. Local advertisers can sometimes earn even lower rates by buying large or repeated amounts of space at *volume discounts*. Such incentives are not offered by all newspapers, however. Many national papers charge *flat rates,* which means they allow no discounts for large or repeated space buys. And some newspapers offer a single flat rate to both national and local advertisers.

Newspapers that offer the advertiser volume discounts have an *open*

*448 lines.

Figure 16–7 Newspaper readership by editorial content

Editoral content	Percent of readers opening average page
Males	
Sports	85
Amusements	84
Radio, TV	83
General news	82
Society	81
Business, finance	77
Food, fashion	73
All other	80
Females	
Society	94
Amusements	90
Food, fashion	88
General news	88
Radio, TV	69
Sports	69
Business, finance	69
All other	85

rate, which is their highest rate for one-time insertions, and *contract* or *earned* rates. Local advertisers can obtain discounts of up to 70 percent by signing a contract for frequent or bulk space purchases. These bulk discounts offer the advertiser decreasing line rates as the number of lines used increases. The contract is renewed annually. Frequency discounts may be earned when a given ad is run repeatedly during a specific period of time (Figure 16–8).

Short rate

If an advertiser contracts to buy a specific amount of space during a one-year period at a discount rate and then fails to buy this amount of space, he or she is charged a *short rate.* This is computed by determining the difference between the standard rate for the lines run and the discount rate contracted. Conversely, if an advertiser buys more lines than the number contracted, he or she is entitled to a rebate.

Combination rates

Combination rates are offered for placing a given ad in (1) morning and evening editions of the same newspaper; (2) two or more newspapers owned by the same publisher; and (3) in some cases, two or more newspapers affiliated in a syndicate or newspaper group. Combination rates are sometimes also offered for placing a given ad in consecutive Saturday and Sunday editions of the same newspaper. At one time, some newspapers were requiring advertisers to buy combinations. Courts have declared this practice illegal and combinations are now optional.

How to compare newspaper rates

One way an advertiser can compare the rates of different newspapers is by computing the cost per thousand readers of each paper. A more common method of comparing newspapers is by computing their *milline rate,* which is the cost per line of space per million circulation.

Here is the formula:

$$\frac{1{,}000{,}000 \times \text{Rate per line}}{\text{Quality circulation}} = \text{Milline}$$

For example, the milline rate of a newspaper with 1 million circulation and a rate of $2 per line would be:

$$\frac{1{,}000{,}000 \times \$2.00}{1{,}000{,}000} = \$2.00$$

In comparison, the milline rate of a newspaper with 500,000 circulation and a rate of $1.50 per line would be:

$$\frac{1{,}000{,}000 \times \$1.50}{500{,}000} = \$3.00$$

Remember: The milline is a means for comparing rates and *not* a unit for buying space (Figure 16–9).

Laboratory application

Compare the milline rate of two newspapers in your area. Based on the milline rate, which is the best buy?

Los Angeles Times

Times-Mirror Square, Los Angeles, Calif. 90053.
TWX 910-321-2460. Phone 213-972-3000.
Sat., Sun., Holidays & after 5:00 p.m. daily, Phone 213-972-5000.

Media Code 1 105 4125 7.00
MORNING AND SUNDAY.
Member: INAME; NAB, Inc.

1. **PERSONNEL**
Pub. & Chief Exec. Officer—W. Thomas Johnson.
Vice-Pres. Sales—Vance L. Stickell.
Display Advertising Director—Donald J. Maldonado
General Advertising Manager—J. Wm. Sinkking.

2. **REPRESENTATIVES and or BRANCH OFFICES**
BRANCH OFFICES
New York 10017—Larry Letters, Mgr., 711 Third Ave. Phone 212-697-6200.
Chicago 60611—Thomas C. Rupp, Mgr., 500 N. Michigan Ave. Phone 312-527-4410.
San Francisco 94111—100 California St., Suite 870. Phone 415-421-6643.
Detroit 48084—John L. Scolaro, Media Rep., 2855 Coolidge Rd., Suite 101. Phone 313-649-4311.
REPRESENTATIVES
The Leonard Company.
Lenha Hawaii, Inc.

3. **COMMISSION AND CASH DISCOUNT**
15% to agencies; no cash discount.

4. **POLICY—ALL CLASSIFICATIONS**
60-day notice given of any rate revision.
Alcoholic beverage advertising accepted.
Our liability for error shall not exceed cost of space occupied by the error. Credit allowed for first insertion only. Notice of errors must be given in time for correction before second insertion, otherwise no credit for repetition shall be allowed.
Copy corrections after 1st revised proof, composition charge 26.30 per hour.
The publisher reserves the right to revise or reject, at its option, any advertisement which it deems objectionable in text or illustration or detrimental to its business.
All ads measured cut-off rule to cut-off rule.
7-column ads not accepted.

ADVERTISING RATES
Effective February 1, 1981. (Card No. NG-12.)
Received December 8, 1980.

5. **BLACK/WHITE RATES**

	Daily	Sunday
Open, per line	6.78	8.22
Full page unit, per line	5.92	7.00

BULK CONTRACT DISCOUNTS

Within 52 weeks:	Daily	Sunday
2,500 lines	6.14	7.28
5,000 lines	6.01	7.14
10,000 lines	5.78	7.01
15,000 lines	5.72	6.84
20,000 lines	5.64	6.70
25,000 lines	5.58	6.63
35,000 lines	5.50	6.56
50,000 lines	5.43	6.50
75,000 lines	5.36	6.41
100,000 lines	5.29	6.36
150,000 lines	5.06	6.20
200,000 lines	4.93	6.07
250,000 lines	4.87	5.91
300,000 lines	4.79	5.84
350,000 lines	4.72	5.76
400,000 lines	4.65	5.70
500,000 lines	4.58	5.62
600,000 lines	4.50	5.57
700,000 lines	4.43	5.48
800,000 lines	4.36	5.41
900,000 lines	4.21	5.34
1,000,000 lines	4.15	5.27

FULL PAGE CONTRACTS

Within 52 week contract periods:	Per line Daily	Sunday
10 insertions	5.43	6.50
15 insertions	5.29	6.36
20 insertions	5.16	6.20
30 insertions	5.01	6.07
40 insertions	4.93	5.97
50 insertions	4.87	5.91

APPLICATION OF DISCOUNTS
Open Space Contract not accepted for discount bulk rate.
Less than full page units take applicable bulk discount contract rate. Full page linage included in computing earned bulk rate. If both full page and fractional units are used, bulk contract and full page contract must be signed in advance.

7. **COLOR RATES AND DATA**
Available: B/w 1 c Monday thru Sunday. Extra charge for special color ink and 14 day lead time is required. No leeway required. All color booked firmly.

	Daily b/w	Daily b/w 1 c
1 page	14,208.00	17,003.00
1,500 lines	10,170.00	12,965.00
1,000 lines	6,780.00	9,575.00

	Sunday b/w	Sunday b/w 1 c
1 page	16,800.00	20,170.00
1,500 lines	12,330.00	15,700.00
1,000 lines	8,220.00	11,590.00

Use b/w line rate plus the following applicable costs:

1,000 lines minimum to 1 page:	b/w 1 c
Daily, extra	2,795.00
Sunday, extra	3,370.00

Closing dates: 2 days before publication date; 4 days for Thursday Food Section.

9. **SPLIT-RUN**
Non-commissionable mechanical charge of 210.00 for black and white and 420.00 mechanical charge plus color premium for black and 1 color. Ads must be of the same size dimension and product.
Established lines rate prevail with minimum 500 lines. Both ads must be same size, dimensions and product.

11. **SPECIAL PAGES, FEATURES**
Best Food Day: Thursday.
Fashion "80" see paragraph 16 for additional information.

12. **MINIMUM DEPTH R.O.P.**
Minimum depth 14 lines. Ads 1 col. and 3 cols. over 150 lines deep charged full column (300 lines); ads 2 cols., 4 cols., 5 cols. and 6 cols. over 252 lines deep charged full column (300 lines); ads 8 cols. over 266 lines deep charged full column (300 lines). 5, 6, and 8 col., 150 lines minimum. Tabloid: 1, 2, 3 cols. over 91 lines deep, and 4, 6 cols. over 140 lines deep charged full column (182 lines).

13. **CONTRACT AND COPY REGULATIONS**
See Contents page for location of regulations—items 1, 2, 4, 5, 6, 9 thru 15, 18 thru 23, 28, 30 thru 36.

14. **CLOSING TIME**
Sunday deadlines: Calendar, View, Travel and Real Estate copy due Tuesday p.m. before publication; reservations by 9:00 a.m.
Main News, Financial, Sports 5:00 p.m. Thursday.
Daily: Monday 9:00 a.m., Friday before; Thursday Food Section, 10:00 a.m. Monday. Other daily editions 2 days before publication.

15. **MECHANICAL MEASUREMENTS**
PRINTING PROCESS: Photo Composition Letterpress & Offset.
For complete, detailed production information, see SRDS Print Media Production Data.
8/9-9/3—8 cols/ach col. 9-9 picas-pts/3 pt. rule.
Lines to: col. 300, page 2400; dbl. truck 4950.

16. **SPECIAL CLASSIFICATION/RATES**
Fashion "80" published Friday.
Open, per line 7.46
R.O.P. Bulk Discounts apply plus 10%.
Deadlines: 2:00 p.m. Wednesday 10 days before publication.
8 columns to page; minimum size ad 300 lines.
POSITION CHARGES
Next to reading 15%; full position, publisher's option 33-1/3%; special pages 15%. First and editorial pages not sold. Minimum depth for full position 56 lines

Figure 16–8 The *Newspaper Rates and Data* listing for the *Los Angeles Times*. Note the variety of rates available to advertisers depending on the volume of their linage.

Run of paper (R.O.P.)

R.O.P. advertising rates entitle a newspaper to place a given ad on any newspaper page or in any position it desires—in other words, where space permits. Most newspapers, however, make an effort to place an ad in the position requested by the advertiser.

Color rates

Color advertising is available in many newspapers on an R.O.P. basis. Since newspapers are not noted for their high-quality color printing because of high-speed presses and porous paper stock, advertisers frequently preprint ads using processes known as HiFi color and Spectacolor. The advertisement is printed on a roll, and the roll is fed into the press by the newspaper, which prints its own material on the blank side.

Figure 16–9 Newspapers: Circulation and rates

Newspaper	Circulation	Open line rate	Milline rate
New York Daily News	1,524,641	$12.60	$ 8.26
Los Angeles Times	1,000,942	6.78	6.78
New York Times	873,275	7.00	8.01
Chicago Tribune	784,388	7.00	8.92
Chicago Sun-Times	655,332	5.80	8.85
New York Post	639,604	7.05	11.02
Detroit News	629,598	6.05	9.61
Detroit Free Press	604,062	4.94	8.18
Washington Post	584,500	6.25	10.35
San Francisco Chronicle	506,600	6.12	12.08
Boston Globe	501,520	4.18	8.33
Long Island Newsday	489,888	5.02	10.25
Philadelphia Bulletin	434,105	6.08	15.66
Philadelphia Inquirer	425,877	5.94	13.95
Newark Star-Ledger	406,728	3.34	8.21
Miami Herald	398,415	5.93	14.88
Cleveland Plain Dealer	395,452	2.75	6.95
Houston Chronicle	356,288	2.59	7.27
Baltimore Sun	348,405	3.36	9.64
Houston Post	331,172	2.59	7.82
Milwaukee Journal	318,723	3.85	12.08
Cleveland Press	304,499	2.35	7.72
Kansas City Times	297,972	3.36	11.28
Los Angeles Herald Examiner	285,371	4.30	15.07

The largest daily newspaper, the national edition of *The Wall Street Journal,* has a circulation of 1,838,891, an open line rate of $27.48, and a milline rate of $14.94.

Preferred position

An advertiser can assure a choice position for an ad by paying a higher *preferred position* rate. For example, a dictating machine manufacturer must pay this rate if it wants to assure that its ad will be on the business or financial page. And a jeweler may do the same to assure a position in the women's pages.

There also are preferred positions on the newspaper page itself (Figure 16–10). The preferred position near the top of a page or on the top of a column next to reading matter is called *full position*. It is usually surrounded by reading matter and costs the advertiser 25 to 50 percent more in many newspapers. Slightly less good, but also a preferred position, is placement "next to reading matter" (N.R.), which generally costs the advertiser 10 to 20 percent more.

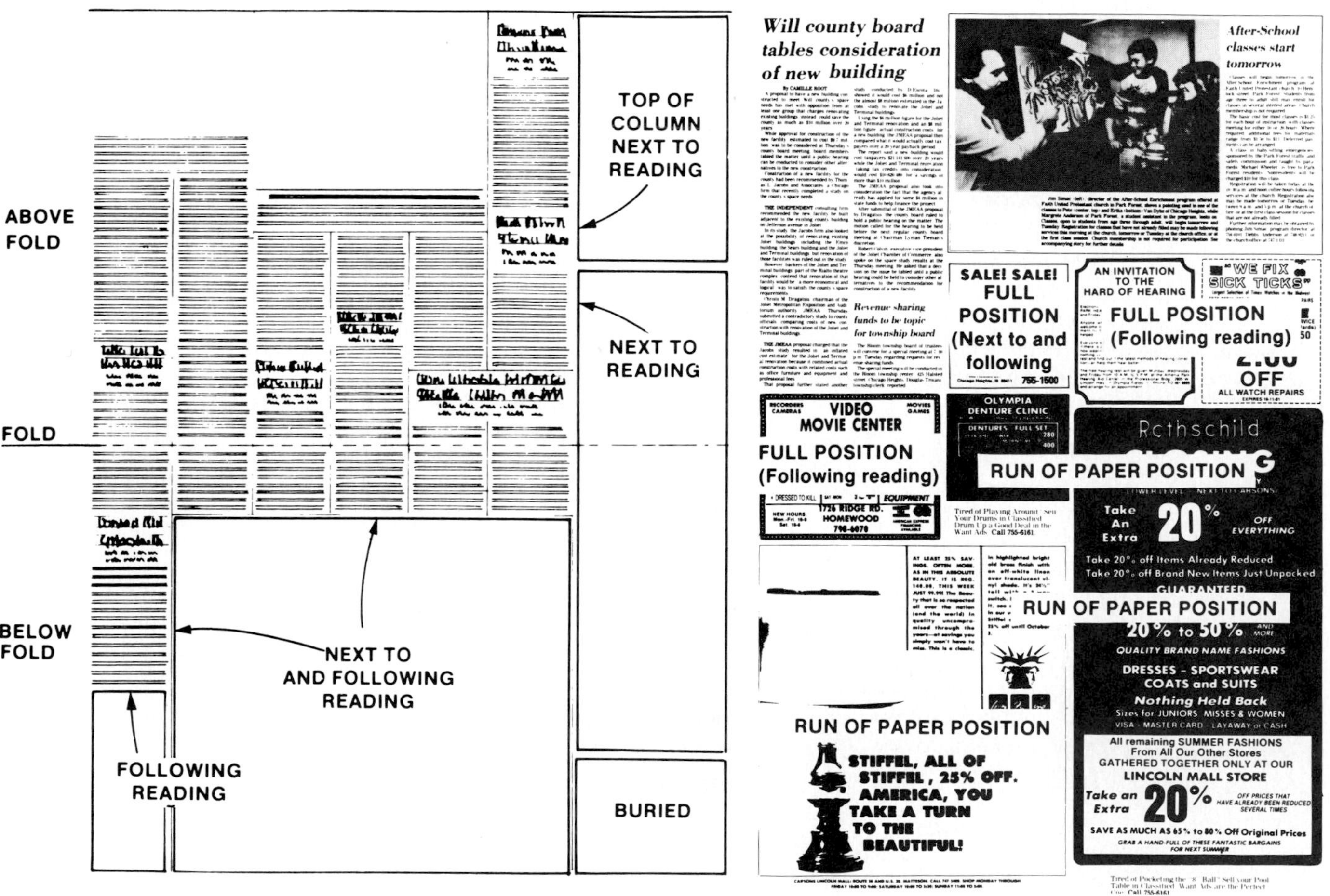

Figure 16–10 This diagram shows the preferred page positions offered by newspapers.

Rate differentials

Newspapers charge different rates for different types of advertising. For example, by law, newspapers—and other media—are required to charge political advertisers no more than the rate offered to any other advertiser for comparable use of space. Some newspapers charge another rate for advertising in the theater or entertainment section. This rate is generally lower than that for general display ads. And some newspapers offer special low rates or other incentives for "In Memoriam" advertisements and religious announcements.

Split runs

Many newspapers (as well as magazines) offer *split runs* to advertisers who want to test the comparative effectiveness of two different advertising approaches. The split run enables the advertiser to run two different ads of identical size, promoting the same product or service, in the same or different press runs on the same day. For example, as the newspapers are printed, half might be printed with one ad while the other half gets a different ad. In this way the advertiser can test the pulling power of one ad against the other. Newspapers set a minimum space requirement and charge extra for this service.

Insertion orders—tear sheets

When an advertiser is ready to run an advertisement, he or she submits an *insertion order* to the newspaper. This form states the date(s) on which the ad is to run, its size, the requested position, and the rate. It also states whether finished art, mechanicals, Velox prints, or mats will be furnished with the ad (Figure 16–11).

When advertising copy and art are created by the newspaper, the advertiser is provided a *proof copy* for checking purposes before the ad is run. In contrast, most national advertising is submitted with the art, copy, and layout in final form. It is important that the agency or advertiser receive verification that the ad has run. Thus, the newspaper tears out the page on which the ad appeared and sends it to the agency or advertiser. Today most *tear sheets* are forwarded through a private central office, the Advertising Checking Bureau.

When a tear sheet arrives, it is examined to make certain that the advertisement ran according to the instructions of the agency or advertiser—particularly with regard to the section of the paper in which it ran, its page position, and its reproduction. If the advertisement did *not* run as instructed, the agency or advertiser may be entitled to an adjustment. This may be a rerun of the ad free of further cost.

Using magazines in the creative mix

What medium do you use if you're an airplane manufacturer and your objectives are: (1) to convince three separate audiences that

TEL.

CABLE: CUNNWALSH, N.Y.

No.

DATE	ADVERTISER	PRODUCT	EST. NO.	TERR. & PROD.	PUBLICATION CODE
7/23/81	THE BANK OF NEW YORK	BANK OF N.Y.	850-375	100	33034

PUBLISHER

PUTNAM COURIER-CORLANDT
45 GLENEIDA AVENUE
CARMEL, N.Y. 10512

NATIONAL ☐ REGIONAL ☐
ORDER NO.
CONTRACT DISC. LEVEL

INVOICE AND CHECKING COPY TO
RATE SUBJECT TO 15% AGENCY COMMISSION
*INDICATES 2% CASH DISCOUNT

INSERTION DATE(S)	SPACE: LINAGE	SPACE: SIZE	CAPTION	AD NO.	RATE
WEEK OF 8/03/81	1000LI		"MY BANK CALLS IT ACTION BANKING"	85489	.60

SPECIAL INSTRUCTIONS

PLEASE SEND TWO(2) TEARSHEETS OF EACH INSERTION TO D. HAMMILL & F. MATHISEN AT C&W.

GROUP INC: CROTON CORLANDT NEWS&CARMEL PUTNAM COURIER.

POSITION REQUEST

ROP-RIGHT HAND PAGE-OPPOSITE A MINIMUM OF ONE COLUMN EDIT. NOT TO BE BACKED UP BY ANOTHER AD CONTAINING A COUPON.

THIS ADVERTISING IS NOT TO APPEAR ON PAGE WITH, PAGE FACING, OR BACKED UP BY THE ADVERTISING OF ANY SIMILAR PRODUCT. THIS ADVERTISING IS NOT TO BE BACKED UP BY COUPON.

PRINTING MATERIAL

HEREWITH FROM REILLY GRAPHIC.
HOLD MATERIAL IN FILE FOR POSSIBLE FUTURE REPEAT INSERTIONS.

RATE BASE

A.A.A.A. CLAUSE 35 YES ☐ NO ☐
SUBJECT TO CONDITIONS ON BACK HEREOF
F75 IBM 22M 8/80

PUBLICATION

BY

Figure 16–11 This insertion order of an advertising agency, Cunningham & Walsh Inc., gives directions for the placement of a newspaper ad for the Bank of New York.

your planes are the best aircraft for their particular needs, (2) to gain market share for your company, and (3) to improve your market position against two very strong competitors?

That was the problem faced by Piper Aircraft Corporation and their new agency Ally & Gargano.[9] The agency accomplished Piper's objectives by using a creative media and message mix that concentrated more on solving the particular marketing problems than on establishing an overall "family" identity.

Magazines were selected that reached one or more of Piper's target audiences. These included general flying enthusiasts who subscribe to various aviation magazines, traveling businesspeople who have never flown and who read a variety of general newsmagazines, and top corporate executives who read business publications like *Business Week, Dun's Review*, and *Nation's Business*. The messages were provocative but factual, with visual presentations that ranged from expressive mood photographs to simple columns of long editorial copy.

For flying enthusiasts, the agency used a full-color photographic poster that ran as a spread in aviation magazines. The brief, dogmatic copy advises that when Piper stops being the best in its class, "we'll change this ad" (Figure 16–12).

A second spread ad encourages corporate sales by using dynamic, in-flight photography and a headline that promises to meet the demand for corporate mobility "without compromising the demands for corporate frugality" (Figure 16–13).

Still a third ad offers a detailed explanation of the advantages of

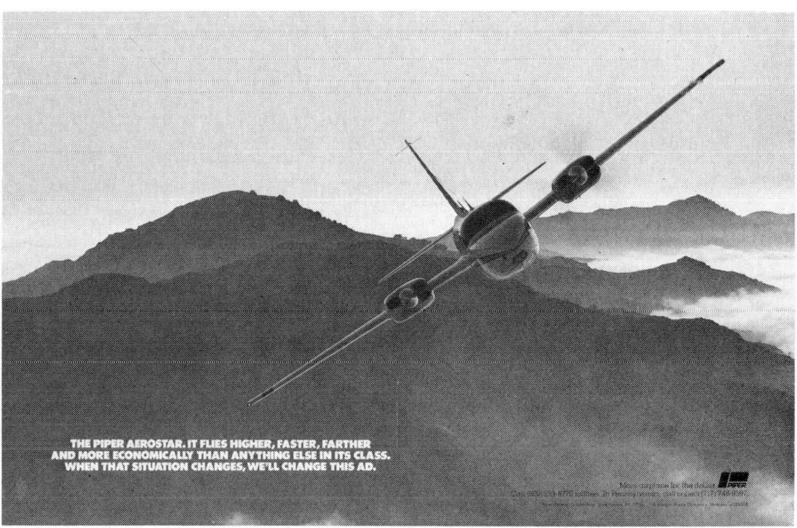

Figure 16–12 Mood photography which captures the feel of flying characterizes this image ad aimed at flying enthusiasts. The objective was to improve Piper's competitive position against other popular aircraft manufacturers.

using a plane for business and an objective, unemotional comparison of the car and the plane as a means of transportation. Set in long, deep columns designed to suggest the magazine's editorial layout, the ad includes a simple visual presentation of the aircraft from top, side, and front views. Rather than treating the plane as a glamorous object, this ad presents it as a basic vehicle for getting someone from one place to another (Figure 16–14).

The campaign's results were impressive. Piper's share of market increased 10 percent in a year and a half. Dollar volume outpaced the industry's growth figures. And direct response from the ad for traveling businesspeople was enormous. One salesman walked into a dealership in Philadelphia carrying the ad in his hand. Inasmuch as Piper had persuaded him to learn to fly, he said he might as well learn from a Piper dealer.

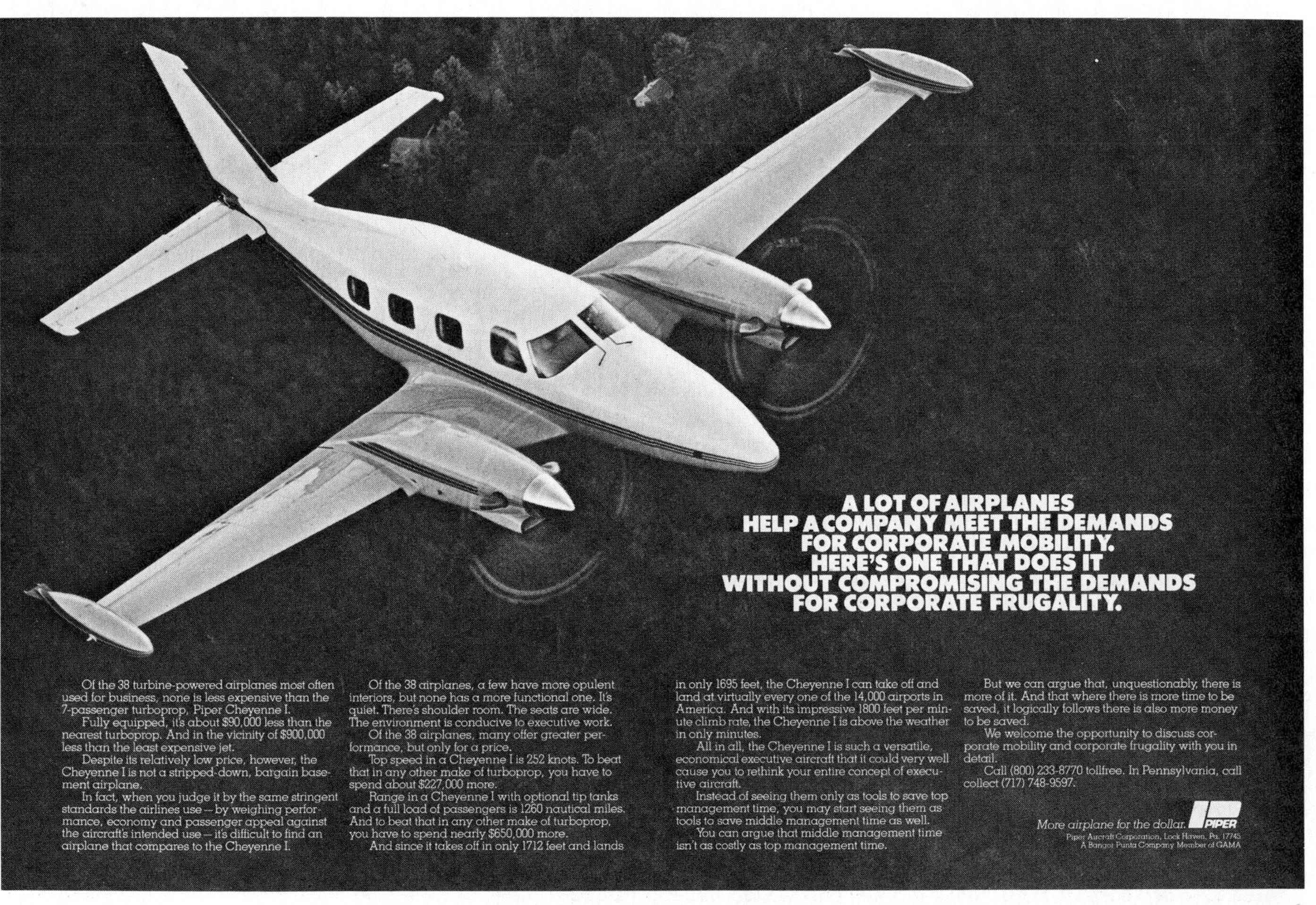

A LOT OF AIRPLANES HELP A COMPANY MEET THE DEMANDS FOR CORPORATE MOBILITY. HERE'S ONE THAT DOES IT WITHOUT COMPROMISING THE DEMANDS FOR CORPORATE FRUGALITY.
Of the 38 turbine-powered airplanes most often used for business, none is less expensive than the 7-passenger turboprop, Piper Cheyenne I.
Fully equipped, it's about $90,000 less than the nearest turboprop. And in the vicinity of $900,000 less than the least expensive jet.
Despite its relatively low price, however, the Cheyenne I is not a stripped-down, bargain basement airplane.
In fact, when you judge it by the same stringent standards the airlines use — by weighing performance, economy and passenger appeal against the aircraft's intended use — it's difficult to find an airplane that compares to the Cheyenne I.
Of the 38 airplanes, a few have more opulent interiors, but none has a more functional one. It's quiet. There's shoulder room. The seats are wide. The environment is conducive to executive work.
Of the 38 airplanes, many offer greater performance, but only for a price.
Top speed in a Cheyenne I is 252 knots. To beat that in any other make of turboprop, you have to spend about $227,000 more.
Range in a Cheyenne I with optional tip tanks and a full load of passengers is 1260 nautical miles. And to beat that in any other make of turboprop, you have to spend nearly $650,000 more.
And since it takes off in only 1712 feet and lands in only 1695 feet, the Cheyenne I can take off and land at virtually every one of the 14,000 airports in America. And with its impressive 1800 feet per minute climb rate, the Cheyenne I is above the weather in only minutes.
All in all, the Cheyenne I is such a versatile, economical executive aircraft that it could very well cause you to rethink your entire concept of executive aircraft.
Instead of seeing them only as tools to save top management time, you may start seeing them as tools to save middle management time as well.
You can argue that middle management time isn't as costly as top management time.
But we can argue that, unquestionably, there is more of it. And that where there is more time to be saved, it logically follows there is also more money to be saved.
We welcome the opportunity to discuss corporate mobility and corporate frugality with you in detail.
Call (800) 233-8770 tollfree. In Pennsylvania, call collect (717) 748-9597.
More airplane for the dollar.
PIPER
Piper Aircraft Corporation, Lock Haven, Pa. 17745
A Bangor Punta Company Member of GAMA

Figure 16–13 Various business publications carried this no-nonsense message about corporate frugality to business executives. Even the tag line promises: "More airplane for the dollar."

What works best in magazines?

The Piper campaign illustrates the best use of magazines as an element of the creative mix. Flexible design, the availability of color, excellent reproduction quality, believability and authority, permanence, prestige, and, most of all, excellent audience selectivity at an efficient cost characterize the opportunities magazines offer advertisers.

1. Magazines are the most *selective* of all media, except for direct mail. The predictable editorial environment selects the audience and enables advertisers to pinpoint their sales campaign. Most magazines are written for special-interest groups. *Golf Digest* helps a golf club manufacturer reach golfers; *Business Week* reaches businesspeople;

TO THE 4,000,000 PEOPLE WHO FREQUENTLY DRIVE OVER 200 MILES ON BUSINESS: THERE'S AN INVENTION YOU SHOULD KNOW ABOUT.

As outlandish, outrageous, ridiculous and totally off-the-wall as the idea may seem at this moment, sooner or later you'll fly your own plane.

No kidding.

BY FEDERAL LAW, IT IS NOW IMPOSSIBLE FOR TRAVELING BUSINESSMEN TO GET RICH QUICK.

With the passage of Public Law 93-643—the law that set the nation's speed limit at 55 mph—businessmen with quotas to reach found themselves hampered by highway patrolmen with quotas of their own.

Accounting, no doubt, for the steady downward trend of the average highway speed.

In an airplane, however, there are no laws governing quick travel. You travel at the speed your machine is capable of attaining.

In something like a Piper Archer II, for example, that's in the area of 150 mph.

Or as fast as a Ferrari driven at speeds guaranteed to attract attention.

IF YOU HAVE A PLANE, YOU MAY NOT NEED A SUITCASE.

At 150 mph, an Archer II can take you 300 or so miles away from home in the span of only a couple of hours.

At that same speed, it follows that an Archer can also take you back home in the same amount of time.

With an airplane flown according to your own schedule, then, a two-day business trip to one of the 14,000 airport-equipped cities in America can become a one-day business trip.

The net result is one of two things, both of which the businessman who drives for a living will find as great luxuries.

More time for more work. Or more time for not working.

If you're one of those people who never seem to have enough time, here's the way to get it.

BELIEVE IT OR NOT, A PLANE IS CHEAPER THAN A CAR.

40,000 miles a year in a large Buick—about the equivalent comfort level of the Archer II, by the way—costs about 13¢ a mile, according to calculations by a major car rental company.

With the cost of an Archer II at 21¢ a mile for 40,000 miles, the real bargain would appear to be driving instead of flying.

What you have to consider in addition, however, is the cost of your own time.

If you make $35,000 a year, for example, every hour in a 40-hour week is worth $17.

40,000 miles in the Archer II takes only about 350 hours. But in a car, 40,000 miles takes about 800 hours.

The true price of a mile in a car, then, is not just the cost of the car, but the cost of 450 extra hours on the road as well.

Or about 32¢ a mile in a Buick.

THE PERFECT CAR FOR BUSINESS TRAVEL ISN'T A CAR AT ALL.

Given the speed of an airplane, the comfort of an airplane and the economy of an airplane, why are you still driving a car for business?

Few things in your business life have the potential to alter your future as dramatically as the ability to use an airplane does.

Which leads to a question that demands an honest answer:

If you could make a decision right now that would change the way you spend the rest of your life, would you do it?

And if it, somehow, seems like too difficult a task to master, how come 784,000 people no different from yourself have already managed to do it?

After all, learning how to fly an airplane is simply a matter of learning how to use a machine.

DECIDING TO LEARN IS THE MOST DIFFICULT PART OF LEARNING.

At Piper, we've made a concerted effort to make learning how to use an airplane, not just how to fly one, easier than ever for traveling businessmen.

Beginning is simple in the Piper Tomahawk, a new single-engine trainer of such advanced design that it stands as the sum total of everything ever learned about learning to fly.

New training materials have been designed.

Instructors at authorized Piper Flite Centers have been trained to use them.

As a result, completing the requirements for a private pilot's license has been made, if not easy, at least a lot less difficult and time-consuming.

You can work your Piper ground and air instruction around your business hours.

In a matter of only months, it's entirely possible to solo and earn a private license for single-engine airplanes like the Archer II, then begin acquiring equal proficiency with multi-engine airplanes and instrument flying techniques.

At this point, there will be little more for you to learn except what experience will teach you.

DON'T JUST SIT THERE. FLY SOMETHING.

Call 800-447-0870 tollfree (800-322-2482 in Illinois). In Canada, call 800-268-7673.

We'll send you what you need to start thinking seriously about the practical use of the remarkable invention called the airplane.

To encourage your call, we'll also give you details about how you can win a $50,000 airplane in the GAMA TakeOff sweepstakes.

It's no idle prediction:

Sooner or later you'll fly your own plane.

INTRODUCING THE AIRPLANE.

PIPER

Piper Aircraft Corporation, Lock Haven, Pa. 17745
A Bangor Punta Company. Member of GAMA

Figure 16–14

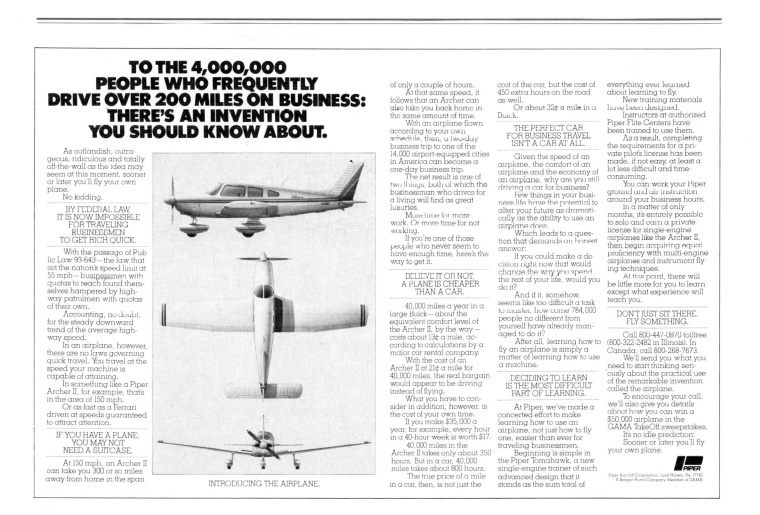

Piper advises the nonflying traveling businessperson about a new invention—the airplane. Simple, long columns of copy are used to convince these people that they ought to at least try flying. An incentive is even offered through an oblique reference at the end of the copy to winning a sweepstakes.

Seventeen reaches teenage girls; and *Ebony,* a black-oriented magazine, helps advertisers reach the black market (Figure 16–15).

2. Magazines offer *flexibility* in both readership and advertising. They cover the full range of prospects—with a wide choice of regional editions as well as national coverage. Each magazine lends itself to a variety of lengths, approaches, and editorial tones. The advertiser, therefore, has the choice of using long copy, black and white, editorial ads, or short copy, colorful poster ads, or humorous cartoons, or any of an infinite variety of approaches (Figure 16–16).

3. Magazine *color* spreads a spectrum of exciting visual pleasure before the reader. Nowhere can better color reproduction be seen than in the slick magazines. Color in such publications as *National Geographic* enhances image and identifies the package. In short, color sells.

4. If the advertiser wants to speak with *authority* and *believability,* magazines can enhance the message. People believe what magazines say. Their influence affects people's ideas, opinions, and desires. This enables magazines to counsel people on child-rearing (*Parents*), financial difficulties (*Money*), marital problems (*McCall's*), and advertising (*Advertising Age*).

5. Magazines offer *permanence.* For the advertiser who wants to communicate lasting information and enjoyment, magazines give the reader more opportunity to appraise ads in considerable detail. Advertisements can deliver a more complete educational/sales message and can effectively communicate the total corporate personality. Magazines also enable advertisers to generate reprints and materials,

Figure 16–15 Kraft targets minority markets for its many food products through special ethnic-oriented media. This half-page spread, created by Proctor & Gardner (see the profile in Chapter 9), ran in *Jet,* a black-oriented magazine.

which further promote and merchandise their corporate advertising campaigns.

6. Advertising a product in such magazines as *Sports Illustrated, Time,* and *House Beautiful* provides the advertiser with *prestige* for the product. The professionalism that publishers strive to maintain can be a great asset in building prestige through institutional advertising.

7. Magazines can be very *cost efficient.* By selecting the specific magazines and editions that reach prospects, the advertiser can keep wasted circulation to a minimum. The selling power of magazines has been proved and results are measurable, so they are the growing choice of many leading advertisers.

There are also other advantages. Magazines have extensive "pass-along" or secondary readership. They generate loyalty among readers that sometimes borders on fanaticism. Magazines also may reach prospects that salespeople cannot because of geographic or other reasons. Hard-to-reach occupational groups such as doctors and entertainment personalities are nearly all reached readily by magazines.

Drawbacks to magazines

Although magazines offer excellent creative capabilities for advertisers in a print medium, they do have their own drawbacks. The immediacy of newspapers, for example, is lost in magazines. Likewise,

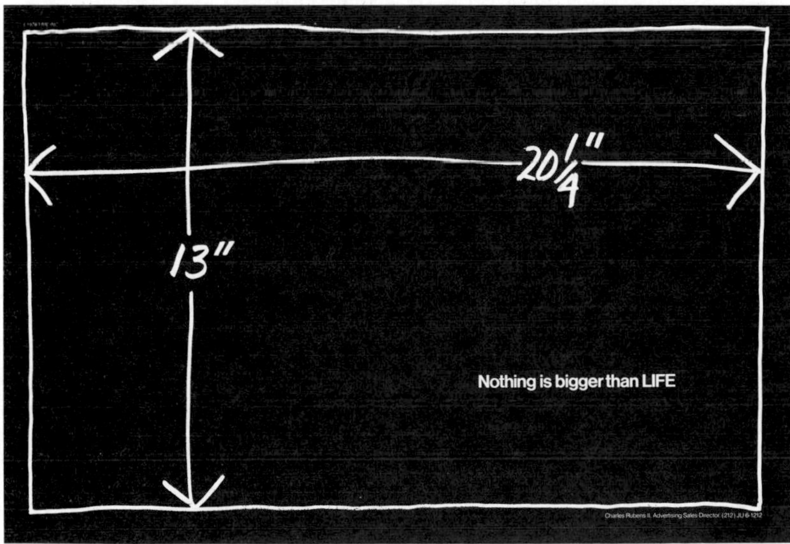

Figure 16–16 Imagine this ad, in bright red, as a gatefold. That's how it ran and how it communicated the message of *Life's* bigness. The ultra-simple, although expensive, concept won many big advertising awards for *Life,* too.

magazines don't offer the depth of geographic coverage or the local reach of newspapers. Nor do they offer the national reach of the broadcast media. They also suffer from the inability to deliver high frequency figures or mass audiences at a low price. The disadvantages of magazines, therefore, are several.

1. Advertising in magazines requires long *lead time*. Space must be purchased and the advertisement prepared well in advance of the date of publication—sometimes as long as three months. Weekly magazines, particularly those that run color advertisements, often require that advertising materials be in their hands weeks in advance of the publication date. And once the closing date has been reached, no changes in copy or art can be allowed.

2. Magazines have problems offering *reach* and *frequency*. It's interesting to note that magazines were the first national medium, yet today their coverage is generally lower (on an individual basis) than that of other media. Where selectivity is not a major marketing consideration, using selective magazines is very costly for reaching broad masses of people. Frequency can actually be built faster than reach by adding numerous smaller audience magazines to the schedule. However, most magazines are issued only monthly, or at best weekly, so building frequency in one publication is very difficult.

3. Magazines that are popular have the problem of heavy *advertising competition*. This can deter other advertisers. Of the 52 magazines that account for 66 percent of total magazine circulation, the average relationship of advertising to editorial linage is 52.4 percent advertising to 47.6 percent editorial matter. Because each advertisement is in so much competition with others, advertisers use a variety of techniques to gain attention, including those discussed in the next section.

4. The *cost* of advertising in magazines can be very high. While national magazines offer an average cost per thousand that ranges from $1.50 to $3.50, some trade publications with highly selective audiences have a cost per thousand of over $20 for a black and white page.

The advertiser naturally must weigh these disadvantages against the advantages mentioned above when determining the appropriate creative mix. Studies have determined that many of these disadvantages can be overcome and campaign effectiveness greatly enhanced by including magazines as part of the mix of media used to communicate the advertiser's message. Then the low-cost reach and frequency of other media can be supported by the permanence, prestige, and selectivity attributes of magazines.

Special possibilities with magazines

Magazines offer advertisers a wide variety of creative possibilities through various technical or mechanical elements. These include bleed pages, cover positions, inserts and gatefolds, and special-size ads such as junior pages and island halfs.

People in advertising

Rance Crain

President and Editorial Director
Crain Communications, Inc.

Publishers should stay "alert and aggressive—and not become smug or complacent," cautioned G. D. Crain, Jr., founder of Crain Communications, Inc. His son Rance listened. At 34 Rance Crain became president and editorial director of the Chicago-based firm that has produced some of the nation's leading trade publications for over half a century. One of them is prestigious *Advertising Age,* which Rance Crain heads today as editor-in-chief.

Crain, whose college-boy appearance belies his 42 years, pursued an early interest in publishing by attending Northwestern University's Medill School of Journalism, where he was graduated in 1960. He soon became a reporter for the Washington bureau of *Advertising Age* and later went on to its New York and Chicago Offices. In 1965 he was named senior editor of *Advertising Age* and the first editor of *Business Insurance.* Crain advanced to editorial director of *Ad Age* in 1971. Two years later, after the death of his father, he became president and editorial director of Crain Communications, Inc.

Under Rance Crain's leadership, the company quickly embarked on an aggressive program of expansion. Within four years it had nearly doubled its circulation. The firm started *Pensions & Investments* and acquired *Rubber & Plastics News* and *Modern Healthcare.* It expanded into the consumer market with *Autoweek* and other titles. In 1978 the company launched *Crain's Chicago Business* with Rance Crain as editor-in-chief and, two years later, *Crain's Cleveland Business* and *The Collector-Investor.* Today the firm publishes 16 titles, including *Automotive News* and *Industrial Marketing.* It also produces books, seminars, and a home-study course. The family-owned company is run by Crain, his brother, Keith, as secretary/treasurer and publisher of *Automotive News* and *Autoweek,* and their mother, Gertrude Crain, as chairman of the board.

Rance Crain continues to be the idea man of the organization. His modest corner office filled with memorabilia is a beehive of activity. Despite administrative demands, Crain spends more than half his time as editor-in-chief of *Advertising Age,* personally overseeing a myriad of editorial and production details.

Ad Age is the leading trade publication of the nation's advertising and marketing industries, a $5-million enterprise with 25 full-time reporters. Widely read by persons in publishing and other allied fields, the slick, attractive illustrated weekly tabloid reports the latest advertising and business news, including information on government actions that affect advertisers, agencies, media, and suppliers. Also covered are advertising campaigns for new and established products, agency appointments, and personnel changes. *Ad Age* data on radio, television, newspapers, magazines, and other media, and its half-dozen or more special issues each year filled with statistical media data are widely read throughout the advertising industry.

Explaining his success, Crain said, "Change and growth have become a way of life in our company. My brother and I pride ourselves on our ability and willingness to constantly build on that philosophy, avoid stagnation, and keep pace with a world which is changing faster than ever before. We intend to keep up with it—and even anticipate it."

That anticipation, he notes, may include acquiring a small, daily newspaper, a radio station, or any other media links that Crain believes will help CCI "keep pace" with a changing world.

A past president of the Chicago Business Publication Association, Crain serves on the boards of directors of the Northwestern Alumni Association, the Better Business Bureau of Metropolitan Chicago, and the Chicago Chapter of the International Advertising Association.

Bleed pages

When the dark or colored background of the advertisement extends to the edge of the page, it is said to "bleed" off the page. Most magazines offer *bleed pages,* but advertisers usually have to pay a 10–15 percent premium for them. By buying a bleed page, though, the artist has greater flexibility in expressing the advertising idea, the printing space is slightly larger, and the ad can be more dramatic than with a white border.

Cover positions

The front cover of American magazines is commonly referred as the "first cover." It is almost never sold. The inside front, inside back, and outside back covers are almost always sold at a premium. They are called the second, third, and fourth covers, respectively.

Inserts and gatefolds

When you turn a page in a magazine and find it extended and folded over to fit into the magazine, this is called a *gatefold.* The gatefold may be a fraction of a page or two or more pages. It may occupy the cover position or the centerfold. Gatefolds, also called *dutch doors,* are useful in making spectacular and impressive announcements. Not all magazines provide gatefolds and they are always sold at a premium.

Often an advertiser will have an ad printed on a special paper stock to add weight and drama to the message. This can then be *inserted* into the magazine at a special price. The same is true for special effects such as *encapsulations* of scents. These ads are normally printed in advance and then inserted. (See the Ad Lab.)

Junior pages and island halfs

One publisher of a large-sized magazine discovered he could generate business with a simple strategy. He accepted the plates for the standard-size magazine page even though the advertisement covered only 60 percent of the page. Then he surrounded it with editorial matter. This saved the advertiser the cost of new plates, which can be considerable. A special flat rate was set for this unit of space, called a *junior* unit or page. The junior unit is usually found on a page with no other advertising. It is an inexpensive method of dominating a page, but not all magazines accept it.

Similar to junior units are *island half-pages,* except that there is more editorial matter surrounding them. The island costs more than a regular half-page, but, since it dominates the page, many advertisers consider the premium a small price to pay (Figure 16–17).

How magazines are classified

Although there are many ways to classify magazines, the most common methods are by content, geography, and size.

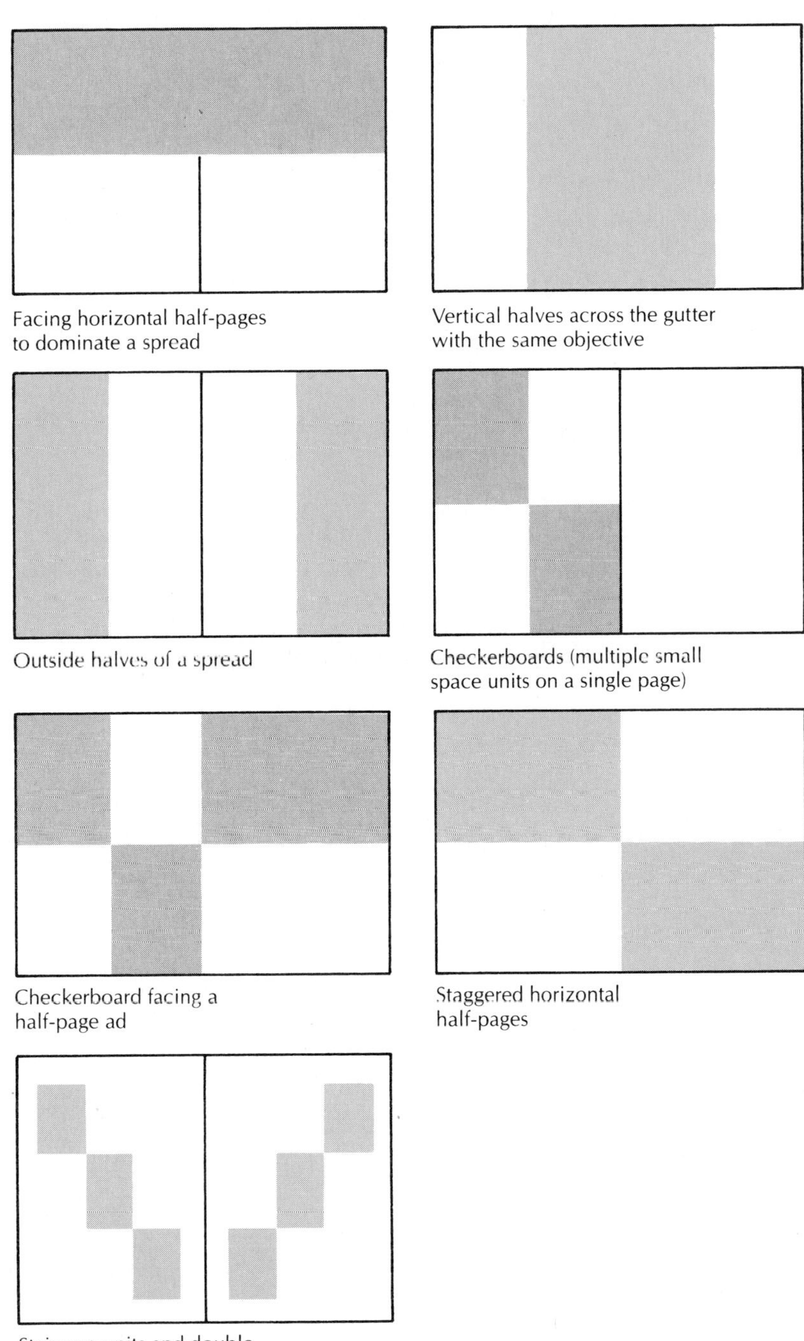

Figure 16–17 Magazine space combinations that can create big impact.

Content

One of the most dramatic developments in publishing during the last three decades has been the emergence of magazines with specialized appeal and content. Although specialization has been no guarantee of success, it has given many publications good prospects for long-term growth.

The broadest classification of content are consumer magazines, farm magazines, and business magazines. Each of these, though, may be broken down into hundreds of categories.

Innovations in magazine advertising

Microfragrence (microencapsulation)

This is a "perfumed" advertisement. "Scratch 'n Sniff" strips use the 3M microencapsulation technique for emitting the odor of perfume, soap, men's cologne, and liquor.

3D illusion printing

Originally introduced by *Look* magazine, Xograph 3D is a process of using a three-dimensional insert in a magazine. Many manufacturers have used this process since its debut, including Pfizer Laboratories, International Harvester, British Overseas Airways, and American Express.

Metallic ink

This is an ink that shines brightly and creates a striking visual effect.

Pop-ups

Illustrated pop-ups have been used by Wm. Wrigley Jr. Company to feature Wrigley zoo animal stars in children's magazines. A manufacturing company ran a three-dimensional pop-up of a prefabricated building in *Nation's Business* and *Better Buildings*.

Recordings

Remington's theme of music-to-shave-by was recorded on vinyl plastic and inserted in magazines. Eva-Tone Soundsheets can be bound into most business and consumer publications. An example of such a soundsheet can be found in this book.

Invisible ink

Ebonite used invisible ink in a four-color spread promoting its bowling balls. The ad carried a coupon of which 5,000 were surprinted with a fluorescent ink. When the special card was presented with the invisible ink, the dealer gave recipients a free bowling ball.

Product samples

Johnson & Johnson's Band-Aids, Scott Towels, Curtis candies, and Vanity Fair Lanolin Facial Tissue have all appeared in magazine advertisements—with samples of the product.

Talking magazines

By 1985 the printed page may talk. *Time* magazine, for example, is working with Microsonics to perfect the technology by which record grooves can be imprinted on a printed page. With the use of a microphonograph, the reader will be able to pass across the page and actually hear the voice of the person whose quotation he or she is reading.

Laboratory application

Pick one of the above innovations. What applications can you suggest in addition to those given? What are the implications for advertisers?

Consumer magazines These are edited for people who buy products for their own consumption. Consumer magazines are purchased for entertainment, information, or both.

Farm magazines The farm publications are magazines directed to farmers and their families or companies that manufacture or sell agricultural equipment, supplies, and services. These magazines include those devoted to dairy and dairy breeds, farm education and vocations, cooperatives and farm organizations, and other specialized agricultural areas. The most widely circulated farm publications are the *Farm Journal, Progressive Farmer, Prairie Farmer,* and *Successful Farming.*

Business magazines These are directed to business readers. They can be classified in the following ways: (1) trade papers (aimed at retailers, wholesalers, and other distributors); (2) industrial magazines (aimed at businesspeople involved in manufacturing); and (3) professional magazines (aimed at lawyers, physicians, dentists, architects, teachers, and other professional people).

Additional information about farm and business magazines can be found in Chapter 21 on "Business Advertising."

Geography

Magazines may also be classified by the amount of geography they attempt to cover.

Local Most major American cities have magazines named after them: *San Diego Magazine, New York, Los Angeles, Chicago, Philadelphia, Palm Springs Life,* and *Crain's Chicago Business,* to name a few. Their readership is usually upscale, professional people interested in the arts, fashion, culture, and business. A few are owned by local chambers of commerce, but most are the products of individual entrepreneurs.

Regional Magazines are not limited by geography like newspapers or broadcast stations. However, it may be more profitable to limit circulation to a certain area. *Sunset* magazine, for example, took editorial techniques from *Better Homes and Gardens* to build up an audience only on the West Coast. Such restrictions are by choice, not necessity.

National magazines sometimes offer advertisers special market runs which allow the selection of specific geographic regions. Many regional editions have been developed largely as a substitution of audience selectivity for size in the face of spot television competition. *Time, U.S. News & World Report, Newsweek, Woman's Day,* and *Sports Illustrated* have developed their coverage to such an extent that an advertiser wishing to buy a single major market can do so (Figure 16–18). Almost 20 percent of all magazine advertising is regional in nature.

National Typically, magazines have been a national medium reaching across the country with varying levels of circulation. The best-known national magazines have large circulations. *Reader's Digest,* with a national circulation of 17,750,000 in the United States, has now been outdistanced by *TV Guide,* which in 1981 had a circulation of over 18,300,000.

There are thousands of lesser-known national magazines with circulations of 100,000 or less. These publications are more often than not trade, industrial, professional, or farm magazines.

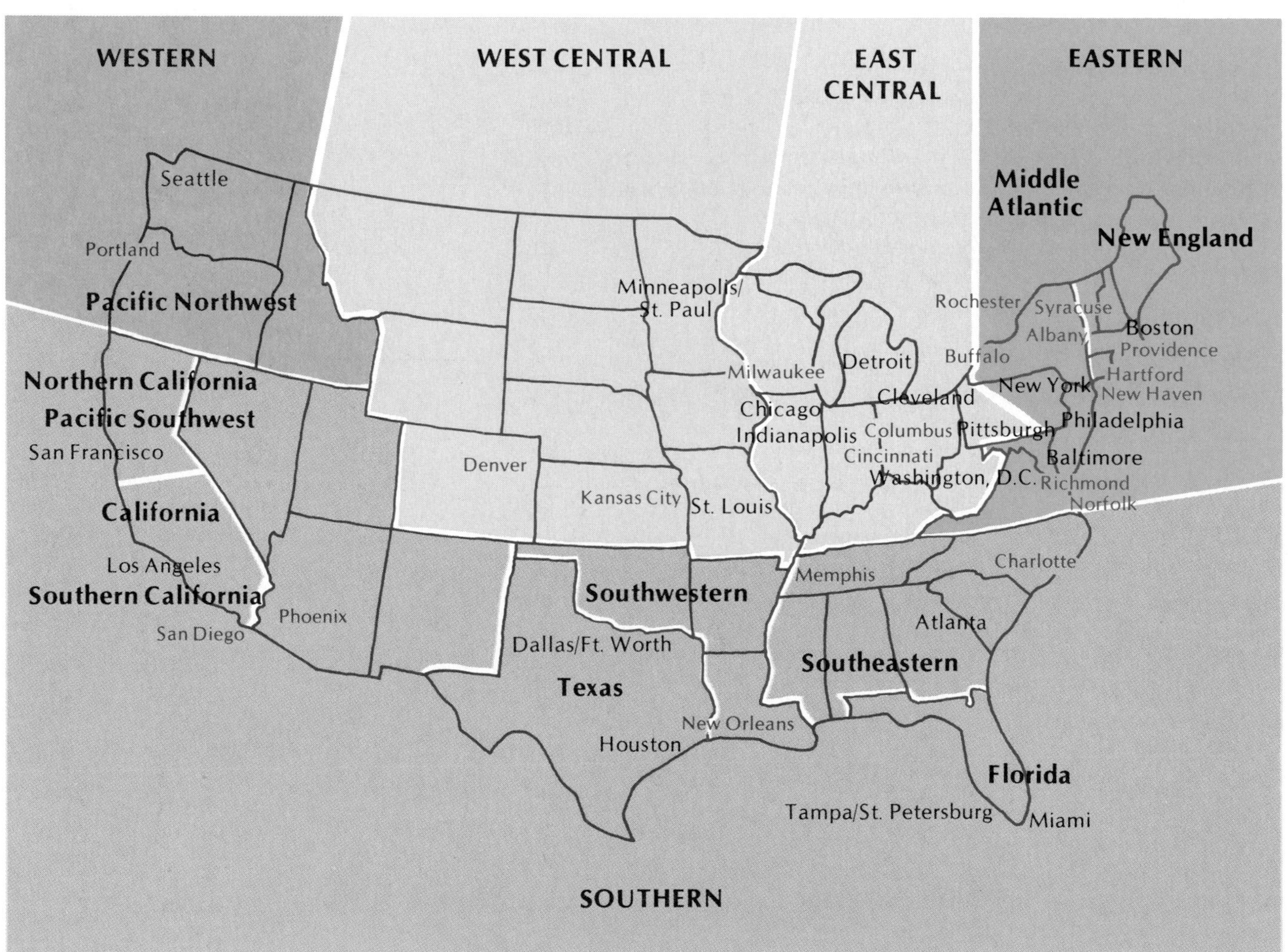

16 REGIONAL EDITIONS – Large Type — **basic regional configurations that can be broadly adapted — individually or collectively — to seasonal and geographic sales efforts.**

20 ADI METRO GROUP I EDITIONS – Small Type — **to concentrate advertising support in the country's topmost consumer, business and industrial markets.**

20 METRO GROUP II EDITIONS — **to enable the advertiser to concentrate in the remaining major U.S. markets.**

Figure 16–18 *Newsweek* promotes its numerous geographic editions in this ad which ran in the Standard Rate and Data Service directory of *Consumer Magazines and Farm Publications Rates and Data*. It also offers demographic editions (not shown here) for such diverse groups as college students and business people.

Size

It doesn't take a genius to figure out that magazines come in different shapes and sizes, but sometimes it takes one to figure out how to get the same advertisement to run in different sized magazines and still look the same. Magazine sizes run the gamut from very large to very small, which makes efforts at production standardization an occasional nightmare. The most common magazine sizes might be grouped as follows:

Classification	Magazine	Approximate size of full-page ad
Large	Life, Ebony	4 col. x 170 lines (9⅜ x 12⅛ inches)
Flat	Time, Newsweek	3 col. x 140 lines (7 x 10 inches)
Standard	National Geographic	2 col. x 119 lines (6 x 8½ inches)
Small or pocket	Reader's Digest, TV Guide	2 col. x 91 lines (4½ x 6½ inches)

At one time most magazines appeared in the standard format, but today few use it. Most magazines now are in the flat format size.

How to buy magazine space

The effective media buyer considers the selection of magazines on the basis of circulation, readership (who reads them), and cost and mechanical requirements. The buyer must understand the magazine's circulation statistics and rate card information.

Understanding magazine circulation

A magazine's audience may be determined by several factors: its primary and secondary readership, the number of subscription and vendor sales, and the number of copies that are guaranteed versus those that are actually delivered.

Primary and secondary readership

The Audit Bureau of Circulations or other verified report tells the media buyer what the magazine's total circulation is. This is *primary circulation,* and it represents the number of households that receive the publication. They may purchase it on newsstands or through a regular subscription. *Secondary* (or pass-along) readership is exactly what the name suggests. After the first reader is finished, he or she may give it to others to read. Pass-along readership can be very important to some magazines since some publications may be read by more than six different people. Multiply that by a million subscribers, and the magazine can boast very substantial readership.

Subscription and vendor sales

Since World War II the ratio of subscription to newsstand sales has increased, and today subscriptions account for the majority of sales for most magazines. Newsstands are still a major outlet for sales of single copies, but no newsstand can possibly handle more than a fraction of the magazines available. Display space is limited and vendors sometimes complain that distributors make them take publications they do not want in order to get others they do want.

From the advertiser's point of view, newsstand sales are impressive because they indicate that the purchaser really wanted the magazine and was not merely taking a subscription out of habit. Single-copy sales in 1980 accounted for an average of 33 percent of all sales, according to the Magazine Publishers Association. Some publications like *Family Circle,* though, are sold entirely through newsstand sales. Others, such as trade publications, are sold entirely through subscription.

Guaranteed versus delivered circulation

A magazine's rate structure is based on its circulation. The advertiser who purchases space is assured of reaching a certain number of people. The *guaranteed* circulation figure is the number of copies of the magazine that the publisher expects will be sold. Since some of these copies are usually sold on newsstands, it is possible that the guaranteed circulation figure may not be reached. If this *delivered* figure is not reached, the publisher will have to give a refund. For that reason, most guaranteed circulation figures (upon which advertising rates are based) are stated safely below the average actual delivered circulation.

Reading rate cards

Magazine rate cards, like newspaper rate cards, follow a standard format so advertisers can readily determine the cost of advertising, the mechanical requirements of the publication, and the additional amount required for special features like color or inserts.

Black and white rates

One means of comparing magazines is to look at the one-time cost for a full-page black and white ad, multiplied by 1,000, and divided by the publication's total circulation:

$$\frac{\text{Page rate} \times 1{,}000}{\text{Circulation}} = \text{Cost per page per thousand (CPM)}$$

For example, in 1981 the page-rate for a one-time black and white ad in *Flying* magazine was $9,240 on a rate base (guaranteed circulation) of 361,000. At the same time *Plane and Pilot* magazine offered a full-page black and white ad for $1,938 on a rate base of 52,000. Can you tell which was the better buy from the standpoint of cost per thousand?

Each of these publications, by the way, claimed substantial pass-along readership, thereby giving *Flying* a total audience of 1,083,000 and *Plane and Pilot* a total of 192,174 readers. If you believed these readership figures, which magazine would then have the better cost per thousand?

Discounts

As with newspapers, discounts are given based on frequency and volume. Frequency discounts are generally based on the number of insertions. Volume discounts are offered on the total space used during a specific period. Almost all magazines offer cash discounts—usually 2 percent.

Color rates

Color, if it is available, normally costs 25–60 percent more than black and white. Some publications, like *Money,* even offer metallic and aluminum-based inks and the use of five colors by special arrangement.

Bleed

Bleed pages add 0–20 percent to regular rates, although the typical increase is about 15 percent.

Covers

Typically second and third cover rates (the inside covers) are less than the rate for the fourth (back) cover. The cover rates usually include color, whether the ad is to be run in color or not. *U.S. News & World Report* charges $38,365 for the second and third covers and $48,965 for the fourth cover.

Special market editions

Magazines offer to publish advertisements in issues that go to a particular market, either geographic or demographic. *Time* offers four-color ads in Portland, Oregon, for $2,720 (32,000 circulation); in Houston, Texas for $3,110 (61,000 circulation); to college students for $17,580 (550,000 circulation), and to the 35 largest metropolitan markets for $53,130 (2,790,000 circulation).

Issue and closing dates

In buying magazine advertising there are three important dates:

Cover date—the date appearing on the cover.
On-sale date—the date the magazine is actually issued.
Closing date—the date when all ad material must be in the hands of the publisher for inclusion in a specific issue.

The closing date is sometimes the first thing the advertiser looks at. After determining whether the advertising materials can be ready by a certain date and which issue would be best, the space can be bought according to the factors we have discussed.

Merchandising services

Like newspapers, magazines often provide special services to advertisers. These include mailings prepared for the advertiser to notify dealers of the impending advertisement. Also, countercards for use in stores stating "As advertised in ______" are sometimes forwarded to retailers. Other services provided by magazines include special promotions to stores; marketing services that help readers find local outlets through a single phone number; aid in handling sales force, broker, wholesaler, and retailer meetings; advance editions for the trade; and research into brand preference, consumer attitudes, and market conditions.

Sources of print media information

There are many general sources of information about newspapers and magazines; more specific, detailed information about the publication itself may be obtained trhough direct contact. Here are some of the principal sources of information that are commonly analyzed by media planners.

Audit Bureau of Circulations (ABC)

The ABC was formed in 1914 to verify circulation and other marketing data on magazines and newspapers. Each publication submits a semi-annual statement, which is checked by specially trained ABC field auditors. They examine all records necessary to verify the figures the publisher reports (Figure 16–19).

The information the publisher supplies includes paid circulation for the period covered. This is broken down by subscription, single-copy sales, and average paid circulation—by regional, metropolitan, and demographic editions. It also analyzes new and renewal subscriptions by price, duration, channel of sales, and type of promotion.

Newspaper Advertising Bureau

Several industry organizations and publications offer helpful aids for planning newspaper advertising. One of them is the Newspaper Advertising Bureau of the American Newspaper Publishers Association, the promotional arm of the nation's newspaper industry. The bureau also provides its newspaper members market information by conducting field research and collecting case histories.

Magazine Publishers Association (MPA)

The MPA has a total membership of 113 publishers who represent 430 publications. This trade group makes available the combined circulation of all ABC member magazines (general and farm) from 1914 to date, with yearly figures related to population. It estimates the number of consumer magazine copies sold by year from 1943. It lists the 100 leading ABC magazines according to circulation and cost of magazine advertising according to circulation.

The association provides the industry with sales, research, and promotion arm that attempts to stimulate greater and more effective use of magazine advertising.

Standard Rate & Data Service (SRDS)

SRDS publishes *Newspaper Rates and Data* and *Consumer Magazine and Farm Publication Rates and Data,* monthly directories that eliminate the necessity for advertisers and their agencies to obtain rate cards for every publication. For the type of information provided, see Figures 16–8 and 16–20.

Audience studies provided by publications

Circulation figures are not enough. Newspapers and magazines also offer media planners many other types of statistical reports. The information contained in these reports details reader income, demographic profiles, percentages of different kinds of advertising carried, and much more.

Reader's Digest, for example, cites research which shows that "more people spend more time with each issue of the *Reader's Digest* than with any other magazine."

The magazine also promotes the quality of their readers. Research shows that 35.6 percent of their readers own two or more cars which were bought new, 36 percent bought a new dishwasher in the last year, 30 percent have passports, and 34 percent spend more than $60 per week on groceries.

These are interesting statistics to the advertiser selling automobiles, household appliances, travel, food, and associated products and services.

Similarly, *Time* magazine promotes its special business edition of *Time B* by citing statistics on its readers. Their average household income, for instance, exceeds $35,000; further, 87.5 percent attended college; and, most importantly, 100 percent are in professional or managerial positions. This underscores the magazine's claim that *Time B* is directed exclusively to businesspeople. And for advertisers of computer equipment, financial services, heavy machinery, or corporate aircraft, this is significant data.

Figure 16–19 Selected consumer magazines: Circulation and rates

		Total paid circulation	Percent subscription	Frequency of issue	Page costs (1 time) Black and white	Four color
General editorial	Ebony	1,271,517	80	Monday	$10,638	$16,443
	Life	1,226,140	46	Monday	15,000	19,860
	National Geographic	10,249,748	99	Monday	54,280	74,365
	People	2,312,444	16	Weekly	19,000	24,300
	Reader's Digest	18,094,192	92	Monday	64,500	77,500
	Saturday Review	526,031	98	Weekly	4,900	6,750
	TV Guide	19,547,763	38	Weekly	55,000	65,000
	US Magazine	848,343	20	Bi-Weekly	6,500	8,330
Selective editorial	Omni	750,000	12	Monday	9,375	14,065
	Psychology Today	1,175,323	85	Monday	14,540	20,990
	Scientific American	685,521	77	Monday	8,800	13,200
Newsweeklies	Newsweek	2,934,083	92	Weekly	29,275	45,665
	Sports Illustrated	2,287,159	96	Weekly	25,900	40,405
	Time	4,314,279	93	Weekly	40,960	63,895
	U.S. News & World Report	2,067,321	96	Weekly	19,800	31,250
Business	Black Enterprise	137,155	99	Monday	6,500	8,310
	Business Week	805,936	97	Weekly	15,560	23,340
	Fortune	676,117	96	Bi-Weekly	14,650	22,270
	Inc.	400,000	*	Monday	8,800	12,760
	Money	845,048	89	Monday	9,890	15,465
Mens	Esquire	651,960	89	Bi-Weekly	8,950	13,400
	Penthouse	4,651,323	5	Monday	22,565	34,075
	Playboy	5,538,559	39	Monday	31,310	43,850
Sports	Golf Digest	970,118	91	Monday	12,815	19,225
	Golf Magazines	709,358	89	Monday	9,275	13,920
	Ski	417,230	76	7xYear	7,990	10,970
	Skiing	464,184	78	7xYear	8,875	12,050
	Sport	1,220,392	87	Monday	10,975	16,016
	World Tennis	336,538	90	Monday	6,175	9,265
Outdoor	Field & Stream	2,064,622	93	Monday	15,400	22,960
	Flying	391,216	81	Monday	8,225	12,345
	Guns & Ammo	488,240	67	Monday	4,870	7,790
	Outdoor Life	1,731,895	87	Monday	13,900	19,800
	Sports Afield	528,793	77	Monday	5,500	7,840

		Total paid circulation	Percent subscription	Frequency of issue	Page costs (1 time) Black and white	Four color
Mechanics Automotive	Car & Driver	727,633	73	Monday	$12,595	$19,935
	Cycle	477,333	70	Monday	9,540	13,215
	Hot Rod	876,193	57	Monday	10,200	16,320
	Mechanix Illustrated	1,751,641	86	Monday	12,920	18,280
	Motor Trend	758,394	71	Monday	11,250	18,000
	Popular Mechanics	1,636,363	76	Monday	12,690	17,990
	Popular Science	1,801,605	83	Monday	14,205	20,150
	Road & Track	592,650	56	Monday	9,115	14,330
Womens	Ms.	518,612	86	Monday	5,910	7,925
	New Woman	1,068,854	29	Bi-Monthly	7,500	10,000
	Parents Magazine	1,441,393	99	Monday	14,780	18,915
Womens Service	Better Homes & Gardens	8,007,202	91	Monday	47,945	57,990
	Family Circle	7,611,578	0	17xYear	44,900	53,700
	Good Housekeeping	5,178,296	67	Monday	33,130	41,575
	Ladies Home Journal	5,633,128	83	Monday	30,240	37,425
	McCall's	6,502,880	87	Monday	38,675	47,500
	Redbook	4,450,806	78	Monday	25,145	33,375
	Woman's Day	7,535,855	0	15xYear	44,960	53,840
Fashion Beauty	Cosmopolitan	2,766,627	4	Monday	14,855	19,990
	Glamour	1,861,818	42	Monday	11,650	16,400
	Harper's Bazaar	622,298	45	Monday	7,300	10,550
	Mademoiselle	930,184	35	Monday	7,375	10,775
	Vogue	970,084	46	Monday	9,300	13,550
Shelter	House Beautiful	863,892	61	Monday	10,395	15,225
	House & Garden	1,035,363	64	Monday	12,725	18,700

* Nonpaid controlled circulation.

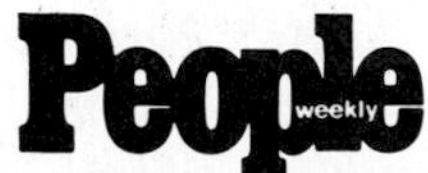

A Time Inc. Publication

(This is a paid duplicate of the listing under Classification No. 36A.)

Media Code 8 364 0983 9.00
Published weekly by Time Inc., Time & Life Bldg., Rockefeller Center, New York, N. Y. 10020. Phone 212-586-1212.

For shipping info., see Print Media Production Data.

PUBLISHER'S EDITORIAL PROFILE

PEOPLE WEEKLY is edited for active, sophisticated women and men. It presents readers with an overview of the pacesetters on the contemporary American scene, focusing on the newsworthy rather than just the news. Articles feature the work and lifestyles of people in the arts, sciences, business and politics as well as stars of television, motion pictures, records and sports. People Weekly also profiles relatively unknown individuals who lead unusual, inspiring, or interesting lives. Rec'd 3/25/80.

1. PERSONNEL

Publisher—Richard J. Durrell.
Managing Editor—Richard Stolley.
Assoc. Pub./Adv. Sales Dir.—Richard B. Thomas.
Nat'l Adv. Sales Mgr.—John J. Crowley.
Production Manager—John J. Gallagher.

2. REPRESENTATIVES and/or BRANCH OFFICES

New York 10020—Franklin S. Roth, Adv. Sales Mgr., James H. Fishman, Richard Newnham, Terrence W. Russell, Divisional Sales Mgrs., Time & Life Building, Rockefeller Center. Phone 212-586-1212.
Boston 02116—Jeffrey C. Ward, Mgr., 277 Dartmouth St. at Newbury. Phone 617-267-9500.
Chicago 60611—Stephen W. Alexander, Mgr., Time & Life Bldg., 303 E. Ohio St. Phone 312-329-7851.
Detroit 48202—Richard T. Flynn, Mgr., 1510 Fisher Bldg., West Grand & Second Blvds. Phone 313-875-1212.
Los Angeles 90010 — R. Michael Carpenter, Mgr., Equitable Bldg., Suite 2000, 3435 Wilshire Blvd. Phone 213-385-8151.
San Francisco 94104—James Shepherd, Mgr., 100 Bush St. Phone 415-982-5000.
Atlanta 30361—Bill Bentz, Mgr., 100 Colony Square, Suite 2130. Phone 404-873-3586.

3. COMMISSION AND CASH DISCOUNT

15% to agencies. Cash discount 2% of net for payment on or before due date. Bills rendered 20th of month of insertion and due within 10 days from date of invoice.

4. GENERAL RATE POLICY

Announcement of any change in rates will be made at least 7 weeks in advance of the issue date of the 1st time to which such rates will be applicable.

ISSUE-BY-ISSUE TALLY (IBIT) PRICING
Effective January 7, 1980.

1) The IBIT System is based on the People Publisher's Statement, which is issued by the Audit Bureau of Circulations for the first and second half of each year, and reports the paid circulation for each issue during each six-month period. The paid circulation for each issue an advertiser uses during a six-month IBIT period will be compared with its published rate base.
2) If the paid circulation of the issue used by an advertiser is lower than its published rate base, the advertiser will receive a credit, relative to the commissionable cost of the advertiser's insertion in that issue, which will be directly proportionate to the amount by which the paid circulation is less than its published rate base.
3) If the paid circulation of the issue used by an advertiser is higher than its published rate base. People will receive a credit relative to the commissionable cost of the advertiser's insertion in that issue, which will be directly proportionate to the amount by which the paid circulation is more than the published rate base.
4) If, at the end of a six-month IBIT period, People has more IBIT credit than does the advertiser, no adjustment will be made.
5) If, however, at the end of such a six-month IBIT period, the advertiser has more IBIT credit than does People, the excess will be credited against future insertions or, upon written request, a cash rebate in the amount of the excess will be issued.
6) Credit to be used against future insertions must be used within twelve months of the end of the six-month IBIT period in which the credit was earned. An advertiser can apply earned IBIT credit to brands, models or campaigns other than those for which the credit was actually earned.
7) Advertisers' insertions will be tallied by a combination of brands, models and campaigns to be agreed upon in advance by the advertiser or its advertising agency and People. The minimum number of insertions separately tallied for any advertiser during a six-month IBIT period will be three, unless that advertiser's total corporate schedule is less than three insertions. Changes cannot be made in the way an insertion is to be tallied subsequent to the Black & White close of the last issue of that six-month IBIT period.
8) In cases involving split runs using three or more brands, models or campaigns, the IBIT tally will be applied to the brand, model or campaign using the largest portion of the split, unless otherwise requested in writing by the advertiser.
9) Agency commissions will be paid at the full card rate for all insertions involving IBIT credits.
10) Cash discounts will not be allowed on that portion of an insertion paid for by IBIT credits.

ADVERTISING RATES

Rates effective January 12, 1981.
Rates received September 29, 1980.

5. BLACK/WHITE RATES

	1 ti	10 ti	13 ti	17 ti	26 ti	39 ti
1 pg	25,700.	25,185.	24,930.	24,670.	23,645.	22,875.
2 col	20,205.	19,800.	19,600.	19,395.	18,590.	17,980.
1/2 pg	16,035.	15,715.	15,555.	15,395.	14,750.	14,270.
1 col	10,695.	10,480.	10,375.	10,265.	9,840.	9,520.
1/2 col	6,000.	5,880.	5,820.	5,760.	5,520.	5,340.

	52 ti	78 ti	104 ti	130 ti	156 ti
1 pg	22,615.	22,360.	22,100.	21,845.	21,590.
2 col	17,780.	17,580.	17,375.	17,175.	16,970.
1/2 pg	14,110.	13,950.	13,790.	13,630.	13,470.
1 col	9,410.	9,305.	9,200.	9,090.	8,985.
1/2 col	5,280.	5,220.	5,160.	5,100.	5,040.

Excluding Year-End Double Issue.
Ads must be inserted within 1 year of first insertion to earn frequency discount.

Schedules composed of mixed space units entitled to earn frequency discounts except when use of least expensive unit lowers the total cost of the campaign below the amount which the other units reached at their earned rate.

SPACE RENEWAL CREDIT PROGRAM

Space credit is earned on a corporate basis. An advertiser must run a minimum of 5 national page equivalents in the prior calendar year and then renew at the same, or greater, level in the following calendar year to earn space credit. Renewed and increased pages receive 2,000.00 per page of space credit. All space credit must be used in the calendar year in which it is earned, and can only be applied to increased (not matching) national page equivalents. Advertisers must pay for at least 51% of an ad in order for it to count towards a frequency discount. (Space credits are not included in determining an advertiser's future renewal base.)

6. COLOR RATES

2 color:	1 ti	10 ti	13 ti	17 ti	26 ti	39 ti
1 pg	28,000.	27,440.	27,160.	26,880.	25,760.	24,920.
2 col	22,010.	21,570.	21,350.	21,130.	20,250.	19,590.
1/2 pg	17,485.	17,135.	16,960.	16,785.	16,085.	15,560.
1 col	11,655.	11,420.	11,305.	11,190.	10,725.	10,375.
1/2 col	6,525.	6,395.	6,330.	6,265.	6,005.	5,805.

2 color:	52 ti	78 ti	104 ti	130 ti	156 ti
1 pg	24,640.	24,360.	24,080.	23,800.	23,520.
2 col	19,370.	19,150.	18,930.	18,710.	18,490.
1/2 pg	15,385.	15,210.	15,035.	14,860.	14,685.
1 col	10,255.	10,140.	10,025.	9,905.	9,790.
1/2 col	5,740.	5,675.	5,610.	5,545.	5,480.

4 color:	1 ti	10 ti	13 ti	17 ti	26 ti	39 ti
1 pg	33,100.	32,440.	32,105.	31,775.	30,450.	29,460.
2 col	28,660.	28,085.	27,800.	27,515.	26,365.	25,505.
1/2 pg	23,145.	22,680.	22,450.	22,220.	21,295.	20,600.
1 col	15,440.	15,130.	14,975.	14,820.	14,205.	13,740.

4 color:	52 ti	78 ti	104 ti	130 ti	156 ti
1 pg	29,130.	28,795.	28,465.	28,135.	27,805.
2 col	25,220.	24,935.	24,650.	24,360.	24,075.
1/2 pg	20,370.	20,135.	19,905.	19,675.	19,440.
1 col	13,585.	13,435.	13,280.	13,125.	12,970.

Excluding Year-End Double Issue.

7. COVERS

4 color:	1 ti	10 ti	13 ti	17 ti	26 ti	39 ti
4th cover	43,030.	42,170.	41,740.	41,310.	39,590.	38,295.

4 color:	52 ti	78 ti	104 ti	130 ti	156 ti
4th cover	37,865.	37,435.	37,005.	36,575.	36,145.

Excluding Year-End Double Issue.

8. INSERTS

Available.

9. BLEED

Extra 15%
No extra charge for bleed across gutter for facing space units.

12. SPLIT RUN

A single advertiser buying the national circulation can split his copy along state or metro lines with a 7-week close at the following rates:

Single Page Units	(*)	(†)
B/W or 2/C	1,000.	475.
4/C	1,450.	675.
4/C Change B/W	1,200.	575.

(*) 2-Way Split (2 Versions)
(†) Each additional Version.

The prices above apply only for full pages. For fractional unit splits add 150.00 per split for each page affected A 5% margin must be allowed in the circulation of split runs.

15. MECH. REQUIREMENTS (Rotary Letterpress)

For complete, detailed production information, see SRDS Print Media Production Data.
Trim size: 8-3/16 x 10-7/8; No./Cols. 3.
Binding method: Saddle stitched.
Colors available: Matched; 4-color Process (AAAA/MPA).

DIMENSIONS—AD PAGE

1	7	x 10	1/2	7	x 5
2 cols			1 col	2-1/4	x 10
	4-5/8	x 10	1 col	4-5/8	x 4-7/8

16. ISSUE AND CLOSING DATES

Published weekly except one double issue at year end. Dated Monday, on sale preceding Monday.
Black and white and black and 1 color closing 3 weeks before issue date. 4 color closing 7 weeks before issue date. Cancellations not accepted after closing dates.

17. SPECIAL SERVICES

A.B.C. Supplemental Data Report released January 1980 issue.

18. CIRCULATION

Established 1974. Single copy .95; per year 39.00.
Summary data—for detail see Publisher's Statement.

A.B.C. 12-31-80 (6 mos. aver.—Magazine Form)

Tot. Pd.	(Subs.)	(Single)	(Assoc.)
2,499,573	449,437	2,050,136	....

Average Total Non-Pd Distribution (not incl. above): Total 57,549

TERRITORIAL DISTRIBUTION 9/80—2,503,957

N.Eng.	Mid.Atl.	E.N.Cen.	W.N.Cen.	S.Atl.	E.S.Cen.
153,145	343,831	442,495	161,932	335,395	93,832
W.S.Cen.	Mtn.St.	Pac.St.	Canada	Foreign	Other
191,917	137,718	458,332	171,678	3,782	9,900

Publisher states: "Effective January 12, 1981 issue, rates based on a six-month circulation rate base 2,300,000 excluding 1980 year-end Double Issue.

(D-C2)

Figure 16–20 The *Consumer Magazine and Farm Publication Rates and Data* listing for *People Weekly*. Note the premium charged for cover position; also the lead time required for color ads as opposed to black and white. The circulation rate base is stated at 2,300,000. Actually the audited circulation is 2,499,573, of which 449,437 are subscriptions.

Summary

The printed page in general and the newspaper in particular provide a unique, flexible medium for advertisers to express their creativity. The newspaper is a mass medium that is read by almost everybody. It offers great flexibility, which assists creativity, and its printed message lasts. In short, there are many advantages to newspapers. However, newspapers also have their disadvantages. These include: lack of audience selectivity, short life span, poor production quality, heavy advertising competition, potentially poor ad placement, and overlapping circulation. Still, the newspaper is the major community-serving medium today for both news and advertising.

The newspaper's rates, mechanical requirements, and other pertinent information are printed on its rate card. This will also tell whether the newspaper's space is sold by the agate line or the column inch. The rates listed vary for local and national advertisers. Also listed are the newspaper's short rate policy, combination rates, frequency discounts, run of paper rates, and other data.

Magazines offer different advantages. They are the most selective of all media. They are flexible in both readership and advertising. They offer unsurpassed availability of color, excellent reproduction quality, believability and authority, permanence, and prestige at an efficient cost.

The disadvantages of magazines, though, are numerous. They require long lead time, they have problems offering reach and frequency, and they are subject to heavy advertising competition. And the cost of advertising in some magazines is very high.

In selecting magazines for advertising, the media buyer must consider the publication's circulation, its readership, and its cost and mechanical requirements. A magazine's audience may be determined by several factors: its primary and secondary readership, the number of subscription and vendor sales, and the number of copies that are guaranteed versus those that are actually delivered.

Magazine rate cards, like newspaper rate cards, follow a standard format so advertisers can readily determine the cost of advertising. The rate card lists black and white rates, discounts, color rates, issue and closing dates, and mechanical requirements.

Questions for review

1. What are the major advantages and drawbacks of newspapers?
2. What are the basic types of newspaper advertising? Describe them.
3. What is a Sunday supplement?
4. What are the meanings of these newspaper terms:
   a. Agate lines.
   b. Retail and general rates.
   c. Short rate.
   d. Combination rate.
   e. Run of paper.
   f. Preferred position.
   g. Rate differential.
   h. Split run.
   i. Insertion order.
   j. Tear sheet.
5. What is the difference between primary and secondary readership?
6. What is the difference between guaranteed and delivered circulation?
7. What are the advantages and drawbacks of magazines?
8. What are the meanings of these magazine terms:
   a. Bleed.
   b. Covers.
   c. Special market editions.
   d. Issue and closing dates.
   e. Merchandising services.
   f. Insert/gatefolds.
   g. Junior pages/island halfs.
9. What function does the Audit Bureau of Circulation perform?
10. What is meant by volume and frequency discounts?

17

Broadcast media

When kids play with toys, they often fantasize about the real world of their parents or other adults. That is the creative premise Bill Kamp and John Russo have worked from in developing television campaigns for Matchbox Cars. As the art director and copywriter on the account, Kamp and Russo constantly seek new ways to promote Matchbox miniature cars like real automobiles.

Says Allen Beaver, one of the agency principals at Levine, Huntley, Schmidt, Plapler & Beaver (LHSP&B), "kids see all the auto advertising that saturates the media, and they live out these experiences vicariously. We've simply borrowed some of the ad approaches and recast them in a child's perspective."

But in many instances these commercials are more than just imitations. They are sly parodies. Beaver admits it. Many automobile ads are so full of clichés and formulas that they are ripe for harpooning.

"The kids may not realize that we're having fun with the Detroit auto makers," he says, "but their fathers—who buy the toys—can't miss it."

One example is a direct take-off on the typical endorsement approach. A series of children discuss what they look for in a car. "Sporty" or "built tough for me," say the boys. "Yet practical for me," says a girl. A voice-over announcer offers the solution: "No matter who you are, Matchbox has a car that says *you.*"

In another commercial, the typical auto demonstration technique is used. Boys in white coats resemble automotive engineers. They put eggs on a toy racetrack to show that the cars can maneuver around them. "They handle like a million dollars," says the announcer, as the tiny cars zoom around a bend and come to a screeching halt in front of a ten-cent piece, "and stop on a dime" (Figure 17–1).

The commercials are normally run during the last three months of the year to support Matchbox's holiday sales. To avoid the clutter of Saturday morning television, the ads are run during fringe time, 4–7 P.M. when children and adults often watch television together.

Says Beaver, "We don't advertise Matchbox like the competition, and we don't want our ads lost in the welter of toy advertising that appears on all the children's shows."[1]

Using television in the creative mix

Although advertising to children has come under severe attack in recent years, no one denies the creative potential of the television medium. In fact, it is television's very potential for creativity and impact that has fueled so much criticism. As a means of reaching the masses, no other medium today has the unique creative abilities of television: the combination of sight, sound, and movement; the opportunity to demonstrate the product; the believability of seeing it happen right before your eyes; and the empathy of the viewer.

In this chapter we want to understand the broadcast media—television and radio—from the standpoint of their roles in the creative mix. We will also study both media through a general overview and then look specifically at how advertisers evaluate broadcast commercial opportunities and how they buy television and radio time.

What works best in television?

Television has grown faster than any other advertising medium in history. From its beginnings after World War II, it has emerged as the medium that attracts the largest volume of national advertising—totaling over $8 billion in 1980. Why is this? It is because of the unique advantages that contemporary television offers advertisers over competing media.

Mass coverage/low cost

A substantial portion of television's national advertising revenue comes from the packaged goods industry (foods and drugs). Procter & Gamble, for instance, has led all other advertisers in spending since 1951. In their nationwide distribution of high-volume, low-profit products in supermarkets, they use television to reach a mass audience and presell their brand names at a very low cost per thousand.

In 1980, 98 percent of all American homes had a TV set, and most had more than one. The average is 1.67 sets per household, and over 80 percent of these are color sets.[2] The overwhelming odds are that at least one person in your family will be watching TV on any given day. This is a safe assumption because, of the homes that own TV sets (television households), 92 percent view TV at least once during the average day. More than 98 percent tune in during an average week.

Typical network nighttime programs reach 20 percent of all television households. The more popular shows and special attractions reach 25 percent and more. For example, over 40 percent are usually reached by a Super Bowl game.

Television, therefore, is a mass medium for mass-consumption products. And despite the often huge initial outlays for advertising, television's equally huge audiences bring the per-exposure cost for each commercial down to a comparatively low level.

Viewer empathy

TV advertising can depict people more realistically than any other medium (Figure 17–2). The subjects are seen to worry over the same problems and cope with the same hardships that the viewer does. With the solutions to these problems occurring in the privacy of the home, television becomes a highly personal medium.

Selectivity

In spite of the fact that television audiences are mass audiences, they can vary a great deal, depending on the time of day and the day of the week. This permits the advertiser to present the message when this potential audience is best. Also, some segments of the population, such as those living in the suburbs, are more easily reached by TV than by other media.

The U.S. distributor of the prestigious Omega watch line had always used print media to reach its rather limited, upper income market. After testing television in three different geographic markets, it

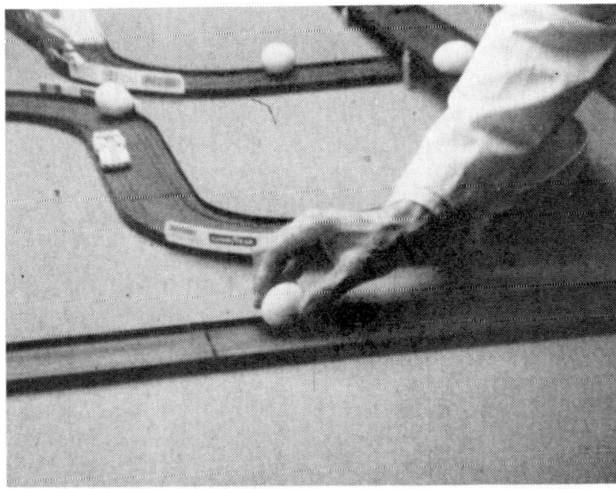

Figure 17–1

Stop on a Dime
30 seconds

Anncr: VO: You're about to see an amazing demonstration. Matchbox Speedtrack RPS will go through some paces no other racing set can. Our system changes lanes the fastest. And on the curves, Speedtrack RPS can stay on the inside track. Matchbox Speedtrack RPS. Cars that handle like a million dollars . . . and stop on a dime.

rapidly switched its print dollars to television and spread its campaign to 30 markets. But they still bought very selectively around the "adult" shows: "Today," "Tonight," various news shows, and serious programming like "Meet the Press." Sales increased 70 percent over the next two years.

Impact

The ability to bring a moving picture with sound into the living rooms of America is practically tantamount to having an army of door-to-door sellers. The sales impact of television was measured by the NBC-Hofstra Study of low-cost, high-volume brands. This study showed that products advertised on TV had an average 30.1 percent sales *increase,* whereas products advertised but not on TV had an average 19.1 sales *loss* among TV viewers. Similar sales differences were found for durable goods.

Figure 17—2 Warmth, sensitivity and drama were all created in 30 seconds in Coke's famous commercial which depicted a weary Mean Joe Green being offered some liquid refreshment by his fan—a timid but adoring little youngster.

Creativity

Television's creative potential is limited only by the commercial creator's talents. The various facets of the TV ad—sound, sight, motion, and color—all permit an infinite number of original and imaginative appeals. For some interesting facts on how to create effective TV commercials, see the Checklist.

Prestige

Hallmark, Bell Telephone, Xerox, and IBM have experienced an increase in prestige and corporate identity by sponsoring dramatic presentations and other cultural highlights. Potential distributors, the company's sales force, and customers are impressed by a product's association with quality programming.

Social dominance

Television has exhibited a power that goes beyond impact and prestige. The entire nation has been emotionally stirred by TV screenings of the Vietnam War, assassinations, the moon landing, and Watergate hearings. The *New York Times* has said of television, "It's impact on leisure, politics, reading, and culture (is) unparalleled since the advent of the auto."

The real relationship of this dominating characteristic to the sale of an advertiser's product is difficult to gauge. However, we can probably safely assume that the magnetic attraction of television events gives this medium a potential for advertising unlike any other.

Drawbacks to television

Although television's power as a creative tool may be unmatched, the medium still has many drawbacks that keep it from being used by most advertisers. Television advertising involves several unique problems. In many instances, television just doesn't "fit" in the creative mix. This may be because of cost, lack of audience selectivity, its inherent brevity, or the clutter of competitive messages.

Checklist of what works best in television

Here is a checklist to help you create effective television commercials.

☐ The picture must tell the story. Forget every other rule in this chapter, and you will still be ahead of the game. It's the most important rule of all! Television is a *visual* medium. That's why the people in front of a set are called *viewers.* They remember what they *see,* not what they hear. Try this trick for looking at a storyboard. *Cover the words.* What is the message of the commercial with the sound turned off? Is there a message at all?

☐ Look for a "key visual." Here's another test to apply to the storyboard. Can you pick out *one* frame that visually sums up the whole message? Most good commercials can be reduced to this single "key visual." A commercial with many different scenes may look interesting in storyboard form but can turn out to be an overcomplicated piece of film. Busy, crowded, fast-moving commercials are hard to understand. The small television screen is not a movie theater. A *simple* storyboard can fool you. It may look hopelessly dull on paper. But film thrives on simplicity.

☐ Grab the viewer's attention. The *first five seconds* of a commercial are crucial. Analysis of audience reaction shows either a sharp drop or a sharp rise in interest during this time. *Commercial attention does not build.* Your audience can only become less interested, never more. The level you reach in the first five seconds is the highest you will get, so don't save your punches. Offer the viewer something right off the bat. *News.* A *problem* to which you have the solution. A *conflict* that is involving.

☐ Be single-minded. A good commercial is uncomplicated. Direct. It never makes the viewer do a lot of mental work. The basic commercial length in U.S. television is 30 seconds. The content possible in that time is outlined in the phrase: "name-claim-demonstration." The name of your product, your consumer benefit, and the reason the consumer should believe it. Longer commercials *should not add copy points.* A 60-second commercial tells the same story as the 30-second one, with more leisure and detail. Or—best of all—*repetition.* The 60-second allows time for a mood to be created; the 30-second generally does not. The 20-second and 10-second commercials are one-point messages. The 10-second registers the brand name and promise. The 20-second makes the promise more explicit. Both these lengths are usually *reminder* messages, run in a media schedule with longer commercial lengths. If your campaign plans include both :60s and :30s, look at the :30s *first.* If the message cannot be delivered in 30 seconds, you are not being single-minded.

☐ Register the name of your product. Too often, a viewer will remember the commercial but not the name of your brand. This is a problem particularly troublesome with new products. Showing the package on screen and mouthing the name is not enough. Take extra pains to implant your product name in the viewer's mind.

☐ The tone of your advertising must reflect your product personality. If you are fortunate enough to have a product with an established brand image, your advertising *must* reflect that image. It takes dedication on the part of advertiser and agency to build a brand personality. Discipline yourself to reject advertising that conflicts with it. (It helps to have a written "personality statement" of your product; if it were a person, what sort of person would it be?) When you launch a new product, the very *tone* of your announcement commercial tells viewers what to expect. From that moment on, it is hard to change their minds. Once you have decided on a personality for your product, sustain it in every commercial. Change campaigns when you must, but retain the same tone of voice.

☐ Avoid "talky" commercials. Look for the simplest, and most memorable, set of words to get across your consumer benefit. Every word must work hard. A 30-second commercial usually allows you *no more* than 65 words, a 60-second commercial twice that amount. Be specific. Pounce upon clichés, flabbiness, and superlatives. Try this discipline. When you ask for 10 words to be added to a commercial, decide which 10 you would *delete* to make room for them.

Figure 17–3

Classy Package
30-second

NORM: Y'know, it does my heart *good* to see a woman of your depth and reception going Natural in public.

MARCIA: It does *my* heart good to see they even let you *out* in public!

NORM: That's nice of you to say. But tell me, why do *you* like Natural?

MARCIA: Oh, this light beer and I have a lot in common. You know. Classy package . . . terrific taste.

NORM: Yeah, natural ageing . . . I mean . . . Natural has the smooth, clean taste that comes from s-l-o-w natural ageing.

MARCIA: Keep trying—

NORM: Really. I have extinct affliction for all women of your gender. I rate you to the highest pinochle!

Cost

Television advertising's greatest handicap is the high expenditures for the production of the commercial and the purchase of airtime. The production costs of a TV spot vary with how the advertiser chooses to present the product. Most national advertisers film their commercials, and they pay as much as $50,000 or more each. In Chapter 13, we discussed how Levi's spent $250,000 to produce its highly effective animated commercials. The cost of professional talent has also become a major expense. Gregory Peck signed for $1 million a year with Travelers Insurance. And Joe Namath enjoyed a $5 million commercial contract. Professional actors and actresses now earn a total of more than $75 million yearly from their work in TV commercials (Figure 17–3).

The second major area of expense is network time. A single minute during prime time may cost $150,000 (Figure 17–4). Special attractions can cost much more. A minute of commercial time during *The Godfather* cost $250,000, for example.

For the large advertiser, television can be relatively efficient, with the cost per thousand viewers running from $3.50 to$4.50. But this cost of large coverage, even at relatively low rates, usually prices the small and medium-sized advertisers out of the market.

Lack of selectivity

Many advertisers are seeking a very specific, small audience. In these cases television is not cost effective and is therefore at a disadvantage. This may change, however. Television seems destined to follow magazines and radio. With the ever-increasing influx of UHF, public, and cable channels, the viewer is offered a larger variety of programming from which to choose. And small advertisers are being offered more selective television alternatives.

Brevity

A television advertising message is brief, usually lasting only 30 seconds. The objective is to get enough viewers' attention and to leave them with a favorable attitude toward the product or at least make them remember it. But in 30 seconds, that's a tall task.

Clutter

One major drawback to television advertising is that a commercial is seldom seen in an isolated position. It is usually surrounded by station-break announcements, credits, public-service announcements, and "billboards" (just the name or slogan of a product), not to mention six or seven competing commercials. With all these messages competing for attention, the viewer often comes away annoyed, confused, and with a high rate of product misidentification.

Looking to the future, the J. Walter Thompson advertising agency has already screened one- and three-second television commercials, predicting they may be commonplace by the 1990s. For example, in a one-second commercial we might hear a phone ring over a flash of a service company logo followed by a flash of a repairman arriving

Figure 17–4

Network TV cost estimates: 30-second announcements

Prime time*	
Cost per 30 seconds	$79,743
Average rating	18.2
Homes (000)	14,030
Cost per rating point	$4,381
Day time*	
Cost per 30 seconds	$12,298
Average rating	6.3
Homes (000)	4,860
Cost per rating point	$1,952
Early evening news (M—F)*	
Cost per 30 seconds	$41,400
Average rating	12.0
Homes (000)	9,250
Cost per rating point	$3,450
Early morning (ABC/NBC)	
Cost per 30 seconds	$8,690
Average rating	4.2
Homes (000)	3,240
Cost per rating point	$2,069
Late fringe (NBC)	
Cost per 30 seconds	$30,000
Average rating	7.5
Homes (000)	5,780
Cost per rating point	$4,000
Late fringe I (ABC/CBS)†	
Cost per 30 seconds	$26,880
Average rating	6.5
Homes (000)	5,010
Cost per rating point	$4,135
Late fringe II (ABC/CBS)‡	
Cost per 30 seconds	$12,320
Average rating	4.6
Homes (000)	3,550
Cost per rating point	$2,678

*Costs reflect an average of all three networks with complete quarterly activity.
†Fringe I: approx. 11:30 P.M.–12:45 A.M.
‡Fringe II: approx. 12:45 A.M.–conclusion.

at a door. Consumers of the future are expected to have faster comprehension to get a one-second message. The effect these new commercial formats will have on the clutter problem is still unknown.

Overview of the television medium

In 1947 five television stations began broadcasting. By 1980 the number had grown to 726 commercial stations. Of these, 516 were VHF (very high frequency—channels 2 through 13) and 210 were UHF (ultra-high frequency—channels 14 through 83).

Until 1952 all stations were VHF. Then the Federal Communications Commission (FCC) authorized 70 more channels (14 through 83) and referred to them as UHF. The original VHF stations developed faster and have been more profitable than UHF for two reasons: (1) they were established fairly early in the major markets, and (2) they have been favored by the networks. Also, in the beginning many TV sets lacked UHF receivers. To equalize coverage, a law was passed in 1965 requiring all new TV sets to be designed to receive UHF broadcasts. This brought on many more UHF stations.

Two additional types of special stations also exist today: *satellite* stations like Ted Turner's WTBS (see Chapter 5), duplicating a major portion of the broadcasts of a parent station and originating some minor programming of their own; and *translator* stations, which rebroadcast regular stations to fringe areas using the higher UHF frequencies but are usually incapable of originating local programming.

Audience trends

Middle-income, high-school-educated viewers and their families are the heaviest viewers of television. There are three possible reasons for this. First, most television programming is directed at this group. Second, those persons with considerably higher incomes and educations usually have a more diversified range of interests and entertainment options. Third, families with less education and income may not emphasize the importance of the home and family as much on the average.

The average number of hours viewed has steadily increased since television was introduced. Children under 12 view an average of 29½ hours per week; middle-aged men 27.3; and middle-aged women, 33.3 (Figure 17–5). By age 18, the average child has watched around 26,000 hours of TV. In 1980 the average household TV usage was about 4¼ hours a day. Older women viewed the most, teenage females the least.

Individual program audiences vary a great deal. A sporting event, for example, attracts proportionately more men in the 18–34 age category than any other group. Adults over 50 show a marked tendency toward westerns, and children rate situation comedy highest (Figure 17–6). Look at the audience composition statistics in Figure 17–6.

How would you describe the primary viewers of network movies? From the information shown, how many viewers comprise the largest TV audience segment? What program on that chart has the largest audience?

The amount of television viewing time varies according to the season and the time of day. The number of viewers rises slowly in the morning, levels off during the afternoon, and increases dramatically in the evening. The audience is approximately two or three times larger in prime time than in the morning. The number of homes viewing is highest in the winter and averages 20–30 percent less in the summer.

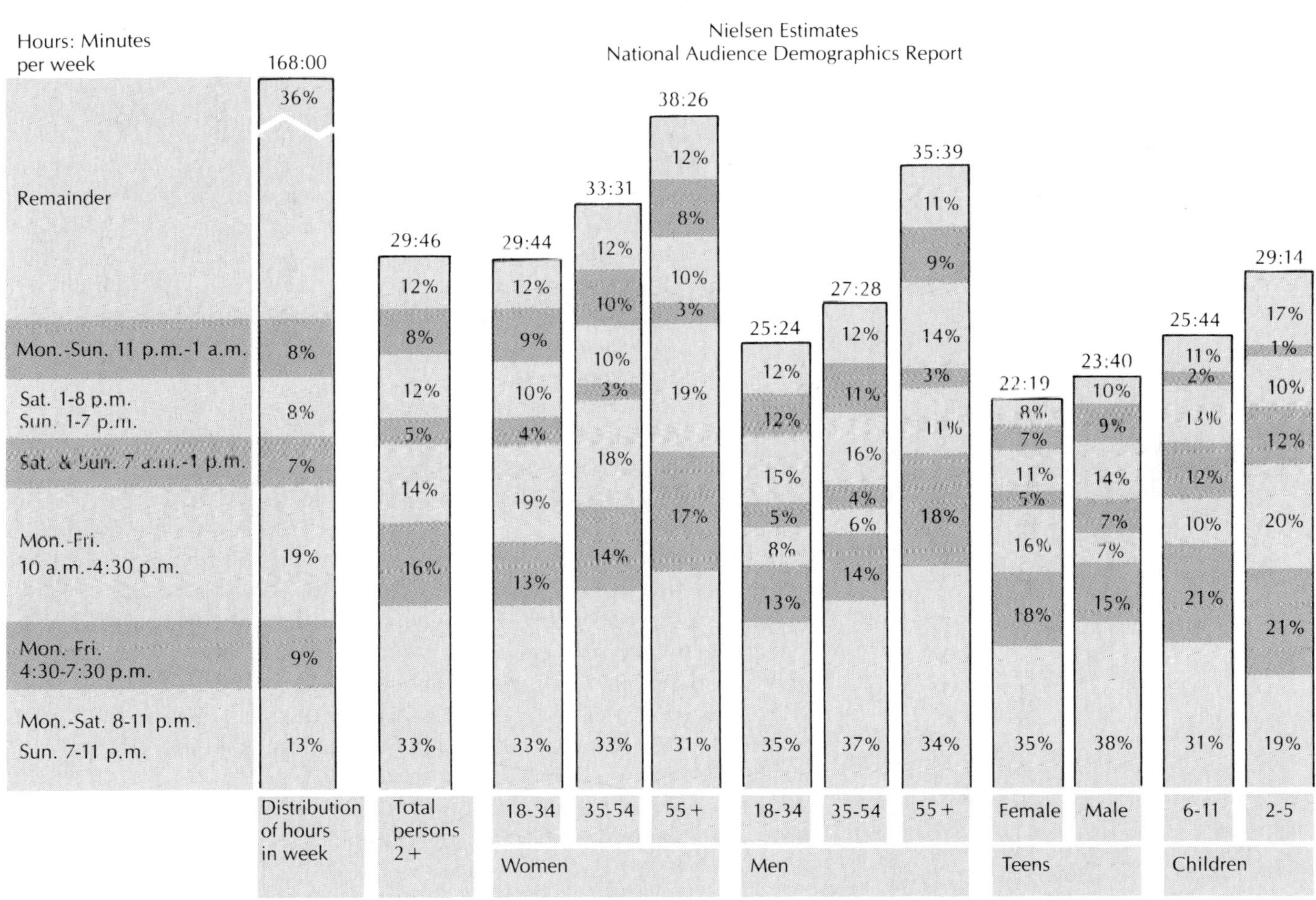

Figure 17–5

The Nielsen Report on Television shows the disproportionate distribution of viewing activity throughout the day by various age groups. For example, more than 30 percent of most people's viewing takes place during prime time (Monday–Saturday 8–11 P.M., Sunday 7–11 P.M.). But those hours make up only 13 percent of the week's total hours (168).

Growth of television advertising

As television viewing has increased over the years, so have the number of advertisers and the amounts they spend. In 1950 only 3 percent of total advertising volume was placed on television. That amounted to $171 million. By 1980 that figure had grown to over $11 billion and accounted for more than 21 percent of all ad spending. Over half of that $11 billion dollars was spent by just the top 100 advertisers.

Types of television advertising

There are three different forms of television advertising: network, spot, and local. Let's discuss each of these briefly.

Network

One way to advertise is to purchase airtime from one of the three national networks: Columbia Broadcasting Company (CBS), National Broadcasting Company (NBC), or American Broadcasting Company (ABC).

Networks telecast their programs and commercials by either a coaxial cable or a microwave relay. Coaxial cables are buried underground and are used to carry both audio and video messages. Microwave relay stations are spaced 25–50 miles apart and beam the broadcast from one station to the next.

Networks offer the large advertiser convenience and efficiency. The message can be broadcast simultaneously throughout the country. The advertiser can have close control over the message and the quality of transmission. It is unlikely, for instance, that a network would follow one ad with one of a competitor. This centralization also simplifies bookkeeping and the advertiser gets only one bill. The total cost per thousand is low—lower even than if time were purchased on a spot basis (discussed later). The network also enhances the advertiser in the minds of retailers and consumers by the prestige attached to sponsoring first-rate network entertainment.

Network advertising also has its disadvantages. An advertiser who desires to buy fewer stations than the full network lineup often finds that preference is given to those willing to buy more. The advertiser who seeks to advertise to a limited market usually finds that the network lineup does not coincide with his or her needs.

Spot

National spot advertising offers the advertiser greater flexibility since commercials can be concentrated on the markets most likely to pay off. Advertisers with limited distribution and budgets find this advantageous. Spots may also be used to introduce a new product into one area at a time.

Spot advertising is more difficult to purchase than network. It involves contacting each station directly. And the complex bookkeeping becomes a headache.

Figure 17–6

TV viewer composition by age*

Program type	Number of men viewing (000)	Percent of total men viewing 18–34	18–49	25–49	25–64	Number of women viewing (000)	Percent of total women viewing 18–34	18–49	25–49	25–64
Morning M–F										
Today										
7:30–8:00 A.M.	1,490	15%	36%	31%	62%	2,790	16%	36%	31%	61%
8:30–9:00 A.M.	1,740	17	40	33	59	3,230	19	39	32	60
CBS News										
7:30–8:00 A.M.	830	23	52	51	72	1,090	15	45	40	69
Good Morning America										
7:30–8:00 A.M.	760	24	47	27	72	1,710	36	58	47	69
8:30–9:00 A.M.	1,170	28	50	35	63	2,610	33	55	41	64
Daytime M–F										
Drama	1,400	31%	45%	29%	59%	5,390	37%	59%	43%	63%
Quiz and audience participation	1,530	29	43	29	54	3,580	32	51	36	60
Situation comedy	2,000	40	56	32	73	3,430	38	59	39	62
All 10:00 A.M.–4:30 P.M.	1,490	32	46	30	57	4,650	36	57	41	62
Early fringe M–F										
Informational										
6:00–7:00 P.M.	6,890	27%	47%	36%	67%	8,550	24%	43%	33%	62%
Evening (Monday–Sunday)										
General drama	8,450	40%	59%	44%	69%	13,190	39%	60%	43%	64%
Suspense and mystery	8,870	34	57	44	70	11,750	36	60	44	68
Situation comedy	9,700	42	64	47	71	13,180	42	65	45	65
Adventure	9,650	43	67	51	73	11,110	44	68	48	67
Variety	7,510	33	59	47	72	10,370	32	56	40	66
Feature films	9,660	40	67	50	73	11,260	39	65	49	71
All 7:00–11:00 P.M.	9,490	39	63	48	72	12,040	39	63	46	67
Late fringe M–F										
Tonight (NBC)	3,460	39%	60%	43%	63%	4,980	36%	59%	43%	67%
Tomorrow (NBC)	980	45	65	41	56	1,540	40	57	32	57
Late movies (CBS)	2,930	39	66	42	62	3,360	37	61	41	64
Saturday Night (NBC)	6,750	63	91	65	74	5,110	56	82	55	69
Sunday Night Late Movie (ABC)	1,580	40	61	51	77	2,070	47	75	47	66

	Total men (000)	Men 18–34	18–49	25–49	25–64	Total women (000)	Women 18–34	18–49	25–49	25–64
Population base:	69,220	28,690	45,380	32,360	47,320	77,060	30,060	47,770	34,010	50,610
(in U.S. TV homes)	100%	41%	66%	47%	68%	100%	39%	62%	44%	66%

*Television viewer composition figures help advertisers understand who watches what and when. Note how percentages tend to increase within higher age brackets for all categories of programs. Note also how many more women are viewing than men during almost all time periods.

Another drawback is that spot advertising during network programming is available only at station breaks and when network advertisers have purchased less than the full lineup. In such cases, the station sells a spot and fits it between network and local ads. Most advertising time of network affiliates is sold in this way.

Local

Retailers, often in cooperation with nationally known manufacturers, are the primary sponsors of local advertising. As a rule, airtime is sold as spot announcements, but sometimes programs are developed and sponsored by local advertisers. Or local firms can buy the rights to a syndicated film series and sponsor it in their own market.

Buying television time

To buy television time the advertiser must first understand the various commercial opportunities that are available. Second, a knowledge of audience measurement techniques and terminology is important in order to evaluate the available commercial time. And, finally, the advertiser needs to know the proper procedures for "making the buy." We shall discuss each of these areas in this section.

Commercial opportunities in TV

There are three ways advertisers can buy advertising time on television. They may sponsor an entire program, participate in a program, or use spot announcements between programs.

Sponsorships

When an advertiser undertakes to present a program alone, it is called *sponsorship*. The advertiser is responsible for the program content and the cost of production as well as the advertising. This is generally so costly that single sponsorships are usually limited to specials.

For companies that decide on this method (AT&T, Xerox, and Hallmark, for example) there are two important advantages. The first is that the public more readily identifies with the product(s) and the company gains in prestige. The second is that the sponsor has control over the placement and content of the commercials. The commercials can be fit to the program and run any length desired as long as they are within NAB regulations. Some major car manufacturers, for example, sponsor an hour-long program in the fall and run a single five-minute commercial that introduces the new line of cars.

The high cost of sponsoring a program has encouraged many advertisers to cooperate. This permits them to realize some of the advantages of sponsorship but at lower cost and risk. They often sponsor on alternate weeks or divide the program into segments. Most sporting events, for instance, are sold as multiple sponsorships.

Participations

Most television advertising is sold on the *participating* basis with several advertisers buying 30- or 60-second segments within the program. Advertisers can participate in a program once or several times on a regular or irregular basis. This allows the advertiser to spread out the budget and makes it easier to get in and out of a program without a long-term commitment. It also enables the small advertiser to buy a limited amount of time and still have nationwide coverage.

Spot announcements

Other than sponsorships and participations, *spot announcements* are the only other means of presenting a commercial on television. Spot announcements are less expensive than participations because they are run in clusters between programs, and they permit the advertiser to concentrate on certain markets. They may be sold either nationally or locally and can be purchased in segments of 10, 20, 30, or 60 seconds. The most common length by far is 30 seconds, and 20-second commercials have virtually disappeared.

Audience measurement

Assume you are the director of corporate advertising for a major international corporation whose stock is traded on the New York Stock Exchange. A study you have commissioned reveals that your company, as large as it is, is suffering from an "identity void"; that is, nobody hates you, nobody loves you, nobody knows you. Furthermore, because of this identity void, your company's stock is rarely recommended by financial analysts, and even your current shareholders are dissatisfied with your stock's performance.

You decide you need to advertise—to inform financial decision makers (analysts, pension fund managers, bank portfolio managers, investment bankers, stockbrokers, and corporate executives) about your company, its activities, its growth, and its future. Would you use television as the mainstay in your creative mix?

A company called TRW did. But first they had to be sure they could reach their target audience efficiently with that medium. That meant studying the audiences of various programs and analyzing their impact and cost effectiveness against those of other media vehicles. To do that, of course, requires an understanding of the audience measurement techniques and the terminology used for television advertising.

Rating services: "The book"

The effectiveness (how many people view or listen) of TV and radio stations is measured by rating services. A number of these firms measure program audiences for advertisers and broadcasters. They pick a representative sample of the market and through various techniques furnish data on the size of the audiences that view the programs.

Several of these research organizations gather the data at their own expense and publish it. Companies interested in their findings subscribe to the service and use it as a basis in making media plans for advertising.

The most commonly used services for TV are *Arbitron* (ARB) and the *A. C. Nielsen Station Index* (NSI). For demographic studies of TV audiences, advertisers also commonly use the *Simmons Reports*.

These services publish their findings two or more times per year, depending on the size of the market, in a publication generally referred to as "The Book." (See the Ad Lab.) The book reports a wide array of statistics on how many people, in what age groups, and of what sex are watching TV at various times of the day within a specific market area.

Television markets

Newspaper and magazine publishers generally report their circulations by state. Television rating services use a more precise definition of their markets to minimize the problem of overlapping TV signals.

Areas of dominant influence (ADI) Arbitron introduced the concept and calls its TV markets *areas of dominant influence* (*ADI*). An ADI is defined as "an exclusive geographic area consisting of all counties in which the Home Market stations receive a preponderance of total viewing hours." Thus, the Charlotte ADI is all counties in which the Charlotte TV stations are the most watched.

Designated market areas (DMA) The Nielsen station index uses a similar method known as *designated market areas* (*DMA*).

When TRW decided to try television advertising as a means to fill up its identity void, the company discovered that approximately half of all its shareholders were in the top 10 DMAs, which include the nation's largest cities from New York to Pittsburgh. Therefore, the company's first ads were scheduled in these top 10 markets with one exception: Houston was substituted for Pittsburgh because of the number of TRW customers in that area.

Dayparts

The next questions for TRW were when to air its commercials and on what programs. Unlike radio, there is little or no station loyalty in television. Viewer loyalty is to programs, and programs continue to run or are canceled depending on the size of their ratings (percentage of the population watching). Ratings also depend on what time of day a program runs.

Television time is divided into *dayparts* as follows:

There are different levels of viewing during each daypart. The highest level is done in prime time (7:30–11 P.M.). Late fringe also ranks fairly high in most markets among adults. Daytime and early fringe tend to be viewed most heavily by women.

To achieve the highest possible reach to the advertiser's target audience within budget while maximizing frequency, a *daypart mix* is determined by the media planner based on the TV usage levels reported by the rating services.

In TRW's initial studies of its target group, they learned that their market watched television for entertainment and information, principally during prime time and late evening news; they listened to the radio on the way to work; and they read trade publications related to their work. When they scheduled their first TV ads, then, they bought enough late evening news from the two top-rated stations in each market to achieve a balance of good reach and frequency totaling a minimum of 50 gross rating points per week. This TV schedule was then supported with additional ads on morning radio and in major business publications (Figure 17–7).

There are numerous other terms that rating services and media planners use to define a television station's audience, penetration, and efficiency. We shall discuss a few more of these before examining the procedures used to buy television time.

	Daytime:	9 A.M.–4 P.M. (EST)
Combine as early fringe	Early fringe:	4–5:30 P.M. (EST)
	Early news:	5 or 5:30–7:30 P.M. (EST)
	Prime access:	7:30–8 P.M. (EST)
	Prime:	8–11 P.M. (EST)
Combine as late fringe	Late news:	11–11:30 P.M. (EST)
	Late fringe:	11:30 P.M.–1 A.M. (EST)

TV households (TVHH)

This term refers to the number of households that own television sets. In the United States over 98 percent, or approximately 70 million, households own television sets. By looking at the number of households that own TVs in a particular market, we can gain a sense of the size of that market. Likewise, by looking at the number of TV households tuned in to a particular program, we can get a sense of how popular the program is and how many people our commercial is likely to reach.

Households using television (HUT)

The percentage of homes in a given area that have one or more TV sets turned on at any particular time is expressed as *households using TV*. If there are 1,000 TV sets in the survey area and 500 are turned on, the HUT figure is 50 percent.

Program rating

The percentage of TV households in an area that are tuned in to a specific program is called the *program rating*.

$$\text{Rating} = \frac{\text{Number tuned to specific station}}{\text{TVHH}}$$

Share of audience

The percentage of homes that have sets in use (HUT) tuned in to a specific program is called the program's *share of audience*. A program with only 5 viewers could have a 50 share if only 10 sets are

Where do those infamous television ratings come from?

Nielsen ratings

The A. C. Nielsen Company uses 50,000 diaries to sample the viewing habits of households in more than 200 markets in order to report ratings in its Nielsen Station Index (NSI) for local television.

The Audimeter, a complex electronic instrument attached to TV sets in 1,200 scientifically selected homes, is used to prepare national estimates of network television audiences for its Nielsen Television Index (NTI). The instrument reports time of day, set usage, and station tuning and transmits this information to a central computer.

Nielsen provides media buyers with information about home audience size and other demographic data, which are used as a basis for determining the time and placement of television commercials for network buyers.

Arbitron ratings

The Arbitron Company gathers information on local television audiences by using diaries in which families record the television viewing habits for each television set in the home. The end result is a viewing report broken down by stations, programs, time periods, and demographics.

Arbitron also uses an electronic meter for audience measurement in the four largest markets, New York, Chicago, Los Angeles, and San Francisco. Data are fed to a computer, which produces instantaneous reports ("overnights").

Arbitron (as well as A. C. Nielsen) reports are used for making spot buying decisions.

Laboratory applications

1. What are the advantages and disadvantages of the television audience measurement methods?
2. Which audience rating method do you consider the best? Why?

A.

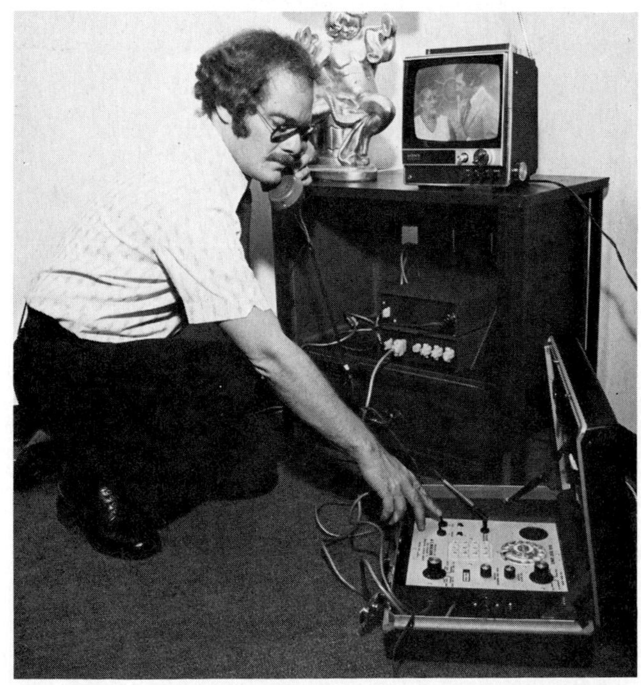

A. A fieldperson installing an instantaneous Audimeter in a Nielsen household.

B.

SAN FRANCISCO–OAKLAND, CA

WK1 10/30–11/05 WK2 11/06–11/12 WK3 11/13–11/19 WK4 11/20–11/26

WEDNESDAY
10.30PM–12.30AM

	Station	Program	DMA HH Ratings Weeks 1	2	3	4	Multi-week avg. RTG	SHR	Share trend May '80	Feb '80	Nov '79
			3	4	5	6	7	8	10	11	12
		R.S.E. THRESHOLDS 25+%	3	3	3	3	1				
		(1 S.E.) 4 WK AVG 50+%	1	1	1	1	LT				
10.30PM	KBHK	BEST-GROUCHO	<<	<<	1	1	1	1	3	3	2
	KGO	VEGA$	12	14	15	14	14	28	27	35	34
	KGSC	MOD SQUAD	1	<<	<<	1	<<		2	3	2
	KPIX	CBS WED-MOV	15	10	9	9	11	22	31	30	24
	KQED	VARIOUS					1	2	2		1
		SONG OF CANARY	<<				<<				
		SOUNDSTAGE		1			1	3			
		1 OF OUR OWN			1		1	2			
		COVER STORY				1	1	2			
	KRON	#QUINCY					11	22	18	15	23
		MOV-WEEK-WED	13				13	25			
		QUINCY		13	9	9	10	22			
	KTVU	10 OCLOCK NWS	7	6	8	8	7	15	13X	11	12
	KTZO	10PM MOV	<<	1	<<	1	1	1		NR	NR
		HUT/PUT/TOTALS *	53	49	46	46	49		54	55	56

Station	Program	DMA Ratings: Persons 2+	Persons 18+	Persons 12-34	Women 18+	Women 18-34	Women 18-49	Women 25-49	Women 25-54	Women WKG	FEM 12-24	PER 12-24	Men 18+	Men 18-34	Men 18-49	Men 25-49	Men 25-54	TNS 12-17	Child 2-11	Child 6-11
		14	15	16	17	18	19	20	21	22	23	24	25	26	27	28	29	30	31	32
	R.S.E. THRESHOLDS 25+%	1	1	2	2	4	2	3	2	3	5	3	2	4	2	3	2	7	7	11
	(1 S.E.) 4 WK AVG 50+%	LT	LT	1	LT	1	1	1	1	1	1	1	LT	1	1	1	1	2	2	3
KBHK	BEST-GROUCHO												1			1	1			
KGO	VEGA$	10	11	11	12	12	12	11	10	12	11	10	10	10	10	10	10	9	2	2
KGSC	MOD SQUAD																			
KPIX	CBS WED-MOV	8	9	7	10	8	10	12	11	10	7	7	8	6	7	7	7	6	2	2
KQED	VARIOUS				1		1	1	1		1									
	SONG OF CANARY																			
	SOUNDSTAGE	1	1	1	1	1	1	1	2	2	1	1						2		
	1 OF OUR OWN																			
	COVER STORY	1	1		1	1	1	1	1		1	1	1		1	1	1			
KRON	#QUINCY	7	8	6	9	6	8	10	10	6	3	4	7	7	7	6	7	3	4	6
	MOV-WEEK-WED	9	10	7	8	3	6	8	9	3	2	5	12	13	11	10	11	2	8	
	QUINCY	6	7	6	9	7	8	10	10	8	3	4	6	5	5	5	5	3	3	4
KTVU	10 OCLOCK NWS	4	5	3	4	2	2	2	2	3	3	3	6	3	4	4	4	4		
KTZO	10PM MOV																			
	HUT/PUT/TOTALS *	32	37	30	39	32	35	37	38	34	27	29	35	30	32	31	31	24	10	12

C.

Weekly Program Estimates

Day and Time / Station	Program	Week-by-week ADI TV HH Ratings WK 1 2/4	WK 2 2/11	WK 3 2/18	WK 4 2/26	ADI TV HH RTG	SHR	ADI TV HH Share/HUT Trends JAN '81	NOV '80	MAY '80	FEB '80	Metro TV HH RTG	SHR
		1	2	3	4	5	6	58	59	60	61	8	9
▲ RELATIVE STD-ERR THRESHOLDS (1 σ)	25%	5	4	5	4	1						1	
	50%	1	1	1	1	–						–	
WEDNESDAY 9:00P– 9:30P													
WJBK	SPC MV PRSNT	19				19	28					20	29
	CBS WD NT MV		18			18	22					17	21
	CBS NW SP RP			24		24	32					25	33
	GRAMMY AWRDS				22	22	32					23	32
	--4 WK AVG--					21	28	30	33	32	29	21	29
WDIV	DFRNT STROKS	23			18	20	30					21	30
	BOB HOPE SPC		23			23	28					24	29
	STATE UNION			20		20	27					20	26
	--4 WK AVG--					21	29	31	25	24	30	21	29
WXYZ	ABC MOVIE SP	18				18	27					19	28
	EAST OF EDEN		32			32	39					33	41
	PRES REAGAN			24		24	32					24	32
	ALOHA PARDSE				17	17	25					18	25
	--4 WK AVG--					23	31	24	34	35	35	24	32

Time Period Average Estimates

TOTAL SURVEY AREA, IN THOUSANDS (000's)

Station	Program	TV HH	Persons 18+	Persons 12-24	Persons 12-34	Women TOT 18+	Women 18-49	Women 12-24	Women 18-34	Women 25-49	Women 25-54	WKG WMN 18+	Men TOT 18+	Men 18-49	Men 18-34	Men 25-49	Men 25-54
		11	13	15	16	18	19	20	21	22	23	24	25	26	27	28	29
▲ Thresholds	25%	16	24	28	25	19	10	26	20	17	17	10	19	19	21	17	17
	50%	4	6	7	6	4	4	6	5	4	4	4	4	4	5	4	4
WJBK	SPC MV PRSNT	314	460	175	263	339	247	76	115	198	234	126	121	87	60	49	72
	CBS WD NT MV	292	370	103	192	198	128	46	84	105	121	38	172	94	53	69	97
	CBS NW SP RP	400	592	36	175	305	161	27	92	137	160	65	287	130	77	123	151
	GRAMMY AWRDS	365	592	184	251	351	211	108	117	144	195	61	241	135	63	90	143
	--4 WK AVG--	343	504	124	220	298	187	64	102	146	178	72	205	111	64	83	116
WDIV	DFRNT STROKS	350	452	183	292	273	162	93	109	120	132	63	179	113	82	74	81
	BOB HOPE SPC	394	578	122	253	333	184	77	117	144	163	96	245	144	61	136	149
	STATE UNION	327	459	94	154	251	141	51	63	113	130	58	208	116	36	104	122
	--4 WK AVG--	355	485	145	248	282	162	79	99	124	139	70	203	121	65	97	108
WXYZ	ABC MOVIE SP	325	547	147	305	253	173	66	111	125	144	58	294	232	152	175	206
	EAST OF EDEN	526	850	283	538	496	368	180	259	265	301	124	354	276	182	194	205
	PRES REAGAN	407	606	111	277	338	218	63	142	176	192	117	268	192	94	162	181
	ALOHA PARDSE	295	410	111	252	224	144	74	118	94	99	69	186	128	88	113	124
	--4 WK AVG--	388	603	163	343	328	226	96	158	165	184	92	275	207	129	161	179

B. Sample material from the Nielsen Television Index for San Francisco/Oakland.

C. A sample page from Arbitron's television rating book for Detroit.

tuned on. For that reason the program rating figures are important because they measure the audience as a percentage of all TV households in the area, regardless of whether their TV set is turned on or off.

Total audience

The total number of homes reached by some portion of the program is referred to as *total audience.* This figure is normally broken down to determine *audience composition* (the distribution of audience into demographic categories).

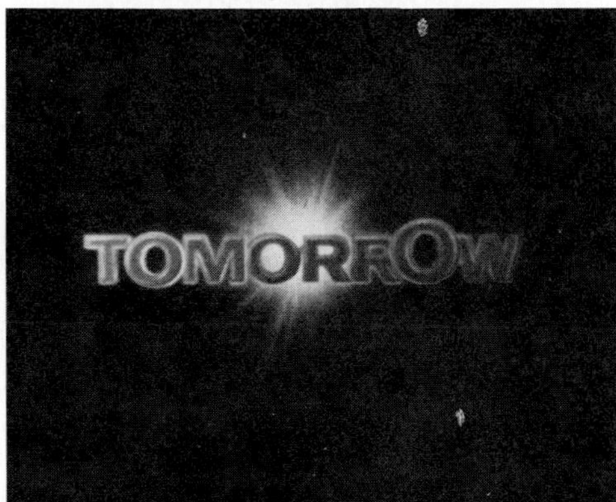

Figure 17–7 Tomorrow is taking shape at a company called TRW.

Gross rating points

In television, *gross rating points* are the total weight of a media schedule against TV households. Thus, a weekly schedule of 5 commercials with an average household rating of 20 would yield 100 GRPs or a total audience equivalent to the total number of TV households in the area.

TRW determined that a schedule of 50 GRPs per week would be sufficient at the beginning of its television campaign. This might have been accomplished by buying 10 spots with an average rating of 5, or only 2 spots with an average rating of 25.

The latter might have been feasible by using a highly rated prime-time program, but then the frequency would have been very low. So TRW opted to use the late evening newscasts, which had lower ratings against total TV households but higher shares of those adults watching; it also afforded the company the ability to gain frequency.

The results of TRW's decision demonstrated the wisdom of their choice. In key markets where the commercials ran, surveys were taken, and the number of respondents who looked upon TRW as an attractive investment alternative increased 20 percent—to more than 60 percent total. In control markets where the TRW commercials did not air, the company's image remained virtually unchanged.

Television buying procedures

The process of buying TV time can be rather lengthy as advertisers try to determine what programs are available to them at what cost, analyze the various programs for efficiency, negotiate with stations or reps on price, determine what reach and frequency they are achieving, eventually sign the broadcast contracts, and then finally review the affidavits of performance to be sure the commercials ran as agreed.

The buying procedures for television are so complex that most large advertisers seek the assistance of professional advertising agencies or media buying services. For the local advertiser, the assistance of station reps also proves invaluable in determining the best buys for the money.

Requesting avails

To find out what programs are available to them, media buyers con-

People in advertising

Jerry Della Femina

Chairman of the Board
and Chief Executive Officer
Della Femina, Travisano &
Partners, Inc.

It was Jerry Della Femina's first day on the job at Ted Bates & Company. Besides himself in the conference room, there were six account, art, and copy supervisors. They were engaged in a life-and-death struggle to dream up a campaign for Panasonic, a Japanese electronics account. During the silent meditation, it hit him. "I've got it! I've got it! How about this headline: From those wonderful folks who gave you Pearl Harbor."

At first there was only stupified silence. The account executive dropped his pipe and an art director started to laugh hysterically. The line was never used in the campaign and the horrified reaction of the agency was one of the reasons that compelled Della Femina to eventually start his own agency.

Jerry Della Femina, who made his mark in American advertising before he was 30 with some of the most provocative—and effective—headlines ever written, is founder, chairman of the board, and chief executive officer of Della Femina, Travisano & Partners, Inc., a Madison Avenue agency.

Della Femina was born in Brooklyn, the son of Italian-speaking, immigrant parents. When he entered school at age six, he was unable to speak English.

After graduating from high school, Della Femina went to work as an advertising messenger for the *New York Times*. He recalls, "I used to deliver proofs of ads to department stores on Fifth Avenue. Wherever I went. . . I used to see guys sitting around with their feet propped up on desks. They were the department-store copywriters. That's when I made up my mind that copywriting was for me." He enrolled in Brooklyn College and took night courses in advertising.

In 1961 Della Femina joined Daniel & Charles, writing ads for Kayser-Roth. Two years later he moved to Fuller & Smith & Rose. He was named creative director of Delehanty, Kurnit & Geller in 1964. Here Della Femina produced award-winning ads for Pretty Feet ("What's the ugliest part of your body?") and for Talon zippers, in which a baseball catcher informs a pitcher, "Your fly is open." His ads won two Gold Keys from the Advertising Writer's Association of New York and two ANDYs from the Advertising Club of New York. Della Femina went to Ted Bates & Co. in 1966 as creative supervisor and produced more attention-getting ads. He persuaded Yogi Berra to appear in Ozone Hair Spray TV commercials alongside copy that read, "Yogi Berra is one of those sissies who uses his wife's hair spray."

In 1967, with Ron Travisano and two other Bates associates, Della Femina launched his own agency. One of the first accounts signed was Squire for Men, a hairpiece manufacturer. For Squire, Della Femina wrote the line, "Are you still combing your memories?"

Three years after launching his agency, Della Femina gained acclaim by writing the book *From Those Wonderful Folks Who Gave You Pearl Harbor: Front-Line Dispatches from the Advertising War,* an industry classic. Later he was named Advertising Executive of the Year. The American Association of Advertising Agencies honored him as one of the nation's top three copywriters in 1978. His name appears in *Who's Who in America*.

Della Femina's startling one-liners, like "Before Hitler could kill 6 million Jews, he had to burn 6 million books" for McGraw-Hill Book Company, not only gripped audiences but sold clients' products and won major advertising awards. They brought Della Femina immediate recognition and success in the industry.

Today Della Femina, Travisano & Partners, Inc. has annual billings of over $100 million and clients that include Airwick, Bekins, Borden, Carte Blanche, Emery Air Freight, Gillette, Lipton, Six Flags, Nalley's, Ralston Purina, and Schlitz. Nearly 60 percent of the agency's media dollars are spent on television advertising.

tact the sales representatives for the stations they are considering. These may be local station salespeople, national media rep organizations that sell for one station in each market, or network reps. The media buyer gives the rep information about the advertiser's media objectives and target audiences and asks the rep to supply a list of available time slots along with their prices and estimated ratings (Figure 17–8).The information supplied by the media buyer includes:

Name of advertiser.

Desired dates of schedule.

Desired daypart mix (e.g., 60 percent prime, 30 percent news, 10 percent late fringe).

Total household GRP goals (e.g., 100 points per week for four weeks).

Demographic target audience.
  Primary: Adults 25–34.
  Secondary: Young adults 18–25.

The information requested from the rep on all the available programs includes:

ADI household ratings.

Total households (in thousands).

Total persons in target audience (in thousands).

ADI HUT (percentage of homes using TV).

Prices for each of available programs.

The avails submitted by the rep should include all the data requested based on the most recent Nielsen or Arbitron book. Many media buyers ask for the information based on the last two or three books in order to see whether a show's ratings are consistent or have an upward or downward trend.

Selecting programs for buys

To determine which shows to buy, the media buyer must select the most efficient ones in relation to the target audience. To do this, a simple computation is made of the cost per rating point (CPP) and the cost per thousand (CPM) for each program, as follows:

$$\frac{\text{Cost}}{\text{Rating}} = \text{CPP} \qquad \frac{\text{Cost}}{\text{Thousands of people}} = \text{CPM}$$

For example assume "Family Feud" has a rating of 25, reaches 200,000 people in the primary target audience, and costs $2,000 for a 30-second spot on station WXYZ in Everittown, U.S.A. Then,

$$\frac{\$2{,}000}{25} = \$80 \text{ CPP} \qquad \frac{\$2{,}000}{200} = \$10 \text{ CPM}$$

Obviously, the lower the cost per thousand, the more efficient the show is against the target audience. The media buyer's task, therefore, is to compare the packages of each station, substituting stronger programs for less efficient ones. For example, prime time may be very strong on one station but news time very weak. The media buyer tries to use the best areas each station has to offer to construct suitable

WAGA-TV
(Airdate March 8, 1949)

CBS Television Network

STS STORER TELEVISION SALES, INC.

NAB TvB

A Storer Station
Subscriber to the NAB Television Code
Media Code 6 211 0100 5.00
Storer Broadcasting Co., 1551 Briarcliff Rd., N. E., Atlanta, Ga. 30306. Phone 404-875-5551. TWX 404-527-2160.
Mailing Address: Box 4207, Atlanta, Ga. 30302.

1. PERSONNEL
Vice-Pres. & Gen'l Mgr.—Paul Raymon.
General Sales Manager—Jack O'Hern.
National Sales Manager—Spencer Koch.

2. REPRESENTATIVES
Storer Television Sales Inc.
Canada—Radio-Television Representatives, Ltd.

3. FACILITIES
Video 100,000 w.; audio 10,000 w.: ch 5.
Antenna ht.: 1,070 ft. above average terrain.
Operating schedule: 6:30-12:30 am. EST.

4. AGENCY COMMISSION
15% commission to recognized agencies; no cash discount.

5. GENERAL ADVERTISING See coded regulations
General: 1a, 2a, 3a, 3c, 4a, 5, 6b, 7b, 8, 9.
Rate Protection: 10h, 11h, 12h, 13h, 14b.
Contracts: 20c, 21, 22a, 24b, 25, 26, 27d, 29, 31b, 32a, 34h.
Basic Rates: 40a, 40b, 41a, 42, 46, 47k, 50.
Comb.: Cont. Discounts: 60a, 60d, 60e, 60f, 61a, 62a.
Cancellation: 70b, †70e, 70f, 71, 72, 73a.
Prod. Services: 80, 83, 84, 85, 86, 87a, 87b, 87c.
(†) or 2 telecasts' notice, but no such cancellation shall be effective until 4 weeks after the start of the schedule.
Affiliated with CBS Television Network.
Station requires 14 days or two telecasts' notice, whichever is longer, for the cancellation of current announcement schedules. The day of notification does not count toward any cancellation notice and no such cancellation shall be effective until four weeks after the start of the schedule. Station requires a 28-day written notice for cancellation of program contracts. No program termination effective until 13 weeks after start of telecasting.
NAB Code: For the purpose of the NAB Code, Prime Time is 8-11 pm Mon thru Sat, 7-11 pm Sun. Station reserves the right to revise its rates at any time without notice.
Firm non-cancellable contracts for uninterrupted existing on confirmed programs or announcement schedules are protected for the remainder of the contract up to a maximum of 52 weeks.
Station reserves right to hold advertiser and its advertising agency and/or media buying service jointly and severally liable for such monies as are due and payable to station.

6. TIME RATES
No. 39A Rev. 6/11/79—Rec'd 8/8/79.
Rates quoted herein apply to single corporate entities only.

7. SPOT ANNOUNCEMENTS
AA1-AA5 Mon thru Sat 7:58-11:01 pm; Sun 6:58-11:01 pm.

30 SECONDS

	I	II	III	IV	V
AA1	6000	5500	5000	4500	4000
AA2	3500	3200	2900	2600	2300
AA3	2000	1900	1800	1700	1600
AA4	1500	1400	1300	1200	1100
AA5	1000	900	800	700	600

10 sec: 50% of 30 sec, rounded to nearest dollar.

8. PARTICIPATING ANNOUNCEMENT PROGRAMS
Rec'd 8/8/79.
DAYTIME
30 SECONDS

MON THRU FRI:	I	II	III	IV	V
CBS Morning News/Captain Kangaroo—7-8/8-9 am	100	80	60	40	20
Phil Donahue/Crosswits—9-10:30 am	210	160	110	90	70
AM Rotator—10:30 am-noon	240	190	140	110	90
PM:					
Noon News Scene—noon-12:30	270	220	170	140	110
PM Rotator—12:30-4:30	260	210	160	130	100
EARLY FRINGE & NEWS					
Merv Griffin—3:30-4:30	295	215	165	135	110
Mike Douglas—4:30-6	400	300	225	175	150
Early Scene News—6-7 Mon thru Fri; 6-6:30 Sun/Late News Scene—11-11:30 Mon thru Sun	1000	800	600	500	400
Weekend Early News Scene – 6-6:30 Sat	650	600	500	400	300
PRIME ACCESS & LOCAL PRIME					
PM Magazine—7:30-8	1200	950	800	650	550
Muppets/$1.98 Beauty Contest—7-8 Sat	1200	950	750	600	550
Access Rotation—7:30-8 Mon thru Fri; 7-8 Sat	1000	800	650	500	350
WEEKEND & FRINGE					
Adam 12—11:30-midnight Mon thru Thurs	400	300	250	200	150
TV5 Late Movie—11:30-concl Fri/Sat; 11:45-concl Sun	210	180	125	90	75
CBS Late Fringe Rotator—midnight-1:15 am Mon thru Thurs	205	175	150	125	100
CBS/Local Late Movie—1:15 am-concl Mon thru Sun	60	50	40	30	20
Kids Block I—6:30 am-noon Sat	450	350	250	200	150
Kids Block II—12:30-2:30 Sat/Sun	350	250	150	75	50
News Scene—noon-12:30 Sat/Sun	220	170	120	100	80
Movies/Various—11 am-6 pm Sat/Sun	300	200	150	100	75
Soul Train—Saturday Afternoon	325	250	175	150	125
Sunday Morning Various—6:30-11 am	150	100	75	50	25
CBS Sunday Morning—9-10:30 am	150	100	75	50	25

9. PACKAGE ANNOUNCEMENT RATES
TWENTY FOUR PLAN
Advertisers will be granted a 10% discount from applicable rate for a single product saturation campaign of 24 spots run within a 7 day period. Twenty four plan is not combinable with other plans.

Preemptibility
All adjacency & participating spots purchased at level 1 classification are considered fixed (4 wk protection). Spots purchased at anything other than level I subject to preemption at discretion of station. All Level I 10 sec spots purchased in a 30/60 sec brk position are subject to preemption at the discretion of the station.

10. PROGRAM RATES
Sun thru Sat 8-11 pm, 1 hr 10000

11. SPECIAL FEATURES
PARTICIPATING SPONSORSHIPS

PER WK:	1 ti			2 ti		
WKS:	13-25	26-51	52	13-25	26-51	52
News Scene—6-7 pm Mon thru Fri; 11-11:30 pm Mon thru Sun; 6-6:30 pm Sat/Sun.						
2 Early	950	900	850	900	850	800
1 Early/1 Late	1000	950	900	950	900	850

Rate includes time, talent, studio production (not to exceed two hours for each 13-week flight), 1 60-sec spot or 2 30-sec spots, plus closing billboard.

COLOR
Schedules network color, film, slides, tape and live. Equipped with high band VTR.

13. CLOSING TIME
4 days for materials required by station prior to telecast.

The *Spot Television Rates and Data* listing for WAGA–TV in Atlanta, Georgia, shows the rate charged on its grid plan for various time slots during the week. The grid used will depend on program audience estimates at the time.

Figure 17–8

packages. Then the bottom line (cost per thousand) for each station is compared for each daypart considered.

	WAAA		WBBB		WCCC	
	GRPs	**CPM**	**GRPs**	**CPM**	**GRPs**	**CPM**
Prime	50	$10.00	55	$9.00	40	$8.50
Fringe	50	5.00	45	6.00	60	4.75

In this situation, WBBB is the first choice for prime time because it is efficient and offers the best audience delivery. WAAA delivers less and costs more. WCCC costs less but doesn't deliver as much. For fringe time, WCCC offers the greatest delivery at the lowest cost. To use two stations' packages for prime and/or fringe, the media buyer tries to negotiate prices to bring the two stations in line with one another.

Negotiating prices

While print media normally stick to rate cards because of their guaranteed circulation, broadcast stations are willing to negotiate prices since their audiences are at best estimated.

The purpose of price negotiation from the advertiser's standpoint is to get the best schedule possible within the budget. The media buyer contacts the rep and tells him or her what efficiency the advertiser needs, in terms of delivery and CPM, to make the buy. The media buyer rarely discloses other stations' prices, but uses CPMs as a negotiating tool in an effort to get the most CPPs within the budget.

Reach and frequency

As we discussed in Chapter 15 on media planning, the objectives of reach and frequency are very important to the media planner. Therefore, once the package has been determined, the media buyer may ask the rep to do a computer run on the schedule to get an estimate of the expected reach and frequency. To do this, the media rep needs to know the total target audience in each of the dayparts, as well as the total GRPs and the number of spots per daypart in the schedule.

Large advertising agencies prepare their own reach and frequency estimates based on their own statistical tables or computer programs. These are too advanced for the beginning advertising student to consider. But it is important to realize that despite the aura of preciseness of these figures, they are really only estimates based on the current state-of-the-art media research principles. Like all statistics, they are subject to potentially great variations caused by immeasurable and uncontrollable factors.

Contracts and affidavits

The station contract is a legal document. As such, it is imperative that the media buyer catch any discrepancies before signing it. The contract indicates the dates, times, and programs on which the advertiser's commercials will run, the length of the spots, the rate per spot, and the total amount. The reverse side of the contract defines in small print the various obligations and responsibilities of the advertiser, the agency, and the station, and the terms of payment.

After the spots have run, the station returns a form to the advertiser or agency, signed and notarized, indicating when spots were aired and what *makegoods* may have run to compensate for spots that were missed or run incorrectly. This *affidavit of performance* is the station's legal proof that the advertiser got what was paid for.

Using radio in the creative mix

Everybody knows what a newspaper coupon is. You clip it, take it to the store, and save 15 or 20 cents on a roll of bathroom tissue or a can of dog food. Advertisers invest big budgets in print coupons, but *Advertising Age* reports that only about 3 percent of the coupons printed are ever redeemed by shoppers.

McDonald's advertising agency, Needham, Harper & Steers, had an idea to use coupons to help promote Big Mac sales. But they gave this idea a creative twist. They introduced radio coupons and used the voices of kids to explain the promotion.

Clara: What are you doing, Glen?

Glen: Making McDonald's radio coupons.

Clara: Radio coupons?

Glen: Don't you listen to the radio, Clara? Place a dollar bill on a piece of paper and draw a dotted line around it.

Clara: Then what?

Glen: Then take a pencil, crayons, whatever, and draw a picture of a Big Mac on it.

Clara: Why, Glen?

Glen: 'Cause everytime you buy a Big Mac, you can turn in your homemade coupon—and get a free regular-size soft drink.

Clara: Why so many coupons, Glen?

Glen: 'Cause I love Big Macs—and I love free soft drinks.

Clara: A free soft drink at McDonald's is great but . . .

Glen: Yeah?

Clara: Glen, your drawings are silly.

Glen: They're impressionistic, Clara.

Clara: Glen, you're a bad artist.

Glen: I'm paid well.

Clara: Glen, you're clipping McDonald's.

Glen: That's the whole idea, Clara.

Clara: Cut it out, Glen!

Glen: OK, Clara!

Anncr.: You heard it on radio, folks! Make your own dollar-bill-sized coupon. Draw a Big Mac on it—pencil, ballpoint, colors—whatever. When you buy a Big Mac, turn in your coupons for a free regular-size soft drink. Get cuttin', Washington. Offer ends September 17th.

Singers: [*music up*] *At McDonald's . . .*

Glen: [*clip-clip-clip*] *Clara, that's a beautiful coupon!*

Singers: We do it all for you.

McDonald's ran the promotion for its 96 stores in Washington, D.C., Virginia, and southern Maryland. Fifteen different radio stations were used to tell listeners to write their own radio coupons, good for a free soft drink with every Big Mac purchased.

When the campaign broke, the general manager of the agency stated that "if successful, the idea would have long-reaching implications for testing the effectiveness of radio as a useful medium for couponing."

After the campaign, Dale Smith, manager of the 96-store co-op, reported that thousands of coupons had been received, like those shown in Figure 17–9. In most promotions a 10 percent sales increase is considered good. But in this one Big Mac sales increased 15–17 percent. Plus the cost of this promotion against the sales generated was excellent. So McDonald's decided to use the coupon promotion with other products.

Since that time, the radio coupon has received wide attention by supermarkets, discount chains, sporting goods dealers, and many other fast-food chains. As a promotional device, radio coupons are just one of the many advantages of using radio in the creative mix. Radio can be fun, it's flexible, it's involving, it's fast, and it can be very inexpensive.

Figure 17–9 Two examples of hand-drawn coupons turned in at McDonald's stores . . . one from a six-year-old, the other from a 25-year-old. As *Ad Media,* the mid-Atlantic advertising business paper, noted in its report on the coupon ideas: "Think of the savings in art charges."

What works best in radio?

Radio is an integral part of our daily lives. We rely on clock radios to wake us in the morning. At breakfast we tune in the morning news. Radio entertains us while we drive to work or school or do household chores. And chances are good that if you work in an office or plant, you enjoy background music supplied by a local radio station. With its unique ability to relax, inform, and entertain, radio has become the daily companion of millions at work, at play, and on the highway.

In short, it is a popular medium. Compared with many other categories of leisure/entertainment/knowledge expenditures, the public spends much more on radio sets. In fact, in 1980 more money was spent buying radios than was spent on stereos and phonographs, or records, movies, spectator sports, musical instruments, or film developing.

In an average week 95.9 percent of all the people in the United States listen to the radio—over 83 percent on an average day. The average adult spends 3 hours and 28 minutes per day listening to the radio. This has tremendous implications for advertisers. As more and more advertisers have learned that radio leads all other media in both daily and weekly reach, radio's advertising revenues have grown steadily.

The largest national advertisers are food producers, auto manufacturers, travel companies, breweries, wineries, consumer services, drug producers, and cosmetics. But the medium's biggest source of revenue is composed of the thousands upon thousands of local neighborhood businesses that use radio to reach out and talk to their local customers. Of the almost $3.7 billion spent in radio in 1980, over $2.8 billion came from local advertisers. Why is that?

Reach and frequency

Radio offers the combination of excellent reach and excellent frequency. With the average adult listening more than three hours a day, radio builds a large audience quickly; and a normal advertising schedule easily allows repeated impact on the listener. The ability to quickly expose the people a sufficient number of times to motivate them to buy makes radio very attractive to local merchants (Figure 17–10).

Selectivity

The wide variety of specialized radio formats available, with their prescribed audiences and coverage areas, enables the advertiser to select just the market he or she wants to reach. Commercials can be aimed at listeners of a specific sex, age group, ethnic or religious background, income group, employment category, educational level, or special interest. Whether commercials are intended for middle-aged homemakers or pro football fans, an advertiser is bound to find a station with just the programming to reach these people.

Efficiency

Radio's strong appeal to advertisers is largely its economy. Radio has the ability to offer its reach, frequency, and selectivity at one of the lowest costs per thousand. Thus, the budget needed for an effective radio schedule is often less than that needed for newspapers, magazines, or television.

In 1980, for example, the cost of buying 25 GRPs on network radio was only $1.70 per thousand. This compares favorably with the cost of daytime network TV, whereas prime-time TV in 1980 cost an average of $3.77 per thousand, national magazines $8.05 per thousand, and newspapers $12.00 per thousand. In fact, only outdoor consistently offers a lower CPM at $0.51 per thousand impressions.

The production of a radio commercial is also relatively inexpensive. National spots can usually be produced for one-tenth the cost of a TV commercial. And in some cases there are no production costs at all since local radio stations frequently produce commercials free for their local advertisers.

Drawbacks to radio

In spite of its great advantages, radio has traditionally suffered from particular limitations in that it is only an aural medium, its audience is highly segmented, the advertiser's commercials are short-lived, and often they are only half-heard, or the listener is interrupted and the advertisers are heard sporadically or out of context.

Limitations of sound

Radio is heard but not seen. This potentially limits the effectiveness of commercials for products that need to be seen to be understood. Advertising agencies usually prefer the freedom of creating with sight, sound, color, and motion, as in television. They see radio as restricting their creative options.

Notwithstanding, many brilliant creative efforts have been achieved with radio through the use of "theater of the mind" techniques. Pittsburgh Paints, for example, conceived a campaign that actually capitalized on radio's aural limitation. "Imagine yellow . . ." the announcer said, and soft music swelled in the background. "This is yellow," he went on, "from Pittsburgh Paint." The campaign, which used the same concept to describe other colors, proved to be highly effective. (See the Checklist.)

Segmented audiences

The ability of radio to deliver highly selective audiences can be a handicap to some advertisers. The large number of radio stations competing for an area audience may make the purchase of effective airtime very difficult for the advertiser. For example, while one city

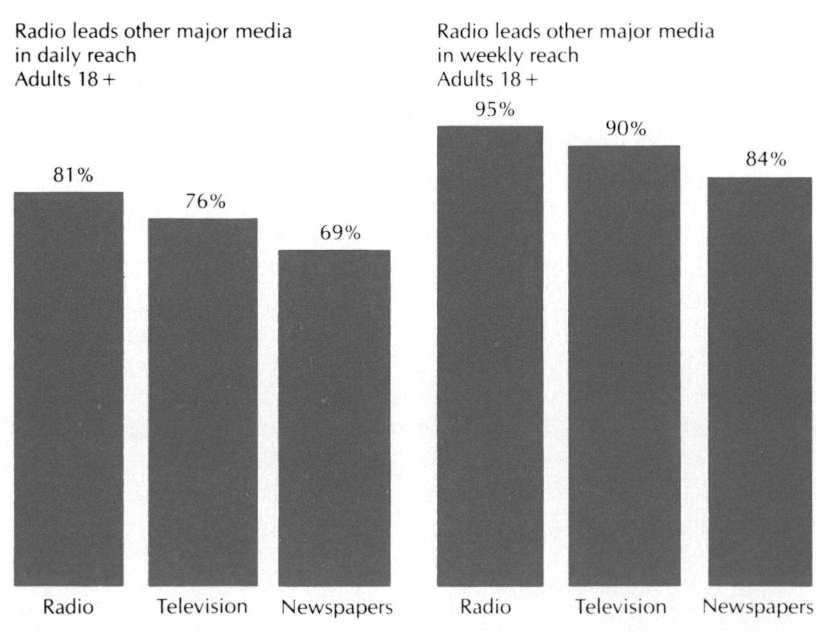

Figure 17–10

may have only three television stations, it may have 20 radio stations competing for a market of, say, 1.5 million people. Each of these stations is distinctive in format and programming, ranging from all news and sports to hard rock to country-western music. Clearly, the advertiser who is seeking to blanket this market will have to buy multiple stations; and this may not be cost effective.

Short-lived and half-heard commercials

A radio commercial is brief and fleeting. You can't clip and keep it like a newspaper or a magazine ad. It lasts only moments, and then it's gone.

For many listeners, radio provides only a pleasant "background sound" while they are driving to work, reading, studying, or entertaining. Thus, radio must compete with other activities for their attention. In such cases it does not always succeed. For these reasons many advertisers shy away from using radio or, at least, are very skeptical of its ability to work for them.

Similarly, it is for these reasons that creativity and production quality are so important to the success of radio advertising. Monotonous or boring radio commercials simply go in one ear and out the other. The astute advertiser, though, will use radio's unique theater-of-the-mind ability to penetrate the listener's consciousness.

Checklist of what works best in radio

Here is a checklist to help you create effective radio commercials.

☐ Stretch the listener's imagination. Voices and sounds can evoke pictures.

☐ Listen for a memorable sound. What will make your commercial stand out from the clutter? A distinctive voice, a memorable jingle, a solution to the listener's problem.

☐ Present one idea. It is difficult to communicate more than one idea in a television commercial. In radio, which is subject to more distractions, it is nearly impossible. Be direct and clear.

☐ Select your audience quickly. It pays to flag your segment of the audience at the beginning of the commercial—before they can switch to another station.

☐ Mention your brand name and your promise early. Commercials that do so get higher awareness. It heightens awareness if you mention the brand name and promise *more than once*.

☐ Capitalize on events. Exploit the flexibility of radio to tie in with fads, fashions, news events, or the weather.

☐ Use radio to reach teenagers. Teenagers don't watch much television. They do listen to a lot of radio. Media experts say it's the best way to reach teens. Some say it's the *only* way.

☐ Music can help. It is particularly effective in reaching teenagers who prefer the "now sounds" offered by music stations. You can give your campaign infinite variety with the same lyrics arranged in different ways and sung by different people.

☐ Ask listeners to take action. People respond to radio requests for action. They call the station to exchange views with the disc jockey or ask for certain music. Don't be afraid to ask listeners to call now, or write in, or send money.

Overview of the radio medium

Radio is the most subjective of all mass media. It offers a wide variety of program formats like rock, easy listening, all news, middle of the road (MOR), sports, and classical music. Within each format, there is a variety of entertainment and information for the station's audience.

Unlike TV or newspaper, though, radio listening is usually done by one person alone. It is a personal, one-on-one medium. And it is mobile. Radio can entertain a person while driving, while walking, and while at home or away from home. Where commuting is done by automobile, radio is an extremely strong medium. In markets like New York, though, where most commuting is done by train, bus, or subway, newspaper is the stronger "drive time" medium.

Radio is also adaptable to moods. In the morning some people may want to hear the news, upbeat music, or interesting chatter from a disc jockey to help them wake up. In the afternoon the same people may want to unwind with classical or easy-listening music. As a result, most people consistently listen to three or four different radio stations representing different types of programming.

For the advertiser, therefore, an appropriate mix of dayparts and formats is important to developing a good radio schedule (Figure 17–11).

Who uses radio?

In increasing number, national advertisers are discovering the reach and frequency potential of radio (Figure 17–12). Maxwell House coffee advertised on television only for many years until they discovered that coffee consumption was in a continuing decline throughout the day. While television reaches most coffee drinkers, it does not do so at the time they are most likely to be drinking coffee. Radio listenership, on the other hand, almost perfectly fits coffee consumption. Also, with radio, Maxwell House could extend its reach from 90 percent to 95 percent, and the cost per thousand was almost a full dollar less than for television.

Exxon's Qwip systems discovered the same thing when they entered the facsimile office products market. With radio they could reach corporate decision makers more precisely and effectively during drive time while work was still on their minds.

Local retailers also like the medium because they can tailor it to their immediate needs, it offers defined audiences, and they can create an identity for themselves by doing their own ads.

In Forest City, North Carolina, Henry Bruegge, the owner of House of Gems, devotes 80 percent of his advertising budget to radio. He gets immediate response, and it gives him a chance to tell about his other services (like watch repair), which are an important part of his business. Using two radio stations, he runs an average of 30 to 35 spots a week. For special promotions, the radio stations come out to his store and broadcast from there. These "remotes" are very successful in drawing traffic and creating an image of activity.

Radio programming and audiences

Stations plan their programming carefully in order to reach specific markets and capture as many listeners as possible. The larger its audience, the more a station can charge advertisers for commercial time.

Figure 17–11 The Radio Advertising Bureau helps its member stations by advertising heavily to prospective radio advertisers. Here the bureau promises to deliver "the impact of television at a fraction of the cost"—a take-off on Western Union's Mailgram slogan. It's interesting to note that the advertising agency for Mailgram is Trout & Ries, which is also the agency of the Radio Advertising Bureau.

Therefore, extensive planning and research go into programming and program changes. When low ratings occur, they are sometimes reversed by a sharp change in programming. Other times stations may test new program concepts to determine the ones that will attract new listeners.

Most stations maintain the same general type of programming

Figure 17–12 Radio's cumulative audience among a range of demographic groups

	Average daily cume	Weekly cume Mon.–Sun.	Average daily time spent listening
Persons 12+	81.4%	95.3%	3:24
Teens 12–17	91.1	99.9	3:01
Men			
18+	81.9	95.8	3:26
18–24	88.7	99.9	3:58
25–34	86.7	99.0	3:49
35–49	83.0	97.2	3:18
50+	74.2	90.4	2:59
Household income			
$25,000+	86.4	99.8	3:28
$20,000–24,999	85.3	98.1	3:42
$15,000–19,999	85.2	97.7	3:45
Under $15,000	73.5	89.1	3:07
College-educated	85.8	97.8	3:22
Women			
18+	78.2	93.6	3:28
18–24	87.1	98.7	3:47
25–34	81.8	97.0	3:36
35–49	80.2	96.1	3:41
50+	70.7	87.8	3:06
Household income			
$25,000+	85.1	99.9	3:39
$20,000–24,999	81.3	96.0	3:34
$15,000–19,999	81.1	95.0	3:42
Under $15,000	71.6	88.1	3:14
College-educated	82.6	96.5	3:32
Adults in Households of			
5+ persons	83.0	96.7	3:38
3–4 persons	81.5	96.1	3:32
1–2 persons	76.9	92.2	3:17

throughout the broadcast week to keep their specific audience. However, they may add special features, such as local sporting events, or contests in which prizes or free tickets are awarded to boost their audience figures.

The most common radio formats are progressive rock, contemporary top 40, middle of the road (MOR), "good" music, classical and semiclassical, country-western, all news, and talk. We shall discuss each of these briefly.

Progressive rock

The perennial favorite of young men and women 18–34 years old, progressive rock stations (also called album-oriented rock) base their programming on current big sounds from well-known groups. Often the trendsetters in musical style, the progressive musicians and DJs usually relate closely to their audiences in social, political, and cultural attitudes as well as music.

Contemporary top 40

These music stations base their programming on current record and album sales. They air the top-selling "hits" throughout the program day. Some feature colorful disc jockeys, with names like Murray the K and Wolfman Jack. Their listeners are chiefly avid, young, black and white teenagers (Figure 17–13), and their music is described in the trade as having a more "bubblegum" sound. These stations naturally do very well with soft drink advertisers, fast-food outlets, movies, and clothing retailers.

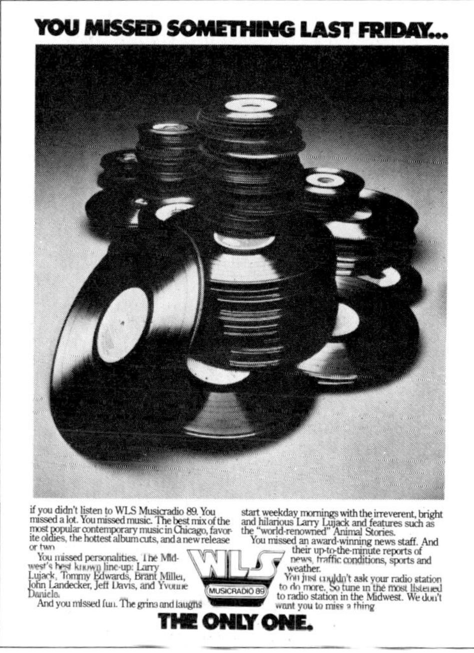

Figure 17–13 Chicago's WLS: 20 years of interest in the young teenager.

Middle of the road (MOR)

These music stations are similar to rock outlets in that they play popular current hits. However, they avoid the harsh rhythm and strident sounds that characterize hard rock. Instead they feature popular music, past and present, and subdued rock and roll, and their audiences tend to be somewhat older (25–49 years) and have proportionately higher incomes.

"Good" music

These stations tend to have older and more mature listeners. They play chiefly instrumental music and some vocal selections limited to ballads.

Classical/semiclassical

Stations of this type offer contemporary classics and music of the "masters" as well as chamber music, opera, and other selections that have endured the test of time. Many such stations lean toward the fuller "concert" sounds.

Classical audiences tend to be considerably older (over 35), have substantially higher incomes, be white or Hispanic, and live in the West.

Country and western

These stations usually feature the "Nashville sounds": ballads, folk, and folk-rock music performed in basic rhythms. There are several types of stations within this category. Some air easy-listening, pop western music. Others tend toward repetitive down-home country ballads.

The largest country audiences are in the Midwest, South, and Southwest. They tend to earn less money, be over 35 years old, and be predominantly white.

All news

Unlike most stations, which offer a brief summary of the news every hour or half-hour, these stations broadcast continuous news throughout the day. Programs are divided into segments devoted to national, international, regional, and local news.

Advertisers tend to favor all-news formats to reach the older, upscale, mature men and women who are deeply involved in business and civic affairs.

Talk

Some stations invite listeners to participate in programming by expressing their views and ideas on the air. Typically a personable announcer encourages listeners to air their views by phoning the station and talking with him or with a featured guest. Such programs tend to emphasize lively and controversial issues, bizarre subjects, and sex. Most have a loyal listenership of older men and women at the lower end of the income scale.

Miscellaneous

In addition to the formats presented above, there are seemingly limitless variations like soft rock, oldies but goodies, disco, and ethnic formats (Spanish, black/soul, etc.), which cater to smaller or more specialized market segments.

Buying radio time

As in television buying, advertisers need to have a basic knowledge in order to buy radio effectively. First, it's important to be aware of the types of radio advertising available for commercial use. Second, a basic understanding of radio terminology is necessary. And finally, the advertiser needs to know the steps in preparing a radio schedule.

Types of radio advertising

Radio time may be purchased by an advertiser in one of three forms: local, spot, or network. Local purchases account for 75 percent of all radio time sold. Spot radio represents another 20 percent, and network 5 percent.

Networks

Advertisers may use one of the national radio networks (ABC, CBS, NBC, Mutual, etc.) to carry their messages to the entire national market simultaneously via the networks' affiliated stations (Figure 17–14). However, radio networks generally provide much less program-

Figure 17–14 Network radio costs: 1 minute/30 second rates, Monday–Friday*

Network	Number of stations	A.M. drive	Housewife time
CBS	275	$3,400/$2,200	$2,100/$1,400
MBS	863	$2,600/$1,300	$2,400/$1,200
NBC	274	$3,100/$2,170	$1,650/$1,155
ABC			
Contemporary	388	$3,680/$1,840	$2,820/$1,410
Entertainment	474	$3,650/$1,825	$3,200/$1,600
FM	195	$1,400/$700	$1,320/$660
Information	497	$3,190/$1,595	$2,380/$1,190
Mutual Black	87	$750/$450	$725/$425
National Black	85	$675/$475	$675/$475
Blair's	104	$4,000/$3,200	$2,900/$2,320
Eastman's	100	$2,800/$2,240	$2,800/$2,240
Katz's	100	$2,800/$2,240	$2,400/$1,920
McGavern Guild's	100	$3,700/$2,800	$3,700/$2,800

Network	P.M. drive	Saturday	Sunday
CBS	$2,100/$1,400	$1,530/$1,010	$1,220/$810
MBS	$2,200/$1,100	$1,960/$980	$1,000/$500
NBC	$2,150/$1,505	$1,980/$1,385	$1,150/$805
ABC			
Contemporary	$3,090/$1,545	$2,100/$1,050	$1,500/$750
Entertainment	$1,790/$895	$1,600/$800	$1,080/$540
FM	$1,820/$910	$1,600/$800	$1,500/$750
Information	$1,790/$895	$1,370/685	$670/$335
Mutual Black	$750/$450	$700/$400	$650/$350
National Black	$675/$475	$675/$475	$675/$475
Blair's	$3,500/$2,800	$3,250/$2,600	$2,800/$2,240
Eastman's	$2,800/$2,240	$2,800/$2,240	$2,800/$2,240
Katz's	$2,800/$2,240	$2,400/$1,920	$2,400/$1,920
McGavern Guild's	$3,700/$2,800	$3,700/$2,800	$3,700/$2,800

* None of these costs are absolute—all are subject to change and negotiation.

ming than the TV networks. Most is in the form of hourly newscasts and special news or sports events.

In addition, there are more than 100 regional radio networks in the United States which operate as state news and farm networks with information oriented toward specific geographic markets.

The use of networks provides national and regional advertisers with simple administration and low effective net cost per station. The amount of paper work and clerical time is greatly reduced, and the cost per station is usually lower than if comparable times were bought on individual stations. However, the disadvantage lies in the lack of flexibility in choosing the affiliated stations, the limitation of the number of stations on the network's roster, and the long lead time required to book time.

Spot radio

When a national advertiser buys airtime on an individual station, it is referred to as a *spot.* Spot commercials can be advantageous because of their flexibility. The advertiser can choose as long or as short a flight as is required. In addition, spot commercials enable the message to be presented to listeners at the most favorable times.

By purchasing radio time in this way, commercials can be tailored to the local market. And they can be put on the air quickly. Some stations require two weeks' notice and others 72 hours, but many are willing to run a commercial with just 20 minutes lead time.

Spot advertising also affords advertisers great flexibility in their choice of markets, stations, airtime and, copy. It enables them to build local listener acceptance of their product or service by using local personalities or by purchasing airtime on locally produced programs.

Spot *advertising* should not be confused with spot *announcements,* which are merely individual commercial messages.

Local radio

Local time denotes radio spots purchased by a local advertiser. It involves the same procedure as national spots. The sole difference is the location of the advertiser.

Radio advertising also can be classified as live, taped, or transcribed (a form of record). In recent years there has been a trend toward recorded shows with live news in between. Nearly all radio commercials today are recorded to reduce costs and maintain broadcast quality.

Radio terminology

Buying radio time requires a basic understanding of radio terminology. Naturally, much of the language used for radio advertising is the same as that used for other media. But radio also has numerous terms that are either peculiar to it or have a special meaning when applied to radio advertising.

The most common of these are the concepts of dayparts, average quarter-hour audiences, and cumes (cumulative audiences). Our purpose here is to define these terms and their importance to the advertiser. The student of advertising should know, however, that volumes have been written on these subjects in the specialized literature of media planning and radio buying.

Dayparts

The radio is divided into five basic dayparts:

6 A.M.–10 A.M.	Morning drive
10 A.M.–3 P.M.	Daytime
3 P.M.–7 P.M.	Afternoon (or evening) drive
7 P.M.–12 P.M.	Nightime
12 A.M.–6 A.M.	All night

The rating services (namely, Arbitron and Burke) measure the audiences for only the first four of these dayparts, as all-night listening is very limited and not highly competitive. (See the Ad Lab.)

The heaviest radio use occurs during drive times (6–10 A.M. and 3–7 P.M.) during the week (Monday–Friday). One exception to this is that easy listening (or "good" music) stations traditionally have their heaviest use during daytime (10 A.M.–3 P.M.). Otherwise, drivetime is radio's prime time.

This is important to advertisers because, as we mentioned in the

The book that makes or breaks radio stations

Two major audience rating services are offered to broadcasters and advertisers. Media buyers use the data obtained by these services as a basis for comparing programs and stations in order to make the right choices.

Arbitron diary

The Arbitron rating service chooses a group of representative listeners and provides them with a diary, which they are instructed to carry with them throughout the day. They are asked to record all the time spent listening to a radio. The diary is returned to Arbitron at the end of the week for tabulation, and a new diary is distributed. The service is available to clients on a subscription basis.

RADAR reports

RADAR (Radio's All-Dimension Audience Research) audience estimates are based on daily telephone interviews that cover seven days of radio listening behavior. The measurements are conducted during four weeks in the spring and four weeks in the fall of each year. The service provides estimates of the audiences of all AM and FM radio stations in total and of several segments of radio use and of the population.

The RADAR studies are jointly sponsored by ABC, CBS, NBC, and the Mutual Broadcasting Company and are available to stations, advertisers, and agencies by subscription.

These rating reports are important not only to advertisers in determining the listenership of a particular station, but to stations as well who may fine tune or completely change their format as a result of the reports.

Laboratory applications

1. What do you think might be the advantages and disadvantages of the two radio audience measurement methods?
2. Which audience rating method would you consider better? Why?

case of Maxwell House Coffee, usage and consumption vary for different products. Television advertising in prime time, for example, is seen when viewers are least likely to consume coffee. On the other hand, radio's morning drive time coincides perfectly with most people's desire for a steaming, fresh cup of coffee.

Radio stations base their rates on the time of day the advertiser wants commercials aired (Figure 17–15). To achieve the lowest rate, an advertiser can order spots on a *run of station* (ROS) basis, similar to ROP in newspaper advertising. However, this leaves total control of spot placement up to the station. Most stations, therefore, offer a *total audience plan* (TAP) package rate, which guarantees a certain percentage of spots in the better dayparts if the advertiser buys the total package of time.

Naturally, the subject of daypart advantages can be exhausting for the sophisticated advertiser who has the time, resources, and facilities to study it in depth.

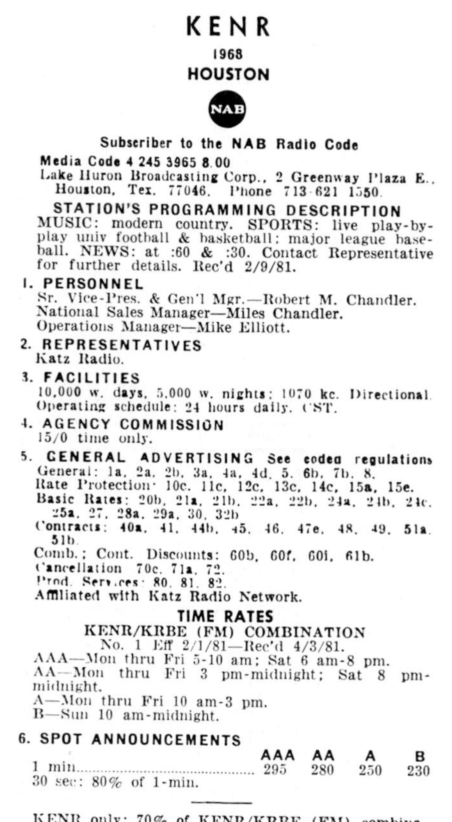

KENR
1968
HOUSTON

NAB

Subscriber to the NAB Radio Code
Media Code 4 245 3965 8.00
Lake Huron Broadcasting Corp., 2 Greenway Plaza E., Houston, Tex. 77046. Phone 713-621 1550.

STATION'S PROGRAMMING DESCRIPTION
MUSIC: modern country. SPORTS: live play-by-play univ football & basketball; major league baseball. NEWS: at :60 & :30. Contact Representative for further details. Rec'd 2/9/81.

1. PERSONNEL
Sr. Vice-Pres. & Gen'l Mgr.—Robert M. Chandler.
National Sales Manager—Miles Chandler.
Operations Manager—Mike Elliott.

2. REPRESENTATIVES
Katz Radio.

3. FACILITIES
10,000 w. days, 5,000 w. nights; 1070 kc. Directional.
Operating schedule: 24 hours daily. CST.

4. AGENCY COMMISSION
15/0 time only.

5. GENERAL ADVERTISING See coded regulations
General: 1a, 2a, 2b, 3a, 4a, 4d, 5, 6b, 7b, 8.
Rate Protection: 10c, 11c, 12c, 13c, 14c, 15a, 15e.
Basic Rates: 20b, 21a, 21b, 22a, 22b, 24a, 24b, 24c, 25a, 27, 28a, 29a, 30, 32b
Contracts: 40a, 41, 44b, 45, 46, 47e, 48, 49, 51a, 51b.
Comb.; Cont. Discounts: 60b, 60f, 60i, 61b.
Cancellation 70c, 71a, 72.
Prod. Services: 80, 81, 82.
Affiliated with Katz Radio Network.

TIME RATES
KENR/KRBE (FM) COMBINATION
No. 1 Eff 2/1/81—Rec'd 4/3/81.
AAA—Mon thru Fri 5-10 am; Sat 6 am-8 pm.
AA—Mon thru Fri 3 pm-midnight; Sat 8 pm-midnight.
A—Mon thru Fri 10 am-3 pm.
B—Sun 10 am-midnight.

6. SPOT ANNOUNCEMENTS

	AAA	AA	A	B
1 min	295	280	250	230

30 sec: 80% of 1-min.

KENR only: 70% of KENR/KRBE (FM) combination.

Figure 17–15 The *Spot Radio Rates and Data* listing for KENR radio in Houston, Texas, shows that spot announcement rates vary from a high of $195 to a low of $140 per minute, depending on the number bought and the dayparts used.

Average quarter-hour

This term is used to identify the average number of people in various age groups who are listening to a specific station during any 15-minute period of any given daypart (Figure 17–16). Following is an example of a quarter-hour listening estimate:

Station	Average 1/4 hour Mon.–Fri. 6 A.M.–10 A.M. Persons 12+
WFAA	2000

This means that any day Monday–Friday, during any 15-minute period between 6 and 10 A.M., it is probable (more than likely) that 2,000 people over 12 years old are tuned in to radio station WFAA.

This same idea can be expressed in terms of rating points if the audience is shown as a percentage of the population. For example, if radio station WFAA is located in a city of 100,000 population, then its average quarter-hour audience could be expressed as an average quarter-hour "rating" of 2:

$$\frac{2{,}000}{100{,}000} = 0.02, \text{ or 2 percent}$$

Determining the gross rating points of a radio schedule, therefore, simply requires multiplying the average quarter-hour rating by the number of spots. For example,

$$2.0 \text{ (rating points)} \times 12 \text{ (number of spots)} = 24.0 \text{ (GRP)}$$

Similarly, the GRPs could be determined by multiplying the average quarter-hour audience by the number of spots and dividing by the population. For example,

$$2{,}000 \text{ (average quarter-hour audience)} \times 12 = 24{,}000 \text{ (gross impressions)}$$

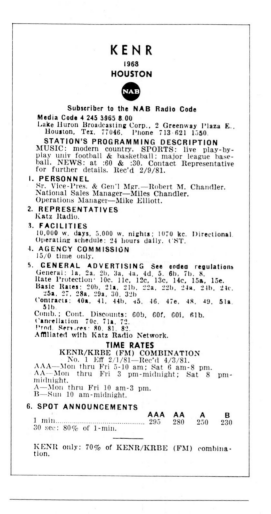

Therefore:

$$\frac{24{,}000}{100{,}000} = 24 \text{ percent, or 24 GRPs}$$

Cume audience

This capsule term for "cumulative audience" describes the total number of *different* people listening to a radio station for at least one 15-minute segment over the course of a given week, day, or daypart (Figure 17–17).

In the example above, we generated 24,000 gross impressions with our schedule on station WFAA. But that does *not* mean that 24,000 *different* people heard our commercials. Many people might have heard our commercial three, four, or five times, depending on how long they stayed tuned to WFAA.

By measuring the cumulative number of *different* people listening

MONDAY–SUNDAY
6:00AM–MIDNIGHT

AVERAGE PERSONS--METRO SURVEY AREA, IN HUNDREDS

STATION CALL LETTERS	TOT. PERS. 12+	MEN 18-24	MEN 25-34	MEN 35-44	MEN 45-54	MEN 55-64	WOMEN 18-24	WOMEN 25-34	WOMEN 35-44	WOMEN 45-54	WOMEN 55-64	TNS. 12-17
KAKZ	42	2	6	6	2	1	2	6	6	1	3	2
KARD	35	1	6	1	4		6	7	3	3	2	2
KBRA	36		4	1	4	4	1	2	3	3	6	
KEYN	55	13	7	2			8	7	3			15
KFDI	51		2	6	7	3	1	2	8	6	7	
KFDI FM	45	7	2	5	2	2	4	5	8	5	2	1
KFH	58		2	7	4	3	1	5	2	6	3	1
KGCS	15	2	1	2				2	3	1	3	1
KICT	71	23	5	1			13	3				26
KQAM	17	1	5	1		1	3	4		1		1
*KSGL	6				1		1	1	1		1	
KWKN	26	2	7			1	3	8	1	1		1
*KJRG	2									1	1	
KOEZ	7									5	1	
KSKU	3	1					1					1
TOTAL LISTENING IN METRO SURVEY AREA	489	53	49	33	27	16	45	54	39	37	30	51

SHARES--METRO SURVEY AREA

STATION CALL LETTERS	TOT. PERS. 12+ %	MEN 18-24 %	MEN 25-34 %	MEN 35-44 %	MEN 45-54 %	MEN 55-64 %	WOMEN 18-24 %	WOMEN 25-34 %	WOMEN 35-44 %	WOMEN 45-54 %	WOMEN 55-64 %	TNS. 12-17 %
KAKZ	8.6	3.8	12.2	18.2	7.4	6.3	4.4	11.1	15.4	2.7	10.0	3.9
KARD	7.2	1.9	12.2	3.0	14.8		13.3	13.0	7.7	0.1	6.7	3.9
KBRA	7.4		8.2	3.0	14.8	25.0	2.2	3.7	7.7	8.1	20.0	
KEYN	11.2	24.5	14.3	6.1			17.8	13.0	7.7			29.4
KFDI	10.4		4.1	18.2	25.9	18.8	2.2	3.7	20.5	16.2	23.3	
KFDI FM	9.2	13.2	4.1	15.2	7.4	12.5	8.9	9.3	20.5	13.5	6.7	2.0
KFH	11.9		4.1	21.2	14.8	18.8	2.2	9.3	5.1	16.2	10.0	2.0
KGCS	3.1	3.8	2.0	6.1				3.7	7.7	2.7	10.0	2.0
KICT	14.5	43.4	10.2	3.0			28.9	5.6				51.0
KQAM	3.5	1.9	10.2	3.0		6.3	6.7	7.4		2.7		2.0
*KSGL	1.2				3.7		2.2	1.9	2.6		3.3	
KWKN	5.3	3.8	14.3			6.3	6.7	14.8	2.6	2.7		2.0
*KJRG	.4									2.7	3.3	
KOEZ	1.4									13.5	3.3	
KSKU	.6	1.9					2.2					2.0

Figure 17–16 Average quarter-hour listening estimates.

to WFAA, the rating services give us an idea of the reach *potential* of our radio schedule.

Thus, *cume* and *average quarter-hour* are important concepts. A high cume figure means that a lot of different people are tuning in to the station for at least 15 minutes. A high average quarter-hour figure usually means that people are listening and staying tuned in.

For the beginning advertising student, it is important to remember one basic concept about these radio audience measurements. They are derived from the manipulation of statistical data, which involves a complex weighting of various members of the station's surveyed audience. These manipulations produce an important result: Generating the average quarter-hour audience figure is dependent on the *length of listening*. The longer the survey respondent listens, the larger the average quarter-hour audience will be. The cumulative audience is dependent on numerous *different* people tuning in to the radio station. The more respondents that tune in, the higher the cume will be.

WICHITA, KS
OCT/NOV 1980

	MONDAY-SATURDAY 6:00 AM-10:00 AM											
		MEN					WOMEN					
STATION CALL LETTERS	TOTAL PERS. 12+	18-24	25-34	35-44	45-54	55-64	18-24	25-34	35-44	45-54	55-64	TNS. 12-17
KAKZ	569	28	96	65	28	27	38	79	67	19	25	44
KARD	354	10	78	11	20	9	78	52	38	14	14	25
KBRA	313		36	16	25	31	8	23	33	40	39	6
KEYN	549	101	78	27	5		78	61	44	4	4	147
KFDI	467		18	71	43	58	15	28	57	36	47	13
KFDI FM	332	36	36	27	20	13	31	42	38	37	14	19
KFH	648	10	24	60	62	58	15	65	34	55	54	6
KGCS	137	18	12	22	10			9	34	15	11	6
KICT	428	138	36		5		46	24	14			165
KQAM	254	27	48	21		13	31	65		10	7	32
KSGL	82		6	11	14		15	14	9		4	
KWKN	413	55	66	21	18	4	38	71	28	11	14	19
KJRG	23				5					6	7	
KOEZ	57				11	4				21	7	
KSKU	35	18						5		6		6
METRO TOTALS	2867	257	323	218	174	141	224	309	230	183	161	353

	MONDAY-SATURDAY 10:00 AM-3:00 PM											
		MEN					WOMEN					
STATION CALL LETTERS	TOT. PERS. 12+	18-24	25-34	35-44	45-54	55-64	18-24	25-34	35-44	45-54	55-64	TNS. 12-17
KAKZ	361	9	65	21	14	13	23	56	58	8	14	18
KARD	200		36	5	16		31	52	28	6	7	19
KBRA	300		24	11	19	22	15	14	14	40	47	
KEYN	413	55	78	11			32	65	29	4		139
KFDI	426	9	18	43	44	44	23	14	57	25	57	6
KFDI FM	305	54	30	32	14	9	38	28	43	8	11	19
KFH	435	9	24	33	36	44	23	33	24	27	39	6
KGCS	133	18	12	21	9			14	24	11	7	12
KICT	404	147	42	11			70	28	5			101
KQAM	174	9	30	11		4	31	52	9	4	7	12
KSGL	68				14		15	9	9		7	
KWKN	321	9	55	11	4	4	48	72	19	6	7	38
KJRG	41				9	4			9	6	4	
KOEZ	85				14	4	8		5	29	11	
KSKU	47	9	12				15	5				6
METRO TOTALS	2407	210	246	152	137	115	232	277	206	137	136	284

Figure 17–17 Cume listening estimates.

Thus, the most stable (accurate) number for estimating the size, scope, and depth of a radio station is the cume. This is because, in the rating service's survey, the cume number is based on a larger sample size!

Preparing a radio schedule

A procedure similar to that discussed in the television section is used by advertisers to prepare their radio schedules. The steps are as follows:

1. Identifying those stations with the greatest concentration (cume) of the advertiser's target audience by demographics (e.g., men 25–34). As we pointed out previously, the cume figure gives us the best idea of the reach potential of our radio schedule.
2. Identifying those stations by format type (e.g., hard rock, MOR), that typically offer the highest concentration of potential buyers. We may know, for instance, that while many men and women between the ages of 35 and 49 may listen to a beautiful music station, the best format for potential tire purchasers in that age group is an all news or sports format.
3. Determining what time periods (dayparts) on those stations offer the greatest number (average quarter-hour) of potential buyers. Here again, it is more likely that our prospective tire buyers will be concentrated in drive time rather than midday.
4. Using the stations' rate cards for guidance, constructing a schedule with a strong mix of these best time periods. (An average weekly spot load per station may be anywhere from 12 to 30 announcements depending on the advertiser's budget.) At this point, it is often wise to contact the station reps, give them a breakdown of your media objectives, suggest a possible budget for their station, and ask what they can give you for that budget. This gives the media buyer a starting point for analyzing costs and negotiating the buy.
5. Determining the cost for each 1,000 *target* people each station delivers. The operation word here is "target." We are not interested in the station's total audience.
6. Negotiating and placing the buy.
7. Assessing the buy (with the help of the agency's or radio station's computer) in terms of reach and frequency.

While these steps are far from all-inclusive, they demonstrate some of the complexity media planners and buyers deal with daily in their efforts to match the advertiser's message with a target audience on radio.

Summary

As a means of reaching the masses, no other medium today has the unique creative ability of television. It offers the combination of sight and sound and movement, the opportunity to demonstrate the product, the believability of seeing it happen right before your eyes, and the empathy of the viewer.

Television has grown faster than any other advertising medium in history because of the unique advantages it offers advertisers: mass coverage at low cost, audience selectivity, impact, prestige, and social dominance.

While television's power as a creative tool may be unmatched, the medium still has many drawbacks. These include cost, lack of selectivity, brevity, and clutter.

The heaviest viewers of television are middle-income, high-school-educated people and their families. Over the years television viewing has steadily increased. By 1980 the average household TV usage reached nearly 4¼ hours daily.

There are three forms of television advertising: network, spot, and local. Within these classifications, there are many commercial opportunities for advertisers in television. These are generally grouped as sponsorships, participations, and spot announcements.

To buy television effectively advertisers need to understand the basics of audience measurement techniques and the terminology used for television viewing by geographic areas, dayparts, and demographic classifications.

To determine which shows to buy, the media buyer must select the most efficient ones against the target audience. The task therefore is to compare the packages of each station, substituting stronger programs for less efficient ones, and negotiating prices to get the best buy.

Radio is also recognized as a highly creative medium. However, its greatest attribute is probably its ability to offer the combination of excellent reach and frequency to selective audiences at a very efficient price. Its drawbacks relate to the limitations of sound, the fact that radio audiences are very segmented, and the nature of short-lived and half-heard commercials.

Radio stations are normally classified by the programming they offer and the audiences they serve. The most common radio formats are progressive rock, contemporary top 40, middle of the road, "good" music, classical, country-western, all news, and talk.

Radio time may be purchased by an advertiser in one of three forms: local, spot, or network.

Buying radio time requires a basic understanding of radio terminology. The most common terms are dayparts, average quarter-hour, and cumulative audiences.

Questions for review

1. What are the advantages and drawbacks of television?
2. What are the types of television advertising? How do they differ?
3. What are the kinds of commercial opportunities? What are the advantages and disadvantages of each?
4. How would you define each of the following terms?
   a. ADI.
   b. DMA.
   c. Television dayparts.
   d. TV households.
   e. HUT.
   f. Program rating.
   g. Share of audience.
   h. Total audience.
   i. Gross rating points.
5. What does it mean to request "avails"? Who are the individuals involved? What information is requested from each?
6. What are the functions of contracts and affidavits in television buying?
7. What are the advantages and drawbacks of radio?
8. What are the most common radio formats? How would you describe their audiences demographically?
9. How would you define each of the following terms?
   a. Radio dayparts.
   b. Average quarter-hour audiences.
   c. Cumes.
10. What is the difference between spot radio and a radio spot?

18

Direct mail and out-of-home media

In the mid-19th century the country stores serving rural America offered a limited variety of merchandise. Much of it was of poor quality, and prices were usually exorbitant. The farmers and ranchers who needed this merchandise and had nowhere else to go resented the treatment they received and banded together into groups called granges to protest the high prices and the inflated rates charged by the railroads for freight. This may have been the country's first consumer movement.

Into the middle of this fray stepped a young peddler in 1872. Responding to their protests, he hit upon a brilliant idea—selling direct to the country people by mail. He had very little money, only $1,600. But with it he bought a stock of dry goods, rented the second floor of a Chicago building, and issued a one-page list of his merchandise. It was the first mail-order catalog.

His contemporaries thought he was mad. Why would those suspicious farmers buy anything they had not seen? But his critics proved to be wrong. That simple one-sheet flyer launched a career, a merchandising empire, and a whole new method of marketing the nation's goods and services. His name was Aaron Montgomery Ward.

By providing a variety of products at reasonable prices, exactly as described in his catalogs, Ward was responding to the expressed needs and desires of his customers. It was perhaps the first broad application of the marketing concept.

Now, over 100 years later, as a wholly owned subsidiary of Mobil Corporation, Montgomery Ward is one of the nation's largest retail chains and catalog merchandisers. In 1980 sales exceeded $5 billion through its coast-to-coast network of over 450 stores and 2,000 catalog centers. And it all started with direct mail[1] (Figure 18–1).

Direct mail as a medium

Direct-mail advertising is the term given to all forms of advertising sent direct to prospects through the U.S. Postal Service or private services. In dollars spent, direct mail is the third-ranked advertising medium today, surpassed only by newspapers and television.

No matter how large or small a company may be, direct mail is nearly always used in its advertising program. When a firm starts in business, its first medium of advertising is generally direct mail. And as it grows, it usually continues to use direct mail, although more dollars may be spent in other media. The reason is clear. The shortest distance between two points is a straight line. And of all the media, direct mail offers the "straightest" line to the desired prospect.

Direct mail versus direct marketing

Several popular terms are frequently confused with *direct mail.* These include *direct marketing, direct response advertising, direct advertising,* and *mail-order advertising.* How are these terms similar and how do they differ?

Direct marketing is the selling of goods or services direct to the consumer without the help of middlemen. No retailer, wholesaler, or dealer is used in the transaction. Some firms, such as Fuller Brush, market their products direct to consumers using door-to-door sales personnel. Others sell through mail-order ads, catalogs, or direct mail. Some direct marketers own their own retail stores. Examples are Goodyear Tire Company and Sherwin-Williams Paint Company. They are called "direct marketers" because they hold title to their products until they are sold to consumers through their own stores. A potential new form of direct marketing is cable television, which is exploring new ways to use two-way communication systems in subscribers' homes for selling products and services direct to the TV viewer.

Direct response advertising is a message that asks the reader, listener, or viewer for an immediate response. A newspaper ad, for example, may ask the reader to fill in and mail the featured coupon to obtain free information about mutual funds (Figure 18–2). Direct response advertising can take the form of direct mail, or it can use a wide range of other media, from matchbook covers or magazines to radio or TV (Figure 18–3).

Mail-order advertising is a method of selling in which the product or service is promoted through advertising and the prospect orders it by mail (Figure 18–4). It involves no intermediate salespeople. As it is practiced today, mail-order advertising is usually received in three distinct forms: catalog selling, advertising in magazines and newspapers, and direct-mail advertising.

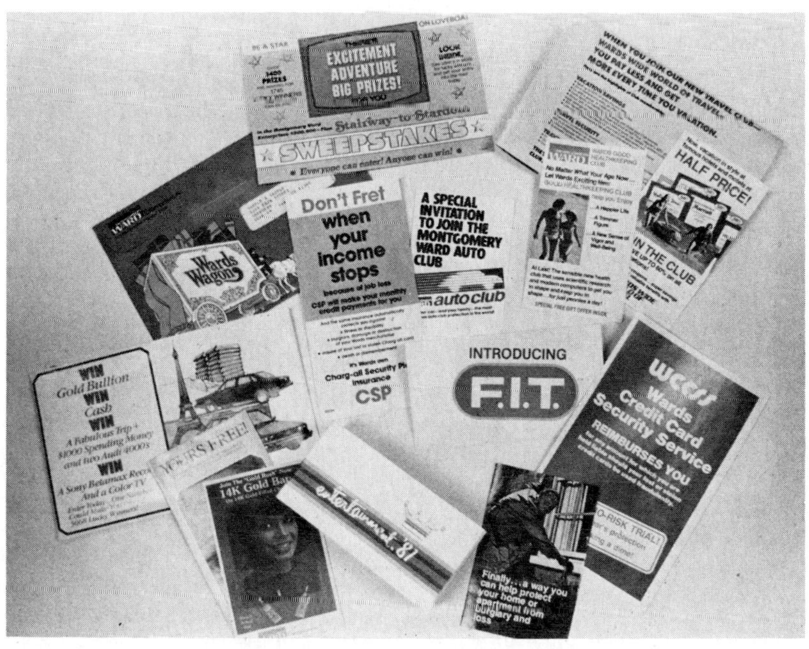

Figure 18–1 A group of Montgomery Ward mailing pieces used to sell insurance, promote sweepstakes, or solicit members for the chain's auto club.

Direct advertising is any form of advertising issued direct to the prospect through the use of the mails, salespeople, dealers, or other means. It does not involve the traditional mass media. Such advertising may take the form of door-to-door circulars, telephone solicitations, handbills, or direct mail.

Direct mail is any form of direct advertising that is sent through

Clipping this coupon may be the best financial investment a woman can make all year.

The Chase Exchange™ is a special resource center at 46th and Madison dedicated to helping women manage their own financial affairs.

Find out about The Chase Exchange for women.

This exclusive Chase program includes personal counseling and referral services, monthly seminars, financial books, a newsletter, telephone hotline and branch banking. Just mail in this coupon, and a Chase Officer will call or send you more information.

THE CHASE EXCHANGE™

NAME ______

PHONE ☐ ______

WRITE ☐ ______

MAIL TO: THE CHASE EXCHANGE
380 Madison Avenue, New York, New York 10017

CHASE

Member FDIC TM © 1981 Chase Manhattan Bank, N.A.

Figure 18–2 Chase Manhattan Bank promotes its services for women through direct response newspaper advertising.

How 30,000 bees (and my mother's medical genius) created one ounce of complexion miracles

How your skin can look 10 years younger than your biological age.

The great beauties of Romania have long been famous for their exquisite, porcelain complexions.. Livia—internationally-known hostess, patron of the arts, Gold Medalist, Woman of Distinction, innovative cosmetologist—is herself, the most convincing proof of this Romanian heritage.

My mother was a doctor in Romania, she had a passion for collecting and analyzing the private complexion recipes used by the seemingly ageless beauties of her time... It was in the products of the bees that she found their secrets for prolonging the youthful appearance of the skin.

She created a totally natural recipe that became a daily regimen for our family. As a self testament to her genius, my mother's complexion at age 73, was clear and flawless.

You can trust this product. Just as I have over the years. It is completely natural—gathered by the most fastidious creature in Nature's kingdom.

A science re-born in the land of bees and beauty

Romanians are also the earliest of beekeepers ... Shipping their beautifying nectars and extracts to the great medieval salons of Florence, Genoa, and Venice—to the harems of the early Turkish empire.

Livia's complexion nectar—first of the new apitherapy products for reducing the appearance of wrinkles

When you consider that a bee can carry only one ten thousandth of a gram of pollen per flight and that hand-harvesting is an incredibly painstaking process, it is understandable why early apitherapy products were limited to very small quantities.

Today's woman is interested in *natural* cosmetic products. She knows petroleum-based products are harmful!

The promise of Apitherapy as an aid in prolonging youthful-looking skin is exciting. Again and again, enthusiastic users have confirmed the revitalizing effect of Livia's Complexion Nectar.

The complete confidence that only a natural product can give you

You can use Livia's Complexion Nectar with complete confidence. All ingredients have been tested by an independent laboratory and are listed on the label as required by the U.S. Government.

Taking the first step towards revitalizing your skin's appearance

Why skin ages
The skin is actually your body's largest organ. An area the size of a quarter contains a yard of blood vessels, 4 yards of nerves, 25 nerve ends, 100 sweat glands and more than 3 million cells!

The appearance of premature aging can occur because the skin is constantly exposed to all types of weather, sun, pollutants, artificial heat and any number of indignities inflicted by ourselves.

The skin requires regular care to maintain its appearance. Neglect your skin and it will pay you back with premature wrinkles!

But, even if neglected, the skin has the uncommon ability to regenerate...

It can replace old or damaged cells with brand new ones... and this capability is maintained no matter what your age!

Why wrinkles form
The outer layer of the skin is constantly sluffing off old cells but, as the skin matures, replacement is slower and cells adhere more tenaciously to form a build-up which creates a coarse, leathery appearance.

Turning back the clock. The new promise of apitherapy.

Livia's Complexion Nectar with Bee Pollen may appear to work miracles... but only if you give it help!

- It helps to retain cell moisture most effectively.
- It provides natural protection better than many heavy oils and grease based protectants... and it lets the skin breathe freely.
- It supplies helpful skin nutrients in a natural form not found in non-Apitherapeutic products.

For mature complexions—how Livia's Complexion Nectar works on outer skin

After cleansing has rehydrated the skin, Livia's Complexion Nectar is applied to hold the moisture in the skin cells. It also lubricates gently to give the skin fresh, youthful lustre.

Treatment of dryness—A medical professor of the Sorbonne once noted: "Bee pollen contains all that is needed by an organism for living and procreation"... It is probably the most perfect nutrient to be found in nature. Aside from the minerals, proteins, vitamins, noted, it contains 20 of the amino acids to help nourish the skin as the body goes through the regenerative process that replaces old cells with new.

The treatment of wrinkle-prone areas:

The Queen Bee's Longevity (98% greater than worker bees) results from an exclusive diet of a concentrated jelly containing most of the vital factors for her existence. In Livia's Complexion Nectar, it is used as an external skin nourishing cream to help minimize the appearance of dry wrinkles.

Premature wrinkles are caused by lessening of the skin's elasticity. Preventative care is most important in the wrinkle-prone areas indicated.

No other skin care product offers this Bee Pollen and Royal Jelly combination in a single skin cream.

FRAGRANCE FREE.

MAJOR CREDIT CARD HOLDERS CALL OUR TOLL-FREE NUMBER 800-221-4978 TO ORDER EASILY

OR SEND CHECK FOR TOTAL TO: LIVIA SYLVA, INC.
111 East 56th Street, New York City 10022

☐ 1 oz. Livia's Complexion Nectar with Bee Pollen #7	$40.00
☐ 8 oz. Bee Pollen Skin Freshener # 7	$13.50
☐ 6 oz. Bee Pollen Cleansing Creme #7	$15.00
☐ 3 oz. Bee Pollen Clay Masque #7	$15.00
☐ 8 oz. Bee Pollen Body Lotion #7	$22.50
☐ 16 oz. Bee Pollen Body Lotion #7	$35.00
☐ 2 oz. Livia's Complexion Nectar with Bee Pollen #7	$65.00

New York State Residents Add Tax. TOTAL QUANTITY
TOTAL $ ENCLOSED

NAME
PLEASE PRINT
ADDRESS
CITY STATE ZIP
PHONE NUMBER (with Area Code)
☐ Check or Money Order enclosed

CHARGE ☐ American Express ☐ Master Charge ☐ Visa

Expiration date
For MASTER CHARGE ONLY: List Interbank Number
(The 4 digits above your name)

Special FREE OFFER with each purchase of $100.00 or more: Deluxe Bottle—QUEEN LIVIA PARFUM

Figure 18–3 In this direct response magazine ad for a skin care product, readers can respond by mail or toll-free telephone number. Typically such ads have a "busy" look and feature a variety of type styles to hold the reader's attention. There is often a free bonus to stimulate trial, and lots of copy to meet consumer need for in-depth details in order to make a purchase decision since there is no opportunity to see or try the product in person.

the mail. It is perhaps the most popular form of direct advertising today. A brochure sent to a prospect by mail is direct-mail advertising. But if the same brochure is distributed door to door, it is not direct mail. (It is still direct advertising.) The difference, then, is the method of distribution.

Growth of direct mail

Direct mail is used to sell everything from rosebushes and wrongway wrenches to investment securities and world cruises. It is successful because it uniquely meets the needs of today's changing lifestyles. Whereas consumers and businesspeople once shopped at local stores, rising fuel costs and parking inconvenience have made at-home and in-office shopping increasingly appealing. Also, shoppers can get more detailed product information through direct mail. While a retail clerk may offer some knowledgeable words about a zoom-lens movie camera, for example, the direct-mail brochure is fully detailed. It has to be if it's going to sell a $300 camera by mail. Added to this, all product claims made "in writing" make the seller liable for their accuracy. (See Figure 18–5.)

The entry of mass marketers into direct-mail advertising has greatly spurred its growth. Food and detergent industries mail cents-off coupons by the millions. Product makers combine their offers in big "package" mailings. More recent has been the debut of free direct-mail "homemaker" magazines that combine interesting recipes and household hints with coupons and premium offers by multiple "co-op" advertisers.

Direct-mail advertising also has boomed as a result of the consumer credit card explosion. Department stores to major oil companies, credit based mass-marketers, have expanded their profit base by stuffing monthly customer statements with tempting mail-order prod-

Figure 18–4 Top 10 mail-order product categories

Rank	Category	Sales ($ millions)
1	Insurance	4,000
2	General merchandising/home furnishings/ housewares/gifts	2,700
3	Magazine subscriptions	1,900
4	Books	1,388
5	Ready-to-wear	1,340
6	Collectibles	920
7	Sporting goods	780
8	Crafts	550
9	Foods	500
10	Records and tapes	478

uct offers from small personal items to major appliances. And the increased availability of credit has enabled them to sell high-priced items to consumers. Whereas once it was difficult to market a direct-mail product priced over $9.95, today major oil companies sell products tagged at $200 or more, urging customers to charge it. Products that are innovative, can be shipped fairly easily, and are not readily available through other distribution channels, are the most likely candidates for direct-mail selling.

Another reason for the success of direct mail is that it gets into your home when a salesperson could not. And it gets your attention. Just as most people come home and check the mailbox or ask, "Was there any mail?" so most businesspeople begin the day by examining their mail. In effect, mail is the most important person-to-person medium.

Direct-mail advertising is being used by most companies across America, from the neighborhood garage to giant industrial leaders like U.S. Steel and Xerox. More than 250,000 firms have third-class mailing permits. And the growing use of direct-mail advertising has spawned scores of private postal services that operate chiefly to deliver advertising mail.

Figure 18–5 Consumer attitudes toward direct response advertising

I would buy more via direct response if:	Percent of all adults
I could be sure I would get what I expected.	79
Offers were from companies I could trust.	78
They offered things I couldn't buy near me.	77
It were easier to return merchandise.	77
They gave me a money-back guarantee.	75
Prices were lower.	74
They offered things that interest me.	71
They sent me receipt or confirmation of order.	70
It were easier to get problems straightened out.	69
Offers were from well-known company.	64
I were offered a free trial period to examine order.	61
I were billed after order is received.	59
I could pay over a period of time.	43
I could use my credit card.	40
They gave me a charge account.	28

Using direct mail in the creative mix

Direct mail is an efficient, effective—and economical—medium for sales and business promotion. Thus, it is used by a wide variety of retail, commercial, and industrial companies, charity and service organizations, and individuals. Direct mail can also increase the effectiveness of advertising in other media if carefully coordinated. The *Reader's Digest,* for example, uses TV spots in conjunction with its direct-mail campaigns to alert viewers to the coming arrival of their direct-mail contest promotions (Figure 18–6).

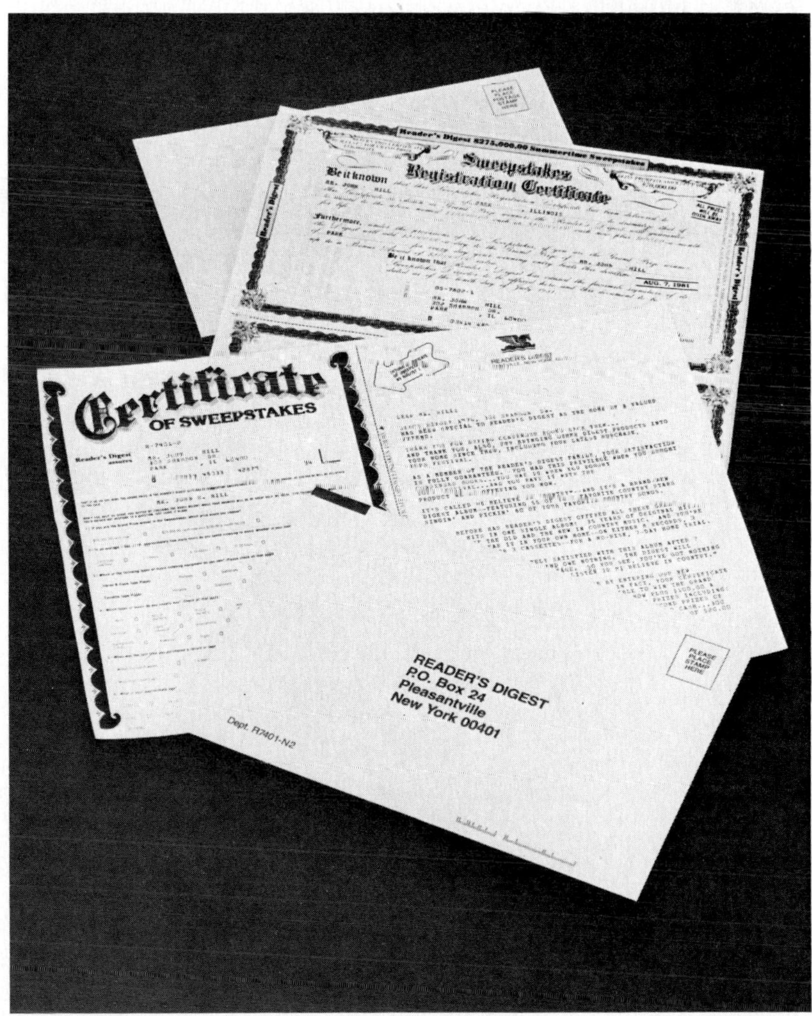

Figure 18–6 An example of the direct mail packages sent by *Reader's Digest* every year for its annual sweepstakes.

What works best in direct mail?

Next to the personal sales call, direct mail is the most effective medium an advertiser can use to put a message in front of a prospect. However, it is also the most expensive on a cost per exposure basis. Therefore, it is important to learn when and when not to use direct mail based on its advantages and disadvantages.

As a medium competing for advertisers' dollars, direct mail traditionally offers several key advantages over its competition. These are selectivity, intensive coverage, flexibility, control, personal impact, exclusivity, and performance.

Selectivity

Direct mail enables the advertiser to select only the prospects he or she wants to reach. By mailing only to these prime prospects—the ones most likely to buy the product or service—the advertiser can reduce sales costs and increase profits.

For example, if you wanted to advertise a 10-gallon paint compressor to professional painters, you wouldn't want to use TV. TV's reach is too broad and you would have to pay for the total audience. But by acquiring a list of professional painters and mailing your message directly to them, you could reach your desired audience more efficiently, at a lower cost, and with greater results. Today the availability of computerized mailing lists enables advertisers to obtain the names of professional painters, doctors, lawyers, construction workers, government employees, teachers, auto mechanics, or a variety of other occupational groups in specific regions or states and in given age groups, income categories, and other classifications. Whatever audience an advertiser wants to reach, he or she can probably obtain a mailing list for it. (See the Ad Lab.)

Intensive coverage

Most of the mass media are limited in the number of readers, viewers, or listeners they can reach. Not all viewers, for example, have their TV sets tuned to the same channel at the same time to see a given commercial. Not everyone in a community subscribes to and reads the local newspaper on the day a given ad is run. And while a billboard posted for 30 days or more is likely to be seen by a large number of motorists in a given area, some people do not own cars. But virtually everyone has a mailbox and, by using direct mail, an advertiser can achieve 100 percent coverage of the homes in a given area.

Flexibility

There are few limitations on direct-mail format, style, or capacity. In addition, the wide variety of materials and processes available enable direct-mail advertising to be uniquely creative and novel (Figures 18–7 and 18–8). The array of sizes, shapes, and formats of direct-mail advertising is limited only by the ingenuity of the advertiser, by the size of the advertising budget, and by the regulations of the U.S. Postal Service.

The direct-mail piece may be a simple postcard or letter, or it may be a large folded broadside or multipage brochure. The advertiser can tell the prospect a little bit or include all the details necessary to understand a complex product.

Moreover, the advertiser can usually produce a direct-mail piece and distribute it in considerably less time than it would take with most other mass media. So when speed is important, direct mail is usually considered.

College grad gets job through mail

A 21-year-old college graduate (B.A. communications/liberal arts) with a desire for a career in direct response marketing sought to get at least two job offers at direct response marketing agencies in New York City, to secure at least 10 interviews at direct response marketing agencies in New York City, to meet leaders of the industry, and to test a direct-mail package and personal sales presentation in the Philadelphia advertising marketplace before rolling out in New York.

His marketing plan included a direct-mail package, a mailing envelope, a letter to get interest, a folder to explain the product, and a reply card to make responding easier. Two weeks following the mail drop, he initiated a telephone call to each nonrespondent. The purpose was to confirm receipt of the direct-mail package and to ask for a personal interview.

Chief executive officers or presidents of direct response marketing agencies, or of direct response divisions of advertising agencies were contacted. The test market was composed of medium to large size advertising agencies in the Philadelphia area who listed direct-mail or direct response advertising as part of their media breakdown.

The Philadelphia list was compiled from an area business publication, *Focus Magazine,* which annually devotes one issue to Philadelphia's advertising agencies. The information listed is basically the same as the Redbook.

The test mailing consisted of 43 units to Philadelphia mailed the first week in June 1978 and roll out of 24 units to New York, mailed the first week of July 1978. The total allocated budget for this program was $723.

The result of this campaign was that the graduate received two job offers in New York City and secured nine interviews in New York City.

Attention Advertising Executives! When You're Ready To Make A Sound Investment . . .

Here Are Five Profitable Reasons Why You Should Hire This Adman

EXPERIENCE:
1. The main reason.

An adman is measured by his track record. Past performance is the best thing he can offer you. Hiring people without experience can be risky and costly. Karl Dentino comes to your firm with one year of part-time agency experience with Serpente, Wharton & Associates Advertising (May 1977 to May 1978). During that year he also worked with the Community Relations Department at Glassboro State College (September 1977 to May 1978).

Karl has previously worked for two retail establishments: Two Guys Department Store (1975-76), and Spencer Gifts (1974-75).

ADVERTISING SKILLS:
2. The tools.

Over the years, advertising has developed a body of research. Proven selling techniques have removed much costly guesswork. Facts, not opinions, make good ads. At Serpente, Wharton & Associates, Karl was taught the facts. He was trained in the direct response advertising philosophy. He learned the tested principles of direct response copywriting, and possesses the necessary ingredients for a career as an up and coming direct response copywriter.

Karl also developed and administered market surveys for a major supermarket account, compiled mailing lists for a direct mail account, and developed media estimates for industrial accounts.

In addition, Karl worked for two years as a retail salesperson for Two Guys Department Store and Spencer Gifts. This experience served as the baptismal ground for a career where persuasiveness, reliability, and the ability to communicate effectively are so vital.

Karl also holds a 3rd Class FCC Broadcasting License.

EDUCATION:
3. Laying the groundwork.

A sound academic background is no longer a luxury for prospective advertising people. Today it's a necessity. Karl Dentino has solid training in the study of advertising. He brings to your firm a B.A. in Communications from Glassboro State College (May 1978), with a concentration in advertising, and a minor in marketing. He graduated with cum laude honors, a 3.50 grade point average.

Direct Marketing Honors!

Karl Dentino was one of thirty-three advertising students from across the country awarded a scholarship to the Direct Mail/Marketing Association (DMMA) Collegiate Institute. The week-long seminar, held in New York, covered all the principles of Direct Marketing and Direct Mail Advertising. This training gives Karl practical knowledge in an area not taught in most universities and colleges in the country.

LEADERSHIP QUALITIES:
4. How to recognize a leader.

A leader is a special breed of person. He accepts that extra responsibility which sets him apart from the others. You would know a leader -- because you are one. And, you will recognize this potential in Karl Dentino.

For three years Karl served as Vice-President of the Advertising Club at Glassboro State College. He helped club membership grow from five to twenty-five. He coordinated field trips to advertising agencies and arranged for advertising professionals to speak at club meetings.

Karl also served as Advertising Director for Student Activities Board Concerts (SAB) for two years. He was responsible for the promotion, logo design, and naming of an annual outdoor music festival held at Glassboro. The "Sunshine Jam" attracts more than 2500 students each year. He also wrote and designed ads for other SAB events.

SELF MOTIVATION:
5. The deciding factor.

Self motivation is the personality trait that separates the superior adman from the mediocre. Mediocre advertising people come a dime a dozen. And they usually don't last too long. The self motivator comes with full realization that hard work gets results. He knows his potential, and he knows how to reach it.

Karl Dentino has the self motivation you are looking for. He is ready to roll up his sleeves and get things done. He seeks a career with your firm, not just a job.

Karl is never satisfied with his present knowledge of advertising and he's always eager to learn more. That's why he is currently enrolled at Charles Morris Price School of Advertising and Journalism in Philadelphia (evening classes). And that's why he served for two years on the Advertising Staff of his college newspaper handling copywriting, layout, and paste-up.

ADVERTISING PHILOSOPHY:

Karl believes that all advertising should be based on a marketing plan. The plan, in turn, should be based on research of the product, its market, and its distribution. The over-all plan objective should be to increase the sale of the product. So advertising is actually selling.

If your advertising meets these selling standards, then Karl Dentino will meet your standards. For a free demonstration of Karl's selling abilities, fill out and mail the enclosed reply card. Or better yet, call Karl today at (609) 662-0387. He'll show you how to make a sound investment.

Do it today! This offer expires as soon as Karl gets a job.

WHAT OTHERS SAY ABOUT KARL DENTINO

"Articulate, enthusiastic, lots of potential." - Joseph Serpente, President, Serpente, Wharton & Associates, Mt. Laurel, New Jersey

"Fine student, bright future in advertising." - Steven Le Shay, President, Le Shay Advertising LTD., Malaga, New Jersey

"Firm grasp on the direct response copy principles." - Frank Grazian, Associate Prof. of Communications, Glassboro State College, Glassboro, New Jersey

KARL G. DENTINO
3330 Hollywood Circle
Pennsauken, New Jersey 08109
(609) 662-0387

6'1"
175 lbs.
September 19 1956
Single

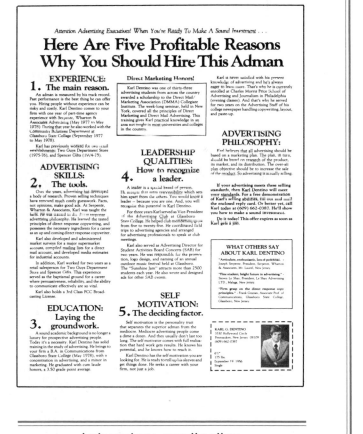

Laboratory application

If you were to prepare a job-hunting direct-mail advertising campaign for yourself, what reader benefits would you include? (See Chapter 10 on copywriting.)

Control

The direct-mail advertiser has a high degree of control over the circulation and the quality of the message. He or she can choose the exact audience desired as well as the number of recipients and their locations, ages, sex, and other factors. These and all other decisions regarding circulation are made solely by the advertiser. There are no limitations, except those imposed by postal regulations. And no media contact is needed.

Preprinted direct-mail pieces enable a large advertiser, such as a department store chain, to control the quality of advertising reproduction for all its outlets. In contrast, a retail organization conducting a chainwide advertising campaign in 16 different newspapers is likely to find significant differences in their quality of printing, page placement, position, and reader responses.

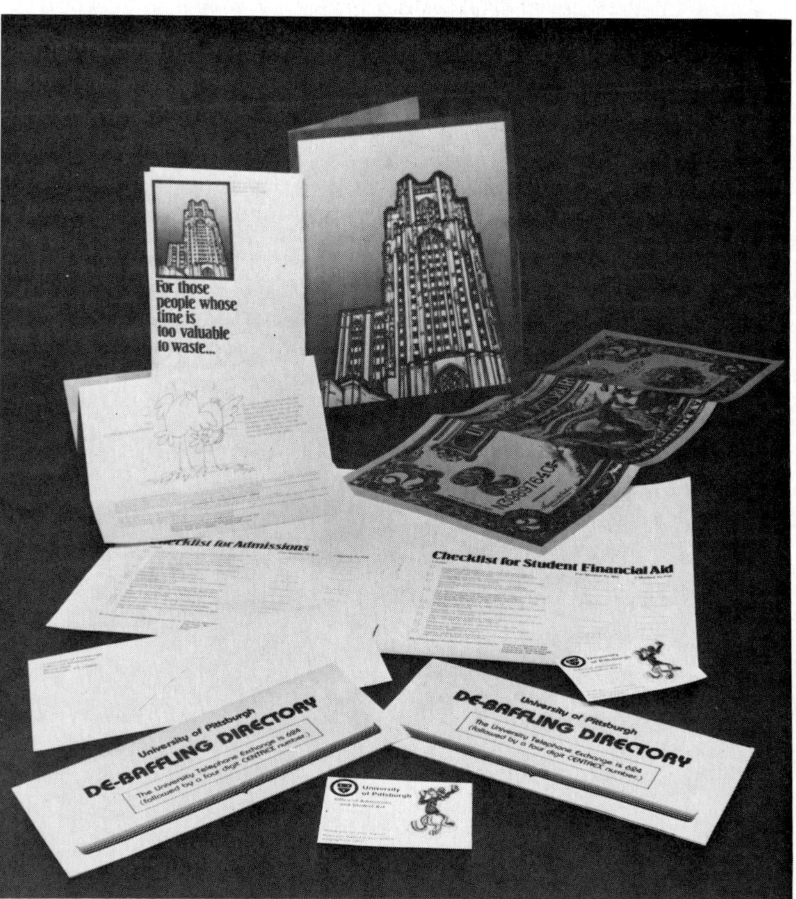

Figure 18–7 The University of Pittsburgh conducted a creative, eight-step sequence of mailings to increase new student enrollment.

Personal impact

Direct mail can be conceived and personalized to the needs, wants, and whims of specific audiences (Figure 18–9). The privacy of direct mail also allows the advertiser to make special offers to a specific group without offending other prospects or customers. A sporting goods manufacturer, for example, can offer golf balls at a discount price to large-volume users, such as golf courses, without offending golfers or sporting goods dealers.

This, however, also makes for occasional mistakes, of which advertisers should be wary. One major airline invited company executives to bring their wives along on their next flight—for just half-fare. After the trip, the airline sent a cordial thank-you note to each "wife." Unfortunately, some of the wives who received these notes hadn't gone on the flights after all. The airline's gracious effort not only unsettled a number of households but also lost at least a few executive customers—perhaps permanently. The personal nature of direct mail requires more caution—and discretion—by the advertiser than most other media. (See the Checklist.)

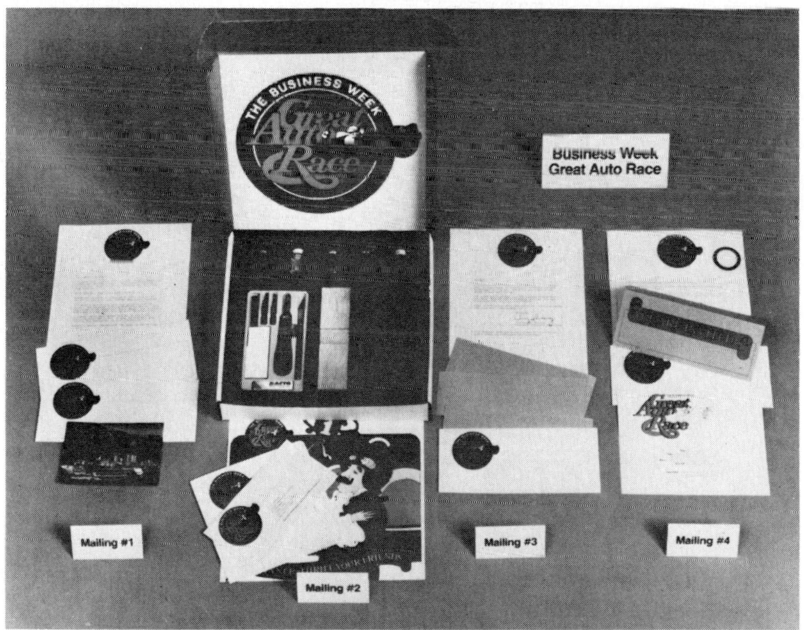

Figure 18–8 *Business Week* created the Great Auto Race, a direct-mail campaign designed to increase its income from automotive advertising. Recipients of the package—500 key decision makers in the auto industry—were invited to build and race a miniature racing car. All materials necessary to build a car were provided. Forty-seven percent (238) built and raced a car. *Business Week* credits its 53 percent increase in automotive advertising to this campaign.[2]

Exclusivity

When the prospect opens the mailbox and takes out a piece of direct-mail advertising, competitive distractions are at a minimum. Thus, the mailer is likely to receive full attention. In contrast, a magazine contains many eye-catching ads as well as articles, stories, and illustrations. These distractions reduce the attention that the reader is likely to give to a single ad.

Performance

Not only does direct mail normally outperform other media in terms of responses, inquiries, and sales, but it also is unique in its ability to measure the performance of a campaign strategy. As a rule of thumb, the direct-mail advertiser receives 15 percent of the responses within

Checklist of what works best in direct response

Here is a checklist to help you create effective direct response advertising.

☐ Make sure your offer is right. More than any other element, what you offer the consumer—in terms of product, price, or premium—will make the difference. Consider combinations instead of single units, optional extras, different opening offers, and commitment periods. *Free* is the most powerful offer you can make, but beware of its attracting lookers instead of buyers.

☐ Demonstrate your product. Offer a free sample, or enclose a sample if you can. Sampling is the most expensive promotion in absolute cost, but is often so effective that the investment is quickly paid back with a larger business base. If you measure response on a profit per piece mailed, it sometimes pays to spend a few more cents.

☐ Use the envelope to telegraph your message. Direct mail must work fast. Your envelope has only seconds to interest the prospect, or go unopened into the wastebasket.

☐ Have a copy strategy. Like any other advertising medium, direct mail will be more productive if you decide *in advance* the important issues of target audience, consumer benefit, and support, tone, and personality. While your promise should relate specifically to your product, experts say the most potent appeals in direct mail are how to make money, save money, save time, or avoid effort.

☐ Grab the reader's attention. Every beginning copywriter in direct mail learns the AIDA formula. The letters stand for the ideal structure of a sales letter: Attention, Interest, Desire, Action. Look for a dramatic opening, one that speaks to the reader in a very *personal* way.

☐ Don't be afraid of long copy. The more you tell, the more you sell—particularly if you're asking the reader to spend much money or invest time. The Mercedes-Benz Diesel car letter was five pages long. A Cunard Line letter for ocean cruises was eight pages long. The key to long copy is *facts.* Be specific, not general. Make the letter visually appealing. Break up the copy into smaller paragraphs and emphasize important points with underlines or handwritten notes. Including several pieces in a direct-mail package often improves response.

☐ Don't let the reader off the hook. Leave your readers with something to do, so that they won't procrastinate. It's too easy to put off a decision. Use action devices like a yes/no token to be stuck on a reply card. *Involvement* is important. Prod them to act *now.* Set a fixed period of time, like 10 days. Or make only a limited supply available. Make it extremely easy for the reader to respond to your offer. But always ask for the order.

☐ Pretest your promises and headlines. Don't guess at what will appeal to the reader. There are many ways to sell your product benefits, and as many inexpensive testing methods. Avoid humor, tricks, or gimmicks. It pays to be serious and helpful.

the first week of a mailing. As a result, he or she knows almost immediately if the campaign is going to be successful. (See Figure 18–10.)

This relatively short-term measurement affords the advertiser still another advantage. The early stages of a campaign can be used to test sales literature ideas and appeals, and to analyze prospect reactions. Often direct-mail advertisers test two or more different approaches to a campaign before deciding on the final format and contents. Direct mail also can be used to determine the most effective appeals for other media.

Drawbacks to direct mail

Although direct mail's advantages are many and unique, it also offers certain disadvantages over other media forms. These include the high cost per exposure, the delays often experienced in delivery, the lack of other content support for the advertising message, and problems with selectivity.

High cost per exposure

Direct mail has the highest cost per thousand prospects of any of the major media. It costs the advertiser about 14 times as much per thousand readers as most magazine and newspaper advertising. The rea-

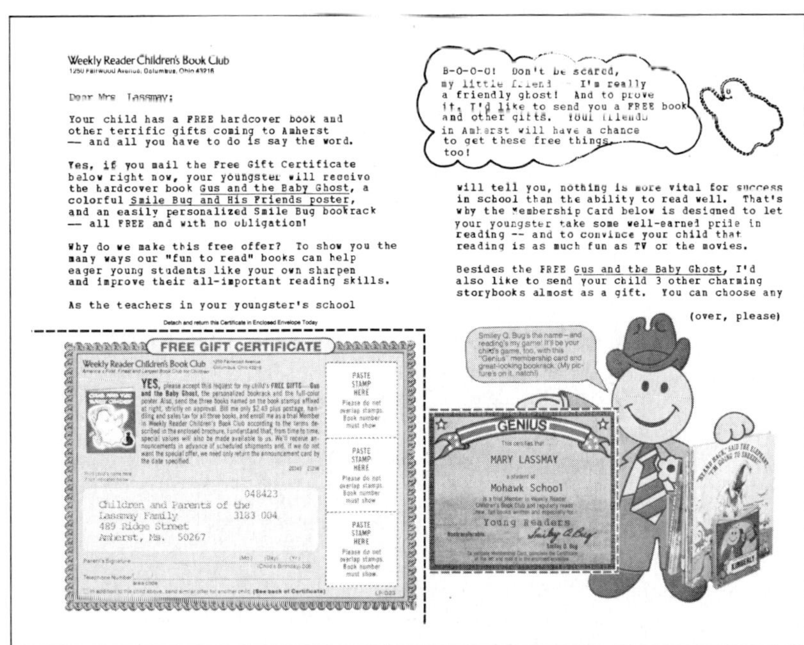

Weekly Reader Children's Book Club
1250 Fairwood Avenue, Columbus, Ohio 43216

Dear Mrs. Lassmay:

Your child has a FREE hardcover book and other terrific gifts coming to Amherst — and all you have to do is say the word.

Yes, if you mail the Free Gift Certificate below right now, your youngster will receive the hardcover book Gus and the Baby Ghost, a colorful Smile Bug and His Friends poster, and an easily personalized Smile Bug bookrack — all FREE and with no obligation!

Why do we make this free offer? To show you the many ways our "fun to read" books can help eager young students like your own sharpen and improve their all-important reading skills.

As the teachers in your youngster's school will tell you, nothing is more vital for success in school than the ability to read well. That's why the Membership Card below is designed to let your youngster take some well-earned pride in reading -- and to convince your child that reading is as much fun as TV or the movies.

Besides the FREE Gus and the Baby Ghost, I'd also like to send your child 3 other charming storybooks almost as a gift. You can choose any

(over, please)

Detach and return this Certificate in Enclosed Envelope Today

FREE GIFT CERTIFICATE

Weekly Reader Children's Book Club

YES, please accept this request for my child's FREE GIFTS—Gus and the Baby Ghost, the personalized bookrack and the full-color poster.

048423
Children and Parents of the
Lassmay Family 3183 004
489 Ridge Street
Amherst, Ms. 50267

PASTE STAMP HERE
Please do not overlap stamps. Book number must show.

PASTE STAMP HERE
Please do not overlap stamps. Book number must show.

PASTE STAMP HERE
Please do not overlap stamps. Book number must show.

Figure 18–9 This personalized direct-mail piece invites a young girl and her parents to join a children's book club.

sons for this are apparent. Postal rates have soared in recent years and are continuing to climb. Paper costs also have risen sharply. Production costs, particularly for full-color mailers, are at an all-time high. Even a one-page sales letter cannot be produced and mailed for much less than $85 per thousand, and that doesn't include postage. (See Figure 18–11.)

Delivery delays

A newspaper offers a precise time of delivery to its subscribers: The Sunday morning paper, for example, is home-delivered on Sunday mornings. Similarly, a radio show is nearly always aired at the time scheduled. Direct-mail delivery, however, has no guarantee. A mailing may arrive days early or late. This is because the U.S. Postal Service makes no delivery commitments on third-class mail. This may pose problems, particularly for "dated" mailers. Large retail stores generally allow 48 to 72 hours for the mail delivery of special "sale" announcements. In some cases, however, "sale" mailers have arrived four to six days after a sale was over. The result is often disgruntled customers—and lost revenues.

Lack of content support

Magazine advertising usually obtains its readership from the articles, stories, and illustrations that surround it. Direct mail, however, has none of these support factors. A sales letter, brochure, or catalog stands alone; it must capture and hold the reader's attention without assistance. For this reason, direct-mail advertising must be conceived very carefully. It must combine strong visual and copy appeals with an attractive format if it is to be successful.

Figure 18–10 Typical mail-order results by month

(base: January = 100)

Month	Rating
January	100.0
February	96.3
March	71.0
April	71.5
May	71.5
June	67.0
July	73.3
August	87.0
September	79.0
October	89.9
November	81.0
December	79.0

Selectivity problems

If the advertiser fails to determine the prime audience for the mailing or does not obtain a bona fide list from a reliable broker or company, the returns from the mailing may be reduced, thereby increasing the cost of sales.

Some groups of prospects are less responsive than others to direct-mail advertising. This may be because they receive large daily volumes of direct mail. Physicians, for example, are the target of many financial, real estate, and insurance advertisers because of their fa-

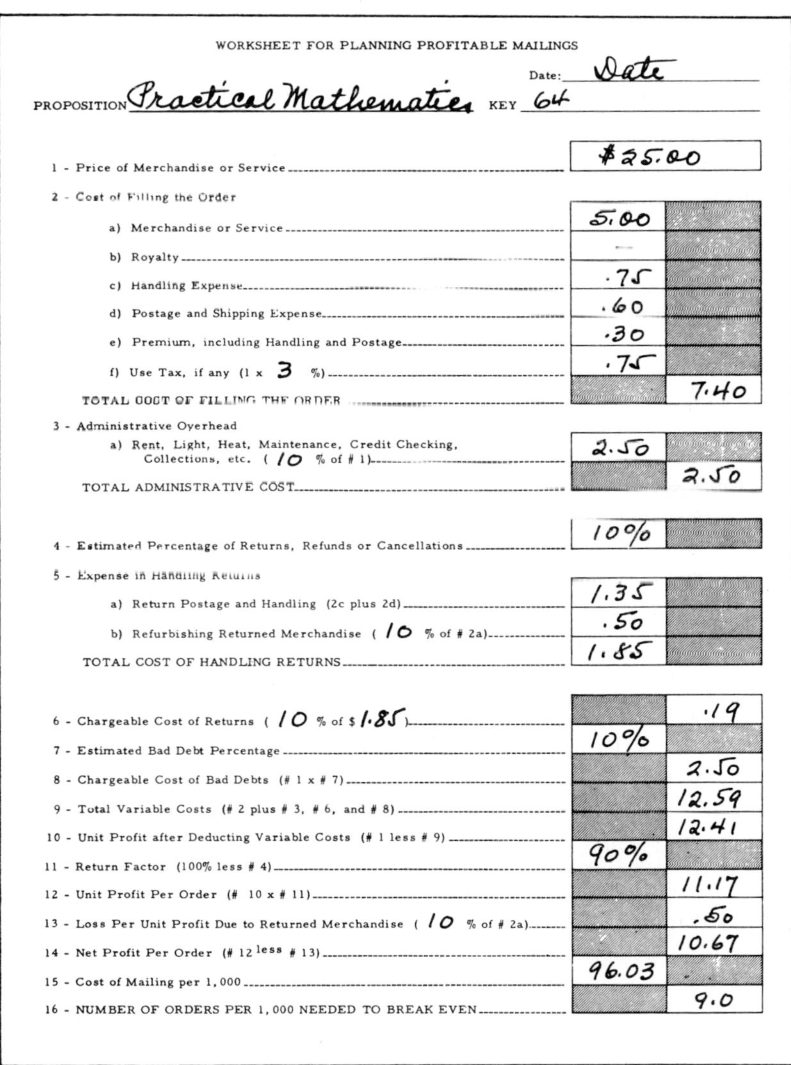

WORKSHEET FOR PLANNING PROFITABLE MAILINGS

Date: Date

PROPOSITION Practical Mathematics KEY 64

1 - Price of Merchandise or Service	$25.00	
2 - Cost of Filling the Order		
a) Merchandise or Service	5.00	
b) Royalty	—	
c) Handling Expense	.75	
d) Postage and Shipping Expense	.60	
e) Premium, including Handling and Postage	.30	
f) Use Tax, if any (1 x 3 %)	.75	
TOTAL COST OF FILLING THE ORDER		7.40
3 - Administrative Overhead		
a) Rent, Light, Heat, Maintenance, Credit Checking, Collections, etc. (10 % of # 1)	2.50	
TOTAL ADMINISTRATIVE COST		2.50
4 - Estimated Percentage of Returns, Refunds or Cancellations	10%	
5 - Expense in Handling Returns		
a) Return Postage and Handling (2c plus 2d)	1.35	
b) Refurbishing Returned Merchandise (10 % of # 2a)	.50	
TOTAL COST OF HANDLING RETURNS	1.85	
6 - Chargeable Cost of Returns (10 % of $ 1.85)		.19
7 - Estimated Bad Debt Percentage	10%	
8 - Chargeable Cost of Bad Debts (# 1 x # 7)		2.50
9 - Total Variable Costs (# 2 plus # 3, # 6, and # 8)		12.59
10 - Unit Profit after Deducting Variable Costs (# 1 less # 9)		12.41
11 - Return Factor (100% less # 4)	90%	
12 - Unit Profit Per Order (# 10 x # 11)		11.17
13 - Loss Per Unit Profit Due to Returned Merchandise (10 % of # 2a)		.50
14 - Net Profit Per Order (# 12 less # 13)		10.67
15 - Cost of Mailing per 1,000	96.03	
16 - NUMBER OF ORDERS PER 1,000 NEEDED TO BREAK EVEN		9.0

Figure 18–11 Projection of costs and profits is essential in planning a successful direct-mail campaign.

vorable income image. The high volume of mail in most physicians' offices causes much of it to go unread. The result is that the response rate among physicians is lower than that among most other professional groups. (See Figure 18–12.)

MORE mail

I want to receive more advertising mail.

Mail to: DMMA
Mail Preference Service
6 East 43rd Street, N.Y., NY 10017

Name (print)

Address

City State Zip

I would like to receive more information in the mail, especially on the subjects below (circle letter):

A All subjects
B Autos, Parts & Accessories
C Books & Magazines
D Charities
E Civic Organizations
F Clothing
G Foods & Cooking
H Gifts
I Grocery Bargains
J Health Foods & Vitamins
K HiFi & Electronics
L Home Furnishings
M Insurance
N Plants, Flowers & Garden Supplies
O Photography
P Real Estate
Q Records & Tapes
R Sewing, Needlework, Arts & Crafts
S Sports & Camping
T Stamps & Coins
U Stocks & Bonds
V Tools & Equipment
W Travel
X Office Furniture & Supplies

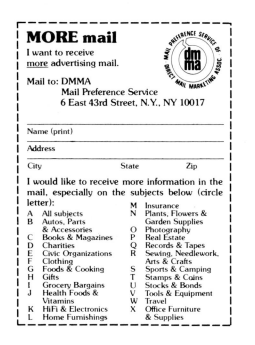

Figure 18–12 For those who want to reduce the amount of direct mail they receive, the DMMA offers a unique service. It has informed more than 30 million readers that they could obtain a Name-Removal Form from the DMMA Mail Preference Service. This form, the ads explain, will enable them to remove their name from advertiser mailing lists. The names and addresses on these forms are recorded on magnetic tape and made available to mailing-list brokers and advertisers. They are encouraged to remove these names from their lists. Direct mail is just too expensive to waste on people who don't want it. The same campaign also offers readers a chance to add their names to lists if they want to receive more direct mail—particularly in their specialized areas of interest. Of all the responses received, over 35 percent have been requests from people to have their names placed on mailing lists.

Types of direct mail

Direct-mail advertising has many forms. These include sales letters, brochures, and even handwritten postcards. The message can be as short as one sentence or dozens of pages long. And within each format—from tiny coupon to giant 100-page catalog—there can be almost infinite variety.

Sales letters are the most common form of direct mail. They can be typewritten, typeset and printed, printed with a computer insert (such as your name), or fully computer-typed. They are often mailed with brochures, price lists, or reply cards and envelopes.

Postcards are generally used by retailers to announce sales, offer discounts, or otherwise generate shopper traffic. They are used for similar reasons by dog groomers, dry cleaners, dentists, and even palmists and astrologers. Postcards may travel by first- or third-class mail. The first-class postcard may feature a handwritten message. Third-class postcards, however, must be printed, and may not contain any handwritten material.

Some advertisers use a double postcard. This enables them to send both an advertising message and a perforated reply card. If the recipient wants the product or service advertised, he or she simply tears off the reply card and mails it back to the advertiser. To encourage this, some advertisers use a postpaid reply card. This requires having a first-class postal permit, which is available for a nominal fee from the local postmaster.

Leaflets or *flyers* are generally a single, standard-size (8½ by 11 inches) page printed on one or both sides and folded one or more times. They usually accompany a sales letter and are used to supplement or expand the information it contains.

Folders are larger than leaflets in most cases and are printed on heavier paper stock. Their weight and size enable them to "take" a printed visual image well. Thus they are often designed with photos or other illustrations, usually in full color. Folders can accommodate a longer, more detailed sales message than most leaflets. Often they are folded and sent as self-mailers, without envelopes, for increased economy.

Broadsides are larger than folders. Though sometimes used as window displays or wall posters in stores, they can be folded to a compact size that will fit into a mail bag.

Self-mailers are any form of direct mail (postcards, leaflets, folders, broadsides, brochures, catalogs, house organs, magazines) that can travel by mail without an envelope. Such mailers are usually folded and secured by a staple or seal. They have a special blank space on which the prospect's name and address can be written, stenciled, or labeled.

Reprints are direct-mail enclosures that are frequently sent by public relations agencies or departments. They are duplications of publication articles that show the company or its products in a favorable light.

Statement stuffers are advertisements that are enclosed in the monthly customer statements mailed by department stores, banks, or oil companies. A wide variety of products—from camping equipment to stereo systems—is sold in this way. To order, all the customer needs to do is write the credit card number on the reply card.

House organs are publications produced by business organizations. They take many forms, including stockholder reports, newsletters, consumer magazines, and dealer publications. Most are produced by the company's advertising or public relations department, or by its agency. Today an estimated 10,000 different house organ publications are mailed in the United States each year and read by more than 3.5 million people.

Catalogs are reference books that list, describe, and often picture the products sold by a manufacturer, wholesaler, jobber, or retailer. Nearly everyone is familiar with the Sears, Roebuck and Montgomery Ward catalogs, but similar catalogs are mailed by the millions each year by industrial, mail-order, and retail firms (Figure 18–13).

Manufacturer's catalogs often have looseleaf formats. This enables the easy insertion or removal of pages as products are added to or withdrawn from the company line. The use of looseleaf catalog sheets also enables the manufacturer to mail them individually as sales literature.

Buying direct mail

Direct-mail advertising entails three basic costs: (1) list rental or purchase; (2) conception, production, and handling of the direct mailer; and (3) distribution. We shall discuss each of these briefly.

Direct-mail lists

Bob Stone speaks of mailing lists as being the "heart" of every direct-mail operation. Each list, he points out, actually defines a market segment. These may be grouped as house lists, mail response lists, and compiled lists.[3]

House lists

A company's customers are its most important asset. It stands to reason, therefore, that the list of names of customers and prospects compiled by the company over a long time is also its most important and valuable direct-mail list. These lists may contain current customers, recent customers, and long past customers or future prospects. They may be further broken down by other demographic or behavioristic characteristics such as size of purchases. Or perhaps they may be broken down by the promotional strategy initially used to attract them: direct mail, TV advertising, newspaper coupon, etc.

Mail response lists

Second in importance are those who have responded to the direct-mail solicitations of other companies, especially those whose efforts are complementary to the advertiser's. For example, if you plan to use

REPLACE BOTHERSOME BED SLATS with sturdy bed spring supports. These supports simply hook over the side rails of the bed and support the mattress and springs. Eliminate bed slats completely. Heavy-gauge steel; will support up to ½ ton. For coil or box springs. Order for wood or metal frames. Set of 6 for each bed.
H5082 Supports for Wood Rails **$5.99**
H5083 Supports for Metal Rails **$4.99**

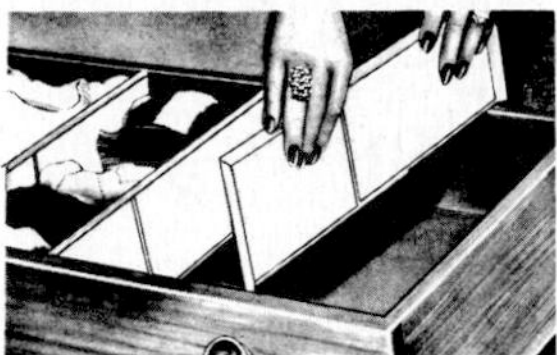

DRAWER DIVIDERS keep all your belongings neatly within reach. No more shuffling through untidy drawers. Quick to install; so handy, you'll wonder how you kept house without them. Expand from 9" to 17" in length. Lightweight metal, smooth finish. They stay in with self-stick tape. For wood or metal drawers. Sizes for every drawer!
H2036 Dividers, 2½" High .... 2 for **$1.49**
H2037 Dividers, 4½" High .... 2 for **$1.99**
H2038 Dividers, 6½" High .... 2 for **$2.99**

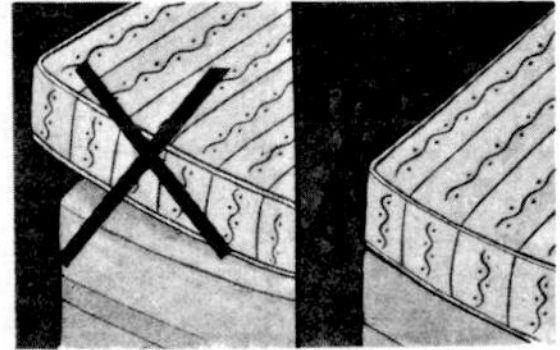

NO-SLIDE™ KEEPS MATTRESS IN PLACE INSTANTLY! No more annoying sliding, slipping, shifting. Just slip No-Slide™ between mattress and springs. Special foam strip grips mattress, ends sliding . . . lets you make bed with ease. 50x12" fits twin, (order 2 for king or queen); 36x12" set of 2 fits double; ⅜" thick. Washable. Saves work —helps lengthen mattress life.
H1346 Twin No-Slide™ Strip **$3.99**
2 Twin Strips for **$7.49**
H1347 Double No-Slide™ Strips **$4.99**

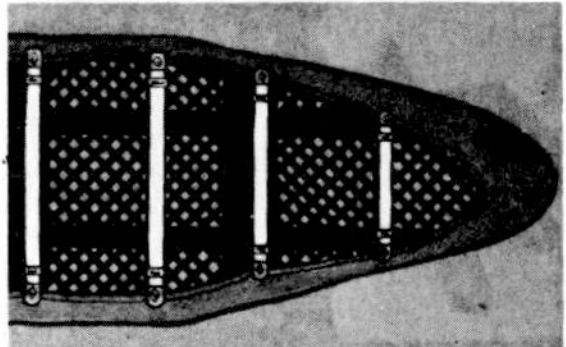

STRAPS KEEP IRONING COVER TIGHT! These elastic fasteners hold your ironing board cover smooth and wrinkle-free . . . your iron will glide over the surface—makes ironing easier! Each strap consists of 2 metal clips and an elastic strap that adjusts automatically to hold your ironing cover tight. Easy to attach to under side of cover . . . won't snag or tear the cover. Set of 4 fasteners fit all standard ironing boards.
K5090 Ironing Cover Fasteners **$2.49**

"FILE" AWAY PANS AND TRAYS in short order with this steel wire organizer. Has 4 wide compartments to store cookie sheets, baking pans, and serving trays. Fits in shelf, cupboard, or oven. A housewife's dream. When you want a pan — just reach for it. No bothersome unstacking or rummaging through the cupboard. Vinyl coating won't chip. 10x10¼", 8" high — holds Corning Ware®, too!
K850 Pan 'N' Tray Organizer **$4.49**

REFRIGERATOR DEFROSTS IN MINUTES with Super-Defroster! No chipping or chopping, no pans of boiling water! Just plug in the unit, set in freezer compartment on metal surface. Heat rays loosen ice, melt away frost before frozen food has a chance to thaw! 7" x 4" lightweight metal heating plate; safety neoprene insulated cord. UL listed. 5½" handle, 6' cord. Cuts defrosting time in half!
K3076 Electric Defroster **$9.99**

TELEVISION AND RADIO NOISE FILTER lets you enjoy your favorite programs without annoying static interference! Special filtering device helps end electrical disturbance caused by appliances, machines, electric razors, etc.! Just plug filter into any outlet . . . plug television or radio into filter for clearer, "static-free" reception. Also works directly on offending appliances. 2⅛x1⅛"; fits standard electrical outlets.
H1438 TV-Radio Noise Filter **$2.99**
2 for **$4.99**

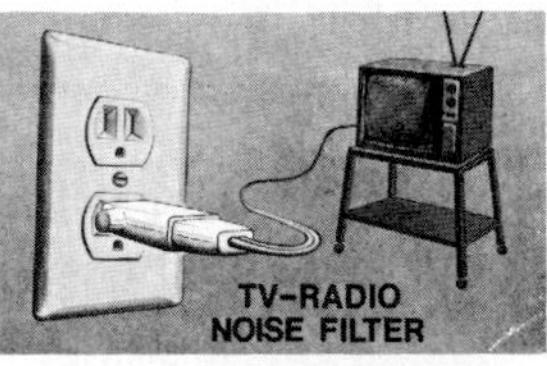

MATTRESS COVER FULLY PROTECTS . . . keeps mattress fresh, clean, and like new! Special envelope design encloses entire mattress . . . protects top, bottom, and sides! Soft, durable plastic cover slips on in a jiffy . . . lets your pretty mattress show through. Waterproof, wipe-clean cover available in all sizes. Ideal for invalid and infant care, storage, rentals, etc.!
H4241 Twin ... **$2.99** **H4243** Queen .. **$5.99**
H4242 Full .... **$3.99** **H4244** King ... **$6.99**

BATHTUB SAFETY RAIL. Here's wonderful, firm support for all the bathers in your family. The elderly depend on its security . . . children can save many slips and spills. Sturdy rail with non-slip rubber grip is a help with the sick or handicapped, too! Fits over the side of most tubs . . . and really takes hold with 4 rubber sleeve-tips. It won't mar your tub either. Supports over 300 pounds. Rustproof, chrome-plated, heavy steel tubing; assembles easily. About 13" long.
H1363 Bathtub Safety Rail **$11.99**

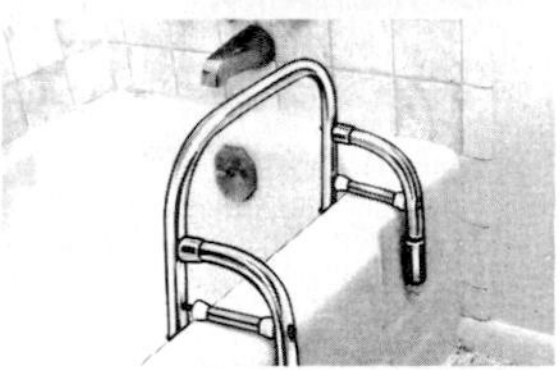

MAKE 2 OUTLETS INTO 6 — INSTANTLY! Just plug this special converter into any regular outlet—no tools or special wiring needed! Lets you plug in up to 6 appliances at once! Great for kitchen, workshop, office —wherever you need extra outlets. Completely safe; UL listed. Durable plastic; 3x4⅝x1". Choose the style for 2-pronged or grounded 3-pronged outlets. So easy—so handy!
H1447 2-Pronged Converter **$2.99**
H1448 3-Pronged Converter **$3.99**

INSTANT HINGES—simply cut to the size you need from a continuous 4-foot roll! Just staple, nail, or screw hinge into place . . . pre-punched ⅛" holes for extra convenience. Absolutely unbreakable—tested to flex over a million times! All-purpose Polyhinge® can't rust or squeak—never needs oiling. Hundreds of uses: box lids, window seats, shutters, doggie doors, drop leaf tables, etc. Heavy-duty, weatherproof plastic; 1½"x4'. Always have the right size hinge on hand!
H6282 Polyhinge®, 4 ft. Roll **$3.49**

NO MORE UGLY TRASH CANS! One Quick Trash™ replaces all your old-fashioned garbage cans. Tubular plastic frame securely holds any bag, 30-gallon or larger. When bag is full, just tie it up, put aside . . . and add another bag! No battered cans to replace . . . no windblown cans to chase . . . no empty cans to put away! Snaps together in seconds; no tools needed. 26" tall. Cover with any standard 30-gallon lid, if you wish. Great when raking leaves or grass, too!
H5355 Quick Trash™ **$9.99**

Figure 18–13 A two-page spread from a Walter Drake & Sons catalog. As this catalog giant has shown, it takes years, capital, and skillful, aggressive merchandising to build a large-volume catalog business. Their selling success is based on their reputation and often their lower prices.

direct mail to advertise wool scarves and sports car caps, you might find the most attractive response list to be held by the company that markets driving gloves.

Thousands of such response lists are available from an endless array of firms. They are simply the house lists of other direct-mail advertisers, and they are usually available for rental with a wide variety of demographic breakdowns.

Compiled lists

The third kind of list is the most readily available in volume but offers the lowest expectation. It is simply a list that has been compiled for one reason or another by a source. These may include lists of automobile owners, new-house purchasers, city business owners, chamber of commerce presidents, union members, or what have you. Compiled lists are often computer merged with mail response and house lists. This "merge and purge" process involves merging all names and purging all duplicates so that no more than one piece of mail is sent to one name.

Direct-mail lists can be purchased or rented. They can be brokered or exchanged with list houses or other noncompetitive companies.

The variety of lists available today is virtually unlimited. The SRDS *Direct Mail List Rates and Data* comes in two volumes: Volume I—*Consumer Lists* and Volume II—*Business Lists*. There are over 50,000 list selections in hundreds of different classifications (Figure 18–14).

The average mailing list changes more than 28 percent a year. One reason for this is that some 22 percent of the nation's population relocates to a new address each year. Large numbers of people also make job changes, get married, or die. Thus, mailing lists must be continually updated. This "cleaning," as it is called, assures that the list is current and correct.

One way for the advertiser to keep a house list up to date is to print or stamp "Address Correction Requested" on the face of the mailer. For a fee, the U.S. Postal Service will enter the new, correct address of the relocated prospect on the mailer and return it to the advertiser.

The prices of mailing lists vary according to their quality. Rental rates average about $28 per thousand, but lists can be secured for as little as $15 per thousand or as much as $300 per thousand. The more stringent the advertiser's selection criteria, the more expensive the list. Spending an extra $10 per thousand is often well worth the savings in wasted mailers and postage that result from using a less precise list.

With the computer, an advertiser can also test the validity and accuracy of a given list. He or she does this by renting or buying every *n*th name and sending a mailer thereto. If the results are favorable, additional names can be purchased, usually in lots of 1,000.

Mailing lists are usually rented for one use only. This means the advertiser agrees to use the list for a single mailing. Most list owners require the advertiser to submit a sample mailer in advance. This enables them to be sure that the advertiser will not mail anything that reflects poorly on them or that conflicts with their own products or services.

Columbia Record & Tape Club

Media Code 3 578 2660 1.00

Member: D.M.M.A.

Participant D.M.M.A. Mail Preference Service.
Columbia House, a Div. of CBS Inc., 1211 Avenue of the Americas, New York, N. Y. 10036. Phones: 212-975-4292/5933/7165.

1. **PERSONNEL**
List Manager—Karen Barry.
Assistant List Manager—Jeannie Wheaton Shaw.
Director, List Marketing Service—Evelyn Deitz.
Broker and/or Authorized Agent
All recognized brokers.

2. **DESCRIPTION**
Active and former members. All names are credit checked. 14% are under 18; 61% are between 18 and 34; 25% are over 35; 51% female.
ZIP Coded in numerical sequence 100%.

3. **LIST SOURCE**
Space ads and direct mail.

4. **QUANTITY AND RENTAL RATES**
Rec'd January, 1981.

	Total Number	Price per/M
Record Club:		
Active members	1,294,389	40.00
Former members	517,327	37.50
Cartridge club:		
Active members	1,017,395	40.00
Former members	651,672	37.50
Casette club:		
Active members	659,146	40.00
Former members	178,658	37.50
Reel to reel:		
Active members	10,020	40.00
Former members	5,305	37.50
Listening preferences:		
Classical:		
Active members	80,836	40.00
Former members	36,646	37.50
Popular Broadway:		
Active members	727,399	40.00
Former members	385,054	37.50
Jazz:		
Active members	68,448	40.00
Former members	26,947	37.50
Country & Western:		
Active members	400,418	40.00
Former members	204,917	37.50
Young Sounds:		
Active members	1,704,749	40.00
Former members	699,398	37.50

Selections: club, listening preference, no extra charge; sex, multi-buyers, hotline, year, SCF, state, ZIP Code, 2.50/M extra; key coding, 1.00/M extra.
Minimum order 5,000.

5. **COMMISSION, CREDIT POLICY**
20% to recognized brokers.

6. **METHOD OF ADDRESSING**
4 or 5-up Cheshire labels. Pressure sensitive labels, 3.50/M extra.
Magnetic tape available.

8. **RESTRICTIONS**
Sample mailing piece required.

Figure 18–14 A typical listing from Standard Rate and Data Service, *Direct Mail List Rates & Data (Consumer Lists)*.

Many lists are handled by list brokers. A list owner who does not want to be bothered with the details of renting it can retain a broker to handle it. For this service, brokers are paid a commission (usually 20 percent) by the list owner. The advertiser also gains: He or she gets the broker's direct-mail knowledge and expertise without paying more than the rental cost of the list.

Production and handling

The advertiser can create his own direct-mail package or retain the services of an advertising agency or free-lance designer and writer. Some agencies specialize in direct mail.

Once the mailing package is conceived and designed, it is ready for printing. The size and shape of the mailing pieces as well as the specified type, illustrations, and colors all influence the printing cost. Special features like simulated blue-ink signatures, cardboard pop-ups, and die cutting (the cutting of paper stock into an unusual shape) add to the cost. The larger the printing volume, or "run," however, the lower the printing cost per unit. For example, printing 1,000 sales letters may cost $40, or 4 cents per unit. However, printing 10,000 copies of the same letter may cost only $25 per thousand, or 2½ cents per unit.

The remaining production tasks can be handled by a local *letter-shop* unless the advertiser prefers to do them internally. Most such firms perform these tasks on a cost per thousand basis. They stuff and seal envelopes, affix labels, calculate postage, and sort, tie, and stack the mailers. Some also offer creative services. If the advertiser plans to use third-class bulk mail, the mailers must be separated by zip code and tied into bundles to qualify for low bulk rates. When these tasks are finished, the lettershop delivers the mailers to the post office.

Distribution

Distribution costs are chiefly based on the weight of the mailer and the method of delivery. The advertiser can choose among several such methods, including the U.S. Postal Service, United Parcel, air freight, and private postal services.

Direct mail has been found to be most effective when it arrives on Tuesdays, Wednesdays, and Thursdays. This may be because some people are affected by Monday back-to-work blues and Friday can't wait-for-the-weekend elation, or because the growing acceptance of the four-day work week and expanded weekends means fewer people are "in town" from Friday through Monday. (See Figure 18–15.)

The most common means of delivery is the U.S. Postal Service. It offers the advertiser a choice of several types of mail delivery.

1. *First-class mail.* Contrary to popular belief, a large amount of direct-mail advertising is sent first class. The reasons are that first class assures fast delivery, returns any mail that is undeliverable, and for-

People in advertising

Robert Stone

Chairman of the Board
Stone & Adler, Inc.

Robert Stone is chairman of the board of Stone & Adler, Inc., one of America's leading full-service direct marketing agencies and an internationally known authority on direct mail/marketing.

Stone & Adler, founded in 1966 with a staff of five, today has 100 employees and annual billings of $25 million. The agency has won numerous "Best of Industry" honors, including the coveted Gold and Silver Mailbox Awards. Its clients include IBM, United Airlines, AT&T, General Electric, Armstrong Cork, Montgomery Ward, Allstate Insurance, and Southwestern Bell Telephone Company. In 1970 Stone & Adler became a division of Young & Rubicam.

Robert Stone recently told an industry audience, "Direct marketing growth in the past decade has been explosive. But growth in the next decade may well come in quantum leaps. Look for clear trends to form within the next three years." Forecasts Stone, "More and more major marketers, seeking new profit centers, will explore and enter the direct marketing stream. Credit card usage for direct marketing offers will continue to grow," he said, "accounting for better than 50 percent of mail-order sales within three years."

New technology will spur even greater direct marketing growth, Stone predicted. "The use of network TV by mass marketers will expand in the face of cable growth. Co-op sponsorship of major TV programming by three or more direct marketers is a real possibility. Worldwide toll-free telephone ordering," he said, "will start to become reality. There will be paid commercials on videodiscs, interspersed between entertainment and educational segments. Printing technology, particularly laser printing," he added, "will lower costs dramatically, keeping ahead of inflation. Electronic mail will become common among business firms." He cited the statement by postal authority John Jay Daly that 40 to 60 percent of postal volume during the next 10 years will be electronic mail.

According to Stone, "The demographics of the 80s will favor direct marketing. The major population group will be between 35 and 39, with vastly increased numbers over 50. More than 54 percent of adult women will work. There will also be more leisure time, with greater discretionary income."

Reflecting the impact of this growth trend, Stone said, "A minimum of 100 universities and colleges will be offering Direct Marketing as an accredited course. The discipline of direct marketing," he added, "will attract an increasing percentage of college graduates."

Stone concluded his observations by predicting, "A 'checkless society,' with automatic funds transfer, will start to take hold."

Stone has been named to the Direct Marketing Hall of Fame. He is the recipient of the International Direct Marketing and Mail Order Symposiums' Bronze Carrier Pigeon Award. Stone was presented the Charles S. Downs Award for outstanding service to the direct marketing industry of Chicago.

Stone is a director of Young & Rubicam Affiliates. He serves on the board of directors of the Direct Mail/Marketing Educational Foundation. Former president of the Chicago Association of Direct Marketing and the Associated Third-Class Mail Users, Stone has also been director and membership chairman of the Direct Mail/Marketing Association. He is a member of the professional division of Alpha Delta Sigma fraternity.

Author of the well-known book *Successful Direct Marketing Methods,* Stone has contributed more than 170 articles to "Stone on Direct Marketing," a column featured in *Advertising Age* since 1967.

wards mail (without additional charge) if the addressee has moved and filed a forwarding address.

2. *Business reply mail.* This type of mail enables the recipient to respond without paying postage. The advertiser must first obtain a special permit number, which is available from the postmaster. Then this number must be printed on the face of the return card or envelope. On receiving each response, the advertiser must pay postage plus a few cents handling fee. Postage and fee are paid only on the responses received. This "postage-free" incentive tends to increase the rate of response.

3. *Third-class mail.* There are four types of third-class mail: single piece, bulk, bound books or catalogs, and nonprofit organization mail. Most direct-mail advertising travels by third-class mail. It represents a significant savings over first-class rates.

4. *Fourth-class mail.* This class applies only to mail that weighs over 16 ounces.

Figure 18–15 Sales response ranking based on the results of 20 mailings offering various types of books and merchandise

Rank	State or district	Rank	State or district
1	Alaska	27	Michigan
2	Washington, D.C.	28	Kansas
3	Hawaii	29	Oklahoma
4	California	30	New York
5	Nevada	31	Rhode Island
6	Arizona	32	Georgia
7	Wyoming	33	Ohio
8	New Mexico	34	Delaware
9	Idaho	35	Virginia
10	Montana	36	Pennsylvania
11	Utah	37	Arkansas
12	Florida	38	Missouri
13	Nebraska	39	South Carolina
14	Louisiana	40	Connecticut
15	Oregon	41	North Carolina
16	Illinois	42	New Hampshire
17	Indiana	43	North Dakota
18	Texas	44	Minnesota
19	Colorado	45	Kentucky
20	Washington	46	Vermont
21	Maryland	47	Tennessee
22	Wisconsin	48	Iowa
23	West Virginia	49	Mississippi
24	South Dakota	50	Massachusetts
25	Maine	51	Alabama
26	New Jersey		

Out-of-home media

In late 1974 Shirley Cothran was crowned Miss America for 1975 on a network television show with an audience of over 50 million viewers. In fact, it was the sixth highest rated television special of the year. Shortly thereafter Shirley appeared on five more network television shows, including a Bob Hope special, as well as dozens of local television and radio programs. The Shirley Cothran name and picture were also shown in hundreds of newspapers and a considerable number of national magazines.

In December 1974 a study sponsored by the outdoor advertising industry was conducted by 25 colleges and universities and 12 independent research organizations. One simple question was asked: "What is the name of Miss America for 1975?" In spite of all the national publicity, all the network TV shows, and all the newspaper and magazine photos, only 1.6 percent of the respondents could give the correct answer.

On January 1 the outdoor industry sponsored a two-month coast-to-coast billboard campaign. Some 10,000 poster panels (billboards) carried a photograph of Miss Cothran and the simple statement: "Shirley Cothran, Miss America 1975" (Figure 18–16). When a second wave of interviews was conducted in February and March, 16.3 percent of those questioned knew who Miss America was.

That is a tenfold increase in awareness. More than 30,000 adults had been interviewed in the two waves of random sample surveys. Projected nationally, that meant that outdoor advertising had communicated a new and difficult name to more than 20 million adult Americans, about one in every seven.

What do you suppose gives outdoor that kind of muscle? On the other hand, if it's really that strong, why doesn't every advertiser use outdoor? Like every other mass medium, outdoor advertising has its advantages and disadvantages.

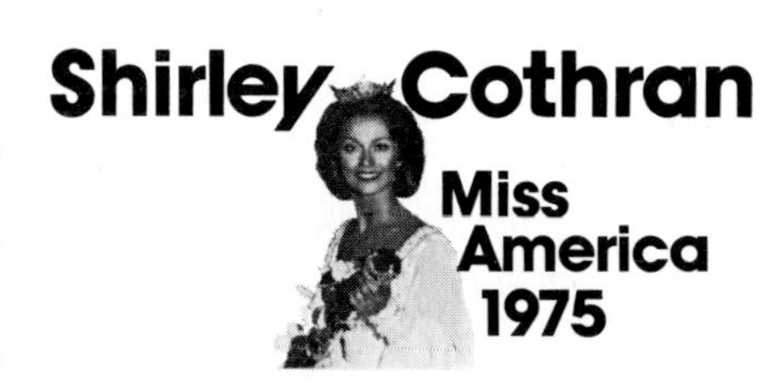

Figure 18–16 Miss America's name was barely known until she appeared on 10,000 poster panels for two months. During that time she achieved a tenfold increase in awareness and demonstrated the advertising effectiveness possible through outdoor advertising.

What works best in outdoor advertising?

The advantages of outdoor advertising are numerous and distinct. They relate to the medium's reach, frequency, flexibility, and cost, as well as its impact. (See Figure 18–17.)

Reach

Often an advertiser requires saturation of a market to accomplish objectives such as the introduction of a new product or feature or a change in package design. Outdoor advertising is a mass medium that makes broad coverage possible overnight.

For example, a 100 gross rating point showing (also called a number 100 showing) covers a market fully by reaching 9 out of 10 adults daily over a 30-day period. Thus, in a single day, with a 100 GRP showing, an advertising message can be given a total number of exposure opportunities equal to the entire population of a market.

Outdoor advertising: A twentieth century art form

A.

B.

C.

D.

E.

Figure 18—17 The billboard gallery of the Sunset Strip in Hollywood, California (page 594), demonstrates how outdoor can be quick and to the point. The best and most generous examples of billboard art are found here for modern music is paving the Strip with gold. (a) the most expensive board ever produced, (b) Chicago packaged in real tin foil, and (c) Christopher Reeves streaks across the Strip promoting Superman. Note how both of the above advertisements also use dynamic illustration enlarged to heroic proportions.

How to use color in outdoor advertising

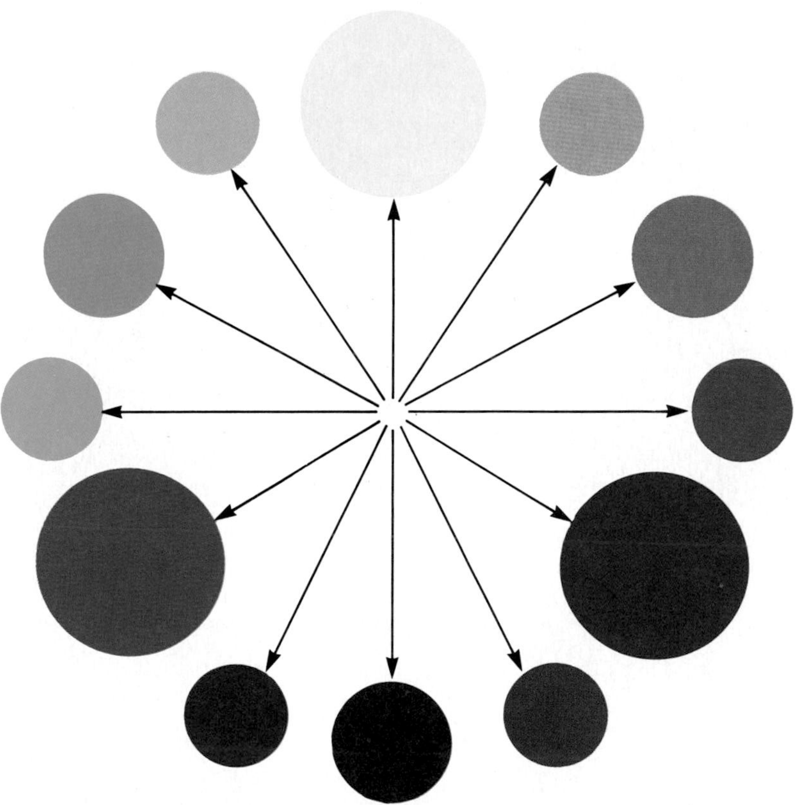

The availability of a full range of colors, vividly and faithfully reproduced, is one of the outstanding advantages of outdoor advertising. A huge poster or bulletin alive with brilliant reds and greens and yellows and blues can produce an effect approached by no other medium.

In choosing colors for outdoor, the designer should seek out those with high contrast in both hue (the identity of the color, such as red, green, yellow) and value (the measure of the color's lightness or darkness). Contrasting colors work well at outdoor-viewing distances, while colors without contrast blend together and obscure the message.

The color wheel illustrates the need for contrast in both hue and value. For example, green and red are opposite each other on the wheel and are therefore complementary colors. They represent a good contrast in *hues,* but in *values* they are very similar. As a result, they set up an annoying vibration. The same is true of blue and orange.

Blue and green and orange and red are especially poor combinations because they are similar in both hue *and* value.

On the other hand, yellow and purple—*dis*similar in both hue and value—provide a strong and effective contrast for outdoor. Of course, white goes well with any dark-value color, while black is good with colors of light value.

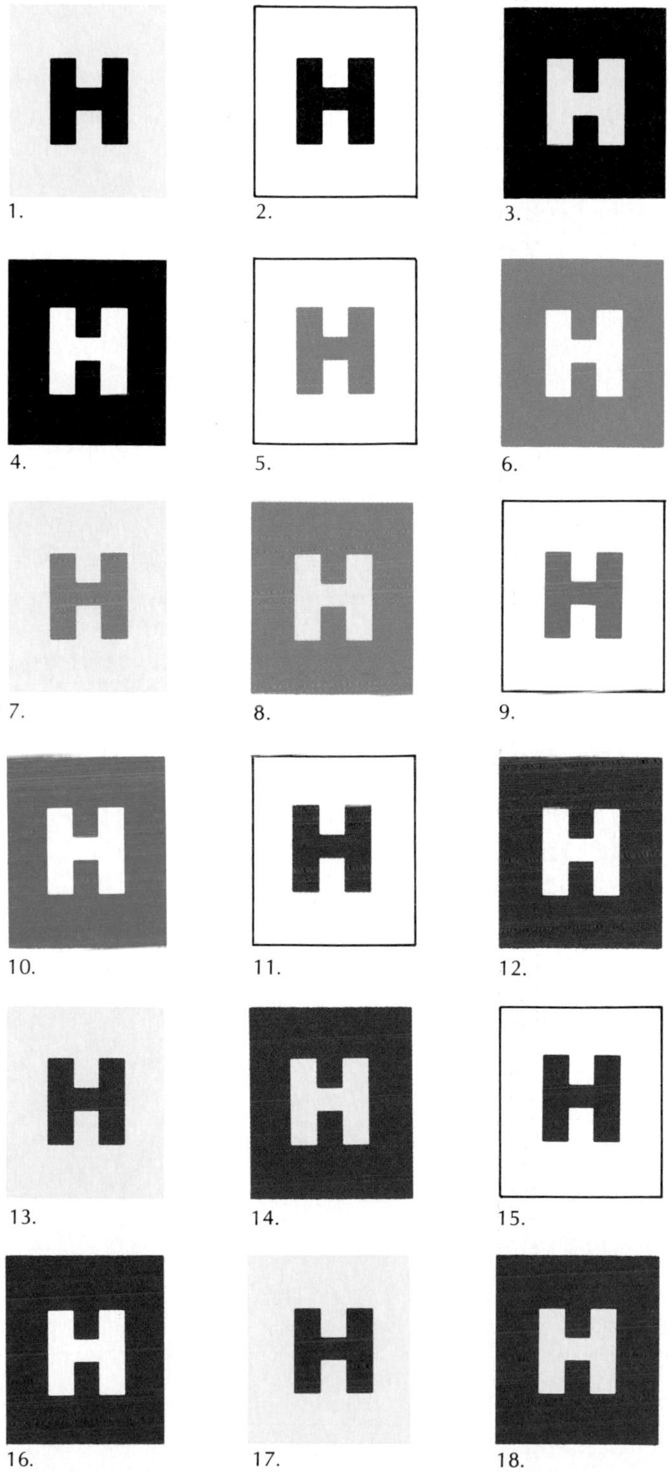

1. 2. 3.

4. 5. 6.

7. 8. 9.

10. 11. 12.

13. 14. 15.

16. 17. 18.

Color impact chart. Among the color combinations shown, legibility ranges from best in combination 1 to poorest in combination 18.

Color combinations illustrate need for contrast in hue and value. Blue and green do *not* work well together; yellow and purple *do* work well. Combinations shown make the same point.

If the advertiser desires even greater saturation, the number of posters can be increased to reach a 200 GRP showing or even 300 GRPs.

Even more important to most advertisers is who is reached by outdoor. For the most part, outdoor's audience is a young, educated, affluent, and mobile population—very attractive to most national advertisers.

Frequency

Outdoor offers frequency of impressions. According to a W. R. Simmons study, the 9 out of 10 people reached with a 100 GRP showing receive an average of 31 impressions each over a 30-day period (Figure 18–18). This frequency increases for groups that are better educated and have higher incomes—again, very attractive.

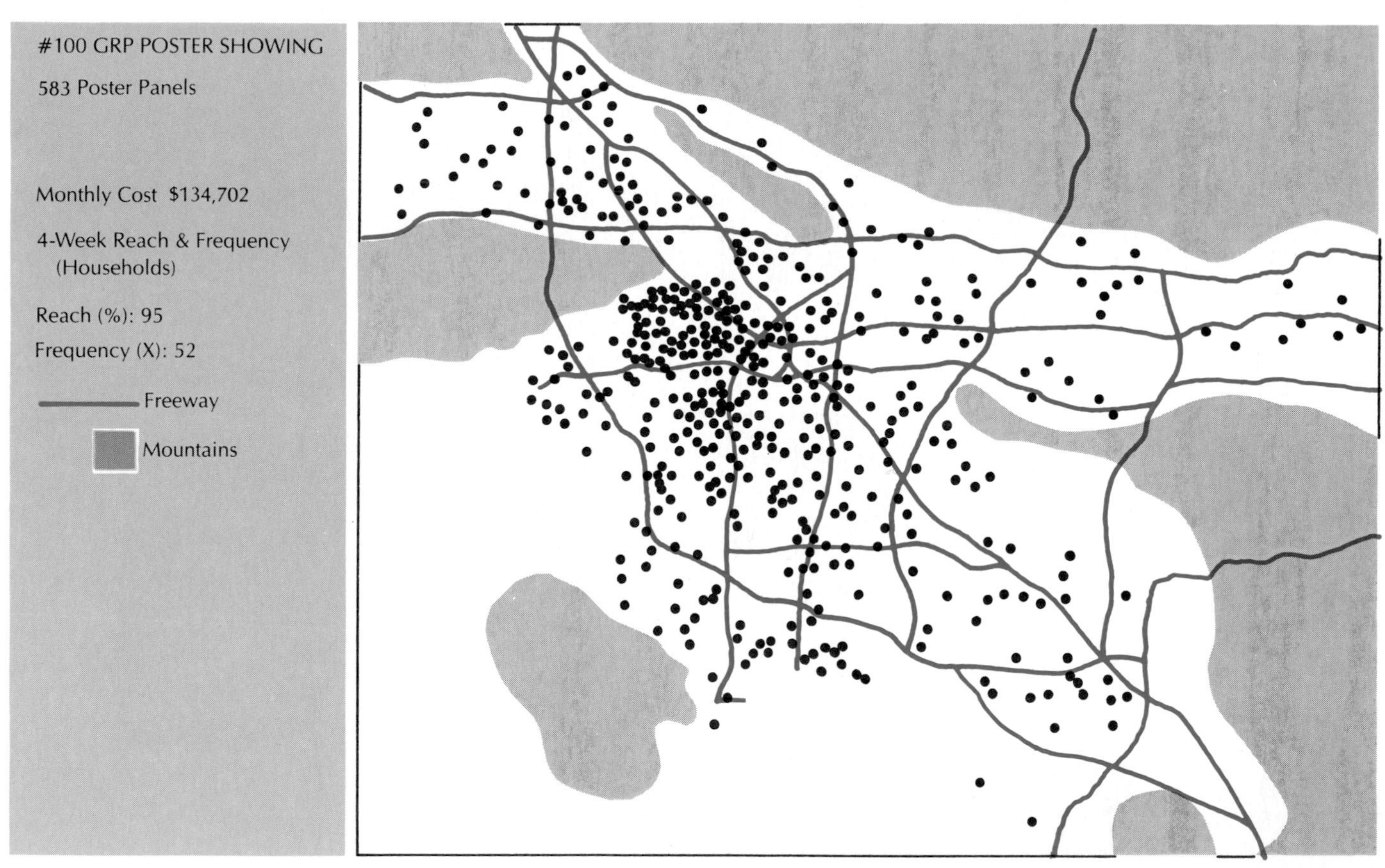

Figure 18–18 A freeway map of Southern California shows that for $134,702 an advertiser can obtain at least 100 GRP's each day for four weeks throughout Los Angeles and Orange counties. While that may sound like a lot of money, the reality is that an advertiser could never obtain that kind of intensity at that price on radio or TV.

Flexibility

In addition, outdoor offers advertisers great flexibility. They can place their advertising geographically where they want it—in any of 9,000 markets across the country—nationally, regionally, or locally. An outdoor advertiser can buy just one city or even a small section of that city.

The flexibility can be demographic. Messages can be concentrated in areas frequented or traversed by young people, upper income people, or people of specific ethnic backgrounds.

Outdoor can even be pinpointed by activity—travelers on their way to the airport, shoppers on their way to the store, businesspeople on their way to and from work.

Cost

Outdoor advertising offers the lowest cost per message delivered of any major advertising medium. Rates vary depending on the size of the particular market and the intensity desired.

The industry uses the term *showing* to indicate the relative number of outdoor posters used during a contract period. Numbers have traditionally been used to indicate the intensity of market coverage. For example, a 100-showing provides an even and thorough coverage of the entire market. A less expensive 50-showing is half as many locations as a 100-showing, a 25-showing one-fourth as many, etc.

Now the industry has largely changed over to the gross rating point (GRP) system similar to that used for TV. If, in a market with a population of 1 million, a showing provides 750,000 total impression opportunities daily, it is said to deliver 75 gross rating points daily. Over a period of 30 days, this showing would earn 2,250 gross rating points. The GRP system makes cost comparison possible from market to market (Figure 18–19).

Local and national advertisers are charged the same rates. These are quoted on a monthly basis for various GRP levels, and they vary considerably from market to market. These differences are due to variations in property rentals, labor costs, and market size. Higher rates are found in larger markets where traffic volume is high.

Detailed rate information may be found in the *Buyers Guide to Outdoor Advertising*. This is published twice a year by the Institute of Outdoor Advertising.

Impact

All this adds up to economical intensity of impressions for the advertiser—impact. With relatively low cost, the advertiser can build up GRPs very fast by hitting a large percentage of the market many times over a very short time. This, of course, is ideal for advertisers who have a short, simple, dogmatic message. It also worked, as we saw, for communicating a not-so-simple name, Shirley Cothran, to a large number of people very quickly.

The inherent features of outdoor add impact to the advertiser's message. It offers the largest display of any medium. Up close, the advertiser's product is seen larger than life. Plus, it offers the spectacular features of lights, animation, and brilliant color. (See the Checklist.)

Finally, whereas other media carry the message to the prospect, outdoor catches people on their way to shop, work, or play, selling continuously day and night. This gives it additional impact for impulse products as well as hotels, motels, restaurants, tourist attractions, and auto-related services.

Drawbacks to outdoor advertising

Just as there are numerous advantages to outdoor, there are also numerous disadvantages. Posters are passed very quickly. To be effective, therefore, outdoor advertising must intrude. The design and leg-

Figure 18–19 Outdoor advertising costs

		Number 25 Showing		Number 50 Showing		Number 100 Showing	
Rank	**Area**	**Panels**	**Cost/month**	**Panels**	**Cost/month**	**Panels**	**Cost/month**
1	New York	386	$78,314	660	$141,115	1,169	$242,309
2	Los Angeles	157	35,392	300	68,802	583	134,702
3	Chicago	163	28,609	284	52,991	529	101,987
4	Philadelphia	221	45,302	367	76,479	655	133,671
5	San Francisco	79	16,889	145	32,151	277	62,153
6	Boston	132	$21,576	223	$38,828	413	$73,937
7	Detroit	120	22,521	176	37,126	315	69,756
8	Washington, D.C.	78	9,214	102	13,089	180	23,041
9	Cleveland	144	21,594	224	37,651	416	72,721
10	Dallas–Ft. Worth	186	19,826	248	29,072	417	51,317
11	Pittsburgh	145	$15,964	197	$23,744	322	$42,032
12	Houston	102	13,494	165	23,018	306	43,968
13	St. Louis	224	24,801	266	33,780	434	59,727
14	Minneapolis–St. Paul	215	25,187	272	35,727	446	61,933
15	Miami	37	7,400	74	14,800	148	29,600
16	Atlanta	134	$18,476	204	$28,499	374	$50,072
17	Tampa–St. Petersburg	74	10,238	114	16,712	204	30,428
18	Seattle–Tacoma	56	10,109	92	17,066	186	34,480
19	Baltimore	56	8,588	95	15,484	177	29,841
20	Indianapolis	166	17,870	201	23,382	325	39,832
21	Denver	50	$7,605	70	$11,470	121	$20,809
22	Portland, Ore.	76	13,998	108	20,218	194	36,478
23	Hartford–New Haven	70	11,411	117	19,283	218	35,862
24	Sacramento–Stockton	57	8,784	89	14,965	160	27,522
25	Milwaukee	107	14,828	159	23,574	277	42,550

end must tell a story briefly and crisply and must sell. Long reason-why copy cannot be used.

Although outdoor advertising is fine for reaching a wide audience, it generally has limitations for reaching a narrow demographic group.

Printing and posting outdoor messages are very time-consuming, so outdoor campaigns must be planned far in advance. Usually a six to eight week lead time is required.

The high initial preparation cost may sometimes discourage local use, although some printing methods such as silk screening require lower preparation costs.

Another disadvantage is the difficulty of physically inspecting each outdoor poster panel (as opposed to checking tear sheets of space advertising or monitoring commercials).

And, finally, the outdoor message is influenced somewhat by its environment. If the billboard is in a depressed or generally run-down area, this will certainly detract from the medium's ability to lend prestige to the product being advertised.

Standardization of the outdoor advertising business

Most advertising that appears out of doors is not *standardized* outdoor advertising but rather consists of on-premise signs that identify a place of business. This type of sign, though certainly helpful to a business, does not provide coverage of a market. On the other hand, standardized outdoor advertising locates its structures scientifically to deliver an advertiser's message to an entire market.

Standardized outdoor advertising is a highly organized medium, which is available to advertisers in more than 15,000 communities

Checklist of what works best in outdoor

Here is a checklist to help you create effective outdoor advertising.

☐ Look for a big idea. This is no place for subtleties. Outdoor is a bold medium. You need a poster that registers the idea quickly and memorably. A "visual scandal" that shocks the viewer into awareness.

☐ Keep it simple. Cut out all extraneous words and pictures, and concentrate on the essentials. Outdoor is the art of brevity. Use only one picture, and no more than seven words of copy—preferably less.

☐ Personalize when you can. Personalized posters are practical, even for short runs. Mention a specific geographic area ("New in Chicago"), or the name of a local dealer.

☐ Look for human, emotional content for memorability. It can be an entertainment medium for travelers who are hungry or bored.

☐ Use color for readability. The most readable combination is black on yellow. Other combinations may gain more attention, but stay with primary colors—and *stay away from reverse.*

☐ Use the location to your advantage. Many new housing developments capitalize on their convenient locations with a poster saying: "If you lived here, you'd be home now." Use outdoor to tell drivers that your restaurant is down the road, your department store is across the street. Don't ignore the ability of outdoor to reach ethnic neighborhoods. Tailor the language and the models to your consumer.

A.

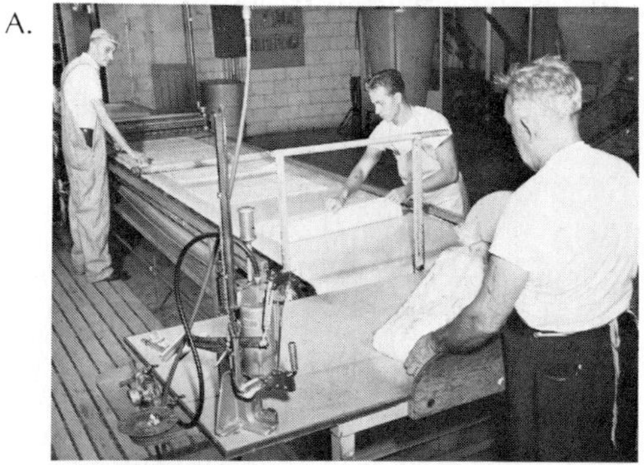

B.

C.

D.

Figure 18–20

across the country. The structures on which the advertising appears are owned and maintained by individual outdoor advertising companies known as "plants." They are built on private land that the outdoor plant operators own or lease and are concentrated in commercial and business areas where they conform to all local building code requirements.

The industry consists of about 600 local and regional plant operators. They find suitable locations, lease or buy the property, erect the outdoor structures, contract with advertisers for poster rentals, and post the panels or paint the bulletins (Figure 18–20). They also have to maintain the outdoor structures so lights are working and torn sheets are replaced, and keep the areas surrounding the structures clean and attractive.

Although national advertising comprises the bulk of outdoor business, about one fourth of the business of a typical outdoor plant is from local advertisers. Usually, the smaller the market, the larger is the percentage of local advertisers. The outdoor firm may employ an art staff to perform creative services for local advertisers, but the creative work for national advertisers is usually handled by advertising agencies.

Standardized outdoor structures

Standardized outdoor advertising structures are in two basic forms: the poster panel and the bulletin. Each has its individual function, yet they work well together to provide coverage of a market and to reach large numbers of people economically in a short time with a high rate of frequency.

Posters

Posters ("billboards") are the basic form of outdoor advertising and the least costly per unit. A poster is a structure of blank panel with a standardized size and border. It is usually anchored in the ground, or it may be affixed to a wall or roof. Its advertising message is first printed at a lithography or silkscreen plant on large sheets of paper. These are then mounted by hand on the panel.

Poster sizes These are referred to in terms of sheets. At one time it required 24 of the largest sheets a printing press could hold to cover a structure 12 by 25 feet. The designation "24-sheet" is still used even though press sizes have changed and most poster sizes are larger. The poster is still mounted on a board with a total surface of 12 by 25 feet, but today there are two basic sizes of posters:

1. 30-sheet poster—with a 9′7″ by 21′7″ printed area surrounded by a margin of blank paper. The 30-sheet provides 25 percent more copy area than the old 24-sheet size of 8′8″ by 19′6″.
2. Bleed poster—with a 10′5″ by 22′8″ printed area extending all the way to the frame. The bleed poster is about 40 percent larger than the old 24-sheet.

Ready-made posters One way some local advertisers get high-quality outdoor advertising at lower than usual cost is to use ready-made 30-sheet posters. These are stock posters and are available in any quantity. They often feature the work of first-class artists and lithographers. The local advertiser simply orders as many as he needs and has his name placed in the appropriate spot. These ready-made posters are particularly suitable for such local firms as florists, dairies, banks, bakeries, and others that have sales stories similar to those of their competitors.

Smaller posters Advertisers of grocery products and many local advertisers like to use smaller poster sizes such as "junior panels." These are also referred to as 8-sheet posters and offer a 5′ by 11′ printing area on a panel surface 6′ wide by 12′ deep.

Painted displays

These are meant for long use and are usually placed in only the best locations where traffic is heavy and visibility is good. They fall into two general categories: bulletins and walls. Painted bulletins may be painted in sections in the plant's shop and then transported to the site for assembly (Figure 18–21). Painted walls obviously must be painted at the site.

Although usually standardized in width and height, actual sizes depend on the available location, the advertiser's budget, and the

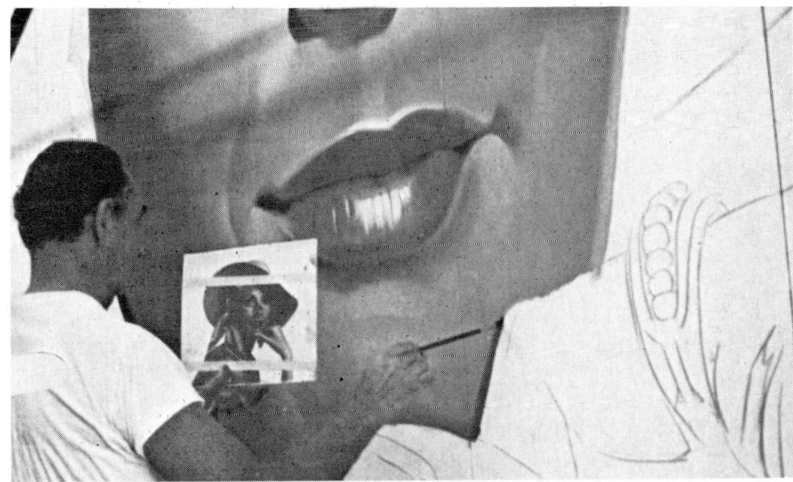

Figure 18–21 Painted bulletins are usually created in the outdoor company's plant. The artist may work from an original photograph or from mechanical art provided by the advertising agency. The bulletin is prepared in sections and is then transported to the location for installation.

(*continued*)

E.

F.

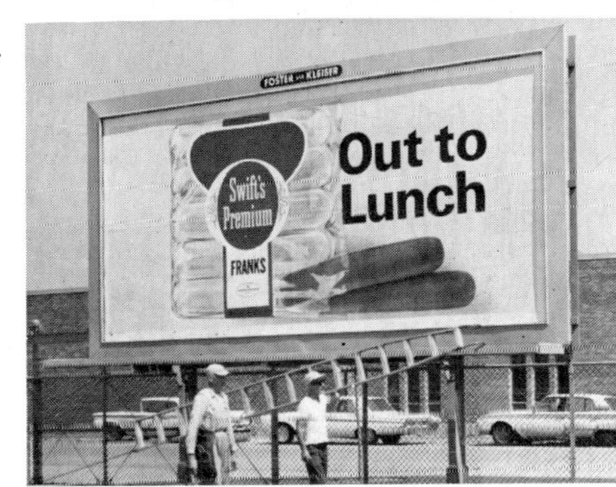

A. Printed poster sheets are collated, prepasted, and vacuum sealed in plastic bags. The glued sheets will remain moist for weeks. Each bag is identified and scheduled for posting routes.

B. First, "blanking paper" is pasted down to form a border. Next, beginning from the bottom, the bill poster takes the prepasted sheets and applies the first section to the panel.

C. By starting at the bottom and working upward, each sheet overlaps the previous section. This forms a "rain-lap" and helps prevent flagging or tearing of the outdoor poster copy.

D. Because the sheets have been prepasted, the bill poster is able to use a dry brush to adhere the paper to the panel. Prepasting techniques eliminate glue streaks from dark backgrounds.

E. Since a poster is a series of sheets, a flexibility of sheet arrangement is possible. The advertiser can localize a campaign to an area, include a dealer's name, or change a package.

F. Sheet by sheet, the giant paper mosaic is assembled to build the advertiser's message into a clean, colorful 25′ by 12′ display. This poster will be exposed to the mass public for 30 days.

character of the message. Bulletins are more custom-made than posters, generally larger, and usually longer. Typical sizes are 14′ by 48′; however, some even extend to 18′ by 62′10″.

Painted displays are normally illuminated and repainted several times each year to keep them looking fresh. Some are three-dimensional and embellished by cut-outs that extend beyond the frames. Variations include the use of cut-out letters, plastic facing, back-lighting, moving messages, clocks, thermometers, electric time and temperature units called "jump clocks," and novel treatment of light and color (Figure 18–22).

Some advertisers overcome the higher expense of painted bulletins by using a *rotary plan*. The bulletins are rotated to different choice locations in the market every 30, 60, or 90 days, giving the impression of wide coverage over time.

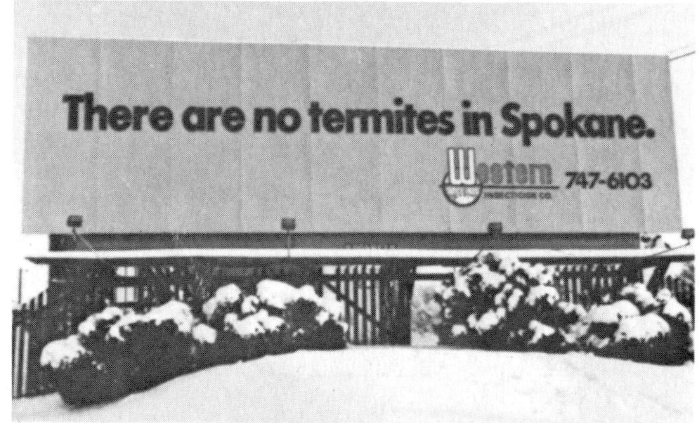

Figure 18–22 The creative opportunities in outdoor are virtually limitless. This award winner from Washington State demonstrates the fun advertisers can have with outdoor.

Transit advertising

Early in the 20th century many famous company names began to emerge. The Campbell Soup Company was one of those; so was Wrigley's Gum. But how did they get their start on the road to becoming household words?

In 1910 Wrigley decided to undertake a new test campaign in Buffalo, New York, because gum had been so difficult to sell there. Wrigley's contacted the Collier Service Company in New York City, which had been established to provide copy and illustration service as well as to sell transit (bus) advertising. At the time Collier employed some of the best writers in America, including F. Scott Fitzgerald and Ogden Nash. Collier's organization developed the famed "spear man," which subsequently became the symbol of chewing gum for generations of Americans.

Wrigley's spear man was then printed on cards and carried on buses throughout Buffalo. The Buffalo program was so successful that it was repeated in city after city across the nation.

In the case of Campbell Soup the company had never used advertising before. Spending its first $5,000 on car card advertising, Campbell contracted to place its advertisements on one third of the surface buses in New York City for one year. After only six months the campaign was so obviously successful that the contract was enlarged to include all surface vehicles in New York City. This produced a 100 percent increase in business, and for 12 years transit advertising was the sole medium used by the company. Campbell had discovered that transit advertising can be "M-m-m-good" (Figure 18–23).

Figure 18–23 Campbell Soup Company started using transit advertising in the early 1900s, and they are still using it 80 years later as shown by this inside card for Campbell's Pork & Beans.

Types of transit advertising

Transit advertising, like standardized outdoor advertising, is referred to as an out-of-home medium. Both include forms of outdoor signs, but they are organized differently. Transit advertising depends on the millions of people who ride on commercial transportation facilities (buses, subways, elevators, commuter trains, trolleys, and airlines) plus pedestrians and auto passengers who see the advertising (Figure 18–24).

Transit advertising actually includes three separate media forms: inside cards; outside posters; and station, platform, and terminal posters.

Inside cards

The standard size of the inside card, placed in a wall rack above the windows, is 11″ by 28″. Four other widths are available in multiples of 14 inches (11″ by 14″, 11″ by 42″, 11″ by 56″, and 11″ by 84″). Cost-conscious advertisers print both sides of the card so it can simply be reversed to change the message, thus saving on paper and shipping charges.

Inside car end posters (in "bulkhead" positions) are usually larger

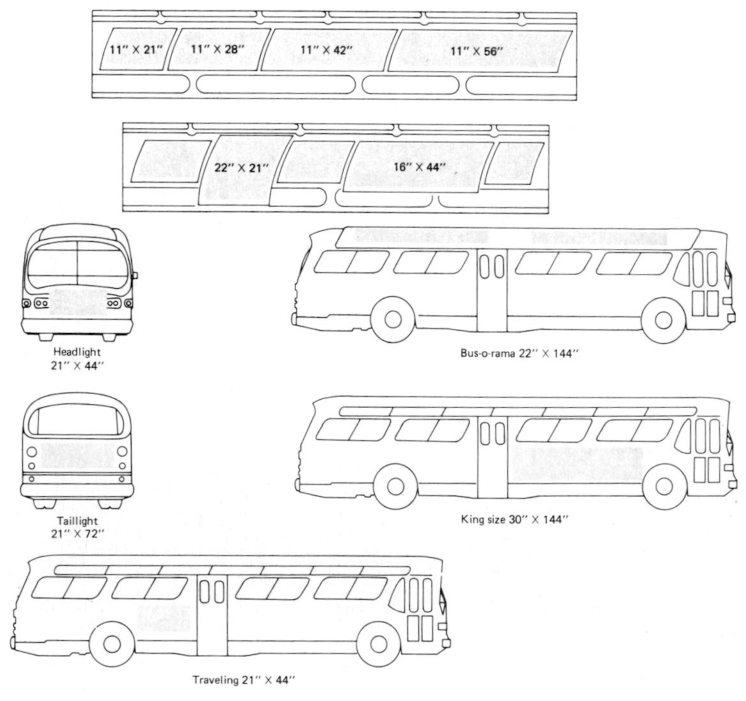

Figure 18–24 Illustrated are the common sizes for inside cards and outside posters available in transit advertising.

and of varying sizes. One common size is 22″ by 21″. Some top-end or over-door cards are 16″ by 39″ or 16″ by 44″. The end and side positions carry a premium rate.

Outside posters

Printed on high-grade cardboard and often varnished to be weather-resistant, the most widely used exterior units are these: (1) side of bus—king size (30″ by 144″), queen size (30″ by 88″), and traveling display (21″ by 72″); (2) rear of bus—taillight spectacular (21″ by 72″); and (3) front of bus—headlights (17″ by 21″ and 21″ by 44″).

Station, platform, and terminal posters

In many bus, subway, and commuter train stations, space is sold for one-sheet, two-sheet, and three-sheet posters. Also, major train and airline terminals offer a variety of special advertising forms that might be compared to outdoor spectaculars. These are usually custom designed and include such attention-getters as floor displays, island showcases, illuminated signs, dioramas (three-dimensional scenes), and clocks with special lighting and moving messages.

Why transit advertising works

Why was Campbell's campaign on bus cards so successful? What was it about transit that helped Wrigley become a household name? The answers to these questions are numerous, and they define the many advantages of transit advertising: high reach, frequency, exposure, and attention values at very low cost.

Transit advertising gives long exposure to the advertiser's message because the average ride is about 25 minutes. It has repetitive value; many people take the same routes day after day. The messages are eagerly read by riders attempting to escape from boredom. Surveys show that readership is high.

The cost is low. This is partly because capital costs are paid for by the fares, with no huge capital investment needed for equipment. The dollar outlay is generally less than for any other medium.

Many riders are on their way to shop downtown and therefore are susceptible to advertising suggestions. Transit cards offer unexcelled color reproduction at relative low cost. Small advertisers are not overshadowed by large ones.

Transit advertising also reaches mass audiences. It offers geographic flexibility and can reach various ethnic or neighborhood groups.

It is a good major market media form that can be used to magnify the total frequency. It permits special constructions and color effects.

While outdoor advertising has been a target of the environmental movement, transit advertising has been one of its beneficiaries. Energy problems have increased social pressure to use public transportation instead of private autos. At the same time, federal subsidies for the transit industry have resulted in larger and better transit systems as well as some new ones.

As the industry has progressed, it has developed more efficient standardization, better research, additional statistical data, and measured circulation, thus making it easier for national advertisers to include transit advertising in their schedules.

National advertisers who have used the medium in recent years have included food and beverage producers, tobacco companies (Figure 18–25), oil companies, financial institutions, proprietary medicines, and of course chewing gum. The medium is especially suitable for reaching middle to lower income, urban consumers, providing supplemental coverage to these groups. Several national advertisers besides Campbell and Wrigley's have used transit advertising for more than 50 years.

Figure 18–25 In this example, More has bought the king size showing, which measures 30″ by 144″. Notice that the smaller traveling display is unsold on this bus.

Transit advertising is about equally popular with local advertisers. Such advertisers as theaters, restaurants, and retailers find it a productive medium for reminders and special announcements.

Disadvantages of transit advertising

Among the weaknesses of transit advertising are its general lack of coverage of some segments of society, such as suburbanites who drive their own cars, rural dwellers, and business and professional people who seldom use mass transportation. Other disadvantages follow:

It lacks the status of an important advertising medium.

Its rush-hour crowds limit the opportunity and ease of reading.

It reaches a nonselective audience, which may not meet the needs of some advertisers.

Cards are so numerous and look so similar that they may be confusing.

The transit vehicle environment, which may be crowded and dirty, may not lend prestige to the product.

The trend to outlying shopping centers means fewer shoppers make trips downtown.

Although transit cards may carry longer messages than billboards, copy is still somewhat limited.

Buying transit advertising

One of the most often cited advantages of transit advertising is the cost per exposure. One of the main reasons Wrigley decided to use transit in its initial Buffalo program was because car card rates were so low. Likewise Campbell's first advertising budget was only $5,000. That wouldn't have gone very far in other media.

Transit advertising's cost per thousand is approximately 13.7 cents in the nation's "A" markets (the 22 largest metropolitan areas in the United States). In fact, outside transit ad costs can be as low as 6 cents per thousand exposures.

The unit of purchase is a showing, also known as a run or service. In transit advertising, a full showing (or no. 100 showing) means that one card will appear in each vehicle in the system. Space may also be purchased as a one-half (or no. 50) showing or a one-quarter (or no. 25) showing. Exterior displays are purchased on a showing basis.

Rates are usually quoted for 30-day showings—with discounts for 3-, 6-, 9-, and 12-month contracts. The advertisers must supply the cards at their own expense.

Cost depends on (1) the length of the showing, (2) the saturation of the showing, and (3) the size of the space. Rates vary extensively, depending primarily on the size of the system.

Rates for specific markets may be obtained from the local transit company, from the American Transit Association's published rate book, or from the SRDS directory, *Transit Advertising Rates and Data*.

Figure 18–26 More cigarettes uses the basic bus approach to transit advertising in this example. That means they have complete domination by buying all the inside space.

Special inside buys

In some cities advertisers may buy all the inside space on a group of buses, thereby gaining complete domination. This buy is called the *basic bus* (Figure 18–26). In addition, pads of business reply cards or coupons (called *take ones*) may be affixed to interior advertisements for an extra charge. This allows passengers to request more detailed information, send in application blanks, or receive some other product benefit.

Special outside buys

Some transit companies offer *bus-o-rama signs*. This is a jumbo roof sign, which is actually a full-color transparency backlighted by fluorescent tubes. Running the length of the bus, it measures 21⅜" by 144¾". Two bus-o-rama positions are on each side of the bus.

A single advertiser may also buy a *total bus*—all the exterior space on a bus including the front, rear, sides, and top. This gives the product message powerful exclusivity.

Some transit companies offer other unique capabilities. With the introduction of new advance-design buses in Houston, for instance, the TDI transit advertising company offered advertisers up to 20 feet of sign space along the street side of the bus. The new, futuristic buses provided a smooth outer surface to which TDI was able to directly apply pressure-sensitive vinyl. Available in several reflective colors and textures, the 30" x 240" vinyl signs offered a versatile alternative to Houston advertisers. In addition, they could be die-cut to any shape within the sign area, so anything from soft drink bottles to carpenter's pencils could travel the streets daily.

To keep advertisers informed of opportunities in transit advertising, the industry has two organizations—the American Transit Association and the Transit Advertising Association. The ATA is the main source of information as it performs research and supplies industry data on the number of vehicles, fares charged, and rider demographics. The TAA is the national trade organization and promotion arm of the industry. Its members represent 80 percent of the transit advertising volume in the United States and Canada.

Summary

Direct-mail advertising includes all forms of advertising sent direct to prospects through the mail. As an advertising medium, it ranks third in dollars spent, surpassed only by newspapers and television.

Next to the personal sales call, direct mail is the most effective way an advertiser can put a message in front of a prospect. It is also the most expensive on a cost per exposure basis. As an advertising medium, it offers several advantages. These include selectivity, intensive coverage, flexibility, control, personal impact, exclusivity, and performance.

The drawbacks to direct mail include the high cost per exposure, the delays often experienced in delivery, the lack of other content support for the advertising message, and certain problems with selectivity.

Direct-mail advertising comes in many forms: sales letters, brochures, and even handwritten postcards all qualify as direct-mail advertising. The message can be as short as one sentence or dozens of pages long.

The direct-mail list is the heart of the medium because each list actually defines a market segment. There are three types of direct-mail lists: house lists, mail response lists, and compiled lists. Their prices vary according to their quality.

Of the major advertising media, outdoor advertising offers the lowest cost per message delivered. In addition, the medium offers other attractive features. These include instant broad coverage (reach), very high frequency, great flexibility, and impact. Drawbacks include the necessity for brief messages, the limitations for reaching narrow demographic groups, and the lead time required. In addition, the high initial preparation costs and difficulty of physically inspecting each billboard discourage some advertisers.

The standardized outdoor advertising industry consists of about 600 local and regional plant operators. National advertising comprises the bulk of outdoor business.

Standard outdoor advertising structures come in two forms: the poster panel and the bulletin. The poster panel is the basic form, the least costly per unit, and available in a variety of sizes. Painted bulletins are meant for long use and are usually placed in the best locations where traffic is heavy and visibility is good. Some advertisers overcome the relative higher expense of painted bulletins by using a rotary plan.

Transit advertising offers the features of high reach, frequency, exposure, and attention values at very low cost. It furthermore gives long exposure to the advertiser's message and offers repetitive value and good geographic flexibility. In addition, advertisers have a wide choice in the size of space used.

Its disadvantages, of course, are numerous. It does not cover some segments of society, it reaches a nonselective audience, it lacks prestige, and copy is still somewhat limited.

Still, transit advertising is very popular because of its extremely low cost per exposure. In fact, in some markets transit advertising can cost as little as 6 cents per thousand exposures. Cost depends on the length of the showing, the saturation of the showing, and the size of the space.

Questions for review

1. What was Aaron Montgomery Ward's contribution to advertising?
2. What are the differences between direct-mail and direct response advertising?
3. Although direct mail offers the advantage of selectivity, what are the associated problems?
4. What are the three types of mailing lists in the order of their importance?
5. What are the costs associated with conducting a direct-mail campaign?
6. What advertising objectives is the outdoor medium mostly suitable for?
7. Do you feel outdoor would be an effective advertising medium for a politician? Why?
8. What is the difference between a poster panel and a painted bulletin?
9. Why is transit advertising considered three separate media forms?
10. What characteristics make transit advertising work for advertisers?

19

Sales promotion and supplementary media

When Thom McAn Shoe Company introduced its JOX line of athletic shoes in the mid-1970s, Americans were buying about 18 million pairs of noncanvas athletic shoes a year. By the late 1970s, annual sales had more than tripled to 61.5 million pairs annually, and the company's JOX brand was then running third in the share of the market.

Thom McAn owns and operates 1,100 "shoestands" and also distributes its products through wholesalers and dealers who carry other lines. Aiming at families with children aged 9 to 12, Thom McAn wanted to build traffic, generate favorable publicity, boost sales and brand awareness, and improve both its corporate and brand image. This major task required substantially more than the basic product advertisements and dealer co-op programs Thom McAn had used in the past. They felt that a major sales promotion campaign was called for to accomplish their objectives.

McAn's advertising agency, Robert Landau and Associates, had developed the concept of a "Pitch, Hit & Run" youth competition for the Major League Baseball Promotion Corporation, which represents all major league owners. The "Pitch, Hit & Run" program was comparable to Ford Motor Company's highly successful "Punt, Pass & Kick" football competition. So Thom McAn decided to tie JOX in with the promotion and sponsor it.

The PH&R competition involved the joint cooperation of the National Recreation and Park Association, the Major League Baseball Promotion Corporation, and the President's Council on Physical Fitness and Sports. Entry forms were made available at 1,500 JOX dealers. No purchase was necessary, but a parent was required to accompany the boy or girl to the store to sign and return the entry form. Research had shown that one of three things happens when a parent and child enter a shoe store. The child gets shoes, the adult gets shoes, or they both get shoes.

Thom McAn staged a full-scale $1 million promotion, with another $750,000 worth of media donated by the networks and major league baseball clubs. The National Recreation and Park Association supervised the competition at local, district, divisional, and final levels. The Major League Baseball Promotion Corporation aided in the divisional competition in major league baseball stadiums and with the final competition held in Yankee Stadium prior to the All-Star game. Each entrant received a 32-page booklet containing a conditioning and warm-up exercise program recommended by the President's Council on Physical Fitness & Sports and playing tips from leading baseball stars. Promotion kits were distributed to participating dealers at $200, less than cost, and the dealers were urged to increase their JOX orders.

The campaign included: "Sign-up" TV commercials featuring baseball star Rod Carew; copy for scorecards, electronic scoreboards, and game programs at major league parks; full-page ads in *Boys' Life* and other publications; tags in Thom McAn newspaper ads; and televising of the competition—all supported by major national publicity (Figure 19–1).

The results were outstanding. Sales of JOX for kids increased 50 percent over the same period in the preceding year, and Thom McAn adopted "Pitch, Hit & Run" as an annual event.[1]

Role of sales promotion

What was the effect of Thom McAn's "Pitch, Hit & Run" promotion? What would have been the effect on JOX sales without the promotion, if McAn had simply advertised the shoes? The answers to these questions are the key to understanding what sales promotion is and how it works.

The purpose of all marketing tools such as advertising, public relations, and sales promotion is to help the company achieve its marketing objectives (see Chapter 6). Specific marketing objectives may include the following:

1. To introduce new products.
2. To induce present customers to buy more.
3. To attract new customers.
4. To combat competition.
5. To maintain sales in off-seasons.
6. To increase retail inventories so more goods may be sold.

As we know, the marketing strategy the company uses to achieve these objectives may include a high degree of personal selling. It may also include nonpersonal selling activities such as advertising the company's products in the national media or in trade journals to its dealers. It may include public relations activities such as feature stories and magazine interviews. Or it may include a major sales promotion campaign such as McAn's "Pitch, Hit & Run" program.

Sales promotion is used to help produce and increase sales. It is sometimes referred to as *supplementary* to advertising and personal selling because it binds the two together, making both more effective. In reality, however, it is far more than supplementary since it may now represent as much as 60 percent of the typical marketing budget versus 40 percent for advertising.

By definition, *sales promotion is a direct inducement offering extra incentive all along the marketing route—from manufacturers through distribution channels to consumers—to accelerate the movement of the product from the producer to the consumer.* Thus, there are three important things to remember about sales promotion.

1. It is an *acceleration tool* designed to speed up the selling process.
2. It normally involves a *direct inducement* (such as money, prizes, extra products, gifts, or specialized information), which provides *extra incentive* to buy, visit the store, request literature, or take some other action.
3. It may be used *anywhere along the marketing route:* from the manufacturer to the dealer, from dealer to consumer, or from manufacturer to consumer.

Sales promotion is used to *maximize* sales volume. It does this, in some cases, by motivating consumers who have been unmoved by other advertising efforts or, in other cases, by motivating particular brand selection when all brands are considered more or less equal. In short, sales promotion ideally generates sales that would not otherwise be achieved.

Figure 19–1 Thom McAn's JOX promotion featured magazine ads, television commercials, and window displays telling youngsters where they could register for the competition.

Studying the Thom McAn example, can you tell what marketing objectives the company wished to achieve? How well did the "Pitch, Hit & Run" promotion satisfy the definition of sales promotion?

Sales promotion: The sales accelerator

S. C. Johnson & Son, manufacturers of Johnson's Wax, has been a leader in the car, floor, and furniture wax business for many years. When that market appeared to level off in the 1960s, Johnson decided to turn to the health and beauty aids market for additional business. It successfully introduced Edge Shaving Creme in the late 60s, but that was followed by a number of dismal failures.

Finally, the company developed a superior hair creme rinse, Agree, with an extra benefit that "helps stop the greasies" (Figure 19–2). It was priced competitively against the market leader, Revlon's Flex, Balsam & Protein.

However, the company was aware that its Johnson's Wax sales force had little experience with this highly competitive, fast-turning, dog-eat-dog product category. And retailers, who had witnessed Johnson's other product failures, would not be inclined to give much shelf space to a new Johnson entry.

Johnson's introductory objectives for Agree, therefore, were rather heady: to rapidly promote enough sales of the new product to (1) achieve and maintain market leadership and (2) create a positive image for Johnson as a marketer of personal care products with its trade customers as well as with consumers. To succeed, Johnson had to develop a sales promotion strategy for Agree that would *push* the product into the dealer pipeline and also induce consumers to try the product, thereby *pulling* it through the pipe. After testing the product's acceptance with consumers and testing possible sampling techniques, Johnson prepared to launch Agree.

Prepacked floor displays, which would hold over 7 million 29-cent, 2-ounce, trial-size bottles, were constructed and shipped to retailers. The dealers were offered introductory price allowances, distribution allowances, and advertising dollar allowances just to stock the product and set up the prepacked displays.

Then samples were distributed to consumers—31 million samples—and 41 million coupons allowing 15 cents off on the purchase of the product. This alone catapulted Agree into a leadership position by generating rapid awareness and trial among its target group of women aged 14 to 30. And to top it all off, the company ran 300 prime-time network TV commercials, ads in 26 leading magazines, and the heaviest creme rinse radio campaign in history.

In all, the company spent over $17 million to introduce Agree. Within five months the product grabbed a 20 percent share of market and was running neck and neck against Revlon's Flex. A consumer attitude study revealed that awareness of Agree was at a whopping 77 percent, with trial of the product at 38 percent and repurchase intent estimated at 78 percent.

As a result, Johnson not only achieved its leadership position with

Agree, but it also earned its spurs with the trade, which should make its next product entry infinitely easier.[2]

Balancing push and pull strategy

How does a company go from 0 to 20 percent share of market in creme rinse conditioners in only five months? Simply by spending lots of money? Hardly.

Johnson started with a superior product. Then they tested it along with the levels of advertising and sales promotion that would make it go. They developed a national strategy based on their test results.

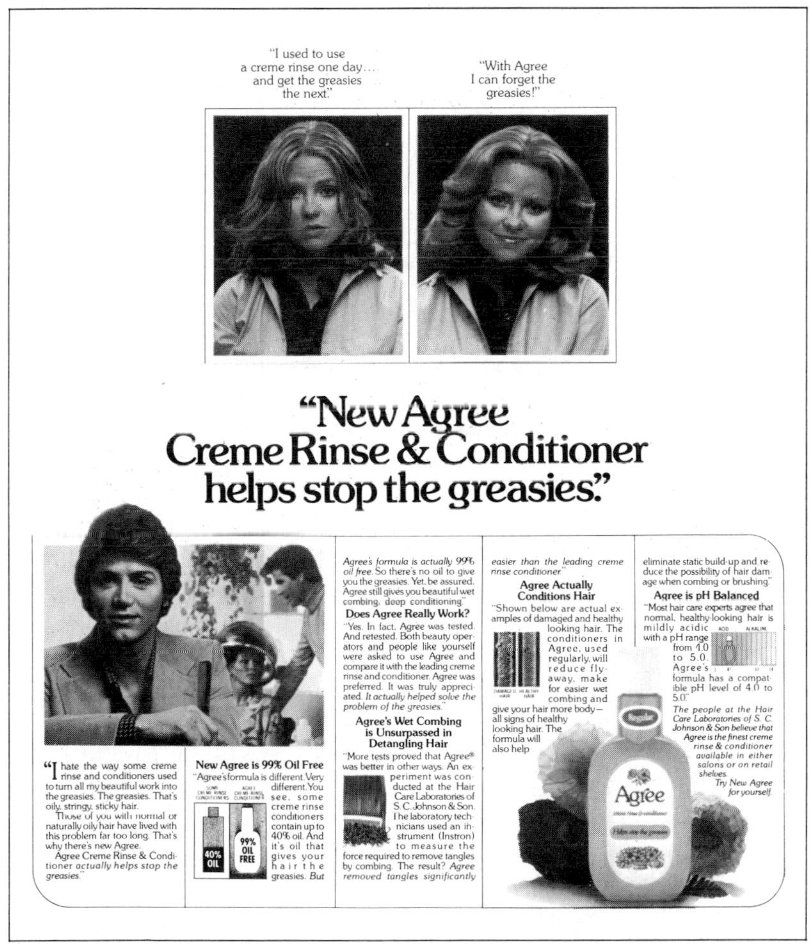

Figure 19–2 S. C. Johnson & Son put $17 million into marketing its new Agree hair creme rinse and conditioner. This effectively catapulted the product into a leadership position. The power of its campaign was as much in its trade promotion as in its consumer promotion.

This strategy would ensure that consumers who sought the product would be able to find it in the stores. And it ensured that dealers who bought the product would have customers wanting to try it.

Then, and only then, did Johnson commit the very big dollars—$6 million in advertising, over $6 million in sampling, and another $5 million in trade promotion—to its assault on the market.

What do you suppose would have been the result if Johnson had not spent money on the trade promotion? On the sampling? On the advertising? How vital was each of these individual elements to accomplishing Agree's success? Do you think any of them could have been left out?

Push strategy techniques

The success of Agree was dependent to a great extent on the cooperation of retail dealers. To get this cooperation, though, S. C. Johnson had to offer substantial inducements in the form of introductory price allowances, other dollar-saving devices, and usable product displays.

Any manufacturer who markets through normal channels must secure the cooperation of retailers. This sometimes is easier said than done because the retailers, in turn, have specific problems of their own. In today's crowded supermarkets, shelf space and floor space are hard to come by. Department stores, in order to maintain their own images, have been forced to set standards for manufacturers' displays. This means that retailers are often unable to use the special racks, sales aids, and promotional literature supplied by the manufacturers. As a consequence, there is substantial waste of material that is thrown away or left unused in a stockroom. Many retailers are pressed for time and lack the personnel to effectively use the flood of manufacturers' sales promotion material. So packages of promotion literature remain unopened, and displays remain unassembled.

Retailers often say their needs are "different," the material does not fit their market, they lack the space for displays and the time to assemble them, and other reasons. True or not, such contentions reveal a need for promotion people to spend time in the field and for distributors' and manufacturers' salespeople to report their findings thoroughly to headquarters.

Despite such problems, many manufacturers do an excellent job of using push strategy in sales promotion, using a wide range of promotional programs closely keyed to retailer needs. One example of this is the dealer plan book used in the automotive industry. Its many color pages present a well-organized and complete selection of advertising and promotion tools—from window and showroom display materials to catalogs, ad kits, wall plaques, and color charts to make the dealer's job easier.

Another example of a far-sighted program was that of an appliance manufacturer who received dealer and distributor complaints that they were under a constant barrage of separate and unrelated bulletins and letters from different factory departments concerning new products, display material, promotion booklets, service problems, policy, ad mats, and countless other topics. The manufacturer solved this

People in advertising

William A. Robinson

President
William A. Robinson, Inc.

Sales promotion specialist William A. Robinson is founder and president of William A. Robinson, Inc., Northbrook, Illinois, one of the nation's leading marketing services agencies. Since its inception in 1961, the Robinson agency has developed successful promotional programs for clients like Procter & Gamble, Heublein, Zenith, Colgate-Palmolive, Lipton, Sara Lee, Borden, and Frito-Lay.

"Our goal is to move products and purchasers closer together," said Robinson. "We begin by examining the client's brand—its marketing strategy, selling proposition, and promotional stance. Next, we look at the brand's objectives—its sales and share projections, distribution, and communications goals." Armed with this, he said, "We determine how to sell more of the product."

Yet sales promotion doesn't always work, Robinson warned. "If a product is unacceptable to consumers," he said, "promotion won't change that. If an established product is experiencing declining sales, promotion won't turn it around. Promotion can't create an 'image' for a brand. And a single promotion won't motivate consumers to buy a product over a long period of time."

What promotion *can* do, Robinson explained, is offer consumers an immediate inducement to buy. It can also prompt a consumer who knows nothing about a product to try it—and to buy it again. Promotion can make current users buy more of a brand or buy larger sizes. And it can motivate salespeople, wholesalers, and retailers to get squarely behind a product.

"Consumers today are exposed to more advertising than ever before," said Robinson. "Thus, it takes more impact to get their attention in the marketplace."

To determine what type of sales promotion works best for a product, the Robinson agency tests the value of various promotion techniques from their inception, using focus groups, interviews, and field surveys. "We set measurable goals and assign specific responsibilities for their accomplishment," said Robinson, citing the 12 promotion techniques most often used. "*Samplings* and *coupons* are best for inducing consumers to try a product. *Price-off* packings can prompt current users to buy more. *Refund offers* reinforce brand loyalty. *Bonus packs* can convert triers to users. *Trade allowances* in combination with *trade communication programs* can increase distribution. *Contests* and *sweepstakes* can enhance brand image. *Premiums* can be used in various ways," Robinson said. "On or near the package, they can attract new triers. Free in the mail, they often increase purchases. When self-liquidated, they can enable low-cost store displays. And *stamp plans* and *continuity premiums*, can create differences among parity products and develop loyal users."

"Every promotion technique has well-defined strengths and weaknesses," Robinson observed. "By maneuvering these techniques, alone or in combination, we determine the most effective strategy."

Author of the column "Robinson on Sales Promotion" featured in *Advertising Age*, Robinson also created the "Best Promotions" program with *Ad Age* that each year highlights the annual EUR-AM Conference and has been shown throughout the United States and abroad. A college educator, formerly on the faculty of Northwestern University, today Robinson teaches a popular course in sales promotion at Michigan State University.

He has participated in Creativity and Promotion Workshops sponsored by *Advertising Age*, the American Marketing Association Spring Seminar, the APAA Annual Show, the National Conference of the American Academy of Advertising, and Boston Ad Club programs. Robinson has also presented numerous seminars for a host of companies on the trends and future of sales promotion.

Honored as Chicago's Sales Promotion Man of the Year in 1965, Robinson is former president of the Chicago Sales Promotion Executives Association.

Figure 19–3 The "General Motors Video Center," reflects the trend toward audiovisuals. By viewing the screen, prospective buyers can receive information on new-model cars through 1985; the unit's special features include random access, multiple languages, and remote control.

problem by incorporating all such necessary information into one compact monthly newsletter, a newsy publication that the dealers and distributors actually looked forward to receiving each month.

Manufacturers use many sales promotion techniques to offer dealers extra incentives to purchase, stock, and display their products (Figure 19–3). Among the more common are the following.

Dealer displays Also referred to as point-of-purchase advertising, these in-store displays, counter stands, and special racks are designed to provide the retailer with ready-made, professionally designed vehicles for selling more of the featured products. A well-designed dealer display can induce a dealer to stock more of the product than he or she normally would (see the L'eggs example in Chapter 14).

Deals Trade deals offer limited discounts on the cost of the product, special displays at reduced charges, or other dollar inducements to sell the product. Trade deals must comply with the Robinson-Patman Act by being offered on an equal basis to all dealers.

Dealer premiums Prizes and gifts are often used to get retail dealers and salespeople to reach specific sales goals or to stock or display a certain product.

Cooperative advertising Local advertising expenses are often shared by the retailer, distributor, and manufacturer through cooperative advertising plans (Figure 19–4). The manufacturer may repay 50 or 100 percent of the dealer's advertising costs or some other amount based on sales. Under the Robinson-Patman Act, the same terms must be extended to all distributors and dealers.

Sometimes special cooperative allowances are made to introduce new lines, advertise certain products, or combat competitive activity.

Advertising materials In addition to sharing the cost of advertising, many manufacturers provide extensive prepared advertising materials: ad mats, slicks, glossy photos, sample radio commercials, preprinted inserts, and others. Most appliance manufacturers, for instance, supply the material and insist that it be used for their dealers to qualify for co-op advertising money.

Push money Retail salespeople are encouraged in many ways to push the sale of particular products. One of these inducements is PM (push money), also called "spiffs." For example, when you buy a pair of shoes, frequently the salesperson will push special cushioned insoles or shoe polish or some other high-profit "extra." For each bottle of shoe polish he or she sells, the salesperson may receive a 25- to 50-cent spiff, depending on the product.

Collateral material In industrial sales and high-ticket consumer product sales, it is usually difficult to get a purchase decision from the buyer without giving considerable data on every aspect of the product. For this reason, dealers request catalogs, manuals, technical specification sheets, brochures, presentation charts, films, audiovisual materials, or other sales aids available from the manufacturer. As a category these are all referred to as collateral sales material.

Company conventions and dealer meetings To introduce new products, sales promotion programs, or advertising campaigns, dealer meetings are held by most major manufacturers. These are also opportune times to conduct sales and service training sessions. Meetings are frequently promoted as opportunities to learn and also share in comaraderie with other company salespeople and executives. As such, they may be used as a dynamic sales promotion tool by the manufacturer.

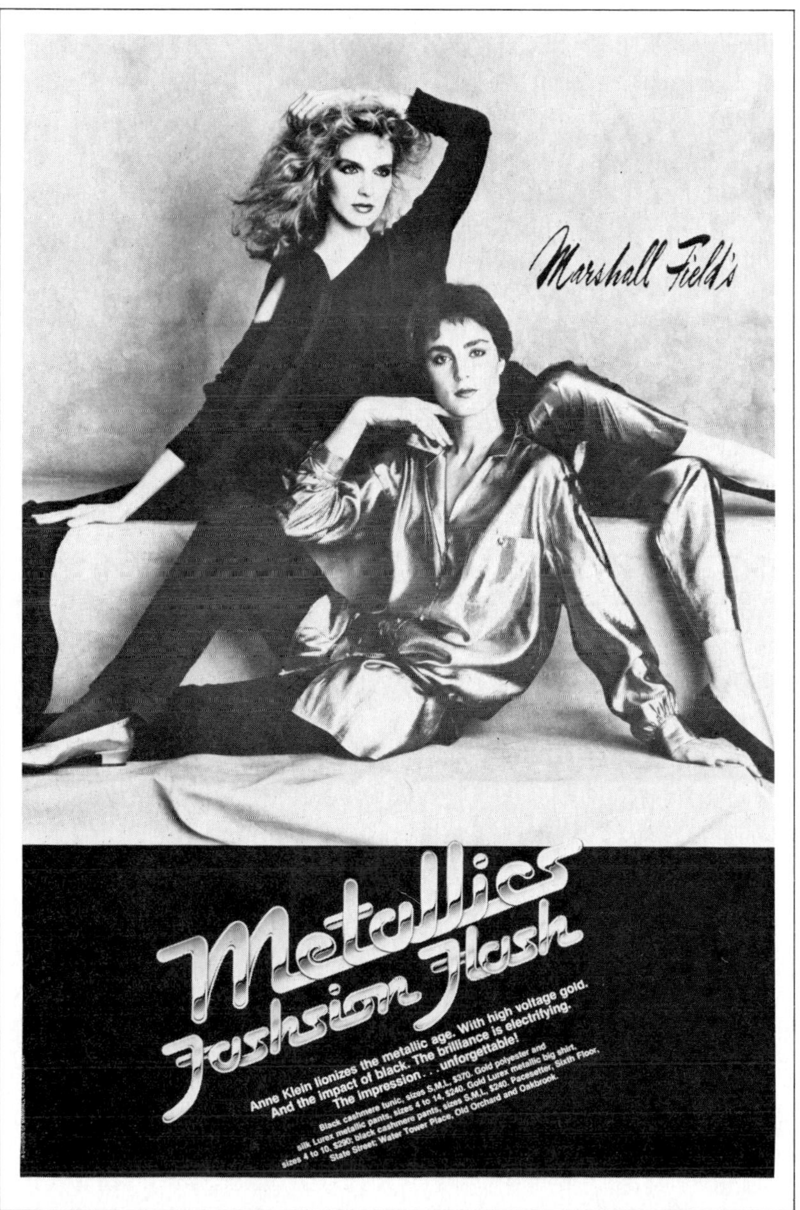

Figure 19–4 Department stores use co-op funds for advertising wearing apparel.

As we shall discuss in Chapter 21, "Business Advertising," much of the advertising created and placed by companies today is invisible to the consumer because it appears only in trade journals read by particular businesspeople. Likewise, the push techniques of sales promotion are usually invisible. These techniques are used to help accelerate sales by offering inducements to dealers, retailers, and salespeople. If the inducements are successful, the product will be given more shelf space, special display, or extra interest and enthusiasm by salespeople. The difference between no interest and extra interest can spell the difference between product failure and success in today's competitive marketplace.

Pull strategy techniques

The most visible forms of sales promotion are those aimed at the ultimate purchaser of the product. In the Thom McAn example at the beginning of this chapter, sales of JOX shoes were accelerated by giving youngsters the incentive to come into the store to sign up for a national baseball competition.

In the case of Agree, 31 million free samples of the product were distributed. That is a very strong, albeit expensive, inducement to try a new product. In addition, 41 million cents-off coupons were distributed—another strong inducement to try the product.

The list of pull techniques used to accelerate the sales or products is long and constantly growing as new ones are always being devised. Some of the most common and successful include the following.

Sampling As in the case of Agree, the success of a sampling campaign depends heavily on the merits of the product. This is the most costly of all sales promotions. It offers consumers a free trial, hoping to convert them to habitual use. To be successful, sampling must deal with a product that is available in small sizes and purchased frequently. Also, the sampling effort should be supported by advertising.

Samples may be distributed by mail, door to door, or via coupon advertising. They may be given free or for a small charge.

Sampling in stores is sometimes less expensive than by mail. But retailers normally are not aggressive in their promotion. Sometimes samples are distributed with related items, but then their distribution is restricted to those who buy the other product.

Many times samples are distributed to specific markets such as cosmetics to college coeds, new drugs to physicians (push), or shampoo to beauty shop operators (push).

Several firms provide specialized sample distribution services, including Welcome Wagon, Gift Pax, and Reuben H. Donnelly Corporation.

Cents-off promotions A common offer is that made by Campbell Soup of 10 cents off on a can of soup. A variation was the L&M cigarette refund of $3 for proof of purchase of a carton. Care must be taken to specify that price reductions are for a limited time only, or it may be difficult to raise the price later. Such offers take different forms including basic cents-off packages, one-cent sales, free offers, and boxtop refunds.

Special problems may be created by cents-off packages where the retailer already has merchandise in stock marked at a higher price or does not want to lower the price.

Cents-off coupons A coupon is a certificate with a stated value, which is presented to the retail store for a price reduction of a specified item. Coupons may be distributed in newspapers, magazines, door to door, on packages, and by direct mail (Figure 19–5). The retailer has to sort the coupons, submit them to the manufacturer or a coupon clearinghouse, and is then reimbursed for the coupon's face value plus a handling charge.

According to Beverly Simonelli, vice president of Coupon Clearing Service, the nation's second largest coupon clearinghouse, manufacturers redeemed over 2.4 billion coupons in 1980 to promote their products to consumers. However, she points out, fraudulent submission of coupons is now costing the industry some $100 million annually.

Coupon fraud comes in a variety of forms, including counterfeiting and submitting coupons for products that were never purchased. The cost of this is borne by the manufacturers at first but ultimately by the consumer in the price paid for products.

Industry concern, according to Simonelli, has risen to such a point that, as a service to grocery manufacturers, Coupon Clearing Service has developed unique, highly sophisticated techniques for detecting misredemption by retailers and consumers. These techniques have greatly aided manufacturers, law enforcement agencies, and postal authorities in their efforts to crack down on coupon cheaters.

Figure 19–5 Even airlines have been known to give coupons especially to encourage customers to return after settlement of a strike.

Combination offers Food and drug marketers have successfully used combination offers such as a razor and a package of blades or a toothbrush with a tube of toothpaste at a reduced price for the two. For best results the items should be related. Sometimes a combination offer may be used to introduce a new product by tying its purchase to an established product at a special price.

Premiums A premium is an item that is offered free or at a bargain price to encourage the consumer to buy an advertised product. Premiums are intended to produce quick sales.

A good premium should have strong appeal and value and be useful or unusual. Also, it should be easily handled and mailed. It may be mailed free, or for a certain amount of money, upon receipt of proof of purchase (boxtop or label). Or it may be given with the product at the time of purchase.

Usually the consumer pays the cost of the premium plus handling charges. This is known as a *self-liquidating premium.* The seller does not attempt to make a profit on such a premium but only tries to break even. Stanley Urlaub, the president of Bentleys Bank Ltd., even recommends the use of premiums to promote major investment programs to investors. He once gave Stetson cowboy hats to participants in a cattle-feeding tax shelter.

A variation of the self-liquidating premium is one distributed by the retailer. It may be a traffic-building or continuity premium given weekly to customers who return to the store to complete their sets of dinnerware or encyclopedias, for example.

In-pack premiums, such as plastic toys for children, are popular in the food field, especially cereals. *On-pack premiums* (those attached to the outside of the package) have good impulse value, but they may encourage pilferage. Another drawback is that they sometimes make it difficult for the grocer to stack the product on the shelves. (See the Ad Lab.)

Coupon premiums, which require customers to save and collect in-pack coupons for later redemption of valuable premiums, can create great consumer loyalty. For instance, one long-time user of this device, Brown & Williamson Tobacco Corporation, consistently receives as many as 2 million Raleigh coupons daily from repeat cigarette customers who send for more than $10 million worth of premiums annually.

The 10 commandments of creative promotion

Spelling out the commandments may help you see why creativity isn't—and shouldn't be—the exclusive jurisdiction of creative directors, writers, and art directors. You'll also find it handy for developing promotions and reviewing them.

1. Thou shalt set specific objectives. Undisciplined or undirected creative work is a frivolous waste. The first step in developing a promotion is to exercise your creativity by setting meaningful goals. And this is the place where brand managers, account executives, and researchers can get into the creative act. Lack of creativity at this stage results in vague and useless directions—and wasted time. You've got to focus. Do you want trial, or to increase brand awareness, off-shelf merchandise displays, build up trade inventories, etc.? Setting realistic, specific objectives is a quarter of the creative battle.

2. Thou shalt know how basic promotion techniques work. Knowing what a promotion technique can and can't do is another quarter of the creative battle. And this is knowledge that clients and account executives should have as well as creatives. You don't use a sweepstakes to encourage multiple purchases or a refund offer to get new users. A price-off deal cannot reverse a brand's downward sales trend. A sweepstakes can increase brand awareness. A refund can get off-shelf merchandise display at modest costs.

3. Thou shalt have simple, attention-getting copy. This is on the head of the copywriter, usually. I say usually because there are times where promotional concepts become so complex it's impossible to write a simple or even understandable headline. It's directly on the writer's head when she or he takes a powerful offer such as "Save 75¢" and tries to get cute, burying the selling proposition in the process.

4. Thou shalt lay out contemporary, easy-to-track graphics. This is on the head of the art director, except when he or she gets 500 words of text and 20 items to illustrate on a quarter-page of a free-standing insert.

5. Thou shalt clearly communicate your concept. This could be redundant to the third and fourth commandments, but there are times when promotion objectives are contradictory, or when a promotional ad is trying to carry a product advertising message plus promotional messages, and things get hairy. In this case, creative failure may not be blamed solely on the "creatives."

6. Thou shalt reinforce your brand's advertising message. When a brand has a big budget, long-term ad campaign it seems sort of dumb not to try to tie a promotion to it. For example, Smirnoff vodka has been running an ad campaign showing unusual party situations—a cookout in the snow with the line "Cookout—Smirnoff Style." Originally, Smirnoff ran a $25,000 contest called, "Contest—Smirnoff Style" and required entries to have a snapshot of an unusual party and a title for it. It takes an extra shot of creativity on everyone's part to tie a prize

Numerous federal and state laws govern premiums. Most important, these laws restrict the use of the word *free*. A free offer must be absolutely that—with no extra cost. Nor can the price of the offering product be increased to cover the cost of the premium. This must be done at the outset—in conjunction with the word *free*.

Food and Drug Administration regulations govern in-pack premiums, and Federal Trade Commission rules apply to in-pack coupons. Other legal factors to be reckoned with are postal laws, sales taxes, misrepresentation of premiums, and lottery regulations.

Contests and sweepstakes A *contest* offers prizes based on the skill of the entrants. A *sweepstakes* offers prizes based on a chance drawing of entrants' names (Figure 19–6). A *game* has the chance element of a sweepstakes but is conducted over a longer time. Games include local bingo-type games designed to build store traffic. Their big marketing advantage is that customers must make repeat visits to the dealer to continue playing.

---

or premium in with advertising, but it sure makes your marketing bucks work harder.

7. Thou shalt support the brand's positioning and image. What would you think about Kraft offering a recipe book of potent drink recipes or Marlboro offering pantyhose free in the mail? Especially for image-sensitive brands and categories—a family-oriented Kraft, a rugged Marlboro, or ultrapremium Chivas Regal—it's important to get creative about supporting positioning and image. You would not, for example, select a pantyhose premium for Marlboro because your purchasing agent located a warehouse full of hose offered at discount prices.

8. Thou shalt coordinate your promotional efforts with other marketing plans. Responsibility for this falls on a lot more people than creatives. I'm talking about things like timing a consumer promotion to break simultaneously with a big trade allowance, or using a promotion to get trial for a product improvement or line extension that's being introduced with a big new ad campaign. Don't schedule a promotion that requires a lengthy sell-in pitch to the trade when your salespeople are scheduled to go to a national sales convention for a week. Let the right hand know what the left hand is doing, and be creative about scheduling and planning.

9. Thou shalt know the mediums you work through. Here we're talking about media directors, brand managers, account executives, and the creatives all getting into the act. Should you run a promotion with only magazine or newspaper ad support, or should you carry the whole thing through point-of-sale display? Or both? Maybe delivering samples through point-of-sale displays—as salable samples—is more effective and efficient than door-to-door distribution. If you're going with point-of-sale material, what's the strongest type of display for your objectives? Motion? Shelf-talkers? In print, what's the best publication to reach your target audience? There are a lot of creative judgments to be made by a lot more than creatives.

10. Thou shalt know when to break the other nine commandments. This is the ultimate creative exercise. It takes a confidently creative person to know when breaking any of the above rules is really the smartest way to go. It will increase redemption rates and sales. Creatively applying a technique or combination of techniques to meet stated objectives is critical to a successful promotion.

Laboratory application

Thou shalt discuss these 10 commandments with specific reference to the Agree story presented earlier in the chapter.

Sailor Jack and the legendary toy surprise

The sale of Cracker Jack packages with toy prizes began in 1912. Early toy surprises included handpainted metal whistles, spin tops, pins, watches, paper games, puzzles, and yo-yos. In 1915, for one year only, baseball cards were inserted into the packages. These rare cards, which include such greats as Ty Cobb, are prized by collectors; a complete set sells for over $500.

Research has shown that the toy surprise idea is the key to the continued popularity of Cracker Jack. The little prizes are the number one reason why most people buy the product. In fact, with production at 400 million boxes annually, Cracker Jack is now the world's largest user of toys, not to mention popcorn. Over the years, Cracker Jack has distributed 16 billion toys worldwide.

Here comes Sailor Jack

According to company sources, the famous Jack the Sailor Boy character first appeared in ads in 1916 as a patriotic gesture, but proved so popular that he was incorporated into the package design in 1919. Over the years, the box has been updated and modernized a number of times, but Sailor Jack has always played a prominent role in packaging and displays.

The super toy surprise

In many ways, Cracker Jack's current "Super Toy Surprise" program is the culmination of its 68 years of toy surprises. Comedians from Amos & Andy on have played with the idea of finding a diamond ring in a Cracker Jack package. Don Jagoda Associates, a Westbury, New York, promotion company, suggested an in-pack sweepstakes which would offer popular toys as prizes plus a grand prize with adult appeal. What emerged was the Cracker Jack $500,000 Instant Winner Super Toy Surprise promotion. Don Jagoda Associates also handled the legal technicalities associated with the sweepstakes, establishing the mechanics for inserting the Instant Winner cards in Cracker Jack boxes, and receiving and processing winning card claims.

During the first half of 1980, 57,000 boxes of Cracker Jack include winning coupons good for five grand prizes of Mazda station wagons filled with Mattel toys and worth over $10,000 each; 100 first prizes of Mattel's "World of Barbie" or "Hot Wheels" toys; other prizes include Mattel's "Spinout" tricycles, "Magical Musical Things," and "Barbie" dolls. All the toys are worth at least $25 each. In sheer value of prizes, it's the biggest promotion ever conducted by a confection or snack company.

The promotion, backed by the biggest advertising budget in confection industry history ($6.5 million), was expected to increase sales and market share significantly in both the snack and confection areas. Cracker Jack TV commercials by Grey Advertising reached 90 percent of U.S. households for a total of 9 billion impressions during prime time, daytime, and children's programming.

Additional marketing support included a Sunday newspaper supplement ad which featured a rub-off instant winner coupon, P-O-P displays, and a nationwide publicity campaign by Ketchum MacLeod & Grove. Supermarket displays (by Warner P. Simpson Company, Columbus, Ohio) featured the world's largest box of Cracker Jack (3 × 5 feet) with sweepstakes forms. In the third quarter, there was a back-to-school display, and retailers received free Cracker Jack lunch boxes.

Cracker Jack case sales (moved through supermarkets) have risen from 26.8 million in 1977 to 31.74 million in 1979. Approximately 400 million boxes are now sold each year. Since entering the candy business over 100 years ago, it is estimated that Cracker Jack has sold more than 18 billion boxes. Nearly every American has sampled Cracker Jack at least once in his or her life—a statistic that any consumer goods marketer envies. Indeed, Cracker Jack is as American as apple pie and baseball. Maybe even more American than apple pie, which was *not* immortalized in the 1908 song, "Take Me Out to the Ballgame": ". . . take me out to the crowd. Buy me some peanuts and Cracker Jack. I don't care if I ever get back. . . ."

Laboratory applications

1. What other products can you name that have successfully used in-pack premiums such as toys to promote sales?
2. What products can you suggest that also lend themselves to this type of promotion?

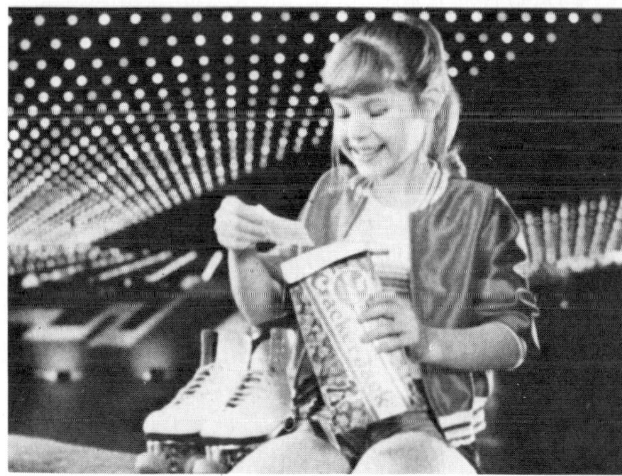

Thirty-second TV ad by Grey Advertising shows Cracker Jack pack in action.

Both contests and sweepstakes have the common purpose of encouraging consumption of the product by creating consumer involvement. These devices are highly popular and pull millions of entries. (See the Ad Lab.) Usually contest entrants are required to send in some proof of purchase such as a boxtop or label. For more expensive products, the contestant may only have to visit the dealer to pick up an entry blank.

In recent years sweepstakes and games have become more popular than contests. They are much easier to enter and take less time than contests and, therefore, have greater appeal for the average person. Sweepstakes require care in following all the laws relating to lotteries. No purchase can be required as a condition for entry, or else the sweepstakes becomes a lottery and therefore illegal. All postal laws must be obeyed in planning contests and sweepstakes.

Figure 19–6 Some advertisers combine coupons with sweepstakes to create instant sales as well as customer involvement with the product.

To encourage a large number of entries, sponsors try to keep their contests as simple as possible. The prize structure must be clearly stated and rules clearly defined. National contests and sweepstakes are handled and judged by independent, professional contest firms.

Contests and sweepstakes must be promoted and advertised. To assure dealer cooperation, many of them require the entrant to name the dealer. In such cases, dealer prizes may also be given.

Lotteries Lotteries are contests in which *prizes* are won by *chance* and where an element of *consideration* is present—for example, the payment of $1 for a lottery ticket. Lotteries and advertisements of lotteries are illegal in most states as well as in interstate commerce. What comprises the *consideration* may be the deciding factor in whether a contest and the advertising for it are legal. For example, some states interpret "consideration" as the requirement that money be paid, such as $1 for a lottery ticket, while other states hold that requiring a person to buy a given product in order to enter a contest is consideration.

Point-of-purchase advertising (P-O-P) As a push technique, good dealer displays may induce a retailer to carry a certain line or promote a new product. However, P-O-P is primarily a pull technique consisting of advertising or display materials at the retail location to build traffic, advertise the product, and promote impulse buying. These may include window displays, counter displays, floor and wall displays to hold the merchandise, streamers, and posters. Often the product's shipping cartons are designed to double as display units. At times, a complete "information center" provides literature, samples, and product photos.

Such material has increased in importance with the trend toward self-service retailing. Even in stores that have clerks, display material can offer extra selling information and make the product stand out from the competition (Figure 19–7).

Trading stamps This promotion device was introduced by the Sperry & Hutchinson Company in 1896. For years the popularity of S&H Green Stamps in department stores, supermarkets, and service stations fluctuated. Finally, as discount stores and suburban shopping centers grew, and with the energy crisis affecting service stations,

The syrup with something extra

The "Dress Up Mrs. Butterworth's" bottle-decorating contest was launched. Designed to boost product awareness, the promotion was supported by magazine ads (in such books as *McCall's, Redbook, Better Homes & Gardens,* and *Southern Living*) and by in-store promotion (created in-house). Consumers were asked to decorate the bottle using common craft items. Then they submitted a photo or sketch of the bottle. Lever selected 200 finalists in each of two age categories (children under 14 and adults).

Prizes included family "dream" vacations to such resorts as Acapulco and Aruba. And consumer response was better than expected. Mrs. Butterworth's bottles were transformed into geishas, spacewomen, and nuns with such materials as paint, yarn, bread dough, seashells, and modeling clay.

Sales in 1980 continued strong—and Mrs. Butterworth's edged out Aunt Jemima to become the second largest selling syrup in the country.

But Lever Brothers executives still credit the original Mrs. Butterworth's packaging designers with much of the product's success. "They were the people who developed a quality glass container that has remained unique all these years," says Coombs. "Now, as then, there are still very few packages on the market that create as much enthusiasm about their contents."

The syrup with something extra *(continued)*

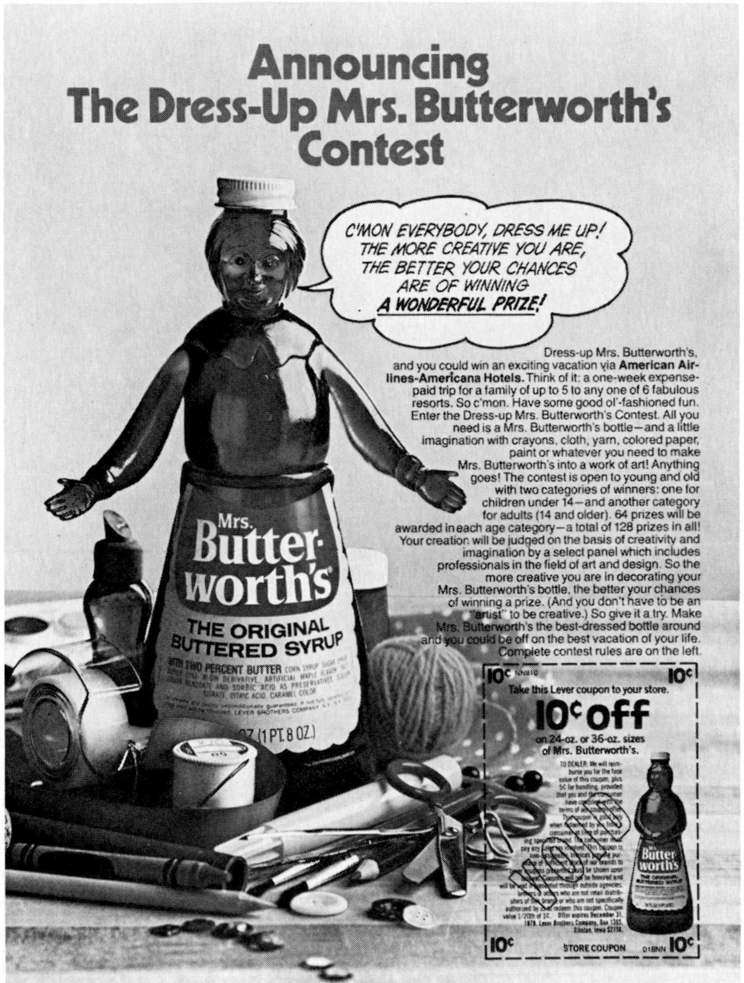

Laboratory applications

1. Generally, how effective do you think creative packaging like Mrs. Butterworth's is?
2. Which do you feel would create greater sales: the type of creative packaging shown here or a price reduction equivalent to the cost of this creative packaging?

interest in trading stamps began to wane. Today the several brands of trading stamps have largely given way to other forms of retail promotion such as games.

Miscellaneous The above is only a partial listing of the bewildering array of sales promotion tools. The choice of which to use in any given instance depends on a combination of factors. Timing is important. Fads and fashions come and go in sales promotion as in anything else. To be successful, sales promotions must take advantage of current consumer preferences.

A promotion needs to be unique to attract attention, but time-tested to ensure probable success. For instance, certain types of sales promotion are known to work well for new products—namely, sampling, couponing, and money-refund offers. Other types have proven helpful in increasing the use of established products, such as premiums, price-off promotions, and contests and sweepstakes. (See the Ad Lab.)

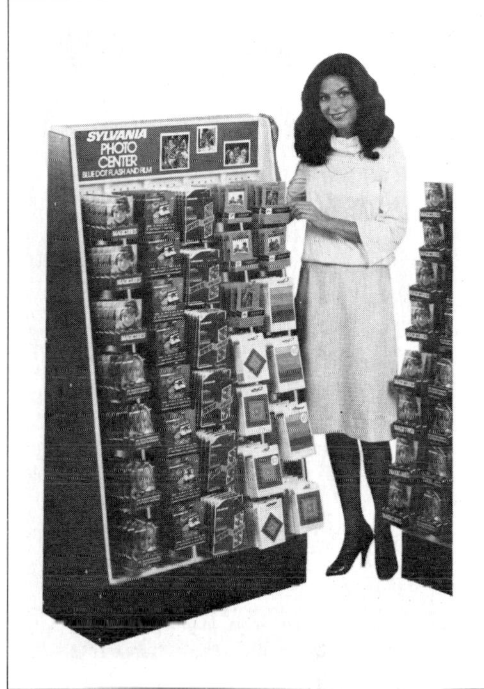

Figure 19–7 The Sylvania Photo Center is designed to merchandise Sylvania Blue Dot Flash Cubes in a one-stop shopping center. Used in department stores, discount stores, and drugstores, the fixture provides adequate space for the display of various photo needs. The purpose is to help shoppers satisfy all their photo requirements in one spot.

Supplementary media

Many miscellaneous promotional media are difficult to classify because they are tailored to individual needs and do not necessarily fall into any major category. They include the following.

Specialty advertising

Today nearly every business uses advertising specialties to some degree. These include everything from key chains, ballpoint pens, and calendars to matchbooks, thermometers, and billfolds (Figure 19–8). They are used by national advertisers, local merchants, banks and insurance companies, industrial firms, and service stations, to name just a few. There are said to be more than 10,000 different items sold, which represent an annual volume of more than $5 billion.

An advertising specialty is different from a premium. The recipient of a premium must give some consideration to the advertiser—buy a product, send in a coupon, witness a demonstration, or perform some other action of advantage to the advertiser. A premium may be an expensive item; therefore, it frequently bears no advertising message.

An advertising specialty is given free. It is an inexpensive, but useful, goodwill gift—a reminder that carries the company or product name or logo. It may feature a new product, a new plant, or some special event or promotion. Some may be kept for years and thereby serve as continuous, friendly reminders of the advertiser's business.

Catalog houses

These include general merchandise houses such as Speigel and Aldens, plus a growing number of specialty and gift houses, such as

Spencer Gifts, Sunset House, and Miles Kimball. These last three have more than 13 million customers who browse through their catalogs' pages to shop for gifts or other products they want or need.

Trade shows and exhibits

Every major industry sponsors annual trade shows and exhibitions where manufacturers, dealers, and buyers of the industry's products can get together for demonstrations and discussion. These occasions can be most productive to exhibitors. They have the opportunity of exposing their new products, literature, and samples to new customers as well as old. At the same time they can meet potential new dealers for their products (Figure 19–9).

As a result the construction of booths and exhibits has become a major factor in sales promotion plans. To stop traffic, booths must be simple in design and attractive, with good lighting, so the attention of passersby will be directed to the booth. The exhibit should also provide a comfortable atmosphere to promote conversation between salespeople and prospects.

Specialists who design exhibits or trade show booths need to consider the following factors in their work:

Smell: Powerful armament in retailers' arsenal

You are strolling past the bakery in your local shopping mall. Isn't that the irresistible odor of fresh-baked chocolate-chip cookies wafting from the ovens?

Maybe not.

International Flavors & Fragrances Inc., has succeeded in synthesizing the mouth-watering aroma not only of chocolate-chip-cookies but also of hot apple pie, fresh pizza, baking ham, and even nongreasy French fries.

IF&F packages the artificial odors in aerosol cans and markets them along with $25 to $30 timed-release devices that periodically fire a burst of scent out into the shopping mall to tempt customers. The sprays are selling briskly, says Ernest Kmites, IF&F's manager of sales services, and cost the owners just "pennies a day."

That surely makes it one of the least expensive tricks in retailing, and doubtless one of the simplest. One favorite of used-car dealers is to rejuvenate an old clunker with a "new-car scent." One popular brand is something called Velvet Touch, made by a company in Wayland, Mass.

Marvin Ivy, president of the National Independent Automobile Dealers Association, a trade group, says he has heard of such a product but disapproves of its use. "I think you shouldn't," Mr. Ivy says. "I think you'll deceive the public. That car could have 60,000 miles on it and smell like hell."

But Joseph Eikenberg, owner of Aero Motors in Baltimore, suggests that the scents may have a legitimate use in used cars, such as when the autos arrive with lingering smells left by dogs or smokers.

Laboratory application

Do you believe using canned, artificial odors is a legitimate sales promotion technique?

1. Size and location of space.
2. Desired image or impression of the exhibit.
3. Complexities of shipping, installation, and dismantling.
4. The number of products to be displayed.
5. The need for storage and distribution of literature.
6. The cost of all of the above.

Audiovisual systems

What once was a standard tool in many promotion programs has almost become a major promotion itself. Audiovisual equipment has now become virtually synonymous with sales training and demonstrations. A variety of available equipment ranges from portable sound-slide filmstrip projectors to small videotape monitors to complex multiscreen equipment for use with small groups or audiences of thousands.

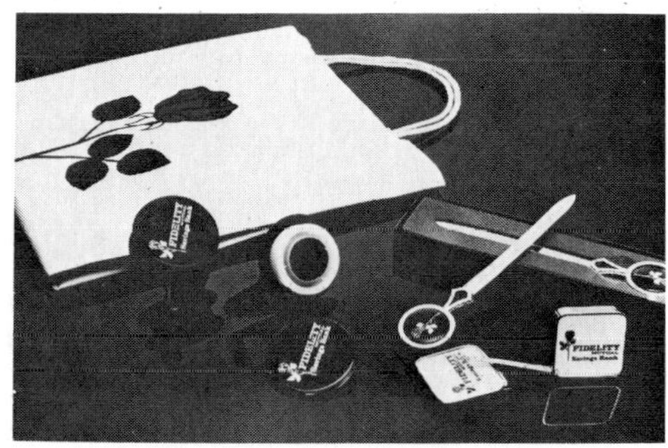

Figure 19–8 Useful advertising specialties, including a tape dispenser, letter opener, tape measure, and shopping bag, were distributed to visitors during the opening day of Fidelity Mutual Savings Bank's new branch in Spokane, Washington. The tape dispenser was used as a teaser—the lid for it was mailed to prospective depositors, who were invited to visit the bank and pick up the article to which it belonged and the other advertising gifts. The bank's symbol, a rose, and the bank name were imprinted on each article. The campaign also incorporated newspaper and radio advertising. The mailing of the tape dispenser lid evoked considerable curiosity. Of the 13,000 persons receiving the mailing, 11,000—or 85 percent—went to the bank to redeem the lid for the complete dispenser.

Directories and Yellow Pages

Literally thousands of directories are published—by trade associations, state and city agencies, chambers of commerce, newspapers, industrial groups, advertising services, and others. While serving mainly as locators, buying guides, and mailing lists, they also carry advertising aimed at their specialized fields.

Figure 19–9 It has been estimated that about $1.5 billion is spent on trade show exhibits every year. This figure, though, does not include the cost of staffing the exhibits or the related travel and hotel expenses. Trade shows are an exciting opportunity for sellers to meet buyers in one location.

In the United States there are approximately 6,000 local telephone directories with a combined circulation of 286 million. They reach 85 percent of the households and every business firm. This gives the national advertisers a choice of the exact territories they need to cover. It is also widely used by local firms. National advertisers may seek the assistance of the National Yellow Pages Service Association for rates and data, creative help, and one-order placement. Such advertising is commissionable to advertising agencies.

Motion picture advertising

Advertising films falls into two classes: theatrical films and sponsored films. *Theatrical films,* usually 10 minutes or shorter, are shown in about 12,000 movie houses in the United States. To be acceptable, they should be entertaining, of high quality, and without obvious "commercials." Such movies are made for advertisers by professional producers. Distribution is handled by film distributors through the film exchanges that supply movie houses.

Sponsored films should be both entertaining and educational. The advertiser engages a film distributing house to arrange bookings for clubs, churches, schools, fraternal societies, airport lounges, resorts, and even TV stations.

Summary

Sales promotion supplements advertising and personal selling for the purpose of stimulating or accelerating sales. It includes widely varied types of promotional activities with unlimited applications aimed at salespeople, distributors, retailers, and consumers. By offering direct inducements such as money, prizes, gifts, or other opportunities, it provides extra incentive to buy a product, to visit a store, to request literature, or to take other action.

Sales promotion techniques are used in the trade to *push* products through the distribution channels or with the ultimate customer to *pull* them through the channel. Manufacturers use a variety of sales promotion techniques to offer dealers extra incentive to purchase, stock, and display their products. These include dealer displays, deals, dealer premiums, cooperative advertising, advertising materials, push money, collateral material, and company conventions and dealer meetings.

The most visible forms of sales promotion aimed at the ultimate purchaser of the product are sampling, cents-off promotions, cents-off coupons, combination offers, premiums, in-pack premiums, contests and sweepstakes, point-of-purchase advertising, and trading stamps.

Supplementary media are so diversified that they defy classification. One type is specialty advertising. There are more than 10,000 different items used as specialties. This includes everything from key chains, ballpoint pens, and calendars to matchbooks, thermometers, and billfolds. Other types are trade shows and exhibits, audiovisual systems, directories and Yellow Pages, and motion picture advertising.

Questions for review

1. How would you define sales promotion?
2. What is the relationship between sales promotion and advertising?
3. What is the difference between push and pull sales promotion strategies?
4. How would you describe each of these push strategy techniques?
   a. Dealer displays.
   b. Deals.
   c. Dealer premiums.
   d. Cooperative advertising.
   e. Advertising materials.
   f. Push money.
   g. Collateral material.
5. How would you describe each of these pull strategy techniques?
   a. Sampling.
   b. Cents-off promotions.
   c. Cents-off coupons.
   d. Combination offers.
   e. Premiums.
   f. Contests and sweepstakes.
   g. Lotteries.
   h. Point-of-purchase advertising.
   i. Trading stamps.
6. What is the difference between an advertising specialty and a premium?
7. What are a trade show and exhibition? How do they aid advertisers?
8. What are audiovisual systems? Describe their usefulness to advertisers.
9. Why should advertisers be interested in using directories and the Yellow Pages?
10. What is the difference between theatrical films and sponsored films?

Part VI

Special Types of Advertising

Where the ACTION is

20

Local advertising

In 1966 Ray Lemke was a barber in the little town of Papillion, Nebraska. His young wife, Gwen, was staying at home, caring for their three small children. But she was bored doing the same thing every day.

That year a survey was published which predicted that by the mid-1980s Papillion would be in the center of the growing metropolitan area around Omaha. The Lemkes decided to go into real estate. They rented a little store-front office next to the barber shop and started listing homes and selling insurance, too. Gwen jumped in with both feet, answering the phone, helping with the contracts, and getting involved in the advertising and the sales. Soon Ray was forced to make a choice. With some trepidation, he sold the barber shop and moved into the real estate business full-time.

They called this business Action Realty. It signified movement and gave them the first position in the phone book. They designed a dynamic "Action" logo to use on signs and in their newspaper ads. They created a standard ad layout which very quickly became recognizable as the Action format: large space, heavy borders, dominant logo, numerous listings of property, and bold type (Figure 20–1). They ran their ads in the local newspaper every week without fail.

They both got involved in local community activities—service clubs, charities, trade associations. They hired additional salespeople who were as service-oriented as they were. They affiliated with a nationwide realty network, Home for Living, and participated in the programs that organization sponsored. They concentrated on developing continuous training programs for their staff. They developed exciting incentives, like vacation trips, for their top producers.

They encouraged their employees to be active in community affairs, and they publicized their successful employees with news releases to the local press. Sometimes they used their ads to communicate goodwill or publicize a new event. They constantly tested new ideas.

Action Real Estate rapidly became the fastest growing real estate firm in Sarpy County. Within 10 years the company was operating six branch offices and selling more real estate than any company in the county. They had a sales staff of over 75 people, 20 secretaries, and an annual gross sales volume of over $40 million.

By this time Gwen had become president of the firm and Ray had retired from active participation so he could pursue his ambition of becoming a personal counselor and motivational speaker. They had both witnessed the potential of consistent, strong local advertising. And they had kept the promise made by their advertising—Action.

Local advertising: Where the action is

Local advertising, as opposed to regional or national advertising, refers to advertising by businesses within a particular city or county to customers within the same geographic area. In 1980, 44 percent of all dollars spent on advertising were for local advertising as opposed to national advertising.

Quite often local advertising is referred to as "retail" advertising because it is commonly performed by retail stores. However, retail advertising is often not local, but regional or national in scope, as witnessed by the volume of commercials run by national fast-food chains, department stores, or jewelry retailers, to mention just a few (Figure 20–2). Moreover, local advertising is also commonly done by insurance agents, real estate brokers, banks, investment houses, professional services, auto mechanics, plumbers, local manufacturers, and many other businesses that are not usually thought of as retail stores.

Local advertising is important because of the arena in which it is performed. It is in the local arena where most sales are made or lost. A national auto manufacturer may spend millions advertising new cars. Local auto dealers as a group spend just as much or more to bring customers into their showrooms to buy the cars. In fact, if they don't make a strong effort on the local level, the efforts of the national advertisers may frequently be wasted. So when it comes to consummating the sale, local advertising is where the action is.

While the basic principles used by national advertisers are applicable to local advertising, local advertisers have special problems which this chapter examines. These problems stem from the simple, practical realities of marketing in a local area. There are therefore many differences between local and national advertisers, including basic objectives and strategies, needs of the marketplace, amount of money available to spend on advertising, heavy emphasis by local advertisers on newspaper advertising, use of price as a buying inducement, and the sources of specialized help in preparing advertisements.

Figure 20–1 The Action ad format may not be very pretty with its extensive use of heavy type and bold reverses. However, it has been very effective in creating a consistent presence for Action Realty and has lent credence to the promise inherent in their name.

Types of local advertising

There are two major types of local advertising: product and institutional. *Product advertising* is designed to sell a specific product or service. It also hopes to get immediate action. *Institutional advertising* attempts to obtain favorable attention for the business as a whole, not for a specific product or service that the store or business sells. The effects of institutional advertising are intended to be long rather than short range.

Product advertising

For most local advertisers, product advertising constitutes the greatest portion of their advertising efforts. Product advertising can be further subdivided into the following types.

Regular price-line advertising The purpose of this type of advertising is to inform consumers about the wide selection or quality of merchandise that a store has available at regular prices (Figure 20–3).

Sale advertising In order to stimulate the movement of particular merchandise, local advertisers advertise items on sale. This type of advertising places the emphasis on special reduced prices.

Clearance advertising To make room for new product lines or new models, or to rid themselves of slow-moving product lines, floor samples, broken or distressed merchandise, or items that are no longer in season, local advertisers may do clearance advertising.

Institutional advertising

Institutional advertising involves selling an idea about the company. The purpose of such advertising is usually to make the public aware of the company and to build a solid reputation of service and good citizenship. An advertisement might stress longer hours of operation, a new credit policy, or store expansion. This type of advertising is expected to reap long-term more than short-term benefits because such advertisements frequently announce the store's concern for the community, local charitable causes, and the customer in particular. Readership of institutional advertising may be lower than that of product advertising. But, if done effectively, institutional ads can be very helpful in building a favorable image for the business and in attracting new customers (Figure 20–4).

Objectives of local advertising

Gerry Smith was a field technical representative for Motorola. He had lived in Mount Holly for many years and had become a local history buff. When the town fathers decided to celebrate the city's 100th birthday in 1979, they turned to Gerry for help. They thought a centennial celebration might be a good stimulus for local business, but they weren't sure who would be interested in visiting this little community in North Carolina 100 miles west of Winston–Salem. They discovered that Gerry Smith was a born promoter.

When he presented his plan to them, they saw that his program would satisfy all the accepted objectives of local advertising (see the Checklist):

1. Introduce new customers to Mount Holly's products and services.
2. Build awareness of the town and its business.
3. Help keep old customers from shopping someplace else.
4. Increase the frequency of visits by regular customers.
5. Reduce the normal cost of selling to large numbers of customers.
6. Help curtail the seasonal dip in business.
7. Accelerate the turnover of retail inventory.

Not only all that, but his plan would cost the city virtually nothing, since he designed it to pay for itself.

First he contacted the local newspaper and arranged for extensive news coverage of the event scheduled for July 14, 1979. He also showed them how they would sell much more advertising that week than ever before. Next he contacted Freightliner Truck Corporation, which had just finished building a new plant in Mount Holly. They agreed to participate by holding a giant open house, running supportive ads in the newspaper, and contributing their largest show vehicles to the centennial parade.

When Smith approached the retailers, they were eager to get involved. They agreed to decorate their stores, run large centennial ads, wear costumes, offer prizes, and help sell centennial souvenirs. Meanwhile he arranged to have a monument erected to honor the founding families of Mount Holly. He had a commemorative bronze coin struck, bumper stickers printed, and even souvenir license plates made. These were put on sale at reasonable prices throughout the retail business district.

To publicize the event, he sent news releases to the community newspapers of all the surrounding towns and followed up with personal calls. Then he called the television station in Winston–Salem and they arranged to have the unique event covered by CBS News.

When July 14 came, it was indeed a day of celebration in Mount Holly (Figure 20–5). A parade led by Freightliner's show trucks kicked

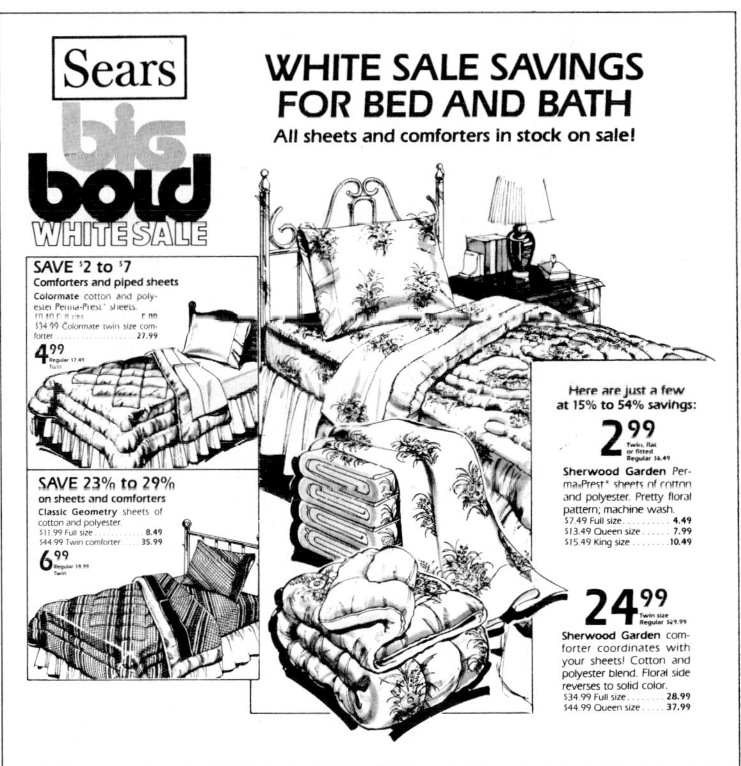

Sears Big Bold White Sale was a major four-week event which ran in the summer of 1981. The magazine ad shown (above left) was just one page of an eight-page section that appeared in July issues of national women's and shelter magazines. The national retail campaign was kicked off by a brief burst of fifteen television spots (page 640) which ran for 5 days in late June. This was supported by an extensive schedule of newspaper ads (above right) which were produced in various sizes and run by local Sears retail stores around the country. The results of the combined local and national campaign were highly successful.

Figure 20–2

off the event. Ending the parade were the town's youngsters on their bicycles, and a prize was given to the best decorated bicycle. Afterward the monument was unveiled by local dignitaries. An old-fashioned fair with contests, bazaar booths, and cotton candy was held all afternoon in the park. Freightliner opened its doors to the public and offered tours, truck rides, balloons, and refreshments. That evening a street dance was held downtown with live bands, and finally the whole event was culminated with a brilliant fireworks show after dark.

Folks came from miles around to join in the fun. Those who couldn't come heard about it on radio and television. The merchants

Figure 20–2 *(continued)*

SEARS TV COMMERCIAL

BIG BOLD WHITE SALE

Sale Dates: 6/21/81-7/25/81
Order Number: SRFA1092(6&7)
Usage Limitation: 7/4/81-10/4/81

VIDEO

WIDE SHOT OF SET. STACKS OF TOWELS, SHEETS, ETC. AROUND BIG BOLD WHITE SALE SIGN. TALENT IN THE MIDDLE.

CUT TO TALENT WITH SHEETS AND COMFORTER.
SUPER: Available in most larger Sears retail stores.
SUPER: Special VALUES GOOD ONLY UNTIL JUNE 27, 1981.

TALENT WALKS TOWARDS STACKS OF SHEETS AND TOWELS.

ZOOM IN TO CU OF SHEETS.
SUPER: Save 50% $1.99 twin size. minimum savings nationally.
SUPER: other sizes also on sale.

TALENT WITH TOWELS.
SUPER: $2.22 bath size. save 40%.

BEGIN REVEAL SET. TALENT PICKS UP MAGAZINE.

TALENT HOLDING MAGAZINE. OPEN TO OUR ADS. CONTINUE REVEAL OF SET.
LARGE SUPER: Big bold white sale. June 24 to July 18. Prices and dates may vary in Alaska and Hawaii.

CONTINUE TO REVEAL SET.

SUPER: C Sears, Roebuck and Co. 1981.
You can count on Sears.

AUDIO

ANNCR: Hurry in to Sears Big, Bold White Sale.

With marvelous values for your bed, kitchen and bath.

And for you early birds, two special values 'til June 27.

Beautiful muslin sheets—Perma-Prest Danberry prints, just $1.99 twin size.

Or, save 40% on Matchmates classic velour bath towels. Now, just $2.22.
And that's just the beginning of Sears Big Bold White Sale.
Look for other values in July magazines.

Remember,

you can count on Sears.

made money, the newspaper made money, the town gained some notoriety, Freightliner earned tremendous goodwill from its new neighbors, and Gerry Smith became a local hero.

The objectives of local advertising differ from the objectives of national advertising in emphasis and time. National manufacturers tend to emphasize long-term objectives of awareness, image, and credibility. On the local, retail level, the advertiser's needs tend to be more immediate. The emphasis is on making the cash register ring—increasing traffic, turning over inventory, and bringing in new customers.

As a result, on the local level there are constant promotions, sales, and clearances, all designed to create immediate activity. The trade-

YOUR KNIT SUIT
BRIGHTENS THE CITYSCAPE
The city suit, classically urbane.
Ripe red, rich navy and crisp white,
keeping you perfectly suited
from boardroom to bistro.
By Venice, tailored of well-mannered
acrylic and polyester knit, for 8 to 14.
Jacket, in red smartened with
checked braid trim;
Blouse, of white polyester
crepe de chine seasoned with
checked necktie: skirt. a flow of
navy pleats. The ensemble, 150.00
Greenbrier Dresses, Fourth,
"F" Street, and all stores.
Garfinckel's

Regular price-line advertising such as this advertisement for Garfinckel's is used to convey an impression of quality merchandise.

Figure 20–3

off, of course, is that the day after the promotion or sale is over the traffic may stop. So to increase traffic again, the merchant may plan another sale or another promotion. Then another and another. What

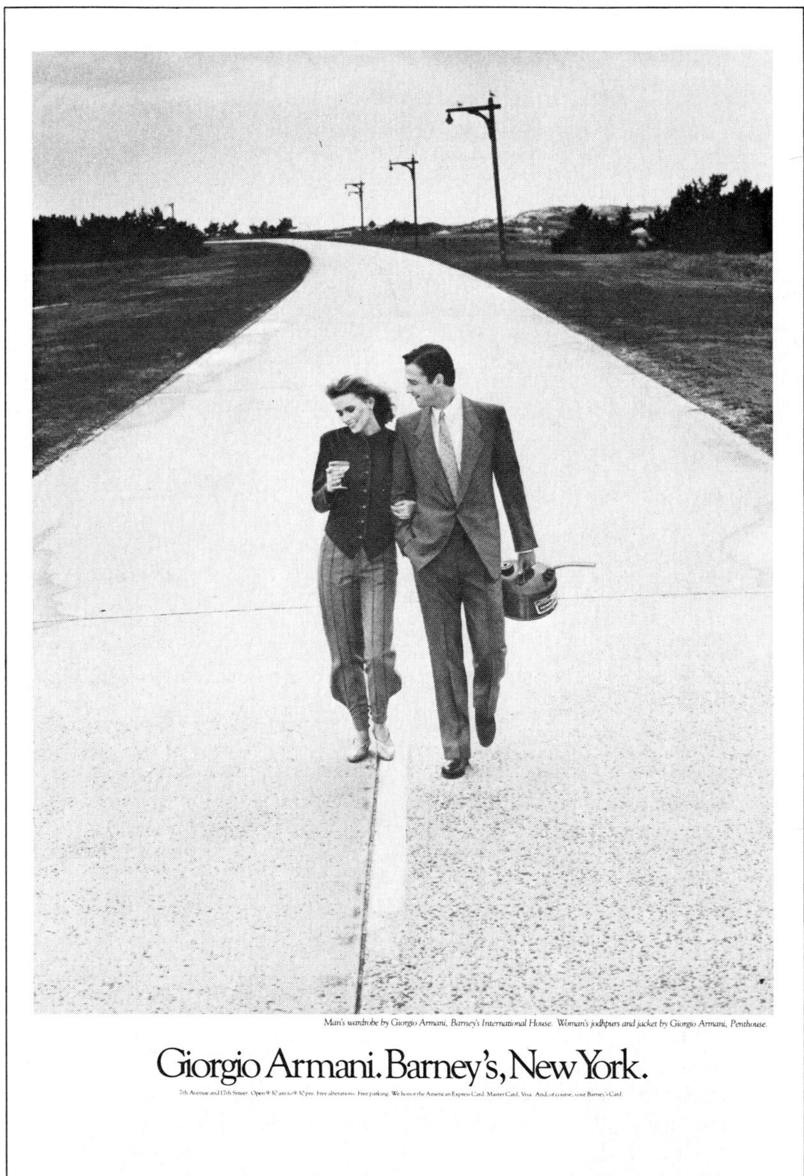

Man's wardrobe by Giorgio Armani, Barney's International House. Woman's jodhpurs and jacket by Giorgio Armani, Penthouse.
Giorgio Armani. Barney's, New York.
7th Avenue and 17th Street. Open 9:30 am to 9:30 pm. Free alterations. Free parking. We honor the American Express Card, Master Card, Visa. And, of course, your Barney's Card.

Figure 20–4 Barney's, New York projects a fine fashion image in its advertising by successfully identifying with its potential customers. Photographs or illustrations are equally concerned with creating the appropriate attitude, whether it be for men's or women's apparel. In this example, the photograph was taken on location on a Long Island causeway to dramatize the sophisticated, "above-it-all" attributes of this couple in their Giorgio Armani fashions.

sometimes results is a cycle of sporadic bursts of activity followed by inactivity, sharp peaks and valleys in sales and a distasteful image of a business that should be visited only during a sale.

Long-term and short-term objectives work against each other when one is sought at the expense of the other. Successful local advertisers, therefore, think of long-term objectives first and then develop short-term goals that are in keeping with their long-term objectives. This usually increases the emphasis on regular price-line advertising and reduces the reliance on sales and clearances for creating traffic (Figure 20–6).

Planning the advertising effort

The key to success in any advertising program, local or national, is adequate planning. Planning is not a one-time occurrence, however. It is a continuous process of research, evaluation, decision, execution, and review.

Mount Holly's one-day centennial celebration was a success because Gerry Smith planned that promotion in detail. Action Realty's 10-year success was due to the fact that Gwen and Ray Lemke made

Checklist of local advertising objectives

☐ To introduce new customers. Every year many old customers are lost due to relocation, death, inconvenience, or dissatisfaction. To thrive, a business must continually seek new customers. Advertising is the best method of use.

☐ To build awareness and image. Many local businesses provide essentially the same services. To distinguish themselves from one another, stores can use advertising techniques to increase awareness and build a unique image.

☐ To help retain old customers and increase their frequency of visits. More customers are lost because of inattention than any other single reason. In addition, a barrage of advertising from competitors may lure customers away. A steady, consistent program of advertising can keep present customers informed and reinforce their desire to remain customers and visit your business more often.

☐ To reduce sales expense. By preselling many customers, advertising lightens the load on sales personnel. By increasing traffic, it allows salespeople to make more sales in a shorter time. These contribute to reducing the cost of sales.

☐ To curtail seasonal peaks. Each year there are dips and swings in the business cycle. One way to level off the peaks and valleys is to advertise consistently.

☐ To accelerate inventory turnover. Some businesses sell all the merchandise in a store four or five times a year. Others turn over the inventory 15 to 20 times. The more times inventory is turned, the more profit can be made. By turning inventory more rapidly, prices can also be kept down. In this way advertising contributes to lower customer prices.

planning a continuous, flexible process, which allowed for change, improvement, new facts, and new ideas.

Several steps are involved in planning the local advertising effort: analyzing the local market, analyzing the competition, conducting adequate research, determining objectives and strategy, establishing a realistic budget, planning media strategy, and determining creative direction.

SATURDAY, JULY 14 A DAY OF MOUNT HOLLY CELEBRATIONS

It's Mount Holly's 100th birthday! It's also the official dedication and open house for the Freightliner Truck Manufacturing Plant.

A full day and night of activities has been planned for your whole family, including a very special Freightliner Open House!

A BIG PARADE

9:30 a.m.—A parade through Mount Holly will kick off all the events. Leading the parade will be Freightliner show trucks. Ending the parade will be bicycles, and a prize will be awarded to the best decorated bicycle. The parade starts at Tuckaseege Road and ends on Woodlawn Road.

TRIBUTE TO OUR FOUNDERS

12:30 p.m.—A beautiful monument to the

founding families of Mount Holly will be unveiled by a special guest. You won't want to miss these ceremonies in front of City Hall on North Main Street.

FUN AND GAMES

1:30 p.m.—An old fashioned "jousting tournament" will be the first in a series of events, contests, games and bazaar booths at Costner Field. The fair atmosphere will be just like the famous old Mount Holly 1890 fairs. The fair will last all afternoon until 8:00 p.m.

FREIGHTLINER OPEN HOUSE

2:00 p.m.—4:30 p.m.—Open House, Freightliner, 1800 North Main Street, Mount Holly, will feature truck rides, balloons and refreshments for the entire family. Take a break from the Fair, and show Freightliner that you're glad they're in Mount Holly!

FREIGHTLINER TRUCKS

You can tour the new truck manufacturing plant and see how trucks are made.

STREET DANCE

8:00 p.m.—An exciting street dance at East Central and Main Streets downtown will last until midnight. A live band and a lively atmosphere will make this dance long remembered.

FIREWORKS

Dark—Fireworks, fireworks and more fireworks will be in full view from the square as soon as it's dark.

There will be fun for the whole family! Let's celebrate Mount Holly's first one hundred years and celebrate the next one hundred with Freightliner.

Figure 20–5 The Mount Holly centennial was a gala event for the local citizenry. Full-page newspaper ads promoted the fun, while souvenir license plates and bumper stickers were used to promote personal involvement.

Figure 20–6 May Company advertising emphasizes a regular price-line approach to inform customers of the type of merchandise carried. Sophisticated retail fashion ads of this genre help the store achieve its long-range objectives of communicating image, quality, and convenience while stimulating short-term traffic goals.

Analyzing the local market

Through careful research, the type of local market in which the business is located must be identified. Whenever possible, local advertising should reflect the needs of the immediate area. Items to consider, therefore, are whether the area is rural or urban, conservative or progressive, high- or low-income, white-collar or blue-collar. A thorough knowledge of the local market and potential customers influences the goods and services the business offers, the prices established, and the design and style of advertising. Accurate analysis at this point prevents advertising misfires later on.

Analyzing the competition

A careful study should be made of all the competitors in the local area. What merchandise and services are offered? What is the pricing strategy? Where are they located? How large are they? What is their advertising strategy? What media do they use? How much do they spend? Do the competitors' places of business invite customers or repel them?

Constant competitive research alerts the advertiser to new ideas, advantages and disadvantages, new merchandising techniques, and new material for advertising campaigns.

Conducting adequate research

The local advertiser usually cannot afford to hire a specialized firm to conduct formal market research programs. However, because of its proximity to the marketplace, a local store or business should be well attuned to the attitudes of customers and be able to conduct informal research to measure customer reaction to merchandise and advertising campaigns. A good local advertising agency might assist in this regard.

Chapter 8 contained a thorough discussion of the field of advertising and marketing research. This chapter will examine those aspects of research that are unique to the local advertiser. As discussed in Chapter 8, there are two types of research. Primary research is data collected firsthand. Secondary research is data accumulated by others that can be adapted to the needs of the advertiser.

Primary research

To be successful, a local advertiser must have the answers to many important questions. Who are our present customers? Who are our potential customers? How many are there? Where are they located? How can our company best appeal to them? Where do they now buy the merchandise or services that I want to sell to them? Can I offer them anything they are not getting at the present time? If so, what? How can I convince them they should do business with me? (See Figure 20–7.) To answer these questions, primary research should be conducted in the following areas.

Customer analysis It is important to keep close track of customers—both charge and cash customers—so that their addresses can be correlated to census tract information. Census information includes such data as average income, family size, education, vehicle and home ownership, and age.

Sales analysis In retail stores, sales should be tabulated by merchandise classification. Careful analysis of this information helps identify changes in consumer buying patterns, which in turn affects the merchandise or services that will be bought and advertised in the future.

Customer attitudes and satisfaction Feedback from sales personnel can provide valuable information about customers. In addition, having salespeople solicit information about customers can forestall problems by locating areas of customer satisfaction and dissatisfaction at an early stage. Customers will also feel that the store cares if it actively seeks information from them.

Analysis of market share and sales potential A comparison should be made of a company's sales by merchandise lines in relation to those of other companies in the area. Information about other companies' market share can be obtained from several sources mentioned later in this section.

Advertising testing Because of the vast number of ads prepared by most local advertisers, it's unusual to test advertisements in advance of their placement. However, posttesting should be conducted to determine the advertising campaign's effect on sales, if any.

Determining the best medium in which to advertise, finding the best mailing lists, determining whether "hard" or "soft" sell works best, and testing music or slogans for broadcast commercials are very worthwhile.

Figure 20–7 Research helps advertisers find the right appeal for their customers. People who live in Santa Barbara, for instance, were found to be very community-minded and proud of their hometown. The appeal in this ad reflects that finding: "keep your money at home in a hometown bank where it can help the community."

Secondary research

Local advertisers should be aware of the many secondary sources of information that are available and can be adapted to their particular needs. These sources include trade publications and associations, local advertising media, manufacturers and suppliers, and various government organizations.

Retail trade publications Trade publications are excellent sources of information for a local advertiser's business. A list of publications is available in *The Standard Periodical Directory* or *Ulrich's International Periodicals Directory*. These publications contain important articles about trends in the business, new technology, and research studies that apply to the particular category of business to which the publication is directed. Just a few of hundreds of such publications are *Stores, The Merchandiser, Progressive Grocer, Automotive News, Farm Supplier, Hotel & Motel Management, Modern Jeweler,* and *Shopping Center World* (Figure 20–8).

Trade associations A glance at the *Encyclopedia of Associations,* available at most libraries, indicates the associations pertinent to a particular area of interest. A short letter will bring membership information as well as research data that may be available with little or no charge.

The National Retail Merchants Association (100 W. 31st Street, New York, NY 10001) publishes an extensive list of materials on research topics of interest to retailers. Also the Mass Retailing Institute's study of shoppers' behavior is available at reasonable cost (579 7th Avenue, New York NY 10018).

Typical of the many associations that are good sources of research information are the National Office Products Association, National Association of Drug Stores, Menswear Retailers of America, United States Savings and Loan League, National Sporting Goods Association, and the American Society of Travel Agents.

Advertising media and media associations The amount of re-

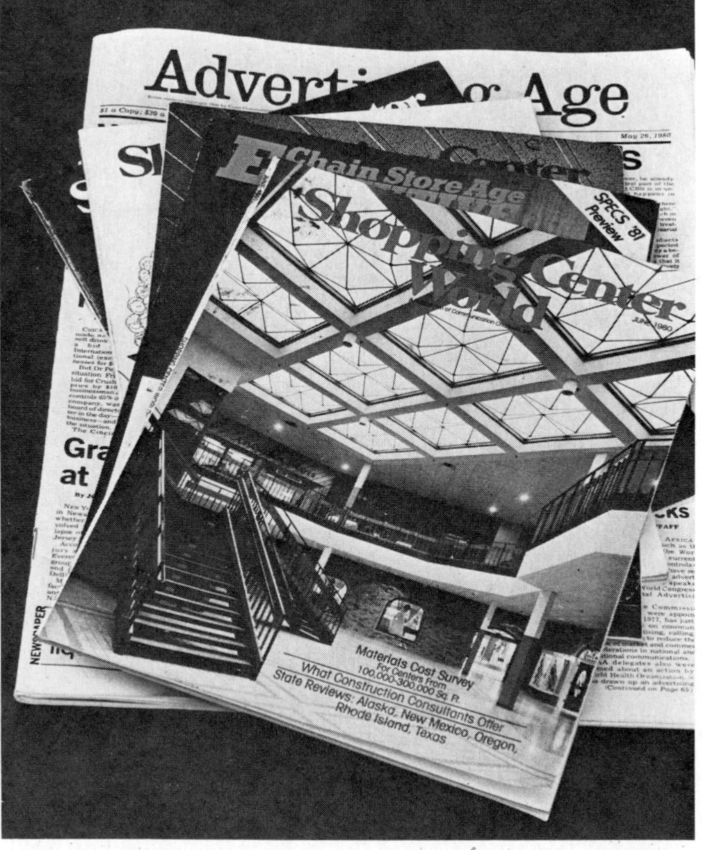

Figure 20–8 A few of the many trade publications available today. These can all be useful to the local advertiser seeking information and ideas on how to run and promote a business successfully.

search data that will be provided by local media depends on the size of the community. In large cities, the newspaper and broadcast stations provide in-depth market data about the communities they serve.

Even if a local advertiser lives in a community so small that the media are unable to provide any research data, the newspaper and broadcasters probably belong to national associations that conduct extensive research. Organizations of particular interest are the Direct Mail Advertising Association, Newspaper Advertising Bureau, Radio Advertising Bureau, Magazine Publishers Associations, Television Bureau of Advertising, and Institute of Outdoor Advertising.

Other publications of importance The most important publication in the advertising field is *Advertising Age.* A weekly publication, it contains articles on all types of advertising written by experts in their respective fields, important data on advertising expenditures, stories on advertising agencies and their clients, and updates on government and its relationship to advertising. Many articles are of a how-to variety—practical, down-to-earth material that can be used by any advertiser whether the budget is large or small.

Advertising is frequently a topic in other publications, too. A glance under "Advertising" in the *Business Periodicals Index* shows the publication source for the various aspects of advertising with which a local advertiser may be concerned.

Manufacturers and suppliers Manufacturers and suppliers want their dealers to suceed. Their dealer-aid programs usually include valuable research on the retail market for their products. Dealer seminars are often conducted in which research results are explained.

County or municipal government Various government bureaus can provide a wealth of useful information to the local advertiser, including data on population projections, birth and death information, marriage license statistics, road construction plans, sewer and water-line extension plans, building permits, zoning and building code changes, and other items that might affect local business.

State government In every state government there is a department in charge of commerce, taxation, labor, highways, and justice, which provide reports and statistical information. These materials can be useful in measuring local markets and making projections. Many states have bureaus in charge of getting new businesses to enter the state and in charge of economic development.

Federal government Of particular interest to most local advertisers is the Small Business Administration (SBA). It publishes a wealth of information, most of it free or available for only a nominal charge.

The Department of Commerce in the U.S. government also has pertinent materials, including: *Retail Data Sources for Market Analysis, Business Service Checklist* (a weekly guide to Department of Commerce reports, books, and news releases), *Bureau of Census Catalog, Census Track Studies,* the annual edition of the *U.S. Industrial Outlook, Current Retail Trade, Survey of Current Business, Monthly Department Store Sales, County Business Patterns,* the annual edition of the *Statistical Abstract of the United States,* and the *County and City Data Book.* Many of these publications are available at local libraries.

Determining objectives and strategy

In Chapter 9, "Marketing and Advertising Planning," the importance of establishing specific marketing and advertising objectives was discussed. The same holds true for local advertising.

When Gerry Smith presented his promotional plan to the city council of Mount Holly, he had very specific objectives in mind. The stated objectives of any marketing and advertising program, local or national, determine the particular marketing mix or strategy to be used. A local advertiser has the same options as a national advertiser when it comes to developing strategy: product, price, place, promotion.

Product

What merchandise should be sold? What services should be offered? Should some lines be expanded or dropped? How wide a selection should be offered? If a store intends to be a discount house, it may want to carry a broad line. If it wants to be a specialty shop, it may opt to carry only selected lines. In short, what is the store's product/service concept? (See Figure 20–9.)

Price

What will the local market support? Should prices be high, low, or moderate? What should be included in the price? What about terms and warranties? Charge cards? What policy should be established on refunds? Are all these policies in keeping with the desired image?

Place

Where should the business be located? What is the trading area? For a bank, how many branches can be established? What kind of areas should we serve? What's the cost of doing business in different areas? Should we limit ourselves to only one location? How large should our facilities be?

Promotion

Should the business be highly promotional, semipromotional, or non-

People in advertising

Jane Trahey

President
Trahey Advertising, Inc.

Popular author, screenwriter, columnist, playwright, and talk show guest Jane Trahey has made her major mark in the advertising world as founder and president of Trahey Advertising, Inc., New York and Chicago, an agency widely known for its retail campaigns.

Jane Trahey has twice been heralded as Ad Woman of the Year. She has been selected among the 100 Most Accomplished Women by *Harper's Bazaar.* Her distinctive copy has won a number of awards. Observed one writer, "Jane Trahey's talent and her independence are her trademark." Both have sparked her rapid rise to success.

Born in Chicago, Trahey received a B.A. from Mundelein College. After graduate studies at the University of Wisconsin, she went to work for the *Chicago Tribune.* Her interest in retail advertising led her to join Carson Pirie Scott, a Chicago department store. She went on to Neiman-Marcus, Dallas, where she became advertising and sales promotion director. Trahey was then named advertising director of a New York manufacturing firm, where she founded and led an in-house advertising agency. Two years later she decided to launch her own agency, and Trahey Advertising, Inc., was born.

Since then Jane Trahey has become a leading name in fashion advertising, serving clients ranging from Elizabeth Arden, Bill Blass, Pauline Trigere, and Adele Simpson to major retailers like B. Altman, Neiman-Marcus, Bergdorf's, and Harzfeld's. She has also created ad campaigns for Lanvin, Charles of the Ritz, Dorsay, and Borghese. Other key accounts have included Union Carbide, Kayser Hosiery, and Olivetti.

In the interim Jane Trahey has continued her education, obtaining an M.A. from Columbia University and a Doctorate in Humane Letters from Mundelein College. She has written 11 books, 2 movies, a play, a monthly magazine column, and a score of newspaper and magazine articles. She has also appeared on virtually every major TV talk show in the nation.

Year after year her agency's campaigns for retail clients have scored impressive success. To achieve this, Jane Trahey first focuses on learning what is unique about the store. "Try to find a uniqueness," she urges, "or help to create one. If a retail account lets you create such a uniqueness," adds Trahey, "chances are it has one."

The next step, says Trahey, is to convey this uniqueness in advertising. "Ads should reflect the heart of the store," she emphasizes. "Ads should tell me what these institutions are—what they mean in their communities—what contributions they make to my life." Do most retail ads do this? No, says Trahey. "I can count on one hand the stores that have that extra readability in their ads that holds me for more than the flip of the page." Defining this "extra readability," Trahey makes clear, "It doesn't matter a lot about the art. It's what the ad *says* that sells the store—and sells the merchandise." Trahey reflects, "You should do the *best* you can for the client. The client trusts you. You want to be worth that trust."

Despite her demanding role as agency president, Jane Trahey still devotes time to her wide-ranging interests. Today she is vice president and a member of the board of the NOW Legal Defense and Education Fund. She serves on the advisory committee of the White House Conference on Families. She is a member of the board of the Mayor's Council on Private Industry, City of Chicago. She also serves on the advisory committee of the Fashion Institute of Technology. In addition, Trahey is a member of the board of directors of Seligman & Latz, New York, and *Executive Woman* newsletter.

promotional? Should we use regular price-line advertising? Sales? Clearances? Or merely institutional advertising and public relations? What is the impact of advertising activities on this type of business? Can we attain our objectives by advertising? How much advertising in what media?

Determining the objectives and strategies of any business—local, regional, or national—is the most important policy decision management ever makes. The decision as to objectives and strategies determines the whole complexion of the business in the years that follow. It gives direction to the enterprise, continuity to its various promotional efforts, and an understanding of the company in the marketplace. For that reason, the decisions regarding objectives and strategies should be highly specific and should be written down. Then they should be reviewed frequently and updated or revised on a regular basis as the business situation warrants. (See the Ad Lab.)

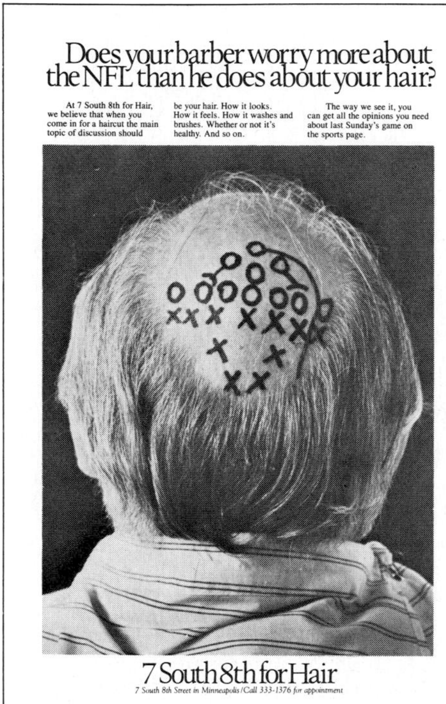

Figure 20–9 Even barber shops can use creative advertising. This ad for a Minneapolis barber won the Award of Excellence in New York's famous Andy Awards competition.

Establishing the budget

How much should a local business invest in advertising? New businesses usually require greater advertising expenditures than established ones. After the public becomes familiar with a company's goods or services, advertising costs should settle at a natural profitable level. But an advertising budget must be precisely designed for a particular business. Figure 20–10 illustrates, by type of establishment, the average percentage of sales invested in advertising. Since these figures are national averages, it is important to remember that they do not reflect the tremendous variety of factors that can affect the budget. The most important of these factors are the policies established when the company's objectives and strategies are determined.

Other influences are the following:

1. Location of the store.
2. Age and character of the firm.
3. Size of the store.
4. Type of product or service sold.
5. Size of the trading area.
6. Amount and kind of advertising done by the store's competitors.
7. Media available for advertising, their degree of coverage of the trading area of the store, and the costs of these media.
8. Results obtained from previous advertising.

If an advertiser's spending is much above or below the averages for that business shown in Figure 20–10, the reasons for this variance can usually be determined by checking the influencing factors listed above.

The local advertiser continually seeks to develop a budget in which the optimum amount of money is spent. If more is spent on advertising than necessary, the advertiser is wasting money. On the other hand, if the advertiser doesn't spend enough money and sales are not generated, then even more money is wasted. Thus, it is easier to waste money by not spending enough than by spending too much.

Budgeting strategy

Advertising programs should be continuous. One-shot ads that are not part of a well-planned program are most often ineffective. Also, advertising money should be spent when prospects are most receptive to buying a local advertiser's goods or services. In practice, this requires that advertising dollars be allocated in relation to sales vol-

Mistakes commonly made by local advertisers

Even the best laid plans for local advertisers may go awry. However, chances of success are much greater if certain potential pitfalls are avoided. The most common mistakes are given here.

1. *Inattention to the advertising effort.* Advertising is sometimes not given the attention it deserves. This sometimes occurs because of distractions, lack of time on the part of the local advertiser, or lack of skill or interest in this aspect of the business.

2. *Ego involvement.* Local advertisers sometimes succumb to the temptation to be a local celebrity by appearing in their own television commercials or placing a photograph of themselves (or their family) in the advertisement. This is dangerous. Most local advertisers are not effective spokespersons.

3. *Inadequate supply of merchandise.* If there is an insufficient supply of merchandise to meet the demand generated by the advertising, the local advertiser loses because potential sales revenue is lost forever, the money spent on the advertising is wasted, and harm is done to customer goodwill.

4. *Unqualified individuals handling the advertising.* Successful advertising requires competent individuals to plan, produce, and implement it. The smaller the establishment, the greater the chance that the person who handles the advertising will be unqualified to do so. Large stores have the advantage of being able to afford an advertising manager.

5. *Compensating for mistakes by advertising.* Even the best advertising efforts cannot compensate for a bad location, poor selection of merchandise, untrained personnel, unreasonable high prices, or a host of other difficulties. A good advertising campaign only speeds up the failure of a poorly run business.

6. *Lack of knowledge about what to advertise.* One of the most important decisions involves what to advertise. If an advertisement is to be successful, it must contain merchandise or services in which people have some interest. A good rule of thumb is to advertise items that are selling well already. Promote items that build traffic, and feature items in advertisements that are nationally advertised brands. These get attention because of the identifiable name, they take less explanation because of national promotion by manufacturers, and they help the local advertiser build a good reputation by association with a well-known name.

7. *Wasting money on charity advertising.* There are always a host of charitable causes waiting for contributors. Particularly difficult to turn down are requests for advertising in high school yearbooks, church bulletins, athletic programs, and fraternal organizations. Rarely do these publications prove cost effective, however. They are very expensive on a cost per thousand basis. If contributions are made by placing advertisements, the advertising expense should be charged to "contributions to charitable organizations" rather than calling it an advertising expense.

8. *Lack of coordination.* Advertising must be coordinated with the buying of the merchandise. Employees should be informed about the advertising so they can answer customers' questions. Merchandise must be properly priced and marked. Displays need to be in position. And local advertising should be coordinated with national advertising by manufacturers so that the advertising efforts reinforce one another.

Laboratory applications

As an observer of local advertisers, identify and describe mistakes you feel they make in addition to those given above? What should they do to correct their mistakes?

Figure 20–10 Average advertising investments of retail businesses

Commodity or class of business	Average percent of sales
Appliance, radio, TV dealers	2.3
Auto accessory and parts stores	0.9
Auto dealers	0.8
Bakeries	0.7
Banks	1.3
Beauty shops	2.0
Book stores	1.7
Camera stores (under $100,000 in sales)	0.8
Children's and infants' wear stores	1.4
Cocktail lounges	0.9
Credit agencies (personal)	2.4
Department stores ($1–$2 million)	2.5
Discount stores	2.4
Drugstores (independent, under $70,000 in sales)	1.1
Dry cleaning shops (under $50,000 in sales)	1.7
Florists	2.1
Food chains	1.1
Furniture stores	5.0
Gasoline service stations	0.8
Gift and novelty stores	1.4
Hardware stores	1.6
Home centers	1.3
Hotels (under 300 rooms)	6.7
Insurance agents, brokers	1.8
Jewelry stores	4.4
Laundromats (under $35,000 in sales)	1.3
Liquor stores (under $50,000 in sales)	0.7
Lumber and building materials dealers	0.5
Meat markets	0.6
Men's wear stores (under $300,000)	2.4
Motels	3.7
Motion picture theaters	5.5
Music stores ($25,000 to $50,000)	1.8
Office supplies dealers (under $100,000)	1.0
Paint, glass, and wallpaper stores	1.3
Photographic studios and supply shops	2.4
Real estate (except lessors of buildings)	0.6
Restaurants (under $50,000)	0.6
Savings and loan associations	1.5
Shoe stores	1.9
Specialty stores ($1 million and over)	3.0
Sporting goods stores	3.5
Taverns (under $50,000)	0.7
Tire dealers	2.2
Travel agents	5.0
Variety stores	1.5

ume month by month or even week by week. To achieve the objective of selling more merchandise at lower unit cost, well-timed advertising should be run to create month-by-month sales and advertising patterns like those illustrated in Figures 20–11 and 20–12.

There are several strategies or methods that local advertisers use to budget their advertising expenditures. Some of these were discussed in Chapter 9. However, most advertisers still use the percent of sales method, since it is the simplest to calculate and the easiest to defend with company bookkeepers and accountants.

For Action Realty, discussed at the beginning of this chapter, advertising has become such a large and complicated activity that Gwen Lemke now uses a computer to determine the advertising budget. The computer analyzes last year's sales along with various influencing factors to determine a budget based on anticipated sales this year. What results is an advertising expenditure curve that month by month slightly precedes the sales curve, as illustrated in Figure 20–12.

Developing the annual sales and advertising plan

Few local advertisers have a computer at their disposal to forecast sales for the coming year. However, by doing some research, a fairly accurate sales forecast can be determined. Some basic questions a local merchant would need to have answered might be: (1) What is the anticipated increase in population for the local area during the next year? (2) What is the anticipated increase or decrease in overall retail sales? (3) What is the outlook for the local employment rate? (4) How are similar businesses doing?

Local accountants, bankers, trade associations, chambers of commerce, and media representatives can be very helpful in answering these questions. After all the factors that affect finance, production, and marketing have been considered, a realistic sales plan for the year, month by month and even week by week, should be developed. From that sales plan an advertising expense plan can be formulated.

Advertising should precede sales. In other words, the most advertising dollars should be spent just before the time when customers are most likely to respond. To determine this, compute the percentage of yearly sales that are anticipated for each month (or, better yet, each week) of the year. Plot this on a graph. Next plot an advertising curve that slightly precedes the sales curve, as in Figure 20–13. (Note that the advertising peaks are slightly lower than the sales peaks, but the valleys are slightly higher.) The advertising curve indicates what percentage of the annual advertising expenditure should be spent each month.

This concept of plotting anticipated sales patterns enables business owners to allot a percentage of the total yearly advertising to each month. By plotting actual sales as the year progresses, the advertiser can compare weekly and monthly expenses to weekly and monthly sales goals. If the business has several departments or services, the same method can be used to allot advertising dollars to each.

A simple device that is commonly used by local advertisers is a monthly promotional calendar. The calendar should be large enough

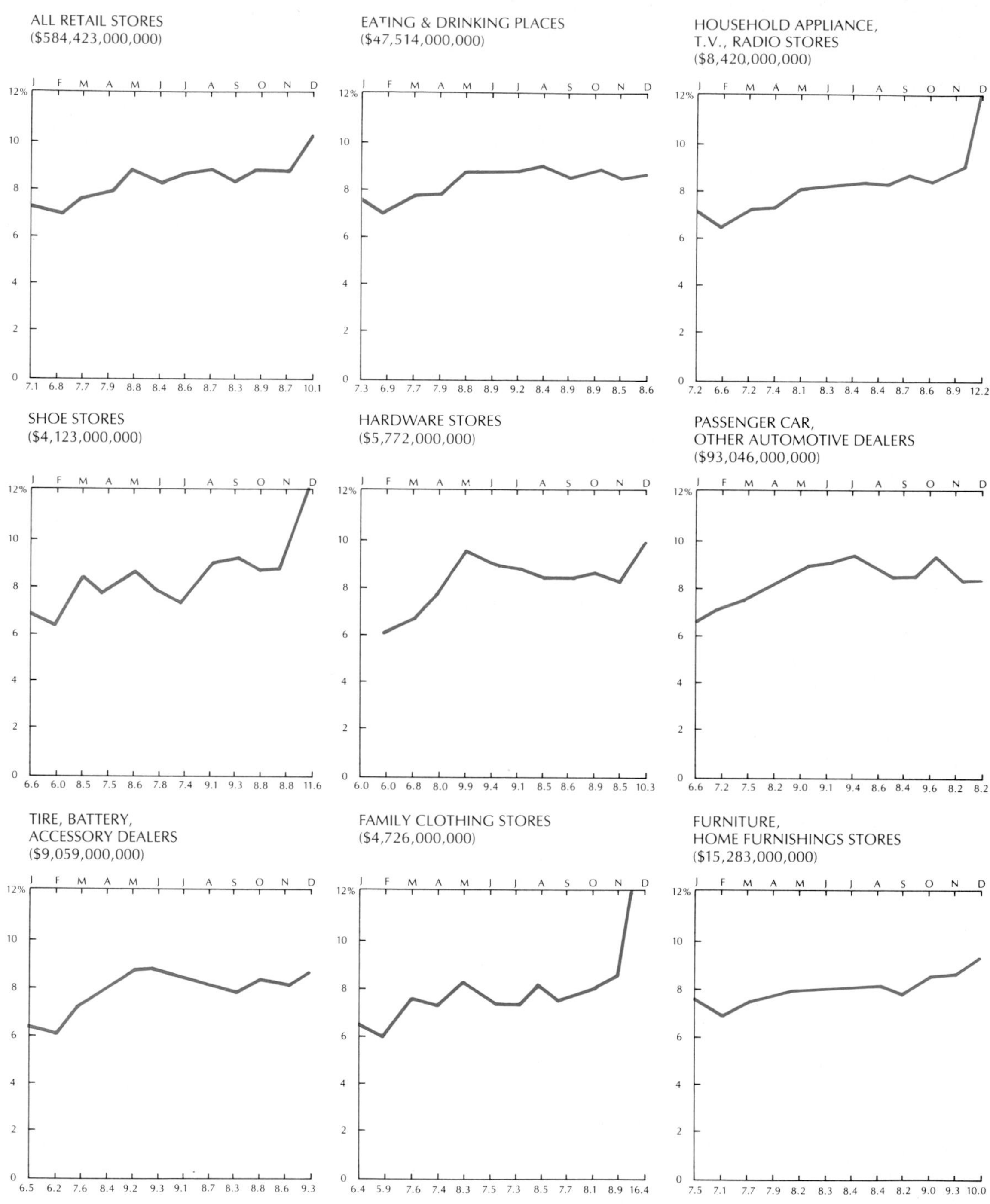

Figure 20–11 Total retail sales by types of stores; percentage of the year's total sales done each month. These tables show how important each month is to the sale of a variety of products and services. These patterns illustrate when customers are most interested in buying. For example, May, contributing approximately 9.9 percent of the year's sales of hardware stores, should logically get about this percentage of the year's advertising budget.

so that it can accommodate information about media schedules, costs, in-house promotions, sales, and special events. The calendar then enables the advertiser to tell at a glance the shape and direction of the advertising program.

To establish such a calendar, the advertiser should enter all the holidays as well as traditional community events like "Washington's Birthday Specials." The local media, trade associations, and trade publications can be especially helpful in supplying this information. (See the Checklist.)

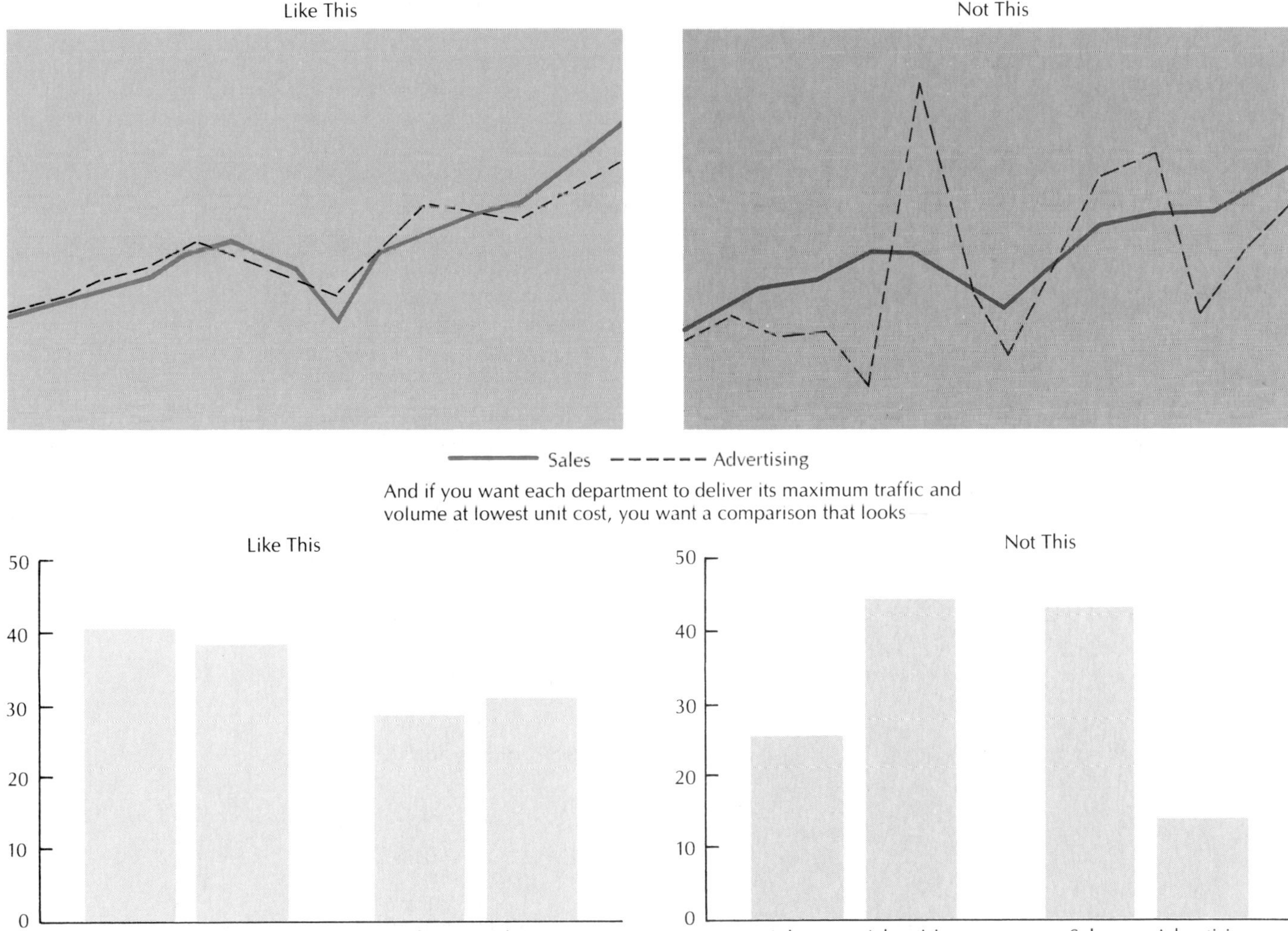

Figure 20–12 Advertising expenditure curves.

Planning media strategy

In the early 1960s Herb Sutton was an advertising sales representative for the *Los Angeles Times*. He had been with the *Times* for 15 years

Checklist for local advertising budgets

Set a sales goal

Write down the sales figures for next month last year—for the whole store and for each department. Then in view of this performance and your own knowledge and judgment of this year's picture, rough in sales goals for next month. Use the profit pointers below as a reminder of the factors to be considered in making your sales goal realistic but challenging.

☐ Your sales last year.

☐ Population, income, employment levels.

☐ New and expanded departments.

☐ Tie-ins with merchandising events.

☐ What competitors are doing, getting.

☐ More aggressive selling and advertising.

Decide how much advertising

Write down how much advertising you used next month last year. Then considering your planned sales goal and what what your competition is likely to do, write in your planned advertising budget for the coming month. Your budget as a percent of sales can be checked against the expenditure of other stores in your classification. The profit pointers below can be used to double check your own thinking on the advertising budget you can afford and need to do the job.

☐ Stores in less favorable locations advertise more.

☐ So do those that are new and expanding.

☐ Strong competition raises the size of the budget needed.

☐ Stores stressing price appeal usually promote more.

☐ Special dates and events offer additional sales opportunities.

☐ Added sales produced by increased expenditure are more profitable . . . more money can be spent to get them.

☐ Co-op support.

Decide what to promote

For instance, if the sales goal of department A is 9 percent of the total store sales objective this month, then earmark for it something like 9 percent of the month's planned advertising space. Your list shouldn't be a straitjacket, but a basic outline. Let your business experience guide you in weighing the advertising you will invest in each of your departments.

☐ Check month's heavy traffic pullers.

☐ Look for departments whose seasonal curve drops next month . . . must be cleared now.

☐ Dig for "sleepers," currently hot, but which don't show up in last year's figures.

☐ Promote newly expanded departments harder.

☐ Calculate co-op support available for each line of merchandise.

Fill in a day-by-day schedule to take full advantage of:

☐ Payroll days of important firms.

☐ Days of the week traffic is heaviest.

☐ National and local merchandising events offering tie-in possibilities.

☐ New or expanded departments.

☐ Current prices and your stock on hand . .. jot down items, prices, and ad sizes for each day.

and had become the company's top salesman. Calling on retail merchants every day in the Orange County area, Herb ran into competitive media salespeople regularly. One day he encountered a man who had recently started a new direct-mail advertising publication called the *Pennysaver*. He explained to Herb the benefits the *Pennysaver* offered the local advertiser:

1. Total weekly coverage of local geographic areas.
2. Direct mail into the home once a week, rather than dropped outside on the driveway every day.
3. Low total cost due to limited circulation.
4. Optional coverage of neighboring locales for minimal "pick-up" rates.
5. High reader interest created by classified-type "reader ads."
6. No competition with editorial readership since the publication is devoted entirely to advertising.

After several meetings Herb decided to accept the offer of his new acquaintance to become partners. He quit his secure job with the *Times* to take over the sales and management of the *Pennysaver* in southern Orange County and northern San Diego County.

He established three publications to start with, covering the communities of Laguna Beach, San Clemente, and Oceanside. For several years he struggled, selling ads all day and supervising art, production, printing, and delivery to the post office at night. At times he and the young advertising salespeople he hired were forced to scurry around to the local merchants to collect enough money to make the Friday payroll.

But as the local communities grew, so did the *Pennysaver* (Figure 20–13). Herb established new publications to cover Laguna Hills, Laguna Niguel, San Juan Capistrano, Capistrano Beach, Vista, Carlsbad, and Escondido. Within five years he had more than 10 *Pennysaver* publications, a new company headquarters and printing plant, over 30 employees, and a frighteningly huge overhead. But with his employees' help, he bought out his partner and forged ahead.

Five years later Sutton had over 40 publications, more than 150 employees, another new company headquarters, several company airplanes, and a personal net worth of several million dollars. The *Pennysaver* had been more than just successful; it had made publishing history. And the reason was simple. As Herb's salespeople were always quick to point out to local advertisers, the *Pennysaver* "pulled."

Choosing the right local advertising media is very important for two reasons: (1) most local advertisers have advertising budgets so limited that not all media that might be appropriate can be used, and (2) certain media are more effective for some businesses than others because the business is restricted either geographically or by type of customer.

Just like national advertisers, local advertisers select media depending on the type of customers the business is attempting to reach, the type of store or business doing the advertising, its location, trading area, competition, size of budget, and the nature of the message to be delivered.

Figure 20–13 A typical *Pennysaver* cover. Each edition covers a relatively small community of 9,000–12,000 homes so that local advertisers may target their messages to those customers within their immediate retail trading area. Rate discounts on neighboring editions allow larger advertisers to increase their circulation at a nominal cost.

Newspapers

For local advertisers, newspapers receive the greatest emphasis for the following reasons (Figure 20–14):

1. Most newspapers are oriented to the local community. This makes it possible for the local advertiser to reach the desired audience with a minimum of wasted circulation.
2. The cost is low considering the large number of prospects reached—so low, in fact, that it is affordable by most businesses. Also, most newspapers have a special rate for local or retail advertisers that is considerably lower than their national rates.
3. Advertising can be placed in the newspaper on very short notice.
4. Some selectivity is possible by advertising in special-interest sections of the newspaper such as sports or business news. For advertisers with very limited budgets, the classified section can even be an appropriate place to advertise.

Drawbacks to newspapers include their limited selectivity and their poor reproduction due to the paper quality.

Newspapers have both display and classified advertising departments. These departments are usually equipped to help advertisers prepare the complete advertisement including copy, art, typesetting, and layout/design. Often the service is given without charge. Large papers even have personnel who will visit an advertiser's place of business to do artwork (clothing is a good example) for advertisements.

For more details on newspapers, review Chapter 16.

Independent shopping guides

A growing number of cities have publications like the *Pennysaver,* which are published as a forum for local advertisers. Some use direct mail to distribute their publications and offer total circulation of a given area. This can be ideal for a local advertiser seeking distribution to the immediate trading area.

Shoppers (as they are called) are normally distributed free of charge, so the local advertiser should be careful to analyze the readership of the publication.

Magazines

The growth of local, slick, special-interest magazines has given local advertisers the opportunity to communicate with upper-income prospects through a prestigious medium. Publications such as *Palm Springs Life, Dallas Home and Garden,* and *Los Angeles Magazine* offer excellent photographic reproduction as well. Local advertisers who seek even greater prestige and selectivity can now use special city editions of major national publications such as *Time, Newsweek,* and *Sports Illustrated* through an organization called Media Networks Inc.

The attractiveness of magazine advertising may be limited because of cost or because a store's trading area may be much smaller than the market reached by the magazine. In addition, magazines require that advertising be submitted weeks before the publication date.

Review Chapter 16 for further information about magazines.

Radio and television

Advertising on local radio and TV stations is used increasingly by local advertisers because it usually reaches a strictly local audience, offers high impact, and actually has a very low cost per thousand. Since it offers so many exposures, though, the total cost may be considered high by some advertisers.

Broadcast commercial time is highly selective, since time slots can be purchased next to the most suitable programs for the product or service being offered. Top-40 radio stations, for example, are ideal advertising media for record dealers.

Immediacy and believability are additional benefits of broadcast media (Figure 20–15), since local personalities, or the advertisers themselves, can present the commercial message personally.

Most radio and television stations gladly offer assistance in the writing and production of commercials for local advertisers. Normally this assistance is provided with just a nominal charge for studio time plus additional fees for talent, special set designs, and tape dubbing.

For additional information on radio, television, and broadcast production, review Chapters 13 and 17.

Signs

The most direct method for merchants to invite customers into their stores is through the use of signs. Three types of signs are used by local advertisers: store signs, outdoor advertising, and transit advertising. Signs offer mass exposure with color, potentially large size, and very low cost per viewer, (Figure 20–16). A disadvantage is the inability to make frequent changes, which limits their use for promotion of many types of merchandise. When signs are used for specific products, it is usually for things that have continuous appeal such as automobiles or fast-food restaurant items.

Sign companies offer copy and art service. Their local representatives frequently provide this service without charge. However, producing signs is usually quite expensive and should be investigated thoroughly.

Chapter 18 gives more complete information on the use of outdoor and transit advertising.

Classified directories

Because the telephone book stays in the home or office as a ready source of information, it is widely used by local advertisers. For some

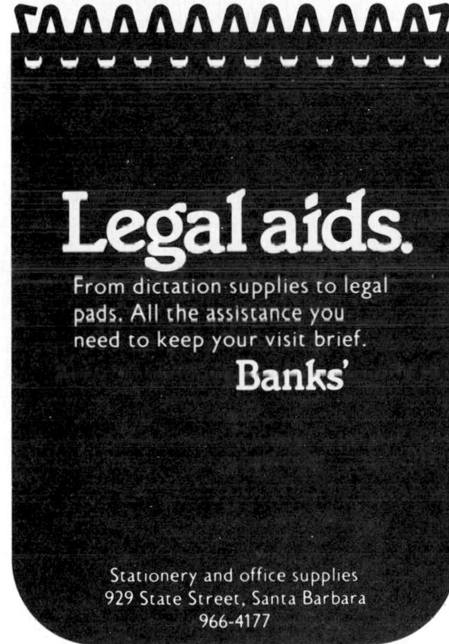

Figure 20–14 Banks' stationery store uses a consistent graphic format and clever headlines to attract attention to its small-space local newspaper campaign.

businesses, it is their sole means of advertising. Every business that has a telephone qualifies for a one-line insertion in the classified section without charge. Additional advertising must be paid for.

For local communities in large urban areas and for military bases, there are usually privately published classified telephone directories, which are less expensive to use than the large telephone company directories. These private directories cater to the special interests of the immediate locale and therefore offer excellent support to the small retail merchant or local professional service.

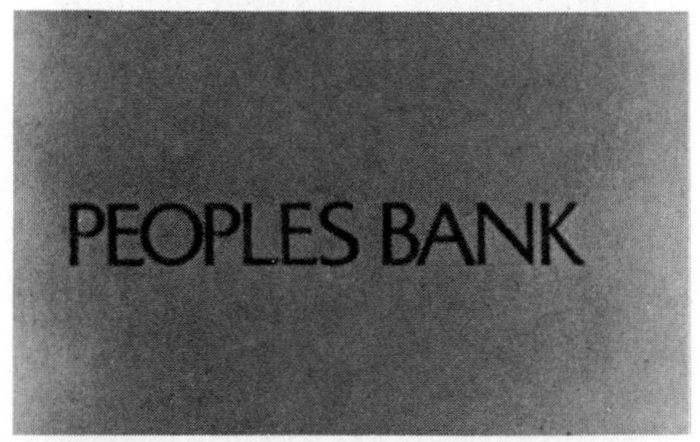

Figure 20–15 To be effective, TV commercials don't have to be expensive or complex, especially for local advertisers. They simply need to be well-written, well-executed, and communicative.

(SOUND OF WEDDING MARCH THROUGHOUT)

ANNCR. (VO): Peoples Bank of South Carolina announces its merger . . .

(Peoples Bank name dissolves into Bankers Trust)

ANNCR. (VO): . . . with Bankers Trust of South Carolina.

(As Bankers Trust name begins moving off screen we hear sound of tin cans)

Handbills

Because of their low cost and their effectiveness, handbills can be an important medium for local advertisers. They are especially useful for making grand opening announcements, advertising sales, and periodically reminding people of the merchandise or service offered (Figure 20–17).

Handbills should be very carefully planned to create a good appearance. Attention should also be given to the message so that effective appeals are built into the headline and body copy.

Although the printer should not be relied upon for advice about the copy, a good printer can provide sound advice about the quality of paper to use, colors, size, cost, and general appearance.

Direct mail

Although it can be used to reach mass markets, the superior advantage of direct-mail advertising is its ability to reach specific market segments. The greatest use of direct mail is envelope stuffers, which accompany monthly bills mailed to charge-account customers.

Direct mail is likely to get the reader's undivided attention because it has no competition from other advertisers at the same time. Local advertisers with limited budgets can use direct mail to great advantage. The number of pieces mailed and the printing costs are simply adjusted to the budget. Unlimited graphic possibilities can be used to meet the requirements for most any product or service. Most local direct-mail houses can offer copy, art, and printing as well as mailing service.

Sales promotion

Many sales promotion methods discussed in Chapter 19 can be uniquely effective for local advertisers.

Sampling Giving the customer a small sample of the product is always effective. Products that lend themselves to this approach are ice cream stores, delicatessens, fabric stores, butcher stores, and bakery shops.

Specialties Specialties, including calendars, rulers, shoehorns, and pens, are inexpensive for the store but can be valuable to the customer. These items generally contain the store name, address, telephone number, and often a brief sales message.

Coupons Coupons provide a special inducement to the customer to make a purchase. Usually a reduction in price is given when the customer presents the coupon, which has been clipped from a newspaper ad or handbill or received in the mail. Coupons can be used to build store traffic, to encourage the use of a product for the first time, and to test the effectiveness of a particular advertisement.

Telephone selling This technique can be used to reach both customers and potential customers. Charge-account customers can be called about a sale, and inactive accounts can be revived by asking the individuals to return to the store once again. New accounts can also be developed with this method.

Demonstrations Local advertisers can develop their own demonstrations according to their product line and their market. Bridal shops can give sessions on how to plan for a wedding, and sporting goods stores can hire a golf pro to give lessons.

Shows Probably the most common type of local shows are the fashion shows given by clothing retailers. Other types include building and home shows given by hardware stores and new-car shows given by local car dealers.

Free publicity The media are always on the lookout for unusual items that may be of interest to their readers or listeners. Stores that

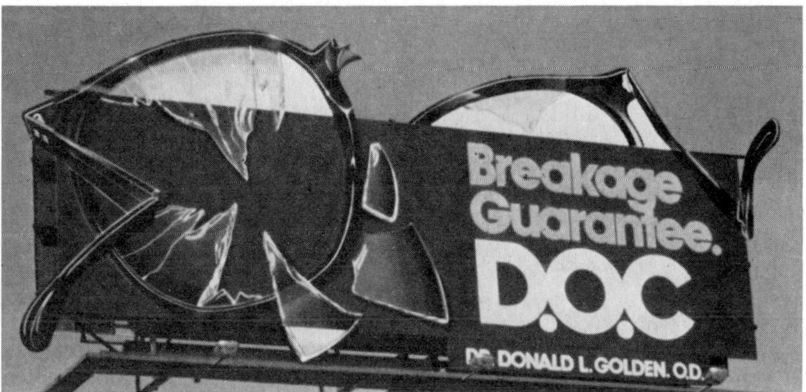

Figure 20–16 Detroit Optometric Centers use the dynamic oversize possibilities of outdoor advertising to communicate the breakage guarantee to eyeglass wearers. Even with poor eyesight, drivers don't have to squint to get Dr. Golden's message.

hold major grand openings, have important personnel changes, or have new and unusual lines of merchandise are newsworthy and might be covered by the local media.

Community involvement This is an effective method of enhancing the image of a business. It can involve sponsoring a local activity such as a baseball team, a summer camp for needy youngsters, or a scholarship. Another way of becoming involved with the community

Figure 20–17 Restaurants are one of the most common users of handbills. Coupons are often included to stimulate store traffic and to give the advertiser some feedback about the handbill's effectiveness.

is allowing store facilities to be used for social of civic organizations for fund-raisers or meetings. Many businesses such as banks and savings associations have rooms specifically designed for community use. (See the Checklist.)

Determining creative direction

One of the most competitive businesses in any local market is the grocery business. Characterized by high overhead, low profit, heavy discounting, constant promotion, and massive doses of food-day advertising, food retailing is a difficult business at best.

The Tom Thumb Page stores in Dallas had an additional problem. They had elected to avoid price competition whenever possible and instead to compete on the basis of quality and service. This policy made it potentially difficult to attract new customers and create store traffic, since grocery customers tend to be very price-oriented.

The Tom Thumb chain had been doing what might best be described as "maintenance advertising" in routine food-day newspaper sections for about four years. When they hired their new advertising agency, KCBN, Inc., the chain's owners, Bob and Charles Cullum, explained their situation and their objectives. They asked the agency to develop a campaign that would show that Tom Thumb was, in fact, very competitive in giving top value even though the prices might be slightly higher.

Barbara Harwell and Chuck Bua, the agency's creative directors, responded by developing a local institutional campaign that made grocery advertising history. They suggested opening the campaign with a television promotion for Thanksgiving turkeys. They convinced the Cullums and Tom Hairston, the chain's president, that to present a truly quality image they would have to create an absolutely outstanding commercial in terms of production quality. (The problems they encountered producing this commercial were discussed in Chapter 13.) Furthermore, to communicate that Tom Thumb's policies truly warranted higher prices, they persuaded them to make such a bold, risky statement that it would actually impress the viewing public. Hairston and the Cullums agreed. Two weeks before Thanksgiving the campaign began.

The commercial opened with a tight closeup of a live turkey. As the off-camera announcer spoke, the camera pulled slowly back and the turkey reacted to the copy with an occasional "Gobble."

The announcer said:

> At Tom Thumb we stand behind everything we sell . . . and that's a promise. It's always been that way. Even when we started, Mr. Cullum said, "We want our customers to be happy with everything they buy in this store. If a woman buys a turkey from us and comes back the day after Thanksgiving with a bag of bones and says she didn't like it, we'll give her her money back . . . or give her another turkey."

The moment he said that, the turkey reacted with a big "gobble" and ran off-camera.The commercial closed on the company logo with the announcer saying, "That's the way we do business at Tom Thumb . . . we stand behind everything we sell, and that's a promise" (Figure 20–18).

The company merchandised the campaign by printing the slogan "We stand behind everything we sell . . . and that's a promise" on grocery sacks, on red lapel buttons for employees, and on outdoor billboards. The audio portions of the commercials were aired as radio spots. Most important, employee orientation meetings were held to explain the concepts to the company's personnel and to make sure that any merchandise returns received a friendly, cordial smile.

The reaction to the campaign was astounding. First it became the topic of local conversation. Then people began to wonder how many turkeys might be returned for the money. Local newspeople began

Checklist for creating local advertising

The increasing complexity of retailing—such as the rapid growth and diversity of competition, changing customer shopping habits, and the continuing squeeze on profits—has made it vitally important that merchants get full value from their advertising investments.

The most important single factor determining how many people will read any newspaper ad is the skill and technique used in preparing the ad. Readership studies have generally indicated that:

Ad noting increases with the size of the ad.

People note more ads directed at their own sex.

Color, particularly for illustrations, increases the number of readers.

Tie-ins with local and/or special news events are effective in attracting readership.

The following suggestions for copy and layout are drawn from several studies. When effectively used, these techniques and rules generally increase readership.

☐ Make your ads easily recognizable. Studies have shown that advertisements which are distinctive in their use of art, layout techniques, and typefaces usually enjoy a higher readership than run-of-the-mill advertising. Try to make your ads distinctively different in appearance from the advertising of your competitors—and then keep your ads appearance consistent. This way, readers will recognize your ads even before they read them.

☐ Use a simple layout. Ads should not be crossword puzzles. The layout should carry the reader's eye through the message easily and in proper sequence: from headline to illustration to explanatory copy to price to your store's name. Avoid the use of too many different typefaces, overly decorative borders, and reverse plates.

☐ Use a dominant element—a large picture or headline—to insure quick visibility. Photographs and realistic drawings have about equal attention-getting value, but photographs of real people win more readership. So do action pictures. Photographs of local people or places also have high attention value.

☐ Use a prominent benefit headline. The first question a reader asks of an ad is: "What's in it for me?" Select the main benefit which your merchandise offers and feature it in a compelling headline. Amplify this message in subheads. Avoid generalized quality claims. Your headline will be easier to read if it is black on white and is not surprinted on part of the illustration.

☐ Let your white space work for you. Don't overcrowd your ad. White space is an important layout element in newspaper advertising because the average page is so heavy with small type. White space focuses the reader's attention on your ad and will make your headline and illustration stand out. When a "crowded" ad is necessary, such as for a sale, departmentalize your items so that the reader can find his way through them easily.

talking about the campaign and showing the commercial in their newscasts. Finally the top disc jockey in Dallas started a contest inviting listeners to guess how many turkeys would be returned to Tom Thumb. The day after Thanksgiving the local television film crews were waiting at the stores to count and interview people carrying bags of bones.

One woman said she returned a turkey and got her money back with no questions asked. Another said she was given her money immediately but that she then gave the money back. She had just wanted to test them to see whether they were telling the truth.

The final score was 30,000 turkeys sold and only 18 returned, a fantastic marketing, advertising, and publicity success. Since that time the story has been reported in numerous grocery and advertising trade journals, and Tom Thumb Page Stores has successfully continued the

---

☐ Make your copy complete. Know all there is to know about the merchandise you sell and select the benefits most appealing to your customers. These benefits might have to do with fashion, design, performance, or the construction of your merchandise. Sizes and colors available are important, pertinent information.

☐ State price or range of prices. Dollar figures have good attention value. Don't be afraid to quote your price, even if it's high. Readers often will overestimate omitted prices. If the advertised price is high, explain why the item represents a good value—perhaps because of superior materials or workmanship, or extra luxury features. Point out the actual saving to the reader and spell out your credit and layaway plans.

☐ Specify branded merchandise. If the item is a known brand, say so in your advertising. Manufacturers spend large sums to sell their goods, and you can capitalize on their advertising while enhancing the reputation of your store by featuring branded items.

☐ Include related items. Make two sales instead of one by offering related items along with a featured one. For instance, when a dishwasher is advertised, also show a disposer.

☐ Urge your readers to buy now. Ask for the sale. You can stimulate prompt action by using such phrases as "limited supply" or "this week only." If mail-order coupons are included in your ads, provide spaces large enough for customers to fill them in easily.

☐ Don't forget your store name and address. Check every ad to be certain you have included your store name, address, telephone number, and store hours. Even if yours is a long-established store, this is important. Don't overemphasize your signature, but make it plain. In a large ad, mention the store name several times in the copy.

☐ Don't be too clever. Many people distrust cleverness in advertising, just as they distrust salespeople who are too glib. Headlines and copy generally are far more effective when they are straightforward than when they are tricky. Clever or tricky headlines and copy often are misunderstood.

☐ Don't use unusual or difficult words. Many of your customers may not understand words which are familiar to you. Words like "couturier," "gourmet," "coiffure," as well as trade and technical terms, may be confusing and misunderstood. Everybody understands simple language. Nobody resents it. Use it.

☐ Don't generalize. Be specific at all times. Shoppers want all the facts before they buy. Facts sell more.

☐ Don't make excessive claims. The surest way to lose customers is to make claims in your advertising that you can't back up in your store. Go easy with superlatives and unbelievable values. Remember: if you claim your prices are unbelievable, your readers are likely to agree.

"We stand behind everything we sell" advertising campaign theme.

In planning the local advertising effort, the last step is the determination of creative direction. Certain elements of the creative direction will have already been determined in the planning process. The local advertiser and its agency will have already decided, for example, who the primary audience is, what the competitive advertising environment is, what policies to follow regarding price competition, what strategies to use to achieve the company's objectives, how much to spend in the advertising effort, and what media are available to use.

Tom Thumb and KCBN had already determined these things before the creative process began. What remained was to determine how to say what they wanted to say and who could help them say it. In the case of Tom Thumb, KCBN provided the answer to both questions. For other local advertisers, the solution might have been considerably different depending on the creative direction and talent used.

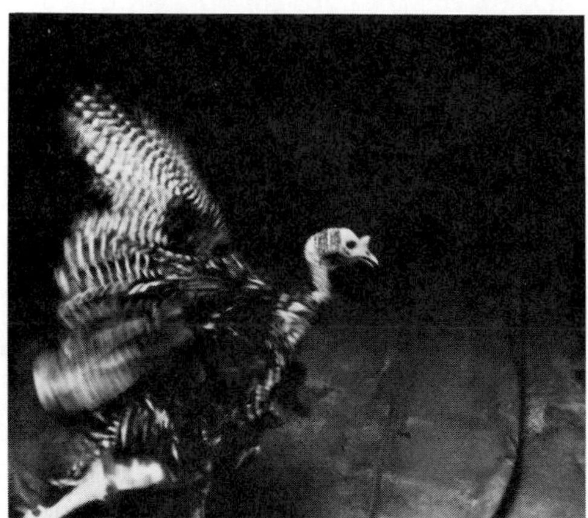

Figure 20–18 Tom Thumb Page Stores talked turkey with customers by promising to stand behind everything they sell.

Seeking creative assistance

Advertisers have a number of sources to whom they can turn for help, including (1) advertising agencies, (2) the local media (3) free lancers and consultants, (4) creative boutiques, (5) syndicated art services, and (6) wholesalers and manufacturers.

Advertising agencies

Because they are usually not equipped to do their own advertising work, local advertisers increasingly turn to agencies for help. One misconception is that all agencies are large and handle only sizable accounts. In many communities there are small agencies that assist local advertisers. Local advertisers find they need help in locating markets, determining media mixes, developing better ads, and following up their advertising with effective evaluation (Figure 20–19). Of course, the quality of agencies varies tremendously, and only the competent agency can be a real aid to an advertiser. Specifically, an agency can help a local advertiser in the following ways:

1. Analyzing the local advertiser's business and the product or service being sold; evaluating the markets for the business including channels of distribution.
2. Evaluating the advertiser's competitive position in the marketplace.
3. Determining the best advertising media and providing advice on the costs and effectiveness of each.
4. Devising an advertising plan and, once approved, implementing it by preparing the advertisements and placing them.
5. Simplifying the advertiser's administrative workload by taking over the complex task of media interviewing, analysis, checking, and bookkeeping.
6. Assisting in other aspects of the advertising and promotion effort

by helping with sales contests, publicity, grand openings, and other activities.

Advertising agencies tend to be used less extensively with local advertisers than with national advertisers. A major reason for this is that most media, including newspapers, have two sets of advertising rates—one for national advertisers and another for retail or local ad-

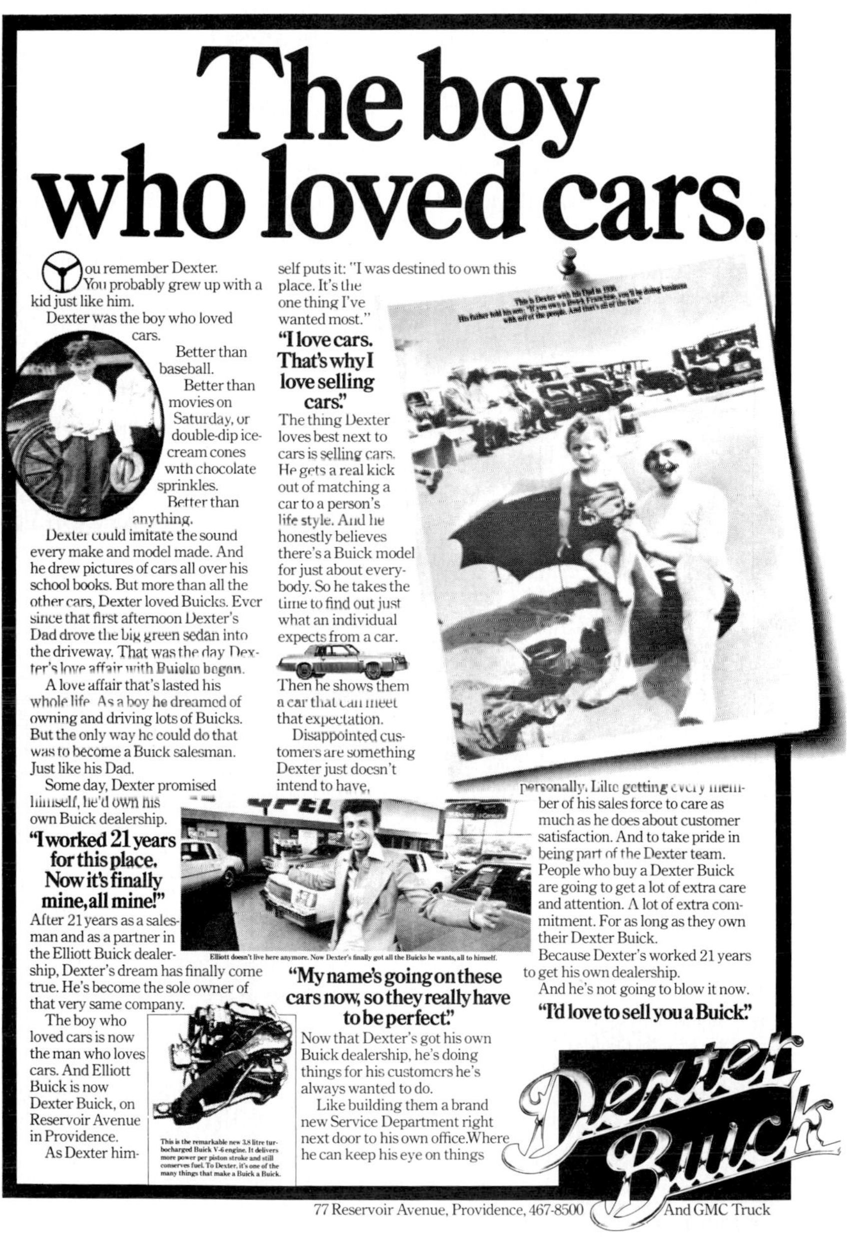

Figure 20–19 An agency-produced ad for a local advertiser. The creativity available from professional advertising people is often worth the extra expense, as this award-winner shows.

vertisers. The local rate is lower, and it is not commissionable. Because the vast majority of local advertising is placed directly by the local advertiser rather than through an advertising agency, the advantage is a lower cost to the retailer for advertising media. Also offered are frequency and quantity discounts that give additional savings to the local advertiser.

Many advertisers simply don't spend enough money on advertising to warrant the hiring of an advertising agency. And many advertising agencies do not accept local advertisers as clients because of low budgets.

For a complete discussion of advertising agencies, see Chapter 4.

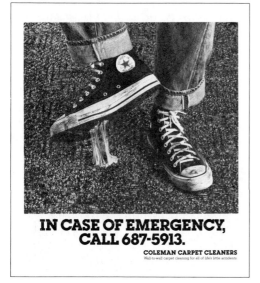

Figure 20–20 Coleman Carpet Cleaners used a creative boutique, Marty Neumeier Design, to create this award-winning advertisement for itself. This was just one of a family of stunning, small-space ads that told the company's story quickly and imaginatively.

Local media

The advertising media, in addition to selling space or time, offer a multitude of advertising services to local advertisers. These services range from planning advertising campaigns to actually preparing the advertisement. Also the media employ research companies to determine the demographic makeup of their readers or listeners.

Free lancers and consultants

Because some advertising people like to be their own boss, they act as free agents who often work out of their home preparing copy, art and layout, photography, or other services. Free lancers often specialize not only in the type of service they perform but also in the type of advertisers, such as car dealerships, clothing stores, or travel agencies.

Creative boutiques

A boutique performs only the creative work. Employees of such shops specialize as copywriters and artists (Figure 20–20). They charge a negotiated fee or a percentage of the media expenditure. Local advertisers who want the best creative work but are not interested in any other services provided by a full-service agency frequently turn to this source for help.

Syndicated art services

Syndicated art services can be useful to local advertisers by offering them a large book of artwork, called *clip art,* ready to be clipped and used in an advertisement. Clip art is available for various types of businesses and is often tied in to seasons, holidays, and other promotional angles. Clip art is available by direct subscription or through the advertising department of a local newspaper.

Wholesalers and manufacturers

As a service to their distributors and dealers, wholesalers and manufacturers sometime provide ready-made advertising (Figure 20–21).

The most common type of help from manufacturers that local advertisers receive is called *vertical cooperative advertising.* The manufacturer normally provides the ad and a percentage of the cost of the advertising time or space (Figure 20–22). The local advertiser only has to have the local newspaper drop in the name and address of the business or have the radio and TV station add a tag line with the name, address, and telephone number of the firm. Because the manufacturer provides the ad, the manufacturer can be sure the ad puts forth the merchandise in the best possible light.

Horizontal cooperative advertising is a joint effort on the part of realtors, insurance agents, pharmacies, car dealers, or travel agents to pay for an institutional ad to create traffic for their type of business rather than for one particular business. Auto dealers in a central area of town often attempt to build traffic for all their business by pooling their advertising dollars and advertising the central area as the place to shop for cars. Shopping centers often do the same thing.

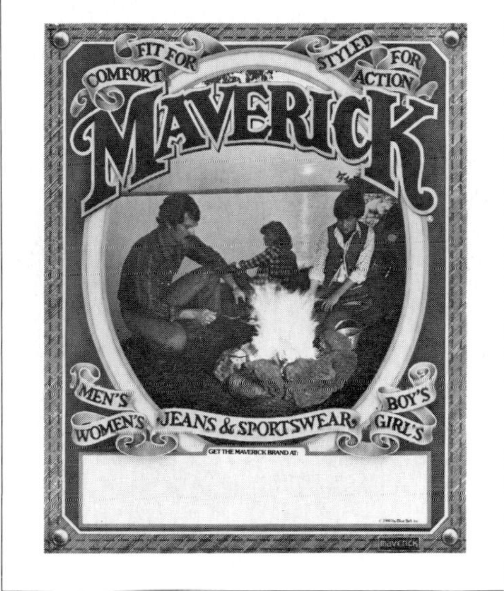

Figure 20–21 This reproduction proof for a newspaper advertisement was provided to the retailer by the manufacturer. Such an advertisement is part of a cooperative advertising program in which the media costs are shared by the manufacturer and the retailer.

Creating the local advertising message

It was 1951 when Cal Worthington first started appearing on Los Angeles television stations to pitch his car dealership. Sponsoring third-rate movies on late-night and Saturday afternoon TV, Worthington appeared in a western outfit and cowboy hat and introduced a variety of hillbilly singers who were on hand all weekend to entertain customers looking at cars.

Thirty years later he was still at it, only the zaniness had increased. He now appears with any of a variety of domesticated wild animals (all of whom are introduced as "my dog Spot") and croons a tune promising to "stand upon his head" to make a deal on your new or used car. Or he offers 2,500 blue-chip stamps or a TV just to "come in and see me first."

Worthington has achieved far more than just sales success. He is ribbed by talk show host Johnny Carson in his monologues, and people stop him in airports all over the country to get his autograph. His fame, therefore, has spread well beyond the local market he serves (Figure 20–23).

The same thing has happened to local advertisers in St. Louis, New York, Des Moines, and around the country. *Dun's Review* refers to these pitchmen as the "Kings of the Tacky Commercials," calling them a "jarring, growing phenomenon on local TV."[1] Some of these low-budget, do-it-yourself advertisers have been so successful that they have engendered a near-cult following of viewers and imitators.

On the other hand, many who have tried the same approach of producing an assortment of low-budget, in-house commercials for viewing on late-night TV have failed miserably and eventually quit trying. Lee Shapiro, owner of Lee's Bars 'n Stools, appeared on Los Angeles TV as many as 60 times a week with his plea "don't judge us by our commercials, folks," which many people obviously did anyway. He's no longer using the medium.

In print advertising many local advertisers have achieved remarkable success using what some professional advertising agency artists might refer to as a "schlock" approach. Heavy bold type, items crowded into advertising space, loud headlines, and unsophisticated

Figure 20–22 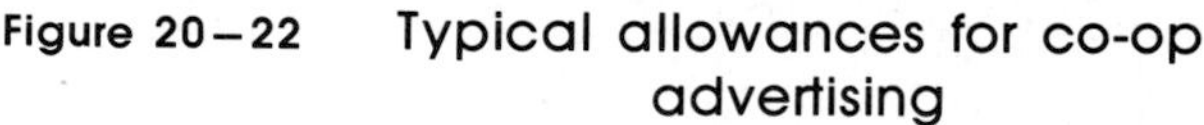
Typical allowances for co-op advertising

Store	Co-op dollars as a percentage of total ad budget
Appliance dealers	80
Clothing stores	35
Department stores	50
Discount stores	20
Drugstores	70
Food stores	75
Furniture stores	30
Household goods	30
Jewelers	30
Shoe stores	50

Figure 20–23 Cal Worthington and his "dog" Spot prove that advertisers who do their own commercials can be highly successful.

graphic design contribute to the "schlock" look, whether it be for a car dealer, a restaurant, or a real estate firm.

As in the case of Action Realty, one has to ask: What are they selling? Is the creative message honest, consistent, and effective? If the answer is yes, then many people say that's all that matters. Invariably the question comes down to whether or not the objectives of the company are being met.

To direct and control the creative aspects of advertisements and commercials, the local advertiser should develop a checklist of creative do's and don'ts for his or her particular business and follow it. This will at least assure consistency.

Summary

Local advertising is placed by businesses within a particular city or county and aimed at customers in the same geographic area. Local advertising is important because it is in the local arena that most sales are made or lost. While the basic principles used by national advertisers are applicable to local advertisers, local advertisers have special problems that they must address. Local advertising appears in either product advertising or institutional advertising. Product advertising can be further subdivided into regular price-line advertising, sale advertising, and clearance advertising.

The objectives of local advertising differ from those of national advertising in terms of emphasis and time. The needs of local advertisers tend to be more immediate. Therefore advertising is usually intended to increase traffic, turn over inventory, or bring in new customers right away.

Successful local advertisers realize the importance of marketing and advertising planning. This includes analyzing the local market, analyzing the competition, conducting adequate research, determining objectives and strategy, establishing a realistic budget, planning media strategy, and determining creative direction.

Local businesses are often highly seasonal. By plotting anticipated sales patterns throughout the year, business owners can allot a percentage of their total yearly advertising to each month. In general, the most advertising dollars should be spent just before the time when customers are most likely to respond.

There are many media normally available to local advertisers. These include newspapers, individual shopping guides, local magazines, local radio and television, and outdoor advertising. In addition, many local advertisers use direct mail, classified directories, sales promotion, and free publicity.

Perhaps the biggest problem for local advertisers is determining creative direction. Fortunately, there are a number of sources to whom they can turn for help. These sources include local advertising agencies, the local media, free lancers and consultants, creative boutiques, syndicated art services, and wholesalers, manufacturers, and distributors.

Questions for review

1. What are the types of local advertising? What are the objectives of each?
2. What does a local advertiser hope to learn by analyzing the local market?
3. How can analyzing the competition give local advertisers the competitive edge?
4. How would you describe the various kinds of primary research?
5. What are some important sources of secondary research data for local advertisers?
6. What are the major factors that influence the establishment of the advertising budget?
7. How should an advertiser go about developing the annual sales and advertising plan? What basic questions would a local merchant need to answer in formulating such a plan?
8. What media should local advertisers consider? Which usually receive the most emphasis? Explain why.
9. What sales promotional tools can be effective for local advertisers? What makes them uniquely useful for local advertisers?
10. What sources can local advertisers turn to for creative assistance? What are the advantages and disadvantages of each?

21

Business advertising

One of the hottest musical groups of the 1970s was the Bee Gees. Maybe you were there on a warm summer evening, sitting in a molded plastic seat, eating a hot dog or sipping a soft drink, as the lights in the stadium were dimmed and thousands of young people started to holler, scream, and clap. Suddenly spotlights fanned the stage in dramatic bursts of color, musical chords exploded through the theater's finely tuned space-age sound system, and the announcer heralded the entrance of the stars of disco: "Ladies and gentlemen, the Bee Gees!" (Figure 21–1).

You stood quickly to get a glimpse of Barry, Robin, and Maurice Gibb as they leaped onstage amid the silver flash of metal guitars and trumpets. In front, behind, and all around you, people had carefully laid their newly purchased record albums on their seats so they could raise their hands above their heads to clap, yell, and shout.

Little did you or they know that as you were standing there enjoying the thrilling sounds of rock and disco, you were actually completing a long chain of business-to-business marketing and advertising that keeps thousands, even millions, of people employed, fed, and housed—and ends up giving rock groups like the Bee Gees an incredible family income.

In 1978 alone, their total record sales, along with their featured musical roles in *Saturday Night Fever* and *Sgt. Pepper's Lonely Hearts Club Band* and their live concert appearances, netted the brothers Gibb over $25 million. The flow of dollars to this family has continued on into the 80s. This might not have been possible without the millions and millions of dollars that had previously been spent in business advertising activities.

The invisibility of business advertising

The reason you and the other people in the audience were unaware of the chain of marketing events leading up to the rock concert is because this chain is largely invisible to you as a consumer. Business marketing and business advertising are activities directed to businesspeople. Unless you are actively involved in some business, it is unlikely that you see it.

The majority of advertising you see as a consumer appears on radio or TV, in the daily newspaper or monthly magazines, and on billboards or transit panels. These are all mass consumer media. Business advertising, on the other hand, is concentrated in specialized business publications or professional journals, in direct-mail pieces sent to business establishments, or in trade shows held for specific areas of business.

There are four distinct types of business-to-business advertising which we shall discuss in this chapter. These include trade advertising, industrial advertising, professional advertising, and farm (agricultural) advertising. Each type represents an important market to some company that wants to sell its goods and services. And each type can be found somewhere in the chain of events leading up to our rock concert.

Trade advertising

In the music business vast amounts of money are spent to advertise record albums to the thousands of retail stores that in turn sell them to consumers. This is called *trade advertising*—the advertising of goods and services to wholesalers and retailers. Generally these middlemen buy the products that are advertised in specialized publications like *Music Trades Magazine* for the purpose of reselling them. However, some advertised items may be bought for use in the middleman's own business such as office equipment, store fixtures, or specialized business services.

The major objective of trade advertising is to obtain greater distribution of the product being sold. That may be accomplished by developing more sales outlets or by selling more products to existing sales outlets.

The success of the Bee Gees' rock concerts depended on how popular the group was (Figure 21–2). Popularity can be measured in terms of record sales in a geographic region before a concert is even scheduled. By the same token, one of the reasons for the concert tour is to promote the sale of more albums. If the Bee Gees had scheduled an appearance in Des Moines, for example, RCA could promote the sale of many more albums to local Des Moines record dealers to satisfy the expected increase in demand before and after the concert.

Other examples of trade advertising are airlines and hotels trying to sell tour ideas to travel agents through special travel agency publications or by direct mail; and Richard D. Irwin, Inc., the publisher of this textbook, distributing its catalog of books to bookstores throughout the United States and the world.

Figure 21–1 A consumer ad for a Bee Gees concert. Unseen is the vast amount of business to business activity stimulated by the consumer activity.

Industrial advertising

The production of a rock concert involves more than a group of musicians standing on a stage playing their instruments. It involves the intricate use of highly sophisticated electronic equipment to produce an exciting array of light and sound designed to complement the performers and fascinate the audience.

The Pacer Corporation is one of several companies that manufacture the expensive ticket-issuing machines used by cashiers in concert hall and theater box offices. "Is your box office out of control? Tame it with Pacer Cashtronic!" says the ad. They use *industrial advertising*—the advertising of goods or services that are used in the production or manufacture of other goods or services.

The ad in Figure 21–3 for Pacer's Cashtronic 600 ticket-issuing machine was run in *Theater Crafts* magazine. It was aimed at theater owners, managers, purchasing agents and others who are responsible for buying this type of equipment. By the same token, designers and engineers at Pacer Corporation may have responded to industrial ads in *Electronic Design Magazine* or *Electronic Product News* for the particular dials, switches, or electronic components they used in the manufacture of their Cashtronic 600.

The objectives of industrial advertising are to (1) reach the person who either directly or indirectly influences the buying of the industrial goods, (2) build awareness of the goods, (3) seek to attain a preference for the goods, (4) identify new customers and develop sales leads by soliciting inquiries, (5) motivate distributors of industrial goods by illustrating to them that you are helping them sell your products, and (6) build company reputation. This type of advertising is especially directed to individuals who make purchase decisions: design

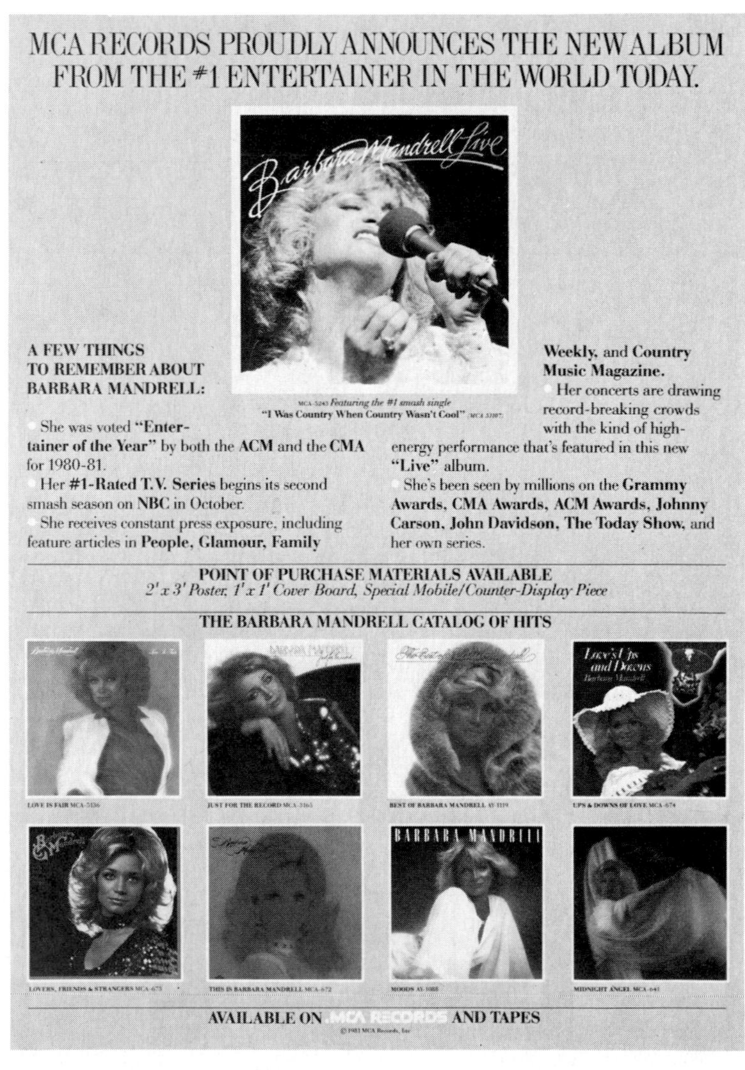

Figure 21–2 MCA Records promotes albums and tapes by Barbara Mandrell in this trade ad which appeared in *Billboard* magazine. Note the offer to dealers of point-of-purchase materials including a poster and counter-display piece. Other popular music trade publications in which recording companies advertise are *Cash Box, Music Retailer* and *Record World.*

engineers, purchasing agents, comptrollers, and plant managers.

Industrial goods include the following:

1. Goods that are used in the production of other goods or become a physical part of another product: raw materials, semimanufactured goods, components, etc. (Figure 21–4).
2. Goods that are used to conduct business and do not become part of another product (as illustrated in Figure 21–3); capital goods (e.g., machinery, desks, operating supplies); and services for which the user contracts.[1]

Figure 21–3 An example of industrial advertising to theater managers.

Industrial advertising can be a way of reaching prospects who are unavailable to sales personnel. Moreover, it is less costly to use advertising to reach people who influence purchasing decisions than to use personal selling. It is also an effective means of paving the way for salespeople when they do call. And it can act as an effective reinforcement or follow-up to the sales call.

Professional advertising

Where do you suppose the performers at rock concerts learned their trade? Almost invariably they have had years of study and coaching

Figure 21–4 This industrial ad is directed to fast-food retailers.

under the guidance of professional music educators. And these professional educators use numerous tools, books, and equipment that they may have learned about through professional advertising.

Professional advertising is advertising that is directed to individuals who are normally licensed and operate under a code of ethics or under a professional set of standards. Teachers, accountants, doctors, dentists, architects, and lawyers are examples. Often the publications used for professional advertising are the official organs of professional societies such as the *Music Educators Journal,* which is published by the Music Educators National Conference whose members are responsible for music education. Similarly, *International Musician* is the professional journal for members of the American Federation of Musicians. Likewise, the architects and engineers who designed the auditorium for the rock concert may have specified building materials advertised in professional architectural or engineering journals. And before the concert the anxiety-ridden concert promoter may have consulted his doctor and been given a sedative advertised to doctors in medical journals (Figure 21–5).

Professional advertising has three objectives: (1) to convince professional people to buy items such as equipment and supplies by brand name for use in their work, (2) to encourage professionals to recommend or prescribe a specific product or service to their clients or patients, and (3) to persuade the person to use the product personally. (See the Ad Lab.)

Since personal selling by salespersons, called "detail" people, is the primary tool used in selling to doctors and dentists, professional advertising is also designed to augment and reinforce sales calls and to act as a reminder between calls.

Farm advertising

Whether it is hot dogs at a rock concert or roast beef at the dinner table, the nation's farmers have to satisfy our need for food. Farming is America's largest single industry. Farmers are consumers, of course, but they are businesspeople, too. Farm advertising is directed to the grower, producer, or dealer of agricultural products (Figure 21–6).

The objectives of *farm (or agricultural) advertising* are to (1) establish a desire for a particular brand with emphasis on quality and performance, (2) build acceptance of the dealer who sells the product because the farmer seeks services that go along with the product, and (3) create preference for products by showing the farmer how the product will increase efficiency, reduce risks, and widen profit margins.

In addition to equipment and machinery, farmers buy a wide range of other products including fertilizers, petroleum, livestock feed, seed, animal health aids, irrigation systems, and chemicals. Farmers also avail themselves of services such as marketing information and economic forecasts; soil testing; crop dusting; insurance, tax, and legal advice; stud service; auctions; banking and financial services; and help on environmental pollution problems that may result from their farming activities.

Today there are fewer farms and larger farms, with more specialization and mechanization. Farmers are better businesspeople and are more knowledgeable purchasers. Advertising directed to farmers must take into account that the farmer wants and demands facts, figures, and results backed by hard-core proof.

It is interesting to note the volume of trade, industrial, professional, and agricultural advertising that is prepared and placed. The Standard Rate and Data Service lists 3,300 farm and business publications that carry business advertising. That's almost four times the number of consumer publications listed.

Even though business advertising may seem invisible to you and your contemporaries at a rock concert, it affects all of us significantly.

The marketing of professionals: Hanging out a shingle via Madison Avenue

One by one, professional organizations have—sometimes unwillingly—relaxed their restrictions. The ever-increasing numbers entering the fields of medicine, law, dentistry, and accounting—professions which more or less guarantee high incomes and prestige—have made advertising almost a necessity for those trying to forge a name for themselves. Young professionals in today's competitive marketplace have no time for the slow-building, country club and personal contact route. In addition, the distrust spawned by high fees and reports of deceptive practices have affected the professional's standing in the public eye. But the question remains: Will advertising—so long taboo to professionals—work?

Arnold Siegel, a San Francisco–based accountant, whose firm Siegel, Sugarman & Seput, was the first to advertise after the American Institute of Certified Public Accountants rejected its 50-year ban on advertising in 1978, says, "I am so sure that advertising works that a question such as 'Will advertising work in the professions?' is like asking if the sun will rise tomorrow. the real question now for professionals is 'Will advertising work for me or my firm?' and I think the answer is that it will *have* to. The environment for the professions is changing so that aggressive marketing will be a fact of life by the end of the decade. The sooner professionals start making advertising work for them, the better chance they will have to survive."

Siegel asserts that since his firm started advertising, "billings have quadrupled, the staff has tripled, the professional staff need spend practically no time making contacts with prospective clients, freeing them to spend their time practicing accounting and developing their own pursuits, and the firm is now widely recognized for quality service in the community, nationally and internationally."

In addition to an increasingly competitive marketplace that forces professionals to advertise, proponents of advertising claim it will force the cost of professional services down (although some opponents wonder where the money to pay for advertising will come from). Advertising's advocates also believe it will remove some of the mystique surrounding practitioners and educate the consumer to be less intimidated and more skeptical.

Educational—not sensational

Educating the public is a sensitive issue. Education has traditionally not only been a right, but a duty of professionals. Advertisers believe that tasteful, informative ads are one means of such education. Others argue that advertising crosses the boundary into the unethical areas of self-laudation and publicity-seeking.

Kantrowitz and Goldhamer, a law firm with offices in Manhattan and Rockland County, N.Y., has taken steps to educate the consumer and at the same time force their name into public consciousness. In addition to twice-weekly newspaper ads, yellow pages advertising, and one short-lived stab at radio, they sponsor occasional seminars on topics such as divorce, buying and selling real estate, or making a will. Walter Kantrowitz states these seminars have drawn a full house every time, and that more are in the works.

More successes

Perhaps the best known example of legal advertising is

What makes business advertising different?

In addition to being relatively invisible, there are several other basic differences that characterize business advertising. Consumer advertising is directly to consumers. Business advertising is directed to businesspeople. Therefore, business markets are different. So are the channels of distribution used by business marketers. And so are the buyers and their requirements. As a result, the entire marketing mix may be different. And the promotional methods used, including advertising, must be appropriately adjusted to the situation.

the campaign for the Legal Clinic of Jacoby & Meyers. The first TV spot ever broadcast for a law firm ran on the CBS Morning News, August 26, 1977. At that time, Jacoby & Meyers was operating four storefront offices in Los Angeles and seeing 80 new clients a month. Today they operate 35 offices in Los Angeles, New York, San Diego, Sacramento, and Stockton, and see over 4,500 new clients each month.

Reservations still exist

Reluctance to try advertising is the result of several factors. The dignified image professionals maintain of both themselves and their professions leads many to consider advertising tasteless, unethical, and inappropriate.

In addition, professionals with established practices are often overworked as it is and have no need for additional business. And there are those who are unwilling to announce publicly they are not quite as busy as they would like to be. Those opposed to advertising also argue that publicizing a "standard service for a standard fee" is impossible because each case is unique and not immune to unexpected problems or costs.

Pitfalls to avoid

There exists a running debate about what information advertising should contain. Some feel a simple listing of services, office hours, and location is sufficient and that price listing is inappropriate.

Dr. Robert Tublin, a practicing dentist and vice president of the International Federation of Health Professionals, stresses education should come before price information. Despite the fact that proponents of advertising emphasize that it can serve to lower prices and provide consistency of rates within the professions, some feel price information will lead to charlatans advertising such things as "Cancer Cured Quik—$25." Tublin would rather see public service-oriented advertising that would relax and inform the patient.

Testimonials and "before and after" pictures are another category of dissension. These are illegal in some states and legislation on this subject is pending in others. One doctor states testimonials are now illegal in California but that she will use them as soon as the law is changed. "I would like to use before and after pictures of a person who actually had the surgery saying, 'Here is what I did and how I went about it.' "

For now, it seems doubtful that professional advertising will change much from its present pattern. Marketing seems to be the key for its future. If professionals are going to use advertising successfully, they will have to be prepared to plan carefully and seek expert advice.

Laboratory applications

1. Have you seen any professional advertising that appeals to you? Discuss.
2. What type of professional advertising would appeal to you the most? Explain.

Business markets

There may be millions of consumers in the market for the record albums of your favorite rock groups. However, the number of record dealers and distributors in the market for these albums is measured only in the thousands. At the same time, while the size of business markets may be small, their gross sales may be large as well as the size of their purchases. For certain goods there is an opportunity for large-quantity purchases and repeat purchases.

The demand for record albums by dealers depends on the demand for these albums by consumers. Similarly the demand for industrial

In moderate anxiety with coexisting depression:

widely useful in office practice

Helps treat the total symptom complex—moderate anxiety and coexisting depression.

The antidepressant component is capable of alleviating such symptoms of depression as early morning awakening, anorexia, poor concentration, and feeling of hopelessness.

The tranquilizer component is capable of alleviating symptoms of anxiety, tension, and psychomotor excitement without apparent dulling of mental acuity. Hypnotic effects appear to be minimal, particularly in patients who are permitted to remain active.

The drug may impair mental and/or physical abilities required for performance of hazardous tasks such as operating machinery or driving.

Depending on the condition being treated, relief of symptoms of anxiety may occur within a few days, but adequate relief of symptoms of depression may take a few weeks or even longer.

Symptomatic relief often increases the patient's ability to return to normal family, social, and vocational activities.

Flexibility of four tablet strengths affords ease of dosage adjustment for better patient management.

Initial therapy for many patients is TRIAVIL® 2-25, containing 2 mg perphenazine and 25 mg amitriptyline HCl, or TRIAVIL® 4-25, containing 4 mg perphenazine and 25 mg amitriptyline HCl, t.i.d. or q.i.d. See full prescribing information for dosage in elderly and adolescent patients.

Treatment with TRIAVIL—a balanced view: TRIAVIL is contraindicated in CNS depression from drugs, in the presence of evidence of bone marrow depression, and in patients hypersensitive to phenothiazines or amitriptyline. It should not be used during the acute recovery phase following myocardial infarction or in patients who have received an MAOI within two weeks. Patients with cardiovascular disorders should be watched closely. Not recommended in children or during pregnancy. The drug may enhance the response to alcohol. Antiemetic effect may obscure toxicity due to other drugs or mask other disorders. Since suicide is a possibility in any depressive illness, patients should not have access to large quantities of the drug. Hospitalize as soon as possible any patient suspected of having taken an overdose.

indicated for a wide range of patients with moderate anxiety and coexisting depression

dual-action Triavil®

containing perphenazine and amitriptyline HCl

prescribe it...with good reason

In moderate anxiety with coexisting depression: widely useful in office practice

dual-action Triavil®

containing perphenazine and amitriptyline HCl

prescribe it...with good reason

Available:
TRIAVIL® 2-25: Each tablet contains
2 mg perphenazine and 25 mg amitriptyline HCl.
TRIAVIL® 2-10: Each tablet contains
2 mg perphenazine and 10 mg amitriptyline HCl.
TRIAVIL® 4-25: Each tablet contains
4 mg perphenazine and 25 mg amitriptyline HCl.
TRIAVIL® 4-10: Each tablet contains
4 mg perphenazine and 10 mg amitriptyline HCl.

INITIAL THERAPY FOR MANY PATIENTS
TRIAVIL® 2-25 (or TRIAVIL® 4-25) t.i.d. or q.i.d.

FOR FLEXIBILITY IN ADJUSTING MAINTENANCE THERAPY
TRIAVIL® 2-10 (or TRIAVIL® 4-10)

CONTRAINDICATIONS: Central nervous system depression from drugs (barbiturates, alcohol, narcotics, analgesics, antihistamines); evidence of bone marrow depression; known hypersensitivity to phenothiazines or amitriptyline. Should not be given concomitantly with a monoamine oxidase inhibitor since hyperpyretic crises, severe convulsions, and deaths have occurred from such combinations. When used to replace a monoamine oxidase inhibitor, allow a minimum of 14 days to elapse before initiating therapy with TRIAVIL. Therapy should then be initiated cautiously with gradual increase in dosage until optimum response is achieved. Not recommended for use during acute recovery phase following myocardial infarction.

WARNINGS: TRIAVIL should not be given concomitantly with guanethidine or similarly acting compounds since TRIAVIL may block the antihypertensive action of such compounds. Use cautiously in patients with history of urinary retention, angle-closure glaucoma, increased intraocular pressure, or convulsive disorders. Dosage of anticonvulsive agents may have to be increased. In patients with angle-closure glaucoma, even average doses may precipitate an attack. Patients with cardiovascular disorders should be watched closely. Tricyclic antidepressants, including amitriptyline HCl, have been reported to produce arrhythmias, sinus tachycardia, and prolongation of conduction time, particularly in high doses. Myocardial infarction and stroke have been reported with tricyclic antidepressant drugs. Close supervision is required for hyperthyroid patients or those receiving thyroid medication. May impair mental and/or physical abilities required for performance of hazardous tasks, such as operating machinery or driving a motor vehicle. In patients who use alcohol excessively, potentiation may increase the danger inherent in any suicide attempt or overdosage. Not recommended in children or during pregnancy.

PRECAUTIONS: Suicide is a possibility in depressed patients and may remain until significant remission occurs. Such patients should not have access to large quantities of this drug.

Perphenazine: Should not be used indiscriminately. Use with caution in patients who have previously exhibited severe adverse reactions to other phenothiazines. Likelihood of some untoward actions is greater with high doses. Closely supervise with any dosage. The antiemetic effect of perphenazine may obscure signs of toxicity due to overdosage of other drugs or make more difficult the diagnosis of disorders such as brain tumor or intestinal obstruction. A significant, not otherwise explained, rise in body temperature may suggest individual intolerance to perphenazine, in which case discontinue.

If hypotension develops, epinephrine should not be employed, as its action is blocked and partially reversed by perphenazine. Phenothiazines may potentiate the action of central nervous system depressants (opiates, analgesics, antihistamines, barbiturates, alcohol) and atropine. In concurrent therapy with any of these, TRIAVIL should be given in reduced dosage. May also potentiate the action of heat and phosphorous insecticides.

Amitriptyline: In manic-depressive psychosis, depressed patients may experience a shift toward the manic phase if they are treated with an antidepressant. Patients with paranoid symptomatology may have an exaggeration of such symptoms. The tranquilizing effect of TRIAVIL seems to reduce the likelihood of this effect. When amitriptyline HCl is given with anticholinergic agents or sympathomimetic drugs, including epinephrine combined with local anesthetics, close supervision and careful adjustment of dosages are required. Paralytic ileus may occur in patients taking tricyclic antidepressants in combination with anticholinergic-type drugs.

Caution is advised if patients receive large doses of ethchlorvynol concurrently. Transient delirium has been reported in patients who were treated with 1 g of ethchlorvynol and 75-150 mg of amitriptyline HCl.

Amitriptyline HCl may enhance the response to alcohol and the effects of barbiturates and other CNS depressants.

Concurrent administration of amitriptyline HCl and electroshock therapy may increase the hazards associated with such therapy. Such treatment should be limited to patients for whom it is essential. Discontinue several days before elective surgery if possible. Elevation and lowering of blood sugar levels have both been reported. Use with caution in patients with impaired liver function.

ADVERSE REACTIONS: Similar to those reported with either constituent alone.

Perphenazine: Extrapyramidal symptoms (opisthotonus, oculogyric crisis, hyperreflexia, dystonia, akathisia, acute dyskinesia, ataxia, parkinsonism) have been reported and can usually be controlled by the concomitant use of effective antiparkinsonian drugs and/or by reduction in dosage, but sometimes persist after discontinuation of the phenothiazine.

Tardive dyskinesia may appear in some patients on long-term therapy or may occur after drug therapy with phenothiazines and related agents has been discontinued. The risk appears to be greater in elderly patients on high-dose therapy, especially females. Symptoms are persistent and in some patients appear to be irreversible. The syndrome is characterized by rhythmical involuntary movements of the tongue, face, mouth, or jaw. Involuntary movements of the extremities sometimes occur. There is no known treatment for tardive dyskinesia; antiparkinsonism agents usually do not alleviate the symptoms. It is advised that all antipsychotic agents be discontinued if the above symptoms appear. If treatment is reinstituted, or dosage of the particular drug increased, or another drug substituted, the syndrome may be masked. Fine vermicular movements of the tongue may be an early sign of the syndrome. The full-blown syndrome may not develop if medication is stopped when lingual vermiculation appears.

Other side effects are skin disorders (photosensitivity, itching, erythema, urticaria, eczema, up to exfoliative dermatitis); other allergic reactions (asthma, laryngeal edema, angioneurotic edema, anaphylactoid reactions); peripheral edema; reversed epinephrine effect; hyperglycemia; endocrine disturbances (lactation, galactorrhea, gynecomastia, disturbances of menstrual cycle); altered cerebrospinal fluid proteins; paradoxical excitement; hypertension, hypotension, tachycardia, and ECG abnormalities (quinidine-like effect); reactivation of psychotic processes; catatonic-like states; autonomic reactions, such as dry mouth or salivation, headache, anorexia, nausea, vomiting, constipation, obstipation, urinary frequency or incontinence, blurred vision, nasal congestion, and a change in pulse rate; other adverse reactions reported with various phenothiazine compounds, but not with perphenazine, include grand mal convulsions, cerebral edema, polyphagia, pigmentary retinopathy, photophobia, skin pigmentation, and failure of ejaculation.

The phenothiazine compounds have produced blood dyscrasias (pancytopenia, thrombocytopenic purpura, leukopenia, agranulocytosis, eosinophilia); and liver damage (jaundice, biliary stasis).

Pigmentation of the cornea and lens has been reported to occur after long-term administration of some phenothiazines. Although it has not been reported in patients receiving TRIAVIL, the possibility that it might occur should be considered.

Hypnotic effects, lassitude, muscle weakness, and mild insomnia have also been reported.

Amitriptyline: Note: Listing includes a few reactions not reported for this drug, but which have occurred with other pharmacologically similar tricyclic antidepressant drugs and must be considered when amitriptyline is administered. *Cardiovascular:* Hypotension; hypertension; tachycardia; palpitation; myocardial infarction; arrhythmias; heart block; stroke. *CNS and Neuromuscular:* Confusional states; disturbed concentration; disorientation; delusions; hallucinations; excitement; anxiety; restlessness; insomnia; nightmares; numbness, tingling, and paresthesias of the extremities; peripheral neuropathy; incoordination; ataxia; tremors; seizures; alteration in EEG patterns; extrapyramidal symptoms; tinnitus; syndrome of inappropriate ADH (antidiuretic hormone) secretion. *Anticholinergic:* Dry mouth; blurred vision; disturbance of accommodation; increased intraocular pressure; constipation; paralytic ileus; urinary retention; dilatation of urinary tract. *Allergic:* Skin rash; urticaria; photosensitization; edema of face and tongue. *Hematologic:* Bone marrow depression including agranulocytosis; leukopenia; eosinophilia; purpura; thrombocytopenia. *Gastrointestinal:* Nausea; epigastric distress; vomiting; anorexia; stomatitis; peculiar taste; diarrhea; parotid swelling; black tongue. Rarely hepatitis (including altered liver function and jaundice). *Endocrine:* Testicular swelling and gynecomastia in the male; breast enlargement and galactorrhea in the female; increased or decreased libido; elevated or lowered blood sugar levels. *Other:* Dizziness, weakness; fatigue; headache; weight gain or loss; increased perspiration; urinary frequency; mydriasis; drowsiness; alopecia. *Withdrawal Symptoms:* Abrupt cessation after prolonged administration may produce nausea, headache, and malaise. These are not indicative of addiction.

OVERDOSAGE: All patients suspected of having taken an overdosage should be admitted to a hospital as soon as possible. Treatment is symptomatic and supportive. However, the intravenous administration of 1–3 mg of physostigmine salicylate is reported to reverse the symptoms of tricyclic antidepressant poisoning. Because physostigmine is rapidly metabolized, the dosage of physostigmine should be repeated as required particularly if life-threatening signs such as arrhythmias, convulsions, and deep coma recur or persist after the initial dosage of physostigmine. On this basis, in severe overdosage with perphenazine-amitriptyline combinations, symptomatic treatment of central anticholinergic effects with physostigmine salicylate should be considered. J7TR16 (DC6613212)

For more detailed information, consult your MSD Representative or see full Prescribing Information. Merck Sharp & Dohme, Division of Merck & Co., INC., West Point, Pa. 19486.

Figure 21–5 The FDA requires pharmaceutical advertisers to include information known as a "Brief Summary of Prescribing Information" in all medical journal advertisements. For TRIAVIL (and many other products) this "brief" summary necessitates buying a full page of advertising space just to get in all the required verbiage.

goods is dependent on the demand for the goods produced by the particular industry. This *derived demand* is typical of business markets.

To locate the fans who would like to attend a Bee Gees' concert might be very difficult. And as a group they might be very difficult to define. On the other hand, to locate and define the market of theater owners and managers for light-control systems is much easier. Moreover this market is covered by specific media, business publications, which provide better coverage than the mass media used for consumer markets. (See Figure 21–7).

GO WITH THE COMBINE LEADER
THIS SEASON:
MASSEY-FERGUSON.
Harvest time — so close to the payoff and yet so far away. Because nothing counts until the crop's in.
Get your crop in fast this year with a new MF 760 or MF 750 Combine from Massey-Ferguson. With its big 60″ hi-inertia cylinder, the MF 760 is the biggest combine in North America. The MF 750, with a 50″ hi-inertia cylinder, also has the kind of capacity you need for big fields.
For a smooth wheat harvest, there are seven table sizes up to 24′. For corn, there's a choice of headers up to 6-row wide for the MF 750 and 8-row narrow for the MF 760.
And MF Quick-Attach headers are on and off in minutes.
New features include an electro-hydraulic system for quick, precise header height adjustment and long 15′ unloader, including optional 4′ extension, for easy unloading on-the-go.
Ask your MF dealer about the many new big capacity features of the harvest-proven Gentle Giants — the MF 760 and MF 750 Combines.
MF
Massey Ferguson
MOVE UP TO
MASSEY-FERGUSON

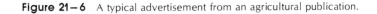

Figure 21–6 A typical advertisement from an agricultural publication.

Figure 21–7 Budget for advertising and sales promotion for the average industrial marketer

Item	Percentage of total budget
Business publications	31.3
Catalog	19.8
Direct mail	9.3
Trade shows	9.1
Administration and salaries	8.4
Dealer and distributor materials	4.4
General magazines	4.1
Publicity and public relations	3.9
Directories	2.0
Television	1.2
Advertising research	1.2
Radio	0.5
Newspapers	0.5
All others	4.9

Channels of distribution

When you are eating a hot dog at a rock concert, you probably have no idea where that hot dog was before you got it. From the farmer who raises the hogs to the packer who manufactures and packages the wieners to the wholesale distributor who sells them to the concessionaire who finally sells one to you, the consumer channel of distribution may involve many middlemen. Business channels, on the other hand, are typically much shorter and goods are more often purchased directly from the manufacturer.

Well-defined geographic marketplaces for business advertising are also common. Detroit is the center for automobile manufacturing. Agriculture dominates the Midwest. This can reduce the cost of distribution and advertising considerably. Where do you suppose is the geographic marketplace for record albums?

Business buyers and their requirements

In industry buyers act as representatives of their firms rather than for themselves. They are therefore not so fickle as consumers. They are well-trained and experienced, and they often state exacting specifications for the goods they buy. As a result, factual or rational appeals are used more often in business advertising, whereas emotional appeals are used more extensively in consumer advertising.

Buying practices are different among industrial firms than among consumers. In industry buying is often influenced by many individuals or done on a committee basis. Negotiation may be required, and some buying is on a bid basis. To close the sale, the seller may have to influence a number of people including users of the product, the purchasing agent, and management.

As a general rule, the manufacturer stays in close contact with the buyer after the sale. This is rarely true of the manufacturer of consumer goods sold through retail outlets.

Computer systems, for example, not only must be installed, but service must be available after the product is in place. The availability of technical help, service, and maintenance agreements are often influential to the sale or are part of the sale package.

Figure 21–8 An unusually beautiful institutional trade advertisement created in-house by a company that prints checks for banks and their customers.

Promotional methods used

The media and promotional methods used in business advertising differ considerably from those used in consumer advertising. There's a reliance on personal, face-to-face selling along with the use of direct mail, exhibits, and catalogs.

The packaging of consumer products places heavy emphasis on appearance. Packaging for business tends to be functional and is likely to serve more as protection than for the promotion of the product.

Price is not often used as a sales device in selling to business. There are no "specials of the week" or loss leaders, as in retail selling.

Organization for business advertising

The industrial advertising department is organized in a similar manner as the advertising department of the consumer goods manufacturer. But there are some differences.

Advertising departments

The advertising department in the industrial goods firm usually has a lower position than a corresponding consumer goods advertising department because, for the industrial advertiser, greater emphasis is placed on personal selling. Another difference is that individuals in the industrial advertising department have greater participation in the actual creation of the advertising. This is necessary because a great deal of industrial advertising and promotion is noncommissionable to advertising agencies—direct mail, catalogs, and exhibits at trade shows. In addition, industrial advertising tends to be quite technical. This frequently requires the expertise of staff members in preparing both copy and art (Figure 21–8).

If business firms do not avail themselves of the services of an advertising agency, they may turn to firms that specialize in services they may not be able to perform for themselves. Art studios, mailing houses, direct-mail consultants, and commercial printers can help in preparing direct mail, for example. There are organizations that produce trade show exhibits. Business publications can also provide advertising counsel.

Advertising agencies

There has been an increase in recent years in the number of agencies that specialize in industrial, trade, professional, and agricultural accounts. There has also been an increase in the number of agencies that offer services on a per-job basis. Both these developments have increased the use of agencies among business advertisers.

Some industrial advertisers do not use agencies because they feel it is uneconomical. Because the cost of advertising space in business publications is quite low, the commissions do not provide a sufficient profit to the agency. Advertisers must therefore pay agencies on a combination commission/fee or straight-fee basis. Some firms feel they realize savings and have greater control by doing their own work. Others maintain that the result is less effective advertising or, in the end, advertising that costs just as much or more than paying an agency. After all, they say, the manufacturers still have to pay for qualified personnel as well as overhead for the advertising staff.

Many industrial firms have found that advertising agencies can be helpful not only in preparing advertisements but also in conducting advertising research, developing advertising plans, devising sales promotion programs, establishing advertising budgets, and providing public relations help, as well as coordinating the advertising program with other marketing efforts. The industrial advertising agency can often bring to the business advertiser a wide range of experience in advertising and marketing, which can rarely be matched by the experience of a single company.

Push/pull: The strategy of business advertising

As we have pointed out, the demand for trade and industrial goods is derived—that is, it depends on the demand for the associated consumer product. Therefore, manufacturers are interested in using advertising that will affect demand by both consumers and middlemen.

Imagine that the channel of distribution is a pipe with the manufacturer at one end and the consumer at the other (Figure 21–9). The manufacturer attempts to "push" products into the pipe by advertising to the retail trade or to the industry that uses his product in the production of theirs. Similarly, the manufacturer may attempt to "pull" his products through the pipe by advertising to consumers.

For example, RSO Records attempted to promote the sale of the soundtrack of the movie *Sgt. Pepper's Lonely Hearts Club Band* by using push strategy to record dealers. Advertisements were run in music trade publications. Banners were distributed to stores, and so were special displays. The placement of the ads was coordinated with concert appearances and local screenings of the motion picture.

People in advertising

Howard G. ("Scotty") Sawyer

Corporate Staff Consultant
Marsteller Inc.

A well-known authority on business advertising, Howard G. ("Scotty") Sawyer is a corporate staff consultant for Marsteller Inc. and a prominent author, columnist, lecturer, and teacher.

Sawyer joined Marsteller in 1960 as vice president of marketing services. Two years later he was appointed executive vice president of Marsteller International. He then served as general manager in Brussels, the agency's first wholly owned office in Europe. Today Marsteller Inc. has 14 offices abroad, 1,405 employees worldwide, and annual billings of $350 million.

Through an agreement with Vneshtorgreklama, the official Soviet state advertising agency, Marsteller became the first United States–based agency authorized to aid American product makers in marketing their goods to the Soviet Union. The agency's long, diversified client list includes Piper Aircraft, Grumman Aerospace, Arthur Anderson Company, United Technologies, and the National Association of Realtors. As corporate staff consultant, Sawyer guides the campaigns of those Marsteller clients who advertise to business and industry. His expertise in business advertising developed from a broad range of experience in advertising and mass communications. Since high school, when Sawyer sold humorous pieces to the old *Life* magazine, his wide-ranging experience has even included being a sportswriter and drama critic. After attending Brown University, Sawyer was hired as a staff radio announcer at station WJAR in Providence. He then joined James Thomas Chirurg Company, Boston and New York, as a copy chief. Sawyer soon advanced to account executive and then vice president. During his advertising career he has performed virtually every type of agency job: copywriter, creative director, research manager, media buyer, and planning chief. He has also bought art and production; written publicity, direct mail, and catalog copy; and directed agency new-business development.

Explaining the key points for selling business readers through print advertising, Sawyer observes in his book, *Business-to-Business Advertising*, that it is essential to give business readers what they are looking for. According to Sawyer, business people are looking for information. They "want to know, right off, if your ad has anything in it" for *them*. They want you to tell them about it in *their* language. They want you to give them the *facts*. And, Sawyer adds, they want these facts expressed in terms of *their* benefit. In business advertising, Sawyer declares, "the reader's viewpoint is paramount."

A popular author, Sawyer is also a featured columnist in *Industrial Marketing* and writes the "Loose Talk" column in *Advertising Age*. He is a frequent contributor to *Sales Management*, *Business Abroad*, *Business Management*, and other publications.

Sawyer has addressed hundreds of audiences at conferences and meetings of major advertising, marketing, research, and business associations and at seminars sponsored by the American Management Association. He has been a frequent lecturer in college marketing and advertising courses and a key speaker at client sales meetings throughout the world.

Former chairman of the board of the Business Publications Audit of Circulations, Sawyer is also past chairman of the International Advertising and Marketing Committee of the AIA. He is an agency representative for the Audit Bureau of Circulations and serves on the AAAA Committee on Telephone Directory Advertising.

At the same time, RSO used pull strategy by advertising the albums to consumers through local newspapers and by seeking the cooperation of radio disc jockeys to play the album. These efforts were coordinated with the timing of concerts, the movie, and the trade ads.

A company's advertising budget is limited. In business advertising, there is a significant trade-off between push and pull strategies. One suffers at the expense of the other. It is far less expensive to advertise to the trade than to consumers. However, dealers may want to know that the manufacturer is going to pull the goods through before they commit to purchases. Careful attention must be paid, therefore, to balancing push and pull strategy.

Media of business advertising

Business and farm publications

There are more than 3,000 business publications and 300 agricultural publications. Listings of these appear in the Standard Rate and Data Service directories. The *Business Publication Rates and Data* directory lists many trade, industrial, and professional publications (Figure 21–10). Listings for farm journals appear in *Consumer Magazine and Farm Publication Rates and Data.*

The information provided includes such items as a statement by the publisher about the magazine's editorial content, the key personnel, media representatives and their offices, commission and cash discount data, general rate policy, advertising rates, mechanical requirements, issue and closing dates, and circulation.

Vertical and horizontal publications

There are two classifications of business publications: vertical and

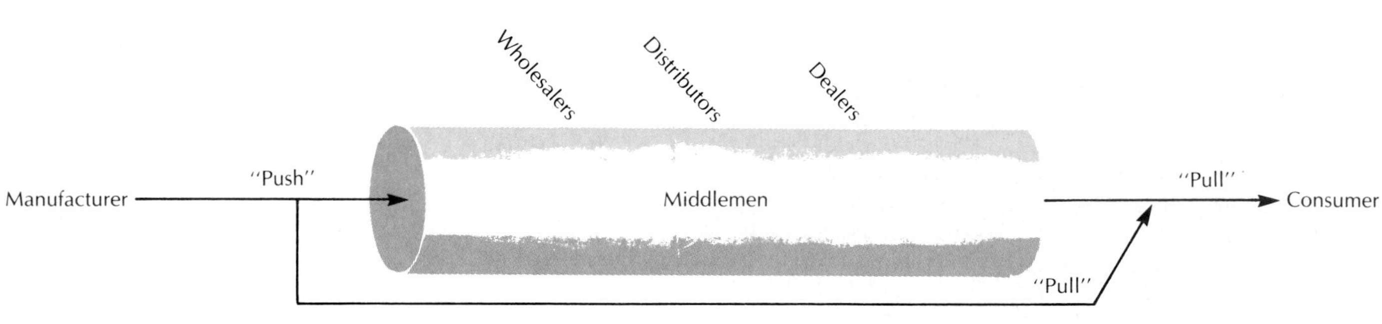

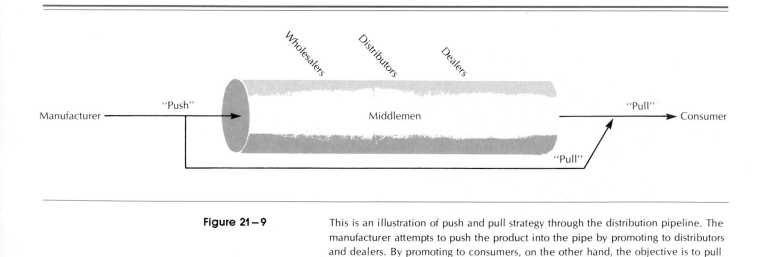

Figure 21–9 This is an illustration of push and pull strategy through the distribution pipeline. The manufacturer attempts to push the product into the pipe by promoting to distributors and dealers. By promoting to consumers, on the other hand, the objective is to pull products through the pipe.

horizontal. A choice of one or the other depends on how deeply an advertiser wishes to penetrate a particular industry or how widely the advertiser wishes to spread the message.

Vertical publications cover a specific industry, such as *Retail Baking Today* aimed only at those people interested in selling baked goods on the retail level. They are read by individuals interested in a specific area of study. *Horizontal* publications deal with a particular job function that cuts across industry lines, such as *Electronic Design* and *Purchasing*.

Billboard

A Billboard Publication

ABC MPA ABP

Media Code 7 560 0800 9.00

Published weekly by Billboard Publications, Inc. **9000 Sunset Blvd., Los Angeles, Calif. 90069.** Phone 213-273-7040.

For shipping info., see Print Media Production Data.

PUBLISHER'S EDITORIAL STATEMENT

BILLBOARD is edited for the international radio/music/record/tape industry. Various news, record reviews, popularity charts in fields, researching and reporting on trends in music, in radio programming, in recording techniques, in equipment, accessories, in the video cassette market, in music publishing, are all part of the weekly coverage. Departmental featurs include: Classical, Country, Disco, Interna-national, Jazz, Music Publishing, Radio, Sound Business, Talent, Video. Rec'd 12/17/80.

1. PERSONNEL

Publisher—Lee Zhito.
Assoc. Pub. & Dir. of Sales—Tom Noonan.
Assoc. Pub. & Dir. of Charts—Bill Wardlow.
National Sales Administrator—John Halloran.
Production Manager—Johnny Wallace.

2. REPRESENTATIVES and/or BRANCH OFFICES

Los Angeles 90069—Harvey Geller, Joe Fleischman, Roni Wald, 9000 Sunset Blvd. Phone 212-273-7040.
New York 10036—Ron Willman, Norman Berkowitz, Ron Carpenter, Jim Bender, 1515 Broadway. Phone 212-764-7300.
Nashville 37203—John McCartney, 1509 Laurel Street. Phone 615-748-8145.
England—Pete Muckler, Philip Graham, 7 Carnaby St., London, W. I. V. 1PG. Phone 01-439-9411.
Milan—Germano Ruscitto, Piazzale Loreto 9. Phone 28-29-158.
Mexico—Marv Fisher, Apartado Postal 11-766, Mexico 11, D. F. Phone 905-531-3907.
Japan—Hugh Nishikawa, Utsunomiya Building 4th Floor, 19-16 Jingunae, 6-chrome, Shibuya-ku, Tokyo, 150. Phone 03-498-4641.
Australia—Geoff Waller & Associates, 64 Victoria Street, North Sydney 2060. Phone 011-61-2-436-2033.

3. COMMISSION AND CASH DISCOUNT

15% to agencies on space, color and position charges only, provided account is paid within 30 days of invoice date. No advertising accepted from agencies acting solely as "agents" for their clients. No discounts on Classified Advertising and such charges as backing inserts, trimming, printing of inserts and other mechanical functions performed by publisher.

4. GENERAL RATE POLICY

Contract advertisers will be short-rated if within a 12-month period of the 1st insertion they do not use the amount of space on which their bills have been based. Contract advertisers will be rebated if within a 12-month period they have used sufficient additional space to warrant lower rate than billed. Advertisers will be protected at their contract rates for 60 days after date of announcement.

ADVERTISING RATES

Effective January 1981 issue.
Rates received December 22, 1980.

5. BLACK/WHITE RATES

	Open	6 ti	13 ti	26 ti	52 ti	156 ti
1 page....	2516.	2390.	2264.	2139.	2013.	1887.
Jr. page....	1738.	1651.	1564.	1477.	1390.	1304.
3/5 page....	1565.	1487.	1409.	1330.	1252.	1174.
1/2 page....	1340.	1273.	1206.	1139.	1072.	1005.
2/5 page....	1098.	1043.	988.	933.	878.	824.
3/10 page....	844.	802.	760.	717.	675.	633.
1/4 page....	712.	676.	641.	605.	570.	534.
1/5 page....	575.	546.	518.	489.	460.	431.
3/20 page....	436.	414.	392.	371.	340.	327.
2/15 page....	390.	371.	351.	332.	312.	293.
*1/10 page....	300.	285.	270.	255.	240.	225.
1/15 page....	202.	192.	182.	172.	162.	152.
1/20 page....	152.	144.	137.	129.	122.	114.
1/25 page....	122.	116.	110.	104.	98.	92.

(*) Minimum rateholder.

Per Issue Rates: Rate earned is determined by number of separate issues used within a contract period. Fractional page ads in a single issue may not be totaled to earn the lowest rate. Contract rates are based on number of issues in 12-month period in which advertiser uses space of 1/10 page or more. 1/10 page (100 lines) minimum rate holder for larger space.

6. COLOR RATES

2-color, extra.......... 495.
3-color, extra.......... 600.
4-color, extra.......... 925.
Special color.......... 620.

7. COVERS

1st cover unit sold to contract advertisers only on following basis:
4-color strip.......... 1410.
4-color artist photo.......... 1095.
*2nd cover.......... 1675.
*3rd cover.......... 1575.
*4th cover.......... 1890.
(*) Includes 4-color.

8. INSERTS

Inserts furnished ready for binding, regular black and white space rates apply.
Special gatefold, dutch-door and other specialized inserts available.
Tip-in, per M.......... 40.
Less than full page inserts are acceptable; in regular binding thay jog to top.
Tip-in inserts can be controlled as to position. Improperly prepared inserts may require handwork at 55.00 per M.

Album slick inserts:
Printed flap, space plus.......... 990.
Publisher prints flap, space plus.......... 1600.

9. BLEED

Acceptable on units of 1/2 page or more at no extra charge for bleed—both black and white and color. Bleeds are not accepted on units of less than full column depth, except for half-page units running across 5 columns.

10. SPECIAL POSITIONS

Premium positions, extra.......... 495.
International Strips, per strip.......... *790.
(*) For International advertisers only.

11. CLASSIFIED AND READING NOTICES

CLASSIFIED
Non-commissionable.
Regular classified, per word (minimum 26.00).... 1.30
International, regular, per word (minimum 20.00).......... .68

DISPLAY CLASSIFIED

	1 ti	4 ti	26 ti	52 ti
Per column inch..........	55.00	49.00	45.00	36.00

Payment must accompany all orders. If box number is used allow 10 words for number and address. Box number service charge 5.00 per insertion, payable prior to date of issue. Reverse ad 10.00 per insertion.

14. CONTRACT AND COPY REGULATIONS

See Contents page for location—items 1, 2, 3, 4, 5, 7, 8, 9, 11, 12, 13, 14, 15, 16, 17, 18, 19, 20, 21, 22, 23, 25, 26, 27, 28, 29, 30, 31, 32, 34, 35, 36.

15. MECH. REQUIREMENTS (Web Offset)

COVERS; SPECIAL SECTIONS; OFFSET, SHEET FED.
For complete, detailed production information, see SRDS Print Media Production Data.
Trim size: 11 x 14-1/2; No./Cols. 5.
Binding method: Saddle Stitched.
Colors available: AAAA/ABP; 4-Color Process (AAAA/MPA); Special Colors.
Cover colors available: AAAA/ABP.

DIMENSIONS AD PAGE

1	10-1/8 x 14		1/5	3-7/8 x 6-7/8
*	8 1/16 x 11-7/8		3/20	1-13/16 x 10-1/2
3/5	6 x 14		3/20	3-7/8 x 5-1/4
3/5	8-1/16 x 10-1/2		3/20	6 x 3-1/2
3/5	10-1/8 x 8-1/4		2/15	1-13/16 x 9-1/4
1/2	8-1/16 x 8-3/4		2/15	3-7/8 x 4-5/8
1/2	10-1/8 x 6-7/8		1/10	1-13/16 x 6-7/8
2/5	3-7/8 x 14		1/10	3-7/8 x 3-1/2
2/5	6 x 9-5/16		1/15	1-13/16 x 4-5/8
2/5	10-1/8 x 5-5/8		1/15	3-7/8 x 2-5/16
3/10	3-7/8 x 10-1/2		1/20	1-13/16 x 3-1/2
3/10	6 x 6-7/8		1/25	1-13/16 x 2-3/4
1/4	3-7/8 x 8-3/4			(*) Junior page.
1/5	1-13/16 x 14			

16. ISSUE AND CLOSING DATES

Published weekly; dated Saturday; issued preceding Monday.

Reservations and ads requiring composition, due Tuesday, 11 days prior to date of issue. Complete negatives or positives (converted to negatives at advertiser cost) accepted in Cincinnati Thursday 4 p.m., 9 days prior to date of issue. For 4-color separations, 15 days prior to date of issue. If proof are desired, copy must be furnished 20 days prior to date of issue. Insert closing date available. Cancellations or copy corrections are not accepted after 4 p.m. Wednesday, 10 days prior to date of issue. Advertiser charged penalty of premium position charge for cancellations of premium position ads, after deadline.

18. CIRCULATION

Single copy 3.00; per year 110.00.
Summary data—for detail see Publisher's Statement.

A.B.C. 6-30-80 (6 mos. aver.—Blue BP Form)

Total	Non-Pd	Paid	(Subs)	[illegible]	[illegible]
43,165	....	43,165	34,130	9,035	....

Average Other Distribution (not included above):
Total 3,402

TERRITORIAL DISTRIBUTION 5/80—44,933

N.Eng.	Mid.Atl.	E.N.Cen.	W.N.Cen.	S.Atl.	E.S.Cen.
1,353	6,051	4,318	1,806	4,233	1,865
W.S.Cen.	**Mtn.St.**	**Pac.St.**	**Canada**	**Foreign**	**Other**
2,546	1,336	5,799	1,707	4,109	9,807

BUSINESS ANALYSIS OF CIRCULATION

TL Total.
1 —Retail merchandisers of records, pre-recorded & blank tapes, playback & communications hardware & accessories.
2 —Rack jobbers, record & tape distrs., one-stops, juke box operators, exporters & importers of records & tapes.
3 —Radio & TV station pers., incl. program & music dirs., air personalities, ind. programmers discotheques.
4 —Record cos., ind. producers, pressing plants & mftrs. of software, hardware, professional equip., recording studios.
5 —Recording artists, performers, attorneys, agents & mgrs.
6 —Buyers of talent, incl. concert promoters, impressarios, clubs, hotels, auditoriums, arenas, & concert facilities.
7 —Schools, colleges, students, faculty, libraries, music fans & audiophiles.
8 —Investment houses, banks, Federal, State & international depts. of govt., embassy officials.
9 —Music publishers, songwriters, performing unions, licensing & rights orgs.
10 —Writers & reviewers, public relations orgs., newspaper & magazine execs., adv. agencies & ind art dirs.
11 —Misc., incl. ind. mgmt. & technical consultants.
12 —Awaiting class.

TL	1	2	3	4	5	6
35333	7121	2544	5873	6033	2453	1260
7	**8**	**9**	**10**	**11**	**12**	
3717	386	1209	901	1293	2543	

(D-C, C-B1)

Figure 21–10 An example of a listing from *Business Publication Rates and Data*.

Paid and controlled circulation

Business publications are published on a *paid* basis or a *controlled* basis. If the publication is available on a paid basis, the recipient must pay the subscription price in order to receive it. Circulation that is free (controlled) means it is mailed to a selected list of individuals whom the publisher feels are in a unique position to influence sales. In order to get the publication they must indicate in writing a desire to receive it and their professional designation or occupation. Ordinarily, to qualify for the subscription list they must also include information about their job title, function, and purchasing responsibilities.

Since advertising rates are based principally on circulation, controlled circulation magazines can characterize their readers as good prospects for the goods and services advertised in the publication's pages. Advertisers are not paying for subscribers who have little or no interest in what they are offering. Publishers of paid circulation magazines say that subscribers who pay are more likely to read the publication than are those who get controlled or free copies. On the other hand, publishers of controlled circulation publications state that giving the publication away without charge is the only way to get good coverage of the market and that there is little or no effect on readership.

In order to avoid confusing these terms, it should be pointed out that some paid circulation publications "control their circulation" in a sense by allowing persons to subscribe only if they represent the kind of circulation they want to build, even though they require the subscriber to pay for the subscription. *Business Week* was historically a prominent example until 1980 when it began to seek newsstand sales.

Business publication audiences

To accurately define the audiences of particular business publications, two devices have become quite useful to business advertisers: the Standard Industrial Classification and circulation statements of business publications.

Standard Industrial Classification This system, developed by the federal government, is useful because it classifies all businesses into broad industry segments and then subdivides each segment into major groups, subgroups, and detailed groups. The numerical categories are assigned based on primary products produced or operations performed. These classifications become useful in analyzing business publications because the circulation audits of the publications give the S.I.C. classifications, enabling potential advertisers to better determine the suitability of the magazine for reaching the desired audience.

Auditing reports Advertisers are particularly interested in the circulation of the publications since the advertising rates are based on it. There are three organizations that audit their member business publications: the Audit Bureau of Circulation, the Business Publications Audit of Circulations, and the Verified Audit Circulation Corporation. Each organization has various criteria for membership. Unaudited publications may not belong to an auditing organization either because they refuse to or because they do not meet the membership requirements. These publications simply issue sworn statements on their circulation.

Direct mail

As shown in Figure 21–7, direct mail accounts for over 9 percent of all business advertising and promotion. It is an especially useful tool for the business advertiser because mailing lists can be established around job titles, function, size and type of company, S.I.C. classification, number of employees, volume of sales, credit rating, and innumerable other factors.

The advantages of direct mail include its low cost relative to other advertising media, its selectivity, its flexibility in timing, the way the message can be tailored to individual companies or people, and the space it offers for telling the full story. The message can be more detailed than most magazine advertising.

Disadvantages include the difficulty of getting the mailing piece past the secretary so that it will arrive on the desk of the intended recipient. Also direct mail is directed to known prospects or customers and may miss entirely those people who may be hidden influences on the buying decision.

For a complete discussion of direct mail, review Chapter 18.

Catalogs

Catalogs are part of the company's direct marketing effort. They can be distributed by mail or directly by a salesperson. The reasons for their use are many and varied.

Few catalogs actually produce orders. The catalog can, however, provide a basis of comparison with other companies' products once a decision has been made that a particular product is needed. If a catalog has been properly prepared, it can speed the buying process by providing information about the product to the individuals who must approve the purchase. If effectively done, it can secure recognition for the company and provide additional opportunities to bid or receive business.

Purchasers frequently consult their files of catalogs to determine how many companies make a particular product. A list of firms is developed and they are then asked to submit bids. Therefore, a well-prepared catalog can help the manufacturer "be in the running" when the buyer needs the product the company sells.

Directories

Each year millions of dollars worth of sales result from listings in directories. Probably the best known industrial directory is the *Thomas Register*. It is available in book form or on microfiche and is a comprehensive listing of American manufacturers. It gives names, telephone numbers, product lines, branch offices, and a host of other information. Purchasing agents rely heavily on directories to determine who makes particular products. As a result, most manufacturers try to have their firms listed, and many buy several pages of advertising in the directories as well.

Trade shows and exhibits

If you owned a theater or a stadium and wanted to stage rock concerts in your facility, how would you know whom to hire and what sort of equipment to install? If you wanted to book the Bee Gees, how would you find them?

One way might be to attend an entertainment industry trade show like the International Talent Forum sponsored by *Billboard Magazine* (Figure 21–11). You could attend seminars and conferences on the best ways to use talent and facilities; you could exchange ideas on security, crowd control, and ticket scalping; and you could see live showcases of new and established performers. At the same time, talent suppliers and equipment manufacturers are available in booths at the trade show to explain face to face what they have to help you in your business as a rock concert promoter.

The trade show is a marketplace of ideas, people, and products and as such is one of the most widely used tools in business marketing and advertising. Some orders may be taken at exhibits, but they are more often designed to lay the groundwork for future sales that will be placed through company buyers.

Some of the most important purposes for exhibitors are (1) meeting potential customers, (2) making lists of visitors to the booth for direct mail and sales calls, (3) building goodwill by meeting present and potential customers person to person, (4) introducing new products and testing their market acceptance, (5) demonstrating products that are too large or complicated to be set up and demonstrated in each prospect's place of business, and (6) expanding distribution by attracting new dealers who attend the trade show. As a central meeting place, the trade show is the least expensive way to meet prospective buyers and dealers face to face. This alone makes it an important marketing tool.

Public relations

Advertisers want to maintain a good image among customers, suppliers, competitors, employees, stockholders, creditors, the local community, and government. This requires a careful analysis of the way in which the company interacts with each of these groups.

The purpose of public relations is to influence the attitudes, opinions, and beliefs of individuals. It should be a planned program on the part of business advertisers to build public confidence and increase understanding about their company. This is important because people may be just as interested in the name and reputation of the seller as they are in the particular product they are buying.

Public relations are discussed in depth in Chapter 22.

Using consumer media for business advertisers

The mass media normally used for consumer advertising are also used at times by business advertisers. These are magazines, newspapers, radio, television, outdoor, and transit (Figure 21–12). Because the audiences of these media have such varied interests, there tends to be wasted circulation for the business advertiser. To reduce such waste, several consumer magazines such as *Time* have demographic editions directed to doctors, lawyers, and businesspeople.

BILLBOARD'S INT'L TALENT FORUM VII

Capture Your Share Of The Live Talent Industry

September 9-11, 1981

New York's Sheraton Centre.

You can't afford to miss Billboard's International Talent Forum VII it's the single industry conference that offers answers to just about every question imaginable, relative to the live talent industry.

Talent Booking Agents
Entertainment Attorneys
Artists
Security Specialists
Talent Managers
Business Managers
Road Managers
College Talent Agents
Talent Promoters
Club and Facility Managers & Owners
Record Company Executives

Billboard's International Talent Forum VII offers three days of panel discussions, problem solving, trouble shooting, workshops, seminars and symposiums.

Here is the perfect opportunity to ask the really tough questions, and get the benefit of some of the best minds in the business.

AMONG THE TOPICS TO BE EXPLORED

"Big Bucks vs. The Long Haul—Short Term Profit Or Long Term Career Development"

"Radio & It's Service To The Music Industry"

"Alternate Methods To Maximize Profits Using Music Industry Skills"

"Demographic Studies—What Can They Do For You"

SPECIAL FEATURES

- **Ken Kragen Keynotes Forum**
- **Miller High Life Beer Presents Opening Evenings Showcase At The Lone Star Cafe**
- **Topping It Off With Those At The Top—President's Panel**
- **One On One Luncheons**

ADDITIONAL TOPICS AND SPECIAL FEATURES SOON TO BE ANNOUNCED

REGISTRATION FORM

Billboard's International Talent Forum VII

THE SHERATON CENTRE, NEW YORK, SEPTEMBER 9-11, 1981

REGISTRATION FEES:
$310—BEFORE AUGUST 5, 1981
$335—AFTER AUGUST 5, 1981
$250—Students/Military/Panelists

Registration does not include hotel accommodations or airfare. Registrant substitutions may be made. Registrations at the door will be an additional $35. Absolutely no refunds after August 24, 1981. Cancellations before August 24, 1981 must be in writing and will be subject to a 10% cancellation fee. Information on hotel accommodations will be mailed to you upon receipt of your completed registration form.

☐ I am enclosing a check in the amount of $ ____

I wish to charge my registration to:
☐ American Express ☐ Diners Club
☐ BankAmericard/Visa ☐ MasterCharge

CARD NUMBER ____ EXP. DATE ____

SIGNATURE ____

MAIL COMPLETED FORM TO: **Billboard's International Talent Forum VII**
9000 Sunset Boulevard
Los Angeles, California 90069
Telephone (213) 273-7040

LAST NAME FIRST NAME INITIAL
TITLE FIRST NAME OR NICKNAME FOR BADGE
COMPANY
ADDRESS PHONE
CITY STATE ZIP

Billboard
BB09091

Figure 21—11 *Billboard* magazine promotes its annual talent forum in this advertisement.

Figure 21—12 Some business advertisers use mass media like television to give their products broader awareness and appeal. Also, many feel that advertisements such as this one for Wang help the corporation in its dealings with the financial and government community.

BUSINESS INFORMATION
30-second

ANNCR: Information. Business is besieged by it. All kinds of equipment have been required to manage it. Until now. Now, with Wang's new Integrated Information System, one person, very simply, can perform data processing, word processing, high speed image printing and worldwide communication. If Wang can create all this today, who knows what the future holds.

Wang. Making the world more productive.

Many media have specialized programming such as early-morning reports for farmers. Newspapers have strong farm and financial sections or supplements that appeal to business advertisers. Consumer media with a business slant—*The Wall Street Journal, Fortune,* and *Time*—are the most likely publications for business advertising because of their editorial content, which appeals to business readers.

Consumer media, in spite of wasted circulation, do appeal to some business advertisers because of their broad coverage. Even with traditional business media, some individuals who influence buying decisions will be overlooked. Approaching them through consumer media is a means of getting the message before them.

Additionally, advertising in such media presents an opportunity to relay an advertising message with a minimum of business competition. Usually exposure to consumer media occurs away from the office when the reader or viewer is less preoccupied with business. Businesspeople are always interested in their companies, however, and presenting an advertising message during off-hours means there is less competition from other businesses.

Firms like to advertise in consumer media because they feel they lend prestige to their organizations. Also, investors who are exposed to such advertising may be stimulated to buy stock in these organizations.

Corporate advertising (discussed in Chapter 22), which is essentially presented to develop goodwill, is often placed in consumer publications to help change the public's attitude in favor of the company.

Business advertisers use consumer media to create derived demand. For example, the Du Pont company advertises Teflon in the hope that you will look for this name when you buy an electric frypan. When consumers seek the name of the fabricated part used in the consumer good, it puts pressure on the manufacturer to buy these parts for the finished products they make.

Creating the business advertisement

More than ever before, there are now fewer differences between business and consumer advertising. The creative principles discussed in Chapters 10–14 apply equally to business and consumer advertising. Here we will examine some of the special aspects that should be considered.

Trade advertisements

Stress the salability of the product and the resulting profits. Offer promotion help and refer to dealer aids that can be supplied, such as advertisements mats and displays. Give product details in terms of consumer demand, and suggest that carrying this product will lead to a high volume of sales. Emphasize the product's consumer appeal.

Industrial advertisements

Stress quality and performance. These are the major factors that industrial buyers consider. Tell what the product does, how it does it, and how well it performs. Industrial copy can be interesting—even exciting. Use technical language when necessary but, where possible, use everyday English. Approach the copy by showing how to solve a problem. Give case histories and testimonials. Write as much copy as necessary, remembering there's nothing wrong with long copy. Technical drawings and graphic aids can be used to illustrate points and to break up the monotony of long copy. Photography should scintillate, showing the product closeup and in detail.

Professional advertisements

Use professional language when addressing a professional audience. Take notice of the reader's desire to progress professionally (Figure 21–13). And, recognize the reader as a user or a recommender of the product.

Agricultural advertisements

Write farm advertisements by using farm language that will make sense to today's technically minded, better educated farmer. Testimonials and case histories can be used effectively. Show illustrations that are authentic, on-the-farm scenes to which a farmer can relate. Most of all, provide proof, demonstrate product use, and offer solid evidence of the value of the product.

Creating international business advertising

National pride is an important consideration in international advertising. Many lower income, less developed countries envy American wealth and technology at the same time that they fear and profess disdain for it. Thus a strange paradox exists in some contries of respect and desire for American products mixed with hidden inferiority feelings and, simultaneously, resentment of American influence and power. Many American advertisers, therefore, toe a careful line to avoid aggravating this understandable national sensitivity in certain foreign markets.

The Ford Motor Company discovered that Germans have a strong positive attitude toward their own technical product. Their research also showed that the Ford name had a strong American association. Many Germans wondered why they should buy an American car when so many Americans who owned Volkswagens and Mercedes obviously thought German cars were better. By introducing the German Ford as an example of cooperation between American ingenuity and know-how and German thoroughness and efficiency, considerable sales success was achieved.

In industrial advertising, Lou Magnani, the general manager of Marsteller International in Brussels, has said that differences in taste and attitude may not be so apparent or important as in the marketing of consumer products. The businessperson's problems, he feels, are fairly universal and so are the appeals. The difference in approach comes down to the economics of the area.

On the other hand, Paul Aass, the president of MarkCom, a Belgian advertising agency, says that "the only thing the European countries and Europe's submarkets have in common is the fact that they are different." This is certainly true when it comes to language.

Figure 21–13 The professional musician is at the mercy of the sound system, and Electro-Voice knows it. Everything in this ad is aimed at talking the musician's language to give him or her the confidence top performers need in their equipment.

The language problem

In Western Europe there are at least 15 different languages and probably twice as many different dialects that are still spoken today. This presents a problem of potentially enormous magnitude to the American marketer entering Europe for the first time. The same is true in Asia, to a lesser extent in South America, and to an even greater extent in Africa. South Africa has a complex multicultural society consisting of four major ethnic groups comprising the white, black, colored, and Asians. These groups in turn are divided into various quite distinct subgroups, most of whom are catered for by separate specifically directed media. For example, the whites have two languages—English and Afrikaans—and most campaigns directed to the whites appear in both languages. The blacks have five basic languages.

Radio and television stations, which are government owned, direct their programs on a carefully worked out time allocation basis—in two languages to the whites and in five languages to the blacks—and commercial content, by regulation, must correspond. An advertiser may not, for example, on radio and television, advertise in English on an Afrikaans program, or vice versa. The same applies in respect to the five black languages. In print media, nearly all campaigns directed to whites appear in English and Afrikaans and most campaigns directed to blacks appear in English. (Figure 21–14)

For years a controversy has raged in international advertising circles over the transferability of campaigns. On the one hand, there are those who feel that it is too expensive to create a unique campaign for each national group. They believe it is acceptable to take one campaign and simply translate it into the necessary languages.

On the other hand, some feel this never works out right and that the only way to assure success is to create a special campaign for each market. In addition, there are a few who feel that both these solutions are uneconomical and unnecessary. They run their ads in English and don't concern themselves with the problems of local markets (Figure 21–15). Shell Oil ran the same campaigns in five different countries. Each ad was produced in the language of that country. The campaigns scored equally well on recall, believability, and persuasion wherever they were used.

Obviously, no one of these solutions is always correct, and the problem of transferability of campaigns remains unsolved. It is indeed unlikely that a different campaign must be created for every country of the world. Moreover, the hard facts of life are that the economics of various promotional strategies must be weighed against the anticipated promotional objectives. Thus each situation must be looked at individually. Identifying the target audience and knowing the cultural and business preferences in that market is basic. For campaigns directed to businesses, English is the universal language used. More and more, English is the language of business people all over the world.

However, even if we are talking to similar audiences and detailing similar product characteristics such that we could use the same basic campaign, we still have the translation problem.

There is a well-known story about the Standard Oil Co. of New

Figure 21–14 This campaign prepared by J. Walter Thompson, Johannesburg, is directed to three markets. Ads for the white markets differ only in language—English (top) and Afrikaans (middle). Copy for the black campaign (bottom), in English, is more feature-oriented and the illustration depicts appropriate subject matter.

Jersey when they tried to market gasoline in Japan under their old brand name of Enco. They couldn't understand why their sales were so low. They sent a team of executives over to investigate the situation. After an exhaustive study of Japanese driving habits, gasoline consumption figures, and service station sites, they decided to interview Japanese consumers. The first person they could find that spoke English gave them a very simple answer to their question. He told them that, in Japanese, "Enco" means "stalled car".

A similar event occurred when General Motors introduced the new Chevrolet Nova to Mexico. In Spanish, "no va" means "it doesn't go." Parker Pen attempted to translate its American billboard campaign in Latin America:

"You'll never be embarrassed with a Parker Pen."

Unfortunately, they were embarrassed when they discovered too late that in Spanish "embarazada" means pregnant.

English is spoken in the United States, Canada, England, Australia, and South Africa, but among these five countries are wide variances of vocabulary, word usage, and syntax. Similarly, the difference in the French spoken in France, Canada, Vietnam, and even Belgium may be as great as the difference in English spoken by a high-brow Britisher and a sharecropper from Tennessee. Even within single countries there is wide variation in the language used.

Translations

Larry O'Neill, the assistant to the president of Ogilvy & Mather, speaks of the five "gears" used in the Japanese language, from haughty and condescending all the way down to fawning and servile. The Japanese translator must know when to change gears.

It is imperative that certain basic rules be followed when translating advertisements:

1. The translator must also be an effective copywriter. Just because the translator speaks a foreign language doesn't mean he or she can write it effectively. The logic of this should be clear. All of us can speak English, yet relatively few of us are good writers, and even less are good copywriters. Still, advertisers all too often fall into the trap of simply having a translation service rewrite their advertisements in the foreign language, and that is rarely a good solution.
2. The translator must have an understanding of the product, its features, and its market. It is always better to use a translator who is a specialist rather than a generalist for particular products or markets.
3. The translator should translate into his or her native tongue and should be a native resident of that country where the ad will appear. Only in this way can you be certain that the translator has a current understanding of the country's social attitudes, culture, and idiomatic use of the language.
4. The English copy submitted to the translator should be easily translatable. Double meanings and idiomatic expressions, which make English such an interesting language for advertising, are usu-

ally totally untranslatable. They only make the translator's job more difficult.

There is perhaps no greater insult to a national market than to misuse its language. The translation must be accurate, but it must also be good copy. Some industrial companies, completely baffled by the translation problem, have simply sent their technical literature and brochures written in English. This is a nonsolution, however, and it may incite the nationalistic feelings of some people against the company. Worse yet, this approach automatically limits a product's market to those people who can read and understand technical English. It also greatly increases the probability of misunderstanding and thus additional ill will toward the company. Therefore, advertisers must use caution in dealing with foreign markets.

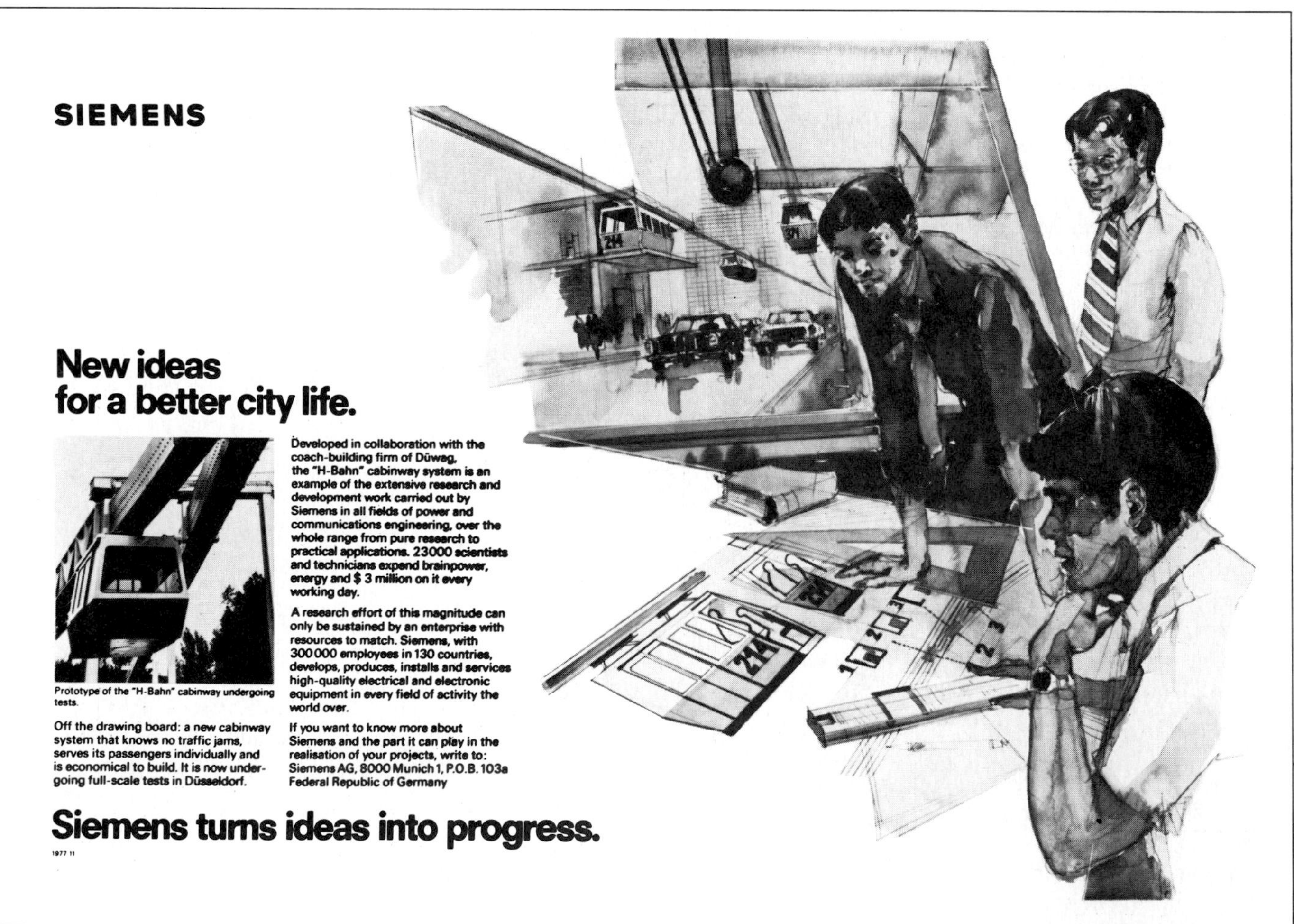

Figure 21–15 Siemens advertises multinationally in 40 publications using six languages. This ad, however, ran in English in Germany and was very successful.

Summary

Business advertising is advertising directed to businesspeople. It includes four distinct types: trade, industrial, professional, and agricultural.

Trade advertising is the advertising of goods and services to wholesalers and retailers who buy these goods and services for resale. Industrial advertising is the advertising of goods and services that are used in the production of other goods and services. Professional advertising is directed to people who are normally licensed or operate under a code of ethics or professional set of standards, such as teachers, accountants, doctors, dentists, architects, and lawyers. Agricultural advertising is directed at the nation's farmers, people who produce, raise, or grow agricultural commodities.

Business advertising differs from consumer advertising in the markets and channels of distribution, buying practices, and advertising and promotional methods used.

Business advertising can be prepared by an in-house department or by an advertising agency. If companies do not avail themselves of the service of an agency, they may turn to firms that offer specialized services such as mailing houses, direct-mail consultants, commercial printers, and the media.

Business advertising strategy can be both push and pull. Push strategy is advertising directed to middlemen. Pull strategy is directed to end users.

The most commonly used media and promotional methods for business are business publications, catalogs, direct mail, and trade shows. Public relations activities are also used to maintain a good image among customers, suppliers, competitors, employees, stockholders, creditors, the local community, and the government.

Although there are some important distinctions to consider, business advertising has more traits in common with consumer advertising than differences.

In foreign markets, American advertisers must be sensitive to national pride. Much controversy still centers on the questions of campaign transferability and language in international business advertising. Certain rules, though, have developed when ads are to be translated. Care should be taken to avoid insulting a market by misusing its language. The translator should be an effective copywriter, should understand the product and the market, and should translate into his or her native tongue. In addition, the English copy submitted should be easily translatable and free of double meanings.

Questions for review

1. What are the four types of business advertising? Describe them.
2. What factors make business advertising different from consumer advertising?
3. How does the industrial advertising department differ from the advertising department of a consumer goods manufacturer? For what reason do industrial advertisers use advertising agencies?
4. What is meant by the push/pull strategy of business advertising?
5. What is the difference between a vertical publication and a horizontal publication?
6. What are paid and controlled circulation publications? From the advertiser's perspective, what are the advantages and disadvantages of using each type?
7. What is an S.I.C. number? Describe its usefulness. On what are the numerical categories based?
8. What are the major auditing organizations? Discuss their importance.
9. What are the primary media and sales promotion vehicles used by business advertisers? Justify their appropriateness.
10. What are some of the special creative considerations in producing business advertising?

22

Corporate advertising and public relations

It was Monday morning and Duane Youngbar was late for work. He had been the director of public relations for a little over a year, and it had become his custom to drift in between 9 and 9:30 if there was nothing pressing. Today was no exception. It was September 25, 1978. He had had a leisurely drive in to Lindbergh Field from his house out in El Cajon. It was one of those typical San Diego fall mornings, crisp, clear, cool, with bright sunlight and unlimited visibility.

Passing the downtown end of the runway, where Laurel Street merges with Harbor Drive, Youngbar noticed that the planes were still taking off eastward instead of westward. This was not uncommon very early in the morning before the land breezes shifted back around to sea breezes, but it was a little unusual this late in the morning. He noticed it but didn't think much about it . . . until later.

Youngbar parked his car and sauntered leisurely across the company lot into PSA's corporate headquarters. He took the elevator up to the third-floor executive offices, greeted the receptionists with his usual Monday morning smile, and strolled into his office.

He had been there only a few moments when a staffer from down the hall poked his head in, grinned, and said, "Hey, how ya doin?"

"Pretty good, for a Monday. What's happening?"

"Nothing much, I guess. I just heard that United had some kind of an accident or something. Have you heard about it?"

"No, not a thing." Youngbar paused as something clicked inside of him, a sixth sense perhaps. "Let's check it out," he said.

He picked up the phone and dialed the company number for the dispatch department.

"This is Youngbar in PR. I just heard United had an accident this morning. That true?"

The relaxed, easy features of Youngbar's face suddenly tightened. His eyes, which only a moment before were twinkling with his casual half-smile, suddenly became moist, red, and deadly serious, darting aimlessly from the telephone to the papers on his desk to the visitor in his office back to the telephone.

"OK," he gulped in a hushed tone. "Thanks."

He pushed the button on his phone to hang up and immediately dialed another number. Covering the receiver with his hand he looked at his visitor.

"It's one of ours," he said. "Flight 182."

"Hello, honey?" The phone had been answered. "I won't be home tonight. One of ours just went in. Talk to you later."

He hung up the phone and tried to mentally prepare himself for the 48-hour day which he knew had just begun.

An incoming PSA jet fully loaded with passengers and employees had just collided with a small private plane taking off to the east. It was the worst air disaster in U.S. history (Figure 22–1).

The role of corporate advertising and public relations

Public relations in a term that is widely misunderstood and misused to describe anything from sales to hostessing, when in fact it is a very specific communications process. Every company, organization, association, and government body has groups of people who are affected by what that organization does or says. These groups might be employees, customers, stockholders, competitors, or just the general consuming populace. Each of these groups may be referred to as one of the organization's "publics." To manage the organization's relationship with these publics, the process called public relations (PR) is used.

When flight 182 went down, Duane Youngbar's small PR staff suddenly became responsible for conducting all of PSA's communication with the press, families of passengers, employees, various government agencies, future customers, and the community at large—not just in San Diego but anywhere in the world someone was touched by this horrible disaster. In addition, myriads of small special-interest groups suddenly popped into the spotlight demanding special attention and care: the private pilots association, the air traffic controllers union, airline pilots associations, local politicians, police groups, the financial community, stockholders, the local press, national networks, and friends and acquaintances of passengers, to mention just a few.

Companies and organizations have learned that they must consider the public impact of their decisions because of the powerful effect of public opinion. This is especially true in times of crisis, emergency, or disaster. But it is just as true for major policy decisions concerning changes in business management, pricing policies, labor negotiations, introduction of new products, or changes in distribution methods. Each of these affects different groups of people in different ways. Conversely, effective administrators can use the power of these groups' opinions to effect positive changes.

In short, the purpose of everything that is labeled public relations is to influence public opinion. In one instance the effort might be to rally public support, in another to obtain public understanding or neutrality, or in still another to simply respond to inquiries.

Put yourself in the position of Duane Youngbar. What do you suppose would be the major purpose of his efforts in the days immediately following the crash of flight 182? What are some things he might have been called on to do? Can you see why airline companies try to hire the best PR professionals in the business?

We shall discuss these and other questions in this chapter. But first it is important to understand the relationship between public relations and advertising since they are so closely allied.

Advertising versus public relations

Advertising is generally described as openly sponsored and paid for media communications between sellers and buyers. Certainly, like public relations, the purpose of advertising is to affect public opinion. However, this is normally accomplished through the open attempt to sell the company's products or services.

Public relations activities, like product advertising, may also involve media communications, but these are not normally openly sponsored or paid for. Usually they appear through news articles, editorial interviews, or feature stories. One means of relaying a public relations message, though, is through corporate advertising, and we shall discuss that later in this chapter.

Advertising versus PR practitioners

Figure 22–1 A startled Hans Wendt captured this picture during the tragic descent of Flight 182 on September 25, 1978. Since that day, the airline has discontinued the use of that flight number.

Another interesting difference between public relations and advertising is the orientation or perspective of professional practitioners in the fields. Advertising professionals tend to be sales- or marketing-oriented (the perspective of this text, for example). They view marketing as the umbrella process used by companies to determine what products the market needs and what means will be required to distribute and sell the products to the market. To them advertising and public relations are primarily tools of marketing used to promote sales of the company's products and services. As a rule, therefore, they tend to use advertising and public relations strictly as "good news" vehicles for the company and its products.

Public relations professionals, on the other hand, consider public relations as the umbrella process that companies should use to manage their continuing relationship with their various publics. From their perspective, marketing and advertising are tools of public relations to be used in the company's sales relationship with customers and prospects. And other tools are used for other publics; among them are program sponsorships, publicity, house organs, newsletters, seminars, and press conferences, to name just a few. The PR orientation, then, is more inclined to use these various PR vehicles to "tell it like it is" even if the company's news might be bad news.

Very few companies are structured with a public relations orientation, but the perspective of the professional public relations person is important and interesting to understand. In times of crisis or emergency, it is normally considered the better perspective to adopt.

To achieve the greatest effectiveness, advertising and public relations efforts should be closely coordinated. As a result, many advertising agencies have public relations departments or perform public relations services. Many company advertising departments also supervise company public relations activities. And students of advertising are frequently interested in the public relations field. It is for these reasons that the topic of public relations is presented in this textbook along with its related counterpart, corporate advertising.

Types of corporate advertising

Advertising textbooks traditionally focus on the subject of product advertising, the primary process used by companies to promote their various products and services. However, successful companies have found that people buy their products and services for a wide variety of reasons. Company reputation and image are important, for example. Conversely, many people choose not to buy a particular company's products, service, or stock if the company is viewed negatively in the marketplace.

An obvious example of this is the airline industry. If a company has a poor safety record or a reputation for being reckless, what do you suppose would be the effect on ticket sales? Or on company stock? Prior to the crash of flight 182, PSA had had a perfect safety record for 29 years. Certainly one of Duane Youngbar's tasks after the crash was to communicate that just as PSA had always been vitally concerned with air safety, it still was, and it was taking every precaution to ensure another 29 years without mishap.

To help manage their reputation in the marketplace, companies use corporate advertising and public relations. As mentioned earlier, one of the basic tools of public relations is corporate advertising. However, there are several types of corporate advertising. These are public relations advertising, institutional advertising, corporate identity advertising, and recruitment advertising. Their use depends on the needs of the particular situation, the audience or public being addressed, and the message that needs to be communicated.

Public relations advertising

PSA was based in San Diego. It was a hometown company. In the days and weeks following the crash, there was a huge outpouring of local community support for the families of passengers, for the employees, and for the company itself. The company felt so moved to express its gratitude to the people of San Diego that it placed the full-page advertisement shown in Figure 22–2 in the local newspaper.

Some months later a financial controversy arose over the attempt by a Texas investor to take control of PSA's stock and board of directors. To communicate its position to stockholders and the financial community, PSA's management ran a series of advertisements that explained in detail the ramifications of the situation.

These examples illustrate what is called *public relations advertising.* In both cases the company wished to communicate directly with one of its important publics in an effort to express its feelings or enhance its point of view to that particular audience (Figure 22–3). Other public relations ads might be used for improving the company's relations with labor, government relations, customer relations, or supplier relations.

When companies sponsor programs on public television, they frequently place ads in other media to promote the programs and their sponsorship. These are designed to enhance the company's general community relations and to create public goodwill.

Corporate advertising

In recent years the term *corporate advertising* has gained popularity in the trade to denote that broad area of nonproduct advertising used specifically to enhance the company's image and increase lagging awareness. The traditional or historic term for this is *institutional advertising.*

Institutional or corporate ad campaigns are used for a variety of purposes, such as to report the company's record of accomplishment;

to position the company competitively in the market; to avoid a communications problem with agents, dealers, or customers; to reflect a change in corporate personality; to shore up sagging stock prices; or to improve employee morale.

David Ogilvy, the founder and creative head of Ogilvy & Mather,

PACIFIC SOUTHWEST AIRLINES

TO THE CITIZENS OF SAN DIEGO:

PSA has always taken pride in its association with this city: The airline was founded here. Our main offices are still located here. And the majority of our employees are based here.

But the depth and true meaning of this association has never been more evident than during the past week.

Minutes after the terrible disaster which befell our Flight 182 shortly after 9 A.M., Monday, September 25, over the North Park area, this city responded in a way that did not seem possible. Concerned law enforcement and fire protection agencies were on the scene within minutes. The American Red Cross, Salvation Army, Blood Bank and other similar agencies were quick to respond. Mayor Pete Wilson and other city officials have been extremely helpful.

But the list does not stop there. It would be impossible for us to name the countless other individuals and agencies who have responded. There have been religious and medical people who offered their assistence. Residents near the disaster area who offered us use of their homes and facilities were very generous. The Federal Bureau of Investigation greatly assisted the county coroner's office in identifying the victims. Commercial businesses of all types volunteered their services. All of our fellow airlines, without exception, volunteered free transportation for relatives traveling to San Diego.

We will never be able to express fully our appreciation.

On behalf of the ENTIRE PSA FAMILY, I extend my sincere thanks to you.

W.R. Shimp

William R. Shimp
President and Chief Executive Officer

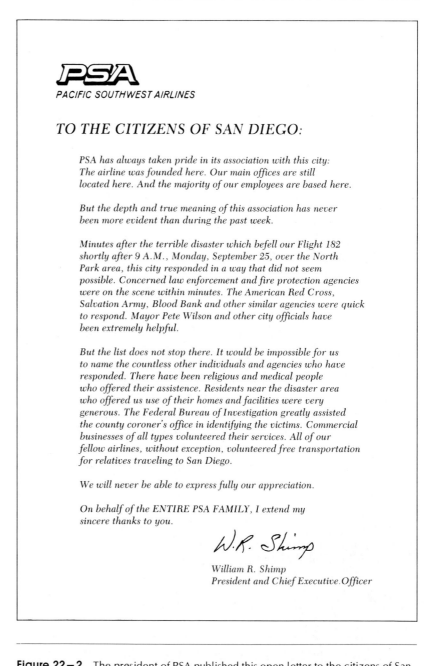

Figure 22–2 The president of PSA published this open letter to the citizens of San Diego to express his heartfelt thanks to the city for its outpouring of warmth and support following the tragic crash of flight 182. This is a very unusual but excellent example of public relations advertising.

has said that most institutional advertising fails to produce results because corporations fail to define the purpose of their campaigns. Good

W.R. SHIMP
CHAIRMAN OF THE BOARD
CHIEF EXECUTIVE OFFICER

Friday, September 26, 1980

Dear PSA Passenger:

No one wants a strike — but there are times when they can't be avoided.

PSA regrets the inconvenience imposed on you, our passenger, caused by the strike called by our pilots' association, the Southwest Flight Crew Association (SFCA). PSA is an important and vital link in the transportation network and the economy of the west. In addition we have almost 3,500 employees, other than pilots, whose lives will be drastically affected by this walkout. With these factors in mind, we bargained hard and in good faith right up to the deadline — we failed. We believe you should know where PSA and the SFCA stand:

- PSA offered a 29% pay increase over a two year period — 15% retroactive to January 1, 1980 — this offer was *rejected* by the SFCA!
- PSA offered to extend company-paid-for overnight rest periods while out of town to the longest in the industry at a cost of 4% loss of productivity — this offer was *rejected* by the SFCA.
- The SFCA demanded a 51% pay increase which includes an override of 7% to fly the advanced and highly automated McDonnell-Douglas DC-9 Super 80.
- The SFCA demanded a reduction in productive flying time of 13% with *no* reduction in pay!
- PSA offered its senior pilots a $89,812 annual income as of July 1981 — the SFCA demanded $105,864 for 13% less work.

PSA has been a low fare leader in the airline industry. We achieved that status by having well paid, hard working productive employees at all levels and departments of the company. We are now being asked to pay more for less work — to pay for featherbedding and loss of that productivity. To do so would require that you, the traveling public, pay much more for your air travel. PSA believes that this is wrong!

PSA will bargain in good faith for fair pay and reasonable working conditions — to be in a position to quickly restore service to you — high quality, *reasonably* priced service.

Sincerely,

W.R. Shimp

Figure 22–3 A common example of public relations advertising is this advertisement by PSA management to communicate to its passengers, stockholders, and the financial community its position on the issues during a strike by pilots.

corporate advertising, he says can hope to achieve one or more of only four objectives. It can build awareness of the company, make a good impression on the financial community, influence public opinion on specific issues, and motivate present employees and attract better recruits.[1] (See the Ad Lab).

Look at the ad in Figure 22–4. What do you feel are the objectives of this corporate advertising campaign? How well are those objectives addressed?

Some firms question the effectiveness of corporate advertising. A market research study sponsored by *Time* magazine and conducted

Corporate advertising by David Ogilvy

I have had some experience with corporate advertising—for Shell, Sears, IBM, International Paper, Merrill Lynch, General Dynamics, Standard Oil of New Jersey, and other great corporations.

Big corporations are increasingly under attack—from consumer groups, from environmentalists, from governments, from antitrust prosecutors who try their cases in the newspapers. If a big corporation does not take the initiative in cultivating its reputation, its case goes by default.

If it were possible, it would be better for corporations to rely on public relations—i.e., favorable news stories and editorials—rather than paid advertising. But the media are too niggardly about disseminating favorable information about corporations. That is why an increasing number of public relations directors have come to use paid advertising as their main channel of communication. It is the only one they can control with respect to *content,* with respect to *timing,* and with respect to *noise level.* And it is the only one which enables them to *select their own battleground.*

So I guess that corporate advertising is here to stay. Why is most of it a *flop?*

First, because corporations fail to define the *purpose* of their corporate campaigns.

Second, because they don't *measure the results.* In a recent survey conducted by *The Gallagher Report,* only one in four of U.S. corporate advertisers said that it measured changes in attitude brought about by its corporate campaigns. The majority fly blind.

Third, because so little is known about what works and what doesn't work in corporate advertising. The marketing departments and their agencies know a good deal about what works in *brand* advertising, but when it comes to *corporate* advertising they are amateurs. It isn't their bag.

Fourth, very few advertising agencies know much about corporate advertising. It is only a marginal part of their business. Their creative people know how to talk to housewives about toilet paper, and how to write chewing-gum jingles for kids, and how to sell beer to blue-collar workers. But corporate advertising requires copywriters who are at home in the world of big business. There aren't many of them.

I am appalled by the *humbug* in corporate advertising. The *pomposity.* The *vague generalities* and the *fatuous platitudes.*

Corporate advertising should not insult the intelligence of the public.

Unlike product advertising, a corporate campaign is the voice of the chief executive and his board of directors. It should not be delegated.

What can good corporate advertising hope to achieve? In my experience, one or more of four objectives:

1. It can build *awareness* of the company. Opinion Research Corporation states, "The invisibility and remoteness of most companies is the main handicap. People who feel they know a company well are five times more likely to have a highly favorable opinion of the company than those who have little familiarity."

2. Corporate advertising can make a good impression on the financial community, thus enabling you to raise capital at lower cost—and make more acquisitions.

3. It can motivate your present employees and attract better recruits. Good public relations begin at home. If your employees understand your policies and feel proud of your company, they will be your best ambassadors.

by the Yankelovich, Skelly & White research firm showed that companies that use corporate advertising register significantly better awareness, familiarity, and overall impression among business executives that those that do not. The corporate advertisers in the study drew higher ratings in every one of 16 characteristics measured, including being known for quality products, having competent management, and paying higher dividends. Of great interest was that the companies with no corporate advertising studied spent far more for total product advertising than did the firms that engaged in corporate advertising.[2]

4. Corporate advertising can influence public opinion on specific issues.

Abraham Lincoln said, "With public opinion against it, nothing can succeed. With public opinion on its side, nothing can fail."

Stop and Go—that is the typical pattern of corporate advertising. What a waste of money. It takes time, it takes *years,* for corporate advertising to do a job. It doesn't work overnight—even if you use television.

A few companies—a *very* few—have kept it going long enough to achieve measurable results.

U.S. Steel ran corporate advertising for 42 years. General Electric for 48 years. Du Pont for 43 years.

One man, George Cecil, wrote the A.T.&T. corporate advertising for 40 years.

Laboratory application

Discuss a corporate advertisement with which you are familiar that demonstrates what David Ogilvy refers to as "the humbug in corporate advertising, the pomposity, the vague generalities, and the fatuous platitudes."

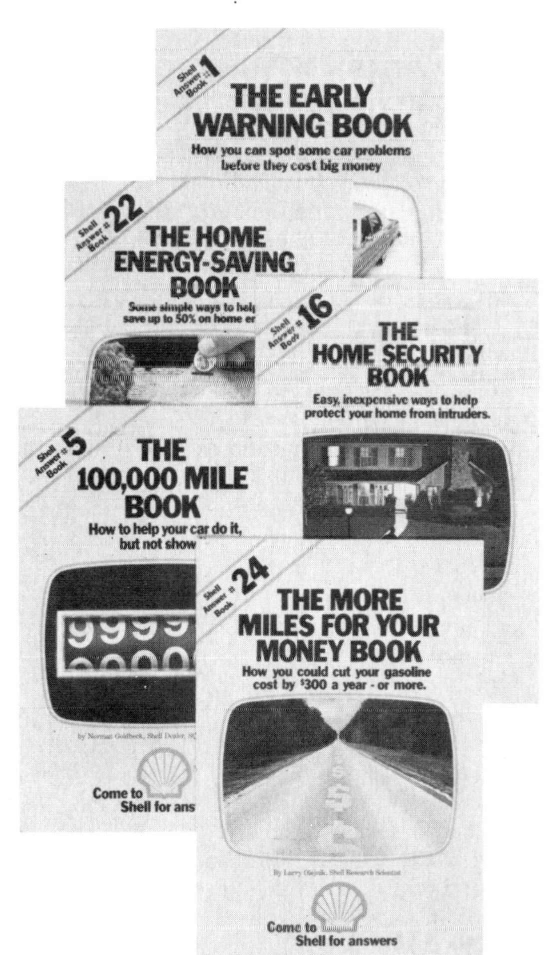

Overwhelming requests have been made for Shell's "Answer" books because of the corporate advertising campaign announcing by Ogivy & Mather their availability.

Corporate identity advertising

In Chapter 14, "Creative Packaging, Labeling, and Trademarks," we discussed that companies take great pride in their logos and corporate signatures. In fact, the graphic designs that identify corporate names and products are considered valuable assets of the company, and great effort is expended to protect their individuality and ownership. What does a company do, though, when it decides to change its logos, trademarks, or corporate signatures? How does it communicate that change to the market it serves and to its other influential publics? This is the job of corporate identity advertising.

In a continuing effort to appear modern and up to date, airline companies traditionally change their corporate logos, airplane graphics, and employee uniforms every few years to reflect current esthetic tastes. In 1971 PSA changed the appearance of its planes as explained in Figure 22–5. To announce the change, corporate identity ads were created and placed in regional magazines, local newspapers, and TV. The "Grinningbird" theme was then carried into the company's product ads to further meet the corporate identity objective. (See Figure 22–6.)

Other well-known examples of corporate identity programs are Exxon Corporation's consolidation of its various previous names (Standard Oil of New Jersey, Enco, Esso, Humble Oil, etc.) to the Exxon name, and the International Business Machines change to the simple, familiar IBM acronym.

Since Dr. Coolidge developed the modern x-ray tube, General Electric researchers have worked to improve it and also develop new kinds of diagnostic equipment. The latest example is Computed Tomography, a totally new kind of x-ray system. It gives cross-sectional views of the body (shown here). This makes it possible to see parts of the body that could never be seen before without surgery.
Progress for People.
GENERAL ELECTRIC

Figure 22–4 Corporate advertising by General Electric accomplishes several objectives at once. As well as relating some of the interesting history of General Electric, it demonstrates the company's optimistic attitude toward the future.

In short, corporate identity advertising may be used when companies need to communicate a name or appearance change, an ownership change, or a change in corporate personality, or when the company is suffering from generally lagging awareness.

Recruitment advertising

David Ogilvy pointed out that one of the prime objectives of corporate advertising is to motivate employees and attract better recruits. Certainly that objective is apparent in the well-known Thomas Edison campaign created by General Electric (see Figure 22–4).

However, when the sole objective is to attract employment applications, companies use recruitment advertising. These advertisements are most frequently found in the classified sections of daily newspapers and are typically the responsibility of the personnel department rather than the advertising department. Recruitment advertising has become such a large field, though, that many advertising agencies now have recruitment specialists on their staff. In fact, some agencies specialize completely in recruitment advertising, and their clients are the corporate personnel managers rather than advertising department managers. These agencies create, write, and place classified advertisements in newspapers around the country as well as prepare recruitment display ads for specialized trade publications (Figure 22–7).

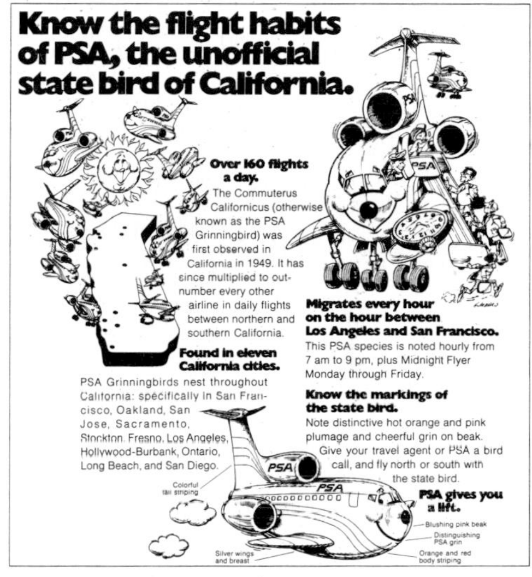

Figure 22–5 Since the initiation of this corporate identity program in the mid 70s, PSA airplanes have come to be called Grinningbirds by passengers and airline employees alike.

Public relations activities

Prior to his appointment as director of public relations for PSA, Duane Youngbar was a member of the public relations staff at Western Airlines for nine years. During his tenure at Western, that airline experienced two accidents and one hijacking. When PSA's flight 182 went down, Youngbar knew what to expect and what had to be done. In fact, he had prepared a formal emergency plan when he first joined PSA. It was now time to put that plan into action.

Hanging up the phone, he ran down the hall to the executive vice president's office. The news was already there and so was the company president. Youngbar quickly outlined what had to be done:

1. Obtain complete flight information from Dispatch.
2. Get passenger manifest and inform all employees of situation.
3. Install emergency telephones and direct all calls to PR.
4. Transport a public relations representative to the accident site immediately.
5. Assign additional personnel to PR to immediately begin notifying families; and numerous other tasks.

Federal aviation regulations place extensive legal restrictions on what an airline may say publicly following an accident. Yet the press is energetic in its demand for answers. Thus, all communications to and from the company had to be channeled through Youngbar's expanded department. His responsibility was to direct and control all press relations, all customer relations, all passenger/family communications, and all government communications. Only in this way could open, clear, consistent, *legal,* and credible communications be maintained. And only in this way could the potentially disastrous effects of rumor-mongering, political backbiting, and corporate defensiveness be minimized.

In the first 48 hours after the crash of flight 182 the calls to PSA were incessant. The moment one line was hung up, the telephone rang again. Employees had to know what to say, what they were not allowed to say, and to whom unanswerable questions should be referred. That, of course, depended on who was calling and what they were asking.

At the same time, the families of passengers had to be notified, authorities had to be contacted, and many others who were important because of the situation had to be reached. And all this had to be planned, coordinated, and supervised efficiently. That was suddenly the job of Duane Youngbar and his staff. It did not matter that every employee had several friends on that flight. They would have to do their crying later.

As unusual as disasters might be, they are still the primary activities of PR professionals and public information officers in highly sensitive organizations such as airlines, police departments, military organizations, chemical and oil companies, and public utilities. These people are all employed in industries characterized by a constant high demand for news information. As a result, their activities are centered around planning, coordinating, and supervising the press relations of their organizations in a variety of pressure-cooker situations.

Most public relations professionals, however, are not occupied in these sensitive, high news-demand areas. Rather they are employed to generate news from basically low news-demand organizations, and the activities they are concerned with reflect that fact.

'OUR SMILES AREN'T JUST PAINTED ON!'

Figure 22–6 Indicative of the success of PSA's corporate identity program is this use of the grinning bird smile and advertising slogan in an editorial cartoon of the space shuttle Columbia which appeared in the *Los Angeles Times.*

Publicity and press agentry

Publicity is the generation of news about a person, product, or service that appears in broadcast or print media and is usually thought of as being "free" because the medium has no publicity rate card. The media do not bill anyone for the publicity they run, and the media cannot be "bought" to run the publicity. The organization that seeks the publicity may go to considerable expense in its effort to get it, but there's no bill for the space or time received.

Press agentry refers to the planning of activities and the staging of events in order to attract attention and generate publicity that will be of interest to the media. Although celebrities, the circus, sports events, politicians, motion pictures, and rock stars come to mind as requiring press agentry, many public relations people use it to bring attention to new products or services or to put their company or organization in a favorable light. For example, if a company makes a donation to a charitable cause, press agentry can be used to bring the donation to the attention of the public.

The most common way to let the media know about an item worthy of publicity is through a news release, which is discussed in greater detail later in this chapter. Often this is accompanied by an appropriate photograph. Many stories in the business pages of a newspaper are either verbatim printings of news releases or stories based on publicity releases. In this case the public relations person acts as a reporter about a client or organization by releasing news that he or she wants published or broadcast. Opportunities for publicity include the introduction of a new product, awards, company sales and earnings, mergers, retirements, parades, and speeches by company executives.

For print media, the publicity person deals with editors and feature writers (Figure 22–8). For broadcast media, he or she deals with a program director or the news editor.

Just as an organization has an advertising program, there should also be a company publicity program. Like the advertising person, the professional public relations practitioner performs careful research, plans a publicity program, and then executes it. A complete program should be tentatively scheduled on a yearly basis and then incorporated into the budget.

Publicity material can have great promotional value. Organizations often reprint publicity received in newspapers or magazines and mail these reprints to appropriate audiences. Photographs of an organization's representative as seen on TV with talk-show host or other celebrity can be sent along with an appropriate story written by the public relations practitioner. Sometimes these materials can even be used in point-of-purchase displays or sent to salespeople to be used in their portfolios as visual aids.

OIL AND GAS ANALYST

Oil and gas analyst wanted for regional brokerage firm. Analyst will evaluate and monitor various oil and gas Limited Partnerships.

Please include salary requirements along with your resume:
Brenda Aston
Foster & Marshall, Inc.
205 Columbia Street
Seattle, Washington 98104

AN EQUAL OPPORTUNITY EMPLOYER

REAL ESTATE ATTORNEY
Must have 4 years experience representing commercial shopping center developers, background in leasing, option, purchase agreements, financing, title insurance. Salary to 45K plus, near LAX.
P.O. Box 92936
Los Angeles, California 90009

Figure 22–7 Recruitment advertising comes in many forms. These two ads from *The Wall Street Journal* were placed by the companies directly and pub set (set by the publication). Others may be prepared by the company's regular advertising agency or an agency that specializes in recruitment advertising.

Public affairs and lobbying

Dealing with community officials and working with regulatory bodies and legislative groups are public affairs work. This means community and government relations and involves encouraging employees to vote or to make political contributions, getting employees to participate in programs for the betterment of the community and the environment, and informing citizen groups of company objectives in order to enlist their support. Perhaps it can best be defined as all activities related to the citizenship of an organization.

Because every organization is affected by the government, there is also an increasing amount of lobbying being done. Lobbying involves trying to inform and persuade government officials in the interests of the client so as to promote or thwart administrative action or legislation.

Promotion and special events management

For profit-making organizations, promotion means using advertising and public relations techniques as a means of selling a product or service as well as enhancing the reputation of an organization. Promotion can be achieved through press parties, open houses, celebrations, issuing of press releases, sponsoring of contests, or a variety of other things.

Special events can take the form of a grand opening of a new store, an autograph party for an author, the announcement of a new product, or the groundbreaking for a new public library. The list is almost endless. The public relations practitioner is responsible for conceiving ideas for special events as well as for planning and staging and all the preparation that must be completed for the event to take place. To capture the attention of the media and, thereby, to favorably impress the public is the responsibility of the public relations person.

Publications

Materials for which public relations persons are responsible often include company publications; new releases and media kits; booklets,

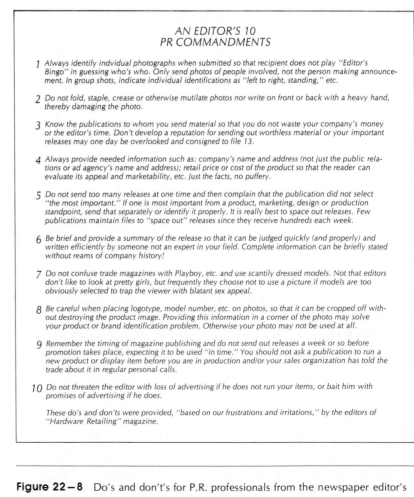

AN EDITOR'S 10
PR COMMANDMENTS

1. *Always identify indvidual photographs when submitted so that recipient does not play "Editor's Bingo" in guessing who's who. Only send photos of people involved, not the person making announcement. In group shots, indicate individual identifications as "left to right, standing," etc.*
2. *Do not fold, staple, crease or otherwise mutilate photos nor write on front or back with a heavy hand, thereby damaging the photo.*
3. *Know the publications to whom you send material so that you do not waste your company's money or the editor's time. Don't develop a reputation for sending out worthless material or your important releases may one day be overlooked and consigned to file 13.*
4. *Always provide needed information such as: company's name and address (not just the public relations or ad agency's name and address); retail price or cost of the product so that the reader can evaluate its appeal and marketability, etc. Just the facts, no puffery.*
5. *Do not send too many releases at one time and then complain that the publication did not select "the most important." If one is most important from a product, marketing, design or production standpoint, send that separately or identify it properly. It is really best to space out releases. Few publications maintain files to "space out" releases since they receive hundreds each week.*
6. *Be brief and provide a summary of the release so that it can be judged quickly (and properly) and written efficiently by someone not an expert in your field. Complete information can be briefly stated without reams of company history!*
7. *Do not confuse trade magazines with Playboy, etc. and use scantily dressed models. Not that editors don't like to look at pretty girls, but frequently they choose not to use a picture if models are too obviously selected to trap the viewer with blatant sex appeal.*
8. *Be careful when placing logotype, model number, etc. on photos, so that it can be cropped off without destroying the product image. Providing this information in a corner of the photo may solve your product or brand identification problem. Otherwise your photo may not be used at all.*
9. *Remember the timing of magazine publishing and do not send out releases a week or so before promotion takes place, expecting it to be used "in time." You should not ask a publication to run a new product or display item before you are in production and/or your sales organization has told the trade about it in regular personal calls.*
10. *Do not threaten the editor with loss of advertising if he does not run your items, or bait him with promises of advertising if he does.*

These do's and don'ts were provided, "based on our frustrations and irritations," by the editors of "Hardware Retailing" magazine.

Figure 22–8 Do's and don't's for P.R. professionals from the newspaper editor's point of view.

leaflets, pamphlets, brochures, manuals, and books; letters, inserts, and enclosures; annual reports; posters, bulletin boards, and exhibits; audiovisual materials; and speeches and position papers. Greater details on these tools of communication will be given in a later section of this chapter.

Research

Research is the process of obtaining reliable and valid information. One common form of public relations research is opinion sampling. Secondary sources of information are directories, the news media, professional journals, and government publications.

Inasmuch as the purpose of all public relations activities is to influence public opinion, it is vital that the public relations person be concerned with measuring and analyzing changes in public attitude and sentiment.

Fund raising and membership drives

A public relations person may be responsible for soliciting money for the organization or for a cause the organization deems worthwhile such as the United Way or a political action committee (PAC).

In order for charitable organizations, labor unions, professional societies, trade associations, and other groups to exist, they must rely on membership fees or contributions as a primary means of support. The public relations specialist must communicate to potential contributors or members the purposes and goals of the organization. Because the public relations specialist is usually considered the chief communicator of the organization, he or she is the person frequently called upon to perform the task.

Public speaking

Public relations practitioners frequently must represent employers at events, so the ability to speak well is essential. The ability to express oneself clearly reflects directly on the organization. Because organization spokespersons are often called upon to be interviewed on TV or to give speeches, organizations are now placing increased importance on the ability to communicate effectively.

Planning and execution

As pointed out at the beginning of this section on public relations activities, probably the most important role of a practitioner is to plan and execute the public relations program. To do this effectively, the practitioner must analyze the relationships between the organization and its public, evaluate public attitudes and opinions toward the organization; assess the organization's policies, procedures, and actions as they relate to the organization's publics; and finally plan and execute a public relations program using any or all of the various PR activities described above.

Public relations tools

The tools of communication at the PR person's disposal are, like in advertising, many and varied—from brochures to photographs to newsletters to audiovisual materials. We shall discuss a few of these here because the same basic techniques of writing, art, layout, and production used in advertising are used in the production of public relations materials.

News releases and media kits

A news release is a typewritten sheet of information (usually 8½ by 11 inches) issued to generate publicity. A large variety of information is put in this form and sent to print and broadcast outlets. Subjects may include the announcement of a new product, promotion of an executive, establishment of a scholarship fund, or signing of a union contract, to name a few.

A media kit is used to gain publicity at staged events such as press conferences or open houses. It includes a basic fact sheet detailing the event, a program for the event or a schedule of the activities, a list of the participants with biographical data, brochures prepared for the event, a news story for the broadcast media, and news and feature stories for print media.

Photography

Like in advertising, a picture may be worth a thousand words. Photographs of events, products in use, new equipment, or newly promoted executives lend credence or interest to an otherwise dull news story.

Photography adds impact, realism, and believability to a news item. However, that impact can be negative as well as positive. On September 25, 1978, Hans Wendt, a staff photographer for the county of San Diego, was taking pictures for an upcoming hearing when he suddenly heard a boom over his head. Looking up, he saw the burning PSA jet plummeting to earth. He pointed his camera and snapped the picture shown at the beginning of this chapter that subsequently appeared in every major newspaper and newsmagazine in the country.

How much negative PR do you feel that photograph might have created for the airline? Are questions of ethics involved when the media run sensational photographs like this?

Booklets, brochures, pamphlets, and books

Printed materials are used extensively in public relations. Materials are written to tell employees how they can aid the public relations program and how the organization started and grew, to teach employees how to go about doing their work, to explain the credit union and safety regulations, and a host of other things.

Frequently books are written on the history of the company or as a biography of the founder of the company. A common item is a presentation booklet describing the organization to visitors, prospective employees, donors, students, and customers.

Letters, inserts, and enclosures

Letters may be written on behalf of the company and sent to customers, legislators, suppliers, retailers, or editors (letters to the editor often rebut a criticism of the company).

Inserts or enclosures may be used for public relations purposes. Inserts are often put in billings from oil or utility companies, for example, to explain rate increases or company views on political issues. These are the types of enclosures for which a public relations practitioner is responsible. Who do you think would be responsible for the type of promotional inserts that offer merchandise at especially attractive prices?

Annual reports

An annual report is a formal document issued yearly by a corporation to its stockholders. It is a reflection of a corporation's condition at the close of the business year. Annual reports contain an ever-expanding amount of information required by either generally accepted accounting principles or specific requirements.* Included in reports are financial statements. While the report is directed to the stockholders of the organization, it is also of interest to potential investors, unions, and legislators (Figure 22–9). Companies usually try to make their reports appealing, readable, and informative.

An annual report can be an important public relations tool because it is really management's justification for its performance. In addition, it can have a strong influence on potential investors who use it to discover the status and prospects of the business. It gives the organization the opportunity to answer questions about itself and to

*For example, Rule 14c-3, of the Securities Exchange Act of 1934 specifies that annual reports furnished to stockholders in connection with the annual meeting of stockholders include the following information: "certified" comparative financial statements, a five-year summary of operations, management's analysis of the summary operations, a brief description of the company's directors and executive officers and their principal occupations, and a statement of the market price range and dividends paid on voting securities for each quarterly period during the past two fiscal years.

offer explanations for its actions. With the government delving into corporate affairs more and more, it can help by giving agencies facts to overcome misconceptions they may have about operations.

Nonbusiness organizations also report to their members or trustees by using reports. These do not necessarily contain financial data, but they present progress on activities and plans for future programs. These reports are used as both internal and external public relations tools.

House organs

A house organ (or house publication) is a company publication. Internal house publications are for employees only. External house

The World of Otis

For more than 125 years, Otis Elevator Company has been designing, building and installing safe, practical and efficient elevators and escalators, carrying millions of people and moving countless tons of goods of all kinds.

Today, Otis is the world's leading producer of elevators and escalators. There are more than 400,000 Otis elevators and escalators in place, worldwide.

Below: Otis escalators provide transportation for millions of visitors and workers each year at Detroit's Renaissance Center. The complex also includes 50 Otis observation elevators.

Above: The traditional "lobby floor" is just one of three in the Trade Center. Otis skylobby systems on the 44th and 78th floors help maximize the nine million square feet of rentable floor space.

Left: The restaurant on the 107th floor of the World Trade Center offers a spectacular view of New York City. Patrons reach it via an equally spectacular 58-second ride on an Otis express elevator.

Figure 22–9 These pages from the Otis Elevator Company's subsidiary report describes the most recent building projects in which it has installations. It is distributed with the annual report of its parent company, United Technologies Corporation. The annual report contains all the required financial data.

publications may go to company-connected persons (customers, stockholders, and dealers) or to the public. They may take the form of a newsletter, a tabloid newspaper, or a magazine (Figure 22–10). Often these company newsletters have the reputation of being simply a gossip sheet or a mouthpiece for management. If that is the case, they will simply be thrown out and not read.

Professional PR people have found that if the company openly talks about controversial issues and admits the negatives, readership of these publications increases and their effectiveness in building morale is strengthened. Their purpose is to promote goodwill, increase sales, or to mold public opinion. A well-produced house organ can do a great deal to get employees or customers to feel they know the people who make up a company. However, writing, printing, and distributing a house organ can be expensive.

Otis is also the industry leader in the aesthetic aspects of elevator and escalator design. The company offers an unusually wide selection of paneling materials, car fronts, ceilings, interiors and exterior control panels, lighting arrangements and colors, balustrade styles and materials, so architects can match elevators and escalators to building decor.

Chicago's Water Tower Place, a 74-story multifunction building and a 12-story commercial center, uses 46 Otis escalators and 44 geared, gearless and hydraulic Otis elevators.

Right: The eight-story atrium of the 73-story Detroit Plaza Hotel, designed by John Portman, in the midst of Detroit's Renaissance Center. More than 90 Otis elevators provide vertical transportation in this five-tower riverfront project.

Below: Soaring 665 feet over Lake Michigan in Chicago, the 70-story Lake Point Tower ranks as one of the world's tallest apartment buildings. It was designed by John Heinrichs and George Schipporeit and built by the Crane Construction Company. Residents are served by 10 Otis elevators.

Speeches and position papers

Company executives give speeches before a great diversity of groups. Writing the speech often falls within the domain of the public relations person. Occasions for speeches may be congressional hearings. annual stockholders meetings, and important conferences and conventions. Practitioners may simply have to do the research for a speech, or they may prepare an outline or write the speech in its entirety for an executive of the company.

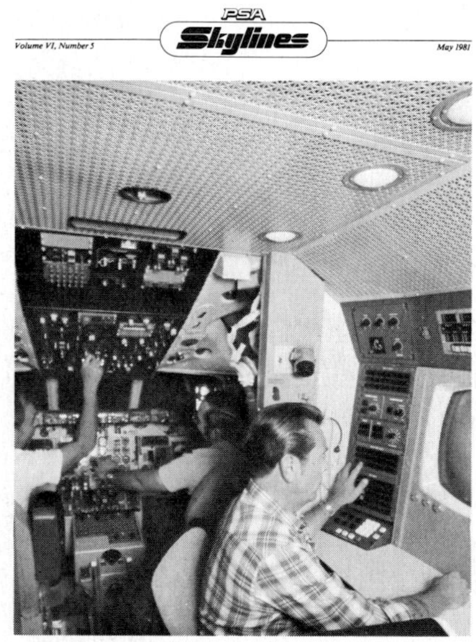

Figure 22–10 *PSA Skylines,* an internal house organ, is published monthly. Typical issues contain employee profiles, reports on company earnings, information about benefits, listings of birthdays and anniversaries, and details about new employee travel packages.

Posters, bulletin boards, and exhibits

Posters can be used to stress safety, security, reduction of waste, courtesy, and other information.

Exhibits can give a history of the organization, present new products, show how products are made, or tell about future plans of the organization (Figure 22–11). Exhibits are often made at local fairs, colleges and universities, and trade shows.

Bulletin boards can announce new equipment, meetings, promotions, new products, construction plans, and recreation news to name just a few possibilities.

Audiovisual materials, films, and closed-circuit TV

These materials can take many forms, including slides, films, filmstrips, and video cassettes used for training, sales, or public relations.

"Nontheatrical" or "sponsored" films are films that are developed for public relations reasons. They are considered a form of corporate advertising. They are furnished without charge to movie theaters, organizations, and special groups, particularly schools and colleges. Examples of these films are *Why Man Creates,* produced for Kaiser Aluminum, and Mobil Oil Corporation's *A Fable,* starring the famous French mime Marcel Marceau.

Through the telephone company, a closed-circuit television system can be leased. It enables the broadcast of live pictures and sound from one point to another. Political parties use these systems for fund-raising dinners. Companies use them for various types of meetings. Colleges use them to teach classes on different campuses.

Open houses, plant tours, and other staged events

There are two kinds of public relations events: (1) events that are designed to create publicity and (2) those whose purpose is to improve public relations through personal contact. Often these two purposes overlap. For example, Macy's Thanksgiving Day parade in New York creates tremendous publicity but also a great deal of community goodwill because of personal contact. Also, an event designed to improve public relations among members of an association—the annual convention of the American Bar Association—can generate vast amounts of publicity.

Open houses and plant tours enable an organization to give the community a greater understanding of its inner workings. They can be instrumental in building goodwill. As part of a tour, companies often give away a sample of their product or a pamphlet about the organization. Organizations that typically give tours are newspapers and TV stations. The public relations person has to be able to plan the event or tour, control it, arrange for the location, devise the program and schedule speakers, send out invitations, and arrange for facilities.

Another type of event that is used as a public relations tool is the company-sponsored art, cultural, or sports event. The sponsorship enhances the identity of an organization. The cultural support creates goodwill in the community. For example, after cigarette companies were no longer able to advertise on radio or TV, they sponsored events such as tennis tournaments in order to reach people via the airwaves.

Figure 22–11 This permanent exhibit at Boeing's Renton, Washington, headquarters was designed to demonstrate the marketing advantages of Boeing's new 757 and 767 airplanes.

The public relations practitioner

In times of corporate emergency, crisis, or disaster, the news media look to the company's public relations director for information. In military or other government organizations, the public relations person is frequently referred to as the public information officer. But the role is the same—to act as the primary communications link between the organization and its various publics.

Government

Before going to work for the airlines, Duane Youngbar had been in the Army where he was assigned to the Office of Public Information at West Point. Here he served as part of a 16-man contingent handling all public relations and protocol for the U.S. Military Academy. This included coordinating the tours of visiting dignitaries, writing stories for local newspapers around the country about their hometown boys as cadets, and answering the constant demand for information from national and international publications, broadcast networks, and special-interest groups.

This is just one example of how government uses public relations. How often do you read about actions by other government organizations—the IRS, SEC, FDA, the state attorney general, the local district attorney, and the police department? All these organizations have highly trained public relations people skilled at presenting their points of view or other information designed to stimulate the desired public opinion.

The government is the largest user of public relations professionals in the country. For the most part, they are all in high news-demand positions.

Business

The demand for news from business organizations is usually much lower except in those sensitive areas previously discussed. As a result, the role of the practitioner is oriented more to creating news that will positively influence public opinion and demonstrate the good citizenship of the particular business. In this regard, public relations is an important tool of marketing and it is in the interest of business to employ public relations people who also have a strong marketing background.

For example, in late 1976, the baby food industry was under attack by consumers and the news media for the amount of sugar and salt added to the food products. Sales were declining, and consumer confidence was at a low ebb. Beech-Nut Corporation along with its concentrated PR firm, Daniel J. Edelman, Inc., launched an intensive public relations program centering around the company's introduction of reformulated products with no added salt and reduced added sugar. The program included press conferences, appearances on national news-talk shows, extensive articles in consumer magazines, consumer education in 50 top markets, and supportive reactions by leading consumer advocates.

After the initial announcement and the PR program were launched, advertising was placed to merchandise the idea of Beech-Nut's naturally good baby food. Continuing public relations and advertising kept the story alive for months, and within a year Beech-Nut's market share had increased several points while the competition had slipped.

Nonprofit organizations

As we shall discuss in Chapter 23, "Noncommercial and Political Advertising," the role of the professional practitioner in nonprofit organizations is to communicate the activities of the group in order to attract contributions as well as to build public awareness and understanding of the group's objectives. Therefore, PR professionals with an understanding of fund raising, direct mail, and advertising techniques are usually sought by these organizations.

Career opportunities

Because of the tremendous diversity in the demands made upon a public relations practitioner, students should explore academic areas that will give them a wide variety of experiences. Newsom and Scott give nine areas of expertise that are desirable:[3]

1. Planning: The scope of this ranges from aiding top management in other than PR problems to the details of the PR department's own organization and functioning. It incorporates the development of policy and procedure and communication of both to other departments.
2. Administration: This goes beyond the administration of the PR de-

partment itself to interpreting top management to the entire organization, participating in association activities, coordinating all outside agencies and activities, accumulating information about the organization, and preparing and allocating the corporate PR budget.

3. Advising: This implies doing the research necessary for authoritative counsel and providing educational and informational materials to stockholders, lobbyists, and others.
4. Industry relations: This means working with personnel in improving employee relations, initiating communication systems with employees, helping to improve labor relations by participating in meetings and conferences with labor representatives, and working closely with labor negotiators in labor contracts and discussions.
5. Economic relations: This involves relations with competitors, dealers, and distributors, and encompasses advertising and promotion, which often means working closely with marketing and merchandising.
6. Social relations: This consists of both human relations, which includes preservation of personal dignity and employee protection (security), and social welfare, which incorporates recreational, medical, and civic activities.
7. Political activities: These extend beyond the community's administrative, educational, and religious groups to legislative bodies and international contacts.
8. Communication: This is knowing how to communicate through both mass and specialized media by advertising and publicity.
9. Educational activities: This encompasses working with employees, the general public, schools, company representatives such as salespeople and dealers, and consumer groups, and arranging appearances and writing speeches for corporate executives.

Inside firms

Internal public relations departments may consist of as few as one person or as many as several hundred persons. The greater the number, the more likely that work will be handled by specialists who are responsible for particular facets of public relations (Figure 22–12).

It is common for internal departments to retain the services of outside suppliers such as artists, printers, mailing houses, and clipping services for monitoring press coverage.

There are many advantages of an internal department. An in-house practitioner is available on a moment's notice, and there is someone who can speak on behalf of the company when needed. It is sometimes less expensive to have someone on the payroll in-house than to hire an outside organization. However, the expertise of outside professionals may offset this minor savings. An in-house person has a more intimate knowledge of the organization than an outsider.

The disadvantages of an internal department include the fact that practitioners may lose their objectivity. It is sometimes difficult for them to step back as a member of the company team. In addition, it is difficult for them to obtain fresh viewpoints and an exposure to other companies with similar problems along with their solutions when they are tied to one company on a full-time basis.

Outside firms

Many advertising agencies offer public relations services. In addition, there are more than 1,600 firms that specialize in public relations

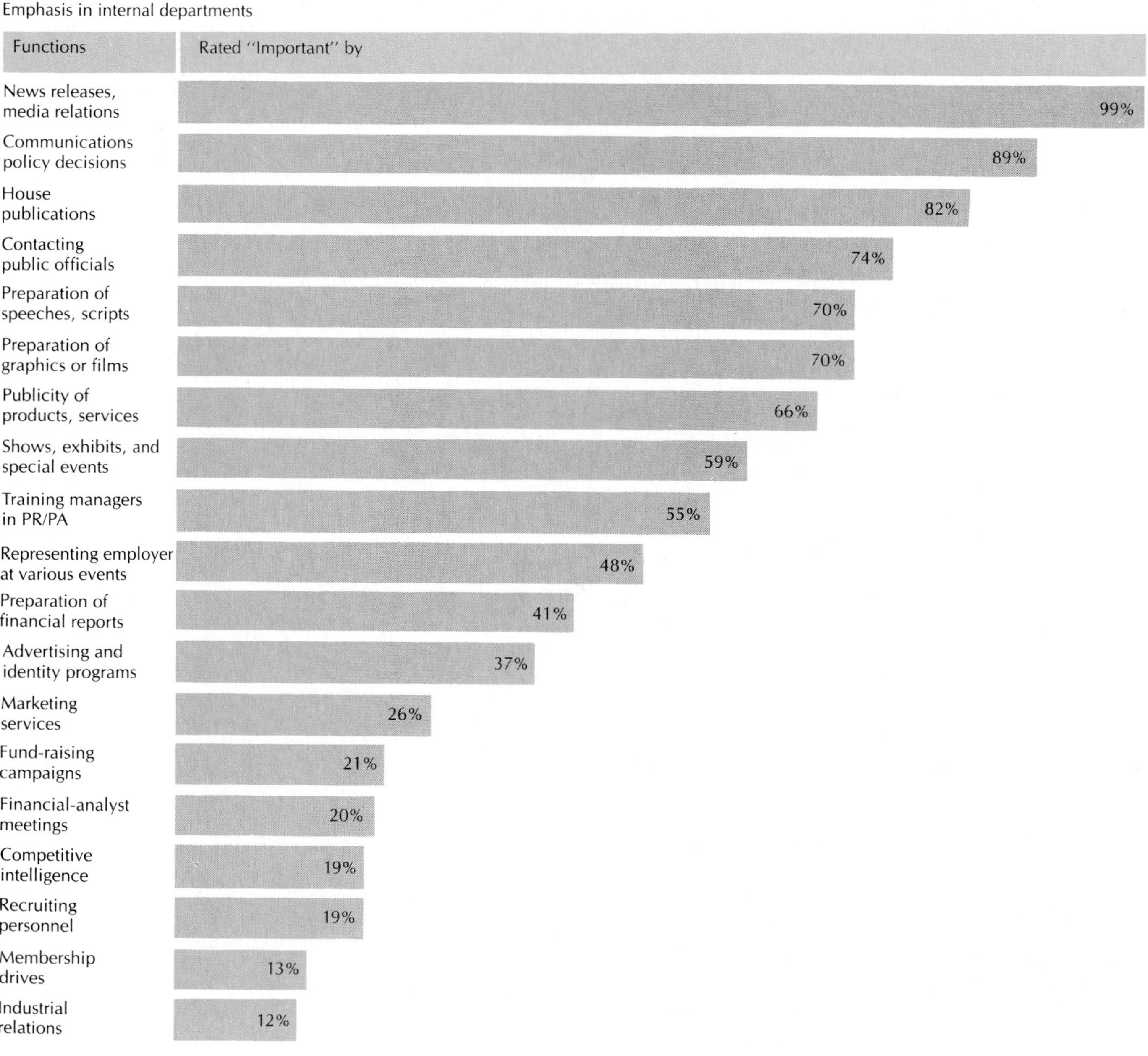

Figure 22–12 Companies use their in-house public relations departments for a wide variety of functions. The most common of these is the preparation of news releases and the coordination of media relations. The least common is labor negotiations (industrial relations).

People in advertising

Dorothy E. Gregg

Corporate Vice President of
Communications
Celanese Corporation

Dr. Dorothy E. Gregg, named one of America's top women business leaders by *Fortune* and *Business Week*, is corporate vice president of communications for Celanese Corporation. She was the first woman ever appointed to the corporate helm by Celanese.

From her handsome executive office, Dr. Gregg oversees all financial, corporate, government, public affairs, marketing, and employee communications for Celanese. She serves as secretary to the Public Responsibility Committee of the Board of Directors and to the Corporate Government Affairs Committee. She is also a member of the Corporate Contributions Committee.

Gregg came to Celanese from U.S. Steel Corporation, where she was assistant staff director of education services and then assistant director of public relations. Earlier she was a consultant to several corporations on management organization, recruitment, training, compensation, and incentive plans. Gregg served as an assistant professor of economics at Columbia University of Texas, and the New School for Social Research. A graduate of the University of Texas with B.A. and M.A. degrees in economics, Gregg earned a Ph.D. in economics from Columbia University. She was awarded an honorary degree of humane letters by Salem College and an honorary LLD by Northwood Institute.

Raised on a ranch in Tempe, Arizona, Gregg recalled, "Ranch life is vigorous. Everyone is a workaholic—you *have* to be to survive. As a child, I was encouraged to be independent, to be a leader. I was expected to take risks and to learn as much from failures as from success. I was always the first to jump from the highest haystack," she added. "If I got hurt, it taught me to make a better jump or to use better judgment next time."

Gregg was appointed by President Jimmy Carter to the President's Management Improvement Council. She has served on the Social Indicators Committee of the American Marketing Association, the UNESCO Committee to improve business education worldwide, and the White House Conference on Children.

President of the Foundation for Public Relations Research and Education, Gregg holds the Professional Chair in Public Relations of the New York Chapter, Women in Communications, Inc. She is a former executive officer of the New York chapter of the Public Relations Society of America, Women Executives in Public Relations, and the Advertising Women of New York.

The only woman on the Civilian Public Relations Advisory Committee of the U.S. Military Academy, Gregg also serves on the Secretary of the Navy's Advisory Board on Education and Training and the Committee on Long-Range Planning of the Public Relations Society of America. She is a member of the Public Relations Committee, Joint Council on Economic Education.

Recipient of the American Advertising Federation National Advertising Woman of the Year Award, Gregg was also one of the first to receive an Economic Equity Award from the Women's Equity Action League. That same year she was presented the Matrix Award in public relations by New York Women in Communications. Gregg is also the recipient of the Theta Sigma Phi Sound of Success Award and the Top Hat Award of the National Federation of Business and Professional Women's Clubs for her "significant contribution toward advancing the status of employed women."

Said Dr. Gregg, "My greatest reward came at an annual meeting of stockholders in Houston. A young woman, a Celanese chemical plant employee, introduced herself to me and said, 'Because of you, I know *anything* is possible.' "

exclusively. Many of these firms specialize in a particular area of public relations such as public affairs, financial public relations, or political public relations (Figure 22–13).

One advantage of an outside agency is the range of services available, which might be prohibitively expensive if maintained internally. A second advantage is objectivity. An outside specialist is above the daily operation of an organization. Third, many public relations firms are in New York City, the communications center of the United States. For some organizations it may be very important to have an outside agency located in the same area. Also, there's the prestige of having a well-known outside firm handle an organization's public relations.

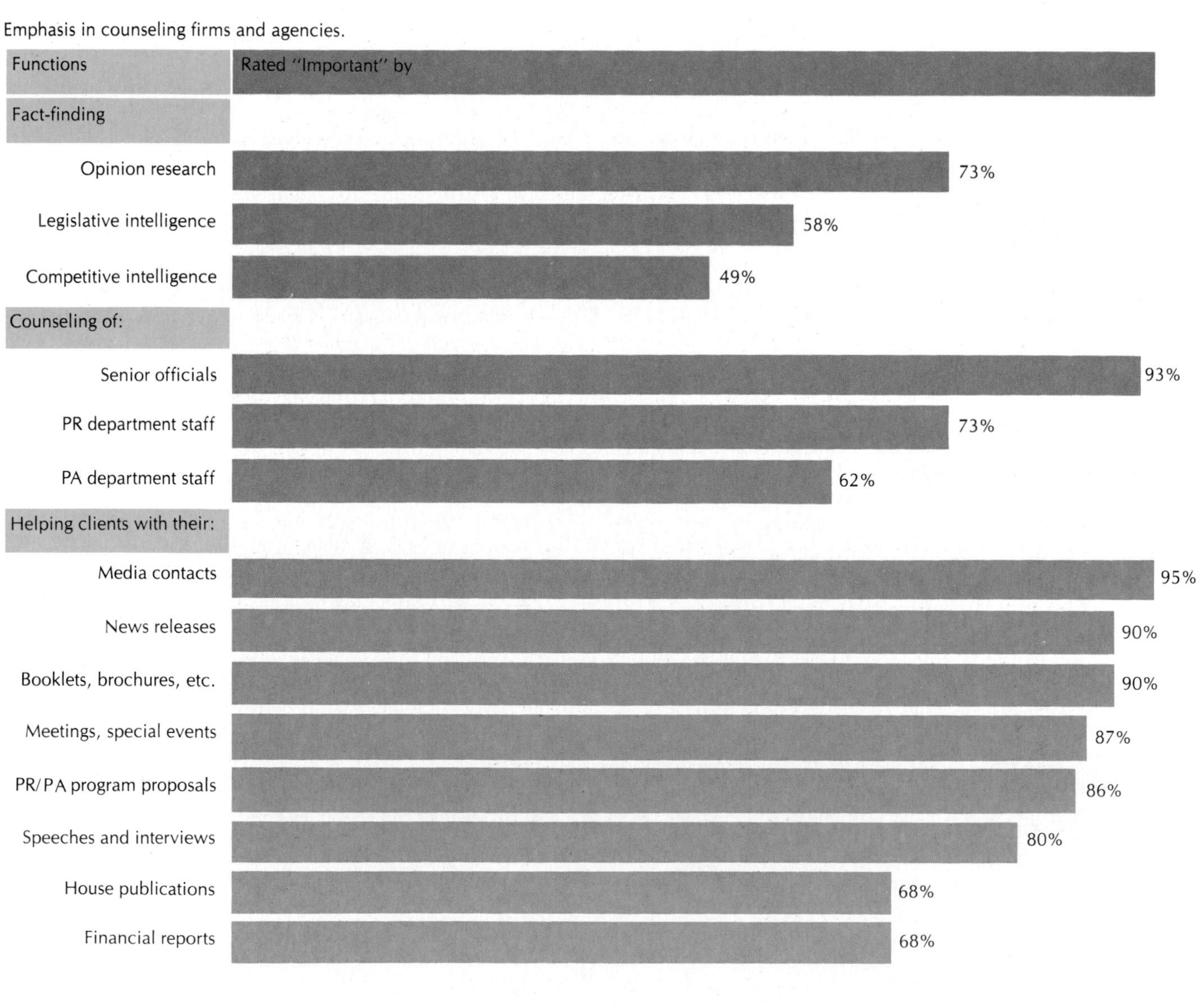

Figure 22–13 Companies look to their public relations firms for research, counseling of senior executives, and preparation of public relations tools—especially the latter.

Summary

Public relations is a process used to manage an organization's relationships with its various publics. These publics include the organization's employees, customers, stockholders, competitors, and the general populace. Many public relations activities involve media communications. However, unlike product advertising, these are not normally openly sponsored or paid for.

To help create a favorable reputation in the marketplace, companies use advertising. There are four types: public relations advertising, corporate (or institutional) advertising, corporate identity advertising, and recruitment advertising.

Corporate or institutional advertising is used to build awareness of the company, make a good impression on the financial community, influence public opinion, motivate present employees, or attract new talent.

Corporate identity advertising is used to communicate a name or appearance change, an ownership change, or a change in corporate personality, or to generate increased awareness.

Recruitment advertising has the sole objective of attracting employment applications. These advertisements are most frequently found in the classified section.

There are many types of public relations activities, including publicity and press agentry, public affairs and lobbying, promotion events management, publication preparation, research, fund raising and membership drives, and public speaking. However, the most important role of the practitioner is to plan and administer the public relations program.

The tools used in public relations are many and varied. These are news releases and media kits, photography, booklets, letters, annual reports, house organs, speeches and position papers, posters and exhibits, audiovisual materials, open houses, and staged events.

In times of emergency, crisis, or disaster, the news media look to the organization's public relations director for information. In government work, the public relations person is frequently referred to as a public information officer. Most government public relations people are in very high news-demand positions.

Except in sensitive areas, the demand for news from business organizations is usually much lower. As a result, the role of the public relations person is oriented more to creating news. In nonprofit organizations the practitioner's role is often to build public awareness and attract contributions.

There are many career opportunities in public relations inside organizations as well as outside in public relations agencies. Areas of expertise that are desirable in perspective employees include planning, administration, advising, industrial relations, economic relations, social relations, political affairs, communication, and education.

Questions for review

1. How would you define public relations?
2. What is the relationship between public relations and advertising?
3. What are the various publics of a company? Discuss their importance to advertisers.
4. How would you describe the following public relations activities? How do they aid advertisers?
   a. Publicity and press agentry.
   b. Public affairs and lobbying.
   c. Promotion and special events management.
   d. Publications.
   e. Research.
   f. Fund raising
   g. Public speaking.
5. What are the tools of public relations? Describe them.
6. In what types of organizations are public relations practitioners usually found?
7. What is recruitment advertising? Why is it under the domain of public relations?
8. What are the various types of public relations advertising? Describe them.
9. What are the reasons for corporate identity advertising?
10. What are the various publics of companies? Discuss their importance to advertisers and the different methods used to deal with them.

23

Noncommercial and political advertising

"There are googols of little creatures squiggling and burrowing, flitting and squishing under the mud, through the swamps and over the sandy marshes. Sea squirts, copepods, lugworm larvae and the babies of little fish. Each with a kind of brain, each with the breath of life. But their life is ebbing. And as they start to go—you do, too.

"You are standing on the threshold of time in as sacred a place as any in the world. It's where the life of the water and the life of the land converge in biological blur. These are the wetlands—the swamps and the mudflats that sometimes smell like rotten eggs. These are the marshes, clogged with weeds, swarming with bugs, teeming with beautiful life. This is where the moon moves the water in shallow ebbs and floods; where the sun pierces down to the ooze and the nutrients flow in a strange and marvelous way. Nowhere else except here in these sopping grounds is there so much life in so much concentration. But the life is dwindling. And as these lands start to go—you do, too.

"These squishy, mushy lands are where most of our fish are born, the fish that feed the fish that feed the fish that fill the sea. These narrow strips of estuarine land are where the birds come to rest and nest and feed; and they are tied inexorably to the life support for the raccoons and the bears and the deer a hundred miles away. And to you . . ."

These are the first three paragraphs of an award-winning advertisement. What do you think is being advertised? A product? A service? Who do you think might have run this ad? A sporting goods store? An oil company? A boat manufacturer?

What do you thing is the objective of this ad? To promote a new fishing area? To persuade people to invest in Florida land? To remind people to buy insect repellent?

Let's consider the last three paragraphs of the same ad.

"In California, most of the wetlands are already gone. In Florida, they're going fast. Once there were 127 million acres of interior and coastal wetlands. Now forty per cent are gone, the precious specks of life in these treasured lands exchanged for yacht clubs and marinas and industrial growth. As we dredge the bays and fill the marshes and cover the mud with asphalt; as we spray our poisons and scatter our waste and spew oil upon the waters—we destroy forever the great forces of life that began millennia ago.

"But now we have gone too far. Because this planet belongs not only to us but to them as well. To the umpteen zillion other things that fly in the sky and roam on the land and swim in the sea and burrow beneath our feet.

"Now, especially now, if we will only stop to think—perhaps we will think to stop" (Figure 23–1).

In recent years the Sierra Club has been the nation's leading advocate for conservation. The club is a nonprofit organization whose primary objectives are to fight the destruction of our natural environment and to communicate the need for conservation to the public. The club has centered its interest on preserving parks and forests, fighting offshore oil drilling, protecting the nation's wild waters and wildlands, promoting energy conservation, and slowing the overdevelopment of urban areas. In the advertisement the club is attempting to communicate the importance of saving our rapidly disappearing marshes and swamplands.

But this advertisement also demonstrates the fine caliber of work often done by noncommercial advertisers. These organizations, which have no profit-making product or service to sell, are concerned only with promoting an idea, a philosophy, an attitude, a social cause, or a political issue. In many respects this is a far more difficult task than promoting the more tangible benefit of a new product or service.

This chapter deals with the difference between commercial and noncommercial advertising and describes the various types of advertising by nonprofit organizations to which we are exposed daily.

Noncommercial advertising

What is the difference between the kind of advertising created for a commercial product or service and the kind we call noncommercial advertising? Is it the way the advertising is written or the media in which it is placed? Is it the type of artwork used or the mix of pictures and music we see on TV? What makes noncommercial advertising different?

The most obvious answer is that the thing being advertised is different; the product is different. Manufacturing companies advertise tangible products: cars, boats, food, soap, soft drinks, industrial equipment, machines, etc. Service companies advertise tangible services: restaurants, income tax services, plumbing, landscaping, etc. In contrast, we see advertisements daily for intangible humanitarian social causes (Red Cross), political ideas or issues (Sierra Club), philosophic or religious positions (Church of Latter Day Saints), or particular attitudes and viewpoints (labor unions). In most cases these advertisements are created and placed by nonprofit organizations. And the product they are advertising is their particular mission in life, be it politics, welfare, religion, conservation, health, happiness, or love.

There is a more subtle difference, however, and that relates to the specific objective of the advertisement. Commercial firms use advertising to stimulate sales by persuading people to buy. In noncommercial advertising the most similar objective would be to stimulate donations or persuade people to vote.

Objectives of noncommercial advertising

In Chapter 6 we learned that the general objective of all advertising is to inform, persuade, or remind people about the specific product being advertised. Likewise, in noncommercial advertising the general objective is to inform, persuade, or remind people about the particular idea, cause, or philosophy being advertised. The difference lies in the specific objectives being sought.

Whereas commercial advertisers may want to stimulate brand loyalty, the noncommercial objective might be to popularize a social cause (Figure 23–2). If a specific commercial objective for a new shampoo is to change people's *buying* habits, the related noncommercial objective for an energy conservation program might be to change people's *activity* habits, such as turning off the lights.

Figure 23–3 shows a variety of related specific objectives for commercial and noncommercial advertisers. Study the table and try to think of examples you may have seen of each objective. Can you think of any other possible specific objectives? Where did you see them? Are the noncommercial objectives usually different or always different?

What was the objective of the Sierra Club ad in Figure 23–1? To

Don't muddy up the googol.*

*Googol: The largest number of things that has a name. Webster defines as the number one followed by a hundred zeroes.

There are googols of little creatures squiggling and burrowing, flitting and squishing under the mud, through the swamps and over the sandy marshes. Sea squirts, copepods, lugworm larvae and the babies of little fish. Each with a kind of a brain, each with the breath of life. But their life is ebbing. And as they start to go—you do, too.

You are standing on the threshold of time in as sacred a place as any in the world. It's where the life of the water and the life of the land converge in biological blur. These are the wetlands—the swamps and the mudflats that sometimes smell like rotten eggs. These are the marshes, clogged with weeds, swarming with bugs, teeming with beautiful life. This is where the moon moves the water in shallow ebbs and floods; where the sun pierces down to the ooze and the nutrients flow in a strange and marvelous way. Nowhere else except here in these sopping grounds is there so much life in so much concentration. But the life is dwindling. And as these lands start to go—you do, too.

These squishy, mushy lands are where most of our fish are born, the fish that feed the fish that feed the fish that fill the sea. These narrow strips of estuarine land are where the birds come to rest and nest and feed; and they are tied inexorably to the life support for the raccoons and the bears and the deer a hundred miles away. And to you.

In California, most of the wetlands are already gone. In Florida, they're going fast. Once there were 127 million acres of interior and coastal wetlands. Now forty per cent are gone, the precious specks of life in these treasured lands exchanged for yacht clubs and marinas and industrial growth. As we dredge the bays and fill the marshes and cover the mud with asphalt; as we spray our poisons and scatter our waste and spew oil upon the waters—we destroy forever the great forces of life that began millennia ago.

But now we have gone too far. Because this planet belongs not only to us but to them as well. To the umpteen zillion other things that fly in the sky and roam on the land and swim in the sea and burrow beneath our feet.

Now, especially now, if we will only stop to think—perhaps we will think to stop.

Figure 23–1 The Sierra Club is one of the nation's leading advocates for conservation. In this advertisement the club attempts to communicate the importance of saving our rapidly disappearing marshes and swamplands.

stimulate donations? To influence votes? To persuade people to like bugs? List all the possible objectives in their order of priority, from most important to least important

Types of noncommercial advertising

The best way to categorize the various types of noncommercial advertising is by the organizations that use them. For instance, advertising is used by churches, schools, universities, hospitals, charitable organizations, and many other *nonbusiness institutions*. We also see advertising by *associations,* such as labor groups, professional organizations, and trade and civic associations. In addition, we witness millions of dollars worth of advertising placed by *government organizations:* the Army, Navy, Marine Corps, Postal Service, Social Security Administration, the Internal Revenue Service, and various state chambers of commerce.

Likewise, every year, as taxpayers and voters, we are forced to witness a massive barrage of advertising and propaganda by *political organizations*. In fact, political advertising has become such a controversial as well as interesting area that we have devoted the second half of this chapter to the subject.

Much of the advertising performed by the organizations mentioned above is referred to as public service advertising. However, the "advertising prepared in the public interest," which is performed by the Advertising Council, is unique, and we shall discuss it here as a separate type of noncommercial advertising.

Advertising by nonbusiness institutions

"It's a matter of life and breath" is a familiar line to anyone who watches television. Every year the American Lung Association places an estimated $10 million worth of advertising on television and radio, in newspapers and magazines, and on outdoor and transit media. All this space and time are donated as a public service by the media involved. In its effort to educate the public about the damaging effects of smoking or the early warning signs of emphysema, lung cancer, and tuberculosis, the Lung Association joins a long list of nonbusiness institutions that use noncommercial advertising to achieve their objectives.

Not all nonbusiness institution advertising is donated, however. If you live in a large metropolitan area and want to place an ad for your favorite charitable organization, you will probably be charged a special nonprofit institution rate by your local city newspaper. Newspaper, radio, and TV advertising departments are besieged by requests from local churches, charity groups, hospital guilds, and other do-good social organizations to donate advertising space and time to these "favorite causes." As a result, out of self-defense, they are forced to charge for most local nonbusiness institution advertising.

The objectives of nonbusiness institution advertising are varied. The Christian Children's Fund uses massive doses of advertising to enlist sponsors for starving orphans in underdeveloped countries around the world (Figure 23–4). A similar organization, the Foster Parents

HOW MUCH OF A WHALE CAN YOU BUY FOR A BUCK?
You may have been thinking that a contribution of one, two, five or even ten dollars would be pretty insignificant when it comes to the enormous task of trying to save the whales.
Think again.
Your dollars may be the difference between our having or not having an essential piece of equipment.
They may buy that one more carton of supplies that lets us stay out one day longer.
It may even be **your** dollars that buy the tank of gas that fuels the inflatable rubber Zodiac at the exact moment it comes between the whales and the harpoon.
Make you feel kind of important? You're right. Your contribution **is** important. It may be the crucial factor that decides between saving or losing forever one of nature's most magnificent creatures.
That's quite a bargain. So don't delay.
Mail your contribution, no matter how small, today!

GREENPEACE
GREENPEACE
1700 Connecticut Ave., N.W. Suite 300
Washington, D.C. 20009

Figure 23–2 The Greenpeace Foundation uses an appeal to humanitarian sympathy to rally support and to raise funds. Similar appeals have been used by this and other groups to protect whales and porpoises. At the same time, opponents in the tuna business have used bumper stickers stating: "Tuna Fishermen Are an Endangered Species."

Plan, asks readers to adopt children from the country of their choice by spending $15 per month for their care and support. Every year these two organizations raise millions of dollars for food, clothing, medicine, and shelter from Americans who care.

This fact that Americans *do* care is in great part the reason nonprofit charitable organizations have proliferated in this country. Another American who cared was Henry Bergh, who in the last century became the father of the humane movement in the United States. In April 1866 Bergh organized the American Society for the Prevention of Cruelty to Animals. Through a long and arduous advertising and publicity campaign, he persuaded state legislatures throughout the nation to pass laws to protect animals and raise the consciousness of Americans to the plight of these creatures.

Today the American Humane Association provides "unity and concert of action as will promote the interests common to SPCAs and humane societies wherever found." In 1914 the association inaugurated its now-famous Be Kind to Animals Week (Figure 23–5). Every year literature is prepared, television and radio commercials are created, and publicity is released during the month of May to remind Americans to take care of their animals and to suggest that they adopt one of the millions of lost pets given shelter every year by SPCAs and other humane societies.

Other familiar names in the long list of nonbusiness institutions that use noncommercial advertising are the United Way, Red Cross, American Cancer Society, American Heart Association, and the Boy Scouts of America, to mention just a few.

Advertising by associations

Attorneys have only recently been allowed to advertise their services. Bar associations, however, have used noncommercial advertising for years as an educational public service tool. Local and state bar associations ads are excellent examples of how business, professional, trade, labor, and civic associations use noncommercial advertising to achieve their individual objectives.

Figure 23–3 Comparison of advertising objectives

Product advertising	Noncommercial advertising
Create store traffic	Stimulate inquiries for information
Stimulate brand loyalty	Popularize social cause
Change buying habits	Change activity habits
Increase product use	Decrease waste of resources
Communicate product features	Communicate political viewpoint
Improve product image	Improve public attitude
Inform public of new product	Inform public of new cure
Remind people to buy again	Remind people to give again

Frequently the purpose of association advertising is simply to create goodwill and a positive impression of the association's members by spotlighting the good works of individuals within the organization. Labor unions, for example, use advertising to inform the public how important union workers are to the nation's economy. By stimulating goodwill in this way they are potentially able to enlist more public support during labor disputes. Other associations use advertising for political impact (Figure 23–6). So, even though the advertiser may be a nonprofit association, and even though the ads may be referred to as "public service announcements" or "noncommercial," the objective of association advertising is often indirectly commercial. This is especially true of the advertising sponsored by trade and manufacturers' associations.

Look at the examples of association advertising in Figures 23–7 and 23–8. What is the objective of the Distilled Spirits Council ad? What is the objective of the Washington Bankers Association ad? Are these ads really noncommercial?

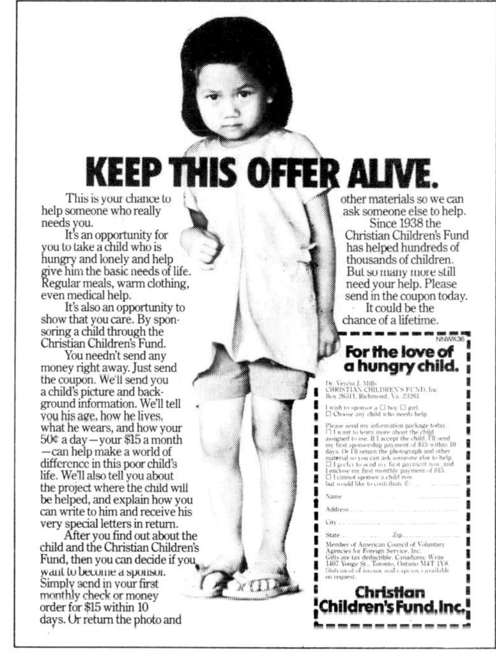

Figure 23–4 Ads like this one for the Christian Children's Fund are run free of charge by many of the nation's media. In the last 10 years, untold millions of dollars of media time and space have been donated to aid the less fortunate.

Advertising by government organizations

During World War II the poster of Uncle Sam pointing his finger and saying "Uncle Sam Needs You" became a famous and effective advertising tool for the Armed Forces. This same graphic theme is used today, 40 years later, in various configurations to remind people of the importance of patriotism.

Government bureaus and departments have been highly effective advertising and propaganda practitioners for years. In its effort to communicate with the voters, the government employs advertising agencies and public relations firms and maintains well-staffed, in-house graphics, communications, and press relations departments.

Much government advertising is to announce the availability of valuable government services such as consumer assistance, welfare aid, or career guidance. Similarly, great effort is given to instructing people on how to use government services correctly. The U.S. Postal Service, for example, has maintained a strong campaign for years to persuade and remind citizens to use zip codes and also to mail early for Christmas.

Frequently government ads are carried free by the media as a public service. In 1973, however, the Postal Service launched its first national paid advertising campaign, spending $4 million in some 370 newspapers to answer common consumer questions about the mail service (Figure 23–9). By 1980 the Postal Service was spending more than $10 million annually to tell people how to use their services.

The 1970s also saw the Army, Navy, Air Force, and Marine Corps enter the paid advertising arena. With the end of the Selective Service draft came the need to recruit more volunteers, so the military pursued the most aggressive advertising techniques to draw young men and women to its ranks (Figure 23–10). Estimated expenditures by the Army in 1980, for example, were $53 million, for the Marines, $13 million.

Many state governments use advertising to attract new businesses, tourists, or workers to aid their economy (Figure 23–11). Ohio, for example, advertises the availability of skilled workers and placement services for industrial concerns. Florida offers warm weather and entertainment. Utah advertises snow and good skiing.

For the most part, government advertising is considered a public service. However, with the resources available to it, government can also use advertising techniques for propaganda purposes, and sometimes the dividing line is very thin. This has given rise to some controversy in the past. For example, at the beginning of every year the

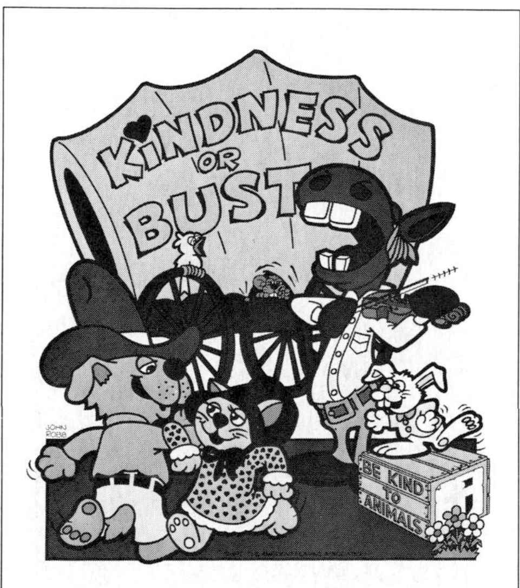

Figure 23–5 Since 1914 the first full week of May has been celebrated as Be Kind to Animals Week. The event is sponsored by the American Humane Association for more than 2,500 local humane societies in an effort to promote the humane treatment of animals.

THE ~~ONE~~ two TRILLION DOLLAR MISUNDERSTANDING:

(While this Ad was being typeset the Social Security Administration admitted that it was another trillion dollars in the hole!)

The One Hundred Dollar Misunderstanding was the basis of a novel by Robert Gover.

The one trillion dollar misunderstanding could be the basis of national bankruptcy. One trillion dollars is the amount that the total financial obligations of the federal government grew last year.

The so-called "national debt" represents a small fraction of the total future financial obligations of the government. It is like the tip of an iceberg floating in a sea of red ink. Consider these Treasury Department figures:

National Debt	$ 596,000,000,000.00
Other Fiscal Liabilities	$ 69,000,000,000.00
Undelivered Orders	$ 130,000,000,000.00
Long-term contracts	$ 12,000,000,000.00
Government Guarantees	$ 175,000,000,000.00
Insurance Commitments	$1,481,000,000,000.00
Social Security Obligations	$2,710,000,000,000.00
Unadjudicated Claims	$ 10,000,000,000.00
International Commitments	$ 10,000,000,000.00
Miscellaneous Commitments	$ 31,000,000,000.00

This isn't even a full list of the federal government's debts. National Taxpayers Union recently completed a computation of the unfunded liabilities of 21 of the federal government's 60 employee retirement plans. This computation shows that taxpayers will pay out $499.155 billion in pensions, even if there is no inflation for the rest of the century. A small inflation rate for a few years would astronomically increase these pension obligations.

Last year alone, *twelve dollars* in unfunded financial obligations were created for every dollar of deficit spending. While the "national debt" increased by $84 billion in 1975, the inflation created by deficits raised the future obligations of government at a rate of about *$83 billion per month*. In all, more than $1 trillion in future obligations were created.

Unchecked, this can mean nothing but disaster. Each new deficit causes greater inflation, which causes greater deficits, which cause still greater inflation.

The longer the situation is allowed to continue, the smaller the likelihood it can be corrected. The Office of Management and Budget has predicted that a continuation of current trends (with no new programs added to the books) would lead to an annual deficit of *$700 billion* by the end of the century.

To figure out what that means, you needn't bother to count ahead 23 fiscal years. Most of your financial assets and those of other Americans would probably be destroyed by inflation long before the deficits actually reached $700 billion annually. Economist Harry Schultz predicts that 50% of the assets of middle class Americans will be lost within the next five years unless something is done now to stop fiscal irresponsibility and its resulting inflation.

The American people understand this. A recent Gallup Poll shows that 78%—an overwhelming majority—favor a constitutional amendment now to force the federal government to balance the budget. Young and old, black and white, rich and poor, Democrat and Republican all agree: we must halt the vicious cycle of deficit spending and inflation which is bringing America to the peril point of disaster.

Led by State Senator James Clark, Finance Chairman of the Senate of Maryland, National Taxpayers Union has been working to prod Congress into passing the Balanced Budget Amendment. This amendment would legally prohibit deficit spending except in genuine emergencies declared by 3/4ths of Congress.

"It is not a question of whether we are to have 'liberal' or 'conservative' government. The issue is more basic than that. Without a constitutional amendment forcing a balanced federal budget, there is little chance we can halt the process which threatens to bury the American way of life under an avalanche of inflation and debt. Balanced budgets are a 'progressive' cause also. Without them, the poor, the weak and the helpless suffer most. This is why I am supporting National Taxpayers Union's efforts . . . it is a matter of common sense."

—Congressman Andrew Jacobs, Jr.
(Democrat-Indiana)
Member, House Ways
and Means Committee

Supporting the effort to require balanced budgets is a matter of common sense . . . and more. It is also a matter of arithmetic. There are fewer than 60 million real taxpayers in America. If you are one of them, you are on the hook for an additional $16,500 as your share of last year's increase in government liabilities.

Each month that passes without a balanced budget generates billions in additional government debts—debts which you may have to pay.

WHAT YOU CAN DO

If you want to help pass a constitutional amendment to Balance the federal budget, now is the time to say so.

It only costs you 13¢—the price of a stamp. That's a good investment, just in terms of the higher taxes it might save you from paying. But it's more than that. By filling out the coupon at the bottom of this ad, or sending a letter of your own directly to your representatives in Washington, you'll be adding your name to the list of those testifying for fiscal integrity by government. Either way, it's well worth 13 cents to let it be known that you oppose national bankruptcy and the human misery it would bring.

Once you've voiced your support for a constitutional amendment to balance the federal budget, get your friends to do the same. The politicians in Washington are slow to learn. With them, it's volume that counts. Each name is a possible vote. The more names, the more votes. Make yours count.

HOW CAN WE AFFORD TO RUN THIS AD?

We can't. It's so expensive that we took a risk in running it. But we thought the issue was important enough to warrant sticking our necks out. And, we thought, given the importance of the issue, that you'd be willing to help.

We hope you'll send a membership contribution along with the coupon so that we can place more ads like this in the papers. We'll send you a copy of our proposed constitutional amendment and petition forms. The more people we can get to oppose fiscal irresponsibility, the greater the chance of stopping it. Your membership will help us get more people involved.

It only costs $15 to become a member of the National Taxpayers Union. We'd like to have you with us.

National Taxpayers Union
325 Pennsylvania Avenue, S.E.
Washington, D.C. 20003

Yes, I agree. Now is the time to pass a Balanced Budget Amendment.

Name ______________________

Address ______________________

City ____________ State ____________ Zip ______

☐ I'd like to make a contribution. Enclosed is a check.
☐ I'd like to join the National Taxpayers Union. Enclosed is my $15 membership fee.

The National Taxpayers Union is a non-profit, non-partisan organization of citizens dedicated to stopping the waste of our tax money.
Your contribution will be used to finance further research into government waste and to help publicize it. A copy of our latest audited financial report is available upon request.

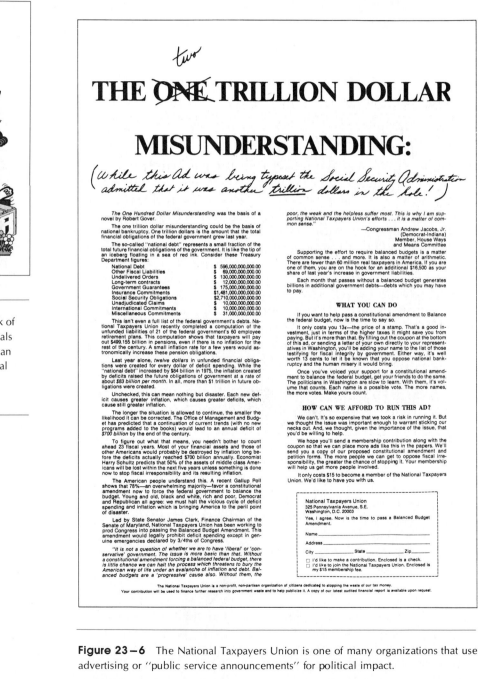

Figure 23–6 The National Taxpayers Union is one of many organizations that use advertising or "public service announcements" for political impact.

IRS places news releases about the new techniques it has developed to catch tax evaders. The objective of this massive annual "public relations" campaign is obvious to many—to intimidate people into filling out their income tax forms correctly.

We have all heard stories about how the Soviet government uses its media to communicate the official party view of world events in the guise of news. While the benefits of government advertising are many (see Figure 23–12), the potential for abuses exists, and for that reason consumer and voter groups rightfully keep a watchful eye.

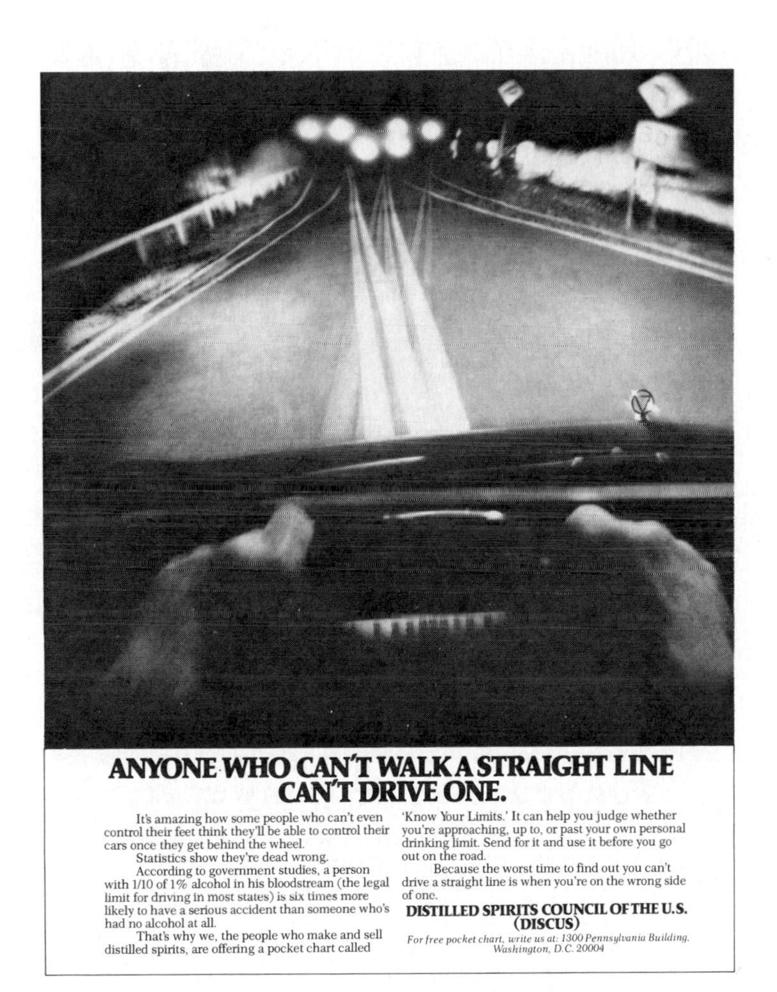

Figure 23–7 The Distilled Spirits Council promotes its good citizens' role by running informational advertisements designed to alert consumers to the dangers of driving while intoxicated. This ad offers a free booklet to help drivers "Know Your Limits."

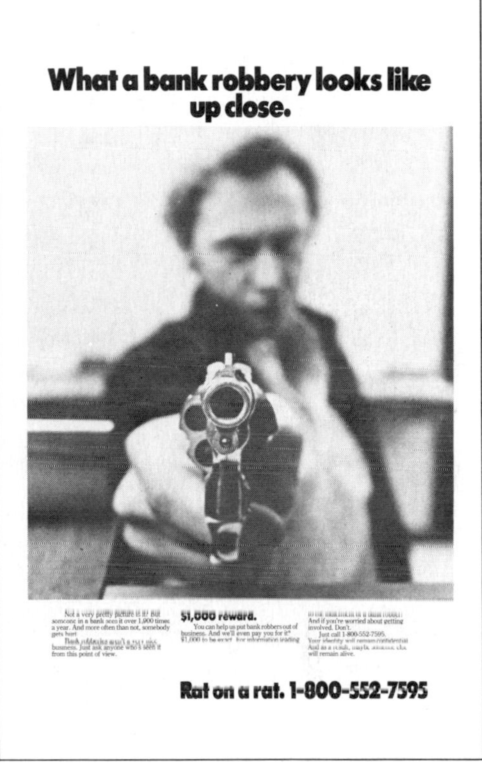

Figure 23–8 If you have ever wondered what a bank robbery looks like up close, the Washington Bankers Association would like you to know. Their hope is that someone will see their ad who also knows the identity of a wanted bank robber.

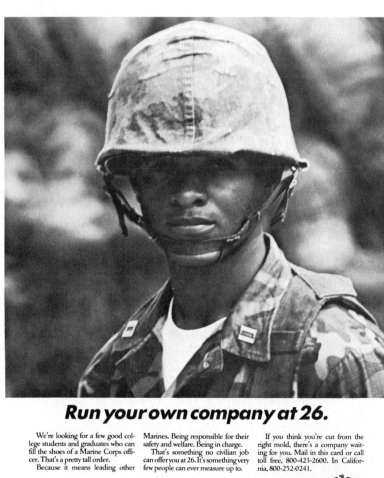

The advertising council

During the early months of World War II a committee of prominent advertising industry figures was formed. They called themselves the War Advertising Council and volunteered to create and place advertising at the service of the government in the national interest.

In conjunction with the Office of War Information, the committee

Figure 23–9 The U.S. Postal Service advertises stamps as a collector's item.

Figure 23–10 In 1980 the Marines spent an estimated $13 million to find a few good men. How does this ad appeal to you?

planned the council's first assignments of promoting the nation's conversion from peacetime to wartime industrial production. By the end of the war more than 100 public service advertising campaigns had been conducted to promote such things as war bonds, victory gardens, venereal disease prevention, and forest fire prevention. American business had donated more than $1 billion worth of advertising media time and space to these campaigns.

When the war ended, rather than disbanding, the committee changed its name to the Advertising Council (Figure 23–13) and began working on the problems of conversion to peacetime. Among the programs continued were the Red Cross and forest fire prevention.

Advertising Age reports that the council's policy today is basically

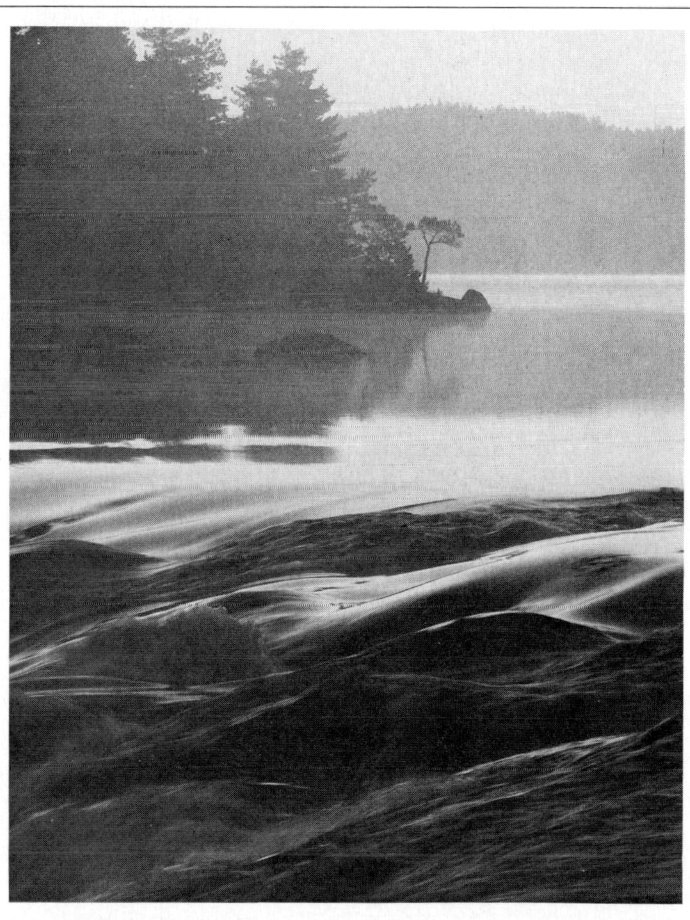

Minnesota—land of 10,000 lakes—advertises its water and a whole lot more. Many state governments use advertising to attract new business, tourists, or workers.

Figure 23–11

the same as when it began: "Accept no subsidy from government and remain independent of it. Conduct campaigns of service to the nation at large, avoiding regional, sectarian, or special-interest drives of all kinds. Remain nonpartisan and nonpolitical. Conduct the Council on a voluntary basis. Accept no project that does not lend itself to the advertising method. Accept no campaign with a commercial interest unless the public interest is obviously overriding."

During America's bicentennial year the Advertising Council conducted 30 major public service campaigns, a record number in its 35-year history. In 1980 the value of donated time and space exceeded $500 million, and the total since 1942 exceeds $10 billion. Three of its earliest projects are still in continuous operation: forest fire prevention, U.S. savings bonds, and the American Red Cross (Figure 23–14).

"People Start Pollution. People Can Stop It." This famous slogan, created by the council for Keep America Beautiful, Inc., was designed to replace the negative attitudes and behavior that lead to pollution with positive attitudes and behavior in order to curb littering and waste. The now-famous picture of the crying Indian, Iron Eyes Cody, has made this campaign one of the most recognized in the council's history (Figure 23–15).

Other familiar campaigns are for the United Negro College Fund ("A mind is a terrible thing to waste"), child abuse prevention ("Help destroy a family tradition"), the U.S. Office of Education "Careers," and the United Way ("Thanks to you, it works") (Figure 23–16).

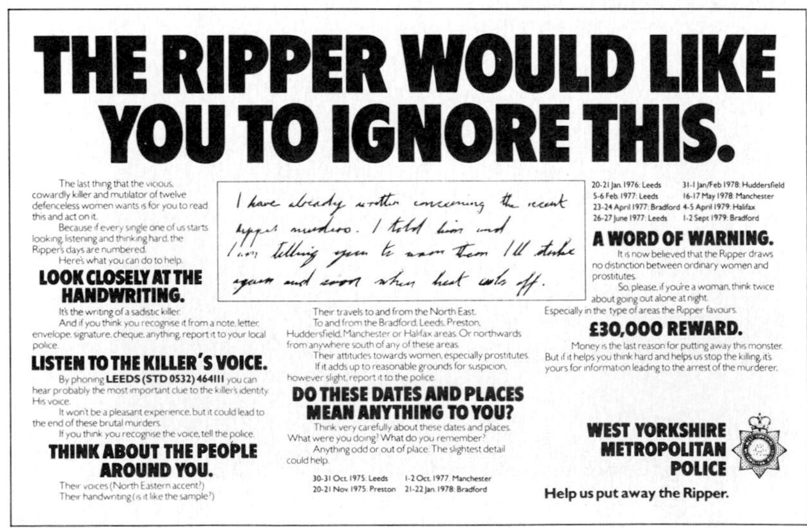

Figure 23–12 "Think about the people around you. Their voices. Their handwriting. Their travels," says copy in this newspaper ad. "Help us put the Ripper away" is the closing line of the ad. They finally did.

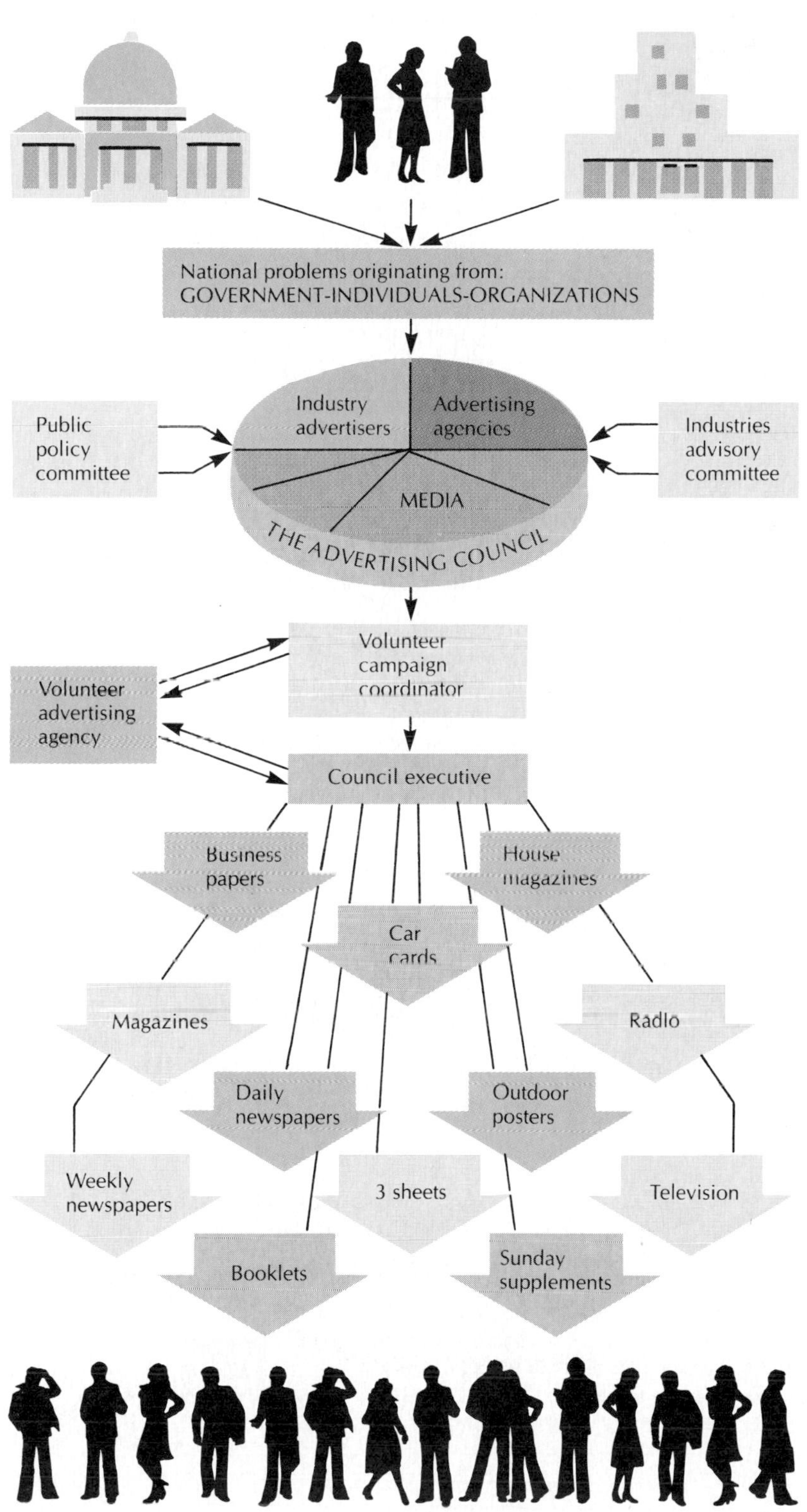

Figure 23–13 How the Advertising Council functions.

Bill Cosby says:
"There's a Red Cross volunteer job that's made for you!"

Call today.

American Red Cross

A Public Service of This Magazine & The Advertising Council

Figure 23–14 Since its beginning in 1942, the Ad Council has created a number of ads for humanitarian organizations such as the Red Cross.

HELP FIGHT POLLUTION CAMPAIGN

KEEP AMERICA BEAUTIFUL, INC.

People working together. Public Service Announcements available in :60, :30, :10 lengths on 16mm film

In America, abandoned cars litter the land.

But the people in Lexington, Kentucky, are removing 100 of them a month.

We discard millions of used tires.

But in New Jersey, they're turning old tires into playgrounds for children.

Our streets and countryside have become dumping grounds for trash.

But all across America, people are now recycling 8-million tons of it a year.

We create staggering amounts of garbage.

But in Virginia Beach, they turned a mountain of garbage into a recreational hillside.

Pollution is destroying our beach-fronts and waterways.

But in Huntington, Long Island, they're planting sea grass which cleanses the water for wildlife and man.

The cure for pollution is people. Working together.

For a brochure on what you can do, write Keep America Beautiful.

A Public Service Campaign of the Advertising Council

Volunteer Advertising Agency: Marsteller Inc.

Volunteer Campaign Coordinator: Marshall C. Lewis, Union Carbide Corporation

CNHF-8160
CNHF-8130
CNHF-8110

Ad Council

Figure 23–15 The Advertising Council with its volunteer advertising agency, Marsteller Inc., promotes the idea of people working together to help fight pollution and keep American beautiful. The famous Indian actor, Iron Eyes Cody, has contributed to making these commercials famous.

Political advertising

It was a warm southern California morning just three weeks before the off-year elections. Seated in the living room of a state assemblyman who was running for reelection were the candidate and his wife, his administrative assistant, his advertising/PR man, and two men from Spencer/Roberts & Associates, the California Republican Party's professional campaign management firm. Stu Spencer and George Young had just flown in from Los Angeles for this urgent meeting with the candidate and his staff. The conversation was intense, the air swollen with emotion.

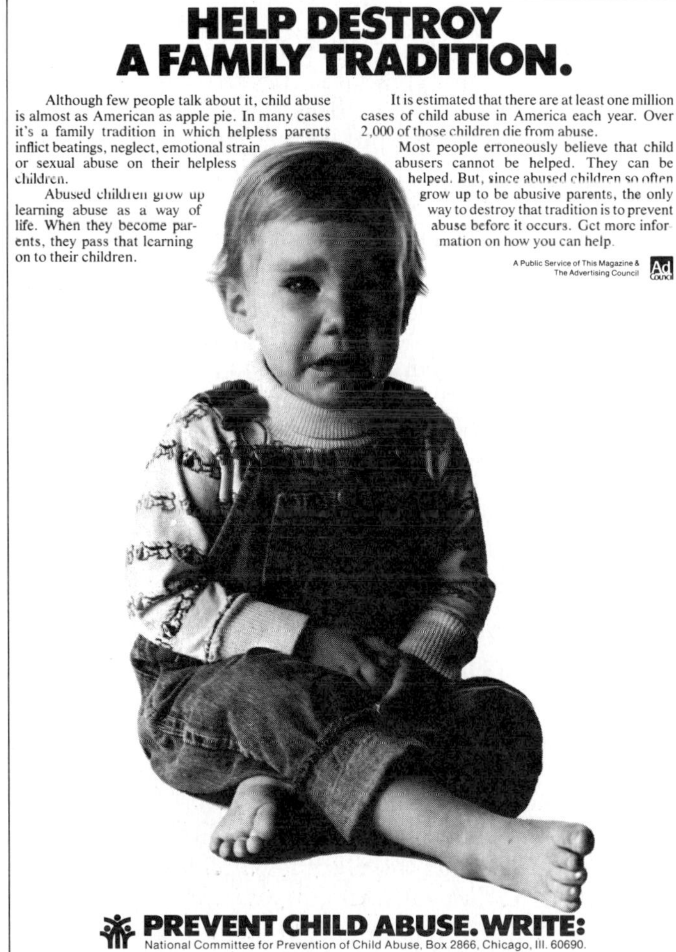

The National Committee for the Prevention of Child Abuse and the U.S. Office of Education have been recipients of a great deal of aid from the Advertising Council for many years. Both advertisements promote the idea of writing for more information to see how you can help kids.

Figure 23–16

Until two days before, the campaign had been flowing smoothly. It was a no-sweat contest. The Republican legislator represented a highly Democratic district, but he was immensely popular. With only three weeks left the latest polls showed him leading with more than 65 percent of the vote. There was ample money, an army of volunteers, and a track record built up over the years of conscientious representation of his constituents. He was the darling of the little old ladies, the quiet but highly principled spokesman for the conservative right, and also a sympathetic symbol for the struggling minorities in need of a leader. In short, he was a shoo-in.

Then out of a clear blue sky, the thunderbolt struck with lightning savagery. The assemblyman and six other men who had served on the local city council four years before were suddenly, without warning, indicted by the county grand jury for bribery and conspiracy in connection with a four-year-old taxicab rate increase for which they had voted. The daily headlines and television networks were screaming the news. Bribery! Conspiracy! Indictments!

Despite his immediate protestations of innocence and no wrongdoing, the assemblyman's volunteer army was deserting, the contributions had stopped, and now the polls were showing a complete reversal, with his popularity suddenly down to only 32 percent and still falling.

So this top-level meeting had been hastily called. The discussion had centered for over an hour on the situation—what had happened, how, why, was it true, and so on.

The conversation turned. "So what are we going to do?"

George Young, one of the men from Spencer/Roberts, had sat silently through most of this, just listening, analyzing, coolly evaluating. He was the epitome of objectivity. The candidate's wife finally turned to him and said, "You haven't said much, George. What do you think?" She was hardly prepared for his answer.

"Well," said George, as he prepared to present his plan to them. "It seems to me that what we have here is a marketing problem."

The political marketing process

George Young was absolutely right. They did indeed have a marketing problem. With only three weeks left before the election, they had to create enough doubt in the voters' minds about the validity of the bribery charges so that they would be willing to vote for this candidate in spite of the indictments.

They could not wait until after the trial. He would be found completely innocent two months after the election was held, but that was too late. In the three weeks that remained, they had to try to convince the voters that, in spite of everything, he was still the best qualified candidate to serve the community's needs in the state legislature.

The old campaign was scrapped, and a new marketing campaign was launched. Flyers were distributed questioning the coincidentally late nature of the charges. Television and radio commercials were produced with local citizens proclaiming their trust. Rallies were held. Interviews were given. Money started pouring in again from party loyals all over the state. In three weeks a marketing blitz was conducted, which showed the candidate as humble, sincere, hardworking, and most of all honest. The slogan, "We believe in you, Tom," was added to all his billboards.

On election day his support had risen to 46 percent. That was not enough to win, but it was a stunning showing nevertheless. Two months later he was found innocent in a court of law and vindicated of all the charges against him. Perhaps if the election had been held only one week later, he might also have been able to retain his seat.

George Young directed an excellent marketing and advertising campaign. He determined the needs of the marketplace and did his utmost to give them what they wanted. Yet this attitude that political advertising is just another marketing function, much like advertising for toothpaste and dog food, has incited unprecedented public outcry in recent years. Why? What's so different about political advertising that people should get so upset?

There are several things that differentiate political advertising from commercial advertising:

1. The product is a person or a philosophy rather than an item for sale or a service.
2. The time period for a political advertising campaign is finite rather than ongoing.
3. The ethical question is larger due to the potentially far-reaching effects of advertising claims.

This section will explore political advertising as a marketing process. In so doing, we will deal with these and other differences as well as the many similarities between political advertising and commercial advertising.

Political product versus commercial product

As we have discussed throughout this text, the first and most important element in any marketing mix is the product. The primary difference between commercial advertising and political advertising is that in politics the product is frequently a human being.

In commercial advertising the effort is to show how a product or service will satisfy a functional, social, or psychological consumer need. If the consumer perceives that the product will be beneficial, she or he may buy it. In politics, similarly, much time and effort are spent determining the needs of the marketplace. If a politician is to represent supporters faithfully, he or she must be tuned in to their desires, wants, and prejudices. The politician strives to relate to and empathize with the voters—to develop that special quality called charisma.

Political advertising, then, needs to communicate those attributes about the politician that relate to the constituents' needs. The candidate gains the voters' confidence—and their votes. In this way the political product is "packaged" much like a commercial product. The problem is that in commercial marketing advertising may move the product off the shelf once, but only satisfied customers will buy it again. In politics, when advertising gets a candidate elected, the voters are stuck with their "purchase" for two to six years.

Political campaigns are not the only places we see political advertising. And politicians are not the only type of political products. We are all exposed daily to forms of political advertising or propaganda that do not relate at all to political elections or campaigns. We see ads and hear speeches supporting myriads of public issues. Special-interest groups print brochures or run ads condemning public policy on a certain issue (Figure 23–17).

During World War II, theaters ran anti-German and anti-Japanese war movies followed by short ads appealing to the citizenry to buy war bonds. The amount of money spent on political advertising during the Vietnam conflict, both pro and con, ran into the millions.

In short, we are confronted with political advertising daily. Much of it is so subtle that we are not even aware of its political nature. But just as in political campaign advertising, which is the primary subject of this chapter, these other forms of political advertising are similarly used to market ideas, attitudes, or political products.

Political market versus commercial market

In Chapter 6 we learned that a market is a group of people who share a common interest, need, or desire. Furthermore, we learned that for commercial products this group must be able to use the product to advantage, and they must be able to afford it.

In political campaigns, the market is likewise a group of people who share a common interest, need, or desire, which may be satisfied by the election of a political candidate. However, unlike commercial products, they don't have to be able to afford him. They only have to be able to vote for him. Therefore, the political market is composed of those people in the candidate's district of influence who are registered to vote. These people are called constituents.

Constituents may be segmented like commercial markets: by geography, age, sex, income, education, race, religion, or occupation. Furthermore, they may be classified by their political affiliation. In some states, when people register to vote, the party they belong to becomes public information.

This information is extremely useful to the political candidate in determining roughly the stance of the community on many important issues. It is also useful because the candidate can assess his or her potential strength by evaluating the number of party loyals in the community. Furthermore, the list of registered party members is the most logical source of both political contributions and campaign workers.

Due to the nature of campaigns and elections, as well as our history of self-government, the political market possesses other unique characteristics. For one thing interest is higher than for commercial products. Politics is news. We are confronted with political stories every day in all the mass media. In the United States about 65 percent of the electorate regularly votes in national elections. Most people are very curious to know as soon as possible who won the election. Compare this with the interest expressed by people in what car is selling best or which brand of detergent cleans clothes the best.

Furthermore, politics generates an emotional level rarely reached in commercial marketing. People either love or hate their politicians; they call them names, picket them. They may be enamored of a certain car or dislike another intensely, but we've never heard of a Cadillac being assassinated.

What this all means is that the political market is a potpourri of Republicans, Independents, and Democrats, hard-hats and white-collar workers, blacks, yellows, browns, and whites, men and women, old people and young people, rich people and welfare recipients, and many more, all of whom express varying degrees of emotion and interest in their political issues and candidates (Figure 23–18). From these groups the office seeker tries to select a target market that will generate enough votes to win on election day.

Political marketing problems

When George Young told the indicted assemblyman and his staff that they had a marketing problem, he knew what he was talking about. In political campaigns the marketing objective is almost always the same: gain a 50+ percent share of market by election day. But the marketing problems faced by political candidates are as varied as those faced by commercial marketers. Which issues appeal to which voters? How can we communicate with the greatest number of voters in the time available? Or, in the case of the indicted assemblyman, how can I improve my image with the voters?

In general, most marketing problems faced by political candidates fall into one of four areas: the party affiliation of the constituency, the candidate's identity and image, the issues, and time and money.

Constituency The politics of the constituency, which is frequently reflected in the percentage breakdown of party membership in a district, is one of the most common as well as difficult problems politicians face. Imagine being a Republican candidate in a district that is 70 percent Democrat in registration, or vice versa. Or, worse yet, imagine being a Socialist Party candidate in virtually any district. Simply by reason of your party affiliation, you have only a small chance of winning a political campaign.

With our two-party system most voters are born into either Republican or Democratic families. Many are raised in their party. As a result, they frequently have a tendency to vote the "straight ticket." They may cross over to vote for a major officeholder like the President, but if they are dyed-in-the-wool party members, they tend to return to the party line-up for the minor offices. Changing parties to many people is almost as serious as changing religions. Thus the minority-party candidate in a district has an uphill struggle to convince voters of the opposing party to cross over and vote for him or her.

The problem of the constituency's politics has become even more complex as the divergence of political viewpoints has increased. In fact, in 1980, those registered as Independents outnumbered Republicans. And politicians have to remind themselves that within both major parties there are both liberals and conservatives. Just paying attention to voter registration, therefore, isn't enough any more.

Identity and image Every candidate faces to some degree the problems of identity and image. *Identity,* or name I.D., as it may be called, means having one's name known by or at least familiar to voters. It is estimated that incumbents automatically pick up 10 percent of the vote because of the good name I.D. they already possess with the voters in the district.

THE WALL STREET JOURNAL, MONDAY, MARCH 23, 1981

"They have labeled Moral Majority the Extreme Right because we speak out against Extreme Wrong!"

Jerry Falwell, President
Moral Majority Inc.

Why do Norman Lear, George McGovern, the ACLU, and others continually attack the philosophies and programs of movements like Moral Majority Inc?

The answer is simple — Moral Majority Inc. is made up of millions of Americans, including 72,000 ministers, priests, and rabbis, who are deeply concerned about the moral decline of our nation, and who are sick and tired of the way many amoral and secular humanists and other liberals are destroying the traditional family and moral values on which our nation was built.

We are Catholics, Jews, Protestants, Mormons, Fundamentalists — blacks and whites — farmers, housewives, businessmen. We are Americans from all walks of life, united by one central concern — to serve as a special interest group providing a voice for a return to moral sanity in these United States of America.

Figure 23–17 The Moral Majority jumped into the spotlight in 1980 with the election of many conservative congressmen and senators whom they had backed. They also came under fire from liberal groups. This ad outlined the group's position and offered a free copy of their newspaper, *The Moral Majority Report.*

On the other hand, *image* refers to what voters think or feel about a candidate, either rightly or wrongly. It is in this area that political challengers try to make up what they may have lost to the incumbent in identity.

The incumbent has a record of votes and actions that he or she must defend. The record may be good, or it may be bad. Either way the challenger attempts to use that record to discredit the incumbent. Thus, while the incumbent tries to paint a self-portrait of a "good guy," the challenger is simultaneously using many of the same facts to paint a picture of the incumbent as the "bad guy."

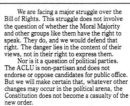

IF THE MORAL MAJORITY HAS ITS WAY, YOU'D BETTER START PRAYING.
MORAL MAJORITY
The Moral Majority—and other groups like them—think that children should pray in school. Not just their children. Your children.
But that's just the beginning.
They want their religious doctrines enacted into law and imposed on everyone.
If they believe that birth control is a sin, then you should not be allowed to use contraceptives.
If they believe that abortion is wrong, then you should not be allowed to have one.
If they believe that the Bible condemns homosexuality, then the law should punish homosexuals.
If they believe that a man should be the breadwinner and the divinely appointed head of the family, then the law should keep women in their place.
If they are offended by the ideas in certain books, then the law should ban those books from your libraries and schools.
And like Joe McCarthy, they believe that anyone who disagrees with them should be barred from teaching in the public schools.
These new groups are on the march and growing stronger each day. Their agenda is clear and frightening: they mean to capture the power of government and use it to establish a nightmare of religious and political orthodoxy.
And they are dangerously deceptive. They appear to represent American patriotism, because they wrap themselves in the American flag and use words like "family" and "life" and "tradition."
In fact, their kind of "patriotism" violates every principle of liberty that underlies the American system of government. It is intolerant. It stands against the First Amendment guarantees of freedom of expression and separation of church and state. It threatens academic freedom. And it denies to whole groups of people the equal protection of the laws.
The new evangelicals are a radical anti-Bill-of-Rights movement. They seek not to conserve American values, but to overthrow them. And conservatives as well as liberals should stand up against them.
THE DANGER POINT.
These groups have already had alarming success. They have been pivotal in blocking passage of the E.R.A. in fifteen states. Public school boards all over the country have banned books and imposed prayer and other religious ceremonies. State legislatures have begun placing increasingly severe restrictions on a woman's right to have an abortion.
They have grown into a rich and powerful force in this country.
How rich? In a week, the Moral Majority raises a million dollars with its television program.
How powerful? In the last election, key members of Congress were successfully targeted by them for defeat, because of their positions on abortion, E.R.A., and other civil liberties issues.
Already there is talk in Congress of constitutional amendments or new laws that would impose prayer in the public schools, outlaw all abortions, and repeal the Voting Rights Act of 1965.
We are facing a major struggle over the Bill of Rights. This struggle does not involve the question of whether the Moral Majority and other groups like them have the right to speak. They do, and we would defend that right. The danger lies in the content of their views, not in their right to express them.
Nor is it a question of political parties. The ACLU is non-partisan and does not endorse or oppose candidates for public office. But we will make certain that, whatever other changes may occur in the political arena, the Constitution does not become a casualty of the new order.
WHAT THE ACLU CAN DO.
For 60 years, the American Civil Liberties Union has protected the Bill of Rights. As former Chief Justice Earl Warren wrote: "Indeed, it is difficult to appreciate how far our freedoms might have eroded had it not been for the ACLU's valiant representation in the courts of the constitutional rights of people of all persuasions…"
We've been there in the past and we'll be there in the days ahead. We will meet the anti-Bill-of-Rights forces in the Congress, in the courts, before state and local legislatures, at school board hearings. Wherever they threaten, we will be there to resist their attempts to deprive you of your liberty and violate your rights.
WHAT YOU CAN DO.
The ACLU, like the Moral Majority, depends on individual contributions. But they raise more money in a few weeks than we raise in a year.
We can only be as strong as the number of people who support us.
In the past, when the Bill of Rights was in danger, enough people recognized the threat, and came together in time to repel it. Such a time has come again.
Please send us your contribution before another day passes.
Without your help, we don't have a prayer.
AMERICAN CIVIL LIBERTIES UNION
☐ I want to join the ACLU and help fight the new anti-Bill-of-Rights movement. Enclosed is my check in the amount indicated below.
☐ I do not want to become a member, but enclosed is my contribution.
☐ I am already an ACLU member; enclosed is an extra contribution.
☐ $25 ☐ $50 ☐ $100 ☐ $1,000 ☐ More
NAME
ADDRESS
CITY STATE ZIP
American Civil Liberties Union: Norman Dorsen, President; Ira Glasser, Executive Director

Figure 23–18 The American Civil Liberties Union, a nonpartisan organization concerned with individual rights, responded to the Moral Majority's attempts to enact legislation based on their religious beliefs. In this ad they suggest that we're going to be in big trouble if the Moral Majority has its way.

Sometimes these roles get reversed. Instead of the challenger attacking the incumbent's record, the incumbent attacks the challenger's. The challenger may then be forced into a defensive position. If the incumbent is successful in changing the traditional focus in this way, repositioning the attacker as a defender, then the challenger faces a serious dilemma and may very likely lose.

In 1964 Senator Barry Goldwater attempted to discredit President Lyndon Johnson's handling of the Vietnam War. The effort was to show Johnson as weak and incapable of satisfactorily ending the conflict, and to show Goldwater as strong, outspoken, and decisive. The roles got reversed, however, and Johnson was successful in discrediting Goldwater's image, painting him as a warmonger who might drop an atomic bomb on women and children. President Johnson meanwhile maintained the image of a man of peace, and he won by a landslide. Richard Nixon did the same thing to George McGovern by questioning his credibility and competency in 1972. McGovern lost. Jimmy Carter, on the other hand, tried to reposition Reagan as a warmonger and failed. Reagan won.

A politician's image may be created by the way he presents himself, by his party affiliation, by his record, by his advertising, by sudden news events, or even by his opposition. The real image is actually the sum of these impressions as they are perceived in the minds of the electorate. In other words, their perception is the reality (to them).

However, the image that took years to create may be destroyed overnight. We saw in the introduction to this section how one politician's image was completely undone by a late-breaking news event. He was accused of having accepted a bribe. It made no difference that he was subsequently found completely innocent. He had already lost the election.

In the case of first-time or minor-office candidates, identity should normally be the primary objective. Many people are elected to school boards and water districts simply because they had more billboards displaying their name than their opponent.

For major-office candidates, image is more important. However, too many would-be officeholders strive for a glowing image without ascertaining first whether the voters even know who they are. What do you suppose is the usual result?

Campaign issues In a marketing sense, the candidate's positions on the various issues are the sales features. The selection of issues as well as one's record on past issues is therefore a major marketing problem for most politicians. This is especially true on the national level or whenever there are major demographic differences within the candidate's voting district.

Unfortunately, the very nature of the politician—seeking approval from the voters—creates internal, psychological pressure to try to be all things to all people. Too many politicians lose sight of their marketing objective: 50 percent of the electorate. In striving to please everybody, they fail to please the half they need.

Similarly, candidates frequently make the mistake of trying to take a major stand on every issue, even insignificant ones. As a result, they blend into the maze of politicians vying for support and fail to achieve any identity or image whatsoever. It is usually better, especially for first-time candidates with low identity, to take a strong stand on one major issue of vital importance to the electorate and hammer away at it. In this way the office seeker gains identity as "the person who backs such and such." In addition, the candidate may even develop the image of someone who "speaks out" or "sticks to his guns," an important quality in elected representatives.

Time and money In 1976 Jimmy Carter might have lost the election if it had been held one week later. In 1980 he might have won if it had been held two weeks earlier. The time element is one of the major differences between political marketing and commercial marketing. And so is money.

In business the marketing campaign is a never-ending effort continuously funded by the company. In politics everything is aimed at election day. You raise as much money through contributions as you can early in the campaign, and then you spend it all on advertising and other activities before a certain date. Timing is crucial. On election day you add up the votes and see who won. This is both the fun and the agony of political advertising.

But it is also one of the biggest problems. Certainly the greatest furor over political campaigns has centered on the subjects of campaign financing and last-minute tactics.

In 1972 a strict federal campaign spending bill went into effect limiting the amount of money federal office seekers may spend to 10 cents per eligible voter. Of this, no more than 6 cents may be spent on broadcast media. Some local governments have even stricter laws. Many people have already been fined or jailed for violating these rules.

In any campaign advertising is the most expensive item. And advertising is as necessary as it is expensive. The candidate may be a great person, but that doesn't help the voters unless they find out.

The way the money is spent on advertising, then, is a major part of the campaign strategy. Most successful candidates design their strategies so that expenditures increase as the election draws nearer. The goal is for the candidate's identity, image, and popularity to all "peak" the day before the election. If they peak too soon or too late, he or she may lose.

Some candidates keep a budget reserve for last-minute tactics. Inevitably, the weekend before the election the voters receive some bit of last-minute "news" about some candidate. This may be sponsored by the candidate or by the opponent. Usually the purpose is to either confuse the voter or smear the opponent when there is no time left for rebuttal.

What would you think if you were a registered Democrat and you received a letter the day before election that read:

> Dear Fellow Democrat:
>
> We have become increasingly alarmed at the efforts of Senator Gluck to buy the upcoming election with illegal contributions from the big oil companies. While we want to support our Democratic Administration in the State Capital, we cannot stand idly by and watch this one Democrat make a mockery of our party and of our democratic system.

As a result, on Tuesday, we urge you as loyal Democrats to write in the name of Admiral Barry Lipschitz on your ballot, so that Governor Weasel's policies may be carried out with honesty and dignity in the Legislature.

We urge this in the name of democracy, in the name of Governor Weasel and in the name of the Democratic Party.

Yours very truly,

Democrats for Honest Government

Who do you think might have sponsored this letter:? Senator Gluck? His Republican opponent? Democrats for Honest Government? And who do you think the Democrats for Honest Government are? Are they really Democrats? And who is Admiral Lipschitz? Do you think he would be a good person to support Governor Weasel's policies?

Also, what do you think of this type of campaign tactic? Is it clever? Is it fair? What do you think Senator Gluck should do?

Political market research

It is vitally necessary to assess several important factors before formulating any specific strategies or advertising plans. This is accomplished through market research. Usually it is best to have an in-depth survey at the outset to discover the relative identity and image of the candidates and to determine the issues as well as the basic attitudes of the voters. From this information the campaign may be planned and budgeted. Toward the end of the campaign, most candidates engage in polling. On this information they may base last-minute decisions for major expenditures or strategy shifts.

More campaign money is wasted because of gut-level market research and seat-of-the-pants planning than any other way. In most cases candidates are well advised to employ a professional market research firm at the outset before spending money on anything else. It is no fun to discover at the end of a campaign that you were on the wrong side of the most important issue.

Use of marketing professionals in politics

Many politicians employ professional campaign managers. These people usually have advertising or marketing backgrounds and have developed an expertise in people management and political strategy.

For a well-financed campaign, money for a skilled, professional manager is extremely well spent. These people understand the importance of fact gathering, planning, organization, and direction, and they are usually instrumental in directing the emotion-ridden campaign coolly and objectively.

In addition to a professional manager, most candidates also find employing an advertising agency worthwhile. The agency is able to implement the strategy of the campaign with brochures, billboards, advertisements, or broadcast commercials. Likewise, if brought in at the beginning, the agency can be helpful in the early planning stages, recommending a reputable market research firm, helping to analyze statistics, and translating objectives into strategy and effective advertising vehicles (Figures 23–19 and 23–20). Forever on tight budgets,

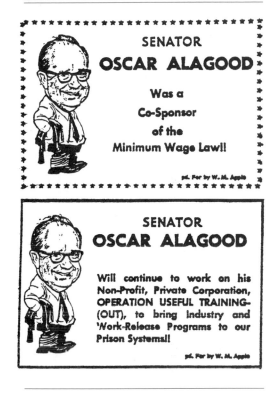

Figure 23–19 Notice the difference between these home-grown, nonagency advertisements for Oscar Alagood and the agency-produced ad for Henry Cisneros in Figure 23–20. The difference is not size, but quality. Which succeeds in offering more appeal to the voters?

political candidates always welcome any friends in the advertising business who are willing to help.

Henry Cisneros talks to San Antonio.

"America is Watching San Antonio."

"This may be the most important mayor's race in the United States this year." –*Texas Monthly*, April, 1981.

"San Antonio has come of age. As America's ninth largest city, we are at a crossroads. The eyes of America are on San Antonio. The country wants to see what we make of our opportunity.

"We can choose to go forward with pride. Confidently. United. Determined to fulfill our dream. Or, we can step backward. Do nothing. Rest on our laurels.

"We can use our energies, our combined resources, our talent, our can-do spirit, to go forward. Or we can attack. Cut down. Belittle. Distort.

"Which road are we taking? America is watching. It wants to know."

Your vote will determine our direction. It will set a tone.

"The way a candidate runs his campaign is an indication of the way he'll run his office. If you evaluate the last month and a half of this mayoral campaign, you'll get an idea of my direction and my opponent's direction.

"I've tried to run my campaign the way I think you want me to. The way I will run the office of the Mayor. Professionally. Objectively. Confidently. Fairly. Concentrating on the issues. The people. The good that is San Antonio. Because I believe when we do that, our appointment with destiny will be met. Our dream for the future fulfilled."

"We have an appointment with destiny."

We must tap the potential we have when we are united.

"If our dream is to be fulfilled, we need a government that is strong enough, fair enough, skillful enough and caring enough to preserve the delicate balance between the neighborhoods, businesses, community organizations, labor, banks, volunteer groups, and other institutions upon whose cooperation the city's prosperity is built. I believe I can help our city prosper and unify as never before."

We need to talk to the issues.

"For too long, we have basked in the glory of other Texas cities. Now, it's up to San Antonio. The job before us is not only to complete what we have begun, but to use our foresight to prepare our city for the new prosperity of the '80's."

- We must develop a surface water supply which will supplement water from the Edwards Aquifer.
- We must continue an orderly process of annexations that protects San Antonio's freedom to grow at its boundaries.
- We must continue to push for the revitalization of downtown. We must press for new bus patterns, historic preservation, enhanced police patrols, sidewalk cleanup, and cooperation on major projects such as Vista Verde South.
- We must build an energy base which assures that we have the generating capacity to meet the growing demand for electricity.
- We must exploit the potential of San Antonio as an international trade center.

"My record is clear on all of these projects. They are the base from which we move into the '80's."

I'm ready to go to work for you now.

"I bring a set of skills, qualifications and ideas. I also bring with them the ability to put them to work. But I need your support. If I can count on your vote this Saturday, you can count on me for San Antonio. Let's show America what a united San Antonio can do."

"I'm making San Antonio my business."

Cisneros For Mayor

- Over 12 years of professional experience in municipal management.
- 6 years on City Council.
- B.A., Texas A&M University. Distinguished military graduate.
- Master of Urban Planning, Texas A&M University.
- Master of Public Administration, Harvard University.
- Doctor of Public Administration, George Washington University.
- White House Fellow.
- Faculty, University of Texas at San Antonio.

Figure 23–20 To Henry Cisneros the question was whether San Antonio would stand still or move forward. As it turned out, the citizens agreed with him, and Cisneros won.

People in advertising

David Garth

President
and Chairman of the Board
Garth Associates, Inc.

Political advertising mentor David Garth has guided 103 political campaigns to date, with a win record of 72 percent, the best in the industry. ". . . even more remarkable," observes *New Times*, ". . . all but 12 of his candidates started out as decided underdogs." Garth is president and chairman of the board of Garth Associates, Inc., a New York–based advertising and public relations firm that has handled some of the toughest fought campaigns in recent years.

Garth even looks like a fighter. His agency occupies offices on the 14th floor of a Fifth Avenue building across from the famed Plaza Hotel. Garth's private office, lined with Emmy citations and autographed photos of clients, contains a three-TV console and a fourth, larger TV set.

The reason for the sets is Garth's emphasis on TV commercials for fighting—and winning—campaigns. His crisp videotape spots usually have the candidate speak for himself. They are crammed with facts, both in the speech and on a printed "crawl" across the bottom of the screen. And they focus on just one issue in each spot. This emphasis on "hard information" sells his political clients, says Garth. He also looks for a candidate who is willing to take strong moral stands. One was Governor Hugh Carey of New York, who firmly supported abortion rights and opposed the death penalty. "For an Irish Catholic father of 11," adds Garth, "that's something."

Raised in a politically active Jewish home on Long Island, Garth was stricken with a severe mastoid infection at age eight and then with rheumatic fever. He spent much of his youth in bed. When Garth heard a doctor tell his parents he would not live past 15, he determined to get well. He did but with exhausting effort. "You become terribly competitive," he said. "You are always testing your own existence." After college, Garth took graduate courses in psychology at Columbia. He was fascinated by the mechanisms of human motivation, tools that he would later put to work in political advertising.

Garth's first big assignment was John Lindsay's successful race for mayor of New York in 1965. Garth had Lindsay filmed strolling through the streets of New York, coat over his shoulder, shirtsleeves rolled up, tie askew. The energetic image invented by Garth was a "first" in the history of TV political advertising.

Along with commercials, Garth Associates does advance work, issues research, polling, speech writing, fund raising, press relations, and campaign management. Once David Garth decides to represent a candidate, his 21-member staff conducts extensive research and polling. Garth and the candidate then select the issues on which they will concentrate in TV spots. From 15 to 35 spots are developed. Garth directs every one of them.

When a campaign is on, Garth and his staff routinely work 15 to 18 hours a day, seven days a week. In his office Garth uses a 31 button computer phone directly linked to candidates, several governors, mayors, members of Congress, and key political reporters.

One of Garth's victories was for New York mayor Edward Koch, who was estimated to have less than 2 percent of the vote when the race began. Garth characteristically recommended exhaustive debating. Koch was drilled for two hours a day on the facts supporting his positions. He completed 62 debates—and emerged victorious.

Garth's other winners include Los Angeles mayor Tom Bradley and Senator Adlai Stevenson III (D-Ill.) He also participated in the 1980 U.S. presidential bid of Senator John Anderson (R-Ill.)

Each year, on the average, more than 50 candidates seek out the services of Garth Associates. What Garth looks for, says *New Times*, "is the scrapper, the tough kid, smaller than the other guys . . ." And to those who think that sounds like David Garth himself, the same article concludes, ". . . this peculiar little man is one of the most powerful politicians in the country."

Advertising solutions to political marketing problems

What an advertisement, brochure, or direct mail piece says frequently has a great effect on the impression the voters get of a candidate. However, what the advertisement says is not merely a function of the words in the ad. Since voters, as people, receive all information subjectively, what an ad says is actually a function of many factors. Who is reading or viewing the advertisement? What words are used and how are they used? What does the ad look like? By what medium is the advertisement communicated? Does the ad ring true? Or is the ad simply a dirty smear of the opposition candidate?

The political office seeker must ask all these questions of every advertisement before it is released to the media. In fact, these questions should be asked and answered before an ad ever even goes into production.

Campaign strategy

The number of different campaign strategies that might be exercised is infinite. Frequently a candidate will mix two or more strategies depending on the particular circumstances of the campaign. Some of the strategies commonly used are listed here:

Popularity (good for creating the bandwagon effect).
Appeal to authority (testimonials from well-known people).
Coat-tailing (using the popularity of a political ally).
Anti-establishment (or anti-special interest, anti-money, etc.).
Successful experience (most common for incumbents).
Appeal to sympathy (good for underdogs, minority candidates, war veterans, etc.).
Appeal to special interest (or special markets).
Appeal to fear or emotion.
Appeal to change.
Appeal to status quo.
Personality (only good for very charismatic candidates).
Bread and butter (jobs, taxes, etc.).
Attack strategy (may be used against incumbents or challengers).
Appeal to truth (or appeal to what people believe is the truth.

Rudy Boschwitz used an effective attack strategy in an effort to win the U.S. Senate seat in Minnesota from Wendell Anderson (Figure 23–21). The Bond Election Support Team pointed out the danger of sending children to school early in the morning to persuade voters to approve needed school bonds (Figure 23–22).

One of the finest examples of an appeal to sympathy was former Cleveland mayor Carl Stokes's ad "Don't Vote for a Negro" (Figure 23–23). By stating the negative, he accentuated the positive in an extremely dynamic, logical manner. The result was to give voters a rational reason to vote for a candidate with whom they probably already sympathized.

The overall campaign strategy the candidate uses determines the mix of the various other campaign activities. It determines the stand on particular issues, the format of speeches, the type of printed materials, the nature of advertising activities, and the priorities for spending money in each area.

Creative strategy

As we have mentioned, the creative strategy in advertising is determined by the mix of market, media, and message. In politics the importance of a well-defined creative strategy cannot be overemphasized. The voters are bombarded every election year with a plethora of appeals from many different candidates running for many

Wendell Anderson says he doesn't have the second worst voting record in the U.S. Senate.
The Congressional Record says he does.
Attendance Record for the 520 U.S. Senate, 94th Congress, Second Session Votes as of End of Session:

1. Proxmire	100%	35. Morgan	93%	69. Biden	87%
2. Jackson	99%	36. DeConcini	93%	70. Bumpers	86%
3. Lugar	99%	37. Garn	92%	71. Long	85%
4. Zorinsky	99%	38. Javits	92%	72. Laxalt	84%
5. Byrd, H.		39. Hayakawa	92%	73. Percy	
6. Byrd, R.	99%	40. Matsunaga	92%	74. Curtis	84%
7. Metzenbaum	98%	41. Packwood	92%	75. Hatfield, M.	83%
8. Glenn	98%	42. Stevenson	92%	76. Scott	83%
9. Leahy	97%	43. Bartlett	92%	77. Young	82%
10. Nelson	97%	44. Hodges	92%	78. Huddleston	82%
11. Stone	97%	45. Bentsen	92%	79. Sparkman	81%
12. Hansen	97%	46. Heinz	92%	80. Gravel	81%
13. Chiles	96%	47. Thurmond	91%	81. Hatfield, P.	81%
14. Danforth	96%	48. Church	89%	82. Mathias	79%
15. Schweiker	96%	49. Moynihan	89%	83. McGovern	79%
16. Hatch	96%	50. Allen, M.	89%	84. Baker	79%
17. Sarbanes	95%	51. Clark	89%	85. Pearson	78%
18. Dole	95%	52. Wallop	89%	86. Humphrey, M.	76%
19.		53. Pell		87.	
20. Williams	95%	54. Sasser	89%	88. Inouye	76%
21. Chafee	94%	55. Burdick	89%	89. Domenici	74%
22. Hart	94%	56. Kennedy	89%	90. McClure	74%
23. Roth	94%	57. Muskie	89%	91. Goldwater	73%
24. Culver	94%	58. Case	89%	92. Griffin	73%
25. Magnuson	94%	59. Eagleton	89%	93. Brooke	73%
26. Cranston	94%	60. Randolph	89%	94. McIntyre	72%
27. Hollings	93%	61. Stevens	88%	95. Hathaway	71%
28. Ford	93%	62. Tower	88%	96. Johnston	69%
29. Melcher	93%	63. Talmadge	88%	97. Eastland	63%
30. Cannon	93%	64. Ribicoff	88%	98. Haskell	52%
31. Durkin	93%	65. Stafford	88%	99. ANDERSON	48%
32. Riegle	93%	66. Weicker	88%	100. Abourezk	43%
33. Nunn	93%	67. Bellmon	88%		
34. Bayh	93%	68. Helms	87%		

Source: Congressional Record
Wendell Anderson says he has a good voting record in the U.S. Senate.
Let's look at what the Congressional Record has to say.
First, for the entire time he's been in the U.S. Senate, only three Senators have worse voting records then Wendell Anderson.
Second, this year in the U.S. Senate, Wendell Anderson ranks 99th out of 100 in voting attendance.
Third, among the 22 U.S. Senators running for re-election this year, Wendell Anderson ranks 22nd.
Who are you going to believe? Wendell Anderson or the Congressional Record?
Rudy Boschwitz for U.S. Senate

Figure 23–21 Rudy Boschwitz used an appeal to authority to justify his attack on Anderson's attendance record in the U.S. Senate. This type of ad is far more effective than the usual mud-slinging attacks which fail to show any substantiation for the charges made.

Figure 23–22 This ad for school bonds has won numerous awards. The message is so simple—and dramatic. The headline and black illustration tell the whole story.

different offices. If candidates do not have a clear, concise, well-defined, strategies, they are seriously handicapped. It is probably in this area of strategy selection and implementation that professional managers and advertising agencies play their most important role.

Audience and geographic considerations In any advertising situation one of the first questions regarding creative strategy must be: Who is the intended audience of the advertisement? On the national level the question might be phrased: Where is this ad going to run?

A liberal candidate might not want to run an ad announcing support of forced busing in some geographic areas. On the other hand, a conservative politician might not wish to run an ad announcing opposition to busing in some other areas.

Figure 23–23 A courageous ad run by Cleveland's black mayor Carl Stokes. He won.

Ronald Reagan was accused of appealing to southern sectionalism during the 1980 campaign, but when the votes were tallied it was evident that he also must have had a western strategy, a northwestern strategy, a midwestern strategy, a north-central strategy, and a mid-Atlantic strategy.

Message and quality considerations The verbal and graphic presentations of the advertisement or brochure are the primary elements that determine what message is received by the audience. This is the one area where most candidates fall down terribly in their efforts at political advertising.

Due to the extreme sensitivity politicians have about raising funds and spending money, the majority find the cost of advertising production distasteful and therefore repeat the same mistake election after election. Most political advertisements are so poorly presented from an esthetic standpoint that it's a wonder many politicians ever get elected. Candidates who run clean, well-conceived, and well-created advertisements are so refreshing in their presentation that they automatically tend to gain prestige in the voters' eyes.

In product marketing, advertising has become such an important element that the quality of the ad is a factor in the quality of the product itself. The same holds true in political advertising. What is the public to think of a candidate whose newspaper advertisements are black, ugly, full of bold, reverse type, and laden with words that seem to scream, "Sale," "Bargain," or "Buy me Cheap?" Yet year after year these political ads appear and reappear.

This is predominantly a problem in local elections where funds are frequently lacking for professional creative talent. But it is not limited to local elections. Ads that lack taste in verbal and graphic presentation are common in statewide elections and sometimes even in national elections. One advertising agency in California became so dismayed by the unprofessional use of advertising by politicians that it began sponsoring Annual Orchids & Onions Awards for the best and worst political ads every year (Figure 23–24).

On the other hand, some of the finest advertising is seen in the political arena. When Delaware governor Pierre du Pont was a congressman, he used an effective play on words to attract attention and simultaneously suggest direct action (Figure 23–25). Following the simple headline were four columns of copy describing in simple detail how Pete du Pont had worked and succeeded for Delaware and the country.

Contrast this with Hedberg's ads for the state senate, which say nothing, offer nothing, and use a hokey, unprofessional approach to gain attention (Figure 23–26). Which of these people would you want to represent you? Which do you think would be most effective as legislators?

In this area of creative presentation, the politician should use a professional advertising agency if at all possible. The American Association of Advertising Agencies publishes a booklet on political campaign advertising that every candidate should acquire. This is a brief but invaluable guide to all the do's and don'ts, complete with pertinent suggestions on how to select and compensate an advertising agency for a political campaign.

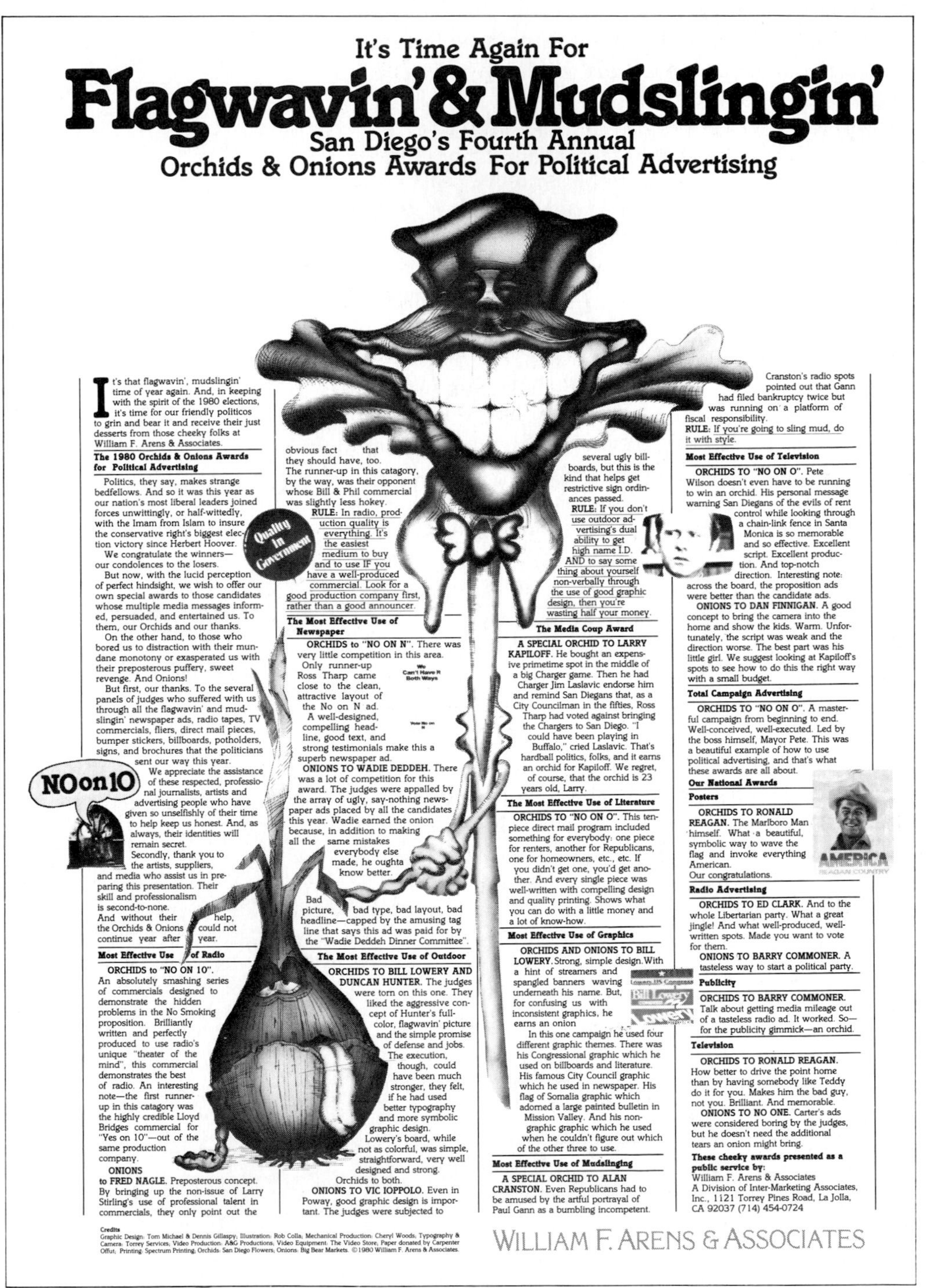

Figure 23–24 Political flag waving and mud slinging are celebrated and roasted in this advertisement, which pays homage to the political ads that truly excel—for better or worse.

Media selection The media selection for political ads depends on the funds available, the strategy of the campaign, the message being communicated, and the audience desired.

Historically, direct mail has been the strongest medium a candidate can use. Most local candidates try to have at least two and preferably three mailings to their district during the campaign. Direct mail is also by far the most expensive medium on a cost-per-exposure basis. With direct mail, however, a candidate may target the message to a specific area or special-interest group. More of the story can be told both graphically and verbally. And fewer total dollars may be spent if the district is small than if mass media were used to reach the same audience.

To gain name I.D., outdoor is the most effective medium. From bumper stickers and small 2 by 2 inch quarter-cards placed on people's lawns to giant illuminated billboards, outdoor is used to communicate very simply the name of the candidate, the office sought, and perhaps one vital issue. Outdoor advertising with good graphic design may also be used to build credibility and show popular support for a candidate. This is especially true of bumper stickers and quarter-cards strategically positioned in residential areas. Some candidates believe that 10 bumper stickers can be as effective as one billboard.

Newspaper ads have always been important to the politician. The space available allows extensive verbal discussion as well as graphic presentation of the issues. The cost is usually far less than direct mail on a cost-per-thousand basis. And, like outdoor, popular support may be shown, in this case by listing influential supporters or picturing people in the community.

Radio and television advertising offers great opportunity to create image. For communicating to large numbers of people, they are by far the most economically efficient media to use. Radio lets the candidate experiment with sound, music, and words to stimulate the imagination of the audience. Television lends motion, color, and sound, all intermingled through professional, albeit expensive, production to create a lasting impression on the electorate.

Fifty reasons to rePete duPont

Count them.

As a member of the Committee on Merchant Marine and Fisheries **(1)**, Congressman duPont has worked hard to preserve our **environment**—to "clean up the rivers, clean up the air."

By sponsoring the 1972 Ocean Dumping Act to protect our oceans, rivers and bays **(2)**.

By voting for the federal Clean Water Act **(3)** and supporting Governor Peterson's Coastal Zoning Bill **(4)**.

By introducing legislation requiring government reports on the ecological impact of any legislation Congress is considering **(5)**.

[illegible] fully opposed a start on the Tocks Island Dam until the dangers to the local ecology can be removed **(6)**.

And he fought for rapid action by the Environmental Protection Agency on Delaware's air quality standards **(7)**, so polluters could be prosecuted.

In the field of **education**, the Congressman voted for the new program of aid to colleges and universities **(8)**.

And for responsible increases in funding for elementary and secondary schools **(9)**.

And against the forced busing of school children away from neighborhood schools **(10)**.

Pete has worked steadily to reduce **crime and drug abuse** by supporting creation of an Action Office on Drug Abuse in the White House to coordinate federal efforts **(11)**.

By insisting on implementation of Turkey's commitment to outlaw and destroy its heroin-producing poppy crop **(12)**.

And by helping obtain $1,200,000 for Delaware drug abuse projects including $500,000 to reduce drug-related street crime **(13)**.

He inaugurated a special study of existing federal drug programs, which helped secure more anti-drug funds for Delaware **(14)**.

And he worked on a Special Task Force on Drug Abuse which authored legislation to meet the drug crisis of Vietnam servicemen and veterans **(15)**.

And he steadily opposed efforts at massive registration of fire-arms **(16)**, as an over-simplified answer to the crime problem.

[illegible] the prestigious House Committee on **Foreign Affairs (17)**, Pete supported the President in his policy of withdrawal from Vietnam, favored leaving the President broad flexibility in negotiations, and constantly opposed escalation of the fighting and bombing **(18)**.

And he also worked on: A Congressional resolution expressing sympathy with the right of Jewish emigres to leave the Soviet Union **(19)**;

Restoration of funds to keep Radio Free Europe in operation **(20)**;

And legislation to limit the war-making powers of the White House without Congressional approval **(21)**.

On the **economy**, Congressman duPont voted to reduce federal spending by backing prudent defense budget reductions **(22)**, opposing the SST **(23)**, opposing the Lockheed loan **(24)**, and supporting a $20,000 limit on the crop subsidy payment to any single farm **(25)**.

And he voted to reduce your federal taxes by supporting the increase in both the exemption **(26)** and the standard deduction **(27)** on your income tax—and by supporting removal of the automobile excise tax **(28)**.

Pete has vigorously supported reform of the non-productive welfare system **(29)**.

And his votes have helped pass the beginnings of revenue sharing **(30)**.

To help hold down prices, he voted for the President's Phase I and II economic measures **(31)**, but he has urged that controls be lifted on small businesses **(32)**.

To help create more jobs, the Congressman voted for the 1971 Emergency Employment legislation **(33)** and co-sponsored a bill to extend tax credits to industries locating in rural areas **(34)**.

Pete has been an outspoken supporter of more **aid to senior citizens** by strongly backing the 20% raise in Social Security benefits **(35)**.

By urging removal of all earnings limitations on benefits **(36)**.

And by working to assure that benefits increase automatically as the cost of living rises **(37)**.

Furthermore the duPont **Congressional office** staff has helped over 400 Delawareans with their Social Security problems **(38)**.

And 600 more concerning their military service or Veterans benefits **(39)**.

With the help of over 50 young Delaware men and women in a student intern program in Washington **(40)**, Pete and his staff have tackled local Delaware projects and produced results.

Like the funds they helped secure for completion of the Luther Towers Senior Citizens apartment complex in Wilmington **(41)**.

Or the heat they kept on the Corps of Engineers to meet the time schedule for repairs on the St. George's Bridge **(42)**.

Or their work to fight beach erosion along Kent County's shores **(43)**.

Or their intervention with FAA to secure a $130,000 grant for the Sussex County Airport **(44)**.

And in Washington Pete has continued his work on **consumer protection**.

By voting for an independent Consumer Protection Agency in the federal government **(45)**.

By persuading the Food and Drug Administration to release to the public their regulations and standards for the production and packaging of certain foodstuffs **(46)**.

By keeping pressure on the Post Office to improve its service in Delaware **(47)**.

And to minimize fraud in the political marketplace by supporting legislation to limit political campaign advertising **(48)** and to require publication of the names of campaign contributors **(49)**.

And he did it all with a voting attendance record of 94% **(50)**.

Whew!

Figure 23–25 Politicians should not be afraid of long-copy ads if they have something interesting and relevant to say. Pete du Pont found this to be true and easily won reelection.

Political advertising as a social issue

The attitude that political advertising is just another marketing function with the same problems and complexities of product marketing is a recent one. The fact is that over the years little has really changed in political advertising except the media used and the skill of the people using them.

In 1952 Dwight D. Eisenhower became the first person to use television spots in a presidential campaign, and he was elected by an overwhelming majority. Suddenly the significance of this new, pervasive medium was realized, and we heard the first protests about packaging politicians like toothpaste and dog food. As the use of television has increased over the years, so have the protests. And so have the art and science of political campaign management and advertising.

There are, however, certain serious ethical problems that must be faced today and in the future by all those involved in political advertising. The first of these relates to campaign financing. As we mentioned earlier, strict laws have been enacted and are being enforced to govern the source and amount of contributions candidates may receive and the way in which these monies may be spent. However, as fast as new laws are created, new ways are discovered to avoid them. One of the strongest criticisms currently prevalent is that these laws enacted by incumbents tend to favor incumbents in future elections.

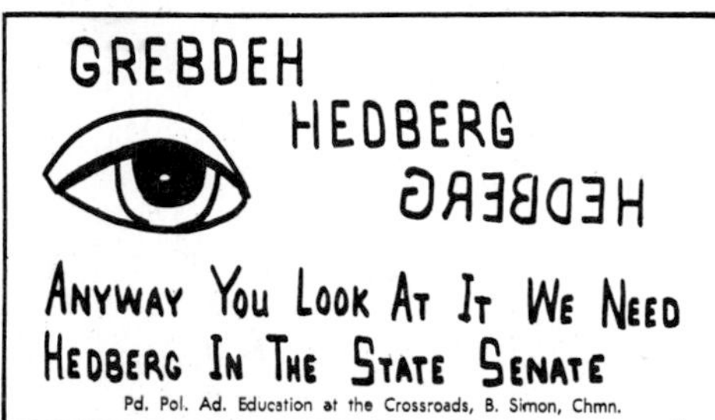

Figure 23–26 In an effort to be clever or cute, political candidates who are unsophisticated about contemporary advertising techniques can sometimes get into trouble by going overboard in their creative attempts.

A second ethical question relates more directly to the style of advertising used in elections. Advertising tends to simplify the important issues at stake. Advertising may oversimplify the personality and the record of the politician. Advertising, the critics say, takes a multifaceted human being and makes him or her appear one-sided—all good. Likewise, well-financed proponents and antagonists of ballot propositions tend to oversimplify the often complex legislative initiatives offered to the voters. How are the voters to know, then, which way to vote if they cannot get the whole story? Defenders of political advertising say that's the role of the press and the responsibility of the voters to investigate both sides of an issue.

A third ethical problem relates to what politicians say in their ads about one another. At what point does an attack on an opponent's record become libelous? What should a candidate be able to say and when does this attack become slander? (See the Ad Lab). Many candidates feel they have been defeated by the mud slinging, distortions, or outright lies of their opponents. And the feat of this keeps many potentially excellent office holders on the political sidelines.

Some of the largest and most respected advertising agencies in the country have declined to handle political advertising because of the tendency of candidates to distort the truth about themselves or their opposition. Doyle Dane Bernbach was very embarrassed in 1971 by the disclosure of certain facts regarding President Lyndon Johnson's secret decisions before and after the 1964 election to increase U.S. military activity in Vietnam. They had been successful, as Johnson's agency, in picturing him as a man of peace and his opponent, Barry Goldwater, as the warmonger. This embarrassment led them to decide not to handle any future political campaigns.

Similarly, J. Walter Thompson's creative director, George Edward Thompson, referred to political ads as the most virulent form of "subvertising"—advertising that subtracts from the total value of advertising.

Other agency executives, though, have suggested that more agencies should enter the political advertising arena to serve as a responsible, balancing force against the questionable practices of unscrupulous political advertising practitioners and the overwhelming power of the news media.

The point made by both these groups is the same. The professional advertising community does not want to be associated with dishonest, fraudulent, or misleading political advertising. The electorate is saying the same thing. And now finally more and more politicians are echoing the feeling. (See Figure 23–27.)

How to tell Republicans from Democrats

Although to the casual glance Republicans and Democrats may appear to be almost indistinguishable, here are some hints which should result in positive identification, according to The Sterling Bulletin:

Democrats buy most of the books that have been banned somewhere. Republicans form censorship committees and read them as a group.

Republicans consume three-fourths of all the rutabaga produced in this country. The remainder is thrown out.

Republicans usually wear hats and almost always clean their paint brushes.

Democrats give their worn-out clothes to those less fortunate. Republicans wear theirs.

Republicans employ exterminators. Democrats step on the bugs.

Democrats name their children after currently popular sports figures, politicians and entertainers. Republican children are named after their parents or grandparents, according to where the most money is.

Democrats keep trying to cut down on smoking, but are not successful. Neither are Republicans.

Republicans tend to keep their shades drawn, although there is seldom any reason why they should. Demorcats ought to, but don't.

Republicans study the financial pages of the newspaper. Democrats put them in the bottom of the bird cage.

Most of the stuff you see alongside the road has been thrown out of car windows by Democrats.

Republicans raise dahlias, Dalmatians, and eyebrows. Democrats raise Airedales, kids and taxes.

Democrats eat the fish they catch. Republicans hang them on the wall.

Republican boys date Democratic girls. They plan to marry Republican girls, but feel they're entitled to a little fun first.

Democrats make up plans and then do something else. Republicans follow the plans their grandfathers made.

Republicans sleep in twin beds—some even in separate rooms. That is why there are more Democrats.

Figure 23–27 The author of this amazing prose is unknown, but the perceptions described are the classic stereotypes which any advertising professional who works with politicians will enjoy.

Presidential candidate commercials: Deceptive or informative?

The candidates and their staffs spend millions of dollars in creating and broadcasting commercials of 30 seconds, 60 seconds, and five minutes to sell themselves and their ideas to a potential 100 million voters. Sometimes they even buy half-hour programs, but the shortforms of 30 and 60 seconds are the real workhorses of campaigns.

Critics often attack the shortform commercials as dangerous to the democratic political process. Some have gone as far as advocating that they be banned from the air, even though such a ban would clearly violate the First Amendment.

Robert Spero, vice president and copy supervisor of a New York–based advertising agency, and author of a new book. *The Duping of the American Voter: Dishonesty and Deception in Presidential Television Advertising,* recently dubbed political commercials as "the principal medium of political deception."

"Today," he wrote, "the use of commercials to camouflage candidates' inexperience is standard fare." Spero's cure for the political disease is free television time made available to all candidates.

Paid political commercials do not lack their defenders. One of them is John Deardourff and Associates.

Deardourff rejects the charge that the makers of political commercials fabricate images. "Good political advertising," he said, "has to bear a very close relationship to information the voters are receiving from other sources, because if it is at odds with the information people acquire on the news, then it will tend to be discounted."

"A candidate running for office is appealing to a mass of voters," he said, "usually in the hundreds of thousands or in the millions. The most effective means of reaching those masses is in prime-time television. When we set out to buy commercials in prime time, the most availabilities are either 30 or 60 seconds. We prefer five-minute periods, but they are not often available. Then, too, television audiences are accustomed to receiving information in short terms. Product commercials are 30 and 60 seconds; television news stories average about 90 seconds."

Marketplace reality

"The new politics which has emerged since Watergate," writes Harden H. Wiedemann, editor of *Campaigns and Elections,* "involves the use of many specialized fields—polling, statistical analysis, computers, media management, fund raising, voter targeting, telephone operations, organizational theory. The combination of new rules and increasing specialization has caused a radical change in political campaigns. . . . The results: elective and party politics will generate an estimated $700 million boom industry in 1980."

The flamboyant Baltimore advertising man, Robert Goodman, has emerged in the last few years as an influential and provocative figure in television political advertising.

"Voting," proclaimed Goodman, "is an emotional experience, not an intellectual one. People tend to vote on honesty, competence, and charisma in that order. We try to show a candidate—he's sensitive, he's attractive, he's nice. The musical background is very important.

Goodman carefully oversees the personal habits of his clients. "Polyester suits and loud ties are out," he said. "You have to worry about the hair. Can't be too short or too long. Slovenliness is not a virtue, but contrived casualness is."

"Feelings decide it all," said Goodman. "We must *like* this human being to vote for him. In most elections, the issue isn't foreign policy or inflation. The issue is really the human being.

"Honesty can't be invented in television commercials. Either it's there or it isn't there. The eyes, emotions, and body language reveal the person. But competence and charisma can't be dramatized."

Five-minute spots

The best buy on the network air is a five-minute segment in prime time. Media buyers request that networks shorten their longer shows, movies, and specials to leave a five-minute hole at the end. Depending on the time, day of the week, and network, a five-minute commercial costs between $22,000 and $30,000, plus production charges, if there are any. In comparison, a 60-second commercial in a top-rated program can cost more than $100,000.

All networks bar political commercials from news, documentary, public affairs, and news special events programs. Payment is required by certified check 72 hours before the broadcast time. Political films, tapes, and scripts are also required 72 hours in advance.

The effect

After a study of news coverage and commercials in the 1972 Nixon–McGovern campaign, two Syracuse University political scientists, Thomas E. Patterson and Robert D. McClure, concluded that television commercials, "scorned by the intelligentsia as too short and too gimmicky to provide an honest basis for political choice," actually furnish voters with more serious information on the issues than all the regular network news programs put together. That opinion is still widely debated in political, news, and academic circles.

But there seems to be little doubt that television has taken over the presidential election process, perhaps starting in 1952 but almost certainly since 1960, the year of the famous Nixon–Kennedy television debates. Three long-time practitioners of the art of political persuasion provide these evaluations:

John Deardourff, of the Ford and Baker campaigns in 1976 and 1980: "The thing that has changed the political process dramatically in this country is television. The ability of a candidate to reach beyond the normal party boundaries right into the homes of millions of voters simultaneously is the most dramatic change in the political process in this country in its whole history."

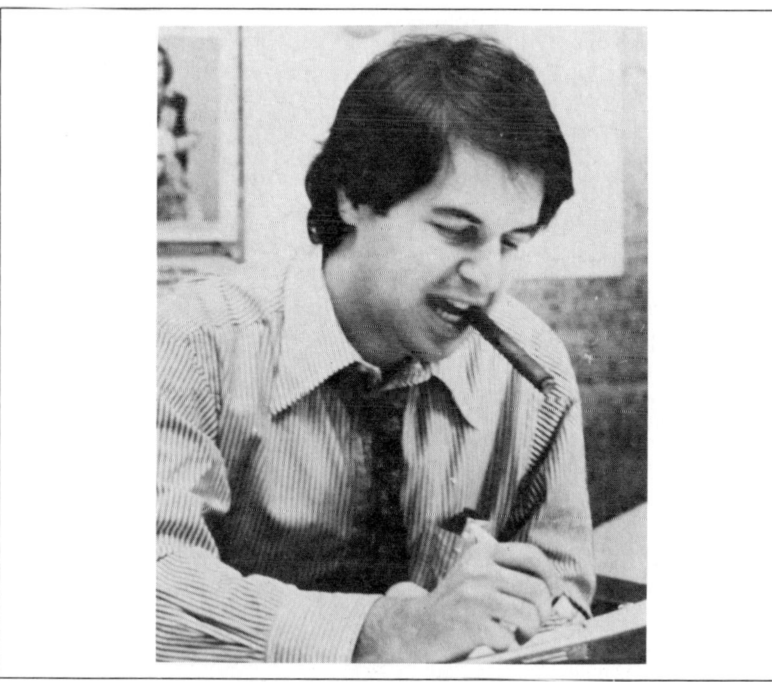

Elliott Curson, Reagan commercials producer: "My philosophy is that when your opponent zigs, you zag. Bush, Baker, and Connally all had Marlboro-man-type commercials—Hollywood-style productions that did everything but tell you what the candidate stands for, what he has done, and what he will do. So I tried to keep mine simple."

(*continued*)

Presidential candiate commercials *(continued)*

Bill Wilson, veteran of Democratic campaigns since 1952 and with the Kennedy forces in 1980: "Television completely ruins political parties, annihilates them. The structure of the ward captain and all the rest is bypassed because of television. The leaders of the political parties in the United States no longer have any power."

Tony Schwartz, creator of political commercials, including the controversial "Daisy Girl" commercial for Lyndon Johnson in the 1964 campaign: "You might say we have three very important parties in this country today—ABC, NBC, and CBS. They are the new political parties, and they are the vehicles for connecting the candidate to the minds of the voter. The [political] parties began to be destroyed when we had media and the secret ballot."

Laboratory application

What is your view of political candidate commercials? Are they deceptive or informative? Base your reasoning on specific examples.

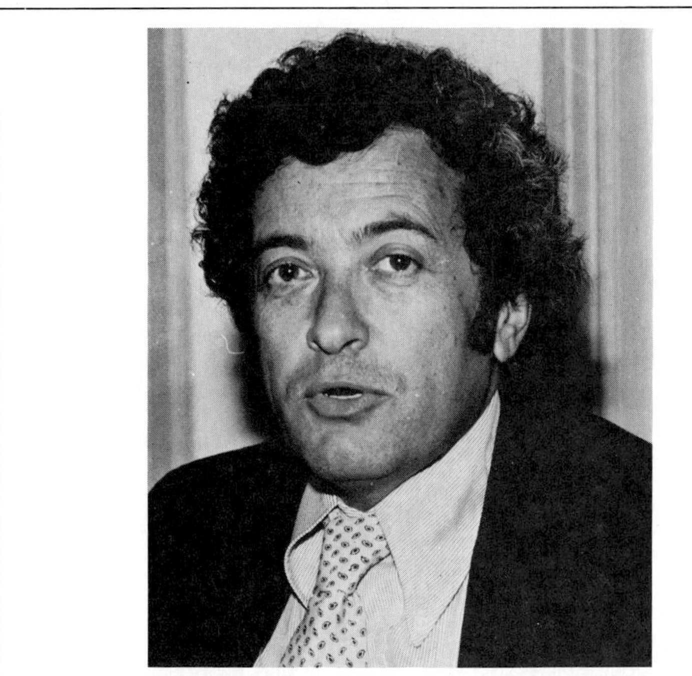

Gerald Rafshoon, Carter media advisor: He made honesty, or lack of it, an issue very early in the 1980 primaries. Trying to put some distance between President Carter and Senator Edward M. Kennedy of Massachusetts, Rafshoon played—not too subtly—on doubts about Kennedy's explanations of his 1969 car accident at Chappaquiddick.

Summary

The most obvious differences between commercial and noncommercial advertising are the sponsors and the things being advertised. Commercial firms usually advertise tangible goods and services, whereas noncommercial advertising by nonprofit organizations usually stresses causes, ideas, attitudes, and viewpoints. A more subtle difference relates to the specific objectives of commercial and noncommercial advertising. One seeks to sell products or services, while the other seeks to change attitudes or popularize a social cause.

Noncommercial advertising may be categorized by its sponsors. These include nonbusiness institutions (churches, schools, universities, charitable organizations, etc.), associations (labor groups, business and professional organizations, civic associations, etc.), government organizations (Army, Postal Service, state departments of tourism, etc.), and political organizations.

To assist certain important causes in the public interest, members of the advertising profession formed the Advertising Council during World War II. During its 40 years of operation it has conducted up to 30 different campaigns a year for such projects as the American Red Cross, U.S. savings bonds, and the United Way. It is estimated that over $10 billion worth of free advertising space and time has been donated by the media to the campaigns created by the council's volunteer advertising agencies.

Political advertising, like product advertising, is a marketing function. The political product, though, is a human being. Or, in the case of noncampaign advertising, it may be the particular ideology or political viewpoint being promoted. Another difference is that the time period for political advertising is limited, rather than ongoing. Third, the ethical question is larger in political advertising.

The political market is the candidate's constituency (i.e., the voters in the district); and the product's "sales features" are the candidate's positions on the issues. In political campaigns, the marketing objective is to achieve a 50+ percent share of market by election day. To do so the politician must overcome marketing problems as diverse as those encountered in product marketing.

Based on the results of market research, a campaign strategy and a creative or advertising strategy must be developed. The strategies used take into consideration the attitude of the constituency toward particular issues, the candidate's stand or record on those issues, the funds available, and the various media that might be used.

Once the strategy has been determined, advertisements may be created. Just as in product marketing, the quality of the advertising reflects the quality of the product—in this case, the politician.

As a social issue, political advertising is confronted by several important ethical problems. Among these are campaign financing, oversimplification in advertisements, libelous claims, and the question of truth in advertising. It behooves the political candidate, therefore, to stick to the facts and base all advertising on truth. Only in this way will there be an opportunity to communicate creatively with the electorate.

Questions for review

1. What is the difference between noncommercial and commercial advertising?
2. What is the Advertising Council? Why is it considered an important organization?
3. What is the most important element in successful political marketing? How is this similar to product marketing? How is it different?
4. What is the difference between identity and image?
5. How does polling help political candidates? What other types of research may be used, and how do they differ?
6. What is the concept of peaking? How can this affect the outcome of an election?
7. What slogan can you think of that you believe was used effectively by a politician?
8. What factors determine the quality of an advertisement? What bearing does that quality have on a candidate's campaign?
9. What is an appeal to authority? Cite one example of its use in politics today.
10. What are some ethical problems in political advertising? Discuss in detail and give your opinion.

Part VII

Advertising Testing

It pays to advertise . . .
SOMETIMES

24

Evaluation of advertising

Seated in a paneled room, a group of men and women linked by electrodes to a monitoring machine watch commercial after commercial speed by on a color television set. After 45 minutes some appear glassy-eyed, as if in a trance. A few fidget nervously. Others yawn and look bored. None of this matters to Dr. Sidney Weinstein. At his NeuroCommunications Research Center in Danbury, Connecticut, he is watching the images of their brain waves lope across a monitoring screen. These waves, he explains, indicate how people *really* respond to commercials—and how effective they are.

But *do* they? Some ad people are dubious. Others believe that factors like light, noise, or a test subject's emotional state can distort the findings. Still others point to possible malfunctions in the monitoring equipment. But Weinstein believes that physiological testing is more effective than the recall method, which asks subjects their reactions to a given advertisement. It also may bare some surprising truths. "One guy," he reports, "said he was repulsed by a commercial that showed a scantily clad young girl." But when this man's reactions to the same commercial were tested with a monitoring machine, "his brain waves went off the charts." How does Weinstein explain this contradiction? "It turned out he was a high school teacher," he reports, "and felt it was unseemly to say he got carried away by her."

Today many companies are turning to similar physiological tests to measure the impact of their advertising. Corporate giants like General Electric and General Foods are investing large amounts in tests that track brain waves or barely perceptible changes in eye movements, voice pitch, or perspiration rates. They hope these tests will remove some of the risk from the costly, hit-and-miss business of making a successful advertisement.[1]

Objectives of advertising testing

When the nation's 100 leading advertisers spend $13 billion a year for advertising, its effectiveness is a major concern. In some instances advertising is the largest single cost in a company's marketing budget. Companies can't stop advertising, nor do they want to. But they *do* want to know what they are getting for their money—whether their advertising works.

Testing is the primary instrument that advertisers have to provide some assurance that their advertising dollars are being spent wisely. Most of the nation's leading advertisers today use some form of testing.

Why test? Because it can help advertisers and agencies achieve a better understanding of their customers. It may prevent costly errors in judging which advertising strategy and what media will produce the greatest results. And it can give the advertiser some measure of the effectiveness of a campaign besides sales results.

In Chapter 8 on marketing research, we presented the four stages of advertising research. The objectives and techniques of the first two stages were discussed in some detail: strategy determination and concept development. In this chapter our goal is to understand the basic objectives of the final two stages: pretesting of print ads and television commercials and campaign evaluation. Then we shall briefly discuss the most common research methods used in each stage.

Pretesting of ads and commercials

The objective of pretesting is to increase the likelihood of preparing the most effective advertising messages. Pretesting can help advertisers detect and eliminate weaknesses or flaws that may ultimately result in consumer indifference or negative audience response.

There are several areas of advertising that may be evaluated in pretesting. These are markets, motives, messages, media, budgeting, and scheduling. Most of these variables are under the advertiser's control.

Markets

Advertisers may pretest advertising strategy and commercials against various market segments or audience groups to measure their reactions. In this process the advertiser may even decide to alter the strategy and target the campaign to a different market.

Motives

As discussed in Chapters 7 and 8, motivation research allows advertisers to learn why consumers behave as they do and what product benefits appeal to customers. In pretesting advertisements, the advertiser is interested in those appeals that might cause people to buy based on their particular motives. The consumer's motives are outside of the advertiser's control, but the messages the advertiser uses to appeal to those motives are not.

Messages

In advertising there are many message variables. Pretesting may be used to determine *what* a message says, or to determine how *well* it says it. On the one hand, the variables tested might be the headline, the text, the illustration, and the typography. On the other hand, the variables might be the message concept, the information presented, or the symbolism inherent in the ad.

Media

There are four levels of media decisions that can be affected through pretesting techniques: classes of media, subclasses, specific media vehicles, and units of space and time.

Classes of media are the broad media categories: print, broadcast, outdoor, and direct mail. Subclasses are radio or TV, newsmagazines or business publications, and so on. The specific media vehicles involve deciding between the all-rock station or the middle-of-the-road music station in Albuquerque. And media units mean half-page ads or full-page ads, 30-second spots or 60-second commercials.

Budgeting

How large should a company's total advertising budget be? How much of this should be allocated to various markets and media? To specific products? Spending too little on advertising can be as hazardous as spending too much, but how much is "too little"—and how much is "too much"? Certain pretesting techniques are used to determine the optimum levels of expenditure before introducing national campaigns. (Refer to Chapter 9, "Marketing and Advertising Planning.")

Scheduling

Advertisers can test consumer response to a product ad during different seasons of the year or days of the week. They can test whether frequent advertising is more effective than occasional or one-time insertions, or whether year-round advertising of, say, a gift product is more effective than advertising concentrated in the Christmas gift-buying season.

Posttesting: Evaluation of campaign results

Determining the effectiveness of an advertisement or campaign *after* it has run is called *posttesting.* The findings obtained from posttesting can provide the advertiser with useful guidelines for future advertising.

Posttesting is generally more costly and time-consuming than pretesting, but it permits advertisements to be tested under actual market conditions and without the unnaturalness of pretest conditions. Advertisers can reap the benefits of both pretesting and posttesting by running advertisements in a few select markets before launching a major nationwide campaign.

Many of the same variables can be tested. However, in posttesting the objective is to evaluate rather than to diagnose. The intent is not to make changes but rather to understand what has already happened.

Markets

The advertiser is interested in determining the extent to which the campaign succeeded in reaching its target markets. Changes in awareness within the market segment may indicate successful advertising exposure, for instance. Or perhaps an increase in market share gives the same information.

Messages

Through posttesting the advertiser can determine to what extent the advertising message was seen, remembered, and believed. Changes in consumer attitude, for instance, indicate success in this area. Similarly, success might be measured by the ability of consumers to fill in the blanks in a campaign slogan or to identify the sponsor.

Media

Numerous tests are used to determine whether the media used were effective in reaching the target audience and in communicating the desired message. With the cost of media soaring, advertisers are demanding greater media accountability.

Overall results

Finally, the advertiser wants to measure overall results to evaluate the extent to which advertising accomplished its objectives. The results of these tests might be used to determine how to continue, what to change, and how much to spend in the future.

All these tests are designed with the hope of discovering to what extent advertising is the *stimulus* and changes in consumer behavior are *responses*. Perhaps the greatest problem for the researcher, though, is to determine which, and how many, of these advertiser-controlled variables to measure and which consumer responses to survey.

Pretesting techniques

Testing the effectiveness of an advertisement *before* it is run has obvious advantages. The advertiser can learn what results an ad is likely to have before spending what may be a large amount to produce it and place it in the media. Although no infallible means of predicting success or failure has been developed, certain pretesting methods can give the advertiser some useful insights if properly applied.

However, it is important to point out the potential pitfalls of some testing procedures. To be useful, the testing method itself must first be evaluated in terms of validity, reliability, and relevance.

Assume a market contains 10,000 individuals, and you want to determine the attitude of that market toward a new advertisement for a new Mattel toy. You show your proposed ad layout to five people, and four say they like it. If you then interpolate that to your entire market, you might predict an 80 percent favorable attitude. Is that test *valid?* Hardly. It is very doubtful that the results of your test reflect the true status of the market.

In addition, if you were to repeat your test with five more people, you might come up with an entirely different response. And if you repeated it again, you might come up with a third result. If that were the case, it would show that your test also lacks *reliability*. For a test to be reliable, it must produce the same result each time it is administered.

Finally, if you reported that your initial test results showed the new toy was going to get an 80 percent share of market, your findings would again be suspect. That's because the test you administered was not *relevant* to determining share of market. This simple example illustrates the importance of evaluating the test itself before administering it in advertising research.

Methods used to test print ads

There are numerous popular techniques used by researchers to pretest print ads. These include order-of-merit tests, paired comparison methods, portfolio tests, mock magazines, direct questioning, perceptual meaning studies, and focus groups. The latter method was discussed in Chapter 8 on marketing research. We shall discuss the others briefly here.

In *order-of-merit tests,* two or more advertisements are shown to a number of potential prospects with instructions to arrange the advertisements in rank order. Sheets are kept on the ranking by each person. It is hoped that some consistency in ranking will emerge. The danger is that none of the advertisements may be particularly noteworthy and the highest ranked advertisements may simply be the best of the worst.

In the *paired comparison method* of testing, each advertisement is compared with every other advertisement in the group. At any one time, only two advertisements are being evaluated. This is a much less cumbersome task than having to rank seven or eight advertisements as called for in the order-of-merit test.

In *portfolio tests,* the test ads are interspersed among other ads and editorial matter in an album-type portfolio. Consumers in an experimental group are shown this portfolio; consumers in a closely matched control group are shown this same portfolio but *without* the test ads. Afterward members of both groups are questioned to determine their recall of the portfolio contents and the advertisements being tested.

In *mock magazine tests* (referred to as "tip-in" by the Gallup & Robinson organization, which conducts such tests), an actual magazine is used instead of a portfolio. These test ads are "stripped into" the magazine, and it is left with the respondents for a time. They are told to read the magazine as they would any other—the articles, features, and ads that interest them. Afterward the respondents are questioned about the test ads. This system is also used as a posttesting technique.

Another method of pretesting, which is designed to elicit a fuller range of responses to the advertising, is *direct questioning.* (Figure 24–1). Respondents are asked such questions as: What does the advertising say? What do you think the advertiser is trying to tell you about the product? Does the advertising say anything new or different about the product? If so, what? Is the advertising believable? What effect, if any, does it have on your perception of the product?

From responses to questions like these, the researcher can infer how well the advertising message conveyed the key copy points. The researcher also takes note of verbatim comments made by the respondents, which often reveal more subtle but meaningful reactions to the advertisement. Direct questioning is especially effective for testing alternative advertisements in the early stages of development. Respondents are virtual participants in ad making at a time when their reactions and input can best be acted upon.

The Starch organization conducts a test to measure the visual impact and communication power of advertisements. They refer to these as *perceptual meaning studies* (PMS). The PMS method uses timed exposures to test the ad. The advertisement is shown on a specially

People in advertising

Charles Ramond

Editor
Journal of Advertising Research

The scientific testing and evaluation of advertising are the forte of Dr. Charles Ramond, president of Predex Corporation and a consultant to the Advertising Research Foundation (ARF).

Dr. Ramond formerly served as technical director of the ARF, a nonprofit trade association that enforces standards of media research. He is editor of its *Journal of Advertising Research,* which he established in 1960. The *Journal* examines advertising and its impact on the individual and society. A prestigious publication, it is prepared by and for teachers of advertising, psychologists, and advertising research and business personnel.

Prior to joining the ARF, Ramond was the first manager of advertising research for Du Pont Corporation. In 1966 he founded Marketing Control, Inc., a worldwide marketing research organization. Four years later he became the first non-Frenchman to win the Prix Marcel Dassault for marketing research. Predex Corporation, launched in 1974 as an outgrowth of the World Data Bank service of Marketing Control, is a major economic research organization devoted to forecasting currency exchange rates.

Ramond was born in New Orleans in 1930. He attended Tulane University, where he was graduated with honors and elected to Phi Beta Kappa. He went on to obtain a Ph.D. in experimental psychology at the University of Iowa in 1953. Later, as an Army lieutenant, Ramond headed the research section of the Voice of the UN Command in Tokyo. In 1966 he was appointed to spend three months in Vietnam as a consultant to the White House.

A leading advocate of advertising testing and evaluation, Ramond says, "Think of the mental clutter accumulated from irrelevant advertising, the time and money lost to ill-planned products, ineffective sales calls, too-high prices, and fruitless searches for poorly distributed brands. Everybody pays—buyer and seller alike—for ineffective advertising."

Citing the reason for this ineffectiveness, Ramond said in the *Journal of Advertising Research,* ". . . a good guess is that less than a billion dollars go each year toward all marketing research; and that of this, no more than a few hundred million is spent to help develop and assess advertising. So we probably spend for guidance no more than one or two percent of the amount we spend for that which should be guided."

As to how well this "one or two percent" investment is used, Ramond declared, "Never before have we spent so much time and money trying to find out what to say, how to say it, where and how often to say it, and how well it is communicated and sold. The trouble is that much of this time is misspent seeking results which, like the tools used to find them, can be shown to be ambiguous, ungeneralizable, or wrong."

Then what is the answer? According to Ramond, "I no longer believe the way out lies in ever larger budgets for research. Instead, it now seems clear that we can get, and have gotten, better research for the levels of money now spent."

Author of *The Art of Using Science in Marketing* (New York: Harper & Row, 1974) and *Advertising Research: The State of the Art* (New York: Association of National Advertisers, 1976), Ramond has also been widely published in major technical journals and anthologies.

He is past president of the Market Research Council and is an active member of ORSA, TIMS, the Academy of International Business, and the New York Academy of Sciences. Ramond is listed in *Who's Who in the World* and *Who's Who in America.*

designed electronic tachistoscopic presentation instrument. Each person sees the advertisement first for a brief exposure. The person is questioned on recall of product, brand, illustration, copy, and the main idea of the ad. Following the questioning, the respondent is shown the advertisement for a longer interval and questioned again.

By analyzing with PMS how much the person sees at controlled exposures and comparing this with norms, the researcher can tell whether the perception of the ad is good, bad, or indifferent. By analyzing what the ad means to the respondent, PMS also suggests what is aiding communication and what may be hindering it.

Methods used to test broadcast ads

A number of other methods are used to pretest radio and television commercials. The most common of these are in-home projection tests, trailer tests, theater tests, and live telecasts. We shall discuss each of these briefly.

In-home projection tests

In this approach, often called the "black box" method, test commercials are run on a 16-mm projector in the respondents' homes. Questions are asked before and after exposure to the commercials. The purposes of this test are to measure the effectiveness of the commercials in increasing brand awareness and to detect weaknesses in the commercials.

Trailer tests

These tests are conducted in a *recruited* natural environment. They are intended to measure actual consumer behavior. Trailers are situated in shopping center parking lots, and shoppers are invited in to be interviewed. Commercials are shown on a rear screen projector. Shoppers are then questioned about these commercials and are given packets of coupons that enable them to purchase products seen in the commercials at reduced prices. A matched sample of consumers who have not viewed the commercials are given identical packets of coupons. The impact of the commercials is measured in part by the difference in coupon redemption rates between the two groups. Although this method is less costly than in-home projection tests, it is also less selective in the types of respondents interviewed.

Theater tests

The most popular *captive audience* method for pretesting television commercials is the theater test. Several techniques are used in special test theaters. Persons randomly selected from phone directories are mailed free tickets to what they are told will be the screening of a proposed network TV series pilot program. Before the screening, each respondent may be given a sheet on which are listed, say, several different brands of canned tuna. They are asked to check "the brand you want most to win." A drawing is then conducted for, say, $10 worth of canned tuna. Then the pilot film is shown, interspersed with several commercials, including one or more for canned tuna. After the screening, another drawing is held for $10 worth of canned tuna. Respondents are again given sheets on which several different brands of canned tuna are listed. Again they are asked to check "the brand you want most to win." The degree of the shift in product choice is presumed to indicate the effectiveness of the commercial.

Some theater tests use electronic equipment that enables respondents to press one button to indicate what they like and another to indicate what they dislike as they see the commercial. (See Figure 24–2.) Another form of theater test uses electronic reaction recorders equipped with dials, which enable respondents to rate commercials on the basis of how interesting they find them. The dials are linked to an electronic device that records the reactions of the entire audience moment by moment throughout the commercial, affording the researchers a detailed breakdown of reactions to every aspect of the commercial.

Figure 24–1 Quick, inexpensive research (street interview lasting from 5 to 10 minutes by Penthouse U., Inc.,) was used to determine the validity of an idea for pet insurance. Some 200 dog owners were shown this full-page newspaper layout. They were asked about the price they would be willing to pay for such a program and the extent of coverage they thought it should provide.

Live telecast tests

Television commercials may be tested under normal viewing conditions, thereby allowing the advertiser to avoid the problems associated with the artificiality of forced exposure. These tests, also called "on-air" or "in-the-market" tests, are conducted by substituting test commercials for regular commercials on established TV programs. They may be conducted on closed-circuit television, CATV stations, or nonnetwork UHF stations. After test commercials are shown, viewers are often interviewed by phone for their reactions. The effectiveness of commercials also may be measured by conducting sales audits at stores in the areas where the commercials were run. Another method using "matched" cities that have CATV consists of running identical test commercials in each city, then phoning each sample of viewers to measure their recall of the test commercials. Although on-air pretesting is costly, it may eliminate the high costs of preparing ineffective commercials since it can be used to test all aspects of advertisement development prior to the making of the commercial. Some agencies, for example, pretest commercials by showing *animatic films,* which are filmed storyboards with an accompanying soundtrack (Figure 24–3).

Other pretesting techniques

Additional pretesting techniques in common use are sales experiments, direct-mail tests, and physiological testing. Psychological testing is also used. Since we discussed those methods in Chapter 8, however we will not repeat ourselves here.

Sales experiments

Another method of pretesting the effectiveness of advertisements is the *sales-area test.* This consists of running one or more ads on a small scale before implementing the entire campaign, with its major costs, in the total marketing area. This test can be used to evaluate the comparative impact of alternative advertising themes, appeals, or copy approaches, as well as different budgeting and scheduling strategies.

Prior to the test two or more different, comparable market areas are selected. These may be two groups of cities. Each market area is checked to determine product sales under normal conditions. The alternative advertisements, say, are then run in these market areas for a prescribed period, usually from one to four months. The volume of attributable sales is checked in each market area to determine which advertisement has been most effective. This test is valid only for advertising that is designed to motivate immediate sales response and for products that are purchased frequently, where the influence of advertising can exert itself rapidly.

Figure 24–2 Consumers push buttons in a hand-held device according to their reactions (positive, negative, etc.) to the picture shown on TV.

The sales-area test requires careful, precise planning and implementation to produce valid results. Selecting matched market areas, maintaining comparable conditions in these areas, and making proper corrective allowances when these conditions vary are vital. This test takes longer than other forms of pretesting. It can be very costly. It also alerts competitors to the promotional activities of the advertiser. They can then revise their promotions in these markets to create unusual or changed conditions that may cloud or confuse the test results.

A greater danger is that a competitor may copy or even improve the test product and bring this product to market before the advertiser's product. Some large companies have actually sent research teams into another firm's test markets to conduct surveys to measure the results of the test. They have then used these findings to aid their own decisions. For these reasons other forms of pretesting are frequently used to check advertising themes or messages, and the sales-area test is then used as the final check on the material selected.

Another form of sales experiments used in pretesting is tests designed to measure copy effectiveness. In one such test, called the *blind product test,* containers of the product with their identifying marks masked or removed are grouped side by side on a table in a store. Behind each group is a card that bears different descriptive copy. The copy that sells the most merchandise is presumed to be the most effective.

These tests provide some insights into the sales effectiveness of alternative copy approaches and may help to eliminate totally ineffective or unbelievable appeals. At best, however, these tests are little more than a preliminary step in advertising evaluation because they are not based on normal, real-life exposure.

Direct-mail tests

Mail-order advertisers frequently pretest the effectiveness of two or more alternative advertisements by mailing each ad to different prospects on their mailing lists. By keying each ad, usually with a different reply address, they can record the number of orders each produces. The ad that generates the largest volume of orders is presumed to be the most effective.

A variation of this is the method used to pretest advertising copy approaches by direct mail. In this test the alternate approaches are condensed and printed on a postcard, letter, or other type of mailer. All these mailers make the same free offer. They are mailed to a large

ANIMATIC	FINISHED COMMERCIAL
1. ANNCR: (VO) The legendary Jeep vehicles	1. (MUSIC UNDER) ANNCR: (VO) The legendary Jeep vehicles.
2. have been putting out forest fires...	2. They've been transporting troops...
3. transporting troops...	3. delivering mail...
4. delivering mail...	4. weathering storms...

Figure 24–3 Compton Advertising Inc.'s television commercial for AMC Jeep began as an animatic (left). Modifications from the original concept are evident in frames from the finished commercial storyboard (right). Commercials can be tested at any of six stages from drawn storyboard with tape soundtrack to finished on-air executions.

representative sample of consumers of the product. The mailer that elicits the greatest consumer response is presumed to feature the most effective copy.

The key advantage of this test is that it measures action rather than opinion. It also minimizes variables since all the consumers receive the message at essentially the same time under the same conditions. It is a relatively inexpensive test to conduct. Also, it measures only general appeal. It does not necessarily follow that the most effective copy approach in mail promotion will be most effective for the mass media. Too, it probably would not be a valid test of copy appeals to building product image rather than to stimulate direct action.

Physiological testing

Physiological methods of pretesting are designed to measure unconscious rather than conscious responses. The researcher here is interested in what the subject *does* as a response to the advertisement rather than what he or she says about it. Furthermore, the researcher wants to know the speed, frequency, and amplitude of these responses.

The most common methods of physiological testing use sophisticated equipment to record the subject's physical responses. These include pupilometric devices, eye-movement cameras, galvanometers, and tachistoscopes. Recently some use has even been made of electroencephalographs.

Pupilometric devices Developed by Eckhard Hess and James Polk, this method is based on the theory that the pupil dilates when interesting or appealing visual stimuli are viewed. The method involves measuring the dilation of the pupil of the subject's eye by instrument. The subject is initially exposed to a neutral or control slide for 10 seconds and then to a test stimulus slide for 10 seconds. The subject's left eye is photographed with an eye camera at the rate of two exposures per second. The percentage change that occurs in the pupil diameter between the two exposures is presumed to indicate the subject's reaction to the illustration. This method has been used to evaluate advertisements, graphic designs, and packages as well as to test various art approaches for subjects about which the respondent may be embarrassed to answer questions, such as feminine hygiene.

Eye-movement camera The eye camera is the only totally accurate means of determining what people look at in an advertisement and how much of the copy they read. It is used chiefly to track the subject's eye movement over the layout and copy of advertisements (Figure 24–4). The route that the subject's eye travels is superimposed over the advertisement to show the paths it has taken and the areas that have attracted and held attention. The eye-movement camera has been used to obtain information on the placement of headlines, the proper length of copy for a given advertisement, and the most satisfactory ad layout.

Galvanometer This method is used to measure changes in body responses as the subject looks at an advertisement. A zinc electrode is attached to the subject's palm and another to the forearm. A 25-milliampere current is then passed through the subject, in at the palm and out at the elbow. When the subject reacts to the advertisement, his or her sweat gland activity increases, electric resistance decreases, and the current passes through faster. These changes are recorded on a revolving drum apparatus (Figure 24–5). it is assumed that the more tension an advertisement creates, the more effective it is likely to be. The galvanometer is best used for testing advertisements for products about which people have strong feelings, such as those designed to combat body odor or bad breath.

Tachistoscope This device is used to measure the physical perception of the subject under varying conditions of speed, exposure, and illumination. It controls the subject's exposure to an advertising message so that the researcher can tell at what point it is perceived. The researcher can thereby learn how long it takes respondents to get the intended point of the headline, body text, and illustration. The device also helps to reveal which of two or more alternative advertising layouts communicates the message faster.

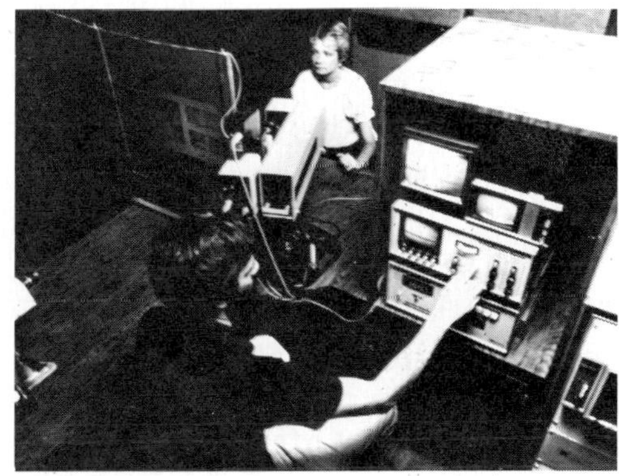

Figure 24–4 The eye-movement camera used in perceptual research can record the manner in which people look at an advertisement. This type of research aids advertisers in adjusting the layout of reading matter and illustrations for maximum legible effect and clarity.

Problems and opportunities with pretesting techniques

By now it should be obvious that there is no one best way to pretest advertising variables. Different methods have been devised to test for different aspects of effectiveness. But each of the methods devised has its own peculiar set of advantages and disadvantages.

Some of the methods we have presented are referred to as *laboratory methods*—where consumers are brought individually or in a group into a studio or auditorium. Laboratory testing offers the advantages of speed, economy, and a high degree of control. The researcher knows for sure that the subject has seen the test advertisement and in fact can control the way respondents are exposed to it. Responses can be measured immediately, and often some information is produced that would be unavailable in other settings. The validity of laboratory findings, though, may be highly questionable since forced exposure in a laboratory setting does not equate with real life.

Field testing, which may actually take place in the respondent's home or in a public place, like a shopping center, still suffers from artificiality. Just as in the laboratory setting, the subject's response is actually a combination of the reaction to the test as well as to the advertisement.

Sales experiments, live telecasts, and direct-mail tests can actually approximate real-life conditions while still offering the necessary controls for experimentation. However, the depth of information available from these methods is usually more limited.

Thus, there are endless trade-offs. Although pretesting is generally conceded to be valuable in distinguishing very strong advertisements from very weak ones, there is still much controversy about the validity of other research findings. Most advertisers, however, are still interested in finding out whether an advertisement is interesting, believable, comprehensible, and memorable to the consumer. Verbatim responses from test subjects can even provide some useful copy ideas, and the contact with consumers can provide the advertiser or agency with beneficial information on consumer buying habits.

Still, there are many limitations to pretesting, and the advertiser should be aware of them. Besides the fact that the test itself is an artificial situation, the test respondents are not typical prospects since most of them tend to assume the role of experts or critics and to give answers that may not reflect their real buying behavior. Consumers who do not have strong opinions about the advertisement shown are likely to invent opinions on the spur of the moment to satisfy the interviewer. Some do not want to admit they could be influenced by the advertisement. Others may try to please the interviewer by voting for the advertisements they feel they *should* like, rather than those they actually do like. Such tests give no indication that the advertisement selected by the consumer as "best" is *really* effective or actually superior to the other ads shown.

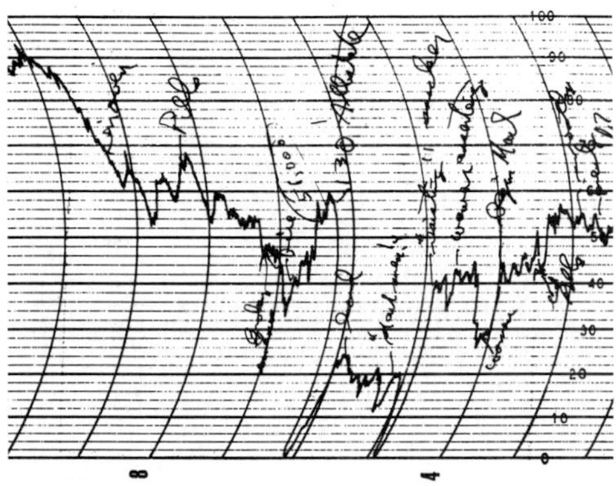

Figure 24–5 A galvanometer chart records the changes in bodily responses as a reviewer watches a television commercial. The greater the response, the more effective the commercial. At least, that is the assumption.

Research has also found that when multiple opinions are sought on alternative advertisements—such as on their interest, personal pertinence, credibility, and comprehensibility—consumers are likely to rank the one or two ads that make the best first impression as the highest in all these categories. This is called the *halo effect.* Also, while the most relevant area of such tests may be questions about the respondent's ultimate buying behavior, responses in this area may be the least valid. Behavior intent, in other words, may not become behavior fact. Most consumer tests are designed to disclose the consumer's opinions and his or her liking and understanding of the advertising message—not whether it will induce attitude change or ultimate purchase.

Posttesting techniques

After an ad or a campaign has run, tests of advertising effectiveness may be conducted. The objective is to determine what awareness or attitude changes have been achieved and what impact the advertising has had on sales results. The most common posttesting techniques fall into five broad categories: aided recall, unaided recall, attitude tests, inquiry tests, and sales tests. Each of these has distinct advantages and limitations.

Aided recall (recognition/readership)

The first recognition or readership tests were conducted many years ago and described in detail by Daniel Starch in his *Principles of Advertising* (Chicago: A.W. Shaw, 1923). Since that time, the Starch Readership Test has become one of the most widely used methods of posttesting print advertising. Its objective is simply to determine how many readers of a given publication have seen and read the advertisement.

Interviewers throughout the United States are supplied with copies of a current issue of the magazine to be tested. These interviewers promptly locate 100–150 women and 100–150 men who have seen the publication. The exact numbers are dictated by the geographic distribution of the magazine's circulation. Interviews begin soon after the sale date of the magazine. The interviewer goes through an unmarked copy of the magazine with the respondents, page by page, and asks them to indicate the ads they have read. The tests may be started at different points in the magazine so that each ad will catch an equal proportion of fresh and tired respondents. When ads are a half-page or larger, respondents are asked whether they saw the headline, the text, the illustration, and other components. No respondent is asked to commit himself or herself on more than 100 ads. The respondents are then classified into the following groups, stated as percentages: "Noted," those who recall seeing a specific advertisement; "Associated," those who saw or read an ad sufficiently to associate the advertiser's name or brand name with it; and "Read Most," those who read half or more of the ad's copy (Figure 24–6).

The results of this test, according to the Starch organization, can be used to answer the following questions: To what extent is an advertisement seen and read? Is an advertiser's current ad better read than previous ones? Are an advertiser's ads better read than those of competitors? Is the reading of a current advertising campaign increasing or decreasing? How can an advertiser tell his or her story so that it will be better read?

Unaided recall

The unaided recall test is intended to measure the penetration of an advertisement. It is more demanding than an aided recall test since respondents are questioned about what they have seen or read *without* having the advertisement in front of them.

The Gallup & Robinson Impact Studies of magazine and television advertisements, for example, ask respondents to recall and describe advertisements they have seen. The only aid given to assist recall is the name of the advertiser. Respondents are asked to tell what the ad looks like, what it says about the product, its key selling points, and whether it made the respondent want to buy the product. Further questions seek to determine whether the respondent is a prospect for the product advertised. The test measures the impression the ad had on the respondents and its meaning to them.

From these findings, three levels of effectiveness are indicated:

1. Proved name registration (PNR) score, which measures the ability of the ad to compel viewer attention and to register the name of the advertiser.
2. Idea communication score, which measures the degree to which viewers who recall an ad can play back the ideas contained in it.
3. Favorable attitude score, which measures expressions of favor toward the advertiser, the message, or the product.

A similar approach used for posttesting television commercials is the "day-after" recall measuring service of the Burke Research Corporation. The day after a commercial has aired, Burke telephone interviewers survey a sample of TV viewers. Their questions seek to measure the extent of brand name recognition among these viewers and their recall of the salient selling points in the commercial. (See the Ad Lab.)

Similar but broader in scope are the Total Prime Time (TPT) Studies conducted by the Gallup & Robinson organization. A sample of TV viewers is asked to recall their television viewing pattern for the previous evening. Their recall of commercials is probed with regard to sales points and persuasiveness. Two scores, commercial recognition (CR) and proved commercial registration (PCR), are reported for every commercial seen during prime time.

The triple associates test developed by Henry C. Link is chiefly

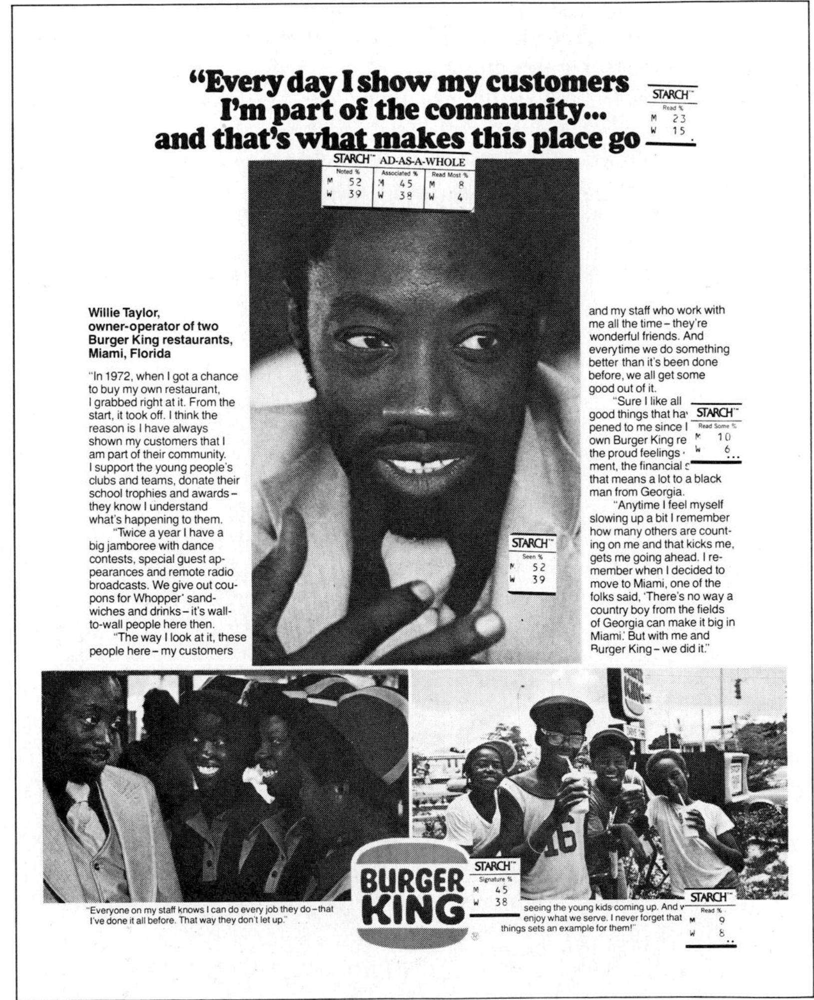

Figure 24–6 A Starch readership report includes a copy of the magazine that has been rated. In this advertisement from *Ebony* is a label that shows ad-as-a-whole and component-part readership (headline, illustration, copy).

used to measure the depth of impression of a sales theme or slogan on consumers. A sample question might be: Which airline advertises "Fly the friendly skies"? The respondent thus has two associates: the type of company and the slogan. It is up to the respondent to supply the third—namely, United Airlines. (See Figure 24–7.)

Should 200 viewers' memories decide whether ads live or die?

Advertisers spent $75 million last year to produce an estimated 4,000 television commercials that will never be seen on the tube. They were duds. In many cases, their debut was also their funeral because 200 consumers participating in a "day-after recall" test couldn't remember seeing them.

Simple? A little too simple, argues Young & Rubicam, the largest U.S. ad agency, which is urging clients to stop depending so heavily on recall tests. Warns Joseph T. Plummer, the agency's research director: "If we rely more on a single-number measure like day-after recall, the effectiveness of advertising will diminish over time." Mr. Plummer calls the technique a "rubber ruler" that often provides unreliable and inconsistent measurements. Like other critics, he also charges that the test results are abused by marketers looking for an easy answer to the difficult question of how well an ad works.

The recall test is the leading method used by advertisers and their agencies to determine whether new commercials—each of which can take months of effort and $50,000 or more to create—are good enough to be shown. In attacking recall, Young & Rubicam is also challenging the cherished beliefs of some of its own major clients, including Procter & Gamble, General Foods, and Johnson & Johnson.

Recall tests are used by marketers who believe that commercials must be memorable to be effective. The tests are relatively uncomplicated, inexpensive, and quick. The leading provider is Burke Marketing Research, Cincinnati, which tested about 1,500 commercials last year at a cost of $4,000 to $4,500 each.

The typical Burke test is made the night after the commercial is shown once during prime time on stations in three cities. Telephone interviewers dial 5,000 to 6,000 numbers to find 200 people who saw the commercial and are willing to talk about it.

The result, phoned to the anxious advertiser and its ad agency by noon the next day, is a single score ranging from zero to 100 that represents the percentage of the commercial's audience that remembers the ad after being given certain clues. The average is 24.

More detailed results—including verbatim comments from consumers and recall scores for specific elements of the commercial—are sent later, but the "top line" or "flash" score is the lightning rod of the recall controversy. "People are looking for a magic number that'll free them from decision-making," says Shirley Young, executive vice president of Grey Advertising. "Those who will defy the numbers are few and far between."

Young & Rubicam critique emphasizes what it claims are other faults of recall tests. One issue is reliability. The agency found that when commercials were retested, scores varied; one spot scored an eight on its first try but a 21 on its second. Scores may also be affected by the type of TV program that carries the commercial.

Certain types of commercials are better than others. Highly structured ads that communicate specific product advantages typically rate higher than "mood" commercials, such as a Pepsi-Cola ad that scored only four. "It's very difficult for consumers to articulate an image message," says an ad executive at Pepsi, which doesn't use recall tests for its cola commercials.

Burke's Mr. Siebert also rejects criticism of recall tests, saying that many marketers overestimate the test's power. "We never said it does everything," he maintains. "The best place to measure the effectiveness of advertising is at the cash register, but that is very difficult to do."

Many advertisers say they'll stick with recall unless a more effective test is demonstrated. Criticizing recall "is as constructive as saying 'I don't like Monday,' " says John R. Andrews, marketing research director at General Foods. "We just can't throw recall out. We've got to find something better."

Laboratory application

Should 200 viewers' memories decide whether ads live or die?

Attitude tests

Attitude measurement tests usually seek to measure the effectiveness of an advertising campaign in creating a favorable image for a company, its brand, or its products (Figure 24–8). It is presumed that favorable changes in attitude predispose consumers to buy the company's product. The key factors attitude tests are designed to measure are consumers' general assessments of a given company, product, or brand, and their preference for, loyalty to, acceptance of, or intention to buy a given product or brand. The tests also seek to measure the comparative ratings of the company and competitors with regard to products, services, and other attributes.

These tests are often conducted in conjunction with consumer awareness or recall tests. The Starch organization, for example, conducts ad impression studies because after an advertiser has learned from readership data whether or not the advertisement succeeded in

1. Unpleasant messages are learned as easily as pleasant messages.
2. Meaningful messages are learned more easily than unmeaningful messages.
3. Ideational learning is faster if massive advertising is followed by distributed advertising.
4. Products requiring mechanical skills are learned best if demonstrated in the ad as though the consumers were doing the task themselves.
5. Product benefits are learned best when presented at the beginning and end of a message.
6. Messages which are unique or unusual are better remembered than commonplace advertisements.
7. Rewarding the consumer who attends to a message enhances learning of the message.
8. Learning by consumers is enhanced when they are told the benefits they will receive from using the product.
9. Active participation in the message enhances learning.
10. Message learning is faster if previous or following messages do not interfere.
11. Repetition strengthens an older idea more than a newer idea.
12. Messages presented closer in time to an intense need are learned faster than those which are presented when the need is weaker.
13. The greater reward a consumer perceives from viewing (or listening to) an ad message, the faster his learning of the message.
14. The less effort required to respond to an ad, the faster learning occurs.
15. The more complex an ad message, the more difficult to learn.

Figure 24–7 Facilitating retention in advertising. While advertisers continue to seek ways to measure advertising effectiveness, M. Wayne DeLozier has compiled a basic list of what does and doesn't work from his own research. While some may appear rather obvious (number 15), any time is the right time to review the basics.

attracting a satisfactory number of readers, the next logical questions are: Is the reader more favorably disposed toward the company, product, or service? What does the ad message mean to readers? Did the ad influence them, and do these readers now want to have the product or service or invest in the company?

In attitude tests a variety of measurement techniques are used, ranging from direct questions (Do you intend to buy this product?) to wholly unstructured questions or depth interviews. The semantic differential test (see Chapter 8) is sometimes used to measure changes in respondents' attitudes after an advertising campaign.

Inquiry tests

Another method that can be used to measure the comparative effectiveness of two or more advertisements is to count the number of inquiries each produces. To do this, the test advertisements must contain identical offers to send something to the reader on request. In print advertisements, this offer may be a coupon to be filled in and mailed, or it may be hidden in the text of the ad so that the reader must read the copy to find the offer.

Broadcast commercials can also be designed to elicit viewer or listener response. These "offers" should not be confused with mail-order advertisements since they do not require the purchase of a product. They may simply offer additional product information, product samples, or premiums. By coding the reply addresses (e.g., Dept. 113) or telephone numbers (e.g., Ext. 701), the advertiser can determine which advertisement generated the most responses. The cost of an advertisement can be divided by the number of inquiries it brings to learn the cost per inquiry, a significant factor if the advertisement is to be used to develop sales leads or produce direct orders.

Sales tests

Several posttesting methods are used to obtain information on the sales-producing value of specific advertisements or whole campaigns. These methods are of six general types: measures of past sales, controlled experiments, matched samples of consumers, mail-order selling, consumer purchase tests, and store inventory audits.

Measures of past sales

Most consumer product manufacturers market items through retail stores. To correlate advertising with sales, they obtain data from research organizations on product sales by brand name and area. They then compare their advertising efforts with sales in the area, seeking to interpret these figures in the light of other variables.

Controlled experiments (field studies)

Most field studies seek to determine the desirability of change in one of four aspects of marketing: price of the product, advertising weight, advertising media, or advertising copy. The simplest, most common form of field study evaluates a proposed change by conducting an experiment in two markets that are closely matched in demographic characteristics, shopping patterns, and media habits. One of these is designated the *control market.* The existing advertising and marketing efforts are continued intact in this market. In the other market, des-

BRC

Please look over these pictures and words from a TV commercial and answer the questions on the right.

(Woman #1) My dog is so big ... we just built him a two-story dog house.

(Singing) brand name dog food, * If you've got a big dog.

(Boy) My dog is so big ... we see eye to eye on everything.

(Singing) brand name dog food, If you've got a big dog.

(Man) Introducing new brand name. The only dog food made for the special nutritional needs of big dogs. Growth food for large-breed puppies and adult food for large-breed adults.

(Woman with sheep dog) My dog is so big ... (rolls over and laughs)

(Singing) brand name dog food, If you've got a big dog.

Do you remember seeing this commercial on TV?

7-1 ☐ Yes -2 ☐ No -3 ☐ Not sure-I may have

How interested are you in what this commercial is trying to tell you or show you about the product? Would you say you were:

8-1 ☐ Very interested -2 ☐ Somewhat interested -3 ☐ Not interested

Please check any of the following if you feel they describe this commercial.

9-1 ☐ Amusing
-2 ☐ Appealing
-3 ☐ Clever
-4 ☐ Convincing
-5 ☐ Dull
-6 ☐ Easy to forget
-7 ☐ Effective
-8 ☐ Gentle
-9 ☐ Imaginative
-0 ☐ Informative

10-1 ☐ Interesting
-2 ☐ Irritating
-3 ☐ Lively
-4 ☐ Original
-5 ☐ Phony
-6 ☐ Pointless
-7 ☐ Silly
-8 ☐ Uninteresting
-9 ☐ Well done
-0 ☐ Worth remembering

* We have blocked out the name. Do you remember which brand was being advertised?

11-1 ☐ Hero
-2 ☐ Mighty Dog
-3 ☐ Mainstay
-4 ☐ Don't know

Do you have:

12-1 ☐ A large dog
-2 ☐ A small dog
-3 ☐ No dogs

13-

Figure 24–8 Bruzzone Research Company uses a direct-mail questionnaire to evaluate recall and attitude toward a dog food commercial in this example. The questionnaires are sent to 1,000 households throughout the country which are chosen at random from either auto registrations or telephone listings. Clients for this service include General Motors, Gillette, Holiday Inns, and Polaroid.

ignated the *test market,* the factor being considered for change is altered. For example, newspaper advertising may be replaced with radio advertising. Sales are then closely audited in both markets.

Matched consumer samples

Just as markets can be matched and then divided into control and test markets, two or more groups of consumers can be closely matched in demographic characteristics such as age, education, and occupation. Group members can also be selected so that all the members of one group have seen the advertiser's message and all the members of the other group have not. The excess of product purchases by the first group over those by the second group may then be attributed to the advertiser's message.

Matched consumer samples of this type are frequently surveyed through CATV. One research organization, AdTel, uses a dual-cable CATV system and surveys two matched consumer panels representing 1,000 households each. Members of these panels regularly record their product purchases in diaries provided. The results of specific commercial copy or intensity are measured by the volume of purchases recorded.

Mail-order selling

Sales results can be measured directly through a mail-order test. This resembles an inquiry test, except that it asks the consumer to *buy* a product by mail rather than merely to write for further information. The sales results of a mail-order advertising effort provide a useful measure of advertising effectiveness.

Consumer purchase tests

These tests are intended to measure the retail sales of a product that result from a given advertising campaign. Such a campaign is normally run in newspapers and regional editions of magazines. Spot radio and TV commercials may also be used. A random sampling of consumers is surveyed to determine how many of them bought the product prior to the campaign, how frequently they have bought it, how much of it they have bought, and how much of the product they still have on hand. After the campaign they are surveyed again to measure the percentage change in purchases of the product immediately following the campaign. An alternate technique is to supply these consumers with diaries in which they are to record all product purchases. That assumes, of course, that there is a known market for the product. Advertising cannot be blamed if there is no market for the advertiser's product.

Consumer purchasing data are available from research organizations such as Market Research Corporation of America. The MRCA National Consumer Panel provides information on consumer buying in terms of the number of households purchasing, size of transaction, quantity purchased, price, type of retail outlet shopped, package size, brand, and varieties. The MRCA consumer sample consists of 7,500 households, which are supplied with diaries for this purpose.

Store inventory audits

The store audit is another measure of sales results. It involves conducting an inventory of retailers' stocks before and after an advertising campaign. Such an audit generally includes not only the advertiser's brand but competitors's brands as well. After the pre-advertising inventory, periodic inventories can be made throughout the advertising campaign to check both the cumulative product sales and the trend of these sales. Post-campaign inventories may be done for some time to test the longevity of the advertising impact and to determine whether a lasting increase in product consumption has resulted.

One organization that does tests of this type is Audits & Surveys, Inc., which conducts a continuous nationwide audit of product sales, inventories, purchases, and product distribution in all types of retail stores.

Problems and opportunities of posttesting techniques

Each posttesting category mentioned above offers unique opportunities for advertisers to study the impact of their advertising campaigns. However, each also has definite limitations that should be understood.

Recall tests

Recall tests are designed to measure specific behavior, not opinions or attitudes. They test advertising under natural conditions of exposure, so they are very helpful in determining whether advertisements are being read, how well they are pulling compared with competitors' ads, and the extent to which they have implanted ideas in consumers' minds. They indicate whether consumers got the point of the advertiser's message. They also can yield useful data on the relative effectiveness of different advertising components, such as size, color, or attention-getting themes. Aided recall tests are fairly simple to conduct, and they can be relatively inexpensive when their cost is borne in part by the media studied.

Recall tests do not measure advertising effect, however, but only what has been noticed, read, or watched. And readership or audience does not necessarily mean product sales. Although more audience members than nonmembers may ultimately buy the product, it does not necessarily follow that the advertisement was the sole motivating force. Recall tests are subject to the variations of individual memory. Some respondents have better memories than others. Some are better able to express what they remember. Respondents are often confused. Some may say they saw an ad merely to impress the interviewer. The techniques used may also encourage guessing.

Attitude tests

Attitude tests are often a better measure of sales effectiveness than recall tests because an attitude change relates more closely to the purchase of the product. Such tests are fairly easy to conduct. They are low in cost because they can be made by phone or mail.

On the other hand, human attitudes represent a complex mix of feelings. Most researchers do not agree on precisely what an attitude is and what is to be measured. Many people find it difficult to determine their attitudes as well as to express them. Deeply entrenched attitudes, like those shaped by religious or philosophical beliefs, are resistant to change even by highly aggressive advertising efforts. Finally, a favorable attitude does not necessarily mean ultimate purchase of the advertiser's product or service.

Inquiry tests

Inquiry tests are fairly easy to conduct. They enable the advertiser to test the attention-getting value of advertisements as well as their readability and understandability. They also permit fairly good control of the variables that motivate reader action, particularly if a split-run test is used. Unlike some methods, the inquiry test can be effective in testing small advertisements.

Unfortunately, though, inquiry tests are valid only when applied to advertisements that can logically make use of an offer to elicit inquiries. When applied to an ad with more indirect purposes, it is questionable whether inquiry tests actually measure the ad's effectiveness or merely its ability to attract inquiries. Such inquiries, in fact, may not even reflect a sincere interest in the product or its purchase. Finally, inquiry tests can be time-consuming since the responses to a magazine offer, for example, may take months to receive.

Sales tests

Since the optimum goal of most advertisers is increased sales, sales tests are logically popular. Unquestionably, sales tests can be a useful measure of advertising effectiveness when advertising is the dominant element, or the only variable, in the company's marketing plan.

Heavy reliance on sales tests has definite pitfalls. It is often difficult to gauge to what extent advertising has been responsible for sales since there are usually many other variables that affect sales volume, such as competitors' activities, the season of the year, and even the weather. Sales response to advertising is usually long range rather than immediate. Sales tests, and particularly field studies, are often costly and time-consuming. And, finally, most of them are useful only for testing complete campaigns, not individual advertisements or the components of an advertisement.

Summary

Advertisers want to know what they are getting for their money—whether their advertising works. Testing is the primary instrument advertisers use to provide some assurance that their advertising dollars are spent wisely.

Pretesting is used to detect and eliminate weaknesses or flaws that may inhibit the success of an advertising campaign. Several advertising variables may be evaluated in pretesting. These include the advertisers' markets, consumer motives, advertising messages, media decisions, advertising budgets, and the way advertisements are scheduled.

Posttesting is used to evaluate the effectiveness of an advertisement or the results of a campaign after it has run. The variables that can be readily evaluated in posttesting are the markets, messages, media, and overall results.

There are many techniques used in pretesting. The most important consideration is that the test be valid, reliable, and relevant.

Methods used to test print advertisements are order-of-merit tests, paired comparison tests, portfolio tests, mock magazine tests, direct questioning, and perceptual meaning studies.

To test broadcast advertisements, the most common methods are in-home projection tests, trailer tests, theater tests, and live telecasts.

Other pretesting techniques include sales experiments, direct-mail tests, psychological tests, and physiological tests. Physiological testing involves the use of sophisticated equipment to record a subject's responses. These include pupilometric devices, eye-movement cameras, galvanometers, and tachistoscopes.

There are numerous problems as well as opportunities with the various pretesting techniques. Often the validity of laboratory findings is suspect due to the forced exposure of advertisements on consumers. In fact, artificiality is the greatest problem with most pretesting techniques. Most advertisers, though, still find pretesting valuable for discovering whether an advertisement is interesting, believable, comprehensible, and memorable to the consumer.

The most commonly used posttesting techniques are aided recall, unaided recall, attitude tests, inquiry tests, and sales tests. Each has opportunities and limitations. Recall tests, for example, can be useful for measuring the readership and memorability of advertisements, but they do not measure the effect of the advertising. Attitude tests are a better measure of sales effectiveness. However, attitudes represent a complex mix of human feelings, which may be resistant to change even by aggressive advertising efforts.

Inquiry tests can be useful in measuring the readability and comprehension of advertisements. However, they are valid only when applied to advertising that can make use of an offer to elicit inquiries. Sales tests are the most popular with advertisers since sales are the ultimate goal. However, advertising is only one of many variables that may be responsible for sales. Therefore, sales tests are useful only for complete campaigns, not for individual advertisements.

Questions for review

1. What areas of advertising are workable for pretesting?
2. In advertising testing, what is the difference between evaluating and diagnosing?
3. What is the difference between the order-of-merit test and the paired comparison test?
4. What are the problems with direct questioning pretests?
5. How might a controlled sales experiment work?
6. What is the difference between a pupilometric device and an eye-movement camera?
7. What do sweaty palms have to do with advertising testing?
8. What is the difference between aided recall and unaided recall?
9. What methods may be used to survey matched consumer samples?
10. What are the opportunities and limitations of inquiry tests?

References

Chapter 1

1. "A New Look for Coca-Cola. A Synopsis of the 70's," Coca-Cola Company, July 1970.
2. Stanley M. Ulanoff, *Advertising in America* (New York: Hastings House, 1977), p. 27.
3. David A. Aaker and John G. Myers, *Advertising Management* (Englewood Cliffs, N.J.: Prentice-Hall, 1975), pp. 559–560.
4. *The Borden Co.* v. *FTC,* 381F. 2d 175, 5th Cir., 1967.
5. Walter Taplin, *Advertising: A New Approach* (Boston: Little, Brown, 1963), p. 106.
6. Charles Yang, "Variations in the Cyclical Behavior of Advertising," *Journal of Marketing,* April 1964, pp. 25–30.

Chapter 2

1. "Afterword," *Madison Avenue,* May 1980, p. 98.
2. Vivian Gornich and Barbara K. Moran, *Women in Sexist Society* (New York: New American Library, 1971), p. 304.

Chapter 3

1. Christian McAdams, "Frank Perdue Is Chicken!" *Esquire,* April 1973, pp. 113–17. Copyright © 1973 by Esquire Publishing, Inc.

Chapter 4

1. "Coors," *Batesworld,* Summer 1979, pages unnumbered.
2. Frederic R. Gamble, *What Advertising Agencies Are—What They Do and How They Do It,* 7th ed. (New York: American Association of Advertising Agencies, 1970), p. 4.
3. Ibid., p. 5.
4. Ibid., pp. 6 and 7.
5. *Communication Arts,* April 1973, pages unnumbered.
6. Franchellie Cadwell and Herman Davis, "Why Is It That Ad Agencies Don't Advertise?," *Advertising Age,* November 19, 1979, p. 51.

Chapter 5

1. "Ted Turner Tackles TV News," *Newsweek,* June 16, 1980, pp. 58–66. Copyright 1980 by Newsweek, Inc. All rights reserved. Reprinted by permission
2. *Current Biography,* 1979, pp. 408–411.
3. "Ted Turner Tackles TV News," p. 58.
4. "The Cable Challenge," *Marketing Communications,* March 1979, pp. 50–53.
5. Dik W. Twedt, *Survey of Marketing Research* (Chicago: American Marketing Association, 1973), pp. 41–44.

Chapter 6

1. "Volks Called Biggest Success; Edsel Gets Booby Prize," *Advertising Age,* April 30, 1980, pp. 130–132.
2. Louis E. Boone and David L. Kurtz, *Contemporary Marketing,* 3rd ed. (Hinsdale, Ill.: Dryden Press, 1980), pp. 142–144. Copyright © 1980 by The Dryden Press, a division of Holt, Rinehart & Winston. Reprinted by permission.
3. Ibid., p. 199.
4. Philip Kotler, *Principles of Marketing* (Englewood Cliffs, N.J.: Prentice-Hall, 1980), p. 48. © 1980 Prentice-Hall, Inc. Adapted by permission.
5. Boone and Kurtz, *Contemporary Marketing,* pp. 207–208.
6. Bert C. McCammon, Jr., *Marketing and Economic Development* (Chicago: American Marketing Association, 1965), pp. 496–515.

Chapter 7

1. Abraham H. Maslow, *Motivation and Personality,* 2d ed. (New York: Harper & Row, 1970), pp. 39–51. Copyright © 1970 by Abraham H. Maslow. By permission of Harper & Row, Publishers, Inc.
2. Ben M. Enis, *Marketing Principles* (Santa Monica, Cal.: Goodyear Publishing, 1980), p. 287.
3. Edward L. Grubb and Gregg Hupp, "Perception of Self-Generalized Stereotypes and Brand Selection," *Journal of Marketing Research,* February 1968, pp. 58–63.
4. Bibi Wein, "Psychographics," *Omni,* July 1980, p. 97.
5. Edmund Faison, *Advertising: A Behavioral Approach for Managers* (New York: John Wiley & Sons, 1980), p. 132.
6. Leon Festinger, *A Theory of Cognitive Dissonance* (Evanston, Ill.: Row, Peterson, 1957), p. 83.
7. Burton Marcus et al., *Modern Marketing Management* (New York: Random House, 1980), p. 83.

Copyright © by Random House, Inc. Reprinted by permission of Random House, Inc.

8. Harold W. Berkman and Christopher C. Gilson, *Consumer Behavior* (Encino, Cal.: Dickenson Publishing, 1978), pp. 226–227.
9. Marcus, *Modern Marketing Management,* p. 86.
10. Peter W. Bernstein, "Psychographics Is Still an Issue on Madison Avenue," *Fortune,* January 16, 1978, pp. 78–84.
11. Everett Rogers, *Diffusion of Innovations* (New York: Free Press, 1962), pp. 168–171.
12. Joseph T. Plummer, "Life Style Patterns and Commercial Bank Credit Card Usage." *Journal of Marketing,* April 1971, pp. 35–41.
13. Philip Kotler, *Principles of Marketing* (Englewood Cliffs, N.J.: Prentice-Hall, 1980), p. 32. © 1980 Prentice-Hall, Inc. Adapted by permission.
14. Ibid., p. 304.
15. William D. Wells and Douglas J. Tigert, "Activities, Interests and Opinions," *Journal of Marketing Research,* August 1971, pp. 27–35.
16. Louis E. Boone and David L. Kurtz, *Contemporary Marketing* (Hinsdale, Ill.: Dryden Press, 1980), pp. 91–92. Copyright © 1980 by The Dryden Press, a division of Holt, Rinehart & Winston. Reprinted by permission.

Chapter 8

1. Philip Taubman, "The Great Soft Drink Shoot-Out," *Esquire,* March 27, 1979, p. 33. Copyright © 1979 by Esquire Publishing, Inc.
2. Edward Buxton, *Promise Them Anything* (New York: Stein and Day, 1972), pp. 218–219.
3. Taubman, "Great Soft Drink Shoot-Out," p. 33.
4. AMA Committee on Definitions, *Marketing Definitions: A Glossary of Marketing Terms* (Chicago: American Marketing Association, 1963), pp. 16–17.
5. Kenneth Longman, *Advertising* (New York: Harcourt Brace Jovanovich, 1971), pp. 177–178.
6. Taubman, "Great Soft Drink Shoot-Out," p. 36.
7. Ibid., p. 36.
8. Don E. Schultz and Dennis G. Martin, *Strategic Advertising Campaigns* (Chicago: Crain Books, 1979), p. 26.
9. Philip Kotler, *Principles of Marketing* (Englewood Cliffs, N.J.: Prentice-Hall, 1980), p. 145. © Prentice-Hall, Inc. Adapted by permission.
10. Kenneth E. Runyon, *Advertising and the Practice of Marketing* (Columbus, Ohio: Charles E. Merrill Publishing, 1979), p. 108.
11. Taubman, "Great Soft Drink Shoot-Out," p. 37.
12. Robert M. Worcester, ed., *Consumer Market Research Handbook* (London: McGraw-Hill, 1972), p. 7.
13. Kotler, *Principles of Marketing,* p. 146.
14. Charles E. Overholser, "Advertising Strategy from Consumer Research," *Journal of Advertising Research,* November 1971, pp. 3–9.
15. Edmund W. J. Faison, *Advertising: A Behavioral Approach for Managers* (New York: John Wiley & Sons, 1980), pp. 664–665.
16. Ibid., p. 665.
17. Ibid.
18. Taubman, "Great Soft Drink Shoot-Out," p. 37.

Chapter 9

1. Speech by Charles Fredericks, executive vice president, Ogilvy & Mather, before the American Association of Advertising Agencies, Eastern Annual Conference, New York, November 1974.
2. Richard Stansfield, *Advertising Manager's Handbook* (Chicago: Dartnell Corporation, 1969), p. 84.
3. Ibid.
4. Philip Kotler, *Marketing Management: Analysis, Planning, and Control* (Englewood Cliffs, N.J.: Prentice-Hall, 1972), p. 369.
5. Burton Marcus et al., *Modern Marketing Management* (New York: Random House, 1980), p. 556. Copyright © by Random House, Inc. Reprinted by permission of Random House, Inc.
6. E. Jerome McCarthy, *Basic Marketing,* 6th ed. (Homewood, Ill.: Richard D. Irwin, 1978), pp. 35–39.
7. Kotler, *Marketing Management,* p. 89.
8. Kenneth Roman and Jane Maas, *How to Advertise* (New York: St. Martin's Press, 1976), p. 2.
9. Speech by Fredericks.
10. Kotler, *Marketing Management,* pp. 360–370.
11. Russell H. Colley, *Defining Advertising Goals for Measured Advertising Results* (New York: Association of National Advertisers, 1961), p. 1.
12. Speech by Fredericks.
13. Leo Bogart, *Strategy in Advertising* (New York: Harcourt Brace Jovanovich, 1967), p. 28. Reprinted by permission of the author.
14. Ibid., pp. 19–23.

Chapter 10

1. "Spreading the Word," *Advertising Techniques,* September 1979, pp. 31–33; and "International Paper Update," *Advertising Techniques,* March 1980, p. 31.
2. F. Allen Foster, *Advertising: Ancient Market Place to Television* (New York: Criterion Books, 1967), pp. 166–167.
3. David Ogilvy, *Confessions of an Advertising Man* (New York: Atheneum Publishers, 1966), pp. 104–107.
4. Ibid., p. 108.
5. Philip Ward Burton, *Advertising Copywriting* (Columbus, Ohio: Grid, 1974), p. 73. Reprinted with permission from Grid Publishing, Inc., Columbus, Ohio 43214.

Chapter 11

1. Joel G. Cahn, *Print Casebooks 3, 1978–79 Edition, The Best in Advertising* (Washington, D.C.: R. C. Publications, 1978), pp. 78–84.
2. J. Douglas Johnson, *Advertising Today* (Chicago: Science Research Associates, 1978), pp. 91–92.
3. Richard H. Stansfield, *Advertising Manager's Handbook* (Chicago: Dartnell Corporation, 1969), pp. 640–641.
4. Stephen Baker, *Advertising Layout and Art Direction* (New York: McGraw-Hill, 1959), pp. 246–247.

Chapter 12

1. Emmett Murphy, "Louis Grubb," *Communication Arts,* May/June 1980, pp. 58–65.

Chapter 13

1. Harry Wayne McMahan, "Levi's," *Advertising Age,* October 31, 1977, p. 58.
2. Joel G. Cahn, *Print Casebooks 3: 1978–79 Edition, The Best in Advertising* (Washington, D.C.: R. C. Publications, 1978), pp. 34–37.
3. Kenneth Roman and Jane Maas, *How to Advertise* (New York: St. Martin's Press, 1976), pp. 79–81.
4. Albert C. Book and Norman D. Cary, *The Radio and Television Commercial* (Chicago: Crain Books, 1978), p. 18.
5. Milton H. Biow, *Butting In—An Adman Speaks Out* (Garden City, N.Y.: Doubleday, 1964), p. 136.

Chapter 14

1. Walter P. Margulies, *Packaging Power* (New York: World Publishing, 1970), p. 62.
2. Ibid., pp. 62–67.
3. Ibid.
4. "How Well Will It Sell?" *Modern Packaging,* February 1970, p. 101.
5. "Is the Packaging Industry Responsible for Solid Wastes?" *Modern Packaging,* March 1971, pp. 38–41.
6. *Idea Special Issue: Saul Bass and Associates* (Tokyo: Seibundo Shinkosha, 1979), pp. 14–25.
7. *Trademarks Promote U.S. Economic Growth* (New York: U.S. Trademark Association, undated), unnumbered.

Chapter 15

1. "Canon Clicks with AE-1 Camera Campaign," *Marketing Communications,* May 1980, pp. 73–74.
2. "Brand Report 45: Cameras," *Marketing and Media Decisions,* September 1979, pp. 176–177.
3. Kenneth Longman, *Advertising* (New York: Harcourt Brace Jovanovich, 1971), pp. 211–212.
4. Ibid., p. 351.
5. Ibid.
6. Ibid., pp. 207–210.
7. Ibid., pp. 371–372.

Chapter 16

1. "Ad Concepts '79," *Creative Newspaper* (Newspaper Advertising Bureau), 1979, p. 26.
2. Ibid., p. 2.
3. Leo Bogart, "Newspapers Fight Off Broadcast Challenge, Survive and Prosper," *Advertising Age,* April 30, 1980, p. 176.
4. "Ad Concepts '79," p. 8.
5. "Ad Concepts '79," p. 26.
6. *1981 Facts about Newspapers,* p. 7.
7. *Newspaper Rates and Data,* January 12, 1981, pp. 156–757.
8. Bogart, p. 177.
9. Joel G. Cahn, *Print Casebooks 4, 1980–81 Edition, The Best in Advertising* (Washington, D.C.: R. C. Publications, 1980), pp. 38–39.

Chapter 17

1. Joel Cahn, *Print Casebooks 4, 1980–81 Edition, The Best in Advertising* (Washington, D.C.: R. C. Publications, 1980), pp. 26–27.
2. *Nielsen Report on Television 1980* (Chicago: A. C. Nielsen, 1980), pp. 1–9.

Chapter 18

1. Richard Cremer, "Innovation Ward's Key to Successful MO Venture," *Direct Marketing,* April 1980, pp. 76, 78–80, 82, 84, 86, 88.
2. *Direct Marketing,* November 1980, p. 2.
3. Bob Stone, *Successful Direct Marketing Methods* (Chicago: Crain Books, 1979), p. 79.

Chapter 19

1. William A. Robinson, *Best Sales Promotions,* 3d ed. (Chicago: Crain Books, 1979), pp. 40–41.
2. Ibid., pp. 22–23.

Chapter 20

1. "Kings of the Tacky Commercials," *Dun's Review,* May 1979, pp. 60–64.

Chapter 21

1. Ferdinand F. Mauser and David J. Schwartz, *American Business: An Introduction,* 4th ed. (New York: Harcourt Brace Jovanovich, 1978), pp. 394–395.

Chapter 22

1. David Ogilvy, "Corporate Advertising," *Viewpoint,* vol. I, 1979, pp. 28–31.

2. *Corporate Advertising/Phase II,* An Expanded Study of Corporate Advertising Effectiveness conducted for *Time* magazine by Yankelovich, Skelly & White, Inc., undated, pages unnumbered.
3. From This Is PR, the Realities of Public Relations, 2d ed. by Doug Newsom and Alan Scott. © 1981 by Wadsworth, Inc. Reprinted by permission of Wadsworth Publishing company, Belmont, Calif. 94002. Pp. 12–13.

Chapter 24

1. John E. Cooney, *The Wall Street Journal,* April 12, 1979, p. 40.

Credits and Acknowledgments

Chapter 1

Figures 1, 2, 4, 5, 6, 23, and Ad Lab. Courtesy The Coca-Cola Company.

Figure 3. Adapted from R. Bartos and T. Dunn, *Advertising and Consumers* (New York: American Association of Advertising Agencies, 1976), pp. 132–34.

Figures 7 and 14. Dick Sutpen, *The Mad Old Ads* (New York: McGraw-Hill, 1966), pp. 9 and 49.

Figure 8. Courtesy Doyle Dane Bernbach Inc.

Figure 9. Courtesy Dancer Fitzgerald Sample.

Figure 10. Courtesy Tracy-Locke Advertising.

Figure 11. Courtesy SSC&B Inc. Advertising.

Figure 12. Adapted from Frank Presbey, *History and Development of Advertising* (Garden City, N.Y.: Doubleday, 1929), p. 361. Copyright 1929 by Frank Presbey. Reprinted by permission of Doubleday & Company, Inc.

Figure 13. Reprinted with permission from the September 10, 1981, issue of *Advertising Age*. Copyright 1981 by Crain Communications, Inc.

Figure 17. Henry Ford Museum/Edison Institute.

Figure 19. Courtesy Volkswagen of America.

Figure 22. International Advertising Association and INRA Hooper.

Figure 24. Courtesy of Union Oil of California.

Figure 25. Photograph by Peter LeGrand.

Figure 26. © Eastman Kodak Company, 1981.

Chapter 2

Figure 1. Courtesy Harvard & Edrick, Inc.

Figure 8. Adapted from H. Keith Hunt, "Decision Points in FTC Deceptive Advertising Matter," *Journal of Advertising* 6, no. 2 (Spring 1977), p. 29.

Figures 17 and 19. Adapted from *The National Advertising Review Board, 1971–1976: A Five Year Review and Perspective on Advertising Industry Self-Regulation* (New York: National Advertising Review Board, 1977).

Figure 20. Adapted from S. Watson Dunn and Arnold M. Barban, *Advertising: Its Role in Modern Marketing* (Hinsdale, Ill.: Dryden Press, 1978), p. 704.

Chapter 3

Figure 1. Courtesy Scali, McCabe, Sloves, Inc.

Figure 2. *Printers' Ink,* December 16, 1960, p. 27.

Checklist. Reprinted with permission from the March 30, 1981, issue of *Crain's Chicago Business*. Copyright 1981 by Crain Communications, Inc.

Figure 3. Courtesy Revlon, Inc.

Ad Lab. *Occupational Outlook Handbook,* 1979.

Figures 5 and 6. Courtesy The Procter & Gamble Company.

Checklist. Adapted from Kenneth Roman and Jane Maas, *How to Advertise* (New York: St. Martin's Press, Inc., Macmillan & Co., Ltd., 1976), pp. 151–56.

Ad Lab. Adapted from Mike Turner, "What Makes a Good Account Executive?" *Viewpoint* 1 (1980), pp. 27–28.

Figures 7 and 8. Courtesy Motorola Semiconductor Group Products, Inc.

Figure 9. Charles J. Dirksen, Arthur Kroeger, and Francesco M. Nicosia, *Advertising Principles and Problems* (Homewood, Ill.: Richard D. Irwin, 1977), p. 647.

Figure 10. Courtesy Bloomingdale's. Artwork by Jan Mathews.

Chapter 4

Figure 1. Courtesy Adolph Coors Company and Ted Bates New York/Advertising.

Ad Lab and Figure 3. Reprinted with permission from the March 18, 1981, issue of *Advertising Age*. Copyright 1981 by Crain Communications, Inc.

Ad Lab. Philip Kotler, *Principles of Marketing* (Englewood Cliffs, N.J.: Prentice-Hall, 1980), p. 522. © 1980 Prentice-Hall, Inc. Adapted by permission. Also courtesy of Pepsico International.

Figure 4. Adapted from Cole & Weber, Inc.

Figure 7. Reprinted with permission from the February 12, 1979, issue of *Advertising Age*. Copyright 1979 by Crain Communications, Inc.

Career Box. Adapted from *Advertising: A Career of Action and Variety for Exceptional Men and Women* (New York: American Association of Advertising Agencies, no date), and *Advertising: A Guide to Careers in Advertising* (New York: American Association of Advertising Agencies, 1975).

Figure 11. Adapted from American Association of Advertising Agencies data.

Figure 14. Courtesy Jack Eagle.

Chapter 5

Figure 1. Photo by Mary Cairns/*Advertising Age*.

Figure 2. Courtesy Turner Broadcasting System, Inc.

Figure 3. Courtesy of Gray & Rogers, Inc.

Figure 4. Courtesy RCA.

Figure 5. Wide World Photos.

Ad Lab. Stephen Baker, *Systematic Approach to Advertising Creativity* (New York: McGraw-Hill, 1979), pp. 176–83.

Figure 6. Courtesy McDonald's International.

Figure 7. Courtesy McGraw-Hill Publications Company.

Figure 8. Courtesy Union-Tribune Publishing Co.

Figure 9. Courtesy John Blair & Company.

Figure 11. Courtesy Arnold & Company Inc.

Figure 12. Photograph by Peter LeGrand.

Figure 14. Courtesy National CSS.

Chapter 6

Ad Lab. Adapted from "Who Were the Top Marketers of the 1970's," *Marketing Communications,* January 1980, p. 20, and "New Freedom in Fragrances," *Marketing Communications,* February 1980, pp. 20–21.

Figure 2. Courtesy Clearwater Federal.

Figure 3. Philip Kotler, *Principles of Marketing* (Englewood Cliffs, N.J.: Prentice-Hall, 1980), p. 297. © Prentice-Hall, Inc. Adapted by permission.

Figure 5. Courtesy Jaguar Rover Triumph, Inc. and American Honda Motor Company, Inc.

People in Advertising. Adapted with permission from *The Positioning Era* by Jack Trout and Al Ries, July 16, 1979, issue of *Advertising Age*. Copyright 1979 by Crain Communications, Inc.

Figure 6. Adapted from Ben M. Enis, *Marketing Principles* (Santa Monica, Calif.: Goodyear Publishing, 1980), p. 351.

Figure 7. Adapted from Elwood S. Buffa and Barbara A. Pletcher, *Understanding Business Today* (Homewood, Ill.: Richard D. Irwin, 1980), p. 37.

Figure 8. Courtesy Black, Starr & Frost and Amtrak-National Railroad Passenger Corp.

Figure 9. Adapted from *Restaurant Hospitality* 16, no. 6 (June 1980), p. 128.

Figure 10. Courtesy Webb & Athey, Inc.

Chapter 7

Ad Lab and Figure 5. Adapted from Burton, Marcus et al., *Modern Marketing Management* (New York: Random House, 1980), p. 66.

Figure 2. Courtesy Peter Rogers Associates. Photo by Bill King.

Figure 3. Adapted from William H. and Isabella C. M. Cunningham, *Marketing: A Managerial Approach* (Cincinnati: South-Western Publishing, 1981), p. 121, and data based on hierarchy of needs in "A Theory of Human Motivation," in *Motivation and Personality,* 2d. edition, by Abraham H. Maslow. Copyright © 1970 by Abraham H. Maslow. By permission of Harper & Row Publishers, Inc.

Ad Lab. Left: Courtesy Warwick, Welsch & Miller, Inc.
Middle: Courtesy Lord, Geller, Federico, Einstein, Inc.
Right: Courtesy Young & Rubicam, New York.

Figure 4. Courtesy McVickers & Benson Ltd.

Figure 7. Adapted from W. Lloyd Warner, Marchia Meeker, Kenneth Eels, *Social Class in America* (New York: Harper & Row, 1960), pp. 6–32.

Figure 8. Adapted from Robert W. Hodges, Paul M. Siegel, and Peter H. Rossi, "Occupational Prestige in the United States, 1925–1963," *American Journal of Sociology,* November 1974, pp. 290–92.

Ad Lab. Left top: © Eastman Kodak Company, 1977.
Left bottom: Courtesy Chiat/Day Advertising Inc.
Right: Courtesy Peter Rogers & Associates.

Figure 9. Adapted from Harold H. Kassarjian and Thomas S. Robertson, eds., *Perspectives in Consumer Behavior* (Chicago: Scott, Foresman, 1968), p. 4. © 1968 by Scott, Foresman and Company. Reprinted by permission.

Figure 10. Adapted from Niles Howard, "More Bang for the Ad Dollar." Reprinted with the special permission of *Dun's Review,* November 1978. Copyright 1978, Dun & Bradstreet Publication Corporation; data from Major Market Index 1977.

Figure 11. Adapted from William D. Wells and George Gubar, "The Life Cycle Concept in Marketing Research," *Journal of Marketing Research,* November 1966, p. 362.

Figure 12. Adapted from David L. Kurtz and Louis E. Boone, *Marketing* (New York: Dryden Press, 1981), p. 146.

Figure 13. Courtesy Chiat/Day Advertising Inc.

Ad Lab. Text: Philip Kotler, *Principles of Marketing* (Englewood Cliffs, N.J.: Prentice-Hall, 1980), p. 303. © 1980 Prentice-Hall, Inc. Adapted by permission.
Illustration. Adapted from Paul Green, "A Multidimensional Model of Product Features Association," *Journal of Business Research,* April 1974, p. 113.

Figure 14. Adapted from Dik Warren Twedt, "How Important to Marketing Strategy Is the 'Heavy User'?" *Journal of Marketing,* January 1964, p. 72.

Figure 15. Adapted from Russell J. Haley, "Benefit Segmentation: A Decision Oriented Research Tool," *Journal of Marketing,* July 1963, pp. 30–35.

Figure 16. Adapted from U.S. Department of Commerce, Bureau of the Census, *Census of Manufacturers Area Statistics* (Washington, D.C.: U.S. Government Printing Office, 1971), p. 39.

Chapter 8

Ad Lab. Adapted from Steuart Henderson Britt, *Marketing Managers Handbook* (Chicago: The Dartnell Corporation, 1973), pp. 286–87.

Figure 2. Adapted from Dik Warren Twedt, ed., *1973 Survey of Marketing Research* (Chicago: American Marketing Association, 1973), p. 41.

Figure 3. Adapted from Philip Kotler, *Principles of Marketing* (Englewood Cliffs, N.J.: Prentice-Hall, 1980). © 1980 Prentice-Hall, Inc. Adapted by permission.

Figure 4. Reprinted by permission from the May 19, 1980, issue of *Advertising Age*. Copyright 1980 by Crain Communications, Inc. Also Thomas C. Kinnear and James R. Taylor, *Marketing Research: An Applied Approach* (New York: McGraw-Hill, 1979).

Ad Lab. Adapted from Natalie Goldberg, "How to Use External Data in Marketing Research," *Marketing Communication,* March 1980, pp. 76–82.

Figure 5. Photograph by Wayne Bladholm.

Figure 6. Courtesy The Seven-Up Company.

Ad Lab. Adapted from Kenneth E. Runyon, *Advertising and the Practice of Marketing* (Columbus: Charles E. Merrill Publishing, 1979), p. 108–9.

Ad Lab. Adapted from *Everything You've Always Wanted to Know about TV Ratings,* A. C. Nielsen Company, 1978.

Checklist. From Don E. Schultz and Dennis G. Martin, *Strategic Advertising Campaigns* (Chicago: Crain Books, 1979).

Figure 10. Photograph courtesy of Kenneth Hollander Associates, Inc.

Figure 12. Adapted from Edmund W. J. Faison, *Advertising: A Behavioral Approach for Managers* (New York: John Wiley & Sons, 1980), p. 664.

Figure 13. Philip Taubman, "The Great Soft-Drink Shoot-out," *Esquire,* March 27, 1979, p. 27. Copyright © 1979 by Esquire Publishing, Inc.

Chapter 9

Ad Lab. Jack Trout and Al Ries, "Marketing Warfare," *Southern Advertising,* July 1978. Photographs by Wayne Bladholm.

Figures 1, 3, 8, 9, and 12. Courtesy Ogilvy & Mather Inc.

Figure 4. Courtesy Waterford Glass, Inc.

Checklist. Adapted from Russell H. Colley, *Defining Advertis-*

ing Goals for Measured Advertising Results (New York: Association of National Advertisers, 1961), pp. 62–68.

Ad Lab. Adapted from William J. Baumol and Alan S. Blinder, *Economics: Principles and Policy* (New York: Harcourt Brace Jovanovich, 1980), p. 335.

Figure 10. Reprinted with permission from the September 10, 1981, issue of *Advertising Age*. Copyright 1981 by Crain Communications, Inc.

Figure 11. Courtesy SSC&B Inc. Advertising. Photograph by Les Goldberg.

Chapter 10

Figure 1. Courtesy International Paper Company.

Checklist. Adapted from *Advertising Today*. © 1978 by J. Douglas Johnson. Reprinted by permission of the publisher, Science Research Associates, Inc.

Figure 2. Courtesy Ally & Gargano, Inc.

Figure 3. Henry Ford Museum/Edison Institute.

Figure 6. Courtesy NW Ayer ABH International.

Figure 7. Courtesy Bozell & Jacobs, Inc.

Checklist. Adapted from Kenneth Roman and Jane Maas, *How to Advertise* (New York: St. Martin's Press, Inc., Macmillan & Co., Ltd, 1976), pp. 32–34, 36–38.

Figure 9. Courtesy Doyle Dane Bernbach Inc.

Figure 13. Courtesy Rosenberg & Co., Inc.

Ad Lab. Prime-Pak: Courtesy Epiphany, Inc.; Jeff Gorman, writer; and Jim Cox, art director. U.S. School of Music: Courtesy BBDO; John Caples, writer.

Ad Lab. Adapted from Robert Gunning, *The Technique of Clear Writing*, rev. ed. (New York: McGraw-Hill, 1968), p. 38.

Chapter 11

Figure 1. Courtesy Scali, McCabe, Sloves, Inc.

Figure 2. Courtesy Ackerman & McQueen Advertising, Inc.

Figure 3. Courtesy Botsford Ketchum Advertising, Inc.

Figure 4. Courtesy Revlon, Inc.

Ad Lab. Adapted from Walter Margulies, "What Colors Should You Use?" *Media Decisions* (New York: Decision Publications).

Figure 5. Courtesy Leo Burnett Company, Inc.

Figure 7. Courtesy of NW Ayer, Inc., and DeBeers Consolidated Mines, Ltd.

Figure 8. Courtesy Leber Katz Partners, Advertising; Peter Paris, designer.

Figure 9. Courtesy DKG Advertising, Inc., Don Ivan Puntchaz, illustrator.

Art Director's Portfolio. A. Courtesy Stan Merritt Inc./Advertising.

B. Courtesy J. Walter Thompson Co.

C. Courtesy Wyse Advertising.

D. Courtesy Koehler Company.

E. Courtesy Ogilvy & Mather Advertising, Robert Rodriguez, illustrator.

F. Courtesy Webb & Athey, Inc.

G. Courtesy Ferrari North America.

H. Courtesy Dancer Fitzgerald Sample, Inc. Photograph by Dennis Gray.

I. Courtesy Kenyon & Eckhardt, S.A. Geneva, Renè Bittel, creative direction, and Bulgari.

J. Courtesy George Lois.

K. Courtesy Margeotes/Fertitta Inc.

L. Courtesy Doyle Dane Bernbach, Inc.

Ad Lab. Left: Courtesy Austin Nichols & Co., Inc.
Right: Courtesy The Martin Agency, Inc.

Chapter 12

Figures 1 and 2. Used by permission of Louis Grubb, 155 Riverside Drive, New York, New York 10024. (212) 873-2561.

Figure 6. Courtesy Scali, McCabe, Sloves, Inc.

Figure 10. Reprinted from U&lc, International Journal of Typographics.

Figure 11. Courtesy AM Varityper, division of AM International.

Figure 13. Courtesy Heidelberg West.

From Concept through Production of a Magazine Advertisement. Courtesy Klaus Schmidt, Young & Rubicam, and Eastern Airlines.

Chapter 13

Figures 1 and 2. Courtesy The Procter & Gamble Company.

Figure 4. Courtesy Genesco, Inc.

Figure 5. Adapted from "The Seven Factors to Creative Successes" by Harry Wayne McMahan. Reprinted by permission from December 17, 1979, issue of *Advertising Age*. Copyright 1979 by Crain Communications, Inc.

Figure 6. Courtesy Doyle Dane Bernbach Inc., James Garner, and Mariette Hartley.

Figure 7. © 1978. Chevron U.S.A. Inc.

Figure 9. Courtesy Leo Burnett Company.

Figure 10. Courtesy KCBN, Inc.

Figure 11. Adapted with permission of Macmillan Publishing Co., Inc., from *Advertising*, by William M. Weilbacher, p. 273. Copyright © 1962 by The Free Press.

Figure 12. Photograph by Peter LeGrand.

From Concept through Production of a Television Commercial. Courtesy Susan A. Irwin, Evelyn Sassoon, Dancer Fitzgerald Sample, Inc., and Yoplait U.S.A.

Ad Lab. Adapted from Wallace A. Ross and Bob Landers, "Commercial Categories," in *Radio Plays the Plaza* (New York: Radio Advertising Bureau, 1969).

Chapter 14

Figures 2 and 3. Photographs by Peter LeGrand.

Figures 4, 5 (bottom), and 12. Photographs by Wayne Bladholm.

Figures 7 and 8. Package design by the Schechter Group of New York.

Figure 9 (bottom). Package design by Selame Design.

Figure 10. Courtesy Morton Salt Division of Morton Norwich.

Figure 11. Adapted from "Packaging Directions: A Survey," *Advertising Techniques*, September 1980. Research by Overlock Howe Consulting Group.

Ad Lab. H. Photograph by Wayne Bladholm.

Ad Lab. Adapted from Corby Kummer, "Bringing up Betty," *Media People*, November 1979.

Figure 17. Adapted from *United States Trademark Association Year End Report, 1970*.

Chapter 15

Figure 1. Courtesy Grey Advertising, Inc.

Figure 2. Reprinted by permission from March 18, 1981, issue of *Advertising Age*. Copyright 1981 by Crain Communications, Inc.

Figure 3. Adapted from Jack Z. Sissors and E. Reynold Petray, *Advertising Media Planning* (Chicago: Crain Books, 1976).

Figure 5. Reprinted by permission from September 10, 1981, issue of *Advertising Age*. Copyright 1981 by Crain Communications, Inc.

Figure 6. Courtesy Doyle Dane Bernbach, Inc.
Figure 7. Courtesy Warner-Lambert Company.
Figure 8. Courtesy Ally & Gargano, Inc.
Figures 11 and 12. Adapted from *Cahners Advertising Research Report.*
Ad Lab. Adapted from Stephen Baker, *Systematic Advertising Research Report* (New York: McGraw-Hill, 1979), p. 154.
Figure 13. From Donald W. Jugenheimer and Peter B. Turk, *Advertising Media* (Columbus, Ohio: Grid Publishing, 1980), p. 90.
Figures 14 and 15. Courtesy Simmons Market Research Bureau: 1980 Study of Media and Markets.
Ad Lab. Copyright 1980 William F. Arens & Associates.

Chapter 16

Figure 3. Courtesy Rose & Brosse Advertising, Inc.; Bill Brennen, illustrator; Evelyn Rose, writer; Bill Sadera, art director; Philip L. Rose, creative director.
Figure 7. Adapted from a 1964 study as listed in *Newspaper and Newsprint Facts at a Glance,* Newsprint Information Committee.
Figure 8. Courtesy SDRS *Newspaper Rates and Data,* April 12, 1981.
Figure 10. Courtesy Star Publications.
Figure 11. Courtesy Cunningham & Walsh, Inc.
Figure 16. Courtesy Geer, Du Bois Inc., Advertising.
Figure 17. Adapted from "Magazine Newsletter of Research," Magazine Publishers Association, vol. 8, no. 1.
Figure 19. Data from ABC and SDRS.
Figure 20. Courtesy SDRS, *Consumer Magazine and Farm Publication Rates and Data,* April 27, 1981.

Chapter 17

Figure 1. Courtesy Lesney Products Corporation.
Figure 2. Courtesy The Coca-Cola Company.
Checklist. Adapted from Kenneth Roman and Jane Maas, *How to Advertise* (New York; St. Martin's Press, Inc., Macmillan & Co., Ltd., 1976), pp. 14–18 and 41–44.
Figure 3. Courtesy D'Arcy-MacManus & Masius, Norm Crosby, and Marcia Wallace.
Figures 4 and 14. Adapted from *Media Facts,* NW Ayer.
Figure 5. *Nielsen Report on Television,* 1981, pp. 8–9. Used with permission.
Figure 6. Adapted from Nielsen Television Index data. Used with permission.
Ad Lab A and B. © 1981 Nielsen Television Index. Used with permission.
C. © The Arbitron Company. Used with permission.
Figure 7. Courtesy Wyse Advertising.
Figures 8 and 15. Courtesy SDRS, *Spot Radio Rates and Data,* April 1, 1981.
Figure 9. Courtesy Radio Advertising Bureau.
Figures 10 and 12. Adapted from Radio Advertising Bureau data.
Figures 16 and 17. © 1981 The Arbitron Company. Used with permission.

Chapter 18

Figure 1. Courtesy Signature Financial Marketing, Inc.
Figure 4. Adapted from Maxwell Sroge Co., Mail Order Industry Annual Report.
Figure 5. Adapted from "A Look before We Leap into the 1980s: A Study of Consumer Attitudes about Direct Response Purchasing" (Speech by Henry P. Bernhard, vice chairman, Ogilvy & Mather).
Figure 6. Photograph by Wayne Bladholm.
Ad Lab. Adapted from *Direct Marketing,* November 1979, p. 63.
Figure 7. Photograph by Peter LeGrand.
Checklist. Adapted from Kenneth Roman and Jane Maas, *How to Advertise* (New York: St. Martin's Press, Inc., Macmillan Co., Ltd., 1976), pp. 60–64.
Figure 9. Courtesy Xerox Education Publications.
Figures 10 and 15. Adapted from Bob Stone, *Successful Direct Marketing Methods* (Chicago: Crain Books, 1979), pp. 92–93.
Figure 11. Reprinted with permission from the August 17, 1970, issue of *Advertising Age.* Copyright 1970 by Crain Communications, Inc.
Figure 12. Courtesy Direct Mail/Marketing Association, Inc.
Figure 14. Courtesy SDRS *Direct Mail Lists Rates and Data—Consumer Lists,* March 2, 1981.
Figure 16. Courtesy Outdoor Advertising Association of America, Inc.
Figure 17. A and C Photos by Robert Landau.
B. Photo by Sally Henderson.
D. Courtesy Foote, Cone & Belding/Honig.
E. Courtesy McCann-Erickson/San Francisco.
How to Use Color in Outdoor Advertising and Figure 21. Courtesy Institute of Outdoor Advertising.
Figure 18. Courtesy Pacific Outdoor Advertising Co.
Figure 19. Adapted from *Media Facts,* NW Ayer.
Checklist. Adapted from Kenneth Roman and Jane Maas, *How to Advertise* (New York: St. Martin's Press, Inc., Macmillan & Co., Ltd, 1976), pp. 50–55.
Figure 20. Courtesy Foster and Kleiser, a Metromedia Company.
Figure 22. Courtesy Corker Sullivan, Inc., agency; Dennis L. Sullivan, creator; and Dick Sperling, writer.
Figures 23, 24, 25, and 26. Courtesy The Transit Advertising Association, Inc.

Chapter 19

Figure 2. Courtesy Walter M. Perls, Inc.
Figure 3. Courtesy DCI Marketing.
Figure 4. Courtesy Marshall Field's, Chicago.
Ad Lab. Reprinted by permission from March 16, 1981, issue of *Advertising Age.* Copyright 1981 by Crain Communications, Inc.
Ad Lab. Adapted from Kenneth Strottman, "Marketing Classics: Cracker Jack's Prized Promos," *Marketing Communications,* June 1980. "Skate/Ski" commerical © Borden, Inc., 1981.
Ad Lab. From "The Syrup with Something Extra," *Marketing Communications,* March 1980, pp. 32 and 34.
Ad Lab. From Bernard Wysocki, Jr., "Sight, Smell, Sound: They're All Arms in Retailers Arsenal," *The Wall Street Journal,* April 17, 1979. Reprinted by permission, *The Wall Street Journal.* © Dow Jones & Company, Inc., 1979. All rights reserved.
Figure 8. Courtesy Specialty Advertising Association, International.
Figure 9. Photograph by Peter LeGrand.

Chapter 20

Figure 1. Courtesy Action Real Estate.
Figure 2. Courtesy Sears, Roebuck and Co.

Figure 3. Courtesy Garfinckel's.
Figure 4. Ad created by ERA Advertising Agency, New York.
Figure 6. Courtesy The May Company.
Figure 7. Courtesy Santa Barbara Bank & Trust.
Figure 8. Photographs by Wayne Bladholm.
Figure 9. Courtesy Martin Williams, Inc.
Figures 10, 11, 12, and Checklists. Data from Newspaper Advertising Bureau, Inc.
Figure 15. Courtesy Thompson, Torchia & Dymond, Inc. Advertising.
Figure 16. Courtesy Sussman Stern & Schafer.
Figure 18. Courtesy KCBN, Inc.
Figure 19. Courtesy Jason Grant Associates.
Figure 20. Courtesy Marty Neumeier Design Studio.
Figure 21. Courtesy Tucker Wayne & Company.
Figure 23. Courtesy Cal Worthington Ford.

Chapter 21

Figure 3. Courtesy Shure Brothers, Inc.
Figure 4. Courtesy J. Walter Thompson Company.
Ad Lab. Adapted from *Madison Avenue,* October 1980, pp. 89–92.
Figure 5. Courtesy Merck Sharp & Dohme.
Figure 6. Courtesy Massey-Ferguson, Inc.
Figure 7. Reprinted by permission from the February 1978 issue of *Industrial Marketing.* Copyright 1978 by Crain Communications, Inc.
Figure 8. Courtesy John H. Harland Company.
Figure 10. Courtesy SDRS, *Business Publication Rates and Data,* April 24, 1981.
Figure 11. © 1981 by Billboard Publications, Inc. Reprinted by permission.
Figure 12. Courtesy Wang Laboratories, Inc.
Figure 13. Courtesy Eddy Graphic Design.
Figure 14. Courtesy J. Walter Thompson Company, South Africa.
Figure 15. Courtesy Siemens Corporation.

Chapter 22

Figure 1. © 1978 Hans Wendt.
Figures 2, 3, 5, 6, and 10. Courtesy Pacific Southwest Airways.
Ad Lab. Adapted from David Ogilvy, "Corporate Advertising," *Viewpoint* 1 (1979). Illustration Courtesy Ogilvy & Mather.
Figure 4. Courtesy BBDO.
Figure 8. Adapted from the *Public Relations Journal,* June 1977.
Figure 9. Courtesy Arnold Saks Design Office.
Figure 11. Courtesy David Strong Design Group.
Figures 12 and 13. Adapted from Scott M. Cutlip, Allen H. Center, *Effective Public Relations,* 5th edition. © 1978, pp. 23 and 24. Reprinted by permission of Prentice-Hall, Inc., Englewood Cliffs, New Jersey.

Chapter 23

Figure 1. Courtesy Sierra Club.
Figure 2. Courtesy Greenpeace International.
Figure 4. Courtesy Christian Children's Fund, Inc.
Figure 5. Courtesy The American Humane Association.
Figure 6. Courtesy The National Taxpayers Union.
Figure 7. Courtesy Scali, McCabe, Sloves.
Figure 8. Courtesy McCann-Erickson.
Figure 9. Courtesy Young & Rubicam.
Figure 10. Courtesy J. Walter Thompson, USA.
Figure 11. Courtesy Minnesota Bureau of Tourism.
Figure 12. Reprinted with permission from the October 22, 1979, issue of *Advertising Age.* Copyright 1979 by Crain Communications, Inc.
Figures 13, 14, 15, 16. Courtesy of The Advertising Council.
Figure 17. Courtesy Moral Majority Report.
Figure 18. Courtesy American Civil Liberties Union.
Figure 20. Courtesy Jill Collins Public Relations and Lionel Sosa & Associates.
People in Advertising. Adapted from material by Robert Sam Anson in October 30, 1978, issue of *New Times.*
Figure 21. Courtesy Bozell & Jacobs Public Relations.
Figure 22. Courtesy Cochrane Chase, Livingston & Company, Inc.
Ad Lab. Adapted from June 2, 1980, issue of *Television/Radio Age.* Photos from Wide World photos.

Chapter 24

Figure 1. Adapted from Stephen Baker, *Systematic Approach to Advertising Creativity* (New York: McGraw-Hill, 1979).
Figure 2. Courtesy Dentsu Inc.
Figure 3. Courtesy Compton Advertising Incorporated.
Figure 4. Photograph courtesy of Perception Research Services, Inc.
Figure 5. From Edmund W. J. Faison, *Advertising: A Behavioral Approach for Managers* (New York: John Wiley & Sons, 1980), p. 681.
Figure 6. Courtesy J. Walter Thompson Company and Starch INRA Hooper.
Ad Lab. Bill Adams, *The Wall Street Journal* July 24, 1980. Reprinted by permission *The Wall Street Journal.* © Dow Jones & Company Inc. 1980. All rights reserved.
Figure 7. M. Wayne DeLozier, *The Marketing Communication Process.* © 1976 by M. Wayne DeLozier. Used with permission of McGraw-Hill Book Company.
Figure 8. Courtesy Bruzzone Research Company.

Illustration Index

Subject Index